TELEPEN

3070337900

D1356259

POPULAR LOAN

This book is in heavy
demand. Please RETURN or RENEW it no
later than the last date stamped below

14 OCT 1994 A	19 FEB 1998 H	8 OCT 1998
12 APR 1995	26 FEB 1998 H	5 FEB 1999 G
19 APR 1995 A		
	5 MAR 1998 H	16 FEB 1999 H
15 SEP 1995 G		
2 SEP 1995 E	11 MAR 1998 H	1 MAR 1999 G
16 OCT 1995 E	17 MAR 1998 H	17 FEB 2000
CANCELLED 1996 D	01 APR 1998 H	28 FEB 2000
15 OCT 1996 D	-7 APR 1998 H	10 MAR 2000
14 OCT 1997 E	CANCELLED 1998 H	21 MAR 2000
CANCELLED 1998	CANCELLED 1998 H	-7 APR 2000
	13 JAN 1998 H	16 NOV 2001

THE CONTENTIOUS ALLIANCE

MARTIN SPENCER : 1939-1990
Secretary to Edinburgh University Press: 1987-1990

Martin Spencer died while the manuscript for this book was still being prepared. The book is closely associated with Martin's work both in Manchester and Edinburgh, and the Committee of Edinburgh University Press would like to take this opportunity to express its sorrow and to pay tribute to all his achievements as Secretary. He was widely recognised as a distinguished publisher of formidable energy, imagination and flair.

H
10.22
042
MIN

THE CONTENTIOUS ALLIANCE
TRADE UNIONS AND THE LABOUR PARTY

LEWIS MINKIN

pop

EDINBURGH UNIVERSITY PRESS

19598
6/92

307033 7900

© Lewis Minkin, 1991

Edinburgh University Press
22 George Square, Edinburgh

Typeset in Linotron Goudy
by Koinonia Ltd, Bury, and
printed in Great Britain by
The Alden Press,
Osney Mead, Oxford

British Library Cataloguing
in Publication Data
Minkin, Lewis
    The contentious alliance: Trade
    unions and the Labour Party
    I. Title
    331.80941

ISBN 0 7486 0301 8

Contents

Part VI. Organisation and Mobilisation

Part VII. Appraisal

There is a legend told of the Emperor Domitian that, having heard of a Jewish family, of the house of David, whence the ruler of the world was to spring, he sent for its members in alarm, but quickly released them on observing that they had the hands of work-people.

George Eliot, *Daniel Deronda*

In view of the far reaching unity of organisation and personalities, and the complete dependence of the Labour Party on the trade unions, the disparity of policy shown between the two bodies in the years 1924 to 1926 would appear to be quite incapable of explanation.

Egon Wertheimer, *Portrait of the Labour Party*, 1929

I want to say to this Congress that there has been no split; there has been no discussion about a split. (Hear, hear.) There had not been the slightest sign of any split. There had been no quarrel in the General Council and Labour Party offices, either between committees, officials or administrative staffs. We have continued throughout the past year, as in previous years, in perfect harmony.

Fred Bramley, TUC Secretary, to the TUC Congress, 1925

Can this immense contradiction continue indefinitely?

Perry Anderson, in Robin Blackburn and Alexander Cockburn, *The Incompatibles*, 1967

The art of living is more like wrestling than dancing.

Marcus Aurelius

Tables

Acknowledgements

At different times, the Nuffield Foundation, with a Research Fellowship, and the ESRC, with a Research Award, have contributed to the opportunities which enabled me to complete this study. The Department of Government and the Faculty of Economic and Social Studies at Manchester University gave me use of their facilities, as did Northern College. The TUC and Labour Party Library staff and archivist, Stephen Byrd, were unfailingly helpful. I am grateful to all of them.

Various academic friends have given me helpful advice, information and discussion of points raised here. These included Mike Campbell, Keith Ewing, Sue Goss, Trevor Griffiths, Anthony Heath, Bill McCarthy, Susanne McGregor, Peter Nolan, Leo Panitch, David Purdy, Patrick Seyd and Eric Shaw. In addition Patrick Seyd discussed with me advance information on the very interesting Labour Party Membership Survey. Arthur Lipow gave me occasional hospitality and belaboured my head with provocative, but beneficial, comment.

I want especially to express my appreciation for the assistance of Bob Fryer of Northern College and David Howell from Manchester University. Bob made a crucial contribution to the completion of this study. Not only did he give me the advantage of his impressive knowledge of trade unionism and his grasp of theoretical arguments concerning the Labour Movement but, in spite of his responsibilities, he repeatedly found time to act as a severely critical filter for the things I wanted to say. David has a wonderfully detailed and nuanced understanding of British labour history. In addition to exchanging information about, and interpretations of, the inter-war years, he read through the manuscript with an eagle eye and the usual constructive comments. It was a pleasure to work with both of them.

I have a rather old-fashioned method of producing manuscripts and I have relied a great deal on the awe-inspiring secretarial skill, good humour and dogged persistence of Jean Ashton, whom I also thank very much. My thanks also go to Barbara Hunter who assisted in a couple of secretarial emergencies. Gina Greenly's support was much appreciated. She helped me to check some of the textual material and also to control the mysterious 'Chinese whispers' effect on the notes.

Daniel Minkin, Tom St. David-Smith and Liz Minkin had a lot to put up with in living with an anti-social hermit who walked around day and night in a world of his own. Daniel helped with some of the tables and Liz found time from chairing uncountable numbers of public bodies to read the draft for clarity and for a more consistent usage of English grammar than I am capable of. I am grateful to the three of them and we are all glad it's over.

I most deeply regret that Martin Spencer did not see the final version. He was a very decent man and a friend who gave me a lot of encouragement.

My much-loved mother and father, Barney 'Bob' and Esther 'Annie' Minkin, have influenced this book to a degree which might have surprised them had they lived to know about it. An experience which took in the Gorbals, the Yorkshire Coalfield, Barnbow, and years of working as 'hands' in Leeds tailoring factories taught them lessons in priorities from which I was slow to learn. In a sense, it is their book.

Finally, my debts in connection with this book go much wider and much further back than indicated here. I have been involved in research on the Labour Movement since the late 1960s. In that time many friends and contacts – trade unionists, Party activists, councillors, Party and union officials and MPs – have shared their knowledge and understanding with me. A lot of information came from this private discussion, which I have respected in a variety of ways. The demands of confidentiality and the uncertainties of derivation for some of the material make it impracticable to list all the names here. But, in the final stages of preparing the manuscript I came across this passage in Robert Louis Stevenson's *Travels with a Donkey in the Cévennes*:

> Every book is, in an intimate sense, a circular letter to the friends of him who wrote it. They alone take his meaning; they find private messages, assurances of love, and expressions of gratitude dropped for them in every corner.

Leeds, December 1990

Introduction

I have not found this an easy book to write. Some of this is unquestionably due to my own limitations. I write with glacier-like speed; architect, bricklayer and painter, moving from drawing board to attic to brick-yard, discarding a foundation here, an upright there, then suddenly hurrying off for more bricks. It seems far removed from the cool flowing logic of completed texts and never destined to get there. Also very much at the mercy of the weather. What begins as one theme is blown to one side and becomes another. The structure changes purpose, the sections change shape. Over time, the whole thing even subtly changes colour.

So much has happened and so many new features have arisen in the trade union–Labour Party relationship since this book was first conceived that my perspectives have twisted and bent, in an effort to understand and follow through the developments.

I first constructed a proposed structure in the early 1980s when the Labour Party and the unions were in the middle of a huge crisis over intra-Party democracy (and many other things). Since that time, as the book painfully took shape, so the subject-matter refused to keep still. Institutions followed each other with great rapidity. Trade Unions for a Labour Victory (TULV) gave way to the Trade Union Coordinating Committee (TUCC) which in turn gave way to Trade Unionists For Labour (TUFL). New institutions were accompanied by new strategies, 'new realism', and then a great deal of new loyalism (see Chapter 5). The Liberal–Social Democrat Alliance threatened the Labour Movement then fell back. It threatened again, fell back again, and then fell to fighting itself. The Miners' Strike came almost out of the blue in 1984, enveloped the Party and the unions for longer than any major dispute in history and then left lasting marks of a kind which few foresaw at its inception. The Political Fund ballots were imposed and devastating consequences threatened in 1985; instead, remarkable victories were won and a new strength was diagnosed. Then, just prior to the 1987 General Election, the new strength appeared to disappear as fast as it had been discovered.

Then came 1989 and the picture changed again. It changed in terms of electoral support, it changed in terms of public attitudes towards trade unionism, it changed in terms of Labour's trade union policies and it changed in terms of major movements for reform in the unions' relationship with the Party.

All these changes (and many more to which reference is made here) perhaps explain why, in spite of many informative books, pamphlets and articles which have dealt with the union–Party relationship in recent years,[1] no one has attempted a comprehensive update of Martin Harrison's pathbreaking *Trade Unions and the Labour Party*, published in 1960. But then, in a sense, neither have I. Limitations of time dictated that I did not explore the grass-roots and regional relationship as much as I would have liked. On the other hand, I chose not to go into the individual union policymaking machinery in detail because I had dealt with it at great length in *The Labour Party Conference*.[2] As for the Miners' Strike and its impact on relations between the NUM and the Labour Party, this became so important and such a story in itself that in the end I made it a separate project (which, in due time, will emerge).

Nevertheless, the study does provide a detailed, wide-ranging and, in some ways, novel exploration of the most crucial features and critical new developments in this, the most important relationship on the Left of British politics.

For over eighty years this relationship has shaped the structure and, in various ways, the character of the British Left. Every major group and party in British politics has had to take account of what Keir Hardie called 'the great alliance', whether they regarded it as 'great' or not.

And many of them did not. From 1901 when the Social Democratic Federation ceased affiliation, Marxist and socialist organisations have often found the union link too constraining and the Party too limited in its aims and strategy. But they always failed, sometimes dismally, each time they attempted to challenge the Labour Party from the outside; repeatedly they sought entry,[3] or re-entry,[4] affiliation, or covert influence via the unions. The older parties of British politics always deeply resented the close relationship; it helped to undermine the old Liberal Party and provided a constant organisational threat to Conservative rule. In recent years, these forces have produced an avalanche of books, articles and speeches which have represented the unions' ties to Labour as a dangerous, industrial–political blockage to their economic programme – *the* problem of the British polity just as the unions were typified as *the* problem of the British economy.[5]

For the Centre and Right it became a priority to seek the destruction of the union–Party relationship either through political defection, the encouragement of trade union separation, or through legislative action – notably the reform of political funding. Often they diagnosed inevitable degeneration or suicide as the future of the Labour Movement. But just as often their anxieties were betrayed in the various desperate attempts they made to commit murder rather than await the predicted death.

In this aim, they were at one with several strands of the revolutionary Left who since the very inception of the Labour Party have seen its form, values and behaviour – Labourism, as some described it – as *the* great obstacle to the development of their socialist project. They too looked to the day when the decisive moment, the great split, took place. This schism was conceived in a variety of forms. For some, it involved a point of departure which would leave both Left and Right with its own distinctive trade union base and its own reinterpretation of the relationship between the industrial and the political. More often it was forecast as a split between the unions and the Party – either a revocation of the federation of 1900, freeing the Leftwing political groups from the strangulation of trade unionism, or an emancipation of newly militant and politicised trade unions from the degenerate political traditions within the Party.

Since the late 1960s, both sets of critics have taken heart from the repetitive difficulties facing the unions and the Party, marked first by the conflict between the unions and successive Labour governments over industrial relations issues, marked also by the destabilisation of relations within the Party following the emergence of a new generation of Leftwing union leaders. The rise of non-affiliated white collar unions added one new dimension to the problems: the decline in the percentage of trade unionists voting Labour added another. Above all, it seemed that the defection of the Social Democrats in 1981 heralded the beginnings of a fundamental realignment in British politics and a potentially fatal blow to the Labour Movement. Diagnoses of impending doom and of 'terminal decline' were very much in vogue.[6]

And yet the relationship survived – a fact which might itself prove to be the most important political feature of the last two decades. Much of this study is preoccupied with how and why the internal conflicts, divergent aims and potential fragmentation came about – and how 'the big split' was avoided. But it is as well before we start to note that many problems were there from the inception of the relationship and particularly from the 1920s. As Martin Harrison noted in 1960, 'the collapse of Labour's relationship with the unions has been prophesied as often as the demise of English cricket'.[7] As I will indicate in Chapter 3, diagnoses of decay were even prevalent in 1944 – twelve months before the Party's greatest success and on the eve of achievements which were to shape British politics for decades to come.

The fact was that the Movement, as I indicate in Chapter 1, always had problems in preserving an ideological and interest-based unity, in managing its social tensions, and in preserving the strategic compatibilities of the unions, the TUC and the Party. Politics was always both a necessary instrument and a problem for the unions. After various attempts to create one structurally unified Movement had failed in the mid-1920s, the relationship was managed – as shown in Chapter 2 and later Chapter 4 – by unwritten rules and protocol derived mainly from trade union values and priorities. These 'rules'* embodied an acceptance of the permanent differentiation of functions and spheres – the political and the industrial.

---

*The existence of 'rules' governing trade union behaviour in the union-Party relationship has been hinted at in various places and was noted specifically by Allan Flanders in an article reproduced in *Management and Unions* (1970) which I am sure must have influenced my own perceptions. But I seemed to come to this via a different process,[8] first watching the behaviour of the Jones/Scanlon generation of union leaders, listening to the comments of ex-Ministers and Shadow Ministers, talking to veteran trade union officials, then observing the Labour Party's multiple conflicts after 1979. The 'rules' as I understand them imply (amongst many other differences) a more explicit set of obligations from the Parliamentary side than is suggested by Flanders.

The 'rules',* only a small number of which were embodied in the Party's Constitution and Standing Orders, and none of which was recognised in the Rules and Standing Orders of the TUC, vitally affected the distribution of power** in the relationship. They acted as boundaries producing inhibitions and constraints which prevented the absolute supremacy of leadership groups in either wing of the relationship.

The consolidation of these 'rules' in the 1950s, at a time of dominating ascendancy by allies from the Rightwing of the Party and unions, was carried through with such vigour and apparent finality that many on the Right – and many influential observers – conceived it as a permanent 'settlement' within the Movement. The assumption was that economic success, political moderation, industrial accommodation and access to Government by the unions would be permanent features of future British politics. Not surprisingly – and this is the underlying reality of the major part of this study – once the terms of the post-war 'settlement' between the parties came under threat, so the 'rules' of the Movement's own 'settlement' (already in difficulties over the 'rules' of democracy) also moved into greater tension and crisis over the 'rules' of freedom. An overview of these developments since 1959 – the forces which pulled the relationship apart and the forces which moved it together – is presented in Chapter 5. It acts both as an analytical structure of conflicting forces and also as context for the later examination of ideology and processes.

The force of the 'rules' can be seen at its clearest in the chapters dealing with the ideological approaches of the trade union Left and the Social Democratic

---

*Throughout the text where I use inverted commas around the 'rules', this is to distinguish regulation derived from unwritten codes. No one refers to them as the 'rules'. This is my terminology.

**Power is defined here as 'the ability to affect outcomes'. It is not an unproblematic definition but it is useful for the purposes of this study. The usual conceptual difficulties are compounded here by the complexity of the union presence (see for example Chapter 19 for the interaction between internal trade unionism and affiliated trade unions) and by the different dimensions of a multidimensional relationship.
The most obvious and arguably the most important dimension of the relationship when Labour is in Opposition concerns the formulation of Labour Party policy. But there are other dimensions of power and there are other outcomes examined in this study – sometimes in passing, sometimes in full focus. Although some of these dimensions interact with Party policy formulation (in establishing resources of policymaking for example), others are virtually independent of implications for Party policy but have important consequences nevertheless. The dimensions include the role of the unions in Party (1) rule-making, (2) sponsorship, (3) elections, (4) organisation, and (5) administration and financial management.
Because these dimensions cover different terrains and institutions, and involve various political and industrial bodies and alignments, they do not invite easy comparison in terms of 'the unions' and 'the Party'. Nevertheless, a full analysis needs to move wider than simply Party policymaking and to take account of these other dimensions. They are dealt with together in the Appraisal (Chapter 20) where I have attempted to summarise each dimension and note the overall pattern, focusing mainly on the period from 1979 to 1990.

Right, particularly in Chapter 6 where I examine the behaviour of the generation of Leftwing union leaders who came to office in the late 1960s. The alliance of Jack Jones and Hugh Scanlon broke the power of the old Rightwing block vote and raised expectations (and myths) of their behaviour which were often at odds with what they did in practice. Were they in their early phase Leftwing ideologues – as critics tended to imply? Or were they, as was also suggested, non-programmatic trade unionists behaving in a manner which would not be out of place in any economistic trade unionism, including the United States? Did they become purely defensive trade unionists with no wider ideological goals or can we detect other political dimensions to their behaviour within the Labour Party after 1974?

Important questions are raised also by the behaviour of the union leaders during the great constitutional revolt after 1979. Some have argued that in this period it was the unions which provided the driving force behind the revolt. I will examine the various forces at work in the unions and the Party as a whole in this period, assessing their complicated interaction. All in all, the experience of Leftwing union leadership from 1968 to 1982 gives us a unique experience from which to reassess some age-old arguments about the relationship between trade unionism and the Labour Party.

In Chapter 8 it is the developing ideological perspectives of the Social Democrats which are explored in relation to trade unionism and the political role of the unions in the Party. By 1979, some of them had come to feel a deep alienation from the Labour Movement and a frustrated antipathy towards the 'rules' of the relationship. I examine their changing attitudes towards trade unionism both before and after defection. I assess their later impact on the Labour Movement. And I also draw attention to some of the reasons which account for their failure to break the Party's relationship with the unions, including a review of the interesting role of the Electricians' union; in a sense a model and a bridgehead for the Social Democrats, but also a highly problematic link to the trade union movement.

In Parts IV, V and VI, the analysis shifts to selected processes, institutions and procedures involving the unions and the Party. One of the most misunderstood areas of the relationship is that which covers union sponsorship of MPs. On the face of it, unions have a crucial leverage over sponsored Members, but here again we find subtle patterns of constraint and inhibition as well as weakness on the unions' side. There were new developments here too with the rise of 'co-option' and of 'political' officers, indicating a new union interest in the work of parliamentary representatives and in their relations with 'the political arm'. But 'Kept Men', 'paying pipers' and 'calling tunes' – as we shall see in Chapter 9 – are not very helpful metaphors of this process.

I move then to a range of processes and problems which can be brought together under the heading of 'The Block Vote'. No feature of trade union procedures arouses more antipathy, and in itself it encapsulates what many see as the heart of all that is wrong with 'the union connection'. It produces a growing range of problems and grievances within the relationship as well as providing a vulnerable target for critics apt to exaggerate some of its features – including the personal power of 'the union barons'.

In Chapter 10 I examine the different meanings and processes of the block vote and explore the problems of representation and power involved in its operation during the making of party policy. In Chapter 11 the focus is on electing the leadership of the Party – broadly defined here to include the NEC. A new 'politicisation' of these processes grew up in the 1980s, affecting the way unions cast their votes for the NEC, involving them in the voting for the Parliamentary leadership and, on three occasions in the 1980s, plunging them into highly politicised battles for the leadership. One of the reactions was to breathe new life into old movements for block vote reform although, oddly, as we shall see, it was the reform of voting at the Women's Conference which provoked perhaps the most significant discussion and seemed most likely to establish the precedent for major change, and there it was a question of *instituting* the block vote, not its abolition. Proposals and movements for reform are analysed in Chapter 12 – a chapter which also includes one set of conclusions to this study.

The proliferation of new committees and linking institutions which appeared in the 1970s and 1980s might be said to raise question marks against the most crude assessments of the way in which the block vote guaranteed union power over the Party's policymaking. If there were this dominance, why seek to re-create it? Yet the Liaison Committee between the TUC and the Party, which some saw as a unique policy innovation, and the TULV organisation which some saw as a covert policymaking body, were both regarded as confirmations of union power over policy. In Chapter 13 the formulation of Party policy will be explored as a formal and informal process, and in Chapter 14 eleven key issue areas are analysed for the period from 1979 to 1987. For a variety of reasons, but particularly because of the Government's attempt at a radical reconstruction of the post-war settlement, virtually the entire field of Party policymaking was open to new formulation and negotiation with the unions. This unique situation gives us the opportunity to examine in detail case studies of policy issues in a period of major new pressures. In what form and with what outcome were the unions involved in Party policy formulation? What distribution of power occurred and why? Major innovations in procedure and some sharp oscillations in policy took place in this period. In an Addendum on the Policy Review of 1987 to 1990, we follow through both the continuities, the developments and the changes, noting particularly the attitudes and responses of the union leadership.

Of all the new linking bodies, the most contentious were Trade Unions for a Labour Victory and its lesser-known offshoot the Voluntary Levy Fund. Some of the animosity which met TULV (and created a significant drag on the Movement's organisational reconstruction) was a product of factional suspicion. But it also arose out of the novelty of the arrangement and the territorial transgression that it involved. There were few precedents for this degree of direct trade union involvement in the Labour Party's organisational and administrative affairs (although in Chapter 3 we uncover an underdeveloped and little-known forerunner). It was deeply resented by the Left on the NEC – even though TULV began to play a role in constructing the campaigning political trade unionism that the Left had always sought.

In the bitter internal row which broke out during the winter of 1983–4, when the NUM attacked its existence and the AUEW seceded from the organisation, a series of charges were made about alleged clandestine operation within the Labour Party. In Chapters 15 and 16, I examine these allegations in the context of an analysis of the organisational and financial role of TULV, and try to provide answers to some of the questions raised. In particular, did TULV act as a neutral trade union assistant to the Party's organisation or as factionally motivated intervention? What objectives did TULV pursue and how successful was it? Was the Party given valuable extra financial assistance by the Voluntary Levy Fund or was it 'drip-fed' for political reasons and guided by political criteria?

These questions take us deep into sensitive territory. The charge of 'drip-feed' engaged strong feelings as it does whenever the question of trade union finance is linked to political power. Both Right and Left in the Party could get very heated over this kind of issue. Outside the Party the criticism was, if anything, even stronger – often as strong as it was ill-informed. For some of the Labour Party's opponents and even for some academic observers of the Labour Party, the unions' use of finance as a lever to maximise power is their most obvious characteristic. Readers of Chapter 16 will find a rather different picture (as they did in Chapter 9). They will ponder the many failures of union leaders to secure their objectives and find it difficult to square the hesitations, divisions and defeats with the image of union 'barons' engaged in crude *realpolitik*.

Certainly, as I will illustrate, at no time in Party history have the union leaders been so concerned with Labour Party finances and so anxious to intervene in matters of organisation and administration. Certainly, also, it was the case that some of the organisational and financial questions had political 'side effects'. But what are we to make of the difficulties encountered by this union leadership and of the power resources which were *not* brought into play? In addition, we need to understand the peculiar and conflicting relationship between an overt trade union leadership involvement from outside the Party office and the resurgence of trade unionism among headquarters staff. Here, an extraordinary network of clashing powers and obligations faced anybody trying to impose their will. Nowhere did trade unionism give the Labour Party more trouble than at its seat of government. How the Party and the unions responded to the crisis at Head Office will be explained in Chapter 19.

Meanwhile, in Chapters 17 and 18, I examine the transmutation of TULV via the TUCC to TUFL, and just as there has been an assessment of the impact of TULV on Labour's electoral organisation in Chapter 15, so there will be an examination of the role of TULV, TUCC and the Labour Party in the Political Fund victories, and then of the role of TUFL in the 1987 General Election.

Crucial questions are raised by the results in the Political Fund ballots of 1985–6. Why, if all the advantages were, as they appeared to be in 1983, on the side of those attacking the political funds, was their defence so successful? If the union connection with the Labour Party was so uniquely unpopular with trade unionists, how are we to account for the move from adversity to comprehensive victory? In Chapter 18 I will offer some answers to these questions.

In the end, what may strike the reader most in looking at the behaviour of

Trade Unionists For Labour is the combination of a strong commitment to the building of the Labour Movement, together with a rule-governed abdication of power within the political wing. In this, it exemplifies the underlying themes of the whole study. It is, broadly speaking, a study of variations on the theme of 'the Movement', variations on the theme of rules, and variations on the theme of power.

What has been learned from these variations will be taken into the two chapters of the Appraisal, where some of the most contentious contemporary questions about the relationship are re-assessed. In particular, what was the distribution and pattern of power? What were the forms and consequences of political mobilisation? How flexible was the relationship? Should there be a detachment of the structural links? Is the relationship breaking down anyway? And, can it survive?

NOTES

1. The relationship is covered or referred to in many different sources. Amongst the most important books which have dealt with the contemporary relationship in some detail since the 1970s have been (in date order): Irving Richter, *Political Purpose in Trade Unions*, 1973; David Howell, *British Social Democracy*, 1976; Leo Panitch, *Social Democracy and Industrial Militancy*, 1976; William D. Muller, *The Kept Men?*, 1977; David Coates, *Labour in Power?*, 1980; Ben Pimlott and Chris Cook, *Trade Unions in British Politics*, 1982; Martin Holmes, *The Labour Government 1974–9*, 1985; Ken Coates and Tony Topham, *Trade Unions and Politics*, 1986; Leo Panitch, *Working Class Politics in Crisis*, 1986; Derek Fatchett, *Trade Unions and Politics*, 1987; John Kelly, *Labour and the Unions*, 1987; Andrew Taylor, *The Trade Unions and the Labour Party*, 1987; Hilary Wainwright, *Labour: A Tale of Two Parties*, 1987; John Kelly, *Trade Unions and Socialist Politics*, 1988. Other references are footnoted where relevant in the text, including the various political positions referred to in the Introduction.
2. Lewis Minkin, *The Labour Party Conference*, 1980, Chapters 4, 6, 7 and 9.
3. See on this John Callaghan, 'The Background to "Entrism", Leninism and the British Labour Party', *Journal of Communist Studies*, December 1986, pp. 380–401.
4. The classic case of failure and re-entry was that of the Independent Labour Party. A pioneer affiliate, it departed in 1932 but, after its support had dwindled, re-entered the Labour Party in 1975 as Independent Labour Publications, still attempting to come to terms with the limitations of trade unionism.
5. Robert Taylor, 'The Trade Union "Problem" since 1960', in Pimlott and Cook, *op. cit.*, pp. 188–214.
6. For example the *Daily Telegraph* editorial 6/7/82, 'An Embrace of Death' and David Steel's description of 'a suicide pact', *Guardian*, 3/9/84. *The Times* editorial comment, 3/9/86, judged: 'This Great Movement of Ours is reaching the end of its useful life.'
7. Martin Harrison, *Trade Unions and the Labour Party*, 1960, p. 344.
8. I presented a paper on these themes to a conference at Leeds University

in 1975, then to a conference at the City University, New York in 1976. The published version first appeared as 'The Labour Party Has Not Been Hi-jacked' in *New Society*, 6/10/77 and the full version as 'Left-wing Trade Unionism and the Tensions of British Labour Politics' in Bernard E. Brown (ed.), *Eurocommunism and Eurosocialism: The Left Confronts Modernity*, 1979, Chapter 7, pp. 210–45.

Part I

Foundations

1

Movement

The trade union–Labour Party relationship has inspired a rich profusion of metaphors. The Party's origins were once colourfully described by Ernest Bevin as out of the bowels 'of the trade unions'.[1] There have since been jocular references to the relations between Cain and Abel and to the link between 'a ball and chain'.[2] In contrast, in recent years, one union leader has likened it to 'a pair of scissors' – a sharp cutting implement when together, useless when forced apart.[3]

Among this wide range of allusions, the most persistent to emerge from within the relationship has likened its history to that of a family's life[4] – symbiotic, intense, at times tragic, but essentially indissoluble. Partial though this is as a representation, it provides us here with a useful entry point for the understanding of a phenomenon which as we shall see has many sides and much complexity.

Thus the Party is seen as an 'offspring' of the TUC through whose affiliates, together with socialist organisations – including the Fabian Society and the Independent Labour Party (ILP) – the Party was created in 1900. The birth took place in conditions of adversity – a dominant and unresponsive Conservative Government, a Liberal middle class reluctant to accept the selection of 'labour' candidates and, particularly, a judiciary whose traditions were unsympathetic to those of organised labour. After the Taff Vale Judgment of 1901, when the court decision threatened trade union freedom of industrial action, the unions increased their affiliation and 'nourished the babe'.[5]

In 1918 the 'adult'[6] party regularised individual membership in constituency parties and, recognising new obligations to its other parent, announced its adoption of Socialism. It was strong enough in 1922 to form the official Opposition, and in 1924 and 1929 formed minority Governments. In 1931 there was a family convulsion: 'betrayal' by some of the Labour Party's leaders, who joined a National Government, and 'desertion' in 1932 by the Independent Labour Party who broke away. The TUC thereupon asserted its right as the parent to create a new protective relationship. Subsequently the relationship was often fraught with conflict and threats of separation. But its family character partially explained its resilience.[7] As Jack Jones indicated in the 1970s, you could imagine murder in this relationship but never divorce.[8]

Others, including some of the participants, saw it in rather more pragmatic terms. The metaphors were of an instrumental transaction, or series of trans-

actions, in which the unions gave financial, electoral and organisational support
in exchange for political protection, and within the Party exchanged affiliated
members for votes and power. There were many variants of this transaction
metaphor. In its favourable form it involved the language of 'contract', 'compact'
and 'partnership'. In its critical and more typical form the *quid pro quo* was
portrayed as permanent subordination of one of the great parties of state to union
'paymasters' and 'bosses' (in Norman Tebbitt's words to 'a politically motivated
Mafia among trade union bosses which buy and sell votes for their political
ambitions'[9]).

What gave substance to this critique were the structural and other formal
features of the Labour Party which indicated its permanent control by the unions,
for the unions.

Thus, although there were always two separate bodies, the TUC and the Labour
Party, the pattern of individual union affiliation to the Party was such that the
large manual worker unions which dominated membership of the TUC also dominated membership of the Party.

Rules of affiliation to the Party also produced a structure which was heavily
weighted towards trade union dominance. Unions could affiliate at local,
regional and national level, with votes which were commensurate with the size of
affiliated membership. Thus at the Labour Party Annual Conference – the
sovereign body of the Party – the blocks of trade union votes soon dwarfed those
available to socialist and, later, constituency party organisations.[10] Similarly, in
elections for the (National) Executive Committee – the Party's administrative
and policy formulating body – trade union votes commanded a majority of the
seats.[11]

The union's weight was also evident in financial terms. The resources of the
Party were always heavily dependent upon the trade union input of affiliation
fees, donations and grants. By sponsoring a large number of parliamentary candidates and subsidising their electoral machinery the unions were also in a position
to affect the composition and, in theory, the policy of the Parliamentary Labour
Party.

And obligations to trade unionism were written into the Party's constitutional
rules. Thus, from 1918, it was a duty for the Party to 'co-operate with the
Parliamentary Committee of the Trades Union Congress'[12] and after 1924 it was
made the rule that individual members of the Party 'if eligible for Trade Union
membership' must be trade unionists.[13] As the mover of the successful constitutional amendment put it, 'The Labour Party ought to be the political expression
of the Trade Union Movement'.[14]

However, much broader allegiances were implied by a third pervasive metaphor. In this view, the relationship was defined in terms of a common loyalty and
a deeply felt commitment to a wider entity and purpose – the Labour Movement.
This 'movement' was both a description and an aspiration. At its most inclusive,
the description involved a triple series of institutions created by the workers to
represent their interests as producers, consumers and political citizens. Each grew
and gained their own victories and achievements in different spheres but they
shared a common purpose and engaged in a common struggle. 'A great move-

ment', said Attlee, 'is like a tide. It will flow later in one place and then in another. It may come in steadily and silently on a low sandy shore, but run violently against the rocks elsewhere. It may be checked by an adverse wind or be deflected by cross currents, but it is the same tide.'[15]

This portrayal of 'the Movement' became a powerful symbol, with description and aspiration often fused into an idealised conception of community. In practice, however, it had rather more mundane features and some inbuilt limitations. It was, most strikingly, a movement shaped around its oldest institutions, the trade unions, and its purposes were most commonly defined in terms of 'the producers'.[16]

This structural and ideological dominance of the producers meant that often the interests of consumers and users were not to the fore in the consciousness of the Movement. Nor were the Co-operative organisations – although seen as genuinely representative of workers' interests – given a full equality of status. For their part, the Co-operative organisations resisted being too far involved in Labour Party activities. Though their own party, formed in 1917, became allied to Labour, it was always distinct from it. Thus it grew to be the case that 'the Labour Movement' was more often defined not as a trinity but as a duality, the connection between two 'arms', 'wings' or 'sides' of the same body – the industrial and the political – trade unions and the Labour Party.

There was also a problematic element in the representation of the unwaged in a producers' party, and a particular limitation concerning the place of women. In formal terms, this was an egalitarian movement committed to equal rights. In practice, women were heavily under represented in its leadership positions and, given the male dominance of manual production, poorly represented in the affiliated unions. There was the usual covert prejudice plus a set of beliefs about the proper domestic role of women. All this produced resistance to the registration of women's issues and to the furtherance of women's interests.[17] The Movement's priorities were focused upon men, even when as in 1918 the Labour Party described itself as 'The Real Women's Party'.[18]

WERTHEIMER'S PUZZLE

If we take the three metaphors – and their implications – together, it is easy to understand why the Labour Party should be so often and so easily characterised as an instrument of the trade unions. Its family history, its resources and its structural features, together with its producer obligations, all weighed in the same direction to a degree which was highly unusual on the European Left.

As Fred Bramley, then Secretary of the TUC, viewed it in 1924:

> The political progress of the Labour Party ... is mainly trade union political progress... The political organisation is kept running by trade union funds, and the Political Labour Party in this Country can be referred to as a Trade Union Labour Party, if we wish to use that term.[19]

Certain endemic features seemed to flow inevitably from these characteristics. The most obvious implication was that the Party would be controlled by its union affiliates. Further, it could be expected that the policy co-ordination of the Party and the TUC would be almost complete, as they were based mainly on the same affiliates. Flexibility would be minimal; closeness would be permanent; autonomy would be negligible. From these features the Party appeared simply as a transmission belt for trade unionism, and it was reasonable to anticipate a developing power structure in which trade union leaders commanded both the party organisation and the determination of policy.

Yet to the close observer of the history of this relationship what is striking are the many deviations from these surface appearances. As the very acute German Socialist, Wertheimer, puzzled in his *Portrait of the Labour Party*:

> In view of the far reaching unity of organisation and personalities, and the complete dependence of the Labour Party on the trade unions, the disparity of policy shown between the two bodies in the years 1924 to 1926 would appear to be quite incapable of explanation.[20]

Further, with the benefit of hindsight from the 1990s, we can see that there has been a remarkable degree of flexibility to the relationship, with an autonomy for both the Party and the TUC, which far exceeded what might have been expected given their common affiliated organisations and membership. Relationships have varied considerably over time: there have been periods of closeness between the TUC and the Party and periods when their separation was more apparent.

As for the power relationship between the unions and the Party, over time no group exercised complete control. Union policies were a foundation of the Party's long term programme up to 1945. The unions exercised a constraining effect on the Parliamentary leadership and showed after 1931 that they could become more assertive in reaction to the past behaviour of a Labour Government, but it was the Parliamentary leadership *not* the union leadership which normally dominated the policymaking process. They were usually pre-eminent in policy formulation and in the production of the programme and the manifesto. Their initiatives regularly carried majorities on the NEC and at the Party Conference. The Parliamentary Labour Party was an autonomous body and through various formulae and mechanisms it was conceded significant discretion in the implementation of the decisions of the Conference. When the parliamentarians formed a Government – as they did in 1924 and 1929 – they were in a position to implement policies, some of which were disliked by the unions, and to some of which the unions were heavily opposed.

One approach to Wertheimer's puzzle, and certainly one partial explanation of these developments, is to be found by focusing on the Parliamentary Labour Party and relating it to those characteristics of mass party organisation and the rules of British political life which encourage the development of Parliamentary elitism. These features, as they were unveiled in general party terms by Robert Michels,[21] and later in the British context by Robert McKenzie,[22] alert us to some of the features of Labour Party experience which enhanced the position of the Parliamentary leadership. As Wertheimer himself described (although not explained) it, the Parliamentary leadership detached itself from the Party but at the same time they, not the unions, controlled the Party organisation.[23]

Yet, we are left with some problems which are difficult to answer satisfactorily within a frame of reference dominated by this focus on the Parliamentary leadership.

If so many features of the Labour Party implied and facilitated the initiative of the unions and their leadership, why did they not control Labour Party policymaking on a permanent basis? Why did the Parliamentary leadership rather than the unions steer the Party organisation? If the degree of overlap of affiliation and personnel was so great, why was there *any* autonomy in the TUC–Labour Party relationship? In casting block votes in both bodies why did union leaders not command similar policies and strategies in both? Paying both pipers why did they not call identical tunes?

Explaining Wertheimer's puzzle and explaining trade union behaviour is a prerequisite for an understanding of the relationship. What happened in the 1920s involved tensions and conflicts which were still a living force half a century later. And what emerged from this period was a reaffirmation of spheres and a pattern of mainly unwritten rules (see Chapter 2) which were to be permanent constraints on the relationship of the two leadership groups. The starting-point of our exploration of this phenomenon is that syndrome of attitudes which trade unions brought to bear upon the spheres of the industrial and the political – particularly upon the activity of 'politics'.

THE INDUSTRIAL AND THE POLITICAL

Although the unions had a long tradition of political action on industrial issues – a tradition which was to lead eventually to the creation of the Labour Party – as they emerged at the turn of the century, British trade unions also had a deep-rooted ambivalence towards 'politics'. This limited their involvement in and shaped the future character of 'the Movement'.

Fundamental to this ambivalence was a distrust of the state, an adherence to customary rights and a tradition of independence. There was an understandable worry by working class organisations that the state might be turned against them. Self-help, the ideological accompaniment of *laissez-faire*, fitted easily with the self-reliance of organisations created by the spontaneous actions of working men and women.

The freedom to uphold unilateral job control, and subsequently free collective bargaining, developed a sacrosanct value. Threats to it generated political action. Only when the courts intervened to handicap the unions in their industrial activities did frustration at the obstacles to labour representation through the existing parties turn into overwhelming support for an independent party of Labour. Even then, as we shall see, the ambivalence remained.

A New Unionism of unskilled workers had, since the 1880s, broadened the policy agenda and upgraded the use of legal enactment, including support for legislative social welfare reforms. But self-reliance, the freedom to bargain collectively and, by derivation, the preservation of the legal immunity from actions in tort granted in the Trade Disputes Act of 1906 were carried forward as fundamental elements of free trade unionism.

These features had both a Rightwing and a Leftwing interpretation (indeed interpretations which varied union by union) but each fed into the Labour Movement a sense of distance from the political wing and created inhibitions upon too close an involvement with its political processes and activities.

On the Right, this focus on free collective bargaining was accompanied by a suspicion of socialist ideology and political policymaking which outlasted the organisational break with Liberalism and the creation of an independent party of Labour. On the Left, self-reliance fed into support for Syndicalism and 'the big strike' as an industrial and political weapon. The fusion with politics was there but as the fusion took place essentially at the point of production it implied at best a suspicion and often a rejection of conventional Labour Party electoral politics.

This emphasis on the primacy of the industrial/production sphere was reinforced by the British state. From the late eighteenth century, judicial pronouncement and legislation produced a line of regulation in which involvement in politics by trade unions bordered on the illegal or illegitimate, or required a special legitimating procedure. Throughout most of the nineteenth century trade unions feared that their trespass into politics might run foul of hostile courts. In the twentieth century their political activities were demarcated and constrained to a degree unknown by most Labour Movements in Western industrial countries. The right of political action regained under the 1913 Trade Union Act required a special fund and special authorisation by the membership. Participation in the Political Fund was even then conditioned by the individual member's right to 'contract out' (or 'contract in' after the 1927 Act). Wariness of the law and the courts contributed significantly towards an internalisation of the distinctiveness of the spheres.

Trade unionism had another cause for concern about the adoption of political goals and the pursuit of political activity. Industrial unity was often fragile in the face of multiple pressures, some of them brutal. Political involvement widened the potential scope of internal conflict and therefore threatened the basic industrial unity. As a result there has always been a strain in trade unionism which resisted politics simply as a means of self-protection. Anti-politics was in this sense a defence against the most acute form of factionalism.

In the period between the two World Wars this perspective was to be accentuated on the Right of the trade unions as a result of the activities of the Communist Party and its international alliances. Communist groups controlled by the party under democratic centralism heightened trade union factionalism and at one stage they threatened to form alternative Left unions into an alternative national trade union centre. Hostility towards the Communist Party became fused with suspicion of the Left as a whole with its advocacy of 'more politics'. One result was often to reinforce trade union resistance to 'politics' and the tendency to see political campaigning, political education and even political discussion as a potential source of infiltration.

Thus, in summary, while the traditions of self-reliance and the industrial power of the strike produced a confident sense of distance from formal political activity, fear of the courts and of political division and manipulation created a nervous sense of its problems. 'Politics' in this context had a variety of meanings. Sometimes it was socialist ideology, sometimes it was revolutionary separatism, sometimes it was political factionalism, sometimes it was political education and open political campaigning, and sometimes it was simply detailed involvement in the political role played by an independent party of labour. Together the meanings fused into a powerful, if ambiguous, demarcation of spheres which fed into the bloodstream of the Movement and underpinned the values and rules of the union–party relationship.

THE POTENTIAL FOR CONFLICT

The existence of an autonomous Labour Party in Parliament tended to further reinforce the sense of there being a political sphere distinct from the industrial world which was the province of trade unionism. And the development of two distinct centres, the Party and the TUC – the one growing out of the other – seemed to imply the acceptance of two orders and two sets of functions. All of this enhanced the possibility of political and trade union role-playing in a way that accounts for much of the subtlety and flexibility of the relationship. As we shall see (Chapter 2), in an important respect this was to produce a range of understandings which lubricated the relationship. But the different institutions and the sense of different functions also produced problems. If the unions and the Party (including the Parliamentary Party) were indeed to be a Movement in practice as well as aspiration, and to sustain a unified momentum, they had to achieve a substantial harmony or accommodation in four problem areas of the relationship.

There had to be a degree of ideological agreement shared by majorities in the industrial and political leadership. There had to be a degree of agreement on the satisfaction of interests represented by the unions. There had to be an element of social affinity between the leadership groups. And, there had to be a degree of compatibility, and preferably convergent trajectories, to the strategic actions of the Party and the unions.

As the following analysis will illustrate, although in practice there was always enough unity of purpose in each of these dimensions in the first forty years to produce cohesion, there was also enough divergence to engender permanent tensions. Many of the problems facing the unions and the Party after 1959 had been there almost from the inception of the Party. Exploring these as deviations from the ideal of 'the Movement' takes us to the strengths of the relationship – and to its crucial vulnerabilities.

IDEOLOGY

It was a fundamental prerequisite of unity in the Movement and of harmony between the trade union leadership and the political leadership that there be a degree of general ideological agreement on aims and values and that a polarisation of purpose did not surface as a permanent feature of the relationship.

In the first instance such an agreement was deeply rooted in the commitment to Parliamentary democracy and in the perception of the state as a neutral and a potentially beneficial instrument of the community. Agreement was also further grounded initially in a diagnosis of the predicament of labour under existing economic and political arrangements. The minimal agreed solution was that there must be an independent representation of labour to protect and advance its interests in Parliament. Most Socialists went further than this in their diagnosis;

some trade unionists went this far only with trepidation. It was not a fundamental unity of purpose but it resulted in a working procedural agreement.

Potentially after 1918, when the Labour Party adopted a socialist goal and programme, the scope for ideological conflict widened. And indeed a range of new tensions did open up over the Party's policies, sometimes feeding upon major reservations about the limitations of trade unionism which could be found in different traditions in the political wing. However, such was the nature of Labour's Socialism, and such were the priorities of both union and party leaders, that these tensions were manageable without major disruption.

Thus, although the Party changed its formal aims from the pursuit of 'trade union principles and ideals'[24] to the goal of Socialism, defined as 'the common ownership of the means of production' and the 'social economic and political emancipation of the people'[25] these could be interpreted in terms which were fully compatible with 'trade union principles and ideals'. Under the new constitution, the Party was to seek 'the full fruits' of the labour of the producers, it was to seek the most equitable distribution of the products of that labour, and it was to seek a system of 'popular administration and control over each industry and service'.

The overlap of purposes was most strikingly demonstrated in the case of those industries – coal and rail – where the unions' adoption of public ownership to protect the interests of their members could be seen in socialist terms as the first stage of social transformation. But the harmonisation appeared even clearer when social and economic emancipation was defined, as it often was, in the broader terms of state intervention on behalf of collective goals. Socialism was, according to Sidney Webb explaining the 1918 constitution, 'no more specific than a definite repudiation of individualism'.[26] In this sense, public intervention and trade union action appeared to fuse in principle. Collectivism was fundamental to both.

Harmony was further facilitated by the tendency of both the Parliamentary and the union leaders to operate ideologically at two levels. Socialism became increasingly a unifying symbol as an ultimate purpose in the inter-war years. But its meaning was not seriously tested in practice because there was no majority Labour Government and Labour was in Opposition for all but four years of the period from 1918 to 1940. Opposition policy formation in the 1920s was viewed by Labour's leaders in the light of the Party's 1918 Programme and through a practical and studiously moderate disposition which fitted well with the priorities of the trade union majority (see Chapter 2, pp. 40–5).

The most serious ideological conflict took place in the 1930s, not over domestic Socialism but over the difficulties and problems of a socialist defence policy in the face of Fascism. The pacifists in the Party, including the Party's Leader, George Lansbury, refused to agree to any national use of arms. Sections of the Left were also opposed to any national armaments while they were in the hands of the government of a capitalist state. But Clement Attlee and Hugh Dalton in the political wing were assertively joined by TGWU leader Ernest Bevin and TUC Secretary Walter Citrine in pushing that there must be a willingness to use force in defence of collective security, and there must be an end to opposition to national rearmament. By 1937, there was a new unity in the leadership of both wings on this position.

As for domestic policy, in the early 1930s, there was initially a widening disagreement on the extent and form of public ownership and sections of the Party moved closer to the Leftwing critique of capitalism – seeing it as on the verge of collapse. But by 1937, there was compromise and agreement on these policies also. *Labour's Immediate Programme* offered the vision of a planned economy with ameliorative measures of social reform, a nationalisation pro- gramme covering basic industries, particularly coal, iron and steel and transport, and a formula for industrial democracy (but see p. 12).

There was unity also at leadership level in the two wings over attitudes towards the Communist Party. The CP was often a major reference point of internal party factionalism and at times in this period was actively involved in it. Issues relating to Communist Party affiliation, Communist Party membership of the Labour Party and alliances with the Communist Party to fight against Fascism always drew out an antipathy unifying a majority of the PLP and the union leaders.

Thus, although there had been periods of ideological conflict and always a tension with the Left in the Party and the unions, by the late 1930s, at leadership level, there was a high degree of unity on basic domestic and defence positions which to some extent covered over various problem areas.

The greatest danger to the union–Party relationship was that ideological issues would be identified with factional positions which reinforced other con- flicts between the unions and the Party – that, for example, majorities ranged on either side over issues of fundamental interest to trade unionism would take on ideological dimensions. At no stage in the inter-war years did this seem likely if only because of the underlying political weaknesses of the Left in the unions. The Left never made headway sufficient to reorder the priorities of the majority of the unions involved in 'the block vote'. For as long as this was the case, then periodic arguments over nationalisation, socialist pacificism, or fronts against Fascism were all containable.

INTERESTS

Inasmuch as the protection and advancement of labour's industrial interests was the anvil upon which the 'labour alliance' was forged, it was the most basic and unifying purpose of the Labour Party. Labour's potential to act as an effective political instrument of these interests seemed confirmed in 1906 when the unions secured the legislative reversal of the Taff Vale Judgment and with it an immunity from prosecution which protected the facility for industrial action.

It was similar with the reversal of the Osborne Judgment and the promulga- tion of the 1913 Trade Union Act; not a total victory but one enabling the unions to sustain a political role. Again after 1927 the Labour Party's commit- ment to reverse or amend the Trades Disputes and Trade Union Act of 1927 was a strongly unifying commitment – a pledge which protected Labour's future finances as much as the unions' political capability.

However, with the Labour Party forming a Government, its ability and its obligations to advance working class interests – particularly the industrial interests of organised labour – became much more problematic. The Labour Governments of 1924 and 1929–31 found themselves operating within a range of powerful pressures unsympathetic or hostile to the claims of the trade union movement. Minority government itself imposed constraints. Thus, the Labour Cabinet of 1929 authorised the repeal of the 1927 Act then had to abandon it because of Liberal Party opposition. But, in addition, the relationship between the Labour Government and the unions ceased to be that of 'political arm'. Labour Ministers perceived their primary obligation to be the protection of the national interest – a view which always made obligations to class, Movement and unions problematic. This was shown with startling rapidity in 1924 over the handling of tramway, rail and dock strikes. The Government even threatened recourse to the Emergency Powers Act in spite of protestations from the TUC and the Party's Executive Committee.

Overcoming unemployment was another source of conflict. In the case of the 1929 Labour Government it involved a clash of economic perspectives between the Chancellor Philip Snowden (an avowed Socialist but in practice a rigid adherent to orthodox economic policy) and a variety of Labour Movement opponents. Prominent among these was the TGWU General Secretary, Ernest Bevin, an advocate of an expansionary monetary policy and public works to soak up unemployment. Ultimately the argument over policies reached crisis point when, under a variety of political and financial pressures, the Labour Chancellor sought a ten per cent cut in unemployment benefit. The proposal was met with a flat rejection by the TUC and a minority of the Cabinet. The culmination of this dispute – the most traumatic in Labour Party history – was the decision of a small group of Labour Ministers to participate in a National Government under Ramsay MacDonald. An alliance of leading trade unionists and political loyalists then forced their expulsion from the Party.

These industrial disputes and economic policies to counter unemployment indicated two critical points in the relationship. Two further important issues surfaced in the period of Opposition. The tension over industrial democracy and neo-syndicalism was a subtext of much of the argument over political strikes in the early 1920s and in a different form fed into arguments over labour representation on the London Passenger Transport Board during the 1929–31 Government. But it surfaced as an open Party–union discussion only for a period in the early 1930s. Then an attempt by the leadership of the two general unions to commit the Party to trade union representation on the boards of nationalised industries met strong opposition from Herbert Morrison, the ex-Minister of Transport, who favoured Boards supervising management by expert administrators but with final control in the hands of a Minister. On the surface, by 1935, the assertive industrial democrats had won the day and a new unity had been achieved. But it was evident that some of Labour's leaders were strongly opposed, and it was also clear the unions themselves were divided.

One other potential source of conflict – more profound than any of the others in its later consequences for the union–party relationship – surfaced briefly in the inter-war years. Free collective bargaining was a fundamental principle to the majority of affiliated trade unions. It was virtually a closed area of Labour Party policymaking, so deeply rooted was the assumption of its virtue. But *The Living Wage* programme of the ILP in 1926 gave warning of some of the difficulties. For impeccable reasons rooted in the socialist commitment to sustain workers' living standards, the ILP advocated a degree of state intervention in the field of wage bargaining in order to produce a minimum wage. The hostility with which this was met by Bevin and many other union leaders gave notice of the problems which would eventually be in store for a Labour Government if it attempted to intervene in 'a very intricate and involved wage system'[27] and particularly if it tried to 'cut across the unions' functions and drag wages into a political programme'.[28] It gave notice also that for the Left as much as the Right the meshing of socialist principles and what trade unions perceived to be their fundamental interests could be a difficult enterprise.

SOCIAL AFFINITY

The most obvious basis for unity in the Labour Movement was the common condition of labour and the similarities of social background and life experience which it produced. Yet from the first this was also the source of the most subtle and persistent friction in the union–Labour Party relationship.

On the one hand the great majority of trade unionists affiliated to the Labour Party, the majority of individual members after 1918, and the majority of trade union leaders came from manual worker backgrounds. Although their lifestyle was sometimes affected by a rise through the union hierarchy and the movement from the provinces to the capital city, union leaders normally retained social outlooks and attitudes derived from their past experience.

But within the Parliamentary Party, on the other hand, the initial similarity of working class background tended to be diluted as the PLP markedly increased in size. The original preponderance of manual worker trade unionists (23 out of 30 in 1906) first began to shift radically with the rise of the Labour Party after the First World War. In 1922 the sponsored trade union proportion had dropped to 87 out of 142 and by 1929 was 115 out of 288. Some readjustment took place in 1931 when a badly depleted Parliamentary Labour Party was forced back into the trade union heartlands and 32 out of the remaining 46 MPs were manual worker trade unionists. But with the rise of Labour again in 1935 the non-trade union sponsored section again rose and the trade union sponsored MPs were only 80 out of 154.

In the Party's first two decades this distinction between trade union sponsored MPs and others on the Labour benches did not necessarily involve a social class difference. The birth of the Labour Party *had* indeed advanced working class representation. Sponsored MPs were overwhelmingly ex-manual workers but so were a significant proportion of the others. In 1906 all 29 Labour MPs elected on behalf of the LRC were from working class backgrounds. In 1918, 64 per cent of the non-trade union sponsored members also came from working class backgrounds. But these proportions changed radically after 1922. Among the non-union-sponsored MPs the manual working class composition was never more than 38 per cent and as low as 20 per cent in 1931.[29]

At leadership level, the differentiation was enhanced by the diminishing overlap of the two leaderships. In the early days of the Party, significant numbers of union leaders became MPs such that in 1906 eight were or had recently been General Secretaries[30] and there were six members of the Parliamentary Committee of the TUC (later called its General Council) in the PLP[31] The tendency to see union leadership as an employment requiring full-time attention caused a change in this pattern and in 1923 the Secretary of the TUC, previously an MP, was barred from Parliamentary work. By 1935, only three trade union General Secretaries were in Parliament and none of these was from a major union.[32]

This compositional differentiation of leadership was also reflected at Cabinet level in the Labour Governments of 1924 and 1929. There were only seven trade union sponsored MPs in the Cabinet of 20 in 1924 and only six in the Cabinet of 19 in 1929,[33] although Guttsman notes that in both Cabinets approximately half came from working class (or working class organisation) occupations. This under-representation of trade unionists and working class backgrounds has to be seen alongside the fact that no fewer than seven Cabinet Ministers in 1924 and five in 1929 came from aristocratic or upper middle class backgrounds.[34]

From one perspective, the changing character of Labour in Parliament was an enormous asset to the Party. It was unique among major parties in the closeness it came to the national profile of the British people. It brought together valuable but different life experiences. And in the diversity of its profile, it came near to its aspiration of being a people's party of workers by hand and brain.

In practice, however, the growing differences of social background and occupation reinforced by differences of institutional affiliation were also sometimes an aggravation on Labour's benches and between the PLP and trade union leaders. Among the non-trade unionists, anti-provincialism, cultural exclusiveness and intellectual snobbery were not unknown. On the other side, the anti-intellectualism of some trade unionists involved a marked distrust of those who had not drawn their understanding from working class experience.[35] For Bevin particularly middle class intellectuals, brought into the Movement out of 'theory' and 'abstract principles', were generally unreliable, volatile and irresponsible.[36]

The relationship of manual worker trade unionists with 'intellectuals' often involved a complex mixture of deference, curiosity and social resentment. In some circumstances it reinforced the tendency for trade unionists to leave politics to 'the politicians', in others it produced an atmosphere in which manual workers could be pulled into the flattering and domesticating embrace. Its most striking expression to foreign observers was the willingness of manual workers to accept middle and even upper class leadership, but differences of social background were also often the source of a resentful prickliness and deliberate negative characterisation which complicated all political alignments.

Of course, social background was never the only factor influencing a sense of affinity, and these differences could be handled by figures on both sides who placed a high value on preserving mutual respect and seeking united action. Arthur Henderson did it for a long time in the triple offices of trade union official, Party Secretary and Member of Parliament – creating the classic role of 'the link man'. Clement Attlee in building a close relationship with Ernest Bevin did it from the position of Leadership after 1935, proving that for some people perspective and priorities were as much a component of being considered 'a trade union man' as was occupational background.

Yet, if anything, the suspicion of intellectuals *increased* from the trade union side in the 1930s. Ramsay MacDonald, like Sir Oswald Mosley, became the symbol of potential 'intellectual' treachery. The alliance sought by Socialist League leaders led by Cripps with non-Labour political forces indicated to trade union leaders their continued disloyalty, their proneness to twists of fashion and their propensity to break away into new groupings. The rise in constituency membership gave greater opportunity for more of the middle class to make 'naïve' demands. The 1935 General Election result again indicated that any Labour Parliamentary improvement would involve an increase in the presence of the 'intellectuals' on Labour's benches. For all these reasons, the close relationship of Labour and the unions in the 1930s masked considerable social tension.

STRATEGIC CONVERGENCE

Ideological differences, conflicts of interest, and social antipathies found their expression also through the mediation of the fourth major difficulty in the relationship. The existence of two centres – an industrial and a political centre, each with its own definition of function – provided an institutional basis for a variety of union–party conflicts to be expressed. But it also provided a source of tension in its own right. Different institutional interests, different perspectives and different strategies flowed from the different centres. Their institutional development and distinctiveness was of such importance to the union–Party relationship that it requires us to probe deeper at this point.

Let us start with affiliations and the Labour electorate. Initially, in the Party's early years, there was no major problem of divergence. The Party represented both organisationally and electorally the Labour interest, drawing support from heavily unionised areas. And as it built up its union membership in the period before the First World War, so the differences in affiliation levels with those of the TUC became very small.

However, a differentiation in the base of the two organisations began during the First World War and continued thereafter. During the War, TUC membership shot up, widening the difference. Largely as a result of the 1927 Trades Disputes and Trade Union Act it widened also in the late 1920s and early 1930s when TUC membership was falling, but the total of Labour's levypayers was falling faster. The differential increased further in the late 1930s when TUC membership began to rise but Labour's political levypaying membership continued to fall. At the outbreak of war in 1939 there were 4,669,186 members of the TUC but only 2,214,070 trade union members of the Labour Party.

The gap also grew between the level of TUC affiliation and the level of Labour Party support, when the Party began to appeal to the expanded electorate which followed franchise reform in 1918. After 1923, the Labour vote passed and was always greater than the level of TUC affiliation. It rose to a peak of 8,370,417 in 1929 when TUC membership was 3,673,144 and then after the downturn of 1931 it rose to 8,325,491 in 1935 at a time when the TUC's membership was less than three and a half million.

What it meant was that for each institution after the First World War there evolved a base which, though it overlapped, was distinctive enough in composition and development to produce differing obligations and concerns. For the TUC, its constituency was its affiliated membership which always ran wider than the Party's membership. For the Party, its constituency included the narrower base of affiliates but consisted also of its wider electoral support.

However, important as they are (as will be shown later), too much should not be read into these disparities of constituency as a guide to the internal politics of the relationship. For example, it offers us little guidance as to the relative closeness, or to the initiating and dominating forces at work.

The relationship was very close, with the Party the more initiating force, in the early 1920s, at a time when the TUC affiliation was not only substantially wider than that of the Party, but was also greater than the Party's vote. On the other hand the TUC leadership became much more interventionist in the Party's affairs in the 1930s, at a time when the Labour vote was far in excess of TUC affiliation and trade union affiliation to the Labour Party was sinking. The push and pull of these movements at these times was determined fundamentally by political factors *internal* to the relationship, not by what was happening to votes, affiliations and membership.

Nevertheless, the different constituencies and the varying levels of membership were always a background factor influencing the perspectives and sensitivities of the leadership of the two 'wings' and shaping their attitude towards the major strategic alternatives that were faced.

Put simply, the major strategic alternatives were these. The Party, seeking after 1918 to become the Government, required as wide an electoral base as possible. In this process it could stress its class character or its broader appeal. It could stress its closeness to the unions or its distance from them. It could seek to exemplify its 'national' commitment, or its role as the political arm of the Labour Movement.

The unions through the TUC, on the other hand, could seek to further their political representations to the Government of the day, or to emphasise their work with the Party. They could stress and use their industrial strength or emphasise accommodation and negotiation: either of these could involve seeking assistance from the Labour Party or protecting their independence from it.

Thus there was no guarantee that the strategies of the Party and the TUC would involve a mutually agreed priority for the union–party attachment and, as will be shown as we examine the development of each of these institutions, there were always many forces at work ensuring that they would not.

THE LABOUR PARTY

Let us first examine the Party's situation. There were always various features of Labour's origins, commitment and structure which gave the Party an unmistakable electoral identity as the voice of labour in its class and organised industrial expression. But after 1918, other features loosened and broadened Labour's appeal, creating new tensions with its original base.

The class identity now involved important elements of ambiguity as Labour's leaders sought to broaden its appeal. 'The workers by hand or brain' implied a wider constitutency than the manual working class, although just how wide was never clear. It could mean the clerical workers, professionals and small traders, all of which were targeted as part of Labour's appeal to rational progressive forces. And it could and sometimes did have an even wider interpretation. Because 'labour … is the lot of mankind', 'the workers by hand or brain' could include everybody, 'the whole community'. In this breadth of usage, it fitted with the differing meanings of 'the People'. At times 'the People' were defined in a radical populist vocabulary which excluded, for example, 'the idle rich'. But often 'the Community', 'the People' and 'the Nation' were interchangeable.[37] Thus although Labour had its special class appeal it had a wider terminology which was often used to enlarge its appeal to the electorate and it had a non-'sectional' identity which turned into a defence of the national interest when Labour was in Office.

This class appeal was further diluted by an ideological approach to the Movement which saw it as 'a movement of opinion', not of a class. As we have seen, until 1922 trade union membership was wider than Labour Party electoral support. From this, political leaders like MacDonald always noted the lesson that class did not guarantee opinion: Labour had to make its appeal wider than the organised producers and to do so on the basis of principles rather than interests.

> The future of the Labour Party is to be determined by its success in making its principles clear to itself and the country. If it narrows itself to a class movement or a trade movement, it will weaken and finally disappear.[38]

The political arm also had distinctive methods. Labour's political leaders throughout the inter-war years after 1923 were at pains to argue not only that parties and unions had different representative obligations but different disciplines and different techniques. The Labour Party was heavily committed to the procedures and norms of Parliamentary democracy, to its tactical exigencies and to its immediate electoral preoccupations.

In these preoccupations strikes were usually unwelcome. It was more than simply a matter of rejecting class struggle as a weapon of political advance or opposing industrial action to bring down an elected Government. Strikes might be an essential element in industrial freedom and occasionally warranted and necessary for industrial purposes, but they always entailed sacrifice and hurt, they exacerbated the emotions involved and they were 'a nuisance to the community'.[39] As such, they could have the effect of rebounding on the political wing.[40]

Some of Labour's leaders (Keir Hardie, pre war, and at times Arthur Henderson after it) were more receptive than others to the need for industrial action. And on the Left of the Party, a very different perspective was evident. Strikes were seen as an opportunity to show solidarity but they were also seen as having potentially advantageous consequences. They were not only an affirmation of Labour's unwillingness to accept subordination, they provided a milieu in which workers could educate themselves about their position in society. Strikes were therefore a crucial means of raising political consciousness and broadening the political base. Thus, in the way the Parliamentary Party handled industrial disputes, there was often a deep-rooted conflict of perspectives, further complicated by union suspicion of political 'interference' (see Chapter Two, p. 28 and p. 38).

In the event, after 1926, with union membership and strength undermined in conditions of mass unemployment, large-scale strikes were not a pressing issue. Thirty years later they were to emerge with growing and increasingly problematic significance.

Labour's leadership also saw it in the Party's electoral interests, as well as an obligation for the Party, to stress its constitutionalism and, especially under MacDonald, to stress its 'fitness to rule'. For this perspective, a majority of the union leaders had much sympathy but it produced immediate problems for them once Labour took Office. In 1924, their expectation that their links with the Party would ensure a much greater degree of access and consultation than they had known from previous governments was to be sadly disappointed. Many things followed from this experience of 1924, but in institutional terms the most important was that the Labour Government dealt a significant blow at the most serious attempt in the history of the Labour Movement to create a more structurally unified movement. We can examine this critical experience as we now follow through the development of the TUC.

THE TUC

The TUC may have been the mother of the Labour Party, but the remarkable thing was that in its early days it was the parent body that nearly passed into oblivion. Since the creation of the political wing there had been repeated attempts – particularly from the Party side – to deal with the overlap of activities and the separation of institutions.[41] In the pre-1914 period it was the infant Party which, in colonising TUC functions, threatened to render its Parliamentary Committee obsolete and to cause the Congress itself to 'fizzle out'.[42] The existence of a General Federation of Trade Unions dealing purely with industrial matters added to the pressure on the TUC and to the uncertainties of its role.

Although it was recognised by leaders of the Labour Party as much as by leaders of the TUC that complete amalgamation or fusion was probably impracticable, there was a continuing belief after 1918 that it was in the best interests of the Movement that there should be more cohesion and if possible a unified central body. Labour's Secretary, Arthur Henderson, and the London Labour Leader, Herbert Morrison, were both impressed with the organisation and methods of the German SPD and saw the advantages of creating joint institutions, cultural auxiliaries and an ethos in which the Movement developed a widening industrial and political base. 'One Movement' rather than two seemed the essential prerequisite. In the industrial circumstances following the First World War they were able for a time to make remarkable headway.[43]

Henderson, an ex-Cabinet member of the Coalition Government and the most senior figure of the Labour Movement, was at the height of his influence as Secretary of the Party. Following the Rail Strike of 1919 the Parliamentary Committee of the TUC appeared to many to be an inadequate instrument for co-ordinating industrial action. It was widely believed that the Movement as a whole needed a greater unity of its two wings and a General Staff on the TUC side to organise its activities. On the Coordinating Committee which set up the new General Council of the TUC, Henderson was able to take advantage of the mood to propose and secure for the first time joint services and supervisory committees between the two centres.

It was a difficult project for the TUC to resist in the circumstances of the time. Joint Press and Publicity, Research and International departments were set up in Eccleston Square and were supervised by joint committees of the Executive of the Party and of the TUC. It was intended, in Henderson's words, 'to make the political and the industrial not two separate movements, but in a real sense two sides of the one movement'.[44]

This unity of the two sides was reflected in other ways which crossed future boundaries of the industrial and the political. The National Joint Council, set up in 1921, which had joint representation from the Party and the TUC, began to play a more wide-ranging role covering both political and industrial isues – including industrial disputes.[45] At local level, amalgamations took place of Labour parties and Trades Councils. And the General Election Manifesto of 1923 went for final approval to a joint meeting of the Party EC, the General Council and the EC of the Parliamentary Committee.[46] There was even an attempt to link the agendas of the TUC and the Party Conference.[47]

But this experiment – a move of potentially historic institutional importance – eventually floundered.

It always faced a range of practical difficulties. Nationally, the TUC was finding a number of administrative problems related to costs, ineffectual supervision under the unified arrangements and salary anomalies; there were difficulties also in combining administrative posts with Parliamentary representation. Locally, there was a growing problem of loss of control and the dangers of penetration; a fusion of local Labour parties and trades councils produced considerable jurisdictional tension and the TUC grew anxious about the intervention of Labour Party, ILP and Communist Party activists in industrial matters.

These strains would almost certainly have led to some re-evaluation of the existing arrangements on the part of the TUC but this re-evaluation became more pressing as a consequence of the experience of the 1924 Labour Government. W.J. Brown of the Civil Service Clerical Association encapsulated most clearly what was eventually to be seen as the key lesson of that experience. As he told the TUC in 1925, the general assumption had been that a Labour Cabinet 'would automatically apply the policy of the TUC in industrial matters'. But they had learned that

> there would be a permanent difference in point of view between that
> Government on the one hand and the Trade Unions on the other: and that
> difference in point of view did not arise from any wickedness on the part of
> the political side, or on the part of the industrial side, but arose from the
> fact that the Trade Unions had different functions to perform than the
> functions of Government ...[48]

Not everybody accepted this diagnosis (see Chapter Two, n. 96) nor was everybody privately convinced that there was a lack of culpability on the part of the Government. Although, as was to be the case with all future Labour Govern-

ments, the TUC endeavoured to contain public criticism, there was a concealed
resentment within the TUC (which was to show itself in the discussions after
1931) about Ministerial reluctance to use the National Joint Council and the
impression given by them 'that consultation with the General Council was in
some sense unconstitutional, unnecessary, or even undesirable'.[49]

In these circumstances, the TUC began to consider other alternatives. In
theory, these alternatives included moving into the Labour Party with greater
assertiveness and purpose so as to establish control over the Labour Party leadership. Yet this was the crucial point in history where a decisive turn was made. Just
as the unions had failed to threaten, let alone activate, party sanctions against an
unresponsive Labour Government (one joint resolution of the TUC and the Party
EC, deploring the threat of emergency powers, was the furthest they moved), so
the union leaders after 1924 moved to the development of the TUC's own structure rather than intervene further in the political wing.

The fact was that there were always elements within the TUC which had
reservations about Henderson's venture with its compromise of the TUC's distinctive character. The belief was that there should be 'a clear delineation of the
political and industrial forces'[50] nationally and internationally. A key figure in
the expanding TUC bureaucracy was Walter Citrine, Assistant Secretary in 1923,
then Acting Secretary from October 1925 to September 1926 when he succeeded
Fred Bramley. Citrine was an innovative leader in the functional reorganisation
of departments, committees and sub-committees which had developed *ad hoc* and
rapidly over the post-war period.

In this process the concern for independent trade union action, which had
been only a sub-theme during the inauguration of joint activity, now became
more strongly articulated. In arguing his case to the 1925 TUC for the ending of
the joint arrangements, Fred Bramley laid out a menu of independent activity
that the TUC was either involved in or was planning: intervention in industrial
disputes, special campaigns, unified educational work and assistance in recruitment. Such activities were 'too big, too various and too distinctly Trade Union to
make it possible for them to be developed as one half of joint departments'.[51] In
April 1926, the two institutions disengaged – apart from a library, a telephonist
and the National Joint Council.

All this pre-dated the General Strike, which in its consequences severely
weakened the trade unions and undermined for many years the appeal of large-
scale militant industrial action. In its place the leadership of the TUC began to
fashion elements of an alternative strategy. Industrially, it involved a new appreciation of the economic gains which could be achieved through rationalisation,
amalgamation and techniques of mass production. There appeared to be immediate benefits to be gained from collective bargaining and accommodation with
the employers in improving this production. The Mond–Turner talks of 1927
signalled the TUC's attempt to engage in a new era of industrial co-operation.

Politically, in the 1930s, the TUC began to look once again towards the
expansion of its direct links with the Government of the day and to broadening
its involvement into the wider economic context of industrial relations – the
fields of economic policy and industrial administration. This was seen as part of a

wider process of democratic involvement. At its most sophisticated – in the writings of the TUC official Milne Bailey – it envisaged an anglicised version of the corporate state with the Government consulting and negotiating with a plurality of independent organisations which would include the unions.[52]

This conception of a pluralistic democracy –a view which became integral to the values and tactics of TUC officials – was seen as the natural product of social and economic development with its growth of a multiplicity of specialised institutions each with its own domain and function. Where Henderson had a vision of 'One Movement' uniting the industrial and the political, Milne Bailey saw only an inevitable functional differentiation. The complexity of industrial civilisation had 'abolished the simple conception of an "omnibus" association which could express all the diverse forms of human fellowship'.[53] The Movement must always be different Movements. The industrial and the political must in this sense always be distinct.

Large trade unions growing now through amalgamations into complex bureaucracies were making more and more demands on the time and energy and expertise of trade union leaders. Less and less could they take on other occupational duties and increasingly they tended to move out of the Parliamentary arena. The departure of the multifunctional Henderson was in a sense the departure of the multifunctional union leader. The 'days of advocacy', as Bevin put it, had turned into 'the day of administration'.[54]

Outside the Parliamentary arena by the 1930s a new role was being envisaged for the central institutions of industrial labour and for the union leadership. Economic planning was being widely accepted by a consensus of intellectual opinion as a means of overcoming unemployment. Whatever the differences in the way that the future society was envisaged in ideological terms it was agreed that the trade unions through the TUC had a crucial place in a national structure of consultative planning based upon functional groupings.

Thus, on one level the 1930s was a period when the unions moved into renewed commitment to the Labour Party: on another level, the ground was already being prepared for a functional pluralism and tripartite planning in which the unions and the Party would to some extent go their own ways.

So it was that although the TUC moved in with the Labour Party at the Transport Workers' new Headquarters, Transport House, in 1927, they were already showing signs of separateness and of a fastidiousness with regard to the protocol of the relationship. This was made clear in relation to fraternal delegates during the joint meeting held with the Labour Party in 1927 to discuss the Trades Disputes and Trade Union Act.[55] Between 1927 and 1930, the TUC made clear its annoyance at any activities within the political wing which it considered to be a usurpation of trade union functions or a venture into trade union affairs.[56]

Slowly, after 1931, the TUC's links to Government began to grow.[57] Though the National Government was not sympathetic to giving the unions a consultative voice in overall economic policymaking, as it became more interventionist, so the TUC's presence on Government bodies, delegations and committees of enquiry began gradually to expand. 'Opposite number' relationships began to grow between the TUC bureaucracy and Government civil servants.[58] A symbol of mutual acceptance was that in 1935 the first trade union knights were created – Sir Walter Citrine and Sir Arthur Pugh.[59] In March 1938, for the first time since 1926, rearmament and the possibility of war once more saw the Prime Minister and the General Council in direct discussion. It was not considered very satisfactory but was welcomed by Citrine. 'The trade union movement', he had said in 1935, 'cannot base its fortunes on one political party.'[60] And, as Bevin recognised, a trade union leader could not confine himself to opposition.[61]

HARMONY AND THE POTENTIALITY FOR CRISIS

Thus, the union–Labour Party relationship was never easy, from the inception of the two wings. Attempts at structural unity were undermined by a range of problems. The management of its ideological, interest-based, social and strategic tensions was always difficult. Ideological problems mattered less than might be thought, given the priorities which underpinned the pattern of factional power, but they were often a feature. Social tensions were ever-present although never of themselves the precipitating cause of major conflict. It was the reconciliation of trade union interests with the policies pursued by the Labour Government and the existence of an alternative neo-corporatist strategy adopted by the TUC bureaucracy which created the most important sources of discord – the one because of the conflict it produced, the other because of the distance and divergence it could involve in Opposition.

Almost all the difficulties which were to appear in acute form in the decades after 1959 were prefigured in this earlier phase – particularly the period from 1924 to 1931. The union–Party relationship at national level always had major problems of sustaining itself as 'a Movement' and there was always the potentiality for crisis.

Much depended on how far the dimensions of conflict reinforced each other and upon how far the leadership of either the Party or the unions were prepared to push a problem at the cost of fundamental division in the Movement. As we have seen, there was not always an easy accommodation, especially in periods when Labour was in Government, but even this experience could be built on in attempting to avoid future conflicts. Managing these potential problems was in part a matter of leadership skill but in great measure it was aided by a range of understandings which produced a framework of mutual restraint. By the 1930s, this restraint was deeply rooted in the ethos of the Party. As we further explore Wertheimer's puzzle, it is the source and form of this restraint that we must now examine.

NOTES

1. *Labour Party Annual Conference Report* (hereafter *LPACR*), 1935, p. 180.
2. Speeches of the fraternal delegates from the TUC to the Labour Party, *LPACR*, 1949, p. 163, a reference by Will Lawther to 'Cain and Abel' and *LPACR*, 1962, p. 153, a reference by Dame Anne Godwin to 'a ball

and chain'.

3. Bill Keys of SOGAT to the author in February 1987.

4. The allusions to parent (usually mother) and child are too numerous to specify but typical of them is Arthur Henderson's fraternal speech to the TUC on behalf of the Labour Party when he referred to the Labour Party as 'the youngest and most innocent and most independent child' of the Congress, *TUC Congress Report*, 1907, p. 177. W.J. Davis, in his Presidential Address to the TUC in 1913, noted that, 'Our Congress is the mother of the greater Labour Movement', *TUC Congress Report*, 1913, p. 56. Fraternal speeches to the TUC and the Labour Party from the earliest days were littered with family references and conceptions of Labour Movement history in terms of family development, 'youngest offspring', 'latest addition to the family', 'parental home', 'filial greetings', etc.

5. J. Compton, Labour Party fraternal delegate to the TUC, 1930, *TUC Congress Report*, 1930, p. 351.

6. Francis Williams, *Fifty Years March*, 1949, p. 284.

7. 'Quarrels are not unknown in family life, but there would not be much left of family life or of our social structure if every quarrel led to separation or divorce', Jack Tanner, fraternal delegate from the TUC, *LPACR*, 1954, p. 90.

8. Jack Jones's speech to a Fabian Society meeting, October 1981, quoted in Panitch, *op. cit.*, p. 258.

9. Reported in *The Observer*, 1/12/85.

10. The proportions have, however, changed over time. On this see Chapter 10, pp. 280–1.

11. Initially, the unions held only seven of the twelve seats. In 1902, the unions took over two seats from the defecting Social Democratic Federation plus one seat from the Trades Councils. In 1918, the unions and socialist societies were given thirteen seats, the local Labour Parties five and women four, and there was an elected Treasurer as before. But from 1918 there were no separate voting sections, so in practice until 1937 the union majority decided all positions.

12. 1918 Constitution, Clause 3(b).

13. 1924 Constitition, Clause 2.

14. J. Fagan (Edinburgh and District Labour Party), *LPACR*, 1924, p. 153.

15. C. R. Attlee, *The Labour Party in Perspective*, 1937, pp. 13–14.

16. Sidney Webb, *The New Constitution of the Labour Party*, 1918, 'The Labour Party of the future, in short, is to be a Party of the producers', p. 3.

17. Information on women's issues supplied by Sarah Perrigo from her manuscript of *Women in the Labour Party*. For union attitudes, see Sarah Boston, *Women Workers and the Trade Unions*, 1980.

18. *Labour's Call to the People*, 1918.

19. D. E. McHenry, *The Labour Party in Transition 1931–1938*, 1938, pp. 304–5.

20. Egon Wertheimer, *Portrait of the Labour Party*, 1929, p. 8. On Page 1, Wertheimer notes that 'the relationship is so close that nothing can receive the slightest blow without its effect being felt by both'.

21. Robert Michels, *Political Parties*, 1911.

22. Robert McKenzie, *British Political Parties*, 1955. For a critique of his view of inevitable dominance by the Parliamentary leadership, see L. Minkin, *The Labour Party Conference*, *op. cit.*

23. Wertheimer, *op. cit.*, pp. 8–9.

24. *LRC Report*, 1900, pp. 11–12.

25. Clause 3(d) of the 1918 Constitution. In 1929, this Clause was renumbered Clause IV(4) and 'distribution and exchange' were added to its common ownership aims.

26. Webb, *op. cit.*, p. 3.

27. Ernest Bevin, *LPACR*, 1929, p. 161.

28. Alan Bullock, *The Life and Times of Ernest Bevin*, Vol. I, 1960, p. 390. The National Joint Council view was that 'The formulation of such a policy involves considerations with which the political Labour Movement, as such, is not concerned', *NJC*, 27/2/27, Appendix II. The TUC, it must be noted, also rejected the accompanying family allowances proposal for fear that it would be used to reduce wages. Hugh Armstrong Clegg, *A History of British Trade Unions Since 1889*, Vol. II, 1985, p. 476. See also Geoffrey Foote, *The Labour Party's Political Thought: A History*, 1985, pp. 132–5.

29. W. L. Guttsman, *The British Political Elite*, 1963, pp. 226, 227 and 238.

30. David E. Martin, 'The Instruments of the People?: The Parliamentary Labour Party in 1906', in David Martin and David Rubinstein, *Ideology and the Labour Movement*, 1979, p. 127.

31. Muller, *op. cit.*, p. 4. Three other MPs on the Parliamentary Committee were 'Lib-Labs'.

32. W. Broomfield (Leek) from the Assistant Textile Workers, Arthur Hollins (Hanley) from the Pottery Workers, and George Isaacs (N. Southwark) from NATSOPA.

33. V. L. Allen, *Trade Unions and the Government*, 1960, p. 225.

34. Guttsman, *op. cit.*, p. 242.

35. Bullock, *op. cit.*, p. 255.

36. *Ibid.*, pp. 531–2 for Bevin's view.

37. These formulations are taken from the 1918 Constitution, the Manifestos and Programmes of the Labour Party in the inter-war years and Sidney Webb, *The New Constitution of the Labour Party*, 1918. See also Stuart Macintyre, *A Proletarian Science: Marxism in Britain 1917–1933*, 1980, pp. 174–7.

38. Ramsay MacDonald, cited in Theodore Rothstein, *From Chartism to Labourism*, 1983, p. 290.

39. J. R. Clynes, cited in Ralph Miliband, *Parliamentary Socialism*, 1972, p. 38.

40. See on this Herbert Tracey (ed.), *The Book of the Labour Party*, Vol. I, 1925, pp. 3, 37 and 91.

41. On this, see particularly Ross Martin, *TUC: The Growth of a Pressure Group 1868–1976*, 1980, Chapter 5, pp. 113–127.

42. Keir Hardie, *TUC Congress Report*, 1911, p. 94. At the 1911 Congress, a motion calling for a central body uniting the TUC and the Labour Party was carried on a show of hands, *TUC Congress Report*, 1911, p. 256. Little came of this.

43. This important experience is well covered in Vic Allen, *The Sociology of Industrial Relations*, 1971, pp. 176–81; Martin, *op. cit.*, pp. 183–91; and in Ross McKibbon, *The Evolution of the Labour Party 1910–24*, 1974, pp. 245–6.

44. Quoted in Martin, *op. cit.*, p. 185.

45. During the Engineers lock-out of 1922, the NJC met union representatives at the House of Commons and Henderson, on behalf of the NJC,

offered the services of the Council as a mediation committee. This was accepted, but with the proviso that all negotiations be conducted by the unions concerned, *NJC*, 9/3/22. The NJC later offered mediation in a shipyard dispute.

46. At a joint meeting of the Party EC, the General Council of the TUC and the Parliamentary Committee, the Party's Election Manifesto 'was circulated, read, discussed, amended and finally approved', *Minutes of Joint Meeting*, 16/11/23.

47. The peak of attempts at fusion came in September 1923 when Labour's EC suggested that the Congress and the Conference be held on consecutive dates with the agendas structured to discuss purely industrial and purely political issues, *Minutes of Joint Meeting of the Party EC, General Council and Parliamentary Committee*, 27/9/23. At a further joint meeting on 1/11/23, the TUC turned the suggestion down.

48. *TUC Congress Report*, 1925, pp. 363–4.

49. *TUC Memo to National Joint Council*, 2/1/32, p. 5.

50. *TUC Congress Report*, 1923, p. 81. The reason given for non-affiliation to the Labour and Socialist International.

51. *TUC Congress Report*, 1925, p. 359.

52. W. Milne-Bailey, *Trade Union and the State*, 1934. Milne-Bailey died in 1936 and was succeeded by George Woodcock as Secretary of Research and Economic Department.

53. Milne-Bailey, *op. cit.*, p. 94.

54. Bullock, *op. cit.*, p. 600.

55. The exchange of fraternal delegates which began in the years of the LRC was discontinued during the One Movement phase. At a joint meeting in 1927 it was suggested that the practice be reinstated 'in view of the special circumstances' of the Trades Disputes and Trade Union Bill. The two sides met separately to discuss the suggestion as it was made clear that the joint meeting could not discuss procedure affecting the TUC, *NJC*, 27/7/27.

56. Among issues brought before the NJC were 'the general question of Parliamentary members and candidates speaking against trade unionism' – this a reference to a speech by Emanuel Shinwell, *Joint Meeting of the EC of the Labour Party and the General Council*, 27/3/29. There was a strong complaint later that year that work undertaken by Labour Party Secretary/Agents, MPs, Councillors and candidates on behalf of unorganised workers was militating against trade union organisation, *Joint Meeting of the EC of the Labour Party, General Council and Consultative Committee of the PLP*, 27/11/29.

57. V. L. Allen, *Trade Unions and the Government, op. cit.*, pp. 32–4, notes that the TUC was represented on only one Government committee in 1931. By 1938, this had risen to twelve.

58. Martin, *op. cit.*, p. 238.

59. *Ibid.*, p. 209.

60. *Ibid.*, p. 232.

61. Bullock, *op. cit.*, pp. 599–600.

2

Regulation

Restraint has been the central characteristic of the trade union–Labour Party relationship. Its most important expression was the way in which trade union leaders focused and limited their activities within the Labour Party, sometimes to the extent of facilitating significant differences between the policy of the Party and the policy of the TUC. On the surface, such differences appeared highly improbable, given the dominant position of the unions in both. As Clement Attlee put it, writing in the 1930s:

> It might be, and indeed, sometimes is, thought that Trade Union opinion must be dominant throughout.

However, as he continued:

> This is to ignore the effect on the mind of the man of the sphere in which he is operating. Men are necessarily influenced in their attitude by the particular function which they are engaged in performing.[1]

In this perception of functions and spheres and in this playing of different roles in the different spheres lay the answer to the puzzle posed by Wertheimer (Chapter 1, pp. 5–7). Those forces which operated upon, and within, the Labour Party, which moved it towards oligarchical dominance (independence combined with control over the Party) by the MacDonald Leadership, fitted into predispositions, precedents and behaviour patterns already evident in the way many union leaders related to the Party. These facilitated the power of the MacDonald Leadership rather than stimulating a direct challenge to it and seeking to bring it under a tight procedural grip.

More, what developed in the late 1920s and early 1930s was neither the divorce of the unions from the Party that disappointed them, nor an active controlling supremacy over its levers of power. There was first a renewed differentiation of functions between the Party and the TUC, and then a renewal of co-ordination. This co-ordination involves the rebuilding of an important bridging committee acting within a pattern of mutual restraint. What is central to this whole period is not any sharp break in union behaviour patterns, one way or another, but the clarification and reinforcement of many of the understandings, obligations and prudential guidelines which regulated the relationship – in effect its 'rules'.

These 'rules' were never brought together in a document. They were only occasionally stipulated as agreements and only rarely given constitutional status. There was, as with all unwritten rules, a degree of looseness and uncertainty, and the usual 'do not be seen' and 'do not get caught' subtext on territorial matters. They were essentially the legacy of the Right rather than the Left in the unions. Nevertheless, it is impossible to understand the trade union–Labour Party relationship (and much else about the Labour Movement) without understanding the powerful and long-lasting restraints produced by adherence to these 'rules'.

Their development within the relationship was, in the main, an organic process, arising from fundamental values of trade unionism and from an industrial experience which included unwritten understandings and a strong sense of the protocol of rule-governed behaviour. The mode of management of the relationship by unwritten rules was equally acceptable to the Parliamentary arm because it harmonised with the style of British Parliamentary democracy. Here, also on a limited base of legislative procedural laws, had been built a flexible and complex superstructure of unwritten conventions often involving discreet and subtle role-playing.

Within the union–Labour Party relationship, the role-playing, the 'rules' and the protocol which went with them produced a syndrome of inhibition and self-control which was the most remarkable feature of a relationship in which all the potential levers of power appeared to lie in the hands of the unions. But they also provided a network of mutual restraint specifying obligations which were a duty on both sides of the relationship.

To understand and delineate these 'rules', we have to see them in terms of their derivation from the trade union values of freedom, democracy, unity and solidarity,[2] and in relation to the operative principle of trade unionism – priority. Each will now be examined.

FREEDOM

If there was a primary value to British trade unionism it was industrial freedom. Trade union organisation was labour's means of contesting the subordination of its position as employee and countering the commanding power of management. Collective organisation afforded both a deterrent and a protection. Through their collective capacity, the liberty of the individual worker was enhanced vis-à-vis the employer. Through the collective, workers increased their control over the work environment. Through the collective, workers advanced living standards without which a simple 'absence of restraint' was often the freedom to go without, to grow sick or to starve.

This view of freedom as collective capacity involved minimising impediments to the operation of the industrial collective, whether they were external or internal to the organisation. By its nature, this involved restricting individual rights in relation to the collective (albeit a democratic collective (pp. 32–5)). Whatever libertarian views trade unionists might hold about individual rights in a wider social and political sphere, they recognised the necessity for the individual *in industrial life* to accept some diminution of choice in one relationship in order to enhance it in another.

Thus trade unionism stressed the need for maximum membership as opposed to the free rider. It stressed the rights of the striking majority against those of 'the blackleg'. It stressed the rights of the union picket to persuade rather than the right of the individual to pass unmolested. And it was unhappy at conceding individual rights of 'contracting out' of the political levy – what the union did with its funds was a matter for majority decision-taking through normal procedures.

These views on collective freedom in the industrial sphere became integral to the Labour Movement; generally accepted by the political leadership of the 1930s[3] but also resolutely protected by the unions. Freedom having been secured, at times tenuously secured, in the face of hostility from employers, the judiciary and, on occasion, the Government and legislature, it was guarded against threats or incursions from *any* source. Thus, in a Party committed to defending the union capacity to organise, bargain, regulate and activate industrial sanctions against employers, it was outside permissible bounds – a basic 'rule' of the relationship – that the Party should restrict what it had been created to protect. Industrial freedom, including legal immunities, became in a sense a 'closed' area of Party policymaking. When, in 1924, the Labour Government sought to activate the Emergency Powers Act to deal with industrial disputes, some union leaders did acknowledge the special responsibility of Government – an acknowledgement which was to grow over time – but the majority reacted angrily. It was made clear that even under a Labour Government, there must be 'complete liberty in regard to strike policy'.[4]

The protection of freedom went even further, to an extent which both Left and Right in the political wing were always to find frustrating. It was made clear that the organisation and conduct of industrial disputes was a matter for the individual union concerned and that union alone. Thus, in the late 1920s, there was growing union resistance at national level to intervention by Labour Party constituency activists, as well as to Communist Party involvement in industrial disputes.[5] Similarly, there was a sharp response to any statements of Labour leaders made in relation to an industrial dispute without the agreement of the union concerned 'as to the line to be taken'.[6] This prohibition against interventions stretched even to a reluctance on the part of unions to involve MPs – even sponsored MPs – in disputes[7] – for fear of loss of control, political interference or clumsy meddling. When, in 1926, CLPs called for 'closer working arrangements' with 'Parliamentary and Local Government representatives over disputes', the TGWU reacted sharply, pointing out that while 'cooperation' was 'welcome', 'the direction and scope of the strike' must continue to be under the control of the unions.[8]

There was a second facet to trade union freedom, which was to have a major shaping effect on the 'rules' of the relationship. Freedom involved autonomy as well as collective capacity. Trade unions had been created by working people without assistance from party or state. Their governmental processes were shaped by distinctive traditions and particular circumstances and they reacted strongly to anybody – within the Labour Movement or outside it – attempting to 'interfere' in their internal affairs. 'Interference' meant, in particular, attempts at regulation but it also involved other political intrusions (see p. 38).

It became of fundamental importance for the future of the Labour Movement that in the mid-1920s, with the ending of the structurally unified relationship, this defence of trade union autonomy became extended to the integrity of the TUC as a distinctive body. Experience of One Movement reinforced the determination to safeguard its distinct function. Above all, the TUC claimed the right to make representation to the Government and to be consulted by Government, regardless of its political complexion, on behalf of the TUC's own constituency – whatever its political allegiance.

Once asserted, this autonomy worked with the grain of structural and financial arrangements. The TUC had no constitutional obligations to the Labour Party. It raised no money from the Labour Party and concern over legal restrictions led it to take great care from the late 1920s that none of its finances could be said to be used for Party purposes. It developed, as we have seen, its own bureaucracy, its own neo-corporatist philosophy – and its own political interests. Autonomy for the TUC became as jealously guarded from the Party as was the autonomy of member unions.

As for the Labour Party, it developed a large measure of autonomy from the TUC – an autonomy which in subtle and complicated ways also placed limitations on the party activity of senior leaders of affiliated unions. The groundwork here was laid down early in the relationship in the TUC's acceptance that the Party had distinctive functions and required the necessary freedom to exercise its own discretion.

Thus, in 1904, the TUC had agreed, in effect, that all questions relating to Party electoral organisation should be left in the hands of the new Labour Representation Committee.[9] Once the LRC became the Labour Party (in 1906), its union majority entertained no suggestion that its programme and policy should be decided by the TUC.[10] At the 1908 Party Conference, a large majority of the trade unions voted to prohibit members of the TUC Parliamentary Committee (later the General Council) from sitting on the Party Executive[11] – a prohibition carried forward in 1918[12] and preserved to this day. All this exemplified a view of roles and duties in which the Labour Party had special functions and responsibilities. In terms of winning a majority, the politicians should be left to 'get on with their job'.[13]

Thus, some of the attitudes which shaped the TUC's response to the problems of 1924 (Chapter 1, pp. 19–20) were already established in the 'rules' and role-playing of the relationship, facilitating both the autonomy of the Parliamentary Leadership and its control over the Party.

There were always some complications to these arrangements, given that union officials on Labour's National Executive were, within their unions, often subordinate to a General Council member. And on issues crucial to the interests of the union it was expected that those interests would be protected on Labour's NEC. But the situation in policymaking was eased by the growing acceptance that the Parliamentary Leadership should receive loyal support for their initiatives (on this, see pp. 36–7). And, most important, a mixture of role-playing defensiveness and status protectiveness provided NEC trade unionists with a measure of insulation as the administrators of the Party. This insulation was reflected in the

agendas of the annual Party Conference. Apart from supportive motions attempting to encourage financial assistance to expand the Party's election effort, unions
rarely submitted resolutions on Party organisational matters.[14]

This acceptance of Party autonomy was to have another crucial consequence.
It became accepted as a 'rule' of the relationship – a rule adhered to with
remarkable consistency in 1924 and 1929 – that neither the affiliated unions nor
the TUC could utilise Party sanctions against a Labour Government in order to
bring it in line with the Movement. A wide variety of such sanctions were
potentially available as a result of the unions' formal dominance of the Party's
organisation and financial resources. As far as is known, none was even threatened, let alone activated. Concern over possible accusations of 'unconstitutionality' (see p. 32) were heavily reinforced by a deepening sense of the
autonomy of the Party and of the TUC. The Party could not be used in this way
without (at least by implication) compromising the TUC to a degree that was
unacceptable.

This respect for the 'territory' of autonomous organisation with distinctive
functions, together with a conscious self-restraint in the use of potential levers of
power, was to become a key feature in the development of the relationship
through critical experiences of the inter-war years.

In terms of the autonomy of the Party, a testing time came after 1931 when
TUC leaders, for a period, appeared to threaten the developing understanding as
they sought to reinvigorate the National Joint Council (later the National
Council of Labour) as a means of ensuring that 'the Labour Movement would
swing in better alignment'.[15] For a period the union leaders also appeared to
reverse the pattern in which the Parliamentary leaders dominated policy initiatives. It was a sharp indication that the unions could not be taken for granted,
and a lasting reminder that the relationships within the Movement had a substantial degree of flexibility. The behaviour of the TUC and union leaders at this
time provides a crucial episode which merits close attention as much for the
limitations of the new arrangement as for the noticeable assertiveness.

There is no doubt that this development involved for a period a major shift of
initiative and power. But it must also be noted that the new arrangements
retained restrictive assumptions about the different spheres and obligations of the
industrial and the political and the autonomy of the two sets of institutions.

The new TUC involvement in the NJC alongside representatives from the NEC
and PLP and the redefinition of its function were only initiated after a legitimating
invitation from the Labour Party Secretary. And they were only pursued after an
elaborate exploration of the distinctive duties of the participants and the assertion of their 'individuality' as industrial and political organisations. The prevention of overlapping activities, and the preservation of autonomous operations,
were, for a time, almost as much a preoccupation as the attempt at cohesion.

It was a complicated business. The TUC asserted its right – as it had done in the
past – to initiate and participate in any political matters of direct concern to its
constituents.[16] And the 'reciprocal side of this question' was that the TUC could
not reasonably object to 'large and important industrial questions' being brought
under review on the initiative of Labour Party representatives.[17]

However, as before, the 'domestic' (i.e. internal) matters of either side were *not* to be part of the operation of the NJC.[18] Further, it was agreed that there were 'matters upon which it will be necessary to preserve a definite Trade Union or Labour Party point of view'. And there would be occasions when either the General Council or the Party Executive would not be able to commit themselves.[19] Two years later the NJC declared again that 'in separate spheres the ... bodies were charged with their own distinctive duties and each must shoulder its own responsibilities'.[20]

For their part the political leaders, Attlee and Morrison prominent among them, were determined to preserve the Party's own autonomy. On the TUC side, the need for this was clearer to Citrine than to Bevin, who, as it happened, was not a member of the National Joint Council until pressed to join in October 1932 and therefore not directly party to the first discussions of role and responsibility. Bevin tended to find the restrictions irksome in the face of his own belief that he was the personal custodian of the rights of working people and that the Party was essentially the instrument of trade unionism.[21]

But even he found it necessary to stress publicly that the Party Secretary, Henderson, had invited the TUC to help revive the NJC[22] and to correct, publicly, the misunderstanding that it had an executive, rather than a co-ordinating, role.[23] And he, like the others, could not escape the logic of the emphasis they now placed on tripartite arrangements and participation in state economic planning. Inasmuch as the TUC sought to ensure its freedom to negotiate and be consulted on behalf of its members regardless of the complexion of the Government, it needed to give indications of the limitations of its involvement in the Labour Party. With the rearmament policy changed and a stronger-based leadership of the Labour Party, Ernest Bevin himself withdrew from the National Joint Council (by then the National Council of Labour) and concentrated on other work – including the Government's Amulree Committee on holidays with pay.[24]

Thus, though it is apparent that the trade union leaders were involved in new political policy initiatives, particularly on defence and foreign policy, through the NJC, we can, in a sense, see the revival of that linking body as itself a recognition of the distinctiveness of the two wings. There was, crucially, no attempt to change Labour's constitution in such a way as to allow General Council members to sit on Labour's Executive Committee. Proposals for a Joint TUC–Labour Party EC Economic Committee were not pursued.[25] Alongside the NJC there continued to function not only the autonomous TUC policymaking process but a Labour Executive Committee process which was independently researched and the source of various initiatives.

There were regular differences of opinion within and between the trade union leaders and those of the Party with no automatic victors. At different times and on different issues both Deputy Leader Attlee and the spokesman of the Transport Workers found themselves having to initiate policy from the floor of the Conference. Bevin's speech at the 1935 Party Conference did in effect secure the downfall of the Leader, Lansbury, but he could not secure the succession for Greenwood.[26] Even on the defence policy issue, where Bevin was at his most assertive in advocacy of collective security and rearmament, it was not until 1937 that the various forums of the Labour Movement moved in accord.

And the scope of TUC involvement has also to be noted. Territorial boundaries were generally respected. Domestic PLP matters were left to the Parliamentary Party. Senior union leaders had no direct involvement in the administration and organisational rebuilding of the Party; this was a matter for the NEC. When it was necessary to consult senior union leaders over the Party's financial income, this was normally carried on through formal meetings between representatives of individual affiliated unions and Party officials.

Thus we have to be careful not to attribute consistent and all-pervasive management by TUC leaders even in this period of what is sometimes seen as a TUC-controlled party,[27] and to note that by the outbreak of war the Labour Movement had come to accept as permanent some important demarcations of industrial and political institutions.

DEMOCRACY

Trade union commitment to the value of democracy was deeply rooted. The 'primitive democracy' – as Sidney Webb termed it[28] – which characterised early local collective activity became transposed into a heritage of delegate democracy. The chain of representation which led upwards to national policymaking reflected a view of proper democratic process in which discussion took place prior to mandating, the conference vote registered the aggregate of predetermined local or regional decisions and union leaders were obliged to carry out the conference decisions.

The form and scope of these procedures were a source of pride to the trade unions – seen as uniquely democratic.[29] It was not surprising, therefore, that such procedures were replicated within the Labour Party. The Annual Party Conference was the sovereign policymaking body, votes of delegates were cast on the basis of mandates, and conference decisions were in principle binding upon the Party's Executive Committee and the Parliamentary Labour Party.

Trade unions were also committed – indeed very heavily committed – to democracy in a second sphere. They had been in the forefront of the struggle for a wider franchise and a Parliamentary democracy. The very birth of the Labour Party was predicated upon the desire to achieve a better representation and the fullest participation of labour within this Parliamentary democracy. When combined with a desire for social acceptability and infused with trade union legalism, this produced a deep unease at the idea of being 'unconstitutional'.

In one sense the values of Labour Movement democracy and Parliamentary democracy were mutually reinforcing – each was hostile to unaccountable power and each embodied a commitment to regular elections involving politically sovereign constituents. But there were also elements of tension and conflict, particularly as Parliamentary representation tended to be governed by assumptions inherited from the older parties and from older traditions. The MP, in Liberal theory, was subject only to his own judgement and conscience – not to prior instructions. The focus was on debate at the level of national representation rather than by local collectivities.

The reconciliation of these two forms of democracy within the Labour Party produced a complicated fusion of practices, obligations and 'rules' which varied area by area and left at least one area of major uncertainty where the 'rules' were for the moment unclear.

The first area of fusion involved union participation in the selection of Parliamentary candidates. Union procedures and union finance dominated the early phase of Labour candidate selection. But by 1933 there was a major reform of practice in the form of the 'Hastings Agreement'[30] – to restrict the level (and, it was hoped, redirect the focus) of union financial sponsorship (see Chapter 9, pp. 242–3)

This restriction upon trade union finance was important in itself – a significant (if limited) union acceptance of the paramount needs of the Party in this area. But what developed, or rather was to a degree imposed by the Party on the basis of the Hastings Agreement, was also very significant. First, initiated by the Party in the wake of 'Hastings', came a prohibition on the mention of any financial support before the selection was made. Eventually, this prohibition became part of the NEC's approved Memorandum on the Selection of Candidates although it was never part of the formal rules. The prohibition was in some ways more symbolic than effective as an attempt to make finance less important; a knowledgeable selector knew from the union background of a candidate what money, if any, was likely to be contributed to the local party. But the symbolism had wider significance. A prohibition had been established in a crucial area and a declaration had been made that it was improper to bring financial resources into play.

The unions at this time were increasingly under attack from the constituency Labour Parties[31] and from the Society of Labour Candidates for the 'dangerous practice of making the selection of candidates depend on cash considerations'.[32] And as 'the paymasters' of the Party they were increasingly sensitive to the charge made by political opponents of 'dictation' to the Party.[33] Hence-forth, union contributions to the Labour Party would be marked by a growing inhibition over threat of financial sanctions in relation to the pursuit of union interests – an inhibition which blended into a 'rule' which was later to guide relations with sponsored MPs (see p. 34). For some in the unions the development of this 'rule' was not accepted with good grace but with feelings of being unappreciated, and often of aggrieved frustration. Nevertheless, it was remarkable how effective the prohibition was.

Another 'rule' also developed in this area. More precisely, some time in the late 1930s or early 1940s, there was initiated from Labour's Head Office a 'rule' enunciated by Party officials at Selection Conferences that delegates were not mandated by their organisations and acted in effect as individuals. Nothing could stop unions from continuing to attempt to instruct their delegates but (as they were often reminded) it was a secret ballot. The interesting feature here was that, as with the 'rule' of no financial mention, the unions made no attempt via the Annual Conference to challenge, clarify or amend it. To this extent, they in effect accepted it – right up to the 1987 reform – in spite of the clear breach of the boundary of union autonomy that it implied. As with the issue of Communist delegates (see p. 47 and n. 99), it indicated the possibility that the boundaries of the industrial and the political could by agreement or quiet acquiescence at leadership level be shifted in favour of the Party's requirements.

A permanent area of tension concerned the responsibilities of sponsored MPs and the rights of the unions and the Party with regard to obligations and sanctions. Gradually, there was to emerge a 'rule' reinforced by Parliamentary privilege which prohibited unions from direct threats related to sponsorship sanctions (see Chapter 3, p. 61 and Chapter 9, pp. 260–1). But in these inter-war years, there was little clarity and consistency in the relationship. Based on a tradition of delegacy and a long-established practice of financial maintenance, unions generally considered sponsored MPs as *their* representatives, and instructions were not considered improper.[34]

For their part, sponsored MPs generally accepted a special responsibility to the unions on trade questions but increasingly the tendency was to accept the primacy of the Party rather than the union and to respect the existing norms of Parliamentary life with regard to the rights and freedoms of Members. In these inter-war years, no conflict was pushed to the point of open crisis but in 1934 it almost came, in the form of an argument between Aneurin Bevan, the TUC, and his sponsoring union, the South Wales Miners Federation. Bevan had joined with two other Leftwing Labour MPs in attempting to ensure that the Unemployment Insurance Bill allowed unorganised workers the same rights of appeal as organised workers – if necessary using the National Unemployed Workers Committee as their representative.[35] In the course of the debate, Bevan made a strong sideswipe at the General Council's attitude.[36] They reported the matter to his sponsoring union who demanded an explanation from Bevan. The form of Bevan's reply indicated his sensitivity to union representation but also involved the clear assertion of independence which was to mark the future development of the relationship. He denied that he had ever voted against the policy of his union or the TUC but also claimed Parliamentary privilege in defence of his rights. Taking note, and increasingly inhibited in the face of charges of 'dictation' and financial control, neither the union nor the TUC took any further action.[37]

The third and central problem area of the two democracies concerned the constitutional authority of the Party – the Party Conference with its built-in union majority.[38] It authorised the Party's constitution and Standing Orders. It laid down the general policy and principles of the Party. And it adjudicated on major issues of contention. In formal terms, the decisions of the Party Conference were followed by their implementation by the Party Executive and the Party in Parliament. A major body of opinion in the unions, socialist societies and growing constituency parties always regarded this Party democracy as integral to the values of the Movement.

However, the rights of the Party Conference had often been contested by sections of the Parliamentary leadership. Indeed, by the late 1920s, MacDonald appeared to have shed all commitment to the tradition of intra-Party democracy and Conference authority. Largely as a reaction to this experience, in the early 1930s there was a reaffirmation of the principle of intra-Party democracy, majority rule and Conference sovereignty.[39]

The unions were as much affected by this mood of renewal as were the constituency parties, but union leaders proved to be much more circumspect in their demands for specific new arrangements. Thus, again, the redefinition of the 'rules' of the relations involved a restraint on the part of the unions based upon precedents some of which had been established in the earliest years of the Party. Anxiety that they might be seen as exercising an improper constitutional role, concern for the stability of the Party, and acceptance of the need for 'the politicians' to have a practicable measure of discretion and initiative, all constrained the reaction to 'MacDonaldism'.

Although it was made clear that the policies to be pursued by the Labour leadership in Opposition and a Labour Government in Office would be made by 'the Party', laid down in resolutions of the Annual Conference and embodied in General Election Manifestos,[40] various qualifications were retained under the 'rules'.

The PLP autonomy was respected as it had been since the formation of a Labour Group in Parliament. The 'rule' established in 1907 that the PLP had 'time and method' discretion in giving effect to Conference decisions[41] was adhered to. The constitutional right of the Parliamentary Leadership to participate with the NEC in *selecting* items for the Manifesto was unquestioned. An enhanced role for the NEC (in practice the MPs who dominated it) in policy formulation had, in practice, been accepted in 1924 and again in 1929 when it was then constitutionally sanctioned.[42] These arrangements continued after 1931. Most significant of all, the unions (who had made virtually no intervention in 1929 at a time when the constitutional obligations of the PLP to the Conference were made more tenuous[43]) made no attempt now to utilise the Party Constitution to tighten union control.[44] This was considered improper as well as unwise. Indeed, from 1924 to 1933 the majority of them acquiesced in the sidelining or defeat of all such proposals for constitutional rule changes coming from the constituency Labour parties.

UNITY

Unity was an essential element of collective action. It was not easily forged or easily preserved for many in the workforce. In sectors of industry and services, managerial antagonism continued to threaten trade union organisation. The unions were riddled with rivalries and hostilities, conflicts over differentials and competition for membership – the latter so bitter that guiding principles and a specialised jurisprudence emerged to deal with it, known as the Bridlington Agreement of 1939.

Yet at national level, what marked the development of the TUC was a remarkable inclusive unity. In the 1920s, with the decline of the General Federation of Labour, the TUC achieved a uniquely strong position as the unified national centre of the industrial wing. Unlike its continental counterparts, it practised no exclusions on political, religious or occupational grounds. It became *the* voice of industrial labour.

Recognition of the value of this national unity was reflected in the 1921 reform which produced a new General Council replacing the Parliamentary Committee. The system of representation by trade groups involving election by the whole of the Congress was intended to ensure both that the full industrial breadth of trade unionism was represented and that the members of the Council were accountable to the Congress as a whole rather than to sections or particular unions. Alongside this pattern of elections in which, according to formal rule, the 'canvassing' and 'bartering' of votes was forbidden, there was in practice an informal set of arrangements in which, as for many years previously, bartering and canvassing began the moment that delegates arrived.[45]

Indeed, there developed unofficial 'rules' of bartering behaviour which were to spread from the TUC to the Labour Party. The first 'rule' covering these arrangements was representation by size. In order to sustain industrial unity, the larger unions supported each other regardless of political stance or other considerations. In many trade groups this meant that contests did not take place at all; in others the winning margins were huge as the big union votes all grouped together. Thus for the largest unions and for others who were, group by group, favoured within the 'understandings', nomination was tantamount to election.

It became a key feature of Labour Party politics that this approach to General Council representation was carried over into representation on the National Executive Committee of the Labour Party and that other arrangements between large unions were sometimes linked in dealing with both executive bodies.

Other customs and industrially-based arrangements also affected NEC elections. There was a 'rule', or custom, of traditional occupancy whereby unions with long-established representation could retain their seat even if their affiliation sank. And there were sectoral agreements and industrial accommodations. There was also a deep respect for 'the law of Buggins' Turn' in establishing a 'next in line', both for individuals and for unions.[46]

These industrially-based 'rules' and arrangements of NEC elections had important political consequences. They restricted the possibility of a full-scale political mobilisation. It became very difficult to achieve a sudden or dramatic political shift in NEC membership. This feature was not generally a problem for the Parliamentary leadership given the dominance of moderate Rightwing and accommodating union officials in so many leading positions, but it was always an obstacle in the path of a major Left radicalisation of the NEC or a sudden *putsch* against the Party Leadership.

The unions took total control over NEC voting in 1917 (until 1937), formally to make the NEC responsible to 'the Conference as a whole' but politically out of antipathy to the anti-coalitionist and pacifist elements on the ILP Left.[47] This control probably involved some heavy filters against Communist Party allies and those judged to be sympathisers in the late 1920s and 1930s, but there was some degree of sensitivity to the representation of political tendencies.[48] And, above all, it was not used to secure union control over the PLP leadership.

One sign of intention here was that the union leaders who had accepted prohibition on their own membership of the NEC would not accept a rule prohibiting or restricting MPs being elected to that body.[49] Ultimately, this situation would work to the advantage of the Left after the Second World War as the constituencies elected critical MPs to their section of the committee, but in the 1920s, it worked as a boost to the position of the Parliamentary Leadership because, in this period, trade-union-sponsored MPs were often represented in the affiliated societies section. In 1924, there were five out of eleven and in 1929 six out of eleven. Indeed, with trade union approval, the committee as a whole was dominated by MPs at crucial periods. During the second MacDonald Government, there were no less than sixteen out of twenty-three NEC members who were MPs in 1929 and sixteen out of twenty-five in 1930.

As these trade-union-sponsored MPs were generally loyalists who placed a great emphasis on unity behind their Parliamentary Leadership, this consolidated a set of behaviour patterns. It reinforced the trade union belief that in the political sphere the PLP 'should hold the strings of the Movement'[50] and it reinforced acceptance that the pre-eminence of the Parliamentary leadership should be accepted on the NEC. The Trade Union Section representatives, both MPs and non-MPs, were generally not the most outstanding union leaders – indeed one historian has described them as 'broadly speaking mediocrities'.[51] Their behaviour established a non-initiating and supportive role-playing tradition in which they 'rarely, if ever, made attempts to control the course of events – even during the fall of the 1931 Government'.[52]

This general behaviour pattern by NEC trade unionists had many long-term consequences for the government of the Labour Party. It encouraged the leading role of the politicians. It enabled the development of a surprising degree of administrative autonomy from the TUC. And it facilitated that phenomenon which was such a puzzle to many – the evolution of policies which could differ significantly from those of the General Council of the TUC, from the decisions of the TUC Congress, and from the sum of the mandates of the unions represented at the Party Conference.

The continuities of NEC membership produced by trade union 'unity' voting patterns helped ensure the passing down of its traditions, and the Trade Union Section members tended to socialise new members into the Group's expectations. This socialisation became, if anything, even stronger later as the Trade Union MPs became fewer and the Group's occupational homogeneity became greater. The trickle of Leftwing MPs always found themselves cross-pressured in their behaviour by this pull to 'the union Group'. In the future, some capable individuals would make their personal mark on important policies. And industrial issues would often stimulate a strong union defensiveness whatever the source of the initiative. A clear, strong union mandate, backed by an alert union constituency, would not so easily be ignored. And it remained to be tested how the Section would respond if the NEC came under the influence of a strong alternative group of politicians. But for the moment, and for a long time to come, the dominant role of the Trade Union Section was that of a supportive base for the Parliamentary Leadership.

The stress that the unions placed upon unity created other restraints within the relationship – particularly restrictions upon political mobilisation from outside particular unions. That such unity as did exist within a union might be put at risk by 'politics' had long been a subtext of mainstream British trade unionism; after the Chartist experience, 'no politics' rules were introduced into many unions.[53] One legacy of this was that political factionalism continued to be disapproved of within the unions even though its development was a growing feature throughout the period after the First World War. Keeping factionalism under control was itself, in part, a political response usually to the activities of the Communist Left but it also reflected a belief that autonomous unions must settle their own internal disputes without interference from outside – in this case again mainly the Communist Party. But, by extension, Labour Party politicians were also forbidden under the 'rules' from entering the territory of the unions for purposes of political mobilisation (unless they were specifically invited).

The value of unity and the consciousness that politics might be divisive was also enhanced by the industrial experiences of the late 1920s. The encouragement by mine-owners and by the Conservative Party[54] of a breakaway Miners Industrial (Non-Political) union from the Mineworkers Federation – 'the Spencer Union' – was seen not so much as a genuine albeit non-political trade unionism, but as a politically-influenced attack on trade unionism from the Right.[55] At the same time, the TUC was facing, from the Communist-led Red International, encouragement for politically-led Leftwing breakaways from affiliated organisations. These developments led to the TUC tightening its rules and outlawing all forms of 'secession'; disciplinary action was taken against unions which aided and abetted the breakaways.[56]

Within the Labour Party, these proscriptions were as powerful as within the TUC. Indeed, in 1929 the Labour Party Constitution was altered to make it clear that not only should Labour Party members ('if eligible') be a member of a union, but that the union should be 'affiliated to the Trades Union Congress or recognised by the General Council of the Trades Union Congress as a bona fide Trade Union'.[57] In practice, the TUC was never happy to make such judgements itself in relation to Labour Party membership but it, and the affiliated unions, were clear that nobody, including Labour MPs, should give support to secessionist unions.[58]

SOLIDARITY

The fundamental ethics of trade unionism involved loyalty to the collective community, the sacrifice, if necessary, of immediate sectional interest, and the extension of assistive strength to those in need. For the trade union movement as a whole, it meant that there was a presupposition that when workers were in dispute with employers, the Movement would give what support and assistance it could, and would do nothing to harm the position of the workers involved.

The application of these principles to the Labour Party relationship was never unproblematic – as we have seen (Chapter 1, pp. 17 and 28). Nevertheless, in Opposition in the 1930s, with few major industrial disputes to focus attention, it was widely accepted that the role of the Party was to be as supportive as possible of unions seeking to defend and advance the position of their members. This perception blended with the fraternal philosophy of the Movement, shoulder to shoulder, the weak assisting the strong, one wing assisting the other.

However, within the union–Party relationship solidarity also took on another implication – solidarity with the Party. Trade Union leaders, conscious of the Party's family history, took on a parental obligation to the Party to play a stabilising role. One clear example of this was trade union attitudes towards

Labour's constitution. Once the 1918 constitution was agreed, the unions made virtually no attempt to change it significantly in the inter-war years[59] *unless requested by the Party Leadership*. The 1929 redrafting was actively contested by the unions only on the issue of 'associated membership' where a majority of the unions thought members should go 'through the proper channels of the Movement'.[60]

It was seen as an extension of this ballast role in 1931, after MacDonald's decision to lead a National Government, that major union leaders moved in to hold the Movement together in opposition to the National Government. For union leaders, this created a precedent which they were to regard in the future as a 'rule' of ballast but it left open the uncertainty as to whether the stabilising intervention was fully legitimate if *opposed* by leaders in the political wing.

At times, this role was defined in even more questionable terms – with union leaders openly encouraging, and even attempting to initiate, action against groups in the Party which threatened to damage the Party's 'constitution', its unity or its role as an independent party of labour. Here the traditional trade union concern with observance of majority decisions could make them insensitive to minority rights in the political wing. At various times and in various ways the ILP, the Socialist League and the supporters of a Popular Front all earned official disapproval, with the trade unions lined up solidly behind the disciplinarians and Ernest Bevin the hammer of the dissidents.[61] Thus there was always room for argument over what circumstances warranted the stabilising function, and Labour's Left never accepted an interventionist union role in initiating disciplinary action.

But this solidarity also involved restraint and discretion on behalf of the unions. It led them generally to restrict the public advocacy of their criticism of Labour Governments[62] and it stimulated a protective loyalty to Labour Governments – however disappointing their performance[63] – in the face of critics from the socialist Left of the Party.

This stabilising and loyalist role, with all its uncertainties of boundary and obligations, was not without its clear quid pro quo. After 1931, there was a strong reinforcement of the precept that the Parliamentary and Party Leadership must 'keep in touch with the Movement' and must abide by the constitutional commitment 'to co-operate with' the TUC.[64] Out of this injunction came the consolidation of four major 'rules' of consultation with the unions.

There had to be a high degree of advance policy consultation. Thus it was agreed in 1932 that there should be close consultation between the departmental officers of the TUC and the NEC which should exchange policy drafts. There should be joint meetings of the comparable committees when occasion arose, and cross-representation when this was not appropriate.[65] The informal network built around these consultative arrangements was to be a long-lasting feature of the relationship, important not only in terms of policy accommodations but also enhancing the process of mutual understanding and influence. It was also agreed that in Government, contact with Ministers should be intimate and that the General Council of the TUC should be fully consulted on proposed legislation 'in which they are directly concerned'. The National Joint Council (later the

National Council of Labour) should provide the machinery for consultation with the Movement as a whole, both in Opposition and in Government.[66]

Alongside this broad consultative 'rule' in relation to policymaking, the unions and the Party operated within a more specific prohibition. In the 1920s, it had become established that the Party did not formulate a policy involving nationalisation of any industry before the union, or unions, in that industry were consulted. Fierce union reaction to any attempted transgression led to the right of consultation becoming in effect a right of veto.[67] These rights guided the formulation of nationalisation policy in the 1930s.

A third rule emerged in the 1930s, apparently as a result of the unions' new shortage of political funds following the 1927 Act, and following a series of embarrassing public discussions (and criticisms) of proposed increases in affiliation fees. There developed a 'rule' of prior private consultation of the unions in connection with any proposed changes in financial levies. This then became extended to all proposals for changes in the financial relationship.

A fourth 'rule' followed 'the great crime' of Ramsay MacDonald. In the hours of crisis before agreeing to form a National Government, 'he never called in his Party'.[68] As a result, the commitment to independence became reinforced as 'a burning conviction'.[69] It became a clear obligation on Labour's leadership, political and industrial, to consult the Movement before any action which could compromise the Party's prized 'independence and freedom'.[70] This was rigorously applied to participation in political fronts or Coalition Governments.[71]

PRIORITY

Perspectives

Alongside these values, and at times ordering and reordering the importance of their application to the Labour Party, was a working principle which regulated union activity within 'the political wing' – the principle of priority. To understand the way that union leaders operated within the Labour Party, it is necessary to appreciate the perspectives and practices of trade union priorities.

In their constitutions, unions were committed to a wide range of 'Objects', some of them far-reaching in their conception of socialist transformation.[72] And most union leaders in the inter-war years were, or became, Socialists – usually defined in terms of opposition to the Capitalist system and of supporting public rather than private ownership – sometimes allied to forms of industrial democracy.

Nevertheless, there was a broad recognition within the unions of the distinction between 'immediate' and 'ultimate' aims and objectives.[73] These immediate objectives – the priorities – were heavily influenced by the character of trade unionism and by the industrial context of their activities.

The unions had been created to deal with the immediate problems faced by industrial workers and their preoccupations continued to be with the terms and conditions of labour.[74] An industrial world increasingly involving collective bargaining and negotiation encouraged a pragmatic approach to problem-solving, a reliance on experience as a guide to appropriate responses, and a stress on the best available outcome – 'a worse or better bargain'[75] rather than a total transformation. The approach was sensitive to the 'world of stern realities',[76] was disdainful of the 'theoretical',[77] was critical of the pursuit of objectives without regard for practicality, time-scale and compromise, and was accustomed to being expected to deliver what was promised.[78]

A predisposition to locate and act upon 'the primary consideration', thus 'putting first things first', was heightened in relation to Labour Party involvement by the way in which union policymaking meshed with that of the Labour Party.

Union policy was made at various forums but essentially as the *union*'s policy (see Chapter 10 for union policymaking) and at some distance and time away from the Labour Party Conference. It was not necessarily made with reference to what the Labour Party should do immediately. If it was on a political issue, it was often the product of a small concerned constituency and it was not necessarily made after extensive discussion or subject to renewed discussion. As a result, although all union policies constituted a mandate upon union delegates at various conferences of the Movement, they had varying status within the union and varying priority for the union's leadership. A union leadership which was effective industrially found more tolerance for the expression of its own political values and purposes than one which was not. But, in practice, a recognition of the membership's own limited political priorities,[79] the difficulty of mobilising them for more Leftwing objectives and the time, effort and expense involved in such mobilisation did normally set boundaries to the actions of union leaders in the Labour Party. It was the members' priorities which generally determined the political issues upon which a union leadership chose to focus and which it chose to pursue vigorously.

Further, the restrictions on the number of resolutions and amendments which could be submitted to Party Conference, the limited opportunities to speak, the necessity to choose which items should be raised and pursued in the committees of the Party, and the *realpolitik* of husbanding pressure and signalling importance all strengthened the tendency to order priorities in a hierarchy ranging from symbolic affirmation to immediate first order concern. What was registered in a vote at a Conference was one thing; what was *pushed* was another.

Thus, as a product of trade union experience, and in response to the practicalities of operating within the Labour Party, the participation of union leaders became regulated by a range of 'rules' of priority which defined 'a trade union point of view', 'a trade union approach' or 'a trade union perspective'. Such 'rules' were precepts, maxims of prudence rather than the normative obligations we have uncovered thus far, but they took on a more binding and normative status as peer groups on the General Council came to pass private judgement on what was proper and responsible behaviour from a 'real' trade union leader.

Among the most important of these precepts were the injunctions: 'Protect the union', 'Defend trade unionism', 'Protect your base in the union', 'Don't move too far ahead of the members; the first duty is to them', 'Face the realities of the situation', 'Focus on the practicable and the deliverable' and, crucially, a precept roughly on the lines of 'Don't sacrifice the union and its obligations for purely political purposes'.[80]

These 'rules' clearly implied a very heavy emphasis on industrial objectives. And industrial concerns were issues where the union leaders could generally be assured of a known army in support. They were also the issues where the room for manœuvre of leaders was normally most limited by this highly motivated constituency, and the issues over which union leaders felt most authoritative, most knowledgeable and most confident.

Practice

It is, therefore, not surprising that in terms of union activity within the Labour Party, the priority of union calls upon sponsored MPs was focused upon trade and industrial matters and the priority revealed year by year on Labour Party agendas was very similar. The Labour Party became the agency, for the unions, of the protection of their industrial rights and the means by which unions pursued industrial objectives which could not be achieved solely or easily by action within the industrial sphere. These had been the major priority since the Party was founded.[81]

For a brief period after 1931 there was enhanced concern among union leaders for a campaign 'for socialism',[82] but proposals for nationalisation continued to be narrowly focused. Union resolutions to Party Conference were almost invariably specific to one industry rather than multiple or general. Normally they came from the union or unions in the relevant industry. This sectional approach was reinforced by the 'rule' of veto already mentioned (p. 40). There was little point in producing a shopping list which had not been the subject of prior consultation.

Allied with this industrial focus was a growing appreciation of the extent to which economic policy affected the terms of trade and the conditions of employment. This was reflected in the creation of the TUC Economic Department in 1929. But, unlike on the immediate industrial issues, the economic involvement of most union leaders was circumscribed by a lack of confidence and a lack of union-by-union expertise in this area.[83] This, plus the absence of an involved 'army' on detailed macroeconomic policy, accounts for the fact that neither the union leaders individually nor the TUC Economic Department appear to have had much influence over the development of Labour Party economic policy.[84] In the slow acceptance of Keynesian policies in the late 1930s, the unions played no role.[85]

Nevertheless, there was always a strong current of concern among union leaders over employment policy – an interest typifying their general preoccupation with industry and its conditions. In this consistent focus, union leaders' behaviour often bore out the common diagnosis of their economism and their limited and often sectional perspectives.

And yet there is much more to be said about the perspectives and priorities of trade union leaders within the Labour Party. The prudential 'rules' were essentially rules of anchorage. That is, they located a base and moorings from which it was dangerous to move too far in pursuit of political purposes. But it did not mean that they could not move at all. The 'rules' were clearer in what they ruled out than in what they prescribed. And there was considerable room for interpretation of the 'realities', the 'practicable' and how far the responsibilities of office legitimised taking a leading role. Although as a product of these 'rules' we can discern general patterns of priority, it is also true that there was sufficient flexibility to allow for the expression of a diversity of union political traditions and a diversity of changing political contexts of Opposition and Government. Within this diversity, union leaders could sometimes find space for the priority of their own national or international political projects. It was, however, much easier to push this priority consistently when it blended into mainstream opinion and objectives than when it was nearer to the Leftwing edge of the Movement's purposes.

The 'rules' were particularly flexible in those areas where the boundaries of the political and the industrial were uncertain or where the policy objective involved a fusion of trade unionists' basic concerns and ideological values. In those areas, if there was a strong body of active opinion within the union, priority involvements could develop a strong head of steam.

The most obvious example concerned the mixture of class-conscious grievance over the conditions of working class life, together with a sense of social justice about their rectification. There is a long history of concern with issues of social reform, including housing, education, and particularly social security, including old-age and widows' pensions. In 1931, it was the issue of not 'sacrificing the unemployed'[86] which drew union opposition to proposed cuts in benefit so strong that it helped precipitate the crisis which brought the end of the Labour Government. The TUC developed its own Social Insurance and Social Welfare Department which, working with the grain of common values, fed into Labour Party policymaking.[87] From this TUC activity would come eventually the creation of the Beveridge Committee in 1941.

The call for industrial democracy was and remains one of the great overlapping issues of the industrial and the political. Industrial considerations produced some inhibitive elements as unions worried about the possible compromise of their freedom under arrangements where they were part of 'management'. Political considerations heightened the priority given to taking control 'out of the hands of profit-seeking proprietors'.[88] TUC policy eventually registered a formal victory for the industrial democrats both within the unions and between some of them and the Party Leadership.[89] But not before an unusual occurrence in the relationship. In 1933, the Party was used by some of the unions allied to a majority of the CLPs to defeat 'the platform' at the Party Conference[90] in an attempt to move past the emerging agreement at the TUC – an indication of the depth of commitment on the issue at that time.

Defending trade unionism could involve a much broader perspective than simply defensive sectionalism. It could be stretched to an involvement in protecting the political context – and that context could itself become a transcendental priority under critical circumstances.

In the 1930s, the sudden new priority given by union leaders – particularly Bevin and Citrine – to collective security and the building of national defence against Fascism was stimulated by an understanding of what Fascism meant to the future of trade unionism. But antipathy to dictatorship also drew upon a deep commitment to democratic government. As Frances Williams pointed out, Fascism 'threw into brightest relief the place occupied by trade unionism as the essential bulwark of democratic freedom and one of the strongest bulwarks against tyranny'.[91] In the minds of many trade union leaders, including Bevin, defence of the one was also defence of the other, and their assertiveness within the Party over defence policy was driven by a much wider concern than simply industrial protection.

Also, how far and in what direction unions were prepared to throw their weight over issues of war and peace varied according to the circumstances of the time and the nature of the threat. The classic involvement (which was to be repeated in 1940) occurred in 1914 when a combination of national patriotism and, again, a concern for 'the preservation and maintenance of free and unfettered democratic government'[92] led most union leaders to full support for the war and subsequently for coalition governments in which Labour was represented. But there was another tradition and another precedent which was to carry down to the 1980s. In 1920, it became for a short period the central priority of most union leaders, backed by a membership weary of war, to prevent an act of British aggression against a government which presented no direct threat to Britain and its institutions – the new Soviet Union.[93]

Not until the late 1940s did a Soviet Communism come to be seen as a military threat requiring armed preparation. Up to that period, a strain of deep sympathy for the new Soviet state was generally insulated from attitudes towards Communism as such. Anti-Communism, which led to the rejection of Communist Party affiliation and then the exclusion of Communist delegates to the Labour Party Conference, was strengthened by the divisive industrial behaviour of the British CP, but it was fostered from inception by a commitment to British Parliamentary democracy – a value which developed a primacy of its own and the deep-rooted support of the mass of British trade unionists.

The obligations that trade unions felt, particularly in war-time, for the national defence of democracy and trade unionism could be built upon to enhance their sense of responsibility for national industrial and economic goals – first within a war effort and then in the development of a peacetime neo-corporatism. In the 1930s, as TUC leaders and particularly the TUC permanent officials slowly became enmeshed within Whitehall, so its influence fed into the Movement influencing perspectives on 'the realities of the situation'. This influence was eventually to provide a permanent counter-definition to some of the narrower industrial interpretations of the prudential 'rules'.

One final qualification – and it is an important qualification – has to be made to the primacy of industrial obligations in the hierarchy of priorities. There was always a tension between this immediate commitment to the union and its members and the duty of solidarity with the Labour Party, its leaders and its Governments. It produced a political dimension to priorities which again could both broaden and complicate any union sectionalism.

Often this was simply an added ingredient in the balance of calculation. Sometimes it was more direct, as when over financial appeals the unions were prepared to give primacy to their assistance: they made considerable efforts in a difficult period to keep up their financial input into the Party after the passing of the Trades Disputes and Trade Union Act of 1927.[94] But most significant was the circumspect union behaviour just prior to the 1929 General Election and in efforts to sustain the Labour Government. Securing and preserving a Labour Government produced its own logic of priorities – a logic sometimes ill at ease with the calculus of prudential union obligations.

Reciprocity

This, then, was the pattern and mixture of trade union priorities. Overall, they reflected a sense of responsible restraint about the exercise and focus of power from what in theory was an omnipotent union position with unrestricted scope for control. And a loose reciprocity was expected. Just as trade unionists understood the language of priorities, so Socialist politicians were expected to speak and act upon it.[95] If that expectation was not realised in the 1930s, then trade union leaders – particularly Ernest Bevin – were apt to remonstrate and point up the comparison with the behaviour of trade union leaders. Out of this dialogue emerged also a view that in the shaping of their priorities within the broad discretion allowed them under the 'rules', the political leaders ought not to offend the basic concerns of the Movement. This, it might be said, was *their* prudential rule.

ROLES AND 'RULES'

These, then, were the roles, and the 'rules' built upon the roles, of the trade union–Labour Party relationship. The role-playing restraint of the TUC leaders and the supportive role played by NEC trade unionists goes a long way to explaining some of the odd divergences of policy which drew the inquisitive attention of Wertheimer. The 'rules' laid down a network of obligations, mutual in form but most restrictive in effect upon the potentially omnipotent trade unions and their senior leaders.

Of course, as we have seen, these 'rules' varied in their status, scope and specificity. Some 'rules' – particularly those relating to the autonomy of the unions – were so integral to 'the Labour Alliance' and so entrenched as to be, for the moment, non-contentious. Some of those relating to solidarity and stability were loose and always problematic in their definition and application. Some 'rules' relating to political interference in industrial disputes were unilaterally imposed by the unions. Some 'rules' relating to union participation in candidate selection were unilaterally initiated by the Party, although in both cases with significant acquiescence by the leadership of the affiliates. And there was at least one area – sponsorship – where the fusion of trade union and Party obligations was yet to develop a clear consensus on the 'rules'. Nevertheless, it was remarkable how comprehensive and pervasive an influence the 'rules' were to exercise over the various transactions, routines and activities of the relationship. And the power relations between the unions and the Party – both in their consistencies and in their variations – cannot fully be understood without appreciating the inhibitions, restrictions and constraints that the 'rules' produced.

The inter-war generation of union leaders passed down this legacy of precedents and guidelines for subsequent generations. The 'rules' were not immutable – as was to be seen in the 1970s – but they constituted a powerful tradition. Those who followed learned some of the appropriate behaviour, as part of the norms and folklore of a trade union career, following the precedents of the past, seeking the respect and recognition of colleagues operating on the myriad committees of the unions and the party. But with the TUC bureaucracy beginning to act as guardians of the rules and protocol, the most potent arena of socialisation was membership of the General Council and particularly its main committees.

The slow advancement of union leaders within the General Council on the basis of seniority was a heavily shaping experience. Accepting the inevitable constraints of time and energy, understanding the customs and role-playing of Parliamentary Government, appreciating the lack of political homogeneity of the trade union membership, and following through the logic of a predominantly industrial vocation, led to a General Council definition of appropriate behaviour becoming part of the process of what was considered political 'maturity'. Thus the 'rules' relating to the union–party relationship came to be accompanied by moral notions of responsibility and propriety. These were reinforced more by embarrassment, guilt and group hostility than by sanctions – although these too were available, particularly when it came to committee positions and elections.

Not all trade union leaders were fully subject to this process. A minority on the Left always retained a belief that the disjunction of industrial and political roles was artificial and an impediment to industrial struggle and political control over a Labour Government.[96] Their voice was much more often heard from the Congress than the General Council. And, in addition, there were occasional maverick General Council members – 'outsiders' within its culture – who, for various reasons, were never fully integrated into its mores, and never fully followed the pattern.[97]

But even the Left and the mavericks were subject to some extent to the influence of the 'rules' which enhanced a consciousness of distinct industrial and political institutions and of distinct industrial and political spheres. A lengthy period in membership of the Council encouraged a general adherence to the fundamental injunction not to act as 'a politician'.

With this differentiation of roles came the development of an intricate protocol, some of it symbolising the fundamental unity of the Movement but much of it recognising and jealously guarding territories and spheres. A routine but significant protocol surrounded the exchange of fraternal delegates from Conference to Congress and of observers from committee to committee. A deeply ingrained protocol governed policy and financial consultations. Rigid and often prickly protocol governed invitations to the sphere of the Parliamentary Party, the TUC and union conferences.

Intervention by union leaders in Parliamentary Party elections was restricted by an etiquette of low profile. Trade union leaders could quietly influence the outcome of elections for the Party's leadership but there was a decorum to observe, respecting Parliamentary autonomy. Conversely, party leaders were expected to 'keep out of the area' when such decisions were being taken in a union. Even the union role in electing Labour's NEC had to be handled by adroit liaison aware of union rights and responsibilities.

The territorial protocol was so sensitive that even addressing a fringe meeting at a union conference could be seen as improper interference if it covered contentious issues in a way that was hostile to the position of a union's leadership. This protectiveness even extended at times to publicly commenting on the internal affairs of a union or even on the behaviour of the unions[98] – a one-sided arrangement given that trade union leaders often felt no inhibition about commenting on the state of the Labour Party.

This pattern of 'rules' and protocol complicated the problems of all reform movements which crossed the boundaries of the two spheres. It was, for example, always a problem for the Labour Party in the 1920s that union delegates to the Party Conference were held to be subject only to the rules of individual unions. Not until 1928 did the Party find it possible to place restrictions on Communist delegates, thus affirming the Party's right to regulate this area.[99] Leftwing attempts to reform the block vote foundered not only on the substantive issues involved but because of uncertainties over territory and the right of the Party to intervene on the question of splitting the vote.

'RULES' AND STABILITY

All in all, the reciprocity involved in the mutuality of restraint – although never fully complied with – was to be a fundamental stabilising element in the relationship encouraging a consciousness of boundaries and the necessity for regular accommodation.

The network of 'rules' also enmeshed both sides in mutual expectations, and obligation. On the Parliamentary side, they provided a powerful counterweight to the pressures which often pulled the Parliamentary leadership away from the Movement. On the union side also, they provided important counter-pressure away from 'business unionism' and 'non-political unionism'.

Adherence to the 'rules' – particularly participation in 'solidarity' consultation with the unions and union solidarity action towards the Party – reinforced existing loyalties and sentiments towards the Movement. Indeed, although there was always a periodic possibility that the union leaders might be pulled into alternative political strategies via the TUC, their involvement within the Labour Party always exercised a significant counter-pull. The more that union leaders rebuilt linkage committees and consultative mechanisms, the more the suction effect worked upon them. The shift towards more involvement in the National Joint Council after 1931 limited any sharp shift towards reliance on neo-corporatism. Protecting the Party against its Left further strengthened their Party identification. It was a dynamic tug which we will note again in 1944, and again in the 1980s.

Ramsay MacDonald, as Ross McKibbon tells us, was rejected in 1931 because he lost his loyalties and no longer adhered to the Party's disciplines and conventions.[100] Conversely, a rejection of MacDonaldism in that sense meant a reacceptance and a reaffirmation of the 'rules'. In the three decades after 1931, for majorities in the major forums and committees of the Labour Movement, the 'rules' became important behavioural guidelines to membership of the Labour Movement. Acceptance became all the more solid and in some areas more specific in the aftermath of the achievements of the 1940s and in the context of the new power structure that emerged in that period – as we shall see in Chapters 3 and 4.

* * *

The Labour Movement of the 1920s had been highly flexible with one event after another acting as a seismic shock exacerbating the dynamics of change and producing new developments. The Rail Strike of 1919, the General Strike of 1926, the First Labour Government in 1924 and the 'betrayal' of 1931 all had significant consequences for the union–Labour Party relationship. The 1930s, by contrast, with few major strikes, no Labour Governments, and an emergent code of 'rules', was a period of slow development and few sharp changes.

By 1939 the trade unions were beginning to regain their industrial strength but they still found access to Government unsatisfactory and their reception unhelpful or condescending. The Labour Party had recovered much of its strength since the trauma of 1931 but appeared to be making its way only to a slightly improved result in the General Election anticipated in 1940. In twelve months, as Britain moved into war, the position of the Labour Movement was suddenly transformed.

NOTES

1. Attlee, *op. cit.*, p. 73.
2. For a classic expression of these values, see the speech of the TUC fraternal delegate W. Kean, *LPACR*, 1935, p. 208.
3. See, e.g., Attlee, *op. cit.*, pp. 67 and 141-4.
4. W. A. Robinson (Distributive Workers), *LPACR*, 1924, p. 146.
5. R. W. Garner, *Ideology and Politics in Labour's Rise to Major Party Status 1918–31*, unpublished Ph.D. Thesis, Manchester, 1988, pp. 148–153, discusses tensions in Lancashire. See also Alan Clinton, *The Trade Union Rank and File*, 1977, Chapter 7 on the reorganisation of Trades Councils.
6. Resolution from the Amalgamated Society of Woodworkers, *1926 Party Conference Agenda*, p. 48.
7. Muller, *op. cit.*, pp. 39–40, Taylor, *op. cit.*, p. 148, and see Chapter 3, p. 60.
8. Resolutions, *1926 Party Conference Agenda*, pp. 28–9.
9. *TUC Congress Report*, 1904, pp. 115–16. The debate was on a procedural motion concerning members of the Parliamentary Committee speaking for or supporting candidates.
10. *LPACR*, 1907, pp. 56–7.
11. *LPACR*, 1908, pp. 61–2. The Conference vote was 608,000 to 202,000.
12. *Standing Orders of the Labour Party*, 1918, 4.6.
13. Bullock, Vol. I, *op. cit.*, p. 286.
14. The exception was the National Union of Clerks and Administrative Workers, whose leadership in the late 1920s and early 1930s had an unusual fixation on Labour Party procedural questions.
15 *Minutes of National Joint Council (NJC)*, 7/12/31. John Bromley speak-

ing from the Chair.
16. Item 6, 'TUC Memorandum Regarding the National Joint Council', NJC, 21/1/32.
17. Item 7, *Ibid*.
18. Item 2, *Ibid*.
19. NJC, 26/4/32, NEC amendments to the Memorandum on Collaboration.
20. NJC, 24/4/34, Appendix II.
21. LPACR, 1935, p. 180 and Bullock, Vol. I, op. cit., p. 235 and p. 255.
22. LPACR, 1935, p. 180. Bevin had been pressed to serve on the NJC by Henderson. Bullock, Vol. I, op. cit., p. 512.
23. LPACR, 1937, p. 174.
24. Bullock, Vol. I, *op. cit.*, p. 598 and p. 601.
25. NJC, 26/1/32.
26. Samuel H. Beer, *Modern British Politics*, 1965, p. 163.
27. Alan R. Ball, *British Political Parties*, 1981, p. 118. After I had completed the draft of this chapter, I came across an excellent article on the role of the NJC and the National Council of Labour, Jerry Brookshire, 'The National Council of Labour 1921–1946', *Albion*, 18, Spring 1986. He also argues that 'neither side controlled the other', p. 67.
28. Sidney Webb, *Industrial Democracy*, 1920, Chapter 1, pp. 3–37.
29. Milne-Bailey, *op. cit.*, pp. 117–18.
30. 'The Hastings Agreement' refers to regulations adopted by the Party Conference of 1933 (then meeting at Hastings) in relation to the financing of Parliamentary candidates. The regulations were drawn up after two consultative meetings with representatives of trade unions and co-operative organisations. In the light of the later development of 'rules' declared to be part of the Hastings Agreement, it is important to note that the Minutes of these consultative meetings (*NEC Minutes*, 28/6/33 and 26/7/33) make no reference to either the mention of finance before selection or the prohibition of mandating. Nor is there any reference to these in the NEC Report to the 1933 Conference, pp. 36/7.
31. The *Party Conference Agenda*, 1933, p. 20 had a wide range of such resolutions, but they were not debated.
32. Resolution of the Annual Meeting of the Society of Labour Candidates, quoted in a special meeting with the Liaison Subcommittee of the NEC, *NEC Minutes*, 15/3/33.
33. See, for example, the fraternal address from the TUC made by W. Kean, LPACR, 1935, p. 209.
34. Harrison, *op. cit.*, p. 293, Muller, *op. cit.*, p. 39.
35. *Hansard*, HC Cols 643–6, Vol. 285, 1/2/34.
36. '... fallen to a pretty low condition when they require the defence of the Parliamentary Secretary', *ibid.*, Col. 657.
37. Michael Foot, *Aneurin Bevan 1897–1945*, 1975, pp. 165–6.
38. An extensive exploration of the role of the Party Conference in the inter-war years is contained in Minkin, *op. cit.*, 1980, Chapter 1.
39. *Ibid.*, pp. 18–19.
40. 'Labour and Government', *LPACR*, 1933, pp. 8–10, Item 7.
41. LPACR, 1907, p. 49.
42. 1924 was the first year that there was a major use of the Party Conference agenda by the NEC to submit policy proposals on key issues where resolutions and amendments had already been submitted by affiliated

organisations. In 1929, Clause 2f of the redrafted constitution formally legitimised the NEC's role.

43. On this see Minkin, *op. cit.*, p. 16.

44. In the whole period of the inter-war years, only one small union (the United Patternmakers) on one occasion (1934) submitted a resolution calling on a Labour Government to carry out Conference policy and no union ever submitted a resolution or a constitutional amendment seeking to tighten control by the Party (NEC or Conference) over the PLP.

45. Will Thorne, *TUC Congress Report*, 1913, p. 290. Between 1913 and 1921, there was election by the different trade groups, not the Congress as a whole.

46. For a detailed analysis of NEC voting practices in the 1950s and 1960s, see Minkin, *op. cit.*, Chapter 9 and for the 1980s, this study, Chapter 11, pp. 322–34.

47. On this see McKibbon, *op. cit.*, pp. 90–1.

48. Although, in the late 1920s and 1930s, there were probably heavy filters exercised against the election of Left and Communist sympathisers, the unions were careful to ensure that the ILP had representation and some on the Left were elected in spite of the generally Rightwing majorities at leadership level in the unions. Among those elected in the 1920s were two from the ILP, Agnes Dollan and Fred Jowett (the latter given a seat in the Societies section which might have gone to the unions), and George Lansbury. See also Bevin's rueful comment on his union's votes for Mosley and for Cripps, *LPACR*, 1937, p. 145.

49. *LPACR*, 1907, pp. 54–5. There was a further attempt in 1908, but this, and an attempt to restrict MPs to one-third of the places, was also rejected, *LPACR*, 1908, pp. 61–2.

50. Speech of John Hodge MP of the Steel Smelters, rejecting attempts to prohibit MPs from membership of the NEC, *LPACR*, 1907, p. 34.

51. Ben Pimlott, *Labour and the Left in the 1930s*, 1977, p. 138.

52. McKenzie, *op. cit.*, p. 520.

53. K. D. Ewing, *Trade Unions, the Labour Party and the Law*, 1982, p. 4.

54. George Spencer was Notts. Miners' leader and a Labour then an Independent MP, but 'Spencerism' was financed by the Conservative Party until about 1935. Keith Middlemas, *Politics in Industrial Society*, 1979, p. 202.

55. See on this also Milne-Bailey, *op. cit.*, p. 107 and General Council pamphlet 'A Union without Politics: A Cripple without a Crutch', 1928.

56. Shirley Lerner, *Breakaway Unions and the Small Trade Union*, 1961, p. 70.

57. *Labour Party Constitution and Standing Orders*, 1929, Clause III 3b.

58. See the protest by the General Council to the Joint Meeting of the NEC and the TUC, *Minutes*, 26/11/1930 and *LPACR*, 1931, p. 166 for a protest from the Shop Assistants.

59. Between 1919 and 1939 only three unions submitted constitutional amendments and these were on minor issues.

60. *LPACR*, 1929, p. 201.

61. On this see Foot, *op. cit.*, pp. 174–80 and Alan Bullock, *Ernest Bevin: Foreign Secretary 1945–51*, 1963, p. 60.

62. In 1930, Mosley's economic proposals largely coincided with Bevin's own ideas but Bevin 'would not compromise with his belief in solidarity', Bullock, Vol. 1, *op. cit.*, p. 450.

63. 'What would the Prime Minister of any other Government give to have the solid loyalty of your followers ready to stand by you in trouble and to forgive you in error as the 4,000,000 Trade Unionists in this country have been ready to do during all this time?' Ernest Bevin to Ramsay MacDonald, reported to the Labour Party Conference in 1937. *LPACR*, 1937, p. 174.
64. Arthur Henderson, *LPACR*, 1932, p. 164.
65. These understandings were agreed at meetings of the *National Joint Council* on 7/12/31, 21/1/32, 29/6/32, and 10/11/32.
66. 'Labour and Government', *NEC Report*, 1933, p. 61.
67. See on this *LPACR*, 1923, p. 200 for MacDonald's guarantee to the Prudential Staff Union in response to their resolution. See also Beer, *op. cit.*, p. 173.
68. Ernest Bevin, *LPACR*, 1935, p. 180.
69. Fred Watkins, Railway Clerks Assn., *LPACR*, 1939, p. 297.
70. Arthur Henderson, *LPACR*, 1932, p. 164.
71. This consultation was carried through impeccably in 1940. See Chapter 3, p. 55 and note 2.
72. W. Milne-Bailey (ed.), *Trade Union Documents*, 1929, pp. 45–6.
73. *Ibid.*, pp. 43 and 46. For a clear statement of this distinction by a trade union leader, see Ben Turner's fraternal address to the Labour Party Conference, *LPACR*, 1928, p. 194.
74. Sidney and Beatrice Webb, *The History of Trade Unionism*, 1920, p. 1. For different perceptions of the character and purposes of trade unionism, see Selig Perlman, *A Theory of the Labour Movement*, 1928; Perry Anderson, 'The Limits and Possibilities of Trade Union Action', in Robin Blackburn and Alexander Cockburn (eds.), *The Incompatibles*, 1967; Allan Flanders, *Management and Unions*, 1970; and Richard Hyman, *Marxism and the Sociology of Trade Unionism*, 1972. See also Chapter 6, pp. 159–61 and notes 1–6 for the relations between trade unions and the Labour Party. For a blunt statement of 'our principal concern' with 'fundamental matters of wages, hours and working conditions' and not 'chimerical notions of ushering in the social milenium', see A. Conley (NUTGW), Pres. address, *TUC 1934 Congress Report*, p. 74.
75. G. D. H. Cole, Trade Unions Today, 1939, pp. 538-9.
76. Lord Citrine, *Men and Work*, 1964, p. 301.
77. Some of the classic statements of this approach come from the very influential Ernest Bevin. For example, 'I visualise that I have a job to do and I say to myself: "What would I do?" That is the difference between a theoretical person and a Trade Union official who has to meet and deal with the practical affairs of everyday life', *LPACR*, 1932, p. 190.
78. 'They had to meet the same members every day of their lives, almost from the cradle to the grave and every word they uttered they were expected to live up to in their Trade Union. That was the difference between politics and the industrial organisations.' Ernest Bevin, *LPACR*, 1925, p. 251.
79. *Ibid.*, also Citrine, *op. cit.*, pp. 300–1.
80. I have taken these rules from the comments of veteran trade union leaders, from references in the autobiographies and biographies of union leaders and from the reported comments of trade union leaders. They are in part interpretative, and they are not exclusive.
81. Beer, *op. cit.*, p. 117. Also Tracey, *op. cit.*, p. 4.

82. Even then they were at pains to defend trade union priorities against those of the socialist intellectuals. See, for example, Cramp of the NUR, *LPACR*, 1932, p. 257.

83. Ernest Bevin, the first Chairman of the TUC's Economic Committee, was unusual in his confident grasp of economic policy, particularly after his service on the MacMillan Committee (1930/1) and the Economic Advisory Council set up under the 1929–31 Labour Government. But in the early 1930s, Bevin was at odds with other union leaders on some key issues of economic policy, Bullock, Vol. I, *op. cit.*, pp. 510 and 513–4.

84. Bullock, Vol. I, *op. cit.*, p. 509.

85. Elizabeth Durbin, *New Jerusalems*, 1985, Chap. 12, pp. 243–264.

86. S. Hurst, TGWU, Chairman's Address to the 1931 Labour Party Conference, *LPACR*, 1931, p. 155.

87. Bevin particularly played a major role in shaping *Labour's Pension Plan for Old Age, Widows and Children* in 1937. *LPACR*, 1937, p. 173 and Bullock, *op. cit.*, p. 597.

88. Resolution moved by the GMWU, *TUC Congress Report*, 1933, p. 371.

89. There was formal agreement on the statutory right of unions to be represented on the boards of socialised industries, *LPACR*, 1935, p. 18, but this agreement obscured continuing uncertainty on the emphasis to be given to expertise in the composition of management boards, on the scope of union representation, and on the role of the unions in relation to the new boards.

90. *LPACR*, 1933, pp. 205–6.

91. Williams, *op. cit.*, p. 413.

92. *Manifesto to the Trade Unionists of the Country*, Parliamentary Committee of the TUC 1914, cited in Clegg, *op. cit.*, p. 119.

93. *Ibid.*, pp. 292–3.

94. Michael Pinto-Duschinsky, *British Political Finance 1830–1980*, 1981, pp. 74–7. Ewing, *op. cit.*, p. 62.

95. In 1949, Aneurin Bevan, speaking 'as a trade unionist' and as a Minister in the Labour Government, summed this up in the statement 'The language of priorities is the religion of Socialism', *LPACR*, 1949, p. 172. That such priorities might have widely differing interpretations is clear from the wartime conflict between Bevan and Bevin. See Chapter 3, pp. 59–61. For the expectation of consultation over priorities, see W. Stott of the Railway Clerks Association moving the resolution to approve *Labour's Immediate Programme* in 1937, *LPACR*, 1937, p. 183.

96. The most clear-cut expression of this alternative perspective came from Communist delegates on the floor of the Congress. In 1924, at the TUC Congress, Harry Pollitt, Communist Party leader and Boilermakers' delegate, challenged the 'tacit agreement to the separation which already exists between the Trade Union movement and the Labour Government'. The Congress 'must be able to control the actions of the Labour Government', *TUC Congress Report*, 1924, pp. 287–8. Pollitt's view was not accepted and the Communist Party was gradually excluded from direct Labour Party activity, but the minority Left position was handed down in the unions alongside the majority and official view. Among union leaders in the Labour Party, it was particularly noticeable in the responses of the National Amalgamated Furnishing Trades Association, whose Secretary was Alex Gossip. He was never a member of the General Council.

97. One such figure was H. H. Elvin of the white collar National Union of Clerks and Administrative Workers. He was in a small minority of union leaders who had opposed the First World War. An ex-Labour candidate, he took detailed interest in Labour Party affairs (see n. 14) and he was never one to show too much respect for traditional demarcations. See the debate on Union Contributions During Unemployment, *TUC Congress Report*, 1934, pp. 267–70.

98. Union leaders even sometimes took to the National Joint Council complaints about MPs 'speaking against trade unionism', for example the TUC criticism of Shinwell, *NJC Minutes*, 27/3/29.

99. Eric Shaw, *Discipline and Discord in the Labour Party*, 1988, pp. 11–15.

100. McKibbon, *op. cit.*, p. 247.

3

Achievement

THE LOCOMOTIVE OF HISTORY

War – 'the locomotive of history' – has been the dynamo of twentieth-century political change. World War II dramatically shifted the balance of industrial and political power in Britain towards organised labour, producing reverberations which went deep into the roots of the Labour Movement and of the society at large. The seven years after 1940 were years of solid achievement. The trade unions grew in size and confidence, and secured a new level of access and consultation from the Government. The Party won a comprehensive victory at the General Election of 1945 and formed the first majority Labour Government. The great bulk of the domestic programme, nurtured through unions and party since the formation of an independent party of labour, was finally implemented. What was created in this period established some of the basic elements of the policy framework of British politics for the next three decades. And the style as well as the substance of this Labour Government's approach to policy encouraged a reinforcement of the 'rules' of the Labour Movement.

Nevertheless, it is important to note that the coming to Office of a successful Labour Government followed a period of acute division and weakness at different levels of the relationship. These have to be understood if we are to place the problems of later decades in perspective. Some of the difficulties sprang from, or were exacerbated by, the unusual circumstances of wartime political life. But there were also problems of a more long-term character. And there emerged from differing political perspectives a growing criticism of the union–Labour Party relationship. The result was a range of prescriptions for dealing with the politics of 'the problem of the unions'.

REGENERATION
'1945'

The political developments of the 1940s are encapsulated in the folklore of the Labour Movement as '1945' – an experience of growing industrial strength and mass radical support accompanied by steadfast realisation of the Movement's objectives. On the Left particularly, each generation looked back at the achievement as an example of Labour Movement power and Democratic Socialist commitment. And, each generation sought to emulate the success. It was, however, a very difficult act to follow – a period unique in its advantages for the Left. Above all, the Labour Movement in the next forty years found it impossible to inspire or benefit from a similar level of radical electoral support, sympathetic to Socialism.

The appeal of Socialism

In the late spring of 1940, the British war position became beleaguered. Chamberlain resigned and was replaced by Churchill. A Coalition Government was formed with Labour as a partner.[1] This compromise of Labour's independence was only agreed after thorough consultations between the Parliamentary leadership, the Party Executive and the General Council of the TUC. In these discussions it was also agreed that there would be a benefit to the Labour Movement as well as to the war effort if the unions were directly involved in the Government.[2] Ernest Bevin became Minister of Labour and National Service.

The change in Government also precipitated changes in ideological perception. The downfall of Chamberlain, and the appointment with Labour support of the Conservative rebel Churchill, involved a repudiation of the Munichites who had dominated the Conservative leadership and had sought appeasement of Hitler. Their lack of military preparation became coupled in the public mind with all the failures of inter-war economic policy. The Conservatives lost some of their normal advantage as *the* party of patriotism but became identified as *the* party of unemployment with, ultimately, damage to their self-confidence which was only restored under Margaret Thatcher in the late 1970s.

For the unions, on the other hand, these political developments gave them not only a new opportunity to influence the conditions of wartime employment but also to be associated with a patriotic national venture. And, as Ernest Bevin told the TUC Special Conference called in 1940 to discuss their attitude to participation in a Coalition Government,

> if ... our class rise with all their energy and save the people, the country will always turn with confidence to the people who saved them ...[3]

Clumsily expressed, but the message of ultimate benefit to the Movement as a whole was unmistakable.

The accumulation of experiences in 1940 generated a new electoral radicalism as yet unfocused upon any party allegiance but hostile to pre-war Conservatism.[4] This radicalism was strengthened in various ways by actions taken on behalf of the Government to sustain the sense of national community and advance the war effort – particularly during and after 'the Blitz'. The People's War was very nearly fought 'on the beaches' and 'in the hills' but for much of the time it was actually fought in the factories and the air-raid shelters with high production the goal and low morale the enemy. 'Demostrategy' (as Professor Falls called it[5]) involved a range of positive steps to safeguard the health and well-being of the people. It involved a consciousness that millions of ordinary people had to be convinced that Britain had something better to offer than its enemies – not only during but after the war.[6] 'Fair Shares' was to become Labour's post-war theme but it was initially a Coalition Government slogan, as a comprehensive rationing system was introduced.[7]

Wartime collectivism was not quite the traumatic break with tradition that it had been in World War I, but its scope and success in this war were a great propaganda boost for the Left and an institutionalised reproach to the failed politicians of the inter-war years. Rational collective organisation by the central Government was seen to overcome a wide variety of obstacles. By all accounts, these measures became for the moment ideologically acceptable even to those who had never shown anything but hostility towards the developing role of the state in peacetime. 'Socialism', defined loosely as the collective organisation of national resources, became even for Conservatives an essential element in national defence.

The appeal of collectivism and planning was reinforced by the sudden national alliance with the Soviet Union in the summer of 1941. From the birth of the USSR (and later in the decades following the Cold War), political and industrial labour had to endure a barrage of propaganda associating the Movement with the 'alien system'. For the moment, the necessities of war after the German invasion of the USSR curtailed the hostile propaganda and to a remarkable degree replaced it with favourable, even eulogistic, support for 'our gallant Soviet allies'. The Government itself took the lead in encouraging hundreds of pro-Soviet committees and societies and as the war progressed and the Germans were turned round at Stalingrad, it became difficult to separate the virtues of heroic defence and patriotic resilience from the advantages of the Soviet economic planning system.

In a sense also this war, fought out for much of the time from the British mainland, was in social terms a war of movement. Significant, if intangible, consequences flowed from the new patterns of geographical mobility and social interaction which undermined old habits of thought and behaviour. Military conscription, waves of evacuation, major shifts of population and the increased employment of women created new political environments and opened minds to new ideas.

The movement of ideas was evident also in a flowering of radical agitation which had new and unusual vantage points; the BBC, the Central Office of Information, the Church of England and even Fleet Street, where a 'revolution' after 1940 had brought into editorial positions a new generation of Leftwing journalists closely attuned to and influencing the popular mood. In the Army, too, there was a new Bureau of Current Affairs which encouraged a mood of criticism which fed off the pre-war record of Conservatism. As the wartime electoral truce closed off conventional party electoral politics, so new independent candidates and new political organisations rose to articulate the new radicalism. In particular, Common Wealth became the wartime party of the idealistic professional middle class.

The rise of industrial labour

As the British Left moved through a unique period of political advantage, organised labour in industry also grew in strength and leverage.

Under the conditions of an economy organised for war on a scale and to an extent unsurpassed by any other nation, manpower became 'the ultimate scarce resource' as the full employment which had proved so elusive in the inter-war years became a reality. The unions grew in membership, expanding chiefly in those occupations like engineering and agriculture which were swollen by war-time exigencies. TUC membership shot up as it had during the First World War. In 1938 it had been 4,460,167. By the end of 1944 it was 6,642,317. For the next thirty-five years it was either stable or growing.

As part of the arrangement whereby in 1940 'the Labour Movement' entered the Coalition, the trade union relationship with Government was put on a new basis. The TUC's longstanding claim 'to represent the working people in all matters affecting their conditions of life and labour'[8] was conceded, as was the principle of equality of representation in a tripartite consultative system. Direct access to Ministers by the unions was confirmed on the instructions of the Prime Minister. Trade unions were given a place on a wide range of Governmental bodies including a high level Joint Consultative Committee.

By mutual agreement, the TUC virtually monopolised trade union consultative access to Government departments.[9] Ernest Bevin's understanding with Walter Citrine at the TUC, while never short on personal friction, shared enough perspectives to help the collaborative process function reasonably smoothly.

Driving to secure a maximum mobilisation of manpower and a high level of morale, Bevin was able to push also for a change in social values and an alteration in the status of working people which would outlast the war. His period as Minister of Labour was marked by a broad range of measures to alleviate working conditions and by a series of legislative reforms. A Determination of Needs Act in 1941, the Catering Wages Act in 1943, the Disabled Persons Act in 1944 and the Wages Councils Act in 1945 were all part of his legacy during this period. Nor was he slow to encourage employers to recognise trade unions. Small wonder that with an easy access to Government, influential friends in high places, and tangible reforms coming through, the TUC particularly should be happy with the wartime arrangements.

The conditions of wartime production enhanced union industrial bargaining power – even though they made major concessions as they redefined priorities. They allowed a measure of 'dilution', industrial conscription and the direction of labour; they raised no objection to the prohibition of strikes under Order 1305. But – and this was a crucial position supported by Bevin and the TUC – collective bargaining was preserved and there were no direct wage controls other than those designed to set minimum wage levels in certain industries. Lockouts were illegal and there was compulsory arbitration in the event of a failure to agree.

In these new conditions of production, local trade unionism thrived. Compulsory arbitration meant that employers were forced to negotiate. Shopfloor control was increased through the growth of Joint Production Committees. The Shop Stewards movement gained a new lease of life – particularly in engineering.

Though officially strikes were illegal and the large-scale national conflicts which marked the First World War were avoided, strikes did take place – usually short unofficial actions over piece-work rates. These strikes increased yearly up to 1945, when there was a record number of such stoppages.[10] They were, however, heavily concentrated in mining (of 2,293 disputes in 1945, 1,306 were in the mines), the docks, passenger transport and engineering, and thus involved mainly three unions, the Mineworkers, the Transport Workers and the Engineers.

This mainly covert but intense pattern of industrial conflict reflected both an increased confidence of working people and the growth of a more vigorous industrial Left – all part and parcel of the new radical mood but not itself a significant cause of it. The waves of radical political opinion in this wartime period were much more attuned to military and national political developments than they were to anything that was happening in industry.

THE STATE OF THE MOVEMENT

Such was the strength of the radical current during the Second World War and so great was Labour's victory in 1945, that in idealised memory it pushes other features into background relief. It is important to be reminded that the two years prior to 1945 were often marked by a deep pessimism about Labour's chances, that internal conflict was often protracted and bitter, and that it was a commonplace of the time that the Labour Party was heavily divided and in political decline.[11] What is also significant is that many of the problems facing the Party in this period affected or arose from the union–party relationship. The relationship may have appeared strong by 1947 and even stronger by 1951, but in 1943 and 1944 it was torn by bitter divisions, often involving questions of representation. And as the war neared its end, its organisational weaknesses became apparent and led to the creation of a unique joint committee. Further, the political weaknesses and limitations of the alliance of the Labour Party and the unions stimulated at this time a range of options for radical realignment or reconstruction of the relationship.

The representation of labour

The conflicts of this period have to be seen in the context of the TUC's new and unique relationship with the wartime Government. The form of these arrangements ensured the TUC would be the authoritative voice of organised labour and, by contrast with the arrangements during the First World War, the Labour Party's position would be correspondingly diminished.

So great was the TUC's new influence that it could, on industrial matters, monopolise discussions with the Government and virtually exercise a veto over the Party's participation. But its interests, its access and its involvement in policy matters, ran much wider than the industrial areas and it was sometimes accorded 'equal or even prior standing' with the Party on other matters in these exceptional conditions.[12]

During this period, the National Council of Labour diminished in importance as a policymaking body (a feature which coincided with an invitation to the Co-operative Union to join it in 1941). Though it met regularly on a monthly basis until 1944, it was rarely involved in major discussions and sent only the occasional deputation to Ministers.

Labour's political leaders in the Coalition appeared to be reasonably happy with these arrangements under the exceptional conditions and at that level there was little in the way of jurisdictional disputes. Not so with the Parliamentary Labour Party where the view began to be articulated that the consultative process with the TUC had gone so far that the Labour Party was ceasing to be a channel at all – simply 'an appendage of the TUC'.[13] This criticism came initially from the Left, but in 1943 and 1944 it involved a much broader spectrum of opinion. Unusually, the PLP in this period became a focal point of the intra-Party 'Opposition'.

Conflicting perspectives on the union–party relationship were exemplified in the different positions of two men, Ernest Bevin and Aneurin Bevan. Both had backgrounds which were impeccably manual working class and each could claim to speak for that class and its political aspirations. In the two years prior to 1945, they were deeply and at times viciously 'at war' in their perspectives and their priorities.

The sharpest impact of this came after a row within the Parliamentary Labour Party over the implementation of the Beveridge Report which had left the party 'in snarling fragments'.[14] An internal crisis 'graver than anything since Ramsay MacDonald's defection', was how Bevan described it.[15] A majority of the PLP actually voted against what was regarded as the Coalition Government's failure to respond adequately to Beveridge. Thereupon Ernest Bevin, in fury, demanded his own expulsion from the Labour Party because he had voted for the Coalition and against the Party.[16]

This being ignored, he then withdrew from all Labour Party meetings and did not reappear for fifteen months. He did not appear at the Party Conference of 1943, nor did he attend the important weekend meeting of Labour's leaders, held from 25 to 27 February 1944, at which policy and attitudes towards a post-war Coalition were discussed.[17] During this time, he apparently regarded himself as the representative within the Coalition Government of the trade unions rather than the Labour Party.[18]

This was not just a public show. It is clear from the minutes that the Transport Workers in 1943–4 did not claim their representative on the Party's Finance and General Purposes Committee – a highly unusual situation for the Movement's largest union and the Party's 'landlord'. Nor did the TGWU involve itself in any of the co-ordinated advance preparations taking place within the unions for the post-war General Election (see below, pp. 62–3).

On one level, these actions can be regarded (or disregarded) simply as the personal quirk of an egotist of great stature. Bevin was still firmly committed to Labour having an independent political voice. But its significance should not be underestimated. There is plenty of evidence to suggest that, after El Alamein, senior Labour Ministers, including Bevin, were sceptical of the chances of defeating Churchill in a post-war election whatever the new polls might say.[19] And they feared the return to 'normality' that might be brought about by such a victorious Conservative Party.

Working people, including unionised labour, had secured many advances from the existence of the Coalition Government. There was much to be said for the view that *the* priority was a continuing Coalition Government which, working in close liaison with the TUC, would be able to protect the advances made and might even be able to continue them. Of course, a reforming Labour Government with a clear majority would be far better, but such a Government had not yet been seen and Bevin was a practical man.

Michael Foot was one of the many on the Left who feared that what was really at stake in 1943 was the unity of the Movement and a split engineered and encouraged by the Tories.[20] In October 1944 the NEC did make it clear publicly that the Party would fight the 1945 election as an independent Party, but even in April 1945, Attlee and Bevin were still arguing that the Coalition should continue until the end of the War with Japan.[21]

More persistent in its consequences for the union–party relationship was Bevin's appreciation that the TUC could offer, in a sense, a political *alternative* to the Labour Party. It was political in its access to Government, political in its representation within the Coalition, and political in its retention of the right it had always claimed to discuss and pronounce upon any policy proposal submitted by one of its affiliates. It would always be a restricted role, given its anchorage in the industrial process. It would always benefit from having a party political 'arm' as a long term safeguard for its industrial functions and freedoms. But as the war years were to illustrate, much could be won via a direct neo-corporatist relationship. Perhaps enough to make the Party seem less than essential. Twenty and forty years on, at the TUC, such thoughts were to surface again.

Bevin moved back into close identification with the Party during the winter of 1944–5, and in March 1945, the Transport Workers agreed to join the Joint Committee co-ordinating election preparations (see below). But meanwhile tensions between Bevin and Bevan, trade union Right and political Left, intensified.

In early 1944 the Coalition Government, preparing for the D-Day invasion, was faced with unofficial strikes in the coalfields, particularly Yorkshire and South Wales. Bevin attributed the strikes to political agitation. Regarding the situation as an emergency, he persuaded a majority of the General Council to support a new Regulation 1AA which would penalise anybody instigating unofficial strikes by fines or imprisonment. Though the disputes were quickly over and the regulation never used, there was a fierce row between the union leaders and the backbench Parliamentary Left led by Aneurin Bevan. In the vote on the Order, only 56 of Labour's 165 MPs voted in favour. Attempts by the union leadership to get Bevan expelled failed, but he was eventually forced to sign an assurance to loyally abide by the standing orders of the Parliamentary Labour Party. However, some idea of the acute divisions within the unions was indicated at the TUC Annual Congress when a motion to refer back the General Council statement was defeated by only 3,686,000 to 2,802,000.[22] At this time also, Citrine wrote to the Labour Party's Secretary, Jim Middleton, that the General Council felt that the Parliamentary Party and, to some smaller degree, the Labour Party and the TUC, 'were drifting into something like opposing factions'.[23]

Bevan, meanwhile, had developed a fierce critique of the new arrangements of British Government – arrangements which not only tied the TUC in with the Coalition Government but diminished the role of public representatives. On the Workmen's Compensation Bill in October 1943, he had described the detailed tripartite arrangements which shaped the Bill before its discussion in the House of Commons as 'the gravest constitutional impropriety'.[24] The deep resentment which Leftwing MPs felt at the accommodating role of the General Council here became a defence of Parliamentary and, to some extent, of Party democracy. In the process, harsh things were said about the way trade unions made their policies and about the solutions offered, which forty years later were to come from a very different section of the Labour Party. Trade union leaders were unrepresentative. Why (on Regulation 1AA) did they not hold a ballot?[25]

Another critique of trade unions which came from the Left but was also eventually to be taken over by the Right concerned the representative role of back-bench sponsored MPs. Bevan's challenge to the role of the unions in their relationship with the Government was coupled with a defence of the independence of MPs. To this end, Bevan resisted, as he had in the past, attempts to put pressure upon him via his sponsoring organisation, and threatened to raise it as a breach of privilege.[26] It was a theme that Bevan was to return to in 1955 when attempts were made to expel him from the Labour Party and it had significance which went further than the immediate issue. It became part of a series of developments in this period which were to strengthen the hand of MPs when faced with union pressure. From Bevan's complaint and the judgments of the Committee of Privileges in the Alderman Robinson (1943–4) and W.J. Brown (1946–7) cases came a much stronger constraint against improper 'instructions' (see Chapter 9, pp. 260–1), and inhibitions which were to affect Leftwing trade union leaders in the 1970s as much as those on the Right in the 1940s.

Organisational decline and the Joint Committee

Conflicts over the priorities and processes of coalition corporatism were not the only source of despondency in this period. The Labour Party's internal life, its local links with the unions and its organisation had all been badly depleted at a time when other Leftwing organisations – particularly the Communist Party and Common Wealth – were thriving. In August of 1943, *Tribune* even noted that it was fashionable on the Left to say that the Labour Party was 'dead'.[27]

Wartime social conditions and the electoral truce led to a major decline in the individual membership of the Party from 428,926 in 1938 to 223,929 by the end of 1942. The number of agents (never large compared with Labour's Conservative opponents) had declined from 132 in 1937 to 58 in 1943. While trade union membership and trade union affiliation to the TUC had risen sharply, Labour's national affiliation from trade unions had first declined and then only marginally increased. In 1943 it stood at 2,672,845 compared with 2,630,286 in 1938. At local level, affiliation from the unions had been very badly impaired. Part of the explanation for these developments was the lack of activity from the Labour Party side. But it was also a reflection of the persistent decline of levy paying which had been going on since the 1927 Act and had *not* been reversed as a result of wartime radicalism. Harrison's information shows that, in 1943, it was at an all-time low of just under 42 per cent of the membership of unions with Political Funds.[28]

In one respect, this weak condition of levypaying did not present a major financial problem. The absence of a General Election in 1940 and the suspension

of electoral activity during the wartime electoral truce had left the unions with
accumulated political fund balances. But the funds were not as great as they
might have been because the levies were very small and had not been adjusted for
many years. It was similar with the level of affiliation fees. The latter could not be
adjusted without an increase in the levies and in 1944, after a survey, the NEC
concluded that an increase in affiliation fees could not be met from existing
Political Funds.[29]

This weakness of organisation and finance, the lack of readiness for a General
Election and the degeneration of the grass-roots links with the unions stimulated
a remarkable and discreet innovation in the closing years of the war – a new
linkage of the Labour Movement, barely visible at the time and long since lost to
view.

In its form – a Joint Committee of the Party and the unions to discuss common
financial and organisational problems – it was a very unusual arrangement. It was
also, it must be noted, a *party*-instigated development – a fact which legitimised
some crossing of delicate territorial boundaries. But in its concerns, its involvement in the preparation of a report on organisational and financial matters, and
its implementational role in organisational reform, it prefigured the creation of
Trade Unions for a Labour Victory by the unions three decades later (see
Chapter 15).

George Shepherd, the Party's National Agent, had been seeking for some time
to involve union executives in joint consultations to discuss areas of finance and
organisation where the union–party relationship was weak and required renova-
tion if the Party was to be prepared for an end-of-war contest with the Conservatives.[30] These discussions, taking place from and on the Party's Finance and
General Purposes Committee, do not appear to have made much headway by the
time of the 1943 Party Conference. At this Conference, a resolution from the
Preston Trades and Labour Council urged the NEC to set up a Committee of
Enquiry into various financial, organisational and electoral problems and to
consult with 'all appropriate interests' in its preparation.[31]

The NEC in response did *not* set up a separate Committee of Enquiry. Instead, it
widened the remit of the Finance and General Purposes Committee discussions
and consequently convened a special conference of senior trade union officers on
12 November 1943.[32] At the conference, after a discussion among the union
leaders, it was moved that a committee of five trade union officers be appointed
to liaise with the Finance and General Purposes Committee on behalf of the
affiliated unions.[33] Subsequently, Joint Committee meetings were held of the F
and GP and the five union representatives, with the Party's National Agent
acting as Secretary. A report from this Joint Committee, covering various financial and related matters, including the Political Levy, was then taken to a further
conference of union officers held on 11 February 1944, with the recommendation
that the Joint Committee continue in office to supervise the implementation of
the draft memorandum embodying its proposals.[34]

Discussions on the Joint Committee appear to have provided the major input
into an *Interim Report on Organisation and Finance* which was taken to the 1944
Party Conference and discussed privately there.[35] Among its proposals were the

raising of permissible payments to Constituency Parties by the unions under the Hastings Agreement, the recommendation of an increase in political levies in the unions, a joint campaign to increase 'contracting in', a greater commitment by the unions to the sponsorship of Labour candidates, and a crash programme of recruitment of agents.

Though held back by the postponement of the 1944 Party Conference and various exigencies of wartime, the Joint Committee continued discreet operation and in March 1945 it was strengthened by the addition of three more union representatives including now the Transport Workers.[36] In November 1944, immediately after the Party Conference, there began a series of twelve regional conferences of trade union branches and the Party's regional officers to stimulate activity between the unions and the Party – particularly levypaying and candidate sponsorship.[37] Special efforts were made in Yorkshire and Lancashire and the East and West Midlands.[38]

The impact of this Joint Committee activity is difficult to assess if only because, as the war neared its end, the General Election released a sudden great burst of pent-up radical energy. But the impact of the committee on levypaying and affiliation was remarkably small.

Political levypaying through 'contracting in' did increase from 1943 to 1945 but by 1945 was only 48 per cent.[39] Perhaps they were concerned with other priorities in 1945, but there was certainly no great rush of trade unionists to volunteer to pay for more trade union political activity. There was a small rise in national affiliation of unions to the Labour Party in 1944 and 1945 – 138,000 then 135,000 – particularly in agriculture and engineering, but affiliation of the Engineers was still at a low level. In most unions, affiliation to the Labour Party in 1945 was under 50 per cent.

As for trade union sponsorship of Labour candidates, although the Transport Workers put on a sudden spurt, overall the number of trade union sponsored candidates was still less than in 1935.[40]

Labour's national financial appeal for its General Election Fund met a much more enthusiastic reception. The target of £250,000 was easily met with the unions contributing the bulk of the income. Indeed, there was a surplus which not only allowed £25,000 to be put towards grants for agents' salaries, but allowed a balance of £60,000 to be carried forward into 1946.[41] This became a regular occurrence.

As for organisation, this was far from being a decisive factor in the 1945 election although, in certain areas, the Conservative machinery was, as Labour's organisers noted, not in as good a condition as it had often been. The Labour Party and local unions scrambled around for agents in the pre-election period and '... men were pulled – in some instances dragged – out of factories, signal boxes and engine cabs' to take up positions'.[42] What mattered rather more than planned organisation in this unique election was the tide of enthusiasm and radical opinion.

In two particular cases, Labour's new industrial strength had a special impact and fed into the Party's organisation. The Labour campaign in rural areas was a revelation; it was based on the reinvigorated Agricultural Workers' Union which provided the organisational core in the Eastern Region and the East Midlands. In the West Midlands, shop stewards in the engineering factories created a vigorous union–Party organisation which lasted well into the 1950s.[43]

But the West Midlands area appears to have been unusual. Over much of the country, the union–Party relationship at the grassroots was not immediately invigorated by the experience of war. Proposals for factory branches (again pioneered in the West Midlands) were rejected nationally and do not seem to have been discussed in the Joint Committee.

Following the victory of 1945, the Joint Committee was reconstituted after a meeting of affiliated unions on 29 March 1946.[44] It aimed to organise the follow-through to the election victory and specifically to discuss increasing the numbers paying the levy. The new Joint Committee (eight from each side) was now packed with trade union heavyweights including Arthur Deakin of the Transport Workers, Charlie Dukes of the General and Municipal Workers and Will Lawther of the Mineworkers, and their influence resulted in an immediate huge increase in affiliation to the Labour Party as soon as the Trades Disputes Act was repealed.

The advantage to the Political Funds of changing the basis of levypaying from contracting 'in' to contracting 'out' was as clear as had been the reverse legislation in 1927. By 1947, the numbers paying the political levy had shot up to 75.6 per cent.[45] It is not necessary to agree fully with the diagnosis of Martin Harrison (that this was almost entirely due to the change in the legislation) in order to accept that the changing onus of action was the major reason for the sudden jump in levypaying.[46] Levypaying, as already noted, had been on the increase between 1943 and 1945. It is not unreasonable to expect that, with the new Labour Government pushing ahead with its programme, and co-ordinated activity through the Joint Committee continuing in 1945 and 1946, a commensurate increase in levypaying would have been achieved from 1945 to 1947, which would have brought it to around 55 per cent. Somewhere in the region of 20 per cent of levypayers were, therefore, involved without active effort and some without conscious approval – a permanent soft underbelly of the Labour Movement.

The long term impact of this inflated increase was to produce a high level of union complacency which did much to create subsequent problems. Although the Joint Committee met again twice in 1946–7 to discuss Labour Party finance and to stimulate income for the new Party Development campaign, there is no evidence of any co-ordinated campaign in the unions after 1947 on the lines of 1943–6. Indeed, after this period, the Joint Committee ceased to function and was lost to history. As for the elected representatives of the Special Conference of affiliated unions, their like was not to be seen for the next thirty years, until the creation of Trade Unions for a Labour Victory.

The short term impact of the increase in levypaying was to give a massive boost to trade union affiliation and to the finances of the Labour Party. In 1946, affiliation had increased by 5 per cent (124,977) over 1945; in 1947, it increased by 53 per cent (1,396,088), of which the Transport Workers contributed no less than 350,000.

This boost to trade union affiliation, which rose from 2,635,346 in 1946 to 4,386,074 in 1947, has also to be seen alongside the development of individual membership in the constituencies. From the wartime low point of 218,783 in 1942, membership had risen to a new high of 645,345 in 1946. As it happened, there was to be a slight dip in individual membership to 608,487 in 1947 before it accelerated in its rise. But at the time when discussions on the future levels of trade union affiliation to the Labour Party were taking place on the Joint Committee, the CLP vote at the Party Conference had reached its highest ever level against the unions at 25 per cent. Given the (inflated) anxieties that there were about the size and activity of the Left and the Communists in the constituency parties, the discussions on raising trade union affiliation in this period had more than financial significance.

Radical alternatives

The scale of Labour's victory in 1945 not only obscures the grassroots deficiencies of the Movement, it hides the alternative paths of political reconstruction which, in the conditions of profound weakness perceived in 1943 and 1944, were being charted for the unions and the Party.

The wartime role of the unions was by no means to the satisfaction of everybody in the large radical camp of these years. The problem of an 'ageing' or 'dying' Labour Party whose potential radicalism was held back by its traditions, its structure and above all by the unions was the subject of diagnosis by forces to both Right and Left of the Labour Party. Each made a radical assessment of Labour's alliance with the unions and concluded that fundamental changes must be made to deal with this problem. Their prognosis was eventually buried in the victory of the Labour Party in 1945 and the sharp consolidation of the two-party system that followed it, but they were to reappear again in a more fluid politics three decades later.

In 1943 and 1944, there was for a while a view emanating from some sections of 'middle opinion' that what was needed in the post-war world was a 'centre party' of reforming progressives. The influential journal The Economist took this prescription further. Labour was held to be in a state of degeneration with out-of-date doctrine and a social base which was ill-fitted to the changing social structure. Above all, Labour dependence on 'the trade union hierarchy' tied it to conservative sectional interests. The 'Labour Coalition' must be ended and a radical regrouping of the non-Conservative forces emerge which could embrace scientific and technical progress.[47]

Trade union conservatism was, of course, seen through very different eyes on the Labour Left. There, for a time, Aneurin Bevan, flirted with a new 'Coalition of the Left' which would involve the Communist Party, the Independent Labour Party and Common Wealth and even some radical Liberals. These would affiliate to the Labour Party and would provide the necessary counterweight to the trade unions who were '... no longer paying affiliation fees to the Labour Party' but 'paying its burial expenses'.[48]

The idea of a realignment of the Left was very common in this period, excited by the electoral success of Common Wealth and independent Leftwing candidates in by-elections, by the growth and new legitimacy of the Communist Party, and by what was felt to be the ineffectual oppositional role of the official party and union leadership. Socialist Unity, Progressive Unity and Left Unity were all variations on this theme.[49] Working with their new-found strength in the Engineers Union, the Communist Party pushed for a 'Unity Conference' of the Left which Labour's NEC rejected.[50] The application for Communist Party affiliation to Labour achieved a new momentum and at the 1945 Party Conference, a reference back (of the Conference Arrangements Committee report) which sought a debate on what was termed 'Progressive Unity' was defeated by a very narrow margin of 1,314,000 to 1,219,000.

There was a third reconstruction position being advocated on the Left, although sometimes it was coupled with support for Left realignment and the strengthening of Leftwing affiliation. This involved Party democratisation. Aneurin Bevan, in 1943, had advocated a major constitutional change which would have restricted trade unions to local affiliation and thus ended the domination over the Party Conference of the trade union block vote.[51] This party 'democratisation' position gained support on the Labour Left and in 1944 became a central plank in the reform programme of the new Victory for Socialism organisation.[52]

However, by the end of 1944, the constitutional reform movement took second place in the priorities of the Left which was seeking to commit the Party leadership to a public ownership programme which already had mandated support within unions, and seeking also the election of a Labour Government which would bring the proposals to fruition.

It remains an intriguing historical question as to whether, in these unique external conditions of electoral radicalism, the Left could have organised and sustained a full-scale constitutional revolt which, like that of 1979, aimed to transform the distribution of power within the Party. Certainly, at no other time in Labour Party history was the wider context so favourable. But here we come to one of the paradoxes of 1945 – the weakness of the organised Labour Left in the constituency parties and in the unions.

Though wartime radicalism created the conditions of Labour's victory and fed the current of support for specific Leftwing policies in the constitutencies, the organised Left in the Party was relatively small. The stand taken by Aneurin Bevan in 1944, the deep antagonism towards the union block vote, and disappointment over the Party leadership's stance over the Beveridge Report, all encouraged a shift to the Left in the constituency section of the NEC in 1944. Harold Laski and Manny Shinwell topped the list and Bevan, standing for the first time, swept into fifth place. But the fact remains that both in 1944 and 1945, the constituency vote (541,000 out of a Conference vote of 2,969,000) was not cast solidly for Leftwing candidates and that four of the seven (Hugh Dalton, James Griffiths, Herbert Morrison and Philip Noel-Baker) were from the centre and Right. And Bevan's position on the realignment of the Left does not appear to have evoked much of a response below. Martin Harrison calculates that the Progressive Unity reference back was supported mainly by the unions but by no more than a third of the constituency vote in 1945.[53]

It might also have been anticipated that the increased industrial militancy of Second World War trade unionism at the grassroots, allied to the broad radical and socialist current of the times, would have led to a major advance for the Left into leadership positions in the affiliated trade unions. Indeed, conditions seemed ripe for the Rightwing block vote to fragment and a powerful Left alliance (of the kind which was to emerge in the late 1960s) to come into being. Signs of such a movement were there in many unions including the Distributive Workers, the Engineers, the Mineworkers, the Railwaymen and the Transport Workers – five of the seven largest unions affiliated to the Party.

But in Labour Party terms, this Leftwing advance suffered from several limitations. It was spearheaded in many cases by a Left outside the Party – the Communist Party whose members were prohibited from participating at the Labour Party Conference. And it noticeably failed to secure major changes in leadership positions in the largest unions. In the highly centralised Transport Workers – the largest union in the Movement – the Left captured positions on the Executive but could neither dislodge nor bypass the firm Rightwing leadership control; in 1945, Ernest Bevin formally gave way to a new hammer of the Left, Arthur Deakin. And the rise of the Left in the Engineers – fastest-growing of the unions during the war – had limited impact on the Labour Party because its levypaying and its affiliation to the Labour Party remained relatively low. At the 1945 Party Conference, the Engineers had only 136,000 votes compared with 679,000 at the TUC.[54]

In any case, changes in political positions within the Labour industrial base always took time to work their way through into National Executive committee positions given the 'rules' of trade union voting. By 1946, when Leftwing currents might have been able to make some impact, there was a Labour Government in office with a record of achievement and a position domestically and internationally that the Right could organise to defend.

Thus it was that during these years of social and political radicalism in British society, its impact on the politics of the unions in the Labour Party was limited and frustrating to the Left. In votes for the majority of places on the Labour National Executive Committee – the trade union and women's sections – the Right was almost as powerful in 1945 as it had been in 1940.

INTO OFFICE

Party, unions, and Labour's appeal

Part of the frustration of the Left with Labour's leadership from 1942 to 1944 arose out of the conditions of wartime politics. Here was sign after sign of the popularity of radical socialist measures. But membership of the Coalition Government and an electoral truce inhibited most of the Labour Party's leadership from any attempt to mobilise support behind a new party programme and from pushing reform disagreements within the Government to a point where it endangered the Coalition. Indeed, in 1942, the Labour leadership even succeeded in winning Annual Conference support for an extension of the electoral truce such that Labour was positively committed to any Coalition Government candidate in by-elections – regardless of whether he or she was a Labour Party member.[55]

Sections of Labour's local activists and PLP deeply resented the interpretation which some Conservatives sought to put on the electoral truce, that is, that it was a political truce, and felt that Labour's leaders were being neutered by processes of Coalition politics. The result was the persistent tension and infighting which have often, before and since, been a handicap to the Labour Party. What is interesting here is that, under the unusual wartime circumstances, the Labour Party was to gain advantage from its confederal structure, its division of authority and its endemic factionalism.

On the one hand it gained public advantage from Labour leaders' senior positions in Government for, unlike in World War I, Labour was not a co-opted minority but an integral part of the Coalition partnership with several of its leaders, particularly Bevin and Morrison, in prominent public positions. They were able to play an influential role in the sub-committees dealing with social and economic aspects of the war effort, to participate in the discussions of post-war plans, and to take on an element of authority which had been lacking in the years since 1931.

At the same time, independent of Labour's Ministerial role, the policymaking machinery of the Party and of the TUC continued to project forward policy, and the affiliated unions continued to express their grievances and aspirations. Labour's dissidents at the Annual Conference and within the Parliamentary Labour Party kept up a running critique of Government policy. Particularly over social security and the Beveridge Report, the Labour Movement outside the House, and Parliamentary Labour Party dissidents within it, associated Labour with a determination to carry through the necessary reforms, even though Labour Ministers were muted in their response.[56] Public opinion began to move behind the Labour Party after this social policy debate.[57] In this sense, the Labour Party had it both ways.

As the war in Europe neared its end, the disunity which had marked Labour's politics and the doubts about its willingness to seek an independent majority Government both evaporated. Agreement and enthusiasm was engendered around the Party's General Election Manifesto *Let Us Face the Future* and the TUC's Manifesto *A Call to the Workers*. Both were substantially in tune with the Party's 1943 Statement *The Labour Party and the Future* and with the TUC's *Interim Report on Postwar Reconstruction* produced in 1944. They carried a programme relevant to the mood and priorities of the time but also one which drew heavily on the policies evolved over decades.

The nation wanted food, work and homes, the Manifesto noted. It promised a planned economy in which there would be 'Jobs for All', a building programme balanced between housing, schools and the urgent requirements of industrial reconstruction and modernisation, and agriculture planned to feed the people. It promised also a high and constant level of purchasing power, 'Social Insurance against a Rainy Day', and a National Health Service.

Alongside these 'bread and butter' priorities there was a vision of a Socialist Commonwealth. It could not come 'overnight' but there was to be a programme of industries 'ripe and over-ripe' for public ownership. These did not include all the industries specified in the resolutions of the 1944 Party Conference, but they did include those where the unions concerned had long indicated their commitment – fuel and power, inland transport and iron and steel. These were, as the TUC's *A Call to the Workers* asserted, 'an immediate necessity'.

Two areas of trade union concern proved to be especially sensitive and in both the unions showed a characteristic degree of understanding of the Party's electoral needs, albeit in different ways. The TUC had sought very specific priority pledges on industrial policy – on shorter hours, the working week and holidays with pay. A joint meeting with the NEC was organised to air their dissatisfaction at the lack of commitment.[58] But in the end, the TUC was persuaded to leave it as an understanding. The commitments went into *A Call to the Workers* but not in *Let Us Face the Future*.

The TUC's restraint was more remarkable over the repeal of the Trades Dispute Act. It was a highly emotive issue covered by long and unsatisfactory discussions with the Conservative leadership during the war. But the TUC, conscious that some elements of the repeal and replacement legislation (that covering General Strikes particularly) might be electorally embarrassing for the Labour Party, was actually prepared to restrict its public claim for repeal to Sections 5 and 6[59] – indeed, those were the terms of the policy in *A Call to the Workers*. In the end, Labour's leaders went ahead with a general commitment to restore 'the freedom of the Trade Unions'.[60]

By this stage, there was growing trust and agreement on priorities. And there was a broad overlap in the social target of their common appeal. The Labour Party's Manifesto appeal was to 'the People's vote', that of the TUC was to 'the Workers', but the two conceptions were not as far apart as later definition was to make them (see Chapter 5). 'The People' were restricted to 'the useful element' – the great majority of the population excluding 'the special interests' – a term which since Dunkirk had come to be identified with the privileged who lived off finance capital – the 'Czars of Big Business' as the 1945 Manifesto described them. And though Labour made a new appeal to middle class radicalism, to 'the suburbs' as Morrison put it, the appeal was often couched in terms of the unity of interest of black-coated *employees* with the manual working class.[61]

And the appeal succeeded beyond the wildest dreams of many. The results of the 1945 election can be compared with that of the Liberals in 1906 and the Reform Bill victory of 1832. Labour's 166 seats at the time of dissolution were increased to 393, against the Conservatives' 213. The first majority Labour Government could take office on an average swing of 12 per cent and a broad response affecting every region of the country – in this sense Labour was more a national party than ever before.

But if we are to appreciate the problems which were to face the Labour Government after 1947 – and for the next forty years – we have to note first that while Labour secured its largest swings in the suburbs and middle class areas, the level of working class support (estimated by Henry Durant of Gallup at 57 per cent of those voting[62]) was still remarkably low for a Party born out of the unions. It was a weakness which has to be viewed alongside the evidence from political levypaying: in 1945, only 48 per cent of trade unionists were volunteering to pay the levy. For these reasons, the underlying political strength of the Labour Movement even in 1945 should not be overestimated. But then neither should its later 'decline'.

The achievement

The legislative programme of the Attlee Government was not in the end to be as sweeping or as fundamental in its redistribution of wealth and power as some on the Left had hoped. But the 1945 Government did steadfastly implement virtually its entire domestic Manifesto commitments. It was a feat which future Labour Governments were to find beyond them.

On the priority objectives, the achievement was comprehensive. The 'Full Employment' objective was attained and then sustained. By the end of 1946, some $7^3/4$ million people had been shifted from military employment and from then on, with the exception of the period of the fuel crisis in the winter of 1947, unemployment was generally under 2 per cent. A 'welfare state' was created involving the complete overhaul of National Health Insurance and social services, envisaged in the Beveridge Report, together with a National Health Service. A mixed economy emerged as the public ownership commitments in the Manifesto were implemented, measure after measure, with only the nationalisation of iron and steel delayed from the first to the second Attlee Governments. Restrictions on trade union activity embodied in the detested Trades Disputes Act were abolished in 1946.

With the passage of time, this reconstruction has come to be viewed in many different lights – some favourable, some highly critical. In retrospect, the changes appear much less radical than was perceived at the time, and their ideological distinctiveness is diminished when placed in the context of the intellectual heritage of Beveridge and Keynes and the plans for the post-war world prepared under the War Cabinet's Reconstruction Committee.

Yet the notion of a political 'consensus' in this period has to be heavily qualified.[63] The post-war 'settlement' was more an acceptance of a new balance of power forged during the Labour Government than a conscious all-party agreement which predated it.

As for the industrial dimension, it is true that wartime tripartism had produced a degree of national accommodation between Government, unions and employers which had its effect on both sides of industry. There were signs, as the war neared its end, that the more progressive employers were prepared to accept a major post-war reform programme and a new approach to industrial co-operation. But leading Conservatives remained deeply divided on industrial policy and attitudes towards the unions, up to and including their return to office in 1951.

The Industrial Charter produced in 1947 was heralded as the new expression of 'One Nation' Disraelian Conservatism but there is some doubt as to how far Churchill felt committed to it.[64] In any case, it is as well to be reminded that even *The Industrial Charter* called for the reintroduction of elements of the Trades Disputes Act. There continued to be also a more 'hawkish' attitude to the unions in the Engineering Employers Federation – dominant in the British Employers Confederation – and this was reflected in support for Rightwing political organisations, the Economic League, and Aims of Industry.[65] For these strands of economic interest and Conservatism, the economic and industrial elements of the settlement were far from being accepted as the new social order. For them, 1945 was always a turning wrongly taken. Twenty years later they began to set about rewriting the post-war settlement – beginning with its industrial dimension.

Government, Party and unions

The gut reaction in the Labour Movement to the victory of 1945 was, as Labour's National Agent put it:

> The working classes hitherto a subject race have succeeded in the organisation of political power and they have become the ruling class in their own land.[66]

But, in practice, this was a government as devoted to the pursuit and protection of the national interest – foreign and domestic – as had been the previous Labour Governments, albeit with some crucial differences of style and achievement. And it was a government resting on a huge Parliamentary Labour Party which was in 'national' terms markedly different from that of the ten year Parliament. The number of ex-teachers was now greater than the number of ex-miners and those with a university education now almost a third. Compared with 1935, the percentage of trade union sponsored MPs had declined from 51 to 31 per cent and it was noticeable that the large general unions had been generous in supporting candidates from a wide variety of social backgrounds.[67]

That the reconciliation of commitments to class and people, to Movement and nation could prove difficult was apparent both from the experience of previous Labour Governments and from aspects of the wartime experience. But the events of 1931 still lingered strongly in the memory, as did the critique of MacDonaldism. From the two central figures, Clement Attlee and Ernest Bevin, in particular, there was a determination that the Government, the Party and the unions should not be pulled apart as the Labour Government tackled the problems of post-war reconstruction and dealt with the recurrent tensions to be expected in the relationship.

Keeping the different elements of the Labour Movement in harmony, or at least securing the optimum cohesion, involved not only ensuring that there was a balanced representation of different elements at Cabinet level but also that there were good links and regular contacts between the industrial and political wings. This linkage was underwritten by the understanding that in the pursuit of unity the basic 'rules' of democracy, solidarity and freedom, as they had developed in the inter-war years, would receive respect from the Labour Cabinet. In the two years after 1945, the processes and the accord were remarkably successful.

At Cabinet level, Attlee made a conscious attempt to balance 'trade unionists' and 'intellectuals' both in number and location. Eleven of the Cabinet of twenty came from working class backgrounds and nine had had a trade union career: of these, two, George Isaacs and Ernest Bevin, had been senior trade union leaders.[68] Though Bevin, who had been on temporary leave of absence from his position as General Secretary of the Transport Workers, continued as a Labour Minister and was, surprisingly, given the post of Foreign Secretary, he kept his contacts with the TUC and his old union and virtually acted as the voice of the unions in the Cabinet.

As for intra-party democracy, the Manifesto of 1945 had been based upon years of Conference decisions, and the Government's domestic policy was based upon and bounded by the Manifesto. As Samuel Beer noted later, 'to an extent unprecedented in British political history, the legislation of a Government was dictated by a party programme'.[69]

In line with the agreement reached in the early 1930s, consultative processes were retained with the unions through the National Council of Labour. The NCL, regularly meeting monthly, heard Ministers on legislative and policy proposals and could question them. It was felt by both sides to be a useful mechanism although not one which dealt with detailed proposals.[70] Attempts to secure representation of CLP and PLP representatives on the NCL were defeated and its operation continued to be dominated by the shared assumptions of the two leadership groups.

Unlike the period following World War I, there was continuity of direct consultation between the Government and the TUC. Initially, the Government favoured more direct links with individual unions rather than a concentration of consultation through the TUC. As in the past, some Ministers and some Departments appeared reluctant to acknowledge the rights and role of the TUC but Attlee, following the precedent set by the war-time Coalition Prime Minister, urged Departments to consult.[71] Generally, by 1951, the relationship had been regularised and the TUC's links to Whitehall and membership of a wide variety of tripartite advisory bodies had been expanded. By the time the Conservatives were to take office again, the consultative access had been in existence for eleven years and had gained a new legitimacy.

There were still occasional grievances.[72] Some important initiatives continued to be taken and announced without specific reference to the TUC, including the pathbreaking Statement on Personal Incomes, Costs and Prices published in 1948. But it is clear from the Cabinet Minutes how sensitive the Government was to complaints of the TUC on this and how anxious it was to point out its respect for the long term consultative process.[73]

There was general agreement not only that the wartime economic controls should be retained but that the free collective bargaining system must be respected and the powers over direction of labour be relaxed. It was the Left, a minority both within the Government and within the unions, which then argued the need for a more rigorous and comprehensive planning system. Ministers Shinwell and Bevan argued for a wages and manpower policy which would have included a minimum wage and an agreed policy relating wages to productivity and the need to induce labour into unattractive industries.[74] Within the TUC at this time, some of the Leftwing led unions, including the Electricians and the Vehicle Builders, were also prepared to support wage planning within a more extensively planned economy.[75]

But the large unions were adamantly opposed to any such interference in what was considered to be not only their legitimate industrial functions but also their right to freedom. At Cabinet level, the ex-trade union leaders George Isaacs, the

Minister of Labour, and Ernest Bevin ensured the defeat of Shinwell and Bevan's proposals.[76]

This commitment to free collective bargaining was not without its incongruities. With TUC agreement, the Government retained the wartime Order 1305 which prohibited strikes. And the Emergency Powers Act, which the unions had in the past seen as a strikebreaking instrument, was renewed in 1946 with Bevin's agreement. But repeal of the 1927 Trade Disputes and Trade Union Act ended prohibition upon local authority employees breaking their contracts of service, and ended the outlawing of 'General Strikes'.

In the short term, little of this mattered in industrial terms. But one could speculate about what the courts might have made of the provisions of the Trades Disputes Act in the 1970s had it not been repealed and it is little wonder that Conservative support for the Act should be passionately asserted for so long after 1946.

The emphasis on free collective bargaining was also in this period an impediment to those who visualised Socialism in more democratic terms than a transfer of ownership. By 1944, in its *Interim Report on Reconstruction*, the General Council had come round to a full acceptance of the Morrisonian position. In the newly nationalised industries there was no internal redistribution of power. Members of the Boards were chosen on grounds of expertise and the TUC leaders were generally content to accept the consultative arrangements rather than advocate anything which would integrate the unions into management processes and possibly compromise their bargaining role. Only a minority of unions and a minority within the unions pushed for an industrial democracy and they often held different views on how it might be implemented. Thus, the Labour Movement in this period never succeeded in evolving a consensual theory of the reconciliation of the public interest, the management function, industrial democracy and trade unionism.

Nationalisation, on which so much visionary hope rested, was experienced by both workers and consumers as something far short of the transformation that had been expected. But on this, as on the other elements in the Manifesto, the Labour Government had, by 1948, delivered the major priorities agreed in 1945. It had also kept faith with the 'rules' of the relationship and it had not moved away from the Movement. It was these features which helped consolidate the leadership alliance which was the most striking characteristic of the politics of the years that followed. And it was these features which further underpinned the belief that the union–Party relationship had a settled political order.

NOTES

1. Labour leaders took two of the five initial positions in the War Cabinet. Clement Attlee became effectively Deputy Prime Minister. Labour leaders often chaired committees dealing with social and economic aspects of the war effort. Paul Addison, *The Road to 1945: British Politics and the Second World War*, 1975, p. 106.

2. At a crucial meeting of the General Council attended by Clement Attlee and Arthur Greenwood from the Labour Party, it was noted that 'it would be an enormous strengthening of Labour's position if the industrial side were represented directly in the Government', *General Council Minutes*, 12/5/40. Attlee had already held private consultations with Bevin about joining the Coalition, Bullock, *op. cit.*, p. 651.

3. Ernest Bevin, Special Conference of TU Executives, 25/5/40, *TUC Annual Congress Report*, 1940, p. 18.

4. Mass Observation Report No. 496, 'Popular Attitudes to War-time Politics', 20/11/40, cited in Angus Calder, *The People's War*, London, 1969, p. 160. Also M.O., 'Social Security and Parliament', *Political Quarterly*, Vol. XIV, 1943, p. 246.

5. Richard M. Titmuss, *Essays on 'the Welfare State'*, 1958, p. 82. The description 'a People's War' was made by Tom Witteringham, Leftwing inspirer of the Home Guard. Calder, *op. cit.*, p. 159.

6. See, for example, the editorials attacking *laissez-faire* and extolling the virtues of a co-operative community in *The Times*, 1/7/40 and the *Yorkshire Post*, 8/7/40.

7. Addison, *op. cit.*, pp. 18–19. Addison and Calder, *op. cit.*, provide a mine of information on Second World War radicalism and the political arrangements on the home front.

8. 'Trade Unions and the War', *General Council Minutes*, 4/10/40, Section B.

9. R. Martin, *op.cit.*, pp. 284–5. The TUC was occasionally by-passed – even by Ernest Bevin.

10. *Labour Party Year Book*, 1946–7, pp. 295–7.

11. On 9 May 1944, in an editorial titled 'Confusion', *The Manchester Guardian* lamented, 'The Labour Party is becoming the delight of its enemies and the despair of its friends … the face it offers to the world is one of petty bickering and disunity. Many have been arguing for some time that the Labour Party has seen its best days and that its future, as the gibe goes, is all behind it'.

12. Martin, *op. cit.*, p. 264.

13. *Tribune*, 4/6/43. This was a regular theme of Bevan's. See also 'Rubber Stamp MPs', *Tribune*, 20/8/43.

14. Aneurin Bevan, 'Labour Must Stay in the Coalition', *Tribune*, 5/3/43.

15. *Ibid.*

16. Bullock, *Bevin*, Vol. II, *op. cit.*, p. 232.

17. *Ibid.*, p. 234.

18. *Ibid.*, p. 234.

19. 'The commonest single belief amongst politicians seems to be that at the next General Election whatever Party or Group Churchill heads will win', Tom Harrison, 'Who'll Win?', *Political Quarterly*, Vol. 15, 1944, pp. 21–32. Bevin, particularly, was thinking of carrying on a partnership with Churchill after the War, Addison, *op. cit.*, p. 234.

20. Michael Foot ('Cassius'), *Brendan and Beverley*, 1944.

21. Bullock, Vol. II, *op. cit.*, pp. 375–6.

22. For two views on this, see Bullock, Vol. II, *op. cit.*, pp. 298–309 and Foot, *Bevan*, *op. cit.*, Chapter 13, pp. 439–62.

23. *Minutes of Joint Meeting of General Council Administration Committee and NEC*, 28/6/44.

24. Foot, *op. cit.*, pp. 415–6.

25. *Ibid.*, p. 452 and p. 457.

26. *Ibid.*, pp. 460–1.
27. *Tribune*, 27/8/1943.
28. Harrison, *op. cit.*, Table on p. 33.
29. *Interim Report on Organisation and Finance*, 1944, p. 3.
30. *NEC Org. Sub Minutes*, 18/3/43. *Labour Organiser*, July/August 1944, p. 11.
31. LPACR, 1943, p. 135.
32. *NEC F & GP Minutes*, 8/11/43, Para. 33.
33. *Special Conference of Trade Union Officers*, 12/11/43, Minutes, Para. 3.
34. *Interim Report on Organisation and Finance*, June 1944, p. 2.
35. LPACR, 1944, p. 142.
36. *Joint Meeting of Trade Union Officers and the Finance Committee*, 6/3/1945, Minutes, Para. 2.
37. LPACR, 1944 Regional Reports, pp. 14-15.
38. LPACR, 1945 Regional Reports, pp. 8-9.
39. Harrison, *op. cit.*, Table on p. 33.
40. Harrison, *op. cit.*, p. 265 shows an overall drop from 130 to 124 but the Transport Workers candidates increased from 11 to 18.
41. LPACR, 1945, p. 88 and LPACR, 1946, Balance Sheet, pp. 46/7.
42. *Labour Organiser*, 1/8/45, p. 9.
43. *Labour Organiser*, 1/8/45, pp. 12-13.
44. LPACR, 1946, p. 14.
45. Harrison, *op. cit.*, Table on p. 33.
46. *Ibid.*, p. 37.
47. See particularly the editorials in *The Economist*, 13/5/44 and 25/11/44 for the most explicit expression of this position.
48. 'A Coalition of the Left', *Tribune*, 18/6/43.
49. On 8 March 1944, a Socialist Unity Conference was held in London. No Left Labour Party members attended. The Communist Party refused to participate because the ILP was there and the ILP and Common Wealth representatives were involved in a major confrontation. *Manchester Guardian*, 8/3/44 and 10/3/44.
50. Joint Meeting of Elections and Org. Subcommittees, Minutes, 5/7/44 and 25/7/44. The NEC took the 'unanimous view that the Party should enter the election as an independent organisation in an endeavour to secure a majority', *NEC Minutes*, 26/7/44.
51. 'Trade Unions and the Labour Party', *Tribune*, 23/7/43.
52. 'Reform of the Labour Party', *Propositions of the VFS Conference of Labour Parties and Trades Councils*, Birmingham, September 1944.
53. Harrison, *op. cit.*, pp. 215–16.
54. The union's leadership was not at this time very committed to the Labour Party and parliamentary action. Richter, *op. cit.*, p. 43.
55. LPACR, 1942, pp. 149–50.
56. Ninety-seven Labour MPs voted against the advice of Labour Ministers in protest against the failure of the Coalition Government to promise early legislation. The NEC's report to the 1943 Party Conference referred to a valuable contribution but 'realised the need for further examination'. It defeated a strong attack at the Party Conference which congratulated the PLP and called for 'immediate legislation', LPACR, 1943, pp. 138–42.
57. Peter G. Richards, 'The Political Temper', *Political Quarterly*, Vol. 16, 1945, p. 65.
58. *TUC General Council Minutes*, 28/3/1945.

59. The General Council was strongly in favour of the Act being removed from the statute book but 'in view of various circumstances which had been outlined, the Labour Party should press at the election for the removal of Clauses 5 and 6 as a preliminary measure'. Clause 5 prohibited members of the Civil Service from belonging to a trade union of which outside persons were members *or* which were affiliated to outside bodies (including the TUC). Clause 6 prohibited local authorities from making membership of a union,a condition of employment, *General Council Minutes*, 28/3/45. Also *National Council of Labour Minutes*, 27/3/45.

60. *Let Us Face the Future*, pp. 3–4.

61. Herbert Morrison, 'Labour Must Capture the East Lewishams', *Labour Organiser*, March 1945.

62. Henry Durant, 'Voting Behaviour in Britain 1945–66', in R. Rose (ed.), *Studies in British Politics*, 1969, pp. 166–7.

63. The view that there was a war-time political consensus which shaped the policies of the Attlee Government was put at its strongest by Paul Addison, *op. cit.* For a criticism of this view and a greater emphasis on the distinctiveness of Labour policies, see Lewis Minkin, 'Radicalism and Reconstruction: the British Experience', in IV ICES Coloquium, Montreal, 1981 (The Reshaping of Europe 1944–1949), *Europa*, Vol. 5, No. 2, 1982, pp. 177–210. As to whether there was a consensus at all in the years since the Second World War, see Ben Pimlott, 'The Myth of Consensus', in L. M. Smith (ed.), *The Making of Britain: Echoes of Greatness*, 1988, Nicholas Deakin, 'In Search of the Post-War Consensus', *LSE Quarterly*, Spring 1989, and Dennis Kavanagh and Peter Morris, *Consensus Politics*, 1989.

64. J. Ramsden, *The Making of Conservative Party Policy*, 1980, quotes Churchill saying of the Industrial Charter (to Maudling), 'but I don't agree with a word of this', p. 114.

65. Keith Middlemass, *op. cit.*, p. 399.

66. George Shepherd (National Agent), 'Independence – The Key to Victory', *The Labour Organiser*, 1/8/45, p. 4.

67. Harrison, *op. cit.*, pp. 266–7.

68. Guttsman, *op. cit.*, p. 242. Henry Pelling, *The Labour Governments 1945–51*, 1984, p. 38 and pp. 42–3.

69. Beer, *op. cit.*, p. 179.

70. Letter from Morgan Phillips, General Secretary of the Labour Party, to Vincent Tewson, General Secretary of the TUC, 23/7/56.

71. R. Martin, *op. cit.*, p. 296.

72. *Ibid.*, pp. 295–6.

73. *CM 11(48) Min. 2*, p. 75.

74. *CM 33(46) Min 5*, p. 264.

75. Panitch, *op. cit.*, pp. 17–18. A Vehicle Builders resolution in 1946, which among other things called for a statutory minimum wage, received 2,657,000 votes; its opponents cast 3,522,000, *TUC Congress Report*, 1946, p. 417. Small, Left-led white collar unions tended to support a planned economy.

76. *CM 33(46) Min 5*, p. 264.

4

Settlement

DEFENSIVE SECURITY

If the years immediately following '1945' became the symbol of 'shining achievement' for the whole Labour Movement, there is a sense in which for the Rightwing majority faction in the unions and the PLP it was rivalled as a golden age by the period that followed it from 1948 to 1959. These were the years of stability, when a heritage was passed from one generation on the Right to another, years of fundamental unity between the Parliamentary Leadership and the majority of senior union leaders, years of mutual appreciation of their different but complementary roles, years when, as Will Lawther put it, 'Between us there is understanding and common sense and adherence to the rules'.[1] As the multiple problems of the union–Party relationship erupted in the late 1960s and 1970s, it was this period to which nostalgic reflection often turned.

Unity between the two wings of the Movement – particularly the close relationship of the leaderships of the PLP and the unions – was based on a willingness of the unions to move fully into a protective, defensive role in the Labour Movement and to sideline attempts to seek a major new political programme for the unions. It was a stance which arose not only out of a profound sense of satisfaction with the Labour Government but also with themselves.

The unions' own efforts had helped secure the objectives of many decades. Their imprint lay on many key features of the post-war settlement.[2] It was there in the initiative which led to the Beveridge inquiry and there also in Bevin's push for the preservation of full employment. The unions had shaped both the content and to some extent the limitations of the nationalisation programme. They had preserved, through both Coalition and Labour Government, the tradition of free collective bargaining. And they had achieved what the TUC had sought assiduously since the late 1920s, permanent and extensive access to the Government of the day. The symbol of their inter-war weakness, the Trades Disputes Act, had been wiped from the statute book. It is only by appreciating the part played by the unions through the wartime administration and the Attlee Government in helping to shape the post-war world that we can understand both the defensive complacency of the 1950s and the disorientation of the 1980s when Margaret Thatcher carried through the first stages of her counter-reconstruction.

The second basis for the unity of the period of settlement was a shared definition of the enemy – the Communists and their allies. With these there could be no accommodation. On the other hand, with the Party's opponents, with the unions' industrial adversaries and with the leading international capitalist states, accommodation was the crucial feature of the age. The entwined accommodations of industrial and political worlds, of domestic and foreign policy, aligned the Labour Movement in a way which neither Party nor unions had hitherto experienced in peacetime. They created a powerful mood and a legacy with lasting consequences for the Labour Movement.

Adjustment – Labour Government

Though the unions in general and Ernest Bevin in particular had played no small part in the distinctive elements of Labour's domestic policy, that distinctiveness was hardly to be seen in foreign policy. Pragmatism, power politics and the national interest were as strongly followed by Foreign Secretary Bevin as they had been by Eden. The pursuit of Britain's 'world role' – undertaken under the immediate illusion that Britain's strength could be re-established – led, by 1947, to a close co-ordination of policy with the only country capable of wielding extensive economic and military power – the United States. And the British Labour Government found itself in conflict with Stalin's Soviet Union in a way which was to reshape international alliances and feed back the resulting divisions into the factionalism of the trade union movement.

In any case, the post-war British economy was increasingly interlocked with that of the United States as the Labour Government sought to rebuild the war-damaged economy and repay the North American loans. Attempting to abide by the Bretton Woods Agreement, to bring the balance of payments into equilibrium and to bridge 'the dollar gap' placed major economic and political constraints on the available options. Productivity and the export drive became preoccupying anxieties.

While these constraints were increasing, the Labour Government came under reinforcing ideological pressures within the domestic environment. As Labour Ministers sought initially to tighten the planning process, so they received a volume of internal and external advice pointing in a different direction. There was, it was argued, an excess of purchasing power and a threat to the export drive from increased costs. The need was now for a policy of 'disinflation' and a relaxation of controls in order to secure the discipline of the market; the planning apparatus must be dismantled not strengthened. The public mood began to change, adding new pressures. Backed by a well-orchestrated campaign against 'shortages', it was relatively easy for opponents of a planned economy to associate planning in the public mind with its more irksome restrictions.[3] And the character of the international 'enemy' led Ministers themselves to elaborate anxiously the ideological distinction between democratic and totalitarian planning.

The Government now began the process of dismantling the legacy of wartime controls. The shift from physical planning to fiscal planning was made clear in the Budget of 1948. For the next decade planning would mean essentially Keynesian demand management.

Other shifts began to take place. There was a movement away from the pursuit of egalitarian redistributive objectives. The mixed and managed economy began to be defined as a permanent achievement requiring no new transfer of power and property. New ceilings were put on public expenditure, including the housing programme. Following a devaluation precipitated by a sustained run on sterling, there was a further cutback involving proposed education and health service expenditure.

In one form or another, this interplay of constraints and pressures was to beset every Labour Government. And the pattern whereby the radical distinctiveness and high public expenditure of the early years was followed by a turn towards economic retrenchment and a marked shift to the political centre was to become a familiar cycle. As was its accompaniment – a pattern whereby a Labour Party which would not, and could not, consider (publicly at least) any form of wages or incomes policy whilst in Opposition, found itself in Government pursuing a stern anti-inflation policy which brought it into direct conflict with the most entrenched of British trade union traditions – free collective bargaining.

Unemployment had been the dominant economic problem discussed by Socialists and trade unionists in the inter-war years: little discussion had taken place of the problem of inflation. And little consideration had been paid to the role of trade unions under a future Labour Government. In 1945, the TUC's *A Call to the Workers* had emphasised the suffering that might be caused by an inflationary boom: 'Wages and salaries will lose their purchasing power. The people's savings, the ex-servicemen's gratuities, payments for sickness and accident, the allowances for children, the pensions of widows and aged people will be reduced in value.' But it had seen the danger in terms of a 'hasty and ill-considered removal of public controls'. There was no examination of the potential problem of rising labour costs.

By 1948, the consciousness that there might be a problem in reconciling traditional trade union behaviour with socialist objectives – a concern that had been articulated in the 1920s by the Left – now also began to be articulated from the Right. Trade union collectivism and Party collectivism did not necessarily lead to a fusion of interests. The one might involve a concern for self and section, the other a concern for community. The fraternity of the union could be at odds with the fraternity of the broader movement, the broader society and the broader vision. These questions were posed now from both a Rightwing and a Leftwing perspective in terms of the goals that trade union sectionalism and traditionalism impeded, but the recognition of potential incompatibility was common to both.

In particular, the new economic problems facing the Labour Government produced a predicament for the union–Party relationship which was to haunt it under every subsequent Labour Government:

> How can the public interest in the outcome of collective bargaining be made effective without destroying the voluntary system or weakening the unions?[4]

From the unions there was to be no satisfactory answer, given that free collective bargaining was, in principle, sacrosanct. But, in practice, as was to be shown time and again, it could, temporarily, be adjusted to the immediate priorities facing a Labour Government, although only after considerable push from the political leadership. Thus, eventually, the Government, after seeking some initiative from the TUC, produced its own emergency policy. The 1948

Statement on Personal Incomes, Costs and Prices was a major landmark in relations between a Labour Government and the unions. With some exceptions, there was to be no increase in wages, salaries or dividends. This intervention ran counter to 'the rules' and according to past attitudes should have stimulated a fierce reaction from the major unions. Instead there was for a time a remarkable turn-around of the positions of Right and Left.

Sharing the political and economic diagnosis of the Labour Government, grateful for the implementation of the programme and the full employment policies, and with that heartfelt loyalty which Labour Governments could evoke from trade union leaders, the General Council majority swung into support for a temporary suspension of full industrial freedom. Conversely, the internal opposition included not only free collective bargaining fundamentalists but some who favoured a more thoroughgoing planned economy. The most outright and fierce opposition came from the Communist Party and the sections of the unions where the CP had its greatest strength.

Here again, the industrial and the political entwined. From 1947, the Communists, now internationally part of the Cominform, moved into more outright hostility to a Labour Government now diagnosed as part of 'the imperialist camp'. Though declining in public support – a decline which continued for the next forty years – the Communist Party's industrial factions and its newspaper were henceforth always the core of opposition to any form of incomes policy.

For three years, the Labour Government had carried through its domestic programme to the advantage of the trade unions and the interests of labour. Now, in 1948, it was the unions who gave the Labour Government the advantage of the union–Party relationship; a cycle which was to repeat itself in the 1960s and 1970s.

Though the TUC was careful to defend the principle of 'free collective bargaining and free negotiations', and to specify the safe-guarding of wage differentials as one of the qualifications of its acceptance,[5] in practice it policed the wage restraint policy with remarkable solidity and success. For two years the majority held. Even after it was rejected at the 1950 Congress, and the TUC moved away from its management with some relief, many of the union leaders attempted to exercise some restraint upon pay claims – particularly as the newly elected Labour Government had a majority of only five.

Seeking now to deal with industrial problems at a time when Ernest Bevin was a sick man and ex-trade union officials in the Cabinet were a declining force, the Government abruptly moved in a direction which threatened a serious rupture in the Labour Movement. The wartime Order 1305, prohibiting strikes, had not been used, in spite of approximately 10,000 stoppages between January 1945 and the autumn of 1950. Suddenly, in November 1950. it was invoked against striking gasworkers and dockers. The strong reaction to this from within the Party and the unions led eventually to the Order being withdrawn.

Whatever divisions had been opened up (and there was still much that consolidated the relationship) were soon dwarfed by other internal political developments. The Korean War, the costs of rearmament and the proposed charges in the National Health Service exacerbated divisions within the political leadership, and in April 1951 Aneurin Bevan, Harold Wilson and John Freeman resigned as Ministers. Their resignation stimulated a new Leftwing factional opposition – the Bevanites – but it also reconsolidated the great majority of the trade union leadership behind the international and domestic policies of the Parliamentary leaders.

Accommodation – the Conservative Government

As the Labour Government slowly adjusted to the various economic, political and ideological pressures, so changes began to take place in the Conservative Party – particularly in a new acceptance of the managed economy and the social legislation consequent upon the implementation of the Beveridge Report. Nevertheless, right up to their return to office in 1951, there were fears in both the Labour Party and the unions that their accession would involve 'the return to normality' that had been feared in 1945.

But the Churchill Government of 1951 was, in practice, remarkably conciliatory – particularly to trade unionism. Although there was a small programme of denationalisation and a further dismantling of some of the egalitarian measures bequeathed by the Labour Government, the Welfare State was protected, full employment was preserved and the nationalisation of rail and mines – the most strongly pursued of the nationalisation measures sought by the unions – was retained. A new term, 'Butskellism', became for a short period a vogue word to describe what was seen as the high degree of consensus which now existed between the two economic spokesmen of the major parties.

The preservation of major policy achievements was accompanied by a preservation of the consultative process bequeathed by the governments of the 1940s. The TUC, in 1951, expressed its hope that the new Government 'would maintain to the full' the pattern of consultation.[6] And so it turned out. Churchill placed a heavy emphasis on avoiding conflict with the TUC. There was no return to any of the provisions of the Trades Disputes Act and no legislative interference in free collective bargaining. Lord Monkton, who was appointed Minister of Labour, tended to urge settlement of any dispute on terms which the unions seldom found too unfavourable. The TUC became seen as virtually a 'Fourth Estate of the realm'.[7]

Trade union anxieties slowly faded. Progress and rationality seemed to dictate a reassessment of old attitudes. The post-war achievement now seemed indeed to be also 'a settlement'. It appeared, as Francis Williams noted, to show

> that neither the degree of consultation with the trade unions on industrial and economic matters nor the acceptance of their essential position in the structure of the national life are likely to be much reduced by political change.[8]

As acute an observer as Ian Mikardo agreed:

> the power-relationship between the government (of any colour) and the trade union movement has changed for all time.[9]

Confidence in the permanence of these new arrangements seemed all the more justified given the emergence of Tory reformers in senior positions in the Conservative Party. As John Strachey, the ex-Marxist theoretician, now Labour revisionist, put it:

> ... if a man were asked to name the greatest single achievement of the British Labour Party over the past twenty five years he might well answer, the 'transformation of the British Conservative Party'.[10]

The dual settlement

This sense of permanent achievement and policy consensus had a significant effect on the unions' relationship with the Labour Party. Just as it was concluded in the unions at this time that there was a settled arrangement of rights and obligations in the relationship between trade unions and the state, so there grew a view on the Right of the Party and the unions that there was now a settled and mature arrangement of 'rules' and protocol in the union–Party relationship

This arrangement rested upon a structure of power which, in its coordination, was unlike anything seen since the Party's foundations. The cabal of union leaders who began to organise their interventions during the Cold War period created a base for the Party's leadership which remained secure in spite of often ferocious internal warfare. The three union leaders at the core of this organisation – Arthur Deakin of the Transport Workers, Will Lawther of the Mineworkers and Tom Williamson of the General and Municipal Workers (plus for a time Lincoln Evans of the Steelworkers) – formed what has been aptly described as a 'praetorian guard'[11] against the Left both in the industrial and the political sphere.

Their commitment had an industrial dimension in the new alignment of pro-'Western' unions within the International Confederation of Free Trade Unions, and had a political element in the new defence alliance of the North Atlantic Treaty Organisation. Both were formed in 1949. Loyalty to Labour's political leadership was reinforced by a general hostility to 'the Left', a Left often undifferentiated from the Communist Party. It led to a deep antipathy towards Bevanism and a determination to secure the future leadership of the Party for an ally they could trust. Eventually they gave their blessing to Hugh Gaitskell who became Treasurer in 1954 and then Party Leader in December 1955.

Their supportive arrangements eventually covered all the major forums of the Labour Movement outside the House of Commons. They also managed to keep close watch on developments in the House. In 1954, Arthur Deakin overcame some misgivings about the revival of the Trade Union Group of sponsored MPs to encourage them to become a stabilising instrument against the Left.[12]

Their confident behaviour within the Party was based on the supremacy of the three Rightwing-led unions at the Party Conference. Together in 1948 they cast together just over 1.8 million of the total Conference vote of 5.4 million, and in 1955, as a deliberate act of political intervention, raised their affiliations and votes to 2.3 million out of 6.8 million votes.[13]

The Left opposition could often call on support in the unions from the Engineers, the Railwaymen and the Shopworkers who together had 1,252,000 votes in 1955 and often on a substantial proportion of the votes of the Constituency Labour Parties whose votes rose to a peak of 1,307,000 in 1953.

But the Right generally could also count on support from most of the middle-sized unions. In all, for the period up to 1956, Harrison calculated a union vote of approximately 2.8 million regularly supporting the NEC, with about 1.8 million going regularly to the Left and around 1 million unpredictable.[14] And although the Bevanites regularly dominated elections for the constituency section, support for Leftwing policies at the Conference was by no means always overwhelming amongst the constituency delegates.

The result was an unprecedented period of 'platform' dominance at Party Conference. After 1948, on only one occasion (a relatively minor defeat in 1950 on food subsidies) was there a defeat for the Party leadership until 1960. The avoidance of defeat was based in part on prior consultation and anticipation of the reaction of the unions but it was, nevertheless, a remarkable tribute to the strength of the Rightwing alliance.

The tight co-ordination tended to diminish in the mid-1950s with the death of Arthur Deakin. Political alignments became more complex in 1956 as first Frank Cousins emerged as a Leftwing General Secretary of the Transport Workers, then Aneurin Bevan moved to a *rapprochement* with Gaitskell after Bevan had become Party Treasurer. Yet the pattern of Rightwing union dominance over the Conference remained a feature. In part, this reflected the political position of a majority of trade union leaders. In part also, it reflected Cousins' inability to quickly change the policies of his own union. But also Cousins' emergence coincided with a shift to the Right in some of the other unions, including the Shopworkers and, most crucially, the Engineers under Bill Carron's leadership.

Dominance of the Right within the Conference resulted in a dominance over the NEC. In the early 1950s, though the Bevanites swept the Constituency section, they could make little headway on the trade union and women's sections which were filled to ensure support for the leadership. Although some loosening up took place after 1955, the Right always had a clear majority. A similar dominance was evident in the Conference Arrangements Committee which, since the Cold War, had been carefully 'carved up' by the major unions. Within this political alignment, Leftwing trade union leaders were in a small minority on every committee of any significance.

THE 'RULES'

Priority

The dominant trade union leadership group which emerged in the late 1940s had a clear, if restricted, set of priorities. Like other union leaders in the past, they were primarily concerned with industrial issues and the immediate needs of their members; they approached problems in a way which stressed practicality and rejected 'theory'. But the key to their position was its defensive mode. Defensive of free collective bargaining, defensive of the post-war settlement, defensive of existing consultative structures, defensive of the TUC and the Party and defensive of the nation and its democratic institutions.

Behind every attack on the Labour Government after 1947 and behind the Bevanite movement against the Party's leadership in 1952, the Rightwing union leadership saw the hands of the Communist Party or those who would weaken the Movement in its struggle against the Communists – Leftwing intellectuals, pacifists and fellow travellers. Organising the defence of the Party leadership on the NEC and at the Party Conference against the coalition of their critics became a routine of their trade unionism.

So regular and so well-defined did this pattern of behaviour become after 1948 that observers judged it to be endemic in the relationship. Allan Flanders, an outstanding scholar of British trade unionism and a member of the Socialist Commentary grouping, developed the view that the unions' supportive but non-initiating role on political issues was itself a part of the traditional terms of the 'marriage' of the unions and the Party.[15]

This interpretation was consistent with post-war developments and the general proclivity of the unions but it ignored the inter-war experience and particularly the political experience of the early 1930s when Ernest Bevin and Walter Citrine played such a forceful role in contesting the position adopted on defence by George Lansbury, the Party's Leader.

After 1956, Cousins' general support for a new nationalisation programme and specific support for unilateral nuclear disarmament involved a significant change of objectives compared with 'the praetorian guard', although he retained a deep sense of the prudential 'rules'. In spite of his reputation as a 'political' General Secretary and a committed Leftwing Socialist, he retained many of the industrial priorities of his predecessors and his colleagues.[16] Thus, though he wanted to see a more socialist Labour Party and in his speeches made this plain, his primary focus was on the wages question. He would never join a Leftwing political grouping and refused a place on the editorial board of *Tribune*. He, too, acted first and foremost with a trade unionist's perspective.

Freedom

The defensiveness of 'the praetorian guard' of union leaders was particularly marked after 1951 over free collective bargaining. Their support for the Government's wages policy from 1948 to 1950 was a temporary expedient. Its problems in practice in these two years had the effect of reinforcing their traditional opposition to governmental interference in the wage bargaining process – even though, in practice, they were prepared to exercise responsible restraint.

Arthur Deakin in his fraternal address to the 1952 Labour Party Conference went out of his way to repudiate the suggestions 'floating about amongst certain people in the political Movement' of a 'National Wage Policy'.[17] It was unworkable and dangerous in that it would be destructive of established channels of negotiation, arbitration and other forms of industrial partnership. There was a serious need for the Party to understand the difficulties faced by the trade unions which have to handle problems which might be inconvenient to the Party in Government. Though the unions must strike a happy medium in dealing with the Party and with their own industrial problems, 'it must be clearly understood that the primary duty of the unions is to carry out those policies and pursue those purposes determined within our own organisations'.[18]

In reaffirming that the unions stood 'four square for freedom of negotiations',[19] the Transport Workers leader virtually closed off this area to party policymaking.

Cousins, in 1956, took a similar line towards the principle of freedom of negotiations but, in addition, he brought forward a new emphasis on the rejection of any form of wage restraint.

Defensiveness of the freedom to carry out industrial functions was also characteristic of the attitude of the TUC. In the early 1950s, nobody doubted the TUC's party alignment and they continued to share fraternal delegates with the Party. But Deakin stamped vigorously on the attempted use of Congress as a 'political' instrument against the Government. In 1952, he told delegates 'Congress is not a political forum; what can and must be said against the Government will be dealt with in another place'[20] (i.e. the Labour Party Conference). What this amounted to was a defence of the TUC's neo-corporate relations with Government and fundamental opposition at this time to any attempts to use the TUC as part of a broader party political campaign.

There was a similar furious reaction from the union leadership at the attempt by delegates to the 1952 Labour Party Conference to support industrial action against the Conservative Government. What seemed to the union leaders as an alliance of Bevanites, Trotskyists and Communists trod into territory that the union leadership regarded as their own and in a way which they regarded as improper. They easily crushed the Left on this issue but the Left's initiative exacerbated the already burning antipathy of the union leadership.

Defending their territory against the Left became a regular ritual, sometimes taken to great lengths. In January 1953, the TUC General Council sent the NEC a message of protest simply because *Tribune* had criticised the Steelworkers Leader, Lincoln Evans, for accepting a peerage from a Government pledged to denationalise steel.[21] At one stage, Crossman likened the letters of protest from the General Council to the NEC as almost a ceremonial 'rather like Black Rod'.[22]

Defensiveness of the industrial sphere – particularly in relation to disputes – was not simply a reaction to the Left, although this was the point of the deepest bitterness. Deakin and the TUC officials believed that the Parliamentary Party, including the Trade Union Group of sponsored MPs, should also keep out of industrial relations matters altogether.[23] These were matters for the individual unions and the TUC, not the Party.

Deakin's demarcation of trade union autonomy was more openly aggressive than was usual from a trade union leader, but the general atttitude which he brought to bear was part of a long tradition and carried over long after he had passed from the scene. Politicians, however senior, learned that there were lines of territory that they must not cross. In 1956, an attempt, supported in principle by the Party's Leader, Gaitskell, to cover trade union procedures in a new document on Personal Freedom, was killed off at the Home Policy committee, after the union representatives voiced their unions' misgivings.[24] That year also, Labour's new Leader, Gaitskell, toothcombed Crossman's Fabian pamphlet *The New Despotism* to erase any 'dangerous' references to the behaviour of trade unions.[25]

Solidarity

The unions' defence of their own internal affairs, of the sphere of industrial relations and of the TUC's independent channel of communication to the Government were all affirmations of the autonomy of 'the industrial'. But their attitude towards 'the political' was much more ambiguous. In principle, they affirmed the independent representative rights of a Parliamentary Labour Party responsible to Parliament, and there were, as will be indicated, major limitations on the scope and effectiveness of their involvement in the Labour Party. But there is little doubt that on grounds of solidarity they sought, and were sometimes invited to play, a heavy supervisory role in relation to the Party's dissidents.

This pattern of intervention was made easier by a confidence that was considered by reputable observers to be a responsible and necessary mode of operation. At this time, critics to the Right of the Labour Party were relatively unconcerned at the practices of the union leaders and in the mass media 'the block vote' was not considered to be a major democratic problem.[26] There was some concern with apathy and low attendance at branch meetings and the opportunities this afforded the Communist Party,[27] but only the Bevanites in this period lamented the unrepresentative behaviour of union leaders.[28]

Their commitment to this protective role had been forged in the circumstances of 1948 going to the aid of 'our Government' in its hour of need over inflation. Indeed, it became a paradox of the way that solidarity was understood that its original purpose was occasionally stood on its head. Under a Labour Government, union leaders spent time and energy attempting to ensure that industrial disputes did not spread and did not become serious. The response of many union leaders to industrial action after 1947 was deeply affected by their worries over the industrial role of the Communist Party, but in general it could be said that solidarity had come to mean primarily understanding the problems of, and giving loyal support to, the Labour Government.

This solidarity carried over from Government to Opposition. Even though the new relationship with the Conservative Government appeared to offer the TUC a permanent consultative arrangement, union leaders felt a deep loyalty to 'our Party' – and 'the Labour Movement'. On the odd occasion when the idea that the unions and the Party might go their separate ways was publicly articulated, it was quickly suppressed or retracted.[29]

Loyalty was given special emphasis after the Bevanite revolt of 1951 was followed by the capture of NEC seats by supporters of Bevan at the 1952 Party Conference in Morecambe. Bevanism they saw as not only prepared to advocate policies which had Communist support – a sin in itself – but as a dangerously irresponsible movement. Aneurin Bevan they saw as ambitious for the Leadership, lacking the necessary self-control and respect for majority decisions which would allow the Movement to survive.[30]

Likening the situation to 'that dark period of 1931'[31] (not an altogether convincing parallel), they sought to impose stability and discipline. The first they helped to achieve, the second proved more difficult than their position of formal dominance over the block votes might suggest. Discipline meant venturing deep into the organisational territory of the Party and even this assertive and at times bullying grouping were circumscribed by the ambivalence of the Parliamentary leadership and, in the end, by their own inhibitions at enforcing their wishes on that leadership.[32]

Their constant pressure for a disciplinary framework helped create an atmosphere of anxiety on the Left and reinforced authoritarian traditions which carried on long after 'the Big Three' were no longer in position. But their main pursuit – the expulsion of the Bevanites – was never secured in spite of one crisis after another in which either the activities of Bevan or the articles in *Tribune* were considered worthy of disciplinary action.

The revolt of 'the 57 varieties' in March 1952 stimulated re-imposition of the Standing Orders of the PLP but no action against the rebels.[33] Deakin's call for disbandment of the Bevanite group at the 1952 Conference was followed by the PLP's prohibition of groups – yet the Bevanites continued their clandestine operation and in some ways were strengthened in their activities.[34] In January 1953, the TUC leaders attempted to get the NEC to act against *Tribune* but their letter was watered down and no action was taken.[35] More pressure on the NEC came in October 1954, but the NEC climbed down and not *Tribune*.[36]

The nearest the Rightwing union leadership came to securing the expulsion that they had been pursuing since 1952 came in March 1955. On the face of it, they had 18 NEC votes dependent upon the unions, plus that of Morrison, who was prepared to vote for Bevan's expulsion. In practice, and in spite of determined pressure, they were defeated by 14 votes to 13 in support of Attlee's compromise.[37]

In the next two years, Deakin died and Bevan and Gaitskell effected a political reconciliation which changed the factional balance on the NEC and in the PLP. The remaining Rightwing union leaders retreated from their interventionism now that the Party had a firmer-based and acceptable leadership.

This period of involvement in the Labour Party with its constant search for discipline and its attempt to oversee the operation of the National Executive Committee left behind a powerful legacy – a folk memory of an authoritarian trade union pressure using the leverage of finance and block votes to ensure the obedience of the Party. Yet the record reveals not only a failure to secure the fundamental disciplinary outcome that the union leadership wanted but an inhibited reluctance to carry out the occasional veiled financial threats.[38] Much more than appeared to be the case, such pressure from the union leaders was constrained and unsuccessful – a fact which partly accounts for their almost permanent state of angry frustration.

Nevertheless, the experience was still being paid in the 1980s. If, for the Right, this was a golden age, for the Left it was a dark age. Those on the receiving end of the disciplinary zealots' activities never forgot it. The reformation in Party discipline in the late 1960s, the dismantling of Party boundaries in the early 1970s and the hesitancy about co-operation with the unions over Party reorganisation in the early 1980s were all heavily affected by the legacy of this experience.

Democracy

The Second World War against Fascism and the Cold War struggle against Communism reinforced the commitment of most trade union leaders to Parliamentary democracy. The coup in Czechoslovakia particularly encouraged the belief that the factional struggle in the Labour Movement was also a struggle against forces that would destroy democracy. This view, together with a new 'insider's' appreciation of corporate consultation, led the union leaders of this era to reject even more vehemently than their predecessors the idea of utilising industrial power for any political purposes, let alone using it for revolutionary aims. The ferocity of their response to the Left in 1952 at the TUC and Party Conferences is partly to be understood in this light.

In this new climate, there was a significant shift of views about the role of sponsored MPs. There was a much clearer affirmation of the independence of these Members from direct pressure by the unions and an acceptance by the TUC that they could not act to instigate disciplinary pressure via the sponsoring unions. This development was accompanied by a general loosening of relationships between sponsored MPs and unions and by a new union focus on contacts with Ministries rather than intervention at the Parliamentary level.

Thus, an MP's freedom from immediate union sanctions now became part of the 'rules' of the relationship. Acceptance of the 'rules' was reinforced by factional considerations. The PLP Left could use it (as Bevan had done in 1944 and was to do again in 1955[39]) to defend their position. The Right in the unions used it to ensure that Leftwing elements did not exert pressure upon sponsored MPs.

This belief in the freedom of 'judgement and conscience' of MPs lived uneasily with the increased pressures being exerted upon MPs by the PLP itself and with the disciplinary measures constantly on its agenda as a result of the promptings of 'the praetorian guard'. It lived uneasily also alongside the consolidation of the authority of the Party Conference.

The belief in 'the final authority' of the Annual Party Conference was a traditional view, coherent with how decisions were legitimised within the unions. But respect for the role of the Party Conference also helped to stabilise the Party

> Firmly based on the millions of workers organised in the trade union movement, the Labour Party could always survive so long as it exerted self-discipline based on full democratic discussion and unswerving obedience to majority decisions once they had been taken.[40]

Upholding the authority of the Annual Conference still left some room for discretion for the Parliamentary leaders in integrating and implementing its decisions. But with every vote secured for 'the platform', Conference authority also became a weapon to be used to bolster the discipline of the Party and the position of the majority faction.[41]

Unity

The paradoxical political character of trade unionism in the late 1940s and early 1950s was nowhere more apparent than in attitude to unity within the Movement. It was a deep commitment linked to the priority of industrial purposes and a hostility to organised political interference within the unions, particularly by factions of the Communist Party. Yet this was a period when union leaders organised on a factional basis which in its tightness and regularity had no precedent. Although committed to representation by industrial criteria within the Movement, they were heavily proscriptive against the Left. And they themselves were organised in a political alignment on a cross-union basis.

In 1947, after the Communists had internationally produced the Cominform, the union leaders on the General Council formed their own organisation (later known as Freedom First) to root out Communists in the trade unions and to encourage the formation of anti-Communist factions. The General Council, in November 1948, issued a circular against the Communists which was followed by probitions against their holding office in several unions – including the Transport Workers which had disregarded a similar circular in 1934. Factional alignments against the Communists took off in several unions in this period including the Engineers and the Shopworkers. At regional level in the Labour Party, in several areas, the Party organisers and the officials of the largest unions combined to tackle what was seen as a joint problem.[42]

The effect of factional anti-Communist mobilisation and proscription within the unions was to make it possible for the Rightwing union grouping to keep off the General Council some of those whom custom and 'rules' would normally have guaranteed a place. In 1948, the Deakin–Williamson–Lawther axis was powerless to keep off the General Council the new NUR General Secretary, Jim Figgins, even though he was seen as very close to the Communist Party. But in 1949 Bert Papworth, who had been on the General Council as the only Communist representative since 1944, was forced off because after the proscription of Communists in the Transport Workers he failed to secure the union's nomination. With the connivance of the NUM's Right Wing, Arthur Horner, Communist General Secretary of that union, was excluded. For smaller and newer unions, including the Public Employees,[43] the exercise of political exclusion was much easier.

A similar pattern was evident in the voting for the Labour Party National Executive, Trade Union and Women's Sections. There was a high degree of political selectivity in the voting for the Women's Section where the union leadership sought to preserve an undeviating and pliable base of support for the Parliamentary leadership and their own aim of disciplining the Bevanites. Eirene White withdrew from her position in 1953 because she had been under so much pressure from Deakin.[44]

The Trade Union Section was rather more difficult. The Engineers, who had begun to show interest in a seat on the NEC after years of political 'distance' from the Party, were kept off until 1955 because their nominee, Leslie Hutchinson, was politically suspect.[45] But again the NUR secured its usual nominee in spite of the fact that on many issues the union voted with the Bevanite Opposition.

The prohibition on 'political' interference remained strong in spite of (and perhaps because of) the anti-Communist factional struggle across the unions. One result was to make it more difficult for the Labour Left to find a space for its own mobilisation. On the one hand, the oppositional role was played in

Rightwing unions by a very efficient Communist machine often led by talented cadres; on the other, Bevanite attempts to mobilise appeared as a transgression against the 'rules' of the union–Party relationship. Bevan's threat in 1954 that he would take the political struggle for the Treasurership into the unions and trades councils caused both anger at the impropriety and some satisfaction that such a course of action was likely to offer grounds for expulsion.[46]

Antipathy to 'political' interference was to remain a permanent feature of the union–Party relationship. But with the emergence of Frank Cousins as General Secretary of the Transport Workers in 1956, the Rightwing alliance at the Conference was weakened, pressure on the NEC was lifted and industrial criteria once more tended to override political considerations in NEC elections. The clearest indication of this came in 1956 with the election of R.W. Casasola of the Foundry Workers. Always considered to be close to the Communist Party, he first took his seat as a replacement for Cousins who had moved to the TUC upon the death of his predecessor. He retained the seat as 'next-in-line' at the 1957 Party Conference.

ACCOMMODATION AND TENSION

But, in general, the application of the 'rules' of the union–Party relationship was an aid to co-ordinated Rightwing control of the Party. They could operate in this way because the overwhelming dominance of the Right within each major forum of the Party was a dominance based on a stronger correlation with the mood and objectives of the working class than that achieved by the Left. And it was a dominance based on a broadly consensual outlook which united the leadership of the Party and the leadership of the majority of the unions.

Ideology

We can sum up this consensual outlook by noting three fundamental foundations which lasted throughout the period of the 1950s and beyond. There was a proud belief that the workers were 'better clad, better shod, better fed and better housed than ever before',[47] and were likely to continue to improve their conditions of life and work under the managed and mixed economy which had emerged in the late 1940s. There was a commitment to the new mix of Parliamentary democracy and corporate consultation – a commitment which involved sensitivity to various rules and responsibilities of inter-Party and interest group conflict. And thirdly there was a view of international Communism as the fundamental enemy of trade unionism, Democratic Socialism, Parliamentary Democracy, and peace; justifying NATO and the US alliance and whatever armaments were necessary for collective security.

This basis of unity crossed the borders of one generation on the political Right to the next, making Gaitskell the 'revisionist' Socialist as acceptable as had been the perspective of the Attlee–Morrison generation.

Viewed in retrospect, we can see that the accession of Gaitskell to the Party Leadership and the ascendancy of 'revisionism' after 1956 marked a major ideological watershed. From this tradition in the next quarter of a century would come a fundamental critique of the union–Party relationship and a rejection of many of the traditional positions held by the unions (see Chapter 8). But in the mid-1960s, this seemed an unlikely possibility. True there was a recognition that there was no inevitability about the link between the labour movement and a revisionist socialism.[48] But:

> Society cannot be changed without the effort of an organised movement. Power must be won, and the labour movement remains the main vehicle in the battle.[49]

Within the unions, apart from the minority of Leftwing union leaders, including Frank Cousins, Jim Campbell of the Railwaymen and Bryn Roberts of the Public Employees, the general domestic position put forward by Gaitskell and his revisionist allies had great appeal, providing that there was no direct challenge to any rule-book tablets of stone.

'Revisionism' argued that almost all the basic characteristic features of traditional pre-1914 Capitalism had been either greatly modified or completely transformed. Capitalist ideology had changed and capitalism had lost elements of its commanding position, to the State on the one hand and to Labour on the other. There had been 'a peaceful revolution' in the relationship between trade unions and the Government.[50] A wholesale 'counter-revolution' by the Conservative Party was now unlikely and not in the nature of that Party.[51] The post-war settlement could not be reversed anyway because 'any Government which tampered seriously with the basic structure of the full-employment Welfare State would meet with a sharp reverse at the polls'.[52]

The economic analysis was equally optimistic. Questions of growth and efficiency were no longer central. The present rate of growth would continue in a society which was on the threshold of mass abundance. The future was more likely to be characterised by problems of inflation than unemployment.

Having redefined Capitalism as a 'mixed economy' whose most fundamental material problems had been solved, the revisionists established an alternative base for the definition of Socialism. It was not to be defined in terms of the structure of property ownership but as a set of values – particularly the values of social justice, equality and personal freedom.

There was much in this new analysis which the trade union Right found acceptable even though, if pushed, as they were to be in 1960, some traditionalists would have quibbled at the loss of common ownership as the ultimate goal. The political analysis seemed to accord with their own experience, and the proposals for a more cautious, selective and specific policy on public ownership appealed to their sense of practicality. Social justice and equality also implied some specific policies which trade union leaders found very appealing. From one there was a promise of high public expenditure on social policy; from the other would come 'large egalitarian changes in our educational system, the distribution of property, the distribution of resources in periods of need, social manners and style of life, and the location of power within industry …'[53]

Above all, the revisionist position on industrial relations was congenial to the trade unionists – so congenial indeed that an authoritative study of the Gaitskellites published as late as 1969 makes virtually no reference to the problems that Social Democrats were saying were fundamental a few years later.[54]

Anthony Crosland accepted the structure of industrial conflict:

> There will thus always be potential conflicts between management and
> labour. The two sides exist, and must to a large extent remain two sides;
> and the workers' side must have an untrammelled Trade Union movement
> to defend its claims. These are harsh facts which cannot be spirited away by
> moral rearmament touring troupes, or luncheons of progressive business-
> men, or syndicalist castles in the air.[55]

It was healthy to have an assertive trade union movement whose ambitions
were wide and whose power rested ultimately on a withdrawal of labour. Unions
should seek to overcome the great disparities of status, privilege and power by
working to 'widen the agenda of collective bargaining' which 'should embrace all
major economic questions affecting an industry; the result would be a significant
further transfer of industrial power'.[56]

Trade union co-operation with management was very important but the
major responsibility for good industrial relations lay with management: '...
within any given framework, greater or lesser harmony is largely a function of the
quality of management'.[57]

In line with contemporary TUC thinking, the revisionist leaders, Crosland and
Gaitskell, favoured joint consultation and 'maximum Trade Union influence'[58]
but not trade union participation in management. So high was the degree of
satisfaction with the pattern of industrial relations and the nature of the two-
party system, that the adversarial character of both was held up as a model of
democracy. Industrial democracy was, it was argued, already produced by the
unions acting as an institutionalised industrial 'opposition'.[59]

There was no conflict here with traditional trade union industrial goals and
practices. Gaitskell, Crosland and the revisionists generally appeared to be well
in tune with the priorities of much of British trade unionism. This unity had so
many points of deep agreement that for the moment it transcended other sources
of friction. However, looking closer at the late 1950s we can see already the
emergence of a range of problems which were to come to the fore later, and were
to appear by the 1980s as fundamental dilemmas.

Interests

One of them concerned the question of wages. In the aftermath of Labour's loss of
Office in 1951 and Deakin's determined assertion of free collective bargaining,
those on both Right[60] and Left[61] who advocated some form of socialist wages
policy tended, after some initial proposals, to leave the issue alone. Gaitskell,
who as Chancellor had sought a further round of wage restraint in 1950, now
moved in line with trade union opinion. Aneurin Bevan, who had favoured a
wages policy as far back as 1945, had moved away from it by the mid-1950s.

In a sophisticated critique of what was fast developing as conventional wisdom
about wage-cost inflation and the role of the unions, Anthony Crosland had
added his intellectual weight against a wages policy. There was, he argued, 'no
definite evidence that a dangerous degree of wage inflation inevitably follows,
under conditions of full employment, from the present method of free collective
bargaining ...'.[62] Further, a national centralised wages policy was impractical and

unwise and went against the British tradition of trade union autonomy. If the unions were too much involved in a change in their traditional function, the result might well be a strengthening of the Left (particularly the Communist Party).[63] It might be desirable for some strengthening of TUC authority and for some clearer exposition of an 'ideal' wages policy by the Government, but otherwise the Government should rely on the sense and moderation of trade union leaders.[64]

Crosland, it must be noted, had speculated that the position might be different if the Communist Left took control within the unions – an outcome he considered unlikely. By 1956, Cousins' election and his emphatic rejection of wage restraint were beginning to cause some in the PLP to begin to reappraise their views; although not, in the first instance, Hugh Gaitskell. He was sympathetic to the position put by Cousins (and generally argued subsequently by other Leftwing trade union leaders) that union pressure for higher wages would, as in the United States, make manufacturers more efficient and stimulate both productivity and growth.[65]

But by 1958 the mood among Labour leaders was also beginning to change – part of a broader intellectual current newly concerned about the increase in union power and rising inflation (see p. 96). Gaitskell and Harold Wilson (the Shadow Chancellor) were becoming greatly concerned at the scale of the commitments projected in the first Budget of a future Labour Government. Privately Gaitskell began to canvass a counter-inflation policy with the unions, involving an agreement on a virtual wage freeze.[66] Union leaders on both Left and Right were adamant that no specific commitment could be given: dissatisfied, but unable to progress further, the Parliamentary Leadership had to be content with the generalities of *Plan for Progress*.[67] It was a story that was to be repeated time and again in the next thirty years.

Social affinity

New, simmering tensions were also being produced as a result of compositional shifts which were beginning to undermine the position of those with ex-manual working class backgrounds within the PLP. Such shifts did not automatically increase tensions with the trade unions. In the Shadow Cabinets of the early 1950s, there were few ex-manual worker trade unionists (only three in 1954) but this was a period of high ideological cohesion and fundamental trade union interests were not at stake. In any case, there was a powerful alliance of Party Secretary Morgan Phillips and the talented miners' leader Sam Watson on the Executive to act as linkage with the unions, with the experienced Dalton and Morrison (to a lesser extent) also able to handle the relationship with the trade unions. If anything, the social tension was between the trade union leadership and the Bevanite 'intellectuals' labelled as a 'group of frustrated journalists' by Gaitskell. The label is said to have endeared Gaitskell to Deakin.[68]

The new PLP of 1955 to 1959 showed little change in the percentage of sponsored MPs and MPs from manual working class occupations[69] but in the Shadow Cabinet there was a small but significant increase in the ex-trade unionists, with Jim Griffiths an ex-miner as Deputy Leader, George Brown and

Alf Robens all prominent members. Jim Callaghan had been a white collar trade union official. And they were joined by Aneurin Bevan, now reconciled to the new Leadership. Sam Watson's status as Chairman of the NEC's International Committee and a 'liaison officer' with the major unions increased during this period.

Gaitskell, who had close personal links with the influential Engineers-sponsored MP Charles Pannell, also succeeded in building his relationship with the new generation of Rightwing figures on the General Council – including the crucial figure of Bill Carron, the Engineers President.

But there was an ominous social undercurrent to the politics of the late 1950s. After the Wilson Report on Party organisation had damaged the prestige of Morgan Phillips, there was a new heightening of tension between his trade union allies and the middle class intellectuals – particularly Wilson.[70]

After the by-elections at Morpeth in 1954 and Wednesbury in 1957, both of which were fought by non-sponsored candidates, the Mineworkers began to feel that their secure, safe seats were under threat and the General and Municipal Workers complained of their diminished representation. On past form, the percentage of trade union sponsored MPs should have risen in 1955 as the Tories increased their majority, but it dropped from 36.6 per cent to 34.3 per cent. At a meeting held in July 1957 to discuss revision of the Hastings Agreement and affiliation fees, the unions voiced their concerns[71] – concerns made all the more acute by reports that Gaitskell was anxious to see some of his younger intellectual protégés in the House.[72]

Their grievances were further fed by a growing resentment within the Trade Union group of sponsored MPs about the exclusiveness of Gaitskell's leadership group of 'intellectuals' labelled 'the Frognal Gardens Set'. Whatever the reality of such a 'set', it became the symbol of trade union hostility to snobbery, real and imagined.[73] They were enraged by public comments of Richard Crossman on the diminished quality of trade union sponsored MPs and his opinion that only four suggested themselves for key jobs.[74] One trade union leader spoke of 'the menacing threat of domination by the party's intellectuals'.[75] Both Crossman and Gaitskell were attacked at the PLP–Trade Union group meetings.[76]

This sudden emergence of social tension was in some respects more sound than substance and had little public effect on the relationship between the Party leadership and the General Council, although it cannot have helped the attempts being made by Gaitskell and Wilson in 1958 to secure trade union cooperation in a wage freeze. And it is also possible that the social prickliness of Gaitskell's relationship with Cousins (together with a failure to consult over nuclear weapons policy) contributed to the beginning of a pre-election crisis over defence in 1959.[77] But, for the moment, social tension appeared more like a new luxury enjoyable because of the end of Bevanism. However, the prospect was there that *combined* with ideological alignments rather than cutting across them, it could provide a bitter cutting edge to Party–union conflict.

Party strategy

Behind the ritual affirmations of fraternity and unity, a quiet questioning began to take place about the Party's proper relationship with its manual worker trade union base. Part of this involved a persistent worry after 1948 about declining support from the radical middle class won in 1945. The anxiety increased even though the results in 1951 showed a consolidation of working class support in the highest vote Labour had ever received: middle class support, and crucial seats, had been lost, putting the Party back into Opposition again. How to reconstruct the 1945 coalition of social forces was a problem pondered for years to come.

Towards the end of the decade, the problem of the appeal to the middle class began to be accompanied by what was seen as also a problem of how to appeal to working class people. By 1958, Gaitskell was convinced that 'week by week' working class people were becoming 'less working-class, less class-conscious and more allergic to such old appeals as trade union solidarity or class loyalty'.[78] Thus, avoiding such old appeals became a new preoccupation – a shift which itself had consequences for the future basis of the Labour Movement.

There were hints of a third problem also. Although Labour's vote and percentage of the poll dropped in 1955 and 1959, and the Conservatives were returned to power, each time with an increased majority, Labour support among trade unionists remained substantial. But it was estimated that in the region of one fifth to one quarter of them voted Conservative or Liberal[79] and there were indications that the Labour vote was not as solid amongst trade unionists as it appeared.[80] Neither were Labour's supporters among trade unionists and union officials as active in electoral terms as was often thought.[81]

New electoral difficulties were also appearing in public attitudes towards the unions and their activities. After 1954, coinciding with the re-emergence of national strikes and a renewed press hostility to the unions, there was a sharp decline in the percentage of the population who considered trade unions to be 'a good thing for the nation'.[82] The threat of an eve of poll rail strike in 1955 was held to be damaging to the Labour Party as was the London Bus Strike of 1958.[83] This public opinion alarmed the Party's leaders at a time when they were beginning to take increased note of opinion polling.

Considerable media and public attention also became focused upon a range of trade union activities, including demarcation disputes, closed shops and the disciplinary practice of 'sending to Coventry'. Both the TUC and the Parliamentary Leadership began to accept that some of these were unnecessary (as well as embarrassing) 'abuses of power'.[84] Within the Parliamentary Leadership a view began to emerge that in electoral terms it would be no bad thing to be seen publicly to be standing up to the union leaders – particularly Frank Cousins,[85] the butt of that character assassination which was to be regularly handed out by the press to militant trade union leaders in the next thirty years.

The TUC as an institution retained a rather different image – a stodgy carthorse, respectable, moderate and accommodating. Thus Gaitskell had few qualms and saw much to be gained by launching the 1959 election campaign at the Congress – a usefully-timed platform from a body of support whose closeness was still defended and welcomed by the Parliamentary Leadership. But the real message lay in how he chose to use the platform. There was an appeal to wavering trade unionists but also a clear declaration of the Party's independence:

We are comrades together, but we have different jobs to do. You have your industrial job and we have our political job. We do not dictate to one another.

And he added:

And believe me, any leader of the Labour Party would not be worth his salt if he allowed himself to be dictated to by the trade unions.[86]

Trade union strategy

At the time, these seemed merely nuances and the indications of vulnerability in the relationship appeared relatively insignificant when placed alongside the overwhelming stability of so many other indicators.

TUC membership reached 7,937,091 by 1949 then rose very slowly up to 8,337,325 by 1958. Labour's affiliation reached 4,946,207 in 1949, rose sharply in 1954 to 5,529,760, then stabilised until the late 1960s. The numbers of unions involved remained very much the same. TUC-affiliated unions declined from 187 to 185 in this period; Labour Party affiliated unions rose from 80 to 87. Levypaying, the basis upon which the unions could affiliate to the Labour Party, was also very stable, rising only marginally (Harrison calculates) from approximately 77 per cent in 1947 to 80 per cent in 1957 – and this rise was attributed mainly to administrative changes.[87]

Stability in one area seemed to be matched by stability in another. TUC membership of Government bodies slowly increased as did access to Ministers. Relationships seemed barely affected by an increase in economic policy differences or the revival of industrial militancy. Although national strikes made their reappearance in 1953 and strike activity moved generally upwards, it was from a very low base and the net total of stoppages in 1959 was still 10 per cent below that of 1946.

But the new wave of union militancy began to feed a shift in the intellectual climate which was already being affected by new concerns over prices, productivity and incomes, and new worries over the balance of payments. In 1958 A Giant's Strength, published by Conservative lawyers, was ahead of its time in its legal prescriptions to curb union power, but was part of a more widely shared view that there was a deep problem of cost-push inflation caused by the strengthening of trade union bargaining power under full employment. Satisfaction over the new affluence was becoming moderated by worries over Britain's competitiveness in the face of emerging international rivals.

At the same time there came a new willingness on the part of some Conservative Ministers to consider industrial confrontation with the unions rather than conciliation and accommodation. The London Bus Strike of 1958 indicated that the Government was not prepared (as it had been in the Engineering dispute of 1957) to step away every time from a conflict. Its new stance raised a question mark over the role of the Ministry of Labour as a mediating department and over the future conduct of Government as a whole in relation to industrial action.[88]

Still, it was a feature of the way the London Bus Strike was dealt with that both the TUC and the Government showed a marked unwillingness to be pulled into the confrontation. Indeed, the covert indications were that the Macmillan

Government, if anything, favoured a closer collaborative relationship with the TUC whatever its attitude towards individual acts of union militancy. All of this confirmed the impression of rule-governed conflict with clear boundaries – a development seen by many observers as an expression of the maturity of Britain's industrial relations system and its Labour Movement.[89]

While this integration within Governmental processes retained its vigour, so on the surface did the TUC's relationship with the Labour Party. The TUC was more involved in Labour Party policy formulation under Gaitskell's leadership than it had been in the period of 'the praetorian guard'. But a closer examination of this period reveals a considerable scepticism and hesitancy about the unions' participation. Largely as a result of union reluctance, the National Council of Labour (apart from during the Suez Crisis) was becoming relatively functionless. With attendances poor and speakers difficult to arrange, the Council went into a decline and after 1956 meetings became quarterly.[90] As for the TUC's involvement in the production of the major policy documents of the late 1950s, there was considerable ambivalence in the attitude of some of the unions' leaders. The TUC staff, particularly George Woodcock and Len Murray, felt more strongly that they should not be there at all.[91]

Yet the TUC was frustrated, as so often, by events in the Party. Cousins's leadership of the growing 'anti-Bomb' campaign, the new revisionist programme on public ownership, *Industry and Society*, and above all the attempt by Labour's leaders to open up the wages question, all had the effect of pulling the TUC into the Party's policy process. TUC staff remember this period as 'disastrous' in that it enmeshed the unions in the give and take of NEC policymaking and resurrected some of the difficulties of the 1948–50 period.[92] Long before the advent of NEDC and the new neo-corporatism, Woodcock could not wait to distance the TUC from these Party exercises.

It was a view which was strongly in tune with much of trade union thinking about Party and political activity. Confident of the permanence of the TUC's new status and of the consensual basis of much of the national policy, most union leaders felt little need to participate in broader campaigns and were much less willing to make financial sacrifices for political action through the Labour Party.[93] They were particularly hostile to proposals which would in any way take activity within the unions – particularly political activity – out of their control. Official proposals from the Labour Party Committee of Enquiry in 1955 which would have allowed the Labour Party's own organisers to mobilise trade unionists from Labour Party regional offices were quietly sidelined.

In this mood of complacency, few union or Party leaders, indeed few observers at this time, had any premonition of the sheer scope and depth of the problems which were to affect the Labour Movement in the next thirty years. On the surface everything seemed to indicate that the difficulties of the Movement were trivial compared to its strengths and that the sources of divergence were dwarfed by the enduring stability of the central relationships. But the problems were there, irritating, simmering, eating away.

There was a symbolic portent. The TUC–Labour Party joint tenancy at Transport House had been the pride of Ernest Bevin and an expression of the united

Movement. In 1956, the TUC moved into new and spacious headquarters in Bloomsbury, intending that the Labour Party should join it as tenants. But the tenancy never materialised. Bloomsbury was too far from Westminster and too expensive. The Labour Party stayed where it was.

And there was, as so often in the Labour Movement, another reality behind the ritual of unity. In 1959, Gaitskell's launch of the General Election campaign from the TUC was met with a chorus of 'For he's a jolly good fellow'. It 'would be superfluous for me to say that you are welcome at this Congress', the TUC President had told him.[94] But Crossman's Diaries tell us another story. There was, he notes, even a row about the protocol of who should meet Gaitskell at the airport. Woodcock, the new TUC General Secretary, made it clear that he 'hated the whole idea'.[95]

NOTES

1. Will Lawther, fraternal delegate from the TUC, *LPACR*, 1949, p. 164.
2. See on this L. Minkin, *Radicalism and Reconstruction, op. cit.*
3. 'An orgy of slander', Philip Williams, *Hugh Gaitskell*, 1979, p. 179. The most scathing academic attack on planning came from John Jewkes, *Ordeal by Planning*, 1948.
4. Allan Flanders, *A Policy for Wages*, Fabian Tract 281, 1950, p. 15.
5. *TUC Congress Report*, 1948, p. 290.
6. *TUC Congress Report*, 1952, p. 300.
7. John Lovell and B.C. Roberts, quoting Churchill in *A Short History of the TUC*, 1968, p. 162.
8. Francis Williams, *op. cit.*, p. 426.
9. Ian Mikardo, 'Trade Unions in a Full Employment Economy', *New Fabian Essays*, 1970, p. 147.
10. John Strachey, Foreword to A.A. Rogow and Peter Shore, *The Labour Government and British Industry 1945–51*, 1955, p. x.
11. Mackenzie, *op. cit.*, pp. 505 and 509. For the industrial sphere, see Henry Pelling, *A History of British Trade Unionism*, 1963, pp. 233–236.
12. On this see V.L. Allen, *Trade Union Leadership*, 1957, p. 151 and Richter, *op. cit.*, p. 137.
13. L. Hunter, *The Road to Brighton Pier*, 1959, pp. 92–3 and P. Williams, *op. cit.*, p. 349. The Miners were already over-affiliated so the increase had to be restricted to the two big general unions who added 415,000.
14. Harrison, *op. cit.*, p. 214.
15. Allan Flanders, *Management and Unions, op. cit.*, pp. 35–6.
16. Geoffrey Goodman, *The Awkward Warrior*, 1979, p. 96.
17. *LPACR*, 1952, p. 126.
18. *Ibid.*
19. *TUC Congress Report*, 1952, pp. 81 and 82.
20. *Ibid.*, p. 82.
21. Janet Morgan (ed.), *The Backbench Diaries of Richard Crossman*, 1981, p. 196.
22. *Ibid.*, p. 359.
23. Harrison, *op. cit.*, p. 296.
24. L. Minkin, *op. cit.*, p. 54. *Crossman Diaries, op. cit.*, p. 467.

25. *Crossman Diaries, op. cit.,* p. 467.
26. In December 1954 and January 1955, the *Manchester Guardian* ran a series of articles which were eventually published as *The Future of the Labour Party.* It made no mention of the problem of the block vote.
27. J. Goldstein, *The Government of British Trade Unions,* 1952.
28. Foot, *Aneurin Bevin 1945–60, op. cit.,* pp. 447, 488, 513.
29. *LPACR,* 1953, p. 194.
30. Their views are well captured in Leslie Hunter, *The Road to Brighton Pier,* 1959.
31. Will Lawther, *LPACR,* 1952, p. 89.
32. 'Not without reason Deakin felt that he could persuade or coerce a majority of trade union votes to uphold any expulsions of which he approved', Hunter, *op.cit.,* p. 48. But he died still waiting for the Parliamentary leadership to act decisively.
33. In a defence vote on 5/3/52, 57 Labour MPs voted against the Government and against the Whip's instructions.
34. Mark Jenkins, *Bevanism: Labour's High Tide,* 1979, p. 171.
35. *Crossman Diaries, op. cit.,* p. 197.
36. *Crossman Diaries, op. cit.,* pp. 359–64.
37. On the attempt to expel Bevan, see Foot, *op. cit.,* Chapter 12, Hunter, *op. cit.,* Chapters 10 and 11 and P. Williams, *op. cit.,* Chapter 11(iv). The Attlee compromise was basically a postponement of decisions until Bevan had prepared a statement and an Executive subcommittee had interviewed him. The Executive later voted to note Bevan's assurances.
38. Trade union leaders normally felt very inhibited at making threats linked to their financial input into the Labour Party (especially if the PLP and its leadership were involved). They tended to retreat immediately if publicly accused of doing so (e.g. Arthur Deakin, *LPACR,* 1952, p. 126). They felt on stronger ground if they were calling for action against the Left because the Left was itself territorially assertive into the industrial field and because of links or associations with the 'anti-parliamentary Left'. Much of the union leaders' resentment in this period was over the failure to act against the Left. This resentment came out at the points where the Party Treasurer and General Secretary were asking for more money (raising affiliation fees) or novel funding (the National Agency Service). It is possible that, on occasions, the response of some union leaders went past the normal protocol of lament to one where financial assistance was linked to action. Hunter, *op. cit.,* p. 105 cites one important case relating to Bevan's expulsion; P. Williams, *op. cit.,* p. 343 doubts it. What is clear is Gaitskell's sensitivity as Party Treasurer to union goodwill, Hunter, *op. cit.,* p. 105 and P. Williams, *op. cit.,* p. 342. However, others on the NEC and in the PLP were not so responsive. As far as I am aware, no financial sanctions were used by the union leaders during this period. There is a very revealing footnote in P. Williams, *op. cit.,* p. 343 – Tom Williamson (GWMU) 'flatly denied such a threat, and others thought that though Deakin might have growled he would not have meant it'. (See also Chapter 7, n. 69 and Chapter 16, pp. 516–19 for union attitudes in the late 1970s, and also the difficulty of applying sanctions.)
39. Aneurin Bevan raised this issue before the NEC meeting which attempted to expel him in 1955, *Crossman Diaries, op. cit.,* p. 408. Attlee informed the meeting that Bevan said that he would raise it in the House and if he did not, the Conservatives would. *Morgan Phillips papers*

for 23/3/55.

40. Hunter, *op. cit.*, p. 47.
41. *LPACR*, 1949, p. 126 re the expulsion of MPs Zilliacus and Solley and M. Jenkins, *op. cit.*, p. 103 re the proscription of Socialist Fellowship in 1951. Attitudes towards the Party Conference are explored in more detail in L. Minkin, *The Labour Party Conference*, *op. cit.*, Chapter 1.
42. On this see Pelling, *The Labour Governments 1945–51*, *op. cit.*, pp. 221–2 and P. Williams, *op. cit.*, p. 336 for the conversation between Gaitskell and Sir Vincent Tewson.
43. Bryn Roberts, 'My Fight with the General Unions', *Tribune*, 23/9/55.
44. Hunter, *op. cit.*, p. 109. She was replaced by Mrs Jean Mann who, as it happened, voted against Bevan's expulsion in spite of Arthur Deakin.
45. Harrison, *op. cit.*, p. 310.
46. Hunter, *op. cit.*, pp. 82–3.
47. Sam Watson, Chairman of the Labour Party, *LPACR*, 1950, p. 77.
48. Socialist Union, *Socialism: A New Statement of Principles*, 1952, p. 46.
49. *Ibid.*, p. 44.
50. Anthony Crosland, *The Future of Socialism*, 1956, p. 32.
51. *Ibid.*, p. 60.
52. *Ibid.*, p. 61.
53. *Ibid.*, p. 216.
54. Stephen Haseler, *The Gaitskellites*, 1969.
55. Crosland, *op. cit.*, p. 346.
56. *Ibid.*, pp. 336 and 519.
57. *Ibid.*, p. 338.
58. *Ibid.*, p. 349.
59. *Ibid.*, p. 346. This view was heavily influenced by the work of Hugh Clegg, particularly *Industrial Democracy and Nationalisation*, 1951. In *A New Approach to Industrial Democracy*, 1960, Clegg noted that 'the essence of democracy is opposition', p. 29.
60. Roy Jenkins, *Plan for Progress*, 1953, p. 180.
61. In *Keeping Left* (1950), Leftwing MPs advocated a form of TUC supervised wages policy. See also Ian Mikardo, *Tribune*, 6/1/50. In 1952, Crossman was still arguing this case, *New Fabian Essays*, *op. cit.*, p. 27, but then he too left it alone.
62. Crosland, *op. cit.*, p. 461.
63. *Ibid.*, p. 346.
64. *Ibid.*, p. 461.
65. P. Williams, *op. cit.*, p. 460.
66. *Ibid.*, p. 465.
67. Which said only that 'some measure of restraint in demands for higher incomes will be needed', *Plan for Progress*, 1958. On this see L. Minkin, *The Labour Party Conference*, *op. cit.*, pp. 51 and 54.
68. Hunter, *op. cit.*, pp. 63–4.
69. Harrison, *op. cit.*, pp. 267–8.
70. On the Wilson Report (*The Interim Report of the Sub-Committee on Party Organisation*, Labour Party, 1955), see *Crossman Diaries*, *op. cit.*, pp. 441–6. See particularly the entry for 7 October, '"It's our Party, not yours"' – George Brown on the intellectuals.
71. *NEC Minutes*, 27/2/57. Report of Conference of Trade Union Representatives, 5/2/57, p. 1.
72. *Manchester Guardian*, 4/7/57 and *Daily Telegraph*, 26/7/57.
73. P. Williams, *op. cit.*, p. 475 and *Crossman Diaries*, *op. cit.*, p. 634.

74. *Daily Mirror*, 5/7/57.
75. Tom O'Brien, *Daily Mail*, 24/7/57.
76. P. Williams, *op. cit.*, p. 475.
77. *Crossman Diaries*, *op. cit.*, pp. 760 and 767.
78. *Ibid.*, p. 688 – Entry for 11 July, 1958.
79. Harrison, *op. cit.*, p. 15. Gallup in August 1959 gave Labour 71 per cent, Conservatives 17, Liberals 4, Others 1 and Don't Knows 7, *Gallup International Public Opinion Polls, Great Britain 1937–75*, 1976, p. 527.
80. See Martin Harrison, 'Trade Unions and the Election', in D. E. Butler, *The British General Election of 1955*, 1956, p. 213. He cites one opinion poll where support for Labour among trade unionists was at 59 per cent just before polling day.
81. *Interim Report of the Sub-Committee on Party Organisation*, *op. cit.*, para. 69, p. 16.
82. George Sayers Bain, *The Growth of White Collar Trade Unionism*, 1970, Table 7.1, p. 89. A high of 70 per cent in 1954 moved to a low of 53 per cent in 1957. Thereafter it rose but did not approach the 1954 level again until 1963/4. See also David Butler and Richard Rose, *The British General Election of 1959*, 1960, p. 28.
83. D. E. Butler, *op. cit.*, p. 164. Williams, *op. cit.*, pp. 463–4.
84. George Woodcock, 'The Trade Unions and Public Opinion', *Listener*, July 1959, p. 120. Eric Wigham, *What's Wrong with the Unions?*, Penguin, 1961, p. 15.
85. *Crossman Diaries*, *op. cit.*, pp. 759 and 764.
86. *TUC Congress Report*, 1959, p. 460.
87. Harrison, *op. cit.*, p. 45.
88. Goodman, *op. cit.*, p. 196–7.
89. The maturity of British industrial relations behaviour was widely accepted at this time, Alan Fox, *Heritage and History*, 1985, p. 370. The most explicit analysis of development towards maturity occurs in the work of Otto Kahn-Freund. An international study by A. M. Ross and P. T. Hartman, *Changing Patterns of Industrial Conflict*, 1960, links this maturity and the new '*modus vivendi*' of industrial relations in the British case with the political relationship to the Labour Party. Clegg, 1960, *op. cit.*, notes that the new political theories 'argue that the political and industrial institutions of the stable democracies already approach the best that can be realised', p. 29.
90. *Minutes of NCL*, 1/11/56 and 17/6/59.
91. Interview with Len Murray, then TUC Deputy General Secretary, July 1969.
92. *Ibid.*
93. Harrison, *op. cit.*, p. 347.
94. Robert Willis, *TUC Congress Report*, 1959, p. 456.
95. Crossman, *op. cit.*, pp. 775 and 777.

Part II

Context and Interaction

5

Dynamics

INSTABILITY

The stability of the union–Party relationship in the late 1950s appeared to be a deeply rooted, almost endemic characteristic. Even those who anticipated the possibility of damaging developments could scarcely have conceived the scale of the problems of the next three decades. Still less could they have envisaged the repetitive oscillations that were to take place following the 1959 General Election. The relationship moved from one period of crisis to another as almost every feature of the relationship became subject to controversy. As one set of forces began to pull the relationship apart, so counter-forces were set in motion which pulled it together again, or at least eased the division. Often a final iredeemable breakdown appeared imminent but just as often new accommodations were found.

As we shall see, one force sustaining the Movement was, ironically, the growth of its enemies. As the consensual and moderate Toryism of the 1950s gave way in the late 1960s to two successive waves of Rightwing Conservatism, so not only the post-war settlement but trade union access to government was threatened in a way which seemed inconceivable in the early 1950s. At crucial moments, the unions were pushed into reliance on the Labour Party.

But if the external threat had unifying consequences, it also produced new dangers and led to new sources of conflict. The breakdown in one settlement encouraged a similar breakdown in the settlement within the Labour Movement; old demarcations between the industrial and the political disappeared or were challenged, and old-established 'rules' of the relationship were contested or broke down at crucial points – particularly the 'rules' relating to democracy and freedom. Integral to these developments – part cause and part effect – was a major realignment of the unions within the Party as the old Rightwing block vote – the ballast of the post-war relationship – was severely undermined. Ultimately, confrontation, constitutional crisis and defection all followed; but then, at other times, so did accommodation, the social contract and 'the Dream Ticket' consensus.

In this chapter I will try to make sense of these oscillations and changes in fortune, by presenting an overview of those forces which have in the past three decades moved the relationship apart and those forces which have moved it together. The chapter will also have the function of establishing the historical context for the analysis of ideological movements, major issues and problem areas which takes place in Chapters 6 to 19. For this reason, to avoid overmuch repetition, the detail thins out as we approach the present day.

Four complete periods will be distinguished in this analysis. Each is characterised by a distinctive feature: 1959 to 1970 a crisis of reinforcing tensions; 1970 to 1979 a new accommodation built upon the idea of the Social Contract; 1979 to 1983 a period characterised by introspection and a high-profile union involvement in Party activity; and 1983 to 1987 a period of managed 'space' and 'distance' by the TUC and a Party Leadership seeking to maximise the chances of defeating the Thatcher Government. The examination of these periods is followed by a summary of key developments in the period of 'reclamation' since 1987.

The analysis will be handled through the framework developed in Chapter 1 involving areas of tension and accommodation over ideology and trade union interests, the social affinity of the leadership groups, and the concordance of strategy. Securing the latter, as embodied in the distinct institutional interests of the Party, the unions and the TUC, was always a central problem of the Labour Movement and was to be the first point of divergence after 1959.

CRISIS – 1959 TO 1970
Strategy

The Labour Party

The 1959 General Election result created its own distinctive aftermath. It was believed to mark a watershed in which socio-economic developments were encouraging more or less permanent Conservative government – a period when 'the pendulum had ceased to swing'. Hitherto, 'the revisionists' under Gaitskell's leadership had been relatively uninterested in the modernisation of the Party and the Movement; now for a while it became a preoccupation. From their analysis of Labour's new predicament came an electoral strategy which tended to undermine the Party's relationship with the unions and to devalue the advantage of its working class base.

It was held that rising material conditions were leading to middle class life styles and to changes in partisanship away from the Labour Party. A parallel theory linked the shift from blue collar to white collar occupations with Labour's declining electoral support in the 1950s.

This dual diagnosis, in the hands of those who had always been unsympathetic to the idea of Labour as a class party, led to the view that Labour's manual worker 'cloth cap' image was socially inappropriate and that it ought to aim at establishing its identity as a broadly based, national people's party.[1] It followed from this that the constitutional structure of the Party with its built-in position of power for the large, manual worker unions provided a permanent electoral liability. This liability increased as the electoral popularity of the unions declined.

One response to this was an attempt to make the Party more representative of the new labour force by encouraging an increase in the affiliation of white collar unions to the Party. The attempt cannot be said to have been a great success in the next quarter of a century. The existing white collar unions did increase their affiliation. But no major white collar union outside the Party in 1960 was affiliated to it in 1970 and not until 1987 was the first such union, The Broadcasting and Entertainment Trades Alliance, brought in.

A second response proved to be far more significant for union–Party relations. The revisionists had always had an ambivalent attitude toward union power within the Party. On the one hand, it had been an asset, in that in the previous two decades it had helped fend off dissidents from the Left and place Hugh Gaitskell as Leader of the Party. On the other hand, it was viewed as yet another sectional (and traditional) force in British politics. When it became clear that the Transport Workers' vote was no longer solidly secure for the Party Leadership, revisionist criticism of the trade union dominance over Party policymaking, its internal methods of deciding policy, and its mechanism for casting votes at Conferences, grew considerably.

The issue became particularly acute in 1960 when the Party Leader found himself in full retreat against the rule-books and long term commitments of the affiliated unions on his proposal to change the Party's historic constitutional commitment to the 'public ownership of the means of production, distribution and exchange'; it rose to crisis point when the Transport Workers threw their support behind unilateral nuclear disarmament and, with the support of other unions, defeated the Party's Leadership at the 1960 Conference.

The adoption of this positive stance against the Party's Leader by the Transport Workers on a major political issue involved a break with the union's postwar practice; the response of the Party's Leader was to break with the 'rules' of the union–Party relationship over Conference authority as reaffirmed after 1931. Gaitskell refused to abide by the Conference decision and successfully reversed it in 1961.

Each side's action was disputed in terms of traditional understandings and constitutional propriety.[2] For the moment, the important fact was that the Leader had won the battle and increased his authority. But the legitimacy of high profile politically assertive trade unionism within the Party and the issue of the democratic authority of the Party Conference were to be permanent sore points in the Movement.

Revisionist perspectives now dominated the Party's appeal, albeit mediated via a new document *Signposts for the Sixties* which integrated some traditional elements in its attack on the 'small ruling caste'; these were impeding the advance of young new executives, engineers and scientists[3] – a new electoral target group. By the time of Labour's election victory in 1964, most commentators agreed that the Party had lost its 'cloth cap' image. It now appeared as a classless and meritocratic party with a special appeal to the new white-collar salariat.

This appeal was carried by a new Leader, Harold Wilson, elected in 1963 after the sudden death of Gaitskell. Initially, Wilson made much of the Party's new deal with the unions over an incomes policy, and a much heralded Concordat of 1965 envisaged a new partnership between Government, employers and unions.

But after the 1964 election, a significant extension of the Party's electoral strategy began to take place. A 'people's party' aimed at increasing its support among the middle class became a 'party of government' aiming to capture the centre ground of British politics and make the Party the normal occupants of office, as their opponents, the Conservatives, had hitherto been. Where the dominant motif of the 'people's party' was 'modernisation', the dominant motif of the 'party of government' became 'responsibility'.

These reinforcing strategies appeared to give a massive pay-off in electoral terms when, after only a narrow victory in 1964, in the 1966 election, the Labour Party share of middle class support attained its 1945 level and its share of working class support reached a new peak.[4] Support for Labour among trade unionists during this period was measured at between 62 and 73 per cent.[5]

From these strategies, however, various detrimental consequences can be traced for union–Party relations in the years that followed. When a section of the Party's traditional working class support, be it electoral or union, was seen as an obstacle to modernisation, the Labour Government felt only a limited obligation to come to terms with it: hence, the rapid closure of many coal mines in spite of the protests of Labour's most loyal electoral supporters and its staunchest union allies. When governmental responsibility involved a direct industrial confrontation with the unions, the Government did not retreat, witness its tough handling of the Seamen's dispute in 1966.

Governmental anxiety that the 'party of government' should not appear to be easily amenable to the pressures of the unions led it to assert a degree of independence in which a positive virtue was claimed for its unwillingness to court popularity, even on issues considered quite fundamental to the purposes of the Movement. Hence, strong and consistent pressure from the TUC after 1968 for an expansionary economic policy that would reduce the level of unemployment was met by governmental assertions that the existing policy was essential; when national and Labour policies clashed, then, in the terms enunciated by Wilson in 1966, the government must 'govern'.[6] When the Party Conference registered its opposition to Government policy, this was consistently disregarded in spite of the adverse effects on Party morale and Party–union relations: thus, even after the 1968 Party Conference had inflicted a series of defeats on the Party Leadership unprecedented in the size of the votes and the importance of the issues,[7] the Prime Minister could tell the Conference that its decisions were merely 'a warning'.[8] As such they could be, and were, ignored.

Above all, with the general backing of public opinion, the Labour Government was prepared in 1969 to push through controversial items of legislation in the field of industrial relations in the teeth of union opposition to some of its provisions (see pp. 17–18). In the end, the Government backed down, but only after a traumatic experience which severely undermined the confidence of many of the union leaders in the Parliamentary Leadership and damaged also the confidence of some of the Rightwing parliamentarians in the traditional relationship.

The trade unions

At the same time as the strategy of the Labour Party Leadership was taking them away from identification with the unions, the TUC under a new General Secretary, George Woodcock, was evolving a strategy which loosened its links and identification with the Party.

In part, the Woodcock strategy was simply reactive. After 1960, there was a shift in Conservative Government attitudes towards economic planning and the involvement of the major economic interests in a new body, the National Economic Development Council. The response of the General Council members was by no means unequivocal. There was friction with the Government over incomes policy. There was a suspicion that its political intention was really to drive a wedge between the unions and the Party. And there was scepticism about the likelihood of being able to influence Government policy. But the TUC bureaucracy under Woodcock was heavily in favour of involvement in what could be seen as a natural development of the TUC's long term relationship with Government since 1940. Accordingly, in 1962, the majority of the Congress went along with the movement 'out of Trafalgar Square' and 'into Whitehall'.

A concomitant of this increasing neo-corporatist activity of the TUC was a sharp increase of white collar, politically 'neutral' unions into affiliation. It was facilitated by the Government's ruling that the TUC alone would represent the labour force on NEDC. It was encouraged by the suggestion of permanent Government intervention in public sector wage bargaining. But most significantly, the white-collar unions were drawn in by a new assertion of the political neutrality of the TUC. Woodcock sought (not always successfully) to ensure that the TUC did not publicly identify itself with Labour's election campaigns. And he affirmed:

> The TUC did not and could not start its examination of any problem as Socialist, Liberal, Conservative or Communist. We start as trade unionists and we end as trade unionists.[9]

Measured purely in terms of composition and growth in the Labour Movement, Woodcockism was a success. The rapidly expanding white collar unions might well have formed their own national centre but did not. Between 1964 and 1970, there was a 75 per cent increase in the affiliated membership of white collar unions, to 2,046,137.[10] By the end of 1971, the 2,916,000 non-manual trade unionists made up 30 per cent of the TUC's total membership.[11] This increased strength led to increased representation on the General Council. By 1972, there were ten white-collar representatives out of a council of thirty eight – twice as many as sat on the thirty-five-member council in 1960.

But hopes for the TUC's role within NEDC were never fully realised. The existence of an NEDC group of TUC leaders ('the Neddy Six') gave the TUC something it had hitherto lacked – an executive grouping who could relate to Government leaders on behalf of the Congress. But hopes that the new body would 'create an agreed development programme for the economy on the basis of tripartite discussion and commitment' were short lived.[12] On the one hand, the forum became downgraded very quickly as power continued to be exercised through the Ministerial Departments. On the other hand, over time it was the

CBI which moved closer to the Labour Government not the TUC. And the pragmatic adjustment of Government economic policy under Wilson was not compatible with the long-term planning envisaged by the TUC. Although the TUC continued to value its access to 'Neddy' and its involvement in a range of training and planning bodies, the general feeling in the last two years of the Labour Government was of 'disillusionment and isolation'.[13]

The TUC's renewed assertion of its functional distinctiveness in this period fitted nicely into the new strategic and political trajectory of the Party Leadership. At national level, after 1961, there were no further Joint Statements and during the period of the Labour Government, the representatives of the Party's National Executive Committee on the TUC's Economic Policy Committee were redesignated as 'observers'. In 1968, the TUC produced an important new innovation – the first of a series of annual Economic Reviews drawn up independently of the Party and directed primarily at Whitehall.

With this new distinctiveness went an atrophy of formal links. The National Council of Labour became a moribund committee. In 1961, there was resistance from Woodcock to its strengthening and in 1963, even opposition to it being called together.[14] Between 1966 and 1970, it met only four times. During the crisis of 1969, no attempt was made to activate it although in the 1930s, this was the body designated to keep the Movement in political harmony.

There was no immediate formal impact on the union–Party relationship but, in retrospect, it is possible to trace a series of changes involving further organisational differentiation. In 1962, for political reasons, there was a constitutional amendment that meant that only trade unionists who were individual members of the Party could be trade union delegates to the Party Conference.[15] In 1965, this was taken a step further when the provision was extended to trade union delegates attending constituency party meetings.[16] And throughout the decade, there was encouragement from both Transport House and Congress House for the breaking apart of local Trades and Labour Councils – often in the face of local wishes.

Less obviously, other consequences flowed from Woodcock's reactive philosophy, his Establishment style and his strategy of moving into Whitehall. Some traditional narrow perspectives were accentuated. A limited view of the unions' political role led the TUC to wind up the National Council of Labour Colleges, to make only token resistance to the transfer of ownership of the *Daily Herald* away from its Labour Movement shareholders, and to take a complacent view altogether of the influence of the mass media and the role of communication and campaigning.

Within the unions also, there was only a weak response to signs of degeneration at the grass roots. The Labour Party's Enquiry into Party Organisation, although chaired by a trade unionist, Bill Simpson, and enthusiastically backed by the Transport Workers' Assistant General Secretary, Jack Jones, arose from disquiet within the Party and not the unions, and it had little to say about the union–Party relationship. The serious problems of the local Labour Movement were only to become clear to the unions in the late 1970s.

Meanwhile, a Leftwing union political strategy, which many in the unions thought had been buried in the 1920s, began its resurrection. In the late 1960s, the growth of membership, the increase in union militancy, the spread of union action, the emergence of the 'flying picket' and the election of militant shop stewards and officers strengthened a new Leftwing and neo-syndicalist current.[17] Its tributaries fed into the TUC and were to feed into the Labour Party but at the time, it involved a new mood of industrial self-sufficiency and the possibility of a more politicised trade unionism able to intervene in a way independent of either the trade union centre or the Party.

Social affinity

Accentuating the new problems of this period was an intensification of the tensions which had always existed between 'the trade unionists' and 'the middle class intellectuals'. These crude categories obscured the growing trade unionism of white collar workers, and the varied elements which made up the middle class, but they were meaningful within the relationship, particularly to the manual worker trade unionists. The trend towards a more middle class Labour Party, described at the time as 'the decline of working-class politics',[18] was to become the source of new friction at all levels of the Party. In the branches and General Management Committees, the older working class element felt on the defensive – a feeling which grew considerably in the next two decades. In the unions, it added to their growing worries at their inability to secure the election of sponsored candidates who had worked at the trade; constituency parties turned increasingly to articulate, higher educated professionals.

The result was that between the elections of 1951 and 1970, there was a marked shift in the composition of the Parliamentary Labour Party, even though the percentage of sponsored MPs changed very little. Ex-manual workers declined from 40.6 per cent to 27.5 per cent. Ex-professionals rose from 30.8 per cent to 45.6 per cent, taking the tensions into the group of sponsored MPs as well as into the PLP as a whole.[19]

At leadership level, a similar shift became more marked as the decade moved on. Although an attempt was made to create the role of link-man for Frank Cousins from the Transport Workers when he was made Minister of Technology in the Labour Government, the experiment soon floundered when the problem of incomes policy moved to the fore.

Cousins's resignation in 1966, and the subsequent resignation of George Brown and Ray Gunter in 1968, sharply altered the social composition of the Cabinet. It was now clearly dominated by the university-educated ex-professionals. Only one member of the twenty-three strong Labour Cabinet at the beginning of 1969, Roy Mason, came from a manual worker occupation and only one other member, James Callaghan, had come up through the trade unions (IRSF – a neutral white collar union).

Of itself, as already noted, this difference in social composition was not necessarily problematic. Much depended on personality, on personal histories and on what styles were adopted by Labour Ministers. Being a trade unionist at Cabinet level did not necessarily make for responsiveness to trade union claims: the career of Roy Mason at the Department of Energy confirmed that. But there was not a Bevin or a Sam Watson (who died in 1962) to bridge the intellectual–trade unionist divide. Informal links weakened. By 1969, the gulf appeared wide to both sides.

Differences in social background, lifestyle and industrial experience were felt at their sharpest over issues relating to the place of work. The readiness of 'the intellectuals' to bring law permanently into the field of industrial relations was seen by union leaders as the action of those out of touch with shopfloor complexities and with the traditions of British industrial labour. Social and educational differences became a reference point for many of the resentments that trade union officials projected on the Party Leadership after 1967.[20]

It was not an ideological or factional matter. The criticism came from both Right and Left in the trade union movement. Only James Callaghan, towards the end of the Labour Government, managed fully to preserve his close links with the unions, playing the role of what Peter Jenkins called 'the keeper of the cloth cap'.[21]

Interests

When the Party was in Opposition, it could hide some of its differences behind ambiguous formulae, but the point of divergence became clear when it moved into Government. Nowhere was this more the case than on issues where fundamental trade union interests were at stake. These interests were most sensitively and most regularly involved over centrally imposed wage norms, over deflationary policies and unemployment, and in the management of strikes. Under the Labour Governments, these were the thorniest problems, and they continued to be a major source of tensions throughout the next two decades.

The fundamental economic problem facing the Labour Government, then and subsequently, was Britain's declining international competitiveness and relatively slow growth. The main industrial objective was:

> To raise productivity and efficiency so that real national output can increase, and to keep increases in wages, salaries and other forms of incomes in line with this increase.[22]

These aims had been part of the incomes policy understanding of 1963, but the agreement had other features. The policy would be voluntary, it would be part of a policy covering salaries, dividends, profits and prices, it would be part of an economic policy of planned expansion, it would chiefly benefit the lower paid and it would be in the context of an overall policy that would be inspired by a sense of social justice.

Verbal agreement on these features, however, masked considerable problems. Each union had its distinct political and industrial traditions, not to mention its place in the ladder of income differentials. Thus, the response to the new Labour Government varied from union to union, as did the degree of commitment to the policy. Also, the policy was vulnerable to a cumulative withdrawal of support in the event of the Government's failure to produce the appropriate economic and social climate, and this failure was to become more apparent with each year of the Labour Government.

Faced with the immediate problem of an estimated £800 million deficit in the balance of payments and a periodic international loss of confidence in the pound sterling, the Government (until forced into a hurried devaluation in November 1967) made defence of the fixed pound axiomatic and turned increasingly to deflationary measures which would reduce domestic demand.

The voluntary incomes policy agreed with the unions in Opposition was rapidly turned into a legislative instrument of wage restraint backed by legal sanctions. This legislation was rejected in principle by the TUC as 'at best irrelevant and at worst a positive hindrance to the development of a coherent policy for incomes'.[23] What the coherent policy might be, under the circumstances, was never clear, except that it must be achieved through willing cooperation. Most union leaders were anxious to sustain the Government and, despite their misgivings, in its first years of office they exhibited a remarkable degree of loyalty to the incomes policy. But the TUC, as a body, although it did briefly introduce a process of 'vetting' wage claims in 1965, was never able to exercise comprehensive control over the wage policies of its affiliated organisations. It also became clear that the union leaders themselves were not in a position to halt the *de facto* passage of power to the shop floor that accompanied the pattern of local collective bargaining under full employment. As the Government's incomes policy moved further away from the original conception, so it became difficult for union leaders to justify their restraining role. Between 1966 and 1968, one union after another came out in opposition to Government policy.[24]

The atmosphere of non-co-operation was fed by the Government's inability to control prices, its inability to sustain expansion, and its failure to sustain a quid pro quo in social policy. Initially, the Government did attempt to implement many of the election commitments that trade unionists welcomed. In 1965, it reversed a judicial decision of 1964 that threatened the unions' industrial immunity (*Rookes* v. *Barnard*), and it carried out a range of social policy reforms ranging from a Redundancy Payments Act to the abolition of prescription charges.

The wage freeze of July 1966, however, was accompanied by deflationary measures that killed the National Plan forecasts, and when in November 1967 the Government was eventually forced into a hurried devaluation, this was accompanied by major cuts in public spending, and a rise in unemployment. The reintroduction of the highly emotive prescription charges added to the resentment within the Party and the unions. In the final two years of the Wilson Government, the rectification of the balance of payments deficit became the central economic purpose: radical measures of income redistribution were regarded as impractical or inopportune, and union pressures for reflationary measures and a higher rate of growth were resisted, even declared 'nearly insane' by the Labour Chancellor of the Exchequer[25] – a judgement he later came to regret.[26]

Conflict between the Government and the unions over incomes and economic policy was crucially related to the industrial strength of the unions, and it was on this issue that attention became focused when, in 1968, the Royal Commission on Trades Unions and Employers Associations reported its findings. The Commission report drew attention to the 'two systems of industrial relations' in Britain. 'The one is the formal system embodied in the official institutions; the other is the informal system created by the actual behaviour of trade unions and employers associations, of managers, shop stewards and workers.'[27]

In the informal system, in which the threat or practice of unofficial strikes played a major part, there was a strong tendency for 'wage drift' from nationally agreed levels. The commission rejected the use of legislation as a means of enforcing adherence to the national pattern of bargaining and of disciplining the shop stewards. Instead, it recommended the voluntary encouragement of an orderly adaptation to this informal system so that the local shop stewards would be more closely integrated within the unions' own authority.

The Government, however, sought instead a legislative solution to the problem. It was conscious of the very damaging strikes by seamen in 1966 and dockworkers in 1967, and, as important, was aware of the need to give the international financial community evidence of the Government's capacity to govern. But, in addition – and another continuing problem for the Labour Movement – there was evidence not only of wide public support but also of support from trade union members for legislative action.[28] The Labour Government thus made a huge break with Party tradition – as clear a breach of the 'rules' of the union–Party relationship as had ever been proposed by any Labour Government.

The 1969 White Paper *In Place of Strife* involved a package which included measures supportive of union recognition, negotiation rights and employment protection, but its most contentious features were three legal powers which departed radically from the Donovan proposals. The Secretary of State would have power to impose a 'conciliation pause' in relation to unofficial strikes. There would also be power to require a union or unions to hold a ballot on an official strike which presented a threat to the economy or public interest. And on inter-union disputes concerning recognition, there would be a power for the Minister to impose a solution. The powers would be backed by penal sanctions which could involve fines deducted from earnings.

In response to this invasion of their traditional freedom, one union after another across the spectrum expressed their strong opposition.[29] The General Council of the TUC took up this opposition but was also pushed into producing its own 'Programme for Action': the Congress would give 'opinion and advice' on unofficial disputes and also take on much stronger powers to deal with inter-union disputes. In spite of this move, the Government produced a short Bill which embodied all the features of the White Paper which the unions found most offensive. The Government then found that it could not carry the Parliamentary Labour Party with it. Eventually a face-saving, 'solemn and binding' undertaking on disputes was made by the TUC, and the Industrial Relations Bill, which the Government eventually produced in April 1970, was emasculated of the offending proposals.

The rejection of penal sanctions by the Parliamentary Party owed much to general union pressure. The parliamentary Trade Union Group of MPs began to play a constraining role upon the Government, and a strong emphasis in the speeches of 'middle-of-the-road' MPs was the need to safeguard 'the Movement'

from a split. A General Election was in the offing, and the result of the implementation of this legislation could have seen the Party fighting an election in
internal turmoil. Whether the policy could have been pushed through at an
earlier stage of the Parliament, when governmental prestige was higher, can only
be speculated. As it was, it led to the widespread belief that this was one area in
which a Labour Government was powerless to act without trade union agreement.

Rejection of the Government's proposals and the relaxation in practice of
incomes policy legislation was followed by an explosion of militancy that included sections of the industrial workforce hitherto noted for their lack of
radicalism: the Ambulance staff, the Dustmen, the Yorkshire Miners, and the
Pilkington Glass workers. This outburst of militancy further nourished the process of factional change and realignment within the unions, producing a climate
in which Leftwing trade unionists advanced within the union structures.

Ideology

The fourth source of tension arose out of two contrary trends at work among the
Parliamentary Leadership on the one hand and the unions on the other. The
trends were interactive and resulted in a formal polarisation of ideology and
institutions to a degree possibly without precedent in Party history. On the one
hand, the Party's official policy, as the result of the dominance of Gaitskell's
supporters, was revised in order to shed the traditional incremental, industry-by-
industry, socialist strategy – and to accept 'that both public and private enterprise
have a place in the economy'.[30] The trend away from traditional socialism was
reinforced by the pragmatism of the Wilson Government in facing the country's
economic problems and by its attempt to capture the middle ground of national
political attitudes. At the same time, a contrary trend was emerging in the trade
unions: a shift to the Left took place in the context of a widening arc of opinion
critical of Government policy and disillusioned with its loss of ideological bearings.

After 1967, new Leftwing union leaders emerged in four of the five largest
affiliated unions. They were Hugh Scanlon, President of the Amalgamated
Engineering Union (elected 1967); Lawrence Daly, General Secretary of the
National Union of Mineworkers (elected 1968); Richard Seabrook, President of
the Union of Shop, Distributive and Allied Workers (elected 1968); and Jack
Jones, General Secretary of the Transport and General Workers' Union (elected
1969).

This Leftwing position was advantaged by amalgamations and occupational
shifts at a time when the union share of the Conference vote was increasing. The
Left was never as dominant as it sometimes appeared but it was clear by 1969 that
the old Rightwing 'block vote' had disintegrated as the dominant entity on the
floor of the Party Conference and the Trades Union Congress. In its place was a
conspicuous new alliance. Although the two largest unions could still be defeated
and Leftwing leadership in the Engineers was precariously based, these two
formed the basis of a Left block more powerful than at any time in the Party's
history (Table 5.1). The pattern of Party Leadership dominance over the Conference was shattered.

Table 5.1 The largest unions and conference voting weight, 1969

Transport Workers	1,000,000
Engineers	777,000
General and Municipal Workers	650,000
Mineworkers	340,000
Shopworkers	292,000
Electricians	275,000
Total of 'Big Six'	3,334,000
Total union vote	5,378,000
Total conference vote	6,110,000

During the final phase of the incomes policy and in the deep split over industrial relations legislation, the Government faced a TUC in which the spearhead of the latter's negotiations was in the hands of two trade unionists who appeared to have few of the loyalist inhibitions of the past two decades.

Further, these union leaders held views which were in sharp contrast with those of the generation of union leaders who had dominated the Party Conference in the early 1950s. They encouraged rank and file militancy, they favoured industrial democracy and they were strong supporters of extending public ownership. On foreign and defence policy they were hostile to many of the Cold War positions and were close to the traditional Left. Their perspectives seemed to place them in a very different political camp to the revisionists and pragmatists who dominated the political leadership of the Party. The political polarisation which had always threatened the future of the Labour Movement now appeared to have arrived.

CONTRACT, 1970–1979

Thus, at the turn of the decade, the union–Party relationship was at a stage where all its most fundamental tensions were reinforcing each other; there was a polarisation on strategy and on ideology and a marked lack of social affinity.

Above all, there had been exposed to full view a disagreement over the management of inflation and the handling of industrial relations which threatened to lock the polarised alignments around issues fundamental to trade union interests. How to deal with these disagreements became a permanent and central problem for the relationship.

Confrontation over *In Place of Strife* expressed and symbolised the depth of division and left a lasting mark on the consciousness of different segments of the Party. It severely diminished the confidence of many union leaders – not all on the Left – in the judgement and reliability of the Parliamentary Leadership. For their part, a section of the PLP saw the retreat of 1969 as unacceptable weakness; they became more ambivalent about the value of the union attachment and increasingly worried about protecting the rights of the Parliamentary Party (see Chapter 8). In turn, a growing body of opinion in the constituencies and in the unions, their suspicions enhanced by the *In Place of Strife* episode, sought new means of exerting democratic control over the Parliamentary Party.

This question of democracy – which was eventually to explode in the constitutional crisis of 1979 to 1982 – appeared on the brink of provoking confrontation in the early 1970s, given the new tensions and the new attitudes brought to bear on the Party by Leftwing union leaders. They openly associated, individually and collectively, with the dissident Left of the Parliamentary and Constituency Parties. They appeared to be bent on extending the trade union political role within the Labour Party. In their affirmation of traditional intra-Party democracy they were hostile to the idea that the Party's policy should be made and implemented by an independent parliamentary 'elite'.

Such a set of attitudes towards activity within the Labour Party – a syndrome never previously shared by so senior a group of trade union officials – raised acute problems of power and authority within the Party. These entwined with the equally acute ideological dilemmas about the Party's purpose and its historic identification with industrial labour. Thus, the Party–union relationship appeared both problematic and fragile.

For the first time for many years there were anticipations and projections of splits and defections, from one wing or the other, as new feelings of estrangement were engendered between union leaders and politicians.

Such feelings were not initially alleviated by the 1970 General Election result; indeed it appeared to heighten the problems indicated by the confrontations of the previous two years and, from one perspective, to bear out the analysis made by the revisionists in 1959. The Conservatives gained (net) sixty-six seats; their largest single advance since the war. Subsequently, critics of the unions over *In Place of Strife* blamed the defeat on their opposition to the proposals and the loss of governmental prestige that the retreat involved:[31] yet neither the opinion poll data after *In Place of Strife* nor during the election itself bore out this interpretation.[32] Critics of the Labour Government noted the damaging drift of working class support from the Labour Party[33] (the first signs of what was to be termed later 'class de-alignment') and diagnosed that one of the factors contributing to defeat was the Labour Government's attitude to industrial relations issues.[34]

Yet in spite of the polarisation and the mixed feelings of bitterness and alienation, there was a remarkably muted post-mortem on the events of the previous four years and the relationship staged a significant recovery in the next eight years. True, at local level, the weaknesses which had been enhanced by the strategies of the 1960s made the relationship increasingly vulnerable: membership, affiliation, delegation and activity were all very low. But at national level in this period there was a real revival which developed into a new convergence of purpose. 'The Social Contract', as it became known, was far from solving all the problems of the union–Party relationship – as was to be shown in the winter of 1978–9 – but for the moment, the divisive factors were diminished or obscured.

There were three reasons why the events of 1969 led to a muted reaction and the *rapprochement* of the early 1970s. The first was that though the Labour Party Leadership had shifted to the Right and contravened some fundamental 'rules' of the Labour Movement stretching back almost to its foundation, this was part of a broader movement of intellectual opinion in which the Conservative Party since

1965 had been making the running. In 1968, *Fair Deal at Work*, the new Conservative Party policy document, threatened a much more comprehensive attack on the system of free collective bargaining and almost immediately after the election, the attack began.

The second element in the situation was the reaction of leading members of the PLP. There was a sense of guilt felt by many ex-Ministers about promulgating such a crisis in the family and breaking the 'rules' of the relationship. Contrition was a marked feature of the response of some of them.[35] In others, it was less obvious than the resentment.

But perhaps the most important factor was that the restraint exercised by the union leaders – a restraint built into the 'rules' of the union–Party relationship – had never been shed during the 1969 crisis (see Chapter 6). None of the intra-Party sanctions which the union leadership might have applied was used. Sensitive to the Party's distinctive role and conscious of the need to protect the TUC's own position, the new Left union leadership fought *In Place of Strife* in a remarkably diplomatic way. And when it was over, they hurried to bury the signs of the discord, were forthright in their expressions of support for the Party, and immediately agreed to *raise* affiliation fees. Within months of the General Election defeat, Jack Jones was feeling his way towards a new accommodation with the Wilson leadership

Strategy

The trade unions

The first priority of the unions after 1970 was to react to the policies of the Heath Government. The new Conservative administration pushed ahead with its plans to introduce a framework of law covering industrial relations – this alongside other policies which moved away from the post-war consensus, including disengagement from industrial intervention and new measures of denationalisation. As bad, as far as the TUC was concerned, was the 'Cold War', which now descended on its direct relationship with the Government – a significant step backwards in the development of a neo-corporate relationship. Neither regular communication nor access broke down but the relationship was halting and embittered after the Government made the consultative document on the new Industrial Relations Bill non-negotiable in its essentials.

Meanwhile, arising from a common opposition to the Industrial Relations Act, the TUC, which under Woodcock had retreated from its Transport House contacts, now began to rebuild them under Vic Feather (1969–73) and Len Murray (1973–84). With Jack Jones a leading influence, the TUC leadership moved to seek commitment from the Labour Party on the repeal and replacement of the legislation. They turned to the precedent of 1931 (see Chapter 2, p. 31). The old forum, the National Council of Labour (which since 1941 had included the Co-operative Union representatives), was bypassed. In its place was instituted a trilateral committee between the NEC, the PLP and the TUC – the Liaison Committee. On this committee, the fundamental industrial and economic policy agreements were formulated between Party and unions in the period leading up to the 1974 General Election. Two policy documents were crucial – a *Statement on Industrial Relations* (1972) and *Economic Policy and the Cost of Living* (1973). In discussions of both, the TUC, particularly Jones, was an assertive force in shaping the broad understanding on policy and procedure which became known as the Social Contract.

This renewed involvement with the Labour Party took place in spite of the continuation (indeed the reinforcement) of some of the factors which had caused the original drift away. At national level, there was a further increase in the white collar membership of the TUC and a new influx of 'neutral' unions. By 1977, almost every significant union was in membership of the TUC, and the non-Party-affiliated membership of the unions was almost a majority of TUC membership.[36] At regional level, reorganisation of the TUC structure and the Trades Council organisations further differentiated their functions.

But these factors were insignificant alongside the determination of the union leadership to secure through the Labour Party the fundamental reform and preferably the abolition of the Industrial Relations Act. In any case, in spite of the changing composition of TUC membership, the General Council was still dominated by officials of unions affiliated to the Party. In addition, most of those from non-affiliated unions were individual members of, or sympathetic to, the Labour Party. And slowly a new radicalisation was beginning to make itself felt in public sector and white collar unions – a product of changing membership and of growing conflict with the Government over incomes and public expenditure. Thus, the threat that a changing TUC composition would pull it away from the Labour Party was slow to materialise.

In the meantime, alongside this national move closer to the Labour Party, a crisis, or rather a series of crisis points, emerged in the relationship between the unions and the Heath Government in the context of an industrial climate in which there was suddenly an evocation of the atmosphere of the 1920s. Unemployment rose rapidly to over a million in January of 1972 and more working days were lost through strikes that year than any since the General Strike of 1926.

Trade union responses to the Conservative Government included a period of sustained protest – back 'into Trafalgar Square' once more. At Upper Clyde Shipbuilders, the work-in campaign against closure aroused a wider political movement and emulative action in other workplaces. As for the Industrial Relations Act, the TUC moved, with some wavering, to a policy of non-registration which became a binding instruction in affiliated unions. Arising out of one application under the Act, five London dockers (the Pentonville Five) were imprisoned and under threat of a General Strike by the TUC, a legal means was found of releasing them.

Under sustained industrial and political pressure, the Conservative Government began to exhibit the collapse to the centre which had hitherto affected all post-war Governments. There was renewed intervention in industry and help to large firms whose businesses were threatened. The trend in unemployment was reversed. The remarkably successful Miners' Strike of 1972 became a symbol of the new power of industrial labour, forcing the closure of depot gates at Saltley, militantly securing a victory which was almost total in its benefits.

Thus, by 1974, the unions were in a powerful political position with all three strategic options available – neo-corporate, militant and Party. But with the Party now suddenly thrust into Government in two quick elections, militant industrial action became more inhibited. The Party connection took on a high profile but the direct neo-corporate linkage of the TUC and the Government was the more important.

Much public attention was drawn to the work of the Liaison Committee which met normally on a monthly basis throughout the period of the Labour Governments. Its role, however, was often misunderstood and just as often overstated. The main purpose of the Committee after 1975 was that of seeking to keep Party, TUC and Government in medium-term agreement on key issues. To this end, the Committee produced for three years from 1976 to 1978 broad thematic statements focused on priorities and even where disagreement existed, expressed it in terms of a collaborative enterprise.

Labour Government Ministers were not anxious to be pulled into any arrangement which might prejudice their independence – trade union 'tutelage' was resented enough. Some on the NEC might, given a different attitude from the unions, have sought a wider role for the commitee, but they, too, were fearful that their own independent policymaking process might be colonised.

Most important, the trade unions through the TUC always had reservations about the operation of the Liaison Committee. On the one hand they did not want sensitive industrial issues – particularly those involving industrial disputes, as in the Fire Service in 1977 – to be put into a forum where the NEC Left could put the unions under pressure; it was, as far as the TUC was concerned, 'none of their business'. On the other hand the TUC valued and wanted to defend, as always, its direct relationship with the Government, both in formal terms and informally through links between senior union leaders and Government Ministers. If there was a priority forum between the the TUC and the Labour Government, it was the regular meetings between the General Secretary, the Neddy Six, the Prime Minister and key Government Ministers.

Further, the TUC's direct relationship with Government was expanding in other ways after 1974. There was a substantial increase in the Congress's representation upon new governmental committees and tripartite bodies at various levels. The most notable area of extension was in the role of the Economic Development Committees and the Sector Working Parties. As a consequence of increased representation, the TUC began to explore new means of internal union consultation. Thus, the Party connection might have been replenished but it was also clear that the TUC was concerned to institutionalise its direct links to Government in spite of a range of policy disappointments.

It was concerned also to differentiate its industrial responsibilities. It was a barely noticed, but, in this context, unsurprising development that the 'Concordat' of February 1979, following 'the winter of discontent', titled *The Economy, the Government and Trade Union Responsibilities*, came out of bilateral discussions between the TUC and Government Ministers – discussions which excluded the Party and the Liaison Committee.

The Labour Party

The unions' move to greater involvement within the Labour Party heightened the Party's electoral identification with them and in doing so ran counter to the electoral strategy evolved in the 1960s. But that strategy was now no longer as respectable as it was. Much of the sociological case for the 'classless' and white collar oriented style was found to be based on mistaken assumptions about social change. The more recent academic studies indicated that for demographic reasons, support from the manual working class electoral base was a growing asset.[37] This, and the evidence of a shift away by manual workers at the 1970 General Election, inhibited those who in the 1960s had been anxious to play down the union and manual worker connection. In the centre of the Party, there was a new readiness to seek support from those 'from whence we came'[38] as the view gained ground that the 1970 election had been lost because of the damage done to union and manual-worker support by the Wilson Government.

This change in electoral approach after 1970 was more a reaction than a worked-out strategy. The highly publicised 'social contract' arose out of the necessity of an understanding with the unions. Some on the Right continued to be sceptical of the value of association with the adverse image of trade unions. Others became increasingly hostile to the new balance of power. Dick Taverne, an ex-Labour MP standing against the Labour Party at Lincoln in 1973, in effect tested the water for a later breakaway Social Democratic Party, with enough initial success for this to be a covert strategy for a minority who shared his critique of the Party and the unions.

But on the Left the response to the unions was much more welcoming. Militant trade unionism appeared to be the dynamo of a new political mobilisation. Tony Benn, impressed by the Clyde Workers' revolt and rapidly moving to the Left after 1971, argued in an important strategy meeting in 1973 that 'the idea of a powerful and really strong policy alliance with the trade union movement would have a wider appeal ...'.[39]

In practice, whether the Labour Party Leadership liked it or not (and some unquestionably did not), the Party's association with the unions was reinforced by the circumstances of the time. As the unions became locked in a series of conflicts with the Government, the Party – encouraged particularly by the Leftward-moving NEC – became ranged alongside them. The Miners' Strikes of 1972 and 1974 evoked widespread sympathy within the Party and a General Election fought in February 1974 around the social contract and the question of 'who rules, Government or unions?' could not avoid bringing the Party's structural links with the unions into the limelight.

However, to the surprise of the Conservative Government, most observers, and not a few in the Labour Party and unions, the public back-up to the Government against the unions was not forthcoming. There was a complex result putting Labour in office but on a vote lower than in 1970 and with reduced support from the trade unionists.[40]

The victory of the Labour Party in 1974, following the Miners' Strike, left two tactical legacies to the Party. One was the knowledge that Labour's ability (compared with their political opponents) to work with the unions in the national interest was a major electoral advantage.[41] Some on the Left took a further view: that what had been achieved in 1974 – a major industrial upsurge followed by the fall of a Conservative Government and the election of a Labour Government pledged to Leftwing policies – was a repeatable exercise.

Certainly the association of the Labour Government and the unions was in the electoral forefront of the politics of the next five years through the Social Contract and various stages of incomes policy. There was a steady media attack on the unions throughout this period, locating threats to the economy, to democracy, and to freedom, from the power-hungry union leaders, shop stewards and activists. Public opinion polls continued to show substantial majorities who believed that the unions were too powerful.[42] In spite of this, the Labour Party continued to be the Party thought best able to deal with industrial relations and strikes[43] and on the basis of a continuing firm unity at national level, an election was awaited in the autumn of 1978.

But the opinion polls were showing a narrow Conservative lead and Callaghan postponed the election. One Ministerial calamity then followed another. The Government 5 per cent pay policy was defeated at the Labour Party Conference in October. A deal negotiated between Government Ministers and the Neddy Six was defeated on the TUC General Council in November. In December, after a dispute at Fords, the Government was defeated in the House of Commons over sanctions to hold back private sector pay claims. The surge of industrial action included the petrol tanker drivers, but its main feature was a revolt by low paid public sector workers unwilling to lose out under the 5 per cent policy, lacking confidence in the Government's commitment to the public sector, and no longer amenable to control from above.

As the winter crisis deepened, the Government's position in the opinion polls fell away. And in 1979, the defeat feared by the GMWU leader as 'potentially of 1931 proportions'[44] came to pass.

Social affinity

The concern to rebuild bridges after 1970 was not simply an institutional matter. There was an awareness that the two leaderships had not talked enough in informal terms during the period after 1967. And there was an appreciation, from Jones particularly, that the growing divide between 'trade unionists' and 'intellectuals' must be made less sharp.

Neither the composition of the Parliamentary Party as a whole nor the composition of the Labour Shadow Cabinet showed any change in the direction of increased manual worker representation, in spite of the hopes expressed by union leaders like Jones. The marked increase in teachers and lecturers continued. But a new axis was forged between the political and industrial wings as a result of the relationship between Harold Wilson, Jack Jones and Michael Foot (a new member of both the Shadow Cabinet and the NEC). Their personal understanding, based on past association with 'Bevanism' and the periodical Tribune, limited the conflict over the Common Market and helped build the accommodation over industrial relations policy. Other political leaders, Tony Benn on the Left, Anthony Crosland and Denis Healey on the Right, also tended to move in closer harmony with the trade union mainstream after 1970.

And though the Labour Cabinets after 1974 were still overwhelmingly composed of the university educated, it was far stronger on personal links with the unions and it was significant that as a result of new appointments there were now four members who were from the important Mineworkers and Engineers unions.[45] With this composition, the Cabinet was more trade-union-sensitive than was the Labour Cabinet of the late 1960s.

But it was Michael Foot rather than any ex-manual trade unionist who became a crucial bridging figure, first as Secretary of State for Employment – a position for which he was suggested by Jack Jones – and then as Leader of the House. His important links to Jones were paralleled by the relationship between Denis Healey and Len Murray. They were the central figures in regular informal discussions alongside the Liaison Committee and through the meetings of Government Ministers and 'the Neddy Six'.

Personal links with the unions were reinforced after the leadership election of 1976 which was, in the final round, fought out by Centre Right and Centre Left candidates each of whom was well thought of in trade union circles. While Callaghan became Leader and Foot Deputy Leader and Leader of the House, another pro-union figure, Albert Booth, became Secretary of State for Employment. Two other figures with increasingly hostile attitudes towards the unions and their role in the Party departed the national Labour stage – Reg Prentice to the Conservative Party, Roy Jenkins to the EEC (there eventually to stimulate a defection from the Labour Movement). So, at a time when policy relations with the unions were becoming more and more difficult, personal linkages were improving.

But Jones and Scanlon retired in 1978. New union leaders, Moss Evans in the Transport Workers and Terry Duffy in the Engineers, replaced them. The linkage of Party and union leaders remained close, but there was not the same personal authority and trust. In any case, the understanding went badly wrong in the period leading up to and following the announcement of the 5 per cent pay policy. The failure to hold an election in the autumn of 1978 after five of the Neddy Six had recommended it, undermined confidence.[46] Above all, for a crucial period, the Prime Minister and the Chancellor failed to heed the warning from their union allies that the pay norm was too low, too rigid and likely to provoke a reaction from the members. After that came disaster.

Ideology

The disaster was all the more significant because the 1970s were marked by ideological developments which were in their consequences momentous for the Labour Party and the unions.

These were difficult years for the ex-Revisionists. Still a majority among the political leadership, they had begun to develop serious differences over strategy and policy in the context of a new climate of opinion, a new economic and industrial situation, and a post-mortem on the 1966–70 Labour Government which focused upon its shortcomings. They now had to face a realigned block vote and a major loss of power in the Party – without obvious issues upon which they could mobilise a counter-assault on the Left.

Table 5.2 The largest unions and conference voting weight, 1974

Transport Workers	1,000,000
Engineers	832,000
General and Municipal Workers	650,000
Electricians	350,000
Shopworkers	293,000
Mineworkers	264,000
Total of 'Big Six'	4,389,000
Total union vote	5,385,000
Total conference vote	6,073,000

The immediate impact of these changes in Opposition from 1972 to 1974 was to curb the assertive confidence of this wing in inner party conflict. Apart from over the EEC, differences with the Leftwing union leaders were voiced with a new discretion. This more muted approach was further encouraged by the pragmatic Harold Wilson, who adopted a style of 'leadership from the rear' in order to facilitate a new unity in the Movement.

From their side, the Leftwing union leaders also behaved with more restraint than their critics often saw or would acknowledge. Although there was a new assertion of the principles of traditional Socialism, unilateral nuclear disarmament and intra-Party democracy, and the union leaders helped swing the NEC to (by 1974) a Leftwing majority, what was remarkable was the extent to which this generation of union leaders continued to abide by the 'rules' of the union–Party relationship (see Chapter 6). The ideological thrust of their activities was limited by a trade union perspective.

When Labour took office after 1974, it was the turn of the Leftwing union leaders to undergo a loss of ideological self-confidence and the beginning of, in some respects, a rapid deradicalisation. The crisis reached a peak in 1975 with the acceptance of an incomes policy followed by a sensational political confrontation between Jack Jones and the veteran Leftwing MP, Ian Mikardo, at the *Tribune* Rally during the Party Conference.

Much more than might have been expected, the three largest unions now moved into closer political harmony in defence of the Labour Government. This, together with changes in affiliation which brought the Electricians temporarily into greater prominence, suggested the possibility of a new 'praetorian guard' emerging to create a stable base for the Parliamentary Leadership at the Party Conference (Table 5.2).

Certainly, on the Liaison Committee, the union leaders were now more often allied with the Parliamentary leadership against the Government's fiercest critics on the Left. There was, they considered, 'a close working understanding' and 'mutual commitment'.[47]

With no signs of the Leftwing movement which had outflanked union leaders in the 1960s and the election in 1978 of Terry Duffy to replace Hugh Scanlon as President of the Engineers' union, the scene appeared set at the close of the decade for a new consolidation of the position of the Right within the unions and a new hope of accommodation with the Parliamentary Leadership. That hope was not to be realised.

Interests

Inasmuch as part of the reaction to the estrangement of 1969 was to build a new accommodation between the Parliamentary Leadership and the unions, then union and workers' interests became central to the discussions. Indeed, such interests were the bedrock of the social contract. The first meetings and the joint statement of the Liaison Committee in 1972 were concerned with the repeal of the Heath Government's Industrial Relations Act and with a variety of industrial relations reforms sought by the unions.

The use of legislation to limit free collective bargaining was dropped completely by the Parliamentary Leadership. The Social Contract involved a general commitment to voluntary restraint by the unions in exchange for a wide range of industrial, social and economic policies which would encourage the quid pro quo.

The delivery to the Labour Movement by the Labour Government in the first phase of office was impressive. A series of measures were introduced which survived the vicissitudes of the latter years of the Government. They included not only the abolition of the whole structure of statutory incomes control and the abolition of the Industrial Relations Act, but a range of new industrial rights consequent upon the Industry Act, the Employment Protection Act and the Trade Union and Labour Relations Acts. Equal Pay and Sexual Discrimination legislation was brought in. There was the nationalisation of shipbuilding and of the aircraft industry. There was a measure of dock work regulation and the long awaited abolition of tied cottages. Tripartite institutions were either strengthened – as in the case of the Manpower Services Commission and the Health and Safety Commission, or created – as in the case of the Advisory Conciliation and Arbitration Service.

To aid co-operation over incomes restraint, price controls were preserved, rents were briefly frozen and food subsidies introduced. But a combination of oil price rises, the legacy of Heath Government threshold agreements and some key catching-up pay settlements, encouraged an escalating inflationary spiral with pay running well ahead of prices. The rate of inflation, which reached 26.9 per cent in August 1975, in turn resulted in a major drop in the value of the pound.

A severe wage restraint policy was introduced, but within the voluntary framework that the union leadership – particularly Jack Jones – wanted, that is, one that protected the low paid. The TUC guided, and to a considerable extent, policed the new policy – a policy which was not significantly breached by any union. Co-operation extended even after the formal ending of the second phase of the policy in 1975–6. The 'twelve months rule' was respected and the TUC evolved a 'nod and wink' understanding with the Government that in spite of its formal opposition to a wage limit it would not seek to mobilise the Movement against Government policy. The rate of inflation had dropped to 7.4 per cent by June 1978 and remained in single figures until the spring of 1979.

This co-operation was achieved in spite of a major drop in average living standards from 1975 to 1977[48] and in spite of the phasing out of food subsidies against TUC wishes. And it was achieved in the face of shifts towards a monetarist approach in the handling of the economy. Ministers became preoccupied with the Public Sector Borrowing Requirement, as well as with reaction of the finance markets and, in 1976, with loan conditions laid down by the International Monetary Fund. Deflationary policies, including cuts in planned public expenditure, exacerbated the employment problems caused by a combination of international recession, lack of competitiveness and a growing labour force. Unemployment, which had reached one and a quarter million by August 1975, went over one and a half million on occasions in the next two years. A considerable gap appeared between Government policy and TUC Congress resolutions. Yet the co-operation continued.

How and why this co-operation was achieved will be explored in Chapter 6 when we examine the motivations of Jones and Scanlon. Here it must be noted that from the Government side throughout the period from 1975 to 1979, the consciousness of union opinion was never an insignificant feature in Cabinet policymaking. Certainly it was sufficient to act as a boundary to a full-hearted acceptance of monetarism, market criteria and supply side incentives[49] where opinion veered in that direction. And union views – particularly those of the TGWU leadership – had a sustained impact on pensions policy.[50]

Further, although the final eighteen months came to be dominated by the clash over incomes policy, there was a continuing, albeit limited, quid pro quo in line with TUC representations,[51] and there was a continuing trickle of progressive industrial legislation.[52] Above all, the Government, deeply concerned over rising unemployment, was committed to job subsidisation and job creation. And in 1977–8 (unlike Roy Jenkins' 'hard slog' period of the last Labour Government) they produced a two-stage mild reflation of the economy. Not as great as that asked for by the TUC, but it contributed to a fall in unemployment in 1979.[53]

All these were signs of shared priorities. In the autumn of 1978, there was some sense of hope that a corner was being turned.[54] Average living standards were rising again.[55] North Sea oil was coming ashore. Sacrifices had been made since 1975. The economy had been strengthened. Expectations were rising. Years later, in both wings, there was a quiet agonising lament over the 'might have beens' of a third successive term of Labour Government – but the chance was lost.

IMPLOSION 1979 TO 1983

The period immediately following 'the winter of discontent' and defeat in the 1979 General Election was unlike anything known before in Labour Party history. In the next four years, the Labour Movement was convulsed by an unprecedented internal schism over Party democracy. Not only did the conflict have important ramifications for the position of the trade unions within the Party but the unions' role was brought into sharp and contentious focus at almost every stage.

Fundamental questions which had simmered below the surface for much of the Labour Party's history were now posed under the most critical of circumstances.

The tensions which had built up within the relationship since the 1960s took on a dynamic so powerful as to stimulate major constitutional changes on the one hand and important Social Democratic defections from the Parliamentary Labour Party on the other.

Meanwhile, the Thatcher Government pushed ahead with its attempt to reconstruct the post-war settlement. This time, there was no collapse to the centre. There was no retreat from the public expenditure constraints, the privatisation programme, and the legislation which restrained trade union action. Indeed, a second stage of trade union legislation brought the curtailment of trade union legal immunities with new limitations on 'secondary' action. Slowly the unions awoke to their political weakness at the grass roots and their loss of political leverage in Whitehall. All the achievements of the 1940s were now under threat. The counter-revolution expected in the 1950s had now begun.

Strategy

The Labour Party

All the evidence indicated that the dispute over the 5 per cent pay limit and 'the winter of discontent' had a traumatic effect on public attitudes towards the Labour Movement. It undermined still further trade union popularity and it increased the number of those who believed the unions were too powerful.[56] It encouraged additional support for legislative restrictions on the unions with even a majority of trade unionists in favour of the Conservative Party's reform programme,[57] and it undermined the Labour Party's claim to be the Party who could best reach an accommodation with the unions.

From the General Election result it was also apparent that new electoral vulnerabilities were emerging within the unions. There was a heavy desertion from Labour among manual workers[58] and among trade unionists support fell, from 55 per cent to 51 per cent.[59] Tory trade unionism now emerged stronger organisationally as well as electorally.[60]

Within the Labour Party, this evidence had a profound effect on the Right of the Party. It heightened their belief that they were in too close a relationship with the unions – in effect that the 1960 diagnosis was correct. Further, the Right warned against the militancy associated with union action in the winter of 1978–9 and viewed with hostility the signs that Leftwing trade unionists were seeking to push the TUC into industrial action against the new Government. It would be both improper and fruitless. A section of the Right went further in their prescription, seeing a growing imperative to freeing themselves from the union connection and its constraining 'rules' (see Chapter 8).

On the Left, a very different view emerged. Industrially, they stressed the precedent of the Pentonville Five and the Miners' Strike in forcing a Conservative Government to retreat and producing a situation where Labour could win a General Election. Where the Front Bench often had reservations at being seen to be too closely identified with militant action, in this period the Leftwing NEC had few such reservations. Open and outright support for trade unionism was seen as an essential element in building up class conscious enthusiasm behind a Labour victory. Politically, the Left blamed the defeat on the failure of the Labour Government to carry out Party policy and there was increased support for the Campaign for Labour Party Democracy in its attempt to change the Party's constitution and induce a higher degree of accountability.

Indeed the Party as a whole was looking inwards rather than looking outwards for much of this period of Opposition. Large-scale demonstrations against unemployment, some of them huge, tended to peter out. And though there was support for CND demonstrations and for the People's March for Jobs in 1981 and 1983, campaigning activities tended to be undermined by the pressure of other priorities, particularly the three constitutional proposals which were debated and voted upon at the Party Conference in 1979 and 1980;[61] and then the Deputy Leadership election which dominated six months of 1981.

Meanwhile, in January 1981 a section of the Right of the Party had broken away to form a new Social Democratic Party and then an Alliance with the Liberals. Labour's big lead in opinion polls disappeared with the defectors. The diagnosis that Labour's vote was less committed and more volatile than it had been in the past was confirmed between 1981 and 1983. The Alliance achieved a series of major by-election successes including running Labour close in Warrington in 1981 and seizing a 'safe' Labour seat at Bermondsey in 1983. As the internal struggle in the Party continued, there was an anxious, although mainly covert, questioning of the unions' affiliation to the Labour Party behind the forthright declarations of loyalty. A major breakdown in the Labour Movement appeared a real possibility.

At Bishop's Stortford in January 1982 the unions did their best to call a halt to the constitutional crisis and to some extent it abated. Through the new organisation, Trade Unions for a Labour Victory, they sought to aid the Party organisationally and financially. Their high profile relationship with the Party continued up to and through the General Election campaign. Their partnership with the Party was stressed in the Manifesto and particularly in the 'National Economic Assessment' – a complicated process which was both a planning concept and a policy in relation to the management of incomes.

The Election campaign and then the result was a bigger disaster than 1979. Labour internal policy divisions erupted in the middle of the campaign, its organisation was generally agreed to be a shambles and there was a major turning away from Labour to the Alliance. In the end, there was a 9.5 per cent drop in the Labour vote and Labour's support among trade unionists dropped to 39 per cent.[62]

The trade unions

The initial response of the unions and the TUC to the Thatcher Government was to look to the reassuring precedent of the Heath Government. There had been an attempt then to place legal restrictions on the unions and to reconstruct the post-war settlement. But eventually Heath had retreated. The same U-turn was hopefully and anxiously expected of Margaret Thatcher. But by the autumn of 1981 it became clear that no such U-turn was likely to take place. The Thatcherite programme was pushed through despite a sharp rise in unemployment to over three million and despite fierce inner city riots.

This administration was determined to reduce trade union industrial and political power. Unemployment cut deeply into trade union membership and finances. Cuts in public expenditure undermined a variety of public and social services and the power of public sector unions. The decline of manufacturing industry bit into some traditional areas of trade union strength. Privatisation was carried through in some key sectors including telecommunications, putting the unions on the defensive in that area also. And through two Employment Acts – in 1980 and 1982 – trade union rights of industrial action were curtailed. Only the National Union of Mineworkers appeared capable of delivering a serious counter-blow; in February 1981, the Government temporarily retreated rather than face a strike over pit closures.

With this shift to the Right in Government policy went a new assertion of Government sovereignty. Corporatism was as criticised on the New Right as it was on the Bennite Left. NEDC, the jewel in the crown of the tripartite kingdom, was downgraded in importance – 'a waste of time' was how Mrs Thatcher had described it.[63] Although some on the Left favoured breaking off TUC–Government relations, the main tradition held as the TUC desperately sought to retain what remained of the access and tripartite structures of the past era.[64]

Once again the unions moved 'into Trafalgar Square' but with much less success than ten years previously. A Day of Action on 14 May 1980, which included demonstrations and some strike action, was generally considered a flop. Unions now began a reassessment of their organisational and mobilisational weaknesses, with the TUC initiating its own investigation into its organisation and services. Slowly, and working against a powerful tide of adverse public opinion, the unions began to rebuild some of their communication and campaigning facilities.

On the Left the memory and myth of 1974 hung on, strengthened by the Government's retreat in the face of a possible Miners' Strike and undeterred by the signs at British Leyland that a new managerial authoritarianism was meeting some receptivity on the shop floor. Aiming to repeat the great victories of 1972, the TUC-affiliated unions as a whole pledged at the 1982 Wembley Conference that the whole Movement would come to the assistance of unions caught up in the effects of the new trade union legislation.

Meanwhile, the TUC and the unions were being pulled more and more into association with the Labour Party. The Liaison Committee for a time became an agency of campaigning co-ordination as the TUC and the Labour Party sought to build the momentum of their campaigns against Government policy. Although there was no early push from the TUC for repeal and replacement legislation to counter the Conservative trade union legislation, the promise was made by the Party just as it had been in 1972.

A second factor at work inducing more trade union involvement in the Labour Party was the state of Labour Party organisation and finance. Aid to the Labour Party channelled through a new organisation Trade Unions For a Labour Victory had revealed to the unions the fragile character of local affiliation and organisation. Their own financial insecurity, coupled with the Party's deficit, heightened anxiety about the Party's handling of financial resources – to which the unions continued to make a heavy contribution. Union pressure led to a Commission of Enquiry unique in its degree of union involvement; and continuing union concern led to the institutionalisation of the TULV organisation (see Chapters 15 and 16).

Much of this novel union involvement was of a non-factional character. But the unions were also being pulled into the Party by a third influence – one which divided them in a very political struggle. The Campaign for Labour Party Democracy split the unions in their attitude towards intra-Party reform; the Electoral College for the Leadership involved them in an immediate and preoccupying political choice of Deputy in 1981. Leftwing organisations sought to build alliances which would strengthen the industrial Left and politicise the unions. A Rightwing alliance sought to end the Left dominance over the NEC by a more politicised pattern of voting (see Chapter 11).

This greater 'politicisation' and greater involvement within the Labour Party was still held back by some traditional inhibitions, but by the beginning of 1982, the development of political conflict appeared to be enveloping the unions and the TUC in ways which further integrated the industrial and the political, and crossed some important previous boundaries of the 'rules'. The TUC did not like it. Many of the union leaders did not like it. Sections of the Parliamentary leadership did not like it. But for the moment they were all pulled into the new behaviour patterns.

Social affinity

For a variety of reasons, the Constituency Labour Party activists played a more significant role in Labour Party politics in these years than they had done before or were to do subsequently. And these developments were complicated by new social changes similar to those taking place at national level. The middle class and white collar element had been strengthened throughout the 1970s. A new active generation of higher educated and mainly public sector employed radicals had now become evident within the local parties. They were assertive of their policy rights and a major initiating force over constitutional reform and over various 'post-industrial' policy issues including nuclear disarmament, the environment and racial and sexual equality.

Social tensions emerged here with older manual worker based groups in the localities and with the more traditional-minded union leadership – particularly in craft employment. This tension persisted even where the new groups took on an assertive 'workerist' approach to politics because their style and wider purpose tended to put them at odds with mainstream manual-worker traditions.

A different kind of tension emerged between the NEC and the unions between 1979 and 1982. In seeking to assert trade union claims, the Leftwing NEC sometimes found itself in conflict with the unions and the TUC themselves. Further, although the leading intellectual figure on the NEC in these years was Tony Benn, the style was set by Dennis Skinner. His aggressive proletarianism was anathema to the middle class Right of the PLP and often a thorn in the flesh of union leaders who found their position under attack and undermined.

At the level of the PLP, on the other hand, there was some adjustment of the social developments of the 1960s. The proportion of the manual working class rose slightly and that of the higher educated professionals declined slightly in 1979.[65] The percentage of trade union sponsored MPS increased.[66] In addition, over half the 1979 intake of MPS were themselves children of manual workers[67] – an important socio-political development.

Among the Shadow Cabinet members there was also an adjustment. Although, as a result of an increase in the Shadow Cabinet in 1981 from twelve to fifteen, the three ex-manual workers, Eric Heffer, Stan Orme and Eric Varley, were a smaller minority in 1982 than in the Shadow Cabinet of 1979, the percentage who were unsponsored rose, as did the percentage who had been children of manual worker parents (from five out of twelve members in 1979 to ten out of fifteen members in 1982).

And the links to the manual worker unions were strong because of the determination of the Callaghan–Foot leadership to keep them that way – to some extent a reaction to the events of 1979 but also integral to the style of the two. Privately, and particularly at the Bishop's Stortford Conferences, the leadership of Callaghan and Foot sought to establish major points of agreement with the unions, now increasingly speaking through TULV, to face the intra-Party crisis. In 1980 the leadership of the Party passed from the hands of one pro-union accommodationist to another. Callaghan's resignation was widely thought to have paved the way for Denis Healey. But Healey had aroused considerable mistrust on the union Left, in part because of his economic policies, in part because of his known belligerency of style. As a result of initiatives encouraged by some of the Leftwing union leaders, Foot became a candidate, then was elected Leader. If his ability to win electoral support was increasingly questioned after 1981, his trustworthiness by the Labour Movement was never at issue.

Ideology

The existence of a Rightwing Conservative Government once again created the circumstances within which a new basis of unity could be forged between the Party and the unions. Underlying the complex organisational and factional politics of the period after 1979 was a developing unity on domestic policy in defence of the post-war settlement. Socialist traditions and union defensive needs were both involved in opposition to denationalisation, hostility to new cuts in public expenditure, and economic policies which led to the sharp rise in unemployment.

Nevertheless, on a range of other issues, there were major disagreements, even an acute polarisation, between majorities in the different forums of the Movement. Although the PLP and the Shadow Cabinet continued to be dominated by the Right – a grouping which was pro-EEC, hostile to unilateral nuclear disarmament and deeply ambivalent about the increased role of the unions within the Party – it was the NEC under the control of the Left which dominated the process of policy formulation.

It was an unprecedented power relationship such that the NEC could push policies on the EEC, defence and the Alternative Economic Strategy based on import controls which ran counter to the positions taken by the Labour ex-

Table 5.3 The largest unions and conference voting weight, 1979

Transport Workers	1,250,000
Engineers	1,019,000
General and Municipal Workers	650,000
Public Employees	500,000
Shopworkers	410,000
Electricians	260,000
Total of 'Big Six'	4,089,000
Total of union vote	6,351,000
Total Conference vote	7,070,000

Ministers when they were in Office. On these, as with, more narrowly, mandatory reselection and an Electoral College for the Leadership, the Party Conference came along in support. Even though there was a new leadership to the Engineers which strove to give support to the Right in the Shadow Cabinet, the Left in the unions still appeared to be impregnably strong. It was this pattern of power – unknown in any previous period of Labour-in-Opposition – which finally provoked the Social Democratic 'Gang of Three', David Owen, William Rodgers and Shirley Williams, together with a group of parliamentary allies, to defect to the side of Roy Jenkins, whose antipathy to the unions and desire to break the mould of British politics had already been widely signalled.

However, the factional alignment which appeared to give a stable base to a Left NEC was much weaker than it appeared. True, the rise of NUPE and increased affiliation by the TGWU (and some smaller unions) had strengthened the core Left,[68] while the reduced affiliation of the EETPU had held back the core Right which was otherwise also increasing affiliation.[69] But the Left's position was often exaggerated by a mass media which tended to view Labour Party developments in cataclysmic and horrific terms. It was often exaggerated by the Left also. Lower down the union hierarchies the Left's support was more shallow than it assumed.

And it was more precarious also at national level. At the time, tactical differences, personal rivalries and conflicts of interest on the Right tended to make their position look weaker than it was. Further, important shifts to the Right in the Engineers' union had yet to work themselves through to the delegation which could swing a million votes. Once the Engineers' delegation had come into line with the factional balance within that union, the Left's strength on the NEC began to wane. In two stages in 1981 and 1982 the Left lost control over the NEC after a period of fourteen years when it had slowly and with only a few setbacks built up its base of support to an extent unparalleled in Party history.

Nevertheless, though strengthened among the major unions as a result of the NEC voting of the Engineers, General and Municipal Workers and the Shopworkers (Tables 5.3 and 5.4), the core Right could not guarantee a permanent base of support, let alone produce a new praetorian guard. Constitutional questions and new policy issues fed into unstable patterns of power at senior levels in several unions. Over a variety of issues in 1980 and 1981, the known position of union leaders on key questions was defeated at union conferences and sometimes

Table 5.4 The largest unions and conference voting weight, 1983

Transport Workers	1,250,000
Engineers	1,008,000
General and Municipal Workers	725,000
Public Employees	600,000
Shopworkers	405,000
Mineworkers	237,000
Total of 'Big Six'	4,225,000
Total union vote	6,189,000
Total Conference vote	6,881,000

in union delegations. The mandates created in this period – including those covering the crucial issues of entry into the EEC and unilateral nuclear disarmament – produced majority votes at the Party Conference which outlasted the Left's dominance of the NEC.

To some extent, policy agreements on the Liaison Committee could circumvent majorities registered at the Conference. And on economic policy, there was a shift of power towards the Front bench after 1981, resulting in a crucial reinterpretation of the Alternative Economic Strategy. On the Register of Non Affiliated Organisations used by the leadership to deal with the problem of Militant Tendency, there was a much heavier union vote in favour than might be anticipated from the strength of the union Left. But on defence policy and the EEC, there was no last minute change of policy – a feature unsatisfactory to the Shadow Cabinet majority although not to the Party Leader.

Interests

Trade union and TUC interests were protected heavily within the Party in this period by a powerful range of forces. Not only did the unions receive parliamentary support for their traditional stance, but the Leftwing NEC developed a high profile public commitment to trade unionism which helped shaped much of the policy from 1979 to 1982 – by which time most of the Party's major positions were established (see the policy analysis in Chapters 13 and 14).

The renewed receptivity by the NEC was marked by an unusual procedure in 1982 whereby the unions were even consulted individually on what they wanted in the Programme. The commitment to repeal and replacement legislation in place of the Tory trade union measures was given without qualification. Through the Liaison Committee, a new level of union involvement in economic planning and industrial democracy was agreed and an attempt to commit the Party to an incomes policy was fended off.

This degree of accommodation to the trade unions – and in the case of the Left, to a particular definition of trade unionism – was not always acceptable either to the TUC or to some of the Rightwing-led unions, let alone the Shadow Cabinet. Over industrial disputes there was a high degree of unity in relation to the Steel and NHS disputes but the NEC also involved itself in some prickly and resented supportive positions – the Derek Robinson case of 1980 and the Rail disputes of 1982 were classic examples – where they were accused of illegitimate interference. Much was expected by the political Left from supporting militant trade unionism. There was a confidence that out of such militancy would come a reinvigorated Left in the unions and a broad move to the Left in the country. Such confidence was undisturbed by the devastating election defeat of 1983.

RECONSTRUCTION, 1983–1987

If the period from 1979 to 1983 was extraordinary in its internal upheavals, the period from 1983 to 1987 was equally remarkable in the oscillations of power and fortune of the unions and the Party. From a General Election defeat heralded by some as a landmark in the demise of the Labour Movement, the Labour Party made a remarkable recovery. A trade union movement which appeared to have accepted the necessities of its weakened industrial strength was suddenly plunged into a Miners' Strike which lasted an extraordinary twelve months. Political Fund ballots arising from legislation which constituted a potentially lethal attack on a political Labour Movement were turned into a sustained series of victories. A TUC which had in the early 1980s looked the stable senior party of the union–Party relationship was suddenly weakened not only in its strength but in its internal cohesion and its strategic unity. And, finally, a Labour Party which under new leadership by October 1986 looked all set for Office after one of the great political turn-arounds in modern history first went into sudden and dramatic electoral decline early in 1987, then made an electoral recovery.

It was a period also when the Party and the TUC moved into a new period of functional distinctiveness. Older conceptions were now given a new language and a change of emphasis. Creating more 'space' for the TUC and the Labour Party to carry out their distinctive functions and representative responsibilities was paralleled by attempts to reassure different political publics of the autonomy of and the 'distance' between the two sets of institutions. This development of 'space' was strongly asserted within both the TUC and the Party Leader's Office but it was the former which developed the most sensitive concessions. 'Space' for TUC officials meant allowing the TUC and the Labour Party to develop some policies independently, even if they diverged occasionally; such divergence should be accepted without anxiety. It meant allowing the Party, as well as the TUC and the unions in other collective forms, to indicate 'distance' in the relationship without embarrassment or recriminations. It meant also (and this emphasis was more original) that the Labour Party leadership in Opposition, as in Government, must be enabled to initiate any policy proposal it considered in the Party or public interest – regardless of past industrial sensitivities and the old 'rules' of freedom.

In the political fund ballots it was the unions collectively which sought to indicate their distance from the Party; in the General Election it was the Party which, in so far as it was able, sought to indicate its distance from the unions – particularly certain features, policies, and past practices of the unions.

Within the new 'space', the Party Leader achieved by 1987 a procedural control and a policy dominance which seemed inconceivable in the democratic implosion of 1979 to 1981. The distancing and the stress on autonomy suggested to some the beginning of a parting of the ways with the unions. Yet, as we shall see later, in the extent of sponsorship, the processes of mobilisation, the development of the Labour Women's organisation, the financial arrangements and the informal mechanisms of consultation, the level of integration of the Labour Movement was higher than it had been for many years.

Strategy

The trade unions

The 1983 General Election was a devastating set-back for the Labour Party which achieved its lowest national percentage poll since 1918.[70] The Government's Rightwing programme, its attack on the post-war settlement and its trade union and industrial relations legislation had to some extent been legitimised by the election result. The surge in support for the Alliance which followed the mid-election split in Labour's campaign had further eaten away at the trade union base of Labour's electoral support.[71]

The TUC, whose membership was now larger than the Labour electorate for the first time since 1923,[72] had to face the fact that only just over a third of trade unionists had voted Labour at this election. Its representational responsibilities obliged the TUC to reconsider its relationship both with the Party and with the Government, particularly as there appeared to be some doubt whether the Labour Party could ever recover its previous status.

At the same time, three years of internal argument over representation on the General Council was finally resolved by a structure which included automatic representation for large unions.[73] The overall result of this reform was an undermining of the Left, an increase in women's representation and a sudden new prominence for the white collar and politically neutral unions, now much better represented.[74] Their rise heightened the TUC's compositional difference from a Labour Party still overwhelmingly dominated by manual worker affiliates. In practice, however, there continued to be a strong Labour Party orientation among officials within many of the 'neutral' unions and a common interest in the protection of the public sector.

Out of the post-mortem on trade union strategy in this situation came a mood labelled 'new realism'. It had several different strands and interpretations but fundamentally involved four dimensions. There was a concern to rebuild contact with the unions' members, and to turn outwards to the other consumers of trade unionism – the public. There was a renewed attempt to stress the TUC's willingness to hold a dialogue with the Government of the day. And there was an attempt to manage what was described as more 'space' for the Party and the TUC to carry out their different functional roles.

Moves on the basis of these perspectives involved negotiating with the Employment Secretaries of State, Tebbitt and then King, reducing the volume of work and meetings of the Labour Party–TUC Liaison Committee, working towards a new Organisational Report on the TUC's activities and (more quietly until the row over the NGA–*Stockport Messenger* dispute in November) downgrading the confrontationist stance of the Wembley Conference of 1982.

As it happened, the TUC's relationship with the Government and the Party was determined as much by others as by strategy and the aspects of 'new realism' were reshaped by events out of their control. The first development – a major benefit to Labour Movement unity – was the election of the 'Dream Ticket' of Neil Kinnock and Roy Hattersley in the Labour Party amid scenes of great enthusiasm and with the Party catapulted once more into contention for Governmental Office. The Party was immediately seen by the TUC as likely to become more sensitive to the needs of working people.

At the same time, although negotiations over the Government's new trade union legislation affecting Political Funds was a sign of union–Government dialogue, it also forced a unity of interest between unions and Party in securing the best outcome and encouraged a tactical agreement between the TUC and the Labour Parliamentary Leadership (see Chapter 17).

But above all, 'new realism' *vis-à-vis* the Government, which had received some quietly encouraging signs of co-operation in the months since the General Election, took a sharp blow when without advance warning to the TUC, let alone consultation, trade unionism was banned at the Government intelligence station, GCHQ, Cheltenham. The TUC–Labour Party Liaison Committee immediately took up the commitment to repeal.

In protest at the Government's 'unprecedented and unilateral decision', the TUC took its own unprecedented action and from March to October 1984 boycotted the National Economic Development Council. A review took place of the TUC representatives on 143 public bodies and in the next three years several attempts were made from the Left to break the TUC permanently from tripartite institutions, particularly NEDC and the Manpower Services Commission. These were successfully resisted. Although the Government was slowly cutting the TUC's representation on governmental bodies, a wide range of formal and informal links continued to operate, albeit with little responsiveness. The TUC, however, was still determined to hold on to what access it had.

Those on the Left who were committed to the Wembley Conference strategy of militant industrial confrontation in the face of the Government's trade union legislation were taken aback by the General Secretary's refusal to pursue that policy in November 1983 over the NGA dispute at Stockport. Five months later, independently of the TUC which was asked by the NUM not to intervene, Left unions swung into support for the miners' strike over pit closures. It was the longest major national dispute in British industrial history and for a whole year took up the energies and finances of many of the TUC's affiliates. But the NUM was not a united union – much of the large Nottinghamshire Area refused to participate, neither did some other sectors. And it was not a united trade union movement which operated alongside it; some union leaderships, particularly the Electricians, the Engineers and Managers Association and the Steelworkers, were politically alienated and heavily and publicly critical of the lack of a ballot and the picketing tactics involved. Only in September of 1984 did the NUM allow the TUC to be involved, but there continued to be problems of mobilising the full trade union movement and the Government proved increasingly determined to outface the NUM. In March of 1985, the NUM returned to work without a settlement.

Immediately, a second front battle began, in a different form, over the unions' Political Funds. Forced under the Trade Union Act of 1984 to ballot their members over maintenance of a political fund (as well as over strikes and for the election of union executives), the unions evolved a degree of unity in action which had evaded them in the Miners' Strike. Independent of the TUC and the Party – but encouraged by both – a Trade Union Co-ordinating Committee, was set up to mastermind the campaign (see Chapter 17). It proved to be a hugely successful operation with every union achieving a majority for its political funds, twenty other TUC affiliates eventually creating new funds and one of those, BETA, voting to affiliate to the Labour Party. It was the first significant new union recruitment for the Party since the Post Office Engineers came in again in 1964.

The campaigns were fought fundamentally over a defence of the right of trade unions to have political funds – the form of the question imposed by the Government – not in defence of the Labour Party. The TUCC publicly distanced itself from the Party. But the Labour Party connection was, of necessity, an element in many union campaigns and the general effect was to encourage and raise morale over Labour Party affiliation.

The campaigns also had the effect of reconstituting the collective organisation designed to encourage trade union mobilisation on behalf of the Labour Party. Trade Unions for a Labour Victory had to some extent been downgraded in its organisational and financial relationship with the Party in the months after the 1983 General Election. After the Political Fund ballot victories, TULV was reconstituted with TUCC into a new organisation, Trade Unionists For Labour (TUFL), whose aim was to organise the input of union support for Labour's General Election campaign (see Chapter 18).

The Government's lack of receptivity, the major defeat for industrial militancy, the election of Norman Willis as TUC General Secretary and the victories in the Political Fund Ballot campaigns all encouraged yet again a turn towards the Labour Party on behalf of the unions and the TUC. It was reinforced by the sharp fall in TUC membership mainly as a result of the catastrophic decline in manufacturing and extractive employment.

The desperation with which the unions viewed their weakening industrial position and the possible return of a Conservative Government facilitated the changing balance of power in the relationship with the Labour Party. The TUC conceded the initiative to the Parliamentary leadership and particularly the Leader, Neil Kinnock. 'New realism' became a new loyalism as the TUC leadership sought to give full support to the Parliamentary leadership. The 'space' of 1983 became almost the subordination of 1986-7 as it became axiomatic that the political running must be left to the Parliamentary leadership, unions must not let their unpopularity rub off on the Party and even on issues as historically sensitive as enforcing union ballots, the TUC must move to accommodate the needs of the Party (and union members).

Alongside these developments, rumbling away, was a potentially explosive fissure as a result of the different industrial strategies with which the unions were now concerned to conduct their operations under adverse conditions. Not since the 1920s had the TUC to face a situation where affiliated unions might diverge to the extent of splitting the TUC itself and as a result damaging the Labour Party. It had become almost axiomatic that the unions were in the end the ballast of the Party. A significant split in the TUC could be devastating to both.

The most delicate and potentially explosive problem which the Party and TUC had to handle related to the defection of the Union of Democratic Mineworkers (centred in Nottinghamshire) following the Miners' Strike. TUC tradition and rules were clear – there could be no acceptance of the UDM into membership. For the Party, precedents were more uncertain and the political situation a danger to Labour's vote in the East Midlands. Eventually, the Party found a formula which tacitly accepted individual UDM members while resisting UDM affiliation.

But there were still pressing problems for the TUC, which in 1985 suddenly found itself in a crisis over an issue which had simmered since 1980 – the issue of accepting Government funding for holding union ballots. In the forefront of the call to accept Government funding were the AUEW and the EETPU, unions which also had deep industrial and political reservations about the drift of union and Party policy on nuclear energy as well as nuclear defence. More (and dangerous for the Party), sections of both union leaderships had some sympathy for the UDM. Out of this crisis might well have come not only the most serious split in TUC history but the formation of an 'alternative TUC' which could provide a new industrial base for the Labour Party's opponents in the Alliance. Eventually concessions were made by the TUC and the unity of the centre was preserved but the nearness of the TUC to the brink and the obvious threat to the Labour Party produced a new dimension to the multiple vulnerabilities of the Labour Movement – vulnerabilities which annually reappeared as the TUC sought to deal with the deviant behaviour of the EETPU.

The Labour Party

Under a new leadership, the Labour Party aimed to broaden its social base and to win back middle class elements who had moved to support for the Alliance. Winning back trade unionists to the Party was also a part of the project, although given the declining membership of the unions, it was not as important as in 1983. The new style of the Party Leadership could be said to have won their approval in that from the time of its election in October 1983, support from trade unionists rose and by February 1984 was running at approximately 10 per cent higher than at the 1983 election; with some variations during and after the Miners' Strike that support was retained for the next three years.[75]

In February 1984, the Labour Leadership's open and enthusiastic support for the workers of GCHQ had put the Party behind a popular trade union protest. But the Miners' Strike presented a much more difficult political operation. The position of the Labour Leadership, as with the NGA dispute of 1983, was to support the strike but oppose violence and illegality. Strategically, the aim was to indicate support for the miners and the case for coal whilst showing distance from the NUM's President, Arthur Scargill, and indicating as far as possible the independence of the Party Leadership from the leadership of the union. Holding this line was not easy – particularly as the NEC spearheaded a strong body of opinion within the Party seeking more support and closer association. Kinnock came under fierce criticism from the Labour Party's opponents for too close an identification with the NUM's tactics but also equally strong criticism from the Left for not giving 100 per cent support.

In the post-mortem on the miners' defeat at the 1985 Labour Party Conference, Kinnock's fighting attack on the conduct of the dispute enhanced his public and Party authority even though he lost the vote. His relationship with the unions began to take on another dimension as they sought to aid the return of another Labour Government. 'Partnership' was redefined to a much broader conception than that of unions and Party. The trade union connection and repeal of Conservative union legislation was played down in Labour Party publicity. And Kinnock's speech to the 1986 TUC was widely read as affirming his independent position *vis-à-vis* the unions.[76]

For a period from the summer of 1985 to the autumn of 1986, the strategy appeared to be leading to one of the more remarkable political recoveries of British politics with Labour performing creditably at Brecon and Radnor, winning an impressive by-election victory at Fulham, and gaining new public support after the Alliance row over defence.

But Labour failed to advance further after the Party Conference of 1986 and the Conservatives suddenly moved into the lead again. Worse, politically, the Labour Party lost the Greenwich by-election in February 1987 to the SDP – its first ever electoral loss to them. In the spring of 1987, Labour's position became dangerously vulnerable. Support by trade unionists for the Labour Party dropped dramatically.[77] The high profile (and media-distorted) 'oppressed groups' strategy of some London Labour Councils took much of the blame but damage was also caused by the sudden reappearance of public disunity and the contrasting fortunes of Kinnock's visit to Washington and Thatcher's visit to Moscow.

In these circumstances, the Labour Party went into the election campaign in a political situation far worse than anticipated since October 1983 and the election result – an increase of only 3 per cent in the Labour vote, and 5 per cent in the support of manual worker trade unionists[78] (though this achieved the psychologically important 51 per cent level) – was deeply disappointing. The overall result – another Conservative landslide (in terms of seats) – was a devastating blow.

And yet the campaign itself did much to cement relations in the Labour Movement. This was in spite of the fact that the Party Leadership made every effort to distance the Party from the least acceptable features of trade unionism and made no attempt to emphasise the value to the Party or the country of the union connection. There was no 1987 version of the social contract. There was an affirmation of Labour independence. A combination of this shift of tactics by Labour's leaders, plus the declining industrial power of the unions, meant that though the Party's opponents did seek to raise the bogy of the violent picket and the role of 'the union bosses', the trade union question was less of an issue in this election than in the previous two.[79]

Above all, it was the way the campaign was organised and conducted that made a big impact – internally as well as externally. It proved to be a remarkable example of self-generated enthusiasm.

It was presentationally and organisationally superior to that produced by the Party's opponents. Its impetus took the Labour Party well past the Alliance in the campaign's early stages and left them on the road to internal turmoil. And in one speech to the Welsh Labour Party and two Party political broadcasts embodying extracts from the speech ('a thousand years' of Kinnocks), the Party Leader brilliantly fused an identification with the Labour Movement with an appeal to those upwardly mobile from the working class. Thus in spite of the distancing tactics and the terrible election result, the campaign was a unifying force in the Labour Movement – viewed even as something of a triumph.

Ideology

Underpinning the new accommodations after 1983 were a range of developments affecting ideology and factional alignments. Though most major unions continued to identify themselves with Right and Left – particularly in NEC voting – the 'Dream Ticket' election indicated a significant body of opinion in the unions (as well as the Party) which was prepared to throw its weight behind a more centrist leadership and leave isolated the 'hard Left' and to some extent the 'hard Right'. This set the tone for the next four years.

Some major elements of the future consensus emerged very quickly. Over the EEC question, union mandates were voluntarily ignored as the Left union leadership tacitly agreed to bury the issue until further notice. On defence, however, the swathe of union opinion was broad and solid enough to give Kinnock the base for a non-nuclear policy which ran against the views of the Shadow Cabinet majority – still overwhelmingly drawn from the *Solidarity* Rightwing faction. On nationalisation, the TUC itself began the process of reappraisal which was to feed consumer consciousness into a new social ownership document which united elements of both revisionist Right and devolutionist soft Left. Crucially, Kinnock found it congenial to work with the Rightwing grouping on the NEC – its largest faction and closely linked to the Shadow Cabinet majority. Thus the leadership developed a workable, if variable, base on the NEC operating an alliance of the Right (including the loyalist Trade Union Section) and a growing soft Left.

The ideological contours of Labour Party policy in this period were rarely explored in depth but there was a clear shift back to the social democratic revisionist framework. There was no critique of Capitalism but criticism of Thatcherism from the values of positive freedom and fairness. This, plus a traditional stress on collectivist solutions, provided a strong unifying set of assumptions linking the Party and the unions. In addition, Kinnock laid a distinctive emphasis on the rebuilding of Britain's manufacturing base and on Labour as 'the party of production', but there was a major shift in industrial policy away from the planning structure evolved in the early 1980s and away from specific proposals for industrial democracy.

In 1983, a simple analysis of the contending forces at the Party Conference suggested that the union Left was moving into a new period of strength – in spite of 'new realism' – at the TUC. There was the huge vote of the TGWU and NUPE, there was a new Leftwing leader, Jimmy Knapp, in the NUR, and Arthur Scargill,

President of the NUM, was consolidating his position. The POEU (later NCU) had for brief periods an Executive under Leftwing control. At the 1984 Conference, in an atmosphere of solidarity with the striking miners, this strength was shown not only in votes on strike-related issues but also on local government campaigning and candidate reselection reform (where the Party Leadership's proposal for one individual member, one vote was defeated).

There were some in the Party who anticipated that the Miners' Strike would produce a further swing to the Left in the unions and the Party. And for a while it appeared to be taking place. But by the spring of 1985 it was clear that a contrary movement was under way – a realignment which in the unions and on the NEC further weakened the position of the hard Left. This weakening in the unions was increased by developments in the Liverpool Labour Party where NUPE was alienated by the employment practices, and the unions as a whole were brought into sharp opposition to the Militant Tendency after redundancy notices were issued to 30,000 workers. This mood gave opportunity for the Parliamentary Leadership to move against Militant with the backing of a huge union majority.

And it set the scene for the Party Leader to lead the opposition to a resolution from the NUM which demanded various commitments in relation to the strike from a future Labour Government.[80] Though defeated in the vote, his stand consolidated his position as Leader and consolidated also the realignment of the Left.

This realignment of 1985 also created the opportunity for a new loose splinter of 'soft Left' union representatives to emerge from Left and Right on the NEC, with specific concern for green, women's and party organisational and procedural issues. They produced a further grouping (albeit very loose) from which new Committee Chairs began to emerge in 1986 and 1987.[81]

It made for a more complex politics on the NEC but in any case trade union alignments after the Miners' Strike were complicated by a new range of issues which brought out different alignments. Union ballots, statutory minimum wage and nuclear energy produced some odd bedfellows. Union positions were further complicated by new uncertainties in the two largest unions. Within the TGWU the election of Ron Todd, a Left General Secretary, was followed by an advance of the Right on the Executive Committee. On some issues the union lined up with the hard Left, on others with the Right but some of its senior officials had strong affinities with the new soft Left. In the GMB a different pattern emerged, with the new General Secretary, John Edmunds, a powerful intellectual force, having some identification with the soft Left but leading a union still with a powerful 'old Right'. It was an uncertain framework of relationships, but one in which the Party Leader was protected from his most determined ideological opponents.

Social affinity

The understanding, particularly after 1985, that there should be more formal space in the relationship between the Party and the TUC meant that informal relationships took on a greater significance. The sense of affinity, the quality of private dialogue and the degree of trust became more important.

On one level the liaison was greater than ever in the past in that an increasing proportion of the PLP and the Shadow Cabinet were sponsored MPS, or became sponsored MPS during the Parliamentary session.[82] Kinnock, the son of a miner, was a sponsored MP of the TGWU. Hattersley became sponsored by USDAW.

But the manual worker composition of the PLP recommenced its decline,[83] as it did in the Shadow Cabinet.[84] Tensions of social background were often a tetchy element in the politics of a period when there was a strategy of increasing distance in the relationship.

A more elitist politics, involving a diminution of the role of the CLPS and the NEC, made for a simplification of the consultative process. An increase in private linkage and informal consultation made for more regular contact. There was, in particular, in 1986, a major increase in the confidential meetings of the Neddy Six group of union leaders and Labour's political leadership. The Kinnock–Willis–Todd relationship, while never the full meeting of minds that appearance would suggest and always cross-pressured by the power struggle within the TGWU, was in general a network facilitating cohesion.

Yet this increased dialogue was not quite accompanied by the degree of trust necessary to make it work well. There was, of course, a political problem. Could anybody guarantee how a Labour Government would behave towards the unions when in Office – particularly a Labour leadership which was anxious to prove its independence and satisfy a strong electoral dynamic? The ghost of the first Wilson Government hovered in the background. But there were other difficult features. There was still from the Rightwing union leaders the sense of unease at dealing with a Leader who was not from their tradition. There was from many union leaders a sense of exclusion and lack of closeness born of the feeling that this most convivial of Labour MPS appeared in this phase to be an aloof leader. And there was some discontent at the operation of his enlarged personal office – the only people who appeared to be in a regular private advisory role. The tension was, in some ways, an inevitable by-product of the Leadership's electoral strategy in relation to the unions and it was fed by media mischief. But it had an aspect as old as the Labour Party. It was not unconnected with social resentments aroused by the fact that the Leader's Office was increasingly staffed by people who were young and middle class and that the unions felt that the Office had nobody who had come from them.[85]

Interests

Once the first phase of 'new realism' was over in 1984, the relationship between the TUC and the unions and the Party Leadership was eased, as in the early 1970s, by the consciousness of a common enemy which had grown confident in its ability to undermine the post-war settlement and change the agenda of British politics. If there was some trimming by the Thatcher Government over the welfare state and a shedding of crude monetarism by 1986, there was no retreat from privatisation, no retreat from trade union legislation, no retreat from parsimony in public expenditure and no major reflation to tackle the problem of a persistent and record level of unemployment.

In contrast to the previous period of Labour in Opposition and a contrast which grew the more marked after 1985, the Labour Leadership in Parliament and even on the NEC was much less prone to give automatic recognition of trade union interests or trade union traditions (see Chapters 13 and 14). Nevertheless, by the time the General Election Manifesto was prepared, there was enough in Labour's policy commitments to preserve a sharp contrast with the Manifestos of the Alliance and the Government in its accommodation with trade union policies and aspirations. Apart from union balloting arrangements, Labour again promised the repeal and replacement of the bulk of the Conservative Government's trade union legislation. The moderate programme of public sector investment, reflation and social reform attuned with the realism which was a growing mood in the unions. The employment goal of a one million reduction in unemployment in two years of a Labour Government was also accepted as a reasonable target. A new mix of individual and collective employment rights satisfied trade union objectives. The new policy on social ownership was formulated in discreet co-operation with the TUC and relevant unions.

Yet there remained a range of sensitive issues where the Labour Leadership was in difficulty with one group of unions while satisfying the interests of others. On two crucial policy issues in 1986, the Parliamentary Leadership had to fight hard, and make concessions, in order to overcome union objections. Retention of the Conservative Government legislation on union ballots was accepted but with very strong reservations from both Right and Left in the unions. A Statutory Minimum wage was approved in the face of an unusual alliance of the Electricians and the Transport Workers.

Industrial disputes were a running sore in the relationship throughout the period with particularly bitter controversy surrounding the NGA dispute at Stockport in 1983, the year-long Miners' Strike in 1984–5 and the year-long News International dispute from 1986 to 1987. Each involved a disagreement about tactics which cut across both wings of the Movement and each left a bitter legacy. And, as usual, proposals for a counter-inflation policy which implied some restraint over incomes produced a persistent war of proposals and formulae. In the end it was agreed that there would be a National Economic Assessment and a National Economic Summit but the Government would be taking its own initiatives. Where this might lead in terms of potential conflict was not explored.

It was not the only area where problems were pushed to one side to await the different relationship with a Labour Government. Indeed, there were many such issues, some of them touching the traditional raw nerves of trade union interests. But another kind of 'new realism' resurrected itself in the period from 1985 to 1987. It was the recognition that more than any time in the past fifty years, the future organisational, industrial, and political interests of trade unionism were at stake in the election of a Labour Government. Defeat in the General Election of 1987[86] left the Labour Movement united but in a state of stunned uncertainty.

RECLAMATION 1987–1990

This uncertainty was followed by a gloomy period of review and reappraisal as the Labour Movement digested the immediate implications – particularly the economic impact on the electorate and the workforce – of two terms of Thatcherism.

While the number of those in poverty had increased, and was increasing, for most people living standards had risen significantly since 1982. Personal taxation had been reduced. And the Government had, for the moment, secured an impressive conjunction; inflation had been under 10 per cent since March 1982 and averaged only 3.4 per cent in 1986, while the number of unemployed claimants was now beginning to fall (helped by a series of statistical adjustments).

The Party initiated a new Policy Review in which it was made clear that nothing was precluded from re-examination. The TUC initiated a wide-ranging Special Review of the role and operation of the unions. For the Party there was one very advantageous element in the context. With the Alliance partners engaged in a damaging fragmentation billed as 'a merger',[87] the political centre ground was now more available than for many years. Reclaiming that terrain and that perspective became the strategic priority which affected virtually every facet of Party activity – procedure, ideology and policy. As for the TUC, its position was even more difficult. There were no welcoming arms for the return to tripartism and, having no clearly defined project, it was left initially to attempt to do better those things it already did, while pondering again George Woodcock's famous question 'Why are we here?' Strategically, it too sought to build upon the centre ground.

Strategy

The Labour Party

Some of the initial gloom sprang from a consciousness of Labour's weakness in the affluent South and the knowledge that the manual working class was continuing to be a declining percentage of the electorate.[88] But also the rise of home and share ownership and the change in consumption patterns were held to be the basis of a new individualism out of step with the Labour Movement's collectivism.[89] Trade unionism was on the defensive and trade unionists now comprised only 36 per cent of the Labour vote.[90] The forecast at advisory level in the Labour Party was that trade unionisation would be less important in the future electorate and that any improvement in union power was likely to be a liability to the Labour Party.[91]

This diagnosis accentuated the defensiveness of Labour's leadership over trade union issues, over industrial disputes and particularly over the unions' relationship with the Labour Party. It was not an easy situation to manage, particularly as the union connection was raised in so many ways and at so many points. It was there in the 1987 reform of candidate selection, there in the steady succession of industrial disputes, and there particularly in 1988 during the Leadership contest and the well-publicised conflict with the TGWU leadership over nuclear defence.

From one perspective, the events of 1989 saw a turning of the tide on some of these questions. Major industrial disputes on the railways and over the ambulance service damaged the Government and not the Labour Party.[92] Labour's climb into a major lead over the Conservatives involved a large increase in trade unionists now supporting Labour.[93] Bad management was rated as far more

important than the unions in creating Britain's economic problems.[94] Those
believing that the unions had too much power had fallen to the lowest for many
years.[95] And those who now believed that trade unions had too much say in the
Labour Party (though still a majority at 53 per cent) were now a decreasing
percentage of trade unionists and of the electorate.[96]

But these changes did not eradicate the problem of public perceptions of the
unions' political role, nor did it diminish the growing belief (now increasingly
accepted within the unions) that there ought to be a major reform of the unions'
position within the Labour Party (see Chapter 12). And it did not halt the chorus
of media advice that the Labour Party should go further by detaching itself or
moving away from the unions. The connection, it was said, was 'out of date and
damaging – to the TUC's prospects as well as to the prospects of the Labour
Party'.[97]

The trade unions

Some within the TUC and the more Rightwing unions were not deaf to this
argument, but the sentiment was not shared by the majority of activists, officials
and union leaders. Aware of the importance of the Labour Party for the future of
trade unionism, they sought to hold up the level of their affiliation to the Labour
Party – sometimes artificially. There was generous assistance for the Party's new
membership campaign and the continuing support of Trade Unionists For Labour. And a tiered system of affiliation fees was introduced in order to secure an
assured electoral fund for the Party.

Union dependence upon the fortunes of the Labour Party was once again
heightened by the remorseless step-by-step limitation of union power embodied
in successive items of legislation, and by adverse judicial interpretations. A new
Employment Act in 1988 made postal ballots obligatory, restricted the unions'
capacity to discipline their own members and created a new post of Commis-
sioner for the Rights of Trade Union Members to enforce complaints. In 1989
came a further Employment Bill covering dismissal and union liability for unofficial action, and further restrictions on secondary action. Strike action became
increasingly hazardous in this legal mine-field. Although strikes at Fords early in
1988, on the railways in 1989 and in the ambulance service in 1989 and 1990
pointed up the continuing possibilities of industrial militancy, other industrial
developments, including the failure of the long Seamen's dispute and the abandoned Dock Strike of 1989, were indications of continuing weakness. A major
dispute between the two largest unions over a new plant at Ford Dundee led to
bitter recriminations over different strategies for dealing with industrial adversity. Similar disagreements lay behind the expulsion of the EETPU from the TUC in
1988 for failing to obey TUC rules.

As for the TUC, it sought anxiously to come to terms with the new political
climate and the continuing hostility of the Government to a revival of neo-
corporatist relationships. There was a renewed stress on 'building stable and
mutually productive relations with employers'[98] and the strategic search for a
more consensual industrial platform with the CBI. Training policy became the
focal point of this neo-corporatism in exile.[99] A second avenue was found in 1989

in the building of new relationships via the EEC,[100] utilising the Social Charter as a means of curbing the free market excesses of the British Government. A third strategic focus was on the rebuilding of the unions. Two reports of the Special Review Body highlighted the need for the unions to concentrate on organising new members, providing good services and promoting the benefits of trade unionism. The decline in union membership had been slowed and some unions were showing gains, but the TUC membership in 1990, 8,404,827, was still well down compared with 12,172,508 in 1980.

Ideology

Aware of this weakness, the TUC exhibited even greater restraint in its dealing with the Party, colluding in a reduction of the importance of the TUC–Labour Party Liaison Committee. This self-effacement was matched in the main by the behaviour of individual unions within the Labour Party. As so often in the past, the union block votes acted in many crucial votes as a loyal, stabilising mechanism even though on the surface, after a swing to the Left in the TGWU, a decline in the affiliation of the AEU, a merger of ASTMS and TASS (into MSF) and the maintenance of the membership of NUPE, there was a strengthened Left at the Party Conference. The loyalty was shown in 1988 when Neil Kinnock and Roy Hattersley were challenged by Tony Benn and Eric Heffer for the leadership, but the Left opposition was badly beaten with the aid of union votes. (John Prescott as an alternative soft Left Deputy Leadership did rather better.) The same pattern was shown in NEC elections where the unions used their weight to avoid candidates who were outright opponents of the Leadership. As a similar movement developed in the CLPs, so the NEC traditional Left which had been in control in 1980 was reduced in 1989–90 to Tony Benn and Dennis Skinner.

These shifts away from the traditional Left were paralleled by the changes in ideology and policy embodied in the statement of *Democratic Socialist Aims and Values* (1988) and the documents *Economic Efficiency and Social Justice* (1988), *Meet the Challenge, Make the Change* (1989) and *Looking to the Future* (1990).

There was a new emphasis on individual freedom, choice, and the realisation of talent. But as freedom was defined in positive terms, involving capacity and opportunity, this still left a vital place for collective industrial activity and for collective public provision. There was a renewed emphasis on a solidaristic community, blended with a recommitment to a reduction of inequality and a charter of rights. Economic and industrial policy involved a mild supply side interventionism with a focus on investment, research and development, and training. A changing attitude towards the role of the state was also reflected in a new stress on regional devolution and a reform of the House of Lords involving the protection of rights. A consolidation of the movement away from planning, public ownership and the producer was coupled with a new stress on the importance of markets, the consumer and the user. On all these changes the Party Leadership succeeded in winning overwhelming support from the unions at the Party Conference. The old non-nuclear defence policy supported ambiguously in 1988 was shed in 1989. On Europe the shift begun in 1983 was reinforced when both the TUC and the Labour Party placed the European dimension at the forefront as they awaited 1992 and the coming of the Single Market.

Interests

These ideological shifts were paralleled by changes in industrial relations policy. As the Government put increasing legislative pressure upon the unions, so the TUC was forced into a position of seeking whatever compromise of position, restraint of claims and acceptance of public (and union membership) opinion would enable them to salvage a workable basis of free trade unionism. There was in the process a marked shift towards the claiming of individual rights for people at work. These would be bolstered by collective organisation and complementary to collective action, but the individual was given primacy. As the Labour Leadership sought to build a progressive anti-Thatcherite electoral majority, so it sought to make some of the no-repeal commitments secure. Over balloting it was now more generally agreed in the unions that the old position could not be restored. Over secondary action and over sequestration it was more a matter of staking out a new 'balanced' position under the law, leaving behind the old platform of immunities.

Making these major changes in the traditional areas of union freedom more palatable was the fact that the Labour Party still gave trade unionism a range of potential gains – over union recognition, over rights of union membership and over protection against victimisation. And there were many issues and circumstances which encouraged a sense of unity. There was the move to advance individual and collective rights at work via the European Social Charter. There was the raising of the importance of the issue of the Statutory Minimum Wage and there was a new emphasis given to health and safety at work.

All this encouraged both well-organised and spontaneous expressions of Labour Movement unity, which appeared to be having its reward as Labour moved into a strong and sustained lead over the Conservatives and its largest opinion poll support since before the defection of 1981.[101] The Conservative Government was now faced with mounting economic problems, including a rising rate of inflation, for which the unions were not responsible, and a new rise in unemployment produced by the Government's interest rate policy. These acute problems in turn focused attention on the consequences of entry into the European Exchange Rate Mechanism and the possibility that the unions could once again be involved in the management of a counter-inflation policy.

Social affinity

The new unity was not without its undercurrents of anxiety, its sense of loss of identity, and a range of grievances and irritations, some of them tinged with social resentments. In 1988 – the most tense year in the period from 1987 to 1990 – what was experienced by the Party leadership and its advisers as a frustration over union conservatism and old-fashioned perspectives (and in the case of the TGWU, unreliability) was seen in some of the unions as a lack of empathy and respect mixed with arrogance.

In the relationship with the TGWU there was a problem building an understanding with the union leadership marked by heavy and personalised faction fighting (see Chapter 10), but what might be called the filofax[102] factor is not to be underestimated in the way TGWU leaders (desperately attempting to reconcile traditional values with new policies) viewed developments within the Party.

Certainly, the sense of estrangement which was felt on occasions in the unions in 1988 was influenced in part by the awareness that the PLP had an increasingly middle class membership,[103] that there had been a further marked decline in the percentage of Shadow Cabinet members who came from manual working-class backgrounds,[104] and that the CLPs, who might be given more votes at the expense of the unions, were now dominated by the salariat.[105]

Few in Labour's political leadership (least of all Kinnock, who was occasionally the butt of Oxbridge snobbery[106]) were unaware of the importance of managing the sometimes subtle (and sometimes crude) hierarchies of British social life – a feature which penetrated the Labour Movement as everywhere else. One yardstick of its significance was that at one point Michael Meacher, the spokesperson for Employment, found himself pursuing a court case over allegations of false claims to working class origins.[107] But old divisions within the Labour Movement were becoming more complicated. The trade unions were themselves changing in their composition, although not as much as the Labour Party in Parliament. The trend to white collar trade unionism,[108] which was most marked at the TUC, was little evident on the Party NEC but it was beginning to show at the Party Conference.[109] And when Meacher was replaced in 1989 by Tony Blair, in the Employment portfolio, his middle class background did not appear to have been a significant factor in his relations with the union leaders.

THE THIRTY YEAR CRISIS

These sensitivities were particularly acute in 1990 as the Party and the unions moved towards new arrangements for dealing with the inbuilt tensions and what amounted to a long term crisis of 'rules' concerning democracy and freedom. Since 1960 there had been a fracturing of attitudes towards intra-party democracy involving the unions. Since 1969 there had been a similar fracture in relation to industrial relations policy and the role of the unions. The Field affair[110] indicated how quickly the democratic question involving the unions could rise to the forefront of political debate. The Blair[111] pronouncement on the closed shop showed how much the unions were prepared to accept in order to adapt to exigencies of the time and particularly the electoral contest. As the Party and the unions sought to manage the multiple tensions of the relationship, so building a new 'settlement' of some outstanding procedural questions became the task of the 1990s.

NOTES

1. Anthony Crosland, *Can Labour Win?*, Fabian Tract 324, 1960, p. 10.
2. Flanders, *Management and Unions, op. cit.*, argued that Cousins had violated a mutual understanding by his intervention on the most political of issues, defence policy – the Party's 'job', pp. 36–7. The Left argued

that the Party Leadership had broken the constitution by defying the Conference. On this, see Minkin, *The Labour Party Conference, op. cit.*, Chapter 10, pp. 272–89. In terms of the future relationship with the unions, it was a crucial factor that the majority of union leaders went along with Gaitskell, leaving the extent of Conference authority, in the eyes of the union leaders, much more a matter of factional perspectives.

3. *Signposts for the Sixties*, 1961, pp. 9–10.
4. Henry Durant gives the working class support for Labour in 1945 as 57 per cent and support among 'the very poor' as also 57 per cent. In 1966, the figures were 61 and 72 per cent. Durant in Rose, *op. cit.*, p. 166.
5. NOP data for 1964 used by Butler and King gives Labour support at 62.2 per cent. David Butler and Anthony King, *The British General Election of 1964*, 1965, p. 296. Blondel used data from the British Institute of Public Opinion which showed, in 1966, 69 per cent support. J. Blondel, *Voters, Parties and Leaders*, 1974 edn, p. 58. Eric Nordlinger, drawing from NOP 1963 data, gives support for Labour among manual worker trade unionists as 73 per cent, Eric E. Nordlinger, *The Working Class Tories*, 1967, p. 198. Richard Rose gives the percentage of manual workers in unions (or where the head of the family held a union card) voting Labour as 65 per cent, 'Class and Party Divisions: The British Case', *Sociology*, 2, 1968, p. 146.
6. Peter Jenkins, *The Battle of Downing Street*, 1970, p. 76.
7. See on this Minkin, *Labour Party Conference, op. cit.*, p. 291.
8. *LPACR*, 1968, p. 22.
9. *Daily Herald*, 1/6/61.
10. R. Lumley, *White Collar Unionism in Britain*, 1963, Appendix I.
11. *TUC General Council Report*, 1973, p. 79.
12. *TUC General Council Report*, 1968, p. 274.
13. Keith Middlemas, *Industry, Unions and Government*, 1983, p. 61.
14. Letter from George Woodcock to the Co-operative Union, 25/10/61 and Letter from Harold Wilson, Labour Party Leader, to Len Williams, Labour Party General Secretary, 12/6/83.
15. *LPACR*, 1962, p. 222. Amendment to Clause VII, Section 1.
16. *LPACR*, 1965, p. 174. Amendment to Model Rules, Clause VII, Section 1.
17. An important initiative during this period was the creation of the Institute for Workers Control at whose large conferences union leaders Jack Jones and Hugh Scanlon were regular speakers. The NUM President after 1982, Arthur Scargill, emerged as a leading militant during this period. For his perspective, see 'The New Unionism' (interview), *New Left Review*, July/August 1975.
18. Barry Hindess, *The Decline of Working-Class Politics*, 1968.
19. Derived from W. L. Guttsman in P. Stanworth and A. Giddens (eds.), *Elites and Power in British Society*, 1974, p. 34.
20. See, for example, Hugh Scanlon's comment on the 'so-called intelligentsia of our party', '… an intellectual is one who is educated above his intelligence', *LPACR*, 1968, p. 142. The comment was made in reference to Barbara Castle's Prices and Incomes Policy. Jack Jones commented: 'Wilson and Castle were basically academics and it was difficult to persuade them to see things from the shop-floor angle', Jack Jones, *Jack Jones: Union Man*, 1986, p. 204. See also Eric S. Heffer, *The Class Struggle in Parliament*, 1973, pp. 106–7 for the reaction of some Rightwing ex-manual worker MPs to *In Place of Strife*.

21. Jenkins, *op. cit.*, Chapter 5, p. 75.
22. *Declaration of Intent on Productivity, Prices and Incomes*, 6/12/64.
23. *TUC Economic Review*, 1969, p. 30.
24. In April 1965, the Transport Workers were the only major union to oppose TUC support for the government's policy. By September 1968, the Electricians and the Railwaymen were the only major unions left in support.
25. Roy Jenkins, *LPACR*, 1969, p. 254.
26. Roy Jenkins, *Hansard* HC 12/3/73, Cols. 939/41.
27. *Royal ('Donovan') Commission on Trade Unions and Employers Organisations*, HMSO, Cmnd. 3628 (June 1968), para. 46.
28. See on this P. Jenkins, *op. cit.*, pp. 144–5. An ORC poll in January 1969 found 62 per cent of union members in favour of Government powers to impose secret ballots and 57 per cent in favour of a cooling-off period. Cited in Stephen Milligan, *The New Barons*, 1976, p. 219. However, by June 1969, 51 per cent of trade unionists were in favour of leaving the problem of unofficial strikes to the TUC, Gallup for *Daily Telegraph*, 14/6/69. Union membership opinion on the imposition of fines for refusal to obey a Government order imposing a solution (the most bitterly resented item among union activists and officials) is unclear but the public as a whole was firmly in favour of all three contentious Government proposals. *Gallup Political Index*, May 1969, Table 4, p. 85 gives 70 per cent (ballots), 59 per cent (cooling-off period), 63 per cent (fines).
29. Among the unions of significant size, only the Electricians struck an ambiguous note in their reaction to the contentious sections. 'ETU agrees to strike reforms', *Guardian*, 23/5/1969.
30. Clause J, *Labour's Aims*, 1960, p. 13. But on this see Minkin, *op. cit.*, pp. 324–6.
31. P. Jenkins, *op. cit.*, p. 164, appeared to suggest this as did his later comments on the union's electoral damage to Labour Governments.
32. The Labour Party standing as the Party best able to handle strikes and disputes was damaged during this whole exercise compared with 1968, but by October 1969, it was back ahead of the Conservatives on this issue 35:33 – a higher approval rating than prior to *In Place of Strife*, *Gallup Political Index*, October 1969. The issue was not central to the 1970 General Election campaign and is not even discussed in the chapters 'The Outcome' and 'An Analysis of the Results' (Michael Steed) in David Butler and Michael Pinto-Duschinsky, *The British General Election of 1970*, 1971, pp. 337–51.
33. The biggest swing against Labour came among the unskilled working class (7.4 per cent). There was a swing against of 2.7 per cent amongst the skilled working class but the Party held its own amongst the non-manual working class (C1 category) (-0.1 per cent swing). NOP, Butler and Pinto Duschinsky, *op.cit.*, p. 342. There was the lowest turn-out in 35 years (72 per cent) seen by Leftwing critics of the Government as a sign of traditional Labour voters' dissatisfaction. Ian Mikardo, *Ian Mikardo: Backbencher*, 1988, pp. 181–2.
34. Heffer, *op. cit.*, 1973, p. 169. Relevant to this is the article by Mark Abrams, 'The Lost Labour Votes', *Socialist Commentary*, February 1969, which notes that the lost Labour voters *of 1968* were inclined against interference with the unions or with unofficial strikes. Panitch, *op. cit.*, p. 139.
35. See on this John Grant, *Member of Parliament*, 1974, pp. 91–2.

36. In 1977, the figures were Labour Party affiliated (59 unions), 5,913,159 members; TUC affiliated (115 unions), 11,515,920 members. The total UK membership of unions at this time was approximately 12,270,000.

37. David Butler and Donald Stokes, *Political Change in Britain*, 1969, Chapter 11, pp. 303–34.

38. At a Joint Meeting of the NEC and the Parliamentary Committee held on 25/1/73 to discuss Party strategy, the Chairman, William Simpson, urged that 'Our appeal should be directed towards our traditional voters'. *NEC Minutes*, 28/2/1973.

39 *Ibid.*, p. 4.

40 In February 1974,for the first time since polling began, under half of all trade unionists (48 per cent) voted Labour. Ivor Crewe, Jim Alt and Bo Särlvik, *The Erosion of Partisanship 1964–1975*, Political Studies Association, 1976, p. 18.

41 In February 1974, next to inflation, industrial unrest was of most concern to voters. Labour led the Conservatives by 12 per cent as the Party best capable of handling strikes. Ivor Crewe, Bo Särlvik and James Alt, 'The Why and How of February Voting', *New Society*, 12/9/74.

42. Gallup Poll Index, August/September 1974–8, gives percentages as 61, 73, 65, 75, 69.

43. Labour had a lead of 41–32 over the Conservatives on this issue. MORI for *New Statesman*, 27/4/79. By May 1979, it was a lead of only 41–39. David Butler and Dennis Kavanagh, *The British General Election of 1979*, 1980, p. 328 and sources cited there.

44. David Basnett, *TUC Annual Congress Report*, 1977, p. 484. See also Ivor Crewe, 'The Labour Party and the Electorate' in Dennis Kavanagh (ed.), *The Politics of the Labour Party*. 1982, p. 10 for the electoral accuracy of this prediction, although Basnett meant much more.

45. The ex-engineers were Albert Booth (from the draughtsmen) and Stan Orme. Booth and Orme were particularly important allies of Foot in Cabinet in responding to the TUC position.

46. Only Hugh Scanlon disagreed. Interview with Hugh Scanlon, 2/9/84.

47. 'The Next Three Years and the Problem of Priorities', *Labour Party– TUC Liaison Committee*, 1976.

48. Average real household disposable income dropped (–0.8 per cent in 1976 and –2.4 per cent in 1977), CSO, *Social Trends*, 18, 1988, p. 84.

49. One interesting facet of this concerned the taxation of wealth and income. The TUC was unable to push the Government into Wealth Tax legislation (although Liaison Committee agreement produced a specific Manifesto commitment in 1979) but union opinion was a powerful constraint over those in the Government who wished to reduce incomes taxation on the wealthy. See Joel Barnett, *Inside the Treasury*, 1982, p. 140.

50. Barnett, *op. cit.*, p. 131 and *TUC Report*, 1978, pp. 99–100.

51. Particularly the new low pay taxation band. Barnett, *op. cit.*, p. 140 and *TUC Report*, 1979, pp. 307–8. And there was a strengthening of price controls.

52. An Industry Act in 1979 gave the National Enterprise Board additional borrowing powers, the Wages and Factory Inspectorate was strengthened, and a Merchant Shipping Act in 1979 extended new safety provisions to shipping. Also in the pipeline in 1979 were an Education Bill with new maintenance allowances, improvements in adult education provision, the national extension of concessionary transport fares,

and a new Company Bill which would have obliged companies to take account of the interests of employees as well as shareholders.

53. The TUC had asked for 2B and 3.8B. The Government injected 1B and 2$\frac{1}{2}$B. Unemployment, which in 1974 had been at 636,000 (3.6 per cent male unemployment), had risen to a peak of 1,636,000 in August 1977 (7.9 per cent) and 1,608,000 in August 1978 (7.5 per cent) but was down at 1,300,000 (6.3 per cent) in May 1979. *Labour Research*, December 1977, December 1978 and December 1979.

54. 'We have come through a period of great economic difficulty', *Into the Eighties: An Agreement*, Liaison Committee statement, 1978, p. 3.

55. Average real household disposable income rose by 7.4 per cent in 1978, CSO, *Social Trends, op. cit.* Still, by September of 1978, most people were no better off in real terms than they had been in March 1975. Paul Ormerod, 'The Economic Record', in Nick Bosanquet and Peter Townsend (eds.), *Labour and Equality*, 1980, p. 59. There was a further rise of 5.4 per cent in 1979.

56. *Gallup Political Index*, February 1979 showed 84 per cent of the electorate agreed that the unions were too powerful. Only 44 per cent believed trade unions to 'be a good thing', probably the lowest ever response recorded to this question.

57. See Chapter 8, n. 59 but also note among the working class electorate a shift away from Government interference in wage bargaining. Crewe in Kavanagh, *op. cit.*, p. 28. This shift is similar to the pattern under the 1964-70 Labour Governments. On this, see Panitch, *op. cit.*, Appendix I, pp. 260-1.

58. Crewe, *op. cit.*, p. 10.

59. MORI for TULV, July 1983.

60. The Conservative Trade Unionists organisation received a big (but brief) boost. Andrew Rowe, 'Conservatives and Trade Unionists', in Zig Layton-Henry (ed.), *Conservative Party Politics*, 1980, pp. 210–30.

61. The three proposals which caused the constitutional crisis were that there should be a mandatory reselection procedure for MPs, that the Labour Leader should be elected on a wider franchise than the PLP, and that the NEC alone (as opposed to the NEC and Shadow Cabinet) should produce the Party Manifesto. The first two were finally won in 1980. The third was defeated on a constitutional amendment in 1981.

62. MORI for TULV, July 1983.

63. Middlemas, *op. cit.*, p. 119.

64. The TUC resisted attempts from the NEC Left to involve them in a policy of non-co-operation with the Conservative Government, *Liaison Committee Minutes*, 22/9/80, para. 301.

65. David Butler and Dennis Kavanagh give the occupations of MPs in 1979 as Professions 117 (43 per cent), Business 22 (5 per cent), Misc. White Collar 36 (13 per cent) and Manual Worker/Clerical as 95 (35 per cent), *The British General Election of 1979*, p. 287.

66. 134 sponsored MPs (49.8 per cent).

67. Andrew Roth (Parliamentary Profiles), *MPs Chart, 1979*, notes that there were 35 sons of miners on the Labour benches, p. 2.

68. The core Left in the unions in this period included the TGWU, the Agricultural Workers and the Dyers and Bleachers (both of which became part of the TGWU), NUPE, ASTMS and TASS. Apart from these larger unions, the Left also included ACCT, ASLEF, the BFAWU, the FBU, FTAT and SOGAT.

69. The core Right in the unions in this period included APEX, the AUEW, the EETPU, the GMWU, ISTC, the NUR, POEU, UCW and USDAW, plus among the smaller unions NUBOCK, NUFLAT and TSSA.

70. Labour's percentage of the UK vote in 1983 was 27.6. David Butler and Dennis Kavanagh, *The British General Election of 1983*, 1983, p. 300. F. W. Craig, *British Electoral Facts 1885–1975*, 1968, gives the 1918 UK percentage as 20.8, the 1922 as 29.7.

71. Trade unionists' support for the Alliance shifted dramatically during the campaign. Support for them at 29 per cent was sixteen per cent higher than support for the Liberals in 1979. *MORI for TULV*, July, 1983.

72. In 1983, the TUC membership was 10,510,157. Labour's General Election vote that year was 8,456,934. In 1987, the TUC membership was 9,243,297 and Labour's support rose to 10,029,778.

73. Under the new rules, the old trade group system was abolished. The General Council would consist of three sections. Section A would have automatic representation according to size for unions with over 100,000 members. Section B would have eleven elected representatives for unions with less than 100,000 members. Section C would have six elected women representatives to take more account of the rising female membership. By 1985, the TUC had 2,345,617 women members out of 9,585,729.

74. In 1982, there were ten white collar representatives out of 44, five of whom were from unions not affiliated to the Labour Party. In 1983, there were seventeen white collar representatives out of 51, ten of whom were from unions not affiliated to the Labour Party. By 1987, there were eighteen white collar representatives out of 48, twelve of whom were from unions not affiliated to the Labour Party. In 1959 there had been only one non Labour-affiliated representative out of a Council of 35. Note that within the labour force, white collar workers now out-numbered manual workers. Robert Price and George Sayers Bain, 'The Labour Force', in A. H. Halsey (ed.), *British Social Trends Since 1900*, 1988, p. 164, give the 1981 figures as 52.3%:47.7%.

75. Information supplied privately drawing on the Labour Party's own polling.

76. See, for example, Geoffrey Smith, *The Times*, 3/9/86 on Kinnock's 'declaration of independence'.

77. One private Labour Party poll at this time touched as low as 36 per cent. Information supplied privately.

78. MORI for *Sunday Times*, 13/12/87.

79. The issue of strikes virtually disappeared. Ivor Crewe, 'Tories Prosper from a Paradox', *Guardian*, 16/6/87. Trade unions came low down in public explanations for Labour's defeat, *Gallup Political Index*, July 1987, Table 2.

80. Composite Resolution No. 69 from the NUM called for the reinstatement of sacked miners, a review of the cases of jailed miners, and reimbursement of 'all moneys confiscated as a result of fines, sequestrations and receivership', *LPACR*, 1985, p. 147.

81. Key figures involved in the realignment to this new grouping were Eddie Haigh (TGWU), Tom Sawyer (NUPE) from the union section and Diane Jeuda (USDAW), a union official from the women's section. See also Chapter 14A, n. 18 and the reference to 'political

unionism' in Chapter 20, n. 22.

82. The percentage of sponsored MPs in 1983 was 56 per cent and rising, due to 'co-option'. See Chapter 9.

83. In 1983, Labour's manual workers composition declined from 35 to 33 per cent. Butler and Kavanagh, op. cit., p. 237.

84. In November 1983, there were three non-university-educated members of the fifteen strong Shadow Cabinet, Gwyneth Dunwoody, Eric Heffer and Stan Orme. John Prescott, like Heffer and Orme, had been a manual worker (a seaman-waiter), but then took a degree as a mature student. In 1984, Heffer failed to gain re-election, as did Dunwoody in 1985. In 1986, Jo Richardson, an ex-secretary with no university education, became the only woman member until 1989.

85. Kinnock's Office was managed first by Dick Clements, an ex-editor of *Tribune*, with many contacts in the unions. In the office also was John Reid, an academic but with strong TULV connections. Reid left in 1985 and Clements was succeeded as Office manager in 1985 by Charles Clarke, who had been Kinnock's personal assistant, having come up via the National Union of Students and the Hackney Council. Clarke was responsible for relations with the Party and the unions. Kinnock always rejected suggestions from the unions that a union official be seconded to the Office. See also Chapter 13, n. 19, and Appendix to Chapter 14, p. 466, for references to policymaking. Also Chapter 16, p. 521 – for union assistance towards the Office – another example of paying pipers and *not* calling tunes.

86. In 1987, Labour won 229 seats, the Conservatives 376, the Alliance 22 and others 23. Labour went up to 30.8 per cent of the vote (from 27.6 per cent), the Conservatives dropped marginally (from 42.4 per cent) to 42.3 per cent and the Alliance dropped (from 25.4 per cent) to 22.6 per cent. David Butler and Dennis Kavanagh, *The British General Election of 1987*, 1988, p. 283.

87. Following the 1987 General Election, accompanied by much acrimony, a section of the SDP moved to form a new party with the Liberals – the Social and Liberal Democrats – a section of the SDP under David Owen retained its identity and a small section of the Liberals attempted to revive the old Liberal Party.

88. There were varying assessments of the scale of this decline, of whether there had been a decline in class-related voting, and of the consequences of both for Labour Party strategy. See on this Anthony Heath, Roger Jowell and John Curtice, *How Britain Votes*, 1985, Chapters 2 and 3, Ivor Crewe, 'On the Death and Resurrection of Class Voting: Some Comments on How Britain Votes', *Political Studies*, Vol. 34, No. 4, December 1986, pp. 620–38 and 'Trendless Fluctuations: A Reply to Crewe', Anthony Heath, Roger Jowell and John Curtice, *Political Studies*, Vol. XXXV, No. 2, June 1987. In 1988 a study by Gordon Marshall, Howard Newby, David Rose and Carolyn Vogler, *Social Class in Modern Britain*, found that the thesis of the decline of relative class voting was *not* supported by the evidence of their survey. They concluded that the Heath *et al.* view was sound; that the slump in the Labour vote and rise of the Alliance were due to political rather than sociological factors (Chapter 9, pp. 225–63). They do not contest the shrinking of Labour's class base.

89. But see on this John Rentoul, *Me and Mine: The Triumph of the New Individualism?*, 1989, for a response to this thesis.

90. ITN/HARRIS, *British Voting Trends*, 1979–1987, p. 12.
91. John Eatwell, Memo, *PD 1205*, December 1987.
92. Gallup/ *Sunday Telegraph*, 3/9/89 on the rail strike and Harris/ *Observer*, 28/1/90 on the ambulance dispute.
93. In the third quarter of 1989, Labour's support among trade unionists averaged 53 per cent. Information from MORI. See also Chapter 20, n. 39, for the improvement in 1990.
94. MORI/*Sunday Times*, 3/9/89. The gap (58 per cent management, 19 per cent unions) had been growing since 1982 when they were almost the same (40 per cent: 38 per cent).
95. *Ibid.* After peaking in 1979 at 82 per cent, the percentage was down to 38 per cent in 1990. MORI/*Sunday Times*, 2/9/90.
96. Gallup/ *Sunday Telegraph*, 4/9/88 – 54 (all), 58 (TU); 3/9/89 – 53 (all), 53 (TU).
97. 'The Speech Neil did not make', *The Independent*, 7/9/88.
98. *Organising for the 1990's*, Second SRB Report, 1989, p. 1.
99. *Skills 2000*, TUC, 1989.
100. *Europe 1992*, TUC, 1989.
101. In May 1989 Labour drew level with the Conservatives in the polls and by September was 8 per cent ahead. ICM/ *Guardian* 17/8/89 and 18/9/89. In March 1990, at the height of controversy over the poll tax, some opinion polls began to show the Labour Party ahead by over 20 per cent. This dropped away in the summer but Labour retained a substantial lead. In October 1990, it was 10 per cent, NOP *The Independent*, 27/10/90.
102. The reference to filofax was contained in Ron Todd's speech to the 1988 *Tribune* Rally. It was a joke but reflected a growing resentment: '... there is a real division in the Party ... It is social as well as political.' 'There is a certain middle class embarrassment in some circles at the idea of belonging to a movement which remains dominated by working class organisations.'
103. In 1987, the percentage of manual worker MPs (29 per cent) sunk to the low point of 1974. Significantly, of 69 new entrants only 12 were ex-manual workers. David Butler and Dennis Kavanagh, *The British General Election of 1987*, 1988, p. 203.
104. In 1988–9, in the Shadow Cabinet, every elected member was now university educated and only one, John Prescott, had experience in a manual occupation. Overwhelmingly, the Cabinet was from grammar school and red-brick university in Wales, Scotland or the North. Only five were the children of manual workers, and John Cunningham was the son of a union official. In 1989 under new rules of positive discrimination, three women were added – Margaret Beckett, Ann Clwyd and Joan Lester. All had been through higher education.
105. A survey by Patrick Seyd, David Broughton and Paul Whitely in 1990 found that more than half of the CLP members were from the 'salariat' with only 20 per cent manual workers. Information supplied privately.
106. See on this the protesting letter from Tom Sawyer to the *Guardian*, 11/1/90 titled 'Right university, right accent, and then the right to lead'.
107. See on this Alan Watkins, *A Slight Case of Libel*, 1990.
108. The proportion of trade unionists in white collar occupations rose from 32 per cent in 1979 to 41 per cent in 1989, MORI for *Sunday Times*, 3/9/89.

109. There are no available figures on this but the decline of the old
      extractive and manufacturing industries, the rise of white collar sec-
      tions of unions and the new affiliation of BETA was slowly affecting
      the balance.
110. In December 1989, Frank Field was deselected as MP for Birkenhead
      although he won a majority of individual votes in electoral college. He
      launched a strong attack on the role of the unions in candidate
      selection and on their 'block vote' within the Party, threatening to
      stand against the Party in a by-election. The NEC agreed to hold an
      investigation into his deselection and moves to change the procedures
      for reselection were brought forward.
111. In December 1989, Tony Blair (under pressure in the House from the
      Government Minister introducing legislation covering the closed
      shop) sent a letter to his CLP which was published as a press statement
      in which he made clear that the Party would now prohibit the refusal
      of a job or dismissal from a job solely on the grounds that an individual
      was not a trade unionist. This was heralded in press briefings as the
      Labour Party's 'abandonment of the closed shop'. Some disquiet was
      expressed privately, particularly on the NEC, about Blair's method of
      policymaking as well as at the substance of the initiative. In practice,
      Blair had privately sounded out a range of union leaders, including
      senior TUC officials, and there was no general move by them to stop
      the change.

Part III

Ideology and reconstruction

6

Leftwing trade unionism, Socialism and party reform

There has been little in the history of the union–Labour Party relationship since 1918 to rival the significance of the changes which took place in the unions in the late 1960s. The emergence of a new generation of Leftwing union leaders and the undermining of the old Rightwing block vote threatened many established relationships, understandings and procedures. And it heightened the possibility of a sharp split between sections of the unions and elements in the Parliamentary Party.

In so far as it tested old patterns of behaviour and institutional loyalties, it raised again some of the questions which have surrounded 'the labour alliance' since its foundation. What was changeable in the Labour Party and what was not? Could the Labour Party undergo a socialist transformation? Would trade unions be the agency of, or the obstacle to, that transformation?

Among writers on the Labour Party, and from the various Leftwing groups, leagues and parties which have come and gone alongside the Labour Party, the question of Labour Party transformation has generally been conceived in terms of two interrelated processes – the adoption of socialist ideology and policies and a change in procedures and power, which would involve undermining the dominance of the Parliamentary leadership and, in effect, compel it to carry out the policies. In discussions of this process of transformation, there have been contrasting attitudes towards the relationship between trade unions, the Labour Party and Socialism. Trade unionism was often recognised as having contradictory features.[1] When these features were related to Labour Party activity they were, from differing perspectives, given emphasis which stressed either their conservative restrictionist role or their dynamic regenerative capacity.

Thus, from one perspective, trade unions were regarded as ultimately a hindrance to socialist activity within the Labour Party. This was argued on the grounds that unions were essentially 'defensive' and 'reactive' instruments shaped by their function within capitalist market relations.[2] Because of their accommodative, compromising, negotiating role and their sectional behaviour, they did not, in practice, pursue socialist goals. Whatever their rhetoric, it was held that they had consistently limited purposes within the Labour Party and therefore could not themselves be a source of regeneration. This perspective has been, for much of the Labour Party's history, the source of calls for structural changes in the Party which would diminish the power of the unions and enlarge that of the 'Socialist element'.[3] It has also been a justification for repeated defections from 'the labour alliance' to an independent Left position where, unencumbered by official trade unionism and the traditions through which it had smothered the Labour Party, the new Socialist Party would make its successful appeal.[4]

An alternative perspective took a more optimistic view of trade unionism and stressed that it would be a radicalising force in the movement towards Socialism.[5] Because it was rooted in the industrial conflicts of the working class, it was bound to be moved to a militant Left position, even if it could not itself act like a political party and had inherent limitations of purpose. From outside the Labour Party it was argued that a time could come when militant trade unionism would withdraw support from the Labour Party.[6] Inside the Labour Party many on the Labour Left took it for granted that a time would come when, following the experience of industrial struggle, working class militants would not only change the union leadership and reshape the aims of the union, they would reinvigorate the links to the Labour Party. Such a movement would be so powerful that it would promulgate a crisis with the Rightwing leadership of the Labour Party. How this crisis then developed was conceived differently by different groups. Some, particularly Marxist 'entryists', saw it involving a split in which a new independent Socialist Party would be reborn leaving the Right in control of a political shell. Others saw the possibility of the Right splitting away – probably into coalition with the Party's political opponents. But most of the Labour Left tended to assume that such would be the underlying condition of working class radicalisation that what the Right did would not be of much significance.

In the light of this prognosis, we will examine in this chapter and the next the processes of change in the Labour Party in the fifteen years after 1967, focusing particularly on the behaviour of union leaders in relation to their socialist and trade union beliefs. Two interconnected developments and periods were involved: first the rise to prominence of Jack Jones and Hugh Scanlon in the two largest unions and second, after their retirement, the constitutional crises of 1979 to 1982 (Chapter 7). There were, as we shall indicate, linkages between the two periods – connections which exemplified the complex relationship of ideology and practice in the behaviour of Leftwing union leaders in the Labour Party.

SOURCES AND PROCESS

Historically, the 'optimistic' view of trade union radicalisation of the Labour Party involved little in the way of detailed exploration of the mechanics of such change, but tended to envisage the process in terms of a broad and coherent movement. Thus, industrial militancy would produce a new Left activism in the unions and, at the same time, encourage currents of change in political consciousness among the wider working class. It was assumed that the same industrial activists would enter the Constituency Labour Parties in great numbers through both increased trade union representation and through individual membership. The Labour Party would be transformed at both local and national levels and the new Socialist Labour Party would appeal to a working class which was already receptive to a Socialist programme.

In practice, the process of change was to be altogether more complicated than was ever foreseen – a fact which accounts for the extent of the crisis which enveloped the Party in the 1980s. And the sources of change were to be rather more autonomous to the Labour Party and its active membership than had been envisaged.[7] This said, there can be no doubt that what happened within the unions was fundamental to the whole experience of this period – an ultimate determinant of success, failure and limitation.

An indication, indeed a test of this, was the attempt by Party activists in 1967 to launch a Campaign for a Democratic Labour Party. It began among activists in Sheffield Trades and Labour Council and then moved briefly on to the national stage.[8] It focused on measures to strengthen the Party Conference as a policymaking body and measures to defend the rights of CLPs in relation to candidate selection. But, at the 1967 Conference, it flopped badly. That Conference was a dull and docile affair. The Right Wing seemed as dominant as ever in the unions. The Parliamentary Leadership seemed impervious to pressure. The constituency activists, rapidly declining in number, appeared an insignificant force.

So for the moment, failure. But it must be noted that a leading sympathiser with the Campaign for a Democratic Labour Party, the MP Frank Allaun, was elected to the NEC for the first time, together with MP Joan Lestor who held similar views. This – the first sign of the fourteen-year rise of the Left on the NEC – was a significant landmark in itself. But, in addition, Allaun was to play a dedicated role in supporting the authority of the Party Conference in these years[9] and he became the first President of the new Campaign for Labour Party Democracy set up by Party activists in 1973.[10]

Between the two 'Campaigns', advocates of intra-Party democracy from the rank and file and NEC received a major boost of support from within the unions by the emergence of a new generation of Leftwing union leaders who both encouraged them and signalled to the Party that they shared the same goals. The link between the two 'Campaigns' was the Socialist Charter organisation of 1968 set up again on the initiative of Sheffield activists but this time with the formal backing of Leftwing union leaders[11] as well as MPs. The simmering revolt within the constituencies was a constant background factor in the politics of the next twelve years before it finally burst out after Labour's 1979 election defeat (see Chapter 7).

But now let us examine the changes which took place in the unions.

THE NEW LEFT UNION LEADERSHIP

As was illustrated in Chapter 5, in a remarkably short period from 1967 to 1969, the political alignment of the block vote at the Party Conference was dramatically changed as new Leftwing union leaders emerged in four of the five largest unions. The old Rightwing 'block vote' was severely undermined in morale and cohesion as a new alliance came to rival it in size and overawe it in assertiveness.

This phenomenon, devastating in its effect on those who had become accustomed to the traditional alignment of the unions, was both unique in its scope and consequences and yet in some respects narrow and limited. It rested much more than appeared to be the case on the fortune of membership, occupational and amalgamation changes which added substantially to the strength of the Left – particularly in the two largest unions. And it arose much more than was subsequently recognised as a result of factional changes in *one* union.

In understanding the strength and weakness of the developing Left after 1967, it is important to appreciate that behind the appearance of fundamental realignment, among the larger unions, only the change in the Engineers' leadership, where Hugh Scanlon replaced Bill Carron, represented a decisive shift from Right to Left. In the largest union – the Transport Workers – Jack Jones replaced Frank Cousins. It involved a shift to more clear-cut industrial and political objectives but was essentially a consolidation of an existing pattern of Leftwing policies.

In the Shopworkers, the election of Richard Seabrook as President, and in the Mineworkers the election of Lawrence Daly as General Secretary (replacing a Communist moderate), were significant changes, but in each case still balanced by senior officials to the Right of the new officers. In the event, Seabrook was replaced in 1972 as the Shopworkers again moved to the Right. And Lawrence Daly, through illness after 1975, played a relatively low-key role until his retirement in 1984; Joe Gormley, elected as President of the Mineworkers in 1971, was the more influential figure as leader of the Rightwing faction. A move to the Right was also evident in the Union of Post Office Workers – the seventh largest union – where Tom Jackson was elected with Leftwing support in 1967 but shifted away after the unsuccessful national strike of 1971.

One other change in the early 1970s indicated an important union shift of position. In the General and Municipal Workers, after 1972, David Basnett replaced Lord Cooper and attempted to pull a Rightwing union into the centre of the Labour Party.

Such cross-currents were important features of the political situation facing Jones and Scanlon, the leaders of the trade union Left. For their entire period of office until their retirement in 1977 and 1978, the two of them were outnumbered 'Leftists' on the important 'Neddy Six' group of union leaders – which meant also among the TUC representation on the Liaison Committee with the Labour Party.[12]

At the heart of all these changes there remained the fact of the clear political realignment of the Engineering union. Even here, after 1972, the Right began to recapture national positions and, as we shall see, fourteen years later it was the consolidation of Rightwing control over the Engineers' delegation which finally marked the end of the advance of the Left and the curtailment of the constitutional revolt.

Policy aspirations

For several years after 1968, Jones and Scanlon were seen as 'the terrible twins' of the Left. And indeed they did share some common industrial and political perspectives. They came to power associated with a wave of shopfloor militancy and with the extension of shop steward bargaining power, and they stressed the need to come to terms with this movement and reflect its aspirations.[13] It was not that they wished to make a direct break with the national operation of the unions through Whitehall, but rather that they saw this development in the context of 'the great tradition of independent working class power',[14] a tradition which involved both militancy and, if necessary, industrial action. Both were open advocates of public ownership and industrial democracy and were regular speakers at the huge conferences of the Institute for Workers Control held during this period.

Their views were also heavily influenced by the experiences of the Popular Front period of the 1930s and of the hostilities of the Cold War. Jones had fought in the Spanish Civil War, Scanlon, together with Daly and Seabrook, had been in the Communist Party. Though they did not challenge NATO as a collective security organisation, all remained suspicious and critical of the US Government's foreign policy and its involvement with the international trade union movement. They were strongly in favour of a reconciliation of the divided international trade union federations, and they had, in various shades, a sympathy for a more independent policy for Britain between two great world power blocs, which they hoped would soon be dissolved. All of the new Left union leaders were supporters of the Campaign for Nuclear Disarmament favouring both unilateral nuclear disarmament and general cuts in arms expenditure.

However, there were always significant differences between Jones and Scanlon, reflecting personal experience, union tradition, union composition *and* ideological values. These affected their perceptions of problems and their definition of priorities. Jones, with views heavily influenced by experience of joint production in the Second World War, was General Secretary of a union with membership across the entire breadth of British industry – including a substantial body of unskilled and low paid workers. Scanlon, in Australia during World War II, was President of a union still predominantly composed of skilled craft workers located in manufacturing industry. Jones brought to bear the coherent programme of industrial and political reform involving an egalitarianism towards wealth and power which always shaped the way he viewed solutions. Scanlon's outlook was shaped initially by elements of Syndicalism and old Communist Party perspectives, plus an unshakeable preoccupation with manufacturing industry.

Power and the Labour Party

However, these differences were not as immediately apparent in the late 1960s as was their similarity, particularly in what appeared to be their common approach to Labour Party activity. Much more than any previous generation of senior General Council union leaders, they were prepared to associate individually, and to some extent collectively, with the Left of the constituency and Parliamentary parties. They appeared regularly on Leftwing platforms – particularly at the Party Conference. Jones joined the board of the periodical *Tribune* and *Tribune*, in turn, moved closer to the trade union leadership. Whilst the Party was in Opposition, they or their representatives attended private pre-Conference discussion meetings with Leftwing members of the NEC.[15]

Their comments appeared to indicate a new interest in formulating political programmes and in using the Labour Party as the channel for implementing those programmes. To do this involved reasserting the role of the Party Conference and reducing the independence of the Parliamentary Party established by Gaitskell and Wilson in the 1960s. In 1968, Jones and Scanlon had little disagreement with the *Socialist Charter*'s commitment to the transformation of the Labour Party into 'an instrument of popular control responsive to the members and their Conference'. They deeply resented what they regarded as the snobbery of Parliamentary elitism. And they were opposed to authoritarian controls over intraparty dissent.

All seemed set, then, for a major transformation of policy and power. As one Labour historian put it:

> At long last the block votes were being turned against the right. This seemed like a fundamental change. After seventy years of waiting, Labour's socialists now began to feel that they were in a position to dictate the terms of 'the labour alliance'.[16]

By contrast, when we come to the period from 1974 when Labour was back in Government, to the retirement of Jones and Scanlon in 1978, their reputation shifted dramatically as did the expectations of the Left about them. There appeared to be a complete shift of political roles, for they were now as defensive of the Parliamentary leadership as they had once been critical; now they appeared as inhibited as they once were assertive; now they appeared to be as hostile to the Left on the NEC as they once were friendly in alliance. For many on the Left, they had now become 'part of the Right', accommodating, protecting and compromising, enveloped completely in the tripartite arrangements surrounding the Government. And yet what we will indicate is a much more complex pattern of behaviour with effects not only on immediate policy but on the future constellation of Party forces. Its exploration takes us to the heart of the union–Party relationship.

There was certainly a series of changes in attitude and a deradicalisation on some issues as they shared the problems of the Labour Government and organised its loyal support. Many of the socio-psychological and political factors which have in the past socialised and educated Leftwing union leaders into the responsibilities of national relationships within British politics affected these union leaders also. But (and it is an important 'but'), there was a much greater degree of continuity to their behaviour than appeared to be the case. If we trace their behaviour back to the late 1960s when they assumed office, we can see that from the first their actions were shaped by a familiar role definition. They were committed to putting forward in policy discussions and in relation to the Party what they saw as 'a trade union point of view'.[17] With this went beliefs about the values and proprieties of industrial and political activity – beliefs as old as the union–Party relationship.

A corollary of this was that purely political or purely ideological considerations were compartmentalised into mainly demonstrative and symbolic activity – in forums where it was appropriate. Did this mean, therefore, as has been suggested,[18] that their ideological beliefs and factional alignments were virtually irrelevant to their behaviour? Here we must take into account two important considerations.

First of all, a 'trade union point of view' and its priorities could involve (as in the past) significant variations of definition and perspective. Scanlon's strict compartmentalisation of the industrial and the political was such that at one point in 1972 he described it to the author in the metaphor of schizophrenia. Jones' trade unionism, on the other hand, was much more directly fused with ideological values of democratic and economic egalitarianism – even though he, too, was respectful of the specific sphere of the political.

Secondly, there was a compartmentalised area of Party activity where ideological and factional identifications could be legitimately expressed. NEC elections were covered by a complicated mixture of industrial-oriented 'rules' and politically-based alignments. The paradox that will be unveiled here is that alongside the growing, and at times bitter, divergence of Jones and Scanlon from the political Left – particularly the NEC Left – was a process whereby Jones and Scanlon strengthened and sustained the Left forces they were opposing! As Scanlon put it to the author in 1972,

> ... we are schizophrenic, but anybody who thinks we do not take our responsibilities seriously doesn't understand.[19]

Let us now examine how Jones and Scanlon related to the 'rules' of the Labour Movement.

PRIORITY

Agreed commitments

Over and above certain basic tenets of free trade unionism, the priority which the trade union leaders gave to particular items had to be read from a range of political signals marked in different forums of the Party. It was in the initiation of proposals and then the extent of involvement in the follow-through which truly reflected the priorities. Jack Jones, for example, always had a two-pronged attack for those issues which he signalled as crucial – a conference resolution proposed by the TGWU to which he or his deputy would speak, and detailed proposals which would also be placed before the Liaison Committee as part of the follow-through. Scanlon was in a more circumscribed position. As President of a union with a complicated constitutional structure and a 'two-party' factional conflict, he was increasingly in the position of carrying forward resolutions about which he had reservations. Signals from Scanlon came 'Kremlinologically' in the emphasis of his speeches but they could also be derived from reports of conflict with members of his delegation.

From the first, Jones and Scanlon were concerned with the priorities established in the Liaison Committee – particularly its 1972 *Statement on Industrial Relations* and its 1973 document *Economy Policy and the Cost of Living*. These covered 'the agreed commitments'[20] to which Government policy was subsequently related. Although it was not apparent at the time, this concern with the statements of the Liaison Committee produced a covert divergence from the political Left which looked to the Party Programme of 1973 and the General Election Manifesto of February 1974 as the benchmarks of policy. Central to the

Liaison Committee's commitments were the repeal and replacement provisions in relation to the Heath Government's industrial relations legislation, and the return to 'free collective bargaining'. The attitude of Jones and Scanlon towards the Labour Government after 1974 was shaped by the fact that the labour law worked out in detail on the Liaison Committee was immediately implemented by the Labour Government. The Employment Protection Act of 1975 was likened by Jones to 'a shop steward's charter'.[21]

The return to free collective bargaining involved the abolition of the Pay Board and the legislative framework of Heath's prices and incomes policy. Both Jones and Scanlon had made it emphatically clear on the Liaison Committee that they would not be party to any form of statutory incomes policy. It was an issue which had helped propel Scanlon into office and had brought both Jones and Scanlon into hostile confrontation with the last Labour Government.

But looking forward to the possibility of a co-operative Labour Government which took the unions into partnership involved the union leaders in private consideration of an understanding over pay. Jones particularly had begun to feel his way towards the guidelines of the relationship in which self-restraint would be an essential element. The question of an agreed level of wage applications and settlements under agreed conditions came up in the talks with the Heath Government in 1972[22] and although Jones rejected specific norms and the talks were abortive, they reinforced the tendency for the union leaders to see the issue of incomes in much broader perspective than they had adopted in the 1960s, and to specify conditions of co-operation.

They became more alert to the need to protect real living standards; thus price controls, rents and food subsidies were all adjudged to be part of the Social Contract. They became sensitive to the idea of the social wage as much as the cash wage.[23] Tax reforms must be supported by a deliberate Government decision to channel resources into the social services. In particular, Jones stressed that pensions must be linked to average earnings – a cause he had espoused for years.

There was also a growing acceptance that, under a Labour Government, union leaders had themselves to offer some alternative 'in place of strife'. Jones' own contribution to a less disrupted industrial relations emerged clearly in this period as a return to something resembling Second World War arbitration arrangements – the Advisory, Conciliation and Arbitration Service.

Thus, though union leaders could not, and would not, give any specific commitments, nor would they involve themselves in detailed discussions about incomes when the Party was in Opposition, the 1973 Liaison Committee document *Economic Policy and the Cost of Living* established in very careful terms their commitment to the pursuit of a 'wide-ranging agreement which is necessary to control inflation'.[24] The crucial proviso was that the unions would be involved in discussing 'the order of priorities'.[25] This procedural agreement to hold discussions on priorities was the solidarity pivot of the social contract – an agreement honoured by the Labour Government to an extent which was to become the dismay of some of those who later defected to the Social Democrats.

It was in recognition of the degree to which this 'Labour Movement' manifesto was being honoured that Jones, his Deputy, Harry Urwin, and Hugh

Scanlon became staunch defenders of the Labour Government in 1974 and fierce opponents of those on the Left who sought further guarantees *before* the unions would deliver co-operation. The Pay Board had been abolished even though Wilson had privately acknowledged to Jones that there was actually a majority in the House in favour of statutory incomes control.[26] The Prices Commission and Price Code, on the other hand, had been retained and were perpetuated throughout the period of Labour Government. Food subsidies were introduced, rent increases cancelled and pensions – always close to Jones's heart – increased. Scanlon, with much less room for manœuvre than Jones at the 1974 TUC Congress, caused a sensation by persuading the TASS delegation and its Communist General Secretary, Ken Gill (part of the Engineers' loose amalgamation), to withdraw its 'conditional' resolution.[27] Following this, with Jones and Scanlon pushing hard, the authority of the TUC was used to encourage unions to adopt negotiating positions which focused on the need to restrain unit costs.

Thus, from the first days of the Labour Government, these union leaders regarded *both* free collective bargaining and restraint as essential priorities. At this stage, they had no intention of moving towards nationally established norms. But, by the summer of 1975, they were faced with a dilemma which called forth a major reordering of priorities and the temporary acceptance of a policy which they had steadfastly opposed for years.

New dilemmas

For a start, in practice, the self-restraint element of the policy, as Jones put it later, 'did not look so good'.[28] As inflation rose, Jones agreed, in discussions with Foot and Healey, that wage claims would be kept in line with price rises. But the TUC's authority alone could not hold the line. While prices were rising at 17 per cent, wage increases were averaging 24 per cent. Jones had never accepted that wage increases were the root cause of inflation, but acknowledged that they could feed the inflationary situation and make it worse.[29]

The problem took on a new aspect when it was related to the sudden sharp rise in unemployment – 643,000 in October 1974, it rose to 940,000 by April 1975. By July it was over one million. All experience since the Second World War had indicated to the union leaders, as well as most economists, that inflationary pressures were a counter to unemployment, not its corollary. Now they had to think again. The solution to unemployment was not necessarily more money in the pocket. If it were, argued Jones, why was there so much unemployment in 1975 when 'we've had more money in our pockets than ever before in living memory'.[30]

The weight of Treasury opinion in 1975 began to shift towards the view that, although the international recession was a factor, unemployment was rising mainly as a result of excessive wage settlements in one area throwing people out of work in another; thus making the unions themselves generally responsible.[31] Jones and Scanlon now also began to accept that money was being traded for jobs.[32] Self-interest and solidarity, therefore, dictated a stricter emphasis on restraint.

Further, the scale of the problem of the inflationary spiral, and the panic in the mass media, appeared to be provoking a massive loss of confidence in the currency – a loss which threatened collapse which would engender mass unemployment. Holding off that mass unemployment and restoring the confidence of the international financial community became the aim, not only of Labour Government Ministers but of the union leaders also – Jones and Scanlon prominent among them. At the same time, there was some cause for optimism that the international recession would be turned in the near future and Labour would reap the benefit, providing it was assisted now.

Alongside these pressing economic priorities, there were also some important political factors to be taken into account. The atmosphere of 1975 led union leaders to fear a Rightwing backlash which could take either of two forms – a Rightwing Conservative Government which in its use of monetarism would allow unemployment to rise and thus 'discipline working people' that way, or a Rightwing coalition 'National Government' which would be fundamentally hostile to trade unionism. Some union leaders, including Jones, even feared a Rightwing coup.[33]

Jones was aware that opinion within the trade unions as well as the Government was rapidly shifting to support for some emergency action which would stem the alarming rise of the inflationary spiral. In the continuous dialogue with allies in the Government, particularly Michael Foot,[34] he worked to secure the most acceptable form of policy for incomes. His view of acceptability was shaped both by the needs of many low paid workers in his own union and by his own egalitarian beliefs about equitable sacrifice. He rejected any statutory element and he rejected the idea of a Government-imposed percentage increase. He turned down proposals also that the TUC re-establish its own wage vetting,[35] and he did not accept the advice of those within the unions (including Scanlon) who said that his alternative could not be delivered. At every stage he responded fiercely to Leftwing criticism that in co-operating in wage restraint, he was betraying his principles.

The principles came in the acceptance of responsibility and the form of the restraint. What became the £6 flat rate increase for all earning up to £8,500 per year, with nothing for those above that figure, was egalitarian in its aid to many of the lower paid and its effect on various differentials. It was also a major contribution towards its objectives. Inflation fell from 25 to 12 per cent in the next twelve months.

Jones always saw these measures simply as a temporary and principled way of dealing with an emergency problem. He thought in terms of a speedy return to free collective bargaining and initially was not even in favour of a second phase of incomes policy. But shared acceptance of the Government's economic problems in dealing with inflation, plus a conviction that Ministers like Michael Foot were absolutely trustworthy and desperately seeking to do their best for the Labour Movement, led Jones in 1976 into acceptance of a further round. The new 5 per cent norm would work within a minimum and maximum flat rate figure thus still involving an egalitarian element.

Scanlon was always less convinced than Jones of the virtue of the flat rate policy. Initially, worried both about the effects on the differentials of his members and the lack of an immediate quid pro quo, he was, in his own words to the author, 'taken along kicking and screaming'.[36] But to the general economic need for restraint he was increasingly committed in 1975 and 1976. Indeed, by 1977 when Jones was hamstrung by the decision of his union conference to return to free collective bargaining, Scanlon put his full weight behind TUC policy over wage restraint and 'the twelve months rule'[37] to the extent of failing to consult his Leftwing-dominated delegation before the crucial vote.[38] In the next twelve months of the TUC's 'nod and wink' acquiescence to the Government-imposed norm of 10 per cent maximum pay increase, Scanlon more than most was nodding and winking. Inflation, he told the TUC in his valedictory address in 1978, was 'the biggest threat to living standards and jobs that we have ever experienced'.[39]

In this sense, the suggestion of a 'toleration' of rising unemployment[40] is an odd way of describing their behaviour. The only validity one can give to it is that the union leadership may have failed to put their weight behind an alternative economic and political strategy which widened the choice. In theory, there was such an available alternative – an 'alternative economic strategy' supported by the Labour Left.[41] What was the response of Jones and Scanlon to this alternative?

Left alternatives

An initial problem was that, among advocates of the alternative economic strategy which emerged in 1975, there was no agreement on the need for a policy for incomes[42] at a time when the union leaders had suddenly become convinced of its (temporary) necessity. But among the agreed elements were a reflation of the economy, a restoration of the public expenditure cuts, a strategy for industrial regeneration based on Labour's Programme 1973 and controls over the flow of trade and capital, with a heavy emphasis on import controls. In TUC terms, the package received its formal legitimacy through long composite resolutions of the 1976 Congress.[43] It was in this sense 'TUC policy'.

Subsequently, Leftwing critics of the Labour Government were to point out, on many occasions, that if TUC Congress or Labour Party Conference decisions were examined, there was a gap between trade union economic policy and that of the Labour Government. In some important academic contributions, this became a test of the limited power of the unions.[44]

But here again we must pose the question of what was real as opposed to formal policy; what was pushed and what was not? In 1974, Jones and Scanlon had no particularly distinctive economic position. There was a general approval of industrial planning and regulation mixed with acceptance of the major tenets of post-war Keynesian economic management. However, it was their misfortune to be in leadership positions at a time when 'stagflation' was producing a new disorientation among Keynesians and the whole intellectual edifice of Keynesian social democracy was moving into a crisis.

The transformation of the economic perspectives of the Prime Minister and of Treasury Ministers towards monetarism appeared to be based on practical exigency – an approach which always appealed to trade union leaders. Lacking any

strong economic facilities within their own unions, Jones and Scanlon were
dependent upon advice from the TUC Economic Department, itself heavily influenced by changing Treasury thinking. Indeed, at this time, on key issues of
macro-economic policy, an avalanche of advice was showered on the union
leaders, all pointing to the common sense of the Government's general approach.

In contrast, there was little regular informal dialogue between the Ministerial
Left around Benn and the Leftwing trade union leaders. They were busy men
working in different spheres, finding it difficult to make time for extra meetings.
After October 1975, relations deteriorated badly as both sides resented a mutual
lack of support. Jones, particularly, was incensed by the failure of the political
Left to appreciate the need for priority action over the pay spiral and by their
demands for an 'unrealistic' immediate quid pro quo. Whatever his reservations
about the Treasury view, he developed more acute reservations about the judgement of Labour's own middle class 'theorists' who struck postures in the face of
acute problems. Certainly he and Scanlon lacked anything near the amount of
confidence required for them to go out on a limb in support of Benn's economic
diagnosis and proscriptions.

Thus, on the one hand there were the cumbersome composite TUC Congress
resolutions in favour of an alternative economic strategy and, on the other, there
were the real views of Jones and Scanlon who regarded the resolutions as at best a
bargaining pressure in relations with the Government, and, at worst, sloganising
impracticalities. For the fact was quietly acknowledged behind the scenes in the
TUC in this period, that in spite of NEC policy and the resolutions of the Congress
'we are not convinced that there is an alternative economic strategy'.[45]

Take one central example. In practice, from 1975 to 1977, there was always a
degree of ambivalence in the way some of the union leaders, including Jones and
Scanlon, approached the idea of a reflation of the economy and a restoration of
the public expenditure cuts.[46] For Jones, the idea that spending power would soak
up unemployment was an idea which ignored 'every hard lesson we have had to
learn in the past two years'.[47] He grew increasingly suspicious of the Treasury's
prognosis about the Public Sector Borrowing Requirement and of the extent of
the cuts, while recognising the special problem of establishing priorities between
the growing demands being made in 1975. His own concern in terms of social
justice was clear. Over pensions, though never fully satisfied with what was
achieved, he regarded Government priorities as 'about right'.

Scanlon, on the other hand, went through a major transformation of views in
this period, not only accepting the primacy of dealing with the country's debts
but also changing his views on public expenditure. Always defensive of manufacturing industry, he accepted the Bacon–Eltis thesis – heavily pushed by economic
journalists and by the Treasury at this time – that high levels of public sector
expenditure were starving the market sector of resources, causing
deindustrialisation and weakening the economy.[48]

Sharing these assumptions, there could be no fundamental alternative to what
the Government was doing. As he told the 1976 Congress, 'We are not asking
the Government for a reversal or a modification of their present economic
strategy'... 'we are in hock to foreign financial interests and speculators ... and

above everything else … we cannot continue to spend more than we are producing.' He went on, 'It is therefore *within these constraints* that we ask, indeed insist, that something shall be done to reduce the present unacceptable and intolerable levels of unemployment'.[49]

Thus out of the dialogues of the social contract, the inter-departmental contacts, the meetings of Ministers and the Neddy Six, the discussions between Murray and Healey and between Foot and Jones, came some common assumptions which cut across the policy criticism of the Left – and the formal TUC Congress commitments. It was on the basis of these shared assumptions that in January 1976 the TUC put forward its own 'five point programme'. This advocated not 'the alternative economic strategy' but a series of proposals dominated by job creation and training measures.[50] That such proposals were, in the main, accepted by the Government reinforced the belief of TUC officials that although the Government would not involve itself in a major reflation, it would give the TUC 'virtually what we ask for'[51] in terms of palliatives – 'selective measures to help keep down the level of unemployment'.[52] It was this aspect of the role of the union leaders via the Secretary of State for Employment which so enraged some on the Right among Government Ministers as 'a habit of mind which amounts to saying "Find out what the TUC wants and tell them they can have it"'.[53]

The unwillingness of the union leadership to push for a major reflationary policy began to change only in 1977 when it became apparent that the economy had been strengthened, that reserves had markedly improved and that there was now a growing trade surplus. As for the political Left's argument that controls over imports would allow the Government to reflate without it provoking severe balance of payments problems, this was rejected by the Government in 1975 and, after early discussions, was not a central part of the TUC–Government dialogue. Official TUC policy, reflecting a strong push from unions in vulnerable industries, favoured *selective* import controls as a means of protecting industries from penetration while (in theory) they restructured and raised performance. The Government was unreceptive (except in clear cases of dumping), fearing the permanent shoring up of inefficient industries. Jones and Scanlon, at different points in the period from 1975 to 1977, publicly supported the call for selective import controls but their shared concern about national competitiveness was always an inhibition on their support, and they too do not appear to have accepted the Left's argument on the balance of payments.

In any case, as the policy was neither part of the original 'contract' of 1973 nor in the Manifesto, it had no special legitimacy. Indeed, given the sectional protectiveness which was very near the surface of trade union concern about imports, the TUC advocacy of this as a macro-economic policy tended to be inhibited. Only Basnett appears to have pushed it.[54] Speaking for his union at the 1976 TUC and Labour Party Conference, Scanlon called (apparently forcibly) for selective import controls but it was noticeable that in his valedictory speech to the TUC in 1978 he made no reference to the question.[55] Jones never took the issue to either Congress or Conference.

More surprisingly, Jones and Scanlon were not really in tune with the Left's 'alternative *industrial* strategy' either. As envisaged in the Party's Programme of

1973, it involved the nationalisation of twenty-five leading firms. The remainder of the large firms would be subject to planning agreements with the Government promulgated by legislation and backed up by sanctions. To the Bennite Left, it was a transformatory programme and a touchstone of socialist commitment. Benn took the Party Programme as his authorisation on industrial policy.

However, there was a very different emphasis in *Economic Policy and the Cost of Living*. On public ownership, it referred only to an unspecified 'development of new public enterprise' and on wider industrial strategy only to 'supervision of the investment policy of large private corporations'. There was no reference to planning agreements but there was a stress on 'agreement and not ... compulsion in one of the most complex fields of our national life'. It was this, rather than the party document, which provided the guidelines of the approach of Jones and Scanlon to industrial policy.

In respect of the public ownership part of it, consistent with their traditional ideological position, both union leaders were prepared, in the period from 1968 to 1972, to support Conference resolutions in favour of a general increase in public ownership and to support, in principle, calls for 'the implementation of Clause IV'.

But they took another perspective on *specific* policy proposals. (See also p. 179 for their response to the 1973 policy and Party unity.) This involved defining as a priority the public ownership of firms and industries *only* where the union concerned regarded it as essential and only where the TUC, not the Party, had agreed the policy development. On the public ownership of finance, banking and insurance, the initial support given by the two union leaders was qualified after the banking unions expressed the firm opposition of the majority of their members. Both accepted the 'rule' of no nationalisation without consent. Though Scanlon moved a composite resolution at the 1976 TUC which included a reassertion of this public ownership policy, he made no reference whatsoever to it in his speech![56]

The only areas where they regarded public ownership as a commitment were the shipbuilding, ship-repairing and aircraft industries where policies had been thrashed out in detailed tripartite discussions between the TUC, the Party and the relevant unions. Certainly, Jones and Scanlon took it as a sign of good faith on the part of the Parliamentary Leadership that shipbuilding and aircraft nationalisation were carried through after a bitter and protracted Parliamentary struggle.

This attitude towards public ownership was carried over into the argument about the purpose and scope of the National Enterprise Board. Again, if asked in the early 1970s to state where they stood in principle, they would have affirmed support for its public ownership potential. The most contentious proposals of the NEC – that 25 leading companies be taken into public ownership – would probably have received their formal support had it ever (in their time) been put to the Conference as a clear choice. But there is little doubt also that they regarded this as an ideological affirmation rather than a practical proposal.

Similarly, the leadership of the two major unions initially regarded it as 'a plus' that the new NEB was able to take within its orbit British Leyland, Rolls Royce and others. But, judging by their later comments to the author, far from resenting the failure of the NEB to expand its public ownership potential, the union leaders developed a new scepticism in the late 1970s about the role of public industries as producers and employers.

As for planning agreements, this new conception of industrial policy had emerged from the Party's 'intellectuals' via the NEC policy process and was fleshed out very late in the period of Opposition. Jones and Scanlon had not been involved, their experience had not been drawn upon and their co-operation had not been won. They had acquiesced in the policy in 1974 but it was never subject to detailed discussion on the Liaison Committee until virtually the eve of the Labour Government, when Jones and Scanlon did not attend.[57] Tony Benn was later to point out that 'there was really no top level support for the industrial policy at that crucial moment when it was reversed'.[58] In truth, there was a lack of convinced top level support for the industrial policy from its inception[59] - as well as a lack of grass-roots mobilisation.[60]

Aside from his lack of involvement in the NEC's formulation of the policy, Jones had other reservations. As a policy process, the inauguration of planning agreements involved a dialogue essentially between Ministers and companies. It was difficult to see where the unions would fit in. Background discussion between Party and union officials in 1973–5 tended to assume the implementation of TUC policy on industrial democracy – that is, parity of power on the boards of companies. But without the implementation of this policy – and it was delayed for years – the trade union stake was uncertain.

Jones mixed sympathy and scepticism in equal proportions. He was conscious of a range of practical problems in dealing with asset-stripping and conglomerates. He doubted whether Governments could enforce compliance over firms without an integrated trade union involvement. And he saw that involvement as *the* priority. He opposed, and grew increasingly critical of, 'the talking shops' involved in the tripartite structure created after the Chequers meeting in November 1975. But locked into this structure, he found it difficult to seize any initiative, and Scanlon showed no interest in doing so. Indeed, on the Left's industrial policy, Scanlon's attitude varied from the evasive to the robustly dismissive.

Jones' egalitarianism

This developing difference in approach between Jones and Scanlon was a feature of several policy areas. Jones's trade unionism was always more in harmony with his ideological values even though he was putting forward 'a trade union point of view'. Scanlon exhibited the clearest rupture of industrial and political perspectives and his more traditional Leftwing trade unionism became, in the end, more an accommodation with established institutions and values.

The difference between them was most marked over industrial democracy. Jones deeply resented criticism from the Left that he was unconcerned with the wider Party purpose of 'a fundamental and irreversible shift in the balance of wealth and power towards working people and their families'. For him, trade unionism and socialist values fused in the proposals for industrial democracy. Socialism involved the widest possible participation in power. The objective here was to redistribute power to the workers through the extended processes of trade union organisation as it had been in the Joint Production Committee of the Second World War. Trade union collective bargaining and democratic participation would be through a single channel of trade union representation, and there would be parity of representation with management over a wide field of decision-making.

Had it been achieved, such measures might well have radically increased the power of shop floor trade unionism. It offered the prospect not only of extended restraint on management prerogatives but a widening scope of trade union activity, education and understanding. In these terms, it is difficult to treat it purely as a category of trade union 'defensive' measures. And it would certainly be difficult to argue that it was not a major priority. There is no doubt that once the first objectives of the TUC (the abolition of the Industrial Relations Act and its replacement by the Trade Union and Labour Relations Act and the Employment Protection Act) had been achieved, then industrial democracy moved to the forefront of Jones' concern.

The measure of the priority that he gave to these proposals was the fact that, with support from Michael Foot, he was prepared to push for an immediate Bill in 1975, despite the fact that he knew that several other trade union leaders were sceptical, despite signs of hostility from sections of the Cabinet, and despite the fact that he knew that there was fierce opposition from the Treasury, from the City and from most employers. The opposition was strong enough to avoid commitment to an immediate Bill and a Commission of Enquiry was instituted as a delaying device. But renewed pressure from the TUC secured favourable terms of reference and a composition which shaped to a considerable extent the outcome of the report. Jones himself was a forceful member of the committee. The majority report with its '2x plus y' formula was not the simple parity which Jones wanted but its principles, particularly of 'the single channel' were near enough to those of the TUC for it to receive a vitriolic response from opponents of 'trade union power'. The Cabinet majority showed their own reservations and the result was a deadlock between the Ministers concerned. By this stage in 1977, Jones' own position was weakening and he could do little. At the time of his retirement, the delayed Government White Paper was still awaited.

For Jones it was a major set-back; for Scanlon it was virtually an irrelevance. Though they had shared the platforms and auspices of the Institute for Workers' Control, there was a sharp difference of view as to what this involved. Scanlon had always doubted that there could be effective workers' control in a nationalised industry without 'the commanding heights of the economy' coming into public ownership.[61] This view, traditional on the Left in the AUEW, was easily compatible with pure oppositional trade unionism in the early 1970s and just as easily shed in its entirety once the commitment to nationalisation itself had receded.

Jones' egalitarianism towards power (an egalitarianism reflected in reforms in his union – see Chapter 10, p. 303) was also matched by an egalitarianism towards wealth and income. He had argued on the Liaison Committee in 1972 that it was the primary role of the Labour Party, not the TUC, to talk about redistribution and equality,[62] but all the way through the period of Opposition and Government, his own egalitarianism was a feature of his priorities. The £6 flat rate policy and the ceiling above those who would receive it was one example. The successful attempt to secure a reduced rate band of income tax for the low paid in 1978 was another example.

The most overtly political of these egalitarian pressures was Jones' attack on the maldistribution of wealth. The idea for a Royal Commission on the Distribution of Wealth and Income had come from him through the Liaison Committee while the Party was in Opposition and he remained a strong supporter of a stiff Wealth Tax. With Labour in Government and the Treasury resistant to the Wealth Tax, pressure from Jones led, unusually, to the establishment of a working party being set up by the Liaison Committee, with Jones as one of the two General Council representatives.

An agreed statement from the Working Party, which brought with it the two Government Ministers on the Committee, Joel Barnet and Gerald Kaufman, was fought strongly by the Chancellor, Healey, in the Liaison Committee. The proposed Wealth Tax threshold was raised from £100,000 to £150,000[63] as a result and though the understanding was that the tax would be introduced in the first session of a new Parliament, Healey's hostility suggested that there would continue to be difficulties. 'We were let down', conceded Jones later. 'They avoided it, I pushed it back on. They avoided it again.'[64]

This egalitarianism was never to the fore with Scanlon, whose preoccupations were heavily focused upon industry and its required differentials. It must also be said that both Jones and Scanlon came from a generation of male trade union leaders who shared limited perspectives about the urgency of what became known as 'women's issues'. But Jones was instrumental in securing a TUC Equal Rights Committee and the £6 pay policy was welcomed by feminists as beneficial to low paid women workers.[65] When it came to the argument over the child benefit scheme and the idea of a family benefit, Jones (with Basnett) was crucial to rescuing the scheme,[66] while Scanlon was much more concerned with the cut in male 'family-wage' packets.

International perspectives

There was a more unified development of their policies in relation to international trade union priorities. Trade union perspectives could lead, as they had in the case of Bevin in the 1930s, from the worldwide defence of free trade unionism to a passionate and assertive involvement in issues of collective security and foreign policy. Jones and Scanlon in one sense followed the Bevin tradition – albeit in a different political direction. Both were, while in Opposition, attentive to major issues of foreign and defence policy. Where Bevin had been a major actor in the Cold War and had a shaping hand in its alignments, Jones and Scanlon defined their political identities in terms of reconstructing the Cold War alignments (particularly the legacy of divided international trade unionism) and achieving unilateral nuclear disarmament.

However, when we examine their behaviour, it is clear that in this area, a consciousness of being in a Leftwing minority plus an anxiety over disturbing too many of the post-war political relationships led them to fall back upon a 'trade union point of view' as a means of insulating rather than as a means of enlarging their initiatives. Thus, Jones became Chairman of the TUC's International Committee and, strongly supported by Scanlon, attempted to prioritise the building of new relationships with unions outside the ICFTU and to seek a *détente* with Eastern European trade unionism. But it meant keeping the TUC clear of some delicate political problems and narrowing the focus to the question of international trade unionism. Similarly, on international human rights, Jones again took a 'trade union point of view' – supporting protests and sanctions against Government policy on trade unions in Bolivia, Chile, South Africa and Spain. Trade union rights internationally were the proper concern of trade union leaders and the TUC International Department. But *not* human rights – that was a matter for Amnesty International.

A narrowing of trade union priorities was reflected also in attitudes towards defence policy. In both 1972 and 1973, the Labour Party Conference supported unilateral nuclear disarmament with both the Transport Workers and the Engineers voting in favour, but neither major union submitted resolutions nor did either of the two leaders speak. Once passed against 'the platform', the 1973 resolution went before the NEC International Committee and stayed there. There were no further representations from the big unions and Jones later admitted that though 'it kept the issue on the agenda', there had been no push from him. It was not a priority because the resolutions of 1972 and 1973 'had no army behind them'.[67]

On the EEC policy, ideological, economic and industrial priorities reinforced each other in the early 1970s. Both Jones and Scanlon felt strongly enough to help reshape Labour Party policy in an anti-market direction and to campaign for a 'No' vote in the 1975 Referendum. But with the 'No' campaign overwhelmingly defeated, Jones and Scanlon regarded the issue as settled for the immediate future and they shifted their priorities and attention elsewhere.

FREEDOM

The emphasis that Jones, Scanlon and other union leaders laid upon trade union conceptions of freedom was marked not only in their rejection of legislative controls over incomes, but also in their emphasis on the extension of the facility for collective action alongside the provision of employment protection *vis-à-vis* the employer. As for union autonomy, this was sacrosanct – not even to be prejudiced by the provision of state finance to assist union ballots.

This perspective was conjoined with a preoccupation with the autonomy of the TUC – and in practice that of the Party also. However much Jones and Scanlon expressed their interest in Party organisation (as Jones had done) or their intention to utilise the Party policy-making machinery (as Scanlon had done), they always regarded the TUC as the primary focus of their attention. They also regarded the protection of the TUC's distinct function and role as their responsibility. The TUC was the voice of industrial labour regardless of the political loyalty of that labour and it had to preserve its direct channels to Government regardless of the political complexion of that Government. The corollary to this, of course, was that they recognised that there were limits to the manner and extent to which they could intervene in the Labour Party against its Parliamentary leadership.

The classic expression of this constraining feature of union involvement in the party came very early in the Jones–Scanlon era, in the behaviour of the unions in 1969 over the White Paper *In Place of Strife*. The fact that in the end the Labour Government retreated from its proposals became part of the mythology of omnipotent trade unionism – the 'barons' of the trade union Left using their attachment to the Labour Party to force a Government to bend to their will.

It is true that consciousness of the trade union connection and of the need to preserve the unity of 'the Movement' was revealed by dissenting MPs. Yet if we look closely at the behaviour of the unions over this issue, what is striking is not their aggression but their restraint in refraining from using the Labour Party as an instrument. In theory, a range of facilities and sanctions was open to the unions – direct threats to individual sponsored union MPs, the threat of curtailment of finance, the threat of withdrawal from the Party, the concerted mobilisation of the national institution of 'the Movement', threats of expulsion by the trade-union-dominated NEC, or support for an alternative Party Leader.

In practice, as Peter Jenkins noted, both Scanlon and Jones took the traditional position that politics was politics and trade unionism trade unionism.[68] None of these sanctions was brought into play.[69] Nor did they support attempts to recall the Party Conference or use the mechanism of a joint meeting of the TUC, PLP and NEC to concert pressure. (See also p. 181 about the relationship with sponsored MPs.)

Some of the Leftwing union leaders not on the General Council favoured more aggressive Party strategy – including Clive Jenkins of ASTMS[70] – but for most General Council members, Right and Left, the same general considerations applied. The Government was to be fought on the basis of a direct relationship. An attempt to use the Party would run counter to a range of 'rules' that governed the union-Party relationship, but most of all, it could seriously undermine the role that the TUC had cultivated for at least a quarter of a century – a direct interest group relationship with the Government of the day.

Similarly, the instigation of the Liaison Committee was not the novel intervention it was often portrayed; there was already the precedent of the National Joint Council in the 1930s. The Liaison Committee represented an attempt at accommodation rather than imposition through the block vote and the Party Conference. Jones came early to the view that such a mechanism was required and had been quietly pushing for it since 1970.[71] He saw it not only in terms of ensuring specific commitments to repeal of the Heath Government's industrial relations legislation, but more generally as a means of ensuring a dialogue of experience creating mutual understanding before Labour went into Government, and thereafter steady consultation.[72] But Jones made no attempt to seek the creation of a subcommittee structure which would in any way rival that of either the TUC or the Party (the 1930s precedent again). He was careful also to protect the TUC from decisions taken on the Liaison Committee which might pull the General Council into a 'party political' role.

A similar concern affected the behaviour of the Liaison Committee when Labour was in Government. Jones, and the NEC Left, made sure it continued in the face of a degree of Government 'forgetfulness'.[73] But on only two issues – Child Benefits and a Wealth Tax – was there a subcommittee of the Liaison Committee to formulate detailed proposals.[74] The emphasis was on dialogue and general priorities rather than detailed policy formulation, on anticipating problems rather than determining immediate Government policy. Most Government Ministers were not keen to see an expansion of the work (and potential pressure) of the Liaison Committee but neither was the TUC keen to move beyond short thematic statements. The Party's controversial 1976 programme was formulated by a procedure which was kept distinct from the Liaison Committee procedures. And, as in 1969, there was no attempt on the part of Jones and Scanlon to utilise the Party and its potential sanctions on policy issues where, on the surface at least, there was a degree of unified opposition from the TUC and the NEC.

The reluctance here had several dimensions including the substantive, if sometimes covert, differences in policy attitudes. But fundamentally, the TUC side always had a sense of its own distinctiveness and its own procedural interests.[75] The fact was that in terms of direct access and consultation, formal and informal, they had done better from this Labour Government than from any previous peacetime administration. This direct relationship to Government had expanded and deepened, through meetings between union leaders and Ministers. It was both an encouragement to a tolerant disposition on the part of the TUC and a feature which constrained the purposes and involvement of union leaders in the Liaison Committee and in the Party.

SOLIDARITY

Alongside this sense of TUC distinctiveness was another subtle set of considerations which in the period after 1974 reinforced the restraints upon the behaviour of the union leaders through the Party and the Liaison Committee. Alongside the sense of 'their show and ours' was a sense of solidarity with the Labour Party and then the Labour Government. The emotional and moral element in this could (in the party sphere no less than the industrial situation) be so great at times to produce a denial of immediate interest.

In one dimension there was an immediate and distinct change from the traditions of the past. Previous generations of union leaders had seen it as their duty to protect the Party against what they saw as disruptive and subversive elements. But as these elements were normally on the Left, and as this generation of Leftwing union leaders had themselves been on the receiving end of Cold War intolerance, they encouraged the opening up and liberalisation of the Party. It was during their phase in leadership that the 'central control regime' was virtually dismantled.[76]

 But in other respects, the new union leadership continued the protectiveness of the past. Immediately following the battle over In Place of Strife, at the consultation meeting they agreed to raise affiliation fees, and they argued 'the need for the movement to throw its weight behind the Party'.[77] In the years of Opposition there were many points at which loyalty to the Party and sensitivity to its electoral needs were dominant considerations. The 1973 Annual Conference (the last one before the General Election) might well have taken a more Leftwing position on public ownership than it did. But the Party Leader's personal appeal that the Party already had an extensive public ownership policy and that, for the sake of unity, 'minimal outstanding differences' should be resolved, met with favourable response from trade union leaders on and off the NEC.[78] Again, the fact that Jones considered himself first and foremost a trade unionist did not prevent him in 1974 arguing publicly on the eve of the second 1974 General Election that 'the election of a Labour Government is more important than a substantial wage claim'.[79]

Then again, there was the way in which the EEC issue – a critical issue on which the Transport Workers' leader felt particularly strongly – was handled so as to minimise the problem for future Party and Government unity. In 1972, the Transport Workers' delegation abstained in the vote on an EEC referendum rather than cause a possible split on a sensitive issue. And when it came to the 1975 Special Conference that rejected the Labour Government's terms of entry, there was no concerted attempt by the Leftwing union leaders to enforce a 'Party' view. For the sake of future unity, an 'agreement to differ' was respected at all levels even though this seriously hampered the referendum campaign of the anti-Marketeers.

The favourable early policy decisions of the 1974 Labour Government and the fact that that Government kept the channels of consultative communication over priorities permanently open to the unions provided a fund of goodwill in the relationship. Most union leaders, even after 1975, felt that whatever its subsequent policies, it had kept faith and had not moved away from the Movement. Subsequently, solidarity with that Government dominated the considerations of Jones and Scanlon to a degree which meant that in the end 'we were almost more concerned to keep a Labour Government in power than was the Labour Government itself'.[80] More loyal even than some Ministers.[81]

Quiet reservations expressed with concern for the Government's problems was one thing; public condemnation was another. Thus, NEC critics of the Government on the Liaison Committee were considered too strident and irresponsible and the union leaders often found themselves less critical and more defensive of the Government as a result.

Attempts from the Left on the General Council to secure a conference of trade union Executives to discuss unemployment in January 1976 were overwhelmed by a majority which included Jones and Scanlon, who were worried that such a conference would be used by the Party's political opponents without achieving anything. Indeed, at a critical juncture in March 1976, Jones and Scanlon initiated with Basnett an expression of loyalty to the Labour Government rather than side with its critics.[82]

It was the Basnett–Jones–Scanlon unity call which led to the Liaison Committee's first joint statement when Labour was in Government. This was no assertive imposition of trade union demands on Government; its title was very appropriate – *The Next Three Years and the Problem of Priorities*. At this time, Jones, Scanlon and the union leadership as a whole appeared bowed down by the weight of responsibility they were being asked to carry in representing the unions on the one hand while loyally sharing the Government's problems on the other.

DEMOCRACY

The public reaffirmation of support for intra-Party democracy and the sovereignty of the Party Conference by this new generation of union leaders fed into, fed from and helped strengthen the movement within the Party which sought to reclaim control over the Parliamentary Party. Their appearance as new union leaders coincided with a growing resentment within the unions and the Party at the way in which the Labour Government appeared to be ignoring one important conference resolution after another. The stress that these union leaders laid upon rank and file activity, participation and a more representative Parliamentary Party gave added legitimacy to the mood within the Party and appeared to be asserting the primacy of intra-Party democracy within the 'rules' of the relationship.

The new union leadership was able to give encouragement to forces which would eventually burst to the fore after they had departed. This encouragement took the form of symbolic alignments including signing the Socialist Charter and of making various statements of support for a democratic Party.[83] It took the form of supporting a resolution in 1970 which upheld the authority of the Annual Party Conference in the face of disfavour from the Party's Leader.[84] And in the period from 1968 to 1970, Jones took the extraordinary step of supporting (unsuccessfully) the redistribution of all the NEC Women's Section seats (controlled by the unions) to the Constituency parties[85] - an action explicable only as a gesture of alliance with constituency activists and a calculated rejection of the historic political packing of that section by acolytes of the Rightwing union leaders and the Parliamentary leadership.

However, alongside this process, we can discern another development as Jones and Scanlon's commitment to intra-Party democracy and Conference authority over the Parliamentary Party became inhibited and constrained. There were two influences here: a growing concern over the propriety of union control via the Party and a preoccupation with the practicality of establishing a co-operative linkage with the Parliamentary leadership.

Since 1960, the defence of the PLP 'rights' against the Conference and against union pressure had received considerable support from commentators and academics, creating an atmosphere of hostility towards political 'interference' by union leaders. Many union leaders had come to feel an increased defensiveness about the position of the Conference in relation to the PLP leadership. There is little doubt that within a short space of time Jones and Scanlon became subject to the same climate of opinion.

In addition, the felt need to seek accommodation and understanding between the industrial and political leadership led to the creation, in 1972, of the Liaison Committee which in its pursuit of agreement at the most senior level in the Movement to some extent sidelined the normal policy-making processes within the Party. Though the Liaison Committee was seen by a section of the PLP as a threat and an imposition, the initiative has to be seen in the context of an alternative procedural strategy available in 1972 – that outlined in the Tribune Group's pamphlet *Party or Puppet?*.[86] Among other things, the latter proposed that the Party Leader should be elected by the Party Conference – a move which would have given the unions a 90 per cent dominance while excluding the PLP entirely. Scanlon was uninterested; Jones was hostile. Both were aware of the public sensitivity of the issue of union control and both sought other means of coming to terms with the Parliamentary Party. At no stage up to retirement did they personally give it the slightest encouragement. So much for 'Jack Jones – Leader of the Labour Party'.[87]

There was a similar sensitivity over the handling of sponsorship. Jones's initial reaction to the performance of most of the Parliamentary Group of TGWU sponsored MPs was one of resentment at their lack of 'energy and interest'.[88] In line with the decision of the 1967 Biennial Delegate Conference, he reminded the MPs that the Conference had supported a review of the panel before the next election. But only two cases occurred during Jones' tenure of office where political positions influenced the departure of MPs from the panel, and they were both unusual. (See Chapter 9, pp. 263–4 for further discussion.) George Brown's removal was the culmination of a thirty-year feud. Reg Prentice's resignation was prior to a union regional interview and not long before he resigned from the Cabinet, totally alienated from the Labour Movement.

There were no comparable cases in the AUEW, where Scanlon did not even meet the AUEW MPs during the crisis of 1969 and no attempts were made afterwards to increase the controls over sponsorship. It is at this point that we return to their attitude towards the Campaign for Labour Party Democracy and particularly the campaign for mandatory reselection of MPs.

Jones had himself been a party activist in Coventry at a time when the local party was involved in a celebrated attempt to get rid of their Rightwing MP, Elaine Burton. He was in favour of reselection, and resented parliamentarians who viewed decision-making as 'the prerogative of a few'.[89] Given these views he would not have dreamt of opposing mandatory reselection in principle, much less organising outside his own union to stop it. This itself was another crucial part of the history of the Campaign for Labour Party Democracy in the mid-1970s. But Jones never joined the Campaign and never appeared on its platform. As between the mandatory reselection and the so-called 'Mikardo compromise' proposal of 1978[90] (the source of passionate argument among Party activists), he cared little – apart from the fact that the compromise would have brought unity while mandatory reselection brought recurrent conflict.

Hugh Scanlon shared similar priorities and, in one of the most famous incidents in Labour Party history, in 1978 he made 'a slip' with the card vote, failing to cast it in line with the delegation decision and therefore ensuring the defeat of mandatory reselection until after the General Election. His exact motives that day will always be disputed, although for years, he himself argued that he had simply made a mistake. He was in favour of some form of reselection. 'It's nothing strange to the AUEW.' But, unlike Jones, he had never been a Labour Party activist and had taken little interest in the complexities of the reselection procedures. His natural inclination in the circumstances of 1978 was to support the Mikardo compromise in order to get the argument out of the way. Compared to the great industrial and economic issues, he considered the question of reselection to be 'chicken shit'.[91]

UNITY

It might be anticipated from these developments that Jones and Scanlon would have worked to secure a major swing to the Left in the composition of the Party's Executive Committee from 1968 to 1975 and then moved to change it as they came into conflicts of priorities and policy with the NEC Left after 1975. Yet this was *not* the pattern, and here we come to one of the most revealing facets of the behaviour of Leftwing union leaders – constrained by 'rules' springing from their trade union definitions, yet still able in this sphere to operate politically, guided by their factional identities.

The shift to the Left on the floor of the Conference – a Left in which the two largest unions provided the central core – was bound also to be reflected in the composition of the NEC. But there were two very remarkable features of this development. The first was that the change in the composition of the NEC was a slow one, with a time lag, and resulted in a Left majority on the NEC only after the 1974 Conference – some six years after the shift of the floor of the Conference was first obvious. The second was that, even after the union leaders, including Jones and Scanlon, had moved apart from the NEC over industrial and economic policy, there was *no* withdrawal of political support from Left candidates for the NEC. Thus, by the time Jones and Scanlon had retired, and on the eve of Labour's electoral defeat, the Left on the NEC was at its strongest in Labour Party history.

This phenomenon, which provides a second connection between the Jones/Scanlon generation of union leaders and the constitutional crisis of 1979, is explicable only in terms of the 'rules' of the union–Party relationship and the schizophrenia to which Scanlon had alluded in 1972. Behaviour over voting for the NEC illustrated *both* their trade unionism with its inhibitions upon factional politics and their continuing socialist ideological identity.

We have already noted how concern for union industrial unity – particularly as it was reflected in elections to representative bodies – was a real inhibition on political activities constraining the behaviour of even the most ideologically committed union leaders. Thus, though political sympathies were a factor in voting behaviour and there have occasionally been political prohibitions and unseatings – particularly on the General Council – these political factors were dwarfed by trade union 'rules' and arrangements. These implied that unions be supported by size, traditional occupancy, and in line with considerations derived from industrial alliances and activity.

The Leftwing union leaders also tended to adhere to these 'rules' and arrangements when they were elected. Even the most political of the unions in terms of voting behaviour – the Engineers – tended to conform sufficiently to safeguard its relationship with other major unions after Scanlon was given a private warning by another union leader in 1968.[92] On the General Council, Jones and Scanlon were eventually instrumental in withdrawing support from leaders of smaller unions – Roy Grantham of APEX and Jack Peel of the Dyers and Bleachers (although there were unusual factors in both cases) – but otherwise they obeyed the 'rules'.

And in elections for the National Executive Committee of the Labour Party from 1967 to 1974, not one sitting tenant of the trade union section was removed. In the Women's Section, only one such unseating took place. Joan Maynard, a Leftwing trade union official and Labour Party activist, replaced Lady White who had retired from the House of Commons. Shifts had to rely on various forms of vacancy. Even in 1974, the trade union section representation of the Left was not as strong as was the Leftwing trade union vote on the floor of the Conference. (See on this also Chapter 11, p. 325 for the strength of the Right.)

So we come to the oddity that the Left was able to take over key committee positions – particularly Benn as Chairman of Home Policy in January 1975 – just at the period when their relationship with the unions was moving into a critical tension over responses to the Wilson and later Callaghan Governments. Passionate feelings were aroused during and after the volcanic confrontation between Jack Jones and Ian Mikardo at the 1975 Tribune Rally. Jones felt that he had been accused of a failure to protect working people; to this day he cannot think of it without anger. It was similar for Scanlon whose open support for the Social Contract of 1975 broke some lifetime friendships.

We have illustrated to what extent the priorities and policies of the Leftwing union leaders and the Leftwing NEC members diverged in the period 1975–8. It was widely diagnosed by close observers of the trade union scene that this marked 'the start of a deliberate attempt by union leaders to find new alliances within the Labour Party and eventually to begin remoulding the party to a shape more to their taste'.[93] Robert McKenzie at this time suggested the rebirth of a 'praetorian guard'.[94] Such a diagnosis drew from many a historical precedent, not least in the career of Ernest Bevin and the factional shift of Jack Tanner.[95] Later it came to be almost a commonplace that 'Scanlon and Jones moved to the right and became the standard bearers of Callaghan and Healey'.[96]

And yet no 'praetorian guard' emerged. Jones and Scanlon continued to cooperate and identify with the Left in NEC voting while involving themselves in divergent policies and some bitter recrimination in other spheres. The full realignment of the union leaders and the organised coup which might have undermined the Left on the NEC (and, in turn, affected the strategic position of the Campaign for Labour Party Democracy after 1979) never took place.[97] This is the fascinating and crucially significant feature of this experience. Jones, after the famous row with Mikardo, stayed on the Board of Tribune and continued to support Leftwing candidates for the NEC where there was room for political considerations to come into play. Not only were vulnerable Leftwing members of the NEC not removed, but Jones nominated and actively organised for Norman Atkinson (a Leftwing MP and ally of Mikardo) against the Secretary of State for Industry, Eric Varley, when the post of Treasurer became vacant in 1976.

Why was there no simple move to the Right? Why no reconstitution of a praetorian guard? Part of this is explicable in terms of Jones's growing suspicion of the political trajectory of some members of the PLP.[98] Much of it goes back to the scars of the Cold War and the fact that Jones and Scanlon retained a suspicion of

Atlanticism in defence policy and as a source of division in the world trade union movement. This world view had been touched very little by the domestic politics since 1974. But probably the crucial feature in all this was the personality of Jones. Throughout this period, he never lost a sense of his political identity and his distance from the Establishment. Few men are determined enough and big enough to move from a position of being labelled 'Prime Minister' to organising pensioners and distributing leaflets in the street. As he saw it, he had fought 'on the Left' and he would die 'on the Left'.

APPRAISAL

Much of the analysis and evidence presented here vindicates the position of those who have argued that the role of trade union leadership within the Labour Party is inherently limited, narrowly focused, and oriented towards defensive industrial positions. In this unique period of Labour Party history, with the two largest unions led from the Left, it was a 'trade union point of view' which guided the behaviour of Leftwing union leaders through the critical conflicts of the decade. And their Labour Party activity was heavily inhibited and constrained by the 'rules' of the relationship, thus limiting their capacity to initiate long term changes in power and policy.

Yet there is something else to be said. Any analysis has to be sensitive to the contingencies of the circumstances faced by Jones and Scanlon. And in important respects they differed greatly from those expected to accompany such an important development of Leftwing union leadership. Those who had held an optimistic scenario of Leftwing transformation of the Labour Party through the unions tended to assume that some of the most acute problems of socialist leadership – how far to represent and how far to seek to broaden the policy horizons of union members and of the potential electorate – would be alleviated by the sheer breadth and scope of the change below and the consequent closing of the gap between the working class, the activists and the leadership.

Occasionally on the Left in the late 1970s and early 1980s, there was a tendency to see the developments since 1967 – particularly the events of 1974 – in these very terms.[99] But support for a radical Socialist industrial policy was much weaker than it appeared to many on the Left of the Party[100] and the Labour Party's victory in 1974 owed much to the advance of the Liberals.[101]

Further, the process of change in the unions was, as with most historical developments, a patchy and, at times, a contradictory phenomenon which left some unions barely touched and others moving to the Right. This Right was always much stronger than it appeared to be. And there emerged some damaging disjunctions between different levels of the Movement involving vulnerable political *weakness* at branch level in the unions which was to show more clearly in 1981.

There might, in Jones' case particularly, have been some reordering of priorities between 1970 and 1974 had it not been that, on key issues which divided Left and Right in the Party, public support was not behind the Left and support at grassroots within the unions was weak. To quote Jones again, there was 'no army'. It could be said that the reluctance of these union leaders (and the past generation) to give greater weight to political education and take more interest in a collective union institution for political mobilisation was itself a contributory factor.[102] But it was simply one factor in a world where union leaders not only inherit 'rules', they inherit much of the context.

This was true in Government as well as Opposition. From 1974 to 1979, with an acceleration after 'the winter of discontent', there was a shift to the Right among the electorate on many issues.[103] It was a development bound to place additional constraints on leaders of unions whose members shared much of the political mood. And it created a tragic context for the Left-led constitutional revolt which will be examined in Chapter 7.

Nevertheless, there were three features of the behaviour of these union leaders which strengthened the ideological pressure upon the Parliamentary leadership, encouraged the movement which would flower after 1979, and sustained the position of the Left in the Party.

First, their public representation of, and identification with, the Left's positions enhanced and encouraged the activities of that Left after 1970 in its general ideological resurgence and in the preservation of traditions like unilateral nuclear disarmament. They gave private and public approval to a liberalisation of Party life in which, at this time, the Left flourished. They also gave an added legitimacy to the new claims for intra-Party democracy and Conference sovereignty – even though they and most union leaders gave it a diminishing priority. Rhetorical affirmations were not insignificant. They were a form of political action and they did have consequences for the Party.

Secondly, in Jones' case, not only was there a consistent pursuit of social justice for pensioners – part of a long history of union concern – but there was an important fusion of industrial priorities with an ideological vision of the redistribution of wealth and power. It was a vision consistent with the steadfast pursuit of industrial democracy and with the egalitarian provisions of Phase I of the incomes policy. It was also a vision embodied in the persistent pursuit of a Wealth Tax. In these fields, Jones' perspectives were always a significant pressure upon Labour Ministers.

Thirdly, and the most significant feature of their behaviour, Jones and Scanlon identified themselves with the Left long after the point of policy crisis in their relationship with that Left, long after they became very disillusioned with nationalisation, and long after they had established alternative definitions of priority. One mark of this identification in 1975 was the refusal to adopt the role of 'praetorian guard' organising against the Left. More striking still, they continued to operate in practice as *allies* of the Left. Trade union 'rules' meant that there were only narrow margins for politics in the elections for the NEC but they were crucial in allowing the union leaders to strengthen the NEC Left at a time when, playing trade union roles, they were in unhappy tension with that same NEC Left. In doing so, they also legitimised the co-operation of Leftwing trade unionists and trade union MPs on the NEC with the alternative Left political leadership.

It was, in a sense, institutionalised schizophrenia but it was a vital element in Labour Party politics and a significant link to the constitutional revolt taking place at a time when the Left on the NEC was uniquely and in some ways fortuitously strong.[104]

NOTES

1. See the very influential chapter by Perry Anderson, 'The Limits and Possibilities of Trade Union Action', *op. cit.* For an excellent analysis of the 'optimistic' and 'pessimistic' interpretations of the role of unions in Marxist sociology, see Richard Hyman, *op. cit.*

2. This is the diagnosis of the Perlman–Richter school of thought which tends to welcome the limited ambitions it identifies. See Richter, *op. cit.* The pessimistic diagnosis had also come down strongly within the ILP tradition. See for example. Barry Winter, *ILP Journal*, Summer 1987. Some of the most perceptive Marxist scholars of the Labour Party, while fully appreciating the two-sided character of trade unionism, were strongly drawn to the pessimistic diagnosis in their analyses of trade union leaders' behaviour within the Labour Party. See on this Ralph Miliband, *Parliamentary Socialism*, 1961, p. 375. Leo Panitch, 'Socialists and the Labour Party: A Reappraisal', in Ralph Miliband and John Saville (eds.), *Socialist Register*, 1979, particularly pp. 56–7.

3. Many of the reforms proposed by the Left during the Second World War were based upon this view.

4. For example the formation of the British Socialist Party. See on this Dylan Morris, *Labour or Socialism? Opposition and Dissent within the ILP, 1906–1914*, Ph.D., Manchester, 1982.

5. There is a strong emphasis on the trade union delegation as 'a transmission belt' into the Party of the demands of an aroused and mobilised working class in the strategy of the Militant Tendency. The Communist Party of Great Britain (until very recently) also took the view that the unions could be an agency for the radicalisation of the Labour Party. (This tradition is now carried on by the Communist Party of Britain and *The Morning Star.*) The Labour Left's 'optimistic' view is best represented by Ken Coates's 'Socialists and the Labour Party', in Ralph Miliband and John Saville (eds.), *Socialist Register*, 1973, pp. 155–178.

6. Tariq Ali, *The Coming British Revolution*, 1972, p. 73.

7. In contrast, some took the view that 'Only huge pressures from the outside have produced certain fissures in what appeared to be an impregnable edifice'. Tariq Ali in conversation with Ken Livingstone, '*Who's Afraid of Margaret Thatcher?*', 1984, Introduction, p. 16.

8. *Tribune*, 11/8/67 and 27/10/67.

9. Allaun pushed consistently on the NEC for a debate on Conference sovereignty in 1969 and in 1970 when the Party Leader, Harold Wilson, was defeated at the Conference on the issue. *LPACR*, 1970, pp. 180–5.

10. Allaun, Lester and Joan Maynard (elected 1972) were the only three members of the NEC to join CLPD at its formation. Eight other MPs gave 'full support' – Norman Atkinson, Lewis Carter-Jones, Eric Heffer, Neil Kinnock, Edward Milne, Stan Orme, Jim Sillars and Dennis Skinner. *Campaign for Labour Party Democracy*, Progress Report, 1973.

11. Among the first Chartists were Lawrence Daly (NUM), Jack Jones (TGWU), Dick Seabrook (USDAW) and Hugh Scanlon (AEU).

12. In 1975, for example the other four trade union leaders were Lord Allen (USDAW), David Basnett (GMWU), Lord Greene (NUR) and George Smith (UCATT). TUC General Secretary, Len Murray was *ex officio* a member.

13. Jack Jones, 'The Unions in 1967', *Tribune*, 23/12/66.

14. '"Woodcockism" meant sacrificing trade union effectiveness at the

point where it was *most* powerful – the place of work – in order to facilitate it operating where it was least influential', in talks with Ministers, Jack Jones, *Labour Weekly*, 7/9/73, p. 15.

15. These meetings began in the late 1960s in discussions of opposition to the Government's industrial relations policy. See on this Ian Mikardo, *Ian Mikardo: Back-Bencher*, 1988, pp. 175–6.
16. James Hinton, *Labour and Socialism*, 1983, pp. 196–7.
17. *Interview* with Jones, LSE, 25/1/83. A similar description was given by Scanlon, Interview, Metropole Hotel, Brighton, 2/9/84.
18. Richter, *op. cit.*, pp. 226–245.
19. Discussion in the bar of the Imperial Hotel, Blackpool, October 1972.
20. Jones's phrase in discussion with the author at the Blackpool TUC, 1981.
21. Jack Jones, *Union Man*, *op. cit.*, p. 285.
22. Whitehead, *op. cit.*, pp. 87–8 and interview with a TUC official present.
23. Harry Urwin, Deputy General Secretary of the TGWU, *TUC Congress Report*, 1974, p. 433.
24. *Economic Policy and the Cost of Living*, 1973, Para. 20.
25. *Ibid.*
26. Jones, *Union Man*, *op. cit.*, p. 284.
27. 'How Ken Gill Won and Lost His Star Rating', *The Sunday Times*, 8/9/1974. 'Murray Swings the Tide for Social Contract', *Guardian*, 5/9/1974. Also 'Pygmies, Giants and Grim Determination to be Heard', *Guardian*, 30/8/85. And interview with Scanlon, Metropolitan Hotel, Brighton, 2/9/84.
28. Jones, *Union Man*, *op.cit.*, p. 285.
29. *Ibid.*, p. 296.
30. *The Record*, September 1975.
31. Adrian Ham, *Treasury Rules*, 1981, pp. 114–8.
32. *Guardian*, 18/10/1974 and Jones, *op. cit.*, p. 288.
33. *Guardian*, 22/1/77. Since the publication of Peter Wright's *Spycatcher*, 1987, the worries of trade union leaders about an unconstitutional assault from the Right no longer look so far-fetched.
34. On this see Jones, *Union Man*, *op. cit.*, p. 297–8. Jones's view of his initiative is on pp. 296-7. Bernard Donoughue, *Prime Minister*, 1987, has Joe Haines as the initiator of the basic proposal with Jones suggesting £6 rather than £5, p. 69. But see also Benn's earlier proposal for a universal threshold and a flat rate rise, Tony Benn, *Against the Tide, Diaries 1973–76*, 1989, p. 166, Entry for 5/6/1974.
35. Both Jones and Len Murray saw the vetting proposal as simply a means of doing nothing. Jones, *op. cit.*, p. 296. Murray interviewed on BBC TV, 3/2/87.
36. Interview, Metropole Hotel, Brighton, 2/9/84.
37. *TUC Congress Report*, 1977, p. 277. Government and TUC policy was for a twelve month gap between pay claims to avoid a risk of 'catching-up' claims.
38. *Guardian*, 8/9/77 and interview, Metropole Hotel, Brighton, 2/9/84. And see *TUC Congress Report*, 1977, p. 467.
39. *TUC Congress Report*, 1978, p. 523.
40. David Coates, *Labour in Power?*, 1980, p. 57.
41. This had various definitions. See for example Brian Sedgemore, *The How and Why of Socialism*, 1977, pp. 30–31. Tony Benn dates the AES

to a paper submitted by him to the economic committee of the Cabinet in January 1975 drafted by Francis Cripps and discussed with Eric Heffer, Michael Meacher and Frances Morrell. Tony Benn, *Parliament, People and Power: Interviews with NLR*, 1982, p. 27.

42. Brian Sedgemore, *op. cit.*, p. 31.
43. *TUC Congress Report*, 1976, Composite Res. Nos. 8 and 10, pp. 638–40. These resolutions were moved in the name of a wide range of unions including AUEW (Engineering), GMWU, NUPE and NALGO (Comp. 8) and NALGO, CPSA, NUPE and COHSE (Comp. 10).
44. For example. D. Marsh and G. Locksley, 'Labour: The Dominant Force in British Politics?', in D. Marsh (ed.), *Pressure Politics: Interest Groups in Britain*, 1983, p. 78.
45. Norman Willis, then Deputy General Secretary of the TUC, in an interview with the author, July 1977. Other TUC officials have since privately expressed similar views about their acceptance of elements of the Treasury case.
46. Note the public rebuke from Jones to Alan Fisher of NUPE over his comment to the press on public expenditure cuts at the forthcoming discussion with the Government, reported in the *Guardian*, 17/7/76. For the public sector unions' campaign against the cuts, see R.H. Fryer, 'British Trade Unions and the Cuts', *Capital and Class*, Summer 1979, pp. 94–112.
47. *Guardian*, 17/7/76.
48. R. Bacon and W. A. Eltis, *Britain's Economic Problem: Too Few Producers*, 1976. The thesis did not stand up well to later scrutiny. For various criticisms, see Geoff Hodgson, *Labour at the Crossroads*, 1981, p. 148; Paul Whiteley, *The Labour Party in Crisis*, 1983, p. 141.
49. *TUC Congress Report*, 1976, p. 527.
50. *TUC Congress Report*, 1976, p. 302. The Council's five-point programme included: the Temporary Employment Subsidy to be doubled; an extra £30m for job creation schemes and an extra £55m for 35,000 training places. In addition, the TUC asked for additional funds for the NEB and import controls 'to protect hard-hit industries'.
51. *Interview* with Norman Willis, July 1977.
52. *TUC Congress Report*, 1977, p. 359.
53. Reg Prentice, quoted in John Burton, *The Trojan Horse*, 1979, p. 59. See also Barnett, *op. cit.*, p. 50 for the Ministerial 'guilt complex'.
54. Healey is reported by Benn as saying privately at this time that Basnett 'was out on his own' on this issue and when Healey had raised it with other TUC people 'they had just smirked', Benn, *Diaries, op. cit.*, p. 531.
55. *TUC Congress Report*, 1978, pp. 523–5.
56. *TUC Congress Report*, 1976, pp. 526–8.
57. Benn, *Diaries, op. cit.*, p. 85, *Minutes of Liaison Committee Meeting*, 4/1/74.
58. Benn, *Parliament, People and Power, op. cit.*, p. 30.
59. David Basnett, Geoffrey Drain (NALGO) and Clive Jenkins developed a stronger interest than either Jones or Scanlon, whose industrial location made them crucial. The three were also more committed to some of the economic aspects of the AES.
60. *State Intervention in Industry: A Workers Inquiry*, 1980, p. 20.
61. Hugh Scanlon, The Way Forward for Workers Control, IWC Pamphlet, 1968.
62. *Notes of a Party official attending a Meeting of the Liaison Committee, 25/9/*

72. Jones is reported as saying that 'the TUC has many non-Labour Party members'.

63. *The Next Three Years and into the Eighties*, Liaison Committee Statement, 1977. *Wealth Tax Working Party Report to the Liaison Committee*, 9/12/1977. *Liaison Committee Minutes*, 19/12/77.

64. Discussion with the author, TUC, Blackpool, 1983. For Healey's view, see Denis Healey, *The Time of My Life*, 1989, p. 404.

65. Beatrix Campbell, 'United We Fall', *Red Rag*, August 1980 for the impact on women's earnings of equal pay and the flat rate policy.

66. Frank Field, *Poverty and Politics*, 1982, p. 42.

67. Interview with Jones at the London School of Economics, 20 January 1983.

68. P. Jenkins, *op. cit.*, p. 136.

69. In the Hansard Society's *Paying for Politics*, July 1981, p. 24, there is a claim that at some point in 1969, Jones warned that union funds 'might be at stake', but no source is cited for this. I have been unable to confirm it and Jones vehemently denied it, Interview, 20/1/83.

70. Jenkins urged the NEC to agree to the recall of the Party Conference and to a joint meeting of the NEC and General Council.

71. Jack Jones, *Union Man*, *op. cit.*, p. 236. In interviews with the author, various other people have claimed that the conception of a Liaison Committee came from them. These included the Party's Research Officer, Terry Pitt, and the then Head of the TUC Economic Department, David Lea.

72. *Ibid.*, p. 237.

73. *Ibid.*, p. 282. See also Mikardo, *op. cit.*, pp. 198–9 for his role in pushing for it to meet.

74. The case of the prolonged impasse over Wealth Tax is dealt with earlier in this chapter, p. 175 – Jones ensured that the Liaison Committee pursued the matter. The Committee's handling of the Child Benefit scheme arose out of embarrassing leaks that the Cabinet was about to abandon it. Barbara Castle, the ex-Social Services Secretary, pushed via the TUC for a Liaison Committee Working Party which set down a compromise timetable for the scheme's introduction. On this see Field, *op. cit.*, pp. 44–45 and 154–7 and Barbara Castle, *The Castle Diaries 1974–76*, 1980, 668 n. and p. 737.

75. Len Murray always saw the Neddy Six meetings with the Government as fundamentally more important than those at the Liaison Committee. Their anxiety about being pulled too far into a politial alignment was one factor which led them to prior agreement on what each was going to say at key meetings of the Liaison Committee. Interview with Lord Murray, 26/3/87.

76. On this see Eric Shaw, *op. cit.*, Chapter 8, pp. 154–84.

77. *Guardian*, 4/3/70.

78. Confidential Memo from Harold Wilson to the NEC, 28/9/73.

79. *Guardian*, 2/9/74.

80. Interview with Jones, LSE, 25/1/1983.

81. Jones, *op. cit.*, p. 309.

82. *Ibid.*, p. 304. The statement followed a rebellion by the Parliamentary Left over proposed cuts in public expenditure.

83. For example, Jones, *LPACR*, 1970, p. 176 and Scanlon, *LPACR*, 1971, Appendix Report of the Special Conference on the Common Market, p. 342.

84. *LPACR*, 1970, Composite Res. No. 16, p. 180.
85. See on this LPACR, 1968, pp. 228–9. He was supporting a Leftwing delegate from the AUEW, Norman Dinning.
86. Frank Allaun, Ian Mikardo, Jim Sillars, *Labour: Party or Puppet?*, 1972.
87. Headline, *Sunday Times* feature article, 1/9/74.
88. Jones, *Union Man, op. cit.*, p. 194.
89. See *LPACR*, 1970, p. 176 for Jones's criticism of the way in which MPs defined their role in relation to the Party – and their 'snobbish' attitude.
90. In 1977, replying to a tactically inept Composite Resolution No. 29 from Brighton Kempton CLP, Ian Mikardo for the NEC secured a remittance by pledging that the NEC would submit its own constitution amendments the following year, *LPACR*, 1977, p. 324. A Working Party chaired by Bryan Stanley of the POEU which included Ian Mikardo and Moss Evans of the TGWU came up with a proposal to provide a reselection procedure but leave it to the management committee of each CLP to decide whether to activate it or not. This formula became known as 'The Mikardo Compromise'.
91. Interview with the author, Metropole Hotel, Brighton, 2/9/84.
92. Interview with the author on a train, Stalybridge to York, 1970.
93. 'Britain's Government: The Role of Union Power', Special Report by Eric Jacobs, *Sunday Times*, 23/4/78.
94. Robert McKenzie, author of the major work *British Political Parties, op. cit.*, argued this point after giving a paper to a meeting of the Political Studies Association, Nottingham, 1976 Notes of the author.
95. Jack Tanner was a Leftwing President of the AEU who eventually became a formative influence in creating the Rightwing machine in that union before he retired in 1954.
96. For example. Tariq Ali and Quintin Hoare, 'Remaking the Labour Party', *New Left Review*, No. 132, March/April 1982, p. 73, n. 29.
97. The Left majority was vulnerable to a coup led by the TGWU leadership in the period from 1975–8. Lena Jeger and Judith Hart would have been the most difficult to move because they had cross-factional support, but a withdrawal of TGWU backing would have been damaging. Norman Atkinson could have been defeated and John Forrester, Joan Maynard and Renee Short could have been removed upon the decision of the TGWU. Short was protected to some extent by TGWU sponsorship, and there would have been a strong reaction from sections of the TGWU Left, but a determined Jones could have done it. Benn's *Diaries, op. cit.* has a report of Jones being restrained within the union in an attempt to ditch Maynard (p. 615) but Jones strongly denies any such move – Telephone conversation with the author, 15/10/89. A realignment of Jones and Scanlon would have been enormously encouraging to the Right in the unions and other sections including the Labour Clubs ('natural Healey territory' as Les Huckfield, their Leftwing NEC representative described it to the author in 1979). See also n. 7. 15.
98. 'The Macdonalds, the Snowdens, the Jimmy Thomas's are lurking around. Their names don't need to be spelt out.' Jack Jones to TGWU Biennial Conference, 1975, *The Record*, August 1975. The Lib–Lab pact was a parliamentary arrangement which did not threaten the 'integrity' of the Party. Jones would have been flatly opposed to any broader agreement or coalition which sacrificed Labour's independence. Discussion with the author, Labour Party Conference, Brighton, 2/10/89.

99. Compare my analysis with Tony Benn, *Parliament, People and Power: Agenda of a Free Society*, 1982, 'there was this industrial militancy and an extraordinary socialist upsurge and they lost control of policymaking on the national executive', pp. 35–6.

100. See *State Intervention in Industry, op. cit.*, p. 31, where 1974 radicalism is compared to 1945 with a 'groundswell of militant support' for a 'radical interpretation' of the Manifesto amounting to 'popular pressure'. But though there was some evidence of a shift to the Left among the *decreasing* number of 'Labour identifiers', the movement in favour of more nationalisation was only from 33 to 50 per cent even in this group. Ivor Crewe, Jim Alt and Bo Särlvik, *The Erosion of Partisanship, op. cit.*, 1976, pp. 22–3. And Labour private polls at this time indicated the very low priority of Labour's industrial policy and nationalisation among Labour voters and trade unionists. Michael Hadfield, *The House the Left Built*, 1978, p. 228.

101. The crucial political shift in 1974 involved a rise in the Liberal vote and a greater drop in the Conservative vote than Labour's, allowing Labour to win more seats. Ivor Crewe, Bo Särlvik and James Alt, 'The Why and How of the February Voting', *New Society*, 12/9/74.

102. Jones and Scanlon considered it to be the Party's responsibility for political education (and Jones had encouraged this via the Simpson Committee in 1967). The two largest unions had in this period low political levies and spent a very low proportion of this on political education and political communication. (In 1974 and election year it was 1.8 per cent Transport Workers, 1.1 per cent Engineers.) Larry Whitty, *Trade Union Political Finances and the Labour Party*, evidence to Fabian Society Study Group on Labour Party Organisation, 1979, Table V. The GMWU spent 3.2 per cent.

103. By 1979, for the first time since 1963, more people favoured privatisation than further nationalisation – a shift affecting all classes (nationalisation 17 per cent, No change 43 per cent, and privatisation 40 per cent). Anthony Heath, Roger Jowell and John Curtice, *How Britain Votes, op. cit.*, pp. 132–3. Support for more nationalisation and for more spending on the social services fell among Labour identifiers. Belief that the unions had 'too much power' rose among the same group. Ivor Crewe, cited in Dick Leonard, 'Labour and the Voters', David Lipsey and Dick Leonard, *The Socialist Agenda*, 1981, p. 48. By 1979, there was only a minority public support for a wealth tax (49–51 per cent) and for trade union representation on boards of major companies (45–55 per cent). S. E. Finer, *The Changing British Party System 1945-1979*, 1980, p. 126. Support for income redistribution fell from 56 to 55 per cent in 1974–9. Heath, Jowell and Curtice, *op. cit.*, p. 134.

104. See n. 7. 15.

7

Trade union leadership, democracy and the constitutional revolt, 1979 to 1982

DIAGNOSIS

A trade union revolt?

After the fall of every Labour Government, there has been some reaction at the Party Conference to the disappointments of Office. In both the early 1930s and the early 1970s, this involved a reassertion of the principle of intra-party democracy. It could be anticipated that a similar development would occur after 1979. But what was unprecedented about the implosion of 1979–82 was the extent to which the issue of democracy and power in the party became dominant almost to the point of making substantive policy issues secondary. And the form of the revolt – an attempt to seek major changes in the constitution of the Party so as to bring the Parliamentary Party under the control of the Labour Party outside the House – was unique in its force and effectiveness.

A strong theme in the literature on the role of the unions in this revolt emphasises their initiating role and their new assertiveness. Ben Pimlott, the editor of an authoritative study, has argued consistently that the changes of 1980 came about because of 'a union decision to move into Labour Party politics more decisively than ever before, and to throw their weight heavily against the Parliamentary leadership'.[1] It was the unions which 'instigated a series of constitutional changes'.[2] A Marxist analyst of the Bennite movement, Alan Freeman, also saw changes in the unions as crucial, albeit at rank and file level: 'This time many Labour voters were unwilling to accept cosmetic policy changes. Now they wanted to ... prevent a repeat of the last Labour Government. Through their unions, they began to seek ways of doing so.'[3] Hilary Wainwright has a similar focus on the unions' 'assertion ... of political power'. 'The unions' concern, or rather the concern of their active members, in supporting the constitutional reforms was to make it impossible for the Parliamentary Party to act as "a party in itself".'[4]

Yet the evidence suggests that this focus on the dynamic role of the unions is considerably overstated – indeed, in key respects, misplaced. The novel initiating feature of union behaviour in this period concerns political mobilisation and party organisation (see Chapters 15 and 16). In this chapter, with an eye on the priorities and 'rules' operating at this time, we will examine the contribution of the unions – particularly the union leaders – to the development of constitutional reform.

Trade union post-mortem

The first thing to be said is that, in a sense, nothing happens at the Party Conference without the unions because their votes dominate all policy decisions and elections for the NEC. Of itself this tells us little in any particular case and it can be used as a catch-all explanation which misses what is significant and what is not. As we have indicated in the previous section, union participation in Conference decisions can involve marked differences of priority. Thus, any approach to understanding the role of union leaders on matters of party control after 1979 has to come to terms with their priorities in response to the 1974–9 Governments.

Unquestionably, in many of the unions – particularly those on the Left and centre-left – there was a build up of resentment towards some ex-Ministers. 'The winter of discontent' was a traumatic period which provoked a lament in the unions about Treasury manipulators,[5] and about the unwillingness of Labour's leaders to heed the advice of their union allies over the 5 per cent policy and over the cuts in public expenditure. These were particularly badly received in the public sector unions, with NUPE at the forefront.

On the Left there was also a more general feeling that the Labour Government had been a failure, lacking the will to pursue radical commitments and being much too ready to succumb to pressure from forces hostile to the Movement. Accusations of 'betrayal' went hand in hand with criticism of some Labour Ministers as aloof and more in tune with the politics of the Liberals than of Socialism. The case for making a priority of new rules of control and accountability appeared immeasurably strengthened.

However, by no means everybody shared this perspective. There were some on the Right of the unions who thought that the Government 'did a good job'[6] – and, more significantly, there was a sub-current stretching well across the political spectrum of the unions which felt deeply uneasy, even guilty, about the fact that union actions in the winter of 1978–9 had contributed to the loss of support for the Labour Government. Bitter recriminations went on within and between unions as well as between unions and ex-Ministers.

The mixture of experiences and memories did not all lead to punishment, counter-weight and control. Alongside what were seen as the failures, disappointments and retreats were the memories of access and procedural understandings. There was an acknowledgement of the major gains made under the Wilson Governments of 1974–6 and, even in the last eighteen months of Office, still a sense of shared values and social priorities with most Labour Ministers. There was certainly more to this last phase of Labour Government than 'wage restraint buttressed by general statements of aspiration'.[7] There were signs of the benefits of an economic upturn and small but significant continuing legislative gains (Chapter 5, p. 126). Further, for reasons explained in the previous chapter, most trade union leaders did not experience the gap between the Party's economic/industrial policy and Government policy in the acute terms felt by the Left in the PLP, NEC and constituencies.

This experience took on a changing definition as the forecasts of unemployment 'shooting up to three million' under the Conservatives proved all too accurate; union leaders could compare this wistfully with the falling unemployment of 1979 and the commitment to a 3 per cent growth rate in the Labour Manifesto of that year. Tax concessions were made to the wealthy. One round of public expenditure cuts followed another. Privatisation began its long incremental course. Government legislation began to eat away at the employment and union rights secured by the Labour Government. As this contrast between the Thatcher and Callaghan Governments began to grow, and there was no sign of a 'U'-turn, so senior union leaders, Left and Right of the Party, became increasingly anxious to restore unity and prepare the Party for Office as soon as possible.

Initially, however, a strong Leftwing element in the unions was prepared to work closely with allies in the Party to secure constitutional changes to make the Parliamentary Leadership more accountable. Within this element, there was a minority group of Leftwing union leaders on the General Council (of which ACTT, ASLEF, the FBU and TASS formed the core). These union leaders were more inclined to see the Labour Government performance in ideological terms, to accept a more root and branch critique of its record and to use the institutions of the Labour Movement to seek greater control over the Parliamentary leadership.[8] Growing in influence and in organisation,[9] for a period after 1979, particularly when linked to a powerful Leftwing grouping in the TGWU, they were a force to be reckoned with on the General Council, albeit never its majority or its senior leaders.

But it remained the case in 1979, as it had been for much of the Labour Party's history, that a majority of union leaders were associated with the Right and centre-Right of the Party. They retained a sense of 'rules' which inhibited intervention within the province of the PLP (including electing the Leader) and considered it improper to use the Party constitution to establish full Conference (i.e. union) control over the Parliamentary leadership. And although appeals to party democracy always had some resonance in this large grouping, they had less force than in the 1950s. There were various causes of this change. Their influence at the conference was more uncertain, the idea of conference sovereignty had lost some legitimacy – particularly as it reflected many weaknesses of composition and procedure – and the Party–TUC Liaison Committee was seen as a more important conduit of policy and forum of consultation. In any case, the Campaign for Labour Party Democracy was seen as a front for the Left, and to be fought accordingly.

These major differences on Left and Right impeded any co-ordinated move in the unions to intervene collectively, let alone to increase their control over the Party. Indeed, if we consider the acute divisions between the unions on the constitutional issues (and most key policy positions), it is difficult to make much sense of 'a union decision' to do anything. Most were, in the end, simply pulled into factional alignments based on general ideological positions.[10]

My sounding of constituency party opinion at this time, and the visual evidence of their responses during the debates, suggest an overwhelming majority of

CLPs in favour of all three constitutional changes. With this in mind, we must note that in 1980 the proposal for bringing the Manifesto under NEC control was defeated by 3,625,000 votes to 3,508,000 and that the proposal for widening the franchise for the Leadership was carried by only 3,609,000 votes to 3,511,000, both of them indicating a union majority against. Even on mandatory reselection, carried by 3,798,000 to 3,341,000, the union majority could only have been very slim and, by my calculations, most likely did not exist.

In any case, the constitutional crisis of 1979 to 1982 was a complex affair and, as we shall indicate, not really explicable in terms of one source, one cause, or one change in behaviour patterns. Further, it is best understood not in terms of a sudden shift in attitudes or a swift seizure of power after 1979, but as the product of a long process beginning in the late 1960s. The coming together of the three constitutional proposals in 1980 masks considerable differences in their gestation and depth of support. Mandatory reselection was near a majority in 1977, long before any post-election reaction, but was thwarted by a range of mishaps and manœuvres.[11]

There is little doubt that the experience of the Labour Government was a catalyst to some attitudinal change at leadership level in the unions, but not as much as might be thought, and the change in union attitudes to the Party was brought out, focused and enhanced by movements taking place in the constituencies and on the NEC, rather than being itself the initiating source of the constitutional revolt.

CLP and NEC initiatives

As we have seen, the constitutional revolt began in 1967 with a campaign from the constituency parties. Its defeat and the general move to the Right in the Labour Government was to result in an exodus of Left activists (including most of the Trotskyist Left) from the Labour Party. However, at the same time, within that section of the Labour Left which stayed in the Party, 1968 was, at local level, what John Gyford has described as the beginning of the Labour Left's 'long march through the institutions and constitution of the Labour Party'.[12]

In 1970, veteran CLP workers were responsible for a Conference resolution reaffirming its own authority over policy. And in 1973, long-serving Party members created the Campaign for Labour Party Democracy.[13] It grew steadily, strengthened in the late 1970s by an infusion of new radical young activists but not by any great wave of manual worker support.[14] The Campaign fed off the anger within the Party over public expenditure cuts, and Reg Prentice's defection, to the point where its resolutions dominated the agendas of the Party Conference. Tactically skilled and growing in its knowledge of Party processes, it was able to contest the tactics of Party managers. In the CLPs it began to draw support from a wide range of age-groups and political positions. In the unions, it aimed at multiple levels of union activity in an attempt to mandate union leadership and bind its conference delegations. In May 1980, the Campaign for Labour Party Democracy joined in a broad Leftwing alliance, the Rank and File Mobilising Committee, to push for the three constitutional amendments.

Coinciding with the development of this Campaign, the Left, led by Tony

Benn (who had taken up the theme of Party democracy in 1971), was strengthening its hold over the NEC, the Party's administrative authority. The Left's majority was provided by the CLP's section, by fortuitous additional representation allowed in the 1970s,[15] and by voting patterns in the union section, the women's section and the Treasurership, most of which dated back to the changes of the Jones/Scanlon era.

This aspect of the Left's influence must not be underestimated. On all previous occasions in Opposition, when the Left had produced constitutional amendments to limit the power of the PLP, the NEC had successfully aided the fight to fend them off. On this occasion, for the first time in Party history, the NEC put itself at the service of the insurrection, using its procedural rights to facilitate the placing of reselection and election of the Party Leadership on the agenda of 1979, to structure the 1980 Conference sequence of votes on the election of the Leadership, and to enable the Special Conference voting procedures in 1981 to produce a clear result.

THE TRADE UNION ROLE

As for the role of the third institutional element directly involved – the trade unions – the first point that is clear is that there was no agreed and consistent drive among union leaders to secure a new constitutional settlement after 1979. The initiatives all came from the political wing and had to be responded to. By the eve of the 1979 Labour Party Conference, it was clear that a major drive was under way from CLPD – a drive which large numbers of constituency parties and the NEC majority were supporting. By contrast, *not a single resolution or amendment was submitted by the unions relating to the three constitutional issues.*

However, in the next two years, there were four ways in which the unions contributed to the victory of constitutional reform after 1979: a diffusion of power in the two largest unions allowed some key decisions to be influenced by an alternative Leftwing union leadership which was relatively unaffected by the norms of General Council membership; there emerged in influential positions in 1979, for different reasons, two hitherto 'outsider unions' less influenced by General Council traditions; for reasons which had little to do with union votes, a Leftwing leader of a relatively small union was able to play a central role in the Commission of Enquiry, and the rule of 'solidarity' was defined by different unions on the Right in ways which involved varying responses to the constitutional reforms, thus enhancing a damaging fragmentation on that wing of the Movement.

The diffusion of power

The exercise of the block vote often has the effect of misleading commentators by obscuring the size of minorities and exaggerating the personal power of the senior official. The forces at work within union governments will be explored in Chapters 10 and 11 but here we must note that union leaders have sometimes been less capable of getting their way in the union delegation than the possession of a block vote might indicate.

For years, the most striking example of this had been the Engineers Union, but even so, in 1979, there was a good reason (a new Rightwing President, Terry Duffy, and a Rightwing-dominated Executive Committee) why the political Right in the Party confidently expected a shift of the Engineers' delegation voting for the National Executive Committee and the first stages of a clear-out of the Left. Yet it did not happen.

Voting for the Engineers' delegation was from the branches – a different procedure from the postal ballot election of the national officers. In both 1979 and 1980, the delegation had a knife-edge Leftwing majority (with links to the CLPD). By establishing and insisting on prior mandates of their National Committee, the new leadership was able to cast the union's vote against all three reform proposals in 1980 after voting the other way on two of them in 1979. But on crucial votes for the NEC, in spite of elaborate preparation, the delegation vote went to the Left on those NEC positions where no inter-union agreement was involved. Only with a change in the Engineers' constitution in 1981, such that the delegation was elected at Divisional level, was a Rightwing majority secured and a change in the political alignment of the NEC brought about.

Thus it was that in a union where the President, General Secretary and virtually the whole Executive Committee were opposed to the constitutional changes, the union cast its votes for an NEC in 1979 and 1980 which was in the forefront of seeking those constitutional changes.

In this period also, a new diffusion of power affected other unions. This was reflected in linkages from the political to the industrial wing below the level of the General Secretary (or President in the case of the NUM).[16] The result on constitutional issues was an input into union decision-making by allies of the Campaign for Labour Party Democracy who instigated resolutions, built up mandates and co-ordinated tactics to a degree that weakened the position of the senior officer. An unusually influential role was played in this period by activists and less senior union officers who did not share the same perspective as senior officers regarding the Liaison Committee, were not as sensitive to the special responsibilities of the PLP leadership or to calls for the autonomy of the Party, and were much more firmly committed to a factional political victory.

Not only is the period from 1979 to 1981 marked by many examples of unions voting at the Party Conference on procedural and policy questions in ways that ran counter to the known wishes of the unions' most senior leader (see Chapter 10, p. 309), but a broad consensus of major union leaders who sought to persuade the NEC to prevent the constitutional changes being voted on at the 1979 Labour Party Conference failed to achieve their objective.[17]

At the centre of the unions undergoing a new pattern of internal power relations was the largest, the Transport and General Workers (see Chapter 10, pp. 301–05 for a full analysis). In this union, there was a crucial interplay between the changing perspectives of the union leader and the powerful constraints on his leadership.

Moss Evans, who replaced Jack Jones as General Secretary in 1978, shared most of the first-phase ideological perspectives of his predecessor. He was a committed supporter of the Left of the Party and in 1978 spoke from the platform of the newly-formed Labour Coordinating Committee. Also, like Jones, he was a believer in a participatory union membership and in the dispersal of power. He saw no reason why leadership in the Party should not operate in a similar style. He had a predisposition, as did Jones, to encourage intra-party democracy – a predisposition which had hardened as a result of his experience of dealing with some of the Labour Ministers during 'the winter of discontent'. Thus, in 1979, he was, in general, sympathetic to the overall thrust of the Left's constitution case. But as a member of the General Council, and of a group of senior union leaders, including Basnett and Jenkins, who were concerned at the financial and organisational drift of the Party, he shared a growing urgency about the need to stabilise the situation. Over reselection, he had favoured the Mikado compromise in 1978. He now favoured broad party agreement on the method of electing the Leader rather than a Left factional victory. And he had serious doubts about the wisdom of sole Executive control over the Manifesto which would exclude the Parliamentary leadership.

But he was not in a position to impose his wishes on the Executive Committee or the union's delegation. A resolution of the 1979 Biennial Delegate Conference of his union put the union four-square behind mandatory reselection and its commitment to 'the extension of the democratic process of our Labour Movement'[18] was used to bind the General Secretary at union meetings where a forceful role was played by the Deputy General Secretary, Alex Kitson, and a lay Leftwing leader, Brian Nicholson. As a result, all attempts at compromise in casting the union's vote were defeated.

Within the confines of the Commission of Enquiry into Party Organisation, there was more room for manœuvre. Evans did consider himself so bound by the decision of his union on mandatory re-selection that his vote swung the Commission on this issue.[19] But he considered himself less bound on the other two questions and it was Evans' own proposal for an electoral college (giving the PLP 50 per cent of the votes), which would both elect the Leadership and supervise the Manifesto, which at one stage carried a 7/6 majority on the Commission.[20] Ultimately, such narrow majorities were of little use and all the three constitutional matters were thrust back to the delegations at the 1980 Party Conference. Here Evans was again tied. The TGWU rejected all compromise and voted for each of the three constitutional reforms. In 1981, they voted at the Special Party Conference to give the PLP only 30 per cent.

The 'outsider' unions

An important contributing factor to the success of the constitutional revolt after 1979 was the increased involvement within the Party during this period of two unions which had not previously played a major role in Party developments. Both in their various ways had been, in the past, 'outsider' unions in the hierarchy of the General Council and the NEC – the National Union of Public Employees and the Association of Scientific, Technical and Managerial Staffs. Of the larger unions (over 100,000 members) NUPE and ASTMS with the TGWU were the only unions to vote consistently for all three constitutional changes at the Conferences of 1979 and 1980.

The rise of the National Union of Public Employees, a rise which accelerated in the 1970s, had been met by a mixture of sectional and political hostility by other General Council union leaders. Its leadership in this period, Alan Fisher and Bernard Dix, had still not achieved the status within the Labour Party commensurate with their union's size. The union had a tradition of Leftwing political trade unionism. It had been deeply involved in the first public sector union demonstrations against the 1974-9 Labour Government and equally deeply involved in 'the winter of discontent'. These events left a bitter legacy of mutual recrimination between the union and ex-Labour Ministers.

By coincidence, Fisher was Chairman of the TUC from 1980 to 1981 and publicly supportive of the Campaign for Labour Party Democracy. Bernard Dix, an unusually assertive and creative second-line union leader, was heavily involved with the Party Left as he had been in the past and critical of the limited political character of trade union activities. Dix, in fact, virtually gave the CLPD organisation *carte blanche* to operate from the union's research department. Further, NUPE's experience of public expenditure cuts led them to seek a much higher political profile within the Labour Party and affiliation shot up from 150,000 in 1974 to 600,000 by 1980 – a product both of membership growth and conscious political commitment. Without these additional votes in 1980, the constitutional change on the election of the Leadership would have been defeated.

Clive Jenkins, leader of the union ASTMS, had been kept out of senior positions in the Party and the TUC for many years as a result of various political, industrial, personal and social resentments. In the late 1970s, he had finally managed to move to a position of greater prominence on the General Council, linking for a while in a grouping with David Basnett, Moss Evans and Geofrey Drain of NALGO.

Working with Basnett and Evans, he also took a leading role in the development of TULV and was an active Chairman of the Commission Panel which dealt with Labour Party finance. Although his union ranked only eleventh in size in the Labour Party, he was, in 1979, very much at the centre of union discussions on the future of the Party. But he remained a maverick and untraditional figure with no history of great respect for the Movement's established customs. At various stages in the past he had been prepared to adopt a more prominent political role than was usual[21] and although in 1979 and particularly in 1980 he was in favour of consensual solutions to the constitutional crisis, he found no difficulty in supporting proposals for constitutional innovation at the Commission of Enquiry or in supporting the three amendments when they were put to the Party Conference in those years.

The intervention of Keys

This unusual prominence of a union leader whose affiliation was markedly smaller than the biggest unions (and also suspect in its size) was rivalled by the sudden and remarkable emergence of the leader of the Society of Graphical and Allied Trades. SOGAT, with only 50,000 affiliated members, ranked as low as twenty-third in size. It had never to this point even nominated for a place on Labour's NEC. The way these things normally happen, it would not have been expected to be central to political decision-making.

Bill Keys, its General Secretary, was a member of the General Council's Left Group and a supporter of the campaign for intra-Party democracy. Highly committed to a more political trade unionism,[22] he was an important figure in the development of TULV. Because of his sustained interest, but mainly because he was willing to give both time and facilities to TULV activity, he became a central figure in TULV liaison with the Party. Efficient, innovative and respected, he, in effect, pushed his way into the quintet of union leaders who made up the TULV component of the 1980 Commission of Enquiry. Thus he was able to tip the balance of that group decisively in favour of accommodating the reformers. Like Evans and Jenkins, he was seeking a broader consensual accommodation but his union, like ASTMS, voted solidly for all the proposals.

The fragmentation of the Right

Looking at the issue of election of the Leader, what is striking is the way in which, unusually for the Left, it managed to evolve a degree of unity in action behind the CLPD and then, in May 1980, the Rank and File Mobilising Committee, while the Right was divided to an extraordinary degree. Mandatory reselection had such a breadth of support by the late 1970s that, given NEC support and the appropriate procedural facility, it was probably unstoppable. But reform of the election of the Leader could have been averted and could certainly have been implemented in ways more advantageous to the Parliamentary Party had the Right been able to secure a measure of agreement on what it wanted, communicate this to its union allies and 'police' the united strategy.

But the Right was heavily affected by conflicts over how to respond to the call for reform of leadership elections. In the PLP, the conflict became acrimonious and personalised and then complicated by threats of defection from the Party. There was an initial split in 1979 between (to put it briefly and rather crudely) accommodationists, die-hards and radicals favouring One Member One Vote (OMOV). In June 1980, the Leader and Deputy Leader, having registered their opposition to change, switched at the Commission to accommodation over an Electoral College in an effort to build understandings with the unions (see p. 198). But other die-hards subsequently switched to OMOV as their total opposition became untenable. Between the Conference of 1980, when the principle was agreed, and the Special Conference of 1981, which would agree the rules and procedures, the Shadow Cabinet was heavily split, first in an election for a new Leader, then over the 50/25/25 proposals to be placed before the Special Conference.[23] Further divisions emerged after TULV leaders judged that a stipulation concerning the involvement of levypayers was impracticable (see Chapter 15, p. 503). As in the summer, the different positions became issues of principle and generated much bitterness.

These splits in the PLP both undermined the capacity to mobilise in the unions but were also to some extent a product of attitudes *within* the unions. In these crisis conditions the unions, by tradition, were expected to stabilise the Party situation. But this generation of union leaders faced major problems in playing such a role. There was first the problem that in all previous crises the union leadership had been able to work with or through a majority on the NEC, but in this period, the NEC was under the control of the Left and deeply hostile to the interventions of union leaders. In this situation (and given a wide range of organisational and financial difficulties facing the Party), there was no agreement on the Right of the unions over what coalition of forces ought to provide the stability. The GMWU leadership favoured preserving the consensual activities of TULV, the AUEW favoured a more robust Rightwing factional alliance which would deal with the Left. These divisions over political strategy were exacerbated by industrial tensions following the Isle of Grain dispute.

The role of the GMWU leadership under David Basnett was crucial to these developments. He had never favoured the union being locked into the trade union Right; he was also seeking to build a working alliance with Leftwing union leaders Evans, Jenkins and Keys on financial and organisational issues in which the Engineers' leader, Duffy, was relatively uninterested. In addition, Basnett's own views had slowly begun to change on the question of electing the Leader, following the experience of the Treasury and its Ministers under the Labour Government and in the light of the arguments being advanced from the Left, from Clive Jenkins and from his Research Officer, Larry Whitty.

Although Basnett was in favour of the Mikardo compromise on reselection and opposed to the NEC having sole control of the Manifesto under the existing party structure, he had come gradually to accept that the present process of electing the Leader was not 'necessarily defensible'.[24] But any change in the method of electing the Leader brought into question many other considerations, some of them far-reaching in their implications. Only if the change was thought through to all its ramifications, and only if broad constitutional agreement were reached, should the leadership electoral method be changed.[25]

No such agreement was reached and in the end the General and Municipal Workers voted against all three constitutional changes at the 1980 conference, as they had done in 1979. Basnett, meanwhile, had voted *against the status quo* on the Commission. The effect of his vote for the Evans electoral college compromise proposal (strongly supported by Keys and Jenkins) was to have major reverberations within the Right. It encouraged a similar shift by the Leader and Deputy Leader, Callaghan and Foot, and their ally, Duffy, causing a devastating shock for some sections of the PLP. This in turn led to a further split within the PLP Right and further uncertainty amongst the Rightwing union leaders.

This uncertainty on the Right made them both vulnerable to mistakes and curiously weak in securing any coordinated mobilisation. One example of this weakness – history-making in its consequence – concerned the failure to monitor developments within the union delegations at the 1980 Conference. At one crucial stage, the leaders of the Boilermakers union, confident at having established the union's policy, simply left the delegation to its own devices while they got on with other things. Members of the delegation, linked to the Rank and File Mobilising Committee, bided their time and then pushed for a reconsideration of the union's position on electing the Leader. The result was a reversal of policy and a shift in the entire Conference alignment in favour of the principle. Without it there would probably have been no reform.

The sudden resignation of Callaghan produced new divisions within the unions, not only in the contest for Leader, but over whether there should be an 'interim' Leadership rather than a contest.[26] Further, the three-way split in the Shadow Cabinet over proposals for the Special Conference, and the plans for defection being laid among the Social Democrats had, together, the effect of leaving the individual unions virtually to their own devices in establishing their policies for the Special Conference. So, in isolation, and with little Leftwing prompting, the Rightwing-led USDAW moved to a formula of 40 per cent for the affiliated organisations (mainly the unions) and 30 per cent each for the PLP and CLPs – a formula which appears to have evolved purely out of the politics of their Executive Committee meeting.[27]

The Campaign for Labour Party Democracy was able to line up other union delegations behind this formula thus binding in the Shopworkers' support. At the same time, other possible alternatives were being undermined by the position of the Engineers. Again without any liaison between the trade union and political Right, the Engineers' leadership had gone their own way by instigating a National Committee resolution which forbade them to vote for a formula which gave the PLP less than 51 per cent of the vote. Presumably they hoped to give the PLP as large a majority as possible, but it meant, in practice, that without a gigantic row in the delegation, they could not vote for the only alternative formula that was viable at the Special Conference – one that gave the PLP just 50 per cent. So the PLP ended up with 30 per cent! It was a tactical blunder of awesome proportions, understandable only in terms of a Right which could not agree on what it wanted to happen in the Party or even in some cases (see Chapter 8) whether it wanted to be in the Party to get it.

Priorities and the Peace of Bishop's Stortford

As the Party crisis moved into its third year, the leadership of the largest unions became preoccupied with action to stabilise the situation and assist the Party to win the next election. They had continuing difficulty in agreeing what the elements of this stability should be but it came about through two processes which contrasted markedly with the position in 1979 and 1980. The union Left – indeed the Left as a whole – began to fragment, while the Right became more unified. Both were the product of a reconsideration of priorities in the face of Benn's leadership campaign.

Some of the Leftwing union leaders who had given active support to the constitutional change, like Bill Keys, expressed their strong opposition to Benn's candidature for the Deputy Leadership as unnecessarily divisive. Clive Jenkins did the same. Alex Kitson, an influential supporter of CLPD on the NEC and for a period in 1981 Acting General Secretary of the TGWU, actively organised against Benn. Even among some on the 'hard' Left on the General Council there were initial misgivings expressed in private meetings with Benn although, in the end, they moved behind his campaign (and it is from this time that Benn began to be invited to meetings of TUC's Left group). But by November 1981, they, too, were strongly counselling unity and a halt to Leadership elections.

Meanwhile, alarmed by the temper and purpose of Benn's campaign, the

GMWU and UCW leaders, Basnett and Jackson, who had distanced themselves from the St Ermin's group of Rightwing union leaders, now moved with the AUEW to secure a change in the composition of the NEC and a halt to the fourteen-year rise of the Left.

The background to these changes was the clear evidence from by-elections, opinion polls and union ballots of the contrast between what was going on at the Party Conference and what was happening to working class opinion and to its political allegiance. The defecting Social Democrats, in alliance with the Liberals, were proving a real threat to the Labour Party in a traditional Labour seat at Warrington, in a marginal at Croydon, and in a Conservative seat at Crosby. Three by-election candidates, all from positions Left of centre in the Labour Party, did substantially worse than expected.

At the same time, the message from grass-roots activists in the soundings and ballots in the Transport Workers' and Public Employees' unions (see Chapter 11, pp. 339 and 341) did not indicate any major groundswell for a new Left initiative – as Benn himself virtually acknowledged.[28] Indeed, the clearest message, after the Party Conference of 1981, appeared to be that the Party should cease its internal upheavals and get on with the job of representing working people. The union leadership was now being heavily pressured from below to 'do something about the mess in the Labour Party' – a mess for which the Left was getting the blame.[29]

The culmination of this change of mood was the meeting of the NEC and TULV held at Bishop's Stortford on 5 and 6 January 1982, a meeting after which, in a sense, a peace was declared focused on two understandings. There would be no further constitutional changes, implying also no attempt to reverse the changes of 1980 and 1981. And there would be no new contest for the Leadership or Deputy Leadership. Some thought that there was an understanding that there would be no organisational action taken against Militant and other Trotskyist groups; others did not. But for the moment what was significant was that the constitutional and Leadership crisis was over.

As to how far the pressure from union leaders secured this stabilisation, this is more problematic than it might seem. Benn had never regarded the views of union leaders – however politically sympathetic they might be – as decisive. His aim, since 1972, had been to encourage rank and file Leftwing movements which would not be dependent upon national trade union leadership. Union leaders had called for a halt to many things at many different times – usually to little avail. Benn's campaign for the leadership was based upon the active support of capable organisers who had experience of guiding the constitutional amendments and had proved time after time their ability to mobilise below the level of General Secretary, sometimes in the face of unremitting hostility

But his own group of organisers had also begun to shift their position slowly after the Party Conference. Many of them had drawn pessimistic lessons from recent events – particularly their failure to win in the union branches. Some – including the shrewdest organiser of the Campaign for Labour Party Democracy, Vladimir Derer – believed that Benn's victories in the TGWU, ASTMS and several other unions were very fragile and might well be turned into a devastating defeat in 1982. Their own trade union and local Labour Party experience was beginning to give them a very different perspective on working class opinion from that held by the Trotskyist groups. These latter were quietly ditched by the Bennite inner group and the CLPD leadership.

Thus, in the final weeks of December 1981, majorities in one group after another of erstwhile 'Bennite' cadres and supporters began to urge caution on the constitutional issues and a halt to Leadership elections.

Benn has since indicated that he had no intention of seeking a second contest for the Deputy Leadership but could not give advance commitments for fear of encouraging the Right to counter-attack on the constitutional issue.[30] It was on this point that the senior union leaders may have been decisive. In early 1982, the new consensus among these leaders involved as strong a determination to stop any attempt at a constitutional counter-attack from the Right as it did to stop Benn and his allies. It was, in fact, on these terms that the Peace of Bishop's Stortford conference turned into an affirmation of 'absolute and total agreement on the need for unity and co-operation'.[31]

Trade unions and the constitutional revolt: an overview

An analysis of the constitutional revolt which emphasises the initiative and assertiveness of the unions has to be qualified to take account of their lack of input into the 1979 agenda, the probability that in 1980 a majority of union votes were cast against all the constitutional proposals, and the evidence that a majority of the union leaders were heavily preoccupied with stabilising the situation as quickly as possible.

The initial dynamism was provided by a movement of CLP activists allied to a section of the NEC Left which had been growing since 1967. Without support on the NEC, that movement would always have been handicapped in managing the procedural obstacles of Conference procedure. It was vital, therefore, that in 1979 the NEC was controlled by a Leftwing majority who assisted the reformers and were remarkably successful in fending off pressures from the major union leaders.

There was a new balance of forces within the unions which also assisted reform. This balance of forces was influenced by resentment against Labour Government policy and particularly 'Treasury power'. But the main factors undermining the old 'rules', which protected the autonomy of the PLP and restricted union control, were (i) the emergence of lay and second rank union leaders who did not fully share General Council orthodoxy about the relationship, (ii) the unusually prominent role of three Leftwing union leaderships prepared initially to support or accommodate the reformers, and (iii) the strategy of the GMWU in seeking to build cross-factional support on a broad range of organisational issues, precipitating a chain reaction which exacerbated the tactical divisions on the Right.

Leftwing union leaders Evans, Jenkins and Keys always tempered their support for constitutional change with a concern that the changes be as consensual as possible. By 1980, this concern was accentuated by anxieties over the stability and viability of the Party. On matters of Party finance, they were unimpressed with the NEC Left's stewardship and not prepared to use financial leverage to secure increased control over the Parliamentary leadership. Just the opposite. (See on this Chapter 16, pp. 520–1.) Such priorities brought them into conflict with the NEC Left and then with the Bennite Campaign for the Deputy Leadership. In this, they were joined in 1981 by another section of the Leftwing union leadership which had been prepared in 1979–80 to give more full-hearted support to CLPD's campaign. Subsequently, by the end of 1981, a broad consensus of opinion stretching across the political spectrum had emerged in favour of 'peace'. It was the breadth of this support, together with the evidence of growing hostility to constitutional reform among trade unionists, not the fiat of union leaders, which produced the Peace of Bishop's Stortford.

NOTES

1. 'Trade Unions and the Second Coming of CND', in Pimlott and Cook, *op. cit.*, p. 231. Also 'How Labour Went Unilateral', *New Statesman*, 8/10/82.
2. Ben Pimlott, Week in Review: Opinion, *Sunday Times*, 21/8/88.
3. Alan Freeman, *The Benn Heresy*, 1982, p. 110.
4. Wainright, *op. cit.*, p. 51.
5. This view was, of course, shared by many in the Labour Government who struggled with the Treasury 'bounce' (as the point was put to me by political staff in Downing Street in 1978). See on this Barnett, *op. cit.*, p. 21 re figure 'fudging' and Joe Haines, *The Politics of Power*, 1977, pp. 27–32. And see Donoughue, *op. cit.*, pp. 66–7 re incomes policy, p. 94 re PSBR, and pp. 99–100 re the Statement of Intent, giving examples of contesting the Treasury's position. See also Healey, *op. cit.*, pp. 376, 381 and 401.
6. Terry Duffy, President of the AUEW, LPACR, 1979, p. 202.
7. Coates, *Labour in Power?*, *op. cit.*, p. 59.
8. At the 1979 TUC, ASLEF leaders attempted to use the TUC 'to ensure that the next Labour Government carries out the policy of the Labour Party as decided by Labour Party Conferences' (Res. 118). The Resolution was withdrawn under pressure. In 1980, a counter-resolution from the EMA which argued that the purpose of the TUC was to represent 'the workers by hand or brain as a whole' was passed by the Congress. *TUC Congress Report*, 1980, p. 569.
9. In 1980, the General Council Left Group appointed a Secretary – Alan Meale, then an officer of ASLEF – and its meetings became more formalised. Union leaders understood to have attended the Left Group meetings in the 1979–81 period included Ray Buckton (ASLEF), Ken Cameron (FBU), Ken Gill (TASS), Walter Greendale (TGWU), George Guy (NUSMW), Doug Grieve (TWU), Bill Keys (SOGAT), Bill Maddox (NUDBT), Mick McGahey (NUM), Alan Sapper (ACCT), Jim Slater (NU Seamen) and Arthur Scargill (NUM).
10. Although the ability of Campaign for Labour Party Democracy supporters in the unions to mandate their reluctant leadership was a crucial element in the changes, it was still the case that most voting was strongly correlated with the factional alignment of union leaders. Fourteen Leftwing-led unions voted in favour of all three constitutional changes at each of the 1979 and 1980 Conferences. Twelve Rightwing-led unions voted against all three in those years. These commitments were very durable. In 1984, in the argument over OMOV, supporters of

the reform proposals were overwhelming on the Right while opponents were overwhelming on the Left. Of the unions of any significant size, only the NUR had shifted general alignment.

11. On this see L. Minkin, *The Labour Party Conference*, *op. cit.*, p. 355.
12. John Gyford, *The New Urban Left: Origins, Style and Strategy*, Town Planning Discussion Paper No. 38, 1983, p. 7. Arguably the first step at national level was taken in October 1967 in the NEC elections which replaced Callaghan and Crossman by Allaun and Lester (see Chapter 6, p. 161).
13. CLPD began in 1973 after an initiative by long-time Labour Party activists Brenda Brett and Ron Heisler following a Troyskyist penetration of Socialist Charter of which Brett was Secretary. They brought with them Stephen Boddington and Vladimir and Vera Derar who from 1974 for years afterwards organised the campaign from their home in Golders Green. The appeal to attend the Campaign's first public meeting at the 1973 Conference was made by 30 activists most of whom had been around on the Labour Left for many years. Subsequently most of the activity was carried out by new young activists including Victor Schonfield as Treasurer and Pete Willsman who was eventually elected to the Party Conference Arrangements Committee. Others who played a leading role from 1975 to 1981 were Francis Prideaux, Chris Mullin, Reg Race, Andy Harris, Jon Lansman, John Bloxham, Walter Wolfgang, Heather Gaebler, Mandy Moore, Frances Morrell and Ann Pettifor. Patrick Seyd, *The Rise and Fall of the Labour Left*, 1987, p. 88.
14. In some areas, including Lincoln and Sheffield, there was a limited infusion of working class trade unionists. See Seyd, *op. cit.*, p. 47, but this was not widespread nor very deep.
15. In 1972, the Left on the NEC was strengthened by allowing the Young Socialists to be represented (ironically on a proposal from Shirley Williams, *NEC Minutes*, 28/4/71). In 1978, they were strengthened by allowing the Labour Clubs to affiliate. The Clubs sent Les Huckfield on to the NEC mainly because nobody else was organising there. When they did, in 1981, he lost his seat.
16. No senior General Council union leader was part of the CLPD organisation or (as far as I know) spoke on its platforms. The early support came from Joan Maynard, then an official of the Agricultural Workers and Ernie Roberts, then Assistant General Secretary of the Engineers. The only union General Secretary to become a 'Vice-President' was Alan Sapper of the small union ACTT. Other Vice-Presidents in 1979 were Walter Greendale, the lay Transport Workers' representative on the General Council, Emlyn Williams, President of the Welsh Miners and Bob Wright, Assistant General Secretary of the Engineers.
17. *NEC Org. Sub. Minutes*, 10/9/79.
18. *Report of T & GW Biennial Delegate Conference*, 1979, Minute 40, p. 27.
19. There were thirteen members of the Commission, Evans voted with the six from the NEC.
20. The five trade union representatives, Basnett, Duffy, Evans, Jenkins and Keys, plus the Leader and Deputy Leader voted in favour.
21. In 1969, when Clive Jenkins sought to convene a special conference of the Labour Party, and to convene a special meeting of the NEC and the TUC, to use the Party to oppose *In Place of Strife*, his calls were not supported by other union leaders.
22. He eventually became Co-ordinator of Trade Unionists for Labour. See

Chapters 17 and 18.

23. At a Shadow Cabinet meeting on 11/11/80, the Electoral College proposal of 50(PLP):25:25 (with just trade union political levypayers participating) – known as the Hattersley compromise – was carried by 8 votes to 7.

24. Interview, House of Lords, 30/4/87.

25. *Ibid*. The proposal that the GMWU eventually came up with was based on the reconstruction of the National Council of Labour which would have a much broader composition including representation from the Party's regional conferences, local authority groups and the PLP. This 61-member body would decide the Manifesto and elect (later changed to 'confirm' the PLP election of) the Leadership. The unions would have 12 members and were to *decrease* their representation at the Annual Conference. The proposal was such a break with tradition that (apart from Clive Jenkins) it gained no senior support. At the Commission, it failed to secure a seconder.

26. Basnett and Jenkins favoured an interim Leadership under Michael Foot. This caused tension with some on the Right in the Engineers, Steelworkers and Railwaymens unions. *Guardian*, 16/10/80. *The Times*, 27/10/80.

27. Interview with Diana Jeuda, USDAW Research officer, 4/3/1982.

28. 'In the non-politically conscious unions and amongst the non-politically conscious members of unions there is a hell of a lot of work to be done... We cannot have a movement too far ahead of the people it represents', Tony Benn, *Morning Star*, 1/10/81.

29. At the time of the Bishop's Stortford Conference, the opinion of trade unionists was becoming increasingly hostile to the Left on inner party questions as well as some of the Left's key policy issues. Asked who was to blame for Labour's troubles, only 2 per cent blamed the record of the Wilson and Callaghan Governments, while 46 per cent blamed Benn and the Labour Left and a further 7 per cent blamed Trotskyists, Communists and Marxists. Only 29 per cent favoured Benn continuing his campaign to reform the Labour Party while 60 per cent were opposed. MORI for *World in Action*, 18/1/82.

30. Interview with the author, 5/9/86.

31. *Labour Party–TULV Accord Summary*, 8/1/82.

8

Rightwing Social Democracy, trade unionism and the Labour Party

In spite of the extraordinary and embittered crisis which split the SDP in 1988 and which has (at least for the moment) marginalised the Centre's challenge to Labour, there can be no doubt that the defection of the Social Democrats in 1981 was the most serious and the most damaging in Labour Party history.

Behind the multiple personal routes to defection and the many different points which individual defectors saw as unacceptable features of 'the new Labour Party' lay a more fundamental estrangement. It is true that there were novel and threatening institutional reforms which they desperately opposed and deeply resented. Deeply held commitments to nuclear defence and to the EEC were also under concerted challenge. In the constituencies, a new Left – aggressive, confident, suspicious and unforgiving – was putting some of them under mounting pressure. On the NEC there was a uniquely powerful Leftwing grouping which appeared impervious to counter-attack. These constituted a web of reasons for defection.

But it was the 'rules' of the Labour Movement which provided the frustrating context of their growing disenchantment and it was the trade union role in society and in the Party which formed a crucial sub-text of their departure. Only when they came to shape their own public policies towards the unions as the SDP would it become clear just how far this alienation had gone.

The roots of this estrangement can be traced back to the latter years of the 1950s. Difficulties that did surface at that time could be ridden because, as has been shown, there was so much else about Labour's traditions, the post-war settlement and 1950s revisionism that formed the basis of agreement. But, in the next twenty years, this agreement was severely undermined as a broad crisis of revisionist social democracy stimulated and coincided with a crisis over power within the Party.

The central economic assumption of the Gaitskellites in the 1950s – that steady assured economic growth would be sufficient to facilitate social objectives through the mechanism of increased public expenditure – proved to be very shaky. Optimism about economic management turned to pessimism in the context of persistent inflation, diminishing international competitiveness and repetitive problems with the balance of payments. Social engineering via the state encountered new difficulties and produced new dilemmas.

The political terrain also took on a shape unanticipated in the 1950s. A new trade union militancy emerged, led from the Left. A new political configuration was established within the Party. A new Rightwing Conservatism made its appearance. The politics of ideology, class and industrial conflict, thought to have been buried by the post-war consensus, suddenly emerged as a dominating element in political life. Outside the Labour Party, a reaction to this new polarisation could be seen, strengthening the Liberals in what had already become a rebirth of third party politics.

Faced with a reappraisal of means and ends, the majority of ex-Gaitskellite revisionists met the new political problems with an uneasy mixture of moderation, adaptation and pragmatism. The early death of two outstanding intellectual leaders, Allan Flanders in 1974 and Tony Crosland in 1977, left Roy Jenkins as the senior ex-Gaitskellite. Flanders and Crosland had sought to preserve their socialist values and Labour's special link with the organised working class but to reorder priorities and reaffirm distinctive institutional responsibilities – and passed on this legacy. But Jenkins was much readier to shed the socialist ascription, some of the main commitments[1] and ultimately the fundamental values and 'rules' of the Labour Movement.

As a group on the now more consciously Social Democratic (rather than Socialist) Right made its continuing reappraisal, so 'the trade union question' began to loom large as the source of problems and as an obstacle to their solution. The shifting, halting, uncertain movement which would eventually lead to defection and to an Alliance with the Liberals was affected in the first instance by the militant activities of Labour's Left. It was shaped also by the blandishments of the Liberal leadership on the one hand and the critique from the New Right of British politics on the other. But the pull and push of these pressures traversed time and time again the terrain of trade unionism, its defects and culpabilities

The fetters on production

Awareness of Britain's relative economic decline led Social Democrats to a series of economic questions, each of which involved trade unionism. How to overcome poor productivity and achieve a measure of international competitiveness? How to keep income rises in line with productivity increases in order to sustain growth without inflation? And how to overcome the regular disruption of economic activity produced by the clash of interests in industry?

It was in seeking answers to these questions that, as the political journalist, Peter Jenkins, put it later, 'The Old Order' – the post-war consensus – 'crumbled' and the first crack occurred in its weakest area – namely over the role expected of trade unions.[2] And it came not under a Conservative Government but from the Labour Government of 1964 to 1970 with its statutory incomes policy and its attempt at legislative reform of industrial relations – *In Place of Strife*. Where once Gaitskell and Crosland had urged that legislation should be kept out of industrial relations, now a significant section of Labour Ministers became quietly sympathetic to a range of permanent legislative solutions to industrial problems.

Constrained by a newly assertive trade unionism within the Labour Party in the early 1970s, the ex-Labour Ministers were unable to pursue either the industrial relations reforms or the detailed incomes policy commitments that they favoured. It was a time of great frustration marked by the first defection – that of Dick Taverne in 1972 and the formation of the Democratic Labour Party in Lincoln.

Subsequently, the experience of Government from 1974 to 1979 reinforced their misgivings about the industrial role of the unions and about union political leverage through the Labour Party. The loose and general social contract appeared in 1974–5 to be incapable of dealing with escalating wage claims and spiralling inflation. For a period, 1975–8, the TUC's co-operation brought a degree of control but the accommodation was always predicated, on the union side, on the assumption of a return to free collective bargaining. This assumption was not shared by some of Labour's Ministers for whom it now represented a dated perspective inconsistent with the pursuit of policies conducive to the prosperity of the economy.

In particular, the critique of the damage done under free collective bargaining was now extended to its impact on unemployment. There was 'a failure', said the Manifesto Group of Rightwing Labour MPs in 1977, to distinguish 'the unemployment which was due to deficient demand', and 'unemployment caused by organised labour using its bargaining power to push wages beyond what the economy could stand'.[3]

The culpability of trade unions went further. In the heyday of revisionism, Crosland and Flanders had both argued that it was management which bore the primary responsibility for industrial success. Now another view was growing – that a major problem of British industry – perhaps *the* major problem – was the assertive power of unions. Power in industry had shifted too far in their direction. Management, by contrast, was too weak, too defensive and too prone to believe that they would lose any confrontation.[4]

Not until after the defection did a comprehensive and pointed Social Democratic critique of the unions surface to public view, but on Labour's Right, long before then, it was beginning to be accepted that the national cultural weaknesses of conservatism and resistance to change were particularly acute in the unions. In 1979 it was sympathetic journalists who conveyed much of what this section of the PLP was really thinking. That it was the unions who were leading the Labour Government down the path of a 'half-hearted statism' where intervention was, more often than not, directed towards the subsidy of the inefficient.[5] The unions, with their present attitudes and procedures, were a drag on industrial modernisation.

Further, the union pressure for reversal of Conservative Government industrial relations legislation and for public ownership locked the political system into a repetitive cycle of industrial change. The discontinuity involved in the interest-based see-saw of two-party politics was itself a major problem in terms of encouraging industrial productivity.[6] Thus, for some on the Right, the problem of how the Labour Party was to lever itself free of the constraints of trade unionism became linked with a second question of how to achieve a realignment of British politics and a change in the adversarial two-party system

The problem of democracy

The problem of trade union attitudes and activities in industry and their behaviour within the Labour Party was seen as closely related to the internal failure of trade union democracy. Ever since the rise of the Left in the late 1960s, the Right in the PLP had become increasingly concerned at the way the unions conducted their internal affairs. The protocol of the Party's relationship with the unions prevented these concerns from being articulated with the ferocity that they were to take on after 1981, but there was a quietly growing contempt for systems of branch delegate representation. Mass meetings taking decisions on industrial action were seen as anachronistic and susceptible to manipulation by unrepresentative minorities of Leftwing activists. Out of the procedures of trade union democracy came union policies which it was said were too militant and too obsessed with class conflict. Through their methods of leadership recruitment came also 'the new Barons'[7] who were increasingly out of touch with their members.

'There is more than enough evidence', declared the Manifesto Group in 1977, 'that in any system those with power tend to use it to their advantage.'[8] Perhaps so, but what was noticeable was that this diagnosis was used much more with reference to the trade unions than to other organisations and institutions. Where once the autonomy of trade unions from governmental interference was seen as a central tenet of liberal pluralism, as well as a fundamental value of the Labour Movement, so now some on the Right of the PLP began to look for ways in which the State might seek to influence the form, as well as financially assist the development of, the democratic procedures of the unions.

In the 1950s and 1960s, Flanders had argued that the unions had an institutional need for a bureaucracy to protect the union against temporary fluctuations in membership opinion.[9] Now Social Democrats began to pick up a new agenda and looked for ways through which they could permanently increase the immediacy of membership influence. The answer they came to was the institution of more ballots and some began to be insistent that *only* postal ballots (with government assistance towards the cost) would avoid the dangers to which trade union democracy was prone. It was even said that society had a 'right to demand' a more representative trade union leadership – a step towards Government claiming a right to regulate.[10]

The right to regulate on behalf of the public interest was made all the more pressing by the political role of the unions as 'an estate of the realm' within a set of neo-corporatist arrangements. These arrangements aroused mixed feelings on the Right of the Parliamentary Party. There were defectors as well as loyalists who continued to argue, during and after the defection, that a Government which endeavoured to govern with consent *had* to evolve such procedures and to involve the unions and their members as social partners.[11] But another view also began to surface. 'Corporatism', with its emphasis on consensus and consultation, produced delay and a lack of decisiveness. This was itself a cause of Britain's decline.[12] Further, it took power away from the democratic Parliament to place it in the hands of those – particularly in the unions – who were often themselves not democratically organised. For Britain's revival, the domination of 'corpor-atism' must be rejected and democracy allowed to flourish.[13]

A similar point could, of course, be made about the institutions of capital involved in neo-corporate arrangements – as Tony Benn often noted – but the experiences of Labour Governments since the late 1960s had convinced many on the Right that a clear and present danger lay in the ability of trade unions to bend Governments to their will over industrial relations policy. In this sense, the retreat over In Place of Strife marked something of a watershed – 'a psychological blow to the whole political system', one of the defectors was to label it later.[14]

In the ten years from 1969 to 1979, the rumbling concern on the Right of the Labour Party about trade union power over Government moved to a climax. It was now said that the Callaghan Government was the third 'to have been destroyed, essentially, by the trade unions'.[15] It was an exaggeration, but it raised a spectre which haunted the Social Democrats

The problem of freedom

They were haunted also by the growing accusation that they were allied to a new authoritarianism. Personal Freedom had been one of the trinity of revisionist values in the 1950s, meriting one of the earliest Party documents of the Gaitskell leadership.[16] The priority in the late 1950s became the removal of legal restraints in connection with a range of personal moral decisions.[17] This turned into one of the few clear success stories of the 1964–70 Labour Government.

In the industrial sphere there was always an unresolved problem of reconciling this individual-focused and negative concept of freedom – absence of restraint – with trade union collectivism and the culture that sustained it. It did not often surface, in part because trade unionists resented interference from the political wing in their industrial affairs, in part because there was some sharing of collectivist perspectives in 'rejecting the view that a good society could be composed out of a mass of unrelated self-seeking individuals'.[18] One strand of revisionism always defined freedom in positive terms as 'something that needs to be enlarged'[19] rather than as simply the absence of restraint. Such a perspective could more readily appreciate the benefits to the individual of collective capacity in the face of the power of the employers.

The problems of these two concepts of liberty became accentuated for the Right of the Party in the 1970s as they discussed the electoral liabilities of various labour institutions. They were now under sustained intellectual criticism from the Conservative Right rediscovering its market and economic libertarian tradi-tions. F.A. Hayek's The Road to Serfdom, first published to an unsympathetic audience in 1944, was reprinted twice in 1976 and pushed with much more vigour by a Conservative leadership anxious to point out the unanticipated and unpleasant consequences of collectivism.[20] A new and introspective awareness grew on the Right of the Labour Party of the trade-off between equality and liberty – a trade-off the older revisionist leaders, 'children of the successes of war-time collectivism', had not fully appreciated. The worry went wider than trade unionism and embraced 'the existence in some sectors of a single employer, the state, and of the sort of problems that arise in small working class towns where there is only one landlord, the local council',[21] but central to the problem was the behaviour of the unions. They had been given new facilities through the 1974 and 1976 Acts, which made it legal for employers who were party to a closed shop agreement to refuse to employ or to dismiss employees who refused to join a trade union (except on grounds of religious conviction). Some highly publicised cases of 'closed-shop victimisation' were brought to light by the press.[22] And a protracted struggle broke out within the Labour Government over the application of the legislation to the National Union of Journalists.[23] In the Cabinet, Roy Jenkins and Shirley Williams were prominent in contesting this aspect of the legislation.[24]

At the same time, the Social Democrats found themselves one of the targets of the vitriolic attack launched by Paul Johnson on trade union collectivism as a totalitarian threat to freedom. In 1972, in a speech critical of the Industrial Relations Act, Brian Walden on Labour's Right had defended the closed shop and collectivist values with 'no weasel words'.[25] Now, in 1977, Johnson described that great dividing line as between 'those who put their trust in the individual and those who insisted on the moral righteousness of the collective', and he found an anxious sensitivity on Labour's Right.[26] He was, initially, strongly criticised by Peter Jenkins for his overstatements and his pessimism but it was acknowledged that the question of freedom was now high on the agenda of politics all over Europe with the ethical credentials of Socialism under scrutiny.[27] If it was for the moment 'unproven that the Labour Party will be incapable of redressing the balance between collectivism and individualism',[28] that it required redressing was not in doubt.[29]

The brooding shadow

As with all changes of belief, there were many nuances and individual differences of focus to the diagnosis on the Right of the Parliamentary Party, and some key points relating to the unions were to be contested up to and long after the defection of 1981. And even if the new diagnosis of the unions was broadly accepted, it did not automatically lead to a path out of the Labour Party. Indeed, it could be argued that the problems of democracy and freedom could best be tackled in a realistic partnership with union leaders and the TUC. Ultimately, that is precisely what did happen. But for the moment this seemed to be out of the question, as the experience of the new pattern of power in the 1970s engendered continuing aggravation in a political grouping used to being in the ascendancy.

'On all too many issues', declared the pioneer defector, Dick Taverne, in 1972, 'the hands may be the hands of Harold Wilson but the voice is the voice of Hugh Scanlon.'[30] As we have seen, such views tended dramatically to overstate the power of union leaders and to ignore the extent to which Scanlon and Jones played by the old 'rules' of the relationship. But the unions and the claims of 'solidarity' were now perceived by many Labour Front Benchers as a brooding, oppressive shadow whose approval was as undesirable as it was deeply resented.[31]

One crucial event which appeared to confirm the constraint was the final leadership ballot of 1976. While both Crosland and Jenkins were decisively beaten, the victory went to 'the keeper of the cloth cap',[32] James Callaghan, and the Deputy Leadership to the 'prisoner's friend'[33] for the unions in the Cabinet, Michael Foot. The road to power and a very different style of Labour leadership now seemed permanently closed for Roy Jenkins and those who shared his perspective. Jenkins moved to a new post as President of the Commission of the EEC. David Marquand, his adviser, joined him in 1977.[34] His supporters and allies within the PLP continued to experience deep frustration within the 'rules' of the Labour Movement.

Whereas for the Left the 1974–9 Government was one in which there was too little respect for what the unions were claiming, for the Right it was a Government where too often they would 'wander through the Lobby, as is our way, in a reluctant position'.[35] If the Liaison Committee was increasingly seen by some on the NEC Left as a means by which the unions co-operated with a Labour Government in disowning radical policies, for many on the Right of the PLP, it remained a disturbing new arrangement – a new way of institutionalising union power and a potential threat to Parliamentary accountability.[36] For the Left, the period after 1976 was one in which the forces of capital reasserted their control over the Labour Government; for the Right it continued to be a Government tied in a connection to the unions by which they were at the beck and call of vested interests and of further excessive demands for public expenditure commitments, while being unable to firm up a certain and lasting arrangement over industrial productivity and inflation.

This assertive trade union presence within the Labour Party was experienced by the Social Democrats not only in the obligations of policy but as an expression of class, style, and culture. The preoccupation with manual worker trade unionism was seen by some on the intellectual Right as a rejection of *their* worth to the Party. There had developed 'a strange, inward-looking proletarianism' whose proponents imagined that the Movement could 'rely exclusively on the strong right arm of the working class'.[37] The 'working class culturalism' that accompanied this proletarianism was epitomised by the cultivated style of 'mindless incivility' adopted by the MP Dennis Skinner, now 'rewarded with a seat on the National Executive'.[38]

The Bill of Rights

The problem of the brooding shadow for the Social Democrats was made most painfully clear in a conflict which received little publicity at the time and was mainly fought in private in the subcommittee of the NEC. It concerned the proposal for a Bill of Rights. The proposal, supported for years by the Liberals, was given new life by Lord Scarman in December 1974.[39] His call was taken up by other legal experts[40] and also by Lord Hailsham, who saw the Bill of Rights as a potential check against the 'elective dictatorship' of a Labour Government.[41] It became increasingly acceptable to a section of the Right in the Labour Party, concerned as in the past with personal freedom from the State but now as much concerned, as were others, at the threat to freedom thought to be posed from the Left by trade union practices, including the closed shop. The Home Secretary, Roy Jenkins, was known to be sympathetic[42] (although, at the time, the Home Office management itself was under attack within the Party for illiberalities over immigration procedures and the operation of the Prevention of Terrorism Act[43]).

By no means everybody was carried along with the intellectual tide. There was a strong reaction to the idea of passing power from a democratically elected parliament to the judiciary – particularly the British judiciary given its record and social composition. Professor Harry Street noted the past failure of the judiciary to fashion the common law in such as way as to protect the citizen.[44] Professor John Griffiths, a scathing critic of the judges, called for 'hard block-letter specific reforms' to deal with specific problems.[45] Within the Labour Party, the Right was divided on the issue, with Roy Hattersley among those strongly opposed. Even among Home Office Ministers, a division emerged. Alex Lyon, particularly, expressed reservations about giving the English judiciary more power.[46]

But Labour's NEC Subcommittee on Human Rights was heavily dominated by sympathisers with a Bill of Rights (most of whom were to be part of the defection of 1981).[47] Shirley Williams was in the Chair.

They produced, in February 1976, a discussion document, *Charter of Human Rights*, which affirmed 'the need to tip the scales away from public and private concentration of power back in favour of the individual'. While they rejected the idea of a Bill of Rights which would be entrenched in the constitution and amendable only by a fixed and substantial majority, they committed themselves to enacting a Charter of Human Rights – in practice the incorporation of rights guaranteed by the European Convention of Human Rights into British law. Existing and future statutes should be interpreted by the courts so as to enforce conformity with the Charter. Parliament would retain sovereignty and would have the right to override judicial interpretation of the Charter, but Governments, it was argued, would be slow to introduce such legislation as the Charter would have 'special authority'.

Though the NEC gave agreement for the publication of the discussion document, it was made clear in the 1976 Party Programme that 'We will not finally commit ourselves to this step until and unless we are satisfied that it has the support of the Party'.[48] Such support was not obviously forthcoming in resolutions to the Party Conferences in 1976 and 1977.[49] At the TUC, alarm bells were ringing at the potential implications, particularly as the *Sunday Times* had welcomed the Charter specifically as a means of dealing with the victims of trade union legislation,[50] and for this reason, support for the idea of a Bill of Rights was growing within the Conservative Party.[51]

In January 1977, the TUC moved into the discussion with a weighty memo prepared by the Head of Industrial Relations, John Monks.[52] This pointed to the contrast between the Charter which emphasised positive rights and the 'immunities' which were central to the present 'highly acceptable framework of British labour law'. It drew attention also to the dangers from the judiciary, given 'their social background' and 'mistrust of collective action'. And it expressed doubts specifically in relation to Labour Party education policy and crucially on issues relating to the right to join or not to join a trade union. Though it simply counselled caution, in effect the TUC decisively thrust its weight against the subcommittee proposals. About this time, Paul Johnson launched one of his blistering epistles on collectivism and 'the brute power of the group', putting more pressure on Williams and Labour's Right.[53]

In the House of Lords, the Liberal Lord Wade now produced a Bill to incorporate the European Convention into British law. This was referred to a Select Committee of the House of Lords which invited evidence. Determined to follow through on their discussion document, the majority on the Human Rights subcommittee prepared their evidence with a Home Office legal adviser to Roy Jenkins, Anthony Lester, as the draftee.[54] Their position was fiercely contested by a minority of the subcommittee

On the Home Policy Committee, however, the majority and minority position was reversed. Shirley Williams found herself virtually without allies from the trade unionists and completely outvoted by the Left led by Michael Foot. In a major snub to the subcommittee, the Home Policy Committee decided not to submit any evidence to the House of Lords Select Committee but to ask the subcommittee to come forward with a package of specific measures.[55]

Thus, the pro-Bill of Rights faction found itself in what appeared to be a political cul-de-sac. The TUC had spoken; its word had been conveyed to the NEC. The NEC with its Leftwing majority agreed that there was a potential threat to party policy and to trade unionism from court intervention. This was decisive. But to change the composition of the NEC required trade union co-operation. Catch 22. Furious at the rebuff, and at their own imprisonment within Labour's power structure, the subcommittee majority broke all precedents and sent their memorandum to the House of Lords under their own names.[56] A portent of things to come

The winter of discontent

The last months of the Callaghan Government left deep emotional scars on the leading participants. For many on Labour's Right, it was an embittering and an embarrassing time exemplifying all they found unappealing and unwelcoming about their structural attachment to the unions. An incomes policy which could not be negotiated to an agreement. Economic dislocation that could not be halted. A union leadership seen as feeble and irresponsible. Violent picketing. 'Rubbish in the streets, disrupted hospitals, closed schools, in some places the dead unburied.'[57] And at the end of it, a shift in public opinion and the Labour Government's asset – that it and it alone could come to an understanding with the unions – badly damaged.[58] Among Labour supporters, there was strong agreement with some of the Conservatives' proposals in relation to strikes and the unions. Among trade unionists, there was a similar measure of support.[59]

The mixture of feelings that the 'winter' left behind included guild. The 5 per cent policy had been arbitrary rather than consultative. Warnings from loyal union allies had been ignored. The General Election had been badly mistimed. Alongside this was also resentment at union industrial behaviour and the inadequate response of the TUC – defensive, willing to reject, but incapable of rising to the need for a new incomes policy agreement. There was resentment also that the guilt feelings produced in conflicts with the unions occurred even where the ex-Ministers felt they were in the right.[60]

Indeed, there was some feeling of righteous indignation. Here were Ministers under constant accusations of 'selling out' and deviating from principles. But was not militant trade unionism in defence of a sectional interest itself in practice a deviation from the objective of social justice? Could any egalitarian Government deal with low pay without starting a war of differentials? Could the unemployed be assisted without a fraternal concern for the level of inflation? Could improvements in living standards be sustained if unions were prepared to defend antiquated work practices?[61]

There was, some considered, 'an underlying tension between the economic aims of trade unionism with their emphasis on self-help, free collective bargaining and rampant individualism and the wider Socialist perspective of Labour with their appeal to fraternity and equality'.[62] These features of trade unionism filled out a growing disenchantment on the Right of the PLP, provoking discreet but urgent discussions on their future within the Labour Movement.

In the event, the first group to move were the expatriate Parliamentarians, returned or about to return from the Brussels headquarters of the EEC. Roy Jenkins and David Marquand, courted by the Liberal Party Leader, David Steel, were now prepared to defect (albeit to a new political formation). The gulf between this most alienated group of Social Democrats and the Labour Movement was now profound. To them, it was now the deepest gulf in British politics.[63] So great indeed that these erstwhile representatives of the Labour Movement now set themselves the task of undermining the Labour Party and creating a permanent shift of power from organised labour to government.[64] It would involve a breakout from the present party system which would strengthen 'the radical centre'.[65] This would enhance the leverage to force proportional representation. It would enable other constitutional changes in the political system to be introduced. It would allow 'compatible coalitions'. It would have the authority to deal with the sectional interests – particularly the power of the trade unions. It would be able to carry through the necessary reforms of the industrial relations system and then ensure the equally necessary continuity of basic industrial policy

Defections

By the time that the Labour Party had been a few months in Opposition, defections had already, in effect, taken place marked by David Marquand's first *Encounter* article[66] and then by Roy Jenkins' *Dimbleby Lecture*.[67] It remained to be seen how far these developments would engender a wider move out of the Labour Party which would involve a significant section of the PLP.

Bill Rodgers, and most of the others who would eventually go in 1981, were still arguing publicly in 1979 that 'there is no salvation for the Labour Party in a break with the trade union movement'[68] although by the time of the *Dimbleby Lecture*, the consideration of a move out of the Labour Party was in some cases at the point of commitment.[69]

There was a continuing pull of tradition and loyalty and still strong voices on the Right of the PLP who argued that the unions were among the Party's greatest assets and that Austria and Sweden indicated the potential for a successful partnership.[70] Indeed, there were occasionally calls for *more*, rather than less, trade union involvement in the Party as a counterweight to the Leftwardsmoving NEC and the Leftwing-dominated constituencies. Whatever was thought quietly about the need for a loosening of ties with the unions, the most marked characteristic of the tactics of the Right of the PLP in 1979 and 1980 was their sense of 'waiting for Terry' or 'waiting for David' – the first a hope that the AUEW President would get his delegation sorted out, the second a hope that the GMWU would be pulled into a new Rightwing 'praetorian guard'.

Thus, from the 'Campaign for Labour Victory' broadsheet, *Labour Victory*, came a call in September 1979 for the unions to insist (with financial threats if necessary) on a Party Commission of Enquiry. And in October 1979, *Labour Victory* urged that the TUC, alongside the PLP, be brought more into policymaking, building upon the machinery of the existing Liaison Committee.

There was much uncertainty about tactics, timing and priorities, even after an open letter to the *Guardian* in August 1980 announced the existence of what became the 'Gang of Three' leading defectors, William Rodgers, David Owen and Shirley Williams. The threatened formation of a new party went with a coded thrust to the unions for 'no compromise with those who share neither the values nor the philosophy of democratic socialism'.[71]

Yet in the eighteen months after Labour's election defeat, union allies failed to deliver. At the Party Conferences of 1979 and 1980, in spite of confident expectations from the Right, the Left continued its advance on the constitutional issues. A political leadership which had historically depended upon the 'fixing' power of union leaders now saw them as having lost the power to 'fix'. Delegations like the Boilermakers changed sides leaving their senior officials and the Parliamentary leadership open-mouthed.

In crucial elections for the National Executive Committee, where the Right had been anticipating its own counter-attack for years, the purge of the Left failed to materialise. In the Engineers delegation, the Right's slate was 'turned over' by a delegation which appeared unpredictable and increasingly unfathomable. Faced with the collapse of their plans, for the second successive year, sections of the political Right began to feel that the trade unions were in the hands of forces which were out of the control of any leaders that they could respect.

They took a similar view of the behaviour of the organisation Trade Unions for a Labour Victory. It was always seen by Rightwing members of the Shadow Cabinet and by the Party Leader, James Callaghan, as a potential block on the activities of the Leftwing NEC and perhaps the foundations of a new 'praetorian guard' which would organise to throw the Left out. Yet while the union leaders were unwilling or unable to perform that task, they were apparently capable of pushing the Labour Leader and his Deputy into acceptance of the principle of extending the franchise for Leadership elections.

On the Right, in the unions, reassuring voices told them to be patient. The Left's advance would run its course. The counter-attack would come. Some even said privately, 'We pay the piper, we will call the tune.' But, in practice, there seemed to be precious little tune-calling going on.

At the same time, among many of the Social Democrats there was a growing and deep ambivalence about this whole process. Some of them had had enough of the unions calling *any* tune – particularly as it was they who were still having to dance. In Parliament, in April 1980, the Right found themselves voting against the Prior legislation on trade unions which involved provision for public money for ballots which many of them supported. They were also called upon to vote against restrictions on secondary union action – a measure for which they had a growing sympathy. But into the Lobbies they went, following the Party and TUC line.

In response to the decisions of the 1980 Party Conference and to the calling of a Special Conference on the procedure for election of the Party Leadership, the Party Leadership appeared unwilling to do anything but seek accommodation with the advancing Left and with the 'unacceptable' union voting arrangements.

Such political subservience seemed inescapable after Michael Foot, pressed into standing by a section of the Left, including union leaders, won an unexpected victory in the Leadership election of November 1980. What for many in the Party was seen as a signal of its integrity was seen by some on the Right as a clear sign that the compromisers would always be in the saddle and the voice of the unions in the Labour Shadow Cabinet would now be heard from the Leader's seat. The faults in the Labour Movement appeared endemic, incurable and worsening fast.

At every turn they felt constrained by the 'rules' of the relationship. They could not initiate the industrial relations policies nor the incomes policy they felt to be necessary; nor could they produce a Bill of Rights. Each in some way breached the 'rules' of freedom. Equally, reform of trade union democracy was (it appeared) prevented by the operation of that same trade union democracy through the Labour Party. Solidarity they regarded as having been in great measure corrupted during the past decade, yet within the Party it meant the unions leaning on *them* in policy formulation through a close consultative process. By contrast, the union leaders seemed incapable of coming to their aid. Indeed, some seemed unwilling to play the role, preferring to co-operate with or to accommodate a range of dangerous new constitutional reforms and damaging new policies with priorities which were miles away from the concerns and perspectives of a moderate Social Democracy. Even the rules of union unity, which had in the past stood in the way of a swift political move to the Left on the NEC, now appeared to stand in the way of a swift shift back to a 'sensible' committee.

Their despondency and pessimism was reinforced by allies in the mass media. Some of the journalists who covered the Labour Party in this period were caught up in their own ideological crisis. Others had more blatant political designs, carrying into their columns the tactics of a Conservative Party leadership which in 1980 and 1981 was desperately unpopular with the electorate. A split in the Labour Party might divide the Opposition for years to come. For both the Right and Centre of British politics, such a split might secure another bonus – the destruction for ever of the unions' ability to reconstruct labour legislation via the Labour Party.[72]

Alongside the doom and gloom portrait of the Labour Party's inevitable future was painted another, more hopeful, scenario. Social and economic changes were creating fertile ground for a new party of the centre. Academic studies were scanned which showed the long-term erosion of Labour's class base and the growth of partisan de-alignment. Support for some of Labour's ideological positions had declined among its own identifiers. There had been a decline in support by trade unionists for the Labour Party. The academics' message was that a new social democratic party would have significant electoral support.[73] It was said that a break from Labour would be a gamble and would face a range of problems, but conditions were more favourable than at any time since the 1920s.[74] Further, polls were beginning to indicate that a breakaway party in alliance with the Liberals might sweep the country.[75] By the end of 1980, for the Gang of Three and a group of Parliamentary supporters, the defection was on.

In terms of the defeat of their wing of the Labour Party, the defectors' tactics produced in the short term its own self-fulfilling prophecy. While it distracted and divided the political Right, it left the trade union Right with no unified tactical direction in preparation for the Special Conference of January 1981 (Chapter 7, pp. 200–02). The disunited Right blundered into almost its worst case scenario of defeat – with the unions having a bigger say in electing the Leader than the PLP had.

In the end, media allies and sympathisers did give the first wave of departing Social Democrats[76] the best platform they could have, typifying the events of the Special Conference as the manipulation of union leaders most of whom had, in practice, been passive victims of the tactical skills of the campaign activists.[77] With this misleading message, the Social Democrats could now make the issue of trade union power – an issue dear to their hearts and the subject of mass political prejudice – the first point of the Limehouse Declaration:

A handful of trade union leaders can now dictate the choice of a future Prime Minister.[78]

THE VANISHING MARK II LABOUR PARTY

There is little doubt that the speed and trajectory of the defection took most of its participants by surprise. For some time (to this day some would say) there was tension and disagreement as to the identity of the new Party and its relationship with the Liberal Party. Certainly there was a strong element which saw the SDP not as a centre party, but as a party whose natural base was the centre-left and the Labour electorate, and its natural allies moderate trade unionism. It would be a party which embodied traditional Labour values[79] – the Labour Party Mark II, some called it later. But it would be a party shorn of its 'extreme' and 'authoritarian' features, it would not have block vote affiliations, and it would have a looser relationship altogether with the unions. For some of them, the model of the relationship between the Democratic Party in the United States and the AFL-CIO would not have been unwelcome, once the break had been made from the old trade union based party.[80]

The project of replacing Labour and reconstructing a new relationship with the major elements of moderate trade unionism was a bold one, given the immediate problems – particularly the first-past-the-post electoral system, and the residual weight of traditional loyalties. But the enterprise was approached with eagerness and vigour and the confident belief that almost every aspect of the

Labour Movement was in a state of decay, degeneration and, some would add, corruption. Its flexibility and its capacity for recovery appeared very doubtful (particularly if you wanted to see it that way).

And, as some of the defectors knew, there was much for the new party to work on in terms of half-severed relationships and shared values with elements who remained in the Labour Party. It was not only in the political wing that there was a nostalgia for something from the 1950s called 'the old Labour Party' and a belief that the unions should leave politics to the politicians. In some of the Rightwing-led unions and within the TUC itself, the same noises could be heard. There were strong personal links with some of the union leaders in APEX, the AUEW, ISTC, and strongest of all in the EEPTU. Political forums existed where old friendships and alliances endured – including the Fabian Society and the Labour Committee for Transatlantic Understanding.

Those who had been sponsored trade union MPs found their sponsorship immediately withdrawn – a fact that did not trouble them given that from the point of their defection they suddenly moved to opposition to the principle of sponsorship. But some kept contact with friends in the sponsoring unions, looking forward to a time when perhaps a new relationship might be forged.

Yet the breakthrough in the unions never came. To understand this failure, we have first to note the evolving policy, style and strategy of the SDP itself before examining the character of union responses

Liberation

One of the first factors which was to undermine the chances of reforging the links with the unions was the attitude of the new Party's leaders in the aftermath of defection. They had used 'the power of the union leadership' as the first element in their explanation of the need to move. Now in pastures new, they discovered the exhilaration of being able to say exactly what they liked about the unions and the Labour Party.

'We are going to be independent, we are going to be free to make our own decisions', Owen told a launch meeting.[81] That sense of 'liberation' was an indication of how far they had come to detest and resent always having to look over their shoulders at the unions and their leadership. The feeling of guilt which was an endemic and pervasive feature of being at odds with the unions and breaking the 'rules' of the Movement was now lifted. And they discovered just how far they had travelled and could travel in their change of values, attitudes and policies.

After (for some) the pain of separation, there was a sense of rebirth – heady days when they could openly discuss their beliefs and criticisms and at times indulge in the most lurid characterisation of a Labour Party in the vice-like grip of the Communist Party in the unions and the Militant Tendency in the constituencies. Ideas inhibited or suppressed for years could now be brought forward – every statement critical of the Party and the unions widely reported and well received in the press.

Most of the SDP leadership would have reacted strongly to any suggestion in this period that they were 'anti-union', but there is little doubt that they were at this time more preoccupied, even obsessed, with the sins of the unions than with almost any other British institution. They wanted as a priority 'a new balance' in industry in which there would be constraints on union behaviour. They also wanted a new legal framework of industrial relations – without shirking in any way the need to insist on the reforms of trade union procedures, which they regarded as a fundamental problem.

This focus became all the more accentuated as the new party sought alliance with the Liberals and a shedding of the rhetorical associations from the past. But in attitudes towards trade unionism it was pulled further by the new influences brought about by an infusion of SDP members, the vast majority of whom had been political 'virgins' with no history of Labour Party activity and therefore with no traces of émigré custom. A survey in November 1981 indicated that 72 per cent of SDP members wanted a curtailment of trade union immunities and 67 per cent the complete abolition of the closed shop.[82] Thus, from a context in which favouring the unions was written into the basic assumptions of Party activity, they had moved into a context in which antipathy to trade union power and concern for the dangers of collectivism pressed and encouraged a new dynamic.

John Cole noted at a conference of the new party: 'Every criticism of union abuse was as fervently clapped as at a Tory Conference'... there was rarely any applause for a tolerant remark about the unions.' 'Trade unionists present noticed the hostility. At a fringe meeting later they staged a revolt: the party's discussion paper was, they said, union bashing".'[83]

Yet, alongside this barely suppressed hostility to the unions and the 'Barons' who controlled them, was also a desire for acceptance in a dialogue by the 'moderate' unions and by the TUC. To some extent this was simply a yearning for symbols of legitimacy and 'clout'. But also there was always an important strand within the SDP on the trade union question which continued to look to a renewal of a national understanding with 'responsible' trade union leaders as part of the evolution of a 'sensible' quasi-corporatism[84] and a new consensus.

However, in practice, the SDP bounded eagerly ahead with its own policy positions as it sought to create its own programme and respond to the Thatcher Government's policies. In this development (apart from over 'the closed shop', where they united with pragmatists who were aware of its appeal to some managements as a mechanism of coherence), the moderates lost out and, over time, tended to go quiet or become increasingly reconciled to the position of the populist hardliners. The first stage of their defeat was the sudden shift of voting by a majority of SDP MPs in the House of Commons.

The Tebbitt 'Employment' legislation which came before the House for its second reading in February 1982 restricted the definition of a trade dispute, further curtailed legal secondary action and secondary picketing, and, by removing the general immunity for action in tort granted in 1906, opened up trade union funds to damages for unlawful action. It placed new restrictions on the closed shop, stipulating an 80 per cent vote to create one, and granting compensation facilities for workers dismissed as a result of the closed shop. Inasmuch as it focused on two issues of direct concern to the defectors – trade union power and the freedom of the individual in relation to the unions – it put the new party's leaders on the spot, before their own policy documents had been completed.

The SDP's spokesman, William Rodgers, admitted to some reservations in his attitude towards the legislation. They would have preferred a more balanced package with some reference to industrial democracy and to the political levy. Nevertheless it was, he argued, a 'modest' measure[85] and he had now been converted to legislation of this kind.[86]

So although all of them had voted in 1980 *against* the weaker Prior trade union legislation, a majority of the 27-strong SDP contingent now went into the lobbies *in favour* of the Tebbitt Bill at the second reading. But five – including Eric Ogden, the SDP's Employment spokesman, and John Grant, later to be the Chairman of SDP Trade Unionists – voted against and three others abstained. It was notable that those hostile to supporting the legislation came from a later wave of defectors and had arguably not yet come to terms with the ethos of the new Party. Certainly, Grant's criticism was comprehensive. It was 'a bad Bill'. It was not going to be good for industrial relations. And it was 'more likely to exacerbate the situation in British industry'.[87]

SDP policy – 1982–1987

When the full policy of the SDP towards the unions emerged in 1982, it was clear that the party envisaged progress towards a 'new model' trade unionism different in significant respects from existing practice and embodying a considerable break with the traditions of the Labour Movement.

The consultative document, *Reforming the Trade Unions*, published in 1982, made clear its belief in the worth of unions as organisations to secure rights, to exercise accountability, to represent grievances and to diminish insecurity. Further, unions were offered a Development Fund to assist mergers, tax exemption to ease the raising of subscriptions and a new law on union recognition. To these were added, in the joint Alliance Manifesto of 1983, *Programme for Government*, public support for union facilities, education and training.

But the break with past traditions was made explicit in the attempt to move towards 'a long lasting legal framework' involving not immunities for unions but positive rights as well as clear obligations.[88] The possibility of this shift had been raised in a Conservative Government Green Paper in 1981, but while the Government decided against the move, it became central to SDP and Alliance policy and, eventually, to the policy of the Labour Party.

On the sections of the 1982 Employment Act which had caused such dissension among SDP MPs, the 1982 document accepted the restrictions on secondary action and picketing but opposed the form of liability to damages, which it said could possibly bankrupt some unions.

Legal restrictions were also to cover public employees who worked 'in services where industrial action threatens life and limb'.[89] Here, strikes and other industrial actions were to be made illegal unless there had been prior reference of the dispute to arbitration.

Alongside this framework of law, the SDP offered a new partnership in industry based upon industrial democracy but there was to be no single channel of representation through the unions as proposed by the TUC and the Bullock Committee. The SDP committed itself to a flexible indicative framework based upon individual employees and independent of the collective bargaining process.

This rejection of trade union based representation was now coupled with the same broad-ranging critique of contemporary trade union democracy mounted by the Conservatives. Britain's trade unions had 'failed their members'. What was worse, 'their present leaders for the most part are totally oblivious of the depth of that failure'. The British TUC had shown a remarkable inability to drag itself into the final quarter of the twentieth century '… most union leaderships … are out of touch and unpopular with their members.' The 'first priority' of industrial relations reform was 'to return the trade unions to their members'.[90] Therefore, there must be secret ballots for the leadership of unions, and the form of these ballots – as with other balloting proposals of the SDP – must be by post to and from the members' homes.

It was a presentation so unqualified as to be unlikely to endear the Social Democrats to the very union leaders they kept asking should talk to them – particularly as it helped prepare the ground for the 1984 Trade Union Act. Four years later, a careful rewording made for a more conciliatory tone in the consultative document of 1986, *Industrial Relations – A Fresh Look* – a fact which led some observers to see it as a move away from the role of 'hammer of the unions'.[91] But, verbally, the level of contempt had diminished very little- as union leaders were well aware.[92]

There was a new stress on strike-free agreements and arbitration, but the most significant feature of the new document was that, on as series of key measures, including compulsory ballots before strikes and before the establishment of a post-entry closed shop, the SDP position had hardened and unified in line with the existing legislation. At a time when the unions had been severely weakened, the legal position on secondary action under the 1982 Act was said to be 'broadly valid and should not be changed'.[93] John Grant, now the Chairman of SDP Trade Unionists, introduced the 1986 document to the SDP Conference, and nobody in the Conference spoke against its provisions. Indeed, as David Owen later made clear, many Social Democrats now regarded this legislation as 'an historic breakthrough'.[94]

As for that old bone of contention in the Labour Movement, incomes policy, there was continuing dispute over this within the SDP and the Alliance up to 1987. One strand of thought which always threatened to come to the surface envisaged a counter-inflation policy in terms of an immediate pay freeze and the statutory incomes policy to which the Liberals had been committed for some time. But the Thatcher Government was managing without legislation, and at the 1982 Social Democratic Conference the statutory view was defeated for a more subtle and, it was thought, more practicable range of devices to deal with a complicated and decentralised bargaining system.[95]

As was to be expected, one area of policy where the SDP's position involved an immediate renunciation of what they had espoused in the Labour Party concerned the trade union funding of the Labour Party. The 1982 document proposed that the procedure of 'contracting out' should be replaced by 'contracting in'. This document, it was said, would be fairer to the individual member but also 'healthy for British politics generally' because it would help to weaken the institutional ties between the unions and the Labour Party. They would thus be able to judge policies more on their merits. Affiliation to a political party should be undertaken only after secret ballots of the membership at (say) five-yearly intervals.[96]

There was, of course, a blatant self-interest in this measure – damaging the Labour Party but perhaps also making more funds available for the SDP itself – possibly earmarked during 'contracting in'. Underpinning the intellectual justification was the evidence that block affiliations and block votes seriously overstated and distorted the extent of real commitment to the Labour Party. It was this soft underbelly of the Labour Movement that the SDP was concerned to make its long term target. With a reinforced 'third party' making demands for reform in this sensitive area, the Conservatives were able to move towards legislation which led to the political fund ballots of 1985–6

Trade union responses

The SDP, from 1982 to 1987, made repeated attempts to participate in a dialogue with union leaders. SDP Trade Unionists, a body set up in 1982, regularly (if very uneasily) held an annual fringe meeting at the TUC. Big name SDP figures like David Owen and Shirley Williams were occasionally seen around the balcony of the Congress proceedings.

Initially, some of the SDP leaders hoped for a rolling process of defections and disaffiliations which would evolve into a broad-ranging but loosely linked Social Democratic Movement which would rival the Labour Party in its ability to speak for organised labour. But eighty years of history, reinforced by the values of unity and solidarity, were not to be immediately broken at the whim of 'politicians'. Not one senior trade union leader went with the defection.[97] And from individual unions the rebuffs were immediate and continuous. They came not just from the Left and centre of the Party, they came from the Right also. The NUR, whose General Secretary, Sid Weighell, was personally very sympathetic to many of the political views of the defectors, had given years of loyal service to the Party and was unprepared to encourage them. In *Transport Review*, the union became one of the first to attack the Social Democrats[98] and the NUR actively sought a wider union statement of opposition. At the ISTC Conference, where Bill Sirs also had good links, attempts by a couple of SDP supporters to get support from the union met no takers.[99] At the APEX Conference, the loyalists were led by ex-Gaitskellite Dennis Howell in opposing any attempt to support candidates other than the Labour Party.[100] In one union after another, the pattern was the same. Loyalty prevailed.

Yet within the unions and the TUC at this time, there was also a deep unease and uncertainty which reached its peak in the period from October to Christmas 1981. At this time, Benn appeared to be considering rerunning the 1981 Deputy Leadership campaign, and the Social Democrats were welcoming one well-publicised defection after another. Support among trade unionists was at one point higher for the new force than it was for the Labour Party.[101] Indeed, not until the Bishop's Stortford meeting in January 1982, when the NEC Left indicated a new willingness to seek some measure of unity, did the leaderships of affiliated unions feel confident enough to make a *collective* pronouncement based on the NUR's original statement. On 13 January 1982, TULV committee declared 'total opposition to the whole basis of the Social Democratic Party'. The SDP, it said, was created by elements deeply hostile to the Labour Party's links with the unions. The SDP had made it clear that it was going down a similar road to the Tories in preparing 'new shackles on the trade union movement'.[102]

One month later, the Tebbitt Bill vote in the House of Commons appeared to confirm the prognosis. Among some of the defectors' old colleagues on Labour's Right, the votes exacerbated the wounds of defection. There were some vitriolic comments from Healey and Hattersley. In Rightwing-led unions and at the TUC, opinion hardened that the SDP, far from becoming an acceptable Labour Party Mark II or a continental version of the Social Democratic model, was to be the stalking horse for Rightwing attacks on the unions. It underlined 'the profoundly anti-union nature of the SDP and of its leading Members of Parliament'.[103] This sharp shift in policy by the defectors, and the tone which accompanied it, coupled with the Peace of Bishop's Stortford in the Labour Party, was decisive in setting the seal on the failure of the SDP relationship with the unions before the 1983 election.

The biggest frustration in these years, when the surges of the Alliance seemed to offer unlimited political prospects, was the reluctance of the EETPU to join them. On the surface at least there was solid ground for believing that the EETPU would be the first to break and would form the basis for 'the new unionism' which would ally itself with the Social Democrats. Frank Chapple, the union's powerful senior official, an Alanticist and anti-unilateralist, shared many of the political perspectives of the SDP. His union, firmly controlled by a Rightwing faction, was deeply hostile to the Campaign for Labour Party Democracy. A copy of the 'Gang of Three' open letter had been sent to EETPU constituency delegates.[104] Chapple was (unusually for a union leader) even a public supporter of the Council for Social Democracy – from which sprang the SDP. Indeed, Bradley reports that for a period, the Council used the union's North London Office.[105]

But Chapple was never impressed with the tactics of the Social Democratic 'politicians'. While prepared to encourage the Gang of Three as allies in confronting the Left, he saw the battle in the Labour Party in terms of forcing the Left out rather than defecting.[106] Such defections were fraught with problems and dangers and required precise timing. And their discussion made the task of a counter-attack against the Left *harder* to achieve. Serious discussions about this timing do not appear to have been held with anybody on the trade union side, including Chapple[107] – an elitism deeply resented on the union Right.

In any case, although he appeared to promise a referendum of his members after the defection,[108] there was deep resistance within the EETPU from Rightwing Labour loyalists (some of them well integrated at local and national level with the Labour Party) as well as Leftwing opponents, and Chapple was never in a position to deliver in this crucial period

Elections, ballots and their consequences

The combination of Labour's dreadful campaign and the Alliance's sudden surge left, in 1983, a major question mark over the future of British party politics and over the future of the Labour Movement. The period from 1983 to 1987 was marked by a major struggle to preserve the Labour Party's position as the alternative Government in the face of a continuous threat from the Alliance parties. Among trade unionists, the period was marked by volatile changes of mood in which the Alliance parties periodically appeared on the verge of major breakthrough. During the General Election campaign of 1983, there was a major swing among trade unionists away from Labour.[109] In the third quarter of 1985, there was another swing which accompanied the Notts. ballot to defect from the NUM, the TUC row over public money for union ballots, and the intense controversy over the NUM's demands upon a future Labour Government.[110] In the weeks following the Greenwich by-election in early 1987, a similar shift took place.[111] But at each point, the Labour Party recovered its unity and its electoral momentum, and the unions rediscovered their confidence in the Labour Party leadership. It was also noticeable that the Labour Party, step by step, made its own electoral adjustment towards that segment of electoral opinion which was providing the Alliance with its votes – including that majority of trade unionists who supported, then wanted to preserve, balloting rights guaranteed to them under Conservative Government legislation.

There was no immediate certainty after 1983 that the pattern of events would ultimately strengthen the cohesion of the Labour Movement. With Labour for the moment holding only 39 per cent of the votes cast by trade unionists, it was a clear vindication of the SDP's reiterated charge that in their total commitment to the Labour Party, the manual workers' unions were out of touch with their membership's opinions. Their message also seemed to have some resonance within the TUC, where one strand of 'new realism' thought in terms of more distance from the Labour Party and affirmed the need for the TUC to talk to any Government, whatever its political complexion.

Once again the SDP leadership looked to the Electricians as the bridgehead. The union had restricted its national affiliation to the Party (see Chapter 10, p. 288) and it had paid no money into the national General Election Fund. Frank Chapple had given public endorsement to an SDP candidate, John Grant, during the election campaign[112] and he later appointed Grant (by now the Chairman of SDP Trade Unionists) as Communications Officer of the union. Chapple made the theme of his final address to his own union conference the need for the TUC to start a dialogue with other parties.[113]

And yet the line held. Letters to the union leaderships from the SDP inviting them to begin a dialogue on the Party's industrial relations policy received generally the same blunt rebuff as had previous ventures. Privately, some SDP leaders thought they detected more receptivity in some of the unions. Shirley Williams claimed that the trade unions were beginning to detach themselves from the Labour Party.[114] Certainly, within the TUC, there was a more measured response – a preliminary public rejection – but one of the annual dinners that the

TUC General Secretary had held for some time with David Steel did now include for the first time David Owen.

However, it does not appear to have been a very happy encounter and in the next two years Owen's flirtation with what Roy Jenkins labelled 'sub-Thatcherite' economic policies,[115] his open and blunt admiration for the Government's position on the Miners' Strike[116] and his disdain for the unions, did little to endear him to the TUC. Further, by 1985, the SDP Conference was openly rejecting 'traditional Labour values' and Shirley Williams was acknowledging failure in the fight to define the Party as a centre-left force whose roots lay in the part of the Labour Party from which she had departed.[117]

In any case, the opportunity in 1983–4 of a double-stage realignment – first break a key union or unions from the Labour Party then come to a new form of political relationship with them – passed because of a range of other developments. In the Labour Party, a new 'dream ticket' swept to victory, raising Labour's electoral standing and quelling the doubts of the Electricians and the Engineers in the enthusiasm of the time. Government action over GCHQ taken without consultation, with the TUC leadership frantically signalling its desire for a new dialogue with the Government, undermined 'new realism' and once again forced the TUC into inescapable reliance upon the Labour Party.

At the same time, the SDP's position *vis-à-vis* the EETPU and other affiliated unions was undermined by another tactical predicament. Since 1981, they had placed a high priority on changing the law on trade union political funding. The Political Fund ballots of 1985–6 gave to the membership of every union a chance to vote on whether or not they wanted to retain a political fund. The opportunity was there for the non-Labour voters (which Social Democrats were convinced were a silent majority) to deal a devastating blow at Labour Party affiliations and finances.

But the specific terms of the Political Fund legislation were not those sought by the Social Democrats: they preferred a change to 'contracting in' and a ballot on the specific issue of affiliation. So they now advocated a 'no'-vote in the unions, unless the members were guaranteed a further vote on affiliation. And it was the SDP, not the Conservative Government, which in 1985 became the political focal point of 'the opposition' in the ballots. It was a huge blunder, giving trade unionists the unpalatable option of denying themselves *any* political funds.

Consequently, in union after union during the politial fund ballot campaigns, SDP trade unionist members found themselves in opposition to the Labour moderates they were hoping to woo into a dialogue. Matters were not helped by the style and content of the SDP campaign with its obsessive focus on union manipulation and malpractice – a focus which was seen as provocative and insulting.

In practice, this was one of many aspects of the political fund ballots which, to the vexation of the Social Democrats, *enhanced* the unions' association with the Labour Party (see Chapter 18). Perhaps the least obvious, but in its own way very important consequence, was what happened at the EETPU Conference; rejection of the SDP's position on the ballot was almost unanimous and for the first time since 1981, the Alliance came under attack from that union, now under

Hammond's leadership much more committed to the Labour Party than under Frank Chapple. The EETPU fought its Political Fund campaign with the emphasis on the right of the union to campaign effectively on behalf of its members and the need for balance in a Parliamentary democracy. But there was no attempt to hide the links with the Labour Party, and the bulletins to the branches from the General Secretary laid heavy emphasis on the achievements of Labour Governments and the value to trade unionists of the Labour Party–TUC Liaison Committee.[118]

The electricians: bridgehead and model

At this point it is time to look in more detail at the role of the Electricians' union – widely admired within the SDP as exemplifying 'the new unionism' – their natural ideological allies, their bridgehead to the unions and the core of the future realignment which would shatter the old Labour Movement.[119]

Yet not only did the defection from the Labour Party fail to materialise when the SDP needed it most, in practice, as an exemplary bridgehead to the Labour Movement, the EETPU had some inherent defects and, increasingly, an off-putting style which aroused growing antagonism among even the moderate unions.

This was, in part, a response to the manner in which the EETPU addressed the rest of the unions. Annually, there were themes which could and did strike a chord – the responsibility to seek power rather than strike postures, the responsibility to avoid illegality, and the responsibility for the unions to reform themselves. And some of the EETPU's positions on controversial issues became part of the common sense of the Movement in the years that followed. These included the critique of the tactics of the NUM leadership during their strike and the EETPU's insistence that it was legitimate and necessary to accept government assistance in connection with balloting. Its record was by no means as unimpressive as its union critics often suggested. It had a devout commitment to the cause of *Solidarnosc* in Poland. It had a principled position on the cause of trade unionists at GCHQ. And it was not averse, where necessary, to exerting a degree of industrial leverage on behalf of its members.

But the typical way it delivered its case to the Labour Movement mixed rectitude with arrogance and criticism with needless insults. Such speeches often came over more as declamatory pronouncements than attempts to persuade; directed, it appeared, to an off-stage audience rather than to their listeners in the hall. And always from a union deeply scarred by the struggle against Communist ballot-rigging from 1957 to 1961, there was a remorseless portrait of the Movement and the world in terms of a Manichaean conflict with international Communism. This deviant and offputting behaviour extended into the private sphere of the TUC. In a trade union movement governed by 'rules' and protocol designed for disparate forces to live together, the EETPU's behaviour was wayward to the point of mystery. It was the working rule of at least one senior 'fixer' within the TUC in this period that 'if you want to get something done, first get the Electricians to do *nothing*'.

Then again, although there was a wary respect for the EETPU's progressive organisational efficiency, its political regime under Chapple was not as admired inside the Labour Movement as it was on the outside – even by convinced believers in balloting. Its balloting arrangements put it close to the SDP's model of future union procedures. But there is more to democracy than postal balloting and referenda (see Chapter 10, p. 295). The EETPU leadership became adroit in handicapping opposition and dissidents by its use of the rule book and Executive power.[120] While this darker side of EETPU political control was widely acknowledged in the unions, it produced a curious blindness in the SDP. The description of the EETPU by its press allies as 'rough and tumble populism'[121] remained uncritical in terms of what roughness was acceptable and what values were allowed to tumble.

The EETPU's behaviour in this period is one of the great historical examples of 'the best laid plans' going astray. Instead of the union spreading its bridgehead to embrace a wide range of moderate unions which would defect from the Labour Party, it became more and more unpopular. And instead of leading a defection from the Labour Party, it so outraged opinion within the TUC that in 1988 it was suspended and then expelled from the TUC. Here again, the example of the EETPU in accepting single union deals, co-operative relations with employers, the breakdown of status distinctions at the place of work, and new financial benefits to its members, were not unpalatable to many in the unions. But its behaviour in the News International dispute at Wapping, its ruthless readiness to push out other unions, and in the end its refusal to accept the adjudications of the TUC disputes committee, met a very different response even from unions solidly on the Right.[122] The attitude of the great bulk of union leaders turned to one of repugnance.[123]

Unlike in 1985 when the issue of money for ballots threatened to take the AUEW and other unions out of the TUC alongside the Electricians, there was no question now of any union going with the EETPU. As for breaking the Labour Party, there the position was transformed. By 1988, not only had the EETPU confirmed its connection with the Labour Party in the Political Fund ballots, but it was seeking merger with the AUEW which had a much greater respect for the Movement's 'rules' and relationships. The AUEW was determined that it would not be bounced out of the TUC and it was equally adamant that it wanted no query over its Labour Party affiliation. Keeping in the Labour Party was now a way of keeping the major unions united. The EETPU, far from being a bridgehead to defection from the Labour Party, was now anxiously shoring up its political affiliation; the union which the SDP once saw as leading others out of the Labour Party now threatened legal action to keep themselves in.[124]

POLITICAL SPACE AND POLITICAL ADJUSTMENT

Between 1987 and 1990, in a series of policy developments, the Labour Party moved decisively away from some of the traditional 'rules' of trade union freedom, accepting a permanent legal framework for industrial relations (see Chapter 14A). And it did so with the agreement of a majority of the unions. In some respects, it took over the agenda created by the Social Democrats between 1982 and 1986 (an agenda itself shaped by a longstanding Conservative critique and then by Conservative Government legislation), but it did so as a result of discussion and negotiations within the Labour Movement and in ways still marked by its traditions.[125] In this shift it retained the support of trade unionists, indeed support for the Labour Party moved back to the levels of the early 1970s.[126] Meanwhile, far from the Labour Movement moving into terminal decline, a much bigger question mark hung over the future of the fragments of the Alliance – particularly the sdp.[127]

NOTES.

1. One major point of division on the Right occurred in 1976 after Jenkins's speech at Anglesey which noted the dangers of further increases in the proportion of GDP taken by public expenditure. Philip Whitehead, *The Writing on the Wall*, 1985, p. 346. Jenkins' alienation from the Labour Party is captured in his diary as he went off to Brussels in 1976, 'something quite new for me and in which I believed much more strongly than the economic policy of Mr. Healey, the trade union policy of Mr. Foot or even the foreign policy of Mr. Callaghan'. *The Observer*, 12/2/89
2. Peter Jenkins, 'The Crumbling of the Old Order', in Wayland Kennet (ed.), The Rebirth of Britain, 1982, pp. 45–6
3. *What We Must Do*, Manifesto Group, 1977, p. 14. In 1981, all but two of the active Manifesto Group leadership (Giles Radice and George Robertson) defected to the SDP, Hugh Stephenson, *Claret and Chips*, 1982, p. 33
4. John P. Mackintosh, 'Britain's Malaise: Political or Economic?', *Scottish Banker Magazine*, May 1978, reprinted in David Marquand (ed.), *John P. Mackintosh on Parliament and Social Democracy*, 1982, pp. 215–7
5. Peter Jenkins, 'Staggering Towards a Socialist Future', *Guardian*, 1/10/79. There are elements of this criticism of the unions in the writings of John Mackintosh. See Marquand/Mackintosh, *op. cit.*, but it was not until after the defection that the full critique emerged. See on this particularly, William Rodgers, *The Politics of Change*, 1983, Chapter 6, pp. 94–106
6. Marquand/Mackintosh, *op. cit.*, pp. 177–8 and 193–4. David Marquand, 'Trying to Diagnose the British Disease', *Encounter*, December 1980, p. 78. David Owen, *Let Us Face the Future*, 1981, pp. 179–80
7. Stephen Milligan, *The New Barons*, 1976, Chapter 16, A Policy for Democracy, pp. 213–27. See also SDP, *Reforming the Unions*, 1982, p. 3
8. *What We Must Do*, *op. cit.*, p. 33.
9. Flanders, *op. cit.*, p. 29.
10. *What We Must Do*, *op. cit.*, p. 33.
11. Shirley Williams, *Politics is for People*, 1981, p. 134. See also n. 84
12. Owen, *op. cit.*, p. 55.
13. *Ibid.*
14. Stephen Haseler, *The Tragedy of Labour*, 1980, p. 121.
15. Peter Jenkins, 'Epitaph for a Prime Minister', *Guardian*, 30/3/79. The accusation is particularly exaggerated in respect of the 1970 election and is one-dimensional in respect of both February 1974 and 1979
16. *Personal Freedom*, Labour Party document debated at the 1956 Party Conference, LPACR, 1956, pp. 82–96
17. See on this Roy Jenkins, *The Labour Case*, 1959, pp. 136–7.

18. Socialist Union, *Socialism: A New Statement of Principles*, 1952, p. 35
19. Stephen Haseler, *The Gaitskellites*, 1969, p. 93 and Socialist Union, *op. cit.*, pp. 32–7
20. F.A. Hayek, *The Road to Serfdom*, 1944, Preface to 1976 edition, p. ix
21. John P. Mackintosh, 'Has Social Democracy Failed in Britain?', *Political Quarterly*, July–September 1978, p. 269
22. See, for example, 'The Fight Over the Ferrybridge Six', *Sunday Times*, 7/12/75 and 'Britain's Liberty: The Role of Union Power', *Sunday Times*, 12/3/78 for the case of 'the Birmingham Nine'. Another important case, that of three BR workers sacked in 1976, was taken up by the National Association for Freedom and fought successfully through the European Court of Human Rights
23. See Nora Beloff, *Freedom Under Foot*, 1976 for a critique of the legislation
24. Shirley Williams, 'Cobwebs of the Constitution', *The Observer*, 14/9/86.
25. *Hansard*, HC 27/1/71, Vol. 810, Col. 682.
26. 'Labour and the New Leviathan', *New Statesman*, 11/2/1977.
27. Peter Jenkins, 'Commentary', *Guardian*, 16/9/77.
28. *Ibid.*
29. See on this John P. Mackintosh,'Liberty and Equality: Getting the Balance Right', in Marquand/Mackintosh, *op. cit.*, pp. 182–9, '... the next drive should be to reassert the value of the freedom of the individual', p. 189
30. Dick Taverne, *The Observer*, 8/10/72.
31. 'British politicians fear union power far more than they fear the power of capitalism', Mackintosh, 'Has Social Democracy Failed in Britain?', *op. cit.*, p. 264. During 'the winter of discontent', 'Even her critics conceded that she [Mrs Thatcher] spoke for the nation while the Prime Minister had demonstrated himself to be the prisoner of the trade union movement', William Rodgers, 'A Winter's Tale of Discontent', *Guardian*, 7/1/84
32. Peter Jenkins's description of Callaghan, n. 5.21.
33. Healey, *op. cit.*, p. 396. Foot was also described as 'the Godfather' in dealings with the unions, Barnett, *op. cit.*, p. 165
34. Marquand had been an MP from 1966 to 1977 and returned to academic life in 1978
35. *Guardian*, 12/11/76 quoting a Labour MP referring to the vote on the Dockwork Labour Scheme
36. For Ministerial perceptions of the Liaison Committee, see Reg Prentice, 'I can explain the procedure. It is for the Labour Party leadership to ask the TUC what it wants and for the Labour leadership to do exactly what the TUC wants, not simply in general terms, but detail by detail, without any original thinking of its own', *Hansard*, HC 19/5/82, Vol. 24, Col. 382, p. 202. Also Shirley Williams, 'something of a surrogate Cabinet', in 'The New Authoritarianism', *Political Quarterly*, Vol. 60, No. 1, January 1989, p. 6. By contrast, see Ian Mikardo, *Ian Mikardo, Backbencher*, 1988, pp. 198–9. Trade union attitudes to the Liaison Committee are noted in Chapter five, p. 120.
37. David Marquand, 'Inquest on a Movement', *Encounter*, July 1979, pp. 13–14
38. *Ibid.*, p. 14, 'a perfectly intelligent and reasonable human being in private'
39. Leslie Scarman, Hamlyn Lecture, December 1974 and *English Law* –

New Dimensions, 1974

40. Michael Zander produced *A Bill of Rights* in 1975. This was followed by Peter Wallington and Jeremy McBridge, *Civil Liberties and a Bill of Rights,* 1976

41. Lord Hailsham, *The Times,* 19/5/75, referred specifically to trade union legislation as likely to be caught by any Bill of Rights Legislation. See also *The Dilemma of Democracy,* 1978, pp. 65–7

42. Under Jenkins, the Home Office produced a Green Paper, *Legislation on Human Rights: With Particular Reference to the European Community* in June 1976. Anthony Lester, a Home Office advisor of Jenkins, was strongly in favour

43. *Minutes of the Human Rights Sub-Committee,* 15/12/1975, Item RE 395

44. *The Times,* 29/9/75.

45. John Griffiths, 'Whose Bill of Rights?', *New Statesman,* 14/11/75.

46. *Minutes of the Human Rights Sub-Committee,* 15/12/75, Item 1.

47. Among the members of this committee in the period 1975–7, in addition to Shirley Williams, were Roger Darlington, Lord Harris, Roy Jenkins, Bruce Douglas-Mann, Edward Lyons, John Lyttle, Ian Wrigglesworth, Michael Zander and the Secretary, Anthony Humphris, most of whom (I understand) defected to the SDP as did Anthony Lester, the Home Officer advisor. Among the minority of critics of the Bill of Rights were Patricia Hewitt, Alex Lyon, Clare Short and the LSE lecturer Joe Jacobs, who presented several critical memoranda

48. *Labour's Programme,* 1976, p. 88.

49. In 1976 there was only one supporting resolution on this issue, Res. 346. In 1977 there was none

50. 'Our Vulnerable Rights', *Sunday Times,* 15/2/76.

51. 'A Bill of Rights', *TUC Memo,* JM/JK, 27/1/77.

52. *Ibid.*

53. Paul Johnson, *op. cit.*

54. *Human Rights Sub-Committee,* RE 1288/September 1977 and letter from the Secretary, 13/9/77

55. *Home Policy Sub-Committee Minutes,* 7/11/77, Item 6.

56. Letter from Michael Zander to members of the Human Rights Sub-Committee, 7/12/77

57. Shirley Williams, 'Why We Lost – How To Win', *The Observer,* 13/5/79

58. David Butler and Dennis Kavanagh, *The British General Election of 1979,* 1980, pp. 85, 155, 263. Labour was still judged best capable of handling the unions, p. 345

59. MORI in February 1979 asked respondents their views on (a) compulsory postal ballots before strikes, (b) prohibition of secondary picketing, and (c) taxation of social security payments to strikers' families. The results were as follows:

	All	Trade Unionists
(a)	89	91
(b)	89	86
(c)	65	57

Bo Särlvik and Ivor Crewe, *Decade of Dealignment,* 1983, p. 18, n. 14

60. Resentment at guilt feelings was an important ingredient in defection – as was a trepidation about the Party's reactions. On the guilt complex, see Barnett, *op. cit.,* p. 50 and William Rodgers, 'When It Comes to the Miners, Labour is Paralysed', *Guardian,* 6/4/84. A Radio 4 discussion programme, *Analysis,* 'Labour's Love Lost', presented by Hugo Young,

11/7/79, brought out the 'sheer terror' at the prospect of future 'fratricidal struggle' over their transgressions

61. Some of these questions and others were posed acutely in the writing of John Mackintosh who died in 1978. See particularly, Marquand/Mackintosh, *op. cit.*, Part 3, 'Social Democracy'

62. Robert Taylor, 'The Future of the Alliance', *Labour Victory*, September 1979. But note the different union constituencies and the differing attitudes of union leaders traced in Chapter 6. See also Chapter 21, n. 46 for evidence of a union 'sword of justice' effect

63. Marquand, 'Inquest on a Movement', *op. cit.*, p. 17.

64. Marquand, 'Trying to Diagnose the British Disease', *op. cit.*, p. 81

65. Roy Jenkins, *Home Thoughts from Abroad*, BBC Dimbleby Lecture, 1979, 22/11/79. According to Jenkins' diary, he initially simply referred to 'the centre' but was persuaded by Marquand to talk about 'the radical centre', *The Observer*, 26/2/89. Even so, the idea of a centre party received 'a cool reception' from Rodgers and others who thought in terms of winning the traditional Labour voter. For Rodgers's view, see 'Why We Must Fight to Save the Labour Party', *Sunday Times*, 15/6/80. Shirley Williams said that a new Jenkins-type centre party would have 'no roots, no principles, no philosophy and no values', Stephenson, *op.cit.*, p. 24

66. Marquand, 'Inquest on a Movement', *op. cit.*

67. Jenkins, *Dimbleby Lecture*, *op. cit.*

68. *Guardian*, 14/5/79.

69. Three MPs, Dick Crawshaw, Neville Sandelson and Tom Ellis, were already in the Jenkins camp, Jeremy Josephs, *Inside the Alliance*, 1983, p. 11. Jenkins' Diary suggests that William Rodgers, John Horam and Ian Wrigglesworth were enthusiastic following the Dimbleby Lecture, *The Observer*, 26/2/89

70. Giles Radice, 'Why the Labour Party Must Not Split', *Guardian*, 12/1/80 and 'Labour and the Unions', in David Lipsey and Dick Leonard, *The Socialist Agenda*, 1981

71. David Owen, William Rodgers and Shirley Williams. Open letter, *Guardian*, 1/8/80

72. This position came out more clearly later in the editorials of the *The Economist* as the SDP, on the crest of a wave, considered its future strategy. 'No government constitutionally or politically dependent on organised labour must again be allowed to rule Britain', 26/9/81

73. Ian Bradley, *Breaking the Mould*, 1981, p. 84. W. Rodgers, *The Politics of Change*, 1983, pp. 166–7. Among the academics consulted in the period of defections were Professors Ivor Crewe and Anthony King of Essex University

74. Peter Jenkins, 'The Plunge into an Ideological Vacuum', *Guardian*, 3/12/1980

75. An ORC Poll for London Television's 'Weekend World' programme indicated that an alliance of the centre parties would receive 31 per cent support. Labour would be on 27 per cent and the Conservatives 24 per cent, *Guardian*, 19/1/81. By March 1981, six polls had shown the Alliance in the lead – before it was created

76. The first wave of defectors were: Tom Bradley, John Cartwright, Richard Crawshaw, Tom Ellis, John Horam, Edward Lyons, Robert MacLennan, David Owen, William Rodgers, John Roper, Neville Sandelson, Mike Thomas, Ian Wrigglesworth. There was also one Con-

servative, Christopher Brocklebank-Fowler. One further MP, James Wellbeloved, defected in July. From September to Christmas, a second wave took place: Michael O'Halleran, Ronald Brown, James Dunn, David Ginsburg, Dickson Mabon, Tom McNally, Bob Mitchell, Eric Ogden, John Grant, Jeffrey Thomas, Hudson Davies. In 1982, they were joined by Brian Magee and George Cunningham

77. For example Adam Raphael and Robert Taylor, 'Labour Left Seize Control of the Party', *The Observer*, 25/1/81. Peter Jenkins, 'The Muddle that ended in a Leap in the Dark', *Guardian*, 26/1/81

78. 'Limehouse Declaration', 25/1/81. Stephenson, *op. cit.*, Appendix I, pp. 185–6

79. William Rodgers, 'My Party – Wet or Dry?', *Guardian*, 17/5/85. Ben Stonham, *Guardian*, 11/9/85. Shirley Williams, *The Independent*, 28/8/87

80. Stephen Haseler, 'Towards a Centre Party', *Encounter*, April 1980, p. 30

81. Quoted in 'Claret and Chips', Channel 4 TV Documentary, 'Social Documents Ltd.', 18/9/83

82. ORC for London Weekend TV, 'Weekend World', 29/11/81.

83. John Cole, 'Shirley Through the Looking-Glass', *The Observer*, 11/10/81.

84. One important example of this emerged later in David Marquand's *The Unprincipled Society*, 1988, see pp. 242–3

85. *Guardian*, 9/2/82.

86. *Hansard*, HC 8/2/82, Col. 757, p. 394.

87. *Guardian*, 6/2/82.

88. *Reforming the Trade Unions*, September 1982, p. 26.

89. *Ibid.*, pp. 27–8.

90. *Ibid.*, pp. 1–4.

91. *Guardian*, 28/8/86 and 1/9/86.

92. A classic example was Sue Slipman's platform speech at the SDP Conference of 1986 in the debate on Industrial Relations, where she confidently forecast that a day would come when the unions would come 'whingeing', notes of the Author. The mainstream union reaction to SDP leaders is best summed up by John Edmunds's comment on Bill Rodgers, 'Not until he left the Party did we find out how ashamed he was of us (the unions). It was a humiliating experience', notes of the Author, taken at the Tribune Rally, 30 September 1987

93. *Industrial Relations – A Fresh Look*, p. 15.

94. Terry Coleman, 'Stand by Your Man', *Guardian*, 1/6/87.

95. These included a Pay and Prices Commission with the power to restrict price increases, and a counter-inflation tax on employers who breached pay limits. It is said that the central question of incomes strategy was never properly addressed in the 1983–7 Parliament, 'the proposal for a tax on inflationary pay rises was out, in, then out again and finally half-heartedly in', Roger Liddle (a member of the Council for Social Democracy), 'Democracy David Owen Style: Heads I Win, Tails I Split the Party' *New Statesman*, 21/8/87

96. *Reforming the Trade Unions*, p. 17.

97. I am told that among those who joined the SDP at this time were David Nott, Treasurer and Deputy General Secretary of Barclays Group Staff Union, Jack Britz, General Secretary of the Clearing Banks Union and Charles Corcoran, Chairman of the Greater London General Staff Assocation, none of which was affiliated to the Labour Party. The most

senior ex-trade union officer was Tom Bradley, one of the defecting MPs, who had been a President of the TSSA. Among TUC affiliates, there was also an NEC member of NALGO, Mike Blick. All of these became members of the committee of Social Democratic Trade Unionists. The Chairman of this committee was the defecting MP and later Communications Officer of the EETPU, John Grant. The hope that the post of Trade Union Organiser would be filled by a 'genuine middle rank blue collar trade union official', John Torode, *Guardian*, 12/8/82, was not realised. Tony Halmos, an ex-academic and ex-TUC official, took the post

98. 'The Real Priority', Editorial, *Transport Review*, 30/1/81.
99. *Guardian*, 18/6/81.
100. Interview with APEX Political Officer, Rodger Godsiff, 23/11/85.
101. A MORI poll of trade unionists in November 1981 showed support for the Labour Party at 33 per cent, the Lib/SDP at 51 per cent. By the end of the first quarter of 1982, Labour was receiving 39 per cent and the Alliance 36 per cent. MORI Memo to Labour Party, 21/4/1983
102. 'Statement on the SDP', *TULV*, 13/1/82. The statement was based on an original draft from the NUR
103. David Basnett quoted in the *Morning Star*, 20/2/82.
104. *The Labour Party and the EETPU Trojan Horse*, Flashlight, EETPU internal opposition leaflet, Autumn 1980
105. Ian Bradley, *op. cit.*, 1981, p. 93. Within the EETPU it is contested that this ever happened
106. Frank Chapple, 'Between Left and Centre', *Encounter*, August–September 1980, pp. 88–92
107. Frank Chapple, Interview, *The Democrat*, 20/12/82, p. 15.
108. On 18/1/81, *The Observer* quoted Chapple as saying that he would ballot his members on whether they should disaffiliate. *The Guardian*, 26/1/81, quoted him as rejecting the suggestion that his union might now disaffiliate but saying that the matter would have to be put to a ballot after being discussed by the political committee. Publicly, no more was heard of it
109. Among trade unionists, there was an increase in support for the Alliance during the campaign of 10 per cent. MORI for TULV, July 1983
110. During this brief period, support for the Alliance among trade unionists rose from 26 per cent to 32 per cent – 4 per cent from the Conservatives and 2 per cent from Labour – now down to 45 per cent. Data supplied by MORI
111. After the Greenwich by-election on 26/2/1987 (the first SDP by-election win from Labour), a private poll for the Labour Party showed Labour Party support as low as 36 per cent with the Alliance the main beneficiary
112. Frank Chapple, *Sparks Fly*, 1984, p. 181.
113. *Guardian*, 8/11/83.
114. *The Times*, 8/9/83. In fact, not until 1985 did the Alliance make any headway. That year, John Lyons of the Engineers and Managers Association joined them and his union urged the TUC to broaden its discussions to include political groups other than the Labour Party. But his union was not affiliated to the Labour Party and no affiliated organisation made any positive response
115. *New Democrat*, September 1985.

116. 'It was one of those rare cases where you must say straight out that somebody must be defeated', David Owen, *Sunday Telegraph*, 29/3/87
117. *Guardian*, 11/9/85.
118. *EETPU Support Democracy ... And Our Union*, Bulletin from the General Secretary (undated), 1985
119. *Interviews with Tony Halmos*, SDP Trade Union Organiser, July and September 1983
120. On this theme, there was a fascinating correspondence in the *Guardian* in 1984 between John Grant, Frank Chapple and Harold Best (a former member of the union's Executive Committee). It began on 7/9/84 with a letter from Grant. Best replied on 22/9/84. Chapple replied on 29/9/84. Correspondence continued involving others on 13/10/84, 18/10/84, 5/11/84 and 10/11/84. On democracy in the EETPU during Frank Chapple's leadership, there is also a very interesting exchange in the *New Statesman*. Patrick Wintour, 'How Frank Chapple Stays at the Top', 25/7/80 and Frank Chapple, 'Frank Chapple Hits Back', 10/10/80. Recently, Newman Smith has completed a very comprehensive study, 'Politics, Industrial Policy and Democracy: The Electricians Union, 1945–1988', Ph.D., Glasgow, 1988
121. John Torode, *Guardian*, 2/8/84. See also Robert Taylor, *Sunday Times*, 9/9/84, who refers to the union under Chapple as 'a model of democratic self-government'
122. John Lyons, an SDP member of the General Council and General Secretary of the Engineers and Managers Association, noted that the awards in the Disputes Committee against the EETPU were 'not beyond criticism (few are) but in my opinion they were not unreasonable on the evidence', *Guardian*, 29/8/88
123. For a typical view, see John Edmunds, 'Bitter Fruits of Sweetheart Deals', *Morning Star*, 8/6/88: '... you can put together a plausible argument for each of these elements (in EETPU policy) but the way it is used is to put forward a form of trade unionism as a service to an employer.'
124. Eric Hammond, 'Channel Four News', 22/6/1988.
125. One important example was that the deep suspicion of the role of the judiciary in industrial relations and antipathy towards giving them more power at the expense of the elected Parliament was reflected in the proposal for an industrial court and the continuing opposition to a Bill of Rights (see Chapter 14A). There was also much less commitment to *postal* balloting compared with the policy evolved through the Alliance
126. A poll by Harris for the GMB in February 1988 had Labour's support among trade unionists at 55 per cent. It continued at around that figure for the next 18 months and then headed upwards as support for the Conservative Government rapidly declined (see Chapter 20, n. 39)
127. On 3 June 1990, after a spectacular by-election failure, the SDP National Committee voted to wind up the organisation, without a ballot of the membership.

Part IV

Representation of Labour

9

Sponsorship

In the next seven chapters the focus of the analysis moves to the unions' links with policymakers and with the policy process in the various national forums of the Party. Much of this is concerned with the formulation of Party policy between one General Election and the next. But first we examine union links to a policy process which is historically and in great measure practically distinct from the policymaking of the *Party*.

Union sponsorship of candidates and MPs centres on the representation of trade interests *within Parliament*. It predates the formation of the Labour Representation Committee but was gradually integrated into the arrangements for the new organisation. The first LRC and then Labour Party candidates were regarded as legitimate only 'if they stood at the invitation of the affiliated labour organisations'.[1] Subsequently, sponsoring arrangements were affected by a range of new developments. As with so much else in the union-Party relationship, these developments were initiated from three sides – by the Party, by the unions and by the State.

PROVISION AND AGREEMENTS
Salaries and maintenance

Sponsorship as a process is often misunderstood. It is a common misconception that it still involves the unions paying substantial amounts of money into the pockets of 'their' MPs,[2] and is often equated with the take-up of directorates or financial retainers for Parliamentary consultancy as MPs 'seek to augment their income'.[3] A great deal of prejudice and myth suggests that sponsored MPs are made financially subordinate in these arrangements and therefore under union control.

There was some historical validity to the equation of sponsorship with maintenance. Early Labour MPs received both contributions towards the expenses of their electoral organisations and maintenance payments at a time when no official salaries were paid. These maintenance payments either came directly from individual unions or through the Parliamentary Fund of the Labour Party which was supported by the unions.[4]

Even the institution of Parliamentary salaries under the Appropriation Act of 1911 did not fully solve the problem. MPs still found it difficult to survive on the low salary and unions continued to pay significant additional sums. According to Muller, the Mineworkers in the 1920s were paying an additional £300 on top of the £400 salary.[5]

The salaries of Members tended to remain static for many years. From 1937 to 1954 they remained at £600 and the additional sums paid by unions continued to be significant. Harrison, for the 1950s, cites the NUM as the largest payers – £225 – but the two general unions, the TGWU and the GMWU, and USDAW all paid £200. Other unions paid less; the NUR gave £100 and NUPE £50.[6] For a later period, 1959 to 1964, Muller gives the GMWU as the largest payers with £250.[7] Alongside an MP's salary of £1,250, these would have provided very welcome additions.

However, in an important but relatively unnoticed development in the past quarter of a century, unions have either phased out personal payments or have frozen them at a low level. The considerable increases in Member's salaries and allowances have meant that the case for paying retainers has diminished. But, in addition, the unions became very sensitive to the attention being paid to Members' outside interests in the mid-1970s at the time of the Poulson affair, and aware of the hostility towards sponsorship among those unsympathetic to 'trade union power'.

Thus there developed a view in the unions that large payments to sponsored MPs were neither necessary nor proper. The practice was discontinued in the TGWU and the NUR. It had not existed in the AEU for many years and, significantly, the rising unions, including ASTMS, COHSE and TASS, did not involve themselves in such transactions. Where the practice remains, the sums are relatively trivial. In 1986–7, the largest payer, the Yorkshire Area NUM, was, I am told, paying £400, the GMWU paid £300, USDAW £250, APEX £150 and NUPE £100. Such sums were paltry alongside a salary (1986) of £17,702 and Secretarial and Research Allowances of £12,000. And they were insignificant in comparison to the sums of money understood to be paid directly to MPs from other interests active around the House of Commons.[8]

Thus, in a period when many observers have noted that standards of acceptable conduct in the House of Commons appear to have made it easier for MPs to accept personal financial rewards from lobbying interests, trade union practice has been moving in the opposite direction. One political editor noted in December 1985 that in the past, MPs 'were committed to the Tower for behaviour which today would not raise an eyebrow'.[9] Yet it is still common for 'sponsorship' payments to constituency parties and direct payment to MPs to be equated and treated in a censorious way in editorials and the polemic of everyday politics. William Muller's comprehensive work on the role of sponsored MPs is titled The Kept Men?[10] But as far as personal rewards for the representation of interests were concerned, by the 1970s these were among the least kept men and kept women in the business.

The Hastings agreement

In 1933, at the Hastings Conference, the Party sought and gained from the unions an agreement which regulated union sponsorship. It has been revised after consultations on five occasions since the Second World War, most recently in

1979 when it specified that:

1. An affiliated trade union could not pay more than 80 per cent of the maximum of election expenses permitted by law.
2. An affiliated trade union could not pay more than £600 per annum in a Borough Constituency and £750 in a County Constituency, in respect of organisation and registration expenses.
3. If a full time agent was employed in a constituency, the affiliated organisation could not pay more than 65 per cent in a Borough Constituency or 70 per cent in a County Constituency, of the agent's salary, superannuation and statutory payments.

In practice, by no means all the unions paid maximum figures. In general, they did pay the maximum annual contributions for organisational expenditure. But ASTMS usually paid much smaller sums and sometimes made no annual payment at all. In terms of election expenditure, the GMB, AEU, NUM and NUR paid the maximum but the TGWU paid a lump sum which in 1983 was less than 30 per cent. ASTMS (later MSF) paid such small amounts that they were on a par with the sums which some unions, including the GMB (which had a 'second panel'), paid to the constituencies of non-sponsored but 'supported' MPs (a feature which makes the definition of a 'sponsored' candidate grey at the edges). Some unions did pay the 65 per cent maximum for agents but most either gave a smaller percentage or donated an annual lump sum which fell far short of the maximum figure.

In practice also, the maldistribution of union resources, in terms of the Party's needs, remained a problem. Unlike the sponsoring agreement which the Party signed with the Co-operative Party, there was no provision in the Hastings Agreement for unions to sponsor a proportion of non-Labour seats and the tendency still was for the money to go to areas where the Party needed it least – to the safest seats. The tendency worsened as unions took on more of the MPs in such seats.

This maldistribution always concerned the Party's officials and various attempts have been made in the past two decades to establish a sponsorship fund which could be directed where the interests of the Movement required it. This received encouragement from some of the unions – particularly at the time of the Commission of Enquiry (see Chapter 16, p.524) but there was always difficulty in overcoming the combined problem of union insecurity, union autonomy and union interest. Nothing came of the proposed reform.

Unions did pay sums of money towards the election expenses of other candidates – often to their own union members and sometimes to individuals seen as politically close to the union. In addition, some of the key marginals could elicit funds or received grants from individual unions on an *ad hoc* basis. And the existence of a regional TULV/TUFL machinery led to some funds being made available at regional Labour Party level. But altogether it was an uncoordinated and unsystematised patchwork of allocations. At Head Office, there was not even a full record of such financial arrangements.

Agreement to sponsor

The Party has no say in which candidates receive sponsorship. This is union territory. The Party keeps an 'A' list of candidates which the unions have agreed to sponsor. This is made available to any constituency party on request; but the Party has no controls over the content of this list other than the general and limited restriction over who can stand as a Labour Party candidate. Each of the 25 unions which, in 1983, sponsored Labour candidates had its own governmental structure and its distinctive regulations governing the procedure and qualifications for sponsorship. In general, there were two procedural stages – one in which a 'panel' was constituted of potential parliamentary candidates, and a second in which a candidate drawn from the panel was put forward by the unions to contest a particular seat (providing they could get a local nomination).

Historically, the process of constituting a panel has involved either elections within the unions or a selection made by the Executive Committee on the basis of branch nomination and interviews. Among those still using elections in 1987 were the NUM, TSSA and USDAW. Selectionists included TGWU, GMB, ASTMS, EETPU and UCW. But there has been a move in a few unions since the 1960s towards specialised testing rather than ballots – a development which acknowledges that the qualities necessary for a long-serving member to win ballots in a manual worker union may not be those necessary to win selection in the constituency parties. Unions with testing arrangements in 1987 included the AEU, NGA, NUPE and the NUR.

One further important development which affected the constitution of the panel was the growth of the practice which might be termed 'co-option'. Most of the large unions now regularly adopt sitting MPs with their agreement. Their constituency party then receives assistance and the MP fights the next election as a sponsored candidate. The choice of targets for 'co-option' is made on a senior level in the union after personal 'soundings' and/or political committee recommendation, and then ratified by the Executive of the union. This is the case even in unions like USDAW which retain a strong commitment to the principle of balloting for union 'panel' members.

The spread of co-option in recent years has also often further weakened union rules regulating qualification for sponsorship. Here, the most significant change is that the number of unions who strictly specify years of service within their own industry for those nominated for the panel has declined considerably. In recent years, some of the most important unions which abided by this provision have had to shed it. These included the Shopworkers, the Railwaymen and the Transport Salaried Staffs. In 1987, among the significant 'sponsors' only the Mineworkers and the Engineers still insisted on trade experience.

However, it may be significant that by 1987 the NUR, which had initiated the recent wave of 'co-option', was beginning to reassess its policy. In the light of their experience with 'co-opted' Members, and in view of new improvements in political organisation within the union following the Political Fund ballot (see Chapters 17 and 18), there was a turn towards the further encouragement of talent from within the union. Six members of the union were brought on to the panel after building up a record of activity representing the union – a partial return to trade experience.[11]

One other development was significant. Over the years, the unions have tended to discourage or prohibit their own salaried union officials – particularly the national officials – from standing for Parliament and holding both offices at the same time. Of the three key exceptions, two – USDAW and the TSSA (which had Presidents in the House) – have recently found it difficult to get their nominees elected, leaving only the POEU (later National Communication Union) with a significant overlap in the person of John Golding MP, and Deputy General Secretary. However, in 1986, when Golding became General Secretary and went on the General Council of the TUC, he was instructed by the union's Conference to vacate his parliamentary seat. In 1988, the only union whose leadership still extended into the parliamentary arena was MSF, where one of the (non-salaried) Joint Presidents, Doug Hoyle, was an MP.

SELECTION AND CO-OPTION
Selection

There is no doubt that a prospective candidate who is known to carry sponsorship is carrying an asset into a selection conference. Yet since the late 1950s, unions have encountered a range of new difficulties in securing seats for their candidates.[12] These difficulties have increased in recent years, in spite of the better quality of union candidates, and in spite of a rise in the number of potential candidates they have made available. This decline in the local importance of sponsorship in candidate selection is an important part of the context of the national relationship between the unions and sponsored MPs.

Historically, sponsorship followed the contours of local trade union strength in industrial areas, even to the point where some unions in areas of occupational strength – coal, railways and engineering particularly – gained something akin to a 'right' of occupancy, which they defended against outsiders, however eminent. This pattern was underpinned, and in some safe seats still is, by understandings between major unions to avoid open conflict over territory.

From the late 1950s, changes began to take place which all moved in the direction of weakening local trade union influence and the importance of sponsorship in securing candidates. Local affiliation declined significantly in the 1960s [13]and, though some improvement took place in the 1980s in the wake of new TULV awareness of the problems (see Chapter 15), there was a major increase only in the NUR (which began to seek 100 per cent affiliation before other unions took up the problem of under-affiliation [14]).

The pattern varied area by area, with Scotland and the North having the strongest links and London and the South East the lowest, but even in areas of strength, the formal affiliation often masked considerable weakness in terms of real activity and commitment. The weak linkage was most clearly exposed in the take-up of delegations. In 1988, a rule was brought in which restricted unions to five delegates per organisation. [15] Only for the heavily concentrated NUM was this really a handicap. For years most unions have had difficulty in finding enough delegates to fill the positions available to them. At local level, there was often a deeply ingrained 'separatism' with priority for the industrial work in the minds of most union activists and busy local officials.[16]

Martin Harrison noted in the 1950s that trade union delegates were notoriously erratic in their Labour Party attendances.[17] Barker and Chandler found the same twenty years later.[18] One result of this weakness was that political activists who were members of affiliated unions found the union branch an easy access point to the General Committee of the local party. Even with this 'padding' of delegates, union participation was usually much weaker than its potential. A survey by Fatchett in 1986 found that of the 202 constituencies which replied, only 18 had a majority of trade union delegates on the GMC.[19]

A procedural change in 1965 involving an obligation upon union delegates to be individual members of the Party may have deepened the problem of securing genuine delegates – particularly for the NUM.[20] Certainly it inhibited the flood of selection year delegates which may in the past have ensured a candidature during selection conferences.[21] Here again, the evidence is that though trade union delegates turned out in larger numbers for selections in safe seats, their attendance was significantly lower than other delegates for all types of seat.[22]

This decline of the unions at local level has been compounded by social changes affecting the unions and affecting the Party's membership. The past three decades has seen cut-backs on the railways, the closing of much of the mining industry, and a massive reduction in manufacturing industry. Old centres of manual worker trade unionism have been badly hit. While this experience has undermined the unions' local strength, the local Labour Parties have been undergoing the changes noted in Chapter 5 – a membership increasingly higher educated, from the white collar salariat.

Although being 'working class' remains in many ways an advantage in the culture of the Labour Party, there has been an increasing tendency to select middle class candidates who are more articulate and able to project themselves to the electorate.[23] The financial benefit of sponsorship has been counterbalanced by concern over possible union domination and by consideration of adverse electoral reactions.[24] In addition, although CLPs are not awash with money, the more affluent membership has been able to raise relatively large sums to fight elections. The decline of paid secretary-agents has also reduced the necessity for union funds.

All these changes have created difficulties for manual worker unions in traditional industries. The most obvious example has been the problems of the National Union of Mineworkers. Andrew Taylor's fine, detailed analysis of the Yorkshire Miners points up their advantage in terms of concentration and organisation but also the continuing erosion of their capacity to place sponsored candidates and the relative insignificance of finance in retrieving their position.[25] The undermining of the position of the NUM – one of the best payers under the Hastings Agreement – has been marked by some spectacular failures to retain old positions[26] in spite of sponsorship money.

This experience highlights the fact that the influence of finance in candidate selection is often very much exaggerated. It is probably most significant where a

CLP stands to lose its secretary-agent without it; but, by 1987, this applied to only eighteen sponsored seats. In his study of the role of unions in candidate selection, Denver found significantly that in the marginal seats only 18 per cent of the selectors preferred a sponsored candidate.[27] His overall conclusion was that unions did not 'control' many selections; their influence, though pervasive, was 'partial, subtle and only one of the factors that determine who gets selected'.[28]

There is still enough concentrated union influence in remaining mining areas for the NUM to be concerned that a shift to an individual-based one-member-one-vote system of candidate selection could deprive unions of representation 'where it really counts'.[29] But the NUM position is unusual and it is now very misleading to see 'the unions' as such as the obstacle to reform.

What was significant about the votes in 1984, when the Party Leadership failed to carry reform, was their overwhelmingly factional character. There was a very large union minority in support of the NEC proposal[30] and the alignment was very similar to that over mandatory reselection in 1980 (see Chapter 7, pp.194–5). As for the union leadership, what was noticeable was their increasing amenability towards reform. On the NEC in 1984, 1986 and 1987 a substantial majority from the Trade Union Section lined up against the status quo and in 1987 reform was backed by a substantial union majority at the Conference.

Some of this support can be attributed to the conscious search by the Party Leadership for a hybrid form which would satisfy some of the Leftwing unions including the TGWU and NUPE.[31] In the new procedure, selection was taken out of the hands of the General Management Committee of the CLP and put under the control of an electoral college split between individual party members and affiliated organisations (mainly the unions) but with the latter restricted to a maximum of 40 per cent. The procedure anchored the unions in the process but did so in a way which left open a range of problems.

It proved to be very cumbersome in operation and time-consuming for the Party officials to supervise. It was based on a pattern of union affiliation which could involve, as in the past, a multiplicity of representation from one local branch. While there was a strict one-member-one-vote system for individual members, there was no party control over the methods of union decision-making and no guarantee of involvement by the mass of levypayers (but see Chapter 12, n. 68). Indeed, in one sense, the system was worse than before. Whereas in the past there was a 'rule' of no mandating, and the votes were cast by delegates who were individual members, now the union votes were cast as 'blocks' and there was nothing the Party could do to stop decisions being influenced by people prohibited from membership of the Labour Party. All this virtually ensured that the procedure would be rediscussed at the 1990 Party Conference.

At this point a new factor began to affect union responses – the fear that 'distancing' from the unions was turning into a move to push the unions out of the Labour Party, step by step. Much digging in of heels took place, although in the proposal put to the 1990 Conference, the Leadership did get an acceptance of the OMOV principle (see Chapter 21, pp. 652–3).

However, too much should not be made of union influence via this procedure and particularly its connection with sponsored MPs. As at December 1989, only two MPs (Ron Brown at Edinburgh Leith and George Galloway, Glasgow Hillhead) had retained their candidature purely because of union votes.* And only one MP (Frank Field at Birkenhead) had been deselected in spite of winning a majority of individual votes. As for the connection with sponsorship, only one sponsored MP at that date (George Galloway sponsored by TGWU) owed his selection purely to union votes and the TGWU was only one component of his support. Ron Brown was readopted after he *lost* his union's sponsorship (see p. 262).

Co-option

Alongside the growing opinion in the unions that the Party needed a clearer and more publicly acceptable form of candidate selection, there was another factor at work encouraging an acceptance of reform. The development of 'co-option' and the practice in some of the unions, particularly COHSE, of sponsoring *after* candidate selection, gave some of the unions a security of representation regardless of selection procedures. It was this co-option, concentrated increasingly on safe seats, which in the main accounted for the small rise in the percentage of sponsored Labour candidates in the 1980s. It varied little between 1950 and 1970 (between 20 and 23 per cent).[32] But, according to the Nuffield general election studies, in 1979 it was 26.5 per cent (165 of 623), in 1983 it was 24.3 per cent (154 of 633) and in 1987 it was 25.9 per cent (164 of 633).[33]

In one respect there was nothing new in the procedure. ASTMS and the TGWU had long had the practice of taking on individual Members of Parliament after their election, the only stipulation being that these had first to be members of the union. In the 1970s and 1980s, first the NUR then COHSE, TSSA and USDAW took on groups of MPs but made no such stipulation – usefulness to the union was the only criterion.

There was and remains some regret at the lessening of 'the shop floor' connection.[34] This regret can be found even in unions like the Transport Workers which had for many years been sponsoring MPs with a wide variety of social backgrounds. A manual working class background could involve a deep sensitivity to the lifestyle and multiple problems of the huge manual workforce. It could produce an experience-based expertise on the practices and difficulties of life at the workplace. And it could enable MPs to empathise with the unions' case and to give it an authentic voice.

By no means all ex-manual workers shared this perspective. Indeed, some of them – particularly in later life – took on a disdain for developments in the union. But the most general lament about the sponsored ex-manual workers – as far as the union was concerned – was that while the knowledge, expertise and sensitivities were often in place, the capacity to make things happen in Parliament was much less developed.

This had something to do with the residue of long-established practice in some unions of putting out long-serving officials to pasture in the House. But in any case, sponsored ex-manual workers were generally less articulate, less adept in

---

* As at October 1990, in only seven contests had the union vote swung selection away from the candidate preferred by the individual members.

handling legal technicalities, and less skilful in handling the intricacies of the legislative process. 'Co-opting' existing middle class MPs generally solved these problems, while avoiding the potential 'waste' of election expenditure. They were generally secure in their seats and sometimes excellent value in pushing the unions' case. A paradigm case was that of Frank Dobson, university-educated son of a Railwayman, and representing Holborn and St Pancras, which covered the stations of Euston, Kings Cross and St Pancras. Adopted by the union in 1975, he was to play a major role as the voice of the union during the political aftermath of the King's Cross Fire of 1987.

Unfortunately, co-option also had its problems. Some unions (COHSE for example) appear to have initially taken on a 'job lot' of MPs after consultation with the Whips Office; as before, commitments and abilities varied considerably. Targeting the most able also meant taking on MPs with expanding obligations and interests, particularly if, as was to be expected, they moved quickly through the hierarchies of Parliamentary and Party life. Work as a sponsored MP, however useful, was not necessarily the most glamorous nor was it necessarily the biggest priority in the life of a busy politician. It was this realisation of the limitations of commitment, time and energy which led the NUR to turn again towards indigenous talent from the industry.

THE PATTERN OF SPONSORSHIP

Although the unions sponsor less than a third of Labour's candidates, these are overwhelmingly located in safe (or nearly safe) seats. Because of this concentration, there has always been a marked tendency for the percentage of sponsored MPs to rise when Labour's Parliamentary strength declines (and – less regularly – to decline when Labour's Parliamentary strength increases). This rise was repeated as the PLP declined in size in 1979 and 1983, but it was reinforced by a general trend to increased sponsorship which focused even more on the safer seats as a result of the co-option of sitting tenants. Thus, the percentage of sponsored MPs was significantly higher in 1979 (49.8 per cent of a PLP of 269) than it was in 1959 (36 per cent of a PLP of 258). The general increase became much more obvious in the late 1980s. In 1983, the percentage of sponsored Members was 56 per cent and in 1987, when Labour's representation rose, it was 56.3 per cent. The rise continued to well over 60 per cent as the session progressed. Not since 1931 has there been a comparable scale of sponsorship on Labour's benches.[35]

Even this increase does not fully capture the extent of trade union group membership in the House. Some unions without officially sponsored representation nevertheless call together groups of sympathetic MPs whose constituencies they support financially in small ways. ASLEF did this for years. Others, including ASTMS, APEX and GMWU, developed the practice of calling together groups which included all their members in the House of Commons – sponsored and unsponsored. Indeed, on this basis, the new GMB group, after amalgamation with APEX in 1988, including the two 'panels',[36] was bigger even than the TGWU which calls together only its sponsored members.

The most striking feature of individual union representation within this

REPRESENTATION OF LABOUR

Table 9.1 Trade union sponsored MPs, 1945, 1959, and 1966–1987

Union	Previously	1945	1959	1966[a]	1970[a]	Feb.1974[a]	Oct.1974[a]	1979[b]	1983[c]	1987[d]
AEU	(AUEW)	3	8	17	16	17	16	17	13	12
APEX	(CAWU)	–	1	4	3	6	6	5	3	3
ASTMS	(ASSET)	–	–	2	3	9	12	8	10	8
COHSE		–	–	–	–	–	–	3	3	4
EETPU	(ETU)	1	–	1	3	3	3	4	3	3
GMB	(GMWU)	8	4	10	12	13	13	14	11	11
NCU	(POEU)	–	–	–	1	2	2	3	3	2
NUM		35	31	26	20	18	18	16	14	13
NUPE		–	1	5	6	6	6	7	5	9
NUR		12	5	7	5	6	6	12	10	8
SOGAT		–	–	–	–	–	–	–	2	2
TASS	(DATA)	–	–	2	4	4	4	4	5	5
TGWU		17	14	27	19	23	21	21	26	33
TSSA		9	5	5	4	3	3	3	–	2
UCATT	(ASW) (AUBTW)	5	1	2	2	2	3	2	1	1
UCW	(UPW)	–	2	4	1	2	2	2	1	1
USDAW		6	9	10	9	6	5	5	2	8
		96	81	122	108	120	120	126	112	124
Other unions		25	12	12	8	9	9	8	5	5
Total		121	93	134	116	129	129	134	117	129
PLP		393	258	363	288	301	319	269	209	229
% Sp'd MPs		30.8	36.0	36.9	40.3	42.8	40.4	49.8	56.0	56.3

Sources: (a) Derived from Muller, *op.cit.*, pp.62–3, and sources cited there (b) Derived from *Labour Party NEC Report*, 1979, pp.10–11, supplemented and amended by information supplied by union offices, MPs and the PLP Office. (c) Derived from *Labour Party NEC Report*, 1983, p.6, supplemented and amended by information supplied by union offices, MPs and the PLP Office. (d)

pattern has been the decline of the National Union of Mineworkers representation – from a peak of 37 in 1950 to just 13 in 1987. Replacing it as the union pre-eminent in its sponsorship has been the TGWU. At its low point of involvement in 1959, it had only 14 sponsored MPs. By 1987 it had 33. The GMB also increased its strength from a low of four in 1959 to eleven in 1987. Two Leftwing white collar unions built up their representatives. ASTMS built up its strength from none to eight MPs. TASS has varied; it too had no sponsored MPs until 1959 but now has five (amalgamated together these two unions move to challenging the GMB, the NUM and the AEU for the second largest sponsored group). A further white collar union, APEX, which also had no representation in 1945 slowly built it up to a peak of six in 1974 and it had three prior to amalgamation.

The AEU, with a low representation of between six and eight from 1950 to 1959, first rapidly increased its sponsored representation in the 1960s, then declined significantly in the 1980s; at its peak, between 1964 and 1974, it had a representation of sixteen or seventeen; in 1987 this was down to twelve.

In decline also for a period were the NUR, TSSA and USDAW but each revived its strength by 'co-option'. The NUR declined from twelve MPs in 1945 to only five in 1970, then shot up from six to twelve in 1979, falling back to eight by 1987. The TSSA, in the same contracting industry, declined from nine in 1945 to the point in 1983 where it had no representation. It 'co-opted' two MPs for the 1987 Election. USDAW declined from ten in 1964 to just two in 1983 but by 1987 had increased to eight.

There has been a striking rise in the representation as well as the membership of the Health Service unions, both of which have become very conscious of the need for a political voice. NUPE had no sponsored MPs in 1945; it had nine by 1987. COHSE had no representation at all up to and including 1979; it now has four.

THE RELATIONSHIP IN PRACTICE
Sponsorship, purpose and role

The past two decades have seen some remarkable changes in union perspectives on the role of sponsored MPs. In the post-war years, it became widely accepted that extensive union access to Government via the TUC was a permanent part of a mature, pluralistic democracy. Given this institutionalised consultation and the ready availability of Ministers to see TUC delegations over particular problems, sponsorship began to look superfluous as a form of union representation. It could be argued that by this stage sponsorship was primarily a matter of helping the Labour Party. Financially, sponsorship funds provided a valuable addition to local organisational and electoral funds. Politically, the great bulk of union-sponsored manual worker MPs were loyalists, influenced by union traditions valuing unity and majoritarian democracy, and after 1954, they often acted in concert through the Trade Union Group, to defend the Labour Leadership against its largely middle class, Leftwing critics.

What did the unions get out of sponsorship in the post-war period up to the late 1960s? They got more than immediately met the eye. First there was the continuing symbolism of a successful political project – the better representation of Labour in Parliament had been the primary purpose of the founding unions in 1900, sponsorship was its vestigal reminder. Second, sponsorship provided the reassuring presence in Parliament of a group of 'men' from manual working class backgrounds – 'real trade unionists' who were available, if need be, to articulate the realities of working class experience. Third, for the overwhelming Rightwing leadership of the unions, they had an acknowledged and immediate political function – they could be counted upon to throw their weight on the side of Party stability, on the side of moderation and anti-Communism, and behind the fundamentals of the post-war achievement, including the preservation of free collective bargaining. Fourth (and never to be underestimated), individual unions achieved a recognition of status by the level of their sponsorship and the presence of a large group of MPs in Parliament – regardless of how badly the group was organised or how little it did in practice.

In addition, there was also a continuing, if minor, instrumental role to be played in defending union interests against Government legislation and policy. Sponsored MPs might be used where TUC policy remained neutral or unsatisfactory.[37] They might be used as a fall-back where initial negotiations had secured only limited success.[38] They could be used occasionally as instruments of tactical pressure upon firms via Ministers.[39] And they could be used to secure information from Ministers useful to the union's purpose.[40] Above all, the House of Commons could be used as a forum of publicity for the union case. If nothing else, sponsored MPs were heavily represented in debates and Question Time on issues of industrial concern to their own union. Miners' MPs were particularly assiduous and knowledgeable in pursuing fuel and power issues which were of interest to the NUM,[41] albeit keeping away from industrial disputes until the official miners' strike of 1972.[42]

Nevertheless, given what appeared to be a permanent post-war settlement and permanent neo-corporate relations between unions and the state, it was not surprising that sponsorship should appear a little outdated and encourage both predictions of its demise and advocates of reform. What was paradoxical about this development was that just at the point in the late 1970s when a radical reform of sponsorship began to gain some powerful allies in the trade union movement – particularly in the GMWU (where there was increasing concern over rationalising Party finance) – so a counter movement began to gather force to strengthen the links between unions and sponsored Members and to build up the effectiveness of sponsorship.

This 'turn back' to sponsorship, though not affecting all unions, became the dominant movement of the 1980s. The causes of this shift were multiple and reinforcing. It began with a dissatisfaction over the performance of some of the sponsored MPs during the arguments with the Wilson Government of 1966 to 1970 over industrial issues. It was deepened by a political gulf which began to emerge between some of the unions and the Right of the PLP – particularly over the EEC. It was strengthened further by evidence of the Labour Government's new austere 'the Party's over' approach to public expenditure in the mid-1970s. Even then the decisive weight was not necessarily behind a general revival of sponsorship. This came about primarily because of the anti-corporatist stance towards the unions by the Thatcher Government – there was a major curtailment of consultation and access at a time when the Government was developing a wide range of legislative inititatives. Finally, the great consolidation and legitimation came through the Political Fund Ballot campaigns of 1985–6 where unions placed the greatest emphasis on the value of 'a voice in Parliament' and attempted to justify the past work of sponsored MPS.

Organisation and liaison

The most marked change as a result of these forces was in the organisation of sponsored MPS and their relationship with the unions. The limited purpose and importance of sponsorship in the period of the post-war 'settlement' had shown itself in the attitude of most of the unions to the work of sponsored MPS. Although MPS from the larger unions met as groups in the House, their working arrangements varied considerably in their scope and effectiveness.[43] Further, liaison with and communication from the unions were generally very poor,[44] even in the case of the large grouping from the TGWU.[45]

In formal terms, several of the union groups in the House met with union officials on a monthly or quarterly basis but these meetings do not appear to have been approached with much rigour or purpose. Some MPS reported to their unions on the work of the group, either to the Conference, Executive or the membership by an article in the union's journal. But these were not treated with much importance and were often more ritualistic than informative.

Contact and effectiveness might be improved on a temporary basis where union interest was aroused by an issue in the House. Even then some MPS complained of the lack of liaison. Ellis and Johnson, writing in the mid-1970s, noted the overwhelming wish of sponsored MPS for a closer relationship.[46] They objected to being ignored by their sponsors! Indeed, often the closeness of the relationship depended not on the unions seeking control but upon the MPS making their own special effort to link to the unions. In one case told to me in the 1970s, a union with two sponsored MPS only met with them when the MPS asked for it; the union normally asked for an annual report but then stopped bothering even to do that.

Between the late 1960s and the early 1980s the complacency which affected trade union attitudes towards sponsorship was slowly transformed. As a result, in a variety of ways but varying union by union, the relationship between sponsored MPS and the unions began to change. It was not entirely a coherent process. In the union which was best known for its organised and communal links to MPS, the National Union of Mineworkers (where the EC could send representatives to the group, and the group was represented on the EC), there was a serious mutual crisis of confidence and very poor linkage during the year-long Miners' Strike of 1984–5. In the Engineers union in the early 1980s, there was no push from the union side to improve either linkage or servicing and the relationship tended to weaken further before it began to improve a little under new group officials after 1983.

In the seven unions which from 1983 to 1987 had just one sponsored MP, the relationships remained extraordinarily diverse. Some unions officials described the MPS (to the author) as 'very close' and 'hard-working for us'. In others, particularly small craft unions, the relationship was 'underdeveloped', involved 'little contact' or 'no obvious purpose'. Yet among the majority of unions there was unquestionably a move towards closer liaison and much more effective parliamentary action.

The big innovation came in 1976, and from the most tradition-conscious of all unions, the National Union of Railwaymen. In terms of political organisation and political mobilisation, it continued to set the pace in the next decade.

Aware of the new Labour Government's stringency in public expenditure and increasingly anxious about the degeneration of the Labour Movement at the grass roots, Sid Weighell, the union's General Secretary, took two immediate steps to strengthen the union's political work.[47] Having taken over four existing MPS who had no direct involvement with the railway industry, the union took the unprecedented step of creating the post of Political Liaison Officer and giving it to an ex-University Lecturer, Keith Hill. Hill was given accommodation in Westminster with NUR MPS. It was a major innovation directed mainly towards strengthening the work of what had become virtually a moribund group and improving its relationship with the unions. However, once in place, Hill's role eventually expanded and fused into wide political developments within the union and the Party.

Meetings of the ten-strong NUR group were regularised, research assistance was provided and Parliamentary Questions were prepared in advance. Hill became the Group's Secretary and after 1979 a senior national official also attended the group meeting. The relationship of the NUR to its MPS – pro rata now the highest number of MPS to union members – was not perceived in terms of control or power but in terms of creating a more powerful voice for the Railways in the House. There was some claim to having secured minor legislative concessions but the biggest advance was in helping to create a climate of opinion more aware of the problems and needs of the railway industry than would have otherwise been the case in an increasingly difficult environment. By the early 1980s, it was recognised that the NUR group was now the most effective in the House of Commons.

The success of the group and, in particular, the successful creation and operation of the new liaison officer role led to other unions seeking to emulate the behaviour of the NUR. At the same time, the growth of Trade Unions for a Labour Victory, which focused both on political mobilisation and on the increasingly serious state of affairs within the Labour Party (see Chapters 15 and 16), meant that linking with sponsored MPS became just one feature of the political liaison role – more stressed in some cases than in others. (Hill later became heavily involved in organising the NUR's campaign in the Political Fund ballots of 1985–6 and in 1987 moved his office back to union headquarters as he shifted the balance of his work.)

The next union to pick up the political officer role was the TGWU, building upon organisational and liaison improvements initiated by Jack Jones. Jenny Pardington was appointed to the new post of Parliamentary Liaison Assistant in 1979. She too began to operate initially within the House of Commons but felt that this, in practice, cut her off from the union and soon moved to an office in union headquarters. Like Hill, she first began to build up the tactical and service functions to the group and to liaise between the group and the national trade group secretaries of the union. Like Hill again, Pardington also became involved in the union's internal politics, its relationship with the Labour Party, and also the work of TULV.[48]

This strengthening of liaison and organisation of sponsored MPs was followed in several other unions, although not all on the same format. APEX, for example, also greatly strengthened its work in the House and its links to MPs. It had only three sponsored MPs in 1983, but made these the core of a wider organisation. Its Group in Parliament consisted of all Labour Members of the House of Commons and the House of Lords who were members of APEX, not necessarily sponsored. Thus it numbered around twenty-five. Its agendas were prepared by Head Office, whose relevant staff, including the Political Officer, joined the meetings (as also did the Secretary of the APEX branch of Secretaries and Researchers in the House). But the Chair and Secretary – the key officials of the Group – were always sponsored Members. Together with this strengthening in the House, after 1984 came a strengthening of links to the union. The officers of the group regularly met officers of the union and minutes of the Group meetings went to the Executive Committee. A wider 'panel' meeting which included sponsored MPs, APEX Members of Parliament and ten lay APEX members met quarterly with national officials.

Improvements in liaison with MPs also occurred in the GMWU and NUPE. Improvements were also noted in COHSE as they built up sponsorship. In all of them, a marked feature, as with the NUR, TGWU and APEX, was an attempt to build up communication and information to the union on the work of the Group. NUPE even created a forum at their annual conference in which the MPs made a report on their activities and then answered questions from delegates.

Looked at overall, what was interesting about these new developments was not just that some of the unions had sought to increase the usefulness of their sponsored MPs in the light of new issues and curtailment of access to the Government. What was striking was the creation under varying titles of the new category of 'political officers'. Out of the differentiation of functions which, in the 1960s and 1970s, saw the rise of research officers and education officers, came a third offshoot whose role was concerned primarily with politics and with representation through the Labour Party. In addition to Hill and Pardington in the early 1980s there was Alan Meale in ASLEF, Roger Godsiff in APEX and later Bill Gilby in NUPE, Angela Eagle in COHSE and John Starmer in the NCU.

In a parallel and similar development, research officers in some of the major unions which did not have political officers began to take on a much higher political profile and political responsibilities. In the early 1980s, the key examples were Barry Sherman in ASTMS, John Speller in the EETPU and the most important, Larry Whitty of the GMWU, who acted as Secretary of TULV. Later, Diana Jeuda of USDAW became the first research officer to be elected to the Labour Party's NEC, her union's first 'political officer', and the first of the political officers to be given a portfolio which emphasised the politicisation and political mobilisation of the members. Similar developments could be found in other Research Departments.[49] What all this meant was that for the first time in the history of the union-Labour Party relationship a category of officers was emerging whose job or whose emphasis was, in part, to service that relationship at various levels.

The appointment of these political officers, apart from providing a new and more efficient linkage to the sponsored Members and improving the unions' capacity for political mobilisation, created something else. There was now for the first time a network of research/political officers who met together formally through TULV, then TUCC, then TUFL (Chapters 15, 17 and 18) and also linked together informally in seeking to improve the unions' political role both within and in liaison with the Labour Party. By 1987, it was taken for granted that when the Party needed to discuss a major procedural question which affected the Party and the unions (such as the implementation of the Electoral College reform of 1987), then the Party's national officials should meet with the Political Officers. It was yet another blending and integrating feature of a relationship growing in its dimensions and complexity.

The work of sponsored MPs

The union groups have always concentrated their attention on trade and industrial issues.[50] Some of these issues came up via the union and the industry but often arose from Government legislation, new regulations and public reports. The interests of the unions' members were pursued through a variety of Parliamentary channels. There was Question Time, there were Early Day Motions, there was examination of legislation in Standing Committee and there were debates in the House. In addition, the rise of the Select Committee since 1979 has added significantly to the forums where sponsored MPs could be effective.

In recent years, the informational role of MPs has become much more important. Unions have realised since 1979 that MPs are in a position to extract information which was often unavailable to the union otherwise. It could provide advance notice of future plans by the Government or public bodies. It could provide useful ammunition in the legislative debates. And it could add to campaigning resources. This campaigning was an increasing part of the unions' activity in the face of unfavourable Government policy, and sponsored MPs, via the Parliamentary processes, could be integrated into these campaigns.

There were few illusions in the mid-1980s that the Government would easily be forced to back down in the face of union pressure but well-briefed MPs who were persistent and committed could sometimes extract what union officers describe as 'marginal changes' or 'minor concessions'. Occasionally these amendments were of more substance. One such example quoted by union officers was the removal of Crown immunity from problems of health and safety within health service premises under the NHS (Amendment) Act 1987. This followed a two-year campaign by sponsored MPs linked to the GMB and COHSE; they had a strong case, they were well-resourced and well-informed and they were active and consistent in their pursuit of the amendment.[51]

Under Margaret Thatcher, union officials at national level, like the TUC, were never fully 'frozen out' of the consultative process or the occasional meeting with Ministers. But the experience of the years since 1979 has caused unions to rediscover some intrinsic advantages of the rights and tactical location involved in Parliamentary representation. It can give opportunities which are *not* open to the union leadership or the TUC. In the face of representations from MPs, as part of their public duties, Ministers *have* to make some reply and often this reply can form the basis of further action.

Further, whereas the status of unions under the Thatcher Government was uncertain and in some ways lacking legitimacy in the eyes of Ministers and Departments, Ministers felt obliged to see deputations which involved MPs – the Parliamentary right to raise grievance. And the discussion tended to take on a slightly different atmosphere. Some saw it as more productive also. In APEX, the view expressed in a 1983 report was that 'Success has been obtained on issues where representations by even the TUC have failed but have been acceded to following representation by a member' (of Parliament). Interestingly, it made a further point which is echoed in some other unions:

It has been said that poachers make good gamekeepers and vice versa. Whether this is true or not, your members who have been Ministers, and many have been for long periods in a whole range of government departments, have not forgotten the experience and skills they acquired as Ministers as to how the machinery of government operates, which button to press, and when, in order to get the right decision.[52]

One very shrewd union official also located the Whip's Office as an important position for sponsored MPs, able to encourage access and also to facilitate representation at key stages of the legislative process.

Conscious of the difficulties of dealing with an ideologically driven and politically dominant Government, unions after 1983 also became increasingly aware of the potential benefits to be gained by picking up the support of Conservative dissidents. The House of Lords became much more of a target for union lobbying as some of its Conservative members proved to be more independent of the Thatcher Government and more consensual in their approach to political problems. It became a feature of union campaigning in this period that consumer and public interest considerations were given much more emphasis than in the past in order to build a wider public support.

In Parliament, this became integrated – on some issues – with a new emphasis on coalition-building among opponents of particular Government measures. It is a form of 'lobby' politics which may well have ramifications for future union assessments of political strategy.

The most successful example of this lobbying was the defeat of the Government over the Shops Bill and Sunday Trading in 1986. A Shops Bill Discussion Group of concerned unions was called into being by the TUC. Amendments were drafted for the Lords Committee stage and Opposition spokesmen briefed, but there was also a wider campaign among possible opponents of the Bill. Eventually it was an amendment moved by the cross-bench peer, Lord Denning, which defeated the Government and retained existing safeguards for shopworkers. When the Bill moved to the Commons, the TUC wrote to *all* Members of

Parliament with their case. USDAW, which had also been very active in the Lords, used its sponsored MPs but also targeted Conservatives and members of the Alliance known to be unhappy about the proposed legislation for a range of industrial, social and religious reasons. From the unions, there was a new stress on the *consumer* case for rejecting the changes. Eventually, a coalition of forces defeated the Government and rejected the Bill.

In the Commons Committees also, a union's coalition building could sometimes be successful. In 1987, the NUR drafted Clause 40 to the Channel Tunnel legislation and initiated it via the sponsored MPs as an amendment. With cross-party support it was accepted by the Government and reintroduced in the House of Lords.[53]

The Trade Union Group of sponsored MPs

While in the late 1970s the groups of sponsored MPs from particular unions were being given new assistance, new effectiveness and closer links with their unions, a very different development was taking place in the Trade Union Group – that organisation which brought together all the trade union sponsored members.

Dormant for a long period after the War, the group had been revived in 1954, not for industrial reasons and thrived as a political instrument.[54] The context was an ideological struggle with the Bevanites for the Party's future and for its leadership. The overwhelming majority of manual worker sponsored MPs was on the Right of the Party and their efforts were mainly directed towards the defence of the Rightwing leadership against 'the splitters' – 'middle class intellectuals' from 'the utopian and fellow-travelling Left' who were undermining 'the Party's unity' and its chances of election victory.

To a lesser extent, the group did have an industrial policy role. It became the repository of trade union tradition and working class experience. For a period after 1957, the group's industrial experience was built into the PLP's formal policymaking process to the extent that issues relating to trade union and industrial questions were automatically passed to the group for discussion.

In the new industrial situation of the late 1960s and early 1970s, the Trade Union Group's industrial background suddenly gave it a new importance within the PLP. Its political composition underwent a small but significant change with the entry of a group of militant Leftwing MPs. The group's antipathy towards the middle class 'intellectuals' became focused on the shortcomings of some of Labour's leaders – particularly the ex-Bevanite Barbara Castle. And its traditional protectiveness of free collective bargaining was aroused by the Labour Government's statutory incomes policy and its White Paper *In Place of Strife*.It became an important barometer of feeling within the PLP and a forum for the reasoned shopfloor experience which was brought to bear by opponents of the short Industrial Relations Bill which the Labour Government proposed, then withdrew, in 1969.[55]

This new active role was sustained by reactions to the Conservative Government's Industrial Relations Bill. It was fought on the floor of the House with considerable vigour by an opposition which was co-ordinated through a committee on which the Trade Union Group was heavily represented.[56]

Yet the flowering of the Trade Union Group was short-lived, with many factors contributing to its decline. As the number of Leftwing ex-manual workers increased, so the Group's political perspective became more fragmented. It also became more uncertain in industrial terms, particularly towards the end of the 1974–9 Labour Government and in the arguments over Government finance for union ballots. Its leadership became older and more conservative. Encouraged by neither the TUC nor Labour's Front bench to take an active role in opposition to the union and industrial relations legislation of the 1980s, the Group was content to go through the limited cycle of meetings and speakers.

To some extent it may have been affected also by the new range of committees and policy groups created under the reorganisation of the Parliamentary Labour Party in 1980. But, more significantly, it was being undermined in social terms. Its strength and *esprit de corps* in the past lay in its distinctive social and industrial experience and the political role that this encouraged.

Considerable efforts were made to preserve both the distinctiveness and the political role. Matters concerned with industrial and trade union questions were usually dealt with on the basis of monthly meetings addressed by a speaker, and these were open to the PLP as a whole. For matters concerned with the political role, however, the group membership appears in the past to have been rather more selective. On the one hand, it appears to have included 'trade unionists' who were unsponsored but in some way recognised by their union.[57] There seems to have been some subtle social selectivity involved in this acceptance.[58] Certainly, even sponsored Members were discouraged from activity, particularly work on the Group committee, if they were not what was regarded as 'authentically' working class.[59] Neil Kinnock, for example, could never get elected in the Group.

Just how important this exclusiveness was when allied to political tendency was indicated in November 1982 in what may prove to have been the Group's last stand. The rise of Neil Kinnock to second place in the Shadow Cabinet elections that year stimulated moves to harness his aggressive oratory to the subject of unemployment. But as part of a mobilisation of the Right to save the Shadow Minister of Employment, Eric Varley, 40 members of the Trade Union Group sent a letter to the Leader, Michael Foot, opposing any such move, and Varley stayed where he was. Kinnock himself was a sponsored TGWU MP but an ex-WEA tutor. 'Kinnock', said a senior member of the Group to the author in 1982, 'is not one of us.' 'Varley is a real trade unionist.' A year later Kinnock was Leader of the Party and Varley was on his way to retirement from politics and into a private sector directorship – and the Trade Union Group had once again gone very quiet.[60]

In any case, strict social exclusiveness was increasingly difficult to practice, given the changing social composition of sponsored MPs. Within the group now, railwaymen became represented by an Old Etonian, and shopworkers by a journalist.[61] When the Group had been revived in 1954 there had been thirty-four miners among them. Now there were only thirteen – one less than the number of sponsored women MPs, a slowly-growing[62] feature that some of the old male chauvinists disliked.

The Group was still different from the rest of the PLP in its core of working class and ex-union official representation. But the signs were that in social terms it was gradually becoming more like the PLP as a whole as 'the professionals' increased and trade union experience declined.[63]

Representation, independence and 'instructions'

The same forces which encouraged a closer liaison between unions and their sponsored Members also produced new difficulties over the obligations of representation. The mechanism of sponsorship within a Parliamentary Labour Party has always thrown up such problems for the sponsored Members. From the unions – even within the same unions – there were contrary perspectives on the role that the Members were expected to play. The old tradition of delegate democracy and the fact that unions paid money to the Party sustained a view of sponsorship in which the trade union MPs had primary loyalties to their unions, especially when the direct interests of the industry were involved.

Alongside this view was another which addressed itself to the division of labour within the Movement – political and industrial spheres in which there were distinct obligations and proprieties. And just as MPs were discouraged, even prevented, from interfering in industrial disputes or in the internal politics of the union, so in this view the union itself recognised an area of political freedom for the sponsored MPs to pursue political issues and follow Parliamentary discipline. Socialisation into the norms and career patterns of Parliamentary life tended to reinforce this division and to ensure that whenever the clash of obligations did make itself felt, loyalty normally went to the Parliamentary Party and to the Parliamentary leadership.

Since 1940 the judgements of the Committee of Privileges in the Alderman Robinson case (1943–4) and the W.J. Brown case (1946–7), have reinforced the protection of MPs. The Committee did accept the legitimacy of sponsoring and similar arrangements. In its report in 1947, the Committee even accepted that action 'calculated and intended to bring pressure on the Member to take or refrain from taking a particular course' was not necessarily a breach of privilege.[64] It recognised also that it was 'inevitable' that if 'an outside body may properly enter into contractual relationships with and make payments to a Member as such, it must in general be entitled to terminate that relationship if it lawfully can where it considers it necessary for the protection of its own interests so to do'.[65] So withdrawal of sponsorship on grounds that the unions' interests were not being served was not itself a breach of privilege. But the Committee also asserted:

> What, on the other hand, an outside body is certainly not entitled to do is to use the agreement or the payment as an instrument by which it controls or seeks to control the conduct of a Member or to punish him for what he has done as a Member.[66]

This indicated that although a union was not precluded from expressing a strong opinion as to the policies that an MP should follow and not precluded from withdrawing sponsorship if it felt that its interests were not being safeguarded, it had to be extremely careful how it conjoined these in terms of sanctions. The greater the threat, the more specific the instruction in relation to a vote in the House, and the nearer in advance to that vote that the threat was made, the more likely it became that a breach had taken place.

Generally in the two decades following the W.J. Brown case, trade union leaders accepted the impropriety of threatening *any* sanctions via sponsorship. On the Left of the Parliamentary Party, this view was strengthened by the vulnerability that Leftwing MPs felt in the face of a Movement so dominated by the Right and by the fierce commitment of Aneurin Bevan and Michael Foot to the freedom of the House. Thus this prohibition became part of the 'rules' of the relationship.

The TUC made it clear that it believed that 'the responsibility of a Member of Parliament is primarily to his party and his constituents'.[67] On the very few occasions when attempts were made from within the unions to express a different view of the obligations of sponsored members, the union leadership weighed in on behalf of 'parliamentary discipline' and the 'higher law' of the PLP.[68]

Yet within the Party and the unions there remained the residue of the older tradition in which mandating and instructions were not considered improper but simply an extension of trade union traditions of class representation and democracy. On the trade union Left, this view had its strongest advocates. But in a period when fundamental industrial issues were closed to the political arena, and a degree of consensus bound the ideas of the industrial and political leadership, issues of control and authority rarely became contentious. When these conditions no longer held, the older traditions of delegate democracy began to be reasserted from within the unions.

Inasmuch as this involved new pressures upon sponsored MPs, it was a significant development in the union–Party relationship. But its significance and the thrust of power behind it must not be exaggerated. There were, as we shall see, continuing and deep inhibitions restraining the actions of senior union leaders and, in any case, in terms of inducing a response from MPs, the new pressures often met a determined resistance.

The fact was that though sponsorship was valued, it was far from being a crucial element in an MP's life. For a small and diminishing number in safe mining seats, withdrawal of sponsorship would almost certainly have led to problems within the constituency party but even here, as we have seen, sponsorship was not necessarily decisive. Many MPs – particularly the more able – were in a position to 'shop around' between unions for the best deal. Among sponsored MPs were some who were 'not bothered' whether they were sponsored or not and had taken sponsorship at the request of the union. For most MPs the advantage of sponsorship was clear but by no means overwhelming.

The provision of resources to the CLP organisation helped ease the local relationship. There was a general advantage to the MP in being associated with a leading union – an expression of value at a time when talent was seen to be 'headhunted' by unions. And a public withdrawal of sponsorship could be a blow to the prestige of the Member and might be seen as symptomatic of a wider divergence from the Movement or a failure of effort and personality. But these were not the most vital considerations.

It may be true that, as Muller suggested in 1977, 'They run the risk of losing their sponsored status at any time because of conflict with their unions ...'[69] but judging by the evidence of the past forty years, the risk is very small indeed, even though sponsored MPs varied considerably in their ability, diligence, and commitment to their sponsoring union. Certainly, as new issues arose in Parliament, and new militancy and new political alignments arose in the unions in the late 1960s, so new tensions emerged in some of the unions in relations with sponsored MPs. On many occasions since then MPs have acted or voted in ways which ran counter to important elements of union policy. Sometimes the mutterings of resentment from within the unions have emerged as public recriminations. More rarely, this has taken the form of warnings in relation to sponsorship. But it was highly unusual for any action ever to materialise.

As union behaviour in 1969 over *In Place of Strife* showed, unions do not put direct pressure on individual MPs, even when what are regarded as fundamental interests are at stake.[70] As for pressure on the Group, sometimes, in the heat of the moment, tongues have run away from heads, but senior union leaders retreat immediately there is any suggestion of the improper. The classic case occurred in 1975 when, in the middle of a bitter controversy concerning the railway policy of the then Labour Government, Sid Weighell, the NUR General Secretary, declared to a protest rally that the union's sponsored MPs would be told to vote against the Government. The press picked it up, the union group of MPs dug in their heels, and Weighell made a full apology to the Speaker before it could be raised in the House – ' ... no such instructions would ever be issued by myself, or any other Officer of the Union'.[71]

Clear and immediate withdrawal of sponsorship for action taken in the House is virtually unknown. I say virtually, because the most striking exception to this was itself a confirmation of union respect for Parliament. In 1988, the AEU suddenly withdrew its sponsorship from the MP for Leith, Ron Brown. But the reasons involved were little to do with policy, let alone union interests. Brown was accused of disrespectful behaviour towards the House of Commons – an action which undermined the public standing of the Labour Party.[72]

This tension between a Leftwing MP and his sponsoring union was unusual also in the factional alignment of the relationship. Normally, in recent years, the tension has been between a union where the Left has moved to a new position of strength and sponsored MPs who were in the main selected during an earlier political era in the union. The new phase of tension began in the later 1960s and was provoked by conflict over incomes and industrial relations policies. This, in turn, was affected by the reappraisal of intra-Party democracy taking place in the 1970s, a reappraisal in which there was much criticism of the extent to which Labour MPs, sponsored and unsponsored alike, had become independent of and unaccountable to the Labour Movement. As the main thrust of this movement for greater accountability came from the Left, it is not surprising that the main conflict over the obligations of sponsored MPs should mainly be concentrated on three Left-influenced unions – the Transport Workers, the Public Employees and the Mineworkers.

In each of these unions there were indications from a section of the union leadership that they wanted both a closer relationship and more sensitivity to union policy. In each of these unions a section of the activist Left and some of the officials pushed for a more 'delegatist' relationship. But in each union there was also a deep wariness of contravening constitutional propriety and of breaking the 'rules' of the relationship. Readers of Chapter 7 will note again the important difference in behaviour which sometimes appears between union leaders on the General Council and less senior national and regional officers of the union. Some of the latter emerged as key figures in the controversies of the 1970s over sponsorship – with again the senior national official playing a restraining and restrained role.

Let us return to the behaviour of Jack Jones, whose emergence was part of, and an encouragement to, a wave of Leftwing opinion at the TGWU Conference which from 1967 to 1971 focused on what was regarded as the poor work-rate of sponsored Members and their disregard of the union's policies.[73] But Jones was to exercise considerable caution and show considerable respect for the proprieties of the 'rules' of the relationship and the privileges of the House of Commons.

Thus, although four TGWU MPs lost their sponsorship after a reconstitution of the panel in 1970,[74] political factors were central only in the case of George Brown. Here, in my view, the crucial feature was not Brown's recent behaviour within the House but his history outside it. The differences between Jones and Brown went back many years and were most heated on defence policy issues[75] (not to the fore from 1966 to 1970). What was deeply resented among the TGWU leadership was Brown's breach of the 'rules' of the relationship in 1961 when, on behalf of the political leadership, he attempted to force himself into the TGWU defence debate at their Conference and, then, failing in his attempt, mounted a factional meeting on the fringes. There was also a deep suspicion of Brown's consultancies from major employers, including the Mirror Group and Courtaulds.[76] Jones personally felt that Brown was potentially disloyal to the Movement. Here was one case where he was unwilling to step in and protect the MP from the pressure to withdraw sponsorship. It was a highly unusual case and has to be judged against the fact that, then and subsequently, MPs who took a very different view from the union's over incomes policy (and much else) retained their sponsorship.

It also has to be judged against the behaviour of Alex Kitson in 1971, an Executive Officer of the union after its amalgamation with the Scottish Commercial Motormen. Kitson made a speech to the 1971 TGWU Conference which appeared to contain a warning to pro-Common Market MPs that sponsorship would be withdrawn if they voted against union policy on the issue. The matter was taken to the House and to the Select Committee on Privileges, but Jones had already acted, alerting Labour MPs to the fact that Kitson had consulted neither the Executive Council nor the senior officers before making his statement – and had made no direct threats.[77] In the light of this explanation, the Committee made no recommendation, simply noting a section of its previous judgement in the W. J. Brown case.[78]

Jones's caution and inhibition in this area can be judged in connection with the treatment of Reg Prentice. If ever an MP was at odds with the policy, style and ethos of his union in the mid-1970s, it was Reg Prentice, a man heavily critical of militant trade unionism and the Left and well into a trajectory which was to take him out of the Labour Party. Yet Prentice remained a TGWU-sponsored MP through both elections of 1974. Attempts from his union branch to force Prentice out were always stymied at Regional level, where Parliamentary privilege was quoted as the reason why no action could be taken. Eventually, after his deselection as a Newham candidate had been confirmed, Prentice indicated that he was no longer interested in sponsorship. In November 1976 he resigned from the sponsored MPs' panel, making a public attack on the union's 'outdated' relationship with the Labour Party.[79] A year later he joined the Conservative Party.

The issue of obligation to the union and displacement from the panel arose again in acute form in 1978 when the new General Secretary of the union, Moss Evans, wrote to all the sponsored MPs pointing out that the union was opposed to incomes policy.[80] This was almost on the eve of an important Commons vote in which the Labour Government was attempting to bring in sanctions against firms which broke the 5 per cent pay guideline. In the event, only three TGWU-sponsored MPs, Syd Bidwell, Roy Hughes and Eddie Loyden (out of 26), abstained, although it was an important abstention given that the Government was defeated by 285 votes to 283.

A week later, one of the sponsored MPs, James Dunn, who had voted for the Government, had his sponsorship withdrawn – an action which was interpreted as a political reprisal. The union leadership gives another view: that there had been regular complaints from both Right and Left in the union that Dunn was not satisfactory in the performance of his duties and that he was not active enough in the House. Moss Evans vehemently denied any connection with the incomes policy vote and strongly affirmed the rights of sponsored MPs to make up their own minds having considered the union's position.[81]

A similar pattern of behaviour could be observed within the National Union of Public Employees in the 1970s, where a strong Leftwing, encouraged by the powerful Deputy General Secretary, Bernard Dix, made it clear that it wanted a much more responsive role from NUPE's panel of sponsored MPs who were very diverse in age, ability and political position. A growing feeling that the Parliamentary 'arm' was not as effective as it might be coincided with policy tensions over the Labour Government's adoption of cuts in proposed public expenditure. Matters came to a head in 1977 when the NUPE Conference passed a resolution which called on its Executive Committee to demand assurances from its six MPs about their voting on public expenditure cuts with an instruction to withdraw sponsorship if the assurances were not forthcoming.[82]

NUPE MPs immediately and totally rejected the resolution and it was taken to the Select Committee. NUPE's General Secretary, Alan Fisher, was already indicating his distance from the resolution and actually wrote to the Committee before it met, asking for its comments so that these could be taken into account by his Executive.[83] In reply, the Committee was clear that for the union to take such action would 'constitute a serious contempt of the House'.[84] Accordingly, Fisher wrote again to say that the Executive, in the light of the Select Committee's letter, would simply let the Conference resolution 'lie on the table'.[85]

As with other unions experiencing a political shift in this period, the adjustment between this union and its MPs was gradual and cautious as its panel was reconstituted. One sponsored MP, Ken Lomas, resigned his sponsorship in 1978 but the others remained in place at the 1979 General Election. In the next eight years a change took place in the relationship between the union and its MPs such that by 1987 it was close and reasonably harmonious. In July 1980, two of the MPs, Peter Hardy and Ted Leadbitter, had their sponsorship for the next election withdrawn, although they remained sponsored for the remainder of the Parliament. Hardy's sponsorship was then taken over by NACODS. Others were taken onto the NUPE panel who were more in tune with the union's style and political perspectives.

The most important case involving trade union attempts to exercise influence over sponsored MPs concerned the National Union of Mineworkers, a union which, according to Harrison, had a long pre-war record of its MPs voting in accordance with Executive Committee instructions.[86] Here again was a strong delegatist view coming from the resurgent activist Left led by Yorkshire Area President, Arthur Scargill. But here again what was noticeable was the sensitivity of the union's senior national officials to the privileges of the House.

The Yorkshire Area of the NUM had been a solid base for the union and the Party's Right Wing in the post-war period. When the union swung markedly to the Left in the 1970s, it created a serious gulf in policy between the union and its sponsored MPs – a gulf which involved industrial issues but which was mainly political. Sponsorship adoption in the union was controlled at area level – an unusual arrangement but traditional in this once federal union.

On 25 June 1975, in response to the behaviour of five Yorkshire Miners' MPs who had deviated from union policy and campaigned for entry into the Common Market, the Yorkshire Area of the NUM passed a resolution which challenged the 'luxury' of independence and threatened a withdrawal of sponsorship if an MP disobeyed 'guidelines' concerning opposition to and campaigning against the union's policy.[87]

There is no doubt that this resolution corresponded with strong feelings in the union's branches and reflected also a more generally assertive mood on the Left about the degree to which Members of Parliament were independent of 'the Movement'. It was a mood with which the Yorkshire President, Arthur Scargill, was very much in tune. At a Press Conference and on ITN's 'News at Ten', he gave interviews on the meaning and significance of the Yorkshire Area's decision. One of his statements was reported in the press and then to the House of Commons by George Cunningham, the Labour MP for Islington and South Finsbury, as 'Miners are entitled by virtue of their sponsorship to tell their Members of Parliament which way to vote'.[88] As a result of Cunningham's complaint, the matter was referred on 27 June to the Committee of Privileges.

The Committee's finding was that the Resolution of the Yorkshire Area 'constituted a serious contempt, which represented a continuing threat to Members' freedom of speech and action and which could not be allowed to remain in existence'.[89] But before the judgement was made, it was noticeable the extent to which the union's national officials made efforts to disassociate or distance the union. On 18 September, the EC of the union (with whom right to withdraw sponsorship lay) passed a resolution nullifying the decision of the Yorkshire Area Council. The President of the union, Joe Gormley, wrote to the Select Committee that

> this Union would never seek to interfere with the freedom of speech or actions of Members of Parliament.[90]

The Yorkshire Area Secretary was at pains to point out to the Committee that the original resolutions were 'watered down' as a result of the intervention of the Area officials.[91] And even Arthur Scargill wrote noting that he was simply reflecting the views of the Area Council.[92]

The significant point here was that the sponsored MPs did not change their political position and (apart from Joe Harper who died in 1978) they fought the 1979 election with NUM sponsorship. Indeed, not until 1986–7, when Frank Haines of Ashfield and Michael McGuire of Makerfield lost sponsorship in the aftermath of the Miners' Strike, did any NUM MP lose sponsorship.[93]

Thwarted via the union's sponsorship process, Scargill moved to a second front. The Yorkshire Area Executive attempted to achieve a greater NUM input into the Labour Party.[94] It was not an easy task and in terms of ridding the coalfields of sitting Rightwing MPs and ensuring their replacement by NUM candidates nearer to the Leftwing position of the union, it was generally a failure. Even in the Barnsley Labour Party, where the NUM was successful in ensuring a dominant Leftwing presence by 1979, Roy Mason proved a tough opponent until 1987 when he retired. Not until 1986 was any sitting MP in the Yorkshire coalfield deselected and even then the MP in question, Alex Woodhall in Hemsworth, was 70 years old. The fact that Kevin Barron, an ex-Scargill organiser, could move to being Kinnock's PPS in 1985 and retain both sponsorship and selection indicated again the freedom of MPs and the constraints operating upon the union's leadership.

The pattern in these unions of assertiveness, warnings and retreats was not without its general impact on MPs, if only because of the increased wear and tear of political conflict. It was part of a growing climate in the 1970s which, as we have seen, had its implosive culmination in the crisis of intra-party democracy after 1979. Strong feelings voiced through the union fed into a series of increasing pressures upon MPs – indirectly from the Party Conference and the NEC and directly from the activists in the MPs' constituencies. It is likely that on some issues MPs not willing to be totally out of 'communion' with the Movement anticipated reactions and went along for a quiet life.

Indeed, it may be, as has been suggested,[95] that some votes on the Common Market in 1971 were affected by the pressure. But it would be a difficult judgement to separate the effect of the individual union, the CLP and the Party at large. Of course, on issues where the unions in general felt strongly in the late 1970s, there would be some inhibition in the PLP at being too far out of step with 'the brooding shadow' (Chapter 8). Occasionally an MP resigned his sponsorship when in disagreement with the union.[96] That option was always open and, with the exception of the mining areas, involved little costs. But no evidence has yet been produced – not even by the defecting Social Democrats, repudiating sponsorship and all similar links to the unions – to indicate improper pressure upon individual MPs. And as for responses to the injunctions from the unions and the general disapproval which was better communicated in the 1970s, it was notable to what extent MPs lived with years of disagreement with union policy – disagreement which stretched from one sponsorship period to the next.

Sponsorship and the Parliamentary leadership

In theory, since 1981 the unions have had a two-track influence over the elections for the Parliamentary leadership. They have (almost) 40 per cent of the votes in the electoral college and in theory they are represented also by those members of the MPs section (30 per cent of the vote) who are sponsored. Yet the evidence from the published lists of votes by MPs indicates little connection between a union's official position and that of its sponsored MPs, and unions made little effort to press it.

Here again, Scargill is the interesting exception of a union leader (albeit from an area position) demanding a vote of the Yorkshire Miners' MPs in 1980 for Michael Foot and in 1981 for Tony Benn against Dennis Healey.[97] And here again all the evidence suggests total failure. As far as is known, the four 'dissident' Rightwing MPs voted in 1980 and 1981 for Healey.[98] Interestingly, a converse situation occurred among the sponsored MPs of the Rightwing union EETPU. As the ex-General Secretary, Frank Chapple, later lamented, only one MP 'could be relied upon to support the union's choice'.[99] In subsequent leadership elections, the voting lists for 1983 and 1988 indicate a wide spread of political loyalties within the sponsored groups with no apparent linkage to the union's vote in the college. Conversely, the unions' votes for Michael Meacher and Eric Heffer in 1983 indicated that sponsorship was no guarantee of union support. As with so many other facets of the union–Party relationship, there are different spheres, different roles and different obligations.

However, sponsorship has changed significantly – as Muller forecast – in the extent to which it embraces the Parliamentary Leadership of the Party.[100] In the Shadow Cabinet of 1973, Labour's last year of Opposition before the election that brought the Party to power, only two of the twelve Shadow Cabinet Members were sponsored. Neither the Leader nor Deputy Leader were sponsored. Indeed, no Leader had been sponsored since the days of Arthur Henderson in the early 1930s.[101]

Signs of change first became apparent during the 1974–9 Labour Government and by 1987 the Leader, Deputy Leader and twelve of the fifteen Members of the Shadow Cabinet were sponsored (Table 9.2).

The transformation was virtually complete by the end of 1989. Denzil Davies and Robert Hughes had been replaced by Tony Blair and Barry Jones, both sponsored by the TGWU. Three women MPs had been added to the committee, Margaret Beckett and Ann Clwyd, also sponsored by the TGWU, and Joan Lester sponsored by the GMB. In addition, Jo Richardson and Jack Straw were put on the GMB's second panel (see p. 243) and their CLPs given assistance. Thus, to one extent or another, all twenty members of the Shadow Cabinet were now 'sponsored'.

Table 9.2 Sponsorship and the
Shadow Cabinet, 1987

N. Kinnock	TGWU
R. Hattersley	USDAW
G. Kaufman	GMB
F. Dobson	NUR
J. Smith	GMB
M. Meacher	COHSE
B. Gould	UCW
J. Cunningham	GMB
R. Hughes	AEU
D. Davies	None
R. Cook	NUR
J. Straw	None
J. Prescott	NUS
G. Brown	TGWU
D. Clarke	NUPE
D. Dewer	NUR
J. Richardson	None

Source: Trade UnionLiaison Office, Labour Party Headquarters,
plus interviews with union officials

The sponsorship of these leading positions was dominated by the two General Unions – the TGWU had six and the GMB also six if we count the second panel support. The NUR had three; COHSE, NUPE, NUS, UCW and USDAW each have one. In contrast to the 1970s, there was noone from the AEU or the NUM – unions still sponsoring mainly ex-manual workers from the industry.

This new linkage between the Parliamentary Leadership and the unions may well have been encouraged initially by the closeness of the unions and the Labour Government after 1974. Becoming sponsored was a harmonious process in a relationship which had seldom been closer since 1918. But it also reflects a change in the composition of sponsored MPs who have increasingly been drawn from the social groups that make up a majority of Labour's leadership. 'Co-option' has accentuated this trend.

This new extension of sponsorship is significant not so much in power terms but in that fusing of identification which gives added depth to the integration of a relationship which is adversely affected by social tension and some acute problems relating to industrial issues. An association with a member of the Shadow Cabinet also gives a union status and some high-flyers have even been 'headhunted' with this in mind. But its implications for access and policy are much less significant than they at first appear.

In practice, a large union can usually find access regardless of sponsorship when it needs a hearing – either at the level of the NEC, the Shadow Cabinet or the Leader's Office. And unions are hesitant (even sometimes hostile) about sponsorship getting involved with Party policymaking. There is a worry lest union groups in Parliament cut across and complicate the communication of the unions' position. And there is the other side of this – that differences over Party policy might undermine the effectiveness of trade representation. All this means that once again lines of protocol are drawn by the unions in terms of appropriate modes of representation and communication at Shadow Cabinet level as well as within the PLP as a whole.

In any case, the Shadow Cabinet is not a collegiate policymaking body. Still less does the wider 'Front Bench' operate in this way. Individual portfolios of sponsored MPs do not necessarily overlap with a union's concerns. Indeed, most Front Benchers are heavily involved elsewhere. In some of the most sensitive positions (in terms of union involvement) – Employment, Industry, Energy and Transport – it would be normal for some of the sponsored MPs to be part of the teams. But this gives reassurance to 'the unions' generally rather than recognition to the interests of a particular union.

Unions may get sympathy, co-operation and commitment from Front Bench MPs who are non-sponsored but they may have a relatively weak relationship with a sponsored MP. Even when a sponsored MP has a strategic portfolio, he or she does not necessarily give priority to one interest group – even to their own union; there have been many examples of this in the history of the Labour Party. John Prescott, though deeply sensitive to the Seamen's problems when he was part of the Transport team, took it to be his responsibility to work for a co-ordinating of the policies of the Transport unions (see Chapter 14, p.442). Stan Orme, as Shadow Energy spokesperson, was to come under severe private criticism from his own union, the AUEW, because of his independent position on nuclear energy and his agreement with a phasing-out policy which ran directly counter to the position of the union.[102] Though Tony Blair was TGWU-sponsored, you would not, in 1990, be able to predict his policy stance on issues connected with the Shadow Employment portfolio from this, nor could you account for the differences be-tween him and his predecessor, Michael Meacher, in sponsorship terms.

As for the Party Leader himself – the first post-war Labour Leader to be a sponsored MP – the fact of Kinnock's relationship with the TGWU was often used by the Party's opponents and critics to suggest his subservience to the union[103] Yet his record after being elected Leader was consistent with his record before. If he was in profound disagreement with his union, then he took his own counsel – as he had done over devolution in spite of the strong views of the Wales Region TGWU. And as Leader he was clear that Party policy was Party policy; the union's policy was something different. On several major issues, including the handling of the Miners Strike and its aftermath in 1985, there was a clear divergence between TGWU policy and that of the Party Leader. The same would apply in the tense circumstances of 1988 to training policy and to the RCN (see n. 11.66 and 11.67). As for the TGWU leadership, it was always deeply sensitive to the proprie-ties. Sponsorship, like the landlordship of Party headquarters, was unmention-able and unemployable as a resource when dealing with the Party Leader. (See Chapter 16, p. 513).

Also, although having one or two sponsored MPs in the Shadow Cabinet and a cluster on the Front Bench gave a union status, there was a feeling within some of the unions that they were better off with good and reliable backbenchers if only because they were able to give more time to the union's main preoccupations over sponsorship, that is, the repetitive presentation of the union's case in a variety of situations. The unavailability of the Front Benchers, plus an accentuation of the sensitivity which inhibited 'leaning on them for anything', meant that there were limited benefits to having too many of them.

The fact was that the Front Bench did rather well out of the sponsoring arrangement. It became occasionally a source of additional funding for research and the employment of political assistance in connection with portfolios which often had little or nothing to do with particular unions. And to some extent it created a career obligation upon the unions in terms of support for the sponsored high-flyer. This was seen not in terms of the allocation of Front Bench portfolios, where Kinnock was deeply protective of his independence as Leader, but in terms of Party elections – particularly for the Women's Section of the NEC (see Chapter 11, pp. 332–3). And though it has yet to be shown to be significant, every aspiring member of the committee was aware that in Leadership elections involving the unions, it was not disadvantageous to be associated with one of the larger unions.

THE DEVELOPMENT OF SPONSORSHIP: AN OVERVIEW

Among the clear patterns to emerge from the recent development of sponsorship has been the major 'turn-back' to sponsorship by the unions and a turn to 'co-option' of existing MPs which has embraced the Leadership of the Party. Although trade union experience has diminished among those sponsored, and union leaders no longer overlap their role with parliamentary representation, there has developed an increasing integration based upon better liaison and the creation of a 'political officer' group. The rise of better-organised individual union groups has been accompanied by the decline of the general Trade Union Group.

For the Party, this increased union interest in sponsorship has been financially beneficial in terms of organisational and electoral funds, although the trend to 'co-option' has further accentuated the maldistribution of such resources. The areas of traditional union strength and the seats with customary occupancy, combined with sponsorship, contribute to the PLP's broad social representation and the preservation of a still valuable and authentic voice for the manual working class.

Sponsorship is often misunderstood in terms of the unions' power relationship with the Party. Sponsorship is not maintenance and unions have either frozen or phased out personal payments. The loss of direct financial influence has also been accompanied by a diminution of union strength at local party level and a decline in influence over candidate selection. What a union can threaten is limited and usually countered by Parliamentarians who value their autonomy. In any case, the striking feature of the sponsoring relationship – a feature borne out during the tensions of recent Party–union experience – is the extent to which union leaders are inhibited and constrained by the 'rules' of the relationship.

NOTES

1. Subcommittee of EC of Labour Representation Committee *Minutes* 31/5/1900.

2. 'Can I thank you for destroying the myth that Labour MPs are paid directly by trade unions.' Dale Campbell-Savours MP to Jimmy Knapp, NUR General Secretary. *Select Committee on Members' Interests*, Parliamentary Lobbying, Minutes of Evidence, 13/12/88, p. 133. Among my third-year politics students in Manchester in 1987 I found an almost universal belief at the beginning of the session that these payments were to the MP.

3. 'The financial support of MPs ... ranges from the trade union sponsorship of some Labour MPs to the directorates offered to so many Conservatives. We pay our MPs so little ... it is unsurprising that many seek to augment their income.' 'One Law for the Rulers?', *Guardian* Editorial, 19/12/85.

4. Labour Party EC Minutes, 12 June 1906, show 28 MPs being paid £200 per annum out of the Parliamentary Fund.

5. William D. Muller, *The Kept Men?*, 1977, p. 7.

6. Harrison, *op. cit.*, p. 92.

7. Muller, *op. cit.*, p. 142.

8. This view was put to me in 1985 by Andrew Roth, an authority on these matters and author of *The Business Background of MPs*, 1981. Investigation by the Select Committee on Members' Interests in 1989 focused on the danger of Parliament being permeated by large sums of money devoted to influencing legislation. The rate for one written question was said to be £200 and for alteration of major legislation £40,000. Adam Raphael, 'A £10m Trade in Influence', *Observer*, 9/4/89.

9. Adam Raphael, 'MPs Prepare Fudge on Cash Sweeteners', *Observer*, 1/12/86.

10. Although Muller's precise and scholarly work notes clearly that payments to constituency parties must not be confused with payments to MPs (p. 55), his own introduction places sponsorship in the context of 'Members who require financial assistance' (p. xiv) and the question mark in the title is not fully confronted in his conclusions. I am grateful to Professor Muller for sending me a copy of his weighty paper 'The Kept Men? Revisited 1975–1986', prepared for the APSA British Politics Panel in August 1986. My own research was independent of his, but it was helpful to be aware of the information contained in his paper.

11. Interview with the NUR Political Officer, Keith Hill, 12/4/89. The six new panel members were all either BR or NUR employees. They included one guard, one railman and one signalman, one travel centre supervisor and two union officers. NUR rules make a distinction between its 'A list' panel comprising members of the NUR prior to sponsorship and its 'Parliamentary' panel comprising candidates or MPs with a proven record of commitment to transport and industrial issues of concern to the unions. Other unions have two different 'panels' for different purposes. See, for example, p. 243 re GMB.

12. Harrison, *op. cit.*, noted the development of this trend, pp. 270–9.

13. Evidence to the Party Commission of Enquiry in 1980 from area conferences brought forth different explanations for the situation but gave a general picture of low affiliation and, in most areas, decline. *Org. Panel Minutes*, 6/5/80. A survey carried out for the Panel produced an average

of 42 per cent of union branches affiliated. The TGWU had 33 per cent of branches affiliated, NUPE had only 37 per cent and the GMWU 52 per cent. Local studies confirm the big decline in the 1960s. Eric McPherson, *Trade Unions as a Local Pressure Group*, unpublished MA thesis, Liverpool, 1973. Andrew Taylor, *The Politics of the Yorkshire Miners*, 1984, pp. 115–17. The Minutes of the Faversham Labour Party, which had a full-time Secretary-Agent until the 1960s, give a revealing portrait of decline through loss of contact. *Labour Party Archives*.

14. At Sid Weighell's insistence, the NUR began to seek 100 per cent affiliation in 1976. By 1980, most of its 490 branches were affiliated and the rest were virtually non-functioning. This was still the position in 1987. The GMWU sought to boost its affiliation after 1979. It was reported to have secured a ten to fifteen per cent increase on approximately 50 per cent (information supplied privately to the author). In contrast, AUEW affiliation declined and the ISTC cut back its affiliation in areas where it could not find delegates. NUPE appears to be one union which increased its affiliation in the early 1980s as a result of a new politicisation of the active membership.

15. Agenda II, Rules and Constitution, 1988, Constituency Parties, Clause IX.1(a). The NEC note alongside the change said 'Analysis shows the maximum laid down locally varies from 3 to 20. More than 80 per cent of constituencies work to the maximum of five', p. 27.

16. On this see McPherson, *op. cit.*, pp. 42–3. M.J. Barker and J.A. Chandler, *The Trade Unions and the Labour Party at the Grass Roots*, Sheffield Polytechnic, 1980, p. 17.

17. Harrison, *op. cit.*, p. 116.

18. Barker and Chandler, *op. cit.*, pp. 15–16.

19. Derek Fatchett, *Trade Unions and Politics in the 1980s*, 1987, p. 54.

20. Interim Report of the Committee of Enquiry into Party Organisation, 1967, Para. 14. See also Andrew Taylor, 'The Modern Borough Mongers? The Yorkshire Area NUM and Grass Roots Politics', *Political Studies*, 1984, 32, pp. 385–400. But cf. Barker and Chandler's, *op. cit.*, finding that for unions in Sheffield it made little difference, p. 14.

21. Barker and Chandler, *op. cit.*, p. 14. See also the comments of John Golding, *LPACR*, 1974, p. 174.

22. D.T. Denver, *Trade Unions and the Selection of Parliamentary Candidates*, European Consortium for Political Science, unpublished paper, 1985, p. 8.

23. J.T. Bochel and D.T. Denver, 'Candidate Selection in the Labour Party: What the Selectors Seek', *British Journal of Political Science*, 13, 1983, pp. 45–69.

24. Denver, *op. cit.*, 1985, pp. 5-6.

25. Taylor, *The Politics of the Yorkshire Miners*, *op. cit.*, Chapters 4 and 5.

26. In 1978 at Castleford, in a by-election selection contest between a sponsored NUM nominee and a non-sponsored miner, Geoffrey Lofthouse, Lofthouse won. In 1981, Eric Ogden, sponsored by the NUM, was deselected as MP for West Derby. In 1983, at Normanton, the NUM-sponsored candidate was defeated by a non-sponsored miner, Bill O'Brien. In 1985, at North East Derby, the NUM-sponsored candidate was defeated by Harry Barnes, a non-sponsored university lecturer.

27. Denver, *op. cit.*, p. 5.

28. *Ibid.*, p. 13.

29. Peter Heathfield, NUM General Secretary, *LPACR*, 1984, p. 56. See on

this also Victor Schonfield of the Campaign for Labour Party Democracy, who speaks of 'depriving millions of affiliated trade unionists of their say', *Morning Star*, 6/7/87. This was a strong theme in the case made by opponents of reform but a range of other arguments were also made for the status quo.

30. The NEC amendment was defeated by 3,041,000 votes to 3,992,000. In general, the Left-led unions voted against it and the Right-led union voted for it.

31. The key union to shift was the TGWU. Producing this was a difficult exercise. In 1987, the electoral college was carried on the TGWU EC by only the Chair's casting vote. At the union's conference there was a vote of 446–331. At the Party Conference, the status quo was defeated by 4,584,000 to 1,851,000 with TGWU and NUPE support, *LPACR*, 1987, pp. 16–23.

32. Data derived from Muller, *op. cit.*, p. 30.

33. Butler and Kavanagh, *op. cit.*, 1979, p. 288; 1983 (Byron Criddle), p. 240; 1987 (Byron Criddle), p. 206.

34. For its importance, see the evidence of Jimmy Knapp (NUR) to the Select Committee on Members' Interests, 1988–9. *Report on Parliamentary Lobbying*, Minutes of Evidence, 13/12/88, p. 131.

35. Apart from 1931 (69.5 per cent), 1922 was the last time that over 60 per cent of MPs were sponsored. Derived from Muller, *op. cit.*, p. 30.

36. At the end of 1989, the union announced its intention of seeking a total panel of 50 candidates. 'Sponsored' and 'supported' panels at that stage amounted to 26. *Information supplied by GMB*.

37. Richter, *op. cit.*, pp. 186–8, cites an example involving ASSET and the threat of a 'company union' in 1962–4.

38. Ellis and Johnson, *op cit.*, pp. 16–17, give a case study of the TGWU and the Merchant Shipping Bill of 1966.

39. Richter, *op. cit.*, p. 188 cites a case involving ASSET and an airline strike in 1965.

40. Muller, *op. cit.*, p. 121, cites a case involving the Agricultural Workers.

41. *Ibid.*, pp. 111–16.

42. See Taylor, *op. cit.*, p. 151 for Roy Mason's complaint about being excluded from raising the issues connected with unofficial strikes.

43. See on this Ellis and Johnson, *op. cit.*, pp. 18–19. Richter, *op. cit.*, pp. 108–122 and 165–189.

44. Muller, *op. cit.*, p. 141. Ellis and Johnson, *op. cit.*, p. 20.

45. Ellis and Johnson, *op. cit.*, p. 18. Richter, *op. cit.*, p. 171.

46. Ellis and Johnson, *op. cit.*, p. 20.

47. Sidney Weighell, *On the Rails*, 1983, pp. 130–1.

48. Pardington moved to TUFL in 1986 as their Assistant National Coordinator and then in 1987 became their National Coordinator. Subsequently her position within the TGWU was given to Sue Rubner who took a lower profile, and occasionally other members of the TGWU staff, including Ian Wilmore, took parts of the expanded political portfolio. Regan Scott, the Research Officer, continued, as in the past, to be very involved on political matters.

49. The political profile of Research Officers depended upon personal motivation and political interest as well as union designation. And unions varied in their formal arrangements covering the operation and supervision of 'the political side'. Arrangements could change quite markedly. In the mid-1980s, the political officer in the GMWU, David

Warburton (a national officer), lost his political responsibilities after some controversial political comments and was replaced, in effect, by his General Secretary, John Edmunds, although Rachel Brooks from the union's Research Department staff dealt with political matters at that level. It was more normally the case that the supervision of the political side was at the level of national officer (e.g. Edward O'Brien, SOGAT and Gordon Colling, NGA) or at the level of Assistant/ Deputy General Secretary (e.g. Tony Clarke, UCW; John Golding, NCU; John Jones, TASS; Tom Sawyer, NUPE and Barbara Switzer, MSF).

50. A Memorandum from the NUR to the Select Committee on Members' Interests, op. cit., p. 127, notes 'the Union has held to a very strict policy whereby its relationship with its sponsored Members is limited to the matters of transport and industrial concern ...'.In the very informative report of the APEX group for in 1983 there were references to discussions of the Energy Bill; the fight to save two British Steel works; the Monopolies and Mergers Committee Report on Charter Consolidated and Anderson Strathclyde; the Shops Bill; the YOP and YTS Schemes; the Report of the Cork Committee on Insolvency Law and Practice; the future of the Aerospace Industry; the Data Protection Bill; the New Meat Regulations; the Age of Retirement; the Job Release Scheme; the Shipbuilding Industry; the Government's Trade Union Legislation; and a number of matters referred to it by the Executive Council which arose at the Union's 1983 Annual Conference.

51. Interview with union officials. MPs mentioned in this connection were Jack Ashley, Dale Campbell-Savours, Alf Dubs and Michael Meacher. See Minutes of Evidence to the Select Committee on Members' Interests, op. cit., p. 135.

52. APEX Parliamentary Report, 1983, produced by the union's Political Officer, Roger Godsiff.

53. NUR Political Report, 1988, p. 6. The Clause related to 'The Railway Board's Plan for International Through Services', particularly collection and distribution centres.

54. See Chapter 4, p. 82 and n. 12.

55. On this see Ellis and Johnson, op. cit., Chapter 3. P. Jenkins, op. cit., 1970, Chapter 4. Eric Heffer, op. cit., Chapters 5 and 6. L. Minkin, op. cit., 1980, pp. 306-7.

56. Heffer, op. cit., Chapters 9-13. Muller, op. cit., pp. 86-7.

57. Muller, op. cit., p. 80 and interview with Eddie Wainwright, Group Secretary, 1982.

58. Richter, p. 129, n. 1, notes the exclusion of Douglas Houghton MP in 1968. At that time, he was General Secretary of the Inland Revenue Staff Federation – a white collar union unaffiliated to the Labour Party – and of course unsponsored.

59. Muller, op. cit., p. 80 and interviews with the Group Secretary, 1983.

60. Under new officials after 1983, some new energy was injected into the Group but it played no part in the Miners' Strike of 1984–5 nor has it been prominent since over other union-related issues.

61. The Guardian reported on 4 July 1987 the formation of a 'working class group' of Labour MPs which appeared to be trying to rescue social exclusiveness.

62. In 1987, there were 21 Labour women MPs of which 14 were sponsored (including six from the TGWU, three from NUPE, three from ASTMS and two from the GMB). There was much pressure on the unions to

improve upon this. In December 1989, the GMB became the first union to introduce quotas on its panel.

63. Those from working class occupations and trade union work still made up 49.5 per cent of the Group in 1983. Trevor Park, Mary Lewis and Paul Lewis, 'Trade Unions and the Labour Party: Changes in the Group of Trade Union Sponsored MPs', *Political Studies*, vol. XXXIV, No. 2, June 1986, pp. 311–2.

64. *Report of the Committee of Privileges*, HC (1946–7) 118, Paras. 11–15.

65. *Ibid.*

66. *Ibid.*

67. *TUC Evidence to the (Donovan) Royal Commission, op. cit.*, November 1966.

68. Harrison, *op. cit.*, pp. 293–4.

69. Muller, *op. cit.*, p. 153.

70. Ellis and Johnson, *op. cit.*, p. 25, 'the most surprising feature of the whole affair is how weak, diffuse and unspecific was the pressure exerted on sponsored MPs by their unions'.

71. *Hansard*, HC 17/12/75, Col. 1392/3, 902. I am informed that the NUR Group Secretary, Peter Snape, was on his way round to NUR Head Office at break of day to ensure that the apology was in the Speaker's mail that morning. See also Sidney Weighell, *op. cit.*, 1983, p. 55.

72. The Ron Brown affair concerned damage to the Mace in the House and then a failure to make an appropriate apology to the House, 19/4/88. On 25/4/88, after AEU officials had publicly criticised his actions, the union's National Committee voted to remove his name from the list of sponsored candidates.

73. The 1967 TGWU Conference called upon the union's Executive to reconstitute the union's panel before the next election – a breach with the past union practice of automatic re-sponsorship. In 1969, the Conference resolved that in future only members 'who fight for union policies and have a proven record of union work' should be supported. In 1971, the Conference accepted one resolution which included the need to take account of 'applicants' political views and previous stewardship' when deciding on sponsorship, *TGWU Biennial Conference Reports*, 1967, Minute No. 48, p. 22; 1969, Minute No. 52, p. 23 and 1971, Minute No. 82, p. 37.

74. In addition to Brown, there was John Lee, Malcolm McPherson and Tom Oswald.

75. Jones and Brown had many bitter rows over nuclear disarmament. See *Jones: Union Man, op. cit.*, p. 169. Brown, in 1962, was also involved in an unsuccessful attempt to expel the philosopher Bertrand Russell (a leader of the Campaign for Nuclear Disarmament) from the Party. All this went into the memory.

76. Brown acted as consultant to the Mirror Group in a period when the *Daily Mirror* opposed the London Bus Strike of 1958. In 1968, Brown took up a consultancy with Courtaulds.

77. See particularly the intervention of Stan Orme, *Hansard*, HC 19/7/71, Cols. 1059/60.

78. *Special Report of the Committee of Privileges*, 'Complaint of a Threat to Withdraw Cash Support from Members of Parliament', XXII, 409, Session 1970–71, 2/8/71.

79. *Daily Express*, 2/12/76. He described trade union procedures within the Labour Party as 'archaic, irrelevant and dangerous', *Guardian*, 3/12/76.

80. Letter from Moss Evans to Eddie Loyden, Chair of the TGWU Group of MPs, 4/12/78.
81. Interview with Moss Evans, 16/12/85.
82. NUPE *Conference Report*, 1977, p. 16.
83. *Fourth Report of the Select Committee of Privileges*, 'Complaint of Action by the National Union of Public Employees', HC Accounts and Papers, 1976–7, XIII, 512, 441, 19/7/77, Para. 2.
84. *Ibid.*, Para. 3.
85. *Ibid.*
86. Harrison, *op. cit.*, p. 292.
87. HC, 1974–1975, 634, *Second Report of the Select Committee of Privileges*, 14/10/75, p. vii. The Resolution said: 'we can no longer tolerate the position where a 'sponsored' MP can oppose his Union's policy on major issues. Therefore, it is agreed that the following guidelines shall apply to MP's sponsored by the Yorkshire Area. (1) No Miners' MP shall vote or speak against Union policy on any issue which affects the Coal Mining industry. (2) No Miners' MP shall actively campaign or work against the Union policy on any other major issue. (3) If any Miners' MP refuses to agree to the 'guide-lines' or violate these guide-lines, the Area Council shall withdraw sponsorship from that MP. We wish to make it clear that the Yorkshire Area will no longer tolerate a situation where a Miners' MP accepts the 'Privilege' of sponsorship and then demands the 'Luxury' of independence from Union policy.'
88. *Hansard*, HC 26/6/75, Col. 677–9.
89. HC 1974-1975, 634, *Second Report from the Committee of Privileges*, 14/10/75, p. iv.
90. *Ibid.*, p. v.
91. *Ibid.*, p. xii.
92. *Ibid.*, p. xii. For Scargill's views on the relationship between the NUM and its MP, see Taylor, *op. cit.*, p. 151.
93. In 1989, there was a peculiar case where Kim Howells, the new MP for Pontypridd (who had not been the official NUM candidate) was first granted sponsorship then denied it in the bitter infighting of post-strike NUM politics.
94. Taylor, *op. cit.*, pp. 122–3.
95. Muller, *op. cit.*, p. 150.
96. The case of Ken Lomas and NUPE in 1978 was one such example, I understand. Muller, *op. cit.*, notes another such case – Peter Doig who relinquished sponsorship from the TGWU in 1972 after an argument over NUM picketing, pp. 152-3.
97. *Morning Star*, 28/10/80.
98. The evidence is clear that in 1981, all the constituencies represented by NUM-sponsored MPs except Hemsworth voted for Benn but all the MPs voted for Healey.
99. Frank Chapple, *Sparks Fly*, 1984, p. 163.
100. Muller, *op. cit.*, pp. 194–5.
101. *Ibid.*, p. 92.
102. Interview with Stan Orme, 24/7/86.
103. For example David Selbourne, who described Kinnock as 'a T and G placeman', New Realism Fails To Revive Unions' *Sunday Times*, 9/4/89.

Part V

Policymakers and Policymaking

10

The block vote: process and policy

SYMBOLS AND MEANINGS

The most familiar feature of the trade unions' role in the Labour Party is their association with the voting procedure known as 'the block vote'. So central, so permanent and so well publicised has this feature become within the Labour Party that it has developed into a symbol of the entire relationship between the industrial and political wings. And it draws to itself all the controversy which surrounds the union connection.

For some, it remains the foundation stone of the Movement, an expression of its trade unionism and its collectivist values and also a security against measures which would cripple Labour's industrial base and undermine the union capacity to pursue effective representation.[1] For others, it is both notorious and obnoxious – an expression of all that is unacceptable about 'Socialism' or 'Labourism'. From Left and Right, opponents of the present Labour Movement focus on its iniquities. On the Left, opponents of the block vote have sometimes given it a disembodied and oppressive quality almost unrelated to the decisions of trade unionists. 'Their arguments were unanswerable', said Tariq Ali in 1983, 'so the bloc [sic] vote was used to hammer them into the ground.'[2] On the Right, the Conservative leadership, never slow to load the terminology of political debate, has taken to using 'the block vote' as a fundamental negation of individuality. 'I care very deeply about individuals', said Mrs Thatcher during the 1987 General Election, 'I don't like treating people as block votes.'[3]

This spread of meanings and associations builds upon ambiguities in the definition of 'the block vote' which have been there since its inception and it reflects a political antagonism which has also been a counterpoint to the procedure since it was first introduced within the TUC. Although it later came to appear as an organic growth deeply rooted in trade union values, the block vote procedure was introduced as a conscious political act at odds with the practice of a quarter-century of TUC Congresses.

Up to 1890, voting at the TUC was by a show of hands – one person, one vote – by delegates from both 'Trade Societies' and Trades Councils. This arrangement involved various anomalies of representation and the largest unions resented the fact that their larger membership did not automatically entitle them to voting rights commensurate with membership.

An argument over representation became entwined with a battle over political strategy. Socialists were making considerable headway through the unions in their efforts to push the TUC towards an independent representation of labour in the House of Commons. The opponents, who were particularly strong in the older and larger unions, were seeking means to hold back the tide. Their answer was the introduction of the block vote system.

But procedural changes did not stop the move towards independent representation. The Labour Representation Committee, which became the Labour Party, took over many existing TUC procedures as it evolved a Constitution and Standing Orders, including 'Voting shall be by a show of hands but on a division being challenged, Delegates shall vote by cards which shall be issued on the basis of one card for each thousand or fraction of a thousand, paid for to the Committee by the Society represented'.[4]

Subsequently, Standing Order 3(1) of the 1918 Constitution simply referred to 'voting cards on the basis of one vote for each 1,000 members or part thereof'. Both wordings were compatible with an organisation splitting its vote. But, in practice, the unions (or most of them – see p. 283) cast their votes as complete units, one way or the other.

As a result of this procedural development, the block vote came to mean two conjoined features of union voting at the Labour Party Conference: (1) a process by which unions were accorded votes in accordance with affiliated membership – thus giving the unions as a whole (but most strikingly the largest unions) preponderance over other organisations and (2) a process by which the unions cast their votes as units which did not register minority opinion in the unions. (See also p. 310 for a further political meaning.)

PROBLEMS OF NATIONAL COLLECTIVE AFFILIATION

Preponderance

In the tentative process of creating a party of labour out of diverse industrial and political organisations, the acceptance of the block voting system was eased by the fact that, because some of the largest unions did not immediately affiliate, disparities of size were nothing like as great as they were to become later.[5] And until 1917 concessions were made by the unions in allowing a composition to the Executive Committee which was remarkably accommodating to the minority from the Socialist Societies while preserving a union majority.[6]

However, by 1918, when the Labour Party was reconstituted, the relationship of forces within the Party had changed significantly. The Mineworkers Federation with its huge vote had affiliated in 1909. The unions had grown considerably in size during the First World War, and in 1917 forced a constitutional change which in effect meant that the Executive Committee, even (from 1918 to 1937) the Local Constituencies section, was under their full control.[7] At the Conference of January 1918, the unions cast 2,471,000 votes, the Socialist Societies 48,000 and the Local Labour Parties 115,000.

Given that determined efforts were now made to build up the individual membership, it could be anticipated that this union predominance would simply be an early-phase feature of the Party of 'the workers by hand or brain'. The tide of history would flood the new Local Labour Parties with members, as political levypayers broadened their commitment.

And indeed some rectification of this huge imbalance in membership and voting did take place in the 1930s as individual membership rose while union affiliated membership declined. And though, as has been shown, union affiliation increased dramatically in the late 1940s after the repeal of the Trade Disputes Act, this was accompanied and followed by a huge influx of individual Party members such that at the peak of the growth in 1952, over a million (594,663 men and 419,864 women) were lined up alongside the 5,071,935 affiliated members. Indeed, because of an element of double counting and topping up, by 1953 the CLPs were actually casting 1,307,000 votes at the Party Conference.[8]

Even with this vote, the CLPs were often deeply antagonistic to the union preponderance and feelings were exacerbated in 1955 when the two largest unions deliberately boosted their affiliation. However, thereafter, the disparity grew because while the union vote stabilised for over twenty years at around five and a half million, the CLP's membership and vote fell away to a low point of only 634,000 in 1970. Even this membership figure was artifically boosted by the stipulation of minimum CLP affiliation to the central Party.

To some extent, grievances against 'the block vote' were assuaged in the 1970s because the large union votes often went to the Left, and Leftwing activists, particularly in the Campaign for Labour Party Democracy, built new linkages within the unions and became adept at 'working the system' of mobilising delegation votes. There was also a practical concession to the CLPs in 1980 when real membership figures were declared and the overall national figure was reduced from 666,091 in 1979 to 348,156 in 1980, but the CLPs were still allowed to cast a minimum of 1,000 votes each at the Party Conference giving them a Conference vote of 689,000.[9]

Nevertheless, the distribution of votes at the annual Conference, in which the unions took around 90 per cent, has come to be central to reform agitation in the 1980s (see Chapter 12), and the resentment has grown rather than diminished. There is little doubt that much of this annoyance was simply the usual factional response to new adversity in Party Conference votes. But, that being said, there were also four features of the Party Conference distribution of votes which in the 1980s acted as a permanent provocation to CLP delegates.

The first was ironically a product of trade union restraint in that they never took up their full right of delegation. They were entitled to send to the Conference 'one delegate for each 5,000 members or part thereof',[10] the same right as the constituencies – and with the same proscriptions. But few unions took full advantage of this if only because the advantages did not warrant the costs in delegations which were in principle subject to mandate. In any case, were they to do so, the Party would have difficulty in finding a conference hall big enough; the TGWU alone would have had 250 delegates!

Hence it was that in terms of the blocks of delegates, the Party Conferences of the 1970s and 1980s looked very similar to the Conferences of the early 1950s. A

50:50 split of delegates between the unions and the CLPs did not change over-much in spite of the growing disparity of votes. In 1953, there had been 651 CLP delegates and 603 trade union delegates; by 1970 these had adjusted to 501 CLP delegates and 605 trade union delegates. Subsequently, there were years when the union majority of delegates was as low as 12 (in 1981) and never greater than 70 (in 1978). In the mid-1980s, in order to save money, the unions began to cut back on their delegations. In 1983, 1985, and subsequently, the number of CLP delegates was again slightly greater than the number of union delegates. In 1989 it was 618 to 589.

Thus it was that the disparity between a hand vote and a card vote increasingly raised the ire of constituency delegates who could only see the immediate fact that about half, or less than half, the hall was casting 90 per cent of the votes. The anger could become acute when hand votes and card votes showed significant differences.[11] To give one such example, in 1981 the hand vote on Composite 33 appeared, according to the Chairman, to show a majority favouring withdrawal from NATO. The card such showed a majority against of 3,587,000.[12] Such contrasts were not unusual and not endearing to the CLP activists.

A second source of resentment grew as feminism became a resurgent force in the constituencies. Union predominance was all the more irksome because many fewer women delegates managed to get to the Conference from their unions than from CLPs. At the 1983 Party Conference, the unions – predominantly manual workers – sent 557 men and only 45 women, the CLPs sent 453 men and 171 women.[13] This disproportion caused some women CLP delegates to view 'the block vote' as a masculine device. Conversely, some union manual worker delegates added a degree of chauvinism to their contempt for the priorities of 'middle class' feminists. This class tension was also sometimes apparent among the women delegates from the two sections and fed into and from arguments over representation at the Women's Conference (see Chapter 12, pp. 369–72).

A third grievance relating to the distribution of votes was concerned with the level of affiliation fees per member. Historically, union and CLP organisations had paid the same fee per member implying in this respect at least an equality of worth. But after 1980, the link was broken and the constituency parties began to pay more per member than the unions. It was a minor boon to Party finances and went some way to rectify the disparity in the national income drawn from the two sources but it became a focal point of a new demand for reform (see Chapter 12, pp. 372–3). By 1986, each affiliated organisation – other than CLPs – was paying 75p per member. CLPs were paying 5.50 per member unless they were on a reduced membership subscription.

But the main provocation arose, as it had done for decades, through the voting preponderance of the largest unions. The existence of a few large unions casting millions of votes was a benefit to a Party Leadership anxious to stabilise the Party through a limited series of understandings which would hold. But it was always a problem for the democracy of the Party Conference and a source of vexation to constituency activists who saw their puny weight dwarfed by the big union delegations.

As the unions slowly amalgamated their membership, so the problem became more obvious and more acute. From a low point in wartime of 68 affiliated unions (1941), the number of affiliated unions rose steadily until it reached a peak of 88 in 1956. Thereafter, it declined steadily, until by 1986 it was only 36.[14] As this decline was almost totally the product of amalgamation, so the increased trade union vote was being cast by fewer and larger units (Table 10.1).

Thus, whereas in 1953 the twelve largest unions cast 77.1 per cent of the trade union vote, by 1986 this was 86.1 per cent. And whereas in 1953, the four largest unions were casting a deeply resented 50 per cent of the union vote, by 1986 this had grown to nearly 60 per cent.

The most striking feature of this concentration was the position of the Transport Workers. The big T and G's vote in 1953, when Arthur Deakin was throwing his weight around, was 835,000, significantly smaller than the CLP's 1.3 million votes. But by 1980, the union's 1,250,000 votes were 561,000 larger than the combined CLP vote. By 1986, with the addition of the Agricultural Workers amd the Dyers and Bleachers, the combined TGWU vote had risen to 1,335,000 and it remained at approximately that level while its largest rival, the AEU, was sinking to 670,000 by 1988 and the General and Municipal Workers was rising to 740,000. Yet the CLP vote in 1988 was only 635,000. The disparity rankled all the more if the TGWU voted 'the wrong way'. If, for some Leftwing CLP delegates, Ron Todd's Tribune rally speech in 1988[15] was seen as 'heroic', for others it brought out all the latent resentment at 'block vote power'.

Unit voting

The procedure whereby unions cast their votes as units which disregarded minority opinion has always caused unease and antipathy and provoked a wide range of reform proposals. Since the drafting of the original constitution in 1918, many attempts have been made to loosen the arrangements. Such attempts have been regularly defeated although not always with the unanimity that its contemporary defenders tend to assume.

Let us note, for example, that in 1918 a large minority of the union votes cast went in favour of union votes being split.[16] It indicates at the very least that many trade unionists did not feel that their industrial solidarity would fall apart if block voting did not extend to every issue in every forum of the Labour Movement.

It is also worth registering that though it was common practice for a union to cast its votes as a unit, there was a Party facility for unions to have cards sufficient for them to split their votes and up to the early 1950s some of them did so. The extent of this practice of split voting is difficult to estimate but it appears that the 'federal' unions – the Mineworkers and the Textile Workers – occasionally did so.[17] And, occasionally, other unions followed the practice.[18] More significantly, one of the oldest craft unions regularly split its vote. The Amalgamated Society of Woodworkers claimed a card for each of its seven man delegation who apparently voted in line with regional opinion.[19]

However, by 1953, a change in procedure initiated by the Party made that facility much less available. Anxiety about the public impact of union leaders appearing on television screens holding up block votes caused Morgan Phillips, the then Party Secretary, to change the voting procedure so that the union received a

Table 10.1 Labour Party Conference:

1953		1974	
Transport and General	835,000	Transport and General	1,000,000
Mineworkers	683,000	Engineers	870,000
Engineers	627,000	General and Municipal Workers	650,000
General and Municipal Workers	400,000	Electricians	350,000
Big four	**2,545,000**	**Big four**	**2,870,000**
Shopworkers	330,000	Shopworkers	293,000
Railwaymen	323,000	Mineworkers	264,000
Post Office Workers	154,000	Construction Workers	184,000
Textile Workers	150,000	Post Office Workers	183,000
Woodworkers	130,000	Railwaymen	164,000
Electricians	120,000	Managerial Staff	151,000
Iron and Steel Workers	89,000	Public Employees	150,000
Transport Staff	79,000	Professional and Executive	100,000
Big twelve	**3,920,000**	**Big twelve**	**4,359,000**
Total union vote	5,086,000	Total union vote	5,385,000
CLPs	1,307,000	CLPs	642,000
Socialist Societies	24,000	Socialist Societies	46,000
Total Conference vote	**6,417,000**	**Total Conference vote**	**6,073,000**

*For data on Conference of 1990, see Appendix 1, p. 663

Trade union voting weight 1953, 1974, 1980, 1986*

1980		1986	
Transport and General	1,250,000	Transport and General (plus amalgamations)	1,335,000
Engineers	928,000	Engineers (all sections)	800,000
General and Municipal Workers	650,000	General and Boilermakers	725,000
Public Employees	600,000	Public Employees	600,000
Big four	**3,428,000**	**Big four**	**3,460,000**
Shopworkers	429,000	Shopworkers	359,000
Electricians	260,000	Mineworkers	208,000
Mineworkers	244,000	Health Service Employees	200,000
Construction Workers	200,000	Construction Workers	188,000
Post Office Workers	187,000	Communication Workers (UCW)	182,000
Railwaymen	180,000	Managerial Staff	153,000
Managerial Staff	147,000	Railwaymen	144,000
Professional and Executive	109,000	Electricians	136,000
Big twelve	**5,186,000**	**Big twelve**	**5,030,000**
Total union vote	6,450,000	Total union vote	5,842,000
CLPs	689,000	CLPs	624,000
Socialist Societies	67,000	Socialist Societies	65,000
Total Conference vote	**7,206,000**	**Total Conference vote**	**6,531,000**

book of cards which were to be placed in ballot boxes.[20]

This change in procedure had several consequences. It speeded up the process and made it more accurate. It also made it more difficult for delegates to see how their colleagues were voting. And it made it more difficult on grounds of practicality and expense for a union to claim a separate vote for each of its delegates. Today, where once there was one card for each voting unit, eighty are issued (40 'for' and 40 'against'). And where once it was accepted custom at Head Office that each union had the right to claim what cards it needed, it has now become conventional wisdom that splitting a delegation's vote between individuals 'just can't be done'.

Thus the block vote became entrenched in the card system of policy voting. As for voting involving elections for the NEC, the Conference Arrangements Committee, and, more recently, the Party Leadership, a ballot form is issued in which the unions were again allotted a specific and undividable vote. In this sphere also, it was institutionalised from the Party side that the individual union vote would be cast as a block. Thus it has become almost axiomatic that the unit voting element in 'the block vote' system is not only a natural but an inevitable element in the trade unions' participation in the Labour Party. Such beliefs produce a huge obstacle to reforms which seek to ensure a more accurate representation of the balance of opinion registered within the unions (but see Chapter 12, p. 383).

Levypayers and 'affiliated members'

These block votes were cast on behalf of millions of 'affiliated members'. This concept of 'affiliated membership' has always been a problem. In law and in practice there was a clear distinction between authorising a political fund and affiliating to the Labour Party. A vote in favour of a political fund was in essence simply that (although it could be said to imply something wider depending upon the case made out in favour of the fund during the ballot and the precedents for how the fund had been used in the past). What it could not be said to do was to declare a Labour Party 'membership'.

Similarly, there was a distinction to be made between agreeing to *pay* the political levy so that the union could pursue its necessary political objectives and agreeing to *participate* in the Labour Party. For some in the unions, the connection was a close one; for many others, it was far too indistinct to warrant the notion of an affiliated 'member'. In a sense, therefore, as became more widely recognised within the unions at the time of the Political Fund ballots, 'a levypayer is a levypayer is a levypayer'.[21] A similar understanding was the root assumption behind the 'Levy Plus' Mass Party campaign inaugurated in 1989 designed to turn levypayers into individual members.[22] For the moment, however, national *Party* categorisations still turned them into affiliated 'members'.

In practice, up to 1986 the adoption of a political fund by a union has normally led to, or confirmed, a Labour Party affiliation. Although the Certification Officer's Report for 1986 listed 50 unions with Political Funds as at 31 December 1985, while the Labour Party Conference of 1986 had 42 unions in attendance, the differences could be explained almost entirely in terms of amalgamated unions subdividing for one purpose but not for another. In 1983, the only union of significant size to hold a Political Fund without affiliation was the Society of Telecom Executives which agreed to authorise political expenditure that year.

However, one significant consequence of the Political Fund ballots of 1985–7 has been to increase substantially the number of white collar unions who have a Political Fund but prefer to retain their political neutrality. By the end of 1989 there were 19 such unions.[23] It was yet another feature of the Labour Movement which enhanced the distinction between political levypaying and Party 'membership'.

In addition, two unions in 1987, the Broadcasting and Entertainment Trades Alliance, and the Amalgamated Society of Textile Workers and Kindred Trades, a past affiliate which had renewed its Political Fund in 1984, made the full passage from adoption of a Political Fund into affiliation to the Labour Party. But this was unusual.[24] It remains to be seen how far the Government's policies will further politicise neutral unions to the point of increasing the range of Labour's affiliations.

Nevertheless, with only two of the fourteen largest unions affiliated to the TUC not in affiliation to the Labour Party (NALGO and the NUT), the custom of Labour Party association was very powerful within the trade union movement and the affiliation provided by these large formations gave the Labour Party its most important source of central and electoral finance.

Though there were some variabilities and uncertainties to this financial input (see Chapter 16, pp. 521–2), the Party was generally spared the problem of sudden withdrawal. Once a union affiliated, it generally stayed in affiliation. In recent years, only the very small unions such as the National Union of Scalemakers (1,250 members in 1983) and the Society of Shuttlemakers (50 members in 1985) – have disaffiliated. Conversely, although the Party in 1961 briefly expelled the ETU when it was under Communist control and accused of ballot rigging, normally it gave no recognition to internal union problems, nor attempted to exclude on grounds of industrial or political behaviour.

Similarly, with applications to affiliate, the Party normally accepted them almost automatically. The only proviso related to TUC acceptability as a bona fide union. According to the Party's Constitution, affiliated members 'shall consist of... Trade unions affiliated to the Trades Union Congress or recognised by the General Council of the Trades Union Congress as *bona fide* Trade Unions'.[25]

In theory, this gave the TUC a veto power over the right to affiliate to the Labour Party. In practice, the TUC bureaucracy, ever mindful of the need to preserve the organisational distinctiveness, from 1980 to 1988 refused to make a judgement to the Party on whether they recognised the union.[26] As a result, the Labour Party had more discretion than was sometimes thought about how it handled the deeply emotive issue of the UDM's breakaway from the NUM – and also the position within the Party of former NUM members, now part of the UDM. In the end, the Party Leadership refused any relationship with the UDM leadership and made clear its opposition to the affiliation of the new organisation (although it opposed expulsions of individual UDM members from the Party).

Even over the issue of the EETPU's expulsion from the TUC in 1988, the TUC was very circumspect in its reply to the Party's enquiry, simply noting that 'there was no reference in the General Council Report adopted at Congress relating to the *bona fide* standing of the EETPU and any consequence for affiliation to the Labour Party'.[27] In practice, this was a deliberate attempt on the part of TUC officials to aid the Party leadership in keeping the EETPU in the Party. At Congress House, in Walworth Road and in the Leader's Office, the agreed view was that the unity of the Labour Movement, not just the unity of the Labour Party, would be best served by a 'stand-off'. Accordingly, with some unease, after receiving the TUC reply and taking legal advice, the NEC majority agreed to take no action.

Levels of affiliation

In theory, the level of affiliation by each union was determined by the total number of union members paying the political levy. In practice, there was a significant degree of flexibility involved. So much so that the process has often been criticised as one in which 'unions cynically buy votes having no relation to the number of levypayers'.[28] As usual, the unions were portrayed as anxious to maximise power at the Conference and therefore eager to use their finances to ensure the largest possible vote.

Now, in a sense, the charge of buying votes was by definition true. All affiliated organisations (not just the unions) paid fees on the number of members affiliated. The larger the affiliation, the larger the payment and the larger the vote. But if the charge is that unions characteristically abuse their affiliation figures and have regularly used their financial resources in order to gain extra voting advantage at the Party Conference, then the criticism is on much weaker ground.

Certainly there have been cases in the past of unions making a sudden increase in affiliations and payments in order to seek additional leverage – the rise in affiliation of the two general unions in 1955 certainly came into this category. There was also the case of the NUM, which for reasons of loyalty regularly affiliated to the Labour Party on a membership greater than that of its TUC affiliation. But alongside these cases, you would also have to consider the fact that for many years in the 1970s, the TGWU *restricted* its affiliation because it did not wish to be over-dominant. And the EETPU, out of disillusionment with developments in the Party, limited its national affiliation and used its political finance for a range of purposes.

Unions have much to consider in relation to affiliation levels other than simply power. There have been times in the past when some unions had a political levy which was less than the Labour Party affiliation fee per member and had to adjust their affiliation to take account of the shortage of money. Even in 1987 (Table 10.2), after years of encouragement to a higher level of levypaying, the variations were such as to give some unions little room for manœuvre – given that they paid to affiliate at other levels of the Party and also had an obligation to pay into the General Election Fund.

However, in spite of these differences in financial resources, it was normally

Table 10.2 Annual poliitcal levy rate of the 16 largest unions, 1987

1.	National Union of Mineworkers	£5.60
2.	Transport and General Workers Union	£3.12
3.	Manufacturing Science Finance	£3.12
4.	Iron and Steel Trades Confederation	£2.80
5.	General Municipal Boilermakers etc.	£2.75
6.	National Union of Public Employees	£2.60
7.	National Union of Railwaymen	£2.60
8.	National Communications Union	£2.50
9.	Society of Graphical and Allied Trades	£2.08
10.	Confederation of Health Service Employees	£1.90
11.	Union of Communications Workers	£1.56
12.	Association of Professional Executive etc.	£1.56
13.	Union of Shop Distributive and Allied Trades	£1.56
14.	Amalgamated Engineering Union	£1.00
15.	Electrical, Electronic, Telecommunication etc.	90
16.	Union of Construction, Allied Trades etc.	80

Affiliation Fee 1987: 75p per member

the case, up to the early 1980s, that most unions attempted to affiliate nationally at a level which approximated to the number of levypayers. As the level of levypaying was normally affected only by changes in total union membership, then when this was stable so was the level of affiliation and voting. Indeed, the most striking feature of the pattern of union affiliation and voting at the Party Conference year by year was its *consistency*. For example, in two years of major political change and controversy – 1969 and 1970 – the level of variation in 29 of the 40 largest unions was less than 2,000. In the explosive years, 1979 and 1980, the level of variation in 31 of the 38 largest unions was also less than 2,000. As for the rest, these can almost all be accounted for by variations in union membership.

ASTMS in its growth years had often declared a membership more akin to what it expected and what it would like to achieve than what was the reality and, subsequently, Clive Jenkins was often accused of 'buying votes'. But if you examine ASTMS affiliation during the years when Jenkins rose to become a major Labour Party figure, that is from 1977 to 1982, the ASTMS affiliation remained the same (147,000) year after year.

This consistency of unions was characteristic even though so lax were the rules of payment up to the 1980s that in theory any union could wait until the eve of the Party Conference, survey the balance of forces, raise *last* year's affiliation, pay its money and get the increased vote at this Conference. When in 1980 NUPE suddenly raised its affiliation by 100,000 and paid just before the Conference opened, it produced a fierce reaction, including an acrimonious correspondence between APEX, the EETPU and the Party's General Secretary. But NUPE *did* have 600,000 levy-payers and its action was within the rules.[29]

However, rule changes followed in 1982 to make the closing date for fees as early as 31 March.[30] These fees, of course, related to the previous year and not until 1988 were the rules tightened to the point that they were payable on 31 December of the year to which they were applicable.[31]

While this potential loophole was slowly being closed, two major anomalies began to develop. Rising unemployment began to affect union membership and therefore the numbers paying the political levy. Yet the affiliations and votes of many unions in the mid-1980s stayed at past levels and in 1986 nineteen unions were casting votes now in excess of the number of levypayers they declared to the Certification Officer. Many of the differences were trivial but some were substantial, particularly the Engineers, the Iron and Steelworkers and the Mineworkers.[32]

There were various factors at work here. There was a question of clout. But there was also an important status anxiety – individual unions did not like to exhibit a sharp fall in the hierarchy of membership strength. There was a factional consideration. NEC voting – particularly in the women's section – was affected by changing levels of union affiliation. But most of all there was a Party dimension. If one is to seek the biggest factor involved in union over-affiliation in this period, it was the Party's pressing need to avoid a sudden loss of regular income.[33] Yet however admirable in terms of solidarity with and assistance to the Party, it undermined the credibility of union representation and exacerbated internal Party grievances over the preponderant union vote. There were signs in 1989 and 1990 that some of the over-affiliated unions were making major adjustments to their votes in the light of a shortage of income, but for the moment the anomalies remain.

A second peculiarity presented itself in the mid-1980s. Broadly speaking, since the 1946 repeal of the Trades Disputes Act, union levels of affiliation bore some correspondence with the electoral support for Labour among trade unionists. It may have been an abstract match and it was, in many cases, a match achieved without active commitment and sometimes in considerable ignorance. Nevertheless, levels of affiliation which involved 5 or 6 million 'members' had some credibility when around 70 per cent of approximately 8 million trade unionists voted Labour in the 1950s and even when it had sunk to 55 per cent of 10 million (1974). But the conjunction in the mid-1980s of a diminished level of electoral support from unionists and a very slow decline in the level of union affiliation left some of the union block votes looking more like 'political dummies'[34] than ever. At the 1987 Party Conference, the unions cast 5,792,000 votes but it was estimated that nearly 3 million of these votes were cast in the name of people who did not vote Labour at all.[35]

UNION POLICYMAKING AND DEMOCRACY
The problem of political participation

Behind the casting of the unions' block votes at the Party Conference there was a complicated pattern of rules and customs which determined who would cast the vote, under what conditions the vote would be cast and usually what policy would guide the decision-makers.

Such procedures were heavily influenced by long-established traditions of union democracy. These trade union traditions were, in terms of age, more deep-rooted than in most other British institutions and indeed predated Parliamentary democracy.

In its original form, it was very much a grass roots democracy based on small participatory gatherings of members. As the unions came to terms with the problems of regional and national organisation, so their 'primitive democracy' spawned and shaped national institutions which retained a commitment to the participatory ideal.

In principle, in the unions, every man and woman member had the right to participate in union affairs and the right to establish the policies of the unions. This participation took place through attendance at branch meetings – the focal point of union democracy. From the branch, there was generally a system of mandating either directly or indirectly to a national assembly of lay delegates whose decisions on the resolutions submitted by the branches constituted the policy of the union.

The dominant tradition, then, was one which placed considerable emphasis on policymaking and control by the members within branches. Issues were debated before decision; delegates and union officials reported back after implementation.

As an ideal arrangement it had much to recommend it. In practice, it was flawed by a range of problems. Not only was it very difficult to exclude the (admittedly often very small) minority of non-levypayers from taking decisions which determined union policy within the Labour Party, but also levypaying itself was surrounded by problems in relation to the commitment to participate.

For one thing, as already noted, the level of political levypaying was strongly affected by the form of the procedure. 'Contracting in' lowered the level; 'contracting out' raised it considerably. Critics have sometimes alleged that this variation can be accounted for in terms of fear or intimidation.[36] Little evidence has been brought into the public domain in recent years to justify this claim,[37] and the level of complaints to the Certification Officer has always been very low.[38] The main factors appear to be membership indifference and inertia and the social 'normality' of the workplace.

However, it is also clear that many unions did not regard it as a priority to remind union members of their right to contract out. Until the Political Fund ballots of 1985–6, there was certainly much ignorance about the levy in some of the unions.[39] In negotiations with the Government over the 1984 Trades Union Act, the TUC agreed to issue guidance to affiliated unions on information to be given to members about their rights in relation to the Political Fund. This was duly complied with.[40] But it was working against the grain of much resentment against what was regarded as an unfair and politically one-sided imposition on a collective organisation (see Chapter 17, pp. 546–7).

Nevertheless, it was significant that the information given to members and the considerable publicity surrounding the Political Fund Ballots led to no significant increase in contracting out; indeed, in most unions levypaying *increased* (Table 10.3). These developments have encouraged some of the unions

Table 10.3 Changes in the level of political levypaying, 1984–1986

| | 1984 | | |
	General Fund	Political Fund	% Paying Levy
ACCT	21,500	2,278	10.6
APEX	94,846	64,069	67.5
ASLEF	22,735	21,164	93.1
ASTMS	375,000	99,132	26.4
AUEW (E.F. and C.)	739,961	542,846	73.3
AUEW (TASS)	187,000	145,765	77.9
BFAWU	36,286	35,574	98.0
CATU	30,297	30,002	99.0
COHSE	214,321	196,523	91.6
EETPU	370,659	279,873	75.5
FBU	43,256	27,108	62.7
FTAT	54,347	33,103	60.9
GMB	846,565	729,108	86.1
ISTC	42,197	36,094	85.5
MU	37,517	30,197	80.5
NACODS	15,848	15,383	97.1
NCU	125,387	94,013	75.0
NGA	111,003	57,725	52.0
NLBD	2,930	600	20.5
NUDAGO	4,000	1,380	34.5
NUFLAT	37,412	36,266	96.9
NUM	208,051***	200,453***	96.3***
NUPE	673,445	653,862	98.0
NUR	136,315	132,133	96.9
NUS	27,700	21,800	78.7
NUTGW	76,699	67,578	88.1
SOGAT	191,130	109,871	57.5
TGWU	1,490,555	1,379,351	92.5
TSSA	52,116	42,713	81.9
UCW	195,374	181,748	93.0
UCATT	241,599	188,005	77.8
USDAW	392,307	358,175	91.3

*Figures affected by amalgamation, including the Tobacco Workers Union which had significantly lower levels of levypaying in 1984 (13,448 Gen. Fund, 7,480 Pol. Fund, 57.5%).
**These figures are completely distorted by the amalgamation with the Civil and Public Services Association (Post and Telecommunications Group) which had no political fund until 1987 when the NCU figure for levypaying was 76.8%, an *increase* on 1984.

| General Fund | 1986 | | |
	Political Fund	% Paying Levy	Increase/Decrease Levypaying 1984–1986
23,500	5,035	21.4	Increase
83,614	56,526	67.6	Increase
21,446	20,093	93.7	Increase
360,000	97,000	26.9	Increase
610,917	444,424	72.7	Decrease
204,850*	159,060*	77.6*	Decrease*
35,988	34,331	95.3	Decrease
30,308	29,508	97.3	Decrease
212,312	194,741	91.7	Increase
336,155	296,845	88.3	Increase
44,919	27,287	60.7	Decrease
41,770	40,839	97.7	Increase
814,084	697,861	85.7	Decrease
42,942	34,638	80.6	Decrease
38,203	33,026	86.4	Increase
12,449	12,107	97.3	Increase
155,643**	89,236**	57.3**	—**
103,607	58,518	56.4	Increase
2,826	1,496	52.9	Increase
3,100	1,380	44.5	Increase
34,782	33,632	96.6	Decrease
104,941	99,790	95.1	—***
657,633	637,072	96.9	Decrease
124,991	121,683	97.4	Increase
22,896	23,093****	100.8****	Increase
75,063	66,296	88.3	Increase
180,752	112,404	62.2	Increase
1,335,245	1,235,456	92.5	No change
45,824	37,888	82.7	Increase
191,959	179,651	93.6	Increase
240,572	199,136	82.8	Increase
381,984	349,133	91.4	Increase

***The NUM figures here are for 1983 as the union was involved in a long fracturing strike in 1984 and gave no figures.
****According to the union and the Certification Officer, the perculiarity of these figures is the result of retired members paying just the political levy. In the 1988 Report, the NUS figure for levypaying is 97.7 per cent.
Sources: Reports of the Certification Officer for 1985 and 1987.

to be bolder and more open in their political activities (see Chapter 18).

Attitudes towards 'contracting out', in the past, were affected by a general 'let sleeping dogs lie' approach to the membership on political questions. Political education and political mobilisation had a low priority in many of the unions. This, plus a traditional 'separatism' in defining the territory of the industrial and the political, meant that committed and knowledgeable participation on political issues, in general, was a minority activity.

Within the branches, discussion of political issues, when it occurred, was often hurried and at best limited. Motions to the national level on political issues tended to come from a minority of branches. At annual conferences of the unions, political issues took only a small part of the total business which was usually heavily dominated by trade questions. Apart from major controversial issues, the amount of time for political debate was limited. There tended also to be a traditionalism about which political issues were taken in which union. Thus, mandates from union conferences were typically limited in range and often dated in applicability. Though such generalisations as have been made here have to be qualified in terms of more politically conscious assemblies, such as the Engineers National Committee or the Railwaymen's long-running Annual Delegate Meeting, the fact was that purely in terms of time and priority, politics was not immediately central to trade unionism and as a result the mandating system was often incomplete. Martin Harrison's appraisal in the 1950s is still relevant thirty years later.

> In general, most large unions will have directly applicable decisions on about one-third of the questions that come before the Party Conference, partially relevant decisions on about a further third, and no appropriate decisions on the remainder.[41]

A second problem of political participation related to the changing character of union branch life. The branch was the basic unit of the whole edifice of union policy-making, yet attendance at branch meetings has seldom involved a majority of eligible members. This was an age-old lament.[42] Over the years, one study after another has indicated a low level of involvement. The authoritative de/psi/ssrc Report, published in 1983, indicated, as had previous studies, a particularly low attendance in manual worker unions which had a geographically-based branch structure, with only about one-twentieth of members estimated to be attending. Workplace branches drew a significantly higher proportion, estimated to be around a fifth for manual workers and as high as a third for non-manuals.[43]

There has been a gradual shift towards industrially-based branches as unions have attempted to come to terms with the priorities and preoccupations of members, but in those unions like the AEU, where the branches are still geographically based, the problem has become even more acute. In 1987 the AEU General Secretary said that attendances at branches involved less than 2 per cent of members.[44] Further, the attendance problem at branches is now affected not only by changing life styles, but by growing distances to work and by the growth of shift work and flexi-time. And as feminists have pointed out, many women continue to have special problems of attendance at meetings. Further, though meetings are essential enabling devices, they are time-consuming, often boring and sometimes off-putting.

This feature of political life, where decisions are taken essentially by those who can or are willing to attend meetings, is not simply a problem for trade unions. Nor is it unique to the present day, or this country. Arguably, it is the normality of trade union politics throughout most of the world. Further, the difference in values and prescriptions on some issues between activists and members – a gap often noted by critical observers[45] – is also not unusual.[46] But whereas on matters close to members' immediate industrial concerns the unions often have alternative channels through which members can make their views heard, and heard decisively, on political questions or on some larger questions of economic and industrial policy, these channels either do not exist or are not utilised by most members. Union government via the branches gives a democratic legitimacy to union conference decisions on such matters but gives a range of problems for the Labour Party attempting to win the support of the non-active trade unionists as well as broaden its constituency of support.

Within the unions there are no easy answers to these problems. The occasional referendum on crucial political issues involving the entire levypaying membership would be in tune with the democratic traditions of both the unions and the Party. But they are not unproblematic mechanisms. They are often difficult to integrate within stable and representative forms of government. And they often produce controversy over the fairness of the wording – witness the arguments within the SDP in 1987 over their ballot on amalgamation with the Liberals, and the arguments in 1989 over the wording of the EETPU ballot in its dispute with the TUC.

Unless they are located within a context of free and balanced communication and access to information, they are susceptible to heavy manipulation from inside or outside the union. As to their more general use, there is much evidence from union history to indicate that such referenda could, in practice, enhance the oligarchic power of union leaderships rather than allowing the membership a real share in government.[47] It was largely for these reasons that the device of referenda diminished in the mid-nineteenth century, and was restricted in a few unions to a few special questions on particular emergencies.[48]

Priority and management

Later in this chapter, union government and union leadership will be examined in detail. But before that, we have to note again that an awareness of the potential gap between union mandates and membership opinion shapes the priorities of union leaders in a variety of ways. Priority issues – particularly industrial issues – which directly concerned the mass membership provided the meat of active union involvement in the Labour Party. On other issues, a degree of 'management' often took place either before, during or after union conferences, or after Labour Party Conference decisions.

This management was a delicate business. It was not just a question of internal relations within the union. The union was often the forum and agency for a plurality of pressure groups and social movements which focused on achieving, preserving and pushing for the implementation of the union's mandate. A plurality of lobbies concerned with environmental, women's, peace, poverty, human rights, national liberation and Labour Party constitutional issues were particularly prominent in the trade unionism of the 1980s.

In an attempt to assist the Parliamentary Leadership and the Party, union leaders – particularly those on the Right – often attempted to keep their union mandates flexible enough to enable them to assist 'Party unity'. In the late 1980s, this accommodationism became evident across a wide spectrum of unions, including the TGWU. Where such accommodation was either not sought or not effective at the level of the union conference, it was sometimes evoked when unions considered the compatibility of their mandates with the Leadership's recommendation (see below p. 308). But its most subtle expression was, after a union mandate had been implemented, in the priority which union leaders gave to pushing for a response.

Union leaders, Left and Right, often related the degree of push in the final stages of Party policymaking to the depth and consistency of union membership commitments (Chapter 2, p. 41 and Chapter 6, p. 184). Conversely, Parliamentary leaders with an eye on the Party's electoral needs registered the depth of commitment in the unions in making decisions on whether and to what extent to respond to Conference decisions. The classic case over the last twenty-five years has been that of public ownership where the pattern has been for Conference decisions to be filtered into a process whereby, over an electoral cycle, commitments get less specific and more restricted but union leaders generally go quiet during this process.

The most remarkable example of the way union leaders co-operate in burying issues which are not considered viable in terms of Labour's electoral appeal concerned the policy of leaving the European Economic Community. In 1983, a consensus emerged in both the political and industrial wings that for the moment the EEC question was over. In spite of the fact that not one major union mandate changed from 1983 to 1986 on this issue, the union leaders aided and abetted a major shift of policy (see Chapter 14, p. 456). Only in 1989 did the TGWU *mandate* come into line.

However, not all issues could be handled by co-operation or a consensus on new policy. Factional differences at leadership level in the unions based on some deeply rooted ideological commitments always complicated the search for accommodation. Some issues in the unions reached a high priority status because of long standing union commitments backed by strong and persistent activist support assisted by an equally committed union leadership. Nuclear defence in the 1980s brought out this commitment, with one side convinced of the transcendent danger of abandoning 'the deterrent', and the other equally convinced of the danger to the human race from the escalation of such weapons.

The most important vehicle of the new unilateralism in the 1980s was the TGWU. Yet polls taken in 1983 and in 1988 indicated that among the membership of the union there was no majority for the policy (28 per cent in 1983 and 33 per cent in 1988).[49] However, there was a further complication which helped in part to account for some of the union's commitment to unilateralism. Among Labour voting trade unionists the gap on this issue virtually disappeared.[50] Unlike the position in Jones's time (see Chapter 6, p. 176), there was 'an army', albeit one which could not give Labour an electoral majority.

What remained to be tested in the years from 1981 to 1988 was the extent to which the unilateralist unions would respond to an alternative definition of priorities supported by the Party's Leadership. The call for new policies was successful in 1989 in NUPE and in a range of other formerly unilateralist unions, although it was less heeded in the TGWU, MSF and the NUR, where the union leadership retained their traditional perceptions and priorities on this issue.

If priority was the clue to much trade union behaviour involving a co-operation and a tendency to accommodation, so freedom was the clue to the major sticking points. Since 1948, the Party and the unions have found the reconciliation of a counter-inflation policy with free collective bargaining to be the most difficult problem of managing the Movement. Union membership opinion has often run ahead of union policies in support of incomes policy – particularly in their willingness to see forms of governmental control. But, broadly speaking, support for incomes policies has peaked in the early years of a Labour government and then declined significantly towards its close.[51] This experience of incomes policy and the acute problems it could cause in terms of union differentials has meant that in the 1980s some key unions on both Left and Right dug their heels in over incomes policies involving imposed norms. The atmosphere in the unions in the early 1980s was also affected by monetarist views on inflation and by Thatcherite attitudes to market bargaining. Only 54 per cent of trade unionists positively supported an incomes policy in 1983 and in the TGWU it was less than half of the membership.[52]

The sharpest contrast between union membership opinion and union mandates from 1979 to 1987 occurred over aspects of Conservative Government legislation regulating trade union government and restricting trade union indus-trial action.[53] Here, the determination of lay activists and union officials – particularly but not exclusively on the Left – to stand firm on traditional freedoms rested on a series of reinforcing arguments and considerations. There was an argument from customary rights which saw concession as the giving away of an historic birthright of self-determination.[54] There was a belief that unions were especially vulnerable bodies whose operation in a hostile environment required protection against temporary fluctuations in membership opinions or pressures which would endanger their long term interests.[55] And there was a view that in any case much of this changing opinion reflected a disjunction between members' own immediate industrial experience and the general experience given to them of other areas of industrial life by the mass media.[56] For these reasons, this area was regulated by a notion of 'responsible government', protective of the union's autonomy and its industrial functions. But such 'responsibility' could not stand permanently unmoved in the face of membership opinion – particularly as the Party had to evoke electoral support from that constituency among others.

Here again, as on some other deeply sensitive matters, the issue has had to be managed at leadership level with regard for deeply held union opinion on the one hand and the Party Leadership's perspectives and electoral needs on the other. Matters were further complicated by the fact that, among Labour supporters, opinion was close to the views of union activists on the 'abolition' of the legislation.[57] Over strike ballots, however, there was a huge majority for retention in both sectors and among active members.[58] These industrial relations issues produced the most difficult area of Labour Party policymaking, albeit one in which slowly the views of the Party Leadership – particularly in relation to regulated balloting – were beginning to feed back into the conference decisions of even the most tradition conscious of unions.[59]

The legend of the barons

The existence of a large trade union membership which was in the main inactive and uninvolved in the political procedures of the Labour Movement was a major vulnerability, a constant source of conflicting obligations for union leaders and an increasingly contentious feature of union affiliation. But it was dwarfed in the preoccupations of the mass media and of opponents of the Labour Party by the attention paid to the power of 'the union bosses' as the most reprehensible feature of Labour politics.

As the block vote was cast in the form of one card, it fell to one member of the union's delegation to cast the vote. Usually this was the most senior member of the delegation present at the time. He, or very occasionally she, who cast the vote tended to be so equated with its use as to be credited with almost a personal possession. Critics of the block vote and of the power of union leaders tended to conflate the two as though trade union decision-making at the Party Conference was simply a matter of 'a handful of union barons who control collectivist block votes'.[60]

This equation of the card carrier with personal power over the vote reinforced an image of union democracy in which everything was decided by 'the union bosses' and a deliberately encouraged caricature of the Labour Party as under the personal control of these bosses. Enough has been said already in this study to indicate how misleading this was. Nevertheless, this almost obsessional critique of the barons and bosses had a revival in the 1980s during a period when union leaders were in their greatest difficulty over the management of Labour Party affairs.

Union government in practice

The role of the union leaders has to be understood in the context of the traditions and structures of union government. There is a rich diversity to the government of British trade unions but there are some common features embodying the unions' commitment to representative democracy. Normally, the centrepiece of union government is a conference of lay delegates elected directly or indirectly to act as the policy-making forum. With rare exceptions, which include the EETPU (which has a distinct political structure based upon Labour Party delegates and Executive authority[61]), this forum is acknowledged to be the supreme policy-making authority. The administrative and executive body of the union is always an elected Executive Committee. This body works closely with the General Secretary of the union. Although most unions have an elected President or Chairman of the Executive, it is the General Secretary who is normally considered to be the senior officer of the union.[62]

Apart from these common characteristics, each union has its own distinctive organisational and governmental structure. Conservative Government legislation in 1984 and 1988 produced some elements of standardisation. Prior to 1984, unions were more or less free to decide how and whether to elect the Executive Committee and the unions' principal officers. As a result, trade union development has been characterised by a multiplicity of procedures, arrangements and tenures of office.[63] Under the 1984 Trade Union Act, voting members of the principal Executive Committee of a union must be elected by a ballot of members at least every five years. This provision only affected senior officials of the union if they had a vote on the Executive but under the terms of the 1988 Employment Act any senior official who had the right to speak at Executive meetings was now subject to five-yearly election; further, all such elections would in future be by postal ballot. This was a major change given that hitherto the most senior union officials had been appointed or elected by a variety of arrangements and the most senior officer had normally been appointed or elected for life.

This attempt to reform what was considered to be the procedural cause of the 'unrepresentative' character of union leadership behaviour has in practice significantly reduced the turn-out[64] and, in any case, was based on an underestimate of the constraining forces upon union leaders which were often at work within the unions.

There *is* a leadership role played in the unions, usually by the General Secretary, and it can be a very powerful role. Setting the tone, focusing on particular objectives, initiating proposals, administering policy and representing the union within the wider public domain, this official took on both a special prestige and an influential capacity to get his or her own way. In this respect, trade unions were little different from most other large organisations. However, the tendency towards the concentration of power was but one strong tendency among others. And the facilities and constraints surrounding the leadership role were affected by many different factors which together shaped a milieu of power which was unique to each union.

There was for a start the structural factor. The unions' governmental institutions varied in the size, form and composition of Conference and Executive; smaller conferences were usually more assertive. Full-time executives were usually able to exert more control than part-time ones. Structure mattered also in terms of areas and regions; decentralisation sometimes allowed regional officers and regional committees a significant degree of autonomy. In the case of the NUM, there was a strong residue of area independence. Then again, the institutionalisation of national positions sometimes involved, as it did in USDAW or for a period the NUM, a dual power in which President and General Secretary were to some extent a check on each other.

Tradition was also an important factor. Some of these traditions are general to the movement and deeply embedded in trade union experience. These include a belief in the ultimate sovereignty of 'the members', a respect for the rule book and a wariness of financial imprudence by the leadership. But, in addition, each union also had its own distinctive culture – particularly in the legacy passed down of the struggles of the past and the precedents established by leaders who were seen to have advanced the union. The culture was often affected by and helped shape a pattern of Left/Right factionalism. In principle, factional organisation was disapproved of in almost all unions as 'divisive' but in many of them it was an inescapable part of the covert internal politics and a factor in the pattern of power around the senior officer. Having the support of an efficient and widely engaged factional machine was an asset at all levels of the policy process. Facing a similar machine could mean permanent war on issue after issue.

In varying degrees the Executive Committee of unions held the authority to put major policy proposals to the union conferences and the senior official was usually closely involved in shaping these proposals. And although the great bulk of union conference notions came spontaneously and unsolicited, the Head Office Secretariat could influence the agenda in a variety of ways through the union's communication network including the union's journal, through the Head Office staff, and through factional support. Close links to the Standing Orders Committee of the Conference were often either built into the union rules and customs or established by factional linkage. Within the Conferences, the senior official acting through the Executive often had, in addition to privileged access to the agenda, the privileged rights of reply. All the skills which brought the man or woman to leadership could be perfected in this environment, drawing on the prestige which normally accrued to those who spoke for 'the union'.

Well-established leaders who had time to reshape both the bureaucracy and the policy could develop a powerful base for personal control until they began to lose touch as a result of taking on other obligations and wider involvement. But new leaders from a different political alignment or factional base did not find it easy to make sudden shifts in policy except perhaps where they were riding the tide of years of industrial discontent. Political policies were often consistent over many years and held in place by a mixture of inertia, tradition and the support of officials appointed by previous incumbents. The union's senior officer might change – from Left to Right or from Right to Left and sometimes in a blaze of publicity which heralded immediate beneficial or catastrophic ramifications. But it was remarkable to what extent the union's policy remained constant in spite of the expected new broom or the new political departure.

The wider the concern over the issue within the union, the tighter the constraint against sudden new departures and the narrower the room for manœuvre. Limitations upon the leadership were generally greatest where the issue was defined as industrial and 'shopfloor' with immediate ramifications upon the members' interests. But they were tight also where the union's commitment was long standing, and they were tight where the pressures coming from the middle levels of the unions and from a range of branches were concerned and persistent.

It is important to stress alongside these generalisations that no two unions were alike in their distribution of internal power and that unions were not static entities either. As they sought to react and adjust to their environments and to new predicaments, so they reorganised and amalgamated procedures and instituted new practices. In the process, the pattern of power could change. Though in a minority of unions, including the EETPU and UCATT, the developments have enhanced centralism, in general the changes have tended to strengthen the decentralisation and diffusion of power.[65]

At the same time, new sources of democratic renewal have made themselves felt in many unions. To a considerable extent, these changes arose in the 1960s and 1970s out of union reorganisation of their own shortcomings. In the 1980s, they have been reinforced by feminism and as a result of new communicational and campaigning projects designed to mobilise and in effect to 'close the gap' with the members. To this has been added the procedural consequences of Government legislation covering balloting arrangements, and the stimulation of consultations following changes in Party procedures – including the election of the Party Leadership (Chapter 11).

Changes have taken place, particularly in the methods of balloting, in the composition of Executives and of delegations to the Party Conference. In addition, new factional alignments, new assertiveness *vis-à-vis* the leadership and the rise of new issues have all played their part in making the role of the senior official more difficult. Significantly, in the 1980s several General Secretaries found themselves in more tension with senior officers in their unions than was normal in the past.

The Transport and General Workers Union

The best and most important illustration of changing power relationships within a union, and their effect upon the Labour Party, concerned the big 'T and G'. This, the largest union in the British Labour Movement, built up to a membership of two million by 1979 and then in the wake of the Thatcherite blitz lost around a quarter of its membership by 1985. Nevertheless, its vote of one and a quarter million at the Labour Party Conference was significantly larger than any other union and twice as big as all the votes of the CLPs together. Its political alignment was therefore of major importance, even if not necessarily always decisive.

For years, the union had been the bastion of support for the Party Leadership at the Party Conference and on the Party's NEC. As we have seen, in the period of 'the praetorian guard', Arthur Deakin, its General Secretary, was the central pillar of the triumvirate of Rightwing union leaders organising on the side of the 'platform' at the Party Conference. Deakin's importance for the Labour Party was based not only on his personal political position but on his ability to bring his union with him on the key issues – a union which was then a by-word for centralisation and 'popular bossdom'.[66]

Its formal structure of government located the sovereign body as the biennial conference of delegates nominated by and from the union's branches. As is normal in trade unions 'for the general administration of the Union's business' and 'within the rules and standing decisions of the Biennial Delegate Conference and of the Appeals Committee to decide the policy of the Union', there was a General Executive Council of lay representatives meeting quarterly and elected to serve two years. Interwoven with this structure and created to improve representation within a multi-industrial organisation was a trade group structure. Each member belonged not only to a region, but to a trade group and 'had a right to representation on both counts'.

There was a potential here for a clash of representation as the BDC delegates were elected by a ballot vote of each regional trade group while the GEC was composed of regional representatives (according to size) and trade group representatives elected by the Trade Group Committees, one for each group no matter how large. If the union was moving clearly in any one direction, the difference was not significant; if it was not, then the difference could be crucial.

The union was still to some extent showing the joins of the complicated series of amalgamations in 1922 which produced the giant structure. New amalgamations in the 1970s and 1980s added to the diversity and problems of cohesion.

A strong force for cohesion was the heavy centralisation of appointments to the regional bureaucracy and a headquarters structure in which the General Secretary's role was highly prestigious and authoritative. But it was not unconstrained. There were always limitations placed upon the General Secretary by tides of opinion within the unions, by the forces and traditions present on the GEC and particularly by the Finance and General Purposes Committee drawn from the GEC. And the decisions of the BDC were a mandate upon the General Secretary and the GEC as to how their votes should be cast in other forums of the Movement. Region by region and trade group by trade group, there were always diverse oppositional forces.

Still, as the office developed from Ernest Bevin to Jack Jones, there could be little doubt of the pre-eminence of the General Secretary. The elected Chairman of the GEC was a lay representative and normally no match for the senior officer. Until the 1988 legislation, the General Secretary was elected until retirement. He was in charge of the union bureaucracy. Through a mixture of skill, weight, drive and bureaucratic situation he could normally command a loyal majority in the inner forums.

His authority was evident at the Biennial Delegate Conference. A large assembly of up to a thousand lay delegates, it met for five days to examine the report of its GEC and to discuss resolutions submitted by the 8,000 branches. Given its biennial character and the multiplicity of resolutions, there was always pressure upon time and considerable work by the Standing Orders Committee to create a manageable agenda of mainly composited resolutions. Though predominantly preoccupied with industrial questions, the BDC always had a fair sprinkling of important political and economic resolutions in front of it. The dominance of the Executive, usually fronted by the General Secretary, was illustrated by the fact that at BDC after BDC 'the platform' was *never* defeated in the days of the 'praetorian guard' nor in the era of Frank Cousins that followed.

A tradition built up under Bevin of accepting the advice of the General Secretary; the custom was facilitated by the union's insistence that delegates to the Conference were not mandated in advance of the debate. But in addition, the procedures of the Conference were very advantageous to the Executive and General Secretary. Executive Statements pre-empted other resolutions on the agenda. The Statements were often skilfully worded but delegates never saw the wording printed, only heard them read out from the platform. In addition, there was a well-established practice that the specific meaning of the Executive Statement was defined on behalf of the committee by the General Secretary in his reply.

Small wonder, then, that with his dominance over the Conference continuing under the new Leftwing General Secretary, Cousins, as it had done under the Rightwing leaders, Bevin and Deakin, it should be taken as axiomatic that the policy of the union changed 'overnight' when one union leader replaced another. This weighty expression of the power of a union 'boss' became part of the mythology of the Labour Movement and almost impervious to evidence to the contrary.[67] The fact was that in industrial terms, the new General Secretary represented a wave from below but in political terms it took four years for the new General Secretary to be able to cast a vote at the Labour Party Conference which was out of line with previous union practice; a new TGWU General Secretary had to operate within many constraints, including incumbent officials and past traditions.[68]

The shift to the Left in the union was a slow and uneven movement not consolidated until Jack Jones became General Secretary in the late 1960s. Even then, the traditional Right in the union was always a significant force.

The union's political stance became further complicated after 1975 by the fact that even in the loyalist phase there was no clear reversal of the union's Leftwing stance. The political legacy that Jones handed on was very much that of his early phase rather than his accommodation with Labour's leaders. And he appeared also to be handing over the tradition of a General Secretary playing a dominant authoritative role. His personal defeat over incomes policy at the 1977 BDC was a sensation in its way and an indication of the constraints operating upon even the most prestigious and well-established union leader in the face of a wages revolt.

But perhaps it was more than that. Jones had initiated via the BDC a range of organisational changes in line with his attempt to decentralise power within the unions. He had strengthened the role of the Regional Secretaries, the new District Committees and the shop stewards. He had encouraged greater participation in union government and collective bargaining processes. At the time, his own authoritative performance of the leadership role of the General Secretary appeared to strengthen a pattern of hierarchical dominance within the union. But within a short time after his departure, the position of General Secretary came to look very much weaker and the assertiveness from below which Jones had nourished became a marked feature of the union. This partial demise of the TGWU 'boss' had enormous ramifications for the stability of the Labour Party.

At the top of the union this new weakness was reflected in the General Secretary's relations with other union officials. Moss Evans's position was contested by a range of other officers (a feature assisted by Evans's absence through illness in 1981). A remarkable degree of autonomy built up around the union's representation on Labour's National Executive Committee through first Alex Kitson and then later Eddie Haigh, both of whom had a distinctive base through an amalgamated union. On the General Council of the TUC there was an unprecedented fragmentation of the union's representation. A lay representative, Walter Greendale, was linked to the General Council Left Group and then the Bennite Left in the Labour Party and acted not only independently of the

General Secretary but in a highly politicised way, pushing the politics of the Labour Left into the union.

The Broad Left in the union created a new and permanent factional presence but in the mid-1980s it became subject to growing internal political disagreement and personality clashes, particularly over the succession to Evans, the Chairmanship of the BDC and over appointments in the regions. Resentment over the Greendale–Benn links and the external influence of the political Left increased the difficulties. The divisions within the Communist Party and the decline of traditional industrial sectors of Leftwing strength added to the problems. Between 1984 and 1986, a new political grouping emerged in the union out of the Broad Left. The dockers' leader, Brian Nicholson, in effect broke with the Left and formed a 'Kinnockite' group which linked with the old Right, kept close contacts with the Party Leader's Office and operated in circumstances of considerable tension with the new General Secretary, Ron Todd. When the Left lost support in 1986, Greendale was ejected from the GEC and lost the Chair of that committee. When the Left advanced in 1988, Nicholson was ejected from the GEC and he lost the Chair.

Leading the union under these circumstances was a difficult business, delivering votes for the Party Leadership even more so. The loss of Jones' project and personality may account for some of the weakness as did the new defensive ethos of the 1980s when for the first time in many years the union began to lose members. By contrast with Jones, Evans was a less authoritative figure, a negotiator rather than a charismatic leader. Todd, too, while gaining from his handling of the leadership election of 1985, found himself in an uncertain industrial and political terrain and losing votes, even in the appointment of regional officials in the face of the assertive Nicholson group.

The divisions at leadership level were paralleled by developments within the Biennial Delegate Conference. Where there was a leadership consensus – over the handling of Northern Ireland, for example – the Conference continued to be adroitly managed. The NEC Statements continued to be important weapons in handling the transfer of mandates from the union conference to the Party Conference – bans, proscriptions and the expulsion of Militant supporters was the best example. But alongside this there emerged in the 1980s a remarkable pattern of defeats for the union leadership, often the General Secretary personally.

In 1981, with Evans absent, the GEC was defeated over a prime element in Jones's project for industrial democracy. Later, in 1983 and 1985, it was brought back in a looser form. That same year, 1981, the GEC was defeated over the handling of local government opposition to Conservative Government cuts.

In 1983, there were repetitive defeats for the Executive – particularly the Women's Officer over women's representation in the Labour Movement and over women's rights. At the same Conference, Evans had to indulge in some dexterous agenda management and a verbal retreat over the National Economic Assessment in order to avoid a rebuff.

At the 1985 Conference, the GEC was defeated on its long-established policy of support for nuclear energy; it was partially revived two years later at the 1987

Conference but only after it had plunged the Labour Party's policy into a pro-tracted crisis. That same year, the GEC was defeated almost unanimously over its handling of the issue of part-time workers and Agency Labour. It led to a major reshaping of policy and the Link-Up campaign of 1987.

All the signs were in 1987 that the pattern of leadership dominance was still under considerable strain. The long-established policy of support for unilateral nuclear disarmament was carried by only 361 votes to 327. And the even longer-established policy of opposition to a *statutory* form of minumum wage was defeated in spite of the GEC majority. The political tone of this Conference was potentially very significant for the Labour Party. The union had been led from the Left now for thirty years and in the early 1980s defeats for the platform had typically been an outflanking from the Left. But now there were signs of a drift to the Right.

It is this context which made the GEC elections of 1988 so problematic for the union. The elections involved a significant shift to the Left and what appeared to be the first clear Leftwing majority since 1985. Some explained this as a by-product of new Government-imposed direct election procedures in the Trade Groups; some in terms of better Leftwing organisation; some in terms of a new wave of industrial militancy. Others saw it as a patchy mix with results which were not as Leftwing as they looked.

Whatever the cause, it had ramifications for the Labour Party and was swiftly followed by a Labour Leadership election (see Chapter 11, pp. 354–6) in which the union's role was once again highly controversial. Defence policy, which had been a major source of contention within the union and between the union and the Labour Leadership under Cousins in 1957, came to the fore again as the union leader dug his heels in against the new Party policy and carried his union with him. But this conflict, important as it was, obscured two other important developments. The union was quietly positioning itself for the maximum of support on other issues.[69] Even on industrial relations, where there were some strongly guarded positions, there was an attempt to assist pre-election unity as the central priority.

Overall, therefore, a significant devolution and diffusion of power had taken place in the TGWU, stimulated, in part at least, by the ideological and procedural consequences of Jones' political egalitarianism. This had placed the General Secretaries of the 1980s in a more difficult position than in the past and in turn made the TGWU a more maverick body in Party affairs than had been known since the 1920s. The precarious balance between Left and Right factions made the result of TGWU elections and conference decisions of vital concern to the Parliamentary leadership, and in various ways the TGWU was intermittently a thorn in their political flesh. But alongside the tensions in 1988-9 it was also apparent that as a matter of electoral priority, the TGWU leadership, backed by sections of the union's Left as well as the Right, was bringing union policy on many issues into line with the development of the Party's Policy Review.

Delegations, Mandates and Leadership

No union leader from a union of significant size went to the Conference unac-
companied; indeed, many unions sent substantial delegations. Among the top
ten unions in 1987, the largest delegation was from the GMWU,who sent 79
people. The TGWU sent 62, the AEU sent 43 and the other delegations varied from
14 (UCW) to 29 (TASS).

As with other aspects of union government, the composition of this delegation varied under each union's rules but typically there was a mixture of lay
members, representatives of the union's Executive Committee plus the union's
senior officials. In some of the unions, including the NUM and the GMWU, the
whole of the Executive Committee of the union was entitled to attend as
delegates. Most unions allowed their sponsored MPs and Parliamentary candidates to attend the delegation meeting on a non-voting basis. Some allowed a
proportion of the sponsored MPs to vote. USDAW made them all voting members
of the delegation. In some unions there was still a strong emphasis on rotation in
the representation of lay delegates from districts and regions but in recent years
there has been an increasing tendency to election. There have also been some
attempts to improve the ethnic and gender composition, particularly the latter.[70]
Nevertheless, the delegations remain overwhelmingly white, male and middle-
aged.

One important compositional example was the delegation of the TGWU, which
has been the centre of many a controversy in recent years (see Chapter 11). In
1988, it had a complex composition of 62 members, involving the four senior
union officers, six members of the General Executive Council elected by that
body, four national officers selected by rota, and two Regional Secretaries also
selected by rota. In addition, there were six representatives of the trade groups
(with the groups participating by rota but the representatives elected by the
committees). There were also 27 lay regional representatives with regions participating by rota and the delegates elected by the regional committees. Ten wom-
en's representatives were also elected from the ten women's regional committees.
Finally, there was also a representation of three from the TGWU-sponsored MPs
elected by the group.

Union delegations were normally the final authority in deciding the way in
which the union's vote would be cast. There were exceptions. In the EETPU, for
example, the Executive Committee, operating through a Political subcommittee,
was the supreme authority. In the NUR, its EC Political subcommittee gave
detailed advice which was almost automatically followed. In the TGWU, the exact
demarcation of authority between the General Executive Council and the delegation was unclear (see Chapter 11, pp. 348–9). But no union of significant size
gave authority to a senior official to make the decision alone, and in most cases, it
was the delegation which made the decision.

However, union leaders were normally skilful, prepared, and at the front of the
meeting making suggestions. To their personal prestige, experience of the Conference procedures, and knowledge of 'what was going on', were normally added
reinforcements including committed support from other union officials and back-

up from Head Office staff. All this gave them a considerable leverage within the delegation in influencing its decision.

But there were major constraints, some of which were built into the representation process. Decisions were normally made within the traditions of delegate democracy and the governing consideration was 'what is the mandate of the union?' The mandate was normally defined by the union's annual or biennial conference and it was a bold person who showed outright disrespect for the mandate where it was clear and up-to-date (see Chapter 11, pp. 328–30 for the case involving Sid Weighell).

If there was no clear mandate, then more discretion could be exercised. Even so, other authoritative precedents came into consideration. What was the past position of the Executive Committee? How did the union vote on previous occasions on this issue? The search for some degree of consistency meant that in the absence of a clear mandate, these precedents were often a strong guide to decision-making in the delegation but they had less authority than a clear union conference mandate and there are examples in the unions of delegations turning round from one year to the next, depending on the composition of the delegation and the context of the issue (see Chapter 7, p. 201 for the crucial case involving the Boilermakers union).

Labour party procedure and its problems

Even when the mandate was well-established, there could be arguments over relevance and situation. The time between a union conference and a Labour Party Conference decision could be considerable, particularly if the union held only a biennial conference, as did the TGWU, and particularly if the issue had not been raised at union conferences for some years. Mandates lasted until they were changed by another union decision. But times changed, situations changed, and meanings were changed by events. The delegation sometimes had much to argue about over the relevance of past decisions.

The lack of up-to-date and relevant mandates was the subject of much complaint, some of it special pleading, by union leaders, that crucial decisions relating to the form of the Electoral College were being pushed at them during the 1980 Party Conference without them being able to have time to consult their members.[71] In fact, most unions were unable to cope with the extraordinary situation. Even after a three month postponement, only seventeen unions engaged in any form of consultation – the rest left it to their leadership and delegations.[72] Usually the unions faced this problem in relation to NEC policy statements without public complaint, although such statements were normally too late for union conferences to declare a position and certainly too late for the membership to be consulted. Almost invariably in such cases, 'the platform', particularly when it was reflecting the position of the Parliamentary Leadership, got the benefit of the doubt and the votes of a union majority.

Even when there had been union discussions, the processes of union policymaking sometimes left the mandates with a degree of ambiguity. The resulting problems were compounded when there were late new initiatives from the Party. Voting on the NEC proposal for a Register of Non-Affiliated Groups of

Party Members in 1982 caused friction and sometimes open rows in many delegations. What did it mean and what did it imply? Those unions with mandates against 'a witch hunt' or against 'bans, expulsions and proscriptions' had to decide whether the Register fitted into these descriptions. The unconstitutionality of Militant's organisational practices, the personal appeal of the Party Leader and the rather vaguer feeling that 'some line had to drawn somewhere' put enormous pressure on the union leaders of the centre left and Left who had qualms about anything which smacked of the authoritarian behaviour of the Right in the 1950s. The result was an interpretation of the Register which allowed crucial votes in the TGWU, USDAW, the NUM and ASTMS to be cast for 'the platform'. The matter did not rest there and there were repercussions in several unions as the NEC began to apply the new Register. Nevertheless, the large majority and the precedent of 1982 made it easier to move unions in line with their previous stance and in 1983 and in 1986 the Conference overwhelmingly backed actions to expel leading members of the Militant Tendency.

The Labour Party Conference agenda procedures added to the problem of representation. Mandates had to be applied in the light of the agenda facing the delegates after a compositing process in which multiple elements were often clumsily linked together. Union delegations had to assess what element of the composite resolution was crucial and what was insignificant – a process in which there was much uncertainty and room for argument. In 1982, for example, Composite Resolution No. 44 moved by NUPE included a wide range of measures 'to eradicate low pay' – among these was the more controversial national minimum of 'no less than two-thirds of the average wage'. This was followed by 'such measures as the 35-hour week with no loss of pay' and 'the implementation of clause IV, part 4, of Labour's constitution'.[73] There was thus a wide discretion over what was the relevant mandate in relation to these different proposals. In the event, the resolution was rejected on a card vote.[74]

Compositing processes sometimes afforded an opportunity for flexibility even when the union itself had a resolution down on the agenda. In 1982 there was a row over the behaviour of the POEU leadership, which apparently took its resolution on 'renationalisation without compensation' into the compositing meeting and there appeared to insist on losing the words 'without compensation', while later reporting to its delegation that 'unfortunately' the compositing meeting had simply expressed its collective view.[75] The POEU official was reported later as claiming that he had simply taken the advice of the Chairman of the compositing meeting (ironically, a prominent Leftwing activist – a nice touch this!).[76] There was some irony also in the fact that by a printer's error, the words 'without compensation' suddenly reappeared in the compositing booklet and the Chairman of the Conference Arrangements Committee had to apologise and take it out.[77]

In the delegations

However, much of what went on in the delegations was consensual, if only because the delegations were normally within the same political traditions as the union's Executive Committee and the union's conference. Where there was uncertainty about mandates, there was often a strong inclination to leave the senior officials to sort it out and to follow their recommendations if only because many of the issues dealt with at the Conference were not at the centre of the delegation's or the union's attention.

Even in the face of determined opposition, an adroit senior official with factional support could sometimes produce a 'coup'. The Construction Workers' leadership managed with just one vote on three issues to avoid supporting the Campaign for Labour Party Democracy in 1979. The Miners' President, Joe Gormley, managed to persuade his delegation to avoid its mandate on mandatory reselection the same year.

However, it was not necessarily all plain sailing for the union leadership. Many delegations had their share of articulate oppositionists anxious to support the platform if the leadership would not, or anxious to defeat it where the leadership might want to go the other way. Indeed, in political terms, from 1979 to 1986, a striking feature of union politics was the *inability* of some of the union leaders to deliver on key votes. In 1980, in six unions, the leadership had to acknowledge defeat over mandatory reselection.[78] And in a further three large unions [79] the union leaderships were defeated over the method of electing the Leader. On unilateral nuclear disarmament and on withdrawal from the EEC from 1981 to 1983 there were many examples of union leaders being forced to cast votes in ways that were opposed to their own positions.[80] On the Register of Affiliated Organisations and over the expulsion of members of Militant, Arthur Scargill, the Mineworkers President, was in the same position.

So much depended on the issue, the union structure, the personality of the union leader and the political composition of the delegation that there was often a degree of uncertainty about the outcome, even when the alignment of union leaders was well known. Among the larger unions, you could count on which way the EETPU or TASS would be voting on almost every issue; others were much less predictable.

For many years, up to the late 1970s, the delegation of the Engineers' union was a law unto itself. Lay members were elected by an independent constituency within the union with a strong 'Left Opposition' that had very much a mind of its own in the interpretation and application of the union's mandate. Not until 1981, when the electoral base of the delegation was changed, was it brought fully into harmony with the majority of the union's Executive Committee, its General Secretary and President.

By contrast, the TGWU delegation had a reputation in the post-war years (sometimes undeserved) for being under the thumb of the General Secretary. But with the departure of Jack Jones, the developing pluralistic features of that union (pp. 303–4) also made themselves felt in the delegation. There was considerably difficulty in handling the delegation over the constitutional issues from 1979 to 1981 although after 1982, over the disciplinary issues concerning Militant, the General Secretary and his allies were able to pull the delegation behind the Parliamentary leadership. Still, the General Secretary's control over the delegation remained uncertain. In 1984, there was a development which some considered unique in the history of the delegation. The General Secretary, Moss Evans, attempted to pull the union behind the Party Leadership over One Member One Vote in Parliamentary candidate reselection. There was no mandate for this change from the BDC and the union's position had been established for years. Evans was virtually isolated in the delegation on this issue and had to back down.

BLOCK VOTES, PLATFORM DEFEATS AND POLITICAL REPERCUSSIONS

The political 'block vote'

Although defeat on an issue where the Party Leader personally put his prestige to the fore became more of a rarity during Kinnock's leadership, defeats for the 'platform' have been by no means unusual in the period of Opposition since 1979. Indeed, since the breakthrough of the Left in the unions during the early days of the Jones–Scanlon alliance, the Party has gone through a deeply unsettled period, the full consequences of which are still being unfolded. Some pivotal union positions – on NATO, for example – remained solid. But alliances have become more unstable, majorities in the different forums of the Movement have often failed to cohere and the Parliamentary leadership has never been guaranteed a firm and persistent majority of support within the unions at the Party Conference.

In these circumstances, among the Parliamentary leadership, fond memory often turned to the era of 'settlement' when relations between the two wings were characterised by a high degree of stability, when functional roles were more consensual and when a loyal grouping of union leaders organised the defence of the Parliamentary leadership on a regular basis.

Underpinning the political arrangements of that period, as we have seen, were deeply held ideological convictions. The generation of union leaders who dominated the 'floor' in the years of 'settlement' were as defensive of the Parliamentary leadership as they were assertive against the Left. So marked was their behaviour in those days that 'the block vote' began to mean more than any procedural definition; it was virtually defined as a political formation. Some called it then 'the Rightwing block vote'; others simply called it 'the block vote', meaning the Right Wing.

Looking backwards to that period there were those on the Left who feared the reinstitution of 'the old block vote' – indeed they sometimes thought in 1977, 1982 and 1986 that it had arrived. Conversely, there have been elements in the unions who have looked with nostalgia on that period and sought means to put together its most basic feature – a regular and organised alignment of the major unions sympathetic to the Parliamentary leadership.

The defeats – 1979 to 1986 (Table 10.4)

But the development was never quite secured. There was continuing instability and a strong Left in the TGWU. The old Rightwing base was declining in its affiliation. New issues and new movements arose to complicate alignments. And until 1987 the nuclear weapons issue continued to divide the Party Leader from some of the strongest 'loyalist' elements in the unions.

This instability of the union vote at the Party Conference becomes apparent with even the briefest examination of 'platform' defeats in comparison with previous periods. The comparison is complicated by the changing political composition of the NEC. It was once a buffer and front for the Parliamentary leadership at the Conference but for a period from 1974 to 1981 it was under Leftwing control and thereafter an uncertain vehicle for the Parliamentary leadership on various issues. Thus from 1979 to 1981, while hand vote Conference defeats for the 'platform' on policy issues were generally from a position further to the Left of the NEC, the organisational and constitutional defeats were generally a curb on the NEC from its Right – a curb often supported by the Parliamentary leadership. Such defeats in the 1980s were made more likely by the abandonment of the procedural device of 'qualified acceptance'.

Statistically the contrast was quite startling. In the period of 'settlement' from 1948 to 1959, only one vote went against 'the platform'. Even in the unsettled and controversial period of Opposition from 1970 to 1973, there were only nine 'platform' defeats in four years. Yet in two periods of Opposition between 1979 and 1986 there were 52 such defeats. From 1987 to 1989 there were 17 defeats.*

The Conferences of 1979 to 1981 were highly unusual in their constitutional and organisational preoccupations. Normally policy issues dominated consideration and, in theory, the Conference decisions authoritatively established 'Party' policy. In practice, these defeats had variable significance and authority depending upon many factors – particularly their salience to the unions – although even on crucial issues there was far from an automatic acceptance by the Parliamentary leadership and the NEC, and there was usually some room for manœuvre.

Some of the defeats were taken to be symbolic (e.g. nationalisation of the arms industry under trade union control) and with little trade union follow-up were pushed to one side. Others (e.g. renationalisation on the basis of proven need) were considered less significant than the agreement on policy forged at leadership level. A similar point can be made about the transport policy. A resolution passed narrowly at the 1982 Conference which was pro-rail was not considered to have altered the existing agreement among the unions. More significant, because they merged with a wider Party concern, were the votes prior to 1985 to support local government resistance against the public expenditure cuts.

More difficult for the Parliamentary leadership to handle because of its image effect on the electorate were the severely critical resolutions on the Police, supported by traditionally law-respecting unions, and for a different reason the

---

* There were six defeats for the platform at the 1990 Party Conference.

Table 10.4 Platform defeats – 1979 to 1989

Year	No. of defeats	Resolution	Issue	Votes*
1979	1	Comp. 19	Procedure for election of Leader	3,033,000 to 4,009,000
1980	8	Comp. 14	Disabled persons taxation	
		Commission Recommendation 5.3	Household membership	
		5.7	Registered Labour supporters	4,717,000 to 2,247,000
		Comp. 33	Council housing sales	
		NEC constitutional amendment	Manifesto	3,508,000 to 3,625,000
		NEC constitutional amendment	Leadership Electoral College proportions – 50 per cent unions	3,322,000 to 3,737,000
		NEC constitutional amendment	Electoral College proportions – 40/30/30	3,235,000 to 3,910,000
		Commission Recommendation 12.4	Three Years Rule: Constitutional Amendment	1,160,000 to 5,882,000
1981	9	Em. Res. 3	Refusal of cuts in services	
		Comp. 37	Unemployment and economic policy	
		Comp. 38	Housing loans	
		Res. 68	Afghanistan	
		Comp. 19	Compaigning: re local government	
		NEC Report reference back	Women's organisation	
		Constitutional amendment	Manifesto	3,254,000 to 3,791,000
		Comp. 47	NHS	
1981		Comp. 6	Freedom of information	
1982	8	Comp. 29	Social security	
		Comp. 63	Tranport	3,679,000 to 3,053,000
		Comp. 25	Renationalisation and compensation	5,131,000 to 1,490,000
		Comp. 50	Nationalisation of arms industry	3,433,000 to 3,263,000
		Comp 27	Recognition of PLO	3,538,000 to 3,263,000
		Em. Res. 4	Middle East	3,318,000 to 3,308,000
		Comp. 47	Shorter working time	
		Comp. 23	Taxation	
1983	4	Comp. 17	Social Security	
		Comp. 20	The Media	
		Comp. 43	Labour daily paper	

Year	No. of defeats	Resolution	Issue	Votes*
		Comp. 5	Youth training	
1984	10	Comp. 66	Policing	
		Comp. 68	Policing	4,117,000 to 2,485,000
		NEC constitutional amendment	Candidate reselection	3,041,000 to 3,992,000
		Comp. 53	NHS	4,555,000 to 2,138,000
		Comp. 62	Social Security	3,632,000 to 2,996,000
		Comp. 43	Local government	
		Res. 43 as amended	Black forums	4,018,000 to 2,019,000
		Comp. 38	YTS	3,750,000 to 2,883,000
		Comp. 28	N. Ireland: justice	3,000,000 to 2,624,000
		Comp. 49	South Africa	
1985	9	Comp. 54	Third World	
		Comp. 55	Third World	
		Comp. 16	Police power and miner's strike	3,639,000 to 2,680,000
		Comp. 40	Reproductive Rights	5,305,000 to 611,000
		Comp. 69	Amnesty for miners, etc.	3,542,000 to 2,912,000
		Comp. 70	Fuel policy and nuclear power	3,902,000 to 2,408,000
		Comp. 35	Women on short lists	1,731,000 to 3,875,000
		Comp. 24	Defence policy: arms production, etc.	4,079,000 to 2,284,000
		Comp. 65	South Africa	3,516,000 to 2,699,000
1986	3	Comp. 47	Women's minister	3,335,000 to 2,905,000
		Comp. 56	Education	
		Comp. 39	Party franchise	3,549,000 to 2,603,000
1987	3	Comp. 41	Welfare, pensioners' rights and allowances	
		Comp. 68	Training	
		Comp. 5	Minimum wage	
1988	9	Comp. 2	One woman on short list	
		Comp. 25	Minimum wage	
		Comp. 4	Block vote reform	
		Comp. 20	Employment Training Scheme	
		Comp. 21	Employment Training Scheme	2,801,000 to 3,117,000
		Comp. 55	Nuclear disarmament	2,942,000 to 3,277,000
		Comp. 56	Nuclear disarmament	3,715,000 to 2,471,000
		Comp. 57	Nuclear disarmament	3,345,000 to 2,868,000
		Comp. 59	Israel and PLO	4,163,000 to 1,943,000
1989	5	Comp. 47	Military spending	4,201,000 to 1,922,000
		Comp. 49	Palestine	4,645,000 to 1,394,000
		NEC Statement	Black society	1,428,000 to 2,893,000
		Comp. 40	Public ownership of water industry (land)	
		Comp. 32	Gay and lesbian equality	3,702,000 to 2,317,000

* Where no vote is given, the voting was by hand.
Source: LPACR, 1979 to 1988 and author's notes, 1989.

defeat on Reproductive Rights – with its challenge to the rights of conscience of Members of Parliament. Given the strong feelings and the large votes accumulated behind the resolution on Amnesty for Miners (calling for legal review, reinstatement and reimbursement) in 1985, it was noteworthy that in the face of Kinnock's defence of legality, it was the union majority which in effect backed down. Most difficult of all to deal with was the shift of policy towards nuclear power which was suddenly boosted by a concerned Party and union opinion in the aftermath of the Chernobyl disaster; vital employment interests clashed here with wider values producing one of the most difficult policy areas to manage.

Year by year the Conference and its delegation meetings registered a range of opinion, a strength of feeling, and a body of commitments. The opinions and the feelings sent messages and warnings. The commitments sometimes established boundaries of policymaking difficult for the Party leadership to move outside. The EEC commitment prior to 1983 was one such issue. Unilateral Nuclear Disarmament, up to 1989, was another. And the 'common sense' of trade union traditions established no-go areas and prickly demarcations where union industrial interests were at stake. If the difficulties of the Parliamentary leadership were apparent in the ambiguities of decisions at the 1982 Party Conference on incomes policy and the national economic assessment,[81] they were less apparent but no less real when there was no discussion of the issue at all at the 1986 Party Conference.

In Kinnock's second period of leadership, although the base of support at the Party Conference was still unstable, there was a series of successes in mobilising union majorities on key issues. These included, in 1987, the reorganisation of Head Office, where union interests were directly at stake, and a loosening of the policy boundaries around industrial relations questions. The defeats on defence policy in 1988 were turned into major victory in 1989 – but with a qualification on the level of defence expenditure.* Active union co-operation in resolutions over economic policy and social ownership also eased the continuing reorientation of Labour's policy. A huge, although ambivalent, union majority was produced in 1987 to support a new statement of *Democratic Socialist Aims and Values*.

Much more 'sticky' were the unions' responses to the Government's Employment Training Scheme and their deep concern for the details of minimum wage legislation. And the unions were prepared to line up consistently for the rights of Palestinians and the equality of gays and lesbians (over which there was some wavering at leadership level). They were prepared also to stand out for one-woman-on-every-short-list in 1988 (although only after three years of NEC recommendations *in favour*). And they were not prepared to accept the botched

---

* A similar resolution was supported against the advice of the platform at the 1990 Party Conference. There were defeats for the platform also over pensions, Pergamon Press and the NUJ, and proportional representation for the House of Commons being included in a new party consultation.

'Black Society' proposal* (although they were still divided in attitudes towards 'Black Sections').

These two defeats for the platform on constitutional and organisational issues were not typical of unions' responses. In general, the unions were consistently supportive of all initiatives on constitutional and organisational questions put to them by the Party Leadership, including the National Constitutional Court and the new Electoral College for Candidate selection, the major change in Youth organisation, the raising of the nomination threshold for leadership elections and a host of minor rule changes in 1988.** As was characteristic of the unions, apart from resolutions designed to be helpful in opening up discussion, they did not seek to play an initiating role in these areas, and in 1988 and 1989 were prepared in principle to vote for a constitutional reduction of their own vote at the Party Conference.

THE BLOCK VOTE, REPRESENTATION AND POLICYMAKING: AN OVERVIEW

The participation of affiliated 'members' within the policy process at the Labour Party Conference and the level of affiliation are determined in accordance with rules and arrangements over which the Party has little control. Further, the policy that unions carry into the Labour Party is established as 'union policy' sometimes in a context divorced from the question of what should be Labour Party policy; yet such union policy decisions always constitute mandates. Labour Party procedures both give the opportunity for flexibility over mandates and yet also often make it difficult for a wider democratic consultation within the unions. The practice of unit voting – a practice reinforced by Party procedures – fails to produce an accurate representation of the balance of opinion registered in the unions. These four features constitute major problems of union–Labour Party policymaking.

In terms of representation, a range of problems arises *within* the unions – problems highlighted by the contrast between the high egalitarian ideals of trade union democracy and the limitations of the real processes. There is more policymaking access for members, there is more pluralism, and there is a more constrained 'Bossdom', than critics usually recognise, but even in the most

---

* In 1990 the Party Conference accepted a proposal (Composite 8) for a Black Society organised on the basis of the working party recommendation which had originally been turned down by the Party Leadership in 1989. In the light of the previous year's decision, the NEC accepted the Composite.

** At the 1990 Party Conference, the NEC Statement on candidate selection, which involved (amongst other things) a new trigger mechanism, was supported by the Conference, but a resolution opposing the introduction of the new mechamism was carried against the platform. This apart, the NEC was remarkably successful in pursuing constitutional changes which included block vote reform, quotas for women, changes in the method of electing the CLP section of the NEC and an overhaul of the policy-making procedures. In addition, Socialist Organister was declared to be 'ineligible for affiliation ... and inconsistent with the Constitutional Rules'.

democratically organised and well-intentioned unions, there are difficulties relating to Labour Party policymaking. In particular, there is too much flexibility in the relationship between levypaying and Party affiliation, and there is too weak an interaction on 'political' issues between the inactive membership and union decision-making processes.

As for the most fundamental problem of trade union representation within the Labour Party – the huge preponderance of union votes alongside those of the individual membership and other affiliates – this problem has grown more rather than less acute. The block vote has become more concentrated, more obvious, and more a source of grievance to the constituency parties. At the same time, it provides a diminished security for the Parliamentary leadership at the Party Conference. As a result, the movements for reform of the block vote became more pressing – particularly after the Deputy Leadership election of 1981 and the conflicts over NEC elections.Before we examine in detail the trajectory of the reform movements, these elections have now to be considered.

NOTES.

1. For example Ken Gill, General Secretary of TASS. 'Block Votes – No Case To Answer', *Morning Star*, 22/2/83.
2. Tariq Ali questioning Ken Livingstone, 'Why Labour Lost', *New Left Review*, 140, July/August 1983, p. 39.
3. *The Independent*, 1/6/87.
4. *Standing Order*, 1903.
5. At the Conference of 1900, the unions, with 545,316 members represented, dwarfed the socialist societies – 22,861. But only five unions cast more than 20,000 votes each while the ILP and the Social Democratic Federation cast 'mini' block votes of 13,000 and 9,000 each.
6. Of twelve Executive Committee seats, the socialist societies were given five (plus in practice the Secretaryship).
7. *LPACR*, 1917, pp. 137–8. The sections, however, retained nominating rights.
8. The unions then cast 5,086,000 as union votes are topped up to the nearest thousand.
9. *LPACR*, 1980, p. 1.
10. *Labour Party Constitution*, 1987, Clause VII 2(a).
11. By implication, from the rules of the Party, S.O. 3(1), a card vote must be held if one is demanded. This has been confirmed time and again, for example. *LPACR*, 1982, pp. 32 and 40; *LPACR*, 1984, p. 157.
12. *LPACR*, 1981, p. 157.
13. Data presented to Women's Committee of the NEC, 6/12/83; see also n. 70.
14. Formally, there were 42 such unions but some unions, including the Transport Workers, Engineers, and General and Municipal Workers, retained separate voting identities for some unions with which they amalgamated. As they operated and voted as units, in practice there were 36 unions.

15. At the Tribune rally on 5 October 1988, the Transport Workers leader criticised both 'modernisers' and 'nostalgics'. This was seen primarily as an attack on the Party Leadership and dominated media attention for the rest of the week. It was labelled the 'Day of the Dinosaur', *The Observer*, 9/10/88. The speech was reprinted as 'Change the party – But Never Forget Labour's Real Values', *Tribune*, 14/10/88.

16. On this, see McKibbon, *op. cit.*, p. 101. The vote was 1,600,000 (to retain) against 757,000. There is no official Labour Party report of this February Conference of 1918, but in January the socialist societies and the Women's Labour League cast 50,000 votes and the local Labour parties cast 115,000. The Trades Councils cast 110,000. It was significant also that when *one* voting card per union was introduced at the 1913 TUC, there were protests from, among others, the Gasworkers union. It was agreed that they could have as many cards as they wished. *Minutes of the Parliamentary Committee of the TUC*, 25/8/1913.

17. *Beatrice Webb Diaries*, 1912–24, p. 182. Ben Pimlott, *Labour and the Left in the 1930s*, 1977, p. 88. Letter from Lord Underhill, 16/5/81, relating to the Textile Workers.

18. Pimlott, *ibid.*, p. 88.

19. *Report of the ASW ADM*, 1950, p. 224. The union was unusual in that its Annual Delegate Meeting was not the designated policymaking authority until 1951. After that date, the practice of splitting the vote ceased.

20. On this, see L. Minkin, 'The Politics of the Block Vote', *New Socialist*, No. 1, September 1981.

21. TULV National Coordinator, Jenny Pardington, to the author in January 1988.

22. See Chapter 12, pp. 375. The project known to some as 'Levy-Plus' arose out of a Tribune Group pamphlet, *A Mass Party*, from an idea by Gordon Brown MP.

23. According to TUFL Office, these were IPCS, CPSA, NUHKW, NULM, SCPS, IRSF, CSU, NCU (Clerical), NUIW, CMA, EIS, AIT, STE, NALGO, NATFHE, HVA and UDM. In addition, the AES and the NASWT also approved political funds in 1989.

24. On this, see Andrew Taylor, 'The Politics of Non-Partisan Trade Unions: The British Case', *Politics*, Vol. 7, No. 1, April 1987, pp. 8–13.

25. *Labour Party Constitution*, 1980, Clause 11(2)(a).

26. The issue was raised in 1980 at the time of the Commission of Enquiry into Party Organisation and raised again in 1983 after queries over the right to individual membership. CE/OM/13/3/80 and letter from David Hughes, the National Agent, to CLPs, 5/7/83. A variety of issues had to be taken into account in making a judgement on a union's acceptability, including whether or not other affiliated organisations or TUC affiliated organisations sat down with the union concerned in joint negotiations.

27. Letter from the TUC General Secretary to the Labour Party General Secretary, 20/9/88, in reply to letter 6/9/88.

28. Alan Watkins, 'Mr. Kinnock's Television Team', *The Observer*, 12/7/87. In 1980, Mike Thomas MP accused trade unions of 'literally buying votes, as many as they can afford', BBC World At One, 22/9/80. Michael Pinto-Duschinsky refers to the 'system which permits trade unions literally to buy power over the party' as 'the most important

single abuse relating to British political finance', *British Political Finance*, 1830-1980, 1981, p. 238. He quotes Tommy Jackson of the UCW, criticising the process as 'simply buying votes and buying influence', p. 305.

29. NEC Org. Sub Minutes, 10/11/80. A resolution simply noting the General Secretary's report on the matter was moved by Tony Benn and seconded by John Golding, the Rightwing representative of the POEU.

30. *LPACR*, 1982, p. 39 and Constitution Clause XI 1.

31. *Labour Party Constitution*, 1988, Clause XI 1(c).

32. According to the Report of the Certification Officer in 1985, the AUEW had 520,000 contributing to its Political Fund. In 1986, it affiliated to the Labour Party on 800,000 votes. The NUM had 129,436 levypayers but affiliated on 208,000 votes. ISTC had 37,664 levypayers but affiliated on 62,000 votes.

33. 'It was an open secret that trade unions over-affiliated to keep this party going'. Sam McCluskie, Labour Party Treasurer, speaking in the debate on Party finances, Labour Party Conference, 1/10/89. Notes of the author .

34. Alan Watkins, 'Kinnock Has A Long Lease', *The Observer*, 14/2/88.

35. Peter Kellner, 'Labour's Head upon the Block', *The Independent*, 21/9/87.

36. This is a very old complaint, see Harrison, *op. cit.*, p. 38. Harrison makes the judgement that such intimidation as existed had declined since the War, p. 40. The complaints were, however, repeated in 1984 by the Director of Aims of Industry, Michael Ivens, in a letter to the *New Statesman*, 6/7/84.

37. On this, see K.D. Ewing and W.M. Rees, 'Democracy in Trade Unions – 1. The Political Levy', *New Law Journal*, February 1983. Also see Keith Ewing, *The Funding of Political Parties in Britain*, 1987, pp. 62–4 and particularly the Report of the Royal (Donovan) Commission, *op. cit.*, Para. 923.

38. It is difficult to give a precise figure for 'contracting out' complaints as the Certification Officer's report does not always provide this information within the general category of 'complaints'. The Annual Report for 1984 – the year of the Trade Union Act – gives total complaints as: 1977 – 18; 1978 – 12; 1979 – 105; 1980 – 20; 1981 – 12; 1982 – 24; 1983 – 21; 1984 – 7. The figure for 1979 includes 76 complaints from one TGWU branch. Since 1984, the figures for complaints relating to the Fund overall have been: 1985 – 7; 1986 – 5; 1987 – 7; 1988 – nil; 1989 – nil. *Annual Report of the Certification Officer 1984–1989*. These figures do not suggest widespread grievance, given that in 1986 there were five and a half million political levypayers in 41 unions. But as Harrison, *op. cit.*, points out, members may be ignorant of the complaints procedure, or they may be unwilling to incur the bother and expense involved in complaining, p. 38.

39. M. Moran, *The Union of Post Office Workers*, 1974, found that 95 per cent paid the political levy but only 51 per cent knew they were paying it, pp. 90–91. See also John Goldthorpe *et al.*, *The Affluent Worker: Industrial Attitudes and Behaviour*, 1968, pp. 110–112.

40. TUC Circular No. 161 (1983/4) and TUC Statement of Guidance. See also Chapter 17, pp. 5–6 and 13.

41. Harrison, *op. cit.*, p. 167.

42. See, for example, G.D.H. Cole, *The World of Labour*, Macmillan, 1913, p. xi.

43. W.W. Daniel and Neil Millward, *DE/PSI/SSRC Survey*, 1983, p. 86.

44. 'We canna' be 16 steps ahead of our members', John Rentoul interview with Gavin Laird, *New Statesman*, 10/7/87.

45. For example Milligan, *op. cit.*, 1976, pp. 218–222; Barry Sherman, *The State of the Unions*, 1986, pp. 108–9.

46. See on this, Marick F. Masters and John Thomas Delaney, 'Union Political Activities: A Review of the Empirical Literature', in *Industrial and Labor Relations Review*, Vol. 40, No. 3, p. 345. See also D.W. Rawson, 'The Paradox of Partisan Trade Unionism: The Australian Case', in *British Journal of Political Science*, 4, October 1974, pp. 399–418.

47. Sydney Webb, *op. cit.*, p. 23. Note also the judgement of Vincent McKee that the SDP constitution with its provision for referenda 'was cleverly designed to create the impression of a member's democracy, whereas in reality it was no such thing'. 'Decision-making was rigidly centralised, leadership exalted and group activity regulated'. 'Factionalism in the Social Democratic Party 1981–1987', *Parliamentary Affairs*, Vol. 42, No. 2, April 1989, p. 169 and p. 178.

48. Webb, *op. cit.*, p. 37.

49. MORI for *Union World*, 3/7/83 and MORI for *Sunday Times*, 2/10/88.

50. MORI for *Sunday Times*, 2/10/88, found 50 per cent of this group favouring removal of all nuclear weapons with 46 per cent either backing an independent or a West European deterrent.

51. On this, see Panitch, *op. cit.*, pp. 137, 161 and 260–1. PEP in Milligan, *op. cit.*, pp. 218–9. MORI for *Sunday Times*, 11/4/76. Ivor Crewe in Kavanagh, *op. cit.*, p. 44 showing that by 1979, 57 per cent of the electorate thought that the Government should leave it to employers and trade unions to negotiate wages and salaries alone.

52. MORI for *Union World* found 54 per cent of trade unionists in support of an incomes policy and 49 per cent of TGWU members, 2/7/83.

53. See Chapter 8, n. 59, for the views of trade unionists in 1979. In 1984 a majority of trade unionists thought that Government legislation on the unions was either about right or should have gone further; only 37 per cent thought that it went too far, Marplan for *Guardian*, 6/2/84. However, in 1989, after further legislation, opinion began to shift and the percentage of trade unionists believing that the legislation had gone too far had risen to 48 per cent, *Guardian*, 23–8 Aug., data supplied privately. See also nn. 57 and 58.

54. For the history of this belief, see Alan Fox, *History and Heritage*, 1985, Chapters 1 and 2, pp. 1–67. And note that the call to protect 'traditional rights' did evoke majority support among trade unionists (55 per cent support, 30 per cent oppose), MORI for 'World in Action', 18/1/82.

55. One sophisticated variant of this can be found in the writings of Flanders, *op. cit.*, pp. 29–30.

56. Academic support for this can be found in Paul Whiteley, *The Labour Party in Crisis*, 1983, p. 94 and Patrick Dunleavy, 'Some Political Implications of Sectoral Cleavages and the Growth of State Employment – Part 2, Cleavage, Structures and Political Alignment', *Political Studies*, 28, pp. 527–9.

57. Harris for *Observer*, 27–29 September 1989. Unpublished data supplied privately by *The Observer*. Labour voters favoured 'abolition' of the trade union laws by 62 – 25 per cent. Trade union activists favoured abolition by 57 – 28 per cent.

58. Labour supporters 73 – 12 per cent, trade union activists 84 – 13 per cent, 'not active' trade unionists 78 – 17 per cent. *Ibid.*

59. This was most significant in the TGWU where, although the union leadership had reservations about the drift of Party policy, a resolution put to the 1989 Biennial Conference which rejected outright the industrial relations section of the Party's policy review was defeated with the backing of the union EC. See also n. 69.

60. 'Labour's Paradoxical Reform', Editorial in *The Independent*, 1/7/87.

61. The sovereign body within EETPU has always been the Executive Council. Following the 1974 General Election, the union was reorganised to create a distinct advisory structure for politial decision-making. EETPU branch delegates to the Labour Party are grouped into regions. They meet annually prior to each regional Labour Party Conference. They also elect a Regional Political Advisory Committee, a member of the National Political Advisory Committee and a delegate to the Labour Party Conference. The national Political Advisory Committee meets twice yearly to advise the Executive Council Political Committee. *EETPU/EESA Fact Sheet*, No. 35.

62. The key exception to this is the Engineers union, where the President is the senior officer. In USDAW and the NUM, there have been periods of parity of esteem, although latterly the NUM Presidency has been the major office.

63. These variations are thoroughly explored in V.L. Allen, *Power in Trade Unions*, 1954; B.C. Roberts, *Trade Union Government and Administration*, 1956 and J. Hughes, 'Trade Union Structure and Government', Evidence to the Royal (Donovan) Commission on Trade Unions and Employers Associations, 1965–8, Research Paper 5. H.A. Clegg, *The System of Industrial Relations in Great Britain*, 1976, pp. 93–109. On political process, see also L. Minkin, *The Labour Party Conference*, 1978.

64. 'Tories' Union Election Law Backfires', *Labour Research*, May 1990, pp. 11–12.

65. R. Undy *et al.*, *Changes in Trade Unions*, 1981, pp. 314–15.

66. H.A. Turner, *Trade Union Growth Structure and Policy*, 1962.

67. On this, see L. Minkin, *The Labour Party Conference*, *op. cit.*, pp. 93–8

68. *Ibid.*, pp. 129–131.

69. On the EEC, on nationalisation, and on industrial relations, the TGWU conference of 1989 rejected critical resolutions from the Left

70. In 1983, 7.5 per cent of TU delegates were women. By 1987, this had risen to 12.9 per cent. (Women delegates were now at around a third of CLP delegates.) A sign of the times in 1989 was that UCATT sent its first woman delegate to the Conference.

71. *LPACR*, 1980, p. 186.

72. 'What About the Workers?', *Sunday Times*, 7/12/80.

73. *LPACR*, 1982, p. 192.

74. *Ibid.*, p. 206.

75. *Tribune*, 4/2/83 and interviews with delegates.

76. *Tribune*, 4/2/83.

77. *LPACR*, 1982, p. 5.

78. ASB, ASTW, AUEW (Foundry), NACODS, NGA and NUM..
79. ASB, COHSE and UCATT.
80. The most obvious examples in 1981 on the EEC were APEX, NUM and NUR, and on unilateral nuclear disarmament COHSE, ISTC, NUM and NUR.
81. The Conference accepted unanimously a Liaison Committee document which included a national economic assessment but defeated composite resolution No. 71 which asked for it to be agreed with the TUC, describing it as 'a socialist social contract', *LPACR*, 1982, pp. 189 and 206.

11

The block vote: electing the leadership

The multiplicity of card votes, and the pause in Conference proceedings which accompanied their casting, always drew attention to the existence of the block vote. Such votes were sometimes crucial in determining the future of the Party – particularly when they dealt with its constitution, rules and standing orders. But there was also another face of the block vote – often highly predictable but also highly significant. Indeed, there were times when the most important exercise of the block votes at the Conference was not by cards but by ballot papers, and not on policy but in elections. The trade unions elected or dominated the election of 18 members of the 29-person NEC which was responsible for the administration of the Party[1] and which, by custom based on constitutional facility,[2] was responsible for the formulation of major policy documents. Thus in a sense the unions were annually involved in electing an element of the leadership of the Party.

However, as we have seen, their role in these arrangements was discreet and politically constrained. The elections were governed by a complicated body of unwritten 'rules' and arrangements derived mainly from industrial considerations. The delicacy of the negotiations involved in the understandings and compacts, plus ingrained diffidence over public displays of anything that looked like union control over the Party, meant that there was considerable secrecy surrounding these processes. And, although there was a strong and sometimes a crucial factional element, the unions' leaders were generally deeply resistant to attempts, particularly from the Left, to make these elections purely political at the expense of the industrial considerations.

Yet the fact remained that in the period from 1979 to 1987, not only was the trade union role in electing the leadership of the Party broadened to encompass the Leader and the Deputy Leader, but NEC elections became subject to new political forces, new political criteria and an enhanced political factionalism. The 'rules' remained in force, affecting and constraining the possibilities of political mobilisation, but the interplay of the industrial and the political took on a new and sometimes unpredictable character.

ELECTING THE NEC

Year after year, close watchers of the Labour Party tried to fathom the complicated pattern of NEC elections – searching for intimations of political change in the way the unions were behaving. Twelve trade union members were directly elected to the Trade Union Section and a further six of the 29 persons on the committee (the five in the Women's Section and the Treasurer) were covered by a majority of trade union votes.

Whereas in the operation of the card votes on policy, organisation, and the Party's Constitution, there was often a lengthy process of policymaking within the unions – imperfect and not comprehensive but involving a much wider constituency than the union leadership – in elections for the NEC those actively involved were very few in number.

With some exceptions, including the nominating elections for the NUM candidate, the politics of NEC elections was carried out almost exclusively at the level of the union Executive and the delegation. Formally or informally, these Executives, and particularly the senior officers, were conceded far more discretion than in the casting of the vote on policy issues. Indeed, in several of the smaller unions, it was common practice simply to allow the union's leadership to make whatever voting arrangements they considered in the best interests of the union.

Most unions – apart from the EETPU[3] – accepted that their delegates should be formally part of the election process but the circumstances under which they decided and the limitations on their participation had many constraining nuances. In the NUR, for example, it was customary for the Political Subcommittee of the NEC to recommend basic decisions on elections before the Conference opened. There was little role for the delegations which almost invariably accepted the recommendations. In the General and Municipal Workers, discretion was, until very recently, informally conceded to the General Secretary personally to make arrangements. In other unions, like NUPE and ASTMS, arrangements made by the union leadership were reported to the delegation and then generally respected. In the huge Transport and General Workers Union, the process was one in which the General Secretary took the initiative after some consultations with other officers and discussions with other unions. His judgement was put to the delegation with a range of justifying criteria if challenged over his choices. Sometimes there was a challenge, but not in recent years has there been a reversal – in part because of the complexity and sensitivity of many of the arrangements.

Unusually, as we have noted (Chapter 7, p. 197), the Engineers delegation for years assertively controlled the casting of their votes. Although the major deals with the larger unions were respected, many of the union's votes – particularly for the Women's Section – were cast in the teeth of determined objections from the union's leadership. By 1981, a change in the method of electing the delegation produced a more factionally agreeable composition and gave the union's President and General Secretary scope for a much more cohesive role working with the other union leaders in a Rightwing factional organisation.

The arrangements and the 'rules'

The basic constraint on political factionalism and on the full 'politicisation' of voting was the 'rule' that in order to facilitate unity, large unions should be represented as of right in major committees of the Labour Movement.

In addition, there were arrangements in relation to particular candidates which spread from the big unions to many of the others. These were at their most complicated prior to 1983 (when automatic representation was introduced for the TUC General Council). They covered nominees for the General Council, for the trade union section of the NEC, and for the Women's Section of the NEC. Some of these understandings were so complicated that they almost defied unravelment. Shirley Williams, when a member of Labour's NEC, was apparently covered by an arrangement negotiated through APEX which made it virtually impossible for the Left in the Transport Workers delegation to withdraw its support and they were still voting for her almost on the eve of her defection.

Some 'unity' arrangements were *ad hoc* deals – 'You vote for our man and we will vote for yours'. A union which was involved in explorations of amalgamations might arrange a vote which ran counter to political factionalism (APEX and ASTMS in 1980, for example). But also, by custom, unions in the same industry (the railways, for example) tended to vote for each other regardless of other conflicts. Unions which sought special industrial accommodations (the 'Triple Alliance' of Miners, Railwayworkers and Steelworkers, for example) would also arrange the exchange of votes in spite of deep political differences.

Apart from these arrangements, there were other 'rules' and customs which regulated the voting patterns. A union with traditional occupancy on the NEC – the NUR, for example – might be held to have more right to a seat than unions which had, as it were, newly arrived; part of the reason why ASTMS and NUPE found it so difficult to break in. A sitting tenant on the NEC from a smaller union developed rights of occupancy over time. When a vacancy occurred, the next in line in the previous year's voting was held to have a special claim.

A candidate must have received the backing of his or her own union before the candidature was legitimate. Within the union, either by custom or rule, a particular position sometimes automatically led to NEC nomination. Where it didn't, 'Buggins' turn' or seniority was a major factor. Almost invariably, a union voted for its own nominee even when the political complexion of the union's leadership changed.

Trade union section and trade union 'rules'

This rule-governed behaviour was apparent in the regular and predictable outcome of elections for the Trade Union's Section of the NEC (Table 11.1). Five unions by size and history made arrangements such as to ensure that they always had representation on the NEC regardless of their leadership at any one time. These were the three largest unions – the TGWU, the GMWU and the AEU – together with USDAW and the NUR. In addition, since 1981 COHSE and, since 1982, NUPE appear to have moved closer to that club. COHSE takes all these unions except the TGWU; NUPE all these unions but not the AEU. Thus, seven of the twelve places in 1988 were virtually settled in advance.

When we move past these seven places, a much more complicated mixture of political and industrial factors come into play. A special claim on these seats was made by unions with a membership of over 50,000; only occasionally, as with the

NGA and the TSSA, did a smaller union get a look in. A politically significant feature of these unions affiliated on between 50,000 and 200,000 which did not have representation on the NEC as of right was that those led from the Right out-numbered those who were led from the Left by about 2 to 1. If you add this factor to the situation whereby the TGWU which had 1,330,000 votes at the Conference only claimed one seat on the NEC (indeed gave up a second seat in 1986), and then note also the loyalist role-playing tendency of NEC 'Trade Unionists', you get near to the explanation of why the NEC was more Rightwing than the Conference on some of the policy issues and more likely to be defeated at the Conference than, say, in the 1950s.

But, in addition, we come to another political factor. Two unions which by size or tradition ought to have had a regular seat on the NEC in this period – TASS and NUM – failed because of the Communist Party or ultra Left association of their leaderships.[4] The NUM moved on and off for reasons which will be noted later. The amalgamation of TASS with ASTMS to form MSF (the sixth largest union) in 1988 has still to result in a guarantee of a seat for this reason.

So there were certainly some political exclusions at work. And from 1981 there was also an enhanced political factionalism behind 'slates' of candidates seeking to win seats other than those taken by the big union arrangements. This slate organisation was at its sharpest in 1981 and 1982 with the General Council Left Group at the core of the Left's organisation (Chapter 7, n. 9) and a 'St Ermin's Group'[5] at the core of the Right. Factional cohesion diminished after 1983 but there were always Left and Right slates.

New politicisation 1981

The deepening conflict over constitutional questions, which involved an asser-tive Left taking the momentum of its victories into a Deputy Leadership election, was always likely to raise the political stakes in terms of NEC elections. And as the Bennite leadership made the politicisation of the unions a central focus of its campaigning strategy (p. 33), this added to the new factional forces at work.

But there was an additional factor – the feedback into the Party of conflicts at the TUC over 'automaticity' and representation on the General Council.[6] This representational conflict slowly became factionalised such that some unions tended to change sides in accordance with ideological alignment rather than immediate union representational interest. Divisions over automaticity began to split the GMWU from ASTMS and TGWU leadership with whom it was working constructively in TULV and by 1981 it was being pulled into the orbit of the organised Right.

These forces generated a Rightwing backlash in 1981. An extension of the 'St Ermin's' alliance took place. The leaders of the AUEW (now under the clear control of the Right), APEX, EETPU, ISTC, NUR, POEU and USDAW (the core of the St Ermin's Group) were now joined by the GMWU and the UCW, which had in recent times kept aloof from the Rightwing grouping. A slate of candidates was produced and a group of Leftwing members of the NEC targeted. Within two years, most of those targeted had been removed.

This political targeting in some cases led to a new fragility in old inter-union

Table 11.1 Representation on trade union section of the NEC, 1979-1989

	1979	1980	1981	1982	1983
TGWU	A. Kitson	A. Kitson	A. Kitson	A Kitson	A. Kitson
AUEW/AEU	G. Russell	G. Russell	G. Russell	K. Cure	K. Cure
GMWU/GMB	N. Nough	N. Hough	N. Hough	N. Hough	N. Hough
USDAW	S. Tierney	S. Tierney	S. Tierney	S. Tierney	S. Tierney
NUR	R. Tuck	R. Tuck	R. Tuck	R. Tuck	C. Turnock
NUPE		B. Dix**		T. Sawyer	T. Sawyer
COHSE			D. Williams	D. Williams	C. Ambler
POW/UCW					T. Clarke
NUS	S. McCluskie	S. McCluskie	S. McCluskie	S. McCluskie	S. McCluskie***
NUM	E. Williams	E. Clarke	E. Clarke		
ASTMS	D. Hoyle	D. Hoyle	D. Hoyle MP		D. Hoyle MP
TSSA	T. Bradley MP	T. Bradley MP			
POEU/NCU	J.Golding MP	J.Golding MP	J.Golding MP	J.Golding MP	
ASBSBSW*	A. Hadden	A. Hadden	A. Hadden	A. Hadden	A. Hadden
APEX	F. Mulley MP			D. Howell MP	
UCATT		C. Kelly			
ISTC			R. Evans	R. Evans	R. Evans
NGA					
SOGAT					

*The Boilermakers amalgamated with the GMWU in 1983 to form the GMB.
**Dix, as runner-up, replaced Bradley in March 1981 after Bradley's defection to the SDP.
***In 1984 McCluskie was elected Treasurer.
****Haigh was General Secretary of the National Union of Dyers, Bleachers and Textile workers which in 1982 amalgamated with the TGWU.
Sources: LPACR, 1979 to 1988 and Ballot Results, 1989.

1984	1985	1986	1987	1988	1989
A. Kitson E. Haigh****	A. Kitson E. Haigh	E. Haigh	E. Haigh	E. Haigh	E. Haigh
K. Cure	K. Cure	K. Cure	K. Cure	K. Cure	P. Burns
N. Hough	N. Hough	N. Hough	N. Hough	T. Burlison	T. Burlison
S. Tierney	S. Tierney	S. Tierney	S. Tierney	S. Tierney	S. Tierney
C. Turnock	C. Turnock	C. Turnock	A. Dodds	A. Dodds	A. Dodds
T. Sawyer	T. Sawyer	T. Sawyer	T. Sawyer	T. Sawyer	T. Sawyer
C. Ambler	C. Ambler	C. Ambler	C. O'Kane	C. O'Kane	C. O'Kane
T. Clarke	T. Clarke	T. Clarke	T. Clarke	T. Clarke	T. Clarke
E. Clarke	E. Clarke	E. Clarke	E. Clarke		
D. Hoyle MP					
				R. Rosser	R. Rosser
A. Hadden					
		J. Rogers	J. Rogers	J. Rogers	J. Rogers
	G. Colling	G. Colling	G. Colling	G. Colling	G. Colling
	E. O'Brien	E. O'Brien	E. O'Brien	E. O'Brien	E. O'Brien

arrangements (in 1981, the Transport Workers voted for the NUR but the NUR did not vote for the Transport Workers) and led particularly to new factional voting for the Women's Section. (As a result, in 1981, the Transport Workers'-sponsored MPs Margaret Beckett and Renee Short were both removed.) This political threat to old-established voting 'rules' looked all the more menacing because of the new aggression of the Engineers' leadership. They took the astonishing step of withdrawing support from their own member and past nominee for the Treasurership, Norman Atkinson MP – very explicable in factional terms but wholly at odds with normal trade union representational behaviour. The Engineers 'lost' their representative and 'gave' the position to an NUM-sponsored Rightwing MP, Eric Varley.

The ruthless political character of the Rightwing's organisation (and its efficiency) stung the TGWU leadership and for a short period there was talk of some of the most basic 'rules' breaking down in the face of the new politicisation. However, the AUEW and GMWU voting pattern continued to include the old understandings with the TGWU. These understandings, aided by the return of Moss Evans and the need to preserve a degree of unity at a difficult time, meant that the basic structure of industrial arrangements among the big unions was preserved, even though the Rightwing organisation virtually achieved a clean sweep of its 'hit list' targets in 1982 when Joan Maynard was removed from the Women's Section and replaced by Anne Davis. The removal of Doug Hoyle of ASTMS and the election for the first time of a NUPE representative, Tom Sawyer, was not so much the result of a political shift but of a deal between the leadership of NUPE and that of the GMWU in which the latter recognised the need to see the fourth largest union represented.

Most striking of all was the removal from the NEC of the representative of the NUM – Eric Clarke. In 1982, the Miners still ranked sixth in the voting weight among the unions. Industrially they were recognised to be among the most powerful of unions. The Party Leader, Michael Foot, wanted them to retain the place they had held on the NEC since before the First World War. But their newly-elected President was Arthur Scargill and in as political a move as one is likely to see in NEC elections, their representative was removed. The case is worth a more detailed examination.

The fall of Sid Weighell

The nature of the arrangements and the extent to which they came under political pressure at this time can be gauged by the dramatic developments in the National Union of Railwaymen. As a result of a crisis of industrial and political obligations, the NUR General Secretary, Sid Weighell – a powerful leader of his union – carried through a manoeuvre which led to his resignation and focused much attention on the deals and slates associated with the block vote.

There was an unusual cross-pressure on the NUR leadership at this time. The publicly owned rail, steel and mining industries were under renewed financial threat from the Conservative Government. They were also involved in pay disputes. A 'Triple Alliance' of the three unions – the NUR, the ISTC and the NUM – set up so that they could come to each other's industrial assistance had been first agreed in 1980 and consolidated in the next two years. At both the 1980 and 1981 Conferences, the three unions had supported each other's candidates on industrial grounds although the candidates were politically very different. It was a symbol of their industrial solidarity, and it was expected it would continue in the immediate future.

But the 1981 Party Conference had also seen a most effective political slate operated by the Right to secure a major change in the composition of the NEC; policies were beginning to change on that body – including a move to tighten up on Party discipline over Leftwing 'entryist' organisations. Clarke, the Leftwing NUM nominee had, in effect, been put on the National Executive with 170,000 NUR votes. The 1982 Rightwing slate aimed to knock him off and produce a stable Rightwing base for the Party Leadership – what Weighell described as a 'nice, sensible, balanced Party Executive'.[7] But the NUR vote stood between them and their purpose and, worse, there were signs in 1982 that the Left would use the NUR Executive Political Sub-committee to increase the NUR's support for Leftwing candidates. Thus Weighell was under political pressure from both Right and Left.

Against all tradition, in July 1982 a Resolution (No. 31) appeared on the agenda from the Bristol No. 3 branch, which urged the Annual General Meeting (Conference) of the NUR to support the *same* nominees as last year. Normally, mandating was unheard of for NEC elections. It was a world, as Weighell pointed out, 'in which we deal for seats on the Party Executive and on.... the General Council there are trade unions that trade votes. That is the world you and I live in.'[8] Normally, strenuous efforts were made by union leaders to avoid opening up the process to discussion by union conferences. In this case, however, not only did Weighell not attempt to keep the offending resolution off the agenda, he welcomed it.[9] Indeed, knowledgeable sources in the NUR suggest that Weighell himself set it up to ensure that the Left were tied up. Instead, as we shall see, it was Weighell himself who got trapped.

The NUR was now committed to voting for the NUM as previously and Weighell wrote to the NUM saying that 'in the spirit of the Triple Alliance, the NUR will be supporting NUM nominees for TUC General Council and General Purposes Committee and for the Labour Party National Executive Committee and Conference Arrangements Committee. I will be pleased to hear that you will be doing the same in the case of the NUR nominees for these positions'.[10] Writing the letter itself was a bit peculiar, given the formal disapproval that exists over 'canvassing and bartering' arrangements. For these reasons Daly, the NUM Secretary, was unwilling, it was said, to put anything in writing but simply gave a verbal agreement.[11] At the TUC, one week following the letter, there seemed nothing amiss.

When it came to the Party Conference, there was one of those freak coincidences which turn the best-laid plans into a nightmare. The votes were duly cast, counted and announced. To the utter consternation of the NUM and those organising the Leftwing slate, including the Secretary of the General Council Left Group (Alan Meale), Clarke's vote – which should have given him a place on the NEC – was found to be many hundreds of thousands short. In 1981, he had

3,307,000 votes; this time apparently only 2,296,000. Where had a million votes gone?

Anxious recanvassing seemed to confirm that Clarke's vote was over three million. Among those canvassed again was Sid Weighell who, according to the NUM, confirmed that he had voted for Clarke.[12] Had the discrepancy been a couple of hundred thousand it is doubtful whether the complaints could have progressed, but the sheer scale of it was bound to raise questions about the accuracy of the scrutineers' count. Accordingly, a recount was held – an unusual event in itself – and it was found that the scrutineers had indeed made a mistake, failing to incorporate 600,000 NUPE votes into the Clarke total.

Arthur Scargill of the NUM went into the scrutineers' room with Moss Evans of the Transport Workers and they were allowed to see the calculations, although not apparently the ballot papers. However, Scargill and Meale had made their calculations and suspected that the NUR vote was missing. A swift glance at the tabulation confirmed that there was a figure of 170,000 missing from the Clarke totals – a figure which could only mean that the NUR vote had *not* been cast for Clarke.

Within the Conference the row progressed to the point where in an unprecedented development, a group of unions led by Clive Jenkins and Arthur Scargill pushed for a second ballot.[13] They were defeated; the precedent this might create was horrendous to think about. So, as a result of Weighell's political manoeuvre, the NUM was not represented on the NEC, the Right was strengthened by this and other changes and regained all the Committee Chairs they had lost in the mid-1970s.

Meanwhile, Weighell had recalled his delegation and admitted that he had not voted for the NUM. He later explained that he had not done so because they had not replied to his letter.[14] Why he had not subsequently spoken to the NUM (whose delegation was sitting a few yards away in the hall) was not explained. Nor was it explained why Weighell had failed to mention the matter to the Executive Committee, the Political Subcommittee, or the NUR delegation meeting on the Sunday prior to the Conference. In the delegation, the news was received with little sympathy even from loyalists who appreciated his political motives. The AGM had been used and then its mandate flouted; that was enough.

Weighell resigned – a move which some saw as a political tactic to turn the issue into one of confidence. Others saw it as a mistake made by a proud man. Certainly, it would have been difficult to force his resignation but at a meeting of the NUR's AGM held later in October, the delegates voted 41–36 *not* to ask him to rescind his resignation.[15]

Trade Union Section, Treasurership and the Dream Ticket leadership

There were those in 1983 who saw the new Leftwing leadership of the NUR (Jimmy Knapp), the continuing Leftwing stance of the TGWU, the sudden shift of the POEU (later NCU) Executive, and the decline of affiliation in the AUEW, as signs that the Left would make a major breakthrough in the Trade Union Section. The shift failed to materialise. Even in 1984, the peak of Leftwing assertiveness at the Conference and the peak of its strength in the Trade Union

Section, there were only three Left-wing representatives in addition to the two from the TGWU. By 1988, the TGWU had voluntarily relinquished one of its seats and the three Leftwing trade unionists had been reduced to Tom Sawyer of NUPE, plus Eddie Haigh of TGWU.[16]

The fact was that the Right continued to dominate leadership positions in the majority of medium-sized and large unions. In addition, the NUR was always represented by an official who happened to be from the Right of that union. And some candidates elected as part of the Left shifted to the centre. But most striking was the unwillingness of the TGWU to vote in purely factional terms. The leadership of that union, particularly between 1985 and 1987, was acutely conscious of the need to ensure a workable base for the Dream Ticket leadership and to avoid political extremities. In fact, the TGWU split its 1,330,000 votes between Right and Left more often than any other union; many on the Left slate were simply ignored as not politically credible candidates. As a result, from 1983 to 1988, the Left slate was reduced, as was the number of candidates in the section (from 22 to 19).

This flexibility of the TGWU leadership was matched in some respects by the GMWU leadership attitude to the Right slate. Although the GMWU vote went much more solidly for the Right than did the TGWU for the Left, the union would never vote for the EETPU (the same was true of USDAW), but would, from 1984 to 1987, vote for the NUM on the grounds that the union ought to be represented. In 1988, when the NUM removed support from their candidate, Eric Clarke (who had returned to the NEC in 1984), and substituted a candidate seen as closer to the NUM President Arthur Scargill, the GMWU and other unions withdrew support and the NUM again lost their representation.

The inability of the Left to deliver a full political vote in the face of union considerations and a covert sentiment in favour of sustaining the Leadership against attacks from the hard Left was shown most strikingly in the voting for the Treasurership.

When Eric Varley left Parliament to work for the Coalite company in late 1983, his position as Treasurer was taken by Albert Booth, runner-up in the 1983 contest. His 'Buggins' turn' status and his loyal relationship with the unions as Secretary of State for Employment from 1976-9 ought to have ensured his election as Treasurer in 1984. But he was faced by a serving union leader from the political centre at a time when the unions wanted financial reassurance (see Chapter 16, p. 511 and Chapter 19, p. 600). This, plus the TASS connection, counted against him sufficiently to ensure defeat.

Thus, at the 1984 Conference, with everything pointing to a Leftwing advance in the shadow of the Miners' Strike, the vote between Sam McCluskie (NUS) and Booth showed some surprising defections from the Left and a narrow vote majority for McCluskie. In 1985, McCluskie, now the sitting tenant, took more union support, including the votes of the TGWU, the NUR and SOGAT. In 1986, Booth withdrew and his position was taken by two Leftwing candidates, Gavin Strang, a TGWU-sponsored MP, and the ex-leader of the GLC, Ken Livingstone. Both were trounced.

However, even when there was both a Rightwing majority in the Trade Union

Section and a covert understanding among trade union leaders that the Parliamentary leadership needed a 'workable' NEC, this did not mean that the Kinnock–Hattersley team could command the election of the NEC they wanted. This was clearer in voting for the Women's Section (discussed below) but it was also true at the margins of the Trade Union Section. Eric Clarke of the NUM was pushed back on in 1984 to replace a steelworker loyalist. John Golding, who worked closely with Kinnock's office, could not get back on the NEC in 1984 or 1985. Nor could Clarke be dislodged in 1986. Further, a quiet realignment began to take place on the NEC involving a shift in strength from the Right to the soft Left; it took Sawyer to the Chair of Home Policy in 1986. The shift began in 1986 as a result of political forces at work in the unions and on the NEC itself. It had little to do with the tactics and preferences of the Party Leadership.

The Women's Section, politics and feminism

Prior to the late 1960s, the Women's Section had, in practice, acted as ballast to the NEC and the PLP leadership – a place where women MPs, viewed as safe in terms of their support for the Parliamentary leadership, were placed by overwhelming trade union votes. To this extent, the section voting had always been covertly political, while covered also by trade union deals and arrangements. In 1981 and 1982, the Rightwing counter-attack which had removed Joan Maynard, Margaret Beckett and Renee Short had produced a Women's Section composition very much in the old mould.

This operation of the block vote enraged the Left who sought subsequently to use the block vote to change it back again. But the politics of this attempt became complicated not only by the narrow margins of Left and Right majorities on particular candidates but also by a new force in Women's Section politics – organised feminism.

The (Labour) Women's Action Committee – an offshoot of the Campaign for Labour Party Democracy – became incensed by the way in which votes piled up in the Women's Section as a result of trade union understandings regardless of the candidates' views on women's issues. One example was Gwyneth Dunwoody, hammer of the feminist Left, who always took the TGWU vote by inter-union agreement. Renee Short, who evoked little confidence among those active in Labour women's politics, stayed on the NEC year after year.

And the Leftwing feminists were increasingly frustrated by the way in which the election processes involved small numbers of male trade unionists in some last minute decisions which they regarded as oblivious to the claims of women within the Party. One problem was that, overall, the base from which candidates were selected for the NEC was much smaller than for men. To be elected, women must be delegates, PPCs or MPs and these were relatively few in number. In both 1982 and 1983, the election of women involved some late casting around for a suitable candidate. In 1982, Dianne Hayter changed occupations and dropped off the Rightwing slate at the last minute. Anne Davis, a little-known delegate who had never stood before, suddenly gained both Rightwing and Leftwing union votes and was swept onto the Executive for a year. In 1983, after the defeated MPs, Ann Taylor and Joan Lester were suddenly ineligible for election, Ann Clwyd was supported by both Right and Left unions; and she, too, was swept on to the NEC for a year – replacing Anne Davis.

This on-off pattern became repetitive and determined by sudden shifts in a small number of unions influenced in this sphere by a relatively small number of people – overwhelmingly men. In 1984, Anne Davis turned the tables after both Leftwing and Rightwing union leaders had withdrawn support from Ann Clwyd. In 1985, Davis was replaced by Margaret Beckett, who was herself removed in 1986 and did not come back until 1988.

These manœuvres caused considerable affront to the Women's Action Committee. Their resentment at male dominance was further increased in 1983 when they were (in their view) deliberately excluded from the process by which the Left decided its slate of agreed candidates for the various NEC positions.[17] The committee demanded that women should decide which women should appear on the slate in the women's section. Rejecting the whole 'tortuous complicated process',[18] WAC developed its own independent slate in what became an increasingly acrimonious business.

Their efforts were not rewarded. The WAC slate was not given much of a priority in most of the unions and the hope that they would build up support was not realised, even when they attempted to give their slate more legitimacy by holding an unofficial vote at the Labour Women's Conference. In 1987, when WAC appeared to be moving further to the Left, all WAC-backed candidates lost votes and the WAC-backed Linda Bellos won only 238,000 union votes. When in 1988 two of them (Margaret Beckett and Clare Short) were elected to the NEC, the reasons had little or nothing to do with WAC or the Women's Conference: only the NUM and NUPE voted the full WAC slate.

If breaking into the pattern of Women's Section arrangements was difficult for the organised feminists, it was also not so easy for the Party Leadership. True, there was no resurgence of support for the hard Left and the majority of those elected on this section from 1983 to 1988 have worked loyally with the Kinnock leadership. But this is not to say that they were always the Leader's choice. He, too, had to operate within the peculiar politics of this section's electoral 'campaigns'. In the establishment of the slates and in the votes, some he supported won; others lost – even in 1986, the year some in the media billed him as 'Master of all he surveys'. Some years there was amicable and co-operative understanding with the TGWU leadership; some years not – and much depended on how that leadership voted. In 1988, the new-comers Margaret Beckett and Clare Short were not the duo which some on the hard Left would ideally have preferred,[19] but then neither was it (at that time) an entrance totally to gladden the heart of the Leader.

Trade unions and NEC representation: the key features

Before we move on to the election of the Parliamentary leadership, let us note again some key features of NEC elections. The first was the small and relatively closed world. Far more than any behaviour associated with policy voting, these were matters purely for the unions' leaderships, and the unions' membership was generally not consulted. The second was that, although it was a political process subject to factional slates, it was also heavily influenced by industrial 'rules', arrangements and *ad hoc* deals. These considerations proved to be remarkably durable in the face of extraordinary pressures at different times, from Right and Left, towards full politicisation.

Within the complex pattern of industrial and political voting, it was possible for the larger unions in the mid and late 1980s to assist the Party Leadership in producing an NEC in which its most unreconciled political critics were reduced in number. This did not mean that the Leadership could pick and choose exactly the NEC it wanted. But in the Trade Union Section elections particularly it had a strong base of support. This was in part, as noted, a representation of the political outlook of the leadership of the majority of middle-sized and larger unions. But also the approach of the trade unionists continued to be one involving, in the main, an acceptance of the initiating role of the Parliamentary leadership. Although this period saw what might well be the final demise of trade union MPs in this section,[20] their old tradition was still a potent influence encouraging a subordinate role.

ELECTING THE PARLIAMENTARY LEADERSHIP

Though the union leadership had often exercised a discreet influence in Labour leadership elections, the boundary of the block vote system stopped at the PLP and it was acknowledged that in the last analysis the PLP, which established its own standing orders and policy, was free to elect its own leadership even though this leadership then became *de facto* the leadership of the Party as a whole.

Suddenly, as a result of the constitutional decisions in 1980 and 1981, the leadership of the PLP became formally the Party's leadership and the unions became directly involved in the election of the Leader and Deputy Leader with 40 per cent of the votes going to affiliated organisations – overwhelmingly (39.5 per cent in 1981) the unions.

This involvement of the unions in elections hitherto seen as the prerogative only of the Parliamentary Party was an unusual crossing of past industrial-political boundaries and in itself, in a sense, a politicisation of union activity. But the politicisation went further in 1981 when Tony Benn unsuccessfully challenged Denis Healey for the Deputy Leadership of the Party in a contest during which old territorial limits were fiercely challenged. Trade union procedures then, and in a further contest in 1983, had to cope with functions for which they were never intended. As a consequence, the problems of block vote decision making were highlighted under conditions of close national scrutiny. The result was to encourage Government legislation covering trade union procedures and also to stimulate a new wave of proposals for block vote reform.

The Deputy Leadership election of 1981

It has been a major concern of those opposed to the reform in 1979 (and some, in principle, in favour of it) that a Labour Government would find itself involved in a repetitive contest over who should be the Labour Prime Minister. In the new provisions for electing the Leader, it was agreed that when Labour formed a Government, an election could only take place if one was requested by a majority of the Party Conference on a card vote[21] - thus placing a major obstacle in the way of a sudden removal.

But no obstacle stood in the way of a contest when Labour was in Opposition and nomination was relatively easy (too easy some thought). Any affiliated organisation, Constituency Labour Party or Labour Member of Parliament could nominate providing the nominee had the consent of 5 per cent of Labour Members and providing, of course, that the nominee was willing to stand.

In April 1981, Tony Benn was determined to challenge Denis Healey; indeed, the decision to stand had been taken in principle at a private meeting held on 25 January – the day after the constitutional conference and the day of the Limehouse declaration which led to the formation of the SDP.

Moves involving some of the unions' leaders to pre-empt Benn's candidature and prevent a contest had been going on since 10 November, when Foot had been elected Leader (see Chapter 15, p. 503). Similar attempts were made within the Parliamentary Party up to the eve of Benn's declaration. All were to no avail. Thus, the candidature began with a wide range of opponents in union leadership and Parliamentary positions – plus evidence of deep reservations from a section of the Left which had supported the constitutional amendments. In this sense, Benn's candidature marked the end of a unified Left campaign.

From the most senior group of Leftwing union leaders, including Moss Evans, Clive Jenkins and Bill Keys, there was outright opposition. Even among the most politically assertive of the Left Group on the General Council, there was some unhappiness with Benn's initiative – although in the end most of them gave it energetic support.

The predominant anxiety among union leaders and others was that the candidature would prove publicly divisive just at the point where the SDP–Liberal Alliance bandwagon was being pushed by a wide range of forces in the mass media. But their concern was deepened by the style of Benn's campaign and its wider aims.

Purpose and style

The fact was that Benn's campaign was unique in Labour Movement history, not simply because it activated a new procedure, but because of the way the campaign was conducted and the purposes it sought to realise. The Left at this stage was moving on the crest of a wave: dominating the NEC, changing policy, carrying through its constitutional reform programme. On both Left and Right there were those who thought the momentum was unstoppable.

Organisationally, the Benn campaign drew its subalterns and its cadres from the Rank and File Mobilising Committee of the constitutional campaign and they went to work with a ferocious energy, utilising the linkage built during the preceding years – linkages often below the level of the General Secretaries. Their activities added to the alarm of union leaders who had been unable to stop the avalanche in 1979 and 1980 and suddenly in the summer of 1981 feared that they would again be shown to be ineffective.

Benn, of course, wanted to win and very nearly did. But victory aside, there was a purpose even in standing. It is easy now to forget how uncertain was the acceptance of the 1981 Special Conference constitutional decision. In March 1981, the PLP had backed a proposal from the Shadow Cabinet to restore at least 50 per cent of the votes to the PLP. Behind it lay not only resentment at the mere 30 per cent of the votes, but some continuing opposition to the whole constitutional package. A range of union leaders on the Right of the Party were still prepared to see the whole thing overthrown. Benn's candidature was an attempt to ensure the permanence of the new method of electing the Leader and a reinforcement of the voting shares. In this he unquestionably succeeded.

But he also had broader objectives. His attempt to take the Deputy Leadership out of the hands of the ex-Minister most associated with the economic policies of the Wilson and Callaghan Governments was to be a means of political education – particularly in the trade unions. Inasmuch as it would draw wide public attention, it would have a wider educational function, but essentially Benn sought the politicisation of the trade unions, if necessary appealing over the heads of union leaders to the activists and branch members in order 'to bridge the gap between the Labour Movement and the PLP leadership'.[22]

Indeed, Benn's announcement of his candidature was timed so that he could intervene at union conferences which began in the spring. In smaller unions, where the Leftwing union leaders supported his candidature, including ASLEF, the Furniture workers and the Fire Brigades Union, Benn was able to use their active support in mobilising the membership. But Benn and his campaign were opposed by the majority of union leaders so they targeted their primary message at the organisational levels immediately below that of the General Secretary – a strategy already evolved in the constitutional campaigns. They aimed at the conference delegates via fringe meetings, sought out sympathetic union Executive members, and, in big urban centre rallies, targeted active union branch members.

It involved a pushing, irreverent, energetic and inspirational campaign which regularly transgressed the 'rules' and protocol of the union-Party relationship, ensuring further animosity from union leaders. Benn's case was heavily oriented to the misdeeds of leadership accommodation during the years of Labour Government, a theme which implied a critique of union leadership as much as it did of Government. Union leaders protested at the various transgressions, but the Bennite campaign pushed on. The TUC found itself submerged in the whole election atmosphere and became unwilling host to a 'New Socialist' fringe debate between the contenders that drew more attention than the Congress itself.

The first priority of the politicisation was, of course, for Benn to win. But how successful the heavy and well-publicised tours of conferences and regional meetings were in this respect is unclear. Only the ASTMS Conference could be acclaimed a triumph for the Bennites when they narrowly (146,840 votes to 140,340 votes) defeated that union's leadership. This decision followed a fringe meeting at which Benn's performance was described as 'brilliant' and followed a Conference speech against Benn from the union's General Secretary described to the author by ASTMS activists as 'poor' and 'terrible'. No further victories were secured at union conferences against the wishes of the union leadership.

As to the reverberations in the branches, this too is difficult to assess, in part because we have limited knowledge of the base of political attitudes that Benn was contesting. Certainly it was the case that the self-selective Bennite meetings, which were unusually packed and enthusiastic, were a poor guide to the state of opinion among ordinary trade union members. Benn supporters often deluded themselves in this respect. A poll of trade unionists taken by Marplan at the height of the Bennite campaign indicated a preference for Healey as Leader of the Labour Party (33 per cent) with Foot second (24 per cent) and Benn supported by only 14 per cent.[23]

It may well be that (as Vladimir Derer has argued) the long Presidential-style campaign drew massive media attention to the *detriment* of Benn's immediate cause.[24] A critique from Healey's supporters and the SDP defectors which associated Benn and his supporters with extremism, violence and dictatorship was carried into the branches by the mass media to the detriment of the Labour Left and the Labour Party. Certainly it was the case that, with the exception of the Mineworkers branches, every time a vote was held at local level it went to Healey. This was true even in the National Union of Public Employees where Benn's views, the union's leadership and the union conference appeared to be in close accord. The branches came up with a majority for Healey. Confident of this kind of response, the managers of Healey's campaign developed a two-level strategy (if one can call it that). By contrast, with Benn's campaign there was a much heavier emphasis on *ad hoc* personal contacts with union leaders and a systematic campaign to call for ballots of the membership. It paid off.

In three crucial ways, Benn did unquestionably raise the level of political organisation. The Bennite campaign gave a major stimulus to Broad Left factionalism, although with an outcome which was unforeseen in 1981. The Labour Coordinating Committee, then supporting Benn, organised a delegate meeting on 18 July 1981 to stimulate the role of the Labour Left in the unions and establish a base of LCC influence. In organisational terms, the result was a success – an encouragement to the emergence and renewal of over 20 Broad Lefts which were eventually co-ordinated by the Broad Left Organising Committee. Bennite meetings at union conferences during the Deputy Leadership campaign and the general atmosphere on the Left which focused considerable attention on union mandates at the Labour Party Conference, helped institutionalise the new organisations. Not only did they take the organisation of the Left in the unions wider than it had been before but they also began to be a dominating alliance in unions where once the Communist Party had been the leading Left force. By 1984, however, it became clear that within the Labour Left it was the Trotskyist groups, particularly the Militant Tendency, which were providing the guiding influence. Although Tony Benn and the Campaign Group strengthened their links with BLOC, others on the Labour Left, including the Labour Coordinating Committee, now kept their distance.

However, this new factionalisation was a double-edged sword – particularly as the support from the real grass roots of the unions was so thin. It stimulated – as it was bound to do – a Rightwing reaction that was much more soundly based. On one level this led to an increased factionalisation of NEC voting, putting considerable strains on union industrial understandings in 1981 and 1982 (as we noted earlier). But the campaign also put new strains on the union Left. In the Transport and General Workers Union, the fact that Benn's links to activists and officials in the TGWU brought them, by the most narrow majority, into supporting his candidature, in spite of the uncertainty of opinion at rank and file level (see below pp. 339–42), stimulated a resentment at 'political nose-pulling' which helped split the Broad Left of that union in subsequent years and later strengthened the Right.

The campaign also had paradoxical implications for Benn's own relationships with Leftwing union leaders. Although by the end of the year they had nearly all moved to a position of wanting Benn to rein in the constitutional campaign and to reject any further leadership contest, the long Deputy Leadership struggle pulled some of them into closer organisational and political linkage. In 1982, Benn was invited to participate in the Left Group meetings of General Council members and subsequently alternative monthly 'political' meetings were held. This oppositional linkage across the industrial/political boundaries has no known parallel in union-Party history and has lasted (albeit loosely and recently with uncertain attendance) to this day. The new formalised politicisation of the General Council Left group added to the range of developments which pushed the Right into the new pattern of politicised voting within the TUC and the NEC which we have already noted.

Decision-making

The speed with which the Deputy Leadership election was thrust upon the unions caused them considerable practical problems. They had voted in early 1981 without preparation for such an eventuality. Now they had to face the difficulties of a political struggle fought out in the full view of the mass media but also some very basic procedural dilemmas. Who should participate in the unions' decision and how was the decision to be made?

As for eligibility for participation, then, if the union used its normal procedures this must – at least in a union representative sense – include all the membership regardless of levypaying or Party sympathies. Union mandates taken to the TUC and the Labour Party Conference were shaped by a process which could in theory involve non-Labour Party members ranging from Communists to Conservatives and members of the National Front. Such an oddity was defended in principle by a view of collective decisionmaking and by a perception of 'the Movement' which assumed that the Party and the unions travelled on convergent paths and that ultimately most union members would support the Labour Party. The position was more or less handleable in practice because among the active and politically concerned core in the union were a majority, in the branches, at the conferences and in the union hierarchies, who were normally sympathetic to the Labour Party.

Political decisions had been taken in the past which directly concerned the Labour Party's organisation – sometimes causing robust exchanges about outside 'interference' by other political groups. But the unions had never taken a decision as important as this for the Party. To many union leaders it seemed unacceptable to throw the election of Labour's Leadership open to all the membership.

The POEU leadership, which had in the past evolved a separate procedure for consulting levypayers, sought to restrict the decision to levypayers. However, the union's own solicitors advised that, because of the wording of the 1913 Act (reproduced in the union's own rules), it would be safest to allow all members to participate.[25] The union then decided to ballot all members and its decision affected others who were considering ballots. Only NATSOPA chose to accept alternative advice (see p. 347 for later practice).

Faced with these legal problems and an innovation for which they had made no preparation, most unions opted for one of two 'normal channels'. Either the union's elected Executive Committee made the decision (over 25 unions used this method, including the AUEW with 850,000 votes, UCATT with 200,000 votes, the EEPTU with 228,000, the ISTC with 85,000 and TASS with 93,000 – (there was no factional pattern, these unions are from both Right and Left), or the union's conference made the decision. These included APEX,with 110,000 votes, ASTMS with 147,000, the NUR with 180,000 and the UCW with 192,000. The remainder of the unions chose either formal balloting, or forms of consultation. Among those half dozen or so who balloted were NUPE (600,000), the NUM (244,000), COHSE (135,000), POEU (79,000) and NATSOPA (26,000). Again, there was no factional pattern to the unions which took a formal ballot. Apart from NATSOPA, which balloted at the workplace, these ballots were held in the branches and although these widened the electorate, in practice they still involved relatively small numbers. In COHSE, for example, the casting of the 135,000 block vote was decided in branches representing 213,000 members. While 83 per cent of the branches made returns *only* 1.7 per cent of the membership actually participated. 3,979 votes were cast, of which Healey took 2,268, Benn 1,356 and Silkin 355.

A mixture of unusual consultations and uncertain authority within the unions on this class of decision, when fused with factional strife, produced some complicated infighting right up to the last delegation meetings. All the union delegations in the end accepted the authority of the ballot result but the hardest to swallow was the NUPE result which ran counter to years of NUPE opposition to Healey's economic policies.

The sensitivity of this decision also highlighted the problem of non-exclusive voting arrangements in the unions. NUPE (600,000 votes) came up with a decision in which non-Labour Party supporters (here, as probably in other unions) strengthened the support for Healey[26] On the other hand, UCATT (200,000 votes) reserved the decision to its seven-strong Executive Committee which included members of the Communist Party; its vote went to Benn by only 4 to 3.

The Transport and General Workers Union

The politial cross-pressures that the Benn campaign produced and the procedural problems that it highlighted, were at their sharpest in the TGWU. It was a union of which Benn was a member and it had, in the final vote, supported most of his constitutional and policy positions in the past two years. But as soon as Benn announced his candidature, the union's senior officials, Moss Evans and Alex Kitson (that year's Labour Party Chairman), expressed their open hostility to a move which they saw as unnecessarily divisive.

This view was not shared by others in the union and a conflict opened up immediately. There was a vote of the Finance and General Purposes Committee against the candidature with its verdict publicised by Alex Kitson (standing in for Moss Evans who was ill).[27] This was later rejected at the union's General Executive Council meeting where support for Benn, led by the union's Vice Chairman, Walter Greendale, was more numerous than on the F and GP.[28] This point and counter-point of pro- and anti-Benn forces was to mark the whole decision-making process.

In an attempt to get the union away from the open choice between Benn and Healey (who had been out of line with much of the union's policy), some officials joined the hunt for an alternative candidate. John Silkin, a TGWU-sponsored MP, with a good record on its major policies, emerged as that candidate, and in various areas of the union – particularly Wales – his candidature was pushed heavily from the Regional Offices.

A unique choice faced the union and it produced a unique problem of decision-making. Who should make the decision? There were those who argued for a wide consultation of the members, even a ballot of all of them. But the union was not geared up for an exercise of this scale covering two million members and the costs were likely to be huge. The main argument was between those who argued for the Biennial Delegate Conference (meeting that year) to make the decision, and those who argued for the traditional method by which the Executive made a recommendation near to the time of the Party Conference and the delegation made the final decision. Supporters of Benn were divided on the question. Most of them favoured a BDC decision but their Executive allies tended to favour the traditional position.

The union's BDC met that August with Benn supporters among the delegates determined to push for a commitment to Benn. They were assisted in procedural terms by the fact that on the agenda were three amendments supporting Benn but none supporting Silkin (his nomination coming rather late in the day).

But it became clear as the week progressed that, working through the Standing Order Committee, the union leadership had crippled the attempt to commit to Benn. In the debate to be held on the Deputy Leadership, the pro-Benn amendments had been composited with a GEC motion which did not mention Benn; an emergency resolution in his favour was declared out of order. By Thursday, the Benn campaign, stimulated by an enthusiastic fringe meeting and the announcement of support from other unions, was running in top gear only to be met with the news that as the GEC motion had been dropped, the Bennite amendments also fell.

Thus, the debate on the Deputy Leadership was dominated by demands that the Conference be allowed to decide.[29] An attempt to refer back to the Standing Orders Committee Report was refused by the Chairman. A delegate then challenged the Chair's ruling and the Chairman (Stan Pemberton) vacated the Chair, making it an issue of confidence. His ruling was then upheld by an enormous majority which suggested that the Bennite campaign was mistaken in its assessment of its support and perhaps, as it turned out, fortunate to be defeated in this way.

However, responding to the feelings expressed vehemently at the Conference and within the union generally, that the members should be consulted, the Finance and General Purposes Committee now agreed a general consultation. This was to be organised through the Regional Secretaries and it left them with the discretion as to how it would be conducted.

What was expected from this consultation is not clear. Some expected Benn to be the dominant choice; others thought that Silkin would come through strongly and that there would be enough 'muddying of the waters' for the union leadership to have the final say. In the event, Silkin made a poor showing and Healey came through much stronger than had been expected – indeed, his was at least the psychological victory.

But given that there were no uniform procedures region by region and no advance agreement on how the result would be assessed, it was a muddy result indeed. And of the union's 7,800 branches less than 900 appear to have participated.

Supporters of Healey and some independent Leftwing observers saw it as a clear Healey victory with seven of the ten regions and 52.2 per cent of the branches (24.6 to Benn and 23.1 to Silkin). They gave the regional aggregate of branch membership as a closer contest, but still a Healey majority over Benn of 885,990 to 845,614. Supporters of Benn countered that Benn had won the vote in three of the four largest regions (Regions 1, 6 and 7) in both the number of branches and the number of members voting. Although Healey had gained a majority of branches in seven regions (2, 3, 4, 5, 8, 9 and 10) he had not always gained the highest number of members' votes. In Region 4 this apparently went to Silkin and in Region 10 to Benn.[30]

In these circumstances, what was certainly clear was that the 'consultation' had been so incoherent and uncertain as to bring the union's procedures into disrepute, and consequently it suffered more hostile comment than unions where decisions were taken purely by the Executive Committee – a point noted for later use.

The decision to consult had not been taken by the General Executive Committee, nor could it be constitutionally binding upon them. After discussing the results and after what amounted to a plea for Silkin from Kitson, the GEC on 21 September then went on to support Benn by 22 votes to Healey's 12, with Silkin receiving only 4 votes.[31] This was now the Executive recommendation to the delegation meeting at Brighton just prior to the opening of the Electoral College.

The 38-strong delegation had a mixed composition of union officers, MPs and 24 lay members. When it met there were many conflicting view-points and a long discussion.[32] Under pressure of time, a secret ballot vote was held which went for Silkin with 18 votes followed by Healey and Benn with 10 votes each. Kitson and Pemberton were apparently content to leave matters like that and had to be reminded by a delegate of the possibility of a second ballot! A further vote was then taken in the delegation on the assumption that Silkin would drop out.

Initially it was agreed that the results of this were to be uncounted and kept secret until the first ballot was completed, just in case there was an outright first ballot result. But it was suddenly realised that they would be in a major dilemma if the secret vote turned out to be a tie. A hurried count showed that the vote was Benn 17, Healey 17 with four abstentions. There was no time for a further delegation meeting and no possibility of a Conference adjournment. So the delegation had to cast its vote after a hurried ballot held in the hall of the Conference.

By this stage, it is important to note, Benn's supporters were aware that the vote in NUPE had gone against Benn and 'a huge disaster'[33] faced his campaign. This may have affected the way the union votes went in the final vote of the TGWU delegation. It came out at Benn 20 votes and Healey 15 with three abstentions.

Thus, in spite of a desperate rearguard action by the union's senior officers, Benn's supporters had triumphed in the end. The TGWU's huge 1,250,000 votes all went for him. It was not enough for victory and Healey still took 1.5 million more union votes than Benn (Table 11.2) but overall in the college, Benn was defeated by only 50.426 per cent to 49.574 per cent.

Consequences

This 1981 Deputy Leadership election left many scars and many problems. It was so all-encompassing in its effect on the Party that many other activities suffered, including Party campaigning. How much new support the campaign had won for the Left from trade unionists by this protracted exercise is unclear but certainly the majority of them were opposed to any further reform campaign and blamed the Left for the Party's troubles.[34] Meanwhile, a more organised factionalism of both Left and Right affected the unions, particularly in relation to NEC elections. But it was the Right which was now unifying and the Left which was beginning to fragment.

The elections drew fiercely critical attention to the unions' methods of decision-making, stimulating plans for reform both inside the Party and from its political opponents. It gave a boost to the Alliance which had a ready target and a preoccupied Labour Party as it sought to establish itself. And, perhaps most unforeseen, so convulsive had been the campaign that large sections of the Party now feared for its use again – at least in the style of 1981. There was an irony to this development. Many on the Left had seen it not only as a mechanism by which they could help bring a greater degree of accountability to the Party Conference, but also in terms of securing the Leadership for Tony Benn. But now they were impeded and inhibited from pushing for a further Deputy Leadership election, let alone bidding for the Leadership.

For the Right, there was a double frustration. They had fought hard against the change in procedure and then against it being used. Yet in the 18 months after the Bishop's Stortford discussions there were repetitive rumblings from Rightwing union leaders about the need to secure a change in Leadership in the light of Labour's poor electoral showing. Certainly, in early 1983, some unions leaders on the Right and Left wanted to push the PLP into action to change the Leadership.

Table 11.2 Trade union votes in the Labour leadership elections of 1981, 1983 and 1988

1981				
	Benn	*Healey*	*Silkin*	*Abstentions*
1st Ballot	(17)* 997,000** (15.5%)***	(28) 3,938,000 (61.2%)	(5) 1,428,000 (22.2%)	(1) 63,000 (0.9%)
2nd Ballot	(21)2,350,000 (36.5%)	(28) 3,938,000 (61.2%)		(2) 138,000 (2.1%)

1983 Leadership				
	Hattersley	*Heffer*	*Kinnock*	*Shore*	*Abstentions*
	(7) 1,644,00 (26.5%)	Nil	(38) 4,335,00 (70%)	Nil	(2) 210,000 (3.3%)

Deputy Leadership				
	Davies	*Dunwoody*	*Hattersley*	*Meacher*	*Abstentions*
	Nil	Nil	(34) 5,317,000 (85.9%)	(11) 689,000 (11.1%)	(2) 183,000 (2.9%)

1988 Leadership		
	Benn	*Kinnock*	*Abstentions*
	(2) 46,000 (0.8%)	(34) 5,544,000 (99.1%)	(2) 2,000 (0.03%)

Deputy Leadership		
	Hattersley	*Heffer*	*Prescott*	*Abstentions*
	(27) 4,379,000 (78.3%)	Nil	(9) 1,211,000 (21.6%)	(2) 2,000 (0.03%)

Source: Derived from data in *LPACR*, 1981, 1983 and 1988
*Number of unions
**Union vote
***% of total union votes

However, there was no broad agreement in the unions on an alternative candidate – that was one problem. And they accepted that the responsibility lay with sections of the PLP to make the first moves – that was another problem. But, in addition, the new procedure was a key obstacle. Whereas in the past the whole thing could have been done by the PLP quickly and with relative discretion, now the unions themselves had to be involved in all the protracted and unpredictable upheavals of the Electoral College. Union leaders were very reluctant to set all that in motion. And there was limited support for a quick 'coup' which would evade the new constitutional mechanism entirely. Either way would have been damaging in its internal consequences. As The *Observer* noted (with only marginal exaggeration):

> Far from involving any threat of foreclosure, Labour's new method of leadership election has, in effect, ended up by offering a virtual freedom to the tenant in possession.[35]

The leadership election of 1983

Labour's severe defeat in the 1983 Election proved to be the end of Foot's leadership – a fact recognised by Michael Foot himself as well as a wide range of others, including the union leadership. Within a few days of the result, Foot's impending resignation was announced and the Leadership election was under way.

In this process, much has been made of the role of ASTMS union leader, Clive Jenkins, as the promulgator of Kinnock's campaign. Some have suggested that his tactics in forcing an announcement of Foot's resignation on the Sunday after the General Election and publicly nominating Kinnock at the behest of his Executive Committee, 'bounced' his fellow 'union bosses' into premature declarations of support,[36] thus giving Kinnock 'a head start' and avoided a compromise candidate. This seems to me highly implausible and a product of the fixation with union 'bosses' and their power which distorted so much reporting in this period.

The fact was that, at all levels of the Labour Party and within 48 hours of the result, it had become a commonplace that the Party must 'move a generation' in its leadership. This could only mean a contest primarily between Roy Hattersley and Neil Kinnock. Kinnock had made a series of powerful and impressive speeches at union conferences and had impressed the delegates and Executives not only at Leftwing conferences such as the Transport Workers but also in centre-Right unions like the UCW and USDAW. Among the important statements made on 'the new generation' theme was one from Alan Tuffin, Right of centre leader of the UCW.[37] The latter took his views to the Executive of his union which decided it would nominate Kinnock on the Friday – the day after the General Election. By the Sunday it was already clear that no union leadership on the Left was likely to nominate an alternative candidate and that support for Kinnock stretched well across the union spectrum. The Kinnock campaign in 1983 was virtually unstoppable. To this extent, what Clive Jenkins did on Sunday was show rather than substance.

As for the other challengers, they were 'also rans' from the very first day. On the Left, a grouping of the Bennites, now without their natural leader since

Benn's defeat in Bristol, recognised that there was no mileage in making a challenge to Kinnock and no obvious alternative candidate. They decided that their position would be advanced by Michael Meacher standing for Deputy Leadership and attempting to force the Right out of that position. Eric Heffer suddenly emerged as a Leftwing challenger to Kinnock but his candidacy stimulated no great groundswell in the constituencies and in the end he took not one union vote in the Electoral College. A similar attempt to challenge the 'Dream Ticket' of Kinnock and Hattersley from the Right by Peter Shore was just as unsuccessful. The key question was whether all of Shore's supporters among Rightwing union leaders would move with the generational tide. Eventually most of them did and Shore, like Heffer, was left with no union support.

Purpose and style

The campaigns within the unions were this time heavily influenced by the known state of opinion at the beginning of the context. Kinnock, unlike Benn, had the support of a broad spectrum of union leaders plus many middle-ranking union officials. Polls of trade unionists showed that they too supported Kinnock.[38] As Kinnock sought no major politicisation from the contest, all he needed to do was to wage a steady low key campaign and not drop too many bricks.

Thus, Kinnock's campaign, managed by Robin Cook, was very different from that waged by Benn in 1981. Kinnock had more direct support from union leaders, he was more circumspect and respectful of union territorial defensiveness, and as very few union conferences remained to be held at this time of the year, he had little need to organise directly for them. There was some difficulty over the ballots issue where Kinnock's personal inclinations came into conflict with union views on non-interference. He made an early noncommital statement and left the matter alone.[39]

A few of the most Rightwing unions were virtually written off in terms of organised effort. Otherwise, the organisation union by union was left to sympathetic union officers – the most senior if they had expressed support, less senior if not.

At rank-and-file level, there was some regional organisation attuned mainly to mobilising the votes in the CLPs. But, although the campaign evoked considerable enthusiasm – although not on the scale of the Benn campaign in 1981 – there was little attempt made to create a distinctive machine or to preserve what had been built once the election was completed. The inability or unwillingness of the new Labour Leader to create his own Leftwing base in the Movement made him that much more reliant on the organised Right at a later stage.

Hattersley's campaign, managed by John Smith, was essentially on the lines of Healey's in 1981, with a stress on encouraging as many ballots as possible, a linkage to the union leaders associated with the St Ermin's Group and Labour Solidarity, and with a regional network in those unions whose leadership was pro-Kinnock and/or pro-Meacher.

Kinnock's popularity at the grass roots was apparent; he won every ballot. And he won support at leadership level in a section of the Right, also further undermining Hattersley's position. The Electricians' leadership on the Right refused Hattersley their support and abstained. The Steelworkers' Executive voted for Kinnock. David Warburton, a key Healey organiser in 1981, offered his *Labour Forward* broadsheet support for Kinnock. The GMWU, which voted for Hattersley, at one point asked him to step down, so strong was the Kinnock current.

The most serious political content of the contest virtually revolved around the question of who would become the Deputy Leader and whether a balanced 'Dream Ticket' of Kinnock and Hattersley would emerge. Much encouragement from both camps, including the union leadership, led Kinnock and Hattersley to agree publicly to serve under each other as Deputy Leader if defeated as Leader. Some of the union leaders were anxious to go further and an attempt was made at a secret meeting on the 26 July to get a common policy among union leaders to stop Meacher and unify behind 'the Dream Ticket'. It proved to be yet another major failure for 'Baronial' tactics. There was apparently a very acrimonious exchange of views and some union leaders took it upon themselves to tell Moss Evans and Clive Jenkins that the days of Baronial 'fixes' were over. Several of the unions represented there eventually voted for Meacher.

Nevertheless, there is no doubt that Meacher's campaign (which at one stage was cleverly 'talked up' and appeared to be very threatening to a Hattersley victory) was handicapped by the obvious desire for unity in the Party, by his association with Tony Benn and by the joint agreement of Kinnock and Hattersley to serve under each other. There is no doubt that attempts were made from the Right to drive a public wedge between Kinnock and Meacher and though Meacher's campaign organisers made a strong attempt to disassociate their campaign from any ultra-Left positions, they were swimming against a powerful current.

In terms of the Party's relationship with the unions, it was in another sense a contest very different from that of 1981. On the one hand, some of the major union leaders of the centre-Left were more directly involved in it as supporters of Kinnock or part of his Campaign Committee.[40] On the other hand, they joined with the Right in attempting to ensure a low-profile political style in the way the campaign touched the unions. Strong representations were made to the candidates not to hold fringe meetings at the union conferences. Hattersley took notice of this as far as the Transport Workers' Conference was concerned, even though Kinnock was being nominated, but Meacher accompanied by Benn ignored it – a fact which did not endear him to that union's leadership.

The TUC were determined not to allow the Leadership contest to invade their territory as it had done in 1981. *New Socialist*, which planned a major debate at the Winter Gardens as it had done previously, was 'warned off' via the Labour Party's General Secretary. Attempts to get some compromise which would allow a debate somewhere else in Blackpool were met with a blanket opposition. For the TUC, Blackpool was their territory during TUC week and they insisted that protocol demanded that 'the Party' keep away and that the TUC not be used as a 'convenience'.[41]

Decision-making

The experience of 1981 and the criticism then aroused by trade union decision-making procedures did have its effect on the 1983 processes.

There was in this leadership election a big shift toward balloting when compared with 1981. The fact that NATSOPA's restriction of the ballot to political levypayers in 1981 had led to no legal complications, plus a new decision of the Certification Officer in 1982 (M.J. Double and EETPU), which seemed to confirm that a non-levypayer excluded from a political contest would have no grounds for complaint (see n. 11.25), might have encouraged more unions to consult only levypayers. In practice, the small numbers of non-payers in the larger unions, the technical problems of locating them, plus a residual unease about legal complications, meant that while the NGA, SOGAT and the Tobacco Workers restricted the ballot to levypayers, most of the others involved everybody attending the branch meetings and, in the case of the National Union of Seamen, a postal ballot of all its dispersed membership.

Among the fifteen unions for which I have records of balloting in 1983,[42] the largest newcomer was USDAW. ASTMS, whose leadership failed in their efforts to push the decision to a ballot in 1981, succeeded in 1983. Even some of the unions who did not move to a ballot attempted to improve the representative quality of their decision. UCATT, heavily criticised from the Right in 1981, moved the decision from the seven-man Executive to the 29-strong elected delegation. The GMWU, which had carried out a very rough regional consultation in 1981, made a more coordinated effort in 1983 before leaving the final decision to the delegation. Two other unions [43] left it to the elected delegates for one or both positions. Seven unions made their decisions at delegate conferences.[44] Alongside this increasing pattern of consultation it must be noted that many unions [45] kept the decision in the hands of the union's Executive Committee, including the second largest union, the Engineers from the Right and also the Leftwing union TASS.

As in 1981, the Leftwing candidates, particularly Heffer, suffered some major reverses in rank-and-file votes in the ballots. In NUPE, NUM and POEU, Meacher was defeated by Hattersley for the Deputy Leadership even though he received Executive Committee support. However, to the surprise of many observers, Meacher took the ballot decision in ASTMS and the National Union of Seamen. In the contests for the Leadership of the Party, Kinnock swept the board, winning every one of the ballots.

The Transport and General Workers Union

Once again, the Transport Workers became the centre of controversy over its methods of decision-making and the focus of considerable political cross-pressure. As in 1981, senior officials – this time Moss Evans, and Alex Kitson – found themselves seeking to hold off the 'Bennite' candidate while winning support for somebody who would maximise Party unity and the Party's electoral impact. Once again the conflict divided the Left in the union and once again the procedures of the union became the subject of tactical political manœuvres – and of severe criticism.

Aware of the damage done to the union's reputation in 1981, the union's leadership had sought in 1982 to re-examine its procedure and evolve a satisfactory method of participating in a Labour Party leadership election. Evans, the General Secretary – now recovered from illness – produced a proposal which would have created a Conference of TGWU Labour Party members to make the decision. In March, this was rejected by the General Executive Council, and over various other proposals no agreement was reached.

Thus, the 1983 contest found the Transport Workers not much better prepared than in 1981 except that there was no inclination to involve itself in the kind of general unstructured consultation which had gone so wrong before. What was left was decision-making by the union's traditional institutions – the union conference, the GEC and the Labour Party Conference delegation.

With the Biennial Delegate Conference about to be held, the GEC recommended (and the Conference accepted) that the Conference when in session should make nominations and that, in between Conferences, the GEC itself should be responsible for nominations for the Labour Party posts of Leader, Deputy Leader and Treasurer.[46] It also agreed to put Neil Kinnock's name forward to the Conference as the nomination for Leadership of the Party but to make no nominations for other positions.[47]

There is no doubt that apart from the external pressures for a ballot in the union and discreet representations from the Hattersley camp, there was a considerable weight of opinion within the TGWU which wanted some form of ballot. MORI for Union World produced a figure of 87 per cent of members in favour of some form of ballot.[48] Among the delegates themselves there were strong feelings that they should extend the decision-making process to the membership. But the General Secretary's argument over the cost (estimated at £260,000) to the Political Fund, and the organisational difficulties of consulting so large a membership in a union with no central register, convinced the majority of the Conference.[49]

It supported overwhelmingly the GEC notion to nominate Kinnock but it rejected a motion to support Hattersley for Deputy Leader.[50] Meacher's supporters in the Broad Left of the union thereupon withdrew the motion that was down to support Meacher before it could be taken to a vote. In doing so, they hoped to be able to utilise a pro-Meacher majority on the GEC to secure a vote for him at the Party Conference.

For their part, the union's leadership was anxious to deliver a vote for the unity ticket of Kinnock and Hattersley in spite of reservations about the policies of the latter. This required them to regard the decision of the Conference as not so much a positive rejection of Hattersley as a 'non-decision' which could be clarified later. By 19 votes to 17 the GEC rejected the leadership's view and voted to support Meacher.[51] They also recommended that their decision be binding upon the delegation as it was in accord with the Conference decision to leave such nominations to the GEC. To one senior officer at least the issue seemed cut and dried: the union would vote for Meacher at the Party Conference.[52]

A sharp constitutional row now erupted within the union over the status of the GEC decision.

It had been the longstanding constitutional custom in the union that the GEC recommended but that the final decision was in the hands of the delegation. Over the years, however, this had meant that the GEC recommended and the delegation accepted its advice. In more recent times, the delegation had affirmed its independence and in 1981 it had, on the first ballot, gone for Silkin after the GEC had recommended Benn. But did the union Conference decision which had given the GEC the right to nominate now mean that its recommendations on the Labour Leadership were binding on the delegation? Evans's ruling, which was accepted by Meacher's major supporters in the union, was that the GEC decision would only be binding if it had actually nominated for that specific office. As it had not nominated in this case, then it was only a recommendation and still a matter for the delegation to decide.[53]

In the two weeks between the GEC decision and the delegation decision at the Party Conference there was a battle for the votes of the delegates which was fierce even by the standards of previous Labour Party Conference cliffhangers. The momentum of a Kinnock–Hattersley ticket began to gather strength throughout the Party, as was to be indicated in the votes of all sections at the Conference. The Transport Workers' delegates were not immune to such influences and they began to find themselves under pressure within the Regions as well as susceptible to the arguments of the senior national officials. Nobody was sure how it would work out but, by the time the delegation emerged, Hattersley had defeated Meacher by 27 votes to 18 (with abstentions)[54] and unlike 1981 the union leadership had 'delivered'

Consequences

The election results – first ballot victory for Kinnock with 71.272 per cent of the college vote and first ballot victory for Hattersley as Deputy Leader with 67.266 per cent – provided a firm new basis for an authoritative leadership. But the honeymoon of the 'Dream Ticket' lasted barely six months. By the early summer of 1984, Kinnock was coming under fierce and increasing attack for his attitude to the Miners' Strike. The 1984 Party Conference was a celebration of Arthur Scargill and the miners, not Neil Kinnock and the Parliamentary Leadership. From then on, a challenge to Kinnock's leadership was always a possibility – particularly as Tony Benn had secured reselection at a by-election in Chesterfield. The remarkable thing is that it took so long to mount. Kinnock himself was one factor – a resilient opponent, he was able to make the 1985 Party Conference his own and later to rise again from the adversity of early 1987. But in broader perspective, the crucial factor was the mood in the unions, and the fact was that since 1985 the Right in the TGWU had been strengthened, Scargill had been weakened in the NUM, and NUPE's leadership had, in general, moved with the realignment of the Left.

The old Bennite alliance which had underpinned Meacher's campaign in 1983 had fragmented badly. There was a strong sentiment against a new leadership challenge after the 1987 General Election and when, in January 1988, John Prescott first announced his intention of challenging Roy Hattersley, he was persuaded to stand down by a wide range of forces including senior Leftwing union leaders, Rodney Bickerstaffe and Ron Todd. The 'hard Left' within the Party appeared to be an increasingly marginalised element, even though able to mount large conferences at Chesterfield.

The leadership election of 1988

What changed the situation for a section of the Campaign Group in the spring of 1988 was a conjunction of two features – industrial and political. A move towards greater militancy, including action by the Transport Workers at Ford, was followed by a shift to the Left in that union's Executive elections. After this came the argument over Ford's new factory at Dundee, an issue on which Benn came out solidly behind the Transport Workers while Kinnock maintained a discreet silence. For the first time for several years the huge TGWU vote appeared potentially available.

As the Party's policy review stimulated a range of procedural and ideological criticisms, so there emerged, apparently 'out of the blue', a draft statement *Democratic Socialist Aims and Values* which, in its commendation of a role for market forces, raised a vulnerable symbolic target for the traditional Left to attack. On Wednesday, 23 March, following an NEC meeting where there was a row over the Ford's Dundee plant and an overwhelming 22 to 4 majority to accept the statement of aims and values,[55] the Campaign Group voted to call a leadership election with Benn and Heffer as candidates.

Purpose and Style

Three immediate weaknesses to the challenge were to cause longterm problems. First, although Benn had strong links with a section of the Broad Left in the TGWU and was still attending the now spasmodic meetings of the TUC General Council Left Group, there were strong sentiments from many on the trade union Left against a contest and some resentment at the lack of consultation before a move which was to put the TGWU leadership under considerable stress. On 29 March, the new Leftwing Chairman of the TGWU GEC signalled publicly his 'guiding priority' concern for the 'members in the workplace' and his denial that the Left victory in his union would threaten Kinnock.[56] Because of these union reservations, as Benn's Campaign Manager, Jon Lansman, was later to lament, 'the leadership election received a relatively low priority even from some of our own supporters'.[57]

Secondly, the Campaign Group meeting at which the decision to contest was made was far from unanimous. One later well-informed account suggests that the vote to contest the leadership was 21 to 7 but with five 'outside' members of the Campaign Group included in the majority vote. The fact that even a majority of the Campaign Group MPs had not voted for the election was eventually to lead to a change in the Party Constitution, making it obligatory to have a twenty per cent nomination among MPs.[58] And the grievance within the Campaign Group led to a further depletion of its Parliamentary strength. A number of talented women MPs withdrew their membership. They included Jo Richardson, the highly-respected elder of Labour Party feminism, Joan Ruddock, Joan Walley and two prominent candidates for the NEC, Margaret Beckett and Clare Short.

The third weakness was the re-emergence of the Prescott candidature, on 30 March. Fighting a narrow front campaign over the role of the Deputy Leadership and the state of Party organisation, Prescott was able to draw out a much more powerful body of opinion worried at the style and emphasis of Kinnock's leadership but alienated from the behaviour, strategy and policy of the Campaign Group.

The Prescott campaign was also a significant problem for the Kinnock–Hattersley leadership. Hattersley was backed 100 per cent by Kinnock and a joint campaign was initiated with the campaign managers of 1983, Robin Cook and John Smith in charge. [In practice, as the campaign progressed, it became clear that the organised Right within the Party was playing a minimal role and the Hattersley campaign as much as Kinnock's was being marshalled from the Leader's Office.] But what might have been a smooth ride to victory was now complicated by the fact that Prescott enabled a substantial protest vote to find a voice – particularly in the large Left-led unions. Prescott's avowal of strong support for Neil Kinnock's leadership, together with the occasional implied criticism, proved to be a difficult act to counter in terms of a Deputy Leadership election.

Even so, initially, as the Kinnock–Hattersley forces and their allies in the union leadership marshalled their forces, it appeared that opposition could be handled in such a way as to minimise embarrassment and maximise the boost to the authority of 'the Dream Ticket'.

Such beliefs were reinforced by the first stages of the Benn-Heffer campaign. The USDAW Conference provided the first set-piece confrontation, with Kinnock invited to speak but Benn holding a Broad Left meeting on the fringe. The result was a defeat for the Left with Kinnock and Hattersley nominated for Leader and Deputy Leader. At Leeds on 7 May, Benn held one of his first campaign meetings in a hall less than half the size of that in 1981 and approximately three-quarters full. The campaign was not biting and Benn–Heffer supporters were discouraged.

This contrast with 1981 was in many ways unsurprising. Although the Bennite campaign had some familiar figures at its helm, including Lansman, it had fewer active organisers and a much narrower base of support at all levels of the Party. In 1981, the Deputy Leadership campaign in the unions followed two years of extensive and successful constitutional campaigning with high morale and a network of union allies at all levels. In 1988, in spite of years of support for workers involved in industrial action, the union base was politically weaker not stronger. Trade unionism understood the language of priorities and this Leadership election, even in the NUM, the TGWU, the NGA and the National Union of Seamen, was not considered a priority by the majority.

The Campaign Group candidates and their organisation produced a wide range of arguments justifying the benefits of a Leadership campaign.[59] It included the belief that such a campaign would strengthen and unite a socialist opposition to the policies of the Thatcher Government, while 'legitimising dissent within the Party and taking the debate on Party policy to thousands of union and Party activists'. At the least, the Campaign Group leadership hoped to give the Left in the Party a higher profile establishing its strength and status. Though few of them thought it likely that either Benn or Heffer would win, there was the hope that Benn, who had confounded many union leaders in 1981, could do so again to a degree that would produce a significant vote.

Crucially, part of the agenda concerned the NEC elections. A sharpening of the ideological issues could, it was thought, make at least two of the NEC CLP representatives occupants, Bryan Gould and Michael Meacher (who had left the Campaign Group), vulnerable to the 'hard' Left. And a sharpening of the factional differences between Left and Right in the unions could cause unions like the TGWU to move against some of the existing Women's Section candidates and strengthen the Left. Thus, if politicisation of the rank-and-file and proselytisation of the electorate were forefront aims, it was factionalisation of NEC elections which offered the best chances of immediate success.

Indeed, examining the Campaign Group targets, it is difficult to escape the conclusion that the covert agenda of the whole exercise was to turn round the realignment of the Left and undermine the soft Left group which was now potentially the most powerful alliance on the NEC. This target appeared to be on course on 19th April 1988 when the Yorkshire Miners, having nominated Kinnock and Prescott for the Leadership, voted to withdraw their support for Eric Clarke (who had moved into the soft Left group) in favour of Ken Capstick, seen as a loyal Scargill supporter. It was this terrain of NEC elections which appeared to be the likely way forward for the 'Bennite' Left in the late spring.

Nevertheless, the Benn-Heffer ticket attempted to resurrect the momentum of 1981 and to use union conferences[60] and union conference fringe meetings alongside regional and city-based meetings. Prescott, with the backing of the *Tribune* newspaper and with Alan Meale[62] as campaign manager, targeted a narrower range of Leftwing and transport unions. Union mobilisation from the Leader's office was left initially to Kinnock's personal contacts and to a range of speeches made by Kinnock to union conferences acting as Labour Party Chairman; there were no union leaders involved in the campaign team as there had been in 1983.

What seemed, in spite of Prescott's candidature, to be a political contest in which the Party leadership barely needed to deviate from normal routine was suddenly transformed in early June by a television interview held four days before a TGWU Executive meeting. Kinnock repudiated 'something for nothing' unilateral nuclear disarmament.[62] The TGWU Executive refused to make nominations for the Leader and Deputy Leader (see p. 55). There was then a sensational resignation by the Shadow Defence spokesperson, Denzil Davies, which focused on Kinnock's failure to consult. Two days later the TGWU General Secretary, Ron Todd, publicly reaffirmed his belief in the collective right of the Party to establish the major policies.[63]

Suddenly, the issues of defence policy, intra-Party democracy and the style of the Leadership were forefront issues of the campaign and the Benn–Heffer campaign took on a new lease of life. So also, and more crucially, did the Prescott campaign, as the votes of the TGWU, NUPE and other unions now seemed more available and there was a tangible groundswell in the constituencies against the style of the Leadership. A range of covert resentments became much more upfront and Prescott was able to broaden his campaign on to the ground of Party democracy.

Meanwhile, a desperately worried Leadership reorganised its campaign team and tactics.[64] Within the unions, the Leader to General Secretary linkage was still crucial but it was now paralleled by contacts from the Leader's Office to other officials within the unions. In particular, the TGWU regions were targeted and sounded out.

Nevertheless, the relationship with the unions continued to be difficult. Though Kinnock unquestionably retreated temporarily over unilateralism in late June[65] and his speech to the TUC in September contained a reassuringly fulsome defence of the rights and benefits of free trade unionism, the style and emphasis of his leadership continued to exacerbate relations with the two unions he was attempting to mobilise on Hattersley's behalf – the TGWU and NUPE. There is no doubt that the Leadership campaign had starkly alerted the Leader's Office to union views and moods but Kinnock made no obvious gestures of policy accommodation. Indeed, over training policy[66] and over facilities for the Royal College of Nursing,[67] the accent seemed to be the other way (see also the case study of the TGWU below, pp. 354–6).

Decisionmaking

Since 1983, and particularly after the Political Fund ballots, the view had grown in the unions that the next Leadership election must be contested in ways which engaged the union and Party membership as much as possible. Some of this was an admission of shortcomings; some of it awareness of the capacity of the mass media to make mischief for the Party. Some of the older craft and industrial unions were still reluctant to shed traditional decision-making. The NUR had bound itself to its Annual Conference decisions as the representative assembly. ISTC and UCATT were still influenced by a strong tradition of Executive government. But overall the stage was set for a further broadening of participation.

In practice, this particular Leadership campaign – particularly Benn's challenge to Kinnock – created so little enthusiasm and so much resentment that it undermined the possibility of a highly participatory campaign. Two of the largest non-balloters of previous campaigns, the AEU and TASS, were now involved in ballots – the former with a postal ballot, the latter with a branch ballot because it had been amalgamated with ASTMS into the MSF. Branch ballots were also held in APEX, COHSE, FBU, NUPE and SOGAT. A workplace ballot was held in the NGA. The NCU regressed to the branch block vote system, a method still used in some of the other balloting unions, the largest of which was NUPE.[68] The GMB continued with its rather patchy method of regional consultation of the branches. However, most unions took the decision in accordance with their normal policymaking procedure, that is, at union conferences or union executive meetings. This included three unions of significant size – the NUM, the UCW and USDAW – which had balloted their branches in 1983. The EETPU as usual produced a distinctive method. It balloted its Party General Committee delegates (part of its 'political' structure) but also took 'a random membership survey'.

The failure to take further the increased participation evident in 1983 was based on two interlocking views. Ballots in an unnecessary contest would take political levy fund money which could be better used to underpin the Party's new two-tier affiliation system. And, secondly, any ballot result was likely to be an overwhelming and probably landslide victory against Benn and Heffer. Thus Prescott, whose campaign had been retriggered by Benn and Heffer, may, in this respect, have suffered from *their* lack of credibility. In practice, although Prescott won ballots in the FBU, MSF and NUPE, Benn and Heffer won no contest that was taken to the branch membership. As in 1983, Heffer won no union support.

The Transport and General Workers Union

A key tactical factor in the promulgation of the Benn–Heffer campaign was a shift of factional strength on the General Executive Committee of the TGWU, a union which would cast the largest of the union votes available. However, it was known already, because of his intervention over the first Prescott candidature in January, that the General Secretary, Ron Todd, was opposed to any election, as was his Deputy, Bill Morris, and the union's NEC representative, Eddie Haigh. Although the TGWU Left had a voting representative, Alan Quinn, on the Campaign Group, he acted there in a personal capacity and in any case is said to have warned of the lack of support on the TGWU Executive. The decision to launch the Leadership contest was taken without general reference to the TGWU Broad Left.

This failure to consult caused considerable aggravation on the Left in the TGWU. There were already serious internal factional and personal conflicts which were causing the Leftwing General Secretary a handful of problems. There was a belief that however worthy some of their campaigning positions might be, Benn and Heffer were not credible Leadership candidates and therefore as a Leadership contest it was not viable. In practical terms, if the union went with Benn and Heffer and they lost, it would simply alienate them further from the Party's Leadership. The Broad Left in the TGWU decided that they would not support the challenge to Kinnock. And though there was much more support for the Prescott challenge to Hattersley, this was tempered by a reluctance to add a destabilising element to the situation – whatever reservations there might be about the present Labour leadership.

As for the form of decision-making, this too was an acute problem. There was no biennial conference this year and a ballot of membership was considered a costly foregone conclusion in the case of the contest for Leader and probably for Deputy Leader also. So, in line with the 1983 decision, the matter would have to be dealt with by the Executive.

As the June quarterly meeting of the General Executive Committee approached, the most informed view in TGWU headquarters was that in spite of the presence of a hard core Left of 17 out of a total Executive Committee of 39, a recommendation from the General Secretary to nominate Kinnock and Hattersley would be accepted on a close vote and would (because they had nominated) bind the delegation. Then came the bombshell of the Kinnock TV interview – and the press briefing that accompanied it. On the Left of the TGWU, defence policy suddenly became the focal point of resentment at the style of Kinnock's Leadership – 'another bunch of politicians who don't know how to consult' – and anxiety over other possible policy shifts – over social ownership, over works councils and over trade union legislation. On the Right and among Kinnock loyalists there was an initial failure to read the situation and prepare properly for the GEC. The Left, on the other hand, gained the advantage of an issue which united the 17 with a small group of more centre-Left allies. They were better prepared than the Right and at the GEC Ron Todd's proposals were defeated 20–17.[69]

This decision of the TGWU Executive, followed very quickly by the Denzil Davies resignation which was focused on Kinnock's personal style, left Todd with considerable problems. He and his immediate supporters and staff were confident that by the time of the Party Conference they would have delivered for the Party Leadership. But he was worried by the policy implications and the reminder from Davies of the possibility that on crucial issues Kinnock might go it alone. After his speech to a TGWU Conference in Ireland, in which he reasserted the traditional view that the Party, not the Leader, established policy, he began to plan a general position speech for the Party Conference which would be true to the policies of his biennial conference and to the traditions of Cousins, Jones and Evans.

Meanwhile, pressure on the TGWU was mounting. It was thunderous in the press. It drew heavily on the 'bully with the block vote' image. It saw the TGWU leadership only as a problem, not as a group of people trying desperately to reconcile support for the Party Leadership with the integrity of their own heavily divided union.

Down below there was a powerful reaction from loyalists who supported Kinnock and Hattersley – a reaction recorded and encouraged by the Kinnock campaign team. Elections and selections for the TGWU delegation to the Party Conference suggested that whatever the Executive decided, there was a majority there for the 'Dream Ticket'; a public clash between the two TGWU bodies seemed a distinct possibility. Meanwhile, key individuals within the TGWU, including the new Chair of the GEC, Dan Duffy (who might be called upon to use a casting vote) were canvassed. And, unusually, representatives on the GEC from the trade group of the Agricultural Workers and the Dyers and Bleachers (known to be Prescott supporters) were mandated to support the Party leadership. It was very intense with much at stake. Senior TGWU officials were gaining confidence about being able to change the GEC decision at the September meeting – in spite of the fact that Kinnock's camp had not warned the TGWU leadership of the critical section of his TUC speech concerning Employment Training.

Then came yet another remarkable turn of events. When it came to the September meeting, the whole Rightwing and Kinnockite section of the GEC walked out in protest at a ruling by the General Secretary over an internal dispute concerning a union election. Numerically, it left Todd with 17 Leftwing Executive members as the decision-making body for the business of dealing with Labour Party matters. Politically, it left a gaping hole through which a politically aggressive Left could have walked in step not only with Prescott but with Benn also. In terms of the public image of the union the walk-out was a damaging blow. In terms of the Party's interest it was an immense gamble taken perhaps in the knowledge that the delegation's factional alignment could salvage a Kinnock-Hattersley vote.

How far and how many on the Left of the TGWU Executive wanted in practice to vote for an alternative Leadership will always be open to question. They could certainly have managed a protest vote for Prescott. As it was, Todd turned the vote for the Party Leadership into an issue of confidence in him and his handling of the union's internal affairs. The result was extraordinary. The TGWU Left voted unanimously to support Kinnock and Hattersley – a support which must have included the TGWU representative on the Campaign Group.[70]

The result of all this was a blow to the Campaign Group ticket and to the Prescott candidature. Prescott did attempt a final ploy (albeit more of a gesture than a serious move) by requesting that the union's delegation hear his case. The union leadership politely told him that they made their own decisions, thank you very much. Indeed they did. In the delegation meeting, Kinnock was supported overwhelmingly over Benn without even a vote. And the vote for the Deputy Leadership gave Hattersley a majority of 'four or five to one'.[71]

Consequences

The defeat of Benn (11.37 per cent of the college) and of Heffer (9.483 per cent of the college) was overwhelming. But their defeat in the unions was particularly devastating. Benn took only two unions and 8 per cent of the union vote, while Heffer received no union votes at all (Table 11.2). Temporarily, their campaign had exposed and in some ways exacerbated Kinnock's relations with Leftwing unions. The contest and its procedures provided a context in which the Leadership was forced into a personally damaging retreat in June, and the problems prematurely exposed in that period were still on display in October. But the final result was a boost to his authority and the opportunity to claim a mandate.

For their part, the Benn–Heffer campaign claimed a legacy of revived organisation as a result of the contest.[72] We shall see. They also noted (correctly) significant minorities in some of the unions, hidden as usual by the block vote system. But the campaign had in practice further undermined their credibility in the unions and limited their capacity to mobilise over the crucial second phase of the policy review. After the 1989 Labour Conference, when the Left suffered major defeats in the NEC elections and over key policy decisions, there was a growing recognition that the 1988 campaign had been a serious tactical error.[73]

It must also be noted that, for years, Benn and Heffer had placed heavy emphasis on the trade union dimension – on full support for free trade unionism, no interference in free collective bargaining, 100 per cent support for workers in struggle and adherence to the 'Wembley' formula of non-cooperation with the Government's trade union legislation. Yet the fact remained that virtually every union which had been 'in struggle', including the National Union of Mineworkers, rejected the Benn–Heffer ticket – a bitter blow to the Left.

The campaign had also, as in 1981, left behind a strong sentiment in the unions that such contests should be rare rather than regular, as some on the Left still argued.[74] The protracted character of the election campaign – particularly one which was widely regarded as an unnecessary distraction – further diminished the willingness of majority opinion in the unions to prioritise such contests if they were waged primarily to induce accountability or to spread a particular political message. Hence their acquiescence in a reform of the rule on nominations.

As for the Prescott campaign, it had come out with credibility primarily because it could partially (but not fully) draw out covert union and Party resentments against the style of the Kinnock Leadership, protectiveness of some long-established principles and aspirations for a broader political vision. In this it fused with a strengthening of the main beneficiaries of the 1988 Conference which, in terms of NEC voting, turned out to be the soft Left, not the Campaign Group.

Finally, as in 1981, a Leadership campaign which had been launched at a time when the unions were unprepared for it had again brought their procedures into the public gaze under circumstances which showed up many of the faults. There were still problems of lack of a wider participation in some of the unions and still problems of who should be allowed to participate in a Labour Party election. Above all, the decision-making procedures in the TGWU still presented a problem – not only in their limited constituency of participants but in the sheer size of a vote which one way or the other was cast as a block. In 1988, the case for a reform of the block vote was strengthened once again.

Trade unions, leadership elections, and Labour in government

What had become even more clear after 1968 was that the electoral college for the election of the Leader and Deputy Leader had become yet another Labour Party procedure in which the appearance of trade union power obscured a relationship of a very different order. Trade union participation in the electoral college had the effect of producing a greater security in office for the Labour Leader, while at the same time broadening his base of authority. With Labour in Government that position was likely to be enhanced. The Constitution and Rules of the Party stipulated that when the Leader was Prime Minister an election could only take place if it was requested by a majority of the Party Conference on a card vote. It is difficult, given their past behaviour, to see the circumstances whereby the majority of unions could be persuaded to vote for months of political crisis, after, in effect, an expression of no confidence in the Labour Government.

NOTES

1. *Constitution and Standing Orders of the Labour Party*, 1989, Clause IX(1).
2. *Ibid.*, Clause IX.2(1) – the right to submit 'resolutions and declarations'.
3. In the EETPU, the decision was made by the EC Political Sub-committee. See n. 10.61.
4. A representative of TASS, John Forrester, was elected to the NEC from 1972 to 1977 while TASS was part of a loose amalgamation – the AUEW. Subsequently, with TASS independent, their nominee was always defeated.
5. The St Ermin's Group was named after the St Ermin's Hotel where they met. Core figures in the group in the period 1979–81 were Roy Grantham (APEX – Whip), Sid Weighell (NUR), Frank Chapple

(EETPU), Hector Smith (NUBOCK), Bill Sirs (ISTC), Bill Whatley (USDAW), Terry Duffy (AUEW) and John Golding/Bryan Stanley (POEU).

6. See Chapter 5, n. 73.
7. *Minutes of 1982 AGM*, 4/115.
8. *Ibid.*
9. *Ibid.*
10. Letter to NUM from NUR General Secretary, 3/9/82.
11. Eric Clarke interviewed by *Newsnight*, BBC 2, 29/9/82.
12. Letter from NUM President, Arthur Scargill, to NUM EC members and Area Secretaries, 1/10/82.
13. *LPACR*, 1982, p. 155 and pp. 161–5.
14. Statement by General Secretary to NUR EC, 6/10/82.
15. In his autobiography, Weighell notes his disappointment that the union did not ask him to reconsider, Weighell, *op. cit.*, p. 165.
16. It was a complicated alignment in that Haigh had a difficult relationship with the TGWU General Secretary and TGWU Left/Right factionalism was not fully synchronised with factional alignment in the Labour Party.
17. *WAC and the NEC*, 1984: A Briefing, Labour Women's Action Committee Secretary, Ann Pettifor, January 1984. Pettifor and her successor as Secretary, Anni Marjoram, were the driving force behind 'WAC'.
18. *Ibid.*
19. Neither Beckett nor Short rejoined the Campaign Group. In 1989, in discussions of the slate, there were attempts to rule out candidates for the CLPD slate who had supported the existing Leader. Beckett, with Jo Richardson, had voted for Kinnock. Short had abstained. See Danny Nichol, *CLPD Bulletin*, No. 18, February 1989. In the event, Beckett and Short were on the Left slate in 1989 but, in the absence of approvable and viable candidates, the slate was abandoned for the Women's Section in 1990. Both were re-elected in those years.
20. See on this Chapter 2, p. 19, for the inter-war years. Since the Second World War, the representation of union MPs has varied between one and three in this section. After 1984 there were no MPs in the section.
21. *Standing Order* 5, 3d(ii).
22. *Minutes of the Rank and File Mobilising Committee*, 13/4/81.
23. Marplan for *Guardian*, 1/6/1981.
24. Vladimir Derer, 'Accountability and the College', *Labour Weekly*, 16/9/83.
25. Letters from Lawford and Co. to POEU, 8/5/81 and 10/6/81. But note that the solicitors also drew attention to the Certification Officer's judgement in the case of Parkin and ASTMS (1979) which indicated that exempt members could be lawfully excluded. The unions were not *obliged* to exclude such members unless there was a duty in their rules to do so. K.D. Ewing, *Trade Unions, the Labour Party and the Law*, 1982, p. 119.
26. A survey of shop stewards in one of the eleven divisions came up with evidence that, though Healey would have won in a ballot of Labour-voting NUPE members, his majority would have been significantly lower. Among NUPE members who were also Labour Party *members*, Benn had a majority in this sample. Stuart Ogden and Derek Fatchett, *Trade Unions and the Labour Party's Deputy Leadership Election*. Unpub-

lished paper, University of Leeds, May 1983.

27. *Guardian*, 4/4/81.
28. *Morning Star*, 5/6/81.
29. Notes of the author, who attended the Conference.
30. For this controversy, see *Guardian*, 22/9/81 and 23/9/81, *Tribune*, 25/9/81 and *Times*, 25/9/81.
31. *Guardian*, 22/9/81, *Morning Star*, 22/9/81 and *TheTimes*, 22/9/81, and notes from a TGWU official.
32. Interviews with TGWU officials. I also had access to an interesting dissertation by Frank Whitelaw, *The Battle for the Block Vote: An Examination of the Role of the TGWU in the 1981 Election for Deputy Leader of the Labour Party*, Northern College Library.
33. Chris Mullin, *Tribune*, 2/10/81.
34. See Chapter 7, n. 29.
35. 'The Future of Mr. Foot', *The Observer*, 22/8/82.
36. Adam Raphael, 'How Kinnock Took the Lead', *The Observer*, 19/6/83.
37. Interview, BBC Radio 4, 10/6/83.
38. MORI for *Sunday Times*, 19/6/83 gave Kinnock approximately 50 per cent and Hattersley approximately 30 per cent. Labour voters were 57 per cent Kinnock, 27 per cent Hattersley.
39. Kinnock made a statement which said: '... where time and union constitutions permit or require a ballot of members, individually or through branches, it is absolutely right that such a process should be undertaken'. But where union constitutions had awarded the duty of reaching such decisions to their executives or conferences, 'it was entirely proper and necessary for them to fulfil that duty'. Reported in *Guardian*, 24/6/83.
40. Tony Clarke, Deputy General Secretary of UCW, and Clive Jenkins, ASTMS, were members of the Committee but it rarely met and the main organising work was done by the campaign manager, Robin Cook, and Kinnock's personal assistant and secretary to the committee, Charles Clarke.
41. Letter from Jim Mortimer, General Secretary to James Curran, Editor of *New Socialist*, 6/7/83. The matter was also raised by the General Secretary at a meeting of the Shadow Cabinet which asked that it not be held.
42. APEX, ASTMS, BFAWU, COHSE, CATU, FBU, NACODS, NGA, NUPE, NUS, POEU, SOGAT, TWU, UCW, USDAW.
43. NUBOCK and the TGWU (for Deputy Leader).
44. ACCT, ASLEF, NUR, MU and TGWU, plus Agricultural Workers and Dyers/Bleachers (for this purpose independent sections of the TGWU) for the Leadership, but not the Deputy Leadership.
45. Among those keeping the decision in the hands of the EC were APAC, AUEW (Engineering and Foundry Workers' sections), FTAT, ISTC, NUFLAT, NUTGW TASS and UCATT.
46. *Minutes of TGWU BDC*, 1983, Min. 23, pp. 10–11.
47. *Ibid.*, p. 10.
48. MORI for Union World, 3/7/83.
49. *Minutes of TGWU BDC*, 1983, p. 11.
50. *Ibid.*, Min. No. 26, p. 11.
51. *Guardian*, 20/9/83, confirmed by union officials.
52. Larry Smith, BBC Radio 4, 19/9/83.
53. *Guardian*, 22/9/83; *Tribune*, 30/9/83, and interview with Moss Evans,

16/12/85.

54. *The Times*, 3/10/83 and interviews with T&GW officials.

55. NEC, *Minutes*, 23/3/88. The Left was highly critical of the procedure by which the NEC dealt with the Statement. See, for example, Dennis Skinner, 'How "Aims and Values" Was Pushed Through the NEC', *Campaign Group News*, April 1988.

56. Dan Duffy, 'My Members Come First', *Morning Star*, 29/3/88.

57. Jon Lansman, 'The Campaign for Socialism moves into higher gear', *Campaign Group News*, October 1988.

58. The amendment to Rule 5(2)(d) was carried by 5,117,000 votes to 799,000 – a devastating union reaction to the Left's challenge. *LPACR*, 1988, p. 160.

59. See for example Tony Benn and Eric Heffer, 'Why the Contest is Necessary', *Campaign Group News*, April 1988.

60. Benn was invited to address the conference of three small Left-led unions: ASLEF, BFAWU and FTAT. Kinnock, as Party Chairman, had the fortunate advantage in 1988 of addressing any conference he wanted as fraternal delegate.

61. Meale's failure to support the Benn–Heffer challenge was another blow to their causes. See Chapter 7, n. 9, for Meale's past position.

62. Neil Kinnock, interviewed on BBC 1, 'This Week Next Week', 5/6/1988, reported as 'Kinnock Ditches peace policy', *Morning Star*, 6/6/88 and 'Kinnock Distances Party from Unilateralist Policy; *Guardian*, 6/6/88.

63. 'Todd's Stern Warning', *Morning Star*, 17/6/88.

64. The Cook/Smith team (more Cook than Smith) was boosted by bringing in a (more or less) full-time worker, Jeanette Gould, Secretary of the *Tribune* group of MPs and a personal assistant to Kevin Barron, Kinnock's Parliamentary Private Secretary.

65. 'Labour's Defence Policy: Neil Kinnock Explains', *The Independent*, 21/6/88.

66. Kinnock's speech to the TUC in 1988 caused a major row with the TGWU leadership over co-operation with the Government's new Employment Training proposals.

67. At the NEC on 20/7/88, Kinnock was in a minority of one in voting to allow the RCN (not affiliated to the TUC) to have a publicity stand at the Labour Party Conference.

68. The branch block voting system involves each branch casting a block vote of the total of local political levypayers in accordance with the local ballot result. It can distort the result (as well as over-state those participating) but I have not found a case where this has definitely occurred.

69. 'Kinnock Rocked', *Morning Star*, 10/6/88, and interviews with TGWU officials.

70. Interviews with TGWU officials.

71. *Ibid.*

72. Lansman, *op. cit.*, 'Left Fights on, Pledges Benn', *Morning Star*, 3/10/88.

73. Among those arguing this view was Ken Livingstone, 'Learning from the Campaign Group's Mistakes', *Tribune*, 27/10/89. The argument continued in correspondence on 10/11/89, 24/11/89, 15/12/89 and 5/1/90. Colin Hughes and Patrick Wintour, *Labour Rebuilt*, 1990, argue (I think correctly) that 'Benn's campaign had only served to expose and exacerbate the weakness of the hard Left', p. 92.

74. This was the position of the Campaign for Labour Party Democracy. 'The mistake" was not that there was a contest in 1988 but that there wasn't one in 1984, 1985, 1986, 1987 and 1989', Danny Nichol, CLPD, *Tribune*, 10/11/89.

12

The trajectory of reform

Before we rejoin the procedural discussion let us note that, in the mid 1980s, the various movements for reform of the block vote began to merge with, and were strengthened by, a changing perception of the position of the unions in society as well as in the Party. The Labour Party's structural connection with the unions is unusual in the international Labour Movement,[1] and its form, involving a preponderant union presence at national level and the casting of block votes, is unique.[2] This position came to be challenged with renewed vigour in the 1980s in the context of a range of social and industrial changes which began to undermine old assumptions – particularly the assumption of inevitable and substantial trade union growth. After 1980, trade union membership dropped significantly.[3] And trade union density – the proportion of employees in unions – also declined.[4]

Too much could be read into this new union weakness. The diagnosis of an inevitable international decline in trade unionism within modern conditions of production, is not entirely borne out by the evidence.[5] And the case that trade unionism is being undermined by an international shift against collectivist values is not convincing.[6] In terms of the union's social and political importance it has to be noted that a union density in 1989 of 39 per cent was only five per cent lower than during the 1950s, when trade unions were regarded as the Fourth Estate of the Realm, and it was higher than the 38.6 per cent density of the Movements' greatest year – 1945.[7]

Future British union membership will depend upon a range of factors including state policy, the European social dimension, the attitude of British management and, perhaps above all, the form, style, tactics and social objectives of trade unionism. There is the important conjecture of whether or not a future Labour Government could facilitate the conditions for union organisation and recognition. Overall, it is reasonable to judge that in various sectors of the British economy trade unions are likely to remain a significant force. Further, within British society as a whole trade unions will continue to constitute a huge network of voluntary association. And there is still the possibility that with a favourable conjunction of circumstances they could become again a growing movement.

However, given the development of temporary, part-time and self-employed occupations, and the contraction of traditional areas of union strength, it must be regarded as doubtful whether trade unions in Britain will again experience the sustained growth of membership that occurred in the 1970s – particularly if membership has to be sought without the aid of a legally sanctioned closed shop or recognition procedure. It is even less likely that the historic Labour Movement assumption that one day trade unions would speak industrially for virtually the entire Labour force will prove to be correct in the foreseeable future.

Alongside these developments, social change has also added three new dimensions to the reconsiderations of union dominance. First, within the Party the rising white collar composition of trade unions has been only slowly registered among affiliates. Second, the social identities which have recently come to the fore – particularly of gender, race, nation and region – have not yet been fully integrated within a structure heavily dominated by the representation of organised labour. Third, though employment-based inequalities remain of major social and political significance, work is now more obviously a limited anchorage in terms of representing the various inequalities evident within a society which had an increasingly complex stratification.[8]

Further, although experience of work affects many aspects of the lives of those in paid employment (and their families) and involves women more than it did in the past, there is now, at least, a question mark over the future centrality of paid employment in the span and perspective of people's lives. With longer life-spans and earlier retirements the period of life-at-work is diminishing. Future flexible forms of education and employment may accentuate the trend. At the same time, as general standards of living rise, they provide the capacity to focus more attention on the varieties (and inequities) of consumption and use. However sensitive grows the awareness of trade unionism of these other dimensions, a party in which there was a dominance of employed trade unionists could still come to look ill-fitting to the character of twenty-first- century society.

In any case, the politics of the 1980s made clearer the fact the that interests of 'the workers', or 'the working class', however defined (let alone a public interest), could not be summed up simply as the aggregate, or the trading off, of the particular interests of those who were employed. The case was most obvious and most vital in relation to the making of nuclear energy policy (see Chapter 14 pp. 448–52). Such policymaking was too important to be established simply by the pressures of two groups of representatives of those who work in the industry.[9] And as the TUC General Secretary was quick to point out after Chernobyl, 'jobs are the beginning of the argument, they cannot be the end of it.'[10]

On all these grounds, over and above any questions of the iniquities or inequities of the operation of the block vote, there was a growing case for the reordering of the position of the trade unions within the Labour Party.

But the way in which trade unions were represented within the Labour Party was also a crucial part of the case. This representation was so contentious an issue within British political life that it aroused fierce passions and was put under a microscope of mass media attention in which every flaw was pointed up and every adverse feature exaggerated.

In this blaze of publicity, the interface of trade unions and the Labour Party was typified as a world of 'bosses'.buying votes' to increase their power, 'dealing and horsetrading' over policy, and 'fixing votes' in the Leadership elections. It was a world where 'the boss' who voted the wrong way was a 'bully' with supreme power. It was a world where the whole process of branch policymaking and union conference mandates tended to drop out of sight. It was a world where the 'union baron' and the block vote become fused. Small wonder that union leaders often became over-sensitive, defensive and resentful.

Nevertheless, as we have seen, there was enough substance to some of the criticism, and enough validity to the caricature, for the critique to be a source of concern to the unions and sometimes an albatross to the Labour Party. Indeed, anyone who looks in detail, as we have done, at the range of problems thrown up by union decision-making within the Labour Party could be forgiven for thinking wistfully that maybe it would be nice to start all over again. But it is not a very constructive thought, and the nearest equivalent – the proposal for a pure individual based Labour Party separated from the unions (OMOV) – would involve (as I shall argue more fully in Chapter 21) significant costs for both the unions and the Labour Party.

What is clear is that the institutional and procedural structures involving formal union domination and a block vote mechanism requires substantial reform. The key question is: How can the reforms be carried through in such a manner as to be least disruptive to the Labour Party and in such a way as to preserve the benefits of the union relationship with the Labour Party?

More than at any time since 1918, this question has moved to the forefront of Party concern. By 1988, it was widely agreed among union leaders that reform of the block vote was 'an idea whose time has come'.[11] In 1989, one union leader even sounded its 'death knell'. [12] And by the turn of that year, a consensus was emerging at leadership level that the immediate future of the block vote would be decided in principle at the 1990 Party Conference, and be followed after the General Election by the necessary constitutional amendments.

In this chapter, it is my objective to examine in some detail the problems and possibilities of block vote reform in the 1990s. In doing so, I will pick up from the analysis in Chapters 10 and 11 and explore the trajectory of recent developments and arguments. My handling of this question will take into account some general conclusions to be drawn about the union–Party relationship – conclusions to be found in Chapters 20 and 21.

THE CONSTITUENCY OF REFORM

Although, as we have seen, the issue of union voting at the Party Conference produces a wide range of problem points, there are two features of the block vote which produce the most aggravation and disquiet – the union preponderance and the practice of unit voting. It was often assumed (and in the past may well have been the case) that the main obstacle to changing either feature was union conservatism reinforced, some would say, by the self-interest of power-hungry national officials. As we explore the trajectory of reform in recent years, we will see a more complicated picture, with much more union flexibility than is usually reported.

Nevertheless, there is still a residual union conservatism, which has a political case. Supporters of this position argue that the union preponderance at the Party Conference simply represents the unions' greater number of members, that there is no conflict with the members in the CLPs who are obliged to be trade unionists anyway, that the union membership roots the Party in the working class, and that reforms to reduce the union preponderance are potentially dangerous in that they are often part of an attempt to break up the Labour Movement.[13]

As for splitting the votes, it is argued that this would run counter to the traditions of the Labour Movement, that these traditions arose out of the necessity for industrial unity, that unions are corporate entities which send delegates, not individual representatives, to the Party Conference, and that in any case, unions have a right of autonomy within the confederal body to establish their own procedures of decision-making.[14]

These positions have come repeatedly under attack since 1979. At the 1979 Party Conference a resolution was carried which called for an inquiry into 'the block vote system'[15] and in 1988 a resolution was carried which instructed the NEC to present to the 1989 Party Conference a number of options for the reform of voting arrangements 'subject to the trade unions retaining over 60 per cent of the total vote in the majority of options'.[16] In between these two votes, as we have seen in Chapters 5, 10 and 11, there was a series of developments highlighting the problematic role of the unions at the Conference.

The constitutional changes, the additional financial contributions of the CLPs, and the problem of women's representation, directed attention to the scale and problematic operations of the block vote. The Party's electoral 'union problem' made abundantly clear the adverse public image of the present voting weight and arrangements. The new Leadership elections exhibited clearly some of the incongruities of unit voting – particularly affecting the votes of the largest union. The Political Fund ballots (see Chapters 17 and 18), though a major success for the unions and the Party, brought into clearer focus the distinction between levypaying and Party membership; as did the Party membership campaign of 1989 which attempted to turn the one into the other.

The grievances of the CLPs were accentuated by the increasing concentration of the block vote into fewer and fewer large units. For their part, the PLP leadership was unable to use this development to reconstitute permanently the 'praetorian guard' of bygone days. The frustration of the Left over the cohesive operation of the Rightwing block vote for NEC elections in 1981, and the frustration of the Campaign for Labour Party Democracy, caused them to intensify the search for new means of re-distributing power; the frustrations of the Right over the nuclear weapons issue and 'the Ron Todd factor' caused them to make a similar search. By the 1989 Party Conference, such was the breadth of agreement in favour of reform of one kind or another, and such was the willingness of the unions to allow the political leadership room to consider the whole issue, that the block vote was even used to defeat a resolution from traditionalist CLPs which *opposed abolition* of the block vote.[17]

ANXIETIES

However, there was certainly little support in the unions for the immediate abolition of the block vote.[18] In general, a problem was recognised, a concession was understood to be necessary, but what that concession would be was very uncertain. Central to the uncertainty were two major anxieties. One anxiety was related to the defence of trade unionism and the interests and social force that they represented. This anxiety was, however, cross-cut by another – a political and factional consideration. Any reduction in the size of the block vote posed a problem of de-stabilisation and could provide a potential threat to the Parliamentary leadership as the more Leftwing CLP activists gained from the new arrangement.

Such anxieties were by no means new. As we saw in Chapter 4, the Right and its media allies overlooked the inadequacies of the block vote and union representation when it benefited the dominant political leadership. The Left, likewise, tended to lose interest in reform when the union alignment shifted in their favour.[19] And sections of the political Left and the political Right were often wary of making proposals which might alienate them from actual or potential union allies.[20]

Thus it was not surprising in 1989 that behind the Leadership's public commitment to the reform of the block vote, and the dangling of abolition in front of commentators' eyes, were the old anxieties – now in some ways accentuated. From sections of the unions there was a worry that it might indeed be the thin end of the wedge of separation. And from the political leadership and its allies there was the worry that it might involve a new loss of political management in a party increasingly projected as 'under control'.

There was one further anxiety which was rarely articulated but nevertheless lurked uneasily alongside the commitment to reform and one-member-one-vote democracy. The *realpolitik* of Labour's flawed representational processes and of the high profile block votes was that they diminished the authority of the Party Conference over the Parliamentary leadership. A new policy process, together with a reform of the block vote, could, in producing more acceptable Conference decisions, also make those decisions more authoritative over the Parliamentary leadership, tightening boundaries in a way which might at some future date prove very problematic.

SOLUTIONS

Technically, the available choice of block vote reforms was enormous, particularly in dealing with the central problem of the union preponderance. Since 1918, the journals and agendas of the Labour Movement have produced a mountain of proposals – some of which were also intended to deal with unit voting. Many of them came back into circulation in the 1980s as reforms of various kinds moved into the forefront of Party debate. In beginning an examination of the new possibilities of reform, it will be useful for the moment to present the various proposals in general categories.

1 **Recomposition** In this proposal, the problem of overwhelming trade union

predominance is dealt with by recomposing the Conference – enlarging the scope of the bodies represented with voting power, including allowing regional representation.[21] Recently, a degree of cross-factional support has been achieved for the introduction of the PLP into the Conference[22](see pp. 376–7).

2 Equalisation In the inter-war years, there were regular attempts to get debated at the Party Conference proposals for methods of voting similar to those appertaining at the TUC before the introduction of the block vote. Equal proportions was the main theme, taking the form sometimes of one vote per organisation (in practice a major redistribution towards the constituency parties) but more regularly a call for one vote per delegate (which would have led either to an enormous increase in delegates or to a redistribution towards the constituencies). This theme of delegate equalisation re-emerged in several of the submissions to the 1980 Commission of Enquiry[23] but they involved various problems for the unions and found few active campaigning supporters even in the CLPs.

3 Synchronisation Another proposal for dealing with the union preponderance, so as to produce a form of equality, was to introduce concurrent voting. Within the Conference, decisions would only be considered as 'approved' if there were a majority both within the CLP section and within the trade union section.[24] Recently, this has been taken a step further with the proposal that the Conference be turned into a bicameral assembly.[25] This has the support of the GMB but is considered to be likely to institutionalise conflict and produce an impasse on some of the key issues.

4 Consolidation One way which has been proposed for boosting the CLP strength within the Conference is by establishing a prior conference of CLP delegates who might agree on a common policy[26] (at its optimum, in effect a combined CLP block vote). Such meetings won a small measure of support in the 1980s.[27]

5 Redistribution A more full-fronted attack on the preponderance of the block vote is contained in proposals for redistribution of the Conference votes so as to alter the balance between the unions and CLPs. This is to be done either by scaling down the trade union vote according to some formula, or by scaling up the CLP vote, or by doing both. In recent years, there have been proposals to limit all votes to 100,000 or scale down each vote over 100,000, and proposals to reduce the trade union vote by such formulae as one vote per 10,000 members instead of the present 1,000. Proposals to scale up the CLP vote have included giving CLPs votes on the basis of *affiliated* local membership, not individual membership, giving them votes pro rata of Labour voters in the constituency, or alternatively multiplying the real CLP membership figures (since 1980 available for the first time in many years) by various percentages.[28]

The two most common positions in recent years have involved either an assertion of parity,[29] or use of the financial contributions as a measure to reorder the voting weight at the Conference. Financial reallocation has, as we shall see (pp. 372–4), recently achieved a significant degree of support.

6 Actualisation In this proposal, only trade unionists who are also individual members of the Party would be counted towards the unions' vote at the Party Conference. It would, however, push out the great majority of political levypayers and involve immediate and drastic reductions in trade union votes within the Party. It has support only from one political tendency on the Left.[30]

7 Localisation A proposal with a long historical pedigree involves abandoning national affiliation by the unions in favour of trade union local affiliation, thus, in theory, encouraging a broadening of the union base of the CLPs while getting rid of the union block vote.[31] It has never won serious consideration by the unions and suffers from the same immediate problems at national level as does 'actualisation'. The organised Left which supported it in the past (see Chapter 3, p. 66) no longer pushes for it.

8 Democratisation In the sense that it fails to address itself to the problem of either union preponderance or the potential misrepresentation of minority opinion by unit voting, this category of proposals is not about the reform of the block vote system but how it is used. It argues for a 'democratisation' of the unions' decisionmaking by introducing more information, more active participation and more accountability, while preserving present modes of voting.[32]

9 Individualisation In this proposal, union affiliation and the union vote are abolished entirely and only the CLPs are represented at Conference on a one member, one vote basis. In a sense, it is not a reform proposal at all so much as a blueprint for a different type of party. It is the favourite solution of Labour's opponents and the bulk of the national press, and it has also received some support recently in the columns of the *New Statesman and Society*.[33] Late in 1989, a group within the Labour Coordinating Committee also proposed that this be an ultimate objective.[34] But within the unions there was significant support only in the EETPU and the AEU (albeit with cautious provisos about destabilisation). Within the PLP, as far as can be ascertained, it was backed by only a small minority. And, within the CLPs, it evoked very little enthusiasm.[35]

APPROACHES TO REFORM

These, then, were the major options which were, in theory, available to reformers in the 1990s. In practice, some were simply non-starters. The trade union relationship with the Labour Party has had a long history, and is surrounded by a range of entrenched interests, collective and personal. It also draws upon collectivist traditions which are still widely respected within the Party. Successful reform had to be managed through a minefield. It cannot simply involve the implementation of ideal solutions or models from other parties of the Socialist International.

What is likely is that the evolution and management of a practicable series of reforms of trade union representation and trade union voting within the Labour Party will draw from the lessons of other recent reform movements, will work with the grain of recent changes, and will be shaped by the outcome of other processes of rebuilding and reconstruction. With this in mind, there are four recent experiences which are crucial in understanding the trajectory of reform of the trade union preponderance and in assessing its likely development. These are (i) the working through of problems relating to the reform of the Labour Women's Conference, (ii) the union responses to the Kitson plan, (iii) the limitations of the 1989 Membership campaign, and (iv) the search for a more integrated and productive role for the Parliamentary Labour Party.

Reforming the Labour Women's Conference

This dispute drew little attention outside the Labour Party but it raised many of the fundamental issues relating to the block vote and the trade union connection, and the form of its resolution was of noteworthy significance for the future direction of the Labour Movement.

The revival of feminism transformed the political alignment and atmosphere of women's sections and the Labour Women's Conference in the early 1980s. By all accounts (and there were some very exaggerated accounts), the Newcastle Conference of 1982 was an angry affair marked by bitter clashes between some of the constituency representatives and the Chair, and with evidence of a clear gulf between many of the trade union women on the one side and an articulate and vociferous section of constituency delegates on the other. Some of the trade union women came away from that conference convinced that the CLP feminists were attacking *them*. But also – as the Secretary of the feminist pressure group, the Labour Women's Action Committee, noted later – much of the resentment from the trade union women was based on the view that 'business cannot be conducted, decisions cannot be reached and the democratic processes of Conference cannot be activated if there is disrespect shown for the rules and procedures of the Conference'.[36]

Out of this tension of experience, styles and tactics came a post-mortem which focused on the composition and operation of the Women's Conference itself. Representation was acknowledged to be very basic. The Women's Sections and Women's Councils in the constituencies could each send two delegates, as could Constituency Parties which had no women's organisation. Nationally, affiliated organisations – mainly trade unions – could send up to twenty delegates, regardless of the size of the union or its women's membership. In practice, most unions sent only token representation and, indeed, approximately half the unions did not even bother to attend. As voting was by hand (with individual card votes simply checks on the hand vote), the trade unions were a minority. In 1982, the CLPs sent 486 of the 606 delegates. Four years later there had been very little change. The CLPs sent 427 of the 586 delegates.

This huge *under*-representation of the unions compared with their position in the rest of the Party produced a fundamental problem for the authority of the Conference. It was calculated in 1986 that had the CLPs and the TUs sent their full potential according to the delegation rules, the CLP women would have numbered 2,380 (73 per cent) and the TU women 880 (27 per cent).[37] But another calculation by the Women's Action Committee suggested that if representation at the Conference was on the basis of women's membership of unions and the Party, the proportion ought to have been trade unions 83.5 per cent and CLPs 16.5 per cent.[38]

In the light of this disparity, an important debate began which had some marked similarities to that waged in the early 1890s prior to the first introduction of a block vote at the TUC. From the Right it was pointed out that the individual delegate's vote bore little relationship to the number of members represented, that there was considerable duplication of CLP representation, and that small ultra-Left, often Trotskyist, groups could exercise a leverage far in excess of their real support on issues which were not a priority for trade unionists. There was one obvious answer to this and some in the unions were not slow to give it. In July, the leadership of the AUEW – not a union to pussyfoot about – wrote directly to the NEC calling for the introduction of a card vote representing the full affiliated membership of the union.[39] In other words, the proposal was to make the Women's Conference a replica of the Party Conference in terms of voting weight and arrangements.

However – and this was the more interesting development – unlike the 1890s, this time an important section of the Left – the Women's Action Committee – also called for the introduction of a trade union block vote, albeit one which was based on women's membership and the decisions of union women's conferences.[40] The reasons they gave were far-sighted. A reformed structure could provide 'a vital link with collectively organised working class women, and act as a means of stimulating trade union involvement in women's issues'.[41] Further, for the Women's Conference to be taken seriously, and women trade unionists to be won to the side of the constituency feminists, the trade union representation at the Women's Conference had to be more meaningful.

Such a change could also then be linked tactically to one of the basic demands of the Women's Action Committee that the Women's Section of the NEC should be elected not by the (male) trade union leaders at the Party Conference but by the Women's Conference.[42] Trade union support at the Women's Conference and at the Party Conference would be necessary to agree the change. And a greater union involvement at the Women's Conference might at the same time reassure the Party Leadership that the delicate factional balance on the NEC would not necessarily be changed overnight.

In the event, the campaign was brought to a halt by practical difficulties and by opposition from various groups who thought they might lose out by the change. The practical difficulties needed time for consideration. Counting male heads to determine Women's Conference votes was unacceptable to feminists. And it was recognised in the unions that as some of the fiercest critics of the feminists were in the Rightwing leadership of unions like the Engineers and the Electricians, giving them additional leverage at the Women's Conference would have been a major provocation.

Even if the weighting was to be on the basis of *women's* membership alone, then the exercise of starting from scratch to construct new voting arrangements was fraught with difficulties – difficulties which were there in discussions of wider block vote reform. How were the different types of 'membership' to be valued? Should affiliated women's membership on the basis of a passive levypaying be treated as though it were the same as the positive commitment to individual membership of the Party? If levypaying women's membership were to be treated as politically equal to individual membership, then the enormous preponderance of women trade unionists would create a similar situation at the Women's Conference as trade union vote did at the Party Conference. The trade unions with a large women's membership – notably the GMB, NUPE, TGWU and USDAW – would replace CLP dominance by union dominance.

There was a further and very sensitive problem. How would individual union policy be decided at the Women's Conference? On what basis would the union block votes be cast? Could they make their decisions in a distinct process or would they, in effect, be taking to the Women's Conference mandates influenced by men? The Party would not be in a position to insist on how the unions decided their policy mandates to the Women's Conference, no more than they could insist on the processes which led up to the Annual Conference. There was, it appeared, no easy answer to this one.

Further, building a consensus among the women and at Party Leadership level was subject as always to the conjectures and anxieties of factional benefit. In particular, if the Women's Conference did eventually elect the Women's section of the NEC, it opened those elections to new and unpredictable influences and cut out almost completely some of the existing power brokers – perhaps to the detriment of the Parliamentary Leadership.

The sheer weight of these problems and the antagonisms within the Women's Conference impeded reform for several years until eventually, after another stormy conference at the Isle of Bute, there was a sudden break in the log-jam. APEX, a white collar union on the Right of the Party, with a significant women's membership, took the step of putting down on the agenda of the Party Conference a resolution which called for the reform of the system of voting at the Women's Conference – a move seen by some as the unions moving in to assert their control. In practice, in the period prior to the Conference debate, discreet discussions between trade union women (from both Left and Right) and the leadership of the Women's Action Committee produced 'a historical turning point'.[43] One immediate result was a formula for reform of the Women's Conference loose enough to win overwhelming support at the Party Conference.[44] But there was more to the discussions than simply a conference formula. It became clear that there was a growing agreement upon the basis of voting reform at the Women's Conference, and that senior trade union women were looking to create a new procedural consensus.

There was an understanding among senior trade union women that if women were to have a more powerful voice in the Labour Party, a degree of unity of trade union women and CLP women was essential. And there developed a broad acceptance of the WAC case that in the absence of an acceptable way of evaluating the importance of CLP women and of union women, of individual membership and collective membership, then working in general harmony with the principle of 'parity of esteem' had much to recommend it. And, further, it was recognised that there was a positive value to the common purpose in drawing together women from different social, political and occupational backgrounds so as to make the Labour Women's Conference a political women's forum unique within British parties. Finally, from feminism was drawn another lesson – that there was value in 'respecting each other's personal experience'.[45]

Thus, in 1988 there emerged an agreement to create an electoral college giving affiliated organisations 50 per cent (including socialist societies 5 per cent) and the CLPs 50 per cent. There was no immediate agreement on the question of electing the women's section of the NEC,[46] but in a move designed to strengthen the voice of women on the NEC, the NEC Women's Committee and the Labour Women's Advisory Committee were amalgamated and the trade union section representatives elected at the Women's Conference.[47] Trade union delegations to the Women's Conference continued to be formally bound by the unions' policy, but it was noticeable that a degree of insulation began to emerge between the arrangements involving trade union women and the general 'rules' and arrangements covering other elections in the Labour Party and the TUC. And occasionally women trade union delegations went their own way in relation to union policy. All in all, by 1990, the atmosphere at the Women's Conference had improved considerably.

As was beginning to be recognised, the adoption of an electoral college mechanism for reconciling different forms of organisation and different types of membership in the Conference had implications for the reform of Party Conference. Significantly, the union majority had *rejected* a full block vote for a weighted vote. In addition, while commentators were generally assuming that the relationship between the unions and the Labour Party was pulling apart, in this area it was moving closer together, even to the point where in 1989 three members of the General Council were elected to sit on an NEC subcommittee. Most significant of all was that while this process of instituting a weighted vote within a federal Electoral College was taking place, a loud campaign was being waged in sections of the press in favour of an individual member one-person-one-vote solution to all Labour's internal problems. In the intense debate over the Women's Conference, *that* solution barely raised its head.[48]

The Kitson Plan

The experience of Women's Conference reform fits into a pattern. It becomes apparent as one investigates the attitudes of the unions towards block vote reform since 1979 that over every aspect of reform there was a degree of flexibility which far exceeded that portrayed by those who typified the unions as conservative and immobile. It is also clear that some of the most determined resistance to immediate change in the unions arises from factional anxiety and fear of destabilising the position of the Parliamentary Leadership rather than the loss of a degree of union leverage.

These features were all evident in the long-running saga concerning the Kitson Plan. The first moves were made by the Left on the NEC in the summer of 1979 when the decision was made to differentiate and increase the affiliation fee per member paid by CLPs. At one stage in July, it was proposed that votes be given in ratio of fees paid to Head Office. In a context where the NEC Left was supporting major constitutional changes in the Party, this proposed change in the balance of votes at the Conference met a wall of opposition from a group of union leaders backed by the Parliamentary leadership. Consequently, the proposal was, in effect, withdrawn.[49]

But pressure for redistribution with reference to finance continued in submissions to the Commission of Enquiry into Party Organisation and via the platforms of the Campaign for Labour Party Democracy. In May 1981, it was Neil Kinnock who resurrected the issue on the NEC, calling for a subcommittee to re-examine representation at the Conference. The Organisation subcommittee rejected any new moves after it became clear that union leaders were hostile to destabilising initiatives from NEC politicians.[50]

There was then a significant new development. The call for redistribution was then taken up by Alex Kitson (an ally of Kinnock) and the Chair of the NEC, in his speech to the 1981 Party Conference and later in *Tribune*.[51] Coming from a trade unionist, who had for months been Acting General Secretary of the TGWU, the proposal had to be taken very seriously – particularly as there were signs in 1981 that some union leaders were appreciative of the new financial case being made. Under the Kitson Plan, the CLPs (which it was anticipated would provide 19 per cent of the income), would get 19 per cent of the vote as opposed to the existing 8 per cent.

However, by the time that the Kitson proposals had been formalised, the Party was adjusting to what, in Labour Party terms at that time, passed for pre-election unity, and there was a growing reluctance at leadership level in both wings to dabble in any constitutional changes – particularly one which might produce a new element of instability. Kitson's letter to the NEC calling for action on his proposal claimed the backing of union colleagues.[52] But such backing was not immediately apparent and the matter was deferred.[53]

And after the General Election, Kitson himself seemed to give it much less priority, as did the new Party Leader, Neil Kinnock. The Organisation subcommittee and the NEC did accept the idea of the change 'in principle' more than once,[54] but consultation followed consultation, discussion followed discussion, and year followed year, without firm proposals being put by the NEC to the Party Conference.

The fact was that the Kitson proposal was held back by three difficulties. First, there were, within even those unions very sympathetic to redistribution, strong ethical (and presentational) misgivings about basing a major reform of representation in the Labour Party on the purely financial criterion of affiliation income. NUPE was one such union. In any case, there were quibbles that the criterion was not really as free from problematic elements and as clear a yardstick as its proponents suggested. The NEC was free (after consultation with union leaders) to propose to the Party Conference new changes in affiliation fees which would then change the balance of Conference voting one way or the other; there was much room for 'politics' there. If financial input was to be the key, why should it not include all inputs at all levels (thus making for a stronger CLP vote) or the unions' contributions to the Election Fund (thus making for a stronger union vote)?

Second, among constituency parties and activists, there was little agreement on what they regarded as their 'rights' in terms of voting weight. The head of steam behind the Kitson Plan was limited because many in the CLPs wanted *more* than in the Kitson formula[55] – a disagreement which the NEC majority used as a delaying device.

But third, and crucial, the redistribution, if implemented, could have immediate consequences for Conference voting on some other nicely balanced constitutional issues – including the reselection franchise and also on some of the most contentious policy issues – including nuclear energy. It could affect also Women's Section representation on the NEC where increases in CLP voting might well be sufficient to change the narrow margins between candidates. For these reasons, the Party Leadership became the most important obstacle to immediate reform and most of the union leaders went along in agreement.

What was discovered, however, as a result of consultation over the Kitson Plan was the scale of union support, in principle, for a redistribution. At various times after 1982, a significant group of large unions, including the GMWU, NUPE, TGWU, UCATT, the UCW and USDAW, all expressed their assent to redistribution.

Indeed, by the late 1980s, there was a huge union majority in favour of a reform which would diminish the size of the union block vote and increase that of the CLPs. There was, however, no agreed criterion by which the redistribution would take place and certainly no majority for the TGWU's financial formula.

Nevertheless, in a series of private discussions between union leaders, the General Secretary and the Party Leader, in the months after the 1989 Conference, a general consensus began to emerge about the first step. It was agreed that any reduction in the union vote had to be by stages beginning after the General Election. And it was found that, by 1989, most of the formulae proposed by, or supported by, the major unions put the CLP vote up from 10 to around 30 per cent. With the GMB and the AEU prepared to join the majority on that figure, an agreement was reached on the basis of an electoral college in which affiliated organisations (unions and socialist societies[56]) would receive 70 per cent of the vote and the CLPs 30 per cent.[57] This proposal was agreed by the NEC[58] and supported by the 1990 Party Conference.

Rebuilding Party membership

It has sometimes been argued that the system of collective union affiliation with its regular financial input has hindered the growth of Labour's local organisation, including individual membership.[59] Yet post-war experience does not indicate such a clear connection and the Houghton Report's investigation of the activity and membership of local parties does not bear it out either.[60] But certainly, as Crouch suggests, the huge union affiliation provided a 'consoling myth'[61] of a mass membership whilst relieving the Party Leadership from the necessity of placing a heavier reliance on local activists to build (or rebuild) local membership.

However, by the late 1980s, the consolation was less and less effective. In 1988, the 265,927 individual members represented a drop of 7 per cent on 1987, the biggest since comparable records began in 1981.[62] Not only was this a particularly damaging blow to the Party's finances (now facing an adjustment of income as trade union affiliation slowly declined), but it also presented a political problem in terms of securing a reform of the block vote. Such reform was bound to place increased voting power in the hands of the CLPs and it therefore became of prime importance in easing the shift that the CLPs should have not only a larger membership but one which had a more representative political and social composition.

The political factor has already been dealt with – basically a fear of the Left –

but the social compositional factor is not to be underestimated in this discussion. Political parties are not simply aggregates of individuals, they are social formations. This factor complicates all proposals for block vote reform although it tends to be ignored by those advocating a simple and comprehensive move to a Labour Party based on individual membership. Union participation within the Labour Party has always been an avenue of representation and mobility for the manual working class; it has been many other things, but it has always been that. Any major reform of the block vote was likely, in practice, to swing voting strength towards the higher-educated middle class (and to accentuate the sectional imbalance towards the public sector). This was one cross-factional source of worry to many in the unions, as much to the EETPU as to the TGWU.

Thus, closely entwined with the argument over reform of the block vote, its scale and timing, was an assessment of the possibility of rebuilding Labour's individual membership on such a scale that it was more broadly representative of Labour's electoral support. In the five formulae of the 1989 consultative document,[63] proportions were estimated on the basis that individual membership of the CLPs might be doubled as a result of the membership drive.

One idea, we have already noted, for increasing the manual working class composition, and perhaps easing an adjustment in the reform of the block vote, came from the MP Gordon Brown and was backed by the Tribune Group. It envisaged a substantial shift of union levypayers into individual membership through a concessionary membership fee. In 1988, a group of unions agreed to underwrite such a campaign which would also create a national membership register for the first time – together with a nationally organised annual renewal procedure. Trade Unionists For Labour became actively involved in encouraging the campaign. And in a fit of enthusiasm, the Party Leader set a target of a million members.

By the standards of any membership drive since the early 1950s, the campaign was a substantial success. The decline of the Party since 1984 was turned round with an increase of 27,786 on the 1988 figure. Given the 20,000 loss which, on the basis of previous trends might have taken place this year, the turn-round (possibly 50,000) was impressive. Judged, however, by the very ambitious target, by the infusion of manual worker union members,[64] and by the internal requirements of the Party, it was a set-back.

There are those in the unions who argue that the target was unrealistic and that the important thing was to establish an efficient long-term project for steady growth. This, it was said, had been achieved. Others note a lack of prioritisation by union leaders who had many other problems on their mind. And it has also been privately argued that there was a political problem. A membership drive, combined with a perspective on reducing the union block vote, and perhaps building new links between the Leadership and the individual members, aroused a degree of suspicion. It was said that too many collectivist turkeys in the unions were being asked to work for the Christmas of an OMOV-based Leadership-dominated Labour Party.

Whatever suspicions there were and whatever anticipations there might have been, in one respect they were significantly off-beam. Some of the CLP General

Commitees might have been well to the Left of the local membership, but the evidence is that the membership is still to the Left of the national political leadership[65] – not surprising really given the sharpness of the swing to the Right.

Thus what became much clearer in the summer of 1990 was that, though the push to build individual membership would continue and there could be a better system of national renewals, this was not going to provide a magic immediate basis for the reduction of union votes. Steadily rebuilding the individual membership would offer the future possibility of more far-reaching reform, but there was no immediate possibility of moving from the 70 per cent union vote to be agreed at the 1990 Party Conference. The only way to reduce the union vote further in the near future was by some other expedient.

The integration of the Parliamentary Labour Party

Historically, the most striking feature of the position of the Parliamentary Labour Party has been its semi-detached situation. It had no statement of aims nor of obligations to the Labour Party. It had no formal representation on the National Executive Committee. It was represented at the Party Conference but could not vote. Its Standing Orders were its own concern and were not endorsed by the Labour Party Conference. Up till 1981, it and it alone elected the Parliamentary Leader and Deputy Leader who, in practice, became Leader and Deputy Leader of the Labour Party.

Although since 1979 direct attempts to bring the PLP within the rules of the Labour Party have been avoided and defeated, the development of the Labour Party and of the Party–union relationship since 1979 has been towards greater integration and this has quietly affected the position of the PLP. In 1979, the Leader of the Parliamentary Party was constitutionally acknowledged as Leader of the Party and in 1981 given an electoral constituency of the whole Party. In 1984, there was a major innovation in policymaking, bringing the PLP (at leadership level) into joint policymaking with the NEC (see Chapter 13, pp. 400–01). In 1988, there came the acceptance, unprecedented in Opposition, of members of the Parliamentary leadership speaking from the Labour Party Conference platform in recommending policy.

As some MPs grew increasingly aware, the natural trajectory of this development was to give the ordinary members of the PLP either representation on the NEC or full membership of the Conference or both. In 1989, a report of a review committee established by the PLP sought to end the 'isolation' and 'remoteness' of the PLP by seeking to bring it within the formal policymaking procedures of the Party.[66] At the same time, there grew a new current of opinion which saw the solution to the reform of the block vote as a tripartite electoral college, something on the lines of 1981, with the PLP as a new voting element. What was significant about this current is that, though in the past sections on the Right had proposed similar changes,[67]a broadening section of the Left had now come to accept it. The ILP accepted it as a possibility in 1982.[68] It was raised in the LCC in 1983 and 1985,[69] and in 1988 Tony Benn gave it his public support.[70] More significantly, among union leaders on the NEC and the General Council there was quiet but increasing support for a measure. And in the 1990 consultation, a significant body of support emerged in the CLPs.[71] USDAW, the union which had produced the decisive 40:30:30 formula for the 1981 Special Conference on electing the Leadership, now produced the same formula for the Party Conference.[72]

These developments take on added significance in the light of the increasing importance of the European dimension to the Party's activities and the need to integrate Members of the European Parliament into the Party's processes of policymaking, communication and accountability.

This integration of the PLP into the Conference had some strong opponents on the Left[73], who saw it as a breach of Conference delegate democracy, and some on the trade union Right who, ever-protective of the PLP, feared a compromise of its political autonomy. Support for it amongst back-benchers waxed and waned, as did back-bench interest in an enhanced policy role.[74]

There were many advantages for the Parliamentary Leadership in such an arrangement. It had a presentational benefit in terms of the diminished prominence of the unions. It enhanced the intra-Party dialogue on a non-adversarial basis, given that the PLP had multiple, but non-commanding, links with all sections of the Party – including the unions. It offered also the possibility that the Front Bench at least, moving in a degree of unity, could act as an additional stabiliser within the Conference. These points were persuasive to many in the PLP and to many in the union leaderships also.

Its problem for the unions – apart from the fact that the central union tradition favoured an uncomplicated upward chain of representation and downward chain of accountability – was over the potential harm to established role-playing. It might, for example, complicate the essentially trade and industrial character of union relations with sponsored MPs. It might also invite more political 'interference' by the MPs as their relations with the unions took on new political dimensions.

For the unions and for the PLP leadership there was also the concern, articulated *sotto voce* but important nevertheless, that a Party Conference, with the PLP represented there, might provide a greater public measure of disunity and would, in the end, be very difficult to ignore. In other words, the stakes of Party democracy would be raised considerably. For this reason alone there was more than a little hesitation.

Nevertheless, it was recognised that moving from a position where the affiliated organisations had 70 per cent of the vote to one where they had approximate parity could take years, unless some other acceptable expedient could be found to reduce the trade union vote. Some possibilities opened up via the 'Division II' organisations, where a broadening of affiliation by Labour-sympathetic, non-employed, user and consumer organisations might change the balance further. But in 1990, the most acceptable way of making the transition to a vote of 50 per cent on policy issues for affiliated organisations appeared to be that of bringing in the PLP and the MEPs with 20 per cent of the vote. Some saw it as a transitional arrangement which might change again when, and if, the CLP base broadened and strengthened. Others saw a strong case for it regardless. But, once instituted, it was likely to take on a permanence whatever the intention.

Union reform and union involvement

There is, as we have seen, one major oddity to the debate on the future of the unions within the Labour Party. Within the mass media and various political journals, a dominating theme has been the advocacy of an individual member one-person-one-vote structure – a structure which by its nature excluded any collective role for the unions. Within the Labour Party, the discourse had a very different emphasis. The commitment to a federal party with collective affiliation remains very strong. Indeed, it is so strong that proposals for the withdrawal or exclusion of the unions became at crucial points counter-productive, setting up such suspicions that they provoked a degree of resistance to reforms which might otherwise have been more acceptable.

However, the constant blast of pro-divorce propaganda, together with the repetitive public debate on the inadequacies of trade union representation, has fed into a period of union self-criticism which has had some valuable consequences.

One major consequence has been a reconsideration of the linkage between union members at the grass roots and the Party in its national policymaking – part of a much broader reawakening of union concern with questions of communication (see Chapters 17 and 18). As we have seen, much of the criticism of union leaders casting block votes exaggerated their capacity to deliver such votes, let alone to command the Labour Party. In reality, their power varied union by union and, much more than was recognised, they had to operate within restraining procedures, established mandates and countervailing power.

However, on political issues, this countervailing power arose out of a dialogue which was mainly (although not exclusively) between a minority of activists and office-holders linked upwards from a branch life of diminishing vitality. Thus, in the late 1980s, a growing concern about the self-exclusion of the majority of levypayers blended in with a parallel concern about the lack of opportunity for ordinary union members to contribute to Labour Party policymaking.[75] Unions made differing responses to this problem, but there was a growing willingness to experiment with new methods of communication, including regional consultations, opinion polling, and direct balloting, alongside the established processes of union policymaking.

A second consequence was more striking. Affiliated unions have always accepted unwritten 'rules' involving obligations within the Labour Party, but they have generally fiercely defended their own territory from intrusions by the Party. There were important exceptions (as we shall note below), but much of union involvement in the Labour Party was considered to be union territory and not subject to Party regulation. Recently, however, a new perspective has begun to emerge based on the need for the Party to ensure the public acceptability of union procedures which are linked to Party decision-making. Basically what is now being argued is that more of the unions' interface with the Party should now be considered *joint* territory, subject either to a code or a series of agreements covering the conduct of union participation.[76]

Of course, trade unions must retain the sovereignty of their own members and their own rule-books. Union leaders must abide by the prudential 'rules' which protect the integrity of their primary function. Unions must have an unimpaired industrial purpose (and, of course, the Party must have the right to 'distance' itself). But it is becoming increasingly clear that, as with many contemporary relationships, the unions involved in the Labour Party have to marry their autonomy with the responsibilities and complexities of wider affiliation.

It is important to stress that this is not quite the major break with tradition that it appears to be. Though the unions have always fiercely defended *their* territory, they have not been averse on occasions to ceding territory to Party regulation if the common interest demanded it. Sometimes this involved agreed Party rules, sometimes simply a voluntary acceptance – a Party innovation followed by informal accommodation.

The Party's regulation of *joint* territory has some significant precedents relating to the composition of union delegations within the Labour Party where, after initial resistance, the unions in the 1920s and 1960s agreed to accept important Party prohibitions. In 1933, there was an even more significant change reflected in what was later known as the Hastings Agreement, where the unions agreed to abide by a limitation on their financial involvement. Other interesting changes followed 'Hastings' as we have seen. The constitutional change took on additional conditions relating to the non-mention of finance during selection, and the prohibition on union mandating, both of which appear to have begun simply as informal 'nod and wink' understandings. In 1990, there seemed to be remarkably little union resistance to the Party specifying quotas for women in union delegations to the Party Conference – a move from prohibitory to stipulatory regulation. There is, in short, much to build upon.

A third consequence is only just emerging, but it is potentially the most far-reaching. Since the Political Fund ballots, with their emphasis on the distinction between levypaying and Party commitment, unions have begun to re-evaluate the role and status of the political levypayer. Levypayers in the different unions, even after the Political Fund ballots victories, were simply that – levypayers. The unions affiliated these levypayers to the Party through the normal processes of collective decision-making. The *Party* then turned them into 'affiliated members', but without many of them being fully aware of the transmutation. Thereafter, most of them voluntarily absented themselves from the union's policy process and therefore to links with the Labour Party. But it was becoming increasingly clear that if the union relationship with the Labour Party was to become more effective, more vigorous and more defensible, then a change had to take place in the awareness, status and facilities of the levypayer.

There was no immediate agreement on how this might be achieved but there were signs within the unions of some creative and flexible approaches to the problem – particularly in the merger discussions which would bring two affiliated unions, COHSE and NUPE, into amalgamation with the non-affiliated union NALGO.[77] My own view, moving parallel to that discussion, is that if collective involvement is to continue on the basis of levypaying then, over time, the unions and the Labour Party have to move towards the concept of associate membership with agreed rights. The form it might take could be that of an automatic entitlement to associate membership for every levypayer (except those who belong to other political parties or organisations not eligible for acceptance on Labour's register), but it would be an entitlement which a levypayer at first membership, and by periodic consultation, should be able to disavow. In effect, there would eventually be a second contracting-out process. And, though the union's constitutionally agreed policymaking body would continue to be the final authority, a range of decisions – particularly those relating to the organisation, constitution and public representation of the Labour Party, would be delegated to the decision-making procedure which involved only Labour Party associate members and, in the case of the delegations to Labour Party committees and conferences, only Labour Party individual members.

It would take time for the unions generally to develop the technical facilities to deal with this, although, as a result of government legislation, they are better geared up than before. It would be expensive for the victors and would have some financial penalties as those contracting out of associate membership reduce the political income, although a measure of state finance for Party organisations could alleviate the financial pressure to retain the status quo. It would reduce the unions' collective affiliation at various levels, but it is doubtful whether the withdrawal would be catastrophic: indeed, it is unlikely to move below the 70 per cent union vote agreed at the 1990 Party Conference. A mixture of core support and an element of inertia would keep the level up. In terms of how unions are obliged to relate to the bulk of non-active levypayers, it would be working against the grain of some restrictive past practices, but it would be moving with the tide of developments during and since the Political Fund ballots. Above all, it would be of major longterm benefit to the Labour Party in terms of public acceptability, a more realistic level of affiliated membership and a greater flexibility in involving 'the associated member' in Labour Party activity. For the unions, the extra contracting-out facility would further enhance the legitimacy of their political funds and could enhance their campaigning capacity if the appropriate communicational facilities are in place.

There was a time when the very suggestion of elements of this project would have been dismissed out of hand in the trade union movement. Even today, some will throw up their hands in horror or quickly draw down the territorial blinds. Others will want to let sleeping levypayers lie. Some will point (quite correctly) to the Party's financial needs and the uncertain possibilities of state finance. Others will focus on the problems for the unions in gearing up for this level of organisation and communication. Of course, such a project cannot be carried through overnight. And it is not unproblematic. But then, the only unproblematic solutions to some of Labour's historic structural problems are offered by those who would prefer the Labour Party to disappear.

The sense of a relationship at an important junction was captured in the background discussions over block vote reform and in the fierce private argument which broke out in 1990 over reform of candidate selection. The case for a union withdrawal here (apart from nominations and shortlisting) was especially persuasive, given the problems of multiple union branch affiliation, the inadequacy of Party controls over union participation[78] and a wide range of problems about the electoral college procedures – including the complex rules. The Party's Leader had given virtually a public promise of individual member OMOV during the arguments over the Frank Field affair. But a fear that what was being proposed might be the thin end of the wedge of separation strengthened opposition in some major unions to the breaking of the federal arrangements – a suspicious response which had been threatening to make itself felt for some time. The form it took, however, was constructive, involving a remarkable series of proposals for more Party regulation of union involvement in the electoral college.[79] From the Leader in turn came an unexpected counter-proposal for an OMOV arrangement which would abolish the electoral college but bring in all union levypayers to a Labour Party selection meeting, albeit with differently weighted votes. There was no agreement on either of these proposals[80] (except the agreement to discuss the future of levypayer involvement at a later date), but it was probably as important a private procedural debate as the Labour Party has ever held.

Party reform and union involvement

There are, as we have seen, some major problems at the interface of union and Labour Party policymaking. There are problems of dated mandates, some of which are the product of a lack of coordinated interplay between union policymaking and Party policymaking. And there is the problem that some union policies which will become the mandate for union delegations are made as 'union policy' in a context often abstracted from the immediate problems facing Labour Party policymakers.

Changes in the unions in dealing with these problems could only be *part* of the solution. Thus discussion on improving communication and participation in relation to Labour Party policymaking became caught up in a broader discussion of the inadequacies of the Labour Party's own policymaking procedures – particularly the flawed processes of a Policy Review which was heralded as a major exercise in participation. It produced a new focus on the relationship between union policymaking and Party policymaking and on the difficulties caused for affiliated organisations by the Party's procedures.

The fact was that even with the best will in the world (which was not always there), consultation of the unions (and the CLPs) was hindered by the tight schedules and pressured deadlines of the Conference policymaking year. At the Party Conference, the procedures were cumbersome and the detailed choices on resolutions often unclear until the last moment. NEC statements and documents, which formed the most important decisions of the Conference, were not normally subject to detailed amendment. The Conference itself was overloaded, bitty and unsatisfactory in its exploration of issues and projection of policy debates. And the formal status of Conference decisions was increasingly problematic now that thirteen years had elapsed since the Party last produced a 'programme'.

A post-mortem on the inadequacies of the policy process which produced the Policy Review documents from 1987 to 1990,[81] led in turn to a search for other models of policymaking. The main focus began to be the practices of other European Social Democratic parties.[82] Here there were examples which appeared to be more conducive to effective, coherent, less confrontational and more participatory policymaking. Thus there emerged in the Party consultations of 1990 an agreement on a Rolling Programme with a two-yearly policy cycle. And there was support also for the introduction of a new intermediary tier of policymaking. This became defined as a National Policy Forum of about 170 people (including the NEC) and breaking down into about seven Standing Commissions.[83]

The extensive discussions within the Party and the unions on the questions of Conference reform, the block vote, candidate selection and quotas for women, all of which were carried out in the period after the 1989 Conference, raised some fundamental concerns and arguments over different models of democracy. The Campaign for Labour Party Democracy saw the whole process as a dangerous subversion of traditional party democracy.[84] They were not the only people to fear oligarchical control masquerading as democratisation.[85] Even in some of the unions highly favourable to the change, there was a determination (shared by the majority of CLPs) that the NEC's position should not be sidelined and that the NEC's accountability to an authoritative conference should be protected.[86]

Nevertheless, it was clear that there were major advantages to be gained in terms of trade union representation, the link to the levypayer and the exercise of the block vote from a reorganisation of Labour's policy process. In 1990, that reorganisation received substantial backing at the Party Conference.

REFORMING THE UNIT VOTE

But an agreement on redistribution of votes and a recomposition of the Conference, together with a reform of the union and Party policy process, would still leave a major question mark over the other problematic feature of the block vote – unit voting. Such voting, while common in federal alliances, creates a major problem of overall representation in that minorities in the larger units could potentially change the overall result if added to the majorities in smaller units. It causes also a permanent aggravation and an acute presentational problem in the way one or two voters in one delegation could be so decisive in the card votes.

The events of 1981, particularly the behaviour of the TGWU, caused a resurrection of one of the oldest of the reform proposals – that the final union votes be split so as to allow minorities to be registered. In the past, this proposal has often come from the Left – from organisations like Victory for Socialism[87] and journals like Tribune.[88] In the early 1980s, however, there was a curiously muted response from the Left as well as the Right in the face of what was thought to be unanimous and unshakable union support for an undeviating union practice carried out on 'union' territory.[89] No-one at leadership level publicly raised the matter and on the Left the Campaign for Labour Party Democracy rejected the reform, the Broad Left Organising Committee was flatly opposed and Tribune avoided the issue.

Aware of this immobilism, a group of Labour MPs, then on the 'soft Left' and centre of the Party,[90] not only took up the issue, they attempted to force a change by the highly unorthodox step of utilising private members' legislation to regulate procedures within the Labour Movement. The first such Bill, embodying consultation of *only* political levypayers in the unions and a vote split proportionately between candidates, was published on 20 July 1982.

Jeff Rooker, the group's organiser, attempted both to consult the unions and to develop union support. The first Bill was amended in the light of trade union anxiety over the possible imposition of *postal* balloting. The second and third Bills were published in July 1982 and in December that year. But no time was allotted for second reading in the House. The Shadow Cabinet, anxious about union sensitivities, did not take the Bill up officially. Some Front Bench spokesmen, with strong union connections on the Right, including John Golding and Eric Varley, sought to block it. Frustrated and disheartened, the sponsoring group drifted on to other priorities.[91]

Yet what was unearthed by the Rooker consultations was a union response which was rather more receptive than was often conveyed by the public face of trade unionism. Some of the most full replies did involve wholehearted opposition – particularly from TASS – but there were also expressions of support.[92] This private flexibility in some of the unions was not quite as surprising as it seemed. John Cole, very knowledgeable on Labour politics, had found a similar response in 1980, with union leaders 'surprisingly self-critical about block votes', discussing even the possibility of splitting the votes.[93]

Nor were these responses and discussions as new or as maverick as they appeared. There is, as has been noted, a tradition (now part-covered by history) involving significant union support for the principle of splitting votes (in 1918) and of votes actually being split at the Party Conference (see Chapter 10, p. 283). Being 'corporate bodies' was apparently no obstacle to *them*.

Further, union internal practices vary considerably in their usage of block votes. Some unions use them to register branch ballot results, some for area or regional conference voting. Others, including the NUR and the AEU, do not require them and it is not that unusual for groups of delegates from the same area to vote differently in national forums. There is no evidence that unions which practise internal block votes are more cohesive than unions which do not. Nor does international evidence suggest that unions who do not cast their votes within 'Labour' parties as blocks are weakened by the experience.

In any case, a Labour Party which did nothing in its voting arrangements about the growing problem of fewer and fewer unions casting larger and larger units stands in the future to come under much fiercer critical scrutiny. Year by year the mergers increase.[94] As a result of amalgamations, the trade unions of the future could even take the form of a few, perhaps only three, giant organisations.[95] This might well facilitate the mobilisation of the Conference votes by the politicians – particularly the Parliamentary leadership – but only at the cost of further reducing the credibility of the Party's procedures.

Although public advocacy of this reform has not been as prominent as redistribution, behind the scenes a growing awareness of its merits now affects even some of the strongest centres of traditionalism. [96]

The arrangements which would be required to create more acceptable procedures should not tax the ingenuity of the Party's managers. The Party itself helped create some of the problem by the 1953 procedures which *impeded* the splitting of votes. At the very least, the Party could (i) recreate the facility, (ii) make this available in the first instance for Leadership elections, (iii) begin discussions around an agreement which might extend split voting into whatever forum or delegation that the *union* itself designates as authoritative, while (iv) producing safeguards for the unions against any pressure to split votes on issues which immediately threatened union industrial interests, or in elections covered by 'rules' of unity.

When it came to applying the reform to policy voting, this would have to involve transitional arrangements to cover issues on which union policy had been 'settled' many years previously. These decisions could, for a limited period, continue to be backed by a full unit vote. But gradually, as the Party's rolling programme focused annually on different priorities, the mandates would be replenished on a proportionate basis.

THE NEC AND THE BLOCK VOTE

It remains a pecularity – explicable, but a peculiarity nevertheless – that the area of block vote operations which involves the least number of participants, NEC elections, was also the most secure and least criticised in terms of reform. It was in these elections that, as we have seen, the behaviour of union leaders comes nearest to the 'horse trading' and 'deals' which are, in general, surprisingly *absent* from other areas where the block vote is used. Yet it is only advocates of the election of the Women's Section by the Women's Conference who have invented a sustained attack on these arrangements. In respect of the Trade Union Section, public proposals for reform were virtually non-existent, and there was a particularly deafening silence within the unions themselves even though there is now a reform current on almost every aspect of the unions' relationship with the Party.

The breadth of the conservative consensus itself gives a degree of legitimacy to the status quo. As far as I am aware, since the Second World War no union conference has ever supported the idea of direct elections or any form of wider participation. The one case in recent years when a union conference was invited to be involved – that of the NUR in 1982 – turned, as we have seen, into a political *cause célèbre* which nobody is anxious to replay. As for the Party Leadership, given the historic role of the Trade Union Section of the NEC, and notwithstanding some of the problems caused recently on industrial relations (see Chapter 14, p. 437 and Chapter 14A, p. 473), there is no particular wish to see reform here given any priority.

And reform of the NEC as a whole has gone on the back-burner.[97] In part, this is because the unions have widely different views on how it should be reformed and in part because that is where the NEC itself wants the debate to be. But in 1990, there was a strong case for conservatism, given the sea of uncertainty surrounding the composition and operation of the new National Policy Forum[98] and the sensitive questions raised by the implementation on the NEC, as in other Party committees, of quotas for women.[99]

There were special uncertainties about trade union representation on the new National Policy Forum. Initially, there is little doubt that the Party Leadership would have preferred national union leaders to stay clear. But the movement of the TUC to allow more space for the Labour Party's policymaking and uncertainties about how the TUC would relate to a Labour Government (given the virtual demise of the Liaison Committee) made it difficult to exclude them from Policy Commissions envisaged as operating in a constructive dialogue with Labour Ministers. The problem was, however, much accentuated by the plan for regional representation on the Commissions. It was one thing to withdraw from direct participation in Labour Party policy formation, it was another to withdraw and leave it to regional union officials.[100]

In the longer term (and it could well be the *much* longer term) the question of the structure, composition and election of the NEC as a whole will come to the fore if only because the issue of quotas is unlikely fully to satisfy the longstanding women's demands over the Women's Section. When it does, it may well be that the procedure of automaticity – automatic representation of the larger unions by size – will be used to accommodate the traditional arrangements within a much wider reform of representation.

THE FUTURE OF REFORM

To summarise. The unions and the Labour Party should aim at a phased reduction of the votes of affiliated organisations to 50 per cent (i.e. the unions casting just under 50 per cent). They should aim to evolve procedures for splitting the unit vote where industrial unity is not a paramount consideration. The arrangements should involve one of a series of agreements on the regulation of *joint* territory and the interface of the relationship; these should also cover policymaking, voting and elections. They should also cover affiliation levels but the unions and the Party should aim also to move eventually towards an associate membership status for levypayers – a status involving facilities, prohibitions – and a right to contract out.

These changes are of such a character that they must evolve in a contingent sequence. The ability of the Party to win a more broadly-based individual membership, the gaining of state finance for Party headquarters' administration and Party organisation, and the evolution of trade union capacity to handle associate membership, will all affect the form and speed of change.

Thus, I am not offering a blueprint for particular areas of the relationship. Changes will be affected by a range of considerations depending upon the development of individual membership and associated membership.

Take, for example, the union role in electing Labour's Leadership. At some future date – particularly if individual membership continues to rise – it may well be that there emerges a consensus that the unions should move out of this electoral college. There was never a union majority for the change and never a majority of union leaders in favour of it. The arguments for it in terms of accountability now look very thin, given the cumbersome and counterproductive character of union involvement. But much will depend on how the unions develop their own internal procedures and their Labour Party membership in the next decade.

Overall, there can be no resting on the basis of the present status quo. There are too many pressures from outside and too many from within the relationship also. The block vote is unpopular not only with the public and with individual members of the Labour Party, but with trade unionists themselves.[101] And there is still a majority amongst trade unionists, as well as the general public, who believe the unions have 'too much say' in the Labour Party.[102]

But to achieve the reforms on the scale I am suggesting will require a commitment from the unions, not simply a passive acquiescence. It will require a degree of mutual trust and some basic unwritten understandings. The abdication of formal power and the change in traditional practice must evoke 'rules' that some core areas of a reformed union participation will remain permanent *and defended* features of the relationship. It may well be the case that in order for the whole package to evolve over the next decade, there will need to be an understanding that whatever the eventual reduction of the union vote in policymaking, unless there is a substantial rise in manual workers' individual membership of the Party, the 70 per cent union vote will continue to cover the constitution and standing orders of the Party. It is a formal power they have always exercised with considerable caution and restraint.

The changes proposed here must not only have the active co-operation of the unions if they are to succeed, they must be dealt with in a sensitive developmental process if they are not to result in an implosion. The experience of 1979–82 reminds us that a diversion of attention and energy towards 'a Conference to refound the Party'[103] can be extremely damaging in terms of Labour's electoral success, not to mention a recipe for years of internal political chaos. The Labour Party already receives too much advice to do this or that 'immediately'[104] from those who want to start it all over again or regard it as 'standing in the way' of various possible political formations of the Left or the Centre.

The developments I envisage here will not make for totally tidy outcomes. They imply the preservation, for the foreseeable future, of two forms of 'membership' and two sets of decision-making structures. The Party and the unions will continue to preserve a distinctive formation with structural pecularities explicable in terms of British historical experience. But, of course, it will not be the first organisation in British politics to look peculiar but to operate effectively.

What is likely to emerge from this trajectory of reform is a consociational democracy involving political egalitarianism within the two memberships but also a power-sharing agreement. Thus the input from the affiliated organisations will be retained and with it a valuable reinforcement of pluralism. But the trade union role will neither be overwhelming nor obtrusive. It will be less commanding in its formal role and more publicly acceptable in its practical operation. It will remain, however, an important element in what is recognisably a federal and union-based Labour Party.

NOTES

1.   Apart from in the United Kingdom there are four major 'Labour' parties

(i.e. parties to which trade unions are collectively affiliated), in Norway and Sweden, Australia and New Zealand. There is also a third party which has governed at provincial level in Canada, and a minor party in Ireland. The affiliation in Norway and Sweden is at local level (and in the latter case, is being phased out). In the Anglo-Australasian cases the unions were instrumental in creating the party.

2. In the New Zealand Labour Party there is an even split of votes at the Party Conference between the branches and representation committees on the one side and the unions on the other – although unions are also represented through the committees. R.S. Milne, *Political Parties in New Zealand*, 1966, pp. 224–5. In the case of the Australian Labour Party the Federal Conference has representation by states (six delegates each). Trade union officials are heavily represented (approximately two-thirds) but voting is not normally along union lines. L.F. Crisp, *The Australian Federal Labour Party*, 1955, pp. 21, 312 and 315. At the conference of the Irish Labour Party there is no block vote. The unions, including the Irish TGWU, are represented per numbers affiliated, but each *delegate* has one vote and union delegates make up usually about ten per cent of the total. Michael Gallagher, *The Irish Labour Party in Transition*, 1957–1982, 1982, p. 256. In the case of the New Democratic Party of Canada, affiliated unions send delegates to the federal convention on a much higher ratio of members to delegates than the constituency organisations, and there is no block voting for policy decisions or the Leadership.

3. According to the Annual Reports of the General Council for 1980 and 1990, TUC affiliated membership hit a peak of 12,175,000 in 1979; since then there has been a drop of over 30 per cent to 8,404,827 by the end of 1989. According to the Annual Report of the Certification Officer for Trade Unions and Employers Association for 1980 and 1989, the total of trade union members in 1979 was 13,212,354. In 1988, the figure had dropped to 10,387,238.

4. John Kelly, *op. cit.*, Table 10.1, p. 261.

5. Kelly points out that recent trade union experience has been very variable, with eight countries showing a rise in density, seven showing a decline, and two recording no change between 1979 and 1985, *op cit.*, p. 269.

6. John Kelly, 'British Trade Unionism 1979-89: Change Continuity and Contradictions', *Work Employment and Society*, Special Issue May 1990, p. 37. For a different view see Henry Phelps Brown, 'The Counter Revolution of Our Time' *Industrial Relations*, Winter 1990.

7. For union density in 1989 see 'Union Density and Workforce Composition', special feature, *Employment Gazette*, August 1990. For the historic record of union density see George Sayers Bain (ed.), *Industrial Relations in Britain*, 1983, Table on p. 5.

8. On this see A.H. Halsey, 'Social Trends since World War II', in Linda McDowell, Philip Sarre and Chris Hamnet (eds.), *Divided Nation*, 1989, pp. 8–24. And, for a comprehensive analysis, see Chris Hamnet, Linda McDowell and Philip Sarre (eds.), *The Changing Social Structure*, 1989.

9. See on this Tony Blair, 'How To Become the People's Party Once More', *Guardian* 24/6/87.

10. Norman Willis in conversation with the author, 22/5/85.

11. Bill Morris, Deputy General Secretary of the TGWU speaking to a working party of the *Tribune* 'Hard Labour' Conference, London, 22/10/88.

12. John Edwards of the GMB made this his theme at the 1989 Conference but its precise meaning was unclear.

13. Taken from discussions with union officials. The traditionalist case on this can be found in its most articulate form in the speeches and articles of Ken Gill, General Secretary of TASS (later MSF), who was associated with the *Morning Star* and not a member of the Labour Party. See, for example, 'Block Votes – No Case to Answer', *Morning Star*, 22/2/83.

14. This is a fusion of two contributions to the 1980 Commission of Enquiry Evidence by TASS (EA 166) and by the GMWU (EA 230) with additions from interviews with union officials. Some of these views are also contained in the Labour Party Consultative Document of 1989, namely 'Arguments for splitting the block vote' are therefore difficult to accept in principle and almost impossible to apply in practice without altering the basic federal structure of the Party', *Voting at Party Conference*, Section 6.

15. Comp. Res. No. 8, *LPACR*, 1979, p. 363.

16. Comp. Res. No. 4, *LPACR*, 1988, p. 169.

17. Comp. Res. No. 4 was defeated by 5,405,000 to 509,000, *LPACR*, 1989, p. 176, but see n. 18.

18. Comp. Res. No. 5 *favouring* abolition was also defeated, on a show of hands, and in the consultations of 1990 no union supported immediate abolition although the AEU and the EETPU favoured abolition in principle.

19. From time to time sections of the Left, particularly *Tribune*, have reminded themselves of the need for consistency in attitudes towards block votes regardless of who was influencing them. See, for example, *Tribune* editorial, 7/8/1959. But neither they nor others found it easy.

20. The most open statement of *realpolitik* on this issue is contained in the contributions of Victor Schonfield, trade union liaison officer for CLPD to the CLPD AGM 1984, *AGM Report*, p. 14, Item 95. But see also Shadow Cabinet responses to proposals for splitting the block vote, p. 383 of this chapter.

21. Eric Hammond, 'Crossed Wires?', *New Socialist*, October/November 1988.

22. See pp. 376–7 and ns. 66–72.

23. For example, Southport CLP (EA 8), Wrexham CLP (EA 110), Derby South CLP (EA 181) and Brent South CLP (EA 306).

24. Frank Hooley MP, *Labour Weekly*, 22/10/82.

25. *Meeting the Challenge*, GMB Discussion Paper, 1989, p. 6.

26. Harrison, *op. cit.*, p. 253. Ben Pimlott, *Labour and the Left in the 1930s*, 1977, pp. 116–121.

27. Meetings were held under the auspices of the Institute for Workers Control in 1983 and 1984 on the day prior to the Party Conference, and on the initiative of the Socialist Organiser group in mid-September of 1988 and 1989.

28. The multitude of such proposals includes Stan Orme, *The Block Vote*, 1973, and Lord Kennett, 'Reshuffling the Card Vote', *Guardian*, 24/4/73. Also proposals to the 1980 Commission by York CLP (EA 224), Ealing North CLP (EA 103), Newcastle North CLP (EA 285), Hallam CLP (EA 4), Nantwich CLP (EA 226) and, interestingly, COHSE (EA 138). In 1990, NUPE proposed consideration of a proposal for CLP votes to be on the basis of local affiliated membership, an old proposal: Pimlott, *op. cit.*, p. 131.

29. See, for example, Ken Coates, *Trade Unions in Britain*, 1980, p. 322, proposals to the Commission from Tooting CLP (EA 33), Castleton CLP (EA 64) and Beeston CLP (EA 123). Michael Meacher, 'Breaking the Block Vote', *New Statesman*, 13/11/81. Also Audrey Wise, 'For voting parity between unions and CLP', *Campaign Group News*, December 1987.

30. This proposal was advocated in the Commission evidence by Eastleigh CLP (EA 175) and by Newton CLP (EA 298). It has recently been advocated by Hilary Wainwright, *op. cit.*, pp. 249–250. It was also advocated in 1990 in a paper prepared by a group called *Labour Party Socialists*, 'Democracy and Power in the Labour Party'.

31. *Who is for Liberty?*, Hugh Ross Williamson, 1939. Aneurin Bevan (see Chapter 3, n. 51), *Tho' Cowards Flinch*, Hugh Jenkins and Walter Wolfgang, 1956. Commission Evidence, Norwich CLP (EA 250).

32. This was the position taken by the Broad Left Organising Committee (BLOC) and by the Militant Tendency. It was argued that 'a struggle has to be conducted' inside the union itself for control over the block vote. Tony Mulhearn (NGA), *LPACR*, 1979, p. 364.

33. The suggestion that 'The party could abolish the present structure entirely and substitute one based on individual membership alone' was one of several proposals by Stephen Howe, 'Unblocking Labour', *NSS*, 24/6/88.

34. The Labour Coordinating Committee Commission on Party Democracy, *Leaders and Members*, 1989. For a different view which appears to have prevailed within the LCC, see Paul Thompson, 'Renewing Party Organisation: An Alternative View', *LCC Mailing*, Winter 1990.

35. The NEC's consultations over national voting arrangements in 1990 produced only *one* CLP (of 144 responses) who wanted the unions to have no vote. Even over candidate selection, the consultation found that in spite of the unpopularity of the electoral college procedures and support for OMOV of individual members, 91 per cent of responding organisations wished the affiliated organisations to *retain* rights of nomination and participation. A survey by Tom Wilson and Martin Lipham came up with similar findings. Letter to *Guardian*, 27/7/90. See also n. 48.

36. Ann Pettifor, *Labour WAC and the Womens Conference*, WAC internal document, 1984.

37. Labour Coordinating Committee *Mailing*, March 1987.

38. 'LWAC Material (For Information)', *Labour Womens' Action Committee*, 1987.

39. The AUEW 'Letter to the Party', 8/7/82, also complained bitterly about the priorities of the Women's Conference, particularly the short debate on anti-union legislation.

40. Labour Women's Action Committee, *1984 Aims*.

41. *Ibid.*

42. Arguments over the composition of the Women's Conference were closely connected with the dissatisfaction noted in Chapter 11 over the way the Women's Section of the NEC was elected. Before feminism was reborn in the Women's organisation, many on the Left had been in favour of the total abolition of Women's Section representation. At this time, and for many years past, both the Women's Section of the NEC and the Women's Conference were preserves of the Right of the Party. Thus it was not surprising (albeit now historically an irony) that the

original proposals that the Women's Section of the NEC be elected by the Women's Conference should come from the Right in 1977, at a time when they were trying to overcome a Leftwing majority on the NEC which included targets in the Women's Section. See *Labour Victory*, No. 2, July 1977, and also Roy Hattersley, 'How Labour Could Prevent its Civil War', *Observer*, 23/9/79.

43. 'A Giant Step Forward for Women', The Ann Pettifor Column, *Tribune*, 31/10/86.

44. *LPACR*, p. 81, 1986, Comp. Res. No. 8 incorporating amendment (B), carried by 5,489,000 votes to 373,000.

45. Margaret Prosser, TGWU, speaking to Labour Women's Conference, 1990. Notes of the author.

46. In the vote on this question at the 1988 Women's Conference, some 60 per cent of union delegates abstained. Anne Davis, *LPACR*, 1988, p. 36. At the 1989 Women's Conference, a resolution which included this claim was carried only narrowly by 39.39 per cent to 38.84 per cent with the unions and the CLPs virtually lined up on opposite sides on the issue. Reform is held back by the over-representation at the Womens Conference of Trotskyist groups, by the potential loss of influence of Rightwing unions with few women members, and by the delicate factional balance in the NEC women's section voting. In any case, there was a growing view in the late 1980s that there ought to be a comprehensive reform involving quotas for women on the NEC.

47. The initiative for this unification came from Margaret Prosser, the TGWU women's officer, in an attempt to strengthen women's influence upon the NEC. The CLP representatives were elected by the regions and not by the Women's Conference for various reasons – including the greater numbers involved.

48. Although there was some sympathy for it within the EETPU. See John Spellar, 'A Party for the Members', *New Socialist*, February/March 1989, where Spellar advocates election of the Women's section of the NEC by the entire female membership of the Party. At the 1990 Labour Women's Conference, a resolution from the EETPU (No. 84), which advocates a 'full democratic members' Party' and the ultimate abolition of separate sections, received only 3.7 per cent of the Conference votes.

49. *NEC Minutes*, 25 July 1979. Adam Raphael and Robert Taylor, 'Left's New Plan worries unions', *Observer*, 17/7/79.

50. Kinnock's proposal was defeated by one vote to four, *NEC Org. Sub. Minutes*, 8/6/81, after Kinnock had given notice of his intention to raise the matter, *Letter to National Agent*, 1/5/81.

51. *LPACR*, 1981, p. 6. 'Fair Shares for the Constituencies', *Tribune*, 5/11/82.

52. Alex Kitson, letter to General Secretary, 1/3/83.

53. Kitson failed to turn up at the Org. Sub. meeting following his letter to the NEC, *Org. Sub. Minutes*, 11/4/83.

54. *NEC Minutes*, 14/12/83 and *NEC Minutes*, 5/3/86.

55. Under the Kitson formula, votes were to be allocated 'in line with the number of individual membership equivalents paid for'. A stipulation of a minimum of 300 votes per organisation was removed in the 1989 version, *Voting at Labour Party Conference*, TGWU Discussion Paper, January 1989. Under either version, the split *on the basis of 1988 fees and members* was likely to be around 70 per cent for affiliated organisations and around 30 per cent for CLPs.

56. The votes of affiliated organisations would be pro rata of membership, so the Socialist societies would receive approximately one per cent.

57. There was a provision for this to change if the CLPs increased their membership 'possibly by 1 per cent for every 30,000'.

58. 'A New Approach to Labour Party Democracy and Policymaking', Paper B, *NEC Minutes*, 25/4/90. Became *Democracy and Policymaking for the 1990s*.

59. See, for example, Michael Pinto-Duschinsky, *op. cit.*, 1980, pp. 77, 79 and 303.

60. In its report the Committee on *Financial Aid to Political Parties* (Houghton), 1976, found that 'there does not appear to be a strong relationship between Trade Union or Headquarters support and the level of activity within constituency organisations', p. 190, and found that 'the average membership for sponsored parties is not significantly different from the average membership for non-sponsored parties', p. 37

61. Colin Crouch, 'The Peculiar Relationship: The Party and the Unions', in Kavanagh (ed.), *op. cit.*, p. 176.

62. *NEC Report*, 1989, p. 21.

63. The Five formulae were (1) Status quo (with the option of counting actual members rather than blocks of 1,000), (2) a formula based upon relative financial contributions, (3) a formula based on aggregate financial contributions, (4) an Electoral College (with the option of incorporating the PLP), (5) a 'Two Houses' approach. Consultative Document, *Future of Labour Party Conference*, Section E 'Voting at Conference', 1989.

64. The target for the unions in turning levypayers into members was 30,000. TUFL records show that from January to December 1989, 7,932 new trade union members were recruited at the reduced rate, plus 4,000 at other rates and 1,927 renewals, giving a total of 13,859. Of these, 2,312 were in the TGWU, 1,596 in the GMB 1,371 in MSF, 1,352 in the AEU and 1,113 in NUPE.

65. Data supplied by Patrick Seyd from the David Broughton, Patrick Seyd and Paul Whiteley Labour Party membership survey, supported by the ESRC, 1989-90. The issues where members' views were to the Left of those of the Parliamentary Leadership included withdrawal from Northern Ireland and unilateral nuclear disarmament.

66. Parliamentary Labour Party. First report of the review committee chaired by Stan Orme MP, 1989, pp. 1–3.

67. See, for example, the Fabian Society document 'Changing the Party of Change', 1979, and the evidence to the Commission of Enquiry, 1980, by Hampstead CLP (EA 193).

68. Eric Preston, *Labour in Crisis*, 1982, p. 44. The ILP support for this became much stronger in 1988 and 1989. See on this Eric Preston, 'Labour's Left must unite against these biased reforms', *Tribune* front page, 14/7/89.

69. In documents by Hilary Barnard, particularly *Labour Activist*, 'New Agenda for Party Democracy', 1984.

70. Tony Benn addressing the 'Hard Labour' conference of *Tribune*, London, 23/10/88.

71. The options with the most support among the CLPs who responded were (1) trade unions 60; CLPs 40 (28 CLP) and (2) trade unions 40; CLPs 30; and PLP 30 (23 CLP and 19 branches – the largest body of organisational support revealed by the consultation).

72. The proposal from the NEC put to the 1990 Conference mentioned the possibility of this development 'over the longer term', *Democracy and Policy-making for the 1990s*, 1990, p. 8.

73. See, for example, the criticism of Tony Benn's proposal in *CLPD Bulletin*, 18, February 1989.

74. In December 1989, the PLP voted not to accept an enhanced role for PLP meetings in policymaking – a rejection of its own review committee report. It was noted that by this stage a record number of Labour MPs now had Front-Bench responsibilities. Phil Kelly, 'Long Haul for Reforms at Westminster', *Tribune*, 8/12/89.

75. In 1989, the GMB held a series of regional political consultations on this question and used the MORI organisation to poll all the delegates.

76. The idea of a voluntary agreement regulating union participation was first discussed (I think) around 1981 over splitting the block vote. It was mooted in background discussion on the Party's regulations over candidate selection after the 1987 reform, but was rebuffed *from the Party side* for a variety of reasons – traditionalism, temerity in the face of past union attitudes, and, to some extent, a 'leave it alone and we'll get OMOV in the end' position. The idea of a code of conduct setting out a broad frame-work of democratic principles for the unions was advocated in Martin Upham and Tom Wilson, *Natural Allies: Labour and the Unions*, Fabian Tract 534, 1989.

77. In the discussion on how to retain the integrity of distinctive traditions of affiliation and independence, one solution offered was of more flexible arrangements in relation to political levypaying, including the adoption of party and non-party political funds. The details of this proposal move quite close to those that I am offering on associate membership, although they start from different problems and were developed independently by advisers to the merger. Information supplied by Bob Fryer (academic adviser to the merger), 18/9/90. It is also worth noting that other unions have discussed or experimented with distinctive union policymaking processes in relation to Labour Party activity.

78. For a strong defence of present arrangements, Martin Upham and Tom Wilson, 'Why Change the System When It's in Good Working Order?', *Tribune*, 6/7/90. Their survey showed that the vast majority of affiliated branches made their decision at a branch meeting after looking at written details. They argued that there was no evidence to support a move to individual member OMOV based on practical difficulties or union malpractice, and that it was not immediately obvious that an individual membership OMOV was more democratic than the college.

79. This was particularly true of submissions from the GMB, NUPE and TGWU.

80. The final version of the document agreed by the NEC at its meeting on 25 July committed the Party to OMOV of individual members when there was next a round of selection contested. 'However, further consideration should be undertaken of the best means of achieving the desire of the party to involve members of affiliated trade unions and socialist societies in the process'. There would not be a constitutional amendment on the reform until the 1991 Party Conference – when the involvement of affiliated members would also be reported upon.

81. See, for example, Walter Cairns, 'Why Labour Must Democratise Its Policy Review Process', *Tribune*, 25/3/88, Martin Linton, 'Swedish Les-

sons for Labour', *Tribune*, 4/11/88, and 'Labour Needs a New Way of Making Policy', Tribune editorial, 9/12/88. There was an important input from the Labour Coordinating Committee to the debate on policymaking held at the 1988 Party Conference, *LPACR*, 1988, pp. 77–80. At fringe meetings of the 1989 Labour Party Conference, the inadequacy of the Policy Review process was a theme of many speeches, including those of Tom Sawyer, Chair of the NEC's Home Policy Committee, and Diane Jeuda, Chair of the Youth Committee.

82. For example, GMB, *Meeting the Challenge, op. cit.*, pp. 4–5.

83. GS: 17/4/90. Future of Party Conference Policy-Making and Party Representational Structure, *NEC Minutes*, 25/4/90.

84. CLPD and Labour Left Liaison, *Has Conference a Future?*, 1989.

85. Eric Preston, *Taking the Party to the Cleaners*, ILP, 1989.

86. The GMB favoured a reformed and expanded NEC being given responsibility for the policy process and the Commissions. The TGWU was adamant that the National Policy Forum should not take away the functions of the NEC. Both stressed the accountability of the NEC to the Conference. The draft proposals were hardened up on this point as they passed through the NEC.

87. *Tho' Cowards Flinch, op. cit.*

88. For example the *Tribune* editorial, 7/8/59.

89. A different view was taken by this author in the first issue of the Party's new journal *New Socialist*. Lewis Minkin, 'The Politics of the Block Vote', September 1981. See also Michael Meacher, *Labour Weekly*, 19/11/82 and Eric Heffer, 'An Agenda for Labour', *New Left Review*, 140, July/August 1983.

90. Prominent among this group were Andrew Bennett, Frank Field, Robert Kilroy-Silk, Jeff Rooker (who became the group's organiser) and David Stoddart. See also Frank Field, 'Personal View', *Solidarity*, October 1981 and Jeff Rooker, 'Electoral College Reform', *Labour Weekly*, 13/11/81.

91. Information supplied by Jeff Rooker.

92. Letters of support came from the ATWU, NUM and NUPE. These were in reply to a draft bill and a letter (20/7/82) which summarised it as 'one person, one vote for those members of trade unions paying into the political fund in certain key elections of a political party with the vote being expressed proportionally'. *Ibid.*

93. John Cole, 'The Safety Valve of Democracy', *The Observer*, 6/7/80.

94. Merging or expected to merge between 1990 and 1992 were COHSE, NALGO and NUPE, NUHKN and NUFLAT, NGA and SOGAT, GMB and NUTGW, and the NUR and NUS.

95. R. Undy *et al.*, op. cit., p. 343.

96. There was a very interesting pointer. The *Morning Star* editorial, 'Labour and the unions', 18/12/89, expressed its support for this proposal after years of supporting the status quo. Less surprising was that the EETPU advocated delegate voting rather than block voting in its submission to the 1990 consultation.

97. In 1990, of the major unions only the GMB favoured immediate reform.

98. The National Policy Forum involved an ambitious attempt to rectify inadequate representation within the current policymaking structure. Pressure for increased representation or direct representation arose from a variety of sources – listed in the General Secretary's Paper B, GS 17/4/90, as women, the regions, and the special Scottish and

Welsh dimensions, the Parliamentary Labour Party and the British Labour Group in Europe, ethnic minorities, particularly black and Asian members, Labour groups on Labour authorities, the Co-operative Movement and the Youth and Student Organisations of the Party.

99.   The 1989 Labour Party Conference carried Comp. 54 which instructed the NEC to bring forward proposals for quotas of women for the constituency and trade union sections of the NEC 'on a realistic but rapid timescale'. *LPACR*, 1989, p. 160.

100. In proposed arrangements for the National Policy Forum, there would be a substantial regional representation (approximately 88 of 170 members) of which three per region from eleven regions would be from the unions. There was no agreement on how these would be elected but it was difficult to imagine that the regional officials of the larger unions would not be well represented. It was agreed that 'National Trade Unions' affiliated to the Party would have to be represented but how many and in what way was left for further discussion.

101. In September 1989, 51 per cent of active trade unionists and 64 per cent of inactive trade unionists disagreed that trade unions should have a block vote at the Labour Party Conference, Harris Research Centre *The Observer*, Table 25, October 1989. Data supplied privately by *The Observer*. What they understood by 'block vote' is, of course, uncertain.

102. See Chapter 5, p. 145 and n. 96.

103. Tony Benn, *Tribune*, 'Hard Labour' Conference, 23/10/88 – notes of the author.

104. 'Breaking the institutional links between the Labour Party and the trade unions is your next, great task, and it needs to be done now'. Open letter to Neil Kinnock from Bill Rodgers, *Guardian*, 17/8/90. Or as Tommy Cooper used to say – 'Just like that!'.

13

Policymaking: procedure, process and role

POWER: PERCEPTIONS AND PROBLEMS.

Perceptions of the power relationship in the Labour Movement have always been dominated by polarised alternatives in which either the union leadership or the Parliamentary leadership were credited with supreme and sometimes total power. Let us note again at this point that post-'settlement' analysis of the Labour Party was for years influenced by the McKenzie thesis – that power was concentrated into the hands of the Parliamentary leadership and that the permanent role of union leaders was that of an assistive, protective 'praetorian guard' of the political leadership.

In spite of some penetrating criticism,[1] this view of the power relationship between Party and union leaders survived well into the early 1970s.[2] But by this stage, perceptions of the Labour Party and its relationship with the unions were beginning to be dominated by a different image, that of the all-powerful unions led by 'the terrible twins', the union leaders Jack Jones and Hugh Scanlon; an image later superseded by that of 'Jack Jones, Leader of the Labour Party'.[3] The result was, for a period, a return to literalism in analysing the Labour Party, with the formal points of trade union dominance interpreted or simply specified as though the formal was always realised in policy terms. From this it was concluded that 'The unions run the Labour Party'.[4] So widespread was this perception of the new Trojan Horse,[5] that even Middlemas, one of the most acute observers of the Labour Movement, diagnosed that the unions had 'established practical as well as policymaking hegemony'.[6]

In Chapter 6, we noted some of the qualifications to be made to this diagnosis. Before moving into an analysis of the period after 1979 in terms of policy, it is important to emphasise again two general analytical points about the assessment of power in the trade union-Labour Party relationship:

1. The polar model of power in the Labour Party, which focused on the oligarchical role of the Parliamentary leadership, tended to understate or ignore trade union power which was reflected in the Leadership's anticipation of the reactions of the unions, adaptation of policy initiatives at drafting stage and the closure of some delicate industrial policy areas in deference to the 'rules'. The fact that unions hold huge majorities of the block votes at the Party Conference or control a majority of the seats on the National Executive

Committee or link to the Party through the TUC-LP Liaison Committee does not of itself determine the distribution of power on any particular policy area, although, when the Party is in Opposition, it can build boundaries to policymaking on issues salient to the unions.

2. The alternative characterisation, in which power was polarised such that the unions were the controllers, tended to play down not only the evasive mechanisms available to the Parliamentary leadership but the crucial inhibitions involved in trade union role-playing and their obedience to the 'rules' of the relationship. In particular, trade union pressure differed, as we have seen, according to the priority of union involvement in particular policy issues. Many different forces contributed to make the politics of each policy area distinctive, but the hierarchy of trade union priorities, and how they were defined, was one major reason why the pattern of power varied issue by issue.

PERCEPTIONS OF POWER: 1979 TO 1987

The characterisation of power in polarised terms was often accompanied by an assumption that power exercised in one area typified a broad front control over all outcomes. In the period following the 1979 General Election, the union dominance model received a boost from two developments: the institution of a new constitutional role for the unions in elections for the Parliamentary leadership, and the creation of Trade Unions for a Labour Victory which played a novel organisational and financial role in relationship to the Party. These developments were seen as exemplifying a broad union intervention which covered all facets of the Party including policy. The union leaders, it was said by Anthony Sampson, had emerged 'much more openly as controllers of the Labour Party'.[7]

Similarly, as noted in Chapter 7, Pimlott diagnosed a sharp union reaction to the experiences of the Labour Government (much as the Bevin–Citrine leadership had behaved after 1931). From this perspective, the changes to policy and to the constitution came about because of 'a union decision to move into Labour Party politics more decisively than ever before'.[8] Peter Jenkins saw this, in an interesting analogy, more in terms of the preservation of order. 'In the way that revolutions usually in the end bring the army to power, so the cultural revolution which blew through the Labour movement after 1979 has brought the trade unions to a still greater pre-eminence.'[9]

In response to these views, we have, first, to differentiate the organisational, financial, constitutional and policy areas – particularly in terms of union concerns. As we shall indicate (Chapters 15, 16 and 19), the union leaders did move into a new concern with Party organisation and finance, but they were pulled rather than pushed into the constitutional mire and with some widely varying solutions (Chapters 7 and 15). As for policy, though there was a climate and an NEC factional composition which constrained the PLP leadership, it is difficult to make much of any generally initiating union role in this period (Chapter 14). Although a small core of Left-led unions now linked with the NEC Left in attempting to set an agenda on some of the key issues, and although union leaders sometimes reacted strongly over a narrow range of priority issues, the tendency was still to accept a differentation of functions and to let 'the politicians' take the initiative. When these politicians were the Front Bench rather than the NEC Left, most trade union leaders found this much more acceptable – *both pre- and post-1983*.

There is a startling contrast between the diagnosis of the post-1979 period and the way the relationship with the unions was perceived in the mid-1980s. By 1986, it was widely recognised that the Parliamentary leadership had moved into a new period of ascendancy – one in which the Leader was even able, in the words of Geoffrey Smith of *The Times*, to make a 'declaration of independence for the Labour Party from the trade unions'.[10] On the Left, Tony Benn and Eric Heffer diagnosed a 'quiet revolution'[11] which was shifting power to the Parliamentary leadership.

This redistribution of power can be, and has been, explained both in terms of a range of new union weaknesses and in terms of the many new strengths of the PLP leadership. The multiplicity of these new factors says much about the reinforcing weight behind the shift. The unions were weakened in this period by a loss of membership, by a dependence upon the Party produced by new limitations upon alternative avenues of influence – industrial and political, by vulnerable weaknesses in policy support among the membership, and by growing awareness of the dangers of public unpopularity – including the unpopularity of union leaders 'controlling' the Labour Party. By contrast, the Parliamentary leadership was strengthened by a broader base of allies on the NEC, by the new assertiveness and personal authority of the Leader, by the dynamics and 'strong leader' image of the new presentational politics, by new policy resources and, in this context, by new procedures of policymaking.

In assessing the behaviour of union leaders in terms of their alleged 'control' over the Labour Party, one of the most important features of the politics of the 1980s was the fact of 'the dog that did not bark'.[12] This was particularly true over the supply and control of new finance for the Front Bench, and over the innovation in policy procedure after 1983 which, without formal constitutional change, brought the PLP leadership into a joint process with the NEC where previously only the NEC had normally been involved. To understand union responses to these changes we have to appreciate how receptive were most union leaders to the better integration of the PLP leaders into policymaking *in the early 1980s* and that the development of financial resources for the Front Bench began *in the period after 1979* with the approval of senior union leaders. These continuities reflected some well-established attitudes on the part of union leaders to the distinctive responsibilities of the Parliamentary leadership. It was this consistent union behaviour which was in some respects pivotal to the whole experience.

Having made these preliminary points, let us now move to the detailed analysis. How, why and to what extent were the unions involved in Party policymaking? How, why and to what extent did they circumscribe or facilitate the policy role of the Parliamentary Leadership? How, why and to what extent did they determine the policy of the Labour Party in the period from 1979 to 1987? These are the questions that I will seek to answer here and in the case studies of Chapter 14.

It must be emphasised again that, as a result of the broad programmatic ambitions of Labour's NEC on the one hand, and the radical reconstructive character of Government policy on the other, a wide field of Party policymaking was now reopened. The breadth of this policymaking, plus a range of new developments in the policy process itself, meant that the policy interaction of the unions and the Party was more complex than at any time since the Party was founded. This complexity has to be explored in order to make sense of the variations in the case studies.

PROCEDURE, INSTITUTIONS AND AUTHORITY

The trade union input into Party policymaking took place within a changing political context (see Chapter 5) and also within changing procedures and institutions which determined the focus of conflicting pressures.

The traditional theory of Labour's intra-Party democracy focused upon the input from below by which resolutions were submitted from affiliated organisations, debated at the sovereign Party Conference and then became party policy as a result of the votes of mandated delegates.[13] Operative practice draws our attention to the NEC as the historical and constitutional body charged with formulating major policy statements and documents.[14] In this process of policy formulation, Conference-delegate democracy became one source of input among others, a source of varying importance depending upon the changing authority of the Conference, and (of more sustained significance) depending upon the priority and scale of union support registered there.

So it was the NEC policy procedures, the headquarters policy staff and the institutional linkage of which the NEC was a part which formed the hub of policy formulation. But there was another set of Party institutions which was also concerned with policymaking. While the NEC was responsible for policy formulation, the Parliamentary leadership, through the Shadow Cabinet, was charged with the duty of implementation. It was a very uneasy distribution of responsibilities. The co-operative fusion of the two depended in great measure on the factional balance in the different bodies and the extent of personal overlap in their composition. An assertive NEC, controlled by a different faction from that of the majority in the Shadow Cabinet, could greatly reduce the role of the PLP leadership in policy formulation – as it did from 1979 to 1981.

Not that the PLP leadership could be fully excluded. The Leader and Deputy Leader were always full and active members of the NEC. And though the Shadow Cabinet was a loose, short-term-focused and essentially Parliamentary co-ordination committee, rather than a policymaking body, its members were, by their involvement in debates in the House, always involved in some form of *ad hoc* policymaking or policy definition. As individual members of the Front Bench became better resourced in terms of administrative and research assistance, so they were in a position to take autonomous policy development much further, if they were so minded. And, although the rest of the PLP was barely involved at all in the Party's policy formulation, sometimes the Chair or Secretary or other specialist from a PLP policy committee was represented on the NEC study groups or subcommittees.

But the procedural tension remained – particularly from 1979 to 1983. The

Parliamentary leadership was in public terms responsible for the Party's policy, yet much of what they did in terms of formulating that policy was either achieved as a side-show to the main theatre or by pushing in from the outside to the main process. This main policy process was, in this period, concentrated upon a network of subcommittees and study groups which fed their decisions, via policy papers, through the NEC's Home Policy and International Committees to the NEC itself. Some of these policy statements went to the Party Conference and were voted upon. Some went to the Party Conference but were not voted upon and some were simply published. As a result, this, plus a constitutional formula covering the relationship between the Conference and a largely fictitious 'Party Programme',[15] left the Party with 'policies' of widely varying status.

Two kinds of policy outputs were, however, much more firmly established than other policies. That the products of the Liaison Committee – the tripartite policy body linking the NEC, PLP and TUC – had a very special status was indicated by the fact that they were not normally subject to an adverse vote by unions at the Party Conference. Partly because of their content and partly because they had been negotiated with the TUC, they became for the unions the most heavily prioritised elements in the Party's policy.

Second, the electoral commitments of the Party were contained in the Party Manifesto produced via a joint meeting of the NEC and the Shadow Cabinet ('The Clause V Meeting').[16] Though in practice the Party's Leader always had an important and sometimes crucial say in shaping this Manifesto, it was a significant feature of the procedure (particularly from 1979 to 1983) that the mountain of policy proposals from which the Manifesto would be drawn had come through a process which was under the formal control of the NEC and not the Parliamentary Party.

This 'semi-exclusion' of the PLP leadership from the earliest stages of policy formulation was felt most acutely after 1979. Not only had they just lost the reins of Government but their presence on a Leftward-moving NEC was badly depleted. At the same time, they experienced the full weight of a remarkable cultural phenomenon within the Party – the reassertion of the value of intra-party democracy and the typification of the PLP leadership as simply an 'arm' of the Party. The primary solution given by the NEC to the problem of policy co-ordination between the Party and its arm was that of the binding commitment – co-ordination by imposition. To this end, there was originated in 1980 a Draft Manifesto which was intended to be redrafted annually – a 'rolling' manifesto – which would take on such a legitimacy that it would be difficult to change substantially at the final 'Clause V' meeting.

These attitudes and the procedural proposals that went with them were deeply resented by the PLP leadership. Largely as a result of pressure from the PLP, the front page layout and foreword to the 1980 Draft Manifesto were significantly altered to reduce its status. And the constitutional amendment, which would have made the NEC alone responsible for the formulation of the Manifesto, was defeated at the 1980 Party Conference and again in 1981. In October 1981, changes in the composition of the NEC undermined the committee's support for the rolling manifesto process.

Another means was now found to co-ordinate. A Policy Coordinating Committee linking the Shadow Cabinet and NEC was used from 1981 to 1983 to discuss major contentious items and to examine areas of the Party Programme which required a degree of policy reconciliation. Working mainly to the policies established via the NEC and the Conference since 1979, the Policy Coordinating Committee took the draft of the Campaign Document and created a degree of formal acceptance such that the final Clause V meeting on the Manifesto yielded few significant open policy disagreements – and also the longest Manifesto in Party history.

And yet not far below the surface some basic disagreements remained – over incomes policy, over the EEC, over the extent of the proposed industrial planning structure, over public ownership – and, crucially as it turned out, over the non-nuclear defence policy. The fact that Labour's defence policy fell apart (some would say was 'sabotaged') during the election campaign not only severely damaged the Party, it changed the minds of some of Labour national officials towards the problem of co-ordination.[17] It also strengthened considerably those forces within the unions which already saw it as a practical necessity that the Parliamentary leadership be involved not only in preparing the Manifesto, but more fully from the earliest stages in the formulation of Party policy. After 1983, within the unions, there continued to be a strong commitment to Party democracy and an understanding that the Leadership would advocate policies evolved through the Party. But a command and, in effect, confrontational form of policymaking, with the Party seeking to impose its will over a wide range of policy items upon a largely uninvolved and unreconciled Parliamentary 'arm', had suffered a serious, and perhaps fundamental, blow.

Further, although it was not fully realised at the time, a longer term transformation was taking place in the facilities available to the Labour Front bench for policymaking. Between June 1979 and July 1983, a major increase took place in MPs' secretarial and research allowances. A further rise took place from 1983 to 1987.[18] In addition, for the first time when Labour was in Opposition, the state-provided 'Short Money' was available for use by the Front Bench: 290,000 in 1979 became 440,000 in 1983. As will be shown in Chapter 16 (p. 520), major union leaders would give no support to attempts by the NEC Left to bring this finance under NEC control; indeed, additional sums were provided by the unions for the Front bench and, particularly after 1983, for the greatly enlarged Leader's Office.[19](Chapter 16, pp. 521). In brief, with the provision from the state and the active co-operation of the union leadership, there were now, for the first time in Party history, resources for a sizeable alternative policy advisory staff available to the PLP leadership.

This provided a new basis for independent policymaking by the Parliamentary leadership and potentially could have produced a new and greater gulf between the policies of the different leadership bodies – the NEC and the Shadow Cabinet. It was felt, therefore, to be all the more necessary to integrate them into the formal processes of Party policymaking.

Thus, after 1983, there was instituted a historic change in procedure. In place of the old subcommittee/study group/NEC process of policy formulation came a

Joint Policy Commitee process involving equal representation from the NEC and the PLP/Shadow Cabinet with joint secretaries from both sides. The new procedure and the old constitutional form were integrated. Canons of Party constitutionalism were respected in that decisions of the joint policy committees had to be reported via the NEC to the Party Conference and only NEC members were allowed to chair the committees.

The consequences of this procedural change for the distribution of power will be assessed below, but here it must be noted that though initially the protocol of joint policymaking was preserved and the committees were still publishing documents right up to April 1987, there also developed in the final stages an unusual looseness in the policy procedures – remarkable, given the normal union-inspired Party respect for procedural regularity. As the Front Bench developed a neo-Ministerial status and Kinnock a neo-Prime Ministerial role, so some of the traditional proprieties went out of the window. The Parliamentary Leadership, now with a modicum of improved policy co-ordination as a result of occasional weekend meetings held away from Parliament, began to develop more of its own independent policy initiatives. Among these was the important new plan for creating one million new jobs – *New Jobs for Britain*. It had been produced in consultation with the TUC, but the NEC was presented with the final draft and not allowed to make amendments.[20] In addition, there was the development of PLP policy statements published during the election campaign at a time when the NEC was not meeting.[21]

These shifts were part and parcel of a development in which, with union acquiescence, the PLP leadership became *the* source of virtually all major initiatives. The Liaison Committee lost important items from its agenda. *New Skills for Britain* (a real mess of a document) was substantially rewritten and abbreviated after the NEC had agreed it. And the Manifesto was actually 'tidied up' under the supervision of the Party Leader, *after* the Clause V meeting. Taking these developments alone as an indicator, it is difficult to find another period in Party history when the Leader had so much procedural leeway to do what he wanted.

INFORMAL LINKAGE

Behind these formal procedures and institutions was a dense pattern of informal links and consultative arrangements between the Party and the unions. Out of these consultations came an awareness of distinctive needs in response to the different industrial and political obligations and out of this interaction came an important process of adjustment. In the period after 1979, the most important feature of this adjustment had been the politicians' anticipation of the reaction of the unions. This was still a significant element in some of the policy areas. But, by 1985, it was beginning to be overlaid by an adjustment the other way, as union and TUC policymaking, and their input into the Party's policy process, anticipated the needs of the Party.

Some of this informal linkage was part of the arrangements forged after 1931 and adhered to more or less ever since. There was, for example, the formal exchange of observers and regular consultation between the NEC and the TUC over economic and industrial policy. For a period in 1982, this was reinforced by a unique sweeping-up arrangement in which all affiliated unions were invited to submit proposals and comments in connection with a draft of the Party's Programme.[22] Even some of the non-affiliated unions – particularly the teaching unions in connection with education policy – were kept in close contact via the co-opting of some of their officials, in their personal capacities as Party members.

There was never the same broad invitation after 1983, although informal contact with the unions remained very strong. Throughout the 1980s there was a regular process of consultation between the Front Bench and the TUC over legislation before the House on such issues as labour law, social security and training, often involving regular weekly meetings during a Bill's progress through the two Houses. In addition, there was a regular (although variable) communication between the Front Bench spokespersons for Employment, Energy, Industry and Transport and relevant union leaders and TUC officials. Similarly with the Shadow Chancellor and the TUC's Economic Committee Chairman and economic specialists. And the Party Leader always kept contact with the TUC General Secretary – a relationship which after 1985 was particularly important in handling the TGWU connection and in dealing with sensitive policy issues including union balloting and nuclear energy policy.

Indeed, although there was far from a full meeting of minds and a satisfactory mutual understanding in this period, it does appear that the informal consultative processes between the Parliamentary leadership and the major union leaders *increased* during Kinnock's leadership. Thus the decline of the Liaison Committee after 1986 (see below, pp. 413) was accompanied by a deepening of private contacts through what was then called the 'Neddy Six' meetings of union leaders, members of the Front Bench, and senior Party and TUC officials. It was an integrative arrangement which underpinned the greater assertion of 'space' and 'distance' in the relationship.

This integration was even more apparent at the level of, and in relation to, the different 'bureaucracies' of the Labour Movement. Here there were three features which were significant. The first was the growth of a new strata of 'political' officers in the unions and of political assistants to the Front Bench. In a sense there were now more people with more time to consult and 'fix'. The second was the growth of the Leader's Office, with a staff of people whose job it was to prepare the ground for the Leader's initiatives and responses. By comparison with all previous periods of Labour-in-Opposition, this preparation expanded considerably in the mid-1980s. And thirdly, the TUC senior officials, whose influence over TUC policy was usually far greater than their Party counterparts, were expanding in number in this period and able to relate easily, in status terms, with the Front Bench as well as with the Leader's advisers.

The policy network of officials and advisers was important, not only in pursuing a general project of 'keeping the show on the road' under various pressures, but also because they were normally responsible for the first drafts of policies submitted within the Party or TUC. In terms of the relationship between Labour Party policy staff and TUC policy staff, the core of the relationship up to 1986 was the Liaison Committee, but there was a broader pattern of contacts, with some significant variations depending upon the preoccupations and traditions of the TUC departments.[23]

The closest and most regular contact was kept between the Research Department (later Policy Development) staff from the Party side and the Economic Department staff from the TUC. There was a similar relationship with the Social Insurance and Industrial Welfare Department of the TUC. This involved a mutual exchange of information and briefings and observer facility for the staff of the two TUC departments (if they wanted it) on the various study groups and joint committees of the Party. Their background liaison was often useful in preparing the ground on 'sticky' issues.

There was a difference of emphasis in the relationship of the Party staff with that of the TUC's Organisation and Industrial Relations Department. In general, there was the same mutual consultation, but the TUC department retained a distinctive character, shaped by its industrial responsibilities and its tripartite links with Government and Employers. It had a strong sense of functional differentiation from the Party, but mixed with a sensitivity to the needs and national obligations of the Parliamentary leadership. Even this department tended to get pulled towards more Party involvement after 1984, given the intensity of the problems over trade union legislation and the Department's take-over (in March 1985) of education and training issues.

In a category of its own was the behaviour of the TUC's International Department – a department which, in 1978, came under fierce attack from an adviser to the NEC's International Department about its relationship with the ICFU and US foreign policy in the Third World.[24] In Labour Movement terms, the department remained the most aloof and secretive, concerned to define its activities in 'trade union' rather than political terms. Not until 1986 (after Norman Willis intervened) did it even exchange observers with the Party, and even then it made clear that the TUC was not going to get pulled into Party arguments over foreign and defence policy.

For a brief period after the 1983 General Election there was some disorientation in relationships between the two bureaucracies as different definitions of 'new realism' fought to become operational. In practice, by 1986, as relations with the Government withered and as the two bodies sought to keep co-ordination on a range of very delicate issues, including labour law, low pay, social ownership and the married man's tax allowance, the informal linkage between the offices was as close as it had been for many years.

One final point about the background work of policy advisers needs to be registered – their role in institutionalising the feminist influence. Since 1980, the women's movement had made a marked advance in terms of ensuring that a programme of 'women's issues' was adopted by the Labour Party. By 1983, only the statutory minimum wage, which had met strong resistance from elements within the unions, was still being *openly* contested (although the conscience issues raised for the parliamentarians by abortion were always a problem, dealt with in 1987 by leaving the issue out of the Manifesto).

But, over and above these 'women's issues', there was a deeper problem of the failure of the policy process to integrate a woman's perspective – a fault not unconnected with the domination of men on the committees. But Party Conference decisions had legitimised a new outlook and research staff in the unions and the Party sought to take account and advantage of it. In 1982, a decision was taken in the Labour Party Research Department that in future an officer would monitor all policy documents and statements to see if this problem could at least be brought to the fore. In 1982, unlike in 1976, the Party's Programme was heavily vetted with this in mind. In 1986, the Transport document, produced in its early stages almost entirely by the unions, was halted within Party headquarters by an alliance of local authority representatives and the Policy Directorate anxious that its treatment of women was still inadequate. It was substantially amended.

TRADE UNIONS, ROLES AND POLICYMAKING

What part did the unions play in the study groups, subcommittees and joint policy process, whose output created the material from which ultimately the Manifesto was drawn? We shall approach an answer to this question in the next chapter by the use of a range of case studies of key controversial issues, but here let us note first the attitudes of the unions generally to the Party's policy process.

Trade unionists intervened in the policy process in ways which were neither unified nor immediately apparent. Once again, role-playing added an important variable to the process. The TUC, for example, was in a sense the voice of 'the unions', but it was also an independent organisation with a specialist bureaucracy that had its own views, interests and role definition. Sometimes its officials played a 'national' role (as over incomes policy) which went further than the individual unions. Sometimes they played an institutional role defending TUC tripartite links (as over the Manpower Services Commission) in a way which brought them into conflict with some of the affiliated unions as well as with some on the Front bench. But most typical, as we shall see, was the restraint that they encouraged in relation to the Labour Party and the discreet assistance that they sought to give to its Parliamentary leadership.

Although, as we have seen, the unions held the great majority of votes at the Party Conference, members of the General Council of the TUC regarded TUC policymaking as the central concern for trade unionists. By extension, they were generally more interested in the formal linking body to the TUC – the Liaison Committee – than they were in the Party's own internal policy process. To some extent, this preoccupation with the TUC was a territorial loyalty dividing senior union leaders from Deputies, Assistant General Secretaries and other second rank union leaders on the Party's NEC, but it also reflected a well-established acknowledgement of the different spheres of the industrial and the political.

This attitude towards distinct responsibilities also affected the behaviour of trade union representatives on the NEC. Historically, the typical Trade Union Section representative was from the Rightwing of the unions, possessed a well developed perception of 'party' and 'union' responsibilities and was unwilling to be brought into other than a temporary conflict with the Parliamentary leadership. There was also a process that in some ways resembled the socialisation process on the General Council of the TUC (Chapter 2). New trade union members, even from the Left, were encouraged to integrate within 'the union group' and play the loyal game as it had been played in the past.[25] This self-denying ordinance was reinforced by industrial priorities and often by a lack of confidence in pursuing some of the wider economic and political issues.

In the late 1970s, the growing strength of Leftwing politicians on the NEC produced problems for the small minority of Leftwingers in the Trade Union Section. They were still pulled towards loyal support and by the priorities of their trade unions, but they also co-operated with the political Left on some of the contentious policy and organisational questions. After the 1980s, their position – indeed the position of the whole Trade Union Section – was further complicated by divisions between the Parliamentary Leaders.

The push and pull of different obligations and different groups of politicians sorely tested the Trade Union Section at this time but cross-pressure was often a feature of their position throughout the 1980s. It produced a curiously semi-detached (and sometimes prickly) relationship with the unions and their General Secretaries which was often crucial to the way that the Party operated at this level. From 1979 to 1981, and subsequently, diplomatic absences, abstentions and apologetic votes were not unknown on the NEC, where union and Party obligations were seen to clash and Trade Union Section members wished to assist the Parliamentary Leadership.

After 1983, a few of them sometimes moved forward on issues of wider political significance – as we shall see over nuclear energy and environmental issues (Chapter 14). And very occasionally in the past two decades, some of them have used the NEC to register fundamentals when it was thought that the Neddy Six had conceded or might concede too much in private discussions with the Front bench (Chapter 14). But, overall, they were generally supportive and accommodative in the development of Party policy. Trade unionists took the Chairs of the Home Policy and International committees but they rarely took independent policy initiatives.

However, there were special sticking points when an issue of priority industrial concern to one or other of the unions was at stake. On such issues, there sometimes emerged a conflict of solidarities as union representatives, anxious to sustain the Party Leadership, also sought to give assistance to a union colleague. This situation was at its most acute over industrial disputes, where some of the less Leftwing trade unionists could be pulled behind the initiatives of the political Left.

Industrial disputes always caused the Parliamentary leaders difficulties, albeit more for some individuals than for others. There were significant differences between Labour's leaders in the way they regarded strike action, and differences of approach often showed themselves in the stances of Front Bench spokespersons – particularly between those linked to the Left and those linked to the Right. But whatever their predispositions, handling such disputes was never easy. On the one hand, under the 'rules' they had no right to offer public advice on timing, negotiating stance and mode of action. On the other, they were constantly pressed by the Government, other parties and the mass media to make judgements. In Opposition, the claim by unions for solidarity support when they were in dispute was strong, and usually precipitated some measure of response by the Parliamentary Party. But matters were further complicated in this period by the behaviour of the NEC which, under Leftwing influence, began after 1979 to play a high profile role in support of workers in dispute – sometimes far past that demanded by either the union concerned or the TUC.[26]

The problem was most acute during the year-long Miners' Strike. In his refusal to be pulled behind '100 per cent support', in his reluctance to attend picket lines and NUM rallies, in his priorities for debate in the House, and in his statements on violence and legality, Kinnock showed his independence of the NUM leadership and of a strong body of opinion in the Party. But the balance of forces on the NEC was often more responsive to the NUM leadership than was the case on the Shadow Cabinet. Consequently, NEC statements and resolutions were sometimes pulled in a direction in which Kinnock would have preferred not to go.

After the strike, Kinnock was able to defy an NUM resolution backed by the 1985 Party Conference calling for amnesty and reimbursement. But, though critical of the NUM leadership's handling of the Notts. miners, Kinnock obeyed the 'rules' of the Movement and refused any association with the breakaway UDM – a stance which further prejudiced the Labour Party's appeal in that part of the world.

A second example of the role of the NEC in establishing constraints on the Party Leadership concerned the News International dispute in 1986. Here (unlike the Miners' Strike), the Parliamentary leadership did have good and co-operative relations with the union's leadership and was able to use the behaviour of the Rupert Murdoch management to highlight the unfairness of the Government's trade union legislation. However, at the NEC on 29 January 1986, the union representatives led calls for a boycott of News International Newspapers – including their journalists. This latter aspect was unwelcome but was respected by the Parliamentary leadership, who refused to accept invitations to discussions with the management and refused to answer questions from News International journalists at press conferences.[27]

This caused some intricate difficulties. The NEC refused to vary its decision to take account of the Party's need for its messages at the Fulham by-election not to be sidetracked onto the issue of who was talking to whom,[28] and the result was at least one very well-publicised and embarrassing press conference as unsympathetic News International journalists sought to make the most of the situation. In response, the Parliamentary Lobby refused to allow Labour's Leader to decide whom he would or would not receive questions from; the result was a significant innovation as Kinnock held his own Lobby press conference but refused to invite News International journalists.

However, usually the majority of NEC trade unionists were sympathetic to any problem faced by the Parliamentary leadership and anxious not to be drawn into 'irresponsible' Leftwing 'posturing'. In this, they saw eye to eye with TUC officials who, often in the period of Leftwing ascendancy and sometimes later, worried about being pulled by the nose by the NEC on issues of central priority to the unions. The result was sometimes manœuvres of a subterranean character by the TUC staff using sympathetic NEC trade unionists and Party staff[29] to defuse potential problems.

Thus, on industrial policy in 1982, a discreet understanding between the TUC, the NEC trade unionists and Party staff sidelined the policy emerging from the Industrial Policy subcommittee, which was a continuation of the Party's industrial policy of the 1970s but now moving out of harmony with the Liaison Committee discussions. NEC trade unionists boycotted the subcommittee and the relevant section of Labour's Programme was put together by Party staff without reference to the subcommittee.

Something similar happened that year in relation to the Employment subcommittee of the NEC – which was (it appeared) prepared to launch itself into delicate areas, including repeal and replacement legislation over industrial relations, and also training policy. The Chairs of the subcommittee, first John Golding of the POEU, then Ken Cure of the AUEW, were used to protect the TUC's position and kill off or side-track any damaging initiatives. The main source of this section of Labour's Programme in 1982 appears to have been the Party Office and the committee Chair (in quiet touch with the TUC office), rather than the subcommittee.

Basically, what the TUC officials and a majority on the General Council wanted and, of course, what the PLP leadership would have preferred also was to deal with these issues either in a process which excluded the NEC Left or in a process in which the PLP leadership dominated the NEC Left. TUC officials grew increasingly irritated and concerned about the process of Party policymaking in the period after 1979. Much of this irritation was simply a covert political critique of the Left but it also took the form of an attack on the Party's lack of 'professionalism'.

The fact was that NEC policy subcommittees and study groups rarely had fixed times of regular meeting, papers often went out at a late stage, membership was large but sometimes changed, meeting by meeting, as individuals found they could or could not attend. Meetings were often held in the House of Commons with division bells ringing and people coming in and out. Trade union officials, used to strict TUC timetabling and attendance, found all this at best non-business-like and at worst 'non-serious', and there was a tendency to 'write off' what was going on and to ignore it unless it needed 'fire brigade' action.

Secondly, a large number of co-optees was not unusual and any relevant Party pressure group with an interest in the area sought, and was usually granted, access in the period after 1979. Their preoccupations and style were often different from that of the trade union representatives and a tension grew up based on the age-old union antipathy to intellectual 'theorists'. Transport policy was one such example where there was dissatisfaction with the composition of the committees. Hence, in this situation, the TUC was not at all averse in 1982 to seeing the transport unions going off to prepare their own arrangements independent of the NEC policy process and of the TUC itself (Chapter 14).

And yet there were also some private regrets. It was recognised that participation by the unions in a party policymaking process could have some benefits which were transferred into the unions. The tendency was for the unions to seek the best available fusion of sectional interests whenever they were left to their own devices. Party policymaking could involve wider criteria, feeding these back into TUC policy formulation and influencing its agenda and climate of discussion.

In the early 1980s, these criteria often involved a Leftwing perspective, but TUC officials looked to the Party to generate a different dynamic. Electoral sensitivity within the Party could feed back into the growing concern within some of the unions and the TUC about putting the unions more in touch with members' opinions. Party sensitivity to the public interest could broaden the outlook of individual unions which had a more self-interested focus. The prospect of a Labour Government could raise questions of how particular interests would fuse with the general and vice versa. The Party's concern with services could heighten producer sensitivity to the user and consumer. As TUC officials sought to reinforce an awareness within the unions of the need to court public, user and consumer opinion, they often looked to the Party as one source of initiative which could 'push us along' and 'demand things of us'. All this would become more apparent after 1983, but there was always a current of opinion within the TUC which was aware that, though trade union sectionalism could be a constraint on the Party, Party universalism could broaden trade unionism.

Of course, the TUC administration was much more appreciative of this educative process when the NEC Left had been undermined. Its senior officers all took the view that both in principle and in practice the Parliamentary Leadership ought to be heavily involved in securing the policy outcome which they would in the end have to implement. These attitudes have to be borne in mind when we assess any characterisation of union 'control' before 1983 and then seek to understand what happened to Labour's policy subsequently.

NEW INSTITUTIONS AND NEW FORCES

It says much about the ingrained norms of the Labour Movement and the 'rules' about consultation that, almost as a reflex (and without any formal decision of the TUC, the NEC or the PLP), no sooner were the joint committees established after 1983 than the TUC was given observer status on any relevant committee, and trade union representation was co-opted on to any committee where this was felt to be appropriate. Thus, of the eleven joint policy committees set up in this period, by 1985 six had TUC observers and only Local Government, Housing and Crime had no co-opted union representatives.

Of course, the TUC, as always, utilised this access with much discretion and restraint. More confident about the Parliamentary leadership, they allowed the issue of planning and industrial democracy to be taken from the Liaison Committee to the Party's Jobs and Industry Joint Committee to give the Party Leadership more room for initiative. They allowed the Social Ownership policy process to be taken independently by a subcommittee of the Jobs and Industry Committee, although having initiated their own review they might have taken it onto the Liaison Committee agenda. They made no attempt to take to themselves the Transport policy rediscussions.

The tendency for the TUC to play a role that was independent but privately supportive of the Parliamentary leadership took on a much clearer tactical perspective after 1985 when Norman Willis became General Secretary and other changes followed in the TUC hierarchy. Publicly, the TUC would do nothing to embarrass the Parliamentary leadership or to imply its subordination in any way. Privately, the TUC would be as helpful as possible in assisting Kinnock to achieve a viable political programme. The unstated quid pro quo was an understanding that the future Labour Government would do its best for organised labour, for working people and for the priority social causes of the Party and the unions.

This position – well understood within the TUC bureaucracy – was only partially implemented by union leaders. There was always the tension of trying to represent their own direct interests while accepting the independence of the Party Leadership. And a trusting relationship was always problematic in the light of past experience of Labour in Government. In addition, there were resentments which emerged from the union leaders' feelings of personal exclusion, and there were tensions provoked by the role of the greatly enlarged 'Leader's Office', full of people who were, it was said, 'young, bright and cocky' but lacking, in the eyes of union leaders, down-to-earth wisdom and a sense of what ordinary people at work were interested in. Indeed, in 1987, it was over the electoral down-grading of place-of-work issues – particularly low pay, employment rights and health and safety – that the simmering grievance was felt most acutely. Nevertheless, all eggs were now in the basket of a future Labour Government and, at any potential crunch, union leaders generally acquiesced.

That being said, one must also note the growing confidence, increasing resources and, at times, ruthless assertiveness of the PLP leaders, as they took full advantage of the mood change brought about by the defeat of 1983. From the first, the key Jobs and Industry Joint Committee was colonised by co-opted supporters of the Shadow Chancellor and Deputy Leader. Key subcommittee Chairs were taken by the Front Bench. An economic strategy emerged not only from the Committee but in public speeches by Hattersley, in which the new direction was charted and new policy departures sometimes announced before they were taken into the Party's procedures.

Through his political and policy advisors, the new Leader was able to exercise a selective but broad-ranging oversight, not only in relation to the management of the Party but to segments and stages of the policy process. In this process, the Leader's assistants sat in on policy committees, formal and informal, taking initiatives, 'fighting fires' and letting others in the unions know 'what Neil wants'.

Alongside this new Front Bench assertiveness – on the part of the 'soft Left' as well as the Right – there has to be registered the collective policy weakness of the NEC Left. They took as many as nine of the thirteen policy committee Chairs in 1985 and every decision of the joint committees had to be confirmed by the Home Policy Committee and the NEC, in both of which the balance of Left and Right was quite fine. But with the passing of 'the alternative economic strategy' there was little agreement on Leftwing economic and industrial policies. And there was a curious mixture of disengagement and negativism in the position of what became known as 'the hard Left' – almost as if they were content to play the role of 'excluded' opposition.

Tony Benn, leading figure in the 'hard' Left grouping, refused to recognise the legitimacy of the new joint committees and failed to attend any meetings. Dennis

Skinner, unofficial 'chief whip' of the Left, played no constructive part in them. Other Leftwing members, apart from those concerned with the Women's Committee, tended to withdraw and leave the initiative elsewhere.

A realignment of the Left, which began in the winter and spring of 1984–5, further divided them and strengthened the Party Leadership. After a while, it became taken for granted on many of these committees, particularly Jobs and Industry, that the Front Bench would take the initiative. Social Ownership apart,[30] only over nuclear energy and, to some extent, the repeal of the trade union legislation, was there a significant input from the NEC Left (see Chapter 14).

THE LIAISON COMMITTEE

If the union relationship with the Party was marked after 1983 by a new reassertion of 'space' and distinct spheres, what happened to the Liaison Committee, the forum that was intended to reconcile the different sets of institutions in the Labour Movement? Here it must be noted that, though the committee had in some ways broadened in its scope, after 1979 there were always some no-go areas (including defence, foreign policy, Northern Ireland and most issues connected with the Home Office). And the continuation of the committee's work after 1979 was not without its uncertainties and reservations.

The uncertainties were to some extent a consequence of the prickly relationship between General Council members and the Leftwing dominated NEC under the Labour Government; in early 1979 the new concordat between the unions and the Labour Government had bypassed the Liaison Committee process altogether. On the NEC there was a growing anxiety about the motives of union leaders who were seeking a major organisational reform of the Labour Party; the concern extended to a worry lest the TUC, encouraged from the political Right,[31] be used to impede a shift to the Left in Party policy.

Some within the TUC still harked back to the second phase of Edward Heath's premiership and thought in terms of the reopening of tripartite talks once the first innocent flush of Thatcherism had been extinguished. The perspective here was to strengthen the Neddy Six talks with the PLP leadership rather than the Liaison Committee. But for the moment it was recognised that relations with the new Conservative Government would be very difficult and though the General Council 'would be adopting a constructive attitude in their relations with the new Government', they would 'also be wishing to maintain, consolidate and build upon the relationship with the Labour Party through the Liaison Committee'.[32] Accordingly, *Planning for Co-operation*, a short exploratory statement on the work of the committee, was put to the Conference and Congress of 1979. This work through the Party became all the more pressing after the failure of the TUC's own political mobilisation in the Day of Action called on 14 May, 1980, and as it became increasingly clear that there was to be no 'U-turn' from the Thatcher Government.

The building process after 1979 did take place, although not without some disagreement on the composition of the Liaison Committee. The TUC always wanted an equal representation of nine representatives from each of the three bodies but in practice, as a result of competition for places on the Party side, the composition varied before 1983 between nine and twelve on each side. Although the occasional disparities of representation indicated nothing about the degree of dominance, size did matter in one respect. The smallest body – the Shadow Cabinet – had most of its members represented on the Liaison Committee and was therefore potentially more confident of its collective voice. This unity became increasingly apparent after 1983. For their part, the TUC members continued to have prior discussions as to their contributions, thus ensuring that they did not fall out in public nor get pulled into sharp Party alignments.

The work of the committee was loosely guided by a programme of work drawn up by the joint secretaries, Geoff Bish, the Party's Director of Policy Development, and David Lea, the TUC Assistant General Secretary. In 1980–81, for example, the Committee had a programme oriented mainly towards problems of economic policy. Some of its work then arose out of papers from the joint secretaries, some was stimulated by consideration of the TUC's A Rescue Plan for the Unemployed and of the TUC's Economic Review (always an important annual discussion). Among the issues discussed were the economic problems facing the next Labour Government, nationalised industries and energy policy.[33]

In the production of major joint statements, the normal form was that the joint secretaries put together a proposal after a 'sounding' process. This was then redrafted and elaborated in the light of the Committee's discussion and then resubmitted.

Each policy statement of the Committee had to be taken back to the NEC Home Policy Committee and then the full NEC. On the TUC side similarly, it went either to the Economic Committee or the Employment Policy and Organisation Committee before going to the General Council. Amendments were regularly made and relayed back in a process which often went on for about three months – sometimes longer. After 1985, these consultative arrangements did not always satisfy the component elements. The EETPU complained of being 'bounced towards acquiescence' on a statutory minimum wage in 1986[34] and some NEC members complained in 1987 that they were not allowed to amend Work to Win (see p. 413).

Though each of the component elements of the Liaison Committee had reasons why they wanted its role restricted, there was a period from 1980 to 1982 when it appeared that the committee was on the verge of a major extension of its structure and authority. Some thought that it was indicative of the TUC's suspicion of the NEC Left in October 1980 that the Committee was asked to endorse the TUC's Rescue Plan for the Unemployed But also, the committee agreed a new document, Private Schools, at the request of the TUC in June 1981 and in 1982 endorsed a new policy document Transport which had (with TUC approval) been produced independently of either the TUC or the Party's procedures. In addition, for the important study Economic Planning and Industrial Democracy, the committee for the first time in its history when the Party was in Opposition spawned a high level subcommittee which involved itself in detailed policy formulation.

By the end of 1982, the Committee secretariat was becoming worried at the possibility that its central priorities could get swamped with demands for further subcommittees and with documents taken to the committee purely to give them extra authority. At this stage, with the NEC now safely under the control of the Right, elements in both the Party and the TUC who thought that the Liaison Committee covered enough ground reasserted themselves.

The lack of *any* Liaison Committee statement to the 1983 TUC or Party Conference was an indication of the new post-election uncertainties not only of strategy but also to some extent of institution. The Liaison Committee 'ticked over' in this period but slowly moved up a gear after the Civil Service unions (one of the sources of 'new realism') had asked that the issue of GCHQ be taken to the committee. In various ways (see Chapter 14, p. 445) training was seen as a suitable issue on which the Liaison Committee might make a statement and in 1984 *A Plan for Training* was published. By November 1984, the mutual confidence of both sides in the usefulness of the committee was reflected in a statement of its role prepared by the joint secretaries.

The form of Liaison Committee publications after 1984 was shaped to some extent by a consciousness that presentation of Labour's policy in short thematic terms and popularisation in terms of values was of more importance in the short run than detailed policy documents. The thematic character (and blandness) of *A New Partnership: A New Britain* in 1985 drew heavily from the past, but there was a subtle refocusing going on.

From the themes of 'Fairness' and 'Rights and Responsibilities', the Parliamentary leadership was able, in 1986, to pursue both the pay question and the issue of trade union ballots. Liaison Committee work (while still interspersed with *ad hoc* discussions on other issues) was primarily focused on these themes leading to the two major documents of 1986: *People at Work: New Rights, New Responsibilities* – a document unprecedented in that it discussed membership participation in unions and prescribed balloting rights. – and the path-breaking statement *Low Pay: Policies and Priorities*, which broke with traditional TUC policy on the statutory minimum wage.

The great advantage of the Liaison Committee as an institution was that it was a co-ordinating body from which basic agreements could be made which would keep the different elements of the Labour Movement in harmony on sensitive issues, and preserve unity when Labour moved into Government. But it also constrained and inhibited all the three sections involved. It was a slow-moving body with internal informal processes of adjustment of sometimes Byzantine complexity. Its secretariat tended to edge forward on the basis of established positions and precedents. Judging how far initiatives could stretch support and how far one year's acceptable terminology could be developed into a new departure the next year became part of the art of 'keeping the show on the road'. On the committee itself, free discussion suffered from the tendency of both the PLP representatives and the TUC side not to break ranks. Private understandings between the Parliamentary leadership and union leaders were sometimes complicated by the presence of members of the NEC who might change the political agenda or bring up wider and more fundamental concerns. And given that the minutes were available to show the general drift of discussion, there was a sense in which the TUC and NEC representatives in particular were always looking over their shoulders.

By the November of 1986, the question privately raised was that if more 'space' was required in the relationship and if the unions could not deliver in terms of an agreement over pay, might not the time be right for a run-down or a discontinuation of the committee? Might this not also be beneficial in terms of signalling 'distance'? Might not adjustments be easier and more discreet? Certainly by this stage private meetings of the Parliamentary leadership with the Neddy Six of TUC leaders were becoming much more important than the Liaison Committee meetings and – it was considered – less encumbered by the interventions of the NEC Left.

Some policy discussions and policy documents expected to evolve on the Liaison Committee now failed to happen. The follow-through on low pay and the construction of a more detailed industrial relations programme were kept off the agenda by the Party Leadership who indicated that they wanted no further documentation. Later it was anticipated that either through Party processes or through the Liaison Committee, a new health and safety document would emerge. This too was pushed to one side.

Only one further document emerged via the Liaison Committee in 1987. The Work to Win document of March 1987 was unprecedented in the form of its production. It was the result not of a draft from the joint secretariat but of a draft put together mainly by the Leader's Office after the offering from the secretariat had come under heavy criticism as being badly structured and dominated by older conceptions of 'partnership'. It was discussed at length in the quiet confines of the Neddy Six meetings then taken to the Liaison Committee for final ratification. The final published version – a much more anodyne document than had been expected – was actually prepared by the Communication Officers of the TUC and the Party.

CAMPAIGNING AND POLICYMAKING

In the period after 1979, not only did Labour Party policymaking involving the unions take on a new breadth and scope, but the campaigning linkages began to be more formalised and integrated. It was a faltering process, beginning first with an adapation of the role of the Liaison Commitee and then, after 1983, involving a new committee – the Campaign Strategy Committee, which had TULV not TUC representation. It is not the purpose here to explore this campaigning itself but to note that, potentially, campaigning (and 'presentational' documents, see note 20) could have indirect policy consequences and could also cause territorial complications.

The initial co-ordination phase on the Liaison Committee involved giving encouragement to the PLP spokespersons and the unions to liaise in opposition to Government policy; their consultations occasionally fed back into the Liaison Committee. But in addition there was an attempt to use the Liaison Committee to synchronise and harmonise Labour Party and TUC campaigns at national and regional level.

The TUC generally welcomed this new role of the Liaison Committee but with a wary eye open for some of the political complications that could arise. The first was the danger that the TUC as an institution might get pulled into Labour Party factional politics and into the Labour Party's own policymaking conflicts. This became a major point at issue over the Party Special Conference which was held in the summer of 1980. On the one hand it was justified as part of a new campaigning stance by the Party – anxious to get maximum publicity for its perspective. Yet there was also an internal Party dimension to the Special Conference. It was seen as a means of pushing the Labour Party policy sharply to the Left through a new policy statement *Peace, Jobs and Freedom*. So great was the division over the Special Conference and the statement that at a special NEC meeting to discuss arrangements for the Conference, ten of the twelve trade union representatives failed to appear although the initial proposal had come from the Transport Workers.[35]

The argument on the NEC had washed over into the Liaison Committee on 31 March 1980 when the NEC representatives attempted to get TUC agreement for a joint statement. It was clear that the Party side was badly divided and the majority of union leaders reluctant to be pulled into the argument. From the TUC, Len Murray made it clear that the *Peace, Jobs and Freedom* statement was the constitutional property of the NEC not the Liaison Committee. It was not for the General Council of the TUC to endorse it, although he conceded that it could be useful for the Liaison Committee to discuss a draft at its next meeting.[36] A month later, the Liaison Committee meeting was suddenly cancelled at the request of the TUC in order, it was said, for union leaders to attend the Scottish TUC.[37] There was no subsequent discussion.

Also worrying for the union leadership was that the NEC Left might use the campaign to pull the unions into industrial action. It was made clear in 1979, in the discussion of the projected campaign against the public expenditure cuts, that there could be no implication that the Liaison Committee would support industrial action – that was a matter for individual unions.[38] Similarly, in February 1980, Len Murray for the TUC made it absolutely clear that the TUC did not want the Liaison Committee commenting on matters to do with a pay dispute.[39] Years later, in early 1987, the TUC established that it was not the practice for the Liaison Committee to discuss disputes at all in the absence of relevant General Secretaries.[40]

Thus the only industrial dispute to be taken to the Liaison Committee in the period from 1979 to 1983 was the Steel dispute and this, as the TUC insisted, was discussed purely in terms of the background problems of the industry and the need to campaign to change Government policy. Thus it was fully in accordance with the past experience and tradition of the Committee that during the Miners' Strike of 1984–5 it should be the NEC representatives who brought it on to the agenda of the Committee and that the TUC was reluctant to see the Committee take any active role, particularly as the NUM had itself requested the TUC to keep out.

It was also recognised at the TUC and on the TULV Executive that the Party must be allowed to fight its own election campaigns. Though in 1983, as a result of TULV pressuring the Party to get a move on in its election preparations, three TULV leaders were put on the large election Campaign Committee,[41] they rarely attended and had no influence over its decisions. Nor did the union leaders interfere in the making of the comprehensive Campaign document of 1983, which became the General Election Manifesto.

After 1983, although the Liaison Committee had some functions in establishing campaign themes, the Party's new Campaign Strategy Committee, with TULV, not TUC, representation, moved to the fore.[42] In practice, union leaders played little or no role in its proceedings. When, in effect, the Campaigns Strategy Committee gave way to the Campaign Management Team set up in 1986, union leaders had no influence over the campaign strategy; the Party was distanced from the unions and there was little emphasis on place-of-work issues. Though as a palliative they were given two places on the Leader's Campaign Committee,[43] there is no evidence that this body had anything but a minimal influence on Labour's election effort. Crucial decisions were made in the Leader's Office and on the Campaign Management Team.[44] As for the Manifesto, that was produced under heavy guidance from the Leader and his office and went through multiple drafts, with the opportunity taken to water down or sideline some commitments which had built up strong union support at times of peak interest. These included the accountability of the police, the treatment of miners and the NUM, and the policy on nuclear energy.

KEY FEATURES

Before we move into the case studies, there are three features of the policy process which need to be emphasised: its complexity, its flexibility, and its growing informal integration.

The main complexity involved a duality in the Party Leadership such that the NEC was mainly responsible for formulation and the Shadow Cabinet mainly for implementation – and there was a multiplicity of entities which constituted 'the unions'. The flexibility was expressed in changing procedural arrangements, in the subtle interaction of formal and informal networks and in the variety of forums through which policy formulation could be processed.

The complexity and flexibility of the relationship was shown particularly in the management of the politics of industrial disputes. 'Rules' regulated important demarcations of territory. Different forums of Labour's leadership dealt with such disputes in different ways. And there was seldom agreement on how they should be processed or even whether they should be processed at all.

The complexity and flexibility of the relationship were also shown in one of the most important but least appreciated features of recent experience. Alongside the assertion of more policy 'space' was the continuing development of mechanisms of policy consultation and liaison which facilitated cohesion. This involved important changes of emphasis from the formal to the informal – from the Liaison Committee to the Neddy Six discussions – but also new liaison personnel in the unions and in the Parliamentary Party.

As for power relations, these will be illustrated in detail in the case studies and assessed at the end of Chapter 14 before we examine the main features of the post-1987 Policy Review. But here let us note again an important confluence of developments which benefited the policy role of the Parliamentary leadership.

In this confluence there were many reinforcing flows, but two interwoven elements are of particular note in terms of the attitudes of senior union leaders to Labour Party policymaking. With their protection, and even additional financial support, new state resources were placed under the control and at the disposal of the Parliamentary leadership. This facilitated the growth of an unprecedented capacity for independent Front Bench policymaking and for the enlargement of what became an 'Executive Office' of the Leader. After 1983, this potential was integrated (albeit not completely) with the normal processes of Party policy formulation, hitherto the province of the NEC. The reform met broad acceptance at leadership level in the unions.

These changes took on a special importance in the mid-1980s, given that they coincided with the undermining of the Left opposition, with a weakening of the unions and with other new strengths of the Party leadership. But, in any case, the change in resources and procedures had potentially profound implications for the traditional form of Party democracy. And the manner of the changes is a reminder, yet again, of some of the crucial continuities in the attitudes of senior union leaders to the operation of the Party. Their behaviour was, as so often in the past, marked by a high level of restraint underpinned by an appreciation of the functional responsibilities of the political leadership.

NOTES

1. The most important criticism was to be found in Beer, *op. cit.*, pp. 86–91, 116–25 and 153–87, Harrison, *op. cit.*, pp. 196, 211, 238 and 255, and in the important correspondence concerning the unions involving Henry Pelling, following a book review by Richard Crossman in the *New Statesman*, 23/6/61, in the editions of 30 June to 28 July 1961.
2. It was briefly reviewed by McKenzie in 1976 after Jack Jones's attack on Ian Mikardo at the 1975 Tribune Rally. See Chapter 6, n. 94.
3. Headline of *Sunday Times* feature article, 1/9/74.
4. For example. Milligan, *op. cit.*, p. 89.
5. John Burton, *The Trojan Horse: Union Power in British Politics*, 1979.
6. Middlemas, *op. cit.*, p. 456.
7. Anthony Sampson, *The Changing Anatomy of Britain*, 1982, p. 98.
8. See n. 7.1.
9. Peter Jenkins, 'Kinnock's Will to Win', *Sunday Times*, 30/6/85.
10. Geoffrey Smith, *The Times*, 30/9/86.
11. *Planning for a Labour Victory*, Memo to the NEC by Tony Benn and Eric Heffer, 1 May 1985. Their main emphasis was on the loss of power by the NEC, to TULV as well as to the Parliamentary Leadership.
12. 'Is there any point to which you would wish to draw my attention?'
    'To the curious incident of the dog in the night-time.'
    'The dog did nothing in the night-time.'
    'That was the curious incident', remarked Sherlock Holmes.
    Sir Arthur Conan Doyle, 'The Silver Blaze', *The Memoirs of Sherlock Holmes*.
13. On this see Minkin, *Labour Party Conference*, *op. cit.*, particularly Chapter 1.
14. Clause IX 2g of the 1979 Labour Party Constitution gave the NEC the right 'to propose to the Annual Party conference... such resolutions and

declarations affecting the Programme, Principles and Policy of the Party as in its view may be necessitated by political circumstances'.

15. The Constitution declares that 'No proposal shall be included in the Party Programme unless it has been adopted by the Party Conference by a majority of not less than two-thirds of the votes recorded on a card vote', 1979, *Clause V* (1). But this Programme was different from the documents titled 'Programme' and issued from time to time by the Party, for example in 1973, 1976 and 1982, which were not open to amendment. Since 1982 there has been no programme of the latter kind.

16. 'The National Executive Committee and the Parliamentary Committee of the Parliamentary Labour Party shall decide which items from the Party Programme shall be included in the Manifesto... ', 1979, *Clause V* (2).

17. Although Neil Kinnock gave the idea its driving force after his speech at Stoke on 12/9/83, it was Geoff Bish, the Party's Research Officer (later Policy Director), who laid out the framework of joint policymaking. *The Failures and Some Lessons*, Heads Meeting 30/6/83; *Future Policy Development*, RD 2806, July 1983; *Programme of Work 1983/84: and a Note on Policy Development*, RD 2889, October 1983. Bish had been a strong advocate of the constitutional changes in 1979 and strongly pursued the theme of Party democracy and accountability in that period. However, the idea of joint policymaking was always part of his thinking; the PLP Leadership had to be more closely involved in policymaking and therefore more committed to the policies that emerged. See on this Ken Coates (ed.), *What Went Wrong*, 1979, p. 169. After 1983, this view began to dominate.

18. The allowance was 4,600 in 1979. By 1983, it was 11,364 and in 1987 it was 21,302.

19. Because of differences in the way the offices were managed, comparisons between the Foot Office and the Kinnock Office cannot be exact. Foot had five members of staff, three of whom were concerned with policy advice and Party liaison – Dick Clements, Henry Neuberger and Elizabeth Thomas (but Neuberger was shared with the Shadow Chancellor, Peter Shore). Under Kinnock, by October 1989 there were twelve members of staff including six on policy and liaison. In addition, Patricia Hewitt, though responsible for the media, was also an important policy influence and continued to be involved when she moved to the Institute for Public Policy in 1988. Charles Clarke was Head of the Office, the Leader's personal assistant and confidant. John Eatwell became senior policy adviser in 1987. Other policy staff were Kay Andrews and John Newbiggin. Late in 1989, Neil Stewart was added to the liaison staff.

20. It contains at least one proposal (cuts in employers' National Insurance contributions) which had, in the past, been rejected by the NEC. For a criticism of the procedure from the Left, see 'NEC Report', *Campaign Group News*, March 1987. Another change in procedure was the categorisation of certain documents as 'presentational'. The NEC was not allowed to vet the defence statement *A Modern Britain in a Modern World*. See on this 'NEC Report', *Campaign Group News*, January 1987, and Eric Heffer, 'Downgrading the Role of the NEC and the Party Conference', *Campaign Group News*, February 1987. 'Presentational' documents could be given the slant the Party Leadership thought most

appropriate.

21. The NEC Report for 1987, p. 37, lists twelve such policy documents.

22. Fifteen unions, replied sending in 104 specific proposals covering 30 different subjects. Many were reaffirmations of existing policy. Many others were not acted upon. A small number of important insertions did go into the Programme including the POEU's proposals on telephone tapping.

23. In linking to the Labour Party, an important role was played by David Lea, an Assistant General Secretary and also a joint secretary to the Liaison Committee with Geoff Bish from the Labour Party. Head of the Economic Department. was Bill Callaghan, of the Social Insurance and Industrial Welfare Department, Peter Jacques, and of the Education Department, Roy Jackson (who became an Assistant General Secretary in 1985). The Head of the Organisation and Industrial Relations Department was John Monks, a rising star, who became Deputy General Secretary in 1987. He was replaced as Head of Organisation and Industrial Relations by Bernard Barber.

24. Don Thompson and Rodney Larson, *Where Were You Brother?*, War on Want, 1978. Thompson was a member of the Development Co-operation study group of the Party's International committee. At a meeting held between TUC and Party officials on 19/9/80, the TUC refused to exchange observers and made specific reference to their unwillingness to attend any meeting where Thompson was a representative, *ID/1980-1/15 November*. Note from Jenny Little.

25. That 'the trade union section always vote together' was made clear to Jack Jones in 1964 'in a friendly fashion' by Len Williams, the General Secretary, and Ray Gunter, the Party Chairman, Jones, *op. cit.*, p. 167. Jones went his own way on the issues which he designated as a priority, including incomes policy.

26. The most angry reaction from the unions concerned the NEC's intervention over the sacking of the BL convenor, Derek Robinson, in 1979 and the NEC's handling of the rail disputes of 1982.

27. 'Why I'm Not Talking to the News of the World', Neil Kinnock, *News of the World*, 23/2/86.

28. *NEC Minutes*, 5/3/86. Withdrawal of first section of Campaign Strategy Committee Minute 9.

29. Roy Green, the member of the Party's policy staff responsible for industrial relations from 1980 to 1986, was an important link and even described to me by a senior member of the TUC as 'more TUC than the TUC'.

30. On the Social Ownership subcommittee of the Jobs and Industry Joint Committee, David Blunkett played an influential role, but it says something about the Left's priorities and attitudes at this time that he was the only regular attender.

31. See for example *Labour Victory*, October 1979.

32. *Liaison Committee Minutes*, 25/10/79, Item 243.

33. *RD 132*, 1980 and TUC *Congress Report*, 1981, p. 271. *NEC Report*, 1981, pp. 60–1.

34. *TUC Congress Report*, 1986, p. 562.

35. *NEC Minutes*, 9/4/80 indicate that only Douglas Hoyle of ASTMS and John Golding of POEU attended.

36. *Liaison Committee Minutes*, 31/3/80, Item 280.

37. Letter to Liaison Committee members, 17/4/80.

38. *Liaison Committee Minutes*, 22/10/79, Item 255.

39. *Ibid.*, 25/2/80, Item 274.

40. *Ibid.*, 26/1/87, Item 527.

41. TULV, anxious over poor Party preparation, had pushed for the committee to be set up. The three representatives were David Basnett, Rodney Bickerstaffe and Moss Evans, but only Basnett attended regularly.

42. The Campaign Strategy Committee was established on 15/11/83. It had twenty-five members plus two secretaries. Trade union leaders were given four places but they rarely attended.

43. On the fifteen-strong Leader's Campaign Committee, there were two union leaders, Ron Todd and John Edmunds, and three NEC trade unionists, Tony Clarke, Tom Sawyer and Diana Jeuda from the Women's Section.

44. This had no union representation. It consisted of the General Secretary, the three Directors, of Policy Development, Organisation, and Campaigns and Communication, two of the Leader's personal advisers, Charles Clarke and Patricia Hewitt, and the PLP policy co-ordinator, Robin Cook (until November 1986) and then Bryan Gould.

14

Policymaking: the key issues

THE ANALYSIS

Policy reviews – even wide-ranging policy reviews – are nothing new in the Labour Party. In a sense, the exercise has been carried on in every period of Opposition. What was remarkable about the period after 1979 was the breadth of the reappraisal. Indeed, for the first time since the formulation of the 1918 programme, virtually the entire field of policymaking was opened up for discussion.

In 1979, the Left (in control of the NEC for the first time in a period when Labour was moving from Government to Opposition) made an attempt to formulate binding commitments over the whole field of policy and in 1982 there was actually a 276-page programme. In 1979 also, the Thatcher Government took its first steps towards breaking the progressive ratchet of modern history, thus opening up over the next eight years a wide range of policy areas where a consensus had been thought to be well established. By 1985, competing views of the character of future industrial relations legislation and of the Party's obligation to preserve legislative balloting rights within the unions were involving the Party Leadership in highly sensitive political interventions. At the same time, new political forces of consumerism, feminism and environmentalism were beginning to affect areas where hitherto policy positions were secure.

The consequences of these dynamic forces, inside and outside the Party, were that Party–union policymaking suddenly broadened its scope and almost every area was subject to re-evaluation. Closed areas were opened, 'settled' questions were reopened and new policy departures began. Further, some sharp shifts in strategic situations – the loss of Left control over the NEC in 1981/2, the electing of a new Parliamentary leadership in 1983 and the defeat of the Miners' Strike in 1985 – were followed by new alignments around several key policy issues. For the student of politics, the opportunities this provides for policy analysis are considerable. On the other hand, the sheer scope of union involvement and labyrinthine and lengthy policymaking make for special problems of comprehension and a measure of selectivity.

In this chapter there follows an analysis of twelve crucial policy areas involving protracted conflict, variations in priority and in most cases major shifts of policy. The cases are broken at the General Election of 1983 although, as will be indicated, other experiences, on occasion, caused sharper changes. The scope and importance of these issue-areas as a representation of Party–union policymaking is, I think, self-evident but there are some initial qualifications to be made.

The first concerns the exclusion of the area of local government policy. It is an area of policymaking where local Labour Groups jealously guarded their own prerogatives from both the PLP leadership and the unions. Nationally, in a sense until the early 1980s, the Party did not have a local government policy at all. However, in the period after 1979, a range of developments began to interlink local and national policymaking in a complicated way. The policy area cannot be dealt with in full here but the most important conflict has to be noted. The crucial question which exercised local authority leaders, the Parliamentary leadership and the many unions with members in Local Government, was how to respond to punitive Conservative Government measures – particularly 'rate capping'. Although unions were now more represented on the Party's Local Government Committee, the 1984 strategy of non-declaration of a rate was constructed independently by local authority leaders. Most unions went along with it in spite of misgivings about the potential threat to jobs and salaries, until in the end, it was clear that the strategy was not working.[1] Then a crisis developed when the Liverpool Council formally issued redundancy notices to its 31,000 employees. A major hardening of opinion took place within the unions against the Liverpool Council policy and against Militant Tendency, which was influential in Liverpool. The union leadership was to prove ineffective in determining the policies of the Liverpool Council but capable of encouraging and supporting the disciplinary measures at national level which led to massive majorities at the 1986 Party Conference in favour of the expulsion of Liverpool's Militant leaders from the Party.

The second qualification is that we need at least to be aware of the existence of suppressed conflict. It is a very difficult assessment to make but it is clear, in general terms, that there were some issues where a union-backed consensus was so broad-based that the opportunity for open policy debate was restricted and pursuing change not worth the effort. Sunday trading was probably one such example, where supporters of reform tended simply to keep their heads down when the USDAW-TGWU case was given full support. Further, as we shall note, though the Parliamentary leadership was able to make a historic advance into hitherto 'closed areas' of the relationship in pursuit of balloting arrangements there is still a question to be raised of how far the Parliamentary leadership might have sought to push other changes were the 'rules' defending union 'freedom' not so heavily policed.

Thirdly, the case studies do not cover areas which were undoubtedly priorities but were also consensual between the Party and the unions and therefore not normally subject to overt conflict. In this period particularly, there was agreement in defending the achievements of the post-war Labour Government. This agreement coincided with the direct interests of many public sector workers, but there was always a value dimension to these objectives. As the Conservative Government increasingly offended against social justice, so the TUC, the NEC and the Front Bench moved together in its defence, healing the rift that had opened up in some areas when Labour was in Government. In the fields of health, social security and education there was broad agreement on funding and fundamentals and only occasional areas of serious tension (see p. 425) on the married man's tax allowance and pp. 444–6 on training). And there was specific agreement that the immediate social justice priorities for the next Labour Government would be, as before, the incomes of pensioners, families with children, and the long-term unemployed.

Moreover, although 'Home Office issues' are missing here, and at NEC level were generally left to the politicians for detailed policymaking, the unions were part of a changing consensus on key issues and could be a significant force in influencing some of the major decisions – most notably in the continuing rejection of a Bill of Rights. Some of the unions had long been linked to the civil liberties lobby and shared a growing concern over, for example, freedom of information, the accountability of the security services, the scope of Crown immunity, press freedom and contempt of court, and public order restrictions on peaceful protest. To this agenda in the 1980s was added, alongside women's issues, a new concern for the rights of minority groups, particularly the disabled, members of the ethnic communities, and lesbians and gays. Of course, concern was one thing, practice and push was another. Some very bitter divisions opened up in relation to the presentation and emphasis of policy concerning the latter two categories – differences which at local level tended to follow class and geographical contours. But it is important to note that over lesbian and gay rights, a supportive union majority at the Party Conference was, in the end, a significant asset in the hands of those attempting to exert pressure upon Labour's political leadership.

Finally, these issues remind the reader also that in setting up a counterpoint of the unions and the Party, we abstract from a context in which a variety of other movements, lobbies and forces are in play, shaping policy. In both the industrial and the political wings, the various meetings and committees provided a terrain on which a plurality of political groups attempted to exert influence. And the whole process was subject, after 1983, to a growing sensitivity of the Parliamentary leadership to the 'opinion formers' in the mass media, to the financial reactions of the City on economic and industrial policy and, over defence policy, to pressure from the US Government.

These qualifications having been made, what is presented here gives us the basis of a broad and detailed appraisal of the unions' role in Labour Party policymaking during a period of extraordinary change in procedures, processes and power relations. Too often this relationship was typified in terms of simply industrial relations policy or whatever topic of high public interest – such as unilateral nuclear disarmament – came into the media gaze. But the unions and the Labour Party were locked in a policy relationship covering a much broader canvas. As we follow developments in these policy areas, it will become apparent that there were significant variations in power relations area by area. Central to these variations was the role played by union leaders and union representatives, and the priority given by them to the different issues.

MACRO-ECONOMIC POLICY

When the Labour Party moved back into Opposition after 1979, it underwent an initial adjustment of economic and industrial policy, much as had happened in the period after 1970. The NEC and the TUC, whose formal policy positions had much in common, found means to reach a new policy accommodation which had few overt points of tension.

At the Party Conferences of 1979 and 1980 there was an immediate attempt by some of the unions (mainly but not exclusively on the Left) to ensure that the Party's economic policy now embraced the Alternative Economic Strategy (see Chapter 6, pp. 169–70). But there was also a significant move by the GMWU to push the discussion into the Liaison Committee (where the trade union Left was weaker), where a dialogue could take place with the Front Bench, and where the TUC's own economic expertise could be brought to bear. In general, most unions (Left and Right) were neither resourced nor motivated to follow through the detailed exploration of macro-economic policy. By contrast, the TUC's Economic Department was annually the source of three major economic statements which became the basis for representations to Government and for public campaigning.

The Budget Statement, the Economic Review and the Commentary on the Autumn Statement became part of Liaison Committee discussions, thus ensuring that there was always a TUC contribution to the dialogue with the Party on key aspects of macro-economic policy. In addition, the TUC after 1982 also developed the use of the Treasury's economic model to test the policies contained in its economic packages. This, too, became part of the dialogue with the Party. Nevertheless, as in the past, TUC officials were prone to see the TUC's primary role as an influence on Government rather than on the Party. Even when the TUC considered itself to have a very strong case, there was a deep reluctance to attempt any imposition of economic policy on the Parliamentary leadership.

With the Home Policy Committee of the NEC chaired by Tony Benn and the Left increasing its strength on the NEC in 1979 and 1980, the committee became very assertive. In these new circumstances, the Party and the TUC deepened their commitment to the expansion of demand and to increased public expenditure. The TUC now shifted emphasis over import controls to a more general planned growth of trade. Both centres accepted the need for exchange controls and a target was established for the reduction of unemployment to below one million within five years of a Labour Government taking office. There would be an egalitarian taxation policy involving a Wealth Tax at the level agreed on the Liaison Committee in 1978.

The Labour Front Bench, which had so strongly contested or qualified these policies in the final years of the Labour Government, now found itself more poorly serviced and in a much less authoritative position to fend them off, particularly as the TUC role had shifted. The adjustment was particularly difficult for the old Treasury team and at various times Healey made known his reservations about the target for unemployment, the trade policy and exchange controls.

However, with the election of Michael Foot as new Leader, there was the beginning of a new accommodation. Foot accepted the Party's target for unemployment and he appointed Shore, a Keynesian opponent of the public expenditure cuts of 1976, to replace Healey as Shadow Chancellor. Nevertheless, there was something of a stand-off on some aspects of macro-economic policy, with the NEC Left reluctant to explore the discussion of inflation and the PLP economic team reluctant to move into detailed discussion of trade and exchange controls.

The stalemate was partially broken after October 1981 when the Left lost its absolute dominance over the NEC and was in a weaker position to take initiatives. At the same time, Shore was developing his links with the Rightwing unions and his differences from the Left over macro-economic strategy were becoming clearer. Shore now felt he was strong enough and had sufficient space to take his own initiatives.

In 1982, this took the form of an *Alternative Budget*, then of a *Programme for Recovery*. These were produced without reference to the NEC and with little reference to the Shadow Cabinet either. They were drawn up with an eye to the problem of raising the incomes policy question outside normal union-influenced channels (see below pp. 427). In spite of their unorthodox origins, it was the Shore *Programme for Recovery* which, together with the TUC's draft *Economic Review*, became the basis of Liaison Committee discussions on the medium term policy for the economy. The TUC, which had partially adjusted to development in the Party after 1979, now partially adjusted to the new centre of political initiative – or at least kept quiet about any reservations.

The Shore programme justified itself as 'within the framework of the Party's economic policy' and occasionally the Front Bench would refer to it as '*the* Alternative Economic Strategy'. Its main continuity involved increasing public expenditure as a means of reflating the economy, accepting the target for reducing unemployment, and supporting exchange controls. But there was a radical change of emphasis over devaluation of the pound. This became central to the strategy and eventually went into the Manifesto under 'Safeguards for Expansion'. Import controls, which had been central to the AES since 1975, were heavily downgraded in importance.

Post 1983

In a dramatically new political context, the Shadow Chancellor's post was taken by the Deputy Leader, Roy Hattersley. Where the previous occupants had developed policy independently of the Party's formal process and secured late adjustments to official policy, Hattersley was in a commanding position from the very first. By packing the Jobs and Industry Joint Committee with sympathetic co-optees, he was able to secure an immediately favourable position. Individual unions made little attempt to set an agenda at the Party Conference. As for the TUC, its leadership stepped back more clearly to leave initiation of Party policy in the hands of the Parliamentary leadership.

In the dialogue between the Front Bench and the Neddy Six, the TUC was receptive to the new emphasis on a more cautious expansion of demand and a phased growth of public expenditure. It is said also to have played an important technical role in working through the consequences of particular economic policies. But each of the major initiatives on economic policy was taken by the Front Bench, including the capital repatriation scheme, the 'one million jobs' target, and the £6 billion reflation figure. Exchange controls disappeared in 1985 and the import controls policy was finally shelved in 1986.

As the position of the Parliamentary leadership strengthened in the run-up to the 1987 General Election, so their ability to determine outcomes increased. One classic example of this was the proposal for a cut in employers' National Insurance contributions; it had been proposed by Hattersley earlier but rejected by the NEC, yet it reappeared and was approved in Labour's *New Jobs for Britain* document. And it was a significant reflection of the position of the Parliamentary leadership at this stage in policymaking that this policy document, concerned with the creation of Labour's one million jobs, should have been produced almost entirely under the control of the Front bench, with Bryan Gould (who was not a member of the NEC) putting together the final version.

On major taxation policy questions, although the TUC was kept fully in touch, it was the Parliamentary leadership again which took the initiatives. The scale of taxation of the rich – raising £3.6 billion from the top 5 per cent – was the product of discussions between Roy Hattersley and Michael Meacher (Front Bench Spokesperson on Health and Social Security). It was Hattersley who declared that there would be no increase in the basic rate of taxation – the Party had officially made no commitment. And although a Wealth Tax was pushed into the Manifesto at the final NEC meeting, its operation was as defined by the Shadow Chancellor.

One taxation problem where the TUC did keep a more active involvement was the thorny question of the abolition of the married man's tax allowance, affecting as it did the income of many members of TUC unions. The TUC, although in favour of independent taxation for men and women and of an increase in child benefits, was deeply conscious that the abolition of the married man's tax allowance amounted to a 'wage cut'. Partly as a result of the TUC's intervention (although with strong support from the Shadow Chancellor), the 1983 Manifesto had a longer time-scale of phasing out than either the 1982 Programme or the draft Campaign Document.[2]

In 1986, the TUC, strongly represented in the discussions which led up to the document *Social Security and Taxation*, made it clear that they expected that the phasing out of the married man's tax allowance in favour of increased child benefit would be accompanied by a reduced rate band of taxation, more progressive National Insurance contributions and special provision for childless working class couples. The TUC's caution over the potential reaction of trade unionists was shared by the Shadow Chancellor's office in terms of likely electoral reactions. There are varying interpretations of how and why the 1987 Manifesto (which included the commitment to increase child benefit) made no mention of the abolition or phasing out of the tax allowance, thus promulgating a small mid-campaign crisis as the Conservatives homed in on the taxation arithmetic, but it is clear that so sensitive was the issue that nobody – particularly the unions – felt like raising a red alert about its absence.

INFLATION, INCOMES POLICY AND STATUTORY MINIMUM WAGE

Whereas on macro-economic policy the TUC and the unions were generally flexible and accommodating in major switches of policy, on issues relating to incomes and collective bargaining the room for manœuvre was much reduced and the boundaries imposed by the unions on policy initiatives were much tighter.

The central policy problem, as Dennis Healey told the 1982 Labour Party Conference, was to find a way of controlling inflation which left real scope for collective bargaining.[3] Seeking the solution to this problem was to be a continuous but mainly covert project of the period in Opposition after 1979 – made all the more difficult by harsh memories of 'the winter of discontent' and deep differences over the lessons to be drawn from that crisis. As with previous periods of Labour in Opposition, the anti-incomes policy tendency had been strengthened, the loyalism which had reinforced adherence had been dissipated, and union leaders now had a wary eye on the Conservative Government in terms of what they were prepared to agree to within the Party.

The result was an impasse, not only at committee level but within the larger forums of the Movement. The stalemate was illustrated all too clearly at the 1980 TUC Congress which voted for apparently contradictory motions about future discussion of the issue.[4] Subsequently, while some Front Bench speakers included occasional references to the need for a discussion of incomes policy, the problem in practical terms was how to keep the item on the agenda of NEC and TUC discussion. In this phase, from 1979 to 1981, the initiatives tended to come from the Party office where there was support for a radical socialist incomes policy. Each such initiative was squashed or referred back by the Leftwing majority on the NEC.

A partial way forward through the difficulties came in 1981 when a list of future problems was brought into the Liaison Committee document *Economic Issues Facing the Next Labour Government*. The fact that inflation was such an issue could not be disputed. The issue was approached by TUC and Party staff by utilising terminology used in the 'concordat' of February 1979, *The Economy, the Government and Trade Union Responsibilities*. The need, the new document said, was for a 'national economic assessment' which had 'to embrace such issues as the share of the national income going to profits, to earnings from employment, to rents, to social benefits and to other incomes'. The formulation was cleverly moved into higher case (a National Economic Assessment or NEA) in the final line of the document. In the new planning framework of *Economic Planning and Industrial Democracy* (1982), this became an annual tripartite appraisal.

In *Partners in Rebuilding Britain*, produced in March 1983, the Assessment became the culmination of a yearly cycle of discussions and collective bargaining and the centrepiece of the planning process. The unstated assumption was that greater bargaining power and new responsibilities would produce greater restraint.

Taking it this far involved a development which was in some tension with the continuing decisions of the Congresses and Party Conferences. At the 1982 TUC, a resolution reaffirming support for free collective bargaining was carried while an amendment affirming the position taken on a national economic assessment in *Economic Issues Facing the Next Labour Government* was lost.[5] Similarly, at the Party Conference, a resolution which linked the national economic assessment to 'a socialist social contract' was lost.[6] But in winning acceptance for what was going on in the Liaison Committee, the pro-incomes policy forces were aided by the fact that the unions had established a tradition of not voting against documents consensually agreed at the Committee.

As previously, with Labour seeking to win the election which would take them into Government, there was a last phase attempt to tighten up the definition of the policy. Incomes policy was the hidden subtext of the *Programme for Recovery*, produced by the Treasury team independently of the normal Party–union channels. Its covert function was to bring the issue of incomes policy once more into the open in the context of the 'hard economic choices' indicated by 'the Treasury model'.

The form of the initiative gave the Front Bench advocates of incomes policy a more flexible instrument than the long, slow, cautious evolution of Liaison Committee documents. But, as always with such ventures, it risked the reaction that it was an attempt to 'bounce' the unions, and its process of initiation crossed procedural boundaries in ways that diminished its effectiveness.

Anticipating likely reactions, the document embodied at its inception an accommodation to the unions in the form of an explicit rejection of a statutory incomes policy – a shift on the part of Shore. But as it went through a series of private consultative drafts, it became progressively amended and its more provocative elements increasingly toned down in the light of complaints and representations from union leaders and the TUC. Explicit references to pay norms were removed.

Nevertheless, the final version produced on 23 November still implied the use of the NEA to restrain wage and salary costs.

> ... if we are serious about containing inflation it will be necessary not just to control price rises and offset their impact, but to contain the costs which prompt the increase in prices. In general, two thirds of total costs consist of wage and salary payments.[7]

At the November NEC, the document was defined by the Leader as 'a contribution to discussion',[8] but at a later meeting of the Press and Publicity Committee, both the trade union Right and the political Left ganged up against it and a decision on whether the Party should officially publish the Programme was deferred until after the Party's own Campaign Document had been finalised.[9] It was never published by the Party.

It had been thought on the Front Bench that as the General Election approached, so some of the union General Secretaries would seek to accommodate the Party's electoral need for a form of incomes policy. In spite of doubts expressed within his union, Moss Evans of the Transport Workers, whose cooperation was considered crucial at such times, had accepted the idea of a national economic assessment. But in the end he pre-empted the final version of the Shore document with an attack on pay restraint and repeated his criticism of a 'pay norm'.[10]

With some exceptions, including Terry Duffy of the Engineers, the general trade union position was to make no concession to the Treasury team's initiatives or to the calls coming from other members of the Front Bench. At the Liaison Committee meeting in February 1983, which discussed *Partners in Rebuilding Britain*, it was John Golding from the NEC Right who spoke for the dominant union position in rejecting the imposition of 'norms or fixed limits on pay'.[11] Michael Foot, it must be noticed, played no direct part in pushing the unions and in this respect was an obstacle to the Shadow Chancellor.

When at the final meeting of the NEC and Shadow Cabinet to discuss the Campaign Document (Manifesto) of 1983, Shore again attempted to raise the issue of incomes policy, his strongest open adversaries were Golding and Michael Foot.[12] If anything, the document was strengthened the other way as a result of an initiative from Tony Benn on the Home Policy committee which was supported by the unions. The section on the National Economic Assessment said, 'we will take a view on what changes in costs and prices would be compatible with our economic and social objectives, and help to ensure that our plan for expansion is not undermined by inflation'. But Benn added, 'We will not, however, return to the old policies of government-imposed wage restraint.'[13]

The necessary balance between consumption and investment would, it was argued, be struck within the collective bargaining process itself, thus rendering governmental constraints unnecessary.[14] It was a position in harmony with trade union traditions and it was the one that Shore had to represent at the 1983 General Election, even though for him there was a gaping hole where an essential incomes policy should be.

Post 1983

The new 'Dream Ticket' leadership was determined to secure a clearer and tighter understanding on pay with the unions than had been achieved in 1983. In his first public speech, the new Shadow Chancellor, Hattersley, made clear his determination to seek a new voluntary agreement with the unions on pay *before* the next General Election.[15] In the next eighteen months there was a steady trickle of such speeches, occasionally by Kinnock, more often by the Deputy Leader.

The speeches had little immediate impact upon policy. Early attempts in November and December 1984 to use the Party's new Jobs and Industry Joint Committee to raise the question of inflation and incomes policy were stalled by union insistence that this issue must be taken to the Liaison Committee. Only the unions could say what was deliverable. At that Committee in December, it was forcefully insisted by the union leaders that at a time when the unions were preparing to campaign in defence of political funds, internal divisions over wage restraint would not be helpful.[16] In line with this, new careful management by the unions ensured that there would be no debate on incomes or the National Economic Assessment at the TUC or Labour Party Conferences of 1984. Front Benchers who attempted to push the issue into the political process were told to 'discuss it informally with the TUC'.

By the summer of 1985, the balance of forces on this question appeared to be going through a major, even a seismic, transformation. The set-back for the miners diminished union emphasis on industrial militancy and refocused trade union attention on the need to elect a Labour Government which would work in harmony with the unions. Looking forward to the new partnership, both Kinnock and Hattersley were explicit in seeking to reopen the question of incomes.[17]

Within the TUC, the senior officers and the policy staff, working closely with the Leader's Office and the Shadow Chancellor's advisers, were urgently looking for 'the X factor' which would open up the discussion and extend the room for manœuvre. That factor was thought by some on both wings to be the question of low pay and the statutory minimum wage necessary to implement it.

For years the tradition of free collective bargaining and anxiety over a possible undermining of union functions had been major obstacles to the Movement's support for a statutory minimum wage. A powerful alliance of Leftwing unions, including the TGWU and Rightwing unions like the AUEW and EETPU, had blocked exploration of the policy on the TUC General Council – where its strongest supporter was NUPE. In the political wing, the policy had some strong adherents including the then Party Leader, Michael Foot, but there was a worry that the policy might prove an inflationary lever as unions attempted to preserve differentials and it was virtually at the last minute (in March of 1983) that, on the initiative of NUPE's Tom Sawyer, a loose commitment to open discussions with the TUC on a Statutory Minimum Wage was pushed into the Party's Campaign Document.

The sheer scale of the Government's attack on existing fair wages mechanisms opened up the space for a more comprehensive discussion of the issue in 1984 and, with trade unions weakened in their industrial role, there was a new willingness to consider a statutory element in relation to low pay. The shift of position of the GMWU towards the NUPE camp strengthened support for the policy in the TUC. The commitment of Hattersley to a Statutory Minimum Wage strengthened the position in the Party.

At the same time, changes in the leadership of the Transport Workers seemed to indicate more amenability over the broader issue of incomes policy. The new General Secretary, Ron Todd, was from the Left but anxious to co-operate with Labour's Leadership. His union conference speech appeared to indicate that a National Economic Assessment was acceptable providing that it went 'much wider than pay policy' and providing that the planning of incomes involved 'active consent'.[18]

Background discussions on Party policymaking moved forward with a close eye on movements in the TGWU. Thus, Kinnock quoted Todd's 1985 speech to his conference at the launch of *A New Partnership: A New Britain* as embodying 'the best definition available of how the next Labour Government would approach the issue of incomes policy.'[19] Although the document made clear that 'statutory norms and government imposed wage restraint offer no solutions', it talked of a National Economic Summit drawing up a wide-ranging agreement, and planning ahead to cover all aspects of economic development including the distribution of income and wealth. More explicitly, Hattersley, accepting at the Party Conference the resolution on low pay and the statutory minimum wage, connected it with joint union and Government planning of the economy and linked that with the Todd statement[20] (but only after some judicious agenda management had taken the Statutory Minimum Wage out of the section on 'Incomes Policy' and put it under 'Low Pay').

Through the Liaison Committee, during the next year the Party and the unions forged an agreement, *Low Pay: Policies and Priorities* – but it required some hard bargaining and some adroit work by the TUC staff to create a majority at the Congress. It still did not carry the TGWU and there were forces on the Right as well as the Left of the trade union movement which were deeply suspicious of the hidden agenda. The EETPU leadership, voice of the skilled craftsman, proud of status and differentials, made it clear that the union did not approve of an incomes policy based on a statutory minimum wage.[21] Theirs was a powerful call for free collective bargaining – a call echoed from the industrial Left, led, as so often before, by TASS.

Nevertheless, there was much in the TUC debate on minimum wage to encourage the political leadership. In urging support for the new policy, Norman Willis had noted that the TUC and the future Labour Government would have to examine the effects on inflation and employment. Ron Todd, though opposing the policy on the grounds that it could undermine union organisation, had argued that the statutory minimum wage need not have an uncontrollable knock-on effect on jobs and inflation.[22] Such encouragement was all the more necessary when it became obvious that Government Ministers were waiting to zoom in on this vulnerable point.[23]

It was expected that the usual pre-election attempt would be made now to tighten up the Party's policy. Accordingly, by agreement between the Shadow Chancellor and the TUC, the National Economic Assessment was put on the agenda for the November Liaison Committee meeting. The stage was set for a final attempt at a pre-election agreement.

At this point, the intervention of the Transport Workers' General Secretary was probably crucial. Ron Todd was still anxious to be supportive – even to the point of antagonising some on his Left within the union, but he was also determined not to promise what he could not deliver. In the Hitachi Lecture on 18 November, Todd argued that collective bargaining was now 'too decentralised, too close to the point of production, too democratic in the broadest sense of the term, to be amenable to the sort of simple wage restraint arithmetic which had been the traditional basis of incomes policies in this country'.[24]

Thereupon, the Parliamentary leadership, which had been hoping that Todd or some other senior union leader would pick up and run much further with the issue, now changed tack and the National Economic Assessment was taken off the Liaison Committee Agenda. Confident of victory, the Leadership believed that there was no point in empty gestures which would collapse to the discredit of a Labour Government. Even the electoral mileage of such an agreement was now less than it had been for the past quarter of a century given the diminished industrial power of the unions and the new emphasis on the 'Presidential' independence of a Labour Prime Minister. Hattersley's economic advisers had always been divided on the need for, and the specificity of, an incomes policy. Hattersley himself had argued that any bargain 'which required the Government to introduce policies which it knew to be wrong and ... obliged unions in return to swallow policies they regarded as undesirable would be disastrous'.[25] The hunt for a new incomes policy was, in effect, called off.

Not surprisingly, the policy of a statutory minimum wage did not loom very large in the campaigning of 1987. This became the source not of unity but of acute tension with those unions like NUPE which had long pushed the concept.

There was a last ditch attempt to rescue an incomes policy of a sort, and it came from the TUC officials. Both before and during the private meetings with the Neddy Six union leaders in early 1987, the Party Leadership was offered a formula which implied an incomes policy. Ironically, the Party Leadership now turned it down as undeliverable. What good would it be to a Labour Government?

Receptivity by the TUC did help to ensure that *Work to Win* was stronger than the 1982 *Partners in Rebuilding Britain* document in terms of general agreement on central guidance. The National Economic Assessment would not only be monitoring inflation (it said twice) but would also be identifying 'the action which must be taken by government, employers and trade unions'. This stress on 'concerted action' was carried over into the Manifesto. But it was nothing like the specific commitment that had been hoped for in 1983.

INDUSTRIAL POLICY AND INDUSTRIAL DEMOCRACY

The reconciliation of national economic planning and industrial democracy had been recognised in discussions on the Left since the mid-1960s to be a central problem of socialist policy. What was new in the late 1970s was that, at senior levels within the TUC and among some union leaders, the problem began to be seen as a practical question as they took on board their experiences of previous Labour Governments and the critique mounted by some of the Trades Councils of Labour's industrial policy.

Further, it was now accepted that the TUC and union leaders had to be fully integrated into the Party's process of industrial policymaking in a way in which they had not been in the last period of Opposition when 'planning agreements' had become party policy with minimal commitment from many union leaders (see Chapter 6, p. 173). Thus followed the idea of a major new detailed policy exercise to be carried out at the highest levels of the Movement through a subcommittee of the Liaison Committee which would draw members from the PLP, the NEC and the TUC.

This initiative was generally supported on all sides, albeit with private hesitation by some of the NEC who feared that there might be a hidden agenda which involved linking planning to incomes (as indeed, from some, there was), and that there might be a watering-down of existing Party policy (see Chapter 13, p. 407).

The conduct of this policy process cannot be understood outside its wider political context. The subcommittee held its first meeting only two days after the momentous Special Conference of 24 January 1981 which agreed a new procedure for electing the Party Leader and precipitated the defection of the Social Democrats. Discussions on the subcommittee went parallel to the bitter fight for the Deputy Leadership, and the final stages of policy agreement ran parallel to efforts made after the 'peace' Conference at Bishop's Stortford to restrain the intra-party battle.

The effect of these contextual factors was to draw Party and union attention away from this policy process at its formative stage, thus allowing the policy staff of the Party and TUC to play a more than usually influential role. Further, a strong desire to downplay the factional infighting that was all-encompassing within the Party led to positive attempts at co-operation and the avoidance of some confrontations which might otherwise have occurred. Add to this the fact that the complicated framework required a heavy emphasis on specialist knowledge and we are left with a major uncertainty. Although in the latter stages of the subcommittee's work some of the union leaders became very enthusiastic about the new policy, it remains a matter of doubt how far, in the end, the majority of them were committed to it.

The new policy envisaged a comprehensive planning framework focused around a new Department of Economic and Industrial Planning and a tripartite national Planning Council chaired by a Secretary of State for Planning. There would be sectoral committees, and agreed development plans with leading companies to put the national plan into effect. Integrated within this planning process would be a flexible process of industrial democracy based on trade union machinery with new rights of information, consultation and representation. The consultative and representational rights could be triggered at various stages, with the workers, through their unions, determining the pace of progress.

Behind the agreement on the overall structure, however, were a range of policy problems, some of which were never fully resolved. On the Left – particularly from the NEC – there was dissatisfaction about the various inducements involved in securing Development Plans from companies. These 'encouragements' were seen by Benn and Heffer as insufficient to induce compliance with national planning. But neither the TUC nor the PLP side saw 'coercion' as practical.

Some of the trade unions had specific misgivings. In particular, there were initially proposals for the participation of multi-union shop stewards' committees within major corporations but in the end this question was treated only in very general terms as it trod too near the toes of major union sensitivities and existing structures – particularly in the case of the AUEW.

Regional planning also produced a problem. Though, under prompting from the Scottish and Wales TUC, the central body had for years supported devolution to elected assemblies in Scotland and Wales, the TUC wanted the main levers of economic power to remain at UK level. In the English regions, it was strongly in favour of appointed tripartite bodies reporting to the national Ministry. This position came under attack from two sources: from the PLP, where the Regional spokesperson, John Prescott, had developed his own plans for democratic regional assemblies, and from the regional consultative conferences, where there was considerable opposition to the creation of *appointed* bodies. Prescott's territorial intervention on this issue at the consultative conferences moved into a political debate which evoked many tensions. On the surface, the argument was about democracy and practicability and about equality and viability. In practice, it was also about the tensions between regions and centres in the national union hierarchies, about the differing regionalist perspectives of North and South trade unionism, and about a challenge to the TUC's Whitehall focus and its centralist preoccupation with NEDC tripartism. From the TUC there was an unusual digging in of heels. In consequence, in the *Partners* document, the issue was fudged behind a commitment to 'flexibility'.[26]

From key figures in the PLP leadership there was considerable concern about the form of the central structure. In particular there were continuing arguments over the power relationship within the new Planning Institutions – particularly the Planning Council and the new Department of Economic Planning – and between the new Department and the Treasury. In general, the TUC position was for a strengthening of the Council *vis-à-vis* the Department and the Department *vis-à-vis* the Treasury. Shore, the Shadow Chancellor, favoured the reverse.

On the first relationship, the end result of negotiations was an element of power sharing rather than the total supremacy of the Ministry. On the second relationship, a final insertion of Paragraph 77 ensured Treasury control.

These issues apart, many on the Front bench had wider misgivings involving both the scope of trade union involvement and their preparedness for such a role (a worry shared within the TUC by Len Murray himself). Privately, some were critical of the complexity of the edifice which had been created on paper but which would have to be implemented in practice in Government. Nevertheless, at the Liaison Committee on 21 March 1983, the Joint Secretaries presented a summary of the main proposals agreed with Lord Wedderburn, the TUC Labour Law adviser, and Merlyn Rees, the Front Bench Industry and Employment Coordinator, which, it was agreed, would form the basis of a draft Bill and 'minimise delay once a Labour Government comes to office'.[27]

Post 1983

This detailed policy document was given little attention during the General Election of 1983 due, in no small part, to the lack of commitment of the Front Bench to its major provisions. However, it remained as 'party policy' for some time after 1983, reaffirmed in both 1984 and 1985 Liaison Committee documents, and formed the basis of an unofficial document produced by the new Shadow Secretary for Employment, John Prescott, in 1985 – *Planning for Full Employment*. In this document, the Treasury role as the central economic department was once again undermined to the benefit of a new Department of Economic and Industrial Planning.

Yet the dominance of this perspective was precarious and was being undermined by changes at several levels of the Movement. In the Shadow Cabinet, Roy Hattersley was antagonistic to this scale of industrial intervention and the Trade and Industry spokesperson, John Smith, pragmatic rather than committed to the established policy. Interest in industrial democracy was much weaker now than in the previous decade and the TUC's own willingness to get involved diminished accordingly. In terms of intellectual and mood currents of the time, one can discern the growing acceptance of Len Murray's 1982 thesis that unions were neither ready nor resourced for extensive industrial democracy functions. Less obvious, but certainly there on the Party side, was a growing awareness of the disturbing implications of the management crisis at Walworth Road (see Chapter 19), and a new consciousness in local government of the need to encourage management expertise.

In the 1986 TUC–Labour Party document, *People at Work: New Rights and Responsibilities*, continuity was claimed with the 1982 document, but alongside the statutory rights to information, consultation and representation was a series of general statements about the form, size and scope of participation which loosened considerably the structure of 1982. And an element of broadening of the 'single union channel' was introduced, in so far as a ballot of the workforce would be used in claiming new representational rights.

At the same time, a subcommittee of the Party's Jobs and Industry Joint Committee (chaired by John Prescott) was also examining planning and industrial democracy. But its rough draft was promptly killed off by a wide range of forces within Party headquarters and the Shadow Cabinet. The important point was that the trade unions and the TUC simply stood aside and let it die. Neither planning nor industrial democracy were priority goals by this stage, if they had been in 1982. In the end, a brief and non-committal conference document – *The Party of Production* – was drafted by the Policy Director, Geoff Bish, in consultation with the Industry spokesperson, John Smith.

In the immediate aftermath of the Conference, there was an attempt from supporters of the 1982 policy to push the whole question onto the agenda of the Liaison Committee, but the Kinnock–Hattersley–Smith team wanted it formulated by the Party's Jobs and Industry Joint Committee and the TUC made no attempt to reclaim it. Indeed, the only TUC contribution of any significance was again a defence of its traditional tripartism – a determined resistance to the idea of widening the composition of NEDC to include regional authorities. Here the TUC felt so strongly that the issue was taken to meetings between the Neddy Six and Labour's leaders and a watered-down formula put in the final version.

What emerged as *New Industrial Strength for Britain* was a pale shadow of the 1982 document. The focus was on rebuilding industry with a strong, efficient manufacturing base and a national strategy spearheaded by a strengthened Department of Trade and Industry. There would be increased investment facilitated by an industrial investment bank, a major expansion of research and development, improved education and training and a special emphasis on regional development. But the national planning structure of 1982 was either loosened or abandoned, and only at the last minute was a reference to the industrial democracy proposals of the 1986 statement inserted in the final draft. Partnership was now portrayed as a relationship between public and private sectors and within industry. The National Economic Assessment and National Economic Summit were broad social forums. As for the trade unions, they now warranted only two passing references in the entire document – a massive transformation of their position.

REPEAL AND REPLACEMENT OF INDUSTRIAL RELATIONS LEGISLATION

From one perspective, the unions' position on the Conservative Government's legislation was no different from that held since the inception of the Labour Party. Government interference in union internal affairs was unacceptable. The shift of legal power benefiting the employers was equally unacceptable. And the Labour Party was the political agent through which the rights of labour would be restored. Congress after Congress called for the Labour Party to give a commitment to repeal of the successive pieces of legislation.

Under the surface, the TUC bureaucracy was far more circumspect in its responses, aware of internal divisions over state funding for union balloting, sensitive to union membership acceptance of the Conservative Government legislation, and increasingly aware also that a blanket attempt to dictate to the Labour Party the terms of a full repeal and replacement bill – as had happened in 1974 – might saddle the political wing with an electoral albatross.

Thus it was the Party's NEC, then under the control of the Left, which in February 1980 gave a commitment, *unrequested* by the General Council, for the 'complete repeal' of the Conservative Government trade union legislation.[28] This pledge was followed in 1981 by the establishment of an Employment subcommittee which might well have developed a 'repeal and replacement' policy ahead of that of the TUC had not Congress House organised against it, and in October 1981 the Left lost their majority on the NEC.

The TUC's position was slow to evolve and required 'careful consultation' with its affiliates.[29] In October 1982, the General Council welcomed the 1982 Labour Party Conference's reaffirmation of the Party's commitment to repeal the 1980 and 1982 Employment Acts and agreed its own priority programme reviewing trade union objectives for future legislation.[30] It ensured that it was the TUC's Employment Policy and Organisation Committee, not the Party's NEC, which produced the repeal and replacement document *Industrial Disputes and Union Membership Agreements*, which was taken to the Liaison Committee and agreed in March 1983.[31]

This became the basis on which, in *Partners in Rebuilding Britain* (1983), the Party and the unions declared that Labour would 'sweep away the present Government's law'. In the 1983 Manifesto, repeal of the 'Tory legislation on industrial relations' became part of the Emergency Programme for Action.

Post 1983

The extent to which the third instalment of Conservative Government legislation in 1984 interfered in the internal affairs of trade unions, particularly in relation to union government and strike ballots, might in the past have produced a united union response to a fundamental challenge to their autonomy. But in the political conditions of the mid-1980s, this aspect of the 1984 legislation accentuated growing divisions within the Movement about union rights and industrial relations procedures.

At a special TUC consultative conference held in March 1986 to discuss a document on industrial relations legislation, two very significant indicators emerged. First, there was no consensus over the content of the unions' response. The crisis of union 'freedom', which had first appeared in the political wing, had now spread to the unions themselves. Second, although there was no agreement on a shift of emphasis from traditional 'immunities' to rights, the line taken by John Edmunds of the GMWU – that unions must in future focus on workers' rights rather than union immunities – began to set an agenda which eased a similar shift in the political wing.

In particular, it eased the unprecedented intervention of Labour's political leadership in defending the balloting rights of union members.

The battle over ballots was fought over a draft document entitled *People at Work: New Rights and New Responsibilities*. Much of the document was consensual and welcome to the trade unions, focusing on 'a better deal at work' – including health and safety – and a positive role for the law in strengthening 'the rights of workers both as individuals and trade unionists'. There was a strong statement of the virtues of collective organisation and collective strength. And although the section on industrial disputes was brief, it sketched out the need not only to strengthen conciliation but to secure comprehensive legal protection for industrial action and the right of peaceful picketing.

It was the final section which contained the contentious proposals. It covered two sensitive areas of balloting – ballots for union executives and ballots in connection with industrial disputes. On the first, it was agreed from the first draft that there must be secret ballots, but unions were later privately assured that a future Labour Government would not require all such ballots to be direct if unions wished to preserve elements of indirect representation. But the question of ballots in relation to industrial disputes was much harder to deal with.

Kinnock was determined from the first that these balloting rights would not be taken away by a Labour Government. TUC officials were supportive and helpful in trying to produce a viable and acceptable electoral policy. Indeed, at one point in a long and complicated interchange of drafts, a draft from the TUC office heavily influenced by prior discussions with Shadow Ministers and the Leader's Office argued, among other things, that there should be a statutory right for union members to have a secret ballot on decisions relating to industrial action, and that the Certification Officer would 'in the first instance' deal with complaints by union members that the union was not meeting the statutory requirements.

This major break with trade union traditions relating to state interference and with the past 'rules' of the relationship in relation to union internal affairs created considerable anxiety within some of the unions and met with considerable hostility from the Left. In their efforts to save the main thrust of the change, the Parliamentary leadership had to make various adjustments to deal with union qualifications and objections. Some of these changes followed meetings with the Neddy Six. The Certification Officer was replaced by an independent tribunal and later, the Front Bench also agreed that the commitment to ballots was *in relation to* strikes and not necessarily a commitment to hold a ballot *before* a strike,[32] – a provision which would have illegalised a multitude of small spontaneous walk-outs.

But the major conflict arose over the role of the independent tribunal and it came, unusually, at Labour's NEC. With the TUC playing an accommodating role and NEC trade unionists excluded from the Neddy Six discussions, the Home Policy Committee of the NEC became the forum where opposition trade unionists, led by Tom Sawyer of NUPE, sought to remove the statutory element. At one stage it appeared as though they had succeeded, but in a fierce defence of his position, Kinnock seized the initiative back and found a formula for getting the statutory element back into the document.[33] But union sensitivities to legal intervention did make themselves felt in an amendment that 'In common with the procedures relating to other tribunals of this kind, appeal to the ordinary courts will only be permitted on a point of law' [34] (although whether the courts themselves would accept that was another matter).

On this basis, the document went back to the TUC, to the Liaison Committee and the Party Conference. At the TUC, aided by some clever compositing (to indicate that the commitment to ballots applied just to strikes, not all industrial action[35]), and a mood of pre-election unity, the document passed the Congress, as it did the Party Conference, with only a few unions voting against.

PUBLIC OWNERSHIP

Historically, Labour's nationalisation programme was both a reflection of the claims of particular unions in their industries and an expression of the general ideological commitment to an extension of 'common ownership'. Conversely, it was a long established 'rule' of the relationship that neither the Party nor the TUC could be committed to a public ownership policy against the opposition of the relevant union or unions. Thus, whatever the push for public ownership from the political wing, the position of the unions in general, and affected unions in particular, was always a crucial factor in determining what would become policy and what would be implemented.

In general, the period from 1979 to 1983 was not one in which public ownership issues were a priority for the political Left let alone the union Left; the constitutional questions, unilateral nuclear disarmament and the EEC drew most of the attention. And significantly, the unions' experience of rationalisation in the public sector was making claims for nationalisation less attractive than in the early 1970s when it was seen as an appropriate defensive policy against unemployment (as in shipbuilding nationalisation). It was not easy now for unions to persuade their members that it gave more security.

Long-established trade union mandates, particularly in Leftwing-led unions, did commit many of them to extensive public ownership programmes, but debates on public ownership were disappearing from union agendas in this period. Hence, though resolutions at the Party Conference favouring extensive new public ownership programmes could, on occasion, gain substantial support, they were given low or no priority. Only on renationalisation, where from 1979 to 1983 individually affected unions were in favour of reacquiring virtually all the industries and services privatised, did the unions generally express firm commitment.

A lack of union interest in extending public ownership was indicated in the TUC's contribution to Liaison Committee policy formulation. Its first draft of the 1981 joint document *Economic Issues Facing the Next Labour Government* contained no reference to public ownership, and a very general reference was finally inserted only after an amendment from the NEC.[36]

On the proposals made from the Left in the early 1970s, that the Party be committed to the public ownership of twenty-five major companies, union opinion had never been tested at the Party Conference, but in 1982 the NEC accepted a resolution to this effect and it was carried by 3,735,000 votes to 2,873,000.[37] However, the lack of any determined union interest was obvious during the period when the Campaign Document was being written and rewritten. The 1983 Manifesto finally referred to 'a significant public stake ... in ... important sectors as required in the national interest'. No union protested.

Nor was there a strong union reaction to other limitations of the public ownership commitments. What the Manifesto amounted to was mainly a mixture of unspecific options together with traditional positions, some of which were watered down. Resolutions might occasionally pass the Conference staking out new territory – as one did in 1982 calling for the nationalisation of the arms industry under trade union control[38] – but they were never followed up and could be ignored with impunity given the unions' attitude.

Indeed, in at least one important case, the unions involved expressed outright hostility. Although the Party Conference had gone on record in support of public ownership of the banking industry in the early 1970s, a revolt within the unions which had members in the banks caused the unions concerned to establish virtually a veto over the public ownership proposals. Some of this opposition was based on disagreement with the analysis of the relationship between finance and investment, some of it on fear of consumer resistance, but much of it sprung from workers' own fears of nationalisation being followed by rationalisation and a threat to jobs.

When the Financial Institutions Study Group was set up to re-examine the financial system in June 1981, there was even an attempt from one of the unions involved, ASTMS, to prevent its operation on the grounds that the issue was already covered by a TUC committee. In spite of a strong body of opinion on the study group and on the NEC in favour of public ownership of the clearing banks, the bankworkers' veto always had to be anticipated. Consequently, references in the Interim Report of the Study Group in 1982 had to be in parentheses and to take the form of a possible public ownership if the banks failed to make changes in line with wider objectives. In the Manifesto, this became a formulation that 'if they fail to co-operate with us fully on ... reforms in the national interest ... we shall stand ready to take one or more of them into public ownership'.

Only in two cases was the general pattern of union involvement different. In the case of the film industry the Left-led union ACTT was very active in the Arts Study Group, even to the unusual point that their General Secretary attended Group meetings. In this case, the final formula in the Manifesto, 'a British Film authority to extend public ownership into film distribution', was probably much less specific a commitment than the union itself would have favoured. The second case concerned microelectronics, where the TUC Economic Department had developed its own view that 'a public stake' could be a strategically important element in industrial policy, and the NEC took up the signal.

Post 1983

In a pamphlet produced by the Campaign for Labour Party Democracy in 1986, it was recognised that the demand for a major extension of public ownership had been 'dramatically marginalised' and that even support for the *principle* had been eroded at all levels of the movement.[39] But CLPD's explanation for this was couched almost entirely in terms of the behaviour of the political leadership, virtually ignoring what was taking place in the unions. At leadership level there, they were responding to the new sets of pressures.

The TUC's private opinion surveys among union members indicated a marked lack of enthusiasm for publicly-owned enterprises and suggested that there must be a new concern with consumer reactions if public ownership was to be defended. Secondly, the scale of Government privatisation meant that there would be a new problem of financial priorities in the policies of a future Labour Government. As a result, the unions were now more prepared to reorder priorities and explore new measures of public control which would involve limited financial outlays. Thirdly, the increasing union worries about rationalisation, job losses and new managerial styles created new anxieties over *any* major changes in ownership – one way or the other.

What this meant was that there was even less positive interest in a new public ownership programme, and even renationalisation lost priority in some of the affected unions. In transport, for example (see p. 443), a policy of reacquisition, it was considered by officials, 'could not be sold' by the unions to the concerned members and was, in effect, dropped. In the case of British Telecom, there was a push to reacquire but accompanied by an anxious attempt to create a more favourable climate of public opinion. It was on the basis of initiatives taken by the Telecom unions that the TUC in 1983 began its own public ownership policy discussions leading in 1984 to the most extensive consultation exercise it had carried out on the subject of public ownership for many years.

It says much about union priorities that by June 1985 only twelve unions replied to the TUC document and of these, only six were affiliated to the Labour Party (APEX, AUEW (TASS), NCU, NUPE, TGWU and UCW).[40] Though these unions favoured an extension of public ownership, there was a marked reluctance to submit lists of industries for the programme and there was a stress on the need to assess priorities. Particularly striking was the renewed awareness of electoral unpopularity and the preoccupation with building consumer representation.

Other signs of changing union attitudes were evident within the Party. There was the defeat of a resolution for the public ownership of twenty-five top manufacturing companies at the 1985 Labour Party Conference.[41] There was also the failure, the following year, of the campaign waged by CLPD for CLPs and unions to submit resolutions urging a new public ownership programme.

The *Social Ownership* document of 1986 had been foreshadowed by developments within the Party as well as the TUC. A *Future that Works*, in 1984, proclaimed a leading role for public enterprise but asserted also two important principles, now broadly accepted by large sections of Left and Right on the NEC and by the TUC: first, that the initiatives taken by Labour local authorities suggested examples of the inherent diversity of socialist structures – municipal, co-operative or joint ventures with the private sector; secondly, that the Party would not allow its public enterprise priorities to be established by the Conservative Government privatisation programme – a position that could herald either a retreat from public ownership or be the basis of a more powerful strategic policy. Either way, the 1984 statement promised a major study of and document on public and common ownership.

This document might have been taken through the Liaison Committee, which did examine the future of nationalised industries in June 1985 on the basis of a paper from the TUC which summarised and analysed responses by trade unions to the TUC's own consultative document. But there appears to have been an agreement between the TUC, the Party's Research Department and the Front Bench that the Party could be more innovative if freed from direct TUC involvement. Accordingly, the social ownership document was prepared by a subcommittee of the Jobs and Industry Joint Policy Committee. It had a creative secretariat and a variety of co-opted members. There were important 'shadow' meetings of officials involving the TUC, the Party and some of the unions – particularly the GMWU and the Telecom unions – thus discreetly holding together policy developments in the unions and the Party.

The outcome was a document associated with both John Smith from the centre right and David Blunkett from the centre left who had worked co-operatively on it, with some give and take from both sides. In harmony with the TUC's policy development, it produced a new populist model of the firm under social ownership in which consumers had major representation on the board and through a National Consumers Agency. There was to be no shopping list of new industries for full public ownership. The industries mentioned, where new or joint ventures or a public stake might be initiated, bore much similarity with past Party and TUC policy, as did the proposal for a new state holding company, British Enterprise. But unlike in the policy documents of the early 1980s, there was now no general commitment to reacquisition of all industries and services privatised, but instead a range of priorities for reacquiring control short of full public ownership.

In line with the proposals coming from the Telecom unions and discussions with the TUC, the document used British Telecom both as an example of the case for social ownership and as a model of the two-stage strategy for bringing about social ownership.

Little noticed at the time, but ultimately the most contentious of the new proposals, was the advocacy of 'democratic employee share ownership' where, drawing from Swedish experience, the aim was 'to enable individual employees to collectively hold shares'. Such plans, 'built upon the collective traditions of the British labour movement', enabled employees to exercise influence as well as receiving income. The proposal was intended to be attractive to the unions but there was little evidence of enthusiasm for the proposal and the TUC remained uncommitted. It was not surprising, therefore, that the Manifesto made no reference to it but simply committed the Party to an extension of social ownership 'by a variety of means'.

COMPENSATION FOR REACQUISITION

Complicating the argument over reacquisition of privatised assets was the problem of compensation. In the wake of the Thatcher Government's first privatisation proposals, the powerful reaction within the TUC and the Labour Party took the form of support for a policy of renationalisation without any compensation under a future Labour Government. The threat of 'no compensation' was intended as a deterrent both to the Government and to investors, although for some on the Left it was also an expression of a wider principle they would have liked to apply. Within the TUC and within Party headquarters, however, there were strong reservations about the practicalities involved in such a policy and doubts (which proved to be well founded) about its effectiveness as a deterrent.

These reservations were to take on an even greater significance when among the investors in sold-off British Rail hotels was the National Union of Railwaymen. On the issue of compensation, therefore, trade union interests worked in conflicting directions.

Because of this conflict on the trade union side, after discussions on the trade union–Labour Party Liaison Committee in September and October 1979, which further highlighted the numerous problems, the whole question was temporarily laid to rest. Reiteration of the policy at the TUC and the Party Conference reinforced the legitimacy of the policy at the same time as doubts grew in the unions as to its feasibility, and it was quietly accepted in several quarters that there would have to be further study. While this further study was being contemplated, the Party's policy became bogged down in a range of incompatible positions which left it very unclear and led in November 1981 to a damaging public clash in the House of Commons involving Tony Benn and Merlyn Rees, both speaking from Labour's Front Bench.[42]

The unsatisfactory state of Party and union policy led to calls (at a conference of nationalised industry delegates held by the TUC in December 1981) for a new policy initiative.[43] Discussions began on the NEC Home Policy Committee and the General Council's Economic Policy Committee. The NUR, initially a vigorous proponent of 'no compensation', was fast becoming the strongest union opponent of existing policy. Fortuitously, in the spring of 1982, discussions taking place among transport unions (then meeting with a Front Bench spokesperson, John Prescott at the NUR's Frant College) led to renewed discussions of compensation. Eventually a formula was worked out with Prescott , which was taken to lengthy discussions on the Liaison Committee before adoption.

The new policy stipulated that shareholders would be paid exactly what the Government had received for them when denationalisation had taken place. This 'refund' or 'no speculative gain' formula was supported at both the Congress and Party Conference of 1982 and went into the 1983 Manifesto.

Post 1983

Party and union policy towards reacquisition now had to take account of the new scale of shareholding which involved not only many union members but also a spectrum of different types of investors. Some had bought at flotation, some after the speculative gains had been made but soon after flotation, and others had bought over the following years.

In the process of producing the Social Ownership document, the Party's research staff, liaising with research officers of the relevant unions, came up with a new, flexible arrangement. This gave shareholders the option of short or long term investment; those not prepared to commit for long term investment would make no speculative gain. Long term shareholders could choose to benefit either from increases in capital value or from secure guaranteed income.

The success of this formula lay in its ability to reconcile different union policy positions, even between the two Telecom unions, which still had wide internal differences of opinion over compensation. The two unions were able to take almost identical resolutions on these lines to the 1986 Labour Party Conference where they received overwhelming support. This became the Manifesto commitment.

TRANSPORT

Formulating and implementing Party policy in areas where trade union interests clashed was always a problem, even when they were desperately anxious to be helpful to the Party. Nowhere was this more the case than over transport, where there were multiple and often intractable problems; under the 1974–9 Labour Government, these problems had, at one point, led to a six-month inter-union dispute between the TGWU and the NUR over the new inland port project at Didcot.

In Opposition, the problems of achieving policy agreement were complicated by the fact that environmental lobbyists and transport specialists tended to produce a different balance of power on the Party's policy subcommittee than that which existed at the TUC: the Party bias towards rail was widely acknowledged, even among rail unions, and twice after 1979 the Transport Workers had forcefully intervened to contest proposals before the Transport subcommittee on lorries and on the Channel Tunnel, because of their 'anti-road' perspectives.

Consciousness of the acute difficulty of normal policymaking over transport led a member of the Front Bench Transport team, John Prescott (an MP with strong National Union of Seamen connections), to seek new policy arrangements which would get the unions themselves to come to terms with each other – away from the interventions of lobbyists and 'theorists'. In the summer of 1981 he managed to get the three rail unions plus the National Union of Seamen and the TGWU to participate in a private policy conference held at the NUR College; its processes were to be independent of both the Party and the TUC, although each policy department sent representatives. The first policy draft was established by sending out a detailed questionnaire to the unions concerned.

In this way, the unions themselves established the basic agenda. They also provided some of the main initiatives in the ensuing discussions as they sought to reconcile their different interests and perspectives under Prescott's chairmanship. It was, by all accounts, a remarkably cordial and constructive process with concessions from both rail and road unions eased by mutual support for increased expenditure. A second conference agreed the final draft.

The document thus produced was taken formally to the NEC and TUC and thence to the Liaison Committee for approval. Few amendments were made. Though groups and interests excluded from the process, including the non-Party-affiliated Merchant Navy Officers, Labour Party transport specialists and the Labour Party Headquarters Research Department expressed some reservations about the procedure, it was generally considered at the time to be a remarkable advance in securing a trade union consensus.

Post 1983

This time it was not the Front Bench but the NUR which forced the pace – an unusual sequence in this period. The first discussions took place in the Party's Joint Committee but, as in 1982, the unions decided to take the basic formulation to private conferences held at the NUR College and with the NUR providing the administrative support; it was thought that the 1982 precedent had been beneficial all round. This time it would finally go through the Party's procedures alone and not through the Liaison Committee – as part of the general inclination of the TUC to 'let the Party get on with it'. But, as before, the TUC and Party staff were represented at the conferences.

Again the process was very productive in terms of reaching agreement, with the Front bench virtual spectators as the unions reached their accommodations. Nevertheless, there were distinct shifts in union attitudes as the unions themselves took more on board user interests and the need to assist the Party's electoral appeal. This was a point made time and time again at the first conference. It involved a new 'economic realism' about the potential scale of future investment and the need – again with the electorate in mind – not to support proposals which lacked economic credibility.

What was also striking was the way in which the unions retreated from older public ownership and planning solutions as they acknowledged public opinion, the views of their own grass roots members, and the new emphasis of Party policy. It affected many of the policy positions adopted in the 1982 document. Commitments to reacquire BR subsidiaries, to the National Ports Authority, to Sealink and to the National Freight Company, were dropped, so was the National Shipping Organisation. The National Transport Authority – pushed in by the TGWU in 1982 and conceived as part of the comprehensive planning framework set out in *Economic Planning and Industrial Democracy* – became a purely advisory body. The proposed creation of a national bus operation was now, following extensive privatisation, to be 'considered in the light of circumstances'.

From the unions involved, there was confidence that a new document would be quickly finalised by the Party and put to the 1986 Party Conference. Instead, there was a sudden intervention to block the document by the Local Government Committee backed by the Women's Committee and the Policy Directorate on the grounds that its treatment of local authorities and women was still inadequate. As a result, the document was for the moment sidelined and a temporary statement put to the 1986 Conference, much to the annoyance of the transport unions. Eventually, the original document was accepted by the NEC but only after significant rewrites which further emphasised the needs of transport users, particularly women, the elderly and the disabled, and an enhanced role for local communities.

TRAINING

Thus far, what has been shown in the case studies is a TUC whose officials (apart from over national tripartite institutions) were remarkably amenable to change, procedurally accommodating to the Party and sensitive not only to affiliates but also to the needs of Labour's Parliamentary leadership – even when deep-rooted union interests were at stake. Training policy, however, was an area where the TUC's own interests as an institution were centrally involved and its accommodation had some strict boundaries.

Key to the issues raised over training was the role of the Manpower Services Commission – a body conceived initially within the TUC itself in the early 1970s. What had begun as a relatively small tripartite body engaged in skills training and employment services had become, by 1981, a rapidly developing institution with a huge and growing budget and functions which penetrated traditional local authority and educational territory. Among its responsibilities were the Youth Opportunities Programme and the Youth Training Scheme introduced in 1983.

A majority of the TUC leaders, and particularly its officials, retained a robust commitment to the MSC. On one level it was a symbol of the tripartite relationships diminished since the advent of Margaret Thatcher – worth preserving for this reason alone. In addition, privately, the TUC contrasted the dynamism of the MSC as an agency of change with the Department of Education and Science and the range of bureaucratic and vested interests surrounding it. But the TUC also argued that it remained a practical source of TUC influence on public policy and to those who noted the loss of influence since 1979, it was pointed out that prior to the MSC, the TUC had no influence over training policy at all. Quietly the staff of the TUC Organisation and Industrial Relations Department sought to build understandings with the CBI which would affect Government policy.

But there were many in the Party (and sections of the unions, particularly NALGO) who did not share these perspectives. There was a strong Left opposition to tripartism which pointed to the complicity of the TUC in the administration of Government policies; there was a quieter Shadow Ministerial view which sought to protect a future Labour Government Department of Education against the hiving off of functions; there was a local authority criticism of the spread of quango control at the expense of local democracy; and there was an educationalist critique of the narrow conception behind MSC training. Some of these positions overlapped and provided a powerful counterpoint to TUC policy from the NEC and the Front Bench where there was some support for the abolition of the MSC. But to a degree which was unusual, the TUC held a clear and determined set of positions and was prepared at crucial points to throw in its weight to defend them.

Post 1983

Because of TUC sensitivities, it was not until after 1983 that this area of policymaking was fully opened up to Party discussion. Training was taken onto the agenda of the Liaison Committee and it was proposed in 1984 that the TUC and the Party should prepare a joint document.

There was a complex mix of motivations involved in this proposal. A document on training opened up many issues of economic policy from which the Liaison Committee could develop its future work. Critics of the Manpower Services Commission favoured the airing of their views; defenders of the MSC sought a new basis of defence against the 'boycottists'. Others simply thought that this crucial area of policy required a Party response: a new policy document might help to avoid polarisation.

In practice the whole process was beset with difficulties and served to highlight differences rather than resolve them. At the June meeting of the Liaison Committee there was a sharp clash of perspectives on the MSC with the document under fire from a political alliance of the NEC Left and the PLP Right. It was attacked for its uncritical attitude towards the Commission and for other failings, including the lack of reference to the needs of women. The combination of a political Left which disliked tripartism (and in some cases favoured a boycott of the MSC) and the political Right which favoured the MSC being brought within departmental control under a future Labour Government met a strong defence of the MSC from a wide range of union representatives. Eventually, it was agreed that there must be substantial amendment in consultation with the Front Bench spokesperson.

These consultations proved to be on a different basis from that anticipated by the TUC and Party staff. At an *ad hoc* meeting involving representatives of the Front Bench, the Leader's Office, the Party and the TUC, the Shadow Minister demanded a complete redrafting of the document – a complete break with Liaison Committee precedent and likened by some to the Peter Shore initiative of 1982. The TUC staff would have none of it and, under pressure from their Organisation Department, the draft returned to its previous form with its previous commitments, albeit couched in less wholehearted terms. The Liaison Commitee then more or less summarily approved it.

Those who felt thwarted or defeated by the Training document made various attempts to reopen the issue without success. One such attempt came in early 1986, but discussions became deadlocked over reconciling education and training and the result was a lengthy hiatus. Because of this, the Joint Committee on Education and Training did not meet for months. Eventually it was decided that the best way forward would be for a series of private discussions to be held among those on the Front Bench, covering Employment, Education and Training, before involving the TUC. For their part, the TUC were prepared to see a new election policy emerge, if only because the Leader himself was a committed educationalist and interested in a new policy development. But unlike most other areas of policy, they were not prepared to cede ground on institutional fundamentals and were confident that the final result in relation to the MSC would look much in line with the 1984 document.

The process by which this document was drafted was labyrinthine – it was a product of many hands, complicated by the range of those involved and the pressure to get the document out in time. Although the TUC conceded over the idea of a separate Research and Intelligence Unit (they wanted the function of Labour Market Intelligence to be carried out entirely by the MSC), the document also pledged that the MSC's own planning and intelligence role should be bolstered. It was agreed that the final version of *New Skills for Britain* required a rewrite to render it presentable in the light of the innumerable alternations and amendments made during drafting. Nearly one-third of the document, including various policy proposals, disappeared at the hands of the Campaigns and Communication Department. The TUC (which was privately kept informed of the editing) was content that the MSC position had been safeguarded.

NORTHERN IRELAND

The issue of Northern Ireland provoked such a distinctive and complex involvement of union interests that it requires some preliminary contextual points. The Province had always been of deep concern to the unions, some of which had a significant membership there. In 1979, 90 per cent of Northern Ireland trade unionists were in unions affiliated to the British Labour Party and approximately 70,000 were 'contracting in' to pay the political levy. Although there were pockets of Republican sentiment in the NUR and UCATT, the fundamental priority of the unions was to avoid any precipitate or sectarian policy which might divide their members. Critics of this stance often suggested that as a majority of Northern Ireland trade unionists were Protestants, the unions, in effect, stood as a barrier to Irish nationalism.

After April 1979 there were attempts by back-bench MPs and in the constituencies to reopen the Northern Ireland policy discussion. The item was forced on to the agenda of the 1979 Labour Party Conference by a snap vote taken just after lunch, while most trade union delegates were still out of the hall. But in the subsequent debate, two resolutions urging a break with bipartisanship and opposing the continuing British military presence were overwhelmingly defeated.[44] However, the International Committee of the NEC had already proposed that a study group should re-examine the issue and both James Callaghan and Michael Foot added to this commitment during the Party Conference. The Party would make a fresh attempt to find a solution.[45]

Given this remit, the NEC moved to establish the appropriate policy committee. One proposal from the Research Department that the TUC Liaison Committee should set up a tripartite working group which would report to both the Conference and the Congress was quietly killed[46] almost immediately. The TUC did not want to get dragged into policymaking on Northern Ireland and the United Ireland supporters did not want the unions to be able to exercise an immediate veto.

So the NEC put the issue to a new Study Group. As it happened, the preparatory meeting of this Group consisted only of NEC members and was dominated by CLP representatives, with only one trade unionist present and no PLP co-optees. Tony Benn sought to establish that the objective of 'an independent and united Ireland' be in the terms of reference of the Group.[47] He carried that meeting but, after strong union representations, he was overruled by the Home Policy Committee which established that this had *not* been a 'first meeting' of the Study Group and that its terms of reference involved 'all possible solutions to end the bloodshed in Northern Ireland'.[48] The Chair of the Study Group was taken over by Alex Kitson of the Transport Workers.

These shifts reflected the narrowness of NEC majorities on this issue at this time, with each side playing to maximise its position in the committees on which it had sometimes temporary advantage. The final stages of the new policy statement to be presented to the 1981 Conference were dominated by a contest between two positions – a United Ireland perspective and a call for the representation of Labour in Northern Ireland.

Both viewpoints made gains in the draft document. There was a rejection of 'a political veto' by Unionist leaders coupled with a commitment to the 'ultimate unification' of Ireland. But there was also a commitment to 'further consultations' towards 'a class based party of Labour in Northern Ireland' and adherence to 'the consent' of 'the two parts of Ireland' before any unification. This latter position was so unsatisfactory to the supporters of Irish unity that they attempted to refer back the entire document, but were defeated.[49]

However, in a series of amendments, Benn's position was very much strengthened. The word 'ultimate' was removed on the casting vote of the Chair. And an attempt to toughen up the section on Labour Representation by calling for a conference to discuss the formation of a Labour Party in Northern Ireland was cleverly neutralised by Benn and Heffer in a way which had the effect of taking out references to the *British* Labour Party both as the organiser of such a conference and as a focus of organisation. It would, of course, be rooted in the unions and they themselves would decide the form and content – a reassurance to them but also a formula for inactivity given divisions at the grass roots. Again on the casting vote of the Chair, the amendment was carried.[50]

Getting such a conference off the ground proved to be impracticable. Whether a majority in the Northern Ireland unions ever wanted such an initiative is uncertain. In any case, sectarian alignments were reinforced by the emotions generated as a result of the deaths of Republican hunger strikers. Trade union organisations in Northern Ireland became even more frozen in their political positions in the new circumstances, and the Labour Party itself was constrained by its policy document in the form of its own initiatives.

A Liaison Committee was set up in July 1982 but no conference of Northern Ireland Labour Organisations was ever held. 'Unification by consent' went into the Manifesto of 1983 but no mention was made of the representation of Labour.

Post 1983

In the period following the General Election defeat, there was little change in the balance of contending forces within the Party and the unions – certainly as reflected in Party Conference votes. The result was that there was no major shift of policy from 1983 to 1986 and the changes that did take place, including the policy of seeking 'harmonisation' between North and South and accepting the Anglo-Irish Agreement of 1985, were established quietly within the Parliamentary arena. However, the new involvement of the PLP in Joint Policy work, and the general shift of power towards the PLP leadership which had taken place after 1984, now worked towards the advantage of Irish unity sympathisers. Although trade unionists took the Chair of the Joint Policy Committee from 1984 to 1987,[51] the trade union members of the Committee were not particularly active, while strong Irish unity sympathisers were now more heavily represented among PLP representatives who became the source of initiatives seeking to move the Northern Ireland policy further towards a nationalist position.

Still the Research Department–trade union axis provided filter and obstacle. In a practical sense, there was a problem in that the long-serving researcher on this issue left Party employment in 1985 and for a year, in the absence of a replacement, the Committee did not meet. There was another practical problem about the congestion of statements to be put to the 1986 Party Conference and a statement on Northern Ireland was postponed. Some on the PLP side saw this as not unconnected with the position put to the NEC that any statement on Northern Ireland 'should not attempt to depart – in any significant way – from the basic approach to existing policy'.[52]

But a majority on the PLP side now *did* want some departures from existing policy. At one point in early 1987, they had even shifted the draft document to the point where it talked of 'a significant degree of consent' to Irish unification – a major loosening of the previous commitment. But no sooner was this leaked to the press than all the old defensive counters were moved into place.[53] The Leader expressed his alarm; the Research Department–trade union axis moved into operation.

The result was that the document emerged with the offending phrase removed and in its essentials it retained the commitment to a united Ireland but on the basis of 'the consent of a majority of the people of Northern Ireland'. As for the organisation of *a* Labour Party, or of the British Labour Party, in Northern Ireland, there was no mention of the project. Defending this position, Kevin McNamara, the Party's principle spokesperson on Northern Ireland, produced a variant of a familiar perspective:

> The trade unions in Northern Ireland have made it clear that any decision by the Labour Party to organise there would seriously embarrass them. The unions would come under considerable pressure to end their agnosticism on the national question and this would damage their ability to represent workers from both traditions and both sides of the border. As a party founded on the trade union movement, it would be inconceivable for us to take a course of action which might wreck the very institutions on which our Party is based.[54]

It may have overstated the balance of opinion in Northern Ireland trade unions,[55] but it was a powerful argument which always evoked majority support among the unions at the Party Conference.

NUCLEAR ENERGY POLICY

Here again there were powerful union interests at stake. Labour's commitment to nuclear power was longstanding, and underwritten by an alliance of trade unions whose members worked in the industry. The TUC's policy was established by its

Fuel and Power Committee, chaired in this period by Frank Chapple of the Electricians. That union and the Engineers were the most assertive pro-nuclear unions but they were supported also by the two big general unions, each of which had members in the nuclear industry. Opponents of nuclear power clustered around the National Union of Journalists and NUPE and (after Arthur Scargill's election as President in 1982) the NUM, but a substantial body of disinterested trade union opinion at the Party Conference as well as the TUC attached itself to the pro-nuclear rather than the anti-nuclear camp, accepting the case that there should be a balanced development of coal and nuclear power and that nuclear energy was a safe, cost-effective contribution to national energy needs.

On the NEC, on the other hand, by 1979, there was now a substantial grouping which, on political and environmental grounds, was inclined to the phasing out of nuclear power. These now included the ex-Secretary of State for Energy, Tony Benn. Among the research staff, there was also a strong grouping which was more sceptical of the benefits of nuclear power. By contrast, the Energy subcommittee of the NEC, although in 1979 it was chaired by Benn, was heavily dominated by trade union representatives of unions in the industry and PLP sympathisers with nuclear power.

In an effort to put a new perspective upon Party policy and to some extent circumvent the pro-nuclear Energy subcommittee, the NEC seized upon a Conference resolution which called for a 'comprehensive discussion' on energy conservation[56] and reconstituted an Environment Study Group to examine nuclear and other problems.[57] Unlike the Energy subcommittee, it was dominated from the first by anti-nuclear NEC representatives, environmentally concerned co-optees and anti-nuclear union representatives from the NUM (Arthur Scargill) and NUPE (Bernard Dix). The TUC, whose staff attended briefly, took note of the alignment, then ceased to participate; other committee members did the same – a factor which contributed to the relatively low attendances.

For three years, the subcommittee and the study group were locked in conflict as they sought to present their different perspectives on Party policy. The result was something of an impasse with three documents produced, each of which gave a different emphasis depending on which group had been its source.[58] Meanwhile, by 1981, the TUC Fuel and Power Committee's own policy investigations had resulted in a reaffirmation of the traditional pro-nuclear position with the qualification of opposition to an immediate new PWR programme. This became the policy of the Movement and attempts by anti-nuclear advocates to contest the position were easily defeated at both the TUC and the Party Conference.

However, the next year, the NUM, now led by Scargill rather than the pro-nuclear Joe Gormley, renewed the pressure for a more anti-nuclear position and at the 1982 Conference it did manage to win support for the call for a harmless-sounding review of nuclear power and energy requirements and a report to the 1983 Conference.[59] The Environment Study Group, now badly depleted, ploughed on with its own policymaking and eventually produced a gigantic, 80-page draft document in March of 1983.

Its antipathy to nuclear power produced a wall of hostility from the TUC and from a majority of the unions. The draft was rejected in is entirety by the Energy subcommittee who felt that the joint committee should not be proceeded with, so great were the differences between them. The Environment draft was referred back (technically to produce a discussion document which contained both sides of the argument). It was effectively buried.

However, with the Leader's agreement, an emphasis was rescued in the final phase of the Party's Manifesto production. There was a commitment to give 'priority to the coal industry' and, alongside the agreement to stop the Sizewell project and scrap the PWR programme, there was also a note that 'the need for a continuing nuclear programme based on the British AGR will be reassessed when we come into office'. Few doubted which way such a reassessment would go, but it was equivocal enough to disturb the pro-nuclear forces.

Post 1983

Just how strong these forces were in the unions was indicated yet again at the 1984 Labour Party Conference. With the miners the heroes of the hour, and the case for coal central to the argument, the union majority at the Party Conference still refused to support a resolution calling for a freeze on further development of nuclear power – in spite of a recommendation from 'the platform'.[60]

But the Miners' Strike did have a crucial impact in the aftermath of its defeat rather than at its peak. At the 1985 Transport Workers Biennial Delegate Conference, the delegates overturned existing policy and an Executive recommendation by calling for the dismantling of all nuclear power stations – effectively calling for the ending of some members' jobs. As a consequence, the first significant realignment took place on energy policy at the Party Conference. By 3,902,000 votes to 2,408,000, the Conference voted to halt the nuclear power programme and phase out all existing plants.[61]

However, the immediate signs were that the Party Leadership thought the resolution impracticable and simply saw it as a one-off Conference decision. The anti-nuclear lobby thought otherwise and the position of Labour's spokesperson for the environment, John Cunningham, became very sensitive at this time. He was the MP for Copeland, a constituency which included the controversial nuclear plant at Sellafield, and an ardent supporter of nuclear power. Cunningham's position, however, was relatively strong. TUC policy had not changed, the nuclear unions were in angry mood – employment was at risk – and the short debate and clumsy compositing involved in the 1985 resolution gave strong grounds for a counter-attack. In April 1986, with Kinnock's tacit support that counter-attack began with key articles in the Labour press.[62]

Then on 26 April came the disaster at the Soviet nuclear power station at Chernobyl and the Labour leadership was thrown completely off balance. In the immediate radio and television responses there was a lack of consistency and in the debate in the House on 13 May there was a difference of view between Cunningham and the Energy spokesperson, Orme, speaking in the same debate.[63] But under strong Party and public pressure,[64] the Shadow Ministers produced *Britain Needs an Energy Strategy*, which moved to Orme's position that Britain's dependence upon nuclear energy would be reduced, albeit with commitments to the existing reprocessing facilities at Sellafield.[65]

The shift was still not in tune with what was happening in the unions, on the NEC and in the CLPs. All the signs were that a major reordering of priorities was taking place in attitudes within the unions and consequently their mandates at the Party Conference. A strengthened body of opinion within the Party was now in favour of the phasing out of nuclear power entirely and opposed to the introduction of new reprocessing plants at Dounreay and Sellafield (Thorpe).

The Party Leadership now needed an agreed statement from the NEC which could be put to the Annual Conference and hold off the more extreme anti-nuclear versions. Tony Benn and Eric Heffer had already submitted proposals to the NEC for a timetable to achieve 'phasing out'.[66] The politics of producing this statement became increasingly complex as Kinnock sought to balance the various forces involved and to preserve his own intellectual consistency; he himself had a crucial hand in the drafting of *Civil Nuclear Power*, a statement discussed by the NEC at a special Home Policy Subcommittee meeting on 14 July. This statement moved even further away from the pro-nuclear camp with a carefully worded paragraph which talked of 'a diminished and diminishing dependence on nuclear power, in a decades-long process of ending its use – and thus the gradual phasing out of existing nuclear plants'.[67]

The position of the Thorpe reprocessing plant which was under construction was particularly sensitive because it directly affected a range of jobs in Cunningham's own constituency. In the original draft, it was proposed that Labour in Office would not go ahead with the construction of the plant, but eventually, at Kinnock's insistence, the statement was amended to read 'We shall proceed with the construction of the plant ... but not commission it for the purposes of reprocessing'.[68] The facilities and scientific skills would be used to develop the technology of waste disposal and storage – a formula which gave some reassurance to the pro-nuclear unions but not much. In these few weeks, the Front Bench, including Kinnock and Orme, were put under strong pressure from representatives of workers affected by the policy who wanted safeguards for their jobs. From Sellafield, a National Campaign for the Nuclear Industry was formed by a wide range of unions with members involved.

In the crucial debate at the Party Conference, in addition to the NEC statement, there was a huge composite resolution to be moved by the National Union of Mineworkers which called on a future Labour Government to halt the nuclear power programme (including the new Thorpe plant) and to phase out all existing nuclear power plants with no loss of jobs in the region.[69] Kinnock thought that elements of this resolution were totally unrealistic but it was clear at the NEC meeting on the Sunday that a majority of the NEC thought differently and that they were transmitting the message of a majority within the Conference. Eventually, after discussions with trade union members of the NEC, including Eddie Haigh (who was replying to the debate) and Tom Sawyer, Kinnock agreed to adopt an old conference device of accepting the resolutions 'with qualifications'.[70]

Scargill refused to accept the qualifications but the procedure allowed him no option and gave Kinnock the room to keep in step with the trade unions' majority. As it happened, it was not quite large enough to command the authoritative two-thirds which would have added to the clamour for its insertion in the Manifesto.[71] By the time the Manifesto was put together the issue had to some extent gone off the boil, and the attention of the anti-nuclear unions were focused on other priorities.

Kinnock could then move back to the position taken by the Shadow Cabinet in *Britain Needs an Energy Strategy* – Labour would initiate 'a major energy conservation programme and ensure that Britain develops the full potential of its coal, oil and gas resources whilst gradually diminishing Britain's dependence upon nuclear energy'; but with an eye on jobs (and on the Sellafield unions) the document also said :'We will ensure a safe future for Sellafield and develop a new strategy for the monitoring, storage and disposal of nuclear waste'.[72]

UNILATERAL NUCLEAR DISARMAMENT AND NON-NUCLEAR DEFENCE

The unilateralist tide that washed through the Party in 1980 was different from that of either the early 1960s or the early 1970s in that it became so powerful that it could neither be successfully confronted, nor headed off or ignored. A non-nuclear defence policy was a feature of the Party's General Election campaigns in both 1983 and 1987.

In seeking to explain this profound shift of policy, the unions have been identified as the key initiating element. The Labour Party's policy changes, it was argued, reflected the new assertiveness of the trade unions. In 1980, 'The decisions at Blackpool came from the unions not the local parties'.[73]

This analysis is plausible but problematic. As we have noted over constitutional reform (Chapter 7), the decisions of the Labour Party Conference were always in one sense the decisions of the unions, if only because unions account for over 90 per cent of the votes cast. In line with this diagnosis, one would certainly have to note a body of opinion in Leftwing unions, particularly the TGWU, whose longstanding sympathy for unilateralism was strengthened into a high priority during this period of growing concern over the dangers of nuclear escalation. But saying more than this and locating *the* source of initiative as the unions would be a weak explanation in several respects.

If the unions were attempting to 'move into Labour Party politics ... decisively' on this issue, they made a rather half-hearted job of it in terms of resolutions and speeches.[74] In fact, four of the six largest unions were opposed to a non-nuclear defence policy at this time. Indeed, the Engineers and the Electricians remained opposed right up to the 1983 General Election. The GMWU was late and reluctant to come into line. USDAW – the 'weathercock' union – swung only in 1981.

If the unions had been as assertive and as in agreement as is suggested, we might have expected the TUC to register it. But the TUC did not pass a resolution in support of a unilateralist defence policy until 1981, a year after the Party had shifted; in 1980 it carried a classic 'fudged' TUC composite resolution, supported by both Right and Left.[75]

A more complicated but more satisfactory analysis of the power relations on this issue would note again the importance of the triadic relationship – involving the NEC – pointed up in Chapter 7. It would be aware of the politics within and between different unions. And it would be sensitive also to the changing balance of opinion in the PLP, including the position of the Party Leader from 1980 to 1987. Above all, it would start from the spontaneous wave of support for the Campaign for Nuclear Disarmament which began in late 1979 and swept the Constituency Labour parties in 1980.[76]

During 1980 the Party began to signal its sympathy for a change of policy through the document *Peace, Jobs and Freedom* put to a Special Party Conference in May, and through the pamphlet *Nuclear Arms No; Peace Yes*, issued at the anti-nuclear march and rally instigated by the NEC in June.[77] In June and July unilateralist resolutions appeared from the CLPs on a scale not seen at a Party Conference since 1960. At the 1980 Party Conference, by a show of hands, and in line with an NEC recommendation, the majority voted to close down all nuclear bases on British soil or in British waters.[78]

Subsequently, the NEC, which in the past might well have confronted, headed off or downplayed the resolution, this time re-established a Defence Study Group which was chaired by the veteran CND activist, Frank Allaun, and packed it with a unilateralist majority. It produced an NEC statement which was fully in line with the 1980 Conference decision.[79] By this stage, Michael Foot was Leader and threw his weight behind it on the NEC. It carried the Conference of 1981 on a show of hands together with a composite resolution moved by the Transport Workers calling for 'an unambiguous commitment'.[80]

In these two years, the wave of support washed through the unions. Still supporting NATO, the union majority retained a commitment to collective security, but there was a marked rise in affiliation to CND. Centrist unions, looking for Party unity, now sought a unifying position close to the unilateralists. The Right in the PLP leadership and in the unions found themselves caught and bound by the mandates built up by this movement. Although the NEC was 'retaken' in 1982, the unilateralist commitment was so strong at this point that there was little basis for a counter-attack.[81]

At the General Election of 1983, the Party was committed in its Manifesto to the removal of all nuclear weapons in the lifetime of a Parliament. The deep frustrations felt by a Shadow Cabinet majority upon whom this policy had been imposed came out during the campaign in a damaging split which badly affected Labour's support.

Post 1983

After the defeat of 1983, a question mark was posed against many of the Party's policies and particularly this one. As we shall see with the case study of policy towards the EEC, it was possible to quietly sideline a policy which was widely considered to be no longer viable. But support for CND in the Party involved a large, active and highly organised series of groupings which were determined to press home the policy in 1983. In addition, TGWU support had been strengthened since 1981 and it was in the forefront of planning for arms conversion and the safeguarding of defence jobs – a factor likely to be crucial in determining whether, when it came to the crunch, the union would pull out all the stops for implementation. Given the jobs issue, the electoral sensitivity and the higher salience of other priorities, the non-nuclear defence policy was not necessarily an unwavering objective for the supporting union. But neither was it an issue which could be easily sidelined.

There was a period of delicate uncertainty in the autumn of 1983 which was marked by the different motions at the TUC and the Party Conference and the contrasting behaviour of the Transport Workers' leadership in the two forums. Their General Secretary's role at the TUC was very diplomatic. Their motion was quietly composited into a resolution which did not mention the removal of nuclear bases or unilateral nuclear disarmament.[82]

But at the Party Conference, a different pattern emerged. Part of the politics here was the role of the Labour Disarmament Liaison Committee, an umbrella grouping of pro-unilateralist organisations working in liaison with Labour Party HQ staff. They agreed in advance a composite which reaffirmed past policy and called for a new NEC statement for the next Party Conference. Not only did the TGWU adopt this composite but Ron Todd, the Transport Workers' official at the compositing meeting (and a future candidate for General Secretary), was determined to hold on to the crucial words 'unconditionally remove all existing nuclear weapons and bases'.[83] He resisted a variety of pressures to remit.

Kinnock also, in the next three years, was to prove as ardent in support of non-nuclear defence policy as he had been in the years before. But he was regularly under pressure from Rightwing colleagues on the Shadow Cabinet and the refusal of the TGWU to remit became in a sense a two-edged sword. It was an important resource in the battle within the Parliamentary leadership to hold off a shift in policy; it was also in the end a real constraint.

The Conference having voted decisively and Kinnock having made clear his continued commitment, defence policy became the first to be processed through a new joint policy committee. In these policy discussions, the unions played little part. The non-nuclear defence policy was confirmed, albeit with a new, strong emphasis on conventional defence. The Conference, in 1984, gave it overwhelming endorsement and it became clear that the Conference and its union majority would not be persuaded otherwise this side of a General Election.

Twice subsequently, a section of the Shadow Cabinet sought to persuade the Leader to make a major adjustment to the commitment. Both times Kinnock did not move, although by the Christmas of 1986 he was apparently beginning to lose his conviction over the unilateralist policy,[84] yet feared that a major shift would produce Party and union convulsions.

In March 1987, Kinnock did make an important adjustment on the basis of discussions with the two key Shadow Cabinet Ministers, and *without* consulting the unions. It was agreed in the light of new arms proposals and a changing international climate that Labour's Cruise missile policy would be dependent upon the outcome of disarmament talks. But unilateralists in the unions were later reassured that this was a diplomatic and presentational adjustment; accordingly no union leaders voiced any criticisms. Labour went through the 1987 election campaign still committed to a non-nuclear defence policy based on unilateral action.

THE EUROPEAN ECONOMIC COMMUNITY

Another policy area where the behaviour of the unions was often misunderstood was that of entry into the EEC. There was always a strong body of opinion – particularly on the Left of the unions – which opposed British membership. But after 1979, in shaping Labour's policy of withdrawal, the initiative again came mainly from the political not the industrial wing.

There was, for example, not even a debate on the EEC at the 1979 TUC, whereas a composite resolution moved by Farnworth CLP, which was strongly anti-Market in tone and raised the question of reconsidering membership, was debated at the Party Conference, accepted by the NEC and supported by the Conference on a show of hands.[85] The major shift of emphasis towards reconsideration of membership was then reflected in the Party's 1980 policy document *Peace, Jobs and Freedom*, greatly alarming the committed EEC supporters.

But at the TUC of 1980, there was a debate on the EEC in which those in favour of withdrawal were defeated by an amendment which committed the TUC to supporting a further referendum.[86] In this debate, unusually, the General Council gave no guidance. It was a different story at the Party Conference where there was an overwhelming vote for withdrawal after the NEC had recommended acceptance. While the TUC made no further policy exploration, the NEC went ahead with a document from an EEC Study Group which was chaired by Tony Benn and packed with anti-Market MPs.

Not surprisingly, the Study Group emerged with a document which pledged the Party to attempt a withdrawal from the EEC within twelve months of there being a Labour Government. When this statement went to the NEC on 21 July 1981, nine of the twelve trade union representatives were *absent* and the matter was virtually left to 'the politicians'. Proponents of the referendum were overwhelmingly defeated, with the three trade unionists splitting 1–2 against.

In the wake of these decisions, the General Council now reconsidered and in September gave its support to withdrawal which carried the Congress on a hand vote. At the Party Conference, card votes registered the overwhelming defeat of the pro-referendum grouping (mainly hard-core pro-Marketeers) and support for withdrawal; the NEC statement got the authoritative two-thirds majority.

Withdrawal from the EEC 'well within the lifetime of the Labour Government' went into the Manifesto's Emergency Programme of Action.

Post 1983

The post-mortem which followed Labour's defeat in 1983 had several consensual features which emerged as if by telepathy and one of them was a fundamental adjustment of policy on the EEC. Within a month of the election result, there developed a view that the Party had to accept EEC entry. The document *Campaigning for a Fairer Britain*, presented to the 1983 Conference, said that the Party must retain the option of withdrawal ('like all member states') but the Party was now committed to membership for the duration of the European Parliament and the emphasis was on working with European socialists to promote a European policy on employment and social justice.[87]

There was, however, no debate on the EEC at the TUC or Party Conferences of that year, or any subsequently, before the 1987 General Election. By an agreement which was virtually universally respected in the unions, no resolutions were submitted on the issue. The reason for this was a simple one. No formal reversal of policy had taken place within the major unions' conferences and, had the argument over the EEC been taken to a vote at the Party Conference or TUC Congress, the mandates pointed to the same decision as in 1981. There was now virtually a consensus at Leadership level that such a decision would be very damaging. Most Leftwing union leaders moved discreetly in line with the rest of the union leadership in attempting to give the Parliamentary leadership room for manœuvre. In spite of occasional complaints from the NEC Left, the line held.

By 1987, the Manifesto, although rejecting 'EEC interference in our policy for national recovery and renewal', stressed working 'constructively with our EEC partners to promote economic expansions and combat unemployment'.[88] There was no reference to the possibility of withdrawal.

APPRAISAL: POLICYMAKING, PROCESS AND POWER

The first point to strike this observer about the interaction of the unions and the Party in the case studies presented in this chapter is that the closer and more detailed the policy analysis, the more the collective entities disappear into divergent elements. The point is relevant to 'the PLP leadership' and to 'the NEC', especially from 1980 to 1982, but it is *particularly* true for the trade unions. Indeed, although for intelligibility's sake it has been and still is often necessary to refer to 'the unions', it is also important to register the reminder that trade unions have distinctive traditions, policies and, to some extent, priorities. They have, in the past, tended to achieve their maximum unity over the defence of fundamental trade union activities and particularly over their own autonomy, yet by 1985 it had become clear that union opinion was even divided over the repeal and replacement legislation covering industrial relations.

Indeed, examining the range of policy issues dealt with in this chapter, it is apparent that on *no* single issue were they united in direct opposition to the position of the Parliamentary leadership. True, there may well have been unity over some covert issues which the PLP leadership might have wanted to raise in terms of trade union industrial activity but in great measure, 'the unions' is simply a convenient shorthand to be used with caution, and received with qualifications.

The qualifications include an appreciation of the scale of the union majority around different policy areas, and the various configurations which constituted the union alignments. It was always a significant feature of union–Labour Party relations that the politicians in the political wing had union factional allies at the Party Conference, at the Trades Union Congress, and on the TUC General Council. But there were, as we have seen in the case studies, many issues where Left/Right alignments were secondary to other political cleavages. The Left/Right division was at the core of conflict over defence policy, the EEC, union balloting legislation, and public ownership. It was broken most sharply over transport policy, nuclear energy, the statutory minimum wage and Northern Ireland.

Further, the qualifications include an awareness of role-playing; even the representation of one union's position sometimes had variations depending upon the official concerned and the forum of activity. Thus the control exercised by unions over the election of a majority of the NEC did not mean that 'the unions controlled policy' because, in general, the trade unionists did not attempt to exert such control. On that committee there were important union interventions over Northern Ireland in 1981, over incomes policy in 1983, and, that same year, over opening new discussions about a statutory minimum wage. *But* each initiative had the support of the then Party Leader. There was a general concern with industrial disputes which sometimes led to decisions problematic for the Parliamentary leadership. And there was an unusually assertive conflict with the Leader involving a section of the union representatives over union balloting and nuclear energy in 1986. But these were exceptions. In the case studies presented here, union representatives were generally passive rather than initiating, and normally highly supportive of the Parliamentary leadership – particularly the Leader.

Also the union role in Labour Party policymaking is inexplicable without an understanding of the complex role of the TUC officials as representatives of 'the unions'. They staunchly defended the formal boundaries of the two territories, and their own distinctive functions, and over some key issues, including foreign and defence policy, they encouraged the General Council to keep away from Party policymaking. Just as important, they were often privately supportive of the Parliamentary leadership, sometimes playing a brokerage role between the political and industrial leadership in an effort to produce a change on sensitive issues, including balloting and the statutory minimum wage. And they needed little encouragement to seek a new formula that would edge the unions gently in the direction of some form of incomes policy. If asked for 'a TUC view' in the mid-1980s they would offer it, but they never encouraged an imposition of the TUC view on the Parliamentary leadership – a restraint which was most marked in the various shifts over macro-economic policy. They were very co-operative in responding to procedural reform within the Labour Party after 1983 – even reform which changed union access. And they would quietly evacuate a joint policy area – as over transport policy, industrial policy and public ownership policy – if this was considered to be in the common interest.

The sticking point for the TUC – a point carefully guarded in this period by TUC officials – concerned its own functions and interests as an institution. Much of this protectiveness worked in harmony with the PLP leadership's anxieties over the radical industrial incursions of the NEC Left, but there were party policy proposals from the Front Bench which occasionally threatened the composition and scope of some of the tripartite institutions involving the TUC. Then, as over regional government and planning and over training, the TUC bureaucracy turned from the role of amenable broker or friendly assistant into a powerful (and successful) defensive agent.

But this was highly unusual. In general, the appearance of trade union 'control' obscured the reality of a more limited passive and supportive role. This was particularly true of union leaders and the block vote at the Party Conference. The unions' huge majority vote at the Conference was often taken as *the* significant indicator of their permanent dominance over policymaking. But the formal authority of the Party Conference and the voting preponderance of the unions drew attention away from the importance of other processes and other union responses. The indicators which mattered in terms of effective power were the signals given by union leaderships before, during and after a Conference decision and these embodied significant variations in the definition of priorities – as the case studies illustrate.

If we take union resolutions submitted to the Party Conference as one important indicator of priorities, we can see that regularly the unions signalled, in a cluster of resolutions, an abiding interest in some of the consensual issues of social policy. But we can also see the magnitude of their interest in industrial issues and in economic and political issues with industrial consequences. The case studies of energy, transport, and industrial relations policy each in their different way highlighted this enduring focus. Enduring also was the concern with reducing unemployment and with the incidence of taxation, although on these, as with other economic policies, individual union involvement was restricted by limited interest in and expertise over the details of policy. Policies which could affect collective bargaining arrangements and incomes were always given high priority – even when rejected. From individual unions – particularly the banking unions – there was determined assertion of the 'rule' of veto over public ownership.

Consistent also with past behaviour was the way priorities were shaped by a sensitivity to movements of opinion among the membership, even when not registered fully through union procedures. Thus there was little support for a new public ownership programme from 1979 to 1983, and then limited support for a renationalisation programme from 1983 to 1987. And though there was continuing strong resistance from sections of the Left to the sacrifice of union autonomy, the reaction of most union leaders to sustained membership opinion on balloting legislation (and the exigencies of Labour's electoral appeal) eventually produced a historic acceptance of Government intervention in this area and a fundamental adjustment of the 'rules' of union freedom.

A concern with practicability also affected the definition of priorities. Between 1982 and 1987 the 'no compensation' and then the 'no speculative gain' formulas for reacquisition had to be adjusted to take account of new investments and new shareholders. And what would 'run' in political terms in the mid-1980s came to be seen in much broader terms than in the period after 1979. Just as the Party leaders have often in the past – particularly on matters affecting union interests – anticipated the reactions of the unions when framing policy, so from the mid-1980s we can see the growth of new anticipations within the unions which affected their priorities over Party policy. These were affected by an increased receptivity to the Party's electoral objectives, but this development was reinforced by a change in the emphasis of union campaigning which sought to enhance public support by locating the unions' cause in the context of consumer and user needs. The development of Social Ownership policy was one key example of the way in which the unions anticipated the reactions of consumers and the electorate. Transport policy was another example, with the wider concerns made even clearer when the union-influenced document passed through Party filters.

Not every such reorientation of union priorities worked to the advantage of the Parliamentary leadership. Support for unilateral nuclear disarmament in the early 1980s was fed by a growing concern over nuclear escalation which found a different response in the unions from that of a majority of the Shadow Cabinet. A sharp rise in alarm at the potential dangers of nuclear power in 1986 caused a reorientation of priorities, even in unions like the TGWU and the GMWU which had members in the industries, as well as a broader spectrum of hitherto pronuclear aligned unions.

These two cases illustrated that, although the formal authority of the Party Conference and the preponderance of the unions was often misleading, it was not necessarily insignificant. The Party Conference provided a measure of temperature on key issues and an indicator of the alignment of union forces. If union majorities were huge and more or less stable and if the informal indicators pointed up to a high union priority, then boundaries were established. In the period from 1979 to 1983, these constrained the NEC Left over Northern Ireland and nuclear energy just as they constrained the Shadow Cabinet over the EEC and nuclear disarmament.

Even after 1983, when the authority of the Conference declined further, its temperature, alignments and majorities (potential and actual) fed into the joint policy formulation, occasionally forcing the Parliamentary leadership either to adjust policy in anticipation (as with nuclear energy), or to forgo a separate statement of policy (the EEC after 1983).

The steady continuities and occasional variations of priority on the part of the unions were major factors shaping the balance of power around any particular issue. Of course, they were not the only factors at work. In a policy process which engaged a variety of pressure groups and social movements, of external pressures and internal divisions, the case studies illustrate the complexity and variety of influences which feed through the Labour Movement. But in most of the case studies, union priority was the key to whether or not there were boundaries to the options available to 'the politicians' and how tight those boundaries were.

Conversely, trade union involvement was itself affected by the interplay with elements in the political wing. In particular it was affected by responses to initiatives taken by others within the Party whose activities could trigger union mandates and draw the unions into commitments. This interaction could at times give a misleading impression of union assertiveness behind a comprehensive project – as was the case from 1979 to 1982.

In Chapter 7 a linkage was discerned between the NEC Left and a core of (mainly small) Left-led unions on the General Council, and a triad of influence over constitutional issues was also noted. On some key issues after 1979 – the AES, the EEC and unilateral nuclear disarmament – this linkage was also significant, and over defence policy the triad involved an important upthrust from the CLPs as well as crucial initiatives and responses by the NEC. However, there was a deep reluctance on the part of a majority of union leaders to see the TUC's authority used to bolster the changes in policy envisaged in the NEC's 1980 document *Peace, Jobs and Freedom*. Over the EEC and over unilateral nuclear disarmament, TUC policy followed in the wake of changes in Party policy and not the reverse. Further, much of the initiative and detailed proposals in 1981 concerning planning and industrial democracy came from the two offices, with some key elements fudged or conceded in the face of representations from the Front Bench. And the proposals for extending public ownership came mainly from the political wing. Where trade unions did play a heavy-handed role – as over Northern Ireland and nuclear energy – this was in harmony with the Shadow Cabinet majority and in response to novel initiatives, again from the NEC Left. Even the union agreement on transport policy, produced independently of the Party's formal procedure, was initiated from the Front Bench. All in all, then, this was far from being the unions seizing the initiative to move decisively into the Party in order to assert their control over policy, as has been suggested.[89]

Alongside these variations of initiative and power between the unions and the politicians, there was another pattern relating to the electoral cycle. There was a general tendency for the Parliamentary leadership to become more assertive and achieve a greater influence over the definition of policy as the election approached. Even in 1982–3, when the constraints were unusually tight in the aftermath of the Left's control over the NEC and the build-up of conference mandates, it was still possible to produce a more acceptable definition of 'the alternative economic strategy', to make less specific the commitments over public ownership, and to flag a possible new receptivity over nuclear energy and the statutory minimum wage.

After 1985, this short term tendency fused with and was accentuated by a longer term shift to the advantage of the PLP leadership produced by the reinforcing factors traced in Chapter 13. In virtually all the case studies, this new policy dominance of the PLP leadership is evident after 1985.

As for the Leadership production of the Manifesto, this has become a strongly-guarded area of Party autonomy, and only once (and then in alliance with the Shadow Chancellor) was there an important TUC representation (in 1983, over the married man's tax allowance). NEC trade unionists sometimes signalled restrictions in the most sensitive industrial areas, particularly incomes policy, but normally left the rest of the Campaign Document and Manifesto to the political Leadership. Even so, the degree of leeway available to the Party Leader in 1987 was remarkable. Never has a Labour Leader had so much discretion as in the months before the 1987 election, dominating both the procedure and the substance of policy, choosing the form of the policy process, and tidying up some contentious issues to his satisfaction, including the policy on nuclear energy.

All in all, it was an astonishing shift in power relations when we are reminded of the constitutional struggle which followed the 1979 General Election. And yet, to put this in perspective, it is important to register some qualifications of the extent to which, in practice, and in Opposition (as distinct from a Labour Government), a Labour Leader at this time could 'declare independence' from the unions.

The Parliamentary leadership was rarely free of the embarrassments, pressures and obligations produced from the unions as a result of industrial disputes. If the characterisation of Kinnock as a puppet of the union leaders – particularly over violence and illegality – was a nonsense, it remained the case that policy on each dispute had to be evolved with some cognisance of the union position, both tactically and in substantive policy. In this respect, the pluralism of the Labour Movement and the duality of leadership centres within the Party added a restric-tive pressure upon the Parliamentary leadership.

It was also the case that in some policy areas, union membership interests, union traditions and TUC strategy still restrained leadership initiatives. Industrial democracy had been sidelined but single channel representation still dominated trade union perceptions of how it might be advanced. Nuclear energy policy had come out in the end, more or less, as a Leadership victory, but only after months of negotiation, shifts and temporary compromises. The compensation for reacquisition formula was satisfactory to the Parliamentary leadership but the union majority had to be kept on board. Further, over anything that challenged tripartite structures involving TUC representational interests, the old 'no-go' line was signalled. And in 1986, the Leadership would dearly have loved to have produced a more convincing counter-inflation policy had union signals, particu-larly those coming from the TGWU, been green rather than red.

Further, there must always be an element of uncertainty about the boundaries of policymaking because we do not know how far, privately, the Parliamentary leadership might have wanted to shift had the balance of forces and the scale of union priorities been different. Certainly over legislation concerning union bal-lots, a vital precedent was created and a Rubicon crossed, but with what agonies of lexical tightrope walking! Such battles could not be fought on a wide front in this period.

NOTES

1. John Edmunds, *LPACR*, 1985, pp. 173–4.
2. Labour's 1982 Programme referred to 'over a period of three years at most', p. 90. The 1983 Manifesto to 'over the lifetime of the Parlia-ment', p. 17
3. *LPACR*, 1982, p. 205.
4. *TUC Congress Report*, 1980, Comp. Res. Nos. 15 and 16, p. 590.
5. Resolution 85 and amendment, *TUC Congress Report*, 1982, p. 653.
6. *LPACR*, 1982, p. 189 and p. 206.
7. *Programme for Recovery*, 1982, p. 38.
8. *NEC Minutes*, 24/11/1982, Item 28.
9. *Press and Publicity Committee Minutes*, 7/12/1982, Item 16. The motion to defer was moved by John Golding and seconded by Eric Heffer.
10. *Morning Star*, 22/10/82. *Labour Weekly*, 10/12/82.
11. *Labour Weekly*, 25/2/83. *Tribune*, 25/2/83. *Liaison Committee Minutes*, 21 February 1983, Para. 406.
12. *Guardian*, 12/5/83.
13. *RD 2725*, March 1983. *NEC Minutes*, 22/3/83. *New Hope for Britain*, p. 9.
14. Roy Green (Labour Party Research Staff), 'Feedback', *New Statesman*, 23/9/83 and *Partners in Rebuilding Britain*, p. 14.

15. *Guardian*, 9/11/83, speech to EETPU Conference.
16. *Liaison Committee Minutes*, 26/11/84, Item 451. It was stressed that the unions and the Party should be identified with issues of concern and interest to trade unions members.
17. Hattersley speech to the AUEW national committee, Guardian, 23/4/85. Kinnock speech to Wales TUC, Morning Star, 4/5/85.
18. *Labour Weekly*, 28/6/85.
19. *Guardian*, 7/8/85.
20. LPACR, 1985, p. 219.
21. *TUC Congress Report*, 1986, Eric Hammond, pp. 561–2.
22. *Ibid.*, Norman Willis, p. 558, Ron Todd, p. 566.
23. Kenneth Clarke, Friday Agenda, *Guardian*, 29/8/86.
24. *Morning Star*, 19/11/86 and 21/11/86.
25. *Guardian*, 23/4/85.
26. Partners in Rebuilding Britain, Para. 14 noted: 'These arrangements must be flexible so that they reflect the wishes of people in the regions and feed into national planning priorities. And … adaptable … to the development of new forms of local government.'
27. Note by Joint Secretaries, *Liaison Committee Minutes*, 21/3/83.
28. *Org. Sub. Minutes*, 11/2/80, Item 73 and NEC Minutes, 27/2/80.
29. *TUC Congress Report*, 1983, p. 25.
30. *TUC Congress Report*, 1983, pp. 32–3.
31. *Liaison Committee Minutes*, 21 March 1983, Item 412.
32. John Prescott, reported Guardian, 19/8/86; Ron Todd, *Tribune*, 29/8/86.
33. *NEC Home Policy Committee Minutes*, 14/7/86, Item 66.
34. *Ibid.*
35. *TUC Congress Report*, 1986, p. 680. Composite Res. No. 1 called for 'a right to strike, and to have a secret ballot in such situations, and to take other industrial actions'.
36. *TUC Congress Report*, 1981, pp. 307–312. 'Economic Issues Facing the Next Labour Government'. Para. 33 was amended to insert 'coupled with an expanding role for public enterprise, including extension of public ownership'.
37. *LPACR*, 1982, Comp. Res. No. 62, p. 95 and p. 108.
38. *LPACR*, 1982, Comp. Res. No. 50, p. 116 and p. 128.
39. *The Case for Public Ownership*, CLPD pamphlet, 1986, Introduction, p. 1.
40. *TUC Economic Committee*, 9/2, 12/6/85.
41. *LPACR*, 1985, Comp. Res. No. 29, p. 225. The resolution was defeated by 3,429,000 to 2,939,000.
42. 'Foot abandons defiant Benn', *Guardian*, 14/11/81. Tony Benn, 'Setting the Record Straight', *Guardian*, 18/11/81. Patrick Wintour, Peter Kellner and Bruce Page, 'Last Tango in Westminster', *New Statesman*, 27/11/81.
43. *TUC Congress Report*, 1982, p. 273, para. 405.
44. *LPACR*, 1979, pp. 232 and 383.
45. *RD 102*, October 1979.
46. *Ibid.*
47. *Minutes of the Northern Ireland Study Group Meeting of Members of the NEC*, ID/1979–80/70, 30 January 80.
48. *NEC Home Policy Sub-committee Minutes*, 11/2/80.
49. *NEC Minutes*, 22/7/81.
50. *Ibid.*

51. Alex Kitson (TGWU) replaced Joan Maynard in 1985. He was succeeded by Tony Clarke (UCW) in 1986.
52. *PD 818*, November 1986.
53. 'How One Little Leak Opened the Floodgates on Labour's Ireland Policy', Clare Short, *Tribune*, 20/2/87.
54. *New Statesman*, 4/12/87.
55. See on this, 'Newsnotes', *Labour and Trade Union Review*, Nov.–Dec. 1990, p. 4.
56. *LPACR*, 1979, Comp. Res. No. 16, p. 242.
57. *RD 87*, November 1979.
58. The interim statement *Nuclear Power and the Environment* was produced initially by the Environment Study Group and was anti-nuclear in tone. The consultative document titled *What Price Energy?* was produced by joint deliberation and therefore balanced in its approach. The discussion document *Energy* came from the Energy subcommittee and was heavily pro-nuclear in tone. All these were published in 1980.
59. *LPACR*, 1982, Comp. Res. No. 60, pp. 216–17 and p. 222.
60. *LPACR*, 1984, Comp. Res. No. 65, pp. 35 and 44.
61. *LPACR*, 1985, Comp. Res. No. 70, pp. 159–61.
62. Allan Rogers, 'Planning for Plenty', *Labour Weekly*, 11/4/86. John Cunningham, 'How Nuclear Power Is Part of a Socialist Energy Programme', *Tribune*, 18/4/86.
63. *Hansard*, HC 13/5/86, Cols. 577–84 and Cols. 637–42.
64. The Welsh Labour Party Conference voted in favour of the decommissioning of all nuclear power stations in spite of a speech from the Party Leader urging avoidance of 'airy declarations'. *Guardian*, 17/5/86.
65. 'Britain Needs an Energy Policy', *Labour Weekly*, 30/5/86, p. 7.
66. Tony Benn and Eric Heffer, *Next Steps in the Phasing Out of All Nuclear Power Stations in Britain*, 12/5/86.
67. 'Civil Nuclear Power', *PD 649 B. Home Policy Sub-committee Minutes*, 14/7/86, item 69.
68. *NEC Statements*, Civil Nuclear Power, 1986, p. 32.
69. *LPACR*, 1986, Comp. Res. No. 63, pp. 72-3.
70. *Ibid.*, pp. 78–79.
71. The vote was 4,213,000 to 2,143,000, *ibid.*, p. 156.
72. *Britain Will Win*, p. 7.
73. Pimlott, *Trade Unions in British Politics*, *op. cit.*, pp. 8 and 231.
74. Apart from SOGAT, of the 149 resolutions favouring unilateral nuclear disarmament at the 1980 Conference, only one other came from a union (the very small ACTT) and Bill Keys of SOGAT (the mover of the composite resolution) was the only trade union leader to speak in favour, *LPACR*, 1980, p. 162. There were also three *multilateralist* amendments from the unions and a resolution from FTAT opposing Cruise missiles in Britain but favouring 'an international pact'
75. *TUC Congress Report*, 1980, pp. 536–40. NB Bill Keys' SOGAT 'opposition' to the motion on the grounds that it did not take the unions 'far enough down … a unilateral path', p. 540
76. At the 1979 Conference, only about twelve people turned up to the unilateralist *Labour Action for Peace* fringe meeting. In 1980 there were over a thousand.
77. At this rally, Party officials noted few trade union banners. Interviews with Party officials in July 1980.

78. *LPACR*, 1980, Comp. Res. No. 45, pp. 162 and 173.
79. *LPACR*, 1981, p. 157. *Nuclear Weapons and the Arms Race*, 1981.
80. *LPACR*, 1981, Comp. Res. No. 31 was carried on a card vote, 4,596,000 to 2,315,000, p. 157.
81. *LPACR*, 1982, Comp. Res. No. 51 moved by Bill Keys of SOGAT was carried by 4,927,000 to 1,975,000, p. 136.
82. TGWU Motion 53, *TUC Agenda*, p. 36. Comp. Res. No. 26, *TUC Congress Report*, 1983, p. 610.
83. *LPACR*, 1983, Comp. Res. No. 40, p. 150.
84. Kinnock's reply to a BBC questioner, Radio 4, 18/5/89. Sources close to Kinnock confirm that his views changed after the Reykjavik Summit in November 1986.
85. *LPACR*, 1979, Comp. Res. No. 40, pp. 327–32.
86. *TUC Congress Report*, 1980, pp. 487–92. TGWU policy was still for a referendum. 1979 *T & GW Biennial Conference*, Minute No. 49, p. 33.
87. *Campaign for a Fairer Britain*, 1983, pp. 12–13.
88. *Britain Will Win*, 1987, p. 15.
89. See Chapter 13, p. 396 and n. 7.1.

Appendix to Chapter 14: trade unions and the policy review 1987–90*

NOVELTIES AND CONTINUITIES

Between 1987 and 1990, the Labour Party became involved in a highly-publicised, three-phase review of policy, leading to the documents *Social Justice and Economic Efficiency* in 1988 and then *Meet the Challenge, Make the Change* in 1989. These were followed in 1990 by a campaign document *Looking to the Future*. This policy review was often portrayed as unique in its breadth and momentous in its contribution to the creation of a 'new model' Labour Party. Its innovations of procedure and its new directions in policy commanded considerable attention in what many considered to be a watershed in Labour Party policy development.

Overall, we can agree that there were certainly novel features in the policy process and some major, even historic, departures in policy. But there were also some strong continuities and developmental features building upon past changes. Most important of all, there were some crucial consistencies of behaviour on the part of union leaders, NEC trade unionists and TUC officials. These were to be of central importance in union acceptance of the mode of policy-making and in creating agreement over, or encouraging acquiescence in, the final product.

PROCEDURE AND COMPOSITION

The fundamental procedural continuity with the way policy was made from 1983 to 1987 was that the Party and the unions did not return to the traditional sole responsibility of the NEC for policy formulation, and the unions, who in theory 'controlled' the NEC, made no claim for any return. Indeed, there was now even a shift in formal supervision. The co-ordination of seven joint Policy Review Groups was given to joint convenors, one from each institution.[1]

Although the wearing of double hats meant that only four of the fourteen convenors were not members of the NEC,[2] only three of these convenors were from the Trade Union Section.[3] The creation of these groups, together with a

---

*Power relations within a policy process can only be assessed adequately in relation to a whole electoral cycle from manifesto to manifesto (as in the two periods covered in Chapters 13 and 14). Nevertheless, here we are able to assess key elements of this Policy Review process in the light of the previous analysis, and to point up some significant characteristics. The evidence from all three chapters is appraised in Chapter 20,

new co-ordination device of a Campaign Management Team,[4] chaired by the
Home Policy Chairman Tom Sawyer, meant that in practice there was a downgrading of the role of the Home Policy and International Committees of the NEC
and the regularity of their meetings declined.[5] However, the final products had to
pass a scrutiny and be agreed by the full NEC before they went to the Party
Conference.

There was a more restricted membership of these groups (approximately nine
per group) than in the past, and the lengthy tail of co-optees disappeared. But,
unusually,[6] the membership of the Groups included four senior union leaders who
were members of the General Council.[7] In 1989, two of them, John Edmunds
(GMB) and Rodney Bickerstaffe (NUPE), were invited to become members of an
Economic Policy PRG subcommittee drawn from the three PRGs whose work
overlapped in their economic aspects.[8]

This innovation (which ran counter to the general public appearance of union
disengagement) arose because in the uncertainty of 1987, when the TUC took its
decision not to be directly involved at all in Labour Party policymaking, some of
the leaders of Labour Party affiliates (particularly John Edmunds) feared that they
would have no say at all at the formulative stage of key policy changes. In practice
it was, however, a very restrained incursion.[9]

The policy groups were again serviced by a Secretariat drawn from the Policy
Directorate and from the political assistants and advisers in the PLP. The Groups
acted with a significant degree of autonomy[10] and with varying complications and
accommodations in the relationship between the Convenors and the Groups.
There was a variety of sources of initiative from the Secretariat and PRG Group
members, but the wider participation which had been promised failed to materialise and was not much encouraged. Increasingly, after the first rather uncertain
year of policymaking, the Groups became dominated by the Front Bench. Usually, one of the Convenors was the Shadow Minister and he became seen as
having the final responsibility for agreeing the most controversial inclusions or
omissions.

The Groups operated under a loose rein from the Leader but, as he chose the
Convenors, and agreed the membership of the Groups in conjunction with the
Convenors, there was a degree of prior control over the likely outcome. In
addition, there was a degree of steering via periodic interventions from the
Leader's Office, the members of which were either part of the Secretariat of the
Groups or attended some of the meetings. The Leadership also exercised an
influence over the themes and general direction of the Groups via the Campaign
Management Team and meetings of the Convenors and Secretariat. There was
also an important network linking the Shadow Communications Agency, the
Director of Campaigns and Communication, Peter Mandelson, members of the
Campaign Management Team, the Leader's Office and the Leader. As Hughes
and Wintour note, 'in the "new model" party, political demands would be
inseparable from the communications imperative'.[11]

The Leadership and Shadow Cabinet input was assisted by a further increase
in financial resources, giving them additional opportunity for advice and research
assistance.[12] A shift towards the formation of a Parliamentary policy substructure

was evident in the creation of an Economic Committee of the Shadow Cabinet.[13] In addition, with union financial backing, an independent Institute for Public Policy Research was created and now linked informally (but closely) to the Leader's Office. Patricia Hewitt, who moved from being Kinnock's Press Officer to being Deputy Director of the Institute, was involved in editing and thematising the final drafts of the second and third policy documents in conjunction with the Leader and his Office.

THE ROLE OF THE UNIONS: PERSPECTIVES AND RELATIONSHIPS

Labour's position as 'the party that listens' to public opinion, and its new strategic search for the centre ground, set much of the boundaries as well as the direction of the policy review. It had clear implications for the role of the unions in the policy process and for the content of policies which involved the industrial behaviour of the unions, especially as the message now going out from the Leader's Office to the media emphasised that the unions would continue to lose power economically and politically.[14] There was an emphatic repudiation of the idea of Labour as the Party which was more concerned with the producer than the consumer.[15] With this went a strong emphasis on 'the Community'[16] and its needs.

These positions in relation to the electorate were broadly accepted by the majority of union leaders, although with some reservations, covert resentments and differences of emphasis. On the Left of the unions there was a significant difference of perspective, as 'the Todd speech' of 1988 showed, but, even there, responses to the political leadership were constrained by the pressing priorities and by a concern for the unity of the Movement.

The fundamental priority was the return of a Labour Government which would at least tilt the balance away from employers to organised labour and would embody a commitment to social justice in its approach to public policy. There was much less consensus in the summer of 1988 than was to emerge in 1990 – or at least a greater proclivity to voice dissent and offer resistance. This was particularly marked after first the Party's defence policy and then its response to the Government's new training policy, were suddenly flung into public dispute. But there were also occasional private set-backs in other areas and some sticky moments over industrial relations policy and industrial democracy on the *People at Work* group.

However, the electoral college landslide of 1988 boosted the Leader's position. In 1989, his own performance improved, as did the Party's electoral standing. A better style and liaison helped change the atmosphere at leadership level. At the same time, new union industrial tactics brought greater benefit to the Party (see below, p. 476). All these developments contributed to the mood in the unions and accentuated accommodation within the relationship.

'Realism' dominated this mood. The unions had accepted with little fuss the major shift away from industrial planning which had taken place since 1983. Now, as the international ideological climate moved steadily in favour of markets, they were in the main[17] content to accept that there would be only limited selective interventionist measures within a predominantly market-based economy. A similar outlook affected the acceptance of a new emphasis on the primacy of *individual* rights at work. Some, like John Edmunds, were to the fore in its advocacy. Others were simply amenable to the shift providing that the collective immunities and/or collective rights remained available.

This amenability dominated union responses to the Policy Review. It was marked at the inception by the helpful initiative of NUPE in calling for the Review and by the changed role of NUPE's Tom Sawyer on the NEC. An ex-Bennite, he had been an influential figure in strengthening the soft Left of the NEC, and occasionally·a thorn in the flesh of the Leader over important items of policy. Now, responding to new priorities, he became a policy co-ordinator, the loyal link to and from the Leader's Office, and the shepherd of the growing 'soft Left' on the NEC.[18] In this behaviour he blended into the dominant ethos of the Trade Union Section and virtually forswore a detailed policy agenda of his own, content that elements of NUPE's agenda on low pay, women and the public services were in the documents.

Union co-operation was also marked in an accentuation of the self-denying ordinance exercised by the TUC. The TUC was never directly part of the Policy Review process and there was a further shift in liaison from the formal to the informal and the less formal. The continuing link between the TUC Economic Committee and the Home Policy Committee of the Party was downgraded to officer level from the Party side[19] and barely taken up at all from the TUC side. Old habits die hard and some of the PRG co-ordinators did attempt to invite a formal TUC contribution, only to be told that the TUC did not want to state a position. Basically, the message on etiquette was 'don't formally ask us what we think or we'll have to tell you'. TUC officials agreed to continue the reduction in the significance of Liaison Committee meetings (a development already under way in 1986). They had once been monthly policymaking gatherings, but from 1987 to 1989 they in effect became half-yearly gatherings for general discussions of the separate institutional reviews and TUC Budget submissions, simply for 'keeping in touch'. No documents were produced through the Committee and no significant decisions were made there. In the session 1989–90, the Committee failed to meet at all.

This reticence on the part of the TUC gave the Parliamentary leadership even more room to initiate, to manoeuvre and to intervene in sensitive areas. It was also understood that the Party might well choose policies with which the TUC disagreed. So be it. But, in practice, as a result of the informal contact and consultations, on most issues the TUC and the Labour Party kept in comfortable tandem.

In fact, in spite of the 'space' and 'distance', there was still a rich and closely-engaged private dialogue between the Party, the TUC and union affiliates. It still covered responses in the House on the old social and industrial union priority issues and it covered some of the key initiatives to be taken within the Policy Review. There were regular contacts at TUC departmental, Party Office, union Research and Political Officer level as well as at the level of union and Party Leadership. Most of the Shadow Spokespersons in key portfolios – particularly Employment – kept open their informal channels of communication with the

TUC over relevant policy initiatives.

The most discreet, but probably the pivotal agenda-setting relationship developed between the Leader's Office and senior TUC officials. Their regular group discussions and telephone contact enabled the TUC to take policy initiatives the Party Leader wanted to happen, to make policy calls the Leader wanted to hear, and to move the unions generally in the direction the Party Leader was pleased for them to take. Following the 1988 TUC, the relationship between Charles Clarke, Kinnock's leading adviser, and John Monks, the TUC's Deputy General Secretary, became pivotal to developments.

In addition, in place of the detailed Liaison Committee discussions (and its place on the calendar of meeting times), there was a new emphasis on the regular private meetings of leading members of the Shadow Cabinet, representatives from the General Council and senior officials of the TUC and the Party. These 'Neddy Six' meetings were now renamed the 'Contact Group' meetings, and for two years (as in 1986–7) that was essentially what they were. Late in 1989, however, as the Liaison Committee was virtually closed down, so the Contact Group discussion became more organised, with both sides now regarding it as a more businesslike arrangement. Even before this, although the meetings were not as systematic in their exploration as they might have been, they allowed for 'understanding' to be reached on problematic elements of some of the key issues – understanding which then fed into the deliberations of the Policy Review Group.

THE ISSUES 1987–90

One important example concerned the proposal for a Statutory Minimum Wage. Again, it was policy which had developed *before* 1987, although one accompanied by a range of practical problems, and industrial and political reservations. Now a broader consensus emerged in the unions in making the policy a central objective. The TGWU's participation guaranteed that it would not easily become a device to produce a legally-bound incomes policy while at the same time broadening a union grouping which could be asked to address the relationship between the statutory minimum wage and issues of pay generally. For the political leadership there was now the added bonus that the policy could be placed at the centre of the Party's new appeal to women, and its anti-poverty programme.

Another policy area where Contact Group discussions assisted common agreement was over public ownership. We have had reasons already to note the unions lack of 'push' behind proposals for more public ownership since 1979. And even renationalisation lost priority. In 1987, 1988 and 1989, all the votes at the TUC and Labour Party Conferences confirmed this position and all attempts to commit a future Labour Government to a major programme of reacquisition were defeated. In the end, there was an affirmation by the Party that the major public utilities ought to be publicly owned, but for the immediate future, with the exception of a public stake in British Telecom and Water, these industries would be dealt with by 'public interest companies' under a regulatory commission. From the unions, adverse reaction was negligible.[20]

Without doubt, the most important single shift of policy discussed on the Contact Group after 1987 concerned the boundaries of trade union industrial freedom. It must be noted that the breakthrough into previously 'closed' territory by the Front Bench had already taken place in 1986 over the regulation of union ballots. And the supportive role of the TUC in 1989 and 1990 had much in common with how its officials had assisted the shift of policy before 1987. However, as we saw then, discussions on the Contact Group, even understandings reached there, did not always lead to the anticipated consequences on industrial relations issues.

By 1989, there was virtually complete agreement among TUC officials, and among a growing number of union leaders (albeit more on the Right than on the Left), that the Conservative Government legislation on union industrial action had built upon and consolidated a more or less permanent body of opinion among union members and in the centre ground of the electorate. Thus, the Labour Party could no longer be saddled with a blanket commitment to repeal and replace the entire legislation. Regardless of the past 'rules' of the relationship, the Labour Party and the TUC had now to accept statutory limitations on the scope of the industrial action of the unions in order to win public support for an agreed area of freedom. This priority was accompanied by, and increasingly overlapped with, an acceptance that there had now to be a historic shift away from the traditional reliance on legal immunities. New rights for employees and unions would accompany the new legal limitations upon trade union actions.

Because there was still a powerful body of support for the unions' traditional positions – particularly within the TGWU – there was no immediate prospect of agreement on what exactly would be the boundaries of trade union freedom. Hence TUC officials played it cautiously. They proposed to prioritise 'an immediate remedy to some of the most unjust elements of the Government's employment legislation'.[21] As for other very complex and contentious issues, the word was, for the moment, given the present union alignments, 'leave well alone'. This view was taken to the Contact Group and, in the perception of the Party Leadership and TUC, 'agreed' there.

By no means all the unions were won over to this tactical position and though there was a consensus among NEC trade unionists that there could not be the blanket repeal of Conservative Government legislation that the political Left was calling for, there were differences of opinion on details, even between representatives of the same union. Although some NEC trade unionists were to the Right of their General Secretaries,[22] and very loyal to the Party Leader, they could be mobilised for a variety of different perspectives on the problems of industrial relations legislation, as in 1986. Then, the leading figure contesting the private TUC 'under-standing' had been a trade union official, Tom Sawyer now it was Michael Meacher, himself Shadow Spokesperson for Employment. Meacher attempted to set his own agenda and did not appear to recognise the signals coming to him from the Contact Group and the TUC, believing Kinnock to have given him and the *People at Work* Group autonomy to sort the problems out.[23]

While accepting the need for a new legal framework with 'a fair balance of power', Meacher's strong commitment was to a positive and assertive trade unionism and his ardent public defence of the trade unions came to be seen as 'the wrong emphasis' both in the Leader's Office and among TUC officials.

This, combined with Meacher's attempt to strike out on his own on the sensitive issues, caused much consternation. He actually took a harder public line against sequestration of union funds than had been envisaged within the TUC. And he produced a formula which gave rights to sympathy action to workers having 'a genuine interest in the outcome of a dispute'.[24] It was a historic contraction of the freedom which unions and the Labour Party had in the past defended, although probably the maximum to be won in the electoral climate of the time and given the attitudes of union members. But these initiatives brought into the public arena a range of problematic issues containing many uncertainties. What had been thought of by the TUC Office as a carefully controlled exercise in *realpolitik* had now been burst apart by what they regarded as 'a loose canon'.

A new ingredient was added to the problems when the TUC Congress passed a resolution emanating from the TGWU which included a call for outright 'immunity from tort for trade unions',[25] thus provoking further public argument over the potential conflict between this position and that arrived at by the Labour Party. Tory attacks on unions being 'above the law' were combined with threats of further controls on union industrial action. While Meacher indicated the compatibility of the TUC decision with Party policy, union leaders grew increasingly alarmed at the effect on Labour's electoral standing.

What happened then tells us much about power relations within the Party, within the Party–union relationship and within the unions on these issues. In effect, the Party Leader simply sidelined Meacher and the PRG membership in the run-up to the Party Conference. Basically, Charles Clarke, from the Leader's Office, took control of the policymaking process and the negotiations with the unions, working in close contact with John Monks from the TUC and taking counsel from sources independent of Meacher and his advisers.[26]

After extensive informal consultation with all the major union leaders, including Ron Todd, the TGWU office and Party officials,[27] the final policy clarification was drafted in the Leader's Office, even though it was issued as a Press release under the names of the co-ordinators of the *People at Work* Group.

It became a very important Note.[28] It made clear that though legal immunities would continue, industrial action outside the ambit of a lawful trade union dispute would not enjoy such immunity. It also made clear that unions would be subject to normal enforcement procedures to obtain damages awarded and to secure compliance with the law – another major break into a sensitive area. For the unions, there were three reassurances. Legislation would prevent '*total*' sequestration of union's funds, thus preventing court action which 'paralyses the union'. There was a promise (already given) to produce more even-handed pretrial injunction procedures. And there was a further movement towards the introduction of a specialist industrial court – seen as a means of part-insulation from the traditional judiciary, although twenty years previously it had been rejected as an unacceptable legal intrusion in industrial relations.

In spite of their virtual exclusion from this policy process, the NEC trade unionists accepted the policy 'clarification'. And attempts from the Left to get NEC trade unionists to support complete repeal of the Conservative Government's legislation met united opposition, as they had done in the summer. At the 1989 Conference, the call for total repeal was defeated by 3,823,000 votes to 2,239,000.[29]

The role played in this affair by the TUC apparently surprised Michael Meacher. But it was consistent with a behaviour pattern noted already in the policymaking process of the Labour Party. After 1987, the TUC simply moved a step further back, publicly a little more distant, a little more distinctive, privately seeking to remove obstructions in the way of the Parliamentary leadership, indeed sometimes moving ahead in order to ensure that there was a clear path.

An invitation to the President of the Commission of the European Community, Jacques Delors, to address the Congress in 1988, and a new emphasis by the TUC on the impact of '1992', helped the Labour Leadership strengthen the Party's Europeanism. In turn, the European dimension gave both the TUC and the Party Leadership the inducement and the opportunity to manage some highly sensitive issues and establish new policy positions.

The most important example in the long run may turn out to be Labour's support for Britain's entry into the Exchange Rate Mechanism of the European monetary system. This policy decision, with major potential consequences for unemployment, was taken virtually at Shadow Cabinet level in the knowledge that a path had been cleared by the TUC officials and the General Council, thus making it that much easier to push it through the NEC to an amenable union vote at Conference.

This pattern was repeated over some of the most sensitive areas left open in industrial relations policy. The European Social Charter offered to trade unionists, increasingly constrained by a Government out of step with much of the EEC, the possibility of comparable facilities to other international trade unionists. Harmonisation gave the TUC officials and Labour's leadership a European frame of reference to argue for further changes in Labour's policy. European traditions gave an extra twist to a conversion to a full framework of law covering industrial relations and rights at work.

The new Front Bench spokesperson on Employment, Tony Blair, was now working in a more favourable climate, including the backing of a majority of the unions for the 1989 Note, a lengthening Labour lead in the polls, and the confident encouragement of TUC officials. The Social Charter's acceptance of a right *not* to belong to a trade union, as well as the right to belong, gave Blair (under pressure from the Tories in the House over closed shop legislation) the opportunity to make a public commitment. The Party would prohibit the refusal of a job, or dismissal from a job, solely on the grounds that an individual was not a member of the union.[30] In effect, he publicly supported the right *not* to belong to a trade union – 'the abandonment of the closed shop' it was said.[31] And there was a major development in policy over secondary action and secondary picketing. The 'direct' interest which Meacher had sometimes verbally used as the legitimating criterion was now turned, using a European example, into 'a direct interest of an occupational or professional nature'.[32] As for picketing, the Leader, the TUC official and the Employment spokesperson were all determined that there would be no return to mass picketing. There would be a right to picket but only 'peacefully, in limited numbers, in accordance with a statutory code of practice', and only where the secondary employer was directly assisting the first employer to frustrate the dispute.[33] These historic changes were developed after consultations which, in general, bypassed the 'People at Work' PRG of the NEC. Only on the scope of picketing was there a substantive reaction by NEC trade unionists, but even this was not sustained in the face of a determination by the Leader to keep the draft as it was.[34]

What was left in the summer of 1990 after the completion of this exercise amounted to a revolution in trade union perspectives on industrial relations policy. A classic reorientation of trade union priorities was now fused with a sea-change in attitudes towards 'law' in industrial relations. It was not without its compensations. Over these past three years the Party, in consultation with the unions, had developed a Charter of Rights for employees – basic minimum terms and conditions of employment protected by law. And for trade unionists there was, for the first time, the benefit of the right to join a trade union and to be protected against blacklisting victimisation, as well as the right not to be sacked for lawful industrial action. In addition, in the last twelve months of the Policy Review, Labour's policy on union recognition was further developed in the Contact Group. If there were a Labour Government, the unions could look forward at least to a strengthening of their position and of the rights of people at work.

The TUC's assistance in this historic process of adjustment, private as well as public, must not be underrated. Although it is clear that the transformation was heavily pushed from the political wing and was, in a sense, electorate-led, it was nurtured by advice and a stance from TUC officials which basically said 'you have to demand things of us'. And in line with this encouragement, the TUC officials sought not to put any impediment of their own in the way of the Labour leadership, not even on the representational issues where the TUC had drawn lines – even in a sense exercised a 'veto' in the past. This development was eased by the fact that the Party leadership and the TUC officials saw eye to eye over much of training policy, including the view that training must be 'a shared responsibility of employers, unions, individuals and government'.[35] The TUC remained heavily committed to the recreation of a 'tripartite national commission along the lines of the Manpower Services Commission'.[36] But there was now a deep reluctance to intervene openly in Party policymaking, even on issues considered to be of special concern to the TUC. One example was the acceptance of probably the biggest innovation of the Policy Review – a comprehensive regional devolution to elected assemblies to be given a range of powers at the expense of Whitehall. It was a proposal which would have been met prior to 1987 with a strongly articulated TUC scepticism about practicability and a concern for the priority of central and regional tripartite relationships.[37] But support for devolution was being pushed from the Northern regions within the unions, had won some national union adherents, and, crucially, had developed a much stronger backing in the political wing. Among TUC officials, the scepticism remained, as did the centre-region tensions within some of the unions. But the TUC made no move to hinder the policy development.

This opening of boundaries was also evident in key policy areas where the consultations took place directly with the officials of major affiliates. In public terms, the most important of these concerned unilateral nuclear disarmament. As in the previous twenty years, the TUC left this area alone in informal and formal liaison. In 1989, the main unilateralist union, the TGWU, was always in a minority on the PRG and, in the end, little concession was made to the unilateralist position. In the past, this would have caused a major reaction on the NEC and at the Party Conference, but the priorities of some of the unions in the unilateralist camp shifted in the light of the new international situation, Labour's electoral predicament and the need to protect and advance their social and industrial objectives. With NUPE, not for the first time since 1987, leading the way, enough unions pulled behind the new policy to secure a major Conference victory.

One other area where from 1985 to 1987 the Parliamentary leadership had edged between boundaries established by the union mandates was nuclear energy policy. The continuing strength of union feeling in favour of 'phasing out' was shown at the TUC Congresses of 1988 and 1989 when the policy was reaffirmed. But the TGWU, whose shift in 1985 had begun the realignment, shifted back again in response to membership pressures in 1987, and, with the anti-nuclear white collar unions much less represented at the Labour Party Conference, the leadership's position was stabilised by a strengthening alliance of pro-nuclear unions.[38]

The formula of 'steadily diminishing dependence', and a promise that most existing stations would close down before the end of the century, achieved a broad measure of acceptability. Nevertheless, it remained a sensitive issue. Only the requirement to sustain unity behind the leadership stood in the way of an anti-nuclear majority on the NEC.[39]

A third area where unions had established the boundaries of policy in the pre-1987 period was over the compensation to be paid on reacquisition of privatised industries. But here the changing interests of union members now reinforced the electoral focus of the Labour Leadership. Reacquisition on the basis of 'no speculative gain' had now to take account of the growing number of workers and trade unionists holding shares.[40] Accordingly, the steer from the political leadership away from the 1987 policy met little open resistance with only the Left in the NCU making it an issue. By 1989, any remaining objectors had gone quiet and there was 'no question of paying other than a fair market price'.[41]

Northern Ireland was dealt with at Parliamentary level rather than through the policy review and there was no basic change of policy in the 1988 document 'Towards a United Ireland'. There was also a Front Bench dominance over policy formulation on constitutional reform. An extensive reform platform emerged, but although a growing number of unions, and a significant body of opinion within the TUC office, were sympathetic to proportional representation for elections to the House of Commons, a majority of the Parliamentary leadership remained in various degrees committed to the present system (but see p. 477).

If there was one policy area which summed up the change in Party policy and the changing flow of influence from 1983 to 1989, it was transport policy. Virtually a union domain in 1982, it retained in 1989 some superficial features of union dominance in the way policy was formulated. As before, there was a distinctive policy process given hospitality by the NUR at its college. But this time the Party's spokesperson on Transport, John Prescott, invited a much broader range of organisations to the first stages of formulation – including consumer groups. Consumer rights, safety and the environment were given a central prominence, as was the particular problem of London transport. Even so, the draft document of *Moving Britain Into the 1990s* was redrafted in the Policy Directorate to further emphasise and clarify these themes.

In two old problem areas there was still an element of impasse, although in each case significant differences within the political leadership complicated the formulation of policy. As so often in the past, it proved very difficult to secure a union–Party consensus over the form of industrial democracy. In its approach to national-level decision-making, the *People at Work* Group took over the formulas of the 1986 Liaison Committee document, but with a further shift of emphasis to the representation of employees and away from the single, union collective bargaining, channel. However, attempts by Michael Meacher to prescribe a form by which employees would be involved in local decisionmaking met strong pockets of union resistance over the Works Council concept. And there was concern by the Party leadership (and within the TUC) over Meacher's 'power sharing' emphasis at company level. The second and third phases failed to deliver the specific formal structure promised in the first document. In the end, the mood became one of waiting for something to turn up (perhaps from Europe) which would change the balance and context of the argument.

Inflation and rising incomes continued to be the subject of spasmodic private discussion in Party–union channels. Entry into the ERM of the EMS was seen as providing an 'anti-inflationary discipline' but one involving a deflationary pressure and the possibility of a sharp rise in unemployment unless wage bargainers responded. The search for an agreed policy on collective pay bargaining was made more difficult by a range of new payment and bargaining arrangements, often decentralised, and by uncertainty over what would now constitute a reasonable quid pro quo.[42]

Nevertheless, as in the past, TUC officials sought to move the discussion forward – their initiatives reflecting both a desire to help the Party and an understanding that any new arrangement over pay was likely to give the TUC enhanced status. As it happened, the most significant initiative appears to have emerged on the Economic Policy Sub-Committee of the PRGS, under the Chairmanship of John Smith and in response to options in an Office paper. Out of these discussions and follow-up consultations on the Contact Group came a proposal from the GMB and UCW leadership for a move towards synchronised annual pay bargaining which could link with the agenda of annual Government economic policymaking. There was no question of 'pay norms' and there was considerable suspicion from some of the oldest critics of incomes policy – particularly in some of the Rightwing-led craft unions and in the Left-led MSF – but by the autumn of 1990 the debate was moving forward. Ironically at this point, it became more obvious that the scepticism of some of Labour's leaders, including the Party Leader, about 'delivery' had hardened in some quarters into a defensive anxiety about bringing the unions back near the centre of the political stage.[43] A deal might lose the Party the electoral advantage of 'distance' and would certainly give the unions some extra political leverage. Front Bench speakers hastened to emphasise that any 'partnership' would be with industry as a whole and not simply the unions. And, in spite of the dire problem of inflation, there was much less public pressure on the unions from the Front Bench than might have been expected.

This rejection of a union-oriented definition of partnership paralleled a range of other shifts – including the consultations with industrialists on Labour's industrial policy. As the Party Leadership gained confidence in its growing supremacy, so many old assumptions and behaviour patterns began to be challenged. The importance of managerial performance began to be restated, particularly in local government, where Labour Party representatives were often the employer. Efficiency, quality and service began to be emphasised as incompatible with rigid employee protectiveness. This change heightened the tensions with white collar unions in the public service but, in terms of the Policy Review, it focused around compulsory competitive tendering which both white and blue collar unions feared could undermine employment, wages and conditions. After much private union consultation and Policy Review discussions, agreement was produced around a Quality Programme policy. Some on the Front Bench saw it as where the political leadership needed to be. Others saw it as a fudge, short of the required element of compulsion in tendering.

Nevertheless, in this area as in others, it marked yet more accommodation with the Party's needs and an attempt to change the balance towards a user and consumer, rather than a producer's, approach to problems. This reorientation was even shown in the most sensitive and prickly area of union–Labour Party relations, that concerning the handling of industrial disputes. Although such disputes continued to raise difficult problems of politics, timing and tactics for the Parliamentary leadership – particularly when there was internal disagreement over responses, as there was in the Docks dispute of 1989[44] – the Party and its Parliamentary leaders were now much more heavily protected by the union leadership. There was much closer liaison than in some of the disputes of 1983–7 and there was a conscious attempt in the unions concerned to ensure that their tactics did not publicly discredit the Party. Conversely, on two important occasions the Party Leader felt able to call publicly for union members' acceptance of the employers' offer.[45] These tactics were understood and assisted by union representatives on the NEC, who neutralised the efforts of the diminishing 'hard Left' to pressure the Party Leader for a more high profile support for the industrial actions. As it happened, and perhaps as a result, in two popular actions of 1989–90 – the rail strike and the ambulance dispute – the Labour Party gained rather than lost from its identification with the union's cause.

Nothing illustrates better the extent to which unions sought to protect the public image of the Labour Party than the way in which they behaved at the 1989 and 1990 Party Conferences in receiving Policy Review documents, some of which evoked deep anxieties – not to mention a more general sense of identity loss. What was remarkable was the extent to which the great majority of union officials and delegates co-operated in supporting the leadership over the direction the Party was taking. In their whole approach to the Party Conference, in the resolutions and amendments submitted, and in the composites agreed in line with 'the Office' draft, the union representatives overwhelmingly aimed to support and unify. Even in the case of differences over nuclear weapons in 1989 and cuts in defence expenditure in 1990,* those unions which stayed in opposition – including the TGWU – attempted to carry it off with restraint.

All this indicated just how far the majority of the unions and their leaders were prepared to accommodate the Party's presentational needs both in terms of the substance of policy and the appearance of unity. The pattern of anticipated reactions had moved overwhelmingly to the advantage of the Parliamentary Leadership and particularly the Leader. Still, it is important to note that there was a persistent consultative dialogue which had to take some account of union opinion. This was still true of industrial relations issues, but also some other issues where there was a sustained majority vote at the Party Conference.[46] It was there in the build-up of support for proportional representation,** and it was particularly notable in 1990 in the argument over the entrenchment of rights.

The proposal for the incorporation into British law of the European Convention on Human Rights had (as we saw in Chapter 8, pp. 214–16) been bitterly contested in the mid-1970s and had met strong union resistance. It suddenly came to the fore again in the late 1980s as a priority of the movement for constitutional reform known as Charter 88. The huge Conference majority against it in 1989[47] reflected both a historical experience of the courts and continuing union suspicion of any proposal to take power from an accountable Parliament and give it to an unaccountable (and virtually irremovable) judiciary. But it also probably reflected a general willingness to give support to the Party Leadership. The Deputy Leader, Roy Hattersley, had long been an opponent of the 'Bill of Rights' concept and favoured specific protective items of legislation and legislative forms of entrenchment.

However, in the summer of 1990, there were strong signals coming via press leaks that a change in policy was about to be launched by the Party Leadership.[48] This appeared to have some support within the TUC Office where the new Europeanism had, as we have seen, secured other significant changes in policy. Incorporation was attractive both as another step towards harmonisation and a practicable electoral gesture to a vocal body of ex-Alliance supporters. According to precedent, one might have expected a new TUC statement clearing the path and winning over key unions. This would be paralleled by a new Party statement changing policy in time for a major debate at the Party Conference.

---

* In 1989 and 1990, the Party leader was defeated over a proposal to reduce defence spending to the West European average. It was noticeable in 1990 that the proposing union did not push for a card vote. It could not have been refused and would have added to the pressure on the Leader if it had been given a two-thirds majority.
** At the 1990 Party Conference, a resolution (Composite 46) was carried, against platform advice, which called upon the NEC to include elections to the House of Commons in the terms of reference of the NEC Committee which was to consider the method of election for regional government, the upper chamber and the European Parliament.

But on this issue things did not go according to plan. In the debate around the NEC and in the unions, the anti-incorporationists were strengthened by a powerful critique of the civil liberties record of the British judiciary.[49] Trade union scepticism about moving away from forms of legislative protection turned into outright majority rejection as the TUC's consultation progressed. At the same time, women, whose rights had generally been left out of the debate, were alerted to the fact that one of their most famous legislative victories – that of a right to choose over abortion – could be threatened by giving new powers to the judiciary. Women on the General Council and on the NEC reacted accordingly. The high profile campaign for incorporation failed to engage publicly with these arguments, failed completely to win a groundswell of opinion from below in the Party, and ultimately failed to convince at national level. As the argument progressed, opinion hardened against the policy change, not only in the unions but in all the significant committees and forums.

Thus there followed a classic piece of anticipated reaction and sensitive leadership. The TUC statement was 'filed' in the General Council Report. The new Labour Party policy statement failed to emerge. And by the Party Conference* of 1990 not a voice was raised on the NEC in its support.

POWER AND POLICYMAKING

Viewing as a whole the policy interaction between the Parliamentary leadership and the unions, by October 1990 it was becoming apparent that, in the distribution of power, the relationship was approaching nearer the polar model of Parliamentary dominance than at any time before when the Party was in Opposition. Private channels of consultation with the union leaders and the TUC remained open and significant, but there was little doubt in the minds of those on the union side where the initiative lay and where the final say in Party policy was expected from.

As for relations between the Front Bench and the NEC, here, as in 1986–7, there were significant departures from the agreed policymaking procedure (albeit sometimes within the protocol of private consultations with the TUC[50]). The first signs emerged that the Shadow Cabinet Economic Committee was being used to formulate an element of the Policy Review – independent of the NEC.[51] The Front Bench ascendancy in policy formulation was reflected in the fact that seventeen policy statements came independently from PLP spokespersons between October 1989 and October 1990 – a development which provoked a new protocol for managing it.[52] With this ascendancy there remained also the possibility that a final policy document and the Manifesto would be used to adjust, to refine, and to omit.

Compared with 1984–6 (and 1988), the NEC trade unionists were by 1990 either sidelined or more pliable on industrial disputes and industrial relations issues and the Liaison Committee had virtually ceased to function (thus keeping

---

* At the 1990 Party Conference, a composite resolution (No. 49) calling for incorporation was easily defeated on a show of hands.

the NEC members away from TUC–Front Bench liaison). Various policy boundaries established and enforced by the Unions before 1983 had been removed or greatly widened. The Parliamentary leadership was less restricted by the unions 'rules' of union freedom than ever before.

Though anticipation of union reactions, particularly on industrial issues, still played a part in the substance as well as the procedure of policymaking, this pattern was dwarfed by the reverse flow as the union leaders and the TUC accommodated and anticipated the needs of the Parliamentary leadership. The political project of securing a Labour Government had in the past evoked solidaristic inhibitions about pushing trade union claims, but the constraints on trade union behaviour were now greater than at any time since the Party's foundations as all attention was focused on electoral victory.[53]

The restraint in private pressure was accompanied by a restraint in public statements. The Party Leader had sought to create a culture of discreet argument rather than public division. This, adding to the unions' concern to protect the Party's image, meant that much more than in the past, union minorities were disinclined to pursue 'settled' arguments and certainly disinclined to pursue them in any way detrimental to the Party's electoral image.

NOTES

1. John Evans MP and Bryan Gould MP, *Productive and Competitive Economy*. Eddie Haigh and Michael Meacher MP, *People at Work*. Diana Jeuda and John Smith MP, *Economic Equality*. David Blunkett MP and Jack Straw MP, *Consumers and the Community*. Roy Hattersley MP and Jo Richardson MP, *Democracy for the Individual and the Community*. John Cunningham MP and Syd Tierney, *Physical and Social Environment*. Tony Clarke and Gerald Kaufman MP, *Britain in the World*. The PRGs were serviced by officials from the Party's Policy Directorate and from the PLP assistants and advisers.
2. John Cunningham, Gerald Kaufman, John Smith and Jack Straw.
3. Tony Clarke, Eddie Haigh and Syd Tierney. Diana Jeuda, a trade union official, was from the Women's Section.
4. The Campaign Management Team included senior Head Office officials, representatives from the Leader's Office and the Campaign co-ordinator from the PLP, which since 1985 had had its own Campaign Officer and campaign unit.
5. The lack of separate meetings of the Home Policy Committee and the International Committee between January and July 1989 was the cause of some complaint at the joint meeting of the Home Policy Committee and International Committee held on 10 July 1989. At this meeting, a promise was made that the normal committee cycle would be respected in future, but it was not adhered to.
6. General Council members had sometimes been members of specialist subcommittees of the NEC – Transport being the most regular example – but it was unusual and they often sent a substitute or failed to appear.
7. John Edmunds (GMB), PCE Group; Rodney Bickerstaffe (NUPE), EE Group; Garfield Davies (USDAW), CC Group; and Ron Todd (TGWU), BW Group.
8. The Economic Policy PRG Subcommittee also included the six PRG convenors (Gordon Brown replacing Bryan Gould and Tony Blair

replacing Michael Meacher in November 1989) plus MPs and NEC members Margaret Beckett, Robin Cook and John Prescott, plus Michael Meacher. Thus there was only one NEC Trade Union Section member and nine from the Front Bench.

9. Only Edmunds was said to have made a distinctive personal contribution, although dialogue with union representatives was always an important element in the Economic Equality Group's work. Ron Todd continued the past practice of his union in relation to Party study groups and subcommittees and sent the union's Research Officer, Regan Scott, to the Britain in the World PRG as a substitute. The union made no attempt to take the initiative.

10. The groups varied in their operation, but most of them established informal sub-groups to examine areas of concern and to prepare first drafts of the relevant sections of the report. These were normally chaired by a Front Bench member.

11. Hughes and Wintour, *op. cit.*, p. 63. The book gives a particularly informative account of the role of the Shadow Communications Agency run by Philip Gould and Deborah Mattinson and of the work of Peter Mandelson, the Director of Campaigns and Communications.

12. MPs' allowances rose to £22,367 in 1989 but the most significant increase was to the Front Bench through the Short Money which rose substantially to £839,000 in 1987. By contrast, in 1988, the Party's Policy Development Department expenditure was £562,000.

13. This had mainly a Parliamentary coordination function during the first two years of the Policy Review, although there were signs that it might play a more important policy role in future, particularly as the PLP now had an Economic Unit with two members of staff. See n. 51 for the third year policy on the replacement of Poll Tax.

14. See, for example, John Lloyd, 'Labour Must Put Unions in their Place', *Sunday Times*, 3/1/88.

15. 'Consumers and the Community', *SJEE*, pp. 25–31.

16. *Ibid.*, pp. 26–8.

17. The Leftwing union opposition was marginalised. Its focal point in the unions was in the NCU and the NUM. See Nicholas Costello, Jonathan Mitchie and Seumas Milne, *Beyond the Casino Economy*, 1989, for a commitment to planning sponsored by the two unions and the Campaign for Labour Party Democracy.

18. The growth of the 'soft Left' was the most marked feature of the composition of the NEC from 1986 to 1990. It was convened as a group by the TGWU representative Eddie Haigh, particularly when committee Chairs were being contested, but it was not encouraged to meet as a policy group by either the Party Leader or by Tom Sawyer, its initial guiding spirit. However, by 1990 the group included some leading Front Bench politicians and was meeting regularly, with Sawyer no longer its most influential figure. Just occasionally by network and meeting, it exercised some collective influence – particularly on organisational and procedural matters, and appointments.

19. The position was complicated by the fact that NUPE's Tom Sawyer was Chairman of the Party's Home Policy Committee, while his General Secretary, Rodney Bickerstaffe, was Chairman of the TUC's Economic Committee and therefore the exchange would have produced role complications, but the downgrading also fitted into the general development of the relationship with the TUC.

20. Composite Resolution No. 11 supporting full renationalisation and taking into public ownership at least one top company in each sector of manufacturing industry was voted down by what was described as 'the biggest margin ever', *CLPD Secretary's Report*, 1990. The vote was 5,597,000 to 459,000.

21. *Employment Law: TUC Priorities*, BB/PM/GS, 9/1/89.

22. Indeed, there may well have been more political differences between NEC trade unionists and their senior officials in this period than at any time previously. It was quietly but significantly a fact of life within NUPE, but it was most marked in the contrasting factional roles of the NGA officials – one organised the Right on the NEC, the other the Left on the General Council.

23. Interview with Michael Meacher, House of Commons, 1/2/90.

24. MCMC, 1989, p. 25.

25. The six words were contained in an amendment to Motion 5 submitted by the TGWU in the light of their experience with the courts during the Docks dispute.

26. Meacher's advisers included Lord McCarthy and Lord Wedderburn, who had assisted the TUC for many years over labour law. Clarke relied on Lord Alexander Irvine.

27. Involved in the drafting were Joe Irvine of the TGWU and Jon Cruddas from Walworth Road.

28. PR 330/89, 'People at Work' Policy Review Group, 29/9/89.

29. Comp. Res. No. 16, *LPACR*, 1989, pp. 167–8.

30. Press Release of a Statement to Sedgefield Constituency Labour Party, 18/12/89.

31. It was, of course, not so much the end of the closed shop as the end of Labour's support for legal protection for it and for the trade union capacity to force a dismissal. *Looking to the Future* included full support for a '100 per cent trade union membership at the workplace', p. 35.

32. *Ibid.*, p. 34.

33. *Ibid.*, p. 34.

34. *NEC Minutes*, 15/5/90, p. 7.

35. MCMC, 1989, p. 17.

36. TUC, *Skills 2000*, 1989, p. 12.

37. See Chapter 14, p. 432. Between 1983 and 1987, apart from a commitment to the establishment of a Scottish Assembly, Labour managed only the production of a last-minute consultative paper, *Local Government Reform in England and Wales*, in February 1987. It argued tentatively that 'a persuasive case can be made for establishing a tier of regional authorities', with a wide range of responsibilities, including regional economic planning. The regional authorities '(eventually) should be directly elected', pp. 12–13. In this period, not only was there strong resistance from various trade union leaders and from the TUC Office but also opposition from some key figures in the political wing. David Blunkett, the Chair of the NEC's Local Government Advisory Committee, was protective of local decision-making, Neil Kinnock was a long-time opponent of devolution for Wales. After 1987, Blunkett joined with the powerful current of support for regional devolution, but Kinnock was known to have retained his major reservations. His continuing scepticism may well have given solace to those with similar views within the TUC.

38. In August 1990, a grouping of six power industry unions deeply con-

cerned about the future of nuclear power began a campaign against Government financial restrictions.

39. The decision to commission power stations at Sizewell, Torness and Hinckley Point was first opposed by 11 votes to 10 on the NEC on 8/5/89, then was supported on a second vote by 13 votes to 11 on 17/5/89, with the assistance of seven of the twelve trade unionists. The context of the argument was constantly changing with new information on costs, safety and the environmental effects.

40. UCW Resolution (No. 307), 1987, *Party Conference Agenda*, p. 39.

41. MCMC, p. 15.

42. TUC officials thought in terms of training policy, infrastructure expenditure, and social policy.

43. An article by Seumas Milne, 'Union Pay Reform Plan Threatens Labour Split', *Guardian*, 3/8/90, located deep unease at 'any whiff of any return to 1960's style corporatism' felt by unnamed 'Labour leaders'.

44. Michael Meacher's high profile support for the TGWU case was not appreciated by the Leader or by a majority of his Shadow Cabinet colleagues.

45. 'Kinnock tells Railmen to call off strike', *Guardian*, 21/7/89. 'Ambulance Leaders Hope For Peace Deal in March', *The Observer*, 25/2/90.

46. It is understood that, after consultation with representatives of the Lesbian and Gay Rights lobby, there was a general acceptance of the formulation that the Party would prohibit discrimination on grounds of race, sex, sexual orientation or disability. *Looking to the Future*, 1990, p. 41. Some of the sympathisers with the cause of the Palestinians found the phraseology of the 1990 document a helpful advance, *ibid.*, p. 44.

47. The vote on Composite 30 was 4,650,000 to 1,358,000. *LPACR*, 1989, p. 172.

48. 'Labour To Back Human Rights Charter', *The Independent*, 11/6/90. 'At Last The Right Turning on Rights', *Guardian* editorial, 12/6/90.

49. K.D. Ewing and C.A. Gearty, *Freedom under Thatcher*, 1990. See also Keith Ewing, *A Bill of Rights for Britain?*, Institute of Employment Rights pamphlet, 1990.

50. The most obvious example was over the closed shop. See Chapter 5, n. 111.

51. The Party's alternative to the Poll Tax was developed within the Economic Committee of the Shadow Cabinet and referred back and forth to the Shadow Cabinet, even though a promise had been given that the Committee would not be used for Party policy formulation. Not until after a press leak of the final version was it taken to the NEC. There was a welcome for the substance of the policy but much aggravation over the policymaking procedure.

52. Draft letter by the Leader (under cover of GS:1/10/90) as amended by the NEC, *NEC Minutes*, 24/10/90.

53. For a classic statement of mainstream opinion, see Bill Morris, TGWU Deputy General Secretary, 'Not Stopping at the Factory Gate', *Tribune*, 31/8/90. 'We should not miss our aim by becoming bogged down in an arcane debate about the margins of Labour's proposals for employment law. Even those who have doubts about Labour's programme must surely see the sense of getting rid of the Tories as a first priority.'

Part VI

Organisation and mobilisation

Party organisation and Trade Unions for a Labour Victory

Mobilisation and intervention

In the past decade, it has been a significant new feature of the trade union relationship with the Labour Party that the unions have created a collective organisation designed primarily to facilitate political mobilisation. From Trade Unions for a Labour Victory (TULV), via the Trade Union Coordinating Committee (TUCC) and through the new fusionTrade Unionists For Labour (TUFL), the Labour Party took on a novel ancillary structure.

It was, in terms of the Labour Party, an important historical development, although not one universally welcomed or even well understood. In the next four chapters, we will examine the form and behaviour of these new bodies beginning here with an exploration of the problems surrounding the birth of TULV, its organisation and political character. This will be entwined with an analysis of the role that TULV leaders attempted to play on Party organisational matters in the 1980 Commission of Enquiry and the problems they faced in securing compliance on the part of Labour's NEC.

The fact that members of the General Council, operating through a new organisation, attempted to play an initiating role in matters of Party organisation amounted to a major breach of the 'rules' and protocol of the relationship. This breach was deeply resented and resisted by the majority of the NEC including some of its trade union members, and the tension was made more acute by the ingrained suspicion that TULV was, in practice, a factional 'Trojan Horse', seeking to undermine or control the political Left. To what extent it operated in factional terms will be assessed at the end of the chapter.

Degeneration

To understand the long term importance of the growth of TULV, we have again to be reminded of the historic political weaknesses of British trade unionism. There was, as has been shown, always an ambivalence about 'politics' such that, although unions varied in their political traditions, it was a general feature that attempts to engender political mobilisation among the mass of the membership were limited and, when initiated, seldom sustained.

The absorption of the 'post-war settlement' accentuated the problem. It encouraged a high degree of complacency and then a new degeneration. 'Woodcockism', which encouraged and accompanied the TUC's movement 'into Whitehall', added a new emphasis on national corporate relationships rather than grass roots mobilisation. Labour Movement media of political communication were run down: the *Daily Herald* was allowed to move away from the unions, the local Labour press was allowed to decline, the National Council of Labour Colleges was wound up – all these developments made it harder to counter the fierce ideological onslaught of the late 1970s.

Even in the period of the shift to the Left in the unions and the growth of a new Left leadership at various levels, the processes of political campaigning and political education remained weak. Much was expected by the Left in the TGWU and the AUEW from the growth of industrial militancy as a spontaneous educative experience; the result was often continuing political weakness at the grass roots where new strength had been expected. At this time also, an expansion of formal trade union education gave priority to training in union and industrial relations functions, leaving a gap where there might have been a broader educational provision.

As for local trade union linkage to the Labour Party, in many areas much of it was ritualistic, empty of vigorous communication, and rarely touched, let alone involved, the bulk of the levypaying membership. Election assistance suffered accordingly. The Wilson Report in the mid-1950s had described beliefs about trade union participation in Labour's election campaigns as 'exaggerated legend'.[1] In 1970, an investigation by the National Agents Department of union–Party liaison at regional level found that there had been a run-down under the Wilson Government.[2] Subsequently, some attempts were made by the NEC and individual unions to produce an improvement, but the continuing weakness remained hidden behind artificially high levels of affiliation, locally, regionally and nationally.

It may well have been the case that Labour's close identification and cooperation with the unions in the 1970s – and the facilities given to trade unionism as a result of Labour Government legislation – strengthened support for the unions' links with the Labour Party among a large minority of trade unionists during this period (see Chapter 18, pp. 560–8). But in terms of the attitudes of trade unionists to issues connected with trade unionism, and to electoral support for the Labour Party, the late 1970s showed, as we have seen, a weakening of traditional positions. And the unions, in organisational and communicational terms, were very poorly equipped to deal with a resurgent Rightwing conservatism and a variety of other perspectives hostile or unsympathetic to the Labour Movement.

The reputation of TULV

In my view, the development of Trade Unions for a Labour Victory represented, potentially, a major breakthrough in the strengthening of the Labour Movement. It became an electoral asset to the Labour Party and, I shall argue, an important organisational precursor for the defence of the unions' Political Funds in the ballots of 1985 and 1986 (Chapter 17). In terms of a potential instrument for the politicisation and mobilisation of trade unionists, it filled a gap which had been there for decades.

And yet it was greatly suspected and unloved all across the Labour Party. Two *Tribune* columnists who in 1986 described it as having 'an inglorious history'[3] would have found agreement in many places. For a start, there was a mixture of hostility and suspicion from sections of a Party bureaucracy which felt threatened by a professional and institutional challenge to their own roles. A section of the Left which included Tony Benn, Dennis Skinner and Arthur Scargill saw the TULV organisation as simply a cloak for the Right and therefore sought to undermine it. Paradoxically, some on the Right of the unions, who saw things rather more clearly, viewed it as an obstacle to an out-and-out factional onslaught by the Right on the Left. Others on the Right disliked it because it pressured them into initiatives and co-operation in political ventures they would otherwise have left alone. Epitomising the two prongs of the factional attack on TULV was the broad-ranging onslaught launched by the NUM in 1983 and the well-publicised defection of the AUEW the same year.

As for the TUC, it was none too keen on another 'infant' in the Labour Movement. Not only was the initiative outside the orbit of TUC control, but it appeared to be threatening their territory when, on 26 November 1980, TULV held a seminar on union pension funds at Congress House itself. It was agreed after this that such involvements were a mistake and should not be part of the work of TULV in future. But for a long period afterwards there was a wariness in that relationship.

In the Central Office of the Conservative Party there was a degree of far-sighted alarm. TULV was seen as an attempt to consolidate and extend support for the Labour Party among trade unionists just at the time when the Conservative Party saw itself on the verge of a significant breakthrough among manual workers. The moment it surfaced to public view, TULV was bitterly attacked as an attempt 'to impose a closed shop on electoral choice'.[4]

The factional complication

If the Conservatives could see further than the end of their noses on this, it must be said that many on the Left could not. This is explicable mainly in terms of misconceptions about the complex mix of motivations on the Right of the unions. Though, as will be indicated, TULV was cross-factional in its composition, and non-factional in its objectives, it began at a time when a section of the Right was attempting a range of moves against the Party's National Executive Committee – a committee controlled, for the first time in the Party's history, by the Left.

For a short period this Rightwing factional attack focused on organisational problems in a way which prejudiced the whole question of organisational reform and placed a 'Rightwing' birthmark on TULV. There is no doubt that there was a genuine and growing worry about the degeneration of the organisational base of the Party and the political vulnerability of the grass roots. Within some of the unions, both Right and Left, a consensus began to develop that the unions must make some new and special effort to reinvigorate the Labour Movement.

Unfortunately, some on the Right began to use the organisational question – particularly after the Labour Party's poor showing in by-elections – in order to blame the Leftwing NEC and to suggest measures which would 'reform' that NEC.[5] For years afterwards, organisational reform and reconstruction was bedevilled by this factional edge – and the equally factional response of sections of the political Left. Time after time necessary organisational changes and major innovations were held back, obstructed or evaded because of suspicions of their factional source or their potential factional consequences.

This fusion of the consensual and the factional was also a feature of the internal politics of the third largest union – the General and Municipal Workers. Under David Basnett – destined to be a 'founding father' of TULV – the union had moved nearer to the centre of the Party's mainstream but it had a Rightwing history and reputation and sectors of 'the old G and M' were still very powerful.

In 1977, within the union, there was a political initiative which was intended (by some at least) to afford an opportunity to counter-attack against the Left and just possibly to weaken their hold on the NEC. At the G and M Conference that year, a motion from the Right sought to criticise the displacement 'of sitting Labour MPs on purely ideological grounds' and proposed an alternative method of reselection to that sought by the Campaign for Labour Party Democracy.[6] In replying to the debate for the G and M Executive, Derek Gladwin (who was also the Chairman of the Labour Party Conference Arrangements Committee and a confidant of the Party Leader, James Callaghan) asked for remittance of the motion and in doing so subtly broadened the terms of reference so as to include the whole question of Labour's constitution and democracy – including the composition of the Labour Party's NEC.[7]

Subsequently, after a discussion on the organisation subcommittee of the G and M Executive, the union submitted to the Labour Party Conference a general resolution which called for 'an enquiry into the structure, organisation, finance and internal democracy of the Labour Party at all levels' and 'relations with affiliated organisations and other Party interests'.[8]

But there was already, in a sense, a factionally tainted element to this resolution. Further, it represented a major break with past protocol and a threat to what was understood to be the 'rules' of the relationship between the unions and the Party.

The senior union leaders could claim strong precedents for 'solidarity' action to assist the Party but there could be little doubt that under the 'rules', the Party's NEC had sole responsibility for Party administration, organisation and finance. If the constitutional clause prohibiting General Council members from sitting on the NEC implied this autonomy, the discussions of the 1930s confirmed it. And Trade Union Section members of the NEC, whatever private argument they might occasionally have with their senior officers over Party policy, were normally among the strongest defenders of this administrative autonomy. This was 'our show'; that was 'theirs'.

The normality was exemplified in the history of the various reorganisation proposals which have been a feature of the Party's life since the mid-1950s. They came from a wide range of sources – but *never* from the unions. And though trade union members of the NEC (a Jack Cooper, a Bill Simpson or a Jack Jones) might individually play important parts in the subsequent enquiries, they in no sense acted as mouthpieces of their unions.

Thus, the General and Municipal Workers' resolution was unprecedented from a trade union and was received with considerable suspicion from the Left in the unions as well as on the NEC. As it happened, the resolution was on its own on the agenda of the 1977 Labour Party Conference and not even the weight of the G and M and the Chair of the Conference Arrangements Committee could secure a debate – such was the suspicion. It was remitted to the NEC.

In the next three months, the union's General Secretary, David Basnett, who was becoming more and more concerned at the organisational weakness at the base of the Labour Movement, sought as a priority to lose the factional taint and to build a broader consensual character to the campaign for an enquiry. He succeeded in persuading ten unions to submit letters to the NEC to back up his own. These unions included the Leftwing TGWU (in transition from Jack Jones to Moss Evans) and SOGAT, led by Bill Keys. Armed with this Leftwing support, Basnett made a personal appeal to the NEC in January 1978 and stressed that the motion was 'not a Trojan Horse' but a genuine organisational concern backed by a wide spectrum of unions.[9]

Basnett's own letter had referred to 'disturbing trends in Labour's finance membership and votes' and to 'enormous problems of organisation, democracy and representativeness at all levels within the Party'.[10] Many of these problems, he conceded, were not recent but long term, and neither the Wilson nor the Simpson reports had produced any significant improvement. Significantly for the future purpose of the TULV, he also noted the acute problems which were now appearing *within* the unions in terms of contracting out, low individual membership of the Party and the lack of political education which was even making it possible for the National Front to make some headway at local level. There was also the longstanding problem of the proper allocation of union finance to where it was most needed by the Party – a problem of maldistribution which involved the sensitive practice of union sponsorship.

Although he secured an NEC enquiry (of a sort), he failed to allay the fears of the NEC Left. In spite of the fact that the enquiry was given terms of reference which precluded issues of Party democracy and representation and was focused purely on organisational matters, there remained suspicion of the motives of the four union leaders on the twenty-two member enquiry team and there was a noticeable lack of interest in its work by members of the NEC. In competition with the Party's practical preparation for a General Election it soon ran into the ground.

Nevertheless, this Party Organisation Enquiry Committee (nicknamed by some 'the Basnett Committee'), though it met only four times, managed – as a result of union prompting – to produce (after only its second meeting) an interim report. Much of it was unexceptional but it contained one huge innovation. It proposed that there be a permanent committee of senior Party and trade union officials acting as a liaison committee on organisational matters, with a co-ordinator and elected representatives from the unions and the Executive[11]

Though the NEC formally accepted the proposal,[12] and in this way could be said to have legitimised a new role for the unions in matters of Party organisation, it was regarded by many on the NEC as a wholly improper innovation. The only body vaguely similar to this proposal had been the secret Joint Committee of 1944 (see Chapter 3, pp. 62–3) but it had been initiated by *the Party* and was focused primarily on the interface of union and Party organisational matters. An organisation involving General Council members overseeing aspects of *Party* organisation was a clear breach of the 'rules'. And it was deeply resented by the NEC, including several members of the Trade Union Section who were by no means all on the Left.

Thus, despite its 'acceptance', it soon became clear that this new committee would never be instituted in practice by the NEC. The union leaders for the moment retired hurt. There was no final report.

The birth of TULV

At this point, another set of developments changed the focus of interest of the union leaders. It has often been said that the origins of TULV lie in the consortium of unions which came together over the redevelopment of Walworth Road as the Party Headquarters. Certainly it deepened their preoccupation with the matter of Party finance. Yet TULV actually arose through a second set of financial discussions concerned with the approaching General Election. In the summer of 1978, it was firmly believed that a General Election was in the offing. At a meeting held in Downing Street between the Party Leader and a group of union leaders, the issue of finance for the General Election was raised and left to the union leaders to see what they could do. In the subsequent private discussions involving a small group of union leaders from both Left and Right, dissatisfaction was expressed with this whole last minute and unstructured 'begging bowl' routine and plans were made to see if the Labour Party could be assisted by placing this aspect of financing on a more rationalised and institutionalised basis.

At the same time, the question of how best the unions might assist the Labour Party was also raised in terms of facilities and personnel. The problem of how to mobilise trade unionists – a problem already part of the dialogue with the Party on the 'Basnett' committee – now also came into the discussion. There are alternative variations on who at this point suggested the TULV-type organisation and its broad function; one locates it with the David Basnett–Larry Whitty axis at the GMWU, another locates it with Ray Buckton, Leftwing leader of ASLEF, following discussion with Geoffrey Goodman, a Leftwing political journalist who had been working in the Downing Street Counter-Inflation Unit until 1978. Whoever it was, it would be difficult to group these four together as a Rightwing union 'plot' but they became the core of the first *ad hoc* committee set up by TULV after an inaugural meeting held at Congress House on 23 August 1978.

Present at this inaugural meeting were the Labour Party General Secretary and representatives of eight unions – four from the Left and four from the Right.[13] The *ad hoc* committee was serviced by Whitty, the GMWU's Research Officer, who became its Secretary and Coordinator, Goodman, who was for a time responsible for liaison with the Press, and Reg Underhill, who as National Agent provided linkage to the Party machine.

The main function of TULV was 'to coordinate union resources during the coming campaign with concentration on marginal seats'. It sought to arrange for trade union speakers to assist the campaign. And it tried to establish 'a parallel all-union Committee to coordinate union action in the election at Labour Party regional level and also at individual marginal constituency level'.[14] These aims were to be fundamental in the developments from TULV in the late 1970s to TUFL in the late 1980s, although it was other activities which often drew more attention.

As it happened, there was no General Election called in 1978. Plans had already been laid to invite other Labour Party members of the General Council to join the TULV committee and in November the Leftwing SOGAT leader, Bill Keys, and the Rightwing Engineers' leader, John Boyd, were brought in – once more keeping a scrupulous balance.

TULV's first effort at national and regional co-ordination of support for the Party was not very successful – indeed, some described it as alarmingly poor. A temporary headquarters was set up in the GMWU headquarters in London with a very limited liaison with Labour Party Head Office. Regional organisation was established by officials of the two big general unions and, in one uncovered region, SOGAT. If there was an improved regional co-ordination with the Labour Party it was only in comparison with a situation where in some areas such co-ordination had become virtually non-existent. The whole show was weakly structured, initiated too late and worked only spasmodically. Activity in most marginals was less than expected and often insignificant. Most TULV publications failed to reach their targets or arrived late. Advertising and press coverage was ineffective. Approximately 82,000 was spent but only the finance-raising aspects of having a national co-ordination mechanism could be said to have worked satisfactorily.

Institutionalisation

There was not a lot of consolation to be gained from the 1979 General Election result, but in retrospect it is possible to see some benefits which came out of the experience. For a start, a precedent had been created of national and regional trade union co-ordination. And, as important, the election taught those participating some harsh lessons. It illustrated very vividly just how little 'the Labour Movement' in the localities actually moved, and how much work needed to be done within the unions and the Party if the relationship was to be reinvigorated. Having taken on a collective responsibility for mobilising trade unionists, the unions had now to face not only the reality of past neglect but the new appeal of an assertive Rightwing Conservatism. There had been a ten per cent rise in support for the Conservatives among trade unionists since October 1974.

Financially, the unions' anxieties continued to grow about the future level of their political funds, and about the demands being made from the Party – particularly in the light of the movement of headquarters from Transport House to Walworth Road. And there was also a surge of complaints about the NEC's handling of Head Office administration (Chapter 19) and of a variety of financial matters. In the next chapter we will explore this financial insecurity and the response of the unions to various financial developments. Here let it be noted simply that the new financial problems fed into the existing organisational concerns and ensured the continuance of TULV.

Ironically, given the political Left's neurotic suspicion of the TULV organisation, it is important to record that at the meeting of the TULV committee on 27 June 1979, when it was decided to institutionalise TULV and also to press the Labour Party NEC for a new enquiry into Party organisation, the union Left were in a clear majority. Basnett was in the Chair; Moss Evans (TGWU), Alan Fisher (NUPE), Bill Keys (SOGAT) and Barry Sherman (ASTMS) outnumbered the sole representative of the Right, Lord Allen (USDAW).[15]

To give TULV a greater legitimacy, a 'report back' session was organised for the eve of the 1979 Labour Party Conference. The thirty unions present at that meeting accepted the committee and discussion began about the inauguration of a constitution and the creation of a permanent organisation. A brief constitution was agreed by the committee in February 1980 and endorsed in September 1980 after a meeting of TULV unions.

Thirty-seven such unions affiliated to TULV covering, at this stage, 90 per cent of the affiliated membership. Among those who did not affiliate, the only important union was the National Union of Mineworkers, who had decided, following the 1979 election, that they wanted no part of another central organisation of trade unionists. Joe Gormley ceased attending committee meetings. 'Too busy watching Scargill, and the NUM Left, over his shoulder' was the privately accepted explanation of the withdrawal.

But developments in TULV now began to be affected also by what was happening over constitutional issues in the political wing. Immediately following the General Election defeat, the NEC and its allies moved to ensure that the two great constitutional issues of mandatory reselection and the procedure for electing the Party Leader would be re-discussed at the Party Conference, and a new constitutional controversy – over the final say on the Manifesto – was opened up.

We have already noted (Chapter 7) the varying trade union responses to these issues and the conflicts that they produced. But over and above any differences was a concern that the Party might be stampeded into fundamental changes which would be impracticable and lacking the legitimacy of a wide spectrum of consent. TULV appeared to most of the major union leaders to provide a useful forum through which they might develop a common set of attitudes to the process of producing constitutional change, if not to the changes themselves. This, however, was to bring them into direct conflict with the Bennite Left on the NEC and lead to further accusations of impropriety.

TULV AND THE COMMISSION OF ENQUIRY

Operation

By the time of the 1980 Labour Party Conference, the TULV Committee, Right and Left, was determined that there should be a comprehensive enquiry into Party organisation and most of the union leaders – now thoroughly alarmed by the upheaval in the Party – were behind an attempt to seek a consensual solution to the constitutional questions through the enquiry. Given the breadth of support for the enquiry and the growing belief that the Party's organisation required both deep diagnosis and surgery, the NEC was no longer in a position to hold out – especially as it was involved in a growing financial crisis which required union assistance (see Chapter 16, p. 517).

However, it was a measure of the different ways in which some of the major issues were approached that the Commission's inauguration should be authorised by two different resolutions at the Party Conference and that these should have significant differences in factional emphasis.[16]

The suspicions of factional purpose, which ran permanently alongside a measure of agreement on the need to explore various organisational problems, burst out almost immediately in a protracted argument over the Commission's composition. Previous enquiries had all taken the form of NEC sub-committees under 'Party' control and the NEC majority could not see why this precedent should not determine that NEC members should have a majority on the new Commission. The union leadership and a majority of the Shadow Cabinet wanted a broader-based membership. Eventually, under very heavy pressure, Alex Kitson, a trade union member of the NEC, withdrew and the composition was agreed. There were six members from the NEC (Frank Allaun MP, Norman Atkinson MP, Tony Benn MP, Eric Heffer MP, Joan Lestor MP, and Jo Richardson MP), five from TULV (David Basnett, Terry Duffy, Moss Evans, Clive Jenkins and Bill Keys), the Leader and Deputy Leader, and the Chief Whip, Michael Cocks MP, as observer. Secretaries were Ron Hayward and Joyce Gould, who organised and collated the vast input.

In its form – basically a joint TULV-NEC Commission – the Enquiry was unprecedented and a major break with the 'rules' of Party autonomy. The role of the union leaders was potentially all the more important because of the sheer scope of the enquiry. Its agreed terms of reference were very wide and covered membership, finance, organisation, electoral arrangements, the policy process, the Party structure and its constitution. In theory, it precluded nothing – not even the question of the block vote, the role of the Parliamentary Party and the composition of the NEC.

A TULV position paper suggested its mode of working and although not all the suggestions were accepted, in the end there emerged a structure in which the main Commission would be fed by three working Panels, each staffed and given facilities by the unions. Two of the three working Panels were chaired and facilitated by trade union leaders, Moss Evans (Organisation and Membership) and Clive Jenkins (Finance), with the third (Political Education) taken by Tony Benn from the NEC with facilities from SOGAT. A triumvirate of Chairmen rotated positions on the main Commission – David Basnett from TULV sharing the position with Eric Heffer from the NEC and Deputy Party Leader, Michael Foot.

There was an enormous input into this Commission, altogether 2,460 pieces of evidence. Nothing on this scale had ever been attempted before. From the trade unions alone came an impressive range of material. Thirty-three different unions submitted evidence in one form or another. It was variable in its scope and depth but some of it – including the evidence produced by Larry Whitty for the GMWU – was farsighted, detailed and comprehensive. TULV itself made no collective input, apart from the organisation of a meeting of all affiliated unions during the work of the Commission, to discuss affiliation fees.

Indeed, one thing became clear immediately. The union leaders, having got their enquiry, had no particular programme to put to it – apart from the fact that something immediate had to be done about the state of Labour's finances (see Chapter 16). The TULV representatives did attempt to act in concert, particularly on financial proposals, and they held prior discussions before important meetings of the Commission, but these were noted to be remarkably non-consensual. As the discussions wore on over the summer, so the difficulties accumulated.

On the three constitutional questions, the TULV leaders believed initially that there should be a comprehensive examination of the constitution and structure. Their main point prior to the 1979 Conference had been that the changes which were then being proposed should be considered in a wider context of reform and with an attempt to construct a wide consensus on the changes. What exactly the consensus should be does not appear to have been discussed within TULV. The union leaders were content that they could negotiate such a consensus away from the 'hot house' of the Party Conference. In the event they failed (see also Chapter 7) and eventually the union leaders simply gave in and threw the issues back to the Party Conference.

This failure, plus the ever-present countervailing pressures of a range of vested interests, led the union leaders to agree that they would not go far into any constitutional issue that was 'hot'. In this sense, the Commission was a major defeat for the union leaders who came to it believing that they could negotiate 'anything' but found that in this party context, facing a resentful NEC and out of their natural territory, they could negotiate very little.

So, although the Commission had received many submissions on the Block Vote, the composition of the NEC, the Parliamentary Labour Party, 'entryism' and other potentially incendiary matters, they were by common agreement pushed to one side. In particular, the occasional attempt by the Party Leader and one of the union leaders, Terry Duffy of the AUEW, to look again at the NEC's structure and membership was given no encouragement.

Nor were the union leaders particularly successful in achieving and securing the implementation of an agreed programme of organisational reform. One hurdle followed another.

There were, to begin with, some self-imposed territorial obstacles from the unions themselves. Speaking for 'the unions' was always problematic. The Organisation Panel found that there was powerful opposition to the revival of joint Trades and Labour Councils which had been a feature of many local Labour Movements until the 1970s. Here, resistance from the TUC, which favoured political autonomy by the Trades Councils, seems to have been the major factor. And the Commission also turned down the Panel's recommendation of a prohibition on payment of expenses for trade union delegates attending the GMC. On this, the Commission seems to have been sensitive to pressure from the NUM – the only major union to be involved regularly in this practice.

A major preoccupation of the Panel was the question of increasing union affiliation at national and local level.[17] But the Commission's sensitivity to union autonomy and an awareness of some of the practical problems involved seems also to have decided it against the encouragement of the exchange between the Party and the unions of lists of branches and officials' addresses!

Another item to be watered down in deference to individual union objections was the Panel's call for each union branch to be a centre of recruitment for the Party. This was considered by some to be too intrusive in relation of the autonomous role of the unions and became instead a call to the unions in general for a membership campaign on behalf of the Party.

Recommendations

Yet in spite of this immobility on some key issues, the Commission did make a range of significant and specific recommendations which marked a new phase in attitudes to the connection between industrial and political activity. One group of such decisions directly concerned the weakness of communication facilities in the Labour Movement.

There were some potentially ambitious recommendations for 'feasibility studies' in connection with a national daily newspaper, for a Press Agency for the Labour Movement and for a national printing and publishing house. There was to be encouragement for improved liaison between the Party and trade union journal editors so that there could be increased space for Labour Party and political matters. And, remarkably, there was support from the unions and from the NEC for a new theoretical journal of the Party.

Political education was to be expanded via an ambitious national, regional and local structure. At the same time, there would be a new interlocking of industrial and political organisation. It was agreed that discussions would take place between the NEC and the affiliated unions 'as to the best practicable means of appointing Trade Union Political Organisers at national and regional level as designated by the NEC'.[18] And workplace Labour Party branches were now given 'the green light' – as Basnett put it.[19]

With these proposals went a range of other recommendations (of differing levels of specificity) for strengthening the interaction and association of the unions and the Party at the grass roots, including the rebuilding of local affiliation and local liaison and the expansion of Party membership among affiliated trade unionists. There were also strongly supported recommendations for broadening the concept of Party 'membership', including the creation of Household Membership and the creation of a new category of Registered Labour Supporters.

In practice, many of these agreed new initiatives were delayed and sidelined in the face of resistance or opposition from individual unions and the Party – but particularly the Party (see pp. 499–500).

Problems of implementation

The first problem in handling the Commission's recommendations was procedural. Given the unique composition of the enquiry, whose report was it? Normally, such reports went before the NEC for approval before they were offered to the Party Conference. But some of this Commission's findings were not acceptable to the NEC, whilst the TULV leaders wanted the whole report put to the Conference. Eventually it was agreed that it would be put to the Conference in its entirety but the NEC would then indicate its own objections.

Normally, only the NEC members spoke from the platform at the Conference, and there had been some tense disputes in the past when Labour Government Ministers, who were not members of the NEC, wanted to address the Conference. Now it was agreed, with some reluctance, that David Basnett from TULV (and a member of the TUC General Council) would introduce the Commission's findings from the platform and that the Chairmen of the Panels, Moss Evans and Clive Jenkins, would also speak on their sections of the Report – an extraordinary territorial intrusion, again deeply resented by many on the NEC.

Thus, for a brief period at the 1980 Party Conference, the result of the new trade union role in Party organisation and administration was a pattern of debate and decision which broke all previous protocol of the union-Party relationship. One example was particularly peculiar. On one recommendation of the Commission – that the three year rule be reintroduced for constitutional changes – the NEC*opposed* the measure but was overwhelmingly defeated by union votes on the recommendation of the Chairman of the Commission from the platform.[20] It has to be noted, of course, that the unions' attitude had the heartfelt support of the Parliamentary leadership.

But if the NEC was straightjacketed on this one, it had much more room for manoeuvre on other recommendations of the Commission and there were repeated and bitter laments from TULV concerning the failure to implement and even to report on action taken. So much for a Party often said to be under the control of 'the union barons'.

From the Conference of 1980, until the joint meeting at the ASTMS college at Woodstock just prior to the 1983 General Election, the TULV leadership took on the frustrating task of pushing for implementation – striving to overcome both NEC resistance and some obstructionism bred by years of trade union complacency. Eventually, after 'the Peace of Bishop's Stortford' in 1982, and after a significant change in the membership of the NEC, more of the recommendations were carried through. But many of the important projects relating to Head Office and to the unions' wider relationship with Party organisation remained contentious and were either never fully implemented or not pursued at all – as we shall see (note also Chapter 16, pp. 527–8 for the financial recommendations).

THE NEW TULV CONSTITUTION AND THE LEVY FUND

Before we examine this aftermath of the Commission and then the attempt to construct a TULV machine for the mobilisation of union support at the 1983 General Election, it is important to note some of the changes taking place within TULV's own organisation. These changes reflected not only the increasing concern of union leaders over the state of the Labour Party, including its Head Office administration, but also their growing resentment and frustration at the resistance of the NEC to a variety of reform and reorganisation proposals.

As a result of the wider role they were now playing in the Labour Party, the TULV leaders again sought means to broaden its acceptability. For a brief period in

July 1980, they decided to change the name of TULV to 'Consortium of Trade Unions for Labour', in order to further differentiate themselves from any association with the Rightwing faction whose acronym was CLV (Campaign for Labour Victory). Little was gained from the change and at the September meeting the name changed back. That meeting also agreed that the annual meeting of affiliated unions should nominate a further three members onto the Committee. By this means, every major union (except the NUM) was represented and the political spectrum stretched from the AUEW (TASS) on the Left to the EETPU on the Right. It was also accepted that there was now a need for a more formal constitution. Consultations on this began almost immediately after the 1980 Party Conference.

Under this Constitution, as it emerged in 1981, the Objectives of TULV were given a wide specification:

> To establish a means by which trade unions can discuss matters of common interest in relation to the Labour Party and make recommendations on matters of finance, organisation and membership with the objective of ensuring the return of a Labour Government.[21]

General Meetings of all affiliated unions would take place twice a year and once a year at these meetings there would be elections for a Committee to serve for twelve months. Interestingly, given the divisive argument taking place at the TUC over 'automaticity' and the composition of the General Council, it was agreed that unions with 75,000 (later 100,000) affiliated members should automatically be represented on the TULV committee. Five or six other places would be subject to election.

This Constitution was agreed by the 1981 meeting of affiliated unions and its implementation resulted in a Committee which consisted of fifteen members, and in 1982 of nineteen members, from a wide spectrum of political viewpoints. Subsequently, there was very little change over the years. In 1985, after the AUEW had withdrawn, there were sixteen members from unions which had all been represented on the Committee in 1980. The attempt to preserve a balanced committee, at a time when TULV was under attack as having masterminded the Rightwing counter-revolution on the NEC, can be seen in the votes for the positions held by six small TULV unions. Four of the positions in 1981 and 1982 were taken by the Left.[22]

In terms of its internal political funding, TULV retained the informal arrangement whereby expenses of the organisation would be borne by those affiliated to TULV pro rata of Labour Party membership. But, in addition, the meeting held on 15 February, 1981 also agreed a remarkable new financial mechanism relating the unions to the Party – a Voluntary Levy Fund which would be used to fund joint agreed projects with the NEC. The proposal was eventually accepted but with considerable reluctance by the Party (see Chapter 16, pp. 529–31). Its operation was always viewed with considerable suspicion not only by those on the NEC who resented union pressure, but also by some of the unions on both the Right (the AUEW) and the Left (the NUM).

How the Voluntary Levy Fund was operated will be examined in the next chapter. Here let us note simply that there was now in place a structure of a kind never seen before in the history of the Labour Party. Norman Atkinson, the Labour Party Treasurer, noted at this time the existence of 'an embryonic political institution'. [23] TULV now had a constitution with wide terms of reference, an executive committee, autonomous sources of finance and a shared, but permanent, bureaucracy strengthened by regular meetings of political and research officers coordinating initiatives.

Aware of the misgivings, and to alleviate the concerns over 'external' pressure, TULV formally agreed that trade union members of the NEC would be invited to the two annual TULV meetings and that the Party's three senior officials, the Chairman, Treasurer and General Secretary, would be invited to all TULV Committee meetings.[24] And 'the bureaucracy' of TULV also began to take its own initiatives to ensure co-operation between the unions on a consensual and non-factional basis. One such meeting, thought to have been of some importance, took place on 5 November 1981 between Larry Whitty, the Secretary of TULV, Alan Meale, the Secretary of the Left Group on the General Council of the TUC, and Jenny Pardington and Regan Scott, the 'Political' and Research Officers of the TGWU. Their understanding then, and subsequently, eased the continuing role of the TGWU within TULV and helped sort out a range of other problems in the next two years.

One further dimension of 'this embryonic institution' is worthy of speculation. Not only did the political/research officers act as a stabilising force within TULV and a 'think tank' in the generation of practical objectives, at this stage they also provided a 'Labour loyalist' infrastructure within the unions. History takes unexpected departure points and sometimes fails to move in likely directions. In the latter months of 1981, the success of the SDP in alliance with the Liberals, and the behaviour of the 'Bennite' Left, were causing enormous strains in the union–Party relationship and raising major, if private, doubts within the TUC. There was one brief moment towards the end of 1981 when some of the most knowledgeable insiders within the Labour Movement noted that TULV provided a form of alternative bureaucracy to that of the TUC – a pro-Labour organisation which might take on a new form in the event of the TUC and more Rightwing unions readjusting their relationship with the Labour Party to a marked degree. It was probably all talk, and in any case by January 1982 and the Peace of Bishop's Stortford, the moment had passed. But it is worth a note.

REPERCUSSIONS

The implementation of Commission recommendations

The changing attitude of Leftwing political and research officers, as with the Labour Party's own research staff, was an important if relatively unnoticed part of the changing tide of opinion over 'Bennism'. It helped produce 'the Peace of Bishop's Stortford'. The joint meeting of TULV and the NEC was momentous both in its short term impact and its long term consequences. Its immediate effect was to produce a crucial pause in the implosive struggle which had engulfed the Party since 1979. Its longer term significance was to establish the continuing role of TULV in Party and union organisational questions, and to lay down some constructive proposals for joint action.

The Bishop's Stortford meeting was felt to have been marked by a 'clear decision by all those who had participated ... to go forward with a new unity and sense of direction'.[25] In line with this it also agreed in general terms a number of important organisational measures 'to continue and strengthen the alliance between the Party and the unions'. Most of these built upon previous discussions and the recommendations of the Commission. Some went ahead; but many important initiatives for reform ground to a halt – highlighting once again some of the obstacles to change in the relationship, as well as the very restricted power of 'the union bosses' to make things happen in Labour's organisation.

The success story (until its decline in 1986) was the creation and expansion of a Party journal, *New Socialist,* and the improvement of liaison between the Party and the union journals. But other plans failed to produce tangible results. The feasibility study of a Labour Movement newspaper (carried out by Lord McCarthy under TUC auspices) encountered adverse economic conditions and in 1984 was sidelined. Similarly, trade union inability to produce financial support led to the abandonment of plans for a Press Agency and for a printing and publishing house.

The concern of the Commission to secure an increase in union branch affiliation to and liaison with the Labour Party was followed through by the Party with a circular in February 1981 and followed through by TULV with repeated exhortations to member unions. Some increase did occur but the prickly problems of autonomy and territory always inhibited concerted action and on the eve of the Political Fund ballots in 1985, the liaison between local parties and local unions was often minimal.

Model rules for workplace branches were promulgated by the Party in 1982 and the project was regularly itemised on the TULV agenda. But the Party gave the new branches limited attention, the unions had very differing views on their acceptability, and TULV leaders had only limited means of pushing. They remained in a weak state for years and were to be insignificant during the Political Fund ballots of 1985/6.

As for individual membership of the Party by levypaying trade unionists, some attempt was made through TULV to instigate or participate in a membership campaign in the autumn of 1982. It was later described in the NEC Report as resulting in 'a large number of new members being recruited'[26] Within TULV and individual unions there was a much more cautious view of its impact – 'negligible' was one comment to the author on its effect. The fact was that neither union nor Party procedures were geared up for a major venture. Not until 1986 was a Provisional Membership card system introduced and not until 1988 were resources, energy and planning put into a Mass Party project. Meanwhile, the proposals for a Household Membership and for a category of Registered Labour Supporters – both proposals pushed strongly by the union leaders and supported by votes at the Annual Conference – were quietly buried by the Party bureaucracy and the NEC.

Reform of the Party's political education facilities and its linkage with the unions was very slow in coming. Not until the summer of 1982 was a National

Education Advisory Panel established with TULV representation, and the complete review of political education asked for that year by the Joint Study of Head Office never materialised. Inertia at Party headquarters, lack of push from the NEC and shortage of finance seems to have been the problem. According to the 1983 NEC Report, the number of political education organisers actually *dropped* between 1982 and 1983. Political Education remained underfunded and poorly regarded.

As for the new and more enlightened perception of political mobilisation which had involved suggestions of union officers being seconded to the Party and of joint regional political organisers, these were resisted by the then General Secretary and the Party officials' union, the National Union of Labour Organisers. The institutionalisation of the TULV–TUCC–TUFL network (see below and Chapter 18) went some way to filling the gap on the union side. But not until the appointment of a Trade Union Liaison Officer at Party headquarters in 1986 was there any official whose prime responsibility within the Party was for trade union linkage.[27]

So, all in all, the follow-through of reform proposals was for some years a failure – as union leaders ruefully noted. Indeed, what was highlighted by this whole exercise, including the financial discussions, was how difficult it was for central bodies of union leaders to deliver action by autonomous union bodies and how seriously the NEC took the issue of Party autonomy – particularly when the issue was laced with a factional defensiveness.

The TULV network

However, probably the most important organisational decisions ratified at Bishop's Stortford were the commitments by the unions to 'back' the Party with 'substantial finance' leading up to the General Election, and the pledge to co-ordinate trade union resources on a long term basis with a view to assisting the Party in marginal seats. There came into being a new and more extensive TULV structure, including the establishment of a regional network of trade unions operating in conjunction with the Regional Labour Party. Much of this regional work was again undertaken in the first instance by the Transport and General Workers' Union together with the General and Municipal Workers and SOGAT. In most areas, their work resulted in a regional co-ordinator and TULV committee which worked on the basis of an extensive list of union contacts. The regional committees sought to make full time officers available for General Election activity in 130 key seats.

There were problems in Yorkshire (where the NUM resolutely opposed and blocked the committee's formation). Eventually, a Yorkshire TULV committee was created but without NUM attendance. Scotland created its own institution, the Scottish Labour Trade Union Committee, but it operated more or less in the same way as TULV and did secure Scottish NUM co-operation.

Unusually, as a result of Bishop's Stortford, the unions involved themselves in a series of political training courses on union premises with facilities and expenses provided by TULV and individual unions. These courses were aimed at lay Party activists who would become election agents and covered a wide range of electoral tasks and processes. However, the numbers catered for in the pre-election period were not substantial.

The General Election campaign

It was no help to the TULV leaders that Party management was in such difficulties in this period (see Chapter 19). The committee of TULV pushed strongly for early preparation by the Party for its election campaign and in early 1983 expressed its concern that little had been done to agree a theme and slogan for the campaign.[28] Eventually, the General Election Campaign Fund Committee (whose work will be described in the next chapter) had TULV representation and three TULV union officials – David Basnett, Moss Evans and Rodney Bickerstaffe – became members of the Party's General Election Campaign Committee.

TULV efforts to secure more publicity for the Labour Party in the union journals bore some fruit. In April 1983, fourteen union journals carried a TULV advertisement and an article by Michael Foot. The joint NEC–TULV meeting at Woodstock on the eve of the General Election campaign noted an excellent coverage of the Labour Party's campaign document in the trade union magazines. During the campaign, almost without exception, they were used to propagate totally committed Labour Party support or, in the case of the non-affiliated unions, to severely criticise Government policy.

During the 1983 General Election, TULV (in its own office in 1979) moved to an office in Party headquarters staffed virtually full time. But their integration within the loosely (and badly) organised head office set-up was not well achieved. However, the office did perform a range of functions which were to establish a precedent for the future. There was an attempt to cover key seats with union assistance, to organise trade union speakers and Speakers' Notes for trade unionists and to liaise with affiliated unions. The financial progress-chasing of unions towards the Party's General Election Fund was also done from this office. Liaison with the TULV regional organisations was also carried out and a limited quantity of leaflets produced for their use.

All in all, the trade union input into the 1983 General Election was very diverse, coinciding with a People's March organised by the TUC and involving a variety of individual union campaigns organised against aspects of Government policy.[29] However, judged in terms of the number of trade unionists who supported the Labour Party at the General Election, these campaigns were all a failure. Trade unionists' support for Labour fell by twelve per cent on the 1979 figure (which was itself a fall of four per cent on October 1974). And the biggest shift actually took place *during* the campaign. Labour support among trade unionists was only two per cent down on 1979 at the start of the campaign. By the end of it, there had been a massive rise in support for the Alliance.[30] Not that any of this can be blamed on the unions or TULV given that the Party fought probably the worst campaign in its history.

There is no doubt that the national organisation and co-ordination of the trade union input into Labour's election campaign worked better than in 1979, in spite of delays in instigating organisation. There was a major improvement in official trade union involvement and the majority of key seats were covered, sometimes by officials who might otherwise have been elsewhere. But the pattern varied from region to region and from seat to seat and there were some strikingly contrasting reports, by those involved, of the usefulness of the operation. The pattern also varied from union to union. Among the big three unions, the Transport Workers' and the General and Municipal Workers' officers were prominent in almost every region, but the Engineers were 'everybody's favourite nominee', as the union that failed to deliver.

Two features of the limitation of TULV stood out. One was that it was often unclear what the function of this assistance was – resource allocation to the Party or the mobilisation of trade unionists. And, overall, the striking failure was a failure to motivate enough active trade unionists to play their part either within the place of work or with the local party.

All the experience of the 1983 General Election tended to confirm the need which had stimulated the TULV organisation and the Commission of Enquiry – the need for a permanent campaigning trade union presence operating with healthy links to the Party and with well-developed lines of communication to the workplace.

THE TROJAN HORSE?

TULV was potentially a major asset to the Labour Party, but from its inception the organisation had to defend itself from a range of critics. The bulk of the public criticism came from the Left although, as we have noted, TULV had opponents in various other groups and places. The Left's critique laid particular emphasis on the lack of accountability of the TULV organisation, its 'dripfeed' financial behaviour (see Chapter 16, pp. 531–2) and, above all, its alleged role as a 'Trojan Horse',[31]directed towards policy issues, the fixing of elections, the prevention of constitutional changes and halting the advance of the Labour Left. In late 1983, all these criticisms were put together in a wide-ranging critique contained in letters and a document from the National Union of Mineworkers.[32]

Time after time, officials of TULV, particularly David Basnett, reiterated that 'TULV has no role in policy issues.TULV is solely concerned with helping the party on finance, organisation and publicity and political education ... '.[33] And Basnett's letter to all Labour-affiliated unions made clear 'it is in no sense intended as a policymaking body or as a body that coordinates union activity or voting on policy or constitutional issues'.[34] Yet still the accusations came in and the mythology built up. Later studies of this period continue to see TULV as part of a factional alignment.[35] These charges of political and factional operations need to be examined before we move into the financial analysis in Chapter 16.

As we have seen, this suspicion dated back to the circumstances of TULV's origins and was also fed by the behaviour of TULV leaders during the constitutional difficulties from 1979 to 1982. Finance and organisation was *the* preoccupation then but, with the Party in turmoil and multiplying crises, TULV became the vehicle through which union leaders expressed their concern to look for a consensual constitutional settlement. For those on the Left (and the Right) who wanted victory rather than a compromise, this union role was an attempt at political restraint – and resented accordingly.

This stabilising role was justified by TULV leaders as inherent in the solidarity which had guided union behaviour in the Labour Party for decades. But, as often with the application of this value, it pulled them into difficult terrain, and into a conflict over territorial rights.

The first example of this occurred in September 1979, when a delegation of TULV General Secretaries (most of whom were on the Left) pressed the NEC strongly (but unsuccessfully) that the three contentious constitutional reforms should not be voted on by the Party Conference pending the deliberations of the Commission of Enquiry.[36]

Once established, this consensual role as 'the voice of the unions' led to a situation where almost any political initiative taken by a large group of union leaders could be associated with 'TULV' and interpreted as factional activity.[37] Such accusations were usually without foundation – apart from one major case where TULV was pulled into consultations which had crucial implications for the factional balance within the Party. This focused around an invitation to meet members of the Shadow Cabinet in December 1980 to discuss proposals to be placed before the Special Conference on electing the Party leadership due to be held in January 1981.

The TULV Committee meeting held on 17 December had – the minutes record – expressed 'the strong view ... that the Party should avoid a contested election this time round and that the current leadership should be maintained in office'.[38] Accounts given to the author of the meeting later that day with Shadow Cabinet members suggest that the PLP leadership made no response to this point, that it was not subject to much discussion and that those attending were concerned with other issues surrounding the constitutional change.[39] Nevertheless, this TULV position went much beyond the acceptable remit of TULV and was later acknowledged privately by its officials to have been a misjudgement damaging to the position of TULV in the eyes of the Left.

However, what also needs to be recorded, to see this in perspective, is that TULV's role at this time and at this meeting was also an impediment to the Shadow Cabinet majority. TULV had been faced with a proposal from the PLP that the CLP's section of the electoral college would be based on one-member-one-vote, that the trade union section vote would include all levypayers, and the vote of the future electoral college should take place outside the Party Conference proceedings. As the TULV minutes baldly state, 'The majority of members of the Committee felt the proposals for trade unions were impracticable, that there was no need to lay down how CLPs would vote and that it was difficult to see why the vote should be taken away from the Conference'.[40] This view was communicated to the PLP leadership and also taken to the meeting on 17 December

Thus, this consensual role of TULV could constrain both factions. Over the NEC elections – contrary to much myth [41] – TULV was never an instrument of the Right. There is no doubt that 'the hard Right', epitomised by the AUEW leadership, and also sections of the PLP leadership including James Callaghan as Leader, would have preferred a more assertive role from the unions in dealing with the Bennite Left. But Basnett made it clear that he would not allow TULV to be used for this purpose. Despite Leftwing suspicion that the successful Rightwing counter-attack which caused a major shift in the composition of the NEC in 1981 was organised under the cover of TULV, the fact was that Basnett kept TULV well away from this development, to the chagrin of some in the Rightwing St Ermin's Group.

There is no doubt that, politics being what it is, TULV meetings prior to the Party Conference proved useful venues where trade union leaders could involve themselves in private bilateral talks involving Conference tactics. But any such meeting would be used in this way and if it were not at that venue it would be another. Again, what went on 'off stage' at TULV could be as useful to Leftwing trade union leaders as to those on the Right. Some of those near to Michael Foot's office in 1982, who were disturbed by stories of a plot by Rightwing trade union leaders in support of Peter Shore, would certainly take this view. It is said that the TULV meeting held prior to the TUC had been a useful place to float privately a pro-Foot loyalist statement which Rightwing union leaders found difficult to refuse. Again, it must be said that this was not on the agenda and had nothing to do with the official TULV.

The truth is that in a body of thirty or so trade unions there were bound to be differences of purpose and occasional confusions of role (deliberate or otherwise) but after 1979, the Chairman and Secretary strove to achieve as non-factional a form of activity as possible and in this they were supported by a majority of committee members and officers. What the TULV committee and officers could not do was prevent its name being occasionally misused at national level or in the regions – sometimes by people utterly unconnected with it.

Potentially, the most damaging allegation made against TULV concerned its alleged intervention in the selection of parliamentary candidates. The allegation first appeared in *Tribune* on 25 June 1982 and was then part of the critical document from the NUM about TULV at the end of 1983.[42] The only case – and it is an important one – to be cited in evidence is that TULV (it is said) was used to organise in Bristol South to ensure that Tony Benn did not become the 1983 candidate. The whole criticism (as far as I can see) hangs on this one instance.

In June 1982, an advertisement appeared in the *Bristol Evening Post* calling on Bristol District Labour Party to vote out its Leftwing Chairman and Secretary and replace them by officials of the Transport Workers' and NATSOPA. This advertisement was placed in the name of 'Bristol Trade Unions for a Labour Victory' and its address was given as that of the GMWU offices in Bristol. As far as I know, no other evidence of 'TULV' involvement has been provided.

But, examined more closely, 'the TULV plot' falls apart. The only official TULV organisation in Bristol was the regional organisation and it, unusually, was organised from the Labour Party's Regional Offices, not from those of the GMWU. Neither the GMWU District official concerned nor the two officers being pushed for the District Party positions were members of the Regional TULV committee nor were they authorised in any way to call themselves 'Trade Unions for a Labour Victory'.

The TULV Regional Secretary, Jean Corston, later described their behaviour (to the author) as 'totally outrageous'. The action of the District GMWU official was repudiated by the TULV committee nationally, and by the union's General

Secretary. Privately, harsh words were said and the District official was later moved from that area. There appears to be no evidence whatsoever linking TULV with this unofficial action nor is there any evidence that I have seen which links TULV with Benn's non-selection.

There seems little doubt that from 1981 some of the union officials in Bristol, including, I am told, members of the GMWU, EETPU, TGWU, APEX, NATSOPA and the POEU, were involved in a Rightwing organisation aimed at countering the Left, and that some of them were also part of the organised attempt to get rid of Tony Benn. But the evidence points to a factional network *independent* of TULV and initiated by John Golding – the Political Officer of the POEU and Rightwing organiser on the Party's NEC.[43]

As for other allegations against TULV from the NUM – that TULV used finance to influence regional parties and that TULV withdrew support from Political Education which was out of line with its own political aims – these again were unfounded. In fact, regional TULV finance was minimal; no evidence was brought forward to substantiate either accusation and they were not followed up in a second NUM letter on the subject.

Critics of TULV eventually found triumphant cause to say 'we told you so' when the AUEW withdrew from TULV,[44] interpreting it as confirmation of political chicanery, that is, 'because it had achieved what it was set up to bring about, namely a "stable" National Executive Committee'[45] Yet, as I have indicated, it is impossible to make sense of this in terms of the history and activities of TULV. And it is difficult to escape the conclusion that the departure of the AUEW from TULV was couched in terms[46] likely to excite comment from the Left because this was one way of ensuring a fragmentation of TULV which the Engineers' leadership had grown to dislike on political grounds and to envy as a source of status for its GMWU rivals.

'RULES', TERRITORY AND POLITICAL ORGANISATION: THE ROLE OF TULV

In summary, then, the reputation of TULV, and to some extent its effectiveness, was influenced by the context and circumstances of its birth. Although at times it had a more powerful Leftwing than Rightwing element in its leadership, suspicion of its ulterior factional purposes on behalf of 'the Right' was a permanent accompaniment to its activities. These activities also occasionally compromised its basic role as a consensual collective organisation for the mobilisation of trade unionists and the stimulation of financial resources for the Labour Party.

Concern for the organisational and financial state of the Party led union leaders into playing a joint supervisory role on the Commission of Enquiry and to the creation of a Voluntary Levy Fund which appeared to shadow NEC administration of the Party. Both initiatives involved an unprecedented breach of the 'rules' of Party autonomy. Concern for the stability of the Labour Party led TULV into initiatives which, on occasions, clashed with the immediate objectives of elements on the political Right and Left – including a majority of the NEC.

But there is little to substantiate the charge of TULV's being a factional 'Trojan Horse' except in the sense that a body which aimed at a balanced political leadership and consensual purposes was a constraint upon factional activity.

Conversely, the territorial intrusions of TULV and its factional taint were a constraint upon its attempts to secure major organisational (and as we shall see in the next chapter, financial) reform. TULV leaders came up against a variety of difficulties engendered by autonomous union organisations on the one side and the NEC's jealous protection of its right to manage the Party, on the other. In a variety of ways, Commission proposals were delayed or sidelined.

This resistance by the NEC appears improbable given the apparent control available to the union leaders as a result of their electoral and financial leverage. But as we have seen many times in this study, 'rules' and roles, as well as practicabilities, constrained the effective power of senior union leaders in relation to the Labour Party. To see this in its full complexity we have to examine the operation (and non-operation) of the financial levers, the motivations of the union leaders in relation to Party finance, and the effectiveness of their intervention in matters of financial management. In Chapter 16 this will be the focus of the analysis before we review again the behaviour of TULV leaders.

NOTES

1. *Interim Report of the ('Wilson') Sub Committee on Party Organisation*, 1955, para. 69.
2. NAD, 13/3/70, pp. 4–5 and Letter from National Agent to General Secretaries of affiliated unions, *NAD*, 17/4/70.
3. Mark Crail and Angela Eagle, 'Finding New Ways for Labour and the Unions to Work Together',*Tribune*, 4/4/86. TULV was a 'focus of Rightwing intrigue'.
4. 'Labour "Seduced" Union Leaders', *Guardian*, 11/8/78 and 'TUC Chief Calls the Tories to Account', *Sunday Times*, 13/8/78.
5. *Labour Victory*, No. 2, July 1977, 'Reform the NEC'.
6. NUGMW, *Annual Congress Report*, 1977, p. 497.
7. *Ibid.*, p. 499.
8. Res. No. 18, 1977.
9. *Minutes of NEC Org. Sub.*, 9/1/78, Appendix.
10. *Minutes of NEC*, 23/11/77.
11. *Interim Report of the Party Organisation Enquiry Committee*, Proposal 3.
12. *NEC Minutes*, 24/5/78.
13. Present at the Meeting were David Basnett (Provisional Chairman), GMWU, Ron Hayward (General Secretary of the Labour Party), Lord Allen (USDAW), Ray Buckton (ASLEF), Moss Evans (TGWU), Joe Gormley (NUM), Clive Jenkins (ASTMS), Sid Weighell (NUR), John Bull (NUPE representing Alan Fisher) and Larry Whitty (GMWU) – the Secretary.
14. *Trade Union Committee for a Labour Victory: Notes of a Meeting* held at Congress House, 23 August, 1978.
15. *TULV Committee Meeting*, 27/6/1979.
16. Comp. Res. No. 29 recognised 'the achievements of the 1974–9 Labour Government' and stressed the need to broaden the Party's base of electoral support. Comp. Res. No. 31 was critical of the failure of the Labour Government to carry out Conference decisions and stressed the need for greater accountability.
17. *Report of the Labour Party Commission of Enquiry 1980*, paras. 7.2, 11.2, 11.3.

18. *Ibid.*, para. 11.2(iii).
19. *LPACR*, 1980, p. 85.
20. *LPACR*, 1980, pp. 210-3. The vote was 5,882,000 to 1,160,000.
21. *TULV Constitution 1981*, 'Objectives'.
22. Ray Buckton (ASLEF), Jack Boddy (Agricultural Workers), Bill Keys (SOGAT) and Jim Slater (NUS).
23. Norman Atkinson, 'Ends and Means', *Labour Weekly*, 26/6/81.
24. Letter from David Basnett (TULV) to Ron Hayward, Labour Party General Secretary, 17/7/81.
25. *Labour Party-TULV Accord*, NEC/TULV Summary, 8/1/82.
26. *NEC Report*, 1983, p. 30.
27. Tom Wilson was given a two-year appointment as Trade Union Liaison Officer. At the end of his appointment, Wilson was not replaced, although the Liaison Office, staffed by a secretary, was preserved.
28. *Campaign Committee Minutes*, 14/3/83.
29. On the role of the unions in the 1983 General Election campaign, see Lewis Minkin, 'Against the Tide: Trade Union Political Communication and the 1983 General Election', in Ivor Crewe and Martin Harrop, *Political Communications: The General Election Campaign of 1983*, 1986, pp. 190–206.
30. All data from MORI for TULV, July 1983.
31. Dennis Skinner, *Labour Weekly*, 30/10/81.
32. Letter and document from the NUM General Secretary, Lawrence Daly, to Jim Mortimer, Labour Party General Secretary, 30/11/83 and letter to Moss Evans, TGWU General Secretary, 5/1/84.
33. *NEC Report*, 1982, p. 3.
34. David Basnett, *Letter to Affiliated Unions*, 18/3/81.
35. For example, Andrew J. Taylor,*The Trade Unions and the Labour Party*, 1987, p. 135, links TULV with the *Labour Solidarity* group of MPs.
36. *NEC Org. Sub. Minutes*, 10/9/79.
37. For example, 'Is TULV Making Political Moves in the Labour Party?', *Tribune*, 23/1/81, for the reference to 'an emergency meeting of TULV' which decided to call for a special conference on the Leadership election procedure.
38. *TULV Committee Minutes*, 17 December, Minute 3(iv).
39. Interviews with Bryan Davies, Secretary of the PLP and Larry Whitty, Secretary of TULV, June 1985.
40. *TULV Committee Minutes*, 26/11/80, Minute 6.
41. *Tribune*, 2/10/81, refers to 'the Rightwing coup' on the NEC being done under cover of TULV.
42. Letter from L. Daly, *op. cit.*, 30/11/83.
43. Transcript of a meeting held at the Dragonara Hotel, 23/11/81.
44. 'TULV: We Told You So', *Tribune*, 9/12/83.
45. *Ibid.*
46. The letter actually referred to 'the financial stability' of the Party, rather than the stability of the NEC, but it did welcome 'the new NEC'. Letter from Terry Duffy to David Basnett, 24/11/83.

16

TULV, TUFL *and the crisis of Party finance*

Crisis

As we have seen, TULV was born out of financial discussions, and it remained preoccupied with issues of Party finance for much of its history. That preoccupation reached its peak in the period from 1979 to 1982, when the union leaders pushed themselves (and were pulled) into an unprecedented level of intervention in the Party's financial affairs, demanding of the Party (and of the unions) major changes in attitudes and procedures.

This experience provides us with unique evidence of trade union responses to a Labour Party crisis. As a case study of financial leverage (and weakness), it has no equal in Labour Party history. It has often been said that 'he who pays the piper calls the tune' in politics. We have already had many reasons to doubt the usefulness of this maxim in understanding the relationship between trade unions and the Labour Party on policy issues. Here we examine the behaviour of union leaders in a situation where financial management was itself the crucial issue.

Provision

That the unions were a major collective source of finance for the Labour Party has never been doubted. At various points in this study we have registered this financial involvement. It came through five main channels: (i) to constituency and district Labour parties through affiliation fees, grants and donations; (ii) to constituency parties through the sponsorship of candidates; (iii) to regional parties[1] through affiliation fees, grants and donations; (iv) to the Parliamentary Labour Party through grants to the Leader's Office and members of the Front Bench; and (v) to the national Party organisation via affiliation fees, grants and donations to particular funds – including the General Election Fund.

The multi-level character and the complexity of the forms of union provision make any calculation of their overall contribution to the Labour Party problematic. There are transfer payments, indirect subsidies, and donations from various sources which might include trade unions. In particular, there has always been a problem of estimating the income generated by wards, constituencies and, latterly, the regions, from non-union sources. Consequently, as all scholars and officials who have entered this area have recognised, any estimate has to be 'treated with caution'.[2] (I agree more strongly with this the closer I examine the evidence and it accounts for the tentative character of some of my judgements later.) Nevertheless, at the time of the Commission of Enquiry and in the subsequent battle over the implementation of its findings, there was a body of informed opinion which not only agreed that unions contributed the majority of the Party's normal annual income, but also was broadly in accord on the level of that contribution.

Martin Harrison in 1960 suggested (with many qualifications) that the unions contributed between 50 and 55 per cent of the Party's total income.[3] Richard Rose estimated that it averaged 57 per cent for the period 1967 to 1970 and in 1972 60 per cent.[4] Michael Pinto-Duschinsky's estimate in his major study of political finance was around 56 per cent in the early 1970s.[5] GMWU evidence to the Commission of Enquiry made a rough calculation that in the late 1970s it was over 60 per cent.[6]

Within this overall union contribution, there were features of the Party's dependency which were much more striking and which were certainly in the minds of the union leaders in 1980. In two respects the Labour Party would be devastated without union finance. The national General Election Fund would be sufficient only for the most minimal campaign – approximately 95 per cent of it came from the unions. And the Party's national organisation would be near collapse without union national affiliation fees; in the late 1970s, this contribution had reached a new post-war peak of 89 per cent in 1978, followed by 86 per cent in 1979.[7]

It was while union contributions were at this high level that union confidence in the Party's management of its financial affairs sunk to a new low. In this chapter we will explore the motivations of the union leaders as they sought to respond. We will examine the nature of the financial crisis and the way the unions proposed to deal with it. We will analyse the major financial decisions of the Commission of Enquiry and then follow them through in terms of implementation and later development. The aim is to assess the use or non-use of financial leverage and the extent of success where financial resources were brought to bear.

Deficit

In his very illuminating study of British political finance, Michael Pinto-Duschinsky casts some doubt on whether there was a financial crisis in this period.[8] Certainly, it is true that the Party's deficit in 1979 was by no means unique.

Since World War II, normal Party income to the General Fund has regularly been outstripped by expenditure. In only eight of the thirty-four years from 1945 to 1979, and in only two of ten years between 1969 and 1979, was this not the case. When the situation deteriorated badly, some self-restraint was exercised and some appeal made to the unions about affiliation fees. There was a particular concern in 1975 when the General Secretary spotlighted 'the gravity of the situation'.[9] Special appeals were made, affiliation fees were raised for the years 1975–7, and economies of one form or another were brought into operation. But the overspending continued and from 1977 the deficits grew again. In 1977 there was a loss of £31, 368. In 1978 there was a loss of £114, 013 and in 1979 a loss of £153, 348.

These deficits may have been 'normal', but they were producing an increasingly serious problem – a long term erosion of Party assets liquefied to meet running costs. These assets had been declining more or less consistently since 1966. By 1979, reserves had virtually run out.

Further, the reality of the Party's borrowing over the years was hidden in the presentation of accounts. 'Deficits' were presented only in terms of the General Fund. Special Funds, such as the Development Fund and the By-election and Deposit Insurance Fund, appeared unimpaired. In reality, most of these Special Funds had nothing in them. Resources had been used up in the running costs of the Party.[10]

Thus, what became clear in 1979 was that, with virtually no reserves, the Party now faced a Treasurer's estimate that the accumulated deficit over a three-year period was likely to be £1.4 million.[11] The Party was 'disastrously' overspending its income.[12]

The incentive to intervene

Here we need to note again the argument in Chapter 15. There was, as will be shown, a diversity and a complexity of motivations involved in this period as the TULV leaders breached the old 'rules' of autonomy. It would be misleading to reduce these motivations to one factor, but the evidence suggests that first an organisational concern, then financial insecurity, rather than political aggression, was the trigger.[13]

Given the mood on the Right of the unions, it would not be too difficult to interpret the new involvement of senior union leaders in the financial management of the Labour Party in the period after 1979 as simply a factional response to the Leftwing NEC (see p. 518), or as part of a broader drive of union leaders to maximise their political control over the Labour Party. [14] But neither of these perspectives seems to me to be adequate. Union leaders in the forefront of TULV's activities included some on the Left, notably Evans, Jenkins and Keys. As for control and power maximisation, we have already indicated at many points in this study how partial a view this is of the complicated union attitudes towards involvement in the Labour Party. This chapter will add further evidence to our portrait.

It is important to register immediately that there was always some tension inherent in a relationship in which the unions raised the bulk of Labour's finances and the NEC spent it – especially as the unions were involved in delicate role-playing and self-restraint. Over time, certain security mechanisms evolved in recognition of the unions' position, but they were usually operated within recognised boundaries.

Under the rules, as we have seen, it grew to be obligatory that the Party never increased its affiliation fees without first consulting union leaders collectively as to their capacity and willingness to pay such increases. (A similar protocol covered changes in the Hastings Agreement.) The increases were *never* imposed, although usually, in the end, they were accepted even in the wake of major upheavals in the relationship, including the raising of fees after the battle over *In Place of Strife* in 1969.

At the consultative meetings, held behind closed doors, it was normal for the unions to register any 'lament' that they had over the Party's general drift or their experience as unions within it. These laments might be procedural or financial but sometimes they were political – a grumbling session directed towards those policies where the unions had a common and priority interest. 'Why should our members be asked to pay … when …', or 'It doesn't help us to put this to our conferences when …'. Normally the form was retrospective and complaining rather than future-oriented and threatening. And there was recognised to be a strong element of 'show' and routine both in the lament and the reaction. Nevertheless, the tone of this meeting was important in that the Party's General Secretary and the Treasurer had to take it seriously and these officials were generally (although not always) very union-sensitive in their operation at leadership level in the Party.

The Treasurer's role here is interesting. The unions, since the mid-1950s, have often indicated that they would prefer that the position be taken by a trade unionist rather than a politician. There are many facets to this preference but mainly it concerns security and not political leverage. In practice, the position has often been held by a politician[15] and the position fought for on factional grounds. Hence, as added security, the unions preferred that the on-the-spot position of Chairman of the NEC's Finance and General Purposes Committee be held by an NEC trade unionist.[16] Thus, even when the Treasurership was taken by a politician with close links to the union leaders (Gaitskell in the mid-1950s or Callaghan in the mid-1970s), there was a union preference that the two posts be kept separate, a preference which also reflected the view of NEC trade unionists – that 'the F and GP' was a status post that ought to be available to *them*.[17]

As a political conduit, the post was not highly significant. Unions recognised certain important and legitimate channels of policy influence and this was not one of them. The post could be held by a trade unionist who was not the most senior on the NEC, and not even from one of the larger unions. On more than one occasion, it has been taken by an official who had a tension-ridden or semi-independent position in his own union hierarchy. In any case, the holder usually developed a strong sense of *Partinost*.

The oddity of this security post in the 1970s (and long before) was that the mechanics of financial administration within headquarters were such that the F and GP never had full control over its operation. (More, the Finance Department did not have adequate control over the general expenditure of the building – this would come out clearly at the 1980 Commission of Enquiry.) Further, the Chair of the F and GP had to work within the overall strategy of the NEC. To this extent, trade union 'supervision' of Party finances was a fiction but the committee arrangement was, nevertheless, a symbolic reassurance. The right person was in the right place.

Norman Atkinson's political election in 1976 dismayed many union leaders on the Right because of its factional significance (see Chapter Six, p.183). But

over and above any factional vindictiveness he aroused, Atkinson heightened
the sense of union insecurity over the NEC's financial prudence and priorities,
particularly as, in an unprecedented move, he took over the Chair of the F and GP
for a short period. By 1978, the post was back in the hands of a trade unionist,
Russell Tuck of the NUR, [18] but by this time a broad-based financial alarm was
spreading among union leaders.

Let us now note a more tangible safeguard for the unions – one which had its
origins in an old tradition of frugality. Some of them procrastinated in affiliation
payments and in the face of pleas from Party officials. And all in a sense 'hoarded'
their political funds until the late stage at which the Party sought to build up its
General Election Funds. This hoarding was an expression of the unions' claim to
possession of the Political Funds; they were the *unions'* funds and not automatically the Party's (a point driven home to advantage in the 1985 Political Fund
ballots). But it was also part of the character of the unions that they should be
concerned with prudent housekeeping – better they kept it safe than somebody
else be tempted to squander it. Signs of such 'squandering' led to a reinforcement
of the tendency to hold on.

This characteristic of trade unionism had always been an irritant at Party
headquarters. But, in the 1970s, their resentment was enhanced by the attention
paid to academic writers who argued convincingly that the Labour Party had a
'Samuel Smiles' attitude to money. It saved to the point of 'madness'. It built up
contingency funds for emergencies which were far larger than prudence dictated. [19]

Contrasting perceptions of financial reasonableness exacerbated the political
suspicions in the relationship. Behind the financial constraints, the NEC suspected political control by parsimony. Behind the financial crisis, the union
leaders suspected that they were being 'bounced' into raising extra finance – in
effect deficit-led expenditure. Both had cause for grievance. The NEC argued that
increases in union affiliation fees since 1977 had not kept pace with inflation and
that the financial crisis was rooted in the failure of income to keep pace with
needs. [20] To the unions this was profligate. 'The Labour Party, along with the
Trade Unions and every sensibly managed business, must only spend what it
receives – if it breaks that rule then the expenditure is excessive and financial
misfortune is inevitable.' [21]

The new headquarters

Here, then, were the attitudinal ingredients of a conflict in which for the first
time in Party history the union leaders pushed into the administration of Party
finance. But, in addition, the union involvement was precipitated by another
development in which they were *pulled* into the financing and removal expenses
of the construction of a new Party headquarters.

Perceptions of trade union financial power in the Labour Party which assume
a drive to power maximisation encounter immediate problems when we examine
the role of the unions as landlord of the Party. A more potentially powerful
position it is hard to imagine. The Party had, since 1928, been tenants of the
Transport and General Workers Union at Transport House. The tenancy was

given at a rent which (it is said) was to the considerable financial disadvantage of the landlord. Yet there is not the slightest evidence that this factor counted as a resource in any internal Party conflict. Neither in terms of anticipating the reactions of the union nor in terms of seeking the favour of the union was this ever a direct factor. To the suggestion that it might be, General Secretaries of the TGWU responded with a mixture of amazement and repugnance.[22]

By the early 1970s, the Transport Workers were in difficulties about the Party's tenancy. There were acute pressures on space in a union expanding to become the largest in the world. In 1972, the union decided regretfully to give the Party notice.[23] The union would ease the transition and, in fact, allowed the Party to hold on to the tenancy for several years. Not until March 1980 did the move take place.

Meanwhile, the Parliamentary leadership and the NEC were slow to make decisions; the appeal for a Building Fund was slow to be launched. In the unions, there was some cynicism that the Party would, in the end, make its decision in the knowledge that the unions would come to the rescue.[24] In 1977, after rejecting options involving expensive office tenancy, the splitting of staff and moving outside central London, the Party decided to restore the derelict property in Walworth Road which had been purchased by Labour Party Properties in 1973.[25]

£1.2 million were targeted in the NEC's 'Build a Brick' building fund but by 1978 only £145,477 had been raised, so, as expected, the union leaders, with some reluctance, stepped in and created their own consortium to raise the money for development.

The unions took from the Party a 999-year lease on Walworth Road and then rented the property back to the Party. Until challenged via the Certification Officer,[26] some of this finance came out of union general, rather than political, funds – on the grounds that it was simply an investment. It is extremely doubtful whether such an investment would have been forthcoming for anybody other than the Labour Party. However, the rental to the Labour Party, while not excessive, was economic and therefore contrasted with the Party's previous tenancy. In 1979, at Transport House, the Labour Party was paying £50 plus rates. In the first year at Walworth Road, it paid £160,000 plus £160,000 rates, thus adding to the financial burdens on the Party at the time when it was under pressure from the unions to cut costs.

Further, there was an extraordinary development in connection with the Building Fund which did little to endear the HQ management to union leaders as they slowly became aware of it. It was decided to utilise the £145,477 in the building fund to cover the removal costs and equipment of the new Party headquarters. The actual removal expenses came to only £35,000 with an additional £19,000 stamp duty on the underlease. But some £116,000 was spent on fixtures, fittings and office equipment. Years later, Head Office staff described this process (to the author) as one where the Administration simply conceded whatever was demanded, department by department, in terms of carpets, cabinets, telephones and whatever else was being competed for. In the end, not only was the £146,000 spent, there was actually a new debt of £22,000 which had to be transferred to the General Funds, [27] thus adding to the Party's overall deficit. The NEC, many of whose members had no idea what this section of the accounts involved, [28] then used 'the cost of moving to Walworth Road' as a part of the explanation why the Party's financial predicament was not rooted in excessive expenditure.[29]

Indeed, one could conjecture that in some unions – particularly the TGWU and APEX – the union leadership knew more of the nitty gritty of the internal workings of Labour Party headquarters than some members of the NEC. A new unionism amongst Labour Party staff was not only causing severe cross-pressures within the unions, it was pulling the national union officials in and alerting them to tales of extraordinary incompetence (see Chapter 19).

Small wonder that as these stories proliferated, the TULV leaders should become more and more pressing and should argue with increasing bad temper:

> Too often in the past it has appeared to the Unions that their principal role, as far as the Party was concerned, was merely to fill the bowl when it was passed around. We can no longer accept that approach … [30]

The expanding centre

It must be said that some of the criticism of the Party's management at this time was unfair and overstated. Alongside the anxiety over inefficiency, waste and maladministration was the more specific charge of maldistribution and unnecessary expansion of staff. A common lament (allied sometimes with an attack on the Research Department – see Chapter 19, p. 595) was that the Party was overheavy at the centre.[31] Academic observers took up the theme. The Labour Party's financial problems, it was argued, sprang from a top-heavy organisation in which there had been a big increase in staffing at the centre and amongst administrators in the national and regional bureaucracy.[32] This diagnosis was contrasted frequently with the decline of Labour Agents in the field.[33]

There is some substance to this criticism. Staff at Labour Party headquarters had risen from 106 to 131 between 1966 and 1979. The staff of the National Agents Department and Regional Organisation combined had risen by 12 in the same period. And there is little doubt that the long term decline of Labour Agents was reinforced in the late 1970s by suspicion on the part of the NEC Left of their past political role. Although no strategic decisions were taken in this direction, there appears to have been an acceptance that resources would be better used elsewhere.

But the extent of the increase in staffing has also to be seen in the context of an increase in functions which, in the mid-1970s, was widely welcomed in the Party and the unions. Of the 25 additional posts at Head Office, 16 at least were accounted for by additional capabilities, including Information, Political Education and Student Organising, but particularly the staffing of a *Labour Weekly* newspaper created with widespread enthusiasm in 1972. As for the additional regional staff employed by headquarters, these are accounted for entirely by the integration of the staff of the autonomous London Labour Party into the London 'region' by the national Labour Party and by extra assistance to the Scottish and Welsh parties as a result of the rise of the devolution issue.

Viewed from this perspective, it does little justice to see the increase in staffing as either simple NEC profligacy or simply the 'expansionist bureaucratic tendencies'[34] of the Party's central organisation (although no doubt such tendencies existed). Fundamentally, the Party sought to come to terms with the campaigning needs of the 1970s – particularly its communicational needs. Arguably, it did not do this particularly well nor was the enterprise followed through successfully. But with union approval, it had willed the ends and required the means.

Nevertheless, the drip-drip of accusations against the expanding centre – part of a sustained attack in which the Right of the Party always had the benefit of opinion-formers in the national media – further undermined confidence among union leaders in the Left's stewardship of the Party organisation. When added to a loss of security, to new demands on their financial beneficence and to rumours of monumental inefficiency, this galvanised the union leaders into a new and more interventionist role – especially as they were beginning to anticipate the undermining of their own financial resources.

The problems of union funding

There is little doubt that factional antipathies between the Leftwing section of the NEC and Rightwing union leaders made it more difficult to approach any of these problems in a reasonable way, and they made the search for a consensual solution all the more problematic. The Leftwing course set by *Labour Weekly*, [35] for example, together with the losses it accumulated under NEC supervision, was always a particular thorn in the flesh of the Right, and added another dimension to the aggression of the leadership of such unions as the AUEW, the EETPU and the NUR.

But factional considerations were relatively insignificant in the motivations of the TULV leadership – particularly Basnett, Evans, Jenkins and Keys – who were responsible for union initiatives within the Commission of Enquiry. They were preoccupied with attempting to safeguard the Party's long-term interests while at the same time registering growing anxiety over the position of their own political funding in the face of an aggressive Conservative Government.

On the face of it, such funds were in a relatively healthy condition. Total funds at the end of 1978 were around £4.5 million compared with around £4.1 million at the end of 1977. Even after the abnormally high expenditure arising from the 1979 General Election, there was still around £4.2 million available at the end of 1979. At the end of 1980, this was £5.3 million.[36]

But underlying this expansion were some major vulnerabilties. The average contribution per member had fallen in real terms from 75 pence per member in 1945 to 59 pence per member in 1977 (in 1980 values).[37] Further, the rise in funds was heavily dependent upon the expansion of two major unions – the Transport Workers and the Public Employees.[38] The increasing anxiety felt by the unions in 1979 and 1980 was that a Rightwing Conservative Government would so stimulate the level of unemployment that their membership would be badly hit (a very reasonable anxiety as it turned out) and that the Political Funds would be correspondingly depleted – perhaps even directly attacked.

This concern for the future was also fed in this period by a new awareness of the need for additional finance to cover political communication and political campaigning (see Chapter 17, p. 545). The flop of the TUC's Day of Action in May 1980 made the need all the clearer. But all this would involve new priorities over political expenditure[39] and, if possible, new political incomes. Certainly, it added to the urgency of union concern about their political finance and explains why, in 1979 and 1980, they considered the Political Funds to be dangerously low.

The concern with new needs and activities should not be underestimated. By the late 1970s, as we have already noted, there was a growing consciousness among the more far-sighted elements in the unions that the Labour Movement was in considerable difficulties and that some trade union traditions and practices contributed to the weaknesses. This new awareness had been evident in the discussions leading to the abortive 1978 enquiry into Party organisation and in the first discussions of TULV. It was given influential expression in Larry Whitty's paper to the 1979 Fabian Society study group on Labour Party organisation, and in the General and Municipal Workers' financial evidence to the 1980 Commission of Enquiry[40] – also prepared by Whitty.

These contained four areas of *self*-criticism which fed into the deliberations of the Commission. First, it was noted that the unions had varied, but generally low, levels of political dues; the need was for a new long term standardisation of the levy upwards. Second, there was a high degree of union hoarding with 'money lying idle' and not available until the General Election 'begging bowl'; it needed to be used when available for earlier campaigning, recruitment and political education and for the overall benefit of the Movement. Third, there were varied and uncertain levels of affiliation at all levels of the Party with late payments creating special cash flow problems; these needed raising and also structuring in such a way as to provide nationally a secure base of income and a growing capital. Finally, there was and always had been a misallocation of union funds into the Party as a result of union sponsorship and grants; these went to where individual unions thought fit, whereas they needed to be redirected away from safe seats to where the Party required the resources. Later on in this chapter, we will examine how far these four objectives were realised.

THE COMMISSION

The financial lever

It has already been pointed out how difficult the union leaders found the task of bringing about a full Commission of Enquiry and of securing the implementations and follow through of its organisational recommendations. What was particularly interesting and significant is that these difficulties were encountered in spite of an unusual readiness on the part of some of the more Rightwing union leaders to make open financial threats in an attempt to secure compliance.

The political target (and the political encouragement) here was crucial. This was not a confrontation between the union leaders and the Parliamentary leadership, and from the Right of the PLP there was an open invitation for the union leaders to use the union money in order to bring the NEC – meaning the NEC Left – to heel.

> 'The trade unions have every right to insist on this and if there is any prevaricating ... the unions should use their financial muscle to do just that – insist.'[41]

Responding to this, a few union leaders felt more confident in making financial warnings of a naked character and of using the financial levers – a confidence unimpaired at this time by any remonstrance from the mass media for this behaviour.

There is little doubt that, the unions having, in 1977, negotiated rises in affiliation fees covering the years 1978 to 1980, made it clear that any further rise in affiliation fees must follow a Commission of Enquiry and would not be conceded before. This was the message given to Labour Party officials at a meeting with TULV held in early September 1979.[42] It was not just a retrospective lament session. Unusually, perhaps even uniquely, it was a session in which the union leaders refused to sanction any increase unless the NEC carried out the specific administrative action that they proposed. It was even accompanied by systematic leaking of the threat to show how much the union leaders were in earnest. In this way, the Commission was clearly forced upon a reluctant NEC by union financial power.

With the Commission authorised by the Party Conference, the union leaders were determined to press home their diagnosis of, and prescriptions for, the Party's financial mismanagement. The Finance Working Panel was chaired by one of the most concerned union leaders, Clive Jenkins, and given secretarial and research facilities by his union. The membership of the Panel was not as large as the other two and consisted of the Party's Treasurer, Norman Atkinson, the Chairman of the Finance and General Purposes Committee of the NEC, Russell Tuck, one Leftwing member of the NEC, Jo Richardson, an MP and management consultant, John Garrett, the former Home Secretary, Merlyn Rees, another union leader, Terry Duffy of the AUEW (who, in practice, played little part) and the Party's Finance Officer.

The Panel was given wide terms of reference to examine the Party's financial situation and to look at the uses of trade union political funds in support of the Party. It took in a wide range of written and verbal evidence, including an important contribution from a group of Trade Union Finance Officers who were a source of independent initiatives and, in effect, background advisers to the Panel.

On the surface, the whole exercise could be seen as an open expression of the political control exercised by union leaders. In practice, things were never so straightforward, either in the determining of the recommendations or in their processing through the network of NEC committees and action by the Party bureaucracy.

To begin with, although the prominent role of Clive Jenkins on the Finance Panel was an innovation and an indicator of earnest intent to improve the financial condition of the Party and the management of its finances, he was far from being in a position to speak for 'the unions' as a whole – as we have seen over organisational matters. There were always some disagreements among the TULV leaders who were directly involved in the Commission and there was wider disagreement among those trade union leaders who were watching from the sidelines. As indicated in the submission of evidence from the unions, if there was a consensus about the need for action over the Party's finances, there were many differences of focus and emphasis in the remedies. Further, the union leaders and the Finance Panel as a whole had to work within 'the rules' of their own adherence to the Party – particularly respect for the autonomy of member unions. This meant that some sensitive areas where the Party's problems arose from the unions themselves could be approached only tentatively.

And there were perpetual problems of securing compliance from the NEC where Party cooperation or action was required. The NEC, as in the past, jealously guarded its autonomy and resented 'being pushed around by union leaders'.[43] On the face of it, financial power was everything and the union leaders could have brought the NEC to heel by simply reducing affiliation. A large cut, and Head Office would have been in serious trouble.

Some of the more Rightwing union leaders made no bones about it. 'At the end of the day', Terry Duffy, President of the AUEW, told the *Sunday Times*, 'the politicians' (meaning the NEC Left) 'have to remember that the unions are the paymasters.'[44] Joe Gormley of the Mineworkers said bluntly: 'We'll keep the cheques in our bloody bank'.[45]

There were, however, some problems in withdrawing financial support. Although they could easily refuse to *increase* the fees and *delay* (or in some cases further delay) payment, their room for manoeuvre in *reducing* affiliation was much more limited. Affiliation gave money to the Party but it also gave votes at the Conference and a pecking order of status. If a cluster of unions acted together, they gave advantage to those who did not. If a union acted alone, it simply diminished its standing. Only the EETPU, a maverick union working to rules and reference groups of its own, reduced its affiliation for political reasons in this period. Some unions, including the NUR, may have specially delayed payment for political reasons in 1980, but union payments were in any case often so tardy that the significance of individual union action or simply of two or three unions working together almost got lost in the general pattern.

In any case, the unions collectively were always torn in tactical terms by clumsy use of financial power. They did not want to cripple the only immediate political alternative to a hostile Conservative Government.

Nor, as has been indicated, were they fully agreed on their tactical objective *vis-à-vis* the NEC. For a section of the Right in the unions, the preoccupation in this period was either a clear-out of the NEC, or the achievement of sufficient political leverage over them to secure 'sanity'. But for Basnett, Evans, Jenkins and Keys, the core leadership of TULV on the Commission, the aim was always a consensual agreement based upon an understanding that the Movement had common problems. This, they considered, involved a responsibility on the part of the union leaders to intervene on behalf of the Movement, even if it took them past the boundaries of what had in the past been regarded as permissible under the 'rules'. Such an intervention had its occasional 'baronial' satisfaction when the union leaders were facing the NEC, but they were never fully at ease in this Party role, uncertain of its legitimacy and nervous about where it might be taking them. Further, from them, their officers and advisers, as we shall see, there came a range of initiatives or support for initiatives which would improve the position of the Party and benefit the Movement, even if it meant *sacrificing* potential union and baronial power.

Thus, what ensued in this period was an intense conflict over Party management and financial administration but one in which the union leaders exhibited a complicated mixture of supportiveness, assertiveness, division and inhibition and were met often by constraint and frustration. There emerged a pattern of politics in which the unions were far from being able to utilise financial leverage to the extent that some would have wanted. And they were far from being able to secure that immediate response which surface appearances suggested might be available to them.

The reader should note that what now follows is, in structural terms, a complicated exercise. To understand fully the political interplay of forces at work within the Party and the unions, we have to follow through some of the key problems of Party finance into the late 1980s. In each section, each problem will take us briefly out of the time frame of the Commission before we return to examine other problems dealt with by the Commission and by TULV.

State finance and collective finance

The supportiveness and the inhibitions produced a significant response to the problem of resourcing the Parliamentary Party. Here, the most obvious characteristic of the Commission in financial terms was not the union pursuit of power but the pursuit of financial resources for the Party from almost any acceptable source. Thus, what the Commission did was to firm up the Party's commitment to State Aid for political parties. The principle of State Aid had hitherto divided the PLP. And some unions, including the NUM, the AUEW and UCATT, had expressed a principled objection to the proposal in their evidence to the Houghton Commission.[46] Even the resource-conscious Group of Trade Union Finance Officers offered their advice to the Finance Panel that State Aid should be approached with caution for a variety of reasons, including the dangers of political control from the State.[47] But the union leaders pushed ahead with their recommendations and urged an improvement on the formula produced by the Houghton Commission. Basnett, Evans and Jenkins were all enthusiastic and their recommendations went into the Commission and through the Party Conference by an overwhelming vote of 5,861,000 to 1,024, 000.

Some doubts were expressed both on the Commission and at the Conference that such a move might undermine links between the Party and the unions, and certainly supporters of this reform in other parties have seen this weakening of the union-Labour Party relationship as one beneficial side effect. But reassured to some extent by foreign experience, and in any case with their eyes firmly fixed on the problem of solvency for the Party rather than the potential of power for the unions, the union leaders committed themselves firmly to the report.

As for the existing form of State Aid (the 'Short Money'), initiated in 1974 by

a Labour Lord President of the Council, Edward Short, and paid to Opposition
Parties since 1975 specifically to enable them to carry out their duties in Parliament, the TULV leaders took very much the same hard-headed financial approach. The Short Money should be substantially increased.

Significantly, the Finance Panel emphasised the need for funds to permit
Opposition spokesmen comprehensively to 'shadow' Government ministers with
the assistance of an experienced back-up team of researchers.[48] In addition, there
was, the Panel said, a strong case for extra PLP staffing, and the needs of the Party
Leader's Office also had to be considered.[49] This perspective (which appears to
have been fully accepted by TULV leaders Basnett, Jenkins and Evans) was very
significant indeed, coming as it did at a time when there was enormous pressure
to assert the right of the Party outside the House to make Party policy (see
Chapter 7). It proved to be one of the most important hidden thrusts of the
Commission.

Significantly also, though they were involved in these discussions on the
Short Money, the TULV leaders made no attempt to interfere in the bitter dispute
which had divided the NEC and the Parliamentary leadership since 1979 over
control of this money, or the question of conditions of service of PLP researchers
which had been a substantive point at issue when the NEC had discussed the
matter at great length in 1979.[50] It might have been assumed that both in terms of
union power and in terms of trade union conditions, the union leaders would
have become more assertive. But, again, what mattered was money for the Party
and the practicalities of making the Party more effective. There was certainly
little desire to get involved in the delicate political question of financial control
in relation to the PLP.

Eventually, in January 1981, under a new leadership, the question of the Short
Money was settled by an agreement in which control over the money would pass
from the Leader to a committee of four – the Leader, the PLP Chairman and two
trustees from the PLP – in effect, a victory for the PLP leadership. All the money
went to the Parliamentary Party with one-third allocated to meet the costs of
Party staff employed in the PLP Office (an NEC responsibility). Some on the
political Left continued to express their dislike for an arrangement in which
(unlike the Conservative Party) the national financial administration of the
Party played no part in the management of a fund which, as we have seen, gave a
significant boost to the capacity of the Parliamentary leadership to involve
themselves in autonomous policymaking.

This issue of financial assistance to the Front Bench was to take on a new
aspect after 1983 when it was argued that the level of Short Money (nearly
£300,000) would still be inadequate to carry out the new tasks envisaged by the
enlarged Leader's Office. TULV agreed to make a lump sum donation to the
Leader's Office for the Leader to deal with it as he thought fit. But, in addition,
discussions over money for the Leader's Office now extended into discussions in
TULV on the funding of the Front bench, whose members, since 1979, had
regularly approached individual unions with which they were connected for extra
financial assistance in employing their research assistants on a full time basis.

In effect, what was offered to the unions here was a unique opportunity to pay the Front Bench piper and call the Shadow Cabinet tune. Or alternatively, they might have agreed with the NEC Left that all union finance for policy assistance should go first to the National Executive Committee – where the presence of trade union representatives might indirectly ensure a degree of union supervision.

They were, however, uneasy with the propriety of this relationship and they did not like the higgledy-piggledy patronage based on no overall assessment of Party needs. On the TULV Committee, Moss Evans moved that single approaches to the unions from the Front Bench should *cease*.[51] As the Committee said later in a letter to the Party's General Secretary, 'the present system of soliciting union money for the Leader's office and the Shadow Cabinet posts is most unsatisfactory ...'. It 'must be rationalised and put on an above the board basis ...'. [52] The TULV Committee insisted that the money be dealt with collectively in one lump sum and distributed not by a union agency or the NEC but by the Leader and his Office. On the NEC, some of the Left returned to their earlier demand that all financial support for the PLP and all TULV contributions should go first to the NEC itself. This proposal was defeated with the aid of union votes as the unions, not for the first time, voted to divest themselves of a major potential lever of power.[53]

Subsequently, the TULV (and later the TUFL) Executive always had to wrestle with individuals on the Front Bench to accept this arrangement, and, occasionally (as a result of the supplications of some Shadow Ministers), some unions were persuaded to pay 'extras'. But the unions collectively always disapproved of this procedure and in 1987 the TUFL Executive, in reconsidering the whole question of the significant amounts of union money now paid to the Front Bench (over £100,000), made it clear that it considered that any move back to individual union payments being made direct to individual Shadow Ministers would be a 'retrograde step'.[54]

A few months later, it became clear that the Short Money would be much greater than anticipated (£839, 000) and consequently TUFL was informed that in future its money for the Front Bench was no longer required.[55] However, there was still a strong request for funds for the expanding Leader's Office – funds which were generously provided to the tune of well over £100,000 per year on a regular basis without application or negotiation. This arrangement was put into practice in spite of regular union grumbles about the composition of the Office and what was considered by some in 1988 to be its poor advice (some even said 'insensitivity') on matters relating to the unions and the Movement.

Closing dates and payments

In as much as the financial crisis of this period was seen as being so acute that it warranted direct intervention by the unions, it also placed upon them an obligation to examine their own role in creating the Party's financial difficulties. In this sense, it provided a unique opportunity – as the GMWU evidence recognised.

One such problem, ludicrous outside its own history, was that, unusually for any organisation, the Labour Party Constitution laid down no closing date for the payment of affiliation fees. Part of the problem of securing change here was one of constitutional inertia. But there was also the difficulty that affiliation fees were considered a sensitive business. Imposing a date of final payment was seen as an intrusion into trade union autonomy. And it was moving into delicate cultural territory, threatening the deep-rooted, neurotic security device of union hoarding.

As a consequence of not having a closing date, there was often an astonishing tardiness and incoherence in the payment of union affiliation fees and a persistent problem for the Party's General Secretary. Nobody knew, month by month, what affiliation fees would arrive, therefore there was always the danger of a problem of inadequate cash flow. Ironically, one of the worst culprits had been ASTMS, whose General Secretary was Chairing the Finance Panel.[56]

Some idea of the problem of securing union compliance on this can be gathered from the fact that in September 1979 at a TULV meeting attended by the General Secretary and Party Treasurer, it had been agreed that the union would try collectively to pay its affiliation fees in January so as to help the Party's immediate problem; yet on 18 April 1980, the Finance Panel was told by the Finance Officer that only a small number of unions had paid by that date.[57] It may be that the continuing dissatisfaction with Party administration had found another outlet, but the problems went deeper and had a much longer history.

The situation was clearly financially unhelpful (and also politically undesirable, see Chapter 10, p. 289). Accordingly, the Panel and the Commission recommended that discussions take place to establish a common date for payment and eventually, in 1982, the closing date of 31 March was written into the Constitution. Yet the problem remained. At the meeting between TULV and the NEC held 6 and 7 May, 1983, the NEC was still complaining of an accumulated shortfall which, by the end of March, was in the region of £300, 000.

Eventually, in 1987, there was a further constitutional amendment aimed at helping the Party's financial stability. The provision of '31st March in the year following that in which they were due' was changed to '31st December of the relevant year'. A logical and reasonable step it might be thought, but it had taken a remarkably long time to achieve – and there was still no way of forecasting the amount and timing of union payments and no guarantee that all the unions would pay by the closing date. The result was an aggravation of the problems of Head Office budgeting – a feature highlighted in a special auditors' report in 1988.[58] Armed with this report, Whitty – the General Secretary – was able finally to persuade the unions to agree not only to the forward planning of affiliation fees (see p. 524) but to place their payment on a quarterly basis.[59] This became part of the package *Promoting Our Values*, which was endorsed at the 1988 Party Conference.

The level of affiliation fees

The payment of union affiliation fees involved a second and more immediate problem dealt with by the Commission. Once the Commission was in being, then the rise in affiliation fees which the unions had evaded at the meeting with Party officials in September 1979 now had to be faced. Here, union leaders were presented both with the evidence that affiliation fees since 1977 had not kept pace with inflation and with the fact that the Party needed guaranteed income sufficient to build a long term capital base. There could be no alternative to an immediate increase in union affiliation fees, but some of the TULV union leaders were keen to do more than simply deal with the immediate problem. They favoured a more assured income for the Party from the unions even if this meant forgoing a position of potential political leverage and doing away with the annual consultative process ('the lament session') which took place before affiliation fee increases were agreed.

Basnett and Jenkins came down in favour of an affiliation fee increase from 32p to 40p per annum in 1981 and a shift to 50p in 1982, and they coupled this with a proposal that the level of political levies be at a single rate and that the level of affiliation fees should, in future, increase automatically with rises in the retail price index.

Not all the union leaders shared this perspective. It raised internal union problems about the size of the levy. It ran counter to the hoarding instinct, and it evoked no sympathy among those who regarded the Leftwing NEC as 'irresponsible'. Consequently, the proposals met resistance all the way.

Strong representations were made by the Trade Union Finance Officers Panel that the scale of fees envisaged was not feasible and some of the reasons they advanced, including the problem of changing some union levies without a union rules revision conference, were also powerful arguments against index linking. Similar arguments were heard at a Special Conference of affiliated unions held to discuss the major financial questions on 31 May 1980. Despite these reservations, the Finance Panel went ahead with the recommendations as 'essential' to the Party.[60] But at a second meeting of affiliated unions held on 20 August, after the Commission had reported, heavy resistance to the new fees came from a wide variety of positions – some of it relating to the unions' own financial and constitutional positions, but much of it affected also by union reservations about the Party's management of its financial affairs.

As a result, the TULV committee was forced into a re-examination of the proposals and agreed to pursue only the 1981 increase and seek deletion of the proposal for a 1982 increase. A letter from Basnett on behalf of TULV carried this amendment to the NEC and agreed not to pursue this part of the Commission's recommendations to the Conference.[61]

As for the recommendation of index linking, this also went through a process of watering down. By the time it had been through all the deliberations of the Finance Panel it had become a more general recommendation that the NEC should be involved in an annual review with authority to determine the level of affiliation fees and subscriptions, 'taking into account the increase in the cost of living'.[62] But in the Report of the Commission, this became simply a statement of the importance of maintaining the value of subscriptions and affiliation.[63] As for the NEC's obligation to make an increase, this was cited only for individual subscriptions and not for affiliation fees.

In the event, with much dissatisfaction being expressed by the unions over the various failures of implementation and the management of Party headquarters, the next two years were not really conducive to an enthusiastic trade union agreement for a general and substantial increase in affiliation fees. In 1982, the increase was a compromise at 47$\frac{1}{2}$p. But in 1983, with the General Election

Fund also making demands, there was a freeze.

Subsequently, with the Party under new leadership and with growing union confidence that under this leadership some of the major problems of Party headquarters would be tackled, there was both a withdrawal of TULV/TUFL's involvement in Party administration and a steady rise in annual affiliation fees by 5p per year. In 1987 it was 75p. And that year the TUFL Convenor recommended that the trade union affiliates provide money to meet the Party annual administrative expenses 'at a percentage no less than at present'.[64] This stimulated long discussions, out of which came in 1988 (again as part of *Promoting Our Values*) an agreement to a three-year plan for affiliation fees – increasing them incrementally in stages to £1.45p by 1991.[65] (See also below, p. 537, for the innovation of a General Election Fund portion of the fees.)

Sponsorship and maldistribution

Overcoming the hoarding instinct in 1988 was a remarkable achievement, particularly as the unions' sense of ownership over *their* funds was reinforced by the terms of the Political Levy Fund campaigns (see Chapter 17). Nevertheless, this possessiveness, allied to a sectional view of what was good for individual unions, still caused one of the Party's most fundamental financial problems. Ever since it was founded, it had relied upon trade union funds to boost its local election machinery and campaigns but it was the unions which in the main decided the location and scale of this finance. As a result, sponsorship and grants were concentrated in safe seats and in particular regions.[66] For many years, before and after the strictures of the Wilson Report, [67] Party officials had wrestled with what, in Party terms, was a gross misallocation of resources.

However, by 1980, a new coalition of forces, including the Tribune Group and the Fabian Society, was beginning to emerge in favour of reforming the sponsorship system. This question of misallocation of union funds to the Party had been raised in early discussions within TULV. Now there was a move within the unions towards 'phasing out'. In the GMWU's evidence to the Commission, 'phasing out' would involve in the first instance a central pooling and reallocation of those proportions of union funds which, under the Hastings Agreement, normally went on agents' salaries and General Election expenditure.

These proposals were strongly contested by other unions although some of them, including TASS and COHSE, did offer alternative solutions to the problem of misallocation. From NUPE and NULO came pressure for unions to pay the maximum of the Hastings Agreement to the constituency they were sponsoring – a move which would have helped the Party financially but ran counter to the reallocation proposals.

After examination of the Party's needs, some agreement on central pooling did take place on the Organisation and Membership Panel, but this was dropped in the Commission's final report. The Finance Panel, although it made sponsorship part of its programme, could find no agreement in the light of union differences and therefore made no reference to it in its report. What the Commission did, in the end, was suggest that the unions 'give consideration to' the support of candidates in seats other than marginal or safe constituencies.[68]

The acute problem in 1980 was that just as one tendency within the unions was moving towards seeking a radical readjustment of the sponsoring system, another tendency was beginning to reappraise the value of the present sponsoring arrangements and to appreciate much more the benefits of a union 'voice' in Parliament. This latter body of opinion was to be reinforced in the mid-1980s as a result of the Political Fund campaigns – campaigns which would have to be fought again within ten years. Thus it became more, rather than less, difficult in the 1980s to raise the question of reform. In this area, territorial protectiveness took on a new lease of life.

Yet while the problem of reallocation was getting more intractable, the problem of overall misallocation was, if anything, getting worse. Not only was the process of union co-option of MPs in safe seats advancing but in Parliament the major increase in back-up funding based on increased Members' allowances, an increase in the Short Money and additional TUFL money were all, in effect, going to safe seat members. Those who had got more.

Through the regional TUFL organisations, and in conjunction with the Party's regional office, some reallocation of resources to needy marginals did take place. But the Party could find few means of influencing the location of individual union grants to whatever constituency was favoured for local, industrial or political reasons. Indeed, years later, the Party headquarters was still very badly informed as to which unions were paying what and to whom.

After 1988, in informal discussions between the General Secretary and the union leaders, the problem of maldistribution and the reform of sponsorship was raised again. But in this period so many other financial and political issues were being raised in relation to the unions that it never attained the priority it merited. There was an agreed new emphasis on maintenance between elections but, on maldistribution, no consensus could be reached privately, and when it was raised within TUFL, the Chairman, Ron Todd, ruled that it was not within the province of that organisation.

The problems of financial management

Those problems of Labour Party financing which stemmed from the attitudes and traditions of its union affiliates were to some extent dwarfed on the Commission of 1980 and, in the subsequent follow-up, by the union leaders' anxieties over the inadequacies of the Labour Party's financial and administrative management.

One of the first tasks of the Finance Panel of the Commission was to produce a clear picture of the state of the Party's finances and a clear diagnosis of the Party's predicament. This proved to be a very difficult operation. The first thing that became clear was that the Party accounts were so badly presented that basic information could only be extracted with great difficulty.

In the course of a special audit of the accounts, it was also revealed that the Special Funds were a presentative fiction and most of the Funds 'did not have any money in them at all'.[69] The Accounts simply registered the amount which had been donated over the years.

Once exploration of the process of financial management took place, it also became apparent that no single officer was responsible for financial management and 'the Finance Officer has little power or influence over decisions which have cost the Party dearly'.[70] On the one hand his time was consumed by other administrative matters; on the other there was a lack of proper budgeting and control at the point of decision-making. A Finance Office note pointed out: 'There have been many instances in the recent past when the office has been required to make payments against firm orders which have been placed by other departments, without any prior knowledge and consultation.'[71] In the Head Office there was, in practice, 'no single person under the General Secretary who has a total control or oversight of all the Party's finances'.[72]

The question of how to re-establish proper internal financial controls was to be one of the long-running sagas of the next decade (see Chapter 19). From the first, opinion was divided between the Finance Panel and the Organisation and Membership Panel as to how the problem might be dealt with. The Finance Panel, particularly Jenkins, thought in terms of 'a new and professional financial administrator' operating under the General Secretary but superior to present Departmental Heads. The Organisation and Membership Panel expressed the view that this would provide 'a superfluous tier of management'. Eventually, the Commission went strongly for a high level post of Director of Finance who would be 'responsible to the General Secretary for all aspects of budgetary control and proper financial planning and reporting'.[73]

The NEC's management of the Party's finances was limited by this lack of control within the Office and by a lack of adequate financial information, but there were problems also in the form of the NEC's own supervision. There was the longstanding, and financially curious, division of responsibilities between the Treasurer and the Chairman of the Finance and General Purposes Committee (to which reference has already been made). There was a lack of co-ordination between the decisions of the F and GP and the decisions of the various sub-committees of the NEC. And there was the special problem at this time of the General Election Fund which was under no clear financial supervision: the Party Treasurer told the Commission and the Party Conference that neither he nor the Finance and General Purposes Committee had been involved in any financial decisions concerning the General Election Fund expenditure.[74]

Seeking to rationalise this organisational mess, the union leaders on the Commission now responded by a discussion of the questions raised by Gaitskell a quarter of a century previously. What was the Treasurer's responsibility? Why wasn't the Treasurer also the Chair of the F and GP? The Group of Trade Union Finance Officers even went so far as to recommend the abolition of the post of Treasurer describing it as 'the post of Honorary Treasurer'. But this was a political hot potato and in the end the Panel's recommendation steered well clear of demarcating responsibilities. However, the TULV leaders on the Commission did eventually decide to recommend that the Treasurer in future be Chair of the F and GP. To improve coordination further, all Chairs of Committees should also automatically be members of the F and GP.[75] Some dispute took place with PLP leaders over the past handling of the General Election Fund, and the Finance Panel's recommendation that NEC budgetary control be 'instituted' became, in the Commission Report, a recommendation that it be 'continued'.[76]

IMPLEMENTATION, THE VOLUNTARY LEVY FUND AND 'DRIP FEED'

Implementation

As we have already seen, shaping the recommendations of a Commission of Enquiry was one thing; securing their implementation was another. With the exception of the proposal for an increase in affiliation fees, none of the financial recommendations involved a change in the Party's Constitution – the maximum point of command for the unions at the Conference. And although the Commission's Report was ratified by the Conference, the degree of control exercised over its implementation was minimal given that the NEC was not obliged to produce a follow-up report. In spite of the NEC's financial difficulties and in spite of the new role of TULV in controlling a Voluntary Levy Fund (see below, pp. 529–31), the NEC largely went its own way.

Part of the negativism of the NEC was based on the belief, shared in Walworth Road, that some of the Commission recommendations were based on an inadequate understanding of the accompanying problems. But it also reflected a deeply hostile response to union leaders transgressing territorial 'rules'. Even after 1981, when there were important changes in the composition of the NEC and then a new General Secretary, trade union leaders found it hard to secure compliance.

One recommendation of the Commission had to be withdrawn almost immediately because of NEC resistance to union encroachment. The Chair of the Finance and General Purposes Committee was held to be a matter for the NEC alone and whatever the rationality of combining the position with that of Treasurer, the Commission's recommendation transgressed strongly guarded boundaries of autonomy. At the Conference of 1980, Clive Jenkins, Chair of the Finance Panel, tactfully retreated.[77] Until 1983, union representatives on the NEC continued to take the F and GP Chair.[78] But with an NEC union leader as Treasurer, and with more union confidence in the management of Walworth Road, the reassurance of the NEC committee post has seemed less relevant.[79]

As for the other recommendations, little seemed to move in the eighteen months following the publication of the Report. Resentment at the new composition and the role played by the NEC Staff Negotiations Committee (see Chapter 19, p. 20) and the continuing annual deficits – £165, 000 in 1980, £320, 000 in 1981 and £141, 000 in 1982 – led TULV leaders to put to the joint meeting with the NEC held in June 1982 a document which listed 17 points from the 22 items of the Finance Panel where progress was, it suggested, 'urgent' and 'valuable time' was being lost.[80]

Some of the items listed, it must be said, depended in great measure on union support as much as Party action. Other items – encouragement of extra trade union national affiliation and State Finance – were either extremely difficult to carry through or dependent on Government action. To this extent, the list was more of a polemic than a reasoned document. Nevertheless, looking at the list and the accompanying comments, it is hard not to see the whole exercise as a scream of frustration. Here they were, the 'Barons' of media legend, controllers of the Party purse-strings, and yet for three years they had been through one rebuff after another. It was, years later, an understandable exaggeration by Barry Sherman (in 1980 Research Officer of ASTMS) to say that the Commission's recommendations were 'neglected and gathering dust somewhere in the Walworth Road basement', [81] but certainly, the process of securing implementation was to be a tardy, tortuous and frustrating experience.

Of eight listed items where the NEC and Party officials could reasonably have acted alone, budgetary control of the General Election Fund was instituted in 1982. A rearrangement of the accounts to improve their public presentation was eventually introduced in 1983 – although there were continuing problems in the way budgets and accounts were presented to the Party's management right up to the calling-in of auditors in 1988. An attempt was made at standardised CLP accounting (with little success) after 1984. National fund-raising was launched in 1984, although not geared to a specific day. But a proposal for a National Membership Lottery was simply buried.

The longest-running battle took place over the most important proposal, which was to appoint a Director of Finance who would be a 'top level financial administrator' with special seniority. The unions cleared the ground by providing redundancy money for restructuring the existing Finance Department. But they could not get any action on the recommendation, which was accepted by the NEC 'in principle' but with deep reluctance.

The reservations were primarily concerned with the envisaged role of the new Director in the Headquarters hierarchy, his high salary and his relationship with the Head of the Finance Department. These difficulties were not resolved for years. In 1983, the new Finance Officer was given only the status and job definition of his predecessor and in 1985 could be said to have lost some relative seniority given the appointment of new Directorates covering other Departments. Not until 1987 was a new post instituted (Chapter 19, pp. 603 and 608) with the appointment of a Personnel Resources and Training Officer.

But by 1983, as we shall indicate, financial management had been improved in other ways which partially reassured the unions. The Finance and General Purposes Committee now included all Committee Chairs. Although there were still problems (see p. 522 and p. 605), various reforms took place in accounting, with one of the trade union finance officers, Fred Jarvest, advising on the Finance Department methods. Most of the accounts were amalgamated and one – the General Election Fund Account – was fully separated. The new General Secretary, Jim Mortimer, placed a heavy emphasis on prudent economy in an attempt to get the Party out of deficit. Under Mortimer's management, and backed by a new Staff Negotiations Committee, the Party actually moved into surplus in 1983, 1984 and 1985.

Nevertheless, the relationship between the NEC and TULV continued to exhibit tensions right up to 1985, after which the Party appointed a new General Secretary (the TULV Secretary – although this was not the reason he was appointed), and the TULV/TUFL Chair was taken by the TGWU. Ron Todd, the new Chair of the union organisation, was much less interventionist than his predecessor, though the G and M leadership continued to see that union as having special responsibilities in relation to the performance of the Party. Its new General Secretary, John Edmunds, did not appear to share Todd's inhibitions, and on Party organisational questions, as with Party policymaking (see Chapter 14A), did not like to be excluded if things were not moving according to expectations. However, Todd's more traditional perspective was much more typical of what was now a much greater propensity to leave Party management to the Party leadership.

While the acute tensions lasted – particularly in the period when TULV leaders were seeking the implementation of the Commission's recommendations – they became focused on and mediated through the new and highly controversial Voluntary Levy Fund. It was, through one set of eyes, a supportive organisation designed to raise extra finance for the Party; through another pair of eyes, it was a unique instrument of financial control for political purposes.

The Voluntary Levy Fund

Its origins lay in the response of the Group of Trade Union Finance Officers to the Basnett and Jenkins plan for a two-stage raising of affiliation fees. Because each union had a distinctive political and procedural character, some were in a position (and willing) to pay for increased affiliation fees twice in the near future; others were either unable or unwilling or both. The unwillingness was related in some cases to factional antipathy towards the NEC but even those eager to help the Party and in a position to pay, were alarmed at the NEC's financial and administrative problems.

The aim of the temporary Trade Union Levy Fund or Labour Alliance Fund (the original alternatives for the name) was that, for a temporary period, money would be drawn from those unions which had a stronger Political Fund base and were willing to use it. As the memorandum from the Group noted:

> There is no long term desire ... to exercise control (of the financial affairs of the Labour Party). However, there is a sad recognition that the oldest international socialist democratic party is in a difficult situation and seems to be prone to inefficiency and indebtedness ... In the short term the trade unions must have positive proof of the efficient use of the additional resources they provide.'[82]

They stressed that their recommendations 'were intended to ensure a proper respect for trade union resources rather than to create a "two masters" situation'.[83]

The proposal was welcomed by the Finance Panel but removed from the Commission Report and instead taken to a meeting of TULV affiliated unions on 20 August 1980. Some unions, including the AUEW, had reservations about the role of an intermediary committee, but the affiliated unions sanctioned what they stressed would be a Voluntary Levy Fund. Each union who volunteered to join would pay a 10p per member affiliation in addition to the TULV affiliation.

By the time that details of the Fund were carried to the NEC in a letter from Basnett, relations with the NEC had deteriorated over a wide field of issues and there were stories of conspicuous waste following the transfer from Transport House to Walworth Road. All this hardened union commitment to the new mechanism, which 'would be administered by the Unions participating, utilising the services of a trade union specialist finance group, who would monitor, and endeavour to ensure effective use of, the resources that are allocated to the Party from the Fund'. Basnett's letter to the NEC carrying this proposal, also suggested that representatives of the Union Finance Officers Group should attend the Party's Finance and General Purposes Committee as 'observers' in order 'To help the Unions to better appraise the financial problems, workings and needs of the Party'.[84]

In what they regarded as an alarming situation, it was another unprecedented intervention by union leaders in the administration of the Party. As such, again it aroused some fierce responses. Indeed, union leaders were met at the NEC with a united and powerful opposition with Benn and Callaghan leading the attack. The proposals were rejected and the Levy Fund was condemned from the Left as being 'undemocratic' and a means of 'drip-feeding' the Party – 'we'll give you money if you do what we want'.[85]

Following this rejection, the multiple tensions between TULV and the NEC were exacerbated rather than diminished. There seemed no end in sight to the Party's deficits. Compliance with the Commission recommendations seemed to be stuck. And pressure on the unions' funds began to increase as unemployment moved ever upwards. TULV was reconstituted and the proposal for a Voluntary Levy was confirmed at another meeting of TULV affiliates on 25 February 1981. The union leaders, feeling powerless to affect the politics of the NEC or its administration of the Party, awaited the inevitable approach as the NEC consulted over new affiliation fees.

It came in July 1981. In a meeting with leaders of affiliated unions on 8 July 1981, the Party's Treasurer again put the case for an increase in the affiliation fee from 40p to 50p for 1982. He coupled this with a plea for the funding of the General Election account and a grant for designated purposes.[86] A number of unions were adamant that an increase in affiliation on this scale was out of the question and they were unsympathetic to the other funding appeals under present circumstances. Eventually, there was a compromise on $47^1/_2$p, but it was in this context that a separate meeting of the Organisational Sub-committee, the Finance and General Purposes Committee and representatives of TULV held further discussions about the relationship between TULV and the Party and about the renewed proposal for a Voluntary Levy Fund.

With deep reluctance but also with some reassuring arrangements (Chapter 15, p. 498), the NEC now agreed to the establishment of the Fund. The Voluntary Levy Fund would be under the control of a Trade Union Management Committee. The levy on unions would be, in formal terms, 10p per member but unions would pay as and when they were able on the basis of any subscription they could afford. Further, any union could at any time give written notice requiring repayment of any funds not spent. The terms for the utilisation of the finance were very wide but it was agreed that the monies would only be used for 'those purposes on which TULV and the Party were agreed'. Where the NEC requested assistance for a particular project, the TULV would have to exercise its judgement, 'but this was in any case the situation at present' when the NEC appealed to the unions on an ad hoc basis to finance particular activities.[87]

The TULV leadership had in view the possibility that they might fund activity within the unions – such as Labour Party recruitment and also joint regional activity with the Party. They already had, in formal terms, three working parties of officers who had been concerned with the three areas of the Party Commission's activities – political education, organisation and finance. It was thought that through a mutual exchange of relevant officers and through joint activity they might aid the Party in ways which were constructive within the unions and reassuring in terms of the expenditure of union funds.

But though they conceded the Fund arrangement, the NEC was reluctant to make any concessions which compromised its own working role. Although TULV agreed to have the Party Chairman, General Secretary and Treasurer on its Committee and to have trade union members of the NEC attend all general meetings of TULV, the NEC refused again to allow union Finance Officers to attend its Finance and General Purposes Committee meetings. And though a formal arrangement for joint working meetings was given some initial assent, this soon fizzled out in the face of opposition from the NEC and the Party Leader.

'Drip feed'?

Although, in practice, the work of TULV through the Voluntary Levy Fund did earn the support of the Party Leader, Michael Foot, and the Party's General Secretary, Jim Mortimer – both from the Left – it stimulated considerable suspicion and resentment from others on the Left. In 1982, it came under strong attack in Tribune [88] and in 1984, the NUM, in a comprehensive political critique, alleged that TULV had 'denied money requested by the Labour Party for specific projects'.[89]

Criticism of the Fund was concerned with three features of its operation. There was a fear that income into the Fund could come to rival in size the income from affiliation fees, and therefore become the method of trade union funding. There was concern also that the TULV now had funds which it was using for its own administration and organisational purposes, some of which might otherwise have come directly to the Party. And there was a strong political fear that TULV now had the power to deny funds for specific political projects which the NEC wanted to pursue – in effect a Rightwing political 'drip-feed'.[90]

In practice, the amounts of money raised by TULV through the Fund were never comparable to those raised through national affiliation. By 30 June 1982 – the date of the annual TULV meeting – twenty-three unions, representing 89 per cent of affiliated membership, had contributed a total of £234, 859, and in the nine months to April 1983 a further £184,615 was raised with three more unions participating. By comparison, affiliation fees in 1982 raised over £2¾ million.

Of £105,706 expenditure in the 1981/2 period, £95,000 was spent on Labour's Campaigns. Of the £263, 448 spent in 1982/3, £100,000 was contributed directly to the Party's General Election Fund, £40,500 was spent on a fund-raising campaign for the General Election and a further £47,252 was spent in support of Labour's election campaign. Whatever method of fund allocation was used, these items would have had to be spent anyway – a fact which has to be borne in mind when considering charges that the Levy Fund could have paid off the Party's debts.

Accusations about factional 'drip feed' have to be judged not only against the small amounts involved but also against the managers of the Fund. The limited company set up as a legal requirement to act as handling agent for TULV had three directors in addition to David Basnett, the TULV Chairman. All three – Moss Evans of the TGWU, Clive Jenkins of ASTMS and Bill Keys of SOGAT – were from the Left. Further, the Rightwing unions, whose leaders were most outspoken about the use of finance to bring a political response from the NEC, were among the most reluctant and smallest payers to the Fund and therefore in less position to exercise any leverage.

In any case, there is no evidence of any political criteria being used to 'drip feed' and most of the time the Party got everything it asked for. Only three categories of request tended to meet a negative response: (i) money which involved taking on additional staff – the overall union view was that Labour Party Headquarters required careful pruning; (ii) money which was requested for what appeared to be general rather than specific purposes; and (iii) (potentially more sensitive) money for projects which TULV thought to be 'unconsidered'. In such cases as came within the latter category, the union leaders proved to be as conscious of the dangers of impropriety as were the NEC. Certainly, there is no evidence whatsoever of a political/factional filter. The union leaders simply took their financial remit literally. The only significant rejection of an NEC request appears to have been a proposal for a Party computer facility which did not cohere with other developments in the building or with trade union facilities.

The Voluntary Levy Fund eventually survived the passing of TULV and was taken over by Trade Unionists For Labour. Although their main fears on its use had not been substantiated, there was still an initial reluctance by some unions on both Left and Right (including the NUM, the AUEW and the EETPU) to have their money used in this intermediary way. However, by 1987, it did not arouse the same animosity. It was used to pay the salary (for two years) of a Trade Union Liaison Officer employed by the Party and under the management of the Director of Organisation. And it was used for the regular unconditional grants to the Front Bench and the Leader's Office, that we have already noted.

After the 1987 General Election, it proved possible to broaden the base of the fund and to use it in a variety of uncontroversial ways which assisted the Party (see Chapter 18, p. 575).

FUNDING THE PARTY

The changing balance

Ironically, although the Finance Panel and the Commission spent much time examining how Party income might be increased at all levels, one of the biggest financial changes took place independently of the Commission. The NEC had already decided prior to the Commission meeting that the national affiliation fees for constituency parties should be unhinged from that of the unions and increased substantially. In 1980, the CLPs were to pay a huge increase from 32p to

£1.25 per member and in the year after £2.50 per member as a means of stimulating national financial income. By 1987, the affiliation fee was £5.50 per member, while the unions were paying 75p.

A similar change has taken place at regional level (each region takes its own decisions on affiliation fees), where CLP affiliation fees have tended to rise more than trade union affiliation fees. Thus, the constituency parties have been placed under more pressure to raise finance and this appears to have led to a renewed emphasis on autonomous fund-raising at that level. An extensive survey by Fatchett in 1986 indicated that the average constituency party raised about 80 per cent of its income from sources other than the unions.[91] This represents a significant shift from the figure of (just below) 70 per cent calculated by Harrison for 1957.[92]

At regional level, there also appears to have been an increase in the proportion of income from non-trade union sources,[93] but it is at national level that this tendency is now most marked.

Although the Commission had discussed fund-raising at considerable length, it had preferred a devolved approach (alongside an annual National Appeal day and a National Membership Lottery). In practice, a national fund-raiser was appointed to Head Office in April 1984 and, for a period, income from this source grew significantly. At the end of 1987 there was a net income from fund-raising of £321,000 and election year donations of £185,000.

Meanwhile, unemployment produced the financial effects that union leaders feared in 1980. Membership declined, as did the numbers paying the political levy. With this came also a slow reduction in national union affiliation to the Party and a change in the relative income from unions and CLPs as the disparity in payments per member compared with the CLPs continued to grow.

Overall, the result of these changes was substantial. The percentage of national income coming to the Party from the unions' affiliation fees (adjusting for the Short Money paid for the PLP office) had sunk to 73 per cent in 1987. If the Short Money is included in the total income, the union contribution that year was 71 per cent.[94]

The 1988 Business Plan

However, by the end of 1987, it had become clear that the Party's income would simply not be sufficient to cope with the demands it was expected would be made on it in future years. And the unions seemed almost to be back with some of the developments they had so deeply resented in 1979. There was a budget deficit, which pulled them into a deep crisis in Party headquarters (see Chapter 19, pp. 605–8). There was a continuing problem in maintaining adequate internal financial control. And as union membership declined, so the reduction in union affiliation (and of course Party income), which had been deliberately slowed down to assist the Party, was steadily progressing and would continue. Further, the CLP membership was declining and with it the affiliation fees from that source. And 1988 was a very disappointing year for fund-raising and donations. The proportion of national income from union affiliation fees was rising again (76 per cent, or 74 per cent if the Short Money is included in the total income).

Within the two big general unions which had been particularly generous in assisting the Party in the past, and seldom slow to respond to its appeals, there was now alarm at the possibility that they might once again have 'to bail the Party out'. The GMB leader was particularly forceful in expressing his exasperation.

These feelings were fed into the deliberations taking place in the Labour Party General Secretary's Department over how the Party could produce a stronger and broader income base. Discussions then proceeding between Larry Whitty, his political assistant Tony Manwaring and Unity Trust led to the creation of a loan to finance a Business Plan which would cover longer term projects for fund-raising, the development of financial services and the promotion of membership campaigns.

The Plan, as it evolved in 1988, involved five major unions – the GMB, NGA, NUR, TGWU and UCW – underwriting £500, 000 from the Unity Trust Bank. It was understood that the Party must have control over anything which concerned Party organisation, but this was a large sum with the unions taking the risk – a risk made more sensitive by the fact that the Party was heavily in debt. Thus the unions demanded the strictest costing and the most careful assessment of performance against budget projections.

To reassure them that this would take place, a joint arrangement was instituted. A Control Group of Guarantor Unions was created with representatives of each of the five unions and Fred Jarvest from Unity Trust as their financial co-ordinator. But the most senior union leaders who had negotiated the conditions now formally stepped aside (although John Edmunds did not step too far away). The managerial co-ordination was done by the Party – by Tony Manwaring. The NEC retained a right of veto and three of the five Control Group members were NEC trade unionists (the other two were finance officers). As the three union representatives (in 1989 Gordon Colling NGA, Andy Dodds NUR and Tony Clarke UCW) were also leading members of the NEC's Finance and General Purposes Committee, a consensus between the Secretariat and the F and GP trade unionists was normally reached before the F and GP met – although very occasionally an NEC veto was registered.

With the assistance of Business Plan activities, income from fund-raising and financial services rose significantly in 1989 and 1990. Though income from affiliation fees also rose in 1989 as fees rose, there was a recommencement in the decline of union affiliation income as a percentage of national Party income. In 1989, it was 75 per cent or 71 per cent (taking the Short Money into account). And though the membership campaign was a financial, as well as a political disappointment, the Business Plan, as a whole, was fast becoming one of the success stories of Labour Party management and trade union co-operation, with a turn-over, by April 1990, of over £1 million and the generation of income sufficient to give near a £500,000 boost to available election funds.

An estimation of overall income received by the Party from the unions at all levels in a normal year now involves an even more uncertain calculation. But what appeared to be the case in 1989 was that, as a result of the changes in party funding, and even taking into account money raised by TUFL, the percentage of Labour annual income overall coming from the unions, excluding the General Election Fund, had dropped to between 45 and 50 per cent.

GENERAL ELECTION FUNDING AND 'THE BEGGING BOWL'

The political levy

One of the first discussions which led to the formation of TULV involved the need to put the accumulation of a General Election Fund for the Party on a proper footing. The *ad hoc* last minute appeals were time-consuming: they inhibited planning of campaigns, and they met with a response which was not always equitable between unions.

To place the Party in a better position required that there be adequate union resources, a funding mechanism at an early stage and a willingness of the unions to overcome their hoarding instinct and release funds early. Part of TULV's more discreet role was to monitor Political Funds and to encourage unions to raise their political levies. In 1980, in a TULV survey, it was found that in the affiliated unions there was an average payment of only 56.5p per year, with some enormous variations ranging from half to double the average. On the Commission of Enquiry, there was a push from Basnett and Jenkins towards standardisation, with Jenkins at one point favouring a common £2 per annum. Although this foundered on the rocks of union rule book distinctiveness and autonomy, the TULV officials kept pushing. Just prior to the 1983 General Election, there was a series of personal representations about the levy which were held to be very successful: '... decisions taken, or in the pipeline, on changes in the level of political levy would significantly improve resources up to 1986 and beyond'.[95]

In 1987, TUFL officials reported that the average political levy had gone up to £1.75 per annum – not yet at the Jenkins figure and still with some very wide variations in levels among the big unions (see Table 10.2), but a major advance on the position seven years earlier. Total political levy income in 1986 at 10.3 million was 13 per cent greater in real terms than the income of 4.67 million in 1979.[96]

Part of the background to the *Promoting Our Values* package in 1988 was the depletion of union political funds following the 1987 General Election.[97] There was an informal agreement that, in accordance with their own procedures and time-scales, the unions should move to a common minimum position on the political levy, thus enabling them both to meet the Party needs nationally and locally and also to expand further their own independent political initiatives which had grown in the 1980s. However, the great bulk of union expenditure from these political funds still went towards Labour Party, or Labour Party related, purposes.[98]

The 'begging bowl'

As an incentive to the unions, but also in some despair at the tardiness of the Party's own election preparations, TULV in 1982 put considerable pressure upon the Party to open its General Election Fund. Eventually, in September, the General Election Campaign Fund was established, with TULV represented on the fund committee. An Appeal Coordinator was appointed from the unions and £25, 000 was set aside from the Levy Fund to organise this appeal. It was initially targeted at £1 million, and then at £2 million.

Not for the first time, the money was slow in coming through, making it difficult to plan ahead. As late as May 1983, the Party officers were lamenting the difficulties of getting the money in. Some of this was the usual cumbersome union response to monetary appeals. Some of it was due to variations in the availability of finance. In addition, reservations felt by many Rightwing-led unions about Labour's policy had financial repercussions. The Engineers, the second largest union, gave only £150,000. The maverick EETPU (flirting with defection some thought) was in a category of its own. It gave nothing to the unions' national appeal, although it sponsored seven Labour candidates.

In the end, with the TULV office in Walworth Road keeping up the appeal throughout the campaign, the target of the national union levy was exceeded by £150,000. Of this, the Transport Workers alone gave £500,000, the General and Municipal Workers £306,000. Although the NUM was outside TULV it gave £234, 000 and NUPE gave £220,000.

In 1987, aware of the disparities and inequities of the union response in 1983 and following an understanding arrived at in 1986, the TUFL organisation agreed a much more structured approach. Each union, it was agreed, would pay 87p per levypaying member, which would have raised a sum of £4,934,325, near enough to the £5 million overall union target. The Victory Fund was established soon after the formation of TUFL and administered by a committee on which sat four representatives of the Party, four from the unions, and one from the CLPs. Bill Keys, the TUFL co-ordinator, became in effect the fund-raiser, a task which he pursued with energy and creativity, establishing at one stage a complicated umbrella scheme whereby unions could lend each other interest-free loans in order to secure the full union payment.

In practice, although no union had objected to the structured payments or the umbrella scheme, there were some very late payments and a shortfall of £1,201,337 from the target figure. With direct mail fund-raising playing a more important role in producing General Election income, the overall contribution of the unions showed a slight fall from past efforts – 93 per cent compared with 98 per cent in 1983.[99] Five unions made no payment and fourteen made only part payment. Much of this was due to financial problems and the costs of the Political Fund ballot campaigns of 1985–6 (a bonus for the Conservative Party here). And there was a reluctance to take advantage of the 'umbrella scheme' if it made a union in any way beholden to the two big general unions. But, again, it was noticeable that the AUEW paid in £250,000 – much less than its affiliated membership, the EETPU paid in nothing nationally, while the NUM (which had a huge Political Fund) paid well over the amount asked – £207,000. UCATT, which was very short of money, also made a low payment of £20,000, but so did USDAW, which had problems of funds which were technically unavailable, and NUPE (which had paid considerable sums to the Party before this financial year). The two big general unions paid almost half of the entire fund (TGWU £1,130, 000, GMWU £631,000).

The incremental election fund

The experience of fund-raising in 1987, and the shortfall in the election fund, led union leaders – particularly Bill Keys from TUFL – to seek union agreement to the principle of incremental trade union contributions to the Labour Party's General Election Fund for the next election. The Fund was set up in May of 1988 (years earlier than the past practice on the election fund) after an agreement on the TUFL Executive on an unprecedented 'two-tier' affiliation fee. This fee now incorporated an element building up to the General Election Fund. Of the £1 fee, in 1990 20p would go to the Fund. Of the £1.20 fee, in 1990 35p would go to the Fund and of the £1.45 fee in 1991, 55p would go to the Fund. The Fund would be supervised by four General Election Fund Trustees from the major unions – but only to ensure that the Fund was still there in its entirety by the time of the next General Election. It was a remarkable break with the 'begging bowl' practices, a breakthrough in terms of union hoarding and yet another major recommitment by the unions to the Labour Party.

More than that, it was yet another example of the individual unions forgoing a potential lever of short term political power. It was, as we have seen, not the only case where paying pipers and calling tunes was a poor guide to the motivations of union leaders in this subtle and increasingly complex and interwoven relationship.

FINANCIAL POWER: AN OVERVIEW

On the surface, a wide range of vantage-points, provisions and facilities seemed to imply a position of tight control by senior union leaders, with the possibility of policy influence linked to financial sanctions. The position, in practice, as we have seen, involved a range of constraints, resistances and inhibitions limiting such control.

Unusually, open financial threats did gain a temporary legitimacy after the 1979 General Election, given that the NEC, not the PLP, was the target, and that a section of the PLP was encouraging the union leaders without adverse media reaction. And, unusually, financial sanctions were clearly brought into play as the consultative sessions moved from *post hoc* lament to responses conditional on future action. As a result, both the Commission of Enquiry and the Voluntary Levy Fund were forced upon a reluctant NEC.

But there is no evidence that this breach of 'rules' or the follow-through of reform proposals was primarily motivated by factional concern, or the pursuit of union policy, or a general attempt at power maximisation by the TULV leadership. Indeed, what was striking about the behaviour of the union leaders was their anxiety over the protection of their funds and a 'solidarity' concern for the financial security and well-being of the Party. What was also striking was that over financial management, as over organisational reform, the union leaders experienced a frustrating sense of their limited capacity to ensure that 'agreed' policy was implemented.

The regular frustration of their efforts, and the obstacles which stood in the path of the Commission proposals, arose from two familiar sources. On the one

hand there was the constraint of autonomous union organisations and the difficulty facing any group of leaders speaking for 'the unions'. On the other hand, the
impropriety of their position under the 'rules' added to the NEC's mood of non-
cooperation – a mood which on occasions enveloped trade union representatives
wearing their 'Party' hats. The sense of propriety also had its effect on the union
leaders themselves, forcing the occasional retreat, inhibiting the form of their
reaction and producing a very circumspect use of the Voluntary Levy Fund –
never a 'drip-feed' in pursuit of factional or union policy goals.

The fact that their intervention was guided not only by financial insecurity
but by a sense of common interest in the future of the Movement was borne out
by the way in which they sought to deal with some of the problems produced by
the unions' own attitudes to the financing of the Party.

Even more significant was that concern for the Party's future needs led the
union leaders to acquiesce in, or even initiate themselves, changes which took
away from the unions key positions of potential financial leverage.

This could be seen in the acceptance of state finance for political parties
which could reduce Party dependence upon the unions, in the encouragement of
policy assistance for the Front Bench, and in the non-intervention of union
leaders in the argument over control of the Short Money. And given the argument made here in terms of the mixture of 'rule' inhibition in relation to the
Parliamentary Party and supportive assistance for their political responsibilities,
it is not surprising that, in the end, the Voluntary Levy Fund, once seen as 'drip-
feeding' the NEC, should in 1987 involve unconditional subsidies to the Parliamentary Leadership. Nor is it surprising that the union leaders should in the late
1980s co-operate in guaranteeing a period of rising affiliation fees (thus sacrificing the 'lament' session). Nor again that they should agree to do away with the
potentially influential 'begging bowl' in connection with the General Election;
they had never used it as a political lever anyway.

Promoting Our Values, the package of financial measures making up a four-year
plan endorsed by the 1988 Party Conference, marked a fitting finale to a decade
of proposals and disputes concerning union involvement in Labour Party
finances. It was fitting that the GMB should act as a pivot of union liaison in
putting together the final package, given the origins of TULV and that union's
input into the 1980 Commission of Enquiry. It was fitting also that the coherent
package sought by union leaders in 1980 should eventually emerge, tying together a plan for the rebuilding of the Party's membership with a range of
proposals to ensure its future solvency. Some of the items in the package were
from more recent initiatives – the Gordon Brown/Tribune proposals for turning
levypayers into members was one key example, the national membership facility
underwritten by TUFL was another. But many of the problems the package
addressed, and some of the solutions it put into effect, were a preoccupation of
TULV leaders in 1980. It was fitting also that Larry Whitty, the ex-Secretary of
TULV, should, as the Party's General Secretary, be responsible for the gestation of
the overall package.

In this package, as with so many developments in the 1980s, the unions were
brought into yet another new form of engagement with the Labour Party. But it

was significant that they should be seeking, as their central objective, means of financial security for the Party, even if it reduced reliance on the unions. And it was significant also that, in the various linkages which tied the Party to the guarantors, whether through Trustees or a Control Committee, the prime motivation should be the safeguarding of union funds rather than the use of financial levers to advance the policy interests of the unions.

NOTES

1. The Party has a structure consisting of eleven regions with an organising staff appointed and paid by the national party. Unions and other organisations affiliate at this level on a financial basis agreed regionally. Each region holds an annual conference and elects a regional executive committee to manage the region's affairs. It also elects, regionally, officials who are normally drawn from the region's larger unions. The regional Treasurer is often from one of the largest unions. The Labour Party regional organiser acts as secretary to the executive committee.

2. Pinto-Duschinsky, *op. cit.*, 1981, pp. 225–6.

3. Harrison, *op. cit.*, pp. 99–100.

4. Richard Rose, *The Problem of Party Government*, 1974, Table on p. 235.

5. Pinto-Duschinsky, *op. cit.*, p. 225. The calculation covers the years 1970–4.

6. GMWU Evidence to the Commission, Finance Section B.3 10. In subsequent discussions with the author, Larry Whitty, who prepared the paper, considered that in the light of Commission evidence from the CLPs, the figure was more probably 55 to 60 per cent.

7. *NEC Report*, 1982, p. 82.

8. Pinto-Duschinsky, *op. cit.*, pp. 173–8.

9. *F and GP Committee Minutes*, 24/4/75.

10. *Finance Panel Minutes*, 18/4/80, Item 31.

11. *LPACR*, 1979, p. 301.

12. *Ibid.*

13. See Chapter 13, p. 396, for some alternative views on union assertiveness during this period.

14. This seems to be implicit in Pinto-Duschinsky's analysis. See particularly p. 226 for references to 'good value for money in terms of their power within the party' and unions investing 'where the political return is greatest'. This is followed by a reference to the unions extending their power by using the block vote at the Party conference to change the procedure for selecting the Party Leader. There is no hint of inhibition or restraint in the behaviour of leaders of the largest unions, who are said to exercise 'a strangle-hold on the Labour Party' (p. 303). The 'only function' of the system of affiliated membership is said to be 'to justify giving power to union leaders' (p. 304).

15. After Bevan's death in 1960, the Treasurership was held by trade unionists Harry Nicholas, TGWU (from 1960 to 1963), and Dai Davies of the Steelworkers (from 1964 to 1967). Jim Callaghan, a politician, took the post from 1967 to 1975. Norman Atkinson took it from 1976 to 1981, when he was replaced by another politician, Eric Varley. Varley resigned to take another post in late 1983 and was replaced temporarily by the runner-up, Albert Booth, an ex-Minister who had lost his seat in 1983. Booth was replaced in 1984 by the National Union of Seamen's

leader Sam McCluskie, who still holds the post. For NEC elections, see Chapter 11.

16. From 1950 to 1975 only six men held this position: M. Hewitson of the General and Municipal Workers to 1952; W. J. P. Webber of the TSSA in 1952–3; A. E. Tiffin of TGWU, 1953–5; H. Earnshaw of the Textile Workers, 1955–61; D. H. Davies of the Steelworkers, 1962–7; A. Cunningham of the General and Municipal Workers, 1967–73; and A. Kitson of the TGWU, 1973–6.

17. See Gaitskell's unsuccessful efforts to take the position away from Tiffin in 1954, P. Williams, op.cit., p. 349.

18. For a brief period from 1977 to 1978, the post was held by a Rightwing representative of the Royal Arsenal Co-operative Society, John Cartwright MP.

19. On this, see particularly Rose, op. cit., pp. 240–2 and H. M. Drucker, Doctrine and Ethos in the Labour Party, 1979, p. 15.

20. Finance Report, issued to Party Conference delegates by the NEC, 1981.

21. TULV document, F29/82.

22. Interviews by the author with Jack Jones and Moss Evans. The question elicited the same angry, incredulous response every time I asked it.

23. Jones, Union Man, op. cit., p. 323.

24. Ibid., p. 323.

25. The Labour Party: A Financial Perspective, from the Treasurer, Norman Atkinson, NEC document, April 1977, Appendix B.

26. Annual Report of the Certification Officer, 1981, W. Richards and NUM, pp. 24–26; Annual Report of the Certification Officer, 1983, E. M. L. Parkin and ASTMS, pp. 57–97.

27. Labour Party Accounts for the year ending 31/12/1980, NEC Report, 1981, p. 74.

28. I make this judgement on the basis of later discussions with some of them.

29. Labour Party Finances, a background note prepared by the Finance Department for Party delegates, 1980.

30. TULV document, F/29/82.

31. Reform and Democracy in the Labour Party, Joint CLV–Manifesto Group Statement, 13/10/79.

32. Pinto-Duschinsky, op. cit., pp. 177–8.

33. S. E. Finer, The Changing British Party System 1945–1979, 1980, p. 102.

34. Pinto-Duschinsky, op. cit., p. 178.

35. It had a Leftwing staff under the editor, Donald Ross. Factional and political factors were a constant source of friction over its deficits (see Chapter 19, pp. 607–8)

36. Annual Report of the Certification Officer, 1980, p. 24, para. 6.8; and 1981, p. 22, para. 6.7.

37. Pinto-Duschinsky, op. cit., p. 216.

38. Larry Whitty, Evidence to the Fabian Society Study Group on Labour Party Organisation, LPR 29, 1980, pp. 3–4.

39. GMWU Evidence to the Finance Panel of the Commission of Enquiry, Section 3.44, argued for 10 per cent of union political funds to be set aside for political education and political recruitment.

40. Whitty, op. cit., pp. 9–10; G and MW Evidence, op. cit., paras. 3.17, 3.25, 3.44, 3.50–56, 3.57–9.

41. Labour Victory, September 1979.

42. Guardian, 7/9/79 and interviews with union officials.

43. Comment to the author by Eric Heffer, Chair of the Org. sub committee of the NEC, during the 1979 Labour Party Conference.
44. *Sunday Times*, 22/6/80.
45. *Sunday Times*, 28/9/80.
46. *Report of the Committee on Financial Aid to Political Parties*, 1976, p. 12, para. 2.30 and LPACR, 1977, Res. 22, pp. 324–5.
47. Finance Officer's Submission 17 to Finance Panel, 29/5/80.
48. *Report of the Finance Panel*, para. 6.19.
49. *Ibid.*, para. 6.20.
50. At the Org. Sub. meeting, 1/6/79, on a resolution from the Treasurer, Norman Atkinson, the committee had voted by 7 votes to 1 that money out of public funds should be paid direct to the Labour Party (rather than the PLP) with equivalent sums disbursed by the NEC to the PLP. Staff paid for out of this fund would be recruited on normal terms and conditions of service. This was supported at the NEC, 25/7/79. The Parliamentary leadership resisted the decision. A similar resolution via the F and GP committee, 24/9/79, was referred back at the NEC meeting of 28/9/79 to allow more time for discussion. *NEC Minutes*, 25/7/79 and 28/9/79.
51 *TULV EC Minutes*, July 1983 and interview with Moss Evans.
52. Letter from TULV Secretary, Larry Whitty, to Labour Party General Secretary, Jim Mortimer, 13/1/84.
53. *NEC Minutes*, 28/11/84. The NEC voted against by 16 to 11. Only three trade union representatives voted in favour.
54. *TUFL EC Minutes*, 13/10/87.
55. *NEC Minutes*, 22/6/1988, Minute 47a.
56. Letter from Ron Hayward, Labour Party General Secretary, to Clive Jenkins, ASTMS General Secretary, 21/8/80.
57. *Finance Panel Minutes*, 18/4/80, Item 31.
58. *The Labour Party. Review of Financial Position*, Peat Marwick McLintock, 6/4/1988, p. 29, Para. 91.
59. Amendment Clause XI(1c), Agenda II, 1988, p. 12.
60. *Report of the Finance Panel*, Para. 5.18.
61. *NEC Minutes*, 26/9/80, Minute 110(a). See also Norman Atkinson, LPACR, 1980, pp. 198–9.
62. *Report of the Finance Panel*, Para. 5.10.
63. *Report of the Commission of Enquiry*, p. 9, para. 5.2.
64. *TUFL Report*, 1987, Part III, p. 4.
65. Amendment Clause XI(1a), Agenda II, 1988, p. 12.
66. See on this Harrison, *op. cit.*, pp. 87–88 and McKibbon, *op. cit.*, pp. 161–2.
67. *Interim Report of the ('Wilson') Sub-Committee on Party Organisation*, 1955, para. 127.
68. *Report of the Commission of Enquiry*, p. 24, para. 13.7 iii.
69. Evidence of the auditors to the Finance Panel, 18/4/80.
70. Note on the organisation and operation of the Finance Department to the Finance Panel, 23/5/80.
71. Office note to Finance Panel, F.227/80.
72. *Report of the Finance Panel*, Para. 2.5.
73. *Report of the Commission of Enquiry*, 3.I(i).
74. Office note to Finance Panel, F.227/80 and LPACR, 1979, p. 301.
75. *Report of the Commission of Enquiry*, 3.I(ii).
76. *Ibid.*, 3.5 and *Report of the Finance Panel*, 2.9.

77. 'When the Executive says that its committee should select their own chairmen that is a very respectable argument and I respect it', *LPACR*, 1980, p. 87.

78. Russel Tuck (NUR), 1980–1; Alex Kitson (TGWU), 1981–2, Alan Hadden (was Boilermakers then General and Municipal Workers), 1982–3.

79. Since 1983, the situation has become much more fluid. In 1983, a failure of factional organisation left the Chair of F and GP in the hands of a CLP representative, Audrey Wise. Albert Booth, an ex-MP, became acting Treasurer when Eric Varley left to take a post in the private sector. In 1984, the unions reacted. Sam McCluskie of the Seamen took the Treasurership from Booth, and Neville Hough of the General and Municipal Workers took the F and GP Chair from Wise in spite of her having done what was recognised as 'a good job'. In 1985–6, briefly, McCluskie took both the positions. In 1986–7, Eddie Haigh of the TGWU took the Chair of F and GP. Since 1987, the Chair has been held by John Evans, a National Union of Labour and Socialist Clubs nominee. Whether this indicates a permanent change in attitudes to the post is uncertain. McCluskie continued to be a Treasurer with strong union connections as a General Secretary.

80. Paper from TULV Finance Officer to TULV-NEC Meeting, 5 and 6 January 1982.

81. Sherman, *op. cit.*, p. 64.

82. Group of Trade Union Finance Officers, *Memo to TULV*, 11/8/80, Appendix B, p. 2.

83. Letter from the Group of Trade Union Finance Officers to the Chairman of TULV, 11/8/80.

84. Letter from Basnett on behalf of TULV to the NEC, 20/9/80.

85. *Morning Star*, 27/9/80, reporting comments of Tony Benn (on democracy) and Dennis Skinner.

86. Norman Atkinson, 'Ends and Means', *Labour Weekly*, 26/6/81.

87. Report of the Meeting between TULV representatives and the Organisation and F and GP Committees of the NEC, 8/7/81. *NEC Minutes*, 10/7/81.

88. *Tribune* editorial, 'Who will speak for the peasants?', 2/7/82. Also Les Huckfield, 'Is TULV trying to drip-feed the Labour Party?', *Tribune*, 22/10/82. Basnett replied 'TULV provides a lifeline for the Labour Party', *Tribune*, 5/11/82.

89. Letter from L. Daly, NUM Gen. Sec. to Moss Evans, TGWU Gen. Sec., 5/1/84.

90. Accusations of TULV political 'drip-feeding' rumbled on for years. See, example, Graham Allen, 'Trade Union Links Must Be Built at the Workplace', *Tribune*, 11/4/86.

91. D. Fatchett, *op. cit.*, p. 50.

92. M. Harrison, *op. cit.*, p. 99.

93. Regional income was in the past always very low with union affiliation fees providing the main source, even though it represented only 2–3 per cent of union political funds. Rose, *op. cit.*, p. 254. Pinto-Duschinsky (from Harrison), *op. cit.*, p. 225. Changes in the 1980s have included the stimulation of more union donations to pay for office equipment no longer provided by Party headquarters, but union funding is now a smaller percentage of total income which has been increased as a result of greater fund-raising and the proceeds of sales. CLP affiliation fees at

regional level have risen faster than union affiliation fees, and since 1984–5, regional union affiliation has been slowly falling.

94. Derived from Labour Party Accounts, presented in or accompanying the *NEC Report* . 'Donations' can include some from unions.

95. *TULV Committee Minutes*, 9/10/83.

96. Michael Pinto-Duschinsky, 'Trends in British Party Funding 1983–1987', *Parliamentary Affairs*, Vol. 42, No. 2, April 1989, p. 207.

97. The total political funds of the 45 unions with such funds in 1987 (affiliated and non-affiliated) was £12,472, 836 at the beginning of the year but only £8, 802, 171 at the end of it. This grew to £11,894, 897 (47 unions) by the end of 1988. Derived from Appendix 8, *Annual Report of the Certification Officer*, 1988, *ibid.*, 1989, p. 55.

98. Pinto-Duschinsky (1980), *op. cit.*, p. 225, used data from Harrison, *op. cit.*, to calculate that 88 per cent of union political funds in the 1950s went to Labour Party purposes, only 3 per cent for purposes not connected with the Labour Party and 9 per cent on tax and administration. I have also found it difficult to update this material in percentage terms. Although the clear trend in the unions was towards more independent political activity and a variety of affiliations to campaigning organisations (Upham and Wilson, *op. cit.*, p. 8), much of this expenditure came out of the general funds. And the categorisation of 'Labour Party purposes' is very problematic in terms of campaigning and political education. Some of the increased independent activity, for example anti-privatisation campaigns, overlapped with Labour Party purposes. The union which had done most to build up its own independent political activity has been the GMB which, in 1990, had ten political officers in the regions. Information supplied by that union indicates that approximately 9 per cent of the political fund expenditure went to independent political activity, including polling, campaigning, political meetings, and the expenses of political staff. It may well be that up to another 2 per cent of political fund expenditure went, at regional level, to independent activity and a further 3 per cent was paid in taxation or administration. So about 86 per cent of GMB Political Fund expenditure probably went either directly to the Labour Party or for purposes connected with the Labour Party. Of course, in the years covered by the Political Fund ballots, there was a much bigger drain of funds away from the Labour Party.

99. Pinto-Duschinsky, *Parliamentary Affairs*, op. cit., p. 201 and 'Financing the General Election of 1983', in Ivor Crewe and Martin Harrop, *Political Communications: The General Election Campaign of 1983*, 1986, p. 287.

17

The Labour Party and the defence of union political funds

THE ATTACK

Vulnerability

In the wake of Labour's traumatic election defeat in 1983, the union–Labour Party relationship came under the most concerted attack in its history and the most serious legal threat since before the First World War. The Political Fund ballots, forced upon the unions in 1985–6, provided a fundamental challenge to union political activity, to the Labour Party's affiliated membership and to the Party's financing. It threatened to destroy not only the individual union's capacity to organise a wide-ranging political intervention on behalf of its members but also the capacity of the affiliated unions to organise collectively on Labour's behalf.

That challenge was met to a degree undreamed of even by political optimists (of which there were not that many in 1983). Far from individual unions having their Political Funds cut off, each received a fresh mandate for their use. And far from a TULV-type organisation being destroyed, the Political Fund ballots gave it a new lease of life and a new form. By the Spring of 1986, not only was the union–Party relationship strengthened but *Trade Unionists For Labour* – born out of the campaign – was in place to build upon its organisational and strategic experience.

Yet in 1983, the situation had looked very different, with all the advantages apparently on the side of those who sought to damage the Labour Movement. As we have noted, trade unionists' support for the Labour Party had sunk to 39 per cent – the lowest since polling began. Academic studies showed 'a loosening of ties' between the Labour Party and those who identified with it in the electorate.[1] Ivor Crewe's General Election post-mortem had argued that the Party's claim to be the party of the working class looked increasingly sociologically threadbare, in the light of its continuing abandonment by manual workers.[2] All opinion polls which asked the question showed a majority of trade unionists opposed to the present relationship with the Labour Party (see Chapter 18, p. 567). Understandably, it became the common sense of many political commentators that the traditional relationship was in a state of broad-based and deep-rooted decline.

Further, in this situation, the Movement also appeared incapable of mounting a successful response. Political mobilisation seemed outside the capacity of the unions and the TUC. All the political campaigns of recent years had ended in failure. The EEC referendum had been lost by the anti-Marketeers. The elections of 1979 and 1983 had been lost despite more co-ordinated union support. The TUC's 1980 Day of Action had been little short of a fiasco. If you were looking for signs that the unions would not be able to defend themselves in a political battle involving the grass-roots membership, these appeared to be plentiful and all pointing in the same direction.

And yet closer examination of the behaviour of the unions in the period from 1976 to 1984 suggested something else – born out of the experience of failure. In these years of adversity, a slow cultural revolution was beginning to take place in trade union attitudes towards communication, media management and campaigning. This can be found in the Labour Party's *Report of the Commission of Enquiry into Party Organisation* in 1980 (discussed in Chapter 15) and also in the TUC's document, *The Organisation, Structure and Services of the TUC* published in 1980 and revised, after consultation, in 1981. Both indicated a union concern with issues of communication and presentation to a degree which was highly unusual. There was renewed interest in the communicational possibilities of the union journals on the one hand and the distortions of the mass media on the other. There were innovative and attractive styles of campaigning, including the People's Marches of 1981 and 1983 and the NALGO and British Telecom campaigns. And there was the new TULV regional and national structure, a break with the complacency of the past and a developing experience of political mobilisation. It was possible, therefore, in 1983, to look more closely at the union performance and envisage circumstances whereby all these features might be pulled together in a successful enterprise. For the moment, however, much of this was obscured by the monumental dreadfulness of Labour's election campaign and by the force of the tide towards the Conservative Party.

Post-mortem

The feelings aroused by this failure in 1983 did nothing to boost trade union self-confidence. A sense of depressive adversity affected the TULV organisation as much as it did the TUC. For a brief period, 'New Realism' seemed to portend a shift to 'business unionism', with the TUC pulling away from the Labour Party and accepting a new accommodation with the Conservative Government. Ambitious plans to expand the role of a political trade unionism associated with the Labour Party appeared out of tune with the times.

The election of Neil Kinnock as Labour Leader, and his encouragement that the TULV organisation should take places on the new Campaign Strategy Committee, provided a small boost to the organisation. But the biting critique of TULV launched by the NUM provided a frontal assault on its legitimacy. Just as this attack from the Left built up, so the Rightwing-led AUEW became the first union to defect from TULV, giving an explanation couched in terms likely to cause further dissension (see Chapter 15).

In short, although at regional level TULV had accumulated a great deal of good will and there were many union officials who stressed its potentiality as an instrument for the encouragement of trade union support for the Labour Party, at national level its future, even its existence, appeared very uncertain. In July 1983, the TULV Secretary, Larry Whitty, did offer an ambitious series of options, including the possibility of a full time secretariat, a permanent presence in the Labour Party headquarters and/or a full time Labour Party national industrial organiser working with both TULV and the NEC. But, as Whitty noted, there was considerable uncertainty even about the continuation of TULV.[3] On both Right and Left there were those in the unions who favoured winding it up.

No specific decisions were taken on any organisational options in 1983. In the end, the position was transformed by events. In the early spring of 1984, the banning of trade unionism at GCHQ delivered a near fatal blow to that strand of 'New Realism' which flirted with forms of disengagement from the Labour Party. And the Political Fund legislation gave a new urgency to the need for co-ordinated trade union political action. The TULV organisation, which had continued to carry out low-key funding and campaigning activities during the period of reflection, was in essence given a new role and a blood transfusion – ironically by a Government which favoured non-political trade unionism.

The historical weakness

The acute vulnerability of the Labour Movement in 1983 was as much historical as it was circumstantial. There had always been a question mark over the extent to which affiliation to the Labour Party represented a political commitment on the part of the unions' membership. The decision to set up the Labour Representation Committee was taken at national level in most of the unions, and only properly tested in 1913, when the Government imposed ballots after the House of Lords had ruled the use of union finances for political purposes illegal.

Under the 1913 Trade Union Act, a union could pursue political objectives if it had a Political Fund which was specifically authorised in a ballot of membership. In these ballots, rejection of a Fund was highly unusual: over 200 unions had held such ballots by 1939 and only 13 had failed to carry them – although some had to try several times.[4]

But behind the ballot successes there were major weaknesses which quickly became further hidden once the ballot was completed. In the ballots held in 28 unions in 1913, the turn-out overall was small, with less than a third of the Labour Party affiliated membership of those unions participating.[5] The total participation was inflated by the performance of the Mineworkers Federation (456,443 of approximately 600,000 members took part), but the turn-out was much lower in many other unions. For example, the Engineers' apparently more impressive 'yes' victory by 20,586 to 12,740 was out of a total membership of around 120,000. Apart from the rail unions, it was very unusual for the 'yes' vote to be an absolute majority of the Labour Party affiliated membership.[6]

These results were not untypical of the ways ballot results went in subsequent years. Between 1945 and 1958, there were twenty-four ballots with seventeen successful – often by narrow majorities on low polls.[7].

Once the majority of those participating had voted for the Fund, the unions generally took it as a once and for all authorisation, resenting the entire process as an unfair and penal restriction placed upon their collective activity by opponents of the Labour Movement. The members had a right to participate in a broad-ranging union democracy which had existed before the 1913 Act. The democracy had registered its majority will over the Fund. It would decide through normal procedures how the fund should be spent. Why should the minority of members have a double right?

'Contracting out' was neither welcome nor normal (see Chapter 10, pp. 291-2). Thus, in spite of the substantial minorities voting against a Fund after the 1913 Act, and in spite of the huge decrease in levypaying after the 1927 Act, only small minorities of union members contracted out before 1927 and after 1946.[8]

After 1946, the unions and the Labour Party could live with this arrangement perfectly happily. It gave the unions a ready source of Political Funds. They did have a tendency to hoard ('our') funds as protection against 'bad times' but the Labour Party nevertheless had regular and legitimate call upon them. The Party could privately negotiate the level of affiliation fees to take account of the unions' funds as well as its own financial state.

But nobody really knew the level of political commitment behind the funding nor was it easy to perceive a shift in the political alignment of the inactive rank and file trade unionist. In this sense, 'false consciousness' about the Labour Movement was built into its character and structure. An ambiguous rhetoric of 'the rank and file' obscured the problem. A lot of committed activity and much changing of hats by delegates creates the image of mass movement. And always concealing the reality was the list of national affiliated membership and card votes cast in the name of millions – many of whom had not positively chosen to be included and some of whom had no idea that they were participating.

The Conservative threat

For seventy years the unions' political role had been carried on with one eye on the courts and another on the Registrar of Friendly Societies (later the Certification Officer) lest the boundaries of legitimate political expenditure be crossed. In relation to the protection of the individual member, such restrictions on the unions were 'without parallel in any of the major labour law systems of the world'.[9].

Even so, they were not as strict as some Conservatives would have preferred. The Conservatives had wanted tighter legislation in 1913. Individual Conservative MPs continued to seek amendment of the legislation for years – particularly the change to 'contracting in' which they achieved in 1927. In 1946, the Conservatives opposed the repeal of the Trades Disputes Act and in 1947 the *Industrial Charter* pledged the Conservatives to restore 'contracting in'. Though they left this well alone in 1951, it remained a resented element of the post-war settlement. Many Conservatives denied that the unions' alignment with Labour was in any sense 'natural', they were hostile to what they regarded as an intimidatory atmosphere surrounding levypaying, and they saw the whole process as an interference with individual rights.

That this view of Labour funding was not entirely disinterested was obvious. The Conservative Party seldom lacked for money from its wealthy corporate and individual supporters. Trade unionism presented the only alternative source of finance which could challenge their monopoly. As we now know, attempting to 'hit the Socialist Party through their pocket' and to 'deplete the funds of the Labour Party' thus financially changing 'the balance of political power' was very much part of the background discussions among Conservatives in the 1920s.[10]

In the consensual mood of the early 1950s, such considerations were pushed to one side and not until the advent of the Thatcher Government did it move to the forefront as a political issue. By then, it was part of a much wider critique of the Labour Movement.

The critique and the opportunity

By the late 1970s, a powerful intellectual challenge was being made to the traditional Labour Movement – a challenge which had its influence within the Party itself (as was shown in Chapter 8). The New Right focused on the detrimental effects of the trade union–Labour Party relationship on the British economy and polity. In Thatcherite terms, the trade unions acted as coercive private monopolies protected by special privileges. They distorted the market and contributed to a range of ideas hostile to economic progress. Their industrial power and privileges were protected by the Labour Party. It was, therefore, more pressing than ever not only to undermine the industrial position of the unions but also to break the link between the unions and the Labour Party and get 'the union leaders out of politics'.

But attacking the Political Funds and the political levy system also meant attacking the funds of the Labour Party. This would cause no great concern in Central Office; indeed it was a bonus, but it could not be handled without some embarrassment. The national Conservative advantage in funding was too well known for legislation which undermined the finances of the Opposition not to be challenged as vindictive and damaging to democracy.

A new and welcome opportunity presented itself in the early 1980s by a constellation of political circumstances. In electoral terms, the decline of Labour's base among trade unionists had strengthened the position of those who argued that trade union political funding distorted the political preferences of trade unionists. The rise in membership of Conservative trade unionists, albeit from a low base, had given the Conservative Party a stronger organisational nucleus from which to mobilise union members. Then came a double bonus. In 1981, the defection of the Social Democrats from the Labour Party and their subsequent attack on trade union funding gave the Conservative Party a wider consensual base from which to initiate reform. And in the Deputy Leadership elections of 1981, the behaviour of the Transport and General Workers Union (Chapter 11, pp. 339–42) drew attention to the problems of trade union political decision-making and the artificiality of 1.25 million votes being placed on only one side of the political choice. This experience was used relentlessly to cast doubt on the legitimacy of the whole involvement of unions in Labour politics.

Trade union political funding was already coming under increasing scrutiny and criticism from the Certification Officer. Although complaints to the Certification Officer about the operation of the Political Fund remained remarkably low, in the years after 1979 they involved some controversial cases in which the

Certification Officer appeared to be tightening the definition of 'political' in ruling that various items which should have been paid out of Political Funds had been paid from general funds.[11] (Two of these cases caused considerable problems for the Labour Party as they involved the financing of Labour Party headquarters.[12]) As a result, in 1981, there was a sudden revival of interest, by some of the unions, in changing the 1913 Act [13] – a response which was understandable but which to some extent further strengthened the climate of opinion that reform was now on the agenda.

It was now a matter of how the Government approached their goals of de-politicisation on the one side and financial damage on the other. In the Green Paper of January 1983, it coupled the issue of political funding with the general question of Democracy in Trade Unions In the section 'The Political Activities of Trade Unions', the Government committed itself to 'the principles' of the 1913 Act which were stated to be: (i) that trade unions should be able to pursue their members' interests through political organisations; and (ii) that no trade union member should be obliged to support financially any political organisation if he or she did not want to. But it argued that the working of major provisions of the Act needed to be questioned. It referred to several problem areas, but its main focus was on the authorisation of political funding.

The Green Paper argued that it was 'not self evident that a majority of the present members of a trade union in which a ballot was held many years ago would wish their union still to pursue political objects or to continue previous political affiliations'.[14] It suggested that there was a strong case for a legal require-ment that unions should, at specified intervals, be required to hold ballots to confirm the support of their members.

Nothing was mentioned of a similar requirement to be placed upon compa-nies. Nor was the discussion of Political Funds placed in a wider context of the distribution of political resources within British party politics. In this sense, it was a blatantly partisan measure very much in tune with the private attitudes of Conservatives in the 1920s who had sought to undermine their opponent's finances.

Such a major political interference in the internal affairs of the unions and the main Opposition party could not easily be pursued without some mandate from the electorate. In the run-up to the 1983 General Election, the Employment Secretary, Norman Tebbit, made clear his intention to legislate on the Political Fund and to force consultations with the TUC under threat of changing 'contract-ing out' to 'contracting in'.[15] Ministers were convinced that the Green Paper as a whole would enhance their appeal to rank and file trade unionists, if not to their leaders, and in this way further undermine the legitimacy of trade union affilia-tion to the Labour Party. In January of 1983, the President of Conservative Trade Unionists launched an appeal for a million more trade unionists to support the Conservative Party.[16]

New realism and new negotiations

It is interesting to note at this point that this aspect of the Conservative appeal failed. Indeed, support among trade unionists for the Conservative Party dropped from 33 per cent in 1979 to 31 per cent at the June 1983 election.[17] But the Alliance had made big gains from Labour among trade unionists and there was now much closer to a three-way split, with the Alliance on 29 per cent and with Labour at only 39 per cent. The Government was thus in a stronger position to argue that the formal union alignment with Labour was illegitimate. And, in terms of its majority in the House, it was in an unchallengeable position to bring forward its legislation. Among its first proposals, in the autumn of 1983, was a Trade Union Bill which covered both union democracy and provisions for Political Funds.

Attitudes towards the tactics of opposition to the Government proposals were initially very divergent among members of the General Council of the TUC. A section of the Left, which still supported the 'Wembley' Conference approach to the Government's legislation, favoured a boycott. When the Government indicated to the TUC that the only aspect of the Bill that it was prepared to negotiate on was the issue of political funding, some of the Left union leaders thought there should be no negotiations at all. For different reasons, other unions were also sceptical of such a narrow base of negotiations – both the General and Municipal Workers and the (non-Party affiliated) Engineers and Managers' Association, from rather different perspectives, thought that the TUC was not the instrument to be involved in negotiations concerning matters of Party funding. Others shared a common scepticism that anything of substance could be won by such negotiations, and feared that the TUC's willingness to negotiate was implicitly conceding what they had always denied – that there was something wrong with the processes surrounding political levypaying.

Negotiations were, however, supported by most unions on the Right of the Labour Party and by Bill Keys, the Leftwing Chairman of the TUC's Employment Policy and Organisation Committee. More significant still, there developed at this point a classic unity of interest between the TUC and the Labour Party. As defined by its General Secretary, the TUC now needed to get into a new and regular negotiating position with the Government of the day – here was a point to start. As defined by the new Leader of the Labour Party, Neil Kinnock, the need was to do anything which would limit the potentially horrendous damage to Labour's finances by the proposed legislation – here was the point to try. Their mutual reinforcement was decisive.

So the negotiations proceeded, and in February 1984 an agreement was reached which was ratified by the General Council. It gave to the Government much of what it sought in the Green Paper – in terms of increasing the facilities for members to become aware of their rights to 'contract out', making clear that non-levypayers should suffer no disability or disadvantage, and tightening control over the Political Fund accounts. Certainly there was a substantial body of opinion in the unions which worried that the TUC had conceded too much.

But, as events were to prove, the agreement still gave the unions an opportunity to fight the Political Fund ballots under circumstances and on grounds which gave them a reasonable basis to make their appeal. They were to poll their members simply on the question of whether or not they were in favour of their union having a Political Fund. There was to be no fixed date for the ballot but a time period of 18 months in which to hold it. It would be won on a simple majority.

There was still the threat from the Government to take further action if the rights to contract out were not properly implemented, but even on the imparting of information on these rights, the unions were not as tightly constrained as some critics favoured. The information sheet to existing members (and all new members in the future) on contracting out was allowed to be prefaced by a statement of the reasons for the Political Fund. The sheet informed members where exemption notices could be obtained but did not itself contain a tear-off section. Further, the notices which had to be given to every new member and available to each member after the Political Fund ballots were one-off events and not institutionalised as a procedure for annual reminder.

As it finally emerged, the Trade Union Act of 1984 stated that a trade union which operated a Political Fund under the 1913 Act must in future ballot its members at least once every ten years if it wished to continue with its Political Fund. These ballots must be through procedures and under conditions approved by the Certification Officer[18] with the understanding that the balloting must be either at the workplace or by post. A Political Fund was necessary if a union wished to pursue 'political objects', as in 1913, but the financial controls were strengthened and the definition of 'political objects' was broadened considerably.

There were tight controls over what resources could be part of the Political Fund and strict specifications forbidding the use of any assets other than from the Political Funds being used to pay 'political' debts. 'Political objects' now covered expenditure in connection with election to office in a political party, the provision of services or property for use by a political party, the holding of meetings or the publication of literature whose main purpose was to persuade people to vote *or not to vote* for a political party or candidate.

The Act and the political agreement that lay behind it by no means met with universal approval. It was strongly attacked by the thwarted Alliance, suddenly aware also that TUC's 'new realism' might not produce a trade union breakaway from the Labour Party.[19] It was attacked from the Right of the Conservative Party where more drastic Government action was favoured, including forbidding unions to engage officially in any party political activity.[20] It was attacked from the Left by those who thought that the TUC had a variety of other tactical positions other than 'Doing Tom King's Dirty Work'.[21]

This reaction from the Left has to be understood against a background of general pessimism about the outcome of the ballots. At Labour Party headquarters, anxious financial and political calculations were being made. How could the Labour Party fight the next election if several big unions lost their Political Funds? Could national headquarters survive in its present form if the 79 per cent of its national income which came from the unions (1983) were suddenly depleted? What if either the Right or the Left in the unions were hit very badly; how would this affect some of the delicate factional balances at the Conference and on the NEC? Whatever disagreement there was on these questions, no one doubted the fundamental danger represented by the Government's legislation.

THE DEFENCE

In organising the response of the Labour Movement to this dangerous political challenge, a wide range of problems presented themselves. In particular, there were three general strategic questions involving the role of the Labour Party:
1. Who was to control the campaign – the Party or the unions?
2. What content should the campaign have and how much should it focus on the relationship with the Labour Party?
3. If the unions were to control the campaign, how was Party activity to be co-ordinated with this campaign?

The role of the Labour Party: control

The input of TULV

In view of the many criticisms which had been levelled at TULV and the wide-spread recognition of the success of the Trade Union Coordinating Committee, it is important to note the influential role of TULV in producing and assisting the development of the new Political Fund organisation. It would be going too far to suggest that TUCC could not have existed without TULV, but that organisation had already broken new ground in securing the co-ordination of most of the affiliated unions in stimulating support for the Labour Party, and had created a permanent regional structure. Further, in a variety of ways it was TULV officers and committees which got the new TUCC committee and organisation off the ground.

The co-ordinated planning of the unions' response over the Political Funds is usually taken by observers of the campaign to have been inaugurated at a meeting held on 1 August 1984, in London, to which all affiliated unions sent representatives.[22] In reality, first discussions on how to respond to the legislation took place on the TULV committee in November 1983,[23] and strategic discussions about co-ordinating the trade union response to the Political Fund legislation began formally on the committee as early as January 1984.[24] These discussions led to the first survey of trade union opinion being commissioned from the MORI organisation.

At a meeting of TULV officers, Party officers and the Party Leader, held in Kinnock's office on 11 April, it was agreed that there should be a consultative conference, with the NEC inviting all the affiliated unions to attend.[25] This conference (scheduled for June) met various timetabling delays, but, in the meantime, the TULV organisation went ahead with briefing sessions in the regions and tactical discussions consequent upon the findings of the MORI polls.[26]

These polls disclosed crucial differences in attitudes towards the potential uses of a Political Fund. Although there was no overall majority in the unions for a union to be 'affiliated and give money to the Labour Party' (38 per cent) there was more support for a union involving itself in 'political activities on behalf of its members' (44 per cent) and a large majority in favour of 'being able to support MPs in the interests of the unions' members' (63 per cent).[27] In other words, there was a large majority in favour of the original concept of 'labour representation' involving no specificity of party. That finding blended with the tactical views expressed privately by the majority of TULV leaders about how the Political Fund ballots should be fought, and discussions on the TULV Executive, and within the Political Officers group (of whom the SOGAT Research Officer, Mike Molloy, was a member), fed eventually into the crucial paper prepared by SOGAT leader Bill Keys for the consultative conference (see below, p. 554).

TULV also provided £50,000 as a contingency fund. The regional organisations of TULV were encouraged to bring in those unions which had attended the national conference of affiliated unions but had not been active in TULV (including the NUM and the AUEW). This regional structure became the basic organisation of TUCC. Thus, in all these ways TUCC was assisted by TULV and was in a sense an offshoot of it.

The exclusion of the Labour Party management

There was never any doubt in these early planning discussions that this was to be a union show. It might not have been this way. In the original Political Fund ballots of 1913, the campaign had been essentially a Party campaign, organised nationally and regionally through subcommittees of the Party Executive and through the National Agents Department which took on extra staff to deal with it.[28] But that was in a period of the Party's supremacy (see Chapter One, p. 18). There had grown since then, as we have seen, a sharper definition of institutional functions, a prototype of trade union collective political organisation (in TULV) and, after years of argument over finance, the union leaders were clearer than ever that these were *union* funds and the unions would decide how to fight for them.

If there was any remaining uncertainty over this, three other considerations consolidated the view that the Party's management must be excluded. From the first sight of the Bill which embodied the new legislation, it was clear that the unions could legitimately separate the question of political from party funding, and that the unions had their powerful case for the possession of a Political Fund strengthened by some of the new definitions and provisions. If the Party relationship was not to be the primary focus of the campaign, there was discreet sense in not having it in control of the organisation.

Secondly, it must be remembered that at this stage the Walworth Road organisation was at rock bottom in terms of prestige, and held by the union leaders in particularly low regard. Officially, the Party was to be sidelined for 'resource reasons', but there were few union leaders to give a second thought to the argument that before the Party headquarters could be associated with anything that affected the crucial interests of the unions, 'the shambles' had to be 'sorted out' (see Chapter 19).

Thirdly, from the moment that the legislation was threatened, there were signs that sections of the NEC Left wanted to respond to it in the only way that they regarded as principled and educative. Either the union members were to be urged to boycott the ballots completely or it was to be treated as a full-scale opportunity to 'campaign for Socialism'. Such declarations caused the stomachs of trade union leaders to sink. The view of most of them – as well as the Party

Leader – was that the conduct of the campaign should be kept as far away from the NEC Left as possible.

If there was to be a separate union co-ordination of the campaign, it needed to be based on as consensual an organisation as could be produced. This, as TULV officials acknowledged, ruled out TULV itself which, in the absence of the AUEW and the NUM and under constant fire from the NEC Left, did not have the necessary status. What was required, it seemed, was something very like TULV, but with full-time staff and a wider base of support.

This organisation, it was understood also, could not be the Trades Union Congress. Although the trade union centre had done the negotiating, it was understood that this function was superseded when it came to campaigning over the Political Funds, where questions of Labour Party affiliation and party issues were bound to be raised. So the TUC gave way to the new Trade Union Coordinating Committee, although in that changing of hats which makes Labour Movement role-playing so complex, Bill Keys, the Chairman of the TUC's Employment Policy and Organisation Committee, and a key negotiator on the provisions of the Act, became Chairman of the TUCC organisation. Thereafter, the TUC took a very low profile.

The planning paper prepared by Keys in the summer of 1984 was presented to, and ratified by, the meeting of all affiliated unions on 1 August. It led to the creation of the co-ordinating unit, with two full time staff, one of whom, Graham Allen, was made the Campaign Co-ordinator. The unit was financed by a levy of affiliated unions which produced £150,000 (in addition to TULV's £50,000). Supervising the unit's work was a Coordinating Committee of fourteen union General Secretaries under the Chairmanship of Keys and a 'working' and strategy committee of Political/Education Officers. For a short period, there was also a smaller strategy committee consisting of Allen, Donald Ross, Editor of *Labour Weekly*, Larry Whitty (then the TULV Secretary), Mike Molloy, the SOGAT Research Officer and Jenny Pardington, the TGWU Political Officer (and later successor to Allen and Keys as Coordinator of TUFL), but this failed to meet after its fourth meeting and all initiatives from that point tended to come from Allen and Keys.

The unit was housed at Transport and General Workers' headquarters in Transport House and was responsible, working with the committee of Political/Education Officers, for a wide range of co-ordinating functions. In a letter to the Labour Party General Secretary,[29] the Chairman of the TUCC specified these as including ballot monitoring, liaison with unions, obtaining legal advice about the conduct and procedure of the ballots, briefing and advising union and party officers and members, liaison with Walworth Road and the PLP on party speakers and resources, press and public relations, commissioning publicity and commissioning polling. But, above all, in practice it co-ordinated the timing – agreeing the order and date of each union's ballot, it liaised with the Certification Officer over the balloting procedure, and it secured an impressive measure of strategic uniformity.

The role of the Labour Party: content

By the time TUCC had come into existence, certain key strategic understandings had already been reached as a result of the discussions in TULV and at the August consultative conference. There would be no boycott of the ballots (although up to December, a small section on the Left were still pushing for this). The ballots would be staged in order to secure the most beneficial timing and, if possible, stimulate a bandwagon of success; the staging of ballots would also have the crucial advantage of making it more difficult for the mass media to intervene with one powerful blast. (In practice, after some initial misrepresentation, the press lost interest. TUCC for its part, under Keys' shrewd guidance, made little attempt to alert the media to anything except successful results.)

This phasing strategy had been discussed in TULV for months, and the proponents of 'one big political bang' were always in a minority.[30] This view was connected with another strategic agreement arrived at before TUCC was founded. As the Keys paper made clear, the campaign would be around the question posed in the legislation – it would be 'to preserve the freedom of political action of trade unions'. Indeed, so well-established was this campaigning emphasis among a majority of unions that when, long before TUCC was under way, USDAW produced an early leaflet defending the unions' links with the Labour Party, it was warned off and for a period desisted.

TUCC never deviated from its original emphasis on (i) the right to a voice in politics – particularly in the House of Commons, (ii) the right of the unions to engage in political campaigning, and (iii) the contrasting treatment of unions and companies under the Conservatives' legislation.

'Say Yes to a Voice' (with its implication that in the absence of a Political Fund the voice could not be heard in the political arena) became the campaign slogan. Attention was focused on the new political restrictions of the Government's legislation. A range of powerful arguments were made in defence of a 'fair' democracy. Information was produced about political funding and about the practical achievements brought through the unions' past Political Funds. Lessons learned since 1979 were turned into attractive and accessible propaganda and educational materials.

In this direct appeal to the members, every union followed both the logic of the question posed in the ballot and the general strategic focus on retention of the political fund. But each union provided its own emphasis and tied it to its own distinctive experience. In most unions, some material was distributed which noted the link with the Labour Party (see also p. 556 for information provided to 'campaign contacts'). The linkage was usually indicated via sponsorship and parliamentary representations. Affiliation was mentioned much less often, and the role of union votes and finance within the Labour Party barely mentioned at all.[31]

How much concentration was placed upon the Labour Party varied considerably union by union. Some unions, like ASTMS and the POEU, concentrated on the union's ability to have its voice heard in Parliament, with little reference to the Labour Party. Others, like NUPE, which had developed a much stronger tradition

of political unionism, were determined from the first to keep the Labour Party
link in high profile. More surprisingly, while the TGWU gave little emphasis to the
Labour Party, the AUEW gave it much more.

Where the Labour Party's role was dealt with, it was treated, generally, in a
non-ideological way and connected with the interests of union members in
place-of-work issues. This was related to the experience of the past rather than to
present party policy or to projects for the future.

In general, as the campaign wore on and the unions gained in confidence and
victories, so the Labour Party connection tended to be introduced with less
anxiety, but given the case that was being argued for the past usage of the
Political Fund, it was difficult for any of the unions, even in the early stages, to
completely avoid mentioning the Labour Party even if they thought it wise not to
emphasise it.

Recognition of this fused into another organisational feature of the campaign.
Previous trade union campaigns – particularly those of TULV in the 1983 General
Election – had failed because they had never secured a steady communication
with ordinary union members. The TUCC campaign avoided all national publicity
and concentrated attention on getting into the place of work and to the home
addresses of those members involved in postal balloting. The crucial locus of the
campaign at work was a 'campaign contact' in every branch and a regular 'two
step flow' of information from the core activists to the ordinary members.

Because the 'campaign contact' had the pivotal role in communication of the
arguments, canvassing support, and mobilisation of the 'yes' vote, they had
themselves to be trained in electoral techniques and educated about the Political
Fund. Activist handbooks were issued by each union with an outline which was
adapted from a basic pattern originated by TUCC. Although the basic text emphasised 'This is a Trade Union Campaign' ... 'It is about retaining the right to have
Political Funds', every handbook carried information and argument favourable to
the Labour Party with model answers to questions which the members might raise
about the party connection. At this level in the unions, the relationship with the
Labour Party was inextricably interwoven into every campaign.

The role of the Labour Party: integration

In its form and composition, TUCC had settled one major question about the
campaign – who was to control it? In its strategy discussions, it had settled
another major question – what would the campaign be about? But there was a
third question to be dealt with. What part should the Labour Party's organisation
and membership play in the campaign?

This question became more than sensitive in these early weeks of the formation of TUCC because on the NEC, the Left, led by Tony Benn and Dennis
Skinner, was, in one phraseology or another, pushing for a General Strike in
support of the miners – and for associating the Miners' Strike with the Fund
campaign. This issue came to the fore in December 1984 when the Labour
Coordinating Committee – first in the field of agitation for an effective response
to the new legislation – called a Conference in London on 'Keeping the Links'.

LCC always held a broader view of the content of the campaign than most union leaders – both in terms of the issues to be raised and the extent of Labour Party involvement. The agenda for the London Conference and its press publicity indicated a strong attempt to link the Political Fund campaigns with the Miners' Strike.[32] LCC Campaign Notes also indicated that they wanted the Party to organise campaign material and to stimulate *ad hoc* Party–union committees at local level.[33]

There was immediately a strong reaction from some of the union leaders who made it clear that having created TUCC they were not very happy with these independent initiatives. They did not agree that the Miners' Strike should be strongly associated with the campaign. And they did not like the idea that Party activists pressing 'the wider socialist case'[34] would have an important role at grassroots level. These messages were strongly communicated to the LCC officers. But the Conference went ahead; to no great effect, it must be said.

But in these first months of the campaign, there was less agreement within the TUCC on the role of the Labour Party than was later to appear. Indeed, Graham Allen and initially, it appears, Bill Keys also were more sympathetic to elements of the LCC's initiative, although not its style. Their views were shared in the early stages by some trade union leaders on the Left, including those from NUPE who saw potential benefits to the Party of a greater practical involvement of the two wings at local level. The main concern of Allen and Keys was that TUCC should keep overall control of the campaign and that its strategic approach should set the dominant guidelines. Within this framework, they were apparently prepared to see and encourage a range of Party activities.

And so, as soon as Allen had been appointed, Keys wrote to Mortimer, the Party's General Secretary, stressing that, while there was no intention to link the Labour Party formally and publicly with the TUCC campaign (because of the need to make a wider political appeal of behalf of trade union Political Funds), he was working on plans to see Labour Party activists 'carrying the message into factories and offices'.[35] At the same time, he requested that the Party approve Donald Ross's membership of the Political/Education Officers Committee, given his expertise as editor of *Labour Weekly*.

Privately, Ross (an old ally of Allen's from his Walworth Road days) and Allen held discussions out of which there emerged a draft strategy paper outlining the role of the Party in the campaign and the organisational guidelines for the contribution of the Labour Party's headquarters. Among its more contentious proposals were: (1) that there should be a total commitment of the Party's resources with every department at Walworth Road making the campaign its top priority for 1985; (2) that the Party should appoint a full-time officer to deal with trade union affairs; (3) that the National Agents Department should produce a plan of action for each region; (4) that there should be a formal regional exchange of addresses between Labour Party and trade union branches; and (5) that Donald Ross himself would be in charge of the Party's own campaign and its liaison with TUCC.[36]

The 'Ross plan', which was to go through several drafts, watering it down, was met with a huge blast of hostility from the senior management at Walworth Road. Its implications for territorial control and seniority within Party headquarters were seen as alarming. And its suggestions for the scope of Party involve-ment roused considerable suspicion and concern among many union leaders, particularly Rightwing union leaders, when they were alerted to its existence. These were – they were adamant – *the unions'* funds. It must be *their* campaign and on themes that *they* would decide. The word was carried to the NEC and the General Secretary.

It was envisaged that the strategy paper would go to NEC meetings in January, but it took some time to find its way on to committee agendas and it was given no encouragement by the Party Leadership. When it arrived, in the middle of February, it was left to 'lie on the table' by the Organisation subcommittee pending further discussion with TUCC.[37] Under pressure from the TUCC office, it did find its way on to the agenda of the NEC that month but accompanied by a 'Covering Note' from the General Secretary which made it clear that the 'Cam-paigns Officer', Joyce Gould, from the National Agents Department, would be co-ordinating the Party's role, and not Ross. There was also a paper from Gould which, in noting the steps being taken to assist the campaign, envisaged a restricted Party role.

The NEC found it diplomatic to agree both the Gould and the Ross papers,[38] but, as he had indicated to the NEC, Mortimer, in his letter to CLPs, was sensitive to union autonomy. He followed the spirit of the Gould paper and not that of the Ross/TUCC office. Although he advised CLPs to appoint trade union liaison officers, he stressed that members should work in their own unions and that the backdrop to the unions' campaign would be the Party's Jobs and Industry cam-paign (not a specific Labour Party Political Fund campaign).[39] There was, in short, to be no independent Party input of organisation, materials or activity. Donald Ross continued to sit in with TUCC planning meetings but without any leverage at Head Office. On 5 April, elements of the Ross plan re-emerged in the pages of *Labour Weekly* underneath a precis of the Mortimer letter but without comment as to their connection. It then sank without trace.[40]

With, at that time, some bitterness the TUCC office tended to see the castra-tion of the Ross plan as a typical piece of Walworth Road bureaucratic conserva-tism. 'If you want to stop anything in the Labour Party HQ tell the Left it's a plot by the Right or the Right it's a plot by the Left.' But the limited activity by Labour's management did have strong parallels with what was happening at every level of the Party. Whenever Party initiatives were proposed, the unions stopped them. Offers to help were turned into advice to 'get active in your own union'. Even proposals to appoint trade union liaison officers were resisted in some branches for fear that they might be too interventionist. Informational meetings were encouraged; activity meetings were not. Even NUPE, running the most committed Labour Party campaign, generally disengaged itself from CLP efforts to give it assistance. At local and regional levels as well as nationally, the Party was, in effect, frozen out. A survey by Derek Fatchet indicated that over 80 per cent of CLPs had played no active part at all in the ballot campaigns.[41]

To some on the Left, this exclusion was frustrating and disappointing, but the process developed a dynamic of its own as the trade union-centred and trade union-oriented campaigns proved successful to a degree which few had envisaged.

The role of the Labour Party

In retrospect, it has been tempting for critical observers to see the preparation for the Political Fund ballots and the TUCC emphasis in its campaign as a concerted manipulative pretence, to hide the Labour Party.[42] However, in the three areas – control, content and co-ordination – the motivations and the political differences were more complex.

Well before TUCC was founded, a consensus was reached in TULV that the unions, not the Party, would control the campaign. Here, the motivation followed logically from trade union attitudes towards their sphere, their funds and their recent collective organisational development. Union control was complementary to the tactical separation of political from Party funding, but it was also heavily reinforced by the union leaders' low regard for Labour Party management and by their alarm at the priorities of the NEC Left.

As for the content, certainly there was an early decision within TULV that the main focus would be on the question posed in the ballot, namely. 'Are you in favour of the union having a Political Fund?', and unions did follow TUCC guidance on the central question. But they also varied considerably in the extent to which they referred to the Labour Party, and in the focus of that reference. In most unions, some material was distributed which mentioned the link with the Labour Party, and in all the campaigns the shop floor 'campaign contacts' received detailed information on the Labour Party relationship.

As for the integration of the Labour Party organisation and membership into the campaign, here there was a major division over tactics, with the TUCC office involved initially in seeking *more* Labour Party activity, but with a coalition of a grouping of union leaders, the Party Leadership and sections of Head Office management involved in stopping it. To some extent, this was a matter of defending union autonomy, but it was also a fear lest the careful campaign of the unions to make the link between industrial interests and political action be compromised or subverted by an inappropriate ideological message or by the interference of political 'outsiders'. In campaigning for their objectives, the unions, as so often in the past, emphasised their control over their own territory and the defence of their own priorities.

NOTES

1. Crewe, in Kavanagh, *op. cit.*, 1982, p. 17 (and footnote 13, where Crewe notes partisanship weakening faster among Labour trade unionists than Labour non-trade unionists).
2. Ivor Crewe, 'The Disturbing Truth Behind Labour's Rout', *Guardian*, 13/6/83.
3. 'Future Organisation of TULV'. Note from TULV Secretary to TULV Committee Members, 12/7/83, p. 2.
4. Harrison, *op. cit.*, p. 23.
5. LPACR, 1914, pp. 46–65 and Appendix V, p. 137.
6. *Ibid.*
7. Harrison, *op. cit.*, pp. 23–4.
8. Pinto-Duschinsky, *op. cit.*, p. 70 and Harrison, *op. cit.*, pp. 36–7.
9. Ewing, *op. cit.*, p. 196.

10. On this see Duff Cooper, *Old Men Forget*, p. 143, cited in Harrison, *op. cit.*, p. 31, fn. 2. *Cabinet Memo PRO CAB 24/182* cited in Ewing, *op. cit.*, p. 51, fn. 42 and Middlemas, *op. cit.*, Chapter 7, p. 203 and fn. 92.

11. *Annual Report of the Certification Officer*, 1980, B. P. McCarthy and APEX, pp. 27–29. *Annual Report of the Certification Officer*, 1981, W. Richards and the NUM and NUM (Nottingham Area), pp. 24–26.

12. *Ibid.* and *Annual Report of the Certification Officer*, 1983, E. M. L. Parkin and the ASTMS, Appendix 9, pp. 57–97.

13. *TUC Congress Report*, 1981, p. 639. Resolution from the POEU with amendments from ASTMS and COHSE. The resolution was not debated.

14. HMSO, Cmnd. 8778, Green Paper, *Democracy in Trade Unions*, January 1983, p. 24.

15. Robert Taylor, 'Tebbit Spells Out End for the Union Barons', *The Observer*, 29/5/83.

16. Donald MacIntyre, 'Tories To Woo Union Voters', *Sunday Times*, 16/1/83.

17. MORI for TULV, July 1983.

18. These involved: (i) submission of draft model rules for preliminary approval by the Certification Officer; (ii) adoption of ballot rules by the union; (iii) submission of ballot rules for formal approval by the Certification Officer; (iv) holding the ballot; (v) sending notices to members about exemption from contribution. The model rules were advisory and unions could submit other rules or modified forms of the models but the guidance resulted in a general standardisation of procedure, safeguarding adequate information, convenience, secrecy, non-interference and the counting of ballots.

19. William Rodgers, 'How Tories Profit When Unions Are Let Off the Hook', *Guardian*, 24/2/84.

20. See on this Joseph Kirwan, 'Trade Unions and Party Politics: The Political Levy is Irrelevant', *Tory Review*, October 1983.

21. Ken Coates and Tony Topham, *Tribune*, 2/3/84.

22. See for example Fatchett, *op. cit.*, pp. 64-5.

23. *Minutes of TULV Committee*, 9/11/83.

24. *TULV Letter*, LW/ATC, 4/1/84 and *Minutes of TULV Meeting*, 11/1/84.

25. Reported in *NEC Minutes*, 25/4/84.

26. *Minutes of TULV Meeting*, 13/6/84.

27. MORI for TULV Committee, 8/6/84.

28. *Labour Party EC Report*, 1913, p. 29 and fraternal address to the TUC by Arthur Henderson; *TUC Congress Report*, 1913, p. 63; *Labour Party EC Minutes*, 6 and 7 May, 1913.

29. Letter from Bill Keys to Jim Mortimer, 20/11/84.

30. Interviews with Larry Whitty, 5/4/84 and Jenny Pardington, 8/8/84.

31. These observations are based on the examination of a wide range of literature from this campaign. Academic specialists who have examined the campaigns all agree that, encouraged by TUCC, the main focus of the campaigns was on maintaining a political voice. But as for the Labour Party links, John W. Leopold, 'Trade Union Political Funds: A Retrospective Analysis', *Industrial Relations Journal*, Vol. 17, No. 4, pp. 187–303 notes that 'allegations of deception and deceit ... cannot be sustained ... in the majority of material examined the link was overt and indeed stressed', p. 299. Richard Blackwell and Michael Terry, 'Analysing the Political Fund Ballots: A Remarkable Victory or the

Triumph of the Status Quo?', *Political Studies*, XXXV, 1987, pp. 623–42, '... all unions were careful to ensure that their campaign material explicitly mentioned the Labour Party and the good historical and contemporary reasons for the link', p. 626. By contrast, David Grant, 'Mrs. Thatcher's Own Goal: Unions and the Political Fund Ballots', *Parliamentary Affairs*, Vol. 40, January 1987, pp. 57–72 argues that 'many unions did not mention their affiliation to the Labour Party', p. 68. Mairi Steele, Kenneth Miller and John Gennard, 'The Trade Union Act 1984: Political Fund Ballots', *British Journal of Industrial Relations*, 24 November 1986, pp. 443–467, put it differently: 'While the question of Labour Party affiliation was not a central theme in all campaigns, certain unions.gave it greater emphasis', p. 454.

32. 'Pits Link Surprise in Levy Campaign', Guardian, 19/11/84. 'McGahey in Defence of Union Freedom', Morning Star, 12/11/86. LCC Campaign Notes, 1/12/84 linked the campaign to victory in the Miners' Strike.

33. LCC, *Action – Labour Party*, November 1984.

34. LCC, *Keeping the Link*, October 1984, p. 4.

35. Letter from Bill Keys to Jim Mortimer, 20/11/84.

36. 'Political Levy Campaign', Donald Ross, NEC, 23/1/85.

37. *Minutes of NEC Org. Sub.*, 11/2/85, Item 40.

38. 'Covering Note to Paper on Political Fund Ballots Campaign by General Secretary, SEC, 3/2/85 and 'Notes on the Supportive Role of the Labour Party in the Political Fund Ballots Campaign', SEC, 4/2/85, *NEC Minutes*, 27/2/85.

39. Letter to CLPs from General Secretary, 27/2/85.

40. 'Full Support for Union Campaign', *Labour Weekly*, 5/4/85.

41. Fatchett, *op. cit.*, p. 78.

42. For example, '... The positive votes, secured by the sedulous pretence that this had nothing to do with the Labour Party ...', Hugo Young. 'After the TUC, Ditch the Labour Party', *Guardian*, 23/6/88.

18

Trade Unionists For Labour

The results

There is little doubt that the Political Fund ballot results will be explored and picked over many times in years to come, if only because they are likely to be refought in 1995–6. In any case, the results were so staggeringly at variance with what was widely predicted to be the likely outcome that they provoke much thought about trade union political behaviour and particularly the thesis that the Labour Movement was in terminal decline.

Of the 37 Labour Party affiliated unions which balloted between 7 May 1985 and 24 March 1986, only TSSA (marginally) and ACTT (by 11 per cent) failed to achieve a 'yes' vote of 70 per cent (Table 18. 1). Twenty-one unions produced 'yes' votes of over 80 per cent and six even managed a 'yes' vote of over 90 per cent. The average 'yes' vote was 83. 6 per cent.

How are we to explain the scale of the successes and how are we to explain the consistency? Unions large and small, industrial and general, Leftwing and Rightwing, public and private sector and even white collar as well as blue collar all registered substantial 'yes' votes. The huge regional variations which had been expected failed to materialise; there was only a slight tendency towards higher 'yes' votes in Scotland and lower 'yes' votes in the East and West Midlands. [1] In ballots which produced very high turn-outs compared with normal union elections, the workplace ballots involved substantially higher participation than the postal turn-outs but with 'yes' and 'no' percentages which were remarkably similar. [2]

Some differences have been discerned between union votes depending on the percentage of women members, the white collar composition and the percentage of members paying the political levy in 1984. [3] But no scholar examining the results has found any significant difference in the result between those unions which emphasised the Labour Party and those which did not. Neither have I. To this extent, the explanation that the unions won simply because they 'hid' or 'covered up' the Labour Party[4] is unsatisfactory as well as, in many cases, clearly untrue.

What follows is an attempt to re-evaluate some of the causes of the victories in the ballots. Although on some points a tentative assessment, it aims to point up the major factors and to remedy some misconceptions.

The case for 'politics'

The main vulnerability of the 'yes' campaign lay in the submerged tradition of hostility to 'politics' which was obscured by the high levels of affiliation to the Labour Party. Poll after poll, survey after survey, decade after decade, has discerned this antipathy. [5] This was true even on the eve of the Political Ballot campaigns, when a MORI poll registered only 31 per cent of trade unionists believing that trade unionists should be concerned with political matters. [6]

But 'politics' takes on a variety of different meanings and associations and the crucial battle was over the meaning to be given to it in this context. There was recognised to be a deep antipathy in the unions to the idea of union leaders giving primacy to political activity and to the subordination of union interests to purely ideological or purely Party political objectives. On the other hand, a powerful case could be made for Political Funds which were concerned primarily with the practical pursuit of the union members' industrial interests through political representation. Put this way, the specific case for a 'yes' vote was much stronger than any abstract case against 'politics'.

Further, these Political Fund ballots were forced upon the unions at a time when the unions' industrial strength had deliberately been undermined by the Government (thus making the political channels all the more important). And – most important – they were forced upon the unions alongside new changes in the definition of 'political' which made the possession of a Fund all the more necessary.

Under the new Act, the definition of 'political objects' was tightened in various ways which made union activity without such Funds more restricted. In particular, there was an important restriction on union campaigning so that not only was it illegal to attempt 'to seek to persuade people to vote for a political party or candidate' without a Political Fund (in line with the 1913 Act), but also it was now illegal if the main purpose was 'to persuade them not to vote for a political party or candidate'. The public sector unions' campaigns against aspects of Government policy during an election period could come under this prohibition. Some ministerial statements appeared to bear out this interpretation. [7]

In any case, 200 years' experience of the judiciary gave unions cause for concern at what *might* be their interpretation of the Act. Such fears may well have been exaggerated, and in some cases deliberately so, in order to maximise the 'yes' vote, but they added a new and powerful argument for the possession of a Fund.

On this terrain, where the arguments for 'politics' were strengthened, the opponents of a Political Fund had few points of leverage to attract the individual trade unionist. There was much to gain from saying 'yes' and not a lot to lose. A 'yes' voter could still, in the end, 'contract out' if he or she were so minded. Even if that person were in two minds about the Fund, the amount of money involved in the political levy was not such as to excite a great fear of monetary disadvantage. In influencing the judgement of how to vote on a Fund, what the union had

Table 18.1 Political Fund ballot results 1985–6, Labour Party affiliated unions

Union	Date	Ballot papers issued	Turn-out %	Yes
SOGAT	07.05.85	208,686	56.8	91,760
ISTC	23.05.85	48,859	67.7	28,633
FTAT	03.06.85	80,194	30.0	11,410
UCW	20.06.85	195,698	69.4	102,546
NCU	28.06.85	121,037	78.7	77,183
GMWU	08.07.85	824,726	61.0	448,426
APEX	22.07.85	90,132	59.9	39,465
BFAWU	29.07.85	35,859	62.0	19,954
AUEW	06.08.85	808,800	37.0	238,604
EETPU	13.08.85	362,047	45.0	140,913
NUR	23.08.85	135,293	61.1	71,907
PLCWTWU	23.08.85	3,350	88.7	2,242
ASLEF	01.09.85	24,211	85.4	19,110
TSSA	03.09.85	49,324	67.2	22,975
NUS	03.09.85	21,040	34.0	6,179
CATU	13.09.85	32,124	73.4	17,967
NUSC	07.10.85	1,095	54.0	460
TGWU	15.10.85	1,307,873	49.5	511,014
COHSE	25.10.85	220,000	40.3	81,012
NUDAGO	30.10.85	4,196	67.7	2,388
NUTGW	30.10.85	66,400	87.4	52,634
NLBD	30.10.85	2,978	82.5	2,218
NUFLAT	03.12.85	32,276	84.0	20,956
USDAW	09.12.85	387,795	39.5	134,592
ACTT	12.12.85	24,900	49.0	7,149
NGA	16.12.85	121,686	72.6	68,559
TWU	17.12.85	11,438	76.0	7,790
NACODS	13.01.86	15,000	76.2	9,930
TASS	15.01.86	219,885	55.0	91,389
NUPE	23.01.86	660,863	59.3	329,442
RUBSSO	03.02.86	3,812	40.0	1,244
GUALO	10.02.86	1,202	92.4	928
MU	03.03.86	37,600	36.5	10,492
NUM	13.03.86	140,276	76.0	96,226
FBU	17.03.86	43,948	87.4	30,607
ASTMS	21.03.86	390,000	32.0	102,334
UGATT	24.03.86	250,000	25.0	56,733

* Percentage 'Yes' and 'No' do not total 100% because of spoiled papers.

Total ballot papers issued	6,984,603
Total 'Yes' vote	2,957,371
'Yes' majority over 'No'	2,376,108
Unions voting 'Yes' 37. Unions voting 'No' Nil.	
Average percentage 'Yes' vote	83.6
'Yes' vote as percentage of total ballot papers issued	42.3

Source: Data provided by TUCC office; ASTMS result taken from *Labour Research*, May 1986, p.

% Yes	No	% No*	Yes vote as % of papers issued
78.0	25,947	21.0	44.0
86.7	4,404	13.3	58.6
72.0	4,269	28.0	14.2
75.5	33,337	24.5	52.4
81.0	17,757	19.0	63.7
89.0	54,637	11.0	54.3
73.0	14,380	26.6	43.7
89.7	2,237	10.1	55.6
84.0	44,399	16.0	29.5
84.0	26,830	16.0	38.9
87.2	10,580	12.8	53.1
75.3	697	24.7	66.9
93.0	1,491	7.2	78.9
69.3	10,017	30.2	46.6
86.5	963	13.5	29.4
76.1	5,383	22.8	55.9
77.0	135	23.0	42.0
78.9	119,823	18.2	39.1
91.3	7,731	8.7	36.8
84.5	439	15.5	56.9
90.7	4,968	8.6	79.3
90.2	221	9.8	74.5
77.0	5,963	22.0	64.9
88.0	17,824	11.0	34.7
59.0	5,043	41.0	28.7
78.2	18,931	21.6	56.3
89.6	905	10.0	68.1
87.0	1,481	13.0	66.2
76.0	29,467	24.0	41.6
84.1	60,332	15.4	49.85
77.5	358	22.0	32.6
83.5	176	16.0	77.2
76.3	3,237	23.5	27.9
90.25	9,958	9.3	68.6
79.6	7,652	11.4	69.6
81.0	23,996	19.0	26.2
91.5	5,295	8.5	22.7

to do was to illustrate the connection between the few pence of the levy, political activity on behalf of the union member and, where necessary, the extended role of the affiliated union through the Labour Party.

All in all, it was difficult to make a very powerful case against it. A 'No' vote was very difficult to argue. This was probably the biggest single factor behind the Political Fund victories.

Misleading conceptions and the mobilisation of the 'yes' vote

On the other hand, mobilising a 'yes' vote had three advantages which were not so apparent in the period of negotiations over the legislation and in the lead-up to the ballots. The commitment to the Labour Party connection was not declining, in spite of the common diagnosis of the time. The core support for affiliation to the Labour Party was more stable than Labour's electoral support. And the unions were better prepared and more capable of a campaign of political mobilisation than even many of their friends realised.

The decay of the Labour Movement

Government Ministers, Alliance politicians and a vast army of critics of the Labour Movement faced the Political Fund ballots with confidence that, in a sense, history was on their side. It was widely believed that the Labour Movement had such inherent and developing weaknesses that they would show up as soon as the great majority of the union membership was allowed to have a voice in ballots, free of the manipulations and intimidations of Leftwing activists and union 'bosses'. The trends were, it was thought, all moving in the same direction – towards decay. The evidence, it was thought, pointed to a new historic level of weakness in support for the unions' affiliations to the Labour Party. All that was needed was a procedure which would allow this decay to be manifest. Give the members the chance and they would precipitate a fundamental blow, perhaps even a terminal crisis, in the Labour Party.

And yet, appearances were deceptive. Or rather many observers hostile to the Labour Movement saw only what they wanted to see – 'disaster for Labour'.[8] This had the effect of making them less than sensitive to counter-evidence. Most crucially, it was assumed that because there was evidence from the 1960s of a reduction in the percentage of the public who favoured close ties,[9] and because there was evidence from the period 1964 to 1974 of a reduction in the percentage of Labour's electoral 'identifiers' who favoured close ties,[10] then a similar decline must have taken place in the 1970s and 1980s in the percentage of trade unionists who favoured close links. Yet the evidence indicated just the opposite.

The issue of trade union affiliation to the Labour Party had not been given much attention in national polls during the thirty years of post-war politics. Regular polls of the attitudes of trade unionists on this issue took place only in the early 1980s. Some of the local polls of earlier periods give varying results with little indication of their typicality. But there was the invaluable Butler and Stokes analysis covering the 1960s. For the years 1963 and 1964 (a time of weak union political communication, a new 'separatism', a new NEDC and, generally, an inter-party consensus on the industrial relations framework) they found only

25 per cent and 31 per cent of trade unionists supporting 'close ties' to the Labour Party. [11]

In the 1970s, the first poll on this question carried out by MORI in August 1977 showed 34 per cent of trade unionists disagreeing with the statement that 'The Labour Party should not be so closely linked to the unions'. [12] This was interpreted as one of the signs that trade unionists were growing increasingly anxious about union political activities. [13] But it was actually higher than that found by Butler and Stokes in favour of 'close ties' in the 1960s. A year later, Gallup, in the *Sunday Telegraph* of 3 September 1978, found the same: 34 per cent of trade unionists saying that close links were a good thing.

Now let us move forward to the data for the 1980s. By then, the Labour Party was plunged into one crisis after another, involving, at times, a haemorrhage of electoral support among trade unionists away from the Labour Party. Further, in the 1980s, the percentage of white collar and women trade unionists had increased and was increasing. Thus, for both these reasons – political and sociological – it was natural to anticipate a major decline in support for the union–Labour Party attachment among trade unionists. And yet what we find is a rather different position. To my knowledge, six reliable[14] polls were taken between February/July 1980 and February 1985 which posed to trade unionists the question of the union links to Labour.

February/ July 1980	MORI/*Sunday Times*	'closely linked to Labour Party'	39%
January 1982	MORI/'World in Action'	'affiliated and give money to Labour Party'	35%
September 1983	Gallup/'Week in Politics'	'affiliate to Labour Party'	36%
January 1984	Gallup/'Weekend World'	'affiliate and give money to Labour Party'	36%
August 1984	MORI/TULV*	'affiliate and give money to Labour Party'	38%
February 1985	MORI/'Union World'	'affiliate and give money to Labour Party'	39%

The first point to register is that the percentage in favour in *all* these polls is significantly *higher* than that found in the 1960s. Further, it would appear that after a decline following the defection and internal upheavals of 1981, support was *growing* from 1982 to 1985. This latter increase is all the more remarkable in

---

* All the polls were of all trade unionists except this one, which was of affiliated trade unionists. The social compositon of affiliated unions suggest to me that one could expect the 'yes' vote in affilated unions to be slightly higher and that this poll (which caused so much gloom in the unions) was on the low side. In the event, the final overall 'yes' vote as a percentage of the total membership of affiliated unions was 42.3 per cent – not very far away from the final MORI poll, adjusting for affiliating membership.

that it takes place during a period of particularly sharp decline in the percentage of manual worker male trade unionists.

It should also be noted that in the final poll of all trade unionists taken before the Political Fund ballots began, support was back at the *highest* level attained in any national poll of trade unionists in the past quarter of a century. Thus the base of support for the campaign was far from being in the state of rapid deterioration that observers often diagnosed.

We can only speculate on the causes of this increased support. It may be attributed to the effects upon trade unionists of over a decade of particularly close identification of the Labour Party with the unions. It was almost certainly assisted by the ability of the unions to win Labour Government support for a variety of union causes. It may, marginally, have been assisted by the creation of TULV and some basic improvements in the communication of the unions' association with the Labour Party. And it may, latterly, have been influenced by a new insecurity in the face of Conservative Government policy. Whatever the cause, in as much as it indicated a hardening of core support for the union–Party relationship, it was a better situation to begin a Political Fund campaign than might have been secured in the 1960s. It was likely that those committed to political affiliation with Labour would also be most inclined to favour a Political Fund, and probably also the most inclined to participate.

Electoral alignment and political linkage

Much of the journalistic comment (and one suspects much of the Government and Alliance assumptions) about the situation of the unions in 1984 and 1985 took it as axiomatic that there was a close relationship between the level of Labour's electoral support and the level of support from trade unionists for the trade union-Labour Party relationship. An even closer relationship was assumed to exist between the level of electoral support by trade unionists for the Labour Party and the level of support by trade unionists for linkage to the Labour Party. It seemed a reasonable assumption. [15] If support went up strongly in the electoral dimension, it would go up strongly in the other. If it went down, the converse would apply.

Now clearly there was a connection, particularly as 'hard core' Labour partisans made up a majority of those in the unions who favoured affiliation. [16] But the relationship between movements in electoral support and movements in support for linkage was significantly looser than was often assumed.

Let us re-examine the figures we have already quoted in relation to support for the Labour Party connection. In 1964, when 31 per cent of trade unionists supported 'close links', Labour's electoral support was significantly higher at 44.1 per cent (General Election) and its electoral support from trade unionists was much higher and estimated at between 62 and 73 per cent (Chapter 5, n. 5). But, by August 1977, when 34 per cent of trade unionists indicated approval for Labour 'being so closely linked to the unions', Labour's electoral support, according to Gallup, was only 37.5 per cent, and indications were that support from trade unionists was down to something in the region of 45 per cent.

From February to July 1980, when MORI found that 39 per cent of trade unionists now favoured unions being 'closely linked' to the Labour Party, Labour's electoral support had risen to an average of 45 per cent. But its electoral support among trade unionists in this period was only 51 per cent. In January 1982, the Alliance surge was still so strong that Labour stood on only 30 per cent of electoral support, and electoral support among trade unionists had slumped to just 39 per cent. But support from trade unionists for affiliation and giving money to the Labour Party (which could be defined as 'close links' but, if anything, involved a stronger commitment) had only dropped to 35 per cent.[17] By August 1983, the Gallup Poll had Labour's electoral support down to 25 per cent and in September it was 24.5 per cent. Among trade unionists it was down to 34 per cent. But support for affiliation to the Labour Party was *higher than both* at 36 per cent.[18]

Thus, there is some evidence here that not only is the fit between these two domains looser than is often thought, but that the commitment to union linkage to the Labour Party was rather more solid in this period than was the commitment to Labour in electoral terms. For all these reasons, Labour's standing in the polls among trade unionists in the years from 1981 to 1984 was not necessarily a good guide to how they would respond to the ballots. On the other hand, how they responded to the ballots in 1985–6 was also not a good guide to how they would later respond to Labour's electoral appeal (see below p. 571).

Trade union competence

The decline in public approval of trade unions, and the growing critique of their role in the economy and polity, was accompanied in some quarters by a view of trade union competence which bordered on contempt. One can trace this perception through much of the writing on trade unionism, even in the serious press and by informed political journalists. Peter Jenkins noted in 1981, about the unions' participation in the electoral college, that they had a propensity to administrative muddle: 'Anyone who knows the trade union world knew that they would be bound to make a hash of it ...'[19] Indeed, it would not be an exaggeration to say that most informed commentators, with a sympathy for the Alliance or the Conservative Party, assumed that the unions would be incapable of mounting a disciplined, co-ordinated and efficient campaign – more likely they would seek to fiddle the ballots.[20]

Anything that pointed in a rather different direction was either not seen or not comprehended, although the evidence was there, as we have indicated, that the unions were beginning to improve their communication and campaigning role. Indications that the Political Fund ballots would be a disaster were eagerly seized; indications that they might succeed were overlooked.

Thus, the votes in NALGO and the CPSA rejecting Labour Party affiliation were normally the only ones cited as relevant.[21] But in early 1983, the Society of Telecom Executives had secured their first Political Fund after a campaign which showed the relevance of the Fund to their interests. And early in 1984, the Amalgamated Society of Textile Workers and Kindred Trades renewed its Political Fund after a similar campaign and ballot of members.

While critics complacently awaited the disaster that would befall the unions, they were actually in a much better condition to fight the Ballots of 1984–5 than their opponents assumed. Their tactics were astute, their co-ordination was very efficient, their communications were better than they had been for many years and their publicity material was of high quality.

Certainly, the powerful case for a Political Fund was put very effectively and with extraordinary success. How far this success was simply a matter of bringing out the 'yes' vote we will never know. The existence of a majority of non-voters in twelve of the unions does not detract from the legitimacy of the result, any more than it does in other ballots and elections. But the results do take on a rather different perspective when we examine the wide variations in the proportion of a union's *membership* which voted 'yes' (Table 18.1). The range was from just over 14 per cent (FTAT) to just under 80 per cent (NUTGW). Seventeen unions, including all the purely white collar unions and 10 of the 11 unions with over 200,000 members, failed to secure a 'yes' vote of over 50 per cent of their members. The average 'yes' vote as a percentage of ballot papers issued was 42.3 per cent. But all succeeded in producing handsome majorities among those who participated.

The lack of counter-organisation

The misunderstanding about the historic level of support for the union–Labour Party relationship, the misconception about the relationship between electoral alignment and attitudes towards union political affiliation, and the contempt with which the unions were held, all fed into the Government's complacent view of the potential effects of the legislation. If you were dealing with a Labour Movement in terminal crisis than you could be confident in dealing it a severe blow. Thus, the consultative process with the TUC could be approached in a relaxed way – with an eye on some essentials, like ensuring that members were informed of their rights to 'contract out', but without a predatory search for blood at every point of vulnerability.

Not all opponents of the Labour Movement were convinced that the blow was struck at the right point or with sufficient force. Both SDP and Conservative backbenchers mounted a call for 'contracting in'. But a subtle observer working within the understanding and expectations of the Conservative leadership might well have thought Ministers to be both ruthless and clever. They were confident that at least some of the unions – particularly the white collar unions – would vote against having a Political Fund.[22] A badly damaged Labour Party operating alongside a financially weak Alliance could appear the best of all possible outcomes.

This restraining confidence operated alongside a degree of inhibition at being seen to be too partisan. The legislation was fundamentally and indefensibly inequitable, but there was considerable difference in presentational terms in offering facilities to the union membership for registering their views and attempting to intervene in a factional sense to ensure the bankruptcy of Her Majesty's Opposition.

For these reasons, the Conservative Party took a decision not to seek a direct organised intervention within individual unions. Just as TUCC distanced its campaign from the Labour Party, so Conservative Ministers distanced themselves from the 'no' campaign. They mounted no overt mobilisation via Conservative Trade Unionists nor did they attempt to form a 'no' front organisation which might have contested 'yes' propaganda at the place of work.

Such a counter-organisation would not have had an easy time, given the weakness of the 'no' case and the difficulty of engaging the continuous attention of the Conservative press in a year-long campaign. The organisers of a 'no' vote would also have had to contend with the resentment produced by what was considered to be partisan Government 'interference' in union internal affairs, further accentuating the mood of 'what bloody business is it of theirs?'. And, although the standing of the parties in the opinion polls was much less significant as a guide to the Political Fund ballot results than was often thought, the loss of popularity of the Conservative Party among trade unionists[23] would probably not have enhanced the authority of its direct recommendations. Be that as it may, by the time that the Conservatives had woken up to the strength of the union 'yes' campaign, the bandwagon was rolling from union to union. Intervention at this later stage threatened to cost the Government a higher political price if it ended in defeat. Surveying the potential for that defeat, Ministers wisely kept aloof.

CONSEQUENCES

With the evidence presented here, I have argued that far from the unions' Political Funds being uniquely vulnerable at this point because of the decline of the Labour Movement, the unions were in a stronger position to defend them than appeared to be the case. They were, crucially, stronger in terms of the case to be made for a Fund, but also stronger in terms of the level and stability of core support for the union–Labour Party relationship – a core support which probably made up a major element of the 'yes' vote in most of the affiliated unions. They were also much stronger in terms of their capacity to organise the defence of the funds and the mobilisation of the 'yes' vote.

I have placed little emphasis in this analysis on the mid-term unpopularity of the Conservative Government, which I do not regard as a major factor in the results. Nor have I made reference to Labour's electoral lead in the opinion polls, which again I do not consider of great significance at this time.[24] Given this analysis, it is, therefore, not surprising that the immediate impact of the series of Political Fund ballot successes on the Labour Party's electoral strength should be so limited, in spite of the romantic belief in some quarters that '83 per cent of trade unionists' had voted 'for Labour'.[25]

Neither public opinion polls, nor the by-elections in the period of the ballots, showed any sharp shift of trade unionists to Labour during and after the Political Fund ballots. The Party's own private polls show some remarkable consistencies over the period from Kinnock's election in 1983 to the autumn of 1986. In the first three quarters of 1986, Labour support among trade unionists averaged 48 per cent – exactly the same as in the first three quarters after Kinnock's election.[26]

Yet, in spite of the limited electoral return, there were some major benefits from the ballots. The resounding success had five different kinds of consequences: psychological, presentational, political, strategic and organisational.

There can be little doubt that the ballots gave an enormous morale boost to a

Labour Movement that had been involved in devastating defeats in both the political and the industrial spheres. It renewed confidence in trade union organising capacity and it did something to undermine the perception of the Thatcher Government as being strategically acute and politically almost invincible.

It also strengthened the presentation of a movement which was, in this respect at least, more in touch with its members and more unified than in the recent past. When, as was to be expected, there was a renewal of pressure for the unions and the Party to go their separate ways, the results in these ballots could be offered in evidence of solid grass-roots support.

It heightened the legitimacy of 'politics' within the unions. Too much should not be made of the extent of politicisation. Large numbers of union members were still relatively untouched by the experience. But the development had created room for a higher political profile, and for more time and expertise to be given within unions to political campaigning.

The success of the venture caused a reorientation of strategy at national level within the unions. Although mobilising trade unionists at the place of work had always been a goal of national union organisations and part of TULV's work, it had, in electoral terms, taken second place to the traditional role of unions within the Party's electoral machinery – providing resources. What was left behind after the Political Fund ballots was a new concern to seek the political mobilisation of trade unionists at the grass roots and to move the emphasis away from resource assistance.

There was an organisational legacy also and in the short term this was the most striking consequence. This legacy had several features. By the spring of 1986, the unremitting success of ballots in the affiliated unions had created such a climate of rationality around the union case for a Political Fund that it affected the mood and balance of argument in non-Labour-affiliated unions. In these unions, the issue was less complicated than in the affiliated unions. There was no political record to offer or defend and no Labour Party association to justify, simply an assessment of the case for having the potential resource of a Political Fund. As a result, a range of politically independent unions sought Funds and won (Chapter Ten, p. 287) and, unusually, one union, BETA, went on to affiliate to the Labour Party – the first major affiliation for over twenty years. And, far from the ballots and the contracting out reminders resulting in a major decline in levypaying, the unions were able to stimulate interest to a point where in most unions the level of levypaying actually rose (see Chapter 10, Table 10.3, pp. 294–5). Further, with the authority of the ballot behind them, many of the affiliated unions felt able to raise the amount of the levy, thus potentially making more money available for politics and for the Labour Party.[27] In terms of national union–Party co-ordination, it encouraged a mood which secured the implementation of an organisational proposal which had been around for years – a Trade Union Liaison Officer in Party Headquarters. And it stimulated the reconstruction and remodelling of a new organisation for the political mobilisation of trade unionists in support of the Labour Party. The much-reviled TULV organisation was married to TUCC to produce a more celebrated offspring – Trade Unionists For Labour.

TULV – TUCC – TUFL

From December 1984 to early 1986, the national TULV operation had adopted a low profile while the TUCC organisation took over its regional structure and carried out the priority task of winning the Political Fund ballots. But TULV preserved its independent national existence and was still assisting other aspects of the Party's activities.

It continued to organise with the Party in by-elections, providing both materials and the secondment of officials. It was still providing the Party with extra financial resources from the Voluntary Levy Fund: in July 1985 it assisted the Party with the purchase of equipment and stationery stores and with the financing of a Social Services campaign. Its central importance as the voice of affiliated unions was shown by the fact that consultative soundings on whether the unions were agreeable to an increase in affiliation were taken first at the TULV committee.

The possibility that TULV activities might become more broadly acceptable, and some old suspicions be alleviated, increased in April 1985 when David Basnett retired and the Chair of TULV was taken by Ron Todd, the new General Secretary of the Transport Workers. The new Leftwing Chairman was balanced by the new post of Vice-Chairman which was taken by Bryan Stanley, a Rightwing leader from the National Communications Union. Jenny Pardington from the TGWU became the TULV Secretary while Larry Whitty took up his new post as General Secretary of the Labour Party.

This more consensual composition was an important move in the aftermath of the Political Fund ballot successes because Whitty's more optimistic plans for TULV in 1983 were now given a new head of steam as the unions became more conscious of the value of TUCC. Should the two now be amalgamated in some way? This question became part of a series of discussions and discreet meetings held as TUCC approached its date of closure in March 1986.

At a joint meeting of TULV and TUCC on 11 December 1985, it was agreed that a subcommittee of union General Secretaries from the main unions – including the NUM and the AUEW – would consider proposals for the development of a 'well organised structure', taking the 'best practices' of the existing organisations.[28]

TUCC had taken a narrow remit and no direct function in relation to the Labour Party, but it had a wide base of *all* affiliated organisations, a full time staff, and a proven record of mobilising grass-roots support through the system of campaign contacts. TULV had a much wider remit (see Chapter 15, p. 497), which included financial and organisational assistance to the Labour Party and the broad purpose of mobilising trade unionists for Labour. But only 29 out of 37 unions were affiliated. The aim of the subcommittee and of the private talks between Keys and Todd, the two Chairmen, was to develop a new fusion. Its main objective would be to assist Labour's General Election effort, but it would be responsible for a wide range of organisational tasks between elections, concerned with strengthening the union–Party relationship – building awareness of the value of the linkage, boosting membership, levypaying and local affiliation, encouraging workplace branches and creating and sustaining a variety of horizontal links at different levels.

To create a new organisation with a broader remit but a consensual base required reassurance being offered to the suspicious unions on Left and Right – particularly the NUM and the AUEW – that it had no factional and no policy intentions whatsoever. The project paper affirmed 'quite emphatically ... policy decisions are for the Party alone'.[29] This process of reassurance and reconstruction was facilitated by the fact that the NUM, now vulnerable to the poaching of the Union of Democratic Mineworkers, was no longer anxious to be outside any of the national institutions, and Terry Duffy, veteran sceptic of TULV's activities, was ill and approaching retirement. In the end, both the NUM and the AUEW[30] joined TUFL and eventually 35 of the Party affiliates became members – virtually all of them.

Trade Unionists For Labour

As it finally emerged, the constitution of Trade Unionists For Labour was significantly more restricted in its avowed aims than had been that of Trade Unions for a Labour Victory. There was no reference to the organisation making 'recommendations on matters of finance, organisation and membership' to the Party – a preoccupation of TULV in its early phase. There was now a specific prohibition on the organisation 'under any circumstances' becoming involved in 'policy matters of the Party'. The ultimate objective was stated as 'the return and maintenance in power of a Labour Government', and the practical priorities in 'giving maximum assistance' to the Party involved 'increasing political aware-ness, strengthening the political links, and raising the level of levypaying and Labour Party membership'.[31]

The existence of this newly-strengthened trade union organisation still led to some perceptions that it was a renewed attempt by the unions to 'enhance their influence in the Party'.[32] Certainly, within the unions it was assumed that if more trade unionists were politically educated and joined the Party, and if the unions were more active locally, its wilder 'middle class intellectual' excesses might be restrained. But influence of any kind was well down the list of immediate priorities of this venture. And the inhibitions consequent on TULV's reputation were considerable. A broad-ranging consensus emerged in the unions that if factional power or policy positions were to become associated with TUFL, it might as well commit suicide. In practice, from this point the constant sniping at 'the Trojan Horse', and the regular accusations of 'drip feed', died away.

The new structure involved a permanent Campaign Unit under a National Campaign Coordinator with a National Administrator and a Deputy Adminis-trator. For a variety of inter-union reasons, Graham Allen, widely recognised to have been a considerable success in the TUCC organisation, was not reappointed and was in formal terms replaced by Jenny Pardington, political officer of the Transport Workers. In effect, however, the Coordinator's job until 1987 went to Bill Keys, now retired as a trade union official.

Partly out of a renewed confidence in its importance and partly to reassure member unions about its activities, the formal structure of TUFL initially involved a much higher degree of formal supervisory activity than did TULV. There was to be a committee of all member unions (the All Trades Union Committee) which would meet on a bi-monthly basis. And there was to be an Executive Committee, also meeting bi-monthly. Much of this committee work seemed unnecessary after a while (particularly as Keys tended to operate what was described in the office as 'a benevolent autocracy') and eventually there was a reduction to just one committee – the Executive – to which every affiliated union could send a representative. Usually this was either the General Secretary or the 'political' officer. The Labour Party General Secretary attended, as did other Labour Party Directors from time to time.

Below this supervisory structure was another 'working level' with a Finance Committee and a Committee of 'Political Officers'. The Finance Committee membership was elected from the Executive. In 1990, the unions involved were GMB, MSF, NCU, NGA, NUPE, TGWU, UCW and USDAW. It was left to the unions who represented them. Sometimes it was a Finance Officer, sometimes again the 'political' officer. They also met bi-monthly and often in attendance were the Labour Party's General Secretary, the Party's Treasurer, the Chair of the Party's F and GP committee and the Party's finance officials.

The 'Political Officers'' meetings (including officials of various designations, portfolios and levels of seniority, depending on the union) had been a very useful link between unions and between the unions and the Party since TULV was first founded. They continued to play an important advisory role over a wide range of organisational/political problems. They met more regularly than the other committees, usually monthly, with a core of about fifteen attenders – although any union could send a representative. TUFL officials from the Campaign Unit attended this meeting and all the others.

The Campaign Unit and its activities were maintained from 1986 to 1990 by an affiliation fee of 3p per affiliated member. In addition, the Levy Fund was continued, at first voluntary as before, but then, from October 1987, as an obligation upon all the unions. The change here reflected the new and mainly non-contentious status of TUFL, and it reflected also the post-General Election mood of appreciation of the style and organisation of Labour's campaign. It also represented, it must be said, a growing feeling among the volunteers that other unions should be paying their share. Subsequently, most unions paid into the Fund but a few unions paid into one fund and not the other and a very few paid nothing at all into either.

TUFL also settled for the moment the vexed question of regional funds. Up to 1986 the TULV regions had no regular source of income. Initially, it was decided in April that year that the regions would receive 7 per cent of Campaign Unit funds to be allocated for special projects. Subsequently, approximately £1,000–£2,000 annually was given from central funds. The eleven regional structures of TULV (which had become the provincial core of TUCC) now became the organisational base of TUFL and their committees were simply renamed. As before, Scotland had a degree of independence and distinctiveness, with its TUFL structure more closely related to the Scottish TUC. In effect, the Scottish TUC's Labour Committee became the TUFL 'branch'. As before also, the TGWU and GMWU dominated the organisational offices; in December 1986 they took eighteen of the twenty-two Chairs'/Secretaries'/ Coordinators' positions. Co-ordination and strategy were facilitated by quarterly meetings of all the regional officials of TUFL with the 'Political' Officers.

Considerable emphasis was laid on the provision of a fund to help the Labour Party fight the coming General Election. A special Victory Fund was established and a committee was set up to supervise its operation. It consisted of four representatives of the Party, four from TUFL plus one CLP member. But TUFL's role (particularly through the Campaign Coordinator, Bill Keys) was crucial. It was agreed at the first annual meeting of TUFL in October 1986 that there would be a target of approximately £5 million and a levy on unions of 87p per affiliated levypaying member to realise a sum of £4,934,325. There would also be attempts to raise voluntary sums through collections and fund-raising events ('Best Party in Town'), and through 'day's pay' (officials) and 'hour's pay' (members) donations. In practice, responses to the voluntary appeals were 'disappointing', in spite of a more co-ordinated approach. And the shortfall on the Victory Fund levy was also considerable (see Chapter 16, p. 536).

TUFL and the General Election campaign

This shortfall in union contributions was paralleled in some ways by a loss of dynamism in the TUFL organisation itself compared with the TUCC organisation and compared with what was expected of it, in the afterglow of the Political Fund ballot successes. There were few close observers of TUFL in this period who thought that it had realised its full potential, although it was recognised that among the varied reasons for this were many which were well outside the control of TUFL officials.

In some ways, the performance of the TUFL organisation centrally reflected wider behaviour patterns within the unions. There was a period of transition after the Political Fund ballot results in which tension slackened and there was a slowness to adapt and develop the networks and processes created during the fight for Political Funds. At the same time, paradoxically, many unions had also developed a new confidence about what they themselves could handle politically – a feeling that led them to a 'do your own thingism' and a tendency therefore to downgrade the importance of the TUFL Campaign Unit. Mixed in with this was a new sense of financial austerity (following the heavy expenditure on the Fund campaign) which led unions into an increased reluctance to let go of funds too quickly.

It was not unexpected that the new organisation – the first institutionalised unit of its kind in Party history – should arouse some of the territorial tensions which are common in one of the most protocol-conscious and rule-governed relationships in British political life. Keys somehow managed the remarkable feat in 1986 of making an appeal for Labour's election funds at the end of a day's session of the TUC Congress. Some in the TUC thought this very 'iffy' in terms of protocol and generally the two organisations kept themselves well apart. But there were particular teething troubles in establishing the relations between the new Unit and the Party at Walworth Road and in the House. Some of this was caused by uncertainty in handling the initiating role of the new organisation, some of it was the product of personality clashes and varieties of tradition.

Certainly, relations between the leadership of the new organisation and the Party Leader's Office were not good and there was less of the mutual respect than ought to have been there. Initially also, there was tension with the Party's Communication and Campaigning staff around the problem of relating TUFL publications to the Party's communicational strategy and style. For a while this caused some 'who does what best?' difficulties. The existence of a new Trade Union Liaison Office within the Labour Party headquarters secured the advantages of better liaison and integration, but it also led to some duplication and strains.

Within TUFL itself all was not sweetness, light and co-operation between the affiliated unions and the centre. Unions varied in their willingness to participate and co-operate with the Unit's initiatives. New tensions emerged, particularly between TUFL and the GMWU which had 'run the show' when it was TULV but which now found considerable fault in the way the new organisation was being handled.

It must be said that some of these difficulties and tensions arose out of a situation where the expected winter surge to Labour, following a successful TUC speech by Kinnock and a 'good' Party Conference, failed to materialise. Scapegoats began to be looked for on all sides and in many offices. Much of this tension was hidden from public view until the defeat in the Greenwich by-election. Not only did that result indicate a new disaffection amongst Labour's working class trade union supporters, it provoked and revealed a short, sharp burst of Party in-fighting over strategy.

Subsequently, a recovery did take place but Labour never, in the pre-election period, regained its steady upper-forties support amongst trade unionists. The unions, like the Party, approached the 1987 General Election at a psychological and political disadvantage that few thought conceivable in 1986. And TUFL began its own campaign aware that there was something of a crisis affecting the trade union vote.

It was given a wide-ranging role in mobilising the trade union vote and assisting the Party with the provision of resources.[33] It ensured that the coverage of Target Seats was actually taking place and monitored the co-ordinators. It provided Trade Union speakers for the campaign. It distributed TUFL literature free of charge to the unions; cards, booklets, leaflets and training packs all produced in co-operation with the Party's Shadow Communication Agency and to a standard far higher than in 1983. And it was responsible for liaison with the Party over the financial resources for the election.

All this was highly integrated into the Party's own campaign and the Liaison Office in Walworth Road became one of the functional units of a well-organised and reconstructed Head Office. Some of the union leaders represented on the TUFL committees were brought formally into the campaign structure by their membership of the Leader's Campaign Committee but this did not play the key role during the campaign which some had expected of it.

The establishment of TUFL as a distinct full time organisation had meant that a wider and more detailed range of preparation had taken place by the time the election unit was formed. Not all of it was successful but the main priority and the biggest improvement on 1983 was an earlier establishment of the campaign organisation in the field.

The TULV regional organisation, taken over by TUFL, was by now a more institutionalised and better prepared operation. Target Seat Coordinators covering offensive and defensive seats were in place in many cases up to eight months before the Election began. In some seats, the Target Seat Coordinators had a team of union helpers. Altogether, some 1,300 names were in place by June, formally linked to the Constituency parties, either through a Trade Union Liaison Officer of the Constituency or its Secretary or Agent.

The regional union contribution, as before, varied in its quality with the North and North-Western areas and the South-West considered 'good', the London area an improvement on 1983 but still not very satisfactory, and the West Midlands the worst, and very difficult to put together.

Each individual union was asked to appoint a senior officer to be responsible for the union's campaign and liaison with TUFL – an integral part of the structure of the TUCC Political Fund ballot's campaign. Getting the linkage fully in place in 1984 had been a problem. It was more difficult in 1987 and a number of unions took no action, with the result that there was some lack of co-ordination.

In their final report, the TUFL organisers made the reasonable judgement that the union input at all levels was better than in previous elections.[34] But, as before, the individual union contributions varied considerably. The AEU was still complained about in terms of its contribution to some of the seats. Of the 29 unions mentioned in reports to TUFL from the co-ordinators, the TGWU and NUPE were the most involved numerically, although close observers noted that the GMWU and USDAW contributions were a big improvement compared with the past. Amongst the middle-sized unions, COHSE and TASS were most active.

The major improvement was, however, still accompanied by a range of weaknesses. TUFL's central organisation reported later that there was a widespread view that the field structure was still set up too late, that in a large percentage of Target Seats the co-ordinators did not begin campaigning until well into 1987 and some not until the Election was called.[35] Although there was evidence of a big improvement in this co-ordination at local level compared with the past, the union contribution was still marred by examples of intra-union chauvinism, and by the tendency for union business to suddenly intrude – even though commitments had been given for time away from the union. In nearly a third of seats, it was reported to TUFL that there was little coordination and planning between the unions.[36]

The problem in making an assessment of the achievements of TUFL is that it suffers by comparison with the union effort in the Political Fund ballots – campaigns fought on a very different terrain. It suffers also from its own aspirations. What the TUFL national officials sought to do was build on the Political Fund ballot's experience and processes. Success then had been based on the network of 'campaign contacts' and the preoccupation with establishing a 'two step flow' of communication from the contacts to the ordinary members. Some union officials detected what they considered to be a lack of clarity in TUFL's main objectives during the General Election campaign, but, certainly in the minds of Keys and Pardington, the aim was to move away from the traditional notion that the job of the unions during an election campaign was simply to provide resources – however valuable. The primary aim was to encourage the political mobilisation of trade unionists. Thus, TUFL nationally sought to encourage the General Election equivalent of the 'campaign contacts'; unions were asked to appoint a person in every workplace who would be responsible for carrying Labour's message. TUFL's material, including 850,000 copies of 'Briefing to Win', was aimed at these contacts as well as a wider rank and file audience.

In practice, it was the provision of resources of manpower, transport and equipment which, as in the past, dominated the local effort. TUFL's own enquiries revealed later that in only 22 per cent of Target Seats was the mobilisation of trade unionists the main union priority.[37] A range of factors contributed to this focus. Local Constituency Party expectations reinforced union traditionalism. The exercise of mobilising trade unionists for a General Election was more difficult and more resisted on the shop floor than similar work in the Political Fund ballots. Unions were still not properly geared up for such a project. Further, although trade union political mobilisation techniques at the centre had improved considerably, conditions for political mobilisation at the grass roots had deteriorated in terms of access and feasibility under new work arrangements and enhanced employers' power.

The difficulties of place-of-work mobilisation were also complicated by the Party's national strategy. The focus of the latter was heavily oriented to national opinion formers and to the national mass media. In addition, the Party's choice of focus for the campaign did not involve a major emphasis on industrial or place-of-work issues such as low pay, rights, and health and safety – issues on which local and national trade union leaders felt most authoritative in communicating with the grass roots. Also, there was a campaign problem that, whilst the unions were seeking to point out to members the benefits of voting Labour, the Party was not anxious to stress its links with the unions – a management of 'distance' in the relationship which was by no means unprecedented but part of a range of difficulties in integrating the campaigns waged by the two wings.

These factors may have affected the level of support by trade unionists for the Labour Party, although they were likely to have been less significant than a range of other considerations which affected electoral behaviour at this time. In terms of TUFL's stated purposes, the result was as the NEC Report for 1987 described it – 'disappointing'.[38] Labour's vote among trade unionists rose by only 3 per cent to 42 per cent and among manual worker trade unionists by 5 per cent.[39] Among this latter group, from which Labour's affiliates are heavily drawn, the Party did regain the psychologically important level of 51 per cent support.

This, plus a pride in the Movement, stimulated by the skill and efficiency of Labour's campaign, encouraged the unions to sustain TUFL's role. There had been some fears in the tense pre-election period that, without Keys' protection, a combination of union factionalism, chauvinism and disappointment might lead to a crisis for this political organisation of unions. In practice, the life of TUFL was extended after the election and after Keys' full retirement.[40]

It continued to provide regular financial assistance to the Leader's Office, it was the forum in which elements of the Business Plan of 1988 were discussed in detail[41] - particularly affiliation fees and the new General Election Fund – and it provided an underwritten loan which enabled the Party's new National Membership system to be introduced. Extra resources available after the termination of assistance to the Front Bench were used to make a donation of £250,000 to the Labour Party's 1988 European election campaign. The TUFL organisation was also involved in the membership campaigns of 1989 and 1990 and in various local government and Parliamentary by-elections. It produced its own materials for trade unionists, explaining relevant elements of the new Party policy review. And, as a matter of course now, it was involved in establishing objectives and gearing up the unions towards preparation for the next General Election.

From TULV to TUFL had been a long and controversial road – a decade of trade union awakening to the need for a new form of political trade unionism. By 1987, that need had been recognised by a broad range of trade union forces and the basic prerequisite – a co-ordinating body – had been institutionalised to a degree which now made it a permanent fixture in the Labour Movement.

NOTES

1. Leopold, *op. cit.*, p. 294.
2. *Ibid.*, pp. 295–6.
3. *Ibid.*, pp. 291–3.
4. See n. 17.42.
5. For example, in 1959, a Gallup Poll asked trade unionists whether unions should be concerned with political matters 'like the H Bomb and foreign affairs'. 36 per cent said 'should', 55 per cent 'should not', *The Gallup International Public Opinion Polls – Great Britain 1937–1975*, 1976, entry for August 1959. David Butler and Donald Stokes found 60 per cent (1963) and 65 per cent (1964) of trade unionists believing that trade unions 'should stay out of politics', *Political Change in Britain*, 1969 edition, p. 11.
6. MORI for *Union World*, 27/2/85.
7. Alan Clarke, Permanent Under Secretary for Employment, cited the NALGO campaign as likely to fall within the new definition of 'political', *Hansard*, HC 12/7/83, Cols. 1307–8. Fatchett, op. cit., p. 27. See also the Government's restrictions on NALGO's 'party political' activities, Leopold, *op. cit.*, p. 290.
8. John Torode, 'Union Levy Poll Spells Disaster for Labour', *Guardian*, 2/3/85.
9. Butler and Stokes, *op. cit.*, second edition, 1964, p. 199.
10. Ivor Crewe, Bo Särlvik and James Alt, 'Partisan Dealignment in Britain 1964–1974', *British Journal of Political Science*, Vol. 7, 1977, Table 9, p. 155. Declining support for 'close ties' also occurred among 'core identifiers' – defined as those with a 'very' or 'fairly strong' Labour identification who belong to a trade union and have a manual occupation (or whose head of household does) – but no data were given for trade unionists as a distinct category.
11. Butler and Stokes, *op. cit.*, 1969 edition, p. 211. No data were provided on the attitudes of trade unionists to this question in the second edition, in 1974.

12. MORI, August 1977, for *Sunday Times*, reproduced in 'Class Geography and the Election', *New Statesman*, 6/4/79.

13. See, for example, Andrew Rowe (Director of Community Affairs at Conservative Central Office with responsibilities for the Conservative Trade Unionist Organisation), 'Conservatives and Trade Unionists', in Zig Layton-Henry, *Conservative Party Politics*, 1980, p. 224.

14. I have omitted one maverick post-Falklands poll done for the BBC by MORI in August 1982 which showed a huge 29 per cent 'don't knows'. The poll was not used. And I have omitted a Marplan poll in 1984 which asked different questions and secured answers which are difficult to compare with the past. In favour of a political fund, 40 per cent. Against 48 per cent. Among blue collar trade unionists the figures were 43:45, and among white collar trade unionists 34:53. Marplan/*Guardian*, 6/2/84.

15. Ivor Crewe's educated guestimate for Granada's 'Union World' of possible disaffiliations following the Political Fund ballot seems to have been based on Labour's electoral support in the opinion polls. Reported in *Labour Weekly*, 24/2/84.

16. Of the 35 per cent of trade unionists favouring 'being affiliated and giving money to the Labour Party' in January 1982, 74 per cent were 'hard core' Labour supporters. MORI for 'World in Action', 18/1/82.

17. MORI for *Sunday Times*, 31/8/80 (survey conducted Feb-July), and information supplied privately by MORI for 1980 and 1982.

18. Gallup Political Index, September 1983, pp. 14 and 18. The poll of trade unionists for 'A Week in Politics' was carried out in August 1983, *Daily Telegraph*, 9/9/83.

19. Peter Jenkins, 'Contracting Out of Reform', *Guardian*, 23/9/81.

20. Informal and formal discussions of my paper to the 1983 Essex Conference on Political Communications, 'Against the Tide', *op. cit.*, drew out these attitudes.

21. As noted in Steel, Miller and Gennard, *op. cit.*, p. 448.

22. Peter Riddell, 'Mrs. Thatcher's Second Term', *Contemporary Record*, Vol. I, No. 3, Autumn 1987, p. 18.

23. Between the first quarter of 1985 and the first quarter of 1986, support for the Conservative Party among trade unionists dropped from 27 to 20 per cent. At the 1983 General Election, it had been 31 per cent. Data supplied by MORI.

24. During the period covered by the 37 ballots, in the polls as a whole, the Labour lead over the Conservatives averaged only 3.2 per cent in a situation where there was a fairly even three-party split.

25. *New Statesman*, heading 28/3/86. In any case, whatever they were voting for, the percentage vote 'of trade unionists' was, strictly speaking, 42. 3 per cent.

26. Information supplied privately to the author. It should be noted again that *retaining* support was against the background of a gradual disadvantageous shift in the occupational and gender composition of trade unionists.

27. The Labour Party, *Promoting our values*, 1988, p. 5.

28. *Organising for Labour*, Working Group paper, 25/03/86.

29. *Ibid.*

30. In October 1987, for 'financial reasons', the Engineers (now the AEU) again withdrew, but this time discreetly, and an unofficial linkage continued at regional level.

31. *Constitution of Trade Unionists for Labour: Objectives.*
32. Steel, Miller and Gennard, *op. cit.*, pp. 462 and 464.
33. The role of TUFL in this election and the conflicts of strategy are explored in more detail in Lewis Minkin, 'Mobilisation and Distance: The Role of Trade Unions in the 1987 General Election Campaign', in Ivor Crewe and Martin Harrop (eds.), *Political Communications: The General Election Campaign of 1987*, 1989.
34. *TUFL Report*, July 1987, 'The General Election', p. 1.
35. *Ibid.*, 'General Election Questionnaire', p. 1.
36. *Ibid.*
37. *Ibid.*, p. 8.
38. *NEC Report*, 1987, p. 4.
39. MORI/*Sunday Times*, 13/6/1987.
40. By the end of 1989, it had three full time members of staff, with Jenny Pardington, since 1987, the National Coordinator.
41. TUFL and its 'political' officers' committee were also involved in consultations over other issues connected with Labour's organisational interface with the trade unions and in 1989 TUFL conducted an important survey as part of the campaign to increase the number of women on trade union sponsorship panels.

19

Trade unionism and the problem of Party Headquarters

THE MORASS

The problem

Though it was normally overlooked by those who studied the politics of the Labour Movement, there was an 'inside' as well as an 'outside' relationship of trade unions with the Labour Party. The Party's own employees at national office and in the regions were members of trade unions which negotiated for them. With the exception of the National Union of Labour Organisers (NULO), these unions were all affiliates of the TUC and, with the exception of the National Union of Journalists (NUJ), the others were also affiliates of the Party itself.

This 'inside' relationship between the Party and the unions provided a political and industrial dimension to the relationship which complicated all dealings over organisation and finance (and all simple models of power).

It was a dimension of the relationships within the Labour Movement of which the outside world was only dimly aware and as far as I know no political scholar has ever examined it. But the Party and the union leadership were conscious of it; indeed, union leaders during the crisis period from 1979 to 1982 were all too aware of it. Its complexity bedevilled all attempts from TULV to seek financial solvency and its pattern of interests appeared resistant to any comprehensive organisational reform.

The problem was especially acute in terms of responsibilities and obligations. Trade unions were both the outside providers of finance and the inside claimants for its use. They were, as members of the NEC, part of the management and yet, through the staff unions, they were representatives of labour. Negotiating these obligations was a delicate problem for the unions involved. It was even more so for the Party, which sought to enhance the efficiency of its organisation as a campaigning and mobilising force, while retaining commitment to industrial democracy and vigorous trade unionism. The reconciliation of these objectives and commitments would have provided acute difficulties at the best of times. But in an organisation with the history of, and in the condition of, the Labour Party headquarters in the late 1970s, it created a long-running crisis which was still not fully resolved a decade later.

The fact was that at the time of the 1979 General Election and the subsequent Commission of Enquiry into Party Organisation, Labour's national headquarters was in a deep-rooted and barely disguised mess. And the anxiety felt by union leaders over the state of Labour Party organisation and finances in the late 1970s was fed not only by their own experience of dealing with the National Executive Committee but by a stream of anecdotes and reports emanating from the union branches within the national headquarters. What the trade union branches had to say about the management of first the Labour Party section of Transport House and then, after 1980, Walworth Road, amounted to a devastating critique. Some of the flavour of this criticism is to be gained from the evidence submitted to the 1980 Commission of Enquiry into Party Organisation.

The Joint Trade Union Committee of Head Office unions wrote: '... the present structure prevents us doing our jobs as well as we could.' As for 'the numerous administrative problems':

> Suffice to say that many internal procedures require clarification, and that lack of clear lines of delegated authority and responsibility lead either to a paralysis of decision-making or to the handling of trivia at the highest levels.[1]

And the Heads of Department lamented their long concern about the weaknesses. 'We believe that at the heart of the administrative problems is the lack of a central focus for the pursuit of efficiency, for coordination and for general planning.'[2]

In private, much harsher words were said. There was poor management, there was inefficiency and there was a lack of coherent organisation. There were individuals in key positions who were notoriously incompetent, there were others who spent much of their time on political business outside the building. Morale was perpetually low. Hours were spent in time-wasting petty conflicts and bickering. Campaigning facilities were underdeveloped, services to members poor. The building was turned in on itself. It was a dreadful morass. Small wonder that union leaders, Left and Right, were alarmed at where a substantial part of their union funds was going.

In defence of the National Executive Committee (and there will be more to say about its responsibility later), it is important to note that no one NEC or one period of rule was the source of the problem. Indeed, the Party headquarters in the late 1970s faced such an accumulation of longstanding problems that discerning their distinct sources was almost as hard as suggesting solutions – although not as hard as getting the solutions implemented.

As far as is known, the Labour Party headquarters has never been the epitome of streamlined efficiency, even under the impressive management of Arthur Henderson. Beatrice Webb's diaries for 1918 refer to a 'ramshackle institution' with 'inferior' and 'decrepit' staff.[3] And though Agnes Hamilton wrote glowingly in the late 1930s of 'an instrument shrewdly adapted to its purpose' and of 'a staff of highly efficient men and women',[4] impressionistic evidence of these years from veterans of the period suggests, as one ex-staff member put it, 'an amiable shambles'.

Under the economic pressure of falling trade union income, a measure of internal departmental reorganisation took place in 1933 (alongside a cut in salaries and wages and a reduction of staff[5]) but it does not appear to have been very successful. An attempt in the late 1930s by Reg Underhill (now Lord Underhill) to seek another reorganisation through the Staff Association (of which he was Secretary) foundered in the face of inertia and was postponed indefinitely because of the outbreak of war.[6] In the period following the great victory of 1945, and during the early years of Morgan Phillips' Secretaryship, Transport House had a high reputation,[7] but by the mid-1950s, the headquarters was again being castigated for its 'low managerial efficiency'.[8] Although under Len Williams there was a greater formal emphasis on administration, the Office remained fundamentally unreformed and heavily criticised.[9]

It was significant that the *Plan for an Efficient Party* which led to the Simpson Committee, 1966–8, came initially from the proposals of dissatisfied staff in headquarters.[10] It was equally significant that there was deep resistance from sections of Head Office management and the NEC to the establishment of a Commission of Enquiry,[11] and it was further significant that the Simpson Reports of 1967 and 1968 should step gingerly around the basic problems of the organisation of the national office.[12]

In 1971, in response to new pressure from the staff and in appreciation of the problems now accumulating in the building, the NEC did commission an Organisation and Methods report by outside consultants. But its major recommendations were not put into operation and the Party fought the elections of 1974 with, as Donoughue later described it, 'a central organisation of almost unbelievable inefficiency'.[13]

Thus, by the mid-1970s, Labour Party headquarters was structured much as it had been since the 1920s. This would not have mattered greatly had there been forces to generate dynamism within the old shell. Such dynamic elements did exist – particularly among the younger staff – but they operated within a power structure which appeared unresponsive to reforming pressure, and within a culture which engendered alienation, conflict and deep-rooted grievance, all features that the Party, in principle, was dedicated to eradicate within the wider society!

Head Office trade unionism

The longstanding problems in Head Office underwent a serious change of form in the late 1970s as the frustrations of the staff led to the birth of a new and aggressively militant trade unionism. Almost parallel to the moves in industry and politics, which led ultimately to the 'winter of discontent' of 1978–9, were similar developments in Transport House where the accumulation of grievances and the emergence of new political forces led to an equally passionate revolt.

The revolt was focused upon levels of pay, upon differentials and upon salary comparisons with other labour organisations. But this resentment was enlarged by, accompanied by, and in some ways legitimised by, a much deeper reaction – against the chaos of Head Office management and the failure of attempts to secure administrative reform. The 1971 report did result in some minor changes but its suggested restructuring into three new directorates (covering Finance and Administration, Research with Press and Publicity, and the National Agents' Department) and its recommendations of reallocations and changes in procedure, were left on the drawing board.

Opposition to the 1971 reform proposals produced a reinforcing series of obstacles which were to become very familiar in the next fourteen years. There was resistance from everybody in the building who had something to lose from the changes. There was a lack of driving interest from the NEC in pushing for the implementation of the report. And there were good practical reasons from the General Secretary why 'in present circumstances' the changes should be postponed – in this case, an impending General Election and a projected move of the Head Office.[14]

In reality, the General Secretary of the time, Ron Hayward, was not impressed by the report and believed that the answer to the problems lay in creating new middle rank deputy heads of department,[15] and in a management style which emphasised departmental autonomy and the importance of regular meetings of Heads of Department. But this style of overall management tended to accentuate the development of baronial fiefdoms, without any improvement in co-ordination and efficiency, and in any case, while Hayward's changes were being implemented, the staff was moving into a classic dispute over pay.

This pay revolt had been a long time coming. It was widely recognised, and had been for years, that Labour Party staff were poorly paid. A major study in 1974 had pointed to the tendency of trade unions and the Party to hoard political finance while the Party paid its 'relatively small staff' ... much less than they might command elsewhere for comparable work'.[16] An ethos of service to the Party meant that the staff themselves had not claimed great material rewards but there were limits to tolerance, and in the early 1970s, these limits were indicated by a new assertiveness from Head Office union branches.

Historically, there had been only a restricted trade unionism in Labour Party headquarters, although by the 1960s many unions were represented. The main staff branch was APEX. Some in the National Agents' Department (like the regional organising staff) were in NULO. There were male and female branches of the print union SOGAT and there was a branch of the TGWU covering mainly manual workers. In addition, the NUJ had a branch covering journalists. But, in practice, negotiations within the building were carried on through a Staff Council – a generally accommodating and non-confrontational forum which met regularly with the NEC's Staff Board (from 1969 the Staff Negotiations Committee).

All this began to change slowly in the 1970s. A new generation of articulate and higher educated white collar staff came into the building. Heavily influenced by the wider climate of industrial militancy, by syndicalist theory and by the Campaign for Labour Party Democracy, they began to push more aggressively for reform of Head Office and for the rectification of their grievances over pay. Making little headway in either direction, they induced and themselves underwent a transformation in industrial relations attitudes. The ethos of 'service to the Party' began to be overlaid by other sentiments. There was new talk of 'exploitation' and there was a growing contempt for the old 'sweetheart unionism'. Suddenly, many of the characteristics of the British industrial relations crisis appeared within the Labour Party itself.

In particular, the growth of the NUJ Chapel brought with it a Fleet Street style of unionism (or at least an aspiration in that direction). As early as 1970, before the advent of *Labour Weekly* strengthened their numbers, the NUJ members were pushing for a 21–42 per cent increase in pay and relating it to Fleet Street national daily scales rather than the scales of magazine branches.[17] They were rebuffed then, and in 1971, and had to accept much less – an experience which reinforced their militancy. With their own distinctive agreement and terms of service, NUJ members were always 'one step ahead' in their demands on management in terms of conditions and provisions. As such, they became both early pace setters in the building and guardians of what was regarded as proper trade union principle, practice and procedure.

But it was 1976 which was the watershed year, with changes in personnel which affected the management, trade unionism and internal politics of head-quarters. That year, Bert Williams, the long-serving Administrative Officer, retired. In the lead-up to the appointment of a replacement, there was a determined push from the Heads of Department for a review of the work-load involved in the post. Because of the broadening of Head Office responsibilities and the increasing political as well as administrative role of the General Secretary, there was felt to be a need for the appointment of a high level Director of Administration with the Administrative Officer carrying out only part of the functions.

But the representations from the Heads were resisted by the General Secretary, Ron Hayward, and unsupported by the NEC. Thus, the new officer, Roger Robinson, was given the redesignated post of Administrative and Personnel Officer – a task which was considered by other Heads of Department to be now almost impossible for one person to carry out.

There were other appointments that year. Nick Seigler became a member of a Research Department which was moving sharply to the Left. He also became a militant new Chairman of the rapidly expanding TGWU branch. In 1976 also, Barrie Clarke, the Youth Officer, was promoted to the post of Political Education Officer. He was both a NULO member and the Rightwing Chairman of the APEX branch.

It was perhaps indicative of Leftwing priorities that Clarke's appointment by a Left-dominated NEC to a potentially crucial post in a Leftward-moving Party went virtually unnoticed on the Left. But then again, there were some curious political oversights to appointments in this period. The appointment of the Youth Officer on 20 September 1976 was made by a badly attended selection meeting at which there was no Left-wing majority. Yet the NEC members present (three of them, with one in the Chair) appointed Andy Bevan, a supporter of the Trotskyist Militant Tendency. When light dawned, there was an outcry over an appointment which was likely to (and did) facilitate Trotskyist control over Labour's youth organisation.

Ironically, the political row was defused on typically trade union terms. The organisers' union, NULO, was angry that the post had not gone to one of their members. In the ensuing negotiations, the political dimensions were used as a trade union lever. NULO accepted Bevan into dual membership (he was already a member of the T and G) but won from the NEC the written confirmation of a past understanding – an agreement which, in practice, virtually guaranteed all future organising jobs, including Head Office senior administrative posts in the National Agents Department, to this very small and declining union.[18]

NULO's success in these negotiations was based on shrewd timing plus accommodating senior officers who were all 'NULO people'. It curbed for the moment the political argument over Bevan but it did so by leaving the Party with a growing political problem and by fanning further the fires of the new unionism. The view grew that if a minuscule union like NULO could exercise such muscle, why could not other staff members do the same – particularly as the NEC continued to show its Leftward shift?

The interesting twist in the saga of Head Office was that NULO's successful leverage appears to have accentuated also the development of trade unionism among the Heads of Departments. Up to 1969 there was not even a procedure for collective consultation with these Heads over their salaries: they tended to get (and be thankful for) what they were given. But in the mid-1970s, all this changed. In 1976, they began a protracted dispute over the compression of their differentials and demanded parity with the TUC (by 1979, the dispute had even been pushed as far as ACAS). Meanwhile, they were forming themselves into a union organisation and in 1977 made an arrangement for a TGWU national official to negotiate for them. In 1979, they reactivated a Heads of Department Trade Union Group and gave themselves new Standing Orders. Thus, 'Heads' trade union meetings joined the growing calendar of meetings and negotiating bodies and the Heads of Department themselves became increasingly subject to that role crisis of 'management or labour?' which was a characteristic of Head Office politics.

While this was going on, the increasingly frustrated and militant members of staff were focusing their resentment on what they regarded as the ineffectual management of the APEX branch and particularly the Chairman, Clarke (who was also increasingly out of tune with the Leftwing ethos of the building). A shift of members began from APEX to the TGWU branch which at that time covered not only Labour Party but also the Transport Workers' own headquarters' staff. As the branch grew in number and assertiveness, so they pressed their union for the status of a separate branch. This was achieved in 1979 and new branch 1/975 was formally established in January 1980. Its formation encouraged a further trickle of members from the APEX branch.

The new overlapping and active multi-unionism required a new mechanism of co-ordination and negotiation and the staff now looked askance at the old Staff Council. In November 1978, a new Joint Trade Union Committee was set up. It was indicative of the neo-syndicalism of the staff unions at this time that in 1980 the body was specifically charged with the constitutional purpose of extending joint staff-management control over executive and administrative questions. As far as they were concerned, all they were doing was applying the policy of the 1976 Party Programme, namely that workers must 'at all levels have a decisive voice in the decisionmaking'.[19]

However, no sooner had the unified trade union representative structure been established than it became locked in an internal dispute over representation. As the TGWU branch was now far bigger than APEX, APEX wanted a system of one union one vote, while the TGWU insisted on representation by numbers – which effectively meant their domination. APEX sought to increase its representation on the grounds that a majority of the Regional staff were its members. This was unacceptable to other Head Office unions and in March 1980, APEX – whose AGM tactics were labelled 'disruptive' by the others – was expelled from the JTUC.

The deadlock eventually led, in February 1981, to national officials of the various unions being called in and they adjudicated over a new constitution for the JTUC. But when it was put to the staff in September 1981, they rejected it. The NUJ branch now also left the JTUC and not until 1985 was the constitution agreed and APEX allowed back in. The NUJ, APEX and the TGWU continued their dispute about representation on the JTUC. The JTUC met only to agree a common negotiating position on some matters which affected the whole staff, while the individual unions also represented their own members to management.

The grievances, conflicts and resentments generated in this period lived on for years later. Militant trade unionism became part of the politics and bloodstream of Labour Party headquarters, further complicating a complex set of relationships and accentuating the range of checks, obstacles and veto points within the building. There was a post-entry closed shop and a remarkably high percentage of the 100-plus headquarters' staff were involved in trade union activity and nego- tiations. Rules and customs were firmly established. Invisible trenches were dug. 'Management' became 'the enemy' almost as though they were the Welsh coal owners of the 1920s, and even though in this period the NEC shared the same Leftwing perspectives as many of the union activists – indeed, were, at crucial points, sympathetic and encouraging to union demands.

Resentment at various past actions, longstanding grievances over pay, aliena- tion caused by the mismanagement or non-management of Head Office, conflicts over representation and dissatisfaction with past trade union achievements pro- duced a classic cumulation of industrial relations disorders. As Phelps Brown has noted, such disorders,

> [s]tarted in the wrong direction … can generate ever new conflicts out of the bitter memories of past ones. Each friendly act is suspect as a trap, each unfriendly one is vital to self defence; and all because that is how it was yesterday.'[20]

Trade unions and management became locked in a damaging dynamic from which they found it almost impossible to escape. Peering above the battlements, some on each side could see possible joint ways forward; locked in their respective roles they could do little about it.

Between 1979 and 1981, militant trade unionism was at its peak – and very successful. In 1979, the Heads of Department Trade Union Group won its comparability with the TUC, albeit with a phased implementation. Pay settle- ments of 28 and 20 per cent were conceded to the staff unions in 1979 and 1980, although only after a protracted conflict which involved industrial action, picket lines and the whole penumbra of industrial disputes. In 1981, the rest of the staff also won comparability with TUC officers who were, until 1980, part of the same TGWU 1/128 branch.

Thus, at a time when union leaders, organised through TULV, were pressing for major economies (Chapter 16), the unions within the Party Office (some of them branches of the same unions as in TULV) were winning their biggest ever pay settlements thus adding to the financial problems. They had done so with a formal agreement to examine future staffing but, in practice, by determined opposition to any suggestion of redundancy, voluntary or otherwise. And they had done so without making any major concessions on the redeployment which the management initially sought to attach to the settlements.

There is no doubt that, over this period, the staff unions secured a series of historically deserved victories in a badly underpaid organisation. But from this point on, the question of the level of Head Office staffing and of the capability of Head Office administration became more of an issue, particularly as, after 1981, the composition of the NEC began to shift away from the Left. From a TULV perspective, it was simply a question of general sensitivity to costs; giving the staff whatever they wanted appeared part of a wider NEC carelessness about who would pay for it – that is, the affiliated unions. But there was also a subtext to this TULV anxiety and one that was to grow in importance throughout the 1980s. How was the Party to deal with those members of headquarters whose incompetence resulted in an inefficient Party organisation on the one hand and the squandering of finance on the other?

This latter problem was a source of anger not only to those raising the finance but to many in the Head Office itself where the existence of incompetence was a source of considerable frustration. The very low salaries paid up to the mid-1970s had resulted in a recruitment which was sometimes not of a high calibre. The appointments system was not very well developed (one of many failures of personnel management) and produced a wide range of abilities – complicated by the tendency for individuals to be 'dumped' at Head Office from other labour movement bodies. Within the headquarters in the late 1970s, across the spectrum of departments, there could be found a wide range of talents and many staff of outstanding ability. But extra energy, commitment and personal achievement were not obviously rewarded and the atmosphere was such as to encourage some of the able to move off, leaving others to block or climb the promotional ladder. Among organisational staff, the NULO agreement affected the range of talent which could be drawn upon for regional positions and for posts within the National Agents' Department, and it appeared to affect the quality of ancillary staff also.

Privately, many union members, including some of the most militant, accepted, and in some cases positively favoured, the weeding out of incompetent staff – particularly as they located several of them in senior positions. When, unusually, at one point, one of the most obvious management problems was given a substantial Golden Handshake, the internal unions simply went through the motions of defending his interest, asking privately – why redundancy, why not just sack him?

Indeed, their case was that the management was weak and incompetent itself in dealing with elementary personnel functions of training and discipline. There were standard disciplinary procedures (applying to Head Office staff but not members of NULO) which somehow the management seemed incapable of utilising. Some people interpreted this weakness as an inhibition built upon a folklore that nobody could be dismissed in the Labour Party. Some recalled an early Industrial Tribunal case which gave the Party adverse publicity. Others saw the problem as a fault of individual department heads and the Administrative and Personnel Officer, who had to be involved in every disciplinary action. Whatever the explanation, though the occasional strikingly bad cases did result in dismissal, stories abounded within the building of examples of gross incompetence and negligence and the inability or unwillingness of management to deal with them.

The Heads of Department and the Staff Negotiations Committee of the NEC tended to blame each other for problems of control. For example, on 26 November 1979, the Staff Negotiations Committee called upon the Heads to deal with the problem of persistent flexi-time unpunctuality. The Heads countered by noting the failure of the Committee to exercise its role as an employer in supporting the Heads in the exercise of discipline.

It was to the credit of the staff union branches that they, more than anybody else in this crisis period, did try to see the wood rather than the trees and did try to seek some constructive overall solution to the quagmire in which they were trapped. This was the hope of Head Office as well as its tragedy.

Head Office staff, in the period after 1979, were the source of several major initiatives aimed at a reorganisation of the Party and its Head Office and were in the vanguard of efforts to turn the Party into a campaigning force. It was from the staff and the Heads of Department in 1979 and 1980 that the initiative was taken which developed into the Office Campaigns Committee. (The Leftwing NEC was pushed into establishing a Campaign Committee to co-ordinate campaigning at their level but 'through lack of interest' the committee ceased meeting.[21]) It was from the JTUC in 1980 that there came one of the most comprehensive and detailed representations to the Commission of Enquiry proposing a variety of organisational reforms. And the unions in the building themselves originated the call for a joint study of the problems of Head Office.

The union branches pressed constantly for a restructuring and reorganisation of Head Office and kept up a running critique of management proposals which failed to embrace a wider perspective. To anybody who would listen (including the author), they pressed their case for root and branch changes. If reminded of the negativism of much of the unions' responses within the building, they lamented the sectional defensive role they were being forced to play and the inflexible industrial tactics that they believed they were being forced into in order to defend their interests.

Chicken and egg, cause and effect, were hard to disentangle here. Certainly the defensive and negative atmosphere fed on itself, creating a union alienation and confrontation reminiscent of the world evoked by Huw Beynon in *Working for Ford*.[22] New members of staff, aghast at the atmosphere, were quickly socialised into the norms, reminded of past concessions, warned against paying the costs of '*their*' mistakes. 'History', as one militant Leftwing NUJ member reminded the author in 1986, 'gets into your blood.'

As individual members of staff or trade unionists sat back discussing the

general interest of the Party Office, many of them could see the overall problem
and the potential overall solutions. But, in as much as they were organised for
defence through the unions, they were increasingly powerful in asserting themselves against management initiatives.

The defensiveness extended to incompetent members of staff who were
threatened with disciplinary action. Capable union negotiators often ran rings
round a hesitant and badly prepared management. Thus, means were usually
found of saving the problem case – sometimes with a heavy heart but also with a
belief that this was 'principled trade unionism'. Where the collective staff interest was at stake, the response was even more defensive. In the financial crisis of
1979, the Party Treasurer, Norman Atkinson, had publicly stated that the NEC
would seek natural wastage solutions and inter-departmental flexibility. In practice, the unions, while always claiming their willingness to be constructive and
flexible, made few concessions and fought their corner with unremitting zeal.
Redeployment took months to negotiate, natural wastage left important posts
unfilled, vacancies were uncovered by colleagues.

Thus, there emerged an extraordinary paradox over Head Office trade unionism and the Party. Union leaders outside the headquarters demanded reorganisation and better management. Unions both inside and outside the Party office
were overwhelmingly in favour of Head Office reorganisation. The most constructive and progressive forces in this respect were the Head Office union
branches. Yet they found themselves constantly in a defensive and reactive role
against particular management initiatives – particularly those concerned with
redeployment. Trade union leaders were also blocked in their efforts to produce a
comprehensive reform and, in unions with members in the building, found
themselves playing an ambiguous role in support of trade union practices within
the building.

These practices involved a panoply of trade union protective devices as the
frustrated, insecure and newly militant Head Office unions resorted to rules and
behaviour which itself became an impediment to the smooth running of the
administration. There was opposition to 'freelancers' and 'volunteers', and suspicion of 'part-timers' and 'trainees'. And although the occasional blind eye was
turned, fear that management would use this as a means of reducing jobs soon
brought the issue to the surface. Union veto power, particularly over the employment of temporary staff,[23] brought forth a multitude of practical problems. The
system was slow to deal with sudden pressures and even when it did adjust, it
moved with agonising slowness. As the Administrative Officer lamented in 1983,
when there was an unsuccessful attempt to renegotiate the Memorandum of
Agreement over the employment of temporary staff, 'Often agreement from the
JTUC takes considerable time to be received; days can pass or even hours [sic]
when a crisis demands instant action to take on staff; there are inevitable
wrangles and a diminution of morale; work is delayed'.[24]

Industrial action and threats of industrial action were part and parcel of the
whole process. 'Blacking' was a frequent practice. Action was taken sometimes in
angry disputes with small regard for the Party's immediate needs. By-election and
General Election preparations were complicated by industrial relations problems.

The management problem

Running Labour Party headquarters in these circumstances involved not so much managing as staggering from one crisis to another. A fundamental problem was that in a sense 'management' lacked any clear focus because there were two 'managements'. The person responsible for the 'in house' administration of Head Office was the General Secretary and with him the Heads of Department. These, in a sense, were 'Management'. But there was also the elected NEC which had ultimate responsibility. Between these two supervisory elements was a complex interaction which was debilitating to the operation of Head Office.

With some exceptions, for much of the time the NEC gave a low priority to the general problems of administering the Party. As criticism of Walworth Road mounted in the 1980s, there was some belated additional involvement. But generally, the preoccupation of NEC members was with policy, with the constitutional crisis, and with the struggle for power in the Party. Sorting out the legacy of organisational decay was not their main priority and it was easy to turn a blind eye to the administrative inadequacies until they burst out into crisis. There were some members of the NEC to whom I spoke in the early 1980s who had only the faintest glimmer of an understanding of the depth of the problem under their noses.

The desire to leave well alone had some justification in that previous General Secretaries had objected to the NEC 'interfering' in their managerial responsibilities. But, fundamentally, as the Joint Study of 1982 was to concede, members of the NEC were not elected primarily for their administrative skill, and the 'dull, colourless chores' that administration entailed did not evoke the same interest as the exciting political issues.[25]

But, whereas there was little sustained interest in the administration of the Office, individual NEC members found themselves caught up in specific problems on an *ad hoc* basis. In particular, they were drawn in by individual relationships with members of staff, many of whom attempted to cultivate a Godfather or Godmother relationship in order to gain leverage and ensure protection. Because the most regular contacts were established at senior levels of the bureaucracy, it was the senior staff who had the best protectors – a feature which enraged those lower down the hierarchy who saw insulated incompetence above them. And it profoundly irritated some of the union leaders in TULV because inherently it worked against their attempts to force rationalisation, reorganisation and economy.

NEC Trade Union Section members had an additional problem. The decisions made could be compared with, and created potential precedents for, the operation of the unions in their outside industrial environment. Hence, individually and sometimes collectively, the NEC trade unionists tended to be pulled in whenever the issue touched on trade union sensitivities over, for example, redeployment or disciplinary procedures.

Problems of special pleading appear to have become more acute in 1979 after the Staff Negotiations Committee underwent a change in composition, bringing on the Chairs of all other committees. Thus, a body which was normally dominated by a small group of Trade Union Section members was suddenly expanded by an infusion of CLP Section members and given a clear Leftwing majority.[26] Via the Left on the NEC, as well as the union branches, there was then an accentuation of the pressure upon NEC trade unionists to abide by 'trade union principles' and the Staff Negotiations Committee became an appeal body which could, and many times did, override the decisions of the General Secretary and the office management.

NEC members – particularly NEC trade unionists – became increasingly involved in a deep ambiguity about the role that they were playing. They had been elected to be 'the administrative authority' of the Party with a wide range of organisational and financial duties. Yet there was little clarity about the extent to which this management role should be regulated by their trade unionism. In the event of any dispute, were they simply 'Management'? Were they, on the other hand, 'trade unionists' offering solidarity to the employees? Or were they, like ACAS, seeking to aid a negotiated settlement?[27] From one perspective they had a democratic responsibility to the Party to act purely as management – and most of them accepted it. But some felt uncertain about the propriety of separating this from 'trade union principles' and put in a certain way, the accusation of 'behaving like Management' was enough to produce apoplectic fury. Even with those who accepted fully the responsibility of management, the contravention of the trade union practices which they supported in other spheres caused some sense of guilt – enough for the staff union representatives to play upon and enough for there to be uncertainties, oscillations, inconsistencies and frequent retreats.

It was not surprising therefore that everything that the management attempted in Walworth Road took an inordinate amount of time. There were four (and after 1984 five) levels of negotiation. There were endless informal meetings to sort out difficulties. There were protracted inter-departmental disagreements. Getting a 'management' team together for negotiations through the Staff Negotiations Committee was often difficult and led to long delays. And, in the end, it was never certain to the administrative management that their proposals or actions would be upheld by the NEC. The result was a debilitating *immobilism* broken through by sporadic management action which, in as much as it sometimes contravened agreed procedure, further enhanced the general sense of grievance.

These grievances fed on the day-by-day experience of living under Walworth Road conditions. With some narrow departmental exceptions – particularly in the Research Department – there was little personal encouragement for the staff and little sense of collective involvement. In the building as a whole there was little on-the-job training and little attempt at career development. The feeling of alienation was so patent that it struck any friendly visitor who made enquiries. The more the financial stringency, the greater the insecurity. The bigger the problems, the more acute became the sense of distance.

The tragic irony of all this was not lost on those members of the research staff concerned with the preparation of documents on *Economic Planning and Industrial Democracy* . Here were two democracies – an elected NEC and elected trade union representatives involved in what ought to have been a productive partnership towards agreed goals. Instead, there was bitter trench warfare, coupled with a poor service to the Party members and its supporters.

Nobody seemed capable of putting together a programme of efficient management and effective involvement. Worse, no individual or group was able to take the fundamental initiative that would break through the impasse. No coalition of forces was available to supply sustained support for organisational change. As for the union leaders – the mythological 'barons' who apparently controlled all this – they were virtually powerless spectators.

Factionalism and the role of the NEC

And yet in the late 1970s up to 1981, and to some extent 1982, the NEC was under the control of a Leftwing majority which in its reforming zeal appeared to be ready to consider almost any constitutional and organisational change. It might have been expected that the NEC would in this period produce a dynamic response to the calls being made from the Head Office union branches. The precedents were there. In 1966, Tony Benn, with Ian Mikardo, had challenged the then Rightwing majority on the NEC for their failure to respond to the *Plan for an Efficient Party*.[28] He had a record of active sympathy for the predicament of the Party staff.[29] He and Eric Heffer (Chair of the Organisation Sub-Committee 1978 to 1982) were committed to enhancing workers' control. And Benn particularly was an innovative as well as an inspirational figure. Here was the opportunity to put ideals into practice, to integrate the traditions of trade union militancy and of industrial democracy in a reconstruction which both enhanced the rewards to the producers, and improved the Party's management and its services to the members in the branches.

But Benn and most of the Left on the NEC were not only preoccupied with other matters, they were obsessed with a factional defensiveness such that their attitude towards Head Office reform varied from the ultra-cautious to the deeply hostile. As we have noted before (Chapter 16), the problem was that attacks on the Head Office organisation from 1977 to 1981 were coming from the most suspect of sources. And they were being combined with attacks on the Research Department. It was said that the Research Department was receiving finance which ought to go on Party organisation, that the Research Department was staffed with the wrong kind of people, 'would-be MPs' and 'philosophers'. It all came down to 'too much policy' coming from Party headquarters – and you did not need to be a philosopher to interpret this as a covert attack on the NEC's independent policy role by Rightwing sections of the PLP.[30]

In defending their position, the Left had the most powerful of cases for rebutting such arguments. To begin with, these complaints appeared very thin when contrasted with years of complaint that the Research Department was *under*staffed – a complaint which in the years when the Right controlled the NEC often came from the Right as well as the Left.[31] Very little change had taken place in the staffing of the Research and International Departments since the early 1970s,[32] and by 1980, it was still small when measured against comparable organisations.[33]

The tragedy was that the patent factional self-interest and mischief of the critics gave the NEC Left an easy ideological justification for a stonewalling and conservatism which was extended to much of the field of Party organisation. Every suggestion for deep-rooted reform was viewed in terms of maneouvres by 'the Right', 'the Parliamentary leadership' and 'the union leaders' to change the balance of power in the Party. Thus, little concession was made to critics of the national organisation.

This, too, added to the irritation of the union leadership who knew all too well what a mess it was. The TULV union leaders were determined that something must be done and if possible done through the 1980 Commission of Enquiry. That the internal administration of Party headquarters was part of the deliberations of the Commission at all was a break with precedent. Neither the Wilson nor the Simpson reports had dared to venture far into this territory. But union leaders, anxious for value for members' money, and assailed by evidence from the Head Office unions which could not be ignored, became increasingly concerned that a major reform should take place. The Organisation and Membership Panel discussed the Head Office department by department. Only the scale of the problem and the demands for full staff consultation persuaded them not to recommend a list of immediate changes. Instead, they went for the option which the staff union branches had proposed – a joint enquiry of Party management, Head Office unions and outside advisers. The Joint Study was paid for by TULV, who also had their own observer present.[34]

There was initially a distinct, but unsurprising, dragging of feet and not until January 1982 did the Joint Study Group have its first meeting. But eventually its report in June 1982 proved to be remarkably honest in its appraisal and criticism of the 'structural defects and gaps' in Head Office organisation. There was, it said, no continuing supervision by the NEC of the Party's administration – no effective matching of activities with the money and manpower available – no effective forward planning – gaps in coordination – an inadequate Finance Department – and a personnel function that did not work well.[35]

The investigation was constrained by the limited time available and the form of the enquiry. There was no plan of overall restructuring and no full organisation and method study: the committee recommended that the NEC consider commissioning such a study. And there was some criticism that the report failed to come up with clear lines of authority and decision-making for the Party's overall propaganda effort.[36] Nevertheless, jointly agreed delineation of the problem was itself an advance and there were various recommendations for improvement. In particular, there was the emphasis on the Party's campaigning work that Head Office staff had been looking for. In dealing with the acute administrative weakness, the Joint Study laid considerable stress, as had the 1971 o and m study, on appointing a new Director of Finance and Administration who would be of sufficient stature to have authority over the staff and the attentive hearing of the NEC.

Although this appointment was made the centre-piece of organisational reform, it was also clear that much was expected from the new General Secretary, Jim Mortimer, in implementing the Joint Study reforms, carrying out a broader restructuring of the Office and introducing a new 'participative and consultative style'. 'His career history', said the Joint Study, suggested that Jim Mortimer would be eminently qualified to carry through this operation.[37]

Mortimer's proposals on the recommendations of the Joint Study did involve acceptance and activation of some of the specific points made in the report but within the existing structure, without the appointment of the recommended senior officer and without the initiation of an organisation and methods study.[38] Restructuring faded into the background, as, within a few months of taking office, Mortimer was completely preoccupied with a financial crisis of such an extremity that at one stage it was thought that the Party's cheques would bounce as it neared its overdraft limit. There was an anticipated annual overdraft of nearly £800,000 and an accumulated deficit of £547,000. More than £400,000 was owed to the staff in arrears of pay and there were no liquid reserves. The Party's bank demanded immediate action.

Redundancy being out of the question at this time, there was a series of emergency moves backed by a newly-composed Staff Negotiations Committee dominated once again by the Trade Union Section.[39] These included a pay freeze, the deferment of capital expenditure, 'natural wastage' cuts in staffing, leaving vacant posts unfilled, and an agreement from the Head of Department to forgo immediate payment of comparability arrears. The overdraft was held within its £500,000 limit.

Even so, and making all allowances for the pressures, it is doubtful whether Jim Mortimer would have been the source of a major reorganisation. As he told *Tribune* later, 'I was clear … when I was appointed General Secretary where my efforts and attention had primarily to be directed. It was towards the finances of the Party'.[40] Reorganisation he regarded from his previous experience as a problematic exercise, as likely to go wrong as to put things right. And it was, in any case, likely to be thwarted by the hydra-headed character of Labour's national power structure.

The staff unions thought differently. At one stage in July 1982 there emerged 'A Workers' Plan for Head Office' in an attempt to produce a major restructuring. It castigated 'years of mismanagement at Head Office, which has alienated the support of our trade union backers' and urged a broader debate within the Party on the problems of the Party's organisation and administration.[41] But as the Party moved closer to a General Election, it was clear that there would be no Party debate and no major restructuring. The dissatisfaction and frustration would remain.

Thus, the Party organisation and Head Office went into the 1983 campaign with some major and longstanding organisational handicaps, apart from the contingent disadvantage that none of the new senior officers had fought a General Election before. One short campaign could not itself make up for years of organisational and campaigning neglect. Preparations for the General Election were delayed by a multitude of political and organisational difficulties. The structural form of Head Office during the campaign was much as it had been for decades. The responsibilities and role of the proposed Director of Finance and Administration had been contested in the building and no appointment had been made. Co-ordination was very poor. There was much uncertainty about who was doing what and some mind-blowing examples of incompetence. Communications and the handling of the media were particularly ineffective.

Above all, it was still an organisation at war with itself. Industrial relations tensions (over temporary staff and 'volunteers') continued during the campaign, the union branches were bitter and alienated, morale was low and degenerated further as the Party campaign floundered. During and after the campaign, the organisation of Head Office became a byword for inefficiency among those whose work brought them in contact with the building. By contrast, the Conservative Party campaign and the Conservative Party organisation seemed to be in a super league.

THE SOLUTIONS

The campaign for reorganisation

The scale and style of Labour's defeat in 1983 produced reverberations which were still being felt seven years later. Not the least important was the stimulation of a sudden wide concern over Labour's national organisation. This concern was to lead within two years to the first major reorganisation of Labour's Head Office since the inter-war years. In the summer of 1987, in the wake of a second restructuring, the Labour Party was to fight an election in which its communication and organisation was acclaimed as superior to all its rivals. And in late 1987 there was a third phase of reorganisation which provoked a major crisis with Head Office trade unionism before its intensive 'surgery' was completed.

That the election result of 1983 would stimulate these changes was not immediately apparent in June 1983. Most observers would have accepted the view of Jim Mortimer that 'the cause of Labour's defeat ... was primarily political and not organisational'[42] and, of course, they were right. But that was not to say that the scale of the defeat was unaffected by it, nor that skilful organisation and communication techniques could not generate its own *élan* (as was to be shown in 1987). Further, the success of the Conservatives and the Alliance in handling the mass media made it essential for the Party to play the same game, at least as well, if not better. Above all, the Party's activists and its supporters deserved something better than the shambles of 1983.

Yet where was the impetus for change to come from? The combined weight of the union leadership in TULV and the branches of unions in Head Office had so far failed to secure a major reorganisation. So much for union power. Securing a radical initiative and creating a coalition of forces to sustain it seemed as far away as ever.

But, as it happened, the General Election had alerted a new audience of people in the Party to the national organisational problems. That the Party's headquarters and its regional 'outposts' were not up to the task became a widely held view in the constituencies at this time, not necessarily because they knew much of what was going on in these offices but because what was seen of their contribution to the election campaign appeared to be so inept and uncoordinated. A few who ventured into Walworth Road after the General Election or received word from its staff were assailed with 'horror stories' of its inadequacy.[43]

Out of these forces suddenly came 'a constituency' of people alert to the need for Head Office and Party organisational reform and anxious to push for it. The Labour Coordinating Committee took up the issue. Numerous resolutions on the 1983 Annual Conference agenda reflected this growing concern.

Crucially, the major contender for the Party Leadership himself took up the matter. In a speech at Stoke on 12 September 1983, he broke precedent and ventured where no senior Party figure had ever trod before, placing himself at the head of a public campaign for organisational reform which included the restructuring of Party headquarters. It was a bold speech whose ten points covered many sensitive areas[44] and was linked to the complaints emerging in many of the Conference resolutions.

Within weeks of his election, some of the ten points were acted upon. In particular, the policy process was reorganised to create a joint machinery (see Chapter 10, pp. 400–01) and a new Campaign Strategy Committee was created. An Appeals and Mediation Committee took some of the pressure from the Organisational subcommittee thus allowing it to spend more time on priorities.

And yet still there was no swift reconstruction of the headquarters. Some internal innovations did take place including the appointment, for the first time, of a Sales and Marketing Officer and a Fundraising Officer. And there was a period of procedural innovation as Mortimer sought to improve the industrial relations atmosphere. A Joint Negotiating Committee was instituted and the Staff Liaison Committee was reconstituted to discuss day-to-day matters. There was a new Negotiation Procedure Agreement in 1984 and a new Disciplinary Procedure Agreement in 1985. But still this failed to stem the grievances of the staff or the demands for a full-scale reorganisation.

The fact was that Mortimer was unwilling to supply the initiating force to an enterprise he viewed with pessimism and some suspicion. And a powerful section of the Left, led by Benn and Skinner, was still adamantly opposed to a major reorganisation, and unable to take its eyes off the factional war. Consequently, criticism of Head Office was played down much as the old Right had done in days gone by. The lament in the constituencies was labelled 'attacks on the staff', 'reorganisation' was 'a code-word for the Right'.[45]

If there was some cause for factional suspicion, there was also a tragic irony in some of this resolute defence of 'the staff'. while Head Office unions called time and again for reorganisation and lambasted the inadequacies of management, a section of the NEC Left simply failed to hear, responding only to calls for 'no sackings'. Then they became the champions of the workers. Every defensive facet of trade unionism was encouraged, its positive features virtually ignored. Small wonder that one Leftwing NUJ member of staff told me sadly in 1986 that 'as employers the Left was worse than useless'.

Some commentators labelled this 'the lost year' in organisational terms,[46] believing that the new Party leadership had sufficient authority to carry through whatever reorganisation it wanted, regardless of the General Secretary and 'the hard Left'. Perhaps so, although any major moves did require a careful sifting of alternatives and a cohesive NEC coalition. Certainly, within Walworth Road, hopes of a new era faded and a new gloom descended. The gloom quickly turned once again to militancy as an archetypal Head Office battle began over plans for a new economy drive and threats of major redundancies.

The immediate problem was that the NEC had committed itself in 1982 to eliminating the Party's overdraft by the end of 1983. The implementation of this had been postponed for a year because of the General Election, but the commitment remained. At the same time, the Party could not now expect the anticipated raising of trade union affiliation fees. Expenditure of Political Funds on the General Election was one reason; the judgement of the Certification Officer in regard to the funding of Walworth Road from Political Funds was another. And it may well be that there was some dragging of union feet given the general dissatisfaction with Head Office administration.

Jim Mortimer, privately criticised by some of the union leaders for the failure to 'sort out' Walworth Road, was still determined to carry through the job he considered he had been put there to do – to make the Party solvent. He was aware that in the next two years the Trade Union Act provisions on Political Funds might deal a devastating blow to the Party's finances – drastic economy was therefore even more desirable. For his part, Kinnock appeared to consider that, in the absence of an attainable reorganisation, a surgery which cut away at some of 'the dead wood' would do no harm.

But the whole exercise only served to indicate that quick surgery was not an easy option given the traditions, relationships and senior officials within Labour Party headquarters. All the defensiveness and resources of Head Office trade unionism were brought out in a fierce and tense conflict in which the unions fought a clever campaign, focusing on first on the budget estimates, then on managerial inefficiency and responsibility and the failure to carry out an overall reorganisation.

In this conflict, the new insecurity of the staff allied, with growing grievances among the secretaries, combined to produce a classic piece of trade union flanking. In December 1983, Nick Seigler, still the Chair of the T and G branch and Secretary of the JTUC, was removed from office and replaced by the more militant (and 'Militant') official Andy Bevan. Although Bevan was to play this role with considerable skill and sensitivity, the election inescapably added a new political dimension to the problem of Head Office industrial relations and to the dilemma of reform.

In a classic series of blocking moves, the Left on the Executive swung behind a 'no-redundancies' policy, trade union members of the NEC moved in support of proper procedures of consultation and the defence of fellow trade unionists, and the case made by the JTUC was conceded.

The result was a fundamental retreat by the Walworth Road management. Not only would there be no redundancies but departing staff would be replaced and *new* posts would be created. Economies would have to be produced by other means. And indeed they were. Surpluses were recorded for 1983, 1984 and 1985. It was achieved by what some described as 'salami-style' prudence but it was a considerable financial achievement nevertheless and, rightly, it gave Mortimer immense satisfaction.

Still there was no major reorganisation. The incompetence, tension and immobilism of Walworth Road was notorious among union leaders who were at this stage feeling their way towards an organisation and strategy for contesting the Political Fund ballots. The state of Party headquarters was noted at the meeting of affiliated organisations held on 1 August 1984 and quietly most of the union leaders determined to ensure that Walworth Road kept its hands off any trade union campaign.

Reorganisation, stage 1: the new Directorates

Meanwhile, moves were underway from Kinnock's office to clear the ground for reorganisation and to find a successor to Mortimer on his retirement. Both of the 'reform' resolutions of the 1983 Party Conference eventually found their way to the new Campaign Strategy Committee – in part because Composite 51 also asked for the setting up of a campaign committee but also because Kinnock was determined to put the initiative into less conservative hands than would handle it on the Organisation Sub-committee and NEC. Rather than set up another Commission or Joint Study, Kinnock chose to have John Garrett, an ex-Labour MP and management consultant, simply produce a 'review of Reviews', that is, an analysis of past reviews since 1967 which had references to Head Office. He was to indicate what had been recommended, what had been implemented and what still required to be done.

The 'review of Reviews' working group was instituted from the Campaign Strategy Committee. It was chaired by Kinnock and composed predominantly of those on the Left who favoured reorganisation.[47] In the summer of 1984, it began its deliberations and its conclusions were available just at the point when a new General Secretary, Larry Whitty, was ready to take over. Among Whitty's qualifications was the fact that he had been a very successful TULV National Secretary and, as such, was very aware of the depth of the problems and difficulties of implementing solutions in the face of Walworth Road's conflicting interests.

The first stage in the process was, therefore, an emphatic statement of intent. Whitty laid out clearly that the Party machine 'has not been seen as meeting the needs of the Party in the country' and that 'there is an overwhelming consensus in the Party that we can and must make a fresh start'.[48] In this fresh start, Whitty was able for the moment to draw upon the active co-operation of the Head Office unions. Around this time, a motion from Roy Green, the Party's industrial relations policy specialist, accepted by the TGWU branch, was particularly strongly worded:

> We have accepted for many years the need for a restructuring of Head Office and have responded constructively to each major exercise on this topic ... We have been disappointed at the lack of action by successive NECs to grapple with this problem ... We accept, however, that the latest review is being undertaken in earnest and in the realisation that there are no grounds for complacency ...

And in a sideswipe against some signs of feet-dragging on the NEC, it said:

> A restructuring which is carried out as part of a shift towards campaigning for power will be of great value to the Party rank and file and will also lift staff morale ... defence of the *status quo* at Head Office is unacceptable.[49]

In the few months before he took up his position, the new General Secretary was able to involve himself in private discussions with the Head Office union representatives and to participate in the final meetings of the Review Committee. In his first weeks in office, he was able to take the plan for reorganisation to the NEC and reconsult with the staff unions on the detailed application.

The NEC, with Kinnock's active support, gave the reorganisation overwhelming approval. Benn's abstention was an indication that in the face of the clear evidence of a broad reform movement, which included the Head Office staff and unions, he was prepared to suspend his political doubts. Only a very small group on the Left, including Eric Heffer and Dennis Skinner, supported reference back of the final Review report.[50]

By the time the Party assembled for the 1985 Labour Party Conference, Whitty, with Kinnock's full backing, had secured what appeared to be a major breakthrough in the national reconstruction of the Party. Head Office had been reorganised with a new and heavy emphasis on the campaigning function. The ten-headed management structure had been reduced to three divisions, each with a Director: Campaigns and Communications, Party Organisation, and Policy Development. At the end of the exercise, new people had been brought in, some capable people had been moved forward, and some, not so capable, sidelined. The General Secretary's Office had been strengthened: a new Political Assistant, Tony Manwaring, was appointed. No redundancies had been involved; staff trade unionism was satisfied and brought into constructive support. Affiliated union leaders now believed that Whitty had Head Office under control and should be left to get on with the job.

A range of improvements and appointments followed. Improvements in services to the CLPs were maintained – particularly in the production of high quality information and campaigning material. Agreement was reached on a new communication to members – *Labour Party News*. Most striking of all was the improvement in the Party's external communications and relations with the national mass media. Observers, by 1985, were already noting the new professionalism of the Jobs and Industry campaign material, and of Labour's handling of the Brecon and Radnor by-election. Under Peter Mandelson, appointed in November 1985, a communications department, notorious for its low morale and accomplishment in 1983, was by 1986 invigorated and full of innovation.

But in truth, some of this improvement camouflaged the fact that the crisis of Head Office management was far from being resolved – indeed, in some respects, it was once again deteriorating. Multiple weaknesses again made themselves evident in 1986, but it was the political problems of Liverpool which necessarily drew most of the energy of the General Secretary and the new Director of Organisation, Joyce Gould. There were difficulties and delays in the preparation of the regional organisation for the General Election, and Head Office still experienced more than its fair share of administrative foul-ups.

As for appointments, by no means all the replacements within the Party machine went to the preferred choice of the Leader and General Secretary. And though the Sex Discrimination Act proved to be a powerful lever in securing a new agreement with NULO over the employment of part time agents, the General

Secretary still wrestled with the problem of organisational appointments made subject to the NULO closed shop. He still could find no practicable way to deal with the problem of 'dead-wood' staff – some of it at senior levels of the organisation. Pressure was also increasing now as a result of growing expenditure – some of it anticipated as a consequence of election preparations, some of it unplanned, particularly from the Party's journals: in 1986, the Party once again moved into deficit.

As these administrative and financial problems grew, so they festered with increasing bad temper and suspicion. As before, every single innovation seemed to require hours of formal and informal negotiation. The management–union relationship, which had gone through a honeymoon period in 1985 after Whitty's appointment, worsened once again. Some in the management despaired of the negativism of the staff unions. Many in the unions returned to their old lament about management inconsistency, incompetence and weakness. The unions protested vigorously over the sacking of a probationary member of the Communications Department. The Directors were dismayed by the abilty of the NUJ branch to win more money from the NEC for the loss-making *Labour Weekly*.

Frustration was increased by a new fragmentation within the Head Office union branches. The rise of the Communications and Campaign Directorate increased divisions within the NUJ branch. The decline in the number of researchers further reduced their impact within the Transport Workers' branch in favour of the lower paid secretaries, the Finance Department and the Organisation Department. Andy Bevan's role as JTUC convenor was expanding, given the multiple issues of conflict. Indeed, ironically, some staff members in the union began to complain that Bevan, a capable man, was spending too much time sorting out 'management's' difficulties!

Two unresolved problems of the 1985 reorganisation once again rose to the surface. The Administrative and Personnel Officer (redesignated Administration and Training Officer in 1986) was still unable to come to grips with the huge difficulties which surrounded his job. Whitty was therefore forced to reconsider one of his decisions of 1985. He had then rejected the idea of a fourth Director who would have overall responsibility for Finance and Administration (a proposal dating back to 1971). The reasoning then was that the General Secretary himself would play a more interventionist role. This had now proved to be virtually a physical impossibility. The political anxiety in 1985 had been that Whitty would be saddled, not with a co-operative new Director, but with a constraining Deputy General Secretary with a different perspective. Now it seemed that this question of a new senior officer must be readdressed.

Further, there was mounting criticism of the operation and rivalries of the new Directorates and the gulf in some departments between the Directors and the staff. Staff unions had always favoured the idea of a second tier of management within departments. An internal memo from two members of the T and G branch complained in November 1986, 'The megadirectorates are more remote than the hopelessly inefficient but more cosy departments they replaced.'[51]

In an attempt to tackle some of the problems afresh, Whitty sought to strengthen the Secretariat and particularly the position of his new Political

Assistant, Tony Manwaring. He also encouraged the formation of a new Training and Equal Opportunities Group and appointed new Training Consultants to investigate and report. Mike Watts, a management specialist, began to give advice on the more fundamental problems. Partly as a result of his role, plus the experience of the dilemmas which constantly faced the Head Office staff, a new interest grew in the professional expertise of management – a development also strongly affecting some of Labour's local government representatives. Early in 1987, members of staff were encouraged to attend management training courses – a development unthinkable in the political and industrial situation of the late 1970s.

Little of this raised morale in the building or increased optimism about the future election campaign. In fact, long before the damaging aftermath of the Greenwich by-election, there was a growing crisis of confidence about Labour's organisation. In the light of subsequent developments, including the remarkable organisational performance of June 1987, it is important to note the depth of despair which was around in Party headquarters at Christmas 1986. The worst feature was that there was now a deep pessimism about any organisational reform, a perplexity about what dynamism could ever provide the opportunity for a revolution in Head Office. There was even a worry in some senior quarters that Labour's election campaign of 1987 might be little better than 1983!

Reorganisation, stage 2: the General Election campaign

Eventually the leverage did come and it came with the General Election itself. Not only did the well-laid communication and campaigning plans produce a dynamism and a flair which left the other parties standing,[52] but the organisational preparations astonished almost everybody by their effectiveness and achievement. Faults could still be found but the election reorganisation of Head Office worked with a degree of co-ordination which was itself the source of great elation.

Whitty built upon the advice and consultations of the past – including the advice of staff unions – to produce a planned move away from the old departmental structures. Spatially and organisationally, Walworth Road was reconstituted into functional units and teams within a comprehensive plan in which everybody involved knew what they were supposed to be doing, with whom and when.

From the staff and unions in the building there was a sudden burst of enthusiasm on Day One of the campaign – a mood which fed into the rise in morale within the Party as a whole. There was a mood of potency at Head Office of a kind which nobody could remember before and with it went a thrilling sense of purpose as the processes interlocked with a new efficiency. A combination of clever deployment and 'sweeping up' dealt with pockets of potential inadequacy. Those who entered Walworth Road in this period and knew something of its history marvelled at the transformation. Those in the building reflected that for the first time anyone could remember, a General Secretary was wandering from department to department listening, talking and encouraging.

During this summer period, the public image of Labour Party headquarters was virtually revolutionised in terms of creativity, competence and energy. Few in the building in early 1987 would have predicted that the Party could match the

Conservative Central Office organisation. In fact, the Party's campaign sent Central Office into a crisis of confidence, highlighting its own organisational weaknesses.[53] Though the Campaign impact on the Tory vote was minimal, the first priority, to kill off the Alliance challenge, was a significant success – and a startling contrast to 1983.

Credit should be given to the Walworth Road management as well as its communications and campaigning specialists for the turn-around. But in a sense, it was also a vindication of Head Office trade unionism. They had always argued that they would respond to a bold and efficient management which was capable of comprehensive planning and reorganisation. Longstanding union militants had argued that trade union negativism was a consequence, not a cause, of the problems. Now, almost without exception, the staff rose to the challenge.

There was a new willingness to live with the frictions of voluntary and part-time labour and all the complications of casual payments and grading comparisons. There was a positive enthusiasm for a pattern of redeployments which broke with old departmental relationships and released a new energy. And there was a highly motivated engagement in the participatory, democratic ethos of the new teamwork. Not for years could anybody remember a mood of confidence, competence and commitment as was evident in Walworth Road during this election campaign.

Reorganisation, stage 3: pruning the administration

However, it became clear immediately after the election that the comradeship and *élan* of the headquarters election campaign was unlikely to last. Too many problems had been left unsolved by the reconstruction of 1985, particularly the continual inadequacies of the administration, training and personnel functions and the existence of pockets of incompetence in key areas of the building. These problems were now caught up in the financial trouble which had built up in the pre-election period. The biggest expenditure problem was the sizeable loss on commercial operations, including the Party's journals.[54] The biggest income problem was the failure to make TUFL's fund-raising target, leading to an unusual deficit on the General Election Fund.[55] The most worrying background anxiety was that future union affiliation levels would be adjusted downwards with a consequent loss of income. As the General Secretary sought to come to terms with the Party's deteriorating overdraft, so he now attempted a third attack on the problem of headquarters' administration. In doing so he become involved in a crisis with headquarters' trade unionism which was to last six months.

On 23 July, Whitty produced his financial diagnosis and his outline plan for the restructuring of Walworth Road. The Party was required, in order simply to return to the overdraft position of recent years, to find savings of £600,000 in this year's budget and £1,150,000 in the projected 1987 budget. To secure this, Whitty recommended, and the NEC agreed, various cost-saving measures including the closure of the publications *Labour Weekly*, *New Socialist* and *Socialist Youth*. A restructuring of the posts in the building involved a reduction of staffing and the possible loss of up to 45 jobs. With this restructuring was promised a major strengthening of the administration involving a new high level post. And there would be the creation of a new second tier of management within the Directorates.

Most controversial of all, formal notification was given to the staff unions of proposed redundancies to be followed by a period of consultation of options before the final decisions were taken. The staff unions had never conceded the necessity of redundancies of any kind. Now it appeared that Whitty and the NEC were prepared to consider targeted and *enforced* redundancies – even of high level officers – in an attempt to produce a solvent and efficient party for the 1990s.

In the next six months, this programme was carried through with a ruthless determination not only to ensure the financial targets, but to complete the restructuring and some of the changes in personnel that had been on the agenda for nearly a decade.

The 'hard Left' group on the NEC fought it all the way. To them, this was 'Thatcherite' management. But there were now only four of them and their case carried little weight. With relatively minor internal disagreement, and with full backing from the Party's Leader and his aide Charles Clarke, a majority on the NEC, including the NEC Trade Union Section, held together throughout the exercise – determined not to be outfaced or sidetracked. A politically balanced F and GP[56] gave solid support. Their view was that the time had come and that here was a General Secretary with the 'bottle' to see the project through.

To the Head Office unions it looked very different. They were, they argued, not opposed to a new reorganisation or reallocation of work. But they had never accepted that it was permissable to declare redundancies, they blamed management for much of the financial problem and for its own inadequacy in dealing with incompetent members of staff; redundancy was an expensive way of dealing with individual incompetence anyway. What was seen as determination and responsibility on the management side was castigated as 'macho management' and disregard for trade union principles on the other. The sense of 'a last stand' and a battle that 'had to be won' affected both sides. It led to a deeply embattled and embittered atmosphere which quickly replaced the euphoria of June.

The General Secretary and his allies were made to fight every step of the way. There was an initial period very similar to that which was experienced in the 1983–4 period when the negotiations were almost entirely concerned with the financial estimates and budgets with charges and counter-charges of over-estimates and under-estimates. A fierce counter-attack on Whitty's financial 'pessimism' and headquarters management was launched by the staff unions, aided by the fact that some of the most militant trade unionists were in the Finance Department, on whom Whitty also relied for his financial information. Arguments over the financial accounting continued all the way through to the Party Conference.

This row overlapped with another about the rights of the unions in the building to use the Party's official communications machinery to campaign against the Head Office management. Bad temper over this episode was accentuated by the proposal to close down New Socialist and *Labour Weekly* – an authoritarian move in the eyes of Leftwing opponents of the Party leadership, an inescapable economy in the eyes of the General Secretary.

In the event, *New Socialist* was saved by organisational changes and outside underwriting of finances. But *Labour Weekly* was in a different category. Its losses were greater.[57] It had been subsidised since its inception. And it had a variety of political enemies. But it was backed by a strong NUJ Chapel. It had long experience of fending off attempts at closure. And, though badly supported in terms of readership (only around 13,500), it could call upon a wider body of sympathisers worried over the question, 'Why close a Labour newspaper?'. *Labour Weekly* became the centre-piece of the whole reorganisation dispute.

Near the centre also, and complicating the general industrial issues involved, were the particular positions of Andy Bevan and Barrie Clarke, two key union representatives. It became clear very early on that their posts were to be abolished and there could be no guarantee that they would be appointed to new posts involving their previous work. Their personal positions were very different. Clarke was politically nearer the mainstream but Bevan's prestige in the building was very high, in spite of his politics. However, these differences were for the moment secondary to the trade union question and, given their positions, they could expect some special sensitivity on the part of NEC trade unionists and the leadership of their own unions. Both Bevan and Clarke were to the fore in agitating for industrial action and there were short strikes by staff in September during protracted negotiations with the NEC. However, more extended industrial action was voted down by union members – an indication that they were unwilling to wage total war against the Whitty proposals.

The staff union branches now threatened to take disruptive action at the Party Conference unless the redundancy 'alternative' was taken off the table completely. An NEC told of this face to face by the JTUC Chair, Andy Bevan, simply dug in its heels, its determination not to back down enhanced by his known political allegiance. Indeed, the high profile Militant involvement in the campaign on behalf of the Head Office staff did them no good at all in terms of winning strategic allies. It increased the stakes in a conflict where the Party leadership could not afford to be defeated.

Within the Conference, there were two distinct levels of political action taking place involving the unions on the question of Head Office reorganisation. There were private negotiations taking place all over the weekend before the Conference, concerning the threat of disruption over redundancy. And there was a public mobilisation aimed at the union delegations to secure support for Composite 15 which focused on *Labour Weekly* in particular but contained an instruction to the NEC that there be 'no forced redundancies' – a commitment which was understood to involve a wider canvas than just *Labour Weekly*.[58]

In the end, the staff unions were defeated in both spheres. The first was in the negotiations between national union officials of the two key union branches involved – APEX and the TGWU – and the General Secretary. In effect, rather than be seen to be aiding a publicly damaging disruption of the Party Conference, the national union officials backed off.

Secondly, the staff unions were defeated within the Conference itself. Composite Resolution No. 15 went down by 3,594,000 votes to 2,556,000. Privately and publicly it involved a deep conflict of responsibilities. What was the priority?

Serving the Party and the Party's members or protecting the Party's employees? Preserving Party communications at any price or facing the constraints of financial life? Signalling a fresh start at Party headquarters or a continuation of the traditions of the past? Supporting the Party leadership or delivering a humiliating rebuff? Solidarity with the Party or with the Head Office unions? Above all, there was the fundamental question of how far the defensive practices of a trade unionism forged in British industrial life against profit-seeking employers were to be applied within the political party of Labour. By this stage, something of the magnitude of the predicament of industrial relations at Party headquarters was widely known at national level in the unions. Which way would the majority go?

As so often since 1979, crucial debates and crucial decisions took place in two Leftwing union delegations – the TGWU, with members in the building, and NUPE, whose Deputy General Secretary, Tom Sawyer, was Chair of Labour's Home Policy Committee. Fought out in the Transport Workers' delegation, the decision was in the end to vote *for* the composite resolution. Fought out in the Public Employees' delegation, the decision was to vote against. With the NUPE vote went the battle and ultimately the campaign.

Their decision not only sealed the fate of *Labour Weekly*, it enabled the General Secretary to claim Conference authorisation for pushing ahead with all the elements of his reconstruction package. In the post-Conference period, a programme of voluntary redundancies and early retirements was carried through.

Much of this was still bitterly contested by the staff unions and there was another short, sharp industrial dispute about conditions of redundancy following the closure of *Labour Weekly*. There was also a background dispute about the designation of the fourth director but Whitty won out on this against attempts from Left and Right to institute a Deputy General Secretary. The new Director of Personnel, Resources and Training was Mike Watts.[59]

Considerable pressure built up in this period at national level within the Transport and General Workers' Union causing a tense cross-pressure to be exerted upon their NEC representative. Eddie Haigh of the TGWU, the Chairman of the Finance and General Purposes Sub-committee until October 1987,[60] had so far backed Whitty virtually all down the line under difficult circumstances to protect the Party's viability. In the complex mixture of industrial and political obligations which had marked the Walworth Road crisis for years, there was a final twist, over the positions of union representatives Bevan and Clarke.

Bevan did not find any supporters of his politics among the TGWU leadership but, as far as they were concerned, his redundancy was a trade union question made all the more sensitive by his position with the JTUC. They could find no *industrial* reason why Bevan should be pushed out, even if his post was to be abolished, and they ensured that he, like Clarke, was offered alternative employment within the building. However, an attempt by Benn and Skinner on the NEC to guarantee Bevan the new Youth and Student Officer's job rebounded when the vote of 4–22 effectively put that job outside any future union negotiations.[61] The situation was finally resolved when Clarke decided to reject alternative employment and take redundancy, and in January 1988, Bevan gave up and took the same course.[62]

PERSPECTIVE

Administrative problems and conflicts at Head Office are not a peculiarity of the Labour Party. Each of the main parties has had its organisational difficulties in recent years. In 1988, the 'ramshackle' Conservative Central Office moved into a phase of change which looked remarkably like the Whitty reforms of 1985.[63] At the same time, the newly formed Social and Liberal Democrats moved into an early financial and managerial crisis which provoked strong demands for reform.[64]

Even some of the features of Labour's administrative crisis, which contrasted with the experience of other parties, have been shared with union, co-operative, and Leftwing organisations in the past two decades. There have been many examples of internal disputes between trade union managers and their staffs also organised in unions.[65] There have been notable occasions in recent years within worker co-operatives when there has been an application of inappropriate trade union practices.[66] And it has come to be recognised that part of the culture of the Left involves a blind spot concerning the skills of management.[67]

One feature which made the Labour Party headquarter's experience distinctive was the highly unusual trilateral dimensions of trade unionism. Trade unions provided the bulk of the resources, trade union representatives made up a section of the NEC management, and trade union branches organised the employees. But uncertainty over obligations and over the hierarchy of authority among these trade unionists made for industrial relations which were, to say the least, highly complicated and difficult to handle.

The complications were brought into sharp focus by the historic legacy of poor management and long-delayed reform, but they were made for a time intractable by the particular mix of industrial and political motivations which affected the staff and the NEC in the late 1970s.

Long-festering grievances over pay, conditions and the organisation of the headquarters stimulated a new militant trade unionism, but politics accentuated the inter-union competition and fed a neo-syndicalist edge into union objectives which was bound to put a fundamental strain on the management's other obligations. Trade unionists as managers are often prone to a role conflict and a sense of uncertainty over criteria, but the strength of the political Left on the NEC and within the staff unions reinforced this uncertainty and strengthened the pressure on NEC Trade Union Section members to abide by 'trade union principles' rather than managerial responsibilities. These principles, in turn, led a section of the NEC Left to defend the staff on the terrain of trade unionism often in opposition to the management's decisions; yet political suspicion froze this same Left into resolute opposition to the reorganisation that the staff union branches were clamouring for. All this made the situation in Head Office a swamp which for years nobody could pull their way out of.

This whole experience gives us yet another perspective on power relations between the Party and the unions, and particularly on the position of the so-called 'union barons'. Even a combination of sustained pressure from the union branches in the building and external leverage from the most senior union leaders failed for years to produce the reorganisation that they were both seeking.

As so often in the decade from the mid-1970s to the mid-1980s, the image of dominance obscured the reality of frustration. Only with changes in political leadership could the reorganisation process begin.

There is also an object lesson in the way in which political leadership in the Labour Party can affect the definitions and priorities of trade unionism. Slowly, under a new Party Leader and a new General Secretary, and with a weakened 'hard Left' on the NEC, the attitude of the NEC changed towards its managerial role. This affected the behaviour of the Trade Union Section, even its more Leftwing members. The traditional loyalty of that Section had often been stretched and qualified by its industrial obligations. Now that loyalty was extended into internal industrial relations during the long conflict over the third phase of Head Office reorganisation. The section's members were prepared to give solid support to the General Secretary and the Party Leader in forcing through a major restructuring, even though it brought them into conflict with Head Office trade unionists – some of them from the same unions as NEC members. In terms of priorities, the broad interests of trade unionists in protecting a viable political instrument weighed more on the NEC Trade Union Section, at this time, than the industrial interests of a particular section. And, at the Party Conference, solidarity went with the Party and not with the union branches.

From this Head Office experience there came also a minor, but noteworthy, influence on Party policy. Though it was appreciated that the position in Labour's head-quarters had some unique features and required solutions that were not necessarily applicable elsewhere, the crisis of Head Office did reshape the perspective of Labour Party management in a way which fed into the Party's changing industrial policy. Supporters of industrial democracy could still focus on the important input which trade union branches had constantly fed into the debate on reorganisation. They could point also to the 1987 election experience that small group democracy had much to recommend it (providing that that was what the group wanted). They could also take the view that, as the NEC was elected by the Party Conference, it was a democratic organisation in which 'joint control' with the small number of Head Office union branch members was an illegitimate interference with the democratic process. But the sour experience of headquarters industrial relations led some past supporters of the 1976 programme to be convinced that, in any case, day-to-day joint control was impracticable, and that poor management skills, defensive trade unions, and unrealistic plans for industrial democracy were among the worst ingredients for an effective industrial policy.[68] All in all, there was now a hard pragmatic edge to the way in which most senior party officials regarded industrial democracy, and an exasperation with the panacea of 1970s-style neo-syndicalism.

CONSEQUENCES

After a tense eighteen months, which included a dispute with the NUJ and a dispute with NULO, there was a growing agreement at leadership level in the Party and the unions that the new management had paid off and that 'the building had been turned round'. In a low key but important step at the turn of 1990, the Finance Department's management was reorganised and it now linked more co-operatively with the senior management. The NEC, with some of the trade unionists in the lead, now began to withdraw from day-to-day management, leaving the General Secretary with more room and more responsibility. The Staff Negotiations Committee met only 'as and when necessary'. The new emphasis on flexible management was accompanied by major improvements in recruitment and training policy. As the Party geared up for the next election, so morale rose and there was a sense of an organisation better prepared than in the past for the time when the challenge would come.

But the reorganisation and the reordering of priorities was not without its costs – in time, in redundancy payments, and in the insecurity of staff who shared the new perspective but were yet to be convinced that the surgery was a one-off action and that the administrative revolution might not in the end claim them. The insecurity was, however, for the moment overlaid by a new mood. One sign was the fact that Heads of Department trade unionism was allowed to wither. Another was that union branch members were disposed to keep their officials in line with the Party's priorities and to accept that union defensive practices inherited from other spheres were not necessarily rigid principles to be applied to the Labour Party. Though privately (and occasionally publicly[69]) some still criticised the redundancies of 1987–8 and adhered to the principle that affiliated unions ought to oppose all redundancies, there were too many other acceptances of economic necessity[70] for that position, respected as it was, to carry much conviction.

And still the problems of the new management were by no means totally resolved. The NULO agreement, which in some ways marked the onset of the years of industrial disputes, proved in practice very difficult to renegotiate and not so easy to bypass.[71] Appointments and reallocations affecting NULO members continued to be heavily constrained by the union – merged in 1989 with the huge GMB. At various levels and in various sectors of the party organisation could be found pockets of resentment and discontent, some of it industrial, some of it political. This was particularly marked in the regions, where officials considered themselves unappreciated and some of them privately attacked what they saw as the downgrading of 'solid, experienced organisation' at the grass roots.[72] In 1989, the Party's General Fund was showing a loss of only £7,000, but in 1990 and 1991, as expenditure on election preparation grew, so a familiar financial gap began to develop. As the overdraft varied between £1.1 and nearly £2 million, there was the prospect of a bleak post-election financial situation. It remained to be seen how far the new management and the new trade unionism would deal with that problem and how far in practice the two sides had moved towards any deep-rooted agreement on the procedures, practices and priorities which should govern the Labour Party's administrative behaviour and its own industrial relations.

NOTES

1. Labour Party Staff Joint Trade Union Committee, *Evidence to the Commission of Enquiry*, 1980, EA 141, Section One, pp. 2–3.
2. Heads of Department, *Evidence to Commission of Enquiry*, 1980, EA/69,

p. 1.

3. *The Diary of Beatrice Webb*, Vol. III, 1905–24, 1984. Entry for 20/3/18, p. 303.

4. Mary Agnes Hamilton, *The Labour Party Today*, 1939, p. 51.

5. *Final Report of the Economy Committee of the F and GP*, 17/1/33. NEC *Minutes*, 18/1/33. F and GP *Minutes*, 21/2/33 and 17/5/33.

6. Interview with Lord Underhill and letter 19/11/84. Memorandum on Office Organisation *undated*.

7. Richard Rose, *Influencing Voters*, 1967, p. 61.

8. This was the judgement of an outside adviser brought in by Gaitskell, P. Williams, *op. cit.*, p. 349. Gaitskell introduced some financial and organisational reforms but met entrenched Head Office opposition. However, Crossman's view was that Gaitskell did not want 'a powerful modern General Secretary' because it might be a threat to his own position. He therefore placed George Brown as the Chairman of the Org. Sub. in 1961 and when Morgan Phillips retired in 1962 Len Williams was appointed. Richard Crossman, *Diaries of a Cabinet Minister*, Vol. II, 1966–8, 1976, pp. 59–60.

9. *Ibid.* Also 'Our Penny-Farthing Machine', *Socialist Commentary*, Supplement, 1965. 'Modern politics require an efficient and professional central office machine. This the Labour Party conspicuously lacks', Section 3, p. xiii.

10. *Plan for an Efficient Party* was a Manifesto launched in 1965 by four editors of Labour journals: Richard Clements, *Tribune*; Rita Hinden, *Socialist Commentary*; Paul Johnson, *New Statesman*; and Dick Leonard, *Plebs*, but the instigator and subsequently the campaign organiser was Jim Northcott, who had been Chairman of the Transport House Staff Council.

11. The General Secretary, Len Williams, argued that an enquiry would be 'a distraction from the task of helping the Government and preparing to fight an election', NEC *Minutes*, 24/11/65. Subsequently, with the General Election out of the way, there was still deep reluctance to hold an enquiry. *The Plan for an Efficient Party Campaign* was refused an entry in the Diary of Events for a Conference fringe meeting but it was packed to overflowing and as a result of this pressure, and an intervention by Harold Wilson, an enquiry was set up. *Plan for an Efficient Party Newsletters*, 1–6, 1966. Richard Crossman, *op. cit.*, pp. 60–1.

12. In his reply to the debate at the Party Conference on the Commission of Enquiry, Crossman promised that it would cover the whole of Transport House but the Commission, after recommending the appointment of a Deputy General Secretary (a post instituted in 1969 then, in practice, abolished in 1972) left the review of 'the work and organisation of the staff' to the new General Secretary expected in 1969. *Report of the Committee of Enquiry into Party Organisation*, 1968, para. 81.

13. Donoughue, *op. cit.*, p. 44.

14. *Finance Panel* of 1980, Commission of Enquiry, 'O & M Report 1971 and Current Position', 18/4/80, p. 3.

15. *Ibid.*

16. Rose, *The Problem of Party Government*, *op. cit.*, p. 274. Drucker, *op. cit.*, 1979, pp. 14–15 also stressed 'It pays its employees shockingly badly', p. 14.

17. *Minutes of Staff Negotiations Committee*, 7/6/71, Item 46.

18. LPACR, 1977, p. 5. Under the Memorandum of Agreement, 1/11/77, it

was stipulated that organising above Grade 1 posts be advertised in the first place 'exclusively to members of NULO' and only subsequently beyond that if the NEC or the employing CLP was of the opinion that no member of NULO was suitable. In 1976 there were approximately 110 non-retired members of NULO.

19. *Industrial Democracy and Joint Control at Party Headquarters*, JTUC, 1982, p. 1, citing *Labour's Programme*, 1976, pp. 33–4.

20. E.H. Phelps-Brown, *The Growth of British Industrial Relations*, 1960, p. 157, cited in Richard Hyman, *Strikes*, 1984, p. 72.

21. *Report of the Joint Study on Labour Party Head Office*, 1982, Section 8.2, p. 23.

22. Huw Beynon, *Working for Ford*, 1975.

23. In 1977, the NEC agreed to the introduction of a new clause (14) in the Memorandum of Agreement which stipulated that there must be agreement from the unions before employing a temporary member of staff.

24. 'Employment of Temporary Staff', *Memo from Admin. Officer*, October 1983.

25. *Joint Study*, p. 5.

26. In 1969–70, the Staff Negotiations Committee had a composition of four Rightwing Trade Union Section representatives plus the Treasurer. In 1978–9, the nine NEC representatives were still all Trade Union Section members, albeit split 6/3 in favour of the Right, even though the NEC itself had a Leftwing majority. In 1979, the committee was expanded to sixteen members of the NEC; it now had five CLP section representatives and one from the Women's section, giving it a Leftwing majority. In 1982, it was reconstituted with eleven members of the NEC; eight were from the Trade Union Section, all but one on the Right. The General Secretary was always a full member of the committee and other relevant senior officers were members without voting rights.

27. In July 1979, the Heads of Department asked the NEC Staff Negotiations Committee whether they should stay at home during the stoppage. The NEC Committee said no, they were part of management – but they should not undertake duties which would normally be done by employees.

28. *NEC Minutes*, 24/11/65. Tony Benn, *Out of the Wilderness: Diaries, 1963–67*, 1987, p. 340.

29. Benn, *op. cit.*, pp. 211, 213 and 225.

30. See, for example, John Cartwright, 'Party Organisation to Win the Election', *Socialist Commentary*, February 1978; also *Labour Victory*, September 1979, where 'a bloated Research and International Department' is compared with the 'meagre' provision for the Party's Agency Service. This damaging coupling of reorganisation with attacks on the Research Department went on for years. See on this Margaret Van Hattem, 'The Labour Party's Second Term of Opposition', *Political Quarterly*, October–December 1984, p. 368.

31. See, for example, *Our Penny Farthing Machine, op. cit.*, pp. xiii and xvi.

32. In 1973, the Research Department had a Research Officer and thirteen research assistants (one more than in 1965) letter from Admin. Officer to author, 9/7/73. In 1979, there were twelve research assistants, 'Head Office and Regional Organisation', CE/OM/29/4/80, *Evidence to Commission of Enquiry*. In 1973, the International Department staff consisted of an International Officer and four research assistants and it was

the same in 1980, same sources. See also, the Houghton Committee judgement that the proportion of Head Office expenditure attributable to research and policy formulation had remained 'fairly static in real terms' since 1967, *Report of the Committee on Financial Aid to Political Parties*, 1976, p. 28.

33. RD 364, April 1980, gives the Conservative Party policy staff as 29 increasing to 50 in the year prior to the General Election.

34. The Joint Study Membership involved seven from Head Office unions plus two from the Heads of Department Trade Union Group and one from NULO. There were four from the NEC and four senior officials including the General Secretary designate. The committee was helped by five outside advisers and there was a TULV observer (John Speller from EETPU). The Chair was the MP Gavin Strang, the Secretary a Councillor Roy Shaw and the research was done by Pauline Bryan of the Fabian Society.

35. *Joint Study*, 3.1, p. 8.

36. Minority Report signed by representatives of APEX, the NUJ and the Heads of Department Trade Union Group.

37. *Joint Study*, 5.6, p. 17. Mortimer's wealth of relevant experience included a variety of positions within the unions, the Prices and Incomes Board, London Transport Executive and the Chair of ACAS.

38. Proposals on the Recommendations of the Joint Study of Head Office, F2/82, NEC, 24/11/82.

39. See n. 26.

40. Jim Mortimer, 'Matching Commitments to Resources', *Tribune*, 15/2/85.

41. *A Workers' Plan for Head Office*, July 1982, p. 1.

42. *NEC Report*, 1983, p. 2.

43. My personal experience of this involves receiving a mountain of complaints and laments as I did my research on other themes connected with the Labour Party.

44. The ten points were: (i) individual membership must be increased and made more socially representative; (ii) Party staffing must be improved in quality, training and allocation; (iii) the NEC must give a higher priority to its organisational and administrative role; (iv) the efficiency of Head Office must be improved; (v) the policy, communication and electoral role of the PLP, the NEC and the Party Office must be better co-ordinated; (vi) there must be closer co-ordination between the Party nationally and the Party in the country and between the Party at all levels and the affiliated unions; (vii) the Party must become more communication conscious and the quality of its communication must be raised; (viii) political education must be upgraded and improved; (ix) the campaigning role must be a permanent activity between elections; (x) there must be clear lines of responsibility for election management.

45. Dennis Skinner addressing a meeting of CLP delegates to the 1984 Party Conference, 30/9/84. Notes of the author.

46. Cover story, 'Labour's Lost Year', *New Statesman*, 1/6/84.

47. The working group consisted of the Party Leader and the General Secretary, plus Alan Hadden, Eric Heffer, Sam McCluskie, Audry Wise plus David Blunkett, Robin Cook, Michael Meacher and the General Secretary designate, Larry Whitty, after his appointment in January 1985.

48. *Guardian*, 31/1/85.
49. *TGWU 1/975 Branch draft submission to Review Committee* . I have been unable to check the date of this motion in the Minutes (which are missing) but I have a copy of the draft and I am assured by branch activists that this was part of their submission.
50. *NEC Minutes*, 26/6/85, Item 219. The vote was lost by 4 votes to 20 with Benn and the YS representative, Frances Curran, abstainers. Benn and others then attempted unsuccessfully to make some specific amendments.
51. Memo.,18 November 1976, Roy Green and Emma MacLennon.
52. See on this Patricia Hewitt and Peter Mandelson, 'The Labour Campaign' and Philip Gould, Peter Herd and Chris Powell, 'The Labour Party's Campaign Communications', in Ivor Crewe and Martin Harrop (eds.), *Political Communications: The General Election of 1987*, 1989, pp. 49–54 and 72–86.
53. Rodney Tyler, *Campaign*, 1987, Chapter 9, pp. 172–194. Bruce Anderson, 'The Myth of Central Office', *Sunday Telegraph*, 7/6/87.
54. Overspends were:

	Variance Against Budget	Total Net Cost
Publishing and Marketing	192,000	312,000
New Socialist	59,000	89,000
Labour Weekly	72,000	147,000

Source: *Briefing Note* from Gen. Sec. to affiliated organisations, August 1987.
55. First estimated at £250,000 then adjusted downwards to £159,000, *NEC Report*, 1988, p. 10.
56. In 1986–7, the Staff Negotiations Committee had a large membership of seventeen NEC members plus the General Secretary. Ten were from the Trade Union Section and seven of these were members of the Rightwing group.
57. The adjusted net deficit for 1986 was £147,000. The accumulated deficit 1979–1987 was £825,000, *NEC Report*, 1987, p. 47. Critics were later to point out that *Labour Party News*, which became in part a replacement for *Labour Weekly*, was by 1988 showing a net loss of £56,000 in the year. Nick Butler, *Fabian Conference News*, 5, 1989. In 1989 it showed a surplus of £36,000 but was still 'some way short of being self-sufficient' without subsidies from membership income. *Labour Party Finances and 1989 Accounts*, 1990, p. 5. The subsidy was £215,000.
58. Comp. Res. 15, 'Party Publications', *LPACR*, 1987, p. 159.
59. Watts' highly qualified appointment was lamented by *Campaign Group News* ' ... we are to appoint a new Director of Personnel and Resources, whose task will be management rather than political', January 1988.
60. In October 1987, Haigh moved to be Chair of the Organisation Sub-committee.
61. *NEC Minutes*, 16/12/87, Item 42. The motion said simply: 'That Andy Bevan should retain his job as Youth Officer.'
62. Overall, 32 members of staff took redundancy out of a total staff of 164. The target of staffing was 125 but with staff leaving for other reasons, it dropped to 109 in 1988. £628,000 was paid out to reduce staff. Auditor's report, *LPACR*, 1988, p. 28.

63. John Carvel, 'The Tories' Memory Man', *Guardian*, 11/10/88.
64. Patrick Wintour, 'Democrats Hit by Cash Crisis', *Guardian*, 28/2/89.
65. In the 1980s, these conflicts have come in unions with very different political traditions, structures and social composition. The unions have included NALGO, NUM, NUPE and TASS.
66. Tony Eccles, *Under New Management: The Story of Britain's Largest Worker Co-operative – Its Success and Failure*, 1981.
67. Charles Landry et al., *What a Way to Run a Railroad: An Analysis of Radical Failure*, 1985, p. 30.
68. This was particularly true of the Policy Director, Geoff Bish. See Chapter 14, p. 434, for changes in policy on industrial democracy.
69. See, for example, the comments of one of the Party's auditors: 'As a party that campaigns for jobs and purports to represent workers, I believe cutbacks of this type at least stretch our credibility as a party who is supposed to be caring for the unemployed in society.' David Hopper (NUM), *LPACR*, 1988, p. 28.
70. For example, in January 1990, the *Morning Star* announced that it 'would have to shed up to 25 jobs by way of redundancies and lay-offs'. Statement to Our Readers, *Morning Star*, 13/1/90.
71. In 1989, the appointment of a South-West organiser first went to a non-NULO member, but he resigned after a short period in the job and was succeeded by a NULO member. Some said that the first appointment represented a victory, in principle, for the management. Some said that his resignation was a victory, in practice, for NULO. Some said that it was 'a draw'.
72. How solid this was in practice was a matter of some contention. At the time of writing (September 1990), a major dispute was beginning over the possible removal from office of the London General Secretary, Terry Ashton (who was also the General Secretary of NULO as it happened), in the wake of Labour's poor performance in the London local government elections. Ashton had a broad range of supporters who argued that he was being scapegoated. On the other side, it was said that the pro-Ashton alliance involved a coalition of those who felt, in various ways, alienated from the Kinnock leadership. It was yet another example of the complex interplay of the industrial and the political.

Part VII

Appraisal

20

'Rules', power and transformation

FROM SETTLEMENT TO CRISIS

If the reader has managed to get to this point in my study then one thing at least will have become very clear. Examined closely, this is not a subject which facilitates simple generalisation – although it often provokes it.

As we have seen, the complexity, peculiarity and paradox of the relationship makes it easy to misunderstand – a puzzle, as Wertheimer noted – with formal features that mask a reality of a very different order. I have examined that order and its historic character as a relationship governed by role-playing in different spheres and by a framework of 'rules' and protocol, based on the values of freedom, democracy, unity and solidarity, and the working principle of priority.

Some of these 'rules', and the main features of trade union role-playing, date back to the earliest days of the Party, but in the late 1920s and early 1930s the 'rules' were clarified as both sides sought to manage the relationship in ways which protected their primary function. By the 1950s, in the wake of the achievements of '1945', they had attained such a status – particularly among the majority factions in the industrial and the political wings – that they appeared to be mature and settled arrangements in a stable relationship.

This stability was neither easily achieved nor easily preserved. There have always been major tensions in this relationship. I have shown how these revolved around conflicts of interest and ideology, how they were at times, exacerbated by problems of social empathy, and how they were also reflected in, and sometimes caused by, differences of institutional strategy. Such tensions were apparent even in the war years, leading up to the great victory of 1945.

But the tensions became much more acute after 1959, with the result that there has been a major breakdown of consensus on the 'rules', first of democracy and then of freedom. It is a predicament which has lasted now for thirty years and is today only part of the way towards a solution.

Contrasting prescriptions for dealing with this predicament, and the various other problems facing the Labour Movement, were located in different wings of the Movement and often accompanied by a broad project for the transformation of the Labour Party in one direction or another. The strongest commitment to traditional 'rules' of freedom and a consistent defence of traditional Labour Movement conceptions of democracy came from sections of the trade union Left.

By contrast, the most assertive supporters of a new industrial relations order and the strongest critics of traditional democracy could be found within the Parliamentary leadership, some of whom in 1981 became Social Democratic defectionists. The interaction of these two positions and their responses to the new forces affecting the relationship in the 1970s provided dynamic sources of changes which are still being felt today.

THE ASCENDANCY OF LEFTWING TRADE UNIONISM

The new generation of union leaders, in the late 1960s, provided a unique test of the 'rules' and of various diagnoses of the role of union leaders within the Labour Party. Their public commitment was to the traditional defence and extension of trade union freedom, to traditional Socialism, and to traditional conceptions of intra-party democracy. But the analysis shows that from the first, Jones and Scanlon accepted in great measure the old 'rules' of the relationship and their functional responsibility to take 'a trade union point of view'. This *immediately* inhibited the part that they could play within the Labour Party and *vis-à-vis* a Labour Government, whether in terms of formulating a Leftwing socialist policy or in terms of redistributing power within the Party. The clearest signal was their acceptance of the 'rule' of no Party sanctions against a Labour Government – a relinquishing of the capacity to enforce. All this did much to confirm the diagnosis that Leftwing union leaders had very restricted political purposes focused upon industrial objectives,[1] that they lacked any 'inclination to bring about sweeping changes in the leadership of the Labour Party',[2] and that under the Labour Government they adopted limited and defensive priorities.[3]

However, there are qualifications to be made, and they are important both in terms of the pressures upon Labour's leadership and the subsequent development of the Labour Party. They concern significant differences between Leftwing trade union leaders and the interactive character of the trade union–Labour Party relationship. 'A trade union point of view' could involve important variations in political purposes. Jones retained a strong commitment to egalitarianism. It enabled him to fuse union obligations and political objectives. He pursued an egalitarian distribution of power in industry to a degree which is difficult to characterise adequately as 'defensive'. And he persisted throughout the Labour Government in seeking to change the unequal distribution of wealth and income.[4] And though the more optimistic Leftwing scenario that these new union leaders might be heralds of a cultural revolution in the Party[5] did not quite come about, they did give encouragement to an alternative leadership from the political Left. They facilitated a climatic change such that Leftwing ideas about policy, procedure and trade union militancy could gain a new status, and they impeded a Rightwing union counter-attack. But in addition and most important of all, the differentiation of roles and 'hats' between individual union involvement in NEC elections and Liaison Committee activities on behalf of the TUC enabled the Leftwing union leaders to enhance the strength on the NEC of those seeking 'sweeping changes' after 1976, at the same time as those same union leaders were themselves criticising and resisting NEC policy. Thus they helped to sustain and handed down a legacy of Leftwing control over the NEC.

A similar diagnosis, with important qualifications, can be made about the behaviour of Leftwing union leaders during the crisis over intra-party democracy after 1979. The evidence of resolutions, votes and behaviour does not support those who argue that 'the unions' or 'the union leaders' were the great initiating, driving force behind the constitutional reform proposals.[6] But again, there are important qualifications to be made, including the vital effects of interaction within the Party. An important triad was at work from 1979 to 1982. It involved the carefully orchestrated use of CLP resolutions as 'detonators' to the union mandate 'bomb',[7] and it involved procedural facilities given by the NEC to allow the union mandates to be registered. The most important effect of this triad was probably the dividing of the Rightwing union leaders – a division made worse by the tactics of the would-be defectionists. And again we have to note the important differences between union traditions and between union leaders. One unusual feature of this period was the prominent role played by some unions and union leaders who were less constrained by the traditional 'rules'. Another unusual feature was the way that, in some of the unions, policy on Labour's constitutional questions in this period was influenced by activists and officials who were less subject to General Council influences and perspectives – including their acceptance of the 'rules'.

SOCIAL DEMOCRACY, DEFECTION AND NEW MODEL UNIONISM

While these tests of the 'rules' were taking place on the trade union Left, another kind of testing of the 'rules' was taking place on the political Right. There were many roads to the defections of 1980–81 but almost all of them crossed the junctions of the Party's relationship with the unions at some point. And for some, the junctions were the feature which made the road out all the more necessary.

On the part of the PLP, union power and union behaviour came to be seen as a major, perhaps *the* major, industrial and political problem. Union democracy and union definition of freedom were seen as both anachronistic and dangerous such that where once 'the petty tyranny of the employer–employee relationship'[8] had evoked a sense of repugnance, by the late 1970s it was primarily the unions' relationship with their members which aroused indignation. Within the Labour Party the unions were seen as acting as agencies for a Left which was, it appeared, in a remorseless momentum towards greater control and the proclamation of undesirable policies. At every turn in the Labour Party the social democrats felt constrained by the 'rules'. Even solidarity came to be seen as involving politically oppressive obligations and relations. The defensive shield of the praetorian guard had apparently gone for ever, but in any case reliance on union leaders heightened the sense of being hemmed in by unacceptable forces. For some on the Right, therefore, challenging the Labour Party from outside seemed the only way to break a stranglehold.

Ten years after their liberation from the 'rules' their position was fraught with paradox and the cause of much chagrin. They had either folded into the mould of the Liberal Party, or had faded away. They had failed to split the Labour Movement, indeed had failed to break even one union away from it. But their defection and subsequent tactical manœuvres had helped to fragment opposition to a

Conservative Government which was busily reconstructing all aspects of the post-war 'settlement'. In one major respect at least – the new laws covering industrial relations and union democracy – this reconstruction was welcomed by them and accepted virtually in full by 1986. The defectionists and their allies also added to the pressures and to the agenda which produced a series of adjustments in policy by the Labour Party and the unions. It was an adjustment which few defectionists had thought possible given the power relations between the Party and the unions.

POWER RELATIONS

These relations have become more complicated than ever in the past fifteen years, given the new links and channels and the multiplicity of informal contacts, but they have always been multidimensional. Let us summarise here what we have uncovered in the different dimensions.

1 Policymaking

The trade union preponderance at the Party Conference often leads to an overstatement of the union role in policymaking. This happened in the period from 1979 to 1982 when commentators located changes in trade union behaviour as central to the politics of policymaking. A much better case can be made for regarding the Leftwing-dominated Party NEC as the hub and generator of change. Certainly, the evidence over the broad range of issues covered in the case studies does not substantiate the diagnosis that in this period after 1979 trade union leaders made a decisive move into Labour Party politics in order to initiate changes in policy.[9]

Policy initiatives and responses by the NEC were sometimes restrained and sometimes reshaped because of the mandates of the unions. Policymaking was also influenced by the hierarchy of priorities of union leaders and as a result of the interaction with the TUC on the Liaison Committee. But the NEC could set the Party agenda and encourage like-minded groups in the unions, and it was NEC policy which laid down the markers of Party unity. The result of this interaction with the unions in the period from 1979 to 1983 was a pattern in which relations and outcomes varied issue by issue, but generally (as Chapter 14 shows) the initiatives of the unions and their leaders were much less significant than appeared to be the case.

The variations issue by issue were also accompanied by a pattern which followed the electoral cycle. The nearer the General Election, the more room for manœuvre there was for the Parliamentary leadership, though the extent was affected by the degree of union commitment behind particular policies. And the process of policymaking was also affected by broader periodic changes which affected the balance of resources. These worked to the disadvantage of the Parliamentary leadership between 1979 and 1982. But after 1983 as the NEC Left and the unions were weakened and the Parliamentary leadership gained new strengths, the changes worked increasingly to reinforce the position of the latter.

By the time of the 1987 General Election the pre-eminence of the Kinnock leadership was evident in three features. The first was the loosening of NEC supervision of policymaking; there was an unusual degree of procedural flexibility – without union reaction. The second was the reordering of the consultative arrangements with the unions; the Liaison Committee was downgraded and a new emphasis was placed on the less formal discussions with 'the Neddy Six'. The third involved the achievement of a range of new policy objectives, including legislation covering union balloting and the proposal for a statutory minimum wage.

Nevertheless the 1987 General Election Manifesto still reflected the inter-action with the unions and important boundaries of policymaking on some key issues. And although Kinnock's personal authority and the unions' dependence upon the political wing had both been boosted in the aftermath of the miners' strike, the leadership was never free of the policy pressures produced during industrial disputes.

It became the central task of the Labour leadership after 1987 to loosen or remove these boundaries and pressures in their strategic attempt to capture the electoral centre-ground. Although union leaders retained their distinctive order-ing of priorities, issue by issue, these now had to be adjusted within the context of acute electoral considerations which in the circumstances became almost over-riding.

Step by step, through various procedures and consultative arrangements, the overall shift of policy was made. The most significant changes included a redefi-nition of the non-nuclear defence policy (abandoning unilateral nuclear disarma-ment) and a new industrial relations policy (abandoning the focus on union immunities and the claim to full autonomy). But there was also a greater neutrali-sation of the problems caused to the Parliamentary leadership by industrial disputes and, less obviously, the lifting of a TUC restraint over policymaking concerning tripartite institutions.

Consultations with the union leaders, and the mandates of the unions, still affected some elements of Party policy, particularly where priority interests, including jobs and conditions of work, were involved and wherever experience of the British judiciary had to be considered. A prudent respect for the build-up of consistent Conference majorities also on occasions fed back into the Policy Review. But this anticipation of the reaction of the unions was heavily overlaid by the way union leaderships now anticipated the needs of the Party and its leadership in the wording of their mandates. This feature added to the policy dominance of the Kinnock leadership which was probably greater than for any previous Labour Party Opposition leadership.

Certainly none had managed to secure trade union acceptance of a permanent framework of law covering industrial relations. Labour Party policy by 1990 constituted a profound break with past definitions of one of the central values of the relationship – trade union freedom. An explanation for this historic shift would have to take account of the permanent pressure on the unions caused by the increasing legal constraints and the threat of more. It would have to take account of the union leaderships' response to the fact that opinion among the majority of non-active trade unionists was consistently in favour of at least a partial adjustment. It would have to take account of union leaders' awareness of the need for a new strategy to deal with the changing composition of the labour force. It would have to take account of the inducements of harmonisation with Europe in countering the attack on trade unions and on employees' conditions of employment. All these together made it essential to move on to a more defensible terrain – a workable area of trade union freedom supported by trade union and public opinion. But it was the drive from the Party – particularly the Leadership – seeking to compete with the Conservatives in the struggle to win Office which most forced the agenda of change.

In securing these changes Labour's leadership transcended ninety years of history and overcame what seemed an impassable barrier in the form of ninety per cent of the Party Conference votes. There could be few stronger tests of power over Labour Party policymaking.

2 Rule-making

The position of the unions was potentially most commanding over rule changes. These had to be implemented in exact form after authorisation by the union-dominated Conference. In theory, it was open to the unions after 1918 to give those unwritten 'rules' which were favourable to them a formal constitutional status, and to enact other rules which would constrain the Parliamentary Party and redress any balance seen as contrary to immediate union interests.

But, as we have seen, there was *no* such pattern of activity. The attitude of union leaders towards Labour's constitution was generally conservative. They saw an obligation of solidarity in the stabilisation of the constitutional rules, unless the Parliamentary leadership were strongly pushing for reform. Then the general tendency for much of Labour Party history has been for a union majority to support them.

For a majority in, and of, the unions, even the exceptional circumstances and interactions of the late 1970s did not fully break this pattern, as we have seen. And the more characteristic union attitude towards Labour's constitution re-emerged from 1982 to 1990. It was a period of unprecedented rule changes; yet no significant change in Labour's constitution arose from union initiative. And the unions accepted virtually all proposals which came from the NEC as a result of the initiatives of the Parliamentary leadership and Party officials. There were only three exceptions to this amenability. Rule changes to candidate selection continued to reflect the deeply entrenched alignments of 1979, and by 1990 had also become a touchstone of union anxiety about being 'pushed out' of the Party. Positive discrimination for women on candidate shortlists was supported against the platform in 1988, in part because the unions had twice supported this proposal in previous years on the advice of the platform. And in 1989 the Leadership's proposal for a Black Society was so hopelessly botched as to undermine its credibility.

3 Sponsorship

Trade union power over the policies of the Parliamentary Party would appear to be at its most immediate and potentially most significant via the practice of sponsorship. This sponsorship has grown in significance as unions have come to revalue their 'voice' in Parliament, as the percentage of union sponsored or union associated Members has increased, and as, in some of the key unions, new liaison personnel and new consultation processes have integrated the work of sponsored groups of MPs.

But this is a much misunderstood relationship. Sponsorship is not maintenance, these are not 'Kept Men',[10] and sponsorship does not involve control. Further, the unions are weaker than they appear at CLP level, their payments to the constituency parties of sponsored candidates are of declining significance in candidate selection, and the evidence indicates that withdrawal of sponsorship is not a 'mighty threat'[11] to the future of a sponsored Member.

This weakness is compounded within the sponsoring unions by prohibitions on a union's right to threaten sanctions and to impose penalties relating to votes in the House. The rules of Parliamentary privilege have become part of the 'rules' of the relationship, sometimes breached by less senior union officials on the Left of the Party, but as we have seen, generally strongly adhered to at the most senior level of the union hierarchy involving General Council members. For their part, sponsored MPs can and do defend their positions robustly and successfully. Overall this relationship is very different from that described by one knowledgeable columnist as 'the muscle of money'[12] and from the increasingly dangerous trend of direct financial relationships with MPs.[13]

Recently, the 'co-option' of existing Members has spread sponsorship, or some other form of union association, to all the members of the Shadow Cabinet. This, plus the added financial assistance given by unions to the Front Bench, appears to have increased the potential for political leverage. But these arrangements are particularly strongly insulated by a sense of propriety and protocol. Nothing indicates this union sensitivity more than their attempt to place a buffer between the unions and union payments for political assistants of individual members of the Front Bench. There are, as we have seen, many policy examples of the independence of sponsored Shadow Cabinet members (including the Leader) from their sponsoring union. The evidence also indicates a deep reluctance by unions to use sponsored MPs for purposes of internal party policymaking. And the record shows how little sponsorship matters in terms of the voting of MPs in internal leadership elections.

4 Elections

Many consequences followed in 1981 from the direct involvement of the unions in Labour leadership elections, but the *least* significant was the extra resource it gave in terms of the power of the unions. The unanticipated consequence of a union involvement which was intended to induce greater accountability of the Parliamentary leadership was that it did just the opposite. Union priorities, union procedures, and the inhibitions of union leaders over their involvement in this sensitive area, produced as much security as any Labour leader had known. A further strengthening of security took place after 1988 with the unions agreeing to raise the nomination threshold. The new constituency produced only minimal policy repercussions – a temporary additional hesitancy during the election period. It was remarkable on how many issues the Party Leader in 1988 was openly at variance with the policies of key unions, including the TGWU, during the election period, let alone afterwards.

As for the union involvement in elections for the NEC, here again roles and 'rules' produced effects which were often very different from surface appearance. Domination of elections for the NEC was not used by the unions collectively to ensure *their* control over the Parliamentary leadership. Indeed the historic role of the Trade Union Section of the NEC has been to act as a loyal base responding to the initiatives of the 'politicians', particularly the Parliamentary leadership. It was a role shaped by a definition of function but facilitated by factional alignment.

The significance of NEC factional composition for Labour's power relations was shown in 1981 when a new political alliance on the Right of the unions effectively ended not only Leftwing control of the NEC but the fourteen-year advance of the Left within the Party. After 1983 a political understanding between union leaders on Left and Right helped to assist in the marginalisation of the NEC Left, and helped to give the 'Dream Ticket' leadership its growing base of support.

But all this political activity – heightened after 1979 by a new politicisation initiated from the Left, by a reactive loyalism and by an assertive feminism – had to operate in a sense along the margins of NEC voting. The 'rules' and arrangements of Trade Union Section voting, and to a lesser extent Women's Section voting, were mainly attuned to industrial criteria – particularly industrial unity. These 'rules' and arrangements were perpetuated under a wide range of pressures and their effect was to restrain factional and Leadership management of the electoral process.

This was a regular frustration to one group or another, to such a degree that, as was shown, one major union leader on the Right who attempted to avoid the 'rules' for the sake of political loyalty was forced to resign. It was a frustration to the Right. On other occasions, it was a frustration to the Left and to the feminists. And it was also a frustration to the Party Leader. The process could be influenced, but could not be controlled, and sometimes did not fully respond to the steering of the Leader's Office. And the emergence of a soft Left loyalist group on the NEC to challenge the position of the rightwing group was mainly a product of union voting and NEC politics, not the Leader's initiative.

5 Organisational and financial management

The unions, it is often said, 'own' the Labour Party and as a result they have complete control.[14] The Party therefore 'dances to the tune' of its union paymasters,[15] whose resources are used to maximise their political leverage.[16]

In practice, in the 1980s as so often in the past, it was the Leader of the Labour Party who was calling the tune: 'He who paid the piper merely played the tuba and the big bass drum.'[17] Appearances were and are misleading because there were and remain unwritten prohibitions against open threats of financial sanctions, and there were and are inhibitions and constraints which limit the implementation of such sanctions. The NEC's responsibility for the government of the Party generally provides a meaningful insulation from direct organisational control by senior union leaders. And financial offices held by trade unionists on the NEC are a reassurance about financial prudence; they are not positions of policy leverage and reciprocity. Propriety and protocol determines appropriate channels and limits acceptable sanctions.

Of course, financial input is not an insignificant feature in terms of inducing a general level of political respect – here as elsewhere in political life. The General Secretary and the Treasurer in particular, had to look over their shoulders at the unions and were often amongst the most sensitive to union grievance. This sensitivity was at its most acute when new affiliation fees were up for discussion. The consultations, mandatory under the 'rules', have often turned into a lament – sometimes over matters of Party management. But rarely was this linked to specific future proposals. In general, the link between finance, power, and future *policy* commitments was loose, almost to the point of non-connection.

However, the inhibition upon financial pressure exercised over MPs and the Parliamentary leadership was always less restrictive in relation to the NEC Left and was relaxed considerably in the early 1980s – particularly when the threats were given encouragement from senior MPs, and union leaders encountered no criticism from the mass media. The period from 1979 to 1982 was highly unusual in the financial threats by some union leaders relating to the general management of the Party. Even so, implementation of the threats was difficult, resented, and often successfully resisted.

There is no doubt that both the Commission of Enquiry of 1980 and the Voluntary Levy Fund of 1981 were imposed on a reluctant NEC, with the threat to refuse increased affiliation fees acting as a significant sanction. But the findings of the Commission of Enquiry were hampered by individual union autonomy on the one hand and the resistance of the NEC on the other. The Voluntary Levy fund was operated with deep inhibition and sensitivity. And all of this financial negotiation was kept well clear of any policy discussion. Throughout this period, and later when union leaders backed a new Business Plan, union leaders were concerned – even at times obsessed – with securing the Party's organisational and financial viability, as well as safeguarding *their* funds from profligacy. But the notion that in policy terms they used their finance as hungry barons seeking to maximise power is difficult to reconcile with their attitude to State Finance for political parties and to control over the state-provided 'Short Money'. It is difficult to reconcile with their willingness to index-link or guarantee rises in affiliation fees. And it is virtually impossible to reconcile with the activation in 1988 of a proposal which dated back to the origins of TULV – the ending of the General Election 'begging bowl'.

6 Administration

Barely noticed by observers of the Party organisation was a trade unionism of Party employees and a highly problematic industrial relations – particularly at Party headquarters. Labour Party administration involved a distinctive triple trade union presence. There was a senior union leadership watching anxiously how 'the members' money' was spent. There was an NEC Trade Union Section with a share in responsibility for Head Office management and there was a range

of internal unions operating a post-entry closed shop and a highly active branch
life.

This head office (and regional party office) unionism was for years an important element in the power relations surrounding Labour Party administration and
its style and attitudes were in part a product, in part a cause of the historic failures
of Labour Party management. However, though the staff union branches were
the base of a powerful defensive unionism and an increasingly assertive militancy,
they were persistently thwarted in their radical and far-sighted organisational
objectives in relation to the management of headquarters.

Indeed, it was a noteworthy feature of the union–Party relationship in the late
1970s and early 1980 that neither pressure from the so-called union 'barons' nor
the representations of the internal union branches could produce the reorganisation that both agreed was desperately needed. The Left-led, and then Left-
influenced NEC resisted.

Reorganisation began eventually under a new Leader and a new General
Secretary and in two phases, ending with the General Election of 1987, produced
an impressive administration as well as a new communications flair. In conditions of new financial adversity a further reorganisation took place, involving this
time a major pruning of Head Office staff. What happened then highlighted the
behaviour of union leaders when the Party's viability was considered to be at
stake.

In new circumstances and responding to new political leadership, NEC trade
unionists and a union majority at the Party Conference expressed its solidarity
with the Party rather than with the militant staff – seeing the Party's viability as
in the general interest, as in the financial interests of levypayers, and as the
greater priority.

The outcome led to a greater dominance by Head Office management, backed
by the Parliamentary leadership, and a new emphasis on efficiency including the
skills of management. There remained, however, a continuing problem in relations with the organiser's union NULO (now merged with the GMB).

THE DISTRIBUTION OF POWER

To understand fully the relationship between trade unions and the Labour Party
we have to appreciate both its consistencies and its variabilities. There are
differences in the power relationship dimension by dimension and, within
policymaking, between the different issue areas and over the electoral cycle.
There are also periodic changes in the overall distribution of power.

These historic changes have encouraged the emergence of two polar models of
power in the way the relationship has been perceived. For a long period in the
1950s and 1960s it was a commonplace to assert that effective power was concentrated around (or 'in the hands of') the Parliamentary leadership. But the moment that a new assertiveness was evident from the union leaders, then commentators easily adjusted to the second polar model because it fitted so well the many
deceptive formal signposts. Given the block voting of the preponderant union
majority and the financial support manifest at all levels of the relationship, who
would not be drawn to the diagnosis of overwhelming 'union control' over the

Party and its Parliamentary leadership?[18]

Both these models were problematic, but particularly in relation to 'union control'. One problem was that, in terms of alignments around particular conflicts, 'the unions' in a sense rarely existed. In recent years, previously unified union positions on constitutional questions and on industrial relations have added to the issue-based and factional conflicts which cut across industrial and political institutions.

But there was a more fundamental problem with the notion of union 'control' in relation to the Labour Party. As illustrated time and again in this study, what we have here is a consistent pattern of behaviour which involves marked inhibitions and constraints derived from a differentiation of industrial and political roles and from the agreed 'rules' of the relationship. An appreciation of this dimension of power relations within the Labour Party has to be integrated with our understanding of those characteristics of mass party organisation which facilitate the development of dominance by the political leadership and, especially in the British context, by the Parliamentary leadership.

Although overall the 'rules' dictated mutual obligations and mutual restraint, and although they derived in great measure from trade union defined values, the most significant feature of the way the rules operated was that they limited the effective power of the group which appeared to have all the key formal levers of power at their disposal – the trade union leadership. And odd though it seems, a polar model of power which looked best fitted to the short periods when the unions were most assertive was, in practice, most applicable to the long periods when the PLP leadership was in the ascendancy.

Thus, whatever the formal features, it is virtually always misleading to say that the unions 'run the Labour Party'.[19] It was misleading in the 1970s when the behaviour of the NEC was the dismay and frustration of most union leaders. It is even more misleading today. Misunderstanding or mischief still bring forth the formal features of the union–Party relationship as evidence, even though any close analysis reveals more party management exercised from the Leader's Office than ever before.

This pre-eminence of the Kinnock leadership owed much to new reinforcing conditions. But it was also based upon a crucial range of consistencies in the attitude of most union leaders to Labour Party activity. This consistency can be found in the behaviour of the most senior union leaders, in the behaviour of NEC Trade Union Section members and in the behaviour of the TUC administration. What appeared to be a quite fundamental change in behaviour turns out on closer inspection to be a change within and alongside patterned continuities. Such continuities were integral to the operation of the trade union–Labour Party relationship.

The continuities could be found in each of the dimensions, before and after 1979, before and after the advent of the Kinnock leadership. Their most remarkable exemplification concerned the relationship between financial provision and policymaking. Union contributions to the Party's finances were heavily insulated from leverage over specific policy outcomes. Union leaders in TULV were for a long time willing to forgo key formal positions of financial leverage. And union leaders throughout the 1980s were concerned with assisting the Front Bench with resources which would increase their effectiveness. Indeed the history of the development of financial assistance to the Front Bench is one where senior union leaders protected the arrangement and gave additional supplements. They did this through mechanisms which, in effect, depleted the possibility of union control while reinforcing the supremacy of the Leader.

It is worth noting that these financial arrangements were beginning to take effect at the time of the revolt over the accountability of the Parliamentary leadership, in 1979. The resources at this point began to strengthen the policy facilities available to the Shadow Cabinet members. In the long term, this was bound to make Labour's double-headed and divided policymaking leadership even more unworkable. In this sense, as some of the NEC Left realised at the time, what was being won in the constitutional dimension was being threatened in the financial field: and being threatened with the co-operation of union leaders, including some who were supporting constitutional reform.

Subsequently, the experience of the 1983 General Election campaign undermined, within the unions as well as at senior levels of the Party, the conception that cohesion between the two heads could be forced by a command democracy based upon the NEC's sole control over policy formulation. The result was an historic adjustment, bringing the Parliamentary leadership into joint policy formulation. This limited the possibility of a public gap opening up between the two leadership bodies and it could, in theory, have been the basis of a new, more co-operative, democratic dialogue. In practice, the procedural change coincided with a variety of circumstances and forces which strengthened considerably the policy pre-eminence of the Parliamentary leadership.

The new financial arrangements also strengthened the capacity of the Party Leader to manage the Party. His Office now housed an unprecedented proliferation of aides, assistants and advisers, with an overview of, and involvement in, all aspects of Party activity and all dimensions of the links with the unions. In effect there was now an Executive Office of the Leader. It was not always successful in this involvement, but there was here the basis of a centralised power structure unique in Labour Party history – likely to be further strengthened if linked to a Downing Street entourage.

And yet there remained a subdued pluralism[20] within this pattern of power – and the unions continued to be key elements in this pluralism. Consultative mechanisms, and mandates backed by a concerned union constituency, still induced a degree of responsiveness by the Parliamentary leadership in 1990.[21] And there were, as we have seen, other influences of the union connection. Trade Union Section elections were never under the full control of the Party Leader, and the Party organisers' union, NULO, retained influence over some appointments and redeployments.

Further, the different dimensions of the relationship still produced distinctive management problems and boundaries of action. Crucially, on constitutional changes the trade union majority at the Party Conference formed the ultimate boundary – the ultimate defence that 'the Party' (as opposed to simply its Leadership) should make policy, and the ultimate union security. Their consistent amenability to leadership initiatives in this area had its limits. Above all, as the argument in 1990 over candidate selection showed, if you proposed that the collective union presence be excluded from any procedure or institution, you were successful only if a majority in the unions could be persuaded to move.

MOBILISATION, POLITICISATION AND FACTIONALISM

Alongside the Left's diagnosis of an industrial militancy which would generate a fundamentally reinvigorated Leftwing political movement in the unions, there has also been, in the past two decades, a Rightwing diagnosis that new affluence and a new acquisitive individualism would lead to a depoliticised form of unionism which would permanently undermine the political Labour Movement. Significant influence on the Movement can indeed be detected from developments in line with both diagnoses, but neither has been hegemonic, and neither has resulted in a decisive change in the form and character of the Labour Movement.

Much more central to recent experience has been the replenishment of a reforming political trade unionism committed to mainstream Labour Movement values and closely identified with the Labour Party.[22] This also failed to realise its potential in the climate and within the Party strategy of the late 1980s. But it left a legacy – the creation of a new agency for mobilising trade unionists in support of the Labour Party and in defence of their political funds.

The political Left – particularly the NEC Left – was often ill at ease with this development. Their primary focus, in terms of political mobilisation, consisted of sustained and unconditional support for industrial militancy, conjoined after 1981 with the use of Leadership elections, to educate, align and bring that militancy into Labour Party activity. In theory a strengthening of the TULV–TUCC–TUFL organisation was not an alternative to the Left's political strategy, and they had overlapping union enthusiasts. But in practice and in emphasis they became for a time alternative modes and priorities of operation in pursuit of a more political trade unionism.

Leadership elections

Only one Leadership election, that of 1983, was a consensual arrangement to produce a successor. The initiating of elections in 1981 and 1988 involved an ambitious political challenge on the part of the Left's political leadership and it met determined opposition from a range of union leaders – including some on the Left – because of a stark clash of priorities and contrasting attitudes towards the 'rules'.

In style and objectives, the 'Bennite' campaigns of 1981 and 1988 were irreverent in their attitude towards the protocol of relations, emphasising a fusion of industrial and political purposes. The 1981 campaign did succeed in entrenching the mode of election and in some respects it was a *factional* success. It generated a new linking arrangement between the General Council Left and the Left's political leader, Benn, and it facilitated the growth of Broad Left factions in the unions. But its politicisation of the trade union membership was minimal, it divided the Left, and it brought upon them further blame for Party disunity. Other costs were also high. It helped to produce a strengthened and unified Party

Right, it damaged the Party's own campaigning, it allowed the defectionist SDP to get off the ground, and it exposed to the advantage of trade union critics the weaknesses of unprepared trade union decision-making processes.

In 1988 it was less damaging to the Party but incurred extra costs to the Left, exacerbating further its fragmentation.[23] As for the response in the unions, moving in the face of the priorities of even some of the closest trade union allies, the Left's campaign diminished its credibility. It gave the opportunity for the Leadership to win union support for a procedural reform which restricted the possibility of further contests, and, as far as can be discerned in terms of its politicising effect on the trade union membership, it was a failure.

TULV–TUCC–TUFL

TULV was a deeply resented organisation, with as wide a range of enemies as one is likely to get in the Labour Movement. And yet it broke through decades of trade union complacency and through some of the rigidities of union–Party boundaries. Its detractors have often been hopelessly prejudiced in judging its political purpose and role in the Labour Party. Initiated by a core of union leaders drawn from the Left and the Right, its primary concern was with the financial and organisational viability of the Party and with its capacity to mobilise trade unionists. In the circumstances of the early 1980s it became preoccupied, as had previous generations of union leaders, with the problem of Party stability, and on occasions became involved in interventions with factional consequences. It also took on a recommendatory role in relation to the Party which was highly contentious and a breach of the 'rules' of Party autonomy. But its political ambitions were often misinterpreted by the political Left. It was not 'a Trojan Horse[24] for the Right'; indeed, it acted as an obstacle to a thoroughgoing Rightwing factional counter-attack. And the Voluntary Levy Fund was not used as a partisan political 'drip-feed'.[25]

Alongside these controversial activities and in the face of much negative and obstructionist criticism, TULV moved forward in the creation of an unprecedented agency of union political mobilisation on behalf of the Labour Party. Even though the end-results never fulfilled expectations, in focusing on the problems of the relationship, in creating structures and above all in establishing union obligations, it provided a beneficial infusion. In the process, it played an important though often unrecognised role in preparing the ground and strategy for the Political Fund ballots campaigns.

These campaigns, co-ordinated by the TUCC, produced an extraordinarily successful defence of the political funds. If it was not the 'victory for the Labour Party' that some diagnosed, neither was it brought about by the contrived total concealment of the Labour Party that others criticised. Indeed the relationship of the union campaign with the Labour Party involved three different questions of political management : who controls?, what content?, with what input from the Labour Party organisation and membership? On the first there was absolute union unanimity that for political and administrative reasons it had to be kept clear of the NEC Left. On the second there was a TUCC line which focused on the union's right to have political funds in order to have a political 'voice'. But the

Labour Party relationship was dealt with in detail in campaign co-ordination material for activists and was mentioned in one way or another in most campaigns, and in some of them prominently. As it turned out there was no significant difference in the result between those which emphasised the Labour Party and those which did not. On the third question there was a hidden struggle between the TUCC office and Chairman and some of the other union leaders, with the Labour Party management and its Leadership also involved. In this conflict the TUCC leaders and Labour Party involvement were both defeated.

The principal reason for the political fund victories was the rationality of adopting a fund given the new definition of political action. Opponents of political funding had also seriously miscalculated the unions' capacity to campaign, whilst the nakedly partisan form of the legislation inhibited Conservative organisation. Yet the most remarkable and unrecognised element in the situation related to the support among trade unionists for Labour Party linkage. Contrary to myth,[26] the success of the campaign was built upon the *solidity* of this support, not its fragility. And there was a *growing* body of such support, not a decline in the period leading up to the Political Fund ballots.

In line with the fact that the results were only weakly related to the electoral position of the major parties, there was no discernible electoral benefit to the Labour Party from the Fund ballot results, although a range of other benefits can be discerned, including the creation of a new body, TUFL. Its disavowal of any recommendatory role in relation to the Labour Party did much to forge a new consensus over its value as a permanent and staffed organisation. In practice, although co-ordinating Labour's union campaign much better than before, it failed to realise its objectives at the grass roots in the election results of 1987, and it has yet to receive the necessary trade union push or to generate the necessary dynamism which accompanied the Political Fund ballots.

Political funding: the next battle

If the political definitions and choices remain the same, and if union communicational vitality is generated to the same degree, then any future Political Fund ballot contest is likely to produce a similar outcome. And it follows from my argument that in any future ballots held under the rules of the 1984 Act, the general mid-term unpopularity of the Government – Conservative or Labour – will not be as crucial as is sometimes suggested in influencing the decision as to whether to support a political fund. The sphere of employment has a political rationality of its own.

The case for a more political trade unionism is being strengthened all the time by the growing connection between industrial concerns and political action. There is, in adversity, a strong sense of the industrial priorities and a general suspicion of unneccesary involvement in 'politics', but much about the politics of the 1990s – the new permanent legal regulation of industrial relations, the feminist perspective on the range of collective bargaining issues, the salience of Government policy for employment conditions, the link between education and training, the environmental dimension, the Europeanisation of British political and industrial life, and the globalisation of economic processes – will demand and encourage a broadening of the horizons of trade unionism.

Further, an awareness of the deeper vulnerabilities and wider concerns of the unions has been heightened by the experience of the past fifteen years. This experience indicates that if trade unions do not seek to strengthen a political dialogue with their members other political forces will. Experience also indicates that the consequences of trade unionism, however narrow in purpose, often involve political reverberations which feed back into the industrial context. And experience further indicates that significant victories are not easily gained, and even less easily protected, unless the views of consumers, users and the community at large are taken into account. These considerations are beginning to become part of the prudential responsibilities of trade union leadership.

These new connections and new responsibilities will require in the end a revolution in the dissemination of knowledge,[27] with union leaders seeking an informed and, in its broadest sense, politicised trade unionism, as part of a wider democratisation in the system of British communication and education. The broader the perspectives of trade unionism, the better for the unions, the Labour Party, the economy, and the public interest.

As for the Labour Party connection and its place in Political Fund campaigns, persistent public 'distancing' may be damaging to the core support if it is not accompanied by more joint local campaigning on issues where the unions and the Party are 'natural allies'.[28] But the crucial question, now and in the future, is the extent to which there are practical advantages which can be offered to trade unionists from the Labour Party connection. If these continue to be evident, and especially if a Labour Government can deliver some of the new facilities and rights and agreed priorities before the next fund campaigns, the case for the relationship will again be strengthened.

FLEXIBITY

The management of the Political Fund campaigns was but one example of a feature of the recent behaviour of the Labour Movement which is often unappreciated – its flexibility. For years it had been characterised in terms of its conservatism – a cart–horse Party slowly plodding its blinkered way forward, unable to modernise, unable to restructure, unable to innovate and unable to take up a variety of radical currents.[29] It is clearly a misdiagnosis and one which proved fateful for the Social Democratic defectionists.

Consider the innovative record revealed in this study of changes in procedure and institution which have either involved the unions or entailed their acquiescence since 1979; new Joint Policy Committees and joint Policy Review Groups; new procedures for candidate selection and Leadership elections; a reorganisation of the Women's Conference and of Women's Executive representation; acceptance of the principle of women's quotas; a new campaign strategy committee, a new organisation for the political mobilisation of trade unionists, TULV transmuting via TUCC into TUFL, new financial and membership arrangements; a new relationship with sponsored MPs involving a new category of 'political officers'; broad agreement on a major reduction in the union vote at the Party Conference, and on a wide-ranging overhaul of the procedures of policymaking, including the procedures of the Party Conference and a new National Policy Forum; a major change in the role of the (much misunderstood) Labour Party – TUC Liaison Committee from a central position in 1982 to a point in 1990 when it had virtually disappeared.

In 1980 what might have struck any observer coming to the Labour Party afresh was that this was a party representing producers (and mainly masculine producers) with a strong emphasis on the collective and a bias towards centralism.[30] Much of this would have been seen as a product of the union connection which limited the possibility of major change. Yet in the late 1980s major changes have actually been taking place. There is a new and marked concern for the user and the consumer. There is a new emphasis on decentralisation, to the nations and the regions of the UK. There is also a new responsiveness to feminism and a new environmentalism.

Although collectivism remains a fundamental and unifying feature of union and Party philosophy (see Chapter 21, p. 657) the balance between the individual and the collective, in terms of rights, is being adjusted as the unions and the Party respond to that desire for moral autonomy and self-expression which is a feature of the age. This shift is underpinned also by a new awareness of the potential dangers of a collectivism which is unreasonable in action or insensitive in policy.

Undoubtedly, the most powerful general influence upon all these changes has been the Parliamentary leadership, as it faced new electoral imperatives. But it would also have to be recognised that there were already receptive currents within sections of the unions and within the TUC office. On some issues at some times, the current was not just receptive, it was jointly activating. And on feminist issues, women in various sectors, including the unions, established and sustained their own agenda.

This adaptability of the unions springs from many sources. There is the influence of a plurality of social movements and lobbies which permeate the unions and link it with the wider society. There is a clash of political traditions which, though they are anchored in the workplace location of the unions and in 'a trade union perspective', allow a flexibility of industrial responses and political goals; even defined as the representation of labour's interests. 'Labourism' is in practice many 'Labourisms'. There is also, interwoven with the pursuit of industrial interests, a persistent internal union and intra-union dialogue couched in terms of equality, freedom and democracy; these are influenced by long-established traditions but they are not insulated from changing interpretations outside the unions. And there is a perpetual reflection on past experience and new problems, some of it internally generated, some of it externally instigated. With this has come a renewed awareness of the need for union policy and union action to appeal to wider audiences and other concerned constituencies as a necessary prerequisite of achieving and retaining a variety of objectives.

What all this indicates, particularly in the light of the interactive effect of movements in one wing on the other, is that the Party can adapt and transform itself to a considerable degree and in a range of different directions.

Certainly, 'Labourism', as some ex-Alliance critics interpret it, has proved to be far less of a suffocating constriction than such critics often diagnosed.[31] Even if we take constitutional reform of the British state as *the* test (as one school of thought now tends to do), neither trade unionism nor 'Labourism' provide irremovable obstacles to radical reform. In the decisions of the Party Conference, and the TUC down the years can be found support for reforms of the second chamber, the legal system, the protection of civil liberties and the opening of government. An old tradition is being replenished as some of the unions become assertive carriers of the Labour Campaign for Electoral Reform. Even the Movement's centralism, reinforced by the magnet of Westminister and Whitehall, has periodically had a counterpoint, and this has been strengthened considerably in recent years by support for a devolution of government to the nations and regions, coupled with reinvigorated support for more autonomy for local government.

Of course, these policies can lose as well as gain priority. Nevertheless, in the 1990s only in two respects are the unions in serious discord with the thrust of British constitutional reform. The first is that years of focusing upon the practicable and the deliverable make most trade union leaders and the TUC administration sceptical of total immediate solutions – particularly those which require a degree of consensual support on thorny procedural issues. There is still a respectful traditionalism to be found in some trade union approaches to British Parliamentary democracy but a written constitution is generally seen as unlikely and problematic rather than intrinsically undesirable. The second is that 200 years of political experience has produced a deep reluctance to qualify Parliamentary democracy by passing more discretion to an unaccountable judiciary – particularly the British judiciary with its distinctive traditions and its unrepresentative social composition.

As for the Marxist critique of 'Labourism',[32] this is in certain features very soundly based. Against the small revolutionary Left, the 'rules' act as a network of checks, filters and obstacles and in critical conditions they act as legitimation of solidarity to protect the Party's constitution and the boundaries of its membership. For this reason, Marxist entryists have been involved in a politics which historically has been more significant for moving them individually towards social democracy than for moving the Labour Party towards a revolutionary strategy. Here I can agree with Leo Panitch that this is a Sisyphus-like task.[33]

This is not to say that the Labour Party cannot be moved significantly to the Left; indeed given its present cautious pragmatic stance it would be surprising if at some stage it did not rediscover the political space for a bolder platform of economic regulation, social justice and planning for social need. As for a reordering of factional strength favouring the organised Left, this could start at any time as a result of electoral trends in the unions and changes in the political composition of union executives and the union leadership. Indeed there were some signs in 1989–90 in some unions, including USDAW, that a shift was beginning to take place. But the speed, scope and form of the Labour Party's adjustment would be, as before, heavily constrained by the 'rules', and heavily affected by counterpressures from the Parliamentary leadership. Crucially, as before, the Left's advance would be limited and constrained by the extent to which changes at the top reflect, or have a resonance, with changes in political attitudes below. Not since the withering away of Second World War radicalism has there been a substantial constituency for the traditional Socialist Left within the population at large or even simply at the grass roots of the unions. It is the trade union membership acting as a section of the Party's electorate which produces the most important restraint on the trade union and Labour Left when it moves too far away from their purposes and priorities. In the future, given the unpopularity and widely perceived crisis of some of the traditional Socialist structures and policies, the restraint is likely to operate more heavily and more immediately than in the past.

REDEFINING THE 'RULES': FREEDOM AND DEMOCRACY

One central task in the management of the relationship in the 1990s is the rebuilding of a consensus on the 'rules' of freedom and democracy.

In terms of union freedom there are very good reasons why some old considerations are still relevant and traditional caution is still appropriate. There is still a need to defend the unions' independence both in terms of democratic sovereignty and the vigour which comes with self-reliance. And there is still a necessary defence of distinct union functions which have to be protected and found means of central representation – regardless of political affiliation. But developments stimulated by the actions of the state, the wishes of union members and the needs of the Party are all challenging the unions to redefine and reinterpret old industrial traditions and old assumptions about the interface between the unions and the Party.

It is doubtful whether there could now be a return to the traditional position of absolute union autonomy and the repudiation of any restraint on collective freedom.[34] Balloting rights given under law, and now embodied in union practice, cannot be taken away without a revolt of trade union members which would find political if not industrial expression. Old immunities cannot simply be recaptured, because the agenda of discussion has moved permanently into a European context of positive rights, of 'fair or unfair laws'.[35] And the beginnings of a sea-change in attitude towards the relationship between the individual and the collective is reducing the acceptability within the Movement of pursuing legal protection for some of the older styles of industrial action

The TUC Congress of 1990 was indeed a 'landmark'[36] meeting, involving a crucial acceptance by the unions of a framework of law in industrial relations. It was a step towards what some in both wings saw as a new 'settlement',[37] much more defensible in the court of public opinion.

However, this 'landmark' meeting has left open a wide range of issues which were not fully explored because of the demands of unity and out of sensitivity to the electoral difficulties. In particular, reservations over the limitations of solidarity action went much wider than the hard Left. The fact was that whatever the law had proscribed in the past, trade union action in support of brothers and sisters in Britain and abroad was still seen as an expression of the Movement's finest values.[38] On this alone there will be much future argument. At some stage also the historic movement for 'participation in power' will be replenished –

taking into account the recent experience of the management function and looking afresh at the various accommodations of trade unionism with employee and consumer democracy. A shift towards industrial democracy in the 1990s is likely to emphasise the motivational benefits of industrial enfranchisement and to harmonise with the most distinctive emphasis of Labour's aims under Kinnock – the liberation and fulfilment of all people's talent.

Whatever its limitations, a fundamental step has now been taken which brings the trade union movement much more into line with its own membership.[39] It is also closer to the trade unionism of a European Labour Movement, which will be the basis of future effective industrial action. And it opens up the possibility that if 'the public interest' justifies this regulation of the unions it can also justify a range of regulatory forms for other British industrial, financial and political arrangements.

A similar important shift is beginning to take place in the agenda, procedures and 'rules' of Labour Party democracy. It is held back by suspicions of a Leadership-dominated party and of any attempt to break the links between the unions and the Party. Nevertheless, the 1990 Conference decisions about the new policy process and an agreement on a formula to reduce the union preponderance at the Party Conference represent the first stage of a historic procedural transformation of the Labour Party.

It is now widely recognised that there is a very weak case for union policymaking processes which operate with no direct regard for the interests of the Party to which they are linked. Labour's internal procedures, involving the unions, are subject to instant public scrutiny via an overwhelmingly hostile press. The Conservative Party's own vulnerabilities over finance, openness and internal democracy do not inhibit its repetitive assaults upon any feature of the relationship with the unions which could cause Labour electoral damage.[40] Under this spotlight, the present arrangements, with uncertain linkage to the levypaying membership, with unit votes, and with a huge union preponderance at the Party Conference, are less and less acceptable to the CLP members, and to trade unionists, as well as to the public. Further, the present procedures maximise internal party frustration whilst encouraging and legitimating behaviour towards the Party on the part of the Parliamentary leadership which destroys trust and undermines morale. In Chapter 12 I have indicated what I believe to be the main trajectory of overall reform and how it might constructively develop.

As with the shift in perspectives and procedures relating to freedom, the shift over democracy is not unproblematic in conception and not without difficulties in practice – including its financial costs. There are dangers that more direct democracy can undermine both debate and accountability. There are dangers of a further loss of political identity if the Party becomes simply a register of waves of levypaying opinion. And there are dangers of a sharp destabilisation if the unions' role is suddenly reduced further. But nevertheless, there is now a prospect of moving towards a more viable, a more healthy and a more publicly acceptable democratic relationship with the unions.

IF LABOUR WINS

These proposals and arrangements will be tested under the most stringent conditions when Labour again forms a Government. All the areas of uncertainty, all the understandings and all the expectations taken on trust will be exposed. And all the old tensions laid out in this study will be present. There will be new acute pressures as an incoming Labour Government faces what is likely to be a bleak economic outlook and a challenging new European economic context.

In these circumstances it is not difficult to envisage a series of calamitous interactions involving the unions. This begins with an avalanche of pent-up financial demands and social grievances. It is faced by Ministers who are less experienced and less ideologically confident than any Labour Government since the 1920s. A potent mix of pressure from the finance markets, resistance from the House of Lords, criticism from the mass media and an avalanche of advice from sources hostile to the Labour Movement encourages measures that put the Labour Government deeply at odds with the Party and the unions. There is a deterioration in relationships and mutual recrimination – from the one side at the loss of disciplined support, and from the other, at the loss of direction. The Government ends with the Labour Movement deeply divided. This is manifested in conflict involving the Government and the law in the industrial sphere, and in disagreement over Party democracy and union consultations in the political sphere.

There is however an alternative scenario, which is rather more optimistic, and involves a two-term Labour Government rectifying some of the underlying weaknesses of the British economy through its supply side policies.[41] But the strains upon the Labour Movement which will accompany this economic project – particularly in the competition for limited public resources – will only be managed by creating and sustaining a consensus on economic objectives and social priorities, and the trust that restraint will not mean simply a permanent sacrifice.

Some of this is at least partially in place. In the past, Labour Governments have been involved in a cyclical pattern – an immediate surge of public expenditure and the satisfaction of outstanding pay claims followed by retrenchment and a tight incomes policy. With this pattern has gone what has been termed a 'cycle of union influence'.[42] In the case of the 1974–79 Labour Governments, union influence was generally overstated from the Right and understated from the Left, but the cycle was undeniable. That experience has affected both the political and the industrial leadership. Less will be promised in the first phase and less will be secured over and above an agreed minimum of priorities. One consequence will be to lessen the recoil of the Movement, the other to diminish the reaction of the finance markets – a reaction already partly assuaged by the absence of socialist rhetoric and the obvious fact that a radical socialist purpose is not on the agenda.

And in managing the restraint of the first phase, the new Labour Government could draw upon three major political assets in its relations with the union leaders. There would be, initially, an enormous boost to morale and a benevolence towards a successful political leadership. There would also be the re-emergence of traditional trade union loyalty and political restraint under the 'rules'. Both these features would give the Labour leaders a stronger base to carry through various party reforms and to gain a sympathetic hearing for the problems which are involved in the implementation of the Party's policies. There is also a significant sharing of economic objectives, with agreement on the priority of securing a productive and competitive economy. It is not just that union *leaders* 'now largely support policies to produce a high technology, high productivity, high wage economy'.[43] An authoritative study of technical change *at the workplace* in the 1980s showed unions at that level much more favourably disposed to technical innovation than critics suggested.[44]

Resistance to change was not simply a matter of historic low trust and traditional oppositionism, although this could be found in many sectors and institutions. It was also affected by the style of management, by the low level of retraining facilities, and by the limited alternative job opportunities. Defensive rigidity was simply one tendency within the trade union movement, and sometimes, as we have seen, one face within a given situation. As for being *the* constraint on productivity growth, 'the union problem' was often misdiagnosed or exaggerated. There is no conclusive evidence that trade unions are associated with lower productivity and some evidence to suggest that strong unions are associated with higher productivity.[45] Workers and their unions were not the crucial constraint upon British manufacturing industry as a whole.[46] British management faced other, more fundamental difficulties. What is now clear is the need to focus on the failures of investment in capital equipment and in employee skills, on the subordination of manufacturing sector investment to the short–term interests of the financial sector, and on the remarkable facilities for merger and take-over.

And the general economic record of the 'union-tied' 1974–79 Labour Governments has begun to look much better when contrasted with the Governments that followed it and in the context of the problems it faced. It did better in terms of unemployment, particularly against the background of world trade. The adjusted growth rates now make that Labour Government's record better than that of the Conservatives since 1979 – in spite of the direct and indirect advantages of North Sea oil.[47]. Further, the reality of the past twenty-five years is that each period of Labour in Office in the 1960s and the 1970s produced an improvement in the balance of payments and in manufacturing investment whereas each period of Conservative Government resulted in a deterioration.

Dealing with the acute problems involving the unions and the next Labour Government has become, in some ways, more difficult because of the new political uncertainty surrounding the channels, forums and weight of trade union representation. Much has changed since 1974. Reminded constantly of the legend of 'the brooding shadow', Labour's Shadow Ministers approach the obligations of Office with a distinct reluctance to emphasise a special relationship with the unions. For their part, wary of the past unpopularity of a trade union leadership which was portrayed as 'running the country' (a mythical arrangement), the TUC now approaches its relationship with a future Labour Government with a range of reassuring negatives, asking only that there will be respect for the views of 'industry', a readiness to listen to the concerns of working people and a sustained commitment to social justice – with priority for pensions and child benefits and the legal minimum wage. Nevertheless, behind all this self-restraint and 'distancing' there is an appreciation on both sides that new arrangements and a new protocol will have to be developed to avoid confrontation and facilitate a close and productive, if low-key, communication and liaison.

How fruitful the interaction is will depend in part on the factional alignments of the major unions. Considerable uncertainty surrounds the future trajectory of three major unions, the TGWU, NUPE (involved in a complex merger with COHSE and NALGO) and MSF. What kind of Labour Left emerges in those unions – indeed whether the Labour Left remains the most powerful force – will have considerable bearing on relations with the Labour Government. But the obverse is also the case. The factional alignments will be heavily affected, as in the past, by the way the Government tackles the most salient problems.

Near the top of the list of such problems is likely to be that of inflation, a problem now given a new dimension as a result of Britain's membership of the ERM – a constraint which is likely to add to the new high levels of unemployment. The serious inflationary situation of 1990–1 could not be blamed on over-assertive trade unions pushing up salary and wage costs; indeed, it was the clearest example since 1948 that such costs were not necessarily the prime cause of inflation. But the level of pay settlements could make it more difficult for a Labour Government to control inflationary pressure and to reduce unemployment. By 1991, a mainstream body of opinion within the unions, this time including NUPE leaders, was looking for a new order in relation to incomes, which would give statutory protection for the lower paid and avert permanent, high level unemployment. It remains to be seen whether, in the absence of other viable or politically acceptable ways of managing inflation, the doubters among the industrial and political leadership and the critics on Left and Right within the unions, aware of the problematic past experience, could be won over to a more co-ordinated pay-bargaining policy. It remains to be seen also whether the National Economic Assessment can produce a consensual approach to a wide agenda connected with Britain's low level of labour productivity, a much broader problem than that of wage costs.

Union co-operation in this exercise will be affected by the problems over the detailed implementation of the policies on industrial relations legislation. There will also be problems over the level of funding to be given to the supply-side programme of investment in education and training compared with the other social commitments of Labour's programme. On the other hand, the relationship can be eased by legislation which deals with the most immediately unacceptable features of Conservative Government policy. It can be eased over a longer term by the facilitation of conditions for union growth. And there is a clear mutual advantage in support of the public sector and the successful revival of Britain's manufacturing industry.

And above all, the relationship will be lubricated by memories of past failures and their consequences. In many ways, the Thatcherite counter-revolution has given a unique and sobering lesson to those in the unions who argued that the differences between Labour and Conservative Governments were relatively unimportant. And there are many in the unions who remember that it was the industrial actions of the winter of 1978–79 which, in the end, fatally undermined the possibility of a third consecutive term of Labour in Office.

The memories are not all of union culpability. If many union leaders are haunted by reminders of their past behaviour, so also, at times, will Labour Ministers be touched by spectres and recollections from other times in Whitehall. There will be the ghost of a Labour Prime Minister who failed to consult his party in a crisis and failed to respect its priorities. There will be the reminders of another Labour Prime Minister whose loss of bearings helped to touch off a long term growth of the union and Party Left and to stimulate a new campaign for Labour Party democracy. And there will be the memory of a third Labour Prime Minister who created an industrial relations crisis by listening closely to the Treasury but failing to heed the advice of his closest union allies.

NOTES

1. Richter, *op. cit.*, pp. 16–18, 178, 226–45.
2. Miliband, *op. cit.*, p. 375 (referring to the previous generation of union leaders).
3. Panitch, in *Socialist Register, op. cit.*, p. 63. See also Minkin, in Brown, *op. cit.*, pp. 229–231.
4. Cp. the diagnosis of Richter, *op. cit.*, p. 234.
5. Ken Coates, in *Socialist Register, op. cit.*, p. 155.
6. See Chapter 7, nn. 1–4.
7. The metaphor was used by Victor Schonfield, a CLPD lobbyist, and quoted in Patrick Seyd, 'The Labour Left', Ph.D, Sheffield, 1986.
8. 'The petty tyranny of the employer-employee relationship – irresponsible, hidden, without redress – is surely not a lovely thing?', Evan Durbin, letter to J.M. Keynes, 29/4/36, quoted in Durbin, *op. cit.*, 1985, p. 158.
9. See Chapter 13, n. 8.
10. Muller, *op. cit.*, title with question mark, and see Chapter 9, n. 10.
11. Pinto-Duschinsky, *op. cit.*, p. 224.
12. Anthony Howard, 'The Unsavoury Enemies of Democracy', *The Independent*, 23/9/89. He was not referring to the unions and sponsorship.
13. 'What Price Democracy?', *The Observer Magazine*, Special Investigation, 14/10/90.
14. 'This is no rhetorical description. The Trade Unions own the British Labour Party … control is … complete.' David Steel, *Labour at 80: Time to Retire*, 1980, p. 4.
15. Ibid., p. 4. Such news can be heard from a wide spectrum of political critics. 'Mr. Todd, as you know, owns the Labour Party … owns and manipulates it.' Norman Tebbit MP, BBC TV 'News At One', 19/4/89; '… who pays the piper must surely call the tune most of the time.' Vernon Richards, *The Impossibilities of Social Democracy*, Freedom Press, 1978.
16. See, for example, Pinto-Duschinsky *op. cit.*, p. 226 and p. 238.
17. Ian Aitken, 'The Structure of the Labour Party', in Gerald Kaufmann (ed.), *The Left*, 1966, p. 29.
18. Such is the mesmeric effect of these features that even the most percep-

tive of political commentators can at times diagnose both that the Labour Leader has 'unprecedented domination of the Party' and that the 'union stranglehold has never been tighter' – a puzzling combination. See, for example, Brian Walden, 'Why Britain Should Not Write Labour Off', *Sunday Times*, 5/6/88.

19. 'The trade unions through their domination of all areas of finance, policy and personnel effectively run the Labour Party.' Conservative Research Department, *Labour and the Unions*, 1990.

20. Apart from the unions, there are many sources of this pluralism, including, at times, pressure from the CLPs, relationships within the Parliamentary Labour Party and the Leader's Office, and the varying positions and covert alliances of Party officials. But, most important, the Parliamentary leadership had its internal divisions and rivalries, as did the NEC, and the two overlapped. Perhaps the most important example of this pluralism concerned the changes in party policy over devolution, but there was also a very important interplay over the Gulf War. But all this is outside the province of this study.

21. Although the 1990 Conference was a stage-managed affair, it should be noted that the platform was defeated over candidate selection, that there was a two-year adjustment of policy over a Black Society, that there was a longer term adjustment over Palestine and that anticipation of union and Conference reactions was a factor restraining a shift of policy on a Bill of Rights. The idea that 'the days of conference controversy are over' is not borne out by the evidence.

22. An important assertion of this renewed political unionism was contained in the evidence presented by Larry Whitty, then GMWU Research Officer and Secretary of TULV, to the Fabian Society's enquiry into Party organisation in 1979 and the GMWU evidence to the Labour Party's Commission of Enquiry into Party Organisation in 1980. Since then union responses to various consultations have produced several important statements of this emphasis on a new political unionism. See also Tom Sawyer, 'When New Realism can Help the Party Activists', *Guardian*, 29/1/87 and Diana Jeuda, 'Remembering the Members', *New Socialist*, March/April, 1988.

23. In 1990, the rapidly diminishing 'hard Left' was divided into adherents of Labour Left Liaison and Labour Party Socialists, with the central bone of contention the question of the emphasis of political activity. Labour Party Socialists favoured a twin-track approach focusing inside and outside of the Party. Labour Left Liaison favoured a concentration on Party work.

24. Dennis Skinner, *Labour Weekly*, 30/10/81.

25. Les Huckfield, *Tribune*, 22/11/82.

26. See for example the emphasis of John Torode, '.they rarely now support the direct and exclusive constitutional link with the Labour Party.' 'The Mood of the Politically Motivated', *Guardian*, 2/8/84.

27. For the role of communication, information and political dialogue in the Swedish experience see Henry Milner, *Sweden: Social Democracy in Practice*, 1989, Chapter 6, *The Dissemination of Knowledge*, and also Martin Linton, *The Swedish Road to Socialism*, Fabian Tract 503, 1985, pp. 15–19.

28. Upham and Wilson, *op. cit.*, Section 7.

29. This diagnosis still comes from a variety of sources, for example Denis

Healey, *op. cit.*, p. 407; William Rodgers, 'Weaknesses in the Thatcher Revolution', *The Independent*, 23/7/87; and Hugo Young, 'Think Now Or Pay Dearly Later', *Guardian*, 3/9/87.

30. See on this the excellent chapter by J.L. Sharpe, 'The Labour Party and the Geography of Inequality: A Puzzle', in Kavanagh, *op. cit.*, pp. 135–170.

31. David Marquand in *The Progressive Dilemma*, 1991, p. 17, and in his articles, adapts Drucker, *op. cit.*, to define Labourism as an ethos – symbols, shared memories and unwritten understandings saturated with trade union influence. It is a very useful definition providing that it is not taken to imply one insulated unchanging culture. We have all been taken by surprise by the speed, scale and direction of some of the developments since 1981. It should make us look for the sources of flexibility and make us hesitant to interpret Labourism (in this usage) in quite the constraining way that Marquand does. On this definition, Labourism has been transcended in a variety of ways since the early 1980s. It is one of the Progressive's Dilemmas to explain that. As for the future, if it is indeed characterised by 'power sharing', 'negotiations and debate', and above all 'politics as mutual education' (Marquand, *The Unprincipled Society*, 1988, pp. 209–247), then the union–Labour Party relationship is surely among the best of nurseries.

32. The devout and generally exclusive commitment to Parliamentary democracy and Parliamentary activity is seen as the major limiting characteristic of 'Labourism' as defined in the works of Ralph Miliband, *op. cit.*, and by John Saville, 'The Ideology of Labourism', in R. Benewick, R.N. Berki, B. Barekh (eds.), *Knowledge and Belief in Politics*, 1973, p. 215. Similar perceptions of Labourism from a Marxist perspective can be found in the work of David Coates, *op. cit.* and Leo Panitch, *op. cit.*

33. Panitch, *op. cit.*, p. 72, referring to the role of Socialists within the Labour Party.

34. For a different view see the various articles by Jim Mortimer, for example, 'Labour Should Make No Concessions to Tory Anti-union Laws', *Tribune*, 1/9/89.

35. *Facing the Future*, 1990, p. 34.

36. Alan Cave, 'New Tack for TUC', *New Socialist*, Aug/Sept, 1990.

37. Tony Blair, Interview with the author 21/8/90, and Norman Willis, Press Conference 1/9/90, reported BBC 1, 2/9/90.

38. There has never been an unrestricted legal immunity for unions to call their members out on sympathy action. Protection only existed where it could be shown that the action was 'in contemplation or furtherance of a trade dispute'. Some of the most treasured historical instances of solidarity action have been outside the law.

39. Although there was some shift in trade union (and public opinion) towards the view that legislation had gone 'too far' and that unions needed 'more freedom' to act in disputes, still only 48 per cent of trade unionists thought 'too far' after years of restrictive legislation. Twenty per cent thought 'not far enough' and 32 per cent believed neither or had no opinion. MORI for NALGO, Aug 1990. Support for the Labour Party among trade unionists showed no adverse reaction to Labour's change in industrial relations' policy. Support was higher than in 1987 at 59 per cent in the first quarter of 1990, and continued at this level through the next two quarters.

40. The 'Stepping Stones' report involved the Conservatives in dragging

'every skeleton out of the union cupboard linking it to Labour', Hugo Young, *One of Us*, 1989, p. 116. It should be noted that, in the past ten years, the Conservative Party has (i) refused to issue full accounts, even to its own members; (ii) refused to give shareholders the same rights as trade unionists in relation to company political donations; (iii) linked to a secret network of companies run by senior Conservatives in order to channel donations to the Conservative Party, *The Independent*, 27/12/ 88 and *New Statesman and Society*, 17/2/89; (iv) opposed state finance for political parties and national ceilings on campaign expenditure. It has also adopted some varying, and at times strange, definitions of democracy internally and in policy, including (in the 1988 Housing Act) a principle according to which abstentions can count as votes in favour.

41. One authoritative study of policy options under a Labour Government concluded that its supply side measures could raise the sustainable level of output, might bring about a lasting reduction in unemployment and could eventually tackle some of the underlying weaknesses of the British economy. But the costs of diverting resources to education and training would reduce those available for other areas of public expenditure. *National Institute Economic Review*, No. 134, November, 1990, Chapter III, pp. 45–63.

42. The phrase is from William Keegan and Rupert Pennant Rea, *Who Runs the Economy?*, 1979, p. 124.

43. 'Thatcher's Parties', *Sunday Times*, editorial, 7/10/90.

44. W.W. Daniel, *Workplace Industrial Relations and Technical Change*, 1987 (based upon the DE/ESRC/PS/ASAS surveys).

45 Bill Callaghan, 'Trade Unions Pay Productivity and Jobs', in *Trade Unions and the Economy: Into the 1990s*. Papers compiled by John Philpott, Employment Institute, 1990, p. 44. David Metcalf had argued that the 'union presence in a workplace or company is associated with lower Labour productivity', *Trade Unions and Economic Performance: The British Evidence*, LSE Quarterly 3 (1), Spring 1989. This was critically examined by Peter Nolan and Paul Marginson, 'Skating on Thin Ice?: David Metcalf on Trade Unions and Productivity', *B.J.I.R.*, Vol. 28, No. 2, July 1990, pp. 227–47. They concluded that serious academic enquiry had failed to provide the 'hard facts' that would support this position. An alternative hypothesis 'that unions may be a source of greater economic dynamism and productivity cannot be ruled out'. A study in 1989 found no significant difference in average productivity growth in union and non-union firms between 1975 and 1978. S. Nickell, S. Wadwhani and M. Wall, *Unions and Productivity Growth in Britain 1974-1986: Evidence from UK Company Accounts Data*, 1989, p. 23, Centre for Labour Economics, London School of Economics, Discussion Paper No. 353.

46. Karel Williams, John Williams and Dennis Thomas, *Why are the British Bad at Manufacturing ?*, 1983, p. 110.

47. Economic growth from 1974 to 1979 averaged just over 2 per cent per annum. Victor Keegan, 'Economics Notebook', *Guardian*, 13/8/90, citing OECD figures. Average annual growth between spring 1979 and the end of 1990 was 1.9 per cent. Giles Wright (ed.), *Facts for Socialists*, A Fabian Special, 1991, p. 4.

21

The contentious alliance

FRAGILITY AND INCOMPATIBILITY: THE DIAGNOSIS

This is, as we have seen, a disputatious and controversial relationship – the most contentious in British political life. So problematic does it appear that, in recent times, it has often been suggested that it would be better for both partners if the direct relationship were ended, that in any case the links are breaking down, and that in the near future it can confidently be expected that there will be a major break in the relationship. In this final chapter I will examine these arguments, drawing from the evidence in this study.

THE COSTS OF SEPARATION OR DIVORCE

Among political centrists there has been a constant urging that there should be 'amicable separation'[1] or an enforced divorce.[2] Advocates of this position can also be found on the Left outside the Labour Party[3] and within the Conservative Party.[4] Even journalists friendly to the Labour Party regularly offer prescriptions for 'at least a semi-detached' relationship,[5] in which the structural links would be ended.

From Labour's opponents it is to be expected, but even from its friends it is understandable in the light of the evidence presented in this study. The close connection complicates life for industrial militants, electoral strategists and moderate lobbyists. It restricts the freedom of manœuvre of Labour's political Left as well as its Right. And in a relationship which is governed, as this one is, by a network of 'rules' and protocol, there is always a degree of frustration which periodically leads one group or another in one wing or the other to wish that they were free of it all. So it has been for generations.[6]

That having been said, I want to show here that the trade union–Labour Party relationship has many benefits which are not so obvious as its well-publicised drawbacks. There is no *one* consideration which is decisive in this argument but too little concern[7] and too little attention has been paid to what might be lost. If the case for agreed separation or enforced divorce had been so overwhelming for so long, neither sentiment nor inertia would have prevented it happening. The fact is that the benefits were, and remain, overwhelming.

First, consider why the unions were originally won to supporting the Labour Representation Committee. How far are those reasons now irrelevant? This peculiar national organisation was created because of a distinctive range of handicaps and obstacles to the influence of organised labour and the representation of 'working-class opinion'. These included an unsympathetic and dominant Conservative Government, a middle class resistance to working class candidates and their priorities,[8] and a judiciary constantly finding new resources of constraint in the individualistic orientation of English Common Law traditions.[9] There was also at the time of Labour's birth a climate of scapegoatism built up by a systematic press campaign against the unions as the obstacles to economic efficiency.[10] It would be difficult to argue that after ninety years all (indeed any) of these features have completely disappeared. They persist just as the Labour Party persists. Consequently they produce justifiable caution on the part of union activists and officials who are being encouraged to cast away their attachment to a labour-sympathetic party in which they have some security of access and influence.

Similarly, if we ask what was the *realpolitik* advantage for the Party from the attachment to the unions then it, too, is still relevant. Union financial support ensured the Party's survival and its continuing viability in competition with the party of the wealthy. As we have seen, in a variety of ways this financial role has been central to much of the Party's recent organisational experience. It has involved extended sponsorship, new funding, including the Business Plan, assistance to the Leader's Office, and a novel mechanism for building the General Election Fund. Until other financial arrangements cover British political life, the unions' financial contribution will continue to be vital. Even then, state finance to party organisations on a scale necessary to make the union contribution unnecessary would be publicly unpopular. (Also, it could have the disadvantage for Labour's Parliamentary leadership of greatly resourcing rival political formations on the NEC, and rival parties; whereas, as we have seen, the union contribution is to a considerable extent politically insulated.)

Moreover the unions provide not just finance but ballast. Though shifts in union political alignments have created new problems for the Labour Party since the late 1960s, and although inter-union strategic conflicts have produced new tensions within the TUC in recent years, the ballast still works. Indeed, in recent years the most significant development has been that this stabilising role has worked not just within the Labour Party but also backwards into the TUC from the Labour Party (as in the crisis over government money for ballots). And the Labour Party's attitude towards the EETPU holds them, for the moment at least, within the Movement, by tacit consent of the TUC. The protected character of Labour Party conflict can be contrasted with the experience of other British political formations. One simply has to ask of the most vociferous critics of 'Labourism', why did the SDP split and not the Labour Party, why did the Liberal Party split (as it has done before) and not the Labour Party? And from a different political tradition, why did the International Marxist Group split and not the Labour Party, etc., etc., etc.? For those anxious to break this or that mould or political structure, these are surely cautionary tales.

Less obvious, but still very important, is the mutual potential benefit of the internal interaction of the relationship. This form of Labour Movement, with its multiple committees, forums and consultative mechanisms where trade unionism and party representation meet, facilitates and in a sense forces a mutual education process. This can be valuable to the Left, as happened at the turn of the 1980s, or to the Right. As we have seen, there is a two-way influence and a two-way anticipated reaction effect, which periodically, and issue by issue, can change flow. In this interaction the Party can prompt and has pushed the unions into greater receptivity to broader social values and to the public interest – a receptivity which inhibits and is a counterweight to narrowly-focused producer sectionalism. And in recent years the Party has also encouraged the unions to seek a closer contact with their inactive members, a section of the electorate to which the Party itself has to appeal. More recently, Party involvement, including the experience of Head Office, has encouraged the unions to a new sensitivity towards the expertise of the management function. It has reinforced their growing awareness of the need for better service, efficiency and competitiveness. And the Party has heavily reinforced the trend in the unions towards greater sensitivity to the user and the consumer.

This is not to say that the trade union input into the Labour Party's policymaking is, could be or should be simply an agency of Labour's leadership or the Party's needs. An important *dialogue* takes place and should continue to take place with a strong union voice. It has elements which have no comparable equivalent in any other major political party. From the unions, their activists and their members, comes a broad social experience, as well as a vital expression of labour's industrial problems. It is an experience relevant to many policy areas and it includes an understanding of poverty[11] and social security as well as of the workplace pressures, insecurity and stress now intensifying in the pursuit of efficiency and competitiveness. Different unions carry different versions of this experience and not all of it is always welcome to the political wing. But its part in the interplay of relations within the Labour Party is an important element in British political representation.[12]

As the proportion of the electorate which is in manual worker occupations declines, and as the working class base as a whole shrinks, so the Labour Party's internal composition and representation will have to adjust accordingly. But it will need to do so without losing the allegiance of its traditional supporters. 'Cutting the link' would not be an adjustment, it would be a metamorphosis, involving the removal of contingents of mainly manual, service and clerical workers – groups who still make up a majority of the working population.[13] And it would accelerate the transformation of the PLP if it involved the loss of local affiliation, of trade union participation in nominating and shortlisting, and of the sponsorship process. The party that has always had the special claim that it was the People's party, more representative of British society than any other major party, would, in practice, become much more of a Party of the middle class, higher-educated, mainly public sector, professional groups. In this situation, the unions would not find it easier to relate to this formation from the outside, the Party would lose an element of its electoral appeal to traditional voters, and the House of Commons would be further flawed in the authenticity of its representative voices. In particular, in the uphill struggle to transform the gender composition of Parliament, the growing army of employed working class women would be likely to find it more, not less, difficult to fight their way through without an organisational base in the Labour Party. In terms of social representation, there is a lot to lose here.

Moreover in assessing its benefits it is important not to overlook the cultural impact of this alliance within British politics. The relationship is more than a policy process and an agency of power, it has considerable symbolic significance. In a society still marked by class inequalities and their 'hidden injuries', it is public testimony to the remarkable political creativity of working people – 'hands' who gave themselves political voices. And it represents a prominent symbolic claim by them for parity of status. In addition, within the elitist political framework of Her Majesty's Government, for all the Movement's flaws it embodies an ideal of a participatory democracy linking the decision-makers of Whitehall with the policy input of millions in offices, shops, factories and other workplaces. There is more to this relationship that can be judged simply in terms of immediate expediency.

Even the electoral advantages of a disconnection have to be assessed alongside other considerations – including the electoral damage which might be done if the links were broken. First it has to be noted that, as has been shown, the links with the unions *need* not have a significantly detrimental effect on voting behaviour at a General Election.[14] Industrial disputes *can* be (and have been) pursued and managed in such a way as to become an asset to the Party.[15] And reforms of the union representative process, coupled with a reduction in the union vote at the Party Conference, can contribute to further diminishing the numbers who believe that the unions have 'too much say in the Labour Party'.[16] As for the advantages of the close links, trade unionism has historically been 'a priceless asset'[17] in terms of creating the base of impregnable seats. It is still an asset in terms of a propensity to vote Labour.[18] A growth of union membership encouraged by a future Labour Government would be to their strong mutual advantage. And it is by no means certain that the advantage which Labour developed in the 1970s from its ability to work co-operatively and consensually with the unions will not reappear in the context of the inflation problem and membership of the ERM.

But more than that, through the TUFL network there is still an underdeveloped potential for what has been called the 'two-step-flow' of communication.[19] In contact with the workplace, the TUFL network could do more to counteract the adverse influence of hostile forces in the mass media. Further, the trade union supporters of close links with the Labour Party – a strengthening body of support (as we have seen) – provide much of the energy and *élan* within the union contribution to the Labour Party. The notion that after a structural divorce the Labour Party would find it easy to draw upon this energy is odd to say the least. A break initiated from the unions would be seen as a sign of the diminished utility of the Labour Party to trade unionists. A break initiated from the political leadership would be read as rejection and perhaps even 'a preparation for them to screw us'.[20] Neither would be a helpful setting for the electoral mobilisation of trade unionists nor for the variety of other discussions and initiatives encouraged and facilitated by the existence of a body such as TUFL.

It is an appreciation of many of these benefits of the relationship which reinforces the traditional support for the union connection within the Party and vice versa. After years of the unions and the Party receiving a torrent of advice to break away or to agree a separation, it is still the case that there are large majorities in favour of the preservation of the federal arrangements in committee of the Movement, with substantial support from the Party membership all the way up to the PLP. What this means is that attempts at divorce, utilising perhaps the levers of state finance and Party reform to push the unions out, will not only meet opposition from within the union – they can, as over In Place of Strife in 1969, quickly produce a fissure running right through the political wing and between Labour Ministers. An attempted divorce would be a very dangerous business.

It would also be a very speculative exercise. The behaviour of parties and pressure groups is shaped, here as elsewhere, by a distinctive social and political system operating within a particular culture – and in some important foreign examples by what Milner describes as a 'complementarity of culture, institutions and policies'.[21] There is much to learn from this foreign experience but there are problems in importing one major political change from its interactive context and then expecting other political forces to react exactly as they do in foreign circumstances. To break up the formal Labour Party–trade union relationship is to gamble on new alliances, new resources and new access in a way which could in practice turn out to be simply a move to permanent and greater weakness.

As to the longer term, beyond the 1990s, a range of forces could radically change perspectives on the form of the British Labour Movement. Many consequences will flow from '1992', including the increasing necessity for close working relationships across the European Labour Movement. Out of this could even develop the embryo of a confederal, European Socialist Party[22] as the Left comes to terms with the development of multinational capital and of European unity. But for the moment what is clear is that the distinctive character of European institutions and power relations, and the problems of economic integration, have enhanced the need for the trade unions, the TUC and Members of the European Parliament to build more effective links.[23] In this situation, divorce, or even a loosening of ties, runs counter to the immediate priorities.[24] As the labour correspondent Robert Taylor has pointed out, under these circumstances and at this level those who want to dilute or ignore the links to the unions may have to think again.[25]

For these reasons the union–Party attachment continues to be a much undervalued relationship, its problems and flaws often noted, its benefits much less so. Consensual reconstruction is necessary to broaden the base of the relationship, to reform its procedures and to reorder the primacy of its national components. It is a large and delicate task, often made more difficult by advocates of a crude structural separation or divorce, and only manageable by negotiation, trust and agreement.

ARE THE LINKS UNCOUPLING?

However, there are many who would say that these arguments over costs and benefits, advantages and disadvantages are of less significance than the inexorable future of the relationship – a gradual loosening of ties leading to a separation, regardless of the sentiments of the participants.

Undoubtedly, a few on the Right of the Labour Party, much of the press, and a vast army of critics of the Labour Movement, hoped that this was indeed the trend. 'Distancing' became the vogue word but what it meant primarily was affirming autonomy, projecting separateness and disassociating from unacceptable behaviour. For many critics, however, 'distancing', 'loosening', 'parting' and 'separation' were seen as essentially the same phenomenon and 'likely to carry on, whether or not it has a conscious will behind it'.[26] Aware of the powerful political pressure from the Right, some on the Left diagnosed a 'progressive uncoupling of the trade union connections of the Party'.[27] If true, whether inexorable or politically motivated, this trend would be the most significant of all the features of the contemporary Labour Movement. But is it true? Is the presentation of more 'distance' in the relationship an indication of substantive changes towards separation?

The substance of this development concerns primarily the TUC, which in a sense has not been directly coupled with the Labour Party since the 1920s. It has recently projected its distance from the Labour Party and the Liaison Committee has virtually been wound up. But as we have seen there is a history of oscillations in this relationship – oscillations both of presentation and of process. The ability to oscillate in this way gives the two organisations the flexibility that allows them to advance and protect their distinctive representational functions. Thus, in the mid-1960s it was the general wisdom that 'the Labour Party may have to make its long-term dispositions without more than vestigial contact and support from the TUC'.[28] That was before new political circumstances led to a move towards a closer and more co-ordinated relationship with the Party. The history of the relationship is a warning against regarding it as inevitable that there will be a culminative parting of the ways.

In terms of effective co-ordination and unity of purpose with the TUC, much depends on how effective are the informal links and the more covert liaison mechanisms. In this, the important feature is that the demise of the Liaison Committee has been accompanied by a more systematic development of 'the Contact Group'.

In any case, whatever is happening to the links with the TUC – even if it involves, in the context of a reformed electoral system, a much greater assertion of political neutrality – does not necessarily involve a disengagement of affiliated unions from the Labour Party. Indeed, it may imply the opposite. It is at least worth noting that a combination of the TUC disengaging from the Liaison Committee policymaking, and the Party considering regional representation on its new National Policy Forum, looks likely to bring union leaders into a *more* formal closeness to Party policy formulation than in the past.

This may well look odd when viewed from the more publicised aspects of

Labour's distance from the unions. But it would not be out of character with some other recent developments. For surprising as it may seem, given all this 'distancing', the evidence overall indicates increasing integration of the links between the Labour Party and its affiliates and *not* a loosening of ties.

The most obvious new area of integration has been the electoral college, which has brought the unions into direct involvement in the election of Labour's Leader and Deputy Leader. But also, as we have seen, there is a new agency of political mobilisation linking closely with the Party at national and local level. There have been new financial arrangements involving a Voluntary Levy Fund, which includes almost all the unions, and a Business Plan, which includes five of the largest unions in a new relationship, concerned with building the Party's financial base, its individual membership, and its services to members. There has been a reorganisation of women's representation which has brought CLP women, trade union women, General Council women and NEC women into a much closer relationship, based in part on a new involvement of the unions in a reorganised Labour Women's Conference. And there has been a marked extension of sponsorship and other arrangements linking the unions with the PLP and the Shadow Cabinet.

To this must be added a less obvious and less measurable, but nonetheless clearly important, increase in liaison and consultation at many levels and in many dimensions of the relationship. It affects the unions and their sponsored MPs. It affects the relationship between the new political officers and the national party organisers. And it affects the policy linkage between the Front Bench assistants, trade unions and the TUC. Altogether, the number of people involved in and responsible for 'networking' between the unions and the Party has increased considerably. The legacy of suspicion surrounding TULV has meant that there is still a gap where there might be a permanent secretariat for liaison between the unions and the Party on the organisational future of the relationship, but the infrastructure is there for creating one.

So far, in spite of 'distancing', and much talk of the slow breaking down of the relationship, there is very little of substance to show for it. What can be seen is a long term tidying-up of the remnants of 'One Movement' in the 1920s as the Party on the one side and the TUC on the other stress their organisational/ functional differentiation in terms of the role of Trades Councils and the boundaries of Party membership. What can also be seen is a phenomenon, which can be dated back to 1937, whereby the unions are eased out of involvement in CLP section elections. By consent, the locally-affiliated unions have recently withdrawn from CLP section elections for the Leadership and from CLP section elections for the NEC, as the Party has instituted direct elections by the individual membership. But the unions have retained their own collective input into both. The idea that this electoral development can be typified as 'weakening the links' is from some a bit of Leftwing special pleading to bolster a weakening case and, from others, Rightwing wishful thinking.

The nearest we have to any sign of 'uncoupling' concerns the union role in candidate selection where the Party leadership has secured conference approval for a proposed rule change in 1991 which will introduce one-individual-member-one-vote participation. Even here, all that can be said at the moment is that there is an honourable impasse on the role of the unions. It is almost certain that they will continue to be collectively involved in nomination and shortlisting and it is also possible given the commitments made by 'the platform' in 1990 that their levypayers will in some way be involved in future selection.

Of course, one conclusion that may be drawn from this analysis is that the relationship is more capable of withstanding a loosening of links in some areas precisely because it is strengthening in others. But for the moment, what is striking to anyone who peers beneath the surface of this relationship is that a trend to separation, which has been anticipated more or less universally by the Movement's citics in the past decade, is hard to discern and nothing like as pronounced as is the new integration of the relationship between the affiliated unions and the Party. Overall, at this level, there is little sign of the 'dissolution of the Labour Movement'.[29] Just the opposite. And it gives yet another powerful reason why any clean 'surgical strike' to cut the links is impracticable.

IS SEVERANCE LIKELY?

Nevertheless, there are many who would argue that this is a fragile[30] relationship, likely soon to result in a major fissure (or several) which would lead to the ending of the structural relationship with the unions. Indeed, it is part of the common sense of the age that this is about to happen. Since the early 1960s it has been difficult to find a period of any significant length when the relationship has not appeared to be approaching or engulfed in a vortex of calamities leading, it would seem inevitably, towards a fundamental crisis when the two 'wings' would be torn asunder.

Among observers the tendency has been to forecast the continuation of whichever particular problematic trend happened to be in the forefront at the time. The TUC would move to political neutrality[31] – this was a diagnosis of the 1960s. Trade unions would be likely to break away to the Left[32] – this was the forecast in the late 1960s and the 1970s. Trade unions would break away to the Right – this was the SDP wisdom of the 1980s.[33] As recently as 1988 it was confidently forecast that after the next General Election the breakup would come, with a section of the PLP joining a realignment.[34] And yet so far, to the considerable annoyance of the pundits and partisans of a host of hostile forces, the damn thing survives – indeed, it has occasionally delivered a swiping blow at its enemies. We can at this point therefore seek to explain why the split has *not* occurred. What overall are the forces which hold it together at times of crisis?

One important source of its resilience is the residual strength which the Movement can fall back upon in situations of adversity and internal conflict. There is still something like a 'family' commitment, accompanied by what critics see as 'a strong lashing of sentimentality'. [35] This is sustained by a range of rituals including fraternal addresses. There is also a Movement consciousness – easy to parody as TIGMOO ('This great Movement of ours') but not so easily ignored. It has its ambiguities but it still evokes a strong sense of participating in a 'Magnificent Journey' of 'The Common People' with 'The People's Flag' carried, as it were, by 'a thousand years of Kinnocks'.

The Movement is of course riven with prickly social resentments particularly around the manual/university educated worker distinction, but it draws unity from a broad sense of a divided society[36] in which the Movement represents 'more particularly' those in social adversity. How this social adversity is perceived varies across the wings of the Movement and often in ways which can swiftly change definition. Thus the Movement has often responded to a workerist call to support 'our class' in industrial conflict with forces backed by capital, but it can just as easily accept a '"no favours" but social justice' appeal, which locates Labour's responsibility to all of the people.[37] And blending and overlapping with both conceptions is a loose radical populism with no consistent definition of class but simply a sense of 'the people' against the 'few' and their political instruments. The flexibility of these appeals allows disparate internal forces to coexist, and gives the Movement considerable adaptability.

And, as our analysis showed, the alliance is preserved and reinforced as much by 'rules' as by sentiment. The 'rules' of solidarity and of unity have proved remarkably resilient in the face of the vicissitudes of the past three decades. The 'rules' of solidarity are not only assistive to the Party and reassuring to the unions, they produce within the unions a sense of responsibility for the Labour Party which acts as a vital counterweight to other strategies and loyalties at critical points. The 'rules' of unity protect the unions' industrial strength but they also help the Party to retain *its* cohesion. The developments of the late 1980s illustrated what complications, industrial and political, can flow from the breakaway of just one union and how important it was for one political centre that the other could be used as an integrating institution. 'Waiting for the EETPU' to break other unions from the Labour Party was not only a strategy based upon a misunderstanding of the potential influence of the EETPU, it underestimated the awareness that unions have of the benefits of all moving together in political alignment. This consideration inhibits breakaways of both Right and Left.

And holding the relationship together there is also a hard-headed appraisal of its benefits – a transactional consciousness which adds a vital contribution to overall unity. It is much less embodied in immediate 'log-rolling' reciprocity and focused deals than is often assumed, and it takes much of its strength from an understanding of shared historic projects. It is rooted in the heritage of a relationship created because the interests of working people were not seen as safe in the hands of Conservatives, Liberals and the judiciary. It is reinforced by the sense of the Party as a practical proven agency of legislation designed to remove or loosen the constraints on trade union industrial and political action. And it has a powerful folk memory of '1945', increasingly idealised, but connected with real achievements – particularly the National Health Service.

From one perspective – the rise in average real incomes under the Labour Governments of the 1960s and 1970s – the record has not been impressive,[38] and there have been times when the relationship appears to people in both wings as an 'immense contradiction'.[39] But the relationship has delivered in other terms, as well as disappointed, even though it faced what has aptly been described as a 'gradient of power'. [40] Since World War II Labour governments have facilitated union growth,[41] and they have produced a wide range of legislation favourable to working people and their conditions of life. Even the disappointing record of the second phase of the 1974–79 Labour Government, as we have seen, was not bereft of legislation and governmental measures welcome to the unions, and during this second phase most of the gains of the first phase were retained. As for the limitations of the performance on social policy, even here, on the agreed priorities – particularly pensions and long term insurance benefits – there was something to show and something to remember.[42] In comparison with what was hoped for in 1974 it was dispiriting. In comparison with what happened after 1979 – to public sector expenditure, inequality, poverty, homelessness and the level of unemployment – it left a growing body of opinion within the unions with a very different sentiment – a yearning for another Labour Government.

Further, the Labour Party began essentially as a procedural revolt against lack of access. Through the Labour Party, union representatives gain local and regional nominating opportunities of various kinds. Locally and nationally, they are assured of a hearing for their case in an industrial dispute. They have a 'voice' in Parliament via sponsorship.[43] They have an integral place in the Labour Party's national policy process. And via the solidarity 'rules' they have the regular availability of consultation. This is not a relationship which guarantees a response to the unions, let alone Jerusalem, but what it gives causes most union officials to think twice before a hazardous fling with something else on Left or Right, and certainly before a move into an uncertain no man's land following structural disengagement.

Of course, sentiment, 'rules', past transactions and present access would not provide a permanent insulation against a union breakaway if the relationship looked permanently incapable of dealing with important political objectives. But the possibility of such a breakaway is only likely when sustained frustration and a sense of alienation within the relationship are combined with the possibility of an available political alternative outside it. Even then, looking back, the evidence is that at such times there are forces in both wings which look to a new reconciliation or an act of compromise (Mr Solomon Binding, The Peace of Bishop's Stortford, The Dream Ticket) which will bind in the disenchanted and 'get on with the job'. In this sense the ultimate clue to the future stability of the Labour Movement lies in the activities of its reconcilers rather than in any external factors.

One possible political option is represented by the TUC, whose longing to recapture 1940 was always a seductive potential alternative to having all eggs in the Labour Party basket. Unfortunately for the TUC, Conservative leaderships from the mid-1960s tended to want to play a different game. 'Selsdon Man' Conservatism, then Thatcherite anti-corporatism, and then the abolition of independent trade unionism at GCHQ, did much at crucial stages to strengthen the TUC's links with the Labour Party – as did the Political Fund ballot negotiations. A shift back towards treating the unions as 'social partners' would again change the atmosphere but it seems an unlikely development.

As for other political alternatives – particularly a break of the most dissatisfied force within the Movement, currently 'the hard Left' – the most significant feature of post-war British politics has been the lack of a sizeable receptive constituancy. For political groups to the Left of Labour, defection has been a path to ineffectuality, obscurity and fragmentation. And there does not look anything remotely viable on the horizon for those recently disenchanted by the Labour Party's redefinition of Socialism and trade union freedom. A reformed electoral system would allow more space for a realignment. But it is unlikely to be introduced under a Conservative Government, and even then there would still be an inclination for trade union allies to want to stay together.

By contrast, the threat from the political centre led by the SDP MPs was much more serious, particularly in 1981, in the summer of 1983 and, perhaps very briefly, early in 1987. But traditional loyalties, 'rules' and procedures inhibited immediate union responses and the SDP defectors did not help this aspect of their cause. They had failed to consult potential union allies before defection. They voted for the Tebbit legislation. Their style and tone of addressing the unions was often derogatory and just as often deeply resented. And their tactics in the Political Fund ballots did not endear them to even the most sympathetic union elements. The 1987 General Election campaign re-established Labour's clear supremacy as *the* Opposition and it enhanced the integration of the relationship. What happened to the Alliance late in 1987 simply set the seal on it. Of course, were the Labour Party to move back into a sustained 'Greenwich mean time' election trough while the Liberal Democrats surged into parity, strategic questions would again be raised in the unions – especially if the surge took in some of Labour's unionised territory. But the signs are that what there was of a chance of a major breakthrough to split the Labour Movement has now passed. In any case the Liberal Democrats still exhibit gut reactions towards trade unions which strike observers as 'depressingly hostile'.[44] And the events of the past decade also suggest that any group of Labour MPs frustrated in the future by the unions and involved in one of the various linkages with the old Alliance forces would think more than twice about going through the hazards of a similar experience.

All in all, then, this is a relationship with major resources, cushioning internal conflict and holding that conflict within certain bounds. It has had periods of vulnerability but it has weathered the storm of the worst of them, and there does not appear to be any immediate prospect of effective political alternatives which might threaten it.

MOVEMENT, PURPOSE AND VALUES

Only time will tell what will have been the longer term side-effects on the Labour Movement of Labour's election and communication strategy[45] in recent years – a strategy which unquestionably paid off in terms of creating a high core vote, a 40 per cent plus position in the polls, and the regaining of electoral support from trade unionists. But the failure to find a consistent role for activist political campaigning did nothing to assist in invigorating the local links to the unions. An apologetic defensiveness about these links did little to encourage union activists to strengthen them. And new uncertainties were created over the common objectives of the two wings after the abandonment of some traditional positions and in the absence of a new vision of the Movement's purpose.

Yet the Movement, locally and nationally, was not without its unifying values.

The traditional definitions of Socialism and of trade union freedom have become more problematic, more disputed and more marginalised than ever. But the contours of such disputes do not follow those of the union–Party boundary, they cut across them.

There is still a high level of agreement on the priority concerns of social justice, and although, in terms of income and wealth, Labour's egalitarianism has been muted in the past four years, there is still a shared perspective that the top earners must bear more of the taxation burden and the lowest paid significantly less. The pursuit of a reduction in inequalities affects the industrial activities of the unions to a degree that is not fully appreciated. Though craft unions particularly protect the skills/earnings differential, overall unions have what has been called a 'sword of justice effect', narrowing the pay structure as between women and men, blacks and whites, manual and non-manual workers, and the disabled and the able-bodied.[46]

Above all, the collectivism which had always provided the basis for the most fundamental sharing of perspectives and purposes remains a central current even though both unions and Party have re-emphasised the ultimate primacy of the individual. A positive conception of freedom defined as capacity, rather than simply the absence of restraint[47] (necessary and fundamental as that is to autonomy), underpins the collective acting as an essential agency for the advancement of liberty in both the industrial and political spheres.[48] With the shift of emphasis on individual rather than collective rights, there is still a recognition that, in part at least, individual rights will depend on collective rights if they are to function effectively.[49] Further, in both wings there is a strong body of opinion which sees collective discussion and collective action as a vital aid in building the confidence of individuals to confront a range of constellations of entrenched economic and political power.[50] Labour feminism in the unions and the Party, with its emphasis on the sharing of experience and on mutual education, has further reinforced this aspect of collectivism. For those reasons, and more, an enduring collectivism can be found at all levels of the Movement,[51] as can a deep-rooted distaste for a society dominated by acquisitive individualism.

In this collectivism, the traditions of union solidarity and Party 'fellowship' can clash at the borders of the public interest, but both draw strongly from a perception of the social nature and mutual obligations of human beings. This can, and for much of the time does, provide the basis for the powerful appeal of a call to social responsibility and the vision of a society where individual and sectional fulfilment is not fundamentally in conflict with the needs of the community.[52]

In as much as we can discern the values and mood of the British people in the 1990s, it is likely that, as they confront problems on a national and international level, their perspectives will prove to be more collectivist than was the case in the 1980s. Even now, public opinion on the necessity for trade unionism[53] and the public provision of welfare [54] is much less individualistic than was often thought to be the case in the heyday of 'Thatcherism'. In social terms the 1990s may well be the decade of a humanism rather than individualism. Certainly, in terms of creating an ideological climate fundamentally uncongenial to the Labour

Movement, the Rightwing Conservative project has failed.

MYTH AND REALITY

Overall, then, though the case for major changes in the relationship between the Labour Party and its affiliate unions is a strong one, the case for separation or divorce is much weaker and would incur unacceptable costs. Further, this is a relationship which, contrary to much mythology, is becoming more not less integrated and is therefore less susceptible to a clean break. This integration adds to the underlying strength of the relationship and to a variety of factors which help to stabilise it in periods of great conflict. As noted in Chapter 20, it has long had weaknesses at local level, but in terms of union members' support for close links, it was stronger in the 1980s than for many years. On these grounds it is arguable that though this is a difficult relationship it is *not* fragile.

Of course, in Government or out, the next ten years will bring new problems. In Government the choices become sharper, in Opposition again the dilemmas become more pressing as the different forces in the Labour Movement seek to build an electable Labour Party. If Labour loses, new industrial militancy, new lobbying strategies, new political alliances and a new national emphasis in Scotland may add to the tensions.

If one focuses on these dilemmas and tensions, then the tasks of maintaining the relationship, managing its consensual reform and securing the election of Labour Governments which build up a record of social and economic achievement look overwhelming. The most likely outcome appears to be dominated by fragmentation and schism.

But then this is the point at which we began the study – a relationship with many difficulties, and the potential for the partners to go their separate ways. Since birth it has produced problems, yet, as we have seen, it has many strengths and many unifying features. It has a rich and much misunderstood internal dynamic, and considerable flexibility. It is not to be underestimated. Nor is it to be undervalued. It has much to recommend it and much to be proud of.

It also has considerable resilience. That too is part of the nature of the beast. Accordingly, no one should be surprised if there is a successful transformation of its structure and procedures in the next decade. Nor should they be surprised if, in its more fundamental features, this contentious relationship outlives many of its contemporary critics. Looking backward from the next century it may well be the judgement that 'these are the trees whom shaking fastens more'.[55]

NOTES

1   Peter Jenkins, 'A Fiction That Has Become a Betrayal', *The Independent*, 8/9/90.
2. Chapter 12, n. 104.
3. See, for example, Panitch, *Social Democracy and Industrial Mililtancy, op. cit.*, p. 257.
4. 'What would please me immensely would be if the TUC was not, and the trade unions were not, a part of the Labour Party, and the Labour Party a part of the trade union movement', Margaret Thatcher, quoted in the *The Observer*, 1/5/83.

5. John Lloyd, 'Parting of the Ways', *Marxism Today*, March, 1988. This was the most influential and thoroughly argued presentation of the case for a separation.

6. See, for example, the discussion within the SDF and within the ILP in the first year of the life of the Labour Party examined in Dylan Morris, *op. cit.*, Chapter 9, 'Towards Socialist Unity', pp. 234–67.

7. See, for example, Lloyd's view that 'the defensible bits' amount only to 'money and power', *ibid.*, p. 39.

8. See on this K.D. Ewing, *Trade Unions, The Labour Party and the Law*, 1982, p. 14.

9. See on this Alan Fox's hugely impressive study, *History and Heritage: The Social Origins of the British Industrial Relations System*, 1985.

10. Ewing, *op. cit.*, p. 13 and Fox, *op. cit.*, p. 181. See also the report of the Labour Party Executive Committee 1901–2, 'a well organised movement to prejudice public opinion against the industrial effects of Trade Unionism', p. 12.

11. By no means all trade unionists can be equated with 'the poor', but low earnings are now a major cause of poverty and trade union members include many who are either living in poverty or move in and out of conditions of poverty. In 1985, the number of people below pension age living in poverty (having an income of less than 40 per cent above supplementary benefit level) was 11.3 million. Of these, the largest single group were those where the head of household received a full time wage. Chris Pond [Director, Low Pay Unit], 'The Changing Distribution of Income, Wealth and Poverty', in Hamnett, McDowell and Sarre, *op. cit.*, p. 67. Trade unions also acted as a major pressure group in support of others in poverty, particularly unorganised low-paid workers and the third of those in poverty who were pensioners.

12. One example is that the Labour Party, above all parties, has the special right to say to its supporters that concern for the environment 'is not some esoteric preoccupation of the well-heeled'. Bryan Gould, quoted in the *Guardian*, 27/7/90.

13. *Social Trends 21*, 1991. *Labour Force Survey*, Department of Employment, 1989, Chart 4.9, p. 70.

14. The trade union question was of marginal significance in 1987 in spite of Conservative Party attempts to make it so. See on this Ivor Crewe, 'Tories Prosper from a Paradox', *Guardian*, 16/6/87 and Gallup Political Index, July, 1987, Table 72.

15. See Chapter 5, n. 92.

16. The percentage of voters who thought that the unions had 'too much say' in the Labour Party declined between 1988 and 1990 from 54 to 50 per cent. *Gallup / Daily Telegraph*, 4/9/88 and 3/9/89, and *Gallup Political Index*, Aug. 1990. Among trade unionists it had declined by 1989 to 50 per cent and only 35 per cent of Labour voters took this view in 1989. In 1990 they do not appear to have been polled on the question, which is significant in itself.

17. Ben Pimlott, 'Labour's Union Marriage Is In Need of Guidance', *Sunday Times*, 17/7/88. For the view that Labour's historic association with the rise of trade unionism may mean a profitable political benefit from any recovery of trade unionism, see Anthony Heath and Sarah K. McDonald, 'Social Change and the Future of the Left' in Linda McDowell, Philip Sarre and Chris Hamnett (eds.), *op. cit.*, 1989, p. 40.

18. How much of a direct asset in terms of independent impact on voting is

unclear. See David Butler and Donald Stokes, *op. cit.*, pp. 190–216. It has been estimated that union membership increases the chances that an individual will vote Labour by 5 per cent. David Lipsey, Andrew Shaw and John William, *Labour's Electoral Challenge*, Fabian Research, Series No. 352, 1989, p. 6.

19. See on this Minkin, in Crewe and Harrop, *op. cit.*, 1986, pp. 193–4.
20. The comment of a union official to the author in Sept. 1990.
21. Milner, *op.cit.*, p. 216. For another very relevant example see Gordon Smith, *Democracy in West Germany*, 1986, Chapter 5, on the distinctive West German political culture and the exceptional constraints upon West German politics since the Second World War.
22. See Ken Coates, 'Editorial: Towards a European Socialist Party?', *European Labour Forum*, Autumn 1990.
23. In 1989 a report on the British Labour Group noted the great value to the unions and the Party of building closer links 'on a working basis'. There needed to be a more organised approach on the Labour side. John Carr, Consultant, *The Organisation and Staffing of the British Labour Group in the European Parliament*, 1989, p. 7.
24. See, for example, on this the GMB resolution No. 289, Labour Party Conference, 1990, re MEPs and Social Action, and see the USDAW workbook, *Europe 1992*, 1990, by Diana Jeuda and Paul Brook, pp. 19, 23 and 30. TUC officials were also anxious for closer working relationships with MEPs. Alongside the improved informal linkage there is now a formal meeting twice a year between the TUC European Strategy Committee and a group of British Labour MEPs.
25. Robert Taylor, 'Let's Get Positive', *Samizdat*, Sept/Oct 1989.
26. Lloyd, *op. cit.*, p. 37.
27. Tony Benn, 'Setting a Socialist Agenda', *Morning Star*, 1/10/88.
28. Ian Coulter, 'The Trade Unions', in Kaufman, *op. cit.*, p. 37.
29. Phelps Brown, *op. cit.*, p. 11.
30. That it was fragile was a commonplace among commentators. See for example the advance publicity for the 'On the Record' programme on BBC 1, 22/4/89. 'Labour and the Unions. How this Fragile Relationship Has Been Affected by the Dock Labour Scheme'. *The Independent*, 22/4/89. See also the thesis of D.W. Rawson, 'The Life Span of Labour Parties', in *Political Studies*, Vol. XVII, No. 3, 1969, pp. 313–333.
31 'All the signs point to a weakening of the Labour alliance and a gradual shift towards a position of neutrality.', John Lovell and B.C. Roberts, A *Short History of the TUC*, 1968, pp. 186–7.
32. See, for example, Tariq Ali, *The Coming British Revolution*, 1972, p. 73.
33. See Chapter 8, pp. 226–7.
34. Paddy Ashdown, the Liberal Democrat Leader, interviewed by Brian Walden, London Weekend Television, 20/11/88. Shirley Williams made the same forecast to the author at the Brighton TUC, 1986, before the 1987 General Election. For a more realistic perspective from that party, see David Marquand, 'Quest for a Pact of the Spirit', *Guardian*, 14/9/90.
35. Lloyd, *op. cit.*, p. 37.
36. Sixty-five per cent of Labour Party members continue to see 'class struggle' (the questionnaire wording) as the central issue in politics. Broughton, Seyd and Whiteley, *op. cit.* For the broader social relevance of this judgement, see the conclusion of Marshall *et al.*, *op. cit.*, that there is nothing in their findings to suggest that class interest has ceased

to be the principal focus of partisanship (p. 246), and their view that 'Social class and social class identities are no less salient today than during earlier periods commonly acknowledged to be characterised by "class voting"' (p. 260). See also 'Greedy, Class-ridden, Ashamed, Unfair', *The Observer* / Harris poll of the 1980s, *The Observer*, 31/12/89 for the voters' view that Britain has become more divided by social class in the 1980s (61 per cent) and between rich and poor (73 per cent).

37. See, for example, Kinnock's very effective reply to Arthur Scargill in his fraternal address to the 1990 Congress of the TUC.

38. This was Leo Panitch's judgement on the 1964–70 Labour Governments, *Social Democracy and Industrial Militancy*, *op. cit.*, p. 264, and it could reasonably be made also about the 1974–79 Governments.

39. Anderson, in Blackburn and Cockburn, *op. cit.*, p. 279.

40. David Coates' illuminating use of the concept 'the gradient of power' tells us a great deal about the environment within which trade unions seek to exercise political power. See David Coates, 'The Question of Union Power', in David Coates and Gordon Johnston (eds.), *Socialist Arguments*, 1983, pp. 55–82. However, if the gradient was quite as steep as is suggested there, and in his other writing, it is not clear how so much was secured *and retained* through the 1974–9 Labour Governments.

41. The legislative framework was particularly favourable under the 1974–79 Labour Governments. George Sayers Bain and Robert Price, 'The Determinants of Union Growth', in *Industrial Relations in Britain*, 1983, pp. 12-33.

42. Social security was largely exempt from the cuts that affected many areas of social policy. The key priority of social security was pensions. In real terms spending on social security (excluding child benefits and family income supplement) rose by 30 per cent between 1973/74 and 1978/79. One half of this increase in expenditure went to the elderly. David Piachaud, pp. 176–7, in Nick Bosanquet and Peter Townsend (eds.), *Labour and Inequality: A Fabian Study of Labour in Power 1974-79*, 1980. See also Frank Field, 'How the Poor Fared' in Ken Coates (ed.), *What Went Wrong?*, 1979, p. 160, on the role of the unions in securing the achievement of a rise in the real value of pensions and other long term national insurance benefits. Retirement pensions rose in relation to average earnings.

43. It is worth noting that the AEU leadership which was the most sympathetic to the withdrawal of the union from national affiliation still favoured means to preserve the representation of 'shop floor' members of the union in Parliament. Gavin Laird, 'Grasping the Opportunity', *Morning Star*, 23/4/90.

44. 'Trading Places', *New Statesman and Society*, editorial, 21/9/90. In their document of priorities up to the year 2,000, the Liberal Democrats make no mention of trade union rights other than that of association. They are heavily critical of 'three decades of stultifying corporatism' (for some a euphemism for trade union influence). And though they place a Bill of Rights at the centre of their priorities they make no mention of reform of the legal system and the judiciary, *Shaping Tomorrow, Starting Today*, 1990.

45. The key communications principle was that there should be 'a shift in campaigning emphasis from 'grass roots'/opinion forming to influencing electoral opinion through the mass media', Hughes and Wintour, *op*.

cit., p. 52. In practice, it became more than a change of emphasis and led to a de-energised atmosphere at the grass roots. Part of the problem was a fear that, whatever was organised, 'the Trots' would grab the headlines.

46. David Metcalf, 'Can Unions Survive in the Private Sector?', in Philpott, *op. cit.*, pp. 12–13.

47. Rodney Bickerstaffe, *Trade Unions and the Future of Socialism*, Northern College Lipman Lecture, 1984. Bryan Gould, *Socialism and Freedom*, 1985, Chapter 2. Roy Hattersley, *Choose Freedom*, 1987, pp. xv–xvii and pp. 21–2; *Democratic Socialist Aims and Values*, 1988, p. 48. For a hostile view by an SDP defector of this perspective on freedom, see Peter Jenkins, 'Bill of Rights for Labour', *The Independent*, 12/7/90.

48. 'It is a matter of historical fact that the liberties most precious to our people have been attained by collective action and are sustained by collective agreement', Neil Kinnock, Foreword to the book by Joyce Marlow on *The Tolpuddle Martyrs*, 1985, p. 10.

49. Text of a statement to his Sedgefield Constituency Party by Labour's Employment Spokesman, Tony Blair, 18/12/90.

50. This position (as seen from the Left) was put very lucidly and forcefully by Audrey Wise MP, Presidential candidate in USDAW, at a meeting organised by *Tribune* on Labour and the Unions during the 1990 Labour Party Conference, 30/9/90. For a passionate assertion that collective action 'has not diminished vitality, it has increased fitness and exposed and fostered talent, inventiveness and self-confidence', see Kinnock, *op. cit.*

51. In their survey of Labour Party members, Broughton, Seyd and Whiteley, *op. cit.*, show an enduring concern of Labour Party members with public expenditure and public enterprise and with trade union bargaining rights and a powerful trade union movement, *Labour Party News*, Sept/Oct. 1990.

52. The sense of this was captured in the contribution of Tom Sawyer (NUPE), Chair of the NEC's Home Policy Committee, speaking to the Labour Party Conference, 1/10/90, when he spoke of a world where 'each human being realises their ability in harmony and solidarity with their neighbour', Author's notes. See also Hattersley, *Democratic Socialist Aims and Values*, p. 6.

53. In 1990, 80 per cent of voters believed that the unions were essential to protect workers' interests – the highest percentage since 1970. MORI / *Sunday Times*, 2/9/90.

54. John Rentoul, *Me and Mine*, 1989, Chapter 11, pp. 156–71.

55. George Herbert, quoted in Elizabeth Gaskell, *North and South*, 1855, p. 119.

Appendix I

Trade union voting weight at the 1990 Labour Party Conference

TGWU	1,250,000	
TGWU: Agricultural Workers	41,000	
TGWU: Dyers and Bleachers	37,000	
	1,328,000	1,328,000
GMB	650,000	
GMB: APEX	54,000	
GMB: Boilermakers	75,000	
GMB: Textile Workers	11,000	
	790,000	790,000
NUPE		600,000
AEU		540,000
	Four largest	3,258,000
USDAW		366,000
MSF		304,000
COHSE		200,000
UCW		188,000
UCATT		160,000
NUR		120,000
EETPU		102,000
NCU		95,000
	Twelve largest	4,793,000
	All other unions (22)	554,000
	Total union vote (34)	5,347,000
	Total Conference vote*	6,038,000

* Estimated with the assistance of the national Labour Party officers; subject to minor amendment depending mainly on absent CLP delegates

Appendix II

A note on names, acronyms, abbreviations and trade union mergers

In the text I have used a range of acronyms and sometimes abbreviations for the individual trade unions. In an analytical work ranging back and forth across different periods, it is difficult to be consistent in usage, particularly as the past quarter of a century has seen a spate of trade union mergers and name changes. I list below the acronyms and abbreviations that I have used, with the name of the union and information on the mergers and name changes which have affected the union concerned.

I. TRADE UNIONS AFFILIATED TO THE LABOUR PARTY

Acronym	Abbreviations used in text	Name and mergers
ACTT		Association of Cinematograph, Television and Allied Technicians
AEF	Engineers and Foundry Workers	Amalgamated Engineering and Foundry Workers' Union – a loose amalgamation of the Amalgamated Union of Foundry Workers and the Amalgamated Engineering Union from 1968 to 1970, when new mergers led to the Amalgamated Union of Engineering Workers (see AUEW).
AEU *	Engineers	Amalgamated Engineering Union. Involved in various mergers (see AEF and AUEW) before reverting to the original name in 1986.
APAC	Patternmakers	Association of Patternmakers and Allied Craftsmen. Merged with TASS in 1984.
APEX	Professional and Executive (Staff)	Association of Professional, Executive, Clerical and Computer Staff. Became APEX partnership – a section of the GMB – after amalgamation in 1989.
ASB	Boilermakers	Amalgamated Society of Boilermakers, Blacksmiths, Shipwrights and Structural Workers. Amalgamated with the GMWU in 1982 to form GMBATU, but retained separate affiliation.

---

* I have used this acronym for any reference to the union which includes the period since 1986 and, of course, before 1967.

ASLEF		Associated Society of Locomotive Engineers and Firemen
ASSET		Association of Supervisory Staffs, Executives and Technicians. Merged with Association of Scientific Workers in 1968 to form Association of Scientific, Technical and Managerial Staffs (see ASTMS).
ASTMS	Managerial Staffs	Association of Scientific, Technical, and Managerial Staffs. Merged with TASS in 1988 to form Manufacturing, Science, Finance (see MSF).
ASTW		Amalgamated Society of Textile Workers and Kindred Trades. Re–affiliated to Labour Party in 1987 after disaffiliation in 1982.
ASW	Woodworkers	Amalgamated Society of Woodworkers. Merged in 1971 with AUBTW to form UCATT.
ATWU	Textile Workers	Amalgamated Textile Workers Union. Merged with GMB in 1986 but retained separate affiliation to Labour Party.
AUBTW	Building Workers	Amalgamated Union of Building Trade Workers. Merged in 1971 with ASW to form UCATT.
AUEW	Engineers (sometimes referred to as AUEW plus the section)	Amalgamated Union of Engineering Workers formed after merger of four unions in 1970s with sections known as AUEW (Construction), AUEW (Engineering), AUEW (Foundry) and AUEW (Technical and Supervisory). In 1985 the Technical section became a separate union (see TASS) and in 1986 the rest of the union reverted to an earlier name, the Amalgamated Engineering Union.
BETA		Broadcasting and Entertainment Trades Union. Affiliated to Labour Party in 1987.
BFAWU	Bakers	Bakers, Food and Allied Workers
CATU		Ceramic and Allied Trades Union
CAWU		Clerical and Administrative Workers Union. In 1972 became Association of Professional, Executive and Computer Staff.
COHSE		Confederation of Health Service Employees
DATA		Draughtsmen and Allied Technicians' Association. Became the Technical and Supervisory section of the Amalgamated Union of Engineering Workers in 1970 and later changed name to AUEW (Technical, Administrative and Supervisory Section) or TASS.
ETU	Electricians	Electrical Trades Union. Merged with Plumbing Trades Union in 1968 to form the EETPU.
EETPU	Electricians	Electrical, Electronic, Telecommunications and Plumbing Union

FBU		Fire Brigades Union
FTAT	Furniture Workers	Furniture, Timber and Allied Trades Union
GMB *	General and MunicipalWorkers	GMB
GMWU **	General and Municipal Workers (sometimes referred to as 'the G and M')	General and Municipal Workers Union. A name change in 1979 from National Union of General and Municipal Workers. Became General Municipal, Boilermakers and Allied Trades Union (GMBATU) after merger with the Boilermakers in 1982. In 1987 became known simply as GMB.
GUALO		General Union of Associations of Loom Overlookers
ISTC	Steelworkers	Iron and Steel Trades Confederation. Merged in 1985 with the National Union of Blast-furnacemen which became a section of ISTC.
MSF		Manufacturing Science Finance. Formed after merger of TASS and ASTMS in 1988.
MU		Musicians Union
NACODS		National Association of Colliery Overmen, Deputies and Shotfirers
NATSOPA		National Society of Operative Printers, Graphical and Media Personnel. Merged with SOGAT in 1982 to form SOGAT 82.
NCU		National Communications Union. Formed in 1985 after merger of the Post Office Engineering Union with the Civil and Public Services Association (Posts and Telecommunications Group).
NGA(1982)		National Graphical Association (1982). Formed after merger of NGA with the Society of Lithographic Artists, Designers, Engravers and Process Workers (SLADE).
NLBD		National League of the Blind and Disabled
NUAAW	Agricultural Workers	National Union of Agricultural and Allied Workers. Became a section of the Transport and General Workers Union in 1982 but retaining separate affiliation to the Labour Party.
NUBOCK	Blastfurnacemen	National Union of Blastfurnacemen, Ore Miners, Coke Workers and Kindred Trades. In 1985 merged into ISTC.
NUDAGO		National Union of Domestic Appliances and General Operatives
NUDAW	Distributive Workers	National Union of Distributive and Allied Workers. One of the components which became, in 1947, USDAW.

---

* I have used this acronym for any reference to the union which includes the period since 1987.
** For simplicity, I have used this acronym for any reference to the union prior to 1987 – including the period when it was the NUGMW.

NUDBT	Dyers and Bleachers	National Union of Dyers, Bleachers and Textile Workers. Became a section of the Transport and General Workers Union in 1982 but retained separate affiliation to the Labour Party.
NUFLAT		National Union of Footwear, Leather and Allied Trades
NUM	Mineworkers (areas referred to as, e.g., Yorkshire Miners)	National Union of Mineworkers
NUPE	Public Employees	National Union of Public Employees
NUR	Railwaymen	National Union of Railwaymen. Merged in 1990 with National Union of Seamen to form National Union of Rail, Maritime and Transport Workers (RMT).
NUS	Seamen	National Union of Seamen
NUSc	Scalemakers	National Union of Scalemakers. Disaffiliated 1983
NUSMW	Sheet Metal Workers	National Union of Sheet Metal Workers, Coppersmiths, Heating and Domestic Engineers. Merged with AUEW–TASS in 1983.
NUTGW	Tailors	National Union of Tailors and Garment Workers. In 1990 agreed a merger with the GMB.
NUVB	Vehicle Builders	National Union of Vehicle Builders. Merged with the TGWU in 1972.
PLCWTWU		Power Loom Carper Weavers' and Textile Workers' Union.
POEU	Post Office Engineers	Post Office Engineering Union (became NCU)
RMT		National Union of Rail, Maritime and Transport Workers. Formed 1990 after merger of NUR with NUS.
RUBSSO		Rossendale Union of Boot, Shoe and Slipper Operatives. Disaffiliated 1983, but affiliated to TUFL.
SOGAT (82)		Society of Graphical and Allied Trades (1982). Formed after merger of SOGAT with NATSOPA in 1982.
SOS		Society of Shuttlemakers. Disaffiliated 1985.
TASS		AUEW Technical, Administrative and Supervisory Section. Became partially independent 1984 and fully independent 1986. Merged with ASTMS in 1988 to form MSF.
TSSA		Transport Salaried Staffs Association
TGWU	Transport Workers (sometimes referred to as 'the T & G')	Transport and General Workers Union. In recent years it has merged with a variety of unions, including, in 1972, Scottish Commercial Motormen's Union; Watermen, Lightermen, Tugmen and Bargemen's Union; Chemical Workers Union; National Union of

		Vehicle Builders; and, in 1982, National Union of Agricultural and Allied Workers; National Union of Dyers, Bleachers and Textile Workers.
TWU	Tobacco Workers	Tobacco Workers Union. Merged in 1985 with TASS.
UCATT	Construction Workers	Union of Construction, Allied Trades and Technicians. Formed in 1971 after merger of Amalgamated Society of Woodworkers and the Amalgamated Union of Building Trade Workers.
UCW		Union of Communication Workers. Changed name from Union of Post Office Workers in 1981.
UPW		Union of Post Office Workers. Changed name to Union of Communication Workers in 1981.
USDAW		Union of Shop, Distributive and Allied Workers.

II. TRADE UNIONS REFERRED TO IN THE TEXT BUT NOT AFFILIATED TO THE LABOUR PARTY

AES	Association of Agricultural Educational Staff
AIT	Association of Her Majesty's Inspectors of Taxes
AUT	Association of University Teachers
CMA	Communication Managers' Association
CPSA	Civil and Public Services Association
CSU	Civil Service Union
EIS	Educational Institute of Scotland
EMA	Engineers' and Managers' Association
HVA	Health Visitors' Association
IPCS	Institute of Professional Civil Servants
IRSF	Inland Revenue Staff Federation
NALGO	National and Local Government Officers' Association
NASWT	National Association of Schoolmasters and Union of Women Teachers
NATFHE	National Association of Teachers in Further and Higher Education
NCU (Clerical)	National Communication Union (Clerical Section)
NUHKW	National Union of Hosiery and Knitwear Workers
NUIW	National Union of Insurance Workers
NULM	National Union of Lock and Metal Workers
NUT	National Union of Teachers
RCN	Royal College of Nursing
SCPS	Society of Civil and Public Servants
STE	Society of Telecom Executives
UDM	Union of Democratic Mineworkers

Index